Yearbook on International Communist Affairs 1973

Yearbook on

International

Communist Affairs

1973

EDITOR: Richard F. Staar

ASSOCIATE AREA EDITORS:

East Europe and Soviet Union	Milorad M. Drachkovitch
Western Europe	Dennis L. Bark
Africa and Middle East	Lewis H. Gann
Western Hemisphere	William E. Ratliff
Asia and Pacific	Robert F. Turner
Front Organizations	Witold S. Sworakowski

HOOVER INSTITUTION PRESS
Stanford University
Stanford, California
1973

The Hoover Institution on War, Revolution and Peace, founded at Stanford University in 1919 by the late President Herbert Hoover, is a center for advanced study and research on public and international affairs in the twentieth century. The views expressed in its publications are entirely those of the authors and do not necessarily reflect the views of the Hoover Institution.

Hoover Institution Publications 135
Standard Book Number 0-8179-1351-3
Library of Congress Card Number 67-31024
Printed in the United States of America
©1973 by the Board of Trustees of the
Leland Stanford Junior University
All rights reserved

Yearbook on International Communist Affairs 1973

Advisory Board

CONTENTS

Western Hemisphere

Asia and the Pacific

International Communist Front Organizations

INTRODUCTION

The objective of the 1973 *Yearbook on International Communist Affairs,* the seventh consecutive volume to be published, is to provide once again a comprehensive survey covering the calendar year 1972 about the organizational structure, internal development, domestic and foreign policies, and activity of communist parties throughout the world. Most of the materials are based on primary sources.

Profiles of individual communist movements include, as far as available data permit, the following information on each party: founding date; domestic conditions under which the party operates; membership figures; electoral support and participation, if any, in government; organization and leadership; the role of auxiliary organizations; domestic political programs and activities; decisions on key problems of communist ideology, strategy, and tactics; views and positions on major international issues; orientation within the international communist movement; and principal party communications media. Pro-Chinese, Castroite, Trotskyist, and other rival communist movements are treated whenever applicable. Insofar as they affect policies and activities of major communist movements, certain pro-communist parties and groups are noted, as are some guerrilla organizations (particularly in Latin America and Africa) and heterogeneous elements of the so-called New Left. In general, the organizational structure and the policies of these groups are treated only peripherally.

In the specific case of Africa, when selecting parties for inclusion in this *Yearbook,* we have only chosen orthodox Marxist-Leninist movements. Groups referred to by Soviet sources as "revolutionary-democratic," like the PAIGC (Partido Africano de Independência de Guiné e Cabo Verde), MPLA (Movimento Popular de Libertação de Angola), FRELIMO (Frente de Libertação de Moçambique) have been excluded, even though these three movements engage in armed struggle with Soviet support, follow a pro-Soviet course in international affairs, and were represented by official delegates at the most recent, Twenty-fourth Congress of the Communist Party of the Soviet Union held in March–April 1971 at Moscow.

Communist-ruled countries present a particular problem as a result of the entwined interrelationship between government and party. In these profiles, therefore, the focus is on the position and functioning of each party, while policies pursued by the communist-ruled states are treated predominantly within the context of official party programs and attitudes.

*   *   *

The most dynamic in regard to world-wide activity during the year under review continued to be the Communist Party of the Soviet Union (CPSU). It launched a campaign that will culminate in an exchange of party cards of its approximately 14.5 million members, to begin 1 March 1973 and to extend over a two-year period. Reissuance of membership cards should achieve the twin objective of expelling undesirable elements from the movement and strengthening the lowest organizational units or primary party organizations. A concomitant and intensified indoctrination drive is aimed at improving the ideological level of non-party elements of society along with that of all CPSU members.

Scientific institutes, together with other centers of higher education, remain the target of this ancillary campaign in order to meet the demands of an increasingly complex technology that requires adaptation to advanced Western managerial systems based on computers and cybernetics. The CPSU leadership has warned repeatedly of the danger stemming from ideological contamination that may result through greater contacts with the West in the form of stepped-up trade and various exchange relations. This struggle against the eroding effects of bourgeois ideology will be the concern of a new department, established at the CPSU Academy of Social Sciences, which will deal with theory and methods of ideological work.

Another preoccupation of the party leadership resulted from failure to achieve many of the annual targets established in the 1971–75 five-year plan. The rate of economic growth declined to its lowest level since 1963, and labor productivity continued to lag. Failures in agriculture necessitated grain purchases, costing some $2 billion, from the West. A projected increase in consumers' goods, that is to say, in the general living standard, had to be abandoned during a general reordering of economic priorities toward the year's end. Improvement of economic administration remained the dominant theme in domestic propaganda.

Apart from the economy, the CPSU leadership is faced with a growing political problem that has manifested itself in a resurgence of nationalism among minorities and dissent in certain elements of the dominant Great Russian ethnic group. The largest minority is comprised of Ukrainians, many of whose intellectuals have been sentenced to prison terms for nationalistic activities. Historians in the Caucasian republic of Georgia found themselves under attack for revisionism. Yet another border area, along the Baltic Sea, witnessed clashes with police after the self-immolation of a student in Lithuania. A large number of Latvian communists protested to their comrades in West European parties against Great Russian chauvinism, and an "Estonian National Front" reportedly demanded a national referendum on self-determination.

One ethnic group, scattered throughout the Soviet Union, received extensive publicity owing to attempts by many of its members to emigrate from the U.S.S.R.; a special tax on these Soviet Jews in effect levies a ransom, the individual amount depending upon the education of the applicant for an exit visa. A resurgence of religious interest among many of the nationalities led to a more militant atheistic campaign and considerable repression. Although arrests of key dissident intellectuals appears to have weakened the civil rights movement, self-published (*samizdat*) materials continued to be circulated. Broader political, social, and economic problems now seem to absorb the attention of those dissidents who still remain outside of prisons.

Despite these domestic difficulties, the Soviet party-state leadership had no major problems with its allies in Eastern Europe. Bloc coordination along politico-military and economic lines continued through the Warsaw Treaty Organization (WTO) and the Council for Mutual Economic Assistance (CMEA). At the end of November, a preliminary conference on European security opened in Helsinki with full WTO participation. Only the Romanians put forward apparently independent proposals that the conference chairmanship rotate and that delegates represent their countries, not blocs or alliance systems. The 26th CMEA session, in July, admitted communist-ruled Cuba as its first overseas member. This may provide Moscow with greater control over the Cuban economy, especially if planned integration of the bloc is attained.

Close ideological alignment with the CPSU did not prevent some of the East European leaderships from pursuing certain distinctive policies that have no counterpart in the Soviet

Union. Bulgaria continued a massive reorganization of its farms into large agro-industrial complexes. Party and government functions were in the process of being merged at all levels in Romania. Integration of central planning with the market mechanism was pursued by Hungary, despite some evidence of Soviet displeasure. Only in Czechoslovakia and East Germany did the orthodox hard line appear dominant. In Czechoslovakia political trials were used to eliminate what remained of the 1968 attempt at liberalization. East Germany announced that its few private entrepreneurs would be forced out of business in 1973.

Although the communists in Yugoslavia claim to be non-aligned, their rapprochement with the Soviet Union included a visit in June by Tito to Moscow, where he was awarded the highest U.S.S.R. decoration, the Order of Lenin. In early November it was announced that the equivalent of $540 million in Soviet credits would help Belgrade to finance various industrial, communications and agricultural projects. These developments were accompanied by an extensive purge of communist leaders in most republics and the two autonomous provinces of Yugoslavia. The party was instructed to assume its command position in political, economic, and cultural affairs.

In Eastern Europe only the small party-ruled government of Albania maintains no relations either with the CPSU or the Soviet Union. Moscow radio has broadcast repeated offers that contacts be resumed, but without result. Tirana even refused an invitation to participate in the Helsinki talks, preparatory to a European security conference. The Albanians have maintained a stance that is more anti-Soviet than that of the Chinese, who do have an ambassador in Moscow.

However, the CPSU has been unable to initiate any party relations with Peking. After President Nixon visited mainland China, the Soviet press attacked the Chinese communist leaders as accomplices of the imperialists. This did not prevent the U.S.S.R. from offering to sign a bilateral agreement with China on renunciation of force and a multilateral collective security treaty for Asia. Apparently fearing an outbreak of hostilities, the Kremlin increased its divisions along the Sino-Soviet border to 44 (including two in Mongolia), totaling almost half a million men, or a fourth of its ground troops. The former commanding officer for the Siberian military district was placed in charge of the U.S.S.R.'s strategic missile forces, and nine ICBMs were fired from the Lake Baikal area over-flying northern China and impacting near the Kamchatka Peninsula. The significance of this act could not have failed to impress the Chinese leadership.

In contrast to such spectacular demonstrations in word and deed, the Soviet "peace program" adopted by the recent Twenty-fourth Congress of the CPSU continued to be projected vis-à-vis Western Europe. Here the local communist parties gave virtually unanimous support for peaceful co-existence and the 1973 European security conference. Détente was emphasized, but not in the field of ideology. On the other hand the West European communist parties called for de jure recognition of East Germany, North Korea, and North Vietnam. They expressed general approval of President Nixon's visits to both Peking and Moscow. Geographic variations existed, however, with certain Nordic parties (in Denmark, Finland, Iceland, and Norway) opposing association of their respective countries with either NATO or the Common Market.

Disagreement over the 1968 Warsaw Pact invasion of Czechoslovakia surfaced again during 1972 in connection with the trials in that Soviet-occupied country. This political repression received clear condemnation by the communist parties of Great Britain, Italy, the Netherlands, Norway, Spain, and Sweden. Endorsement of the CPSU, as leader of the international communist movement, again raised the question of independence and the so-called Brezhnev Doctrine of limited sovereignty. The Soviet defense minister reiterated the latter in an article published by *Kommunist* (no. 15, October, p. 38). Although no overt criticism of it appeared in West European communist publications, the article could not have gone unnoticed.

This silence may have been due to the fact that most of these parties are represented in their respective parliaments (notable exceptions being the Federal Republic of Germany and Great Britain). To raise the issue of limited sovereignty could have worked against détente and served the "enemies" of peaceful co-existence. It also might have frightened other left-wing parties away from possible electoral alliances. Unity of the left had to be preserved, particularly in France where elections were scheduled for March 1973. French communists hoped to increase their representation (34 seats out of 486) in the National Assembly.

A common front not only with socialists but also with "progressive" Christians is the policy advocated by the Communist Party of the Netherlands. Using the unification program in France as a model, the party issued a manifesto calling for establishment of a government at The Hague based on communist-socialist cooperation. Similar advocacy of unity of action appeared in Belgium, Greece, Italy, Luxembourg, Spain, and Switzerland, where the local movements (clandestine in Greece and Spain) hope to emulate the French Communist Party in future elections.

If the West European communists may have some realistic expectation of participation in government, this cannot be said in general about the parties active in the Middle East and Africa. Among the Maghreb countries, only Algeria provides legal status (but with numerous restrictions). Many party members are Frenchmen living in the country or Algerians residing abroad. Egyptian communists were forced to join the only legal political organization, the Arab Socialist Union—which underwent an extensive purge beginning in December 1972, with the avowed goal of expelling Marxist-Leninists.

In Syria de facto legality through the short-lived National Progressive Front also ended abruptly. Banned communist parties have little popular appeal in either Jordan or Iran. The same is true of Lebanon, where the movement operates legally. Only the Iraqi communists have been able to obtain portfolios (two) in the government. In Israel the legal but miniscule communist parties, one pro-Arab and the other pro-Jewish, have no influence on or hope of controlling the government.

The South African Communist Party leadership operates from exile in London. Its allies include the Anti-Apartheid Movement and the African National Congress, both of which have made more of an impact abroad than in South Africa. The small groups comprising this organization seem to consist of a political army of officers, with few in the rank and file. However, its London journal *African Communist* appears to be the leading Marxist organ for the continent, perhaps because it is the best known. The party in Lesotho, allied with that in South Africa, remains minute. The movement in Sudan has yet to recover from the execution or flight of its leaders, following the abortive 1971 coup d'état.

Much more promising is the communist outlook in the Western Hemisphere, especially in certain parts of Latin America. Here too, as in some of the West European countries, electoral fronts have been organized with non-Marxist political parties. The Popular Unity government in Chile apparently serves as a model for emulation by communists in Colombia, Costa Rica, Uruguay, and Venezuela. Plagued by Castroite, pro-Chinese, pro-Soviet, and Trotskyite splinter groups, the Marxist-Leninists in Latin America have succeeded in attaining unity among themselves only in Bolivia and Uruguay.

In the latter country, the urban guerrillas called Tupamaros have been crippled severely by police and army countermeasures. About half of the hemispheric countries have Maoist as well as Trotskyite parties that appeal mainly to young persons. More extensive are Castroite groups, which may not necessarily follow the lead of Havana. The pro-Soviet parties have shown hostility toward military governments, except in the cases of the "progressive" regimes in Ecuador and Peru.

Communists registered poor results in Canadian and U.S. elections. In October the pro-Chinese group in Canada fared better than the pro-Soviet party by the simple device of running more candidates. The following month, the Communist Party, USA came in seventh during the U.S. presidential election, with 25,000 votes out of 77.5 million cast. The Socialist Workers Party, a Trotskyite movement, received more than twice that number. The CPUSA probably has hopes of more support in the future because of making Angela Davis a member of its Central Committee.

During another election, held across the Pacific Ocean in Asia, the Japan Communist Party won 11 percent of the popular vote in December and increased its seats in the House of Representatives from 14 to 40 (out of 491). It is the third strongest group in parliament and, totaling approximately 300,000 members, vies with the French party for second place in size among non-ruling communist movements.

Although claiming the largest ruling organization in the world, with some 30 million members, the Chinese communists still have not recovered from their Great Proletarian Cultural Revolution and its almost total destruction of the party apparatus. At the end of 1972 there existed only five departments in the Central Committee—those concerned with international liaison, organization, united front work, general administration, and publications. The Standing Committee of the Political Bureau consisted of Mao Tse-tung, Chou En-lai, and Kang Sheng (with the last of these incapacitated by illness or old age). The seven-member Military Commission of the Central Committee appeared to be the only active organization at the top level.

A noteworthy decline occurred in the number of pro-Maoist leaders to visit China. During 1972 they included representatives from Australia, Italy, Ceylon (Sri Lanka), and two U.S. groups—the October League and the Revolutionary Union. The Soviet trade union newspaper *Trud* on 16 August alleged that the world proliferation of national pro-Maoist groups had declined from a high of 79 in 1967 to only 25 some five years later. Included among the latter are the factions of communist parties in Burma, Indonesia, Malaysia and Thailand which still have offices or delegations in exile at Peking.

Even relations with the two ruling parties which have maintained close contacts with Peking, those in Albania and North Vietnam, apparently became somewhat strained. The differences with Albanians arise from the stress placed by them on the "two-front" struggle against both the United States and the Soviet Union. President Nixon's visit to Peking initially aroused resentment in Tirana. Continuing high-level contacts between North Vietnamese and Soviet communists may have contributed to the cool reception given Hanoi's chief ideologist and second-ranking Politburocrat, Truong Chinh, when he stopped at Peking en route home from Moscow in December.

The North Vietnamese, despite the indications of a cease-fire at the year's end, made it clear in their party publications that "complete victory" remained their strategic objective for all of Indochina. The Khmer Rouge claimed more than 90 percent control of Cambodia (while Western observers credited them with only 60 percent) and refused in advance to be bound by any cease-fire. Despite reports indicating that Prince Sihanouk, in Peking exile, had lost some power to the communists, the North Vietnamese allegedly assured him of Chinese weapons and supplies through their country even after a cease-fire.

In neighboring Thailand, the government reported about 1,000 casualties in the North inflicted by Thai communists armed with Chinese and Soviet weapons. A Malaysian white paper announced serious communist activity in Sarawak, and Indonesia also was confronted with a small-scale but increasing guerrilla insurgency on Borneo. President Marcos of the Philippines stated that in Isabela Province the communist party (Marxist-Leninist) and its New People's Army controlled 33 of the 37 municipalities.

Two other movements in Asia experienced internal difficulties during the year. In Ceylon (Sri Lanka) hard-liners won a power struggle and lost their financial support from the Soviet Union. A newly formed Socialist Party of Australia split away from the communist movement in that country. Australian communist candidates received less than two percent of the vote in December elections, while the socialists did considerably worse.

The interests of the international communist front organizations appeared to differ, according to the responsibilities assigned to each. Nevertheless certain themes were common to them all. During the year, European security absorbed most of the attention of these groups. The fronts gave full support to all Warsaw Pact and individual Soviet proposals, sponsoring assemblies designed to rally public opinion and particular groups or professions behind the European security conference proposed for 1973.

Interwoven with all activities of the fronts was a continuing denunciation of U.S. policy in Indochina. Without exception, these organizations also gave verbal support to the Arabs against Israeli "aggression." However, the main thrust of their propaganda concerning the Middle East increasingly centered on nationalization of the Iraq Petroleum Company. Chile also received considerable attention, with meetings in Santiago which registered unqualified approval of the Allende government in its struggle against "U.S. imperialism." The problem of Northern Ireland seemed to preoccupy the fronts more than previously, with strong criticism of British "restrictions" on civil rights.

Of particular significance appeared to be a concerted move by the front organizations to improve contacts with their non-communist counterparts. This was especially true of the World Federation of Trade Unions and the World Peace Council. The latter's secretary-general, Romesh Chandra of India, probably spoke on behalf of all fronts when he called for broader association with other organizations which have common interests.

Although loud and direct criticism of the fronts by Chinese communists became somewhat muted, Albania repeatedly attacked these organizations for their subservience to the Soviet Union.

* * *

Members of the staff and several associate editors were responsible for much of the research and writing of the *Yearbook*. Profiles were contributed also by a total of 41 outside contributors, many of whom wrote more than one essay. Full names and affiliations of each outside contributor appear at the end of his or her profile. Mrs. Ica Juilland assisted in the processing and filing of research material; most of the final typing was done by Mrs. Julia Austin.

Special appreciation is due to the Curators of the Hoover Institution and to members of its Readers' Services and Serials Department, as well as to all those organizations—government and private—which made available source material and translations. We are indebted particularly to the copy editor, Jesse M. Phillips, for putting the manuscript in its final form.

February 1973   Richard F. Staar

* * *

Sources are cited throughout the text, with news agencies normally identified by generally accepted initials. Abbreviations are also used for the following widely quoted publications:

Foreign Broadcast Information Service	*FBIS*
World Marxist Review (Toronto, Canada, edition)	*WMR*
and its *Information Bulletin*	*IB*
Yearbook on International Communist Affairs	*YICA*

EASTERN EUROPE AND THE SOVIET UNION

Albania

The Albanian Communist Party was founded on 8 November 1941. At its First Congress, November 1948, the name was changed to Albanian Party of Labor (Partia e Punës e Shqipërise; APL). As the only legal party in Albania, the APL exercises a monopoly of power. All 264 seats in the national legislature, the People's Assembly, are held by representatives of the Democratic Front, which is the party-controlled political alliance of the APL and the mass organizations.

In November 1971 the APL claimed a membership of 86,985. Some 68,000 were full members and 18,000 candidates. Laborers comprised 36.4 percent, peasants 29.7 percent, and white-collar workers 33.9 percent. (*Zëri i Popullit,* 4 November). Party members constitute about 4 percent of the 2.2 million population (estimated 1972)—the smallest ratio among the East European ruling parties.

Although APL size remained relatively stable between 1948 and 1966, a rapid growth of 20,658 members occurred between 1966 and 1971. It appears that the APL is continuing its efforts, especially in the 25–35 age bracket, to expand its ranks (Tirana radio, 23 October 1972).

Organization and Leadership. There were no major changes in the Albanian leadership during 1972. Enver Hoxha, the party's first secretary since its founding, is the dominant personality in the ruling elite.

The APL exercises power through its Politburo (13 members, 4 candidates), Central Committee (71 members, 39 candidates), and Secretariat. (For Politburo names see *YICA, 1972,* p. 4.)

In March, the second ranking member of the Albanian leadership, Politburo member and premier Mehmet Shehu underwent surgery in France. By late spring the 60-year old Shehu had resumed his normal schedule of activities.

Mass Organizations. The Seventh Congress of the United Trade Unions of Albania met in Tirana on 8–11 May. In a keynote address (*Rruga e Partisë,* May), Hoxha called for renewed efforts to implement the program of "workers' control" launched in April 1968. He stressed that "workers' control" did not mean direct or shared administration of factories or enterprises by workers. Rather, it required workers to take the initiative in uncovering problems that hindered production and help to develop solutions. The major responsibilities of the working class under this doctrine are to maintain discipline and morale in their own ranks, and to serve as a check on bureaucrats and technocrats. Hoxha warned the trade unionists that the party had no intention of allowing "workers' control" to evolve into a system resembling Yugoslav self-management.

It was revealed at the congress that trade union membership had risen 58 percent since

3

1967, reflecting the rapid increase during the past five years in the size of the industrial labor force, which in 1972 was estimated at 320,000 (Tirana radio, 12 May). There were no significant changes in the leadership of the organization. Rita Marko, who was named president upon the death of Gogo Nushi in April 1970, was elected to this post by the congress. Tonin Jakova was reelected secretary-general. In his report to the congress, Jakova noted that in 1972 the United Trade Unions of Albania maintained ties with 130 national trade unions and trade union federations in 80 countries. (Ibid., 8 May.)

The Sixth Congress of the Union of Albanian Labor Youth met in Durrës on 23–26 October. Ramiz Alia, the APL expert on ideology and culture, spoke at the session attended by the entire membership of the Politburo. Alia stressed (ibid., 23 October) the crucial role which Albanian youth would play in determining the outcome of the Ideological and Cultural Revolution and the fifth five-year plan (1971–75). He appealed to the youth of the country to resist the "harmful" social and cultural influences which are apparently beginning to infiltrate Albania from abroad. Alia indicated that the Union of Albanian Labor Youth would play a major role in preserving "Marxist-Leninist purity" among the younger generation. The congress elected Rudi Monari as first secretary (ibid., 26 October). Monari had served in this capacity since March 1972 when he replaced Agim Mero, who had been appointed rector of Tirana State University. Monari reported that the organization's membership had risen from about 200,000 in 1967 to 300,000 in 1972 (ibid., 23 October).

Enver Hoxha, as president of the Democratic Front (DF), presided over the 19 April meeting of its general council. DF vice-president Ramiz Alia reported to the council that only 27 percent of those elected to offices in DF local organs in 1972 were APL members (*Zëri i Popullit,* 21 April). This development, which is in line with the campaign to allow greater responsibilities to non-party members, has not weakened APL control over the DF, since the party holds all key positions.

The Ideological and Cultural Revolution ("Revolutionization" Movement). On 26 February 1972 Enver Hoxha launched a new phase of the Ideological and Cultural Revolution with his speech entitled "The Masses Build Socialism, the Party Raises Their Consciousness." This address, distributed in pamphlet form throughout Albania, ranks as a major pronouncement of the country's "revolutionization" movement. In it, Hoxha conceded that his efforts in 1966–72 to reduce the size of the bureaucracy had not been entirely successful. While the central bureaucracy has shrunk, bureaucracy at the local level has grown rapidly in conjunction with the government's decentralization policy, especially in the economic sector. A study of 26 industrial establishments in early 1972, for example, disclosed that one out of every seven employees of these concerns held either a supervisory or an administrative position. (Ibid., 7 June.)

Hoxha also observed that a disproportionately high percentage of communists held such posts in government agencies and economic enterprises. This situation had produced resentment on the part of the masses and threatened to create a gulf between the party and the people.

To deal with these problems, Hoxha by early spring had launched a vigorous campaign to prune the bureaucracy and to reduce significantly the percentage of party members in administrative or supervisory positions (see, e.g., *Rruga e Partisë,* May). There seem to be at least three major factors behind the latest phase of the Albanian "revolutionization" movement. First, the APL leaders appear to be genuinely alarmed by the difficulties they have encountered in raising production in the agricultural sector of the economy and in improving the quality of output in the industrial sector (see below). Second, the leadership seems to have become sensitive to the growing popular resentment against the favored positions enjoyed by the party and state cadres (see, e.g., *Zëri i Popullit,* 20 January; 29 April; 19, 23, 27 May). Third, the leadership has become deeply concerned about the "revisionist" and "reactionary" influences within the country which threaten to "corrupt" both the nation's youth and the older generation (see *Drita,* Tirana, 6 February, 25 June; *Rruga e Partisë,* August).

To combat these most recent threats to the successful construction of their own brand of socialism, Albanian leaders continued to place heavy emphasis on the ideological education of the masses. During early 1972 the first comprehensive Albanian-prepared theoretical text-book, *Materializmi dialektic dhe historik* (Dialectical and Historical Materialism), was placed in circulation. It is intended to free Albanian students from the necessity of relying on foreign works in their ideological studies (*Zëri i Popullit,* 8 January). The second National Congress on Pedagogical Studies, 2–4 March, sought to develop a program of "further revolutioni-zation" of the school system "in accordance with directives of party and government" (Tirana radio, 3 March).

Economy. During the first year (1971) of the fifth five-year plan, industrial production in-creased by 11.5 percent and agricultural output rose by approximately 5 percent (*Ekonomia Popullore,* May–June; *Zëri i Popullit,* 12 January 1973). Although the industrial sector ex-ceeded its planned growth of 7.5 percent, the agricultural sector failed by a wide margin to meet its assigned increase of 25.8 percent. The poor performance in agriculture was obviously a grave disappointment to the leadership, which had given high priority to this matter during 1971. In an attempt to resolve their agricultural difficulties, the Albanians turned to the Chinese for assistance. In April, Albania obtained a long-term, interest-free loan from China (NCNA, 11 April). Reportedly, the loan will be used to buy agricultural machinery, seeds, herbicides, and pesticides, and to underwrite construction of greenhouses and other facilities (*Zëri i Popullit,* 21 June). While preliminary data indicate that agricultural output for 1972 increased by approximately 12 percent (ibid., 12 January 1973), it is too early to determine whether the Albanians are finally on the road to the solution of their farm problem.

Although Albanian industry appeared to be surpassing its assigned targets for the first two years of the current five-year plan (*Ekonomia Popullore,* May–June; Tirana radio, 30 Octo-ber), the domestic press complained on numerous occasions (e.g., *Zëri i Popullit,* 1 July) about the poor quality of workmanship, especially in the manufacture of consumers' goods. While the government seemed to recognize the importance of improving quality and increas-ing the output of consumers' goods to combat worker apathy and alienation (ibid., 30 Au-gust), it does not appear to have taken any significant steps to meet these concerns.

Political Developments. In November 1972, Shenasi Dragoti, who had served as minister of construction since September 1963, was relieved of his post "for reasons of health" (Tirana radio, 17 November). It was also announced that Dragoti, a candidate member of the APL Central Committee since the party's Sixth Congress, November 1971, would be assigned "other important duties." Rahman Hanku, a deputy minister of construction and Central Committee member since 1966, replaced Dragoti.

The drive to decentralize political and economic administration continued as the party leadership called for strengthening and expansion of the "socialist democracy," that is, greater popular participation in decision-making at the local level (*Zëri i Popullit,* 20, 21 April).

Society and Culture. According to recent data (ibid., 8 July 1972), the Albanian intelli-gentsia in 1970 numbered 97,489. Of these, 34 percent were professionals employed as engi-neers or technicians, 57 percent were engaged in teaching or scientific research, and 9 percent were administrators. The majority of the intelligentsia came from a "petty-bourgeois" social background, 65 percent lived in the cities, and 35 percent were women. The average salary of the intelligentsia was only 7 percent above the workers' average. The Albanian National

Academy of Sciences was established in June 1972 to promote and coordinate scientific and intellectual activities in the country (ibid., 21 June). Some 725,000 students, about a third of the population, were enrolled in schools on either a full or a part-time basis (Tirana radio, 1 September).

Foreign Relations. During 1972 Albania established diplomatic relations with Luxemburg (Tirana radio, 15 February), Nepal (ibid., 23 May), and Equatorial Guinea (ibid., 1 December). At year's end, Albania had diplomatic ties with 56 countries.

Albania rejected the invitation extended by the Finnish government to attend the preparatory meeting for a conference on European security and cooperation (ibid., 20 November), the only invited country that declined to participate. The Albanians charged that the conference had been planned and promoted by the United States and the Soviet Union for the sole purpose of legalizing the status quo in Europe. They further claimed that, with their respective positions in Europe secured, the "two superpowers" would be free to pursue their "aggressive, imperialistic" policies toward China and Albania as well as the peoples of Asia, Africa, and Latin America (ibid.).

For the first time since the end of World War II, Albania participated in the Olympic Games. It thus reversed a long-standing policy of refusing to take part in the Olympics so long as Taiwan was permitted to compete. The government scheduled direct daily television coverage of the Olympics (*ibid., 20 August*). While Albania condemned the acts of terrorism perpetrated by Palestinian guerrillas at the Games (*ibid., 7 September*), it also reaffirmed general support for "the national liberation struggle of the Palestinian people" (ibid., 10 September).

Tourism continued to grow at a modest rate during 1972, and there were tourist hotels in various stages of construction in all of the country's major cities and resort areas (*Liria,* Boston, 15 September). Although they recognize that tourism is an important source of much needed foreign exchange, the Albanian leaders appear to be somewhat distressed over the potential impact from a large-scale influx of foreigners on the masses, especially the younger generation (*Christian Science Monitor,* 28 July).

Albanian-Chinese Relations. During the first half of 1972, there were a number of reports that serious tensions had developed in Sino-Albanian relations (e.g., *Time,* 24 April; *Christian Science Monitor,* 6 March, 1 May). It was noted that Tirana and Peking differed over such matters as the visit of U.S. President Nixon to China, the extent to which the "Marxist-Leninist" parties and movements should be supported, the expansion of the European Common Market, and several other issues.

There was little doubt that President Nixon's visit displeased the Albanian leadership. While the Albanians did not publicly criticize the Chinese on this score, they made their feelings known in a variety of ways. An Albanian correspondent was one of the two foreign journalists stationed in China who declined to apply for special credentials to cover the Nixon visit (Reuters, 25 February). The Albanian press limited its coverage of this event to brief factual accounts of Nixon's activities in China (e.g., *Bashkimi,* 22 February, 1 March). Before, during, and after the Nixon trip, the Albanian press continued its vigorous criticism of U.S. foreign and domestic policies (e.g., *Zëri i Popullit,* 16, 28 February, 2, 8 March). Indirectly criticizing the Chinese for conducting negotiations with the "head of the imperialist camp," the Albanians emphasized the doctrine enunciated by Hoxha at the APL's Sixth Congress, November 1971, that "it is impossible to use one imperialism to oppose another." On the other hand, they publicly and staunchly defended the Chinese against the Soviet charge that the Nixon visit marked the beginning of "Chinese-American collusion to destroy world communism" (ibid., 7 January). The Chinese gave immediate and wide publicity to this Albanian statement (NCNA, 8 January).

Subsequently, Sino-Albanian relations noticeably warmed. Both nations apparently were anxious to dispel the rumors that a rift had developed. The Chinese press, after a brief pause, began to reprint strong Albanian editorials concerning the Vietnam war and the Middle East situation (e.g., ibid., 15 March; 4, 6 April). In an obvious gesture to reassure the Albanians of their support, the Chinese condemned the Soviet Union and the United States for their continuing efforts to dominate the Mediterranean and lavishly praised the APL for its "correct stand" on this issue (ibid., 9 April). On 28 March, China and Albania concluded a civil aviation agreement which established air service between the two countries. The following month, agriculture minister Pirro Dodbiba, a candidate member of the Politburo, traveled to China to sign the Sino-Albanian long-term agricultural loan agreement (see above) and to make a brief good-will tour (NCNA, 18 April).

In his address to the congress of Albanian trade unions, Hoxha warmly endorsed China's domestic and foreign policies. In his first major pronouncement concerning Sino-Albanian relations, in the aftermath of the Nixon visit, Hoxha declared:

> The friendship and cooperation between the Albanian and Chinese peoples and between our two parties and governments are ever strengthening. This friendship has been built up and grows on the firm bases of Marxism-Leninism, proletarian internationalism, and common interests and aims. Since this is so, it has resisted and will continue to resist all tests. It will be ever more tempered for the benefit of our two peoples and the cause of revolution and socialism in the world. (Tirana radio, 8 May.)

Albanian-Chinese exchanges appear to have increased during 1972. Mindful, perhaps, of the conjecture regarding the state of Sino-Albanian relations that their failure to send a delegation to the APL's Sixth Congress had inspired, the Chinese sent representatives to the trade union and Labor Youth congresses (ibid., 4 May, 24 October). The Chinese minister of agriculture toured Albania during July, as did a "good will" military delegation (Shqiperia e re, Tirana, July).

The highest-ranking Albanian leader to visit China was Beqir Balluku, Politburo member, deputy prime minister, and defense minister. During a month-long stay (5 November–8 December), Balluku visited Peking and several provincial areas and met with Chou En-lai (NCNA, 9 December). Albania's minister of trade headed the delegation that concluded the 1973 Sino-Albanian trade protocol in Peking (ibid., 9 November).

Mao Tse-tung, Chou En-lai, Tung Pi-wu, and Chu Teh all signed the warm message of greeting to the Albanians on the occasion of their national holidays in late November (ibid., 27 November). During the round of banquets and celebrations in honor of these events, various Chinese spokesmen were lavish in their praise of the Albanian leaders and their policies and of Sino-Albanian friendship (ibid., 27, 28, 29, 30 November).

While it appeared that the Albanian leadership still had some misgivings concerning China's growing contacts with the United States (Tirana radio, 29 November), the Sino-Albanian relationship remained firm. The Chinese were apparently fulfilling their economic commitments to the Albanians (ibid.) and were reportedly providing them with military aid (NYT, 5 March).

Soviet Union. There was no significant change in Albanian-Soviet relations during 1972. The Albanians continued to criticize harshly both Soviet foreign and domestic policies.

They charged that President Nixon's visit to Moscow represented "a new stage in Soviet-U.S. global strategy against the freedom and independence of the peoples" (Zëri i Popullit, 27

May). Nixon's visit to a Moscow church was viewed as "a link in the chain of imperialist-revisionist counterrevolutionary strategy" (*Drita,* 25 June). The United States and the Soviet Union were accused of engaging in "gunboat diplomacy" in the Mediterranean (*Zëri i Popullit,* 27 May). Tirana castigated the Soviets for pursuing a "two-faced" policy toward the Arabs (*Bashkimi,* 30 January) and hailed the expulsion of the Russian military force from Egypt as a blow to Moscow's false imperialism" (*Zëri i Popullit,* 25 June). According to the Albanians, the Warsaw Pact had become a "tool" of the "Soviet-American holy alliance" to preserve the status quo in Europe (ibid., 29 January), while the Council for Mutual Economic Assistance was described as a Soviet agency whose main function was to "facilitate" Moscow's plunder of the revisionist countries (Tirana radio, 17 July). The Albanians also sought to embarrass the Soviets by broadcasting an account of an alleged mutiny aboard a Soviet submarine that had reportedly taken refuge in Norwegian territorial waters (*Chicago Tribune,* 26 November). Despite the broad front on which they waged their propaganda war against the Soviet Union, the main Albanian concern centered upon Moscow's intentions and moves in the Balkans (e.g., *Zëri i Popullit,* 29 March, 1 April, 15 June).

Owing, perhaps, to the leaders' apprehensions about growing manifestations of "revisionist attitudes" within the country, the Albanian press devoted much space to exposing the "evils" that had become prevalent in Soviet life. It was reported that "criminality," "vagabondage," "hooliganism," and other forms of anti-socialist behavior had become common in the Soviet Union (*Zëri i Rinisë,* 7 February). The revival of popular interest in religion (*Drita,* 25 June) and the "degeneration" of contemporary Russian literature were attributed to Soviet abandonment of Marxism-Leninism (ibid., 30 January).

The Albanians continued to spurn all Soviet offers of reconciliation (e.g., Moscow radio 8, 28, 29 November). Hoxha maintained that the Albanian people, who were "building socialism by relying on their own efforts and with Chinese aid which [was] being given in the spirit of proletarian internationalism," were not deceived by Soviet promises of aid and professions of friendship (Tirana radio, 29 November).

Albanian-Greek Relations. Albanian-Greek relations continued to improve during 1972. Both governments evidenced a desire to persevere in efforts to normalize and strengthen their ties. In October a three-year (1973–75) trade agreement was signed. Unlike the Greek-Albanian trade pacts of 1966 and 1970, which were negotiated by the chambers of commerce of the two signatories, the 1972 agreement was concluded at the government level (Athens radio, 16 December). In addition, Greece and Albania signed a pact establishing a permanent mixed commission to resolve any border disputes that may arise between them. In his speech commemorating the 60th anniversary of Albania's independence, Hoxha declared that the Albanian people would never permit their country to serve as a base that "would bring harm to the fraternal Greek people" (Tirana radio, 29 November). This conciliatory gesture did not go unnoticed. The Greek foreign minister stated that Hoxha's remarks constituted "a useful indication of the spirit of good neighborliness which must govern the relations between the two countries" (Athens radio, 16 December.)

Relations with Eastern Europe. With the exception of Yugoslavia, Romania, and Hungary, Albania's ties with the nations of Eastern Europe were both limited and cool. Tirana was somewhat unnerved by the Soviet Union's moves to improve relations with Yugoslavia and by what the Albanians perceived to be its moves to curb the independence of Romania and Hungary (*Zëri i Popullit,* 1 April).

During 1972 Albanian-Yugoslav economic and cultural ties were strengthened. For the most part, however, the Albanians continue to be primarily concerned with cementing relations with their compatriots in Kosovo, Macedonia, and Montenegro. While there is no evidence to indicate that Tirana is in any manner encouraging "separatism" among the Albanians of Yugoslavia, Belgrade has warned its neighbor that it will not tolerate the development of an "irredentist ideology" which calls for the creation of a greater Albania (i.e., the union of Albania and Kosovo) (*Rilindja,* Prishtina, 24 July). The Yugoslavs were also irritated by the scathing Albanian criticism (*Zëri i Popullit,* 25 June) of their foreign and domestic policies occasioned by Tito's visit to Moscow. They warned that continued attacks of this nature threatened the "orderly development of relations between the two states" (*Borba,* Belgrade, 24 June.) Despite the periodic Albanian-Yugoslav polemics, the volume of trade between the two countries continued to grow. It was expected that Yugoslavia would be Albania's third-ranking trading partner at the end of 1972. (*Rilindja,* 22 December).

As the Soviet Union appeared to be strengthening its hold over Romania, Albania again pledged to help the Romanians defend their independence should the need arise (*Zëri i Popullit,* 22 August). It was revealed that, after almost a decade of steady decline, Albanian-Hungarian trade had registered increases during 1971 and 1972 (MTI, Hungarian press agency, 12 October). It was not clear whether this development would lead to a significant improvement in relations between the two countries.

Relations with Western Europe and the United States. During 1972 Albania's relations with Austria, France, Italy, Sweden, and Turkey continued to improve. These countries provided a large share of Albania's tourists, and they were among the most important of its non-communist trading partners. Italy was expected to be Albania's second-largest trading partner, after China (*Rilindja,* 22 December). In April, Albania and Austria signed a five-year commercial pact calling for an increased volume of trade between the two countries (*Wiener Zeitung,* 14 April). Albanian-French cultural contacts were greatly expanded during 1972. An Albanian-French Friendship Society was established (*Shqipëria e re,* July). Albania again participated in many of the major European trade fairs and international expositions. In August, the Albanians indicated they were not yet interested in establishing diplomatic ties with the Federal Republic of Germany (*Zëri i Popullit,* 19 August). Although Great Britain expressed a desire to resume relations (*Christian Science Monitor,* 27 April), Albania apparently did not respond favorably to this overture.

In line with President Nixon's efforts to improve relations with the Soviet Union and China, as well as those states which it does not currently recognize, the United States discreetly indicated its willingness to take the necessary preliminary steps to normalize its relations with Albania (*Chicago Daily News,* 23 October). For this reason the U.S. Department of Commerce authorized the sale to Albania of scientific equipment valued at $800,000. What little hope there was for a U. S.-Albanian reconciliation was dashed on 11 October, when the Albanian chargé d'affaires in North Vietnam was injured during a U.S. bombing raid on Hanoi (NCNA, 12 October). The Albanian Council of Ministers formally condemned this act on 12 October, and anti-U.S. protest rallies were held in schools and factories (*Shqipëria e re,* October). Alleged collusion to dominate the world on the part of the two "superpowers," the United States and the Soviet Union (e.g., *Zëri i Popullit,* 13 May, 13 June), together with U.S. involvement in the Vietnam war (e.g., *ibid.,* 8 March, 18 May) remained major roadblocks to the normalization of U.S.-Albanian relations. The Albanians attributed President Nixon's re-election to his having "a weak opponent" and predicted his second term would see "a continuation of his past policy of aggression and war abroad, plus brutal repression and exploitation at home" (*ibid.,* 10 November).

International Communism. The Albanian leadership made it clear during 1972 that it had no intention of turning its back on the anti-Soviet "Marxist-Leninist" forces within the communist movement. The APL publicly (ibid., 13 February) rejected an invitation to send a delegation to the congress of the Italian Communist Party. In its response to the Italians, the APL argued that there existed an "indelible demarcation line" between the forces of "Marxism-Leninism" and "modern revisionism." To attend the congress, the Albanians claimed, would compromise their integrity. The APL's strong stand on this matter and its formulation of the doctrine that, "as it is impossible to rely on one imperialism to oppose another, it is just as impossible to rely on one group of revisionists to oppose another group" (ibid.) was probably intended to serve as a warning to the Chinese, who had begun to show an increasing interest in improving their relations with several "revisionist" European parties.

Albania continued to serve as a meeting ground for "Marxist-Leninist" and other "revolutionary" forces. Prince Norodom Sihanouk, head of the Cambodian Royal Government of National Union (headquartered in Peking) visited Albania on 22–28 June. At the conclusion of his stay, Sihanouk and his Albanian hosts issued a joint statement in which they pledged to work together to expel the "Lon Nol clique." (Tirana radio, 29 June.) The Albanian trade union congress in May attracted 39 foreign delegations, 12 more than attended the 1967 meeting. Only China, Romania, and North Vietnam among party-ruled states sent representatives (ibid., 12 May). The Labor Youth congress drew 27 foreign delegations, including four from party states—China, North Vietnam, Romania, and North Korea (ibid., 26 October).

Albania by the early 1970s had become the major propaganda center for the "Marxist-Leninist" movement. In 1972 Tirana radio broadcast a total of 479½ hours per week in 17 languages over powerful transmitters erected by the Chinese. In addition to its own programs, it relays several Chinese broadcasts into Europe, Africa, and the Middle East (*Christian Science Monitor*, 1 May). Tirana radio reputedly has a large audience in Eastern Europe, which the Albanians claim has caused the Soviet Union to jam their broadcasts into this region (*Zëri i Popullit*, 3 August).

In February the Albanians began to publish a new periodical, *Albania Today*. This bimonthly, in English, French, and Spanish editions, contains translations of materials from Albanian newspapers and periodicals that present the Albanian viewpoint on major issues confronting world communism.

Publications. The APL central organ is the daily newspaper *Zëri i Popullit,* with a claimed average circulation of 101,000. The party's monthly theoretical journal is *Rruga e Partisë*. Another major publication is *Bashkimi,* the daily organ of the DF (circulation 30,000). The Union of Albanian Labor Youth publishes *Zëri i Rinisë* twice weekly. All together, the country in 1972 had 22 newspapers (total circulation, some 39,000,000) and 43 journals (4,590,000). Television broadcasting was begun in November 1971, with a daily four-hour schedule.

Western Illinois University   Nicholas C. Pano

Bulgaria

The Bulgarian Communist Party (Bulgarska Komunisticheska Partiya; BCP), which assumed the name "BCP (Narrow Socialists)" in 1919, dates its origin from 1891 when the Bulgarian Social Democratic Party was formed. In 1903, a faction split off in a conflict over the "narrow" versus "broad" interpretation of Marxism. Since 1891 the party has also had the designations "Bulgarian Workers' Social Democratic Party," 1894–1903; "BWSDP (Narrow Socialists)," 1903–19; "BCP (Narrow Socialists)," 1919–38; "Workers' Party," 1938–44; and "Bulgarian Workers' Party (Communists)," 1944–48. The Workers' Party, formed in 1927 as a front for the BCP, was outlawed between 1934 and 1944. The BCP dates its "transition to Leninism and bolshevization" from the 1917 revolution in Russia.

A negligible organization of 1,923 members in 1912, the BCP became Bulgaria's second-largest party by 1920 as a result of the debacles the country had suffered in the Balkan wars and World War I. Under the regime of the largest party, the Bulgarian Agrarian People's Union (Bulgarski Zemedelski Naroden Suyuz), the BCP took the position that the Union represented the "rural bourgeoisie," and fought it as implacably as it did the urban parties. In the rightist coup d'état against the peasant government of June 1923, the BCP decided on a course of "neutrality" but was quickly reversed by the Comintern and ordered to stage an uprising in cooperation with the Union's left wing. The abortive insurrection of September 1923 resulted in decimation of BCP cadres throughout the country and flight of its leading functionaries (Vasil Kolarov, Georgi Dimitrov, et al.) to the Soviet Union. During the underground period it recovered some strength and by 1942, under Dimitrov's guidance from Moscow, it joined the left wing of the Agrarian Union, the "Broad" Socialists, and other groups in forming the so-called Fatherland Front (Otechestven Front; FF) coalition as a vehicle for seizing power. This occurred on 9 September 1944, mainly because of the Soviet declaration of war against Bulgaria only four days earlier and the arrival of the Red Army. The coalition began to break up almost immediately over BCP policies aimed at monopoly rule. By 1948 only one other party, a fragment of the Agrarian Union under leaders subservient to the BCP, still survived. Since then the FF has been retained by the BCP as an umbrella organization over the Agrarian Union (120,000 members), the Dimitrov Communist Youth Union (Dimitrovski Komunisticheski Mladezhki Suyuz, 1,161,000 members), the central body for the trade unions, and other mass organizations. Since 1954 the first secretary of the BCP has been Todor Zhivkov.

Membership and Composition. The most recent figures for the BCP's membership and composition date back to the party's Tenth Congress, in April 1971. According to the BCP's daily organ *Rabotnichesko Delo* (21 April), the party had 699,476 members—about 8 percent of the total population of Bulgaria. Of these, 40.1 percent were blue collar workers, 28.1 percent white collar workers, and 26.1 percent peasants.

Leadership Changes in 1972. Despite the fact that the Tenth Congress had taken place as recently as 1971, there were several important changes in the party leadership during 1972. Perhaps the most important was the release of Venelin Kotsev from his position as Central Committee secretary in July. Kotsev had been responsible for matters pertaining to ideology and culture and was generally considered a coming man in the Bulgarian hierarchy. He was made a deputy premier and, although he retained his candidate membership of the Politburo, the move was generally interpreted as a downgrading. In his new position he seems generally to have devoted himself to problems of trade and services. Kotsev's place as a Central Committee secretary was taken by Alexander Lilov (born 1933) who had been head of the Central Committee Arts and Culture Department since the spring of 1970. In February 1972 another Central Committee secretary had been appointed. This was Konstantin Tellalov, who since 1967 had headed the Central Committee's International Department. In July 1972 Tellalov replaced Ivan Abadzhiev as chairman of the Central Committee's Commission on International Relations and clearly emerged as the most active Bulgarian official in relations with other communist parties. (Abadzhiev's replacement by Tellalov did not, however, signify any demotion for him. He has continued to be one of the most prominent and active Bulgarian leaders.)

An important change took place at a level one lower than the Secretariat. In March, Krum Vasilev was replaced as head of the Central Committee Department for Agitation and Propaganda by Dimitar Dimitrov, who until then had been first secretary of the Smolyan district party committee. The change was necessitated by the appointment of Vasilev at the end of 1971 as chairman of the new Press Committee attached to the Council of Ministers.

A notable change in the Bulgarian government took place in December 1971. Foreign Minister Ivan Bashev was killed in a skiing accident near Sofia and was replaced by Petar Mladenov, a former Komsomol secretary and, since 1969, first secretary of the Vidin district party committee. At 35, Mladenov became the youngest foreign minister in Europe. Certain other changes took place in public life affecting party notables. Politburo member Boyan Balgaranov (died on 26 December) was replaced in April by the agrarian leader and former titular head of the state, Georgi Traykov, as chairman of the National Council of the Fatherland Front. Traykov's position as chairman of the National Assembly was taken by Vladimir Bonev, a member of the Central Committee Secretariat since 1966.

Main Party Activities. After the important events of 1971, related to the party congress, very little of note took place in 1972. Only three Central Committee plenums were held during the year. The first, in February, was devoted to trade union affairs. This was obviously the necessary prelude to the seventh national congress of Bulgarian trade unions, which took place in March. This congress had originally been scheduled for November 1971 but was obviously postponed to give time for the Central Committee to hold a plenum on trade union affairs first. Any serious expectations, however, that the congress might produce important changes in the government's workers' or social policy were disappointed. The congress turned out to be an uneventful reiteration of the trade unions' classic role as transmission belt, production agent, and paternalistic defender of the marginal interests of the workers. The second plenum, in July, dealt routinely with the work of the Politburo and Secretariat. (It was this plenum which approved and announced the replacement of Kotsev as Central Committee secretary by Lilov.) The third plenum was much more important. It took place at the beginning of December and dealt with the living standards of the population. A preliminary appraisal of the plenum documents revealed a comprehensively reformist approach to consumer problems and needs, with shorter- and longer-term plans for higher wages, better housing, and higher consumer investments. It was one of the most innovative proposals yet made in Bulgarian communist history and only the future would show how far the promises contained in it would be implemented.

Party Publicity and Propaganda. Two important anniversaries highlighted the BCP's propaganda celebrations during 1972. The first was the ninetieth anniversary of Georgi Dimitrov's birth in June. Important representatives from practically all the foreign communist parties gathered in Sofia for the celebration, and the party exploited the occasion to remind the younger generation of Bulgarians of the BCP's romantic and heroic past. The second anniversary—the fiftieth anniversary of the founding of the Soviet Union—took place at the very end of the year. Here the occasion was used to remind Bulgarians—yet again—of the firmness and the benefits of the Soviet alliance.

Throughout the year, the party's agitation and propaganda work mainly concentrated on two themes: the need for more effective and enthusiastic "socialist competition," and the ideological struggle against the West. This latter, as in other East European states, assumed the dimensions of a major campaign by the end of 1972. The reason for it were the brightening prospects for East-West détente in general and for the holding of a European security conference in particular. Bulgarian official media strongly opposed Western proposals for a freer flow of peoples, ideas, and information within the framework of a European security arrangement and constantly stressed that détente on the state level did not mean any lowering of the socialist countries' ideological guard.

Important Events and Developments in Public Life. Bulgarian economic development was characterized generally in 1972 by the efforts to fulfill the annual target laid down in the Five-Year Plan approved by the BCP's Tenth Congress in April 1971. No information was available by the end of the year on annual plan fulfillment. The quarterly results published, however, showed an overall fulfillment of the targets set down, although a major agitprop campaign was conducted in the last four months of 1972 and was aimed at overcoming the delay in completing certain large construction projects. A similar campaign was mounted because of serious delays in the gathering in of the harvest. In general, the 1972 harvest appears to have been very good, but the deficiencies in gathering it led to a tone of serious alarm in many of the public exhortations on the subject.

In agriculture, the massive reorganization of the farm units into agro-industrial complexes continued. This development, unique in East Europe, began as an experiment in early 1969. By 1970 it had passed the experimental stage, and agro-industrial complexes began to be introduced throughout the country. By April 1972 their number had risen to 170. Their average size was 24,000 hectares of arable land and their average personnel strength was 6,500 people, a size equivalent to that of some of the largest industrial enterprises in Bulgaria. In fact the motive behind this unique development was precisely to "industrialize" agriculture and this Bulgarian organizational example could be followed—at least in part—by other communist states, including the Soviet Union, in the future.

Two other congresses of important public organizations were held (in addition to the trade union congress in March—see above). The first was the Twelfth Congress of the Dimitrov Union of Communist Youth (Komsomol), held in late May. As with the trade union congress, this was a relatively uneventful gathering devoted mainly to organizational questions and to harnessing the youth for socialist work in the age of the scientific-technological revolution.

The party leadership's preoccupation, however, with the need for a more effective ideological preparation and orientation of the youth was evident throughout the congressional proceedings.

The other congress was that of the Bulgarian Writers' Union—its second—which took place in October. The importance of this congress was that it took place under the aegis of a completely new leadership, which had been elected at a meeting of the administrative council of the Union the previous June. George Dzhagarov, president of the Bulgarian Writers' Union since 1966, was replaced by Panteley Zarev and the Union's entire bureau—its leading body —was also changed. The election of a new leadership raised hopes among many Bulgarian writers that a period of cultural relaxation would be ushered in. By the time the Writers' Union congress took place in October it was, indeed, possible to detect a slight relaxation and the congress itself took place in such an atmosphere. Whether such a relaxation would further develop was the most important question for the Bulgarian cultural milieu at the end of 1972.

Foreign Affairs. The role played in Bulgarian foreign policy by the Soviet alliance continued as preponderant as ever in 1972, and Bulgaria's close relations with other East European communist parties were maintained and even enhanced. Bilateral as well as multilateral contacts—(through the Council for Mutual Economic Assistance and the Warsaw Pact) were intensified. All facets of communist inter-party and inter-state relations were covered.

In view of Romania's unique position and behavior within the Warsaw Pact alliance, Sofia's very close relations with Bucharest were particularly noteworthy. The highlights of these close bilateral relations were the unofficial visit of state president and party leader Zhivkov to Romania in August and a visit to Bulgaria in late September by Romanian leaders Ceauşescu, Maurer, and Verdeţ. The most important tangible outcome of these consultations was the agreement to build jointly a vast new hydroelectric project on the Danube—an undertaking which, when completed, will be roughly the Bulgarian-Romanian equivalent of the Romanian-Yugoslav "Iron Gates" project.

Perhaps of even more significance was the perceptible improvement of Bulgarian relations with Yugoslavia. This was obviously a by-product of the rapprochement between the Soviet Union and Yugoslavia which began with the Brezhnev visit to Belgrade in September 1971. The polemics between the two countries over the Macedonian issue virtually ceased in 1972 and both state and party contacts noticeably increased. The most important Bulgarian visitor to Yugoslavia was Central Committee secretary Ivan Abadzhiev, whose tour of the country in August–September included Macedonia. The most important Yugoslav visitor was Iganc Golob, head of his party's International Relations Department, who conferred with Bulgarian officials in Sofia in May. There was even considerable speculation about a possible Zhivkov-Tito "summit" meeting, but this had not materialized by the end of the year.

Bulgaria also stepped up its contacts with a number of non-communist states. In the Balkans, relations with the military government in Athens proceeded briskly and in November the first session of the mixed Greek-Bulgarian economic cooperation commission took place in Sofia. A jarring note crept into Bulgarian-Turkish relations caused by two hijackings of Turkish planes to Sofia in May and October which led to rather acrimonious exchanges between the two governments. But a visit to Ankara by Foreign Minister Mladenov in November appeared to restore the previous cordiality.

More novel was the improvement in relations with the Federal Republic of Germany. The ratification of West Germany's treaties with Poland and the Soviet Union, the subsequent establishment of diplomatic relations between Warsaw and Bonn, the *Grundvertrag* between West and East Germany, the socialist-liberal triumph in the West German elections, the ambassadorial meetings on European security in Helsinki, and, above all, the obvious Soviet wish for improved relations with Bonn—all these factors steadily and progressively removed the impediments to better relations between the two countries. By the end of the year, the only remaining obstacle to the establishment of diplomatic relations between Sofia and Bonn was the need for a normalization of relations between the Federal Republic and Czechoslovakia. But since, through Soviet pressure, the Czechoslovak government had obviously begun to revise its previous stand on the 1938 Munich agreement, it now seemed only a matter of time before this apparently final obstacle was removed.

Even with the United States, Bulgaria's relations showed signs of improvement—another consequence of the evolution of Soviet foreign policy. In September, Foreign Minister Mladenov, in New York to attend the annual session of the U.N. General Assembly, had a conversation with U.S. Secretary of State Rogers and it was reported from Washington that a Bulgarian delegation would visit the American capital in 1973 headed by a deputy premier.

International Party Contacts. Besides those already noted, important contacts in 1972 included the following. In May, Fidel Castro visited Bulgaria during his tour of Eastern Europe and the Soviet Union. Polish party leader Edward Gierek headed a party-government delegation to Bulgaria (he also spent a vacation there in August.)

In February, Todor Zhivkov made an unofficial visit to Poland. During March, Abadzhiev headed a party group to the congress of the Italian Communist Party, Zhivkov led a party-government delegation to Czechoslovakia, and Kotsev took several ideological officials to Moscow. Kotsev also headed a party delegation that visited East Germany in May; Boris Velchev another one to Denmark and Norway. Zhivkov made unofficial visits, as head of a party-government delegation, to the Ukraine and Moldavia in June and appeared at the Warsaw Pact "summit" in the Crimea during July. Velchev led the party delegation that visited Italy in October. Zhivkov was in Moscow in November with a party-government group on an official visit and in December as head of the official delegation to the fiftieth anniversary of the Soviet Union.

Publications. The daily *Rabotnichesko Delo* (Workers' Cause) is the central organ of the BCP. The Central Committee publishes also *Novo Vreme* (New Times), a theoretical monthly, and *Partien Zhivot* (Party Life), a monthly journal on internal party matters. More specialized nationwide publications are *Politicheska Prosveta* (Political Education) and *Ikonomicheski Zhivot* (Economic Life), biweeklies of the Central Committee, and the youth publications *Narodna Mladezh* (People's Youth) and *Mladezh* (Youth), organs of the DCYU.

Radio Free Europe   James F. Brown
Munich, Germany

Czechoslovakia

Like most European communist parties, the Communist Party of Czechoslovakia (Komunistická strana Ceskoslovenska; KSČ) originated from the split which had occurred in the socialist movement under the impact of the October 1917 revolution in Russia. Initially a dissident wing of the Social Democratic Party, it was formed as an independent organization at a constituent congress in Prague, in November 1921. In contrast to other "people's democracies," in Czechoslovakia communist rule was imposed by a coup d'état in February 1948, which put a sudden end to a pluralist parliamentary system. Since then the communist party has maintained a monopoly of political power. The constitution of the Czechoslovak Socialist Republic of 1960 explicitly recognizes the leading role of the KSČ. The mechanism by which the party exercises its rule is the National Front of Working People, a formalized coalition of political parties and mass organizations, where the KSČ commands absolute majority. President Ludvik Svoboda and Premier Lubomír Štrougal are both members of the communist party.

A constitutional amendment, adopted in October 1968, part of a more ambitious but never implemented political reform, transformed Czechoslovakia into a federation of two ethnic units: the Czech Socialist Republic and the Slovak Socialist Republic. This change, however, was inconsistent: the organizational structure of the communist party does not correspond to the federal type of the Czechoslovak state. Although there is a separate party unit in Slovakia—the Communist Party of Slovakia (Komunistická strana Slovenska; KSS)—there is no parallel organization in the Czech Socialist Republic. The attempt to set up a special party component in the Czech provinces, started in 1968, never passed the stage of a provisional coordination bureau and was eventually abandoned in 1971. The paradox of the Czechoslovak political order is that a polity, federal in form, is ruled by a communist party, centralist both in fact and in form.

Party Organization. The top governing organs of the KSČ are the Central Committee and the Presidium. The latest party congress, held in Prague in May 1971, was by official count the fourteenth because the leadership does not recognize the congress convened in August 1968 which condemned the occupation of Czechoslovakia by the troops of five Warsaw Pact countries. The next congress is due in 1976.

Leadership. The composition of the main party organs has not changed since the 1971 congress, which had been preceded by a vast purge both of the party apparatus and of the rank-and-file membership. The present leadership imposed by the pressure of the Soviet occupying power in April 1969 is committed to the policies of the so-called "normalization," which in principle means the return to the centralist and Soviet-obedient line of the era before the "Prague Spring" of 1968. The Presidium consists of 11 full members and 2 candidates.

The Secretariat is led by the KSČ secretary-general, Gustav Husák, and consists of 7 secretaries and 2 members. The first secretary of the KSS is Jozef Lenárt. For names of other officials see *YICA, 1972*, p. 21.

Membership. Not many details on the size of the new enrollment and on membership turnover were made public during 1972. It can be assumed, however, that the total of some 1,200,000 members to which the effectives were reduced after the great purge of 1970 has not changed radically. In 1971, for example, only about 25,000 applicants were admitted, according to official sources (*Život strany*, 7 February). On the other hand, the class background and the age of the membership were matters of serious concern for the party leaders. The Fourteenth Congress advised the top officials to reinforce the blue-collar element, now constituting barely a fourth of the effectives. It was disclosed that among the newly recruited adherents about 55 percent were workers by profession, but it was admitted, at the same time, that this was still very far from the desired improvement in the party structure (ibid., 12 June). Despite an extensive purge and very selective recruitment, the Czechoslovak party remains among the largest communist parties in the world, measured per capita, with 8.4 percent of the total populace carrying membership cards (Czechoslovakia had 14,467,000 inhabitants at the 1970 census). The mass character of the party inhibits the application of the criteria of "political awareness" and "ideological reliability" which have been repeatedly stressed as important in cadre work by the Central Committee and the Presidium and which mean chiefly unqualified loyalty to the Soviet Union and to the present Soviet-supported leadership (*Tribuna*, 1 March).

Domestic Affairs. Among the internal Czechoslovak events in 1972, followed with great attention both at home and abroad, was a wave of trials of "subversive elements." These trials concerned, without exception, persons associated in one way or another with the reform movement of the "Prague Spring" of 1968: journalists, artists, educators, sportsmen, and scientists. About 50 were given stiff jail sentences. The trials aroused very lively reaction everywhere, partly because they were seen as contradicting the pledge given by Secretary-General Husák that no one would be prosecuted for "actions or opinions held in 1968" (Prague radio, 17 February). Formally, this appears to be the case, as no defendant in the trials was accused explicitly of any such action or opinion; instead, "subversive activities" engaged in after the invasion, such as distribution of tracts and leaflets hostile to the leadership, or contacts with émigrés in the West, were charged. However, most observers viewed the trials as an attempt on the part of the present rulers to intimidate the population not reconciled, four years after the event, to the Soviet-led invasion and its consequences. Another indicator of the lack of self-confidence on the part of the leadership could be seen in the resumption of the anti-religious campaign and various restrictive measures against churches, particularly against the Catholics (*Nová mysl*, no. 4). The Catholic-inspired People's Party, one of the KSČ's partners in the National Front, held its national congress in June. The "normalization" was endorsed without reservations at this congress. Earlier in the year, the People's Socialist Party had its national conference, with a similar result (*Svobodné slovo*, 15 January).

Mass Organizations. The trade unions, more than any other mass organization, were in the center of the attention of the party during 1972. The leadership was anxious to see the last vestiges of the will for independence, awakened in 1968, eliminated from the ranks of the unions. Their organization was to return to its role of "transmission belt" for the party, serving the increase of work productivity and a better fulfilment of planned targets rather than the interests of the workers. It was in this spirit that the Czech and Slovak congresses of trade unions were held (*Práce,* 12 May; Bratislava radio, 18 May). The national congress of the federal body, the Revolutionary Trade Union Movement, held in Prague the following month, confirmed the party line and elected individuals unreservedly committed to this line to leading positions (Radio Hvězda, 15 June). Another mass organization which held a national congress during 1972 was the Union of Czechoslovak Agricultural Cooperatives (kolkhozy). This congress, its eighth, met in Prague in April. The prevailing climate was radically different from the February 1968 congress which became the first mass platform of the reform movement, after the suspension of the censorship. The 1972 congress was a well-prepared, party-steered event which adopted, without opposition, current policies in agriculture. At this meeting, the party representatives made public their intention to collectivize the remaining 9 percent of arable land in private hands and to restrict the holdings of private plots in the cooperatives (*Rudé právo,* 29 April).

Culture, Education, and Youth. The tense relationship between the party leadership and the intellectual and cultural elite continued all through 1972. The mistrust manifested towards these circles by the party dates from the period of the experiment with "socialism with a human face" of 1968. In spite of harsh measures taken in the cultural domain by Husák and his associates the resistance seems to continue. In 1972, dramatic art appeared to be in the first line of fire. The authorities intervened several times to prevent performance of dramatic works which were not in agreement with the official, Soviet-sponsored course (*Rudé právo,* 16 February; Prague radio, 2 March). Later in the year, a new Czech Union of Dramatic Artists was constituted which is meant to become an instrument of more efficient political control (*Rudé právo,* 3 October). The Ministry of Culture also initiated an action the purpose of which was to stop or to limit publication of literary works by Czech and Slovak artists in the West by withholding or confiscating the royalty payments (*Neue Zürcher Zeitung,* 4 June). The programs of the Czechoslovak publishing houses were further "streamlined" politically (*Tvorba,* 5 April). Education continued to be exposed to ideological pressures. Regulations for admission to the universities stressed the class background of applicants as one of the most important criteria (Prague radio, 13 March). In this atmosphere, the First Congress of the only youth and children's organization, the Czechoslovak Socialist Youth Union, took place in Prague in September. Apart from the expected demonstration of adherence to the present party line, the officials of the organization had to admit that a large percentage of the membership had taken a "passive attitude." The newly elected functionaries appear all to be docile instruments of the party leadership. (*Mladá fronta,* 2 October.)

Armed Forces. In 1972 Czechoslovakia was the site of two important events in the history of the Warsaw Pact. In January a summit meeting of foreign ministers of pact countries was held in Prague. The meeting approved all basic principles of present Soviet military and foreign policies and expressed the readiness of the pact members to negotiate arms reduction with the representatives of NATO (*Rudé právo,* 27 January). On 12–15 September large military maneuvers were carried out in Czechoslovakia, engaging some 100,000 troops of four Warsaw Pact nations. Considering that the theme of the maneuvers—labeled "Shield '72"— was a mock attack on Czechoslovakia by a simulated enemy force coming from the west and southwest (i.e., from the Federal Republic of Germany and Austria), and that the operation ended in wiping out the strongholds of the alleged enemy on the border of West Germany, the political meaning was unmistakable. The conclusion of the maneuvers by a large military parade in Prague on the Letná plain, not far from the location of the Stalin monument, demolished in 1962, supported this interpretation. The population of Czechoslovakia was obviously to be shown from what danger their country was saved by the 1968 military intervention. Significantly, as in 1968, Romanian units did not participate in the exercises. Prior to the maneuvers, no less than 3,000 meetings between the troops and Czechoslovak citizens were organized in different parts of the country, for the obvious purpose of bringing home the political message (Prague radio, 12 September).

Economy. By official figures, the economic progress of Czechoslovakia in 1972 was, on the whole, satisfactory. The overall increase in industrial production during the first half of the year was 7.3 percent as compared to the same period of the previous year. The performance, however, appears to be rather uneven. The high priority projects, such as the construction of the natural gas pipeline from the Soviet Union, with branches to East Germany, West Germany, and Austria, were completed on time, or sooner, while other sectors, for example the building industry, lagged seriously behind the plan. The average productivity of labor rose by 6.6 percent, which was 2.1 percent more than the plan had foreseen. Czechoslovak agriculture achieved only a moderate output, partly due to weather conditions. Shortages were felt particularly in dairy production, where they had to be offset by imports from hard currency areas. Exports to countries with free convertible currencies rose only by 2.1 percent, which was in accordance with the policy of expanding foreign trade chiefly with the CMEA nations; exports to the latter were increased by 11.2 percent. The percapita cash income grew by 5.8 percent and the average nominal wages in the industry reached 2,040 crowns per month. Retail trade turnover increased by 5.7 percent while the retail price level dropped by 0.7 percent, as a result of price reductions introduced in 1971, and the index of living costs for an industrial worker was reduced by 7.0 percent. (*Svět hospodářství*, 25 July).

The Czechoslovak economy seems to face several serious problems, among which the difficulty in implementing decentralization of management and planning—an inconsistent remnant of a far more systematic economic reform from the pre-invasion period—appears to loom large (*Hospodářské noviny*, 30 June). The shortage of labor in certain key sectors is another problem; it could be only partly solved by importing unskilled workers from Poland and Yugoslavia (Belgrade radio, 9 October). The labor shortage also appears to favor what the Czechoslovak media call "the abuse of overtime"—that is, frequent recourse to overtime work to catch up with the production targets (*Tribuna*, 7 June). An even more acute ill is seen in the alarmingly large absenteeism. Every worker in Czechoslovakia is reported sick at least once a year, and an average absence from the workplace due to an illness is 15 days. Stricter control of the labor force was demanded by the press on many occasions (*Večerník*, 22 September.)

Foreign Affairs. In matters of foreign relations, the continuing negotiations with the Federal Republic of Germany on establishing full diplomatic relations, were among the priority topics. However, 1972 could not, any more than the previous year, bring a successful conclusion of the talks, despite visible improvement of the general political situation in Central and Eastern Europe. The dealings appeared to be deadlocked because of the insistence of the Czechoslovak negotiators that the 1938 Munich treaty be declared invalid *ab initio* by the West Germans (*Rudé právo*, 1 November). For the rest, foreign policies of the present party leadership followed the line adopted by the Soviet Union, favoring an early convening of an European security conference, strategic arms limitations, and giving a positive reception to the U.S. initiative in Moscow (ibid., 31 May). Israel, on the other hand, remained a target of bitter attacks by Czechoslovak mass information media. The campaign linked Israel with the alleged attempt at "counterrevolution" in Czechoslovakia in 1968, and often used arguments closely similar to anti-Semitic propaganda of worst kind (*Tribuna*, 24 May).

International Communist Movement. The controversy stirred among the communist parties of the world by the Soviet-led intervention in Czechoslovakia in 1968 did not quiet down even in 1972, four years after the event. On several occasions the two most important West European communist parties, the French and the Italian, felt compelled to reiterate their negative position on the Soviet action. As a consequence, the relations of the Czechoslovak party with these and other similarly oriented "fraternal" parties suffered serious strain. The party leadership showed its displeasure by sending only a second-rate delegation to the congress of the Italian Communist Party (Prague radio, 12 March). The conflict was exacerbated by the wave of arrests and political trials in Czechoslovakia later in the year. When, in addition to the condemnatory declarations of the French and Italian parties, Dutch, Norwegian, British, and Australian communists declared the trials to be examples of political justice, the KSČ described their criticism as "anti-Sovietism" and "hostile propaganda" (*Rudé právo*, 30 August). However, consistent with the tactics previously adopted in this matter, Czechoslovak officials kept their reactions to an absolute minimum. Unwilling to let the "Czechoslovak question" continue to be an issue at dispute in the international communist movement, they were at great pains to show tolerance and neutrality concerning internal affairs of the "fraternal" parties. It was for this reason that a Presidium member and Central Committee secretary publicly denied having ever criticized officials of the Polish, East German, Hungarian, or other parties; he was referring to reports which had appeared during late 1971 in the Western press (ibid., 20 April). This neutrality, however, was only qualified. In relation to the People's Republic of China, for example, Czechoslovak media took a position which was identical with the Soviet line and condemned the rapprochement with the United States as a concerted U.S.-Chinese attempt to "disrupt the unity of the Socialist community of nations" (ibid., 7 February). Concerning Yugoslavia, economic cooperation was promoted, but political and ideological reservations remained as strong as ever (*Tvorba*, 5 January; Zagreb radio, 17 January). Relations with the Communist Party of Cuba, on the other hand, which had considerably cooled off during the "Prague Spring," were greatly favored. Presidium member and KSS first secretary Jozef Lenárt visited Havana at the head of a party delegation in January. The party leadership stood up to its commitment to aid North Vietnam. In January, an economic delegation headed by the federal deputy premier traveled to Hanoi to conclude two new economic agreements (*Rudé právo*, 17 January). "Full understanding in a spirit of unwavering fraternal relations" was proclaimed between the KSČ and the Communist Party of Bulgaria during the visit of the latter's first secretary Todor Zivkov to Prague (CTK, Czechoslovak press agency, 17 March). Similar unity of views on all important political problems was stated at the occasion of the visit of a Czechoslovak party and governmental delegation, led by Gustav Husák, to the German Democratic Republic (*Rudé právo*, 25 September). Husák also participated in a conference of the party heads of the CMEA countries in the Crimea in July. This meeting, according to official comments, provided an opportunity to work out collectively the strategy and the tactics of the international communist movement. Among the specific questions on the agenda was also "further development of cooperation among socialist countries" (*Rudé právo*, 3 August). An authoritative interpretation to this point which, at the same time, shed some light on the Soviet perceptions of Czechoslovak-Soviet relations, appeared in the Czechoslovak press some six weeks later in the form of an article by the counselor of the Soviet embassy in Prague. According to the article, the cooperation among communist nations should aim at the integration of the economic systems of the smaller CMEA countries with the economy of the Soviet Union, much in the terms of the theory of the "international socialist division of labor" promoted by Nikita Khrushchev at the beginning of the sixties. The article seemed to indicate that a still closer intertwining of the Czechoslovak and Soviet economies is the goal of the Soviets, with the resulting possible reinforcement of the political ties, which could prevent repetition of the 1968 experience, so traumatic for the Soviet partner (*Svoboda*, 13 September).

Publications. The central organ of the KSČ is the daily *Rudé právo*, published in Prague. The official daily of the KSS *Pravda* (Bratislava). There is no special press organ addressed to members in the Czech provinces. The semiofficial theoretical party weekly is *Tribuna;* its Slovak counterpart is *Predvoj.* In the time before World War II, the weekly *Tvorba* was taking the place of today's *Tribuna;* at present, it is oriented chiefly to matters of international politics. The fortnightly *Život strany* brings news and disseminates information about the organizational life of the party. The Revolutionary Trade Union Movement has a Czech daily, *Práce,* in Prague and a Slovak version, *Práca,* in Bratislava. The Union of the Czechoslovak Agricultural Cooperatives publishes the daily *Zemědělské noviny;* with a Slovak counterpart *Rol'nícke noviny.* The Czechoslovak Socialist Youth Union sponsors the daily *Mladá fronta* in Prague and *Smena* in Bratislava.

University of Pittsburgh   Zdenek L. Suda

Germany: German Democratic Republic

The Socialist Unity Party of Germany (Sozialistische Einheitspartei Deutschlands; SED) was founded on 21 April 1946, in the Soviet-occupied zone of East Germany. By order of Soviet authorities the Communist Party of Germany (KPD) and the Social Democratic Party of Germany (SPD) were merged, or, more correctly, the SPD elements (who were in the majority) were ordered to subordinate themselves to a "unity" party. By now, the distinction between former KPD and SPD members within the party has become virtually meaningless. The Soviet zone was formally instituted as the German Democratic Republic (GDR) in October 1949. The SED is linked to its offspring, the Socialist Unity Party of West Berlin (SEW), and to the German Communist Party (DKP) in the Federal Republic of Germany (FRG). It claims authority over the entire Moscow-oriented communist movement in all of Germany.

The SED has more than 1.9 million members. Of those, 56.8 percent are blue-collar workers and 76.5 percent are of proletarian stock; more than 29 percent are women (*WMR,* November 1972, p. 88).

Four additional parties are allowed to operate in the GDR, and together with the SED they form the "National Front": the Christian Democratic Union of Germany (CDU); the National Democratic Party of Germany (NDPD); the Liberal Democratic Party of Germany (LDPD); and the Democratic Peasant Party of Germany (DBD). These organizations send representatives into the GDR's unicameral legislature—the Volkskammer, or People's Chamber—but lack effective power. For the most part, they are controlled by communist sympathizers. Their activity is by permission only. They serve as "transmission belts" from the SED to the non-communist elements of the population, facilitate control over the opposition, and are occasionally used for contacts with "parallel" parties in the FRG. They also may be regarded as one of the tools which would be available to facilitate reunification of Germany under the aegis of the SED-GDR.

Party and Government. *The SED Leadership.* The Politburo elected by the SED's Eighth Congress (15–19 June 1971) was still in office at the end of 1972. The 16 full members are Hermann Axen, Friedrich Ebert, Gerhard Grüneberg, Kurt Hager, Erich Honecker, Werner Krolikowski, Werner Lamberz, Günter Mittag, Erich Mückenberger, Alfred Neumann, Albert Norden, Horst Sindermann, Willi Stoph, Walter Ulbricht, Paul Verner, and Herbert Warnke. The 7 candidate members are Georg Ewald, Walter Halbritter, Werner Jarowinsky, Günter Kleiber, Erich Mielke, Margarete Müller, and Harry Tisch.

Full members Axen, Grüneberg, Hager, Lamberz, Mittag, Norden, and Verner and candidate member Jarowinsky comprise the Secretariat, together with Horst Dohlus, who is styled "member of the Secretariat."

The Politburo and Secretariat are organs of and are elected by the Central Committee. In reality, the Central Committee apparatus serves as a staff for the two directing organs. The Eighth SED Congress in June 1971 elected 135 full members and 54 candidates to the Central Committee.

Erich Honecker is first secretary and the most powerful person in the party and state. Former first secretary, Walter Ulbricht, is chairman of the State Council, with Ebert and Stoph serving as deputy chairmen. Stoph, as chairman of the Council of Ministers is the GDR premier, with Sindermann and Neumann both as first deputy premiers (see below).

Mückenberger is chairman of the Central Party Control Commission. Warnke heads the Free German Trade Union Federation (FDGB). Ewald is in charge of agriculture and agricultural industry; Halbritter manages prices; Kleiber, a computer expert, is a deputy premier; Mielke has been minister of state security since 1957.

The Volkskammer and the State Council. Gerald Götting of the CDU is the president of the 500-member Volkskammer. Ebert is the first deputy and leader of the SED segment. At present 127 seats are allotted to the SED and 52 each to the four other parties. The FDGB (membership estimated at 7 million) holds 68 seats; the Free German Youth (FDJ) 40; the Democratic League of Women (DFB) 35; and the German Union of Culture (Deutscher Kulturbund) 22.

Although reportedly "elected" by 99.85 percent of the voters, the Volkskammer is not a democratic legislature, since it is not constructed to represent the popular will as composed by individual votes. The SED incorporated into the legislature its concept of social groups to be represented (by party members or sympathizers) and the proportion to be alloted each. The practice of voting unanimously was broken for the first time in March 1972, when a few abstentions and a handful of negative votes were registered on a bill for abortion; but party permission had been granted beforehand.

The State Council, which has 24 members plus one secretary, handles Volkskammer business when that body is not in session. It was modeled after the USSR's Central Executive Committee of the Supreme Soviet. As noted earlier, it is headed by former SED first secretary Ulbricht as chairman, with Ebert and Stoph as deputies—apparently representing the "socialist" and "communist" wings of the SED, and each of the four other parties providing a deputy chairman. Other representation includes the National Front, municipalities, and professions. (For details on governmental organization see R. F. Staar, *The Communist Regimes in Eastern Europe,* 2d ed., Hoover Institution Press, 1971, pp. 86–90.)

Key Positions. Several SED officials, most of whom hold membership in the Central Committee but have not yet been promoted to the Politburo or Secretariat, are close to First Secretary Honecker and have been entrusted with significant responsibilities. Wolfgang Rauchfuss, an expert in foreign trade and deputy premier was acting premier during Stoph's illness early in 1972. Gerhard Schürer, chairman of the State Planning Commission and deputy premier, is concerned with long-range planning of U.S.S.R.-GDR economic relations. Klaus Steinitz of the same commission works on preliminary economic plans for the 1976–90 period. Margot Honecker, wife of the first secretary, is minister for public education; she visited North Vietnam in December 1971 and maintains contacts with foreign parties. Hans Modrow directs the propaganda department of the Central Committee.

Security affairs are in the hands of Colonel General Erich Mielke, a Politburo candidate member; Colonel General Herbert Scheide, former chief of the air force and head of the Central Committee's security department; and Colonel General Friedrich Dickel, minister of the interior. Manfred Feist candidate member of the Central Committee and Honecker's brother-in-law, is in charge of foreign intelligence for the party.

Army General Heinz Hoffmann is minister of national defense; Colonel General Heinz

Kessler and Admiral Waldemar Verner act as deputy ministers. Verner is also a head of the Main Political Administration of the armed forces and comments on strategic questions.

Foreign policy is entrusted to Otto Winzer, minister of foreign affairs. Winzer, who is 70, is assisted by four deputy foreign ministers: Oskar Fischer, Ewald Moldt, Ernst Scholz, and Georg Stibi. However, there is reason to believe that foreign policy is largely in the hands of Secretary of State Peter Florin, who is also a member of the Central Committee and the Volkskammer.

The Central Committee's department of international relations is directed by Paul Markowsky, with Harry Ott serving as his deputy. Michael Kohl, secretary of state in the Council of Ministers, was the main negotiator with the FRG.

The Soviet Presence. The USSR evinces great interest in the GDR. As CPSU Politburo member A. N. Shelepin pointed out (*Trud,* 29 June) the GDR is inhabited by only 0.5 percent of the world's population but ranks among the ten most developed industrial countries. (According to U.S. estimates, the GDR ranks about fourteenth.) The U.S.S.R. and the GDR are close economic partners. The strategic significance of the GDR for Soviet power is enormous, regardless of whether the U.S.S.R. pursues an offensive or a defensive strategy. Moscow probably regards the GDR as its single most important satellite or ally. Certainly the Soviet presence there is very noticeable. Soviet armed forces in the country, commanded by Colonel General E. F. Ivanovskiy, include an estimated 20 divisions (of which ten are armored), supplementing the GDR's 2 armored and 4 motorized rifle divisions.

Party Internal Affairs. *The Ulbricht Succession.* For a quarter of a century, Walter Ulbricht was the dominant figure in East Germany. For many years he had been grooming Erich Honecker as his successor. In April 1971 he resigned as first secretary and thereby facilitated the transition. Advanced age was given as an explanation, and Ulbricht (b. 1893) was weakening physically and mentally, but also he had been somewhat at odds with the Soviet policy of normalizing the situation in Berlin and improving Soviet-GDR-Polish relations with the FRG.

There is little doubt that the Kremlin prepared the change in the course of the Twenty-fourth Congress (30 March–9 April 1971) of the Communist Party of the Soviet Union (CPSU), which was attended by Ulbricht, Honecker, Stoph, Axen, and Verner, with the CPSU and the SED reaching consensus on the matter around 3 April. Officially, however, the decision was made by the 16th Plenum of the SED Central Committee, and was announced on 3 May. On 24 June Ulbricht turned over the chairmanship of the National Defense Council to Honecker. Soon thereafter, the negotiations with the FRG for a treaty, which had been stalled, began to gather momentum.

It is presumably a mistake to assume that Honecker's views differ materially from Ulbricht's or that Honecker in any manner can be regarded as a "revisionist," let alone as a person who wants a live-and-let-live understanding with the FRG. Ulbricht's policies still are in force. Honecker is simply a more alert and flexible practitioner than his predecessor, and has a better grasp of current realities and opportunities.

Throughout 1972 Honecker's allegiance to the Kremlin was letter perfect and his convictions about the necessity for the GDR alliance with the U.S.S.R. remained utterly firm. Like Ulbricht, Honecker is a Soviet-trained strategist; before his ascension to the "summit" he was for a long time the SED secretary in charge of security and military affairs. Furthermore, Honecker is experienced in working together with Soviet authorities. Initially an admirer of Stalin, he studied during 1955–56 in Moscow and thus became familiar with the reasons for de-Stalinization. Ulbricht never was comfortable with this policy. It should be added that after the war Honecker rebuilt and ran the communist youth organization (FDJ). (See Heinz Lippmann, *Honecker, Porträt eines Nachfolgers,* Cologne, 1971.)

Honecker is believed to be a poor administrator, though as Ulbricht's close collaborator he learned to be an accomplished bureaucratic in-fighter and manipulator. He enjoys strong Kremlin support, but his power base within the SED is not yet completely secure. Besides, Ulbricht's power was not completely broken when he ceased performing as first secretary and became SED chairman, a position of honor especially created for him; he also retained, and on 26 November 1971 was reelected to, the chairmanship of the State Council. Thus, he remains the GDR's titular head of state. Till October, he probably retained an effective veto power over party and government policies (see below).

Honecker's Actions. During the Eighth Congress (15–19 June 1971), Honecker moved with deliberate caution and limited himself to minimal changes. Krolikowski, first secretary of the Dresden district and thus one of the 15 regional party bosses, moved into the Politburo. Lamberz, a propaganda expert, was promoted from candidate to full membership. Mielke was promoted to Politburo candidate, as was Harry Tisch, first secretary of the Rostock district, who may be groomed as successor to the aging Warnke as boss of the FDGB. In addition, about half of the newly selected Central Committee candidates and close to half of the full members are deemed to be Honecker men. (See Fred Oldenburg, *Konflikt und Konfliktregelung in der Parteiführung der SED 1945/46–1972,* Cologne, Bundesinstitut für Ostwissenschaftliche und Internationale Studien, 1972, chap. 7.)

Naturally, Honecker had been exerting influence on personnel selection for years, but several Politburo members do not seem enamored with the new leader. For example, it is not believed that Premier Stoph is in his camp, but Stoph may be ailing and may become Ulbricht's successor in the State Council.

In 1971 Sindermann was appointed first deputy premier despite the fact that there already was a first deputy premier and only one such post was provided for; yet he is not regarded as a Honecker adherent. Indications are that during 1972 Honecker was preparing Rauchfuss to take over as premier. Significantly, Sindermann is a political-ideological specialist, while Rauchfuss is an expert in foreign trade.

While most of the candidate members are his followers, Honecker seems to have less than half of the full Politburo membership firmly on his side. But at least three members are over 70 (Ulbricht, Ebert, Warnke) and Norden (68) has little power. The main Politburo event during 1972 was, therefore, the fact that Honecker did not see fit to move more of his men into the top policy-making body. Since his position in the Secretariat appears to be comfortable, and since he exercises effective control over the security apparatus, and furthermore enjoys good relations with the military, he was not lacking in power and authority.

But the new first secretary did find it necessary to reduce the residual influence of his predecessor. As it was inadvisable to demote Ulbricht formally, the authority and prerogatives of the State Council were diminished. A law of 16 October, signed by Ulbricht himself, transferred most of the Council's executive responsibilities to the Council of Ministers which, as a result, became the sole GDR government or action agency under Politburo direction. In particular, the Council of Ministers assumed duties in foreign policy and henceforth will represent the GDR under international law. The Council of Ministers also was charged with implementing GDR foreign policy on the basis of SED decisions—specifically to contribute to the political, economic, ideological, and military strengthening of the community of socialist states, to enhance the alliance with the U.S.S.R. and other bloc countries, and to pursue coexistence with non-socialist states. (The law appears in FBIS, 2 November, pp. 22–28.)

The law also appears to have done away with the position of first deputy premier. If so, Neumann and Sindermann are now only deputies to the premier, except that they are members of the Politburo, whereas the other ten deputies are not.

The precise long-term meaning of this law cannot be elucidated at this time. It is possible that the decree will be amended or rescinded after Ulbricht's departure; but it is equally possible that the State Council will remain an ornament.

At any rate, by the end of 1972, Honecker had made considerable progress in consolidating his position as SED leader. This consolidation of personal power was in part based on accomplishment. The agreements on West Berlin, the new arrangements with the FRG, and the improved GDR international position were in no small measure due to Honecker's policy. Moreover, the economic situation of the GDR was improving; and while the U.S.S.R. suffered from a disastrous harvest, the East German harvest turned out to be excellent.

Domestic Affairs. *Nationalization.* In line with the continuing emphasis on "class struggle," Honecker urged nationalization of the remnants of private enterprise (*NYT,* 23 February). This suggestion was taken up by spokesmen of the other parties and the last capitalists "volunteered" to sell to the government. It was announced by the official East German news agency (ADN, 7 July) that the last 16.1 percent of the enterprises had been nationalized and only 0.6 percent still remained in private hands. The private and semi-private sector which was concentrated in the fields of light industry and housing accounted for 5.7 percent of the GNP, some 8.7 percent of the enterprises, and 10–11 percent of gross industrial production. There were about 9,000 semi-private and 3,000 small private firms, but figures vary (See FBIS, 2 August, p. E 4, citing *Pravda,* 25 July). The differences suggest that in actual fact probably two-thirds of the semi-private firms were fully nationalized.

Whatever the exact figures, the so-called private firms had been under control of the bureaucracy anyway. The main effect of the change was that the erstwhile owners—most of whom were retained as "managers"—were put on a salary. From an economic point of view, the operation meant that the former owners lost half or more of their incomes and that the export trade was rendered more difficult.

Agro-industry. In connection with the drive against residual capitalism, Honecker is intent on advancing socialism in agriculture. The GDR has reached a very high level of collectivization, but this particular accomplishment has not resulted in any of the miracles which were promised. Paralleling the trend in the U.S.S.R., the main effort is to transform collectivized peasants into wage earners. It is hoped that this will change peasant mentality.

More important is the program to introduce advanced industrial methods into agriculture and to interrelate agricultural production with the industrial processing of agricultural products. Collectives are to enhance their specialization and restrict themselves increasingly to the output of only one or a few commodities. In addition, "multiple cooperative relationships" are to link farms with technical support, maintenance, supply, and storage units, processing facilities, trade societies, and construction agencies. For example, milk farms would be related to plants manufacturing milk products and to shops selling milk. The scheme could be enlarged to include transport, road building, and irrigation.

Such vertical integration is expected to achieve a "concentration of the means of production." There remain, however, technical, economic, and organizational uncertainties of the undertaking because most collective farms still are below optimal size and would need additional equipment to advance specialization. The program calls for amalgamation of units, but shortages of capital are precluding rapid progress.

GDR agriculture is characterized by a comparatively high consumption of chemical fertilizers. Yet yields still are substantially below those in the FRG. To increase output, a shift toward production and use of compound fertilizers has been put in motion. Within the bloc, the GDR is apparently taking the lead in this new technology. The SED's agricultural policies may not lead to dramatic successes—it is too early to judge. But they are interesting in that new approaches are being tried out within the Stalinist framework of collective farming.

Social Policy and Economy. Honecker recognized that the housing situation has provoked numerous complaints. He announced a program of low-rent housing construction and has employed the military to carry out urgent repair work. The prospects of this program are doubtful. Rents already are so low that the cost of public housing must be covered from taxes. Payments of many tenants are in arrears, and the government, which pursues a cautious financial policy, lacks the capital to step up building activity to a meaningful level. Hence most of the effort will be on repair rather than construction. Nevertheless, Honecker's concern with the housing problem is politically astute.

Steady increases in industrial production, labor productivity, and GNP were reportedly achieved. Figures were presented, for example, by Warnke to the trade union congress (26–30 June) in percentage increases over the averages for 1968–1971, but statistically useful data were not disclosed. (Ibid., 3 August, pp. 5 ff.)

In 1971 the SED's Eighth Congress had promised social reforms, and Honecker later asserted "that the policy of the . . . congress has succeeded in ushering in an economic upswing" (ibid., p. 39). By the end of the year, the party claimed that the 1972 plan had been overfulfilled. Apparently, consumption did increase. Pensions and salaries were raised, with the maximum pension standing at 240 and the highest salaries at about 1,500 marks per month. On 7 December, before the Eighth Plenum, Honecker disclosed that instead of 3.4 million pensions, "as had been originally assumed," 3.9 million pensions were paid out and increased (ibid., 21 December, p. 28). The official exchange rate is $1 = 3.9 marks. The black market discounts the mark substantially. FRG authorities estimate a purchasing power of one West mark to equal three East marks or $1 = 10 East marks (*Die Welt,* 10 January 1973).

Despite the rise in monetary income, the practice of manufacturing high-quality products for export and servicing the internal market with shoddy products continued with little change. In other words, there still is much progress to be made but, by showing interest in the living conditions of the people, Honecker has to some extent improved the political atmosphere.

Population Growth. The party is worried by the fact that for the last ten years, there has been complete demographic stagnation: the GDR had 17 million inhabitants in 1962, and this has not increased. The population declined by 15,000 in 1971. About one-fifth of the population is above retirement age, but the labor shortage is so severe that every third male and every sixth female pensioner continues to work. The GDR publishes no statistics on suicides. It may be mentioned in this context that, according to Honecker, some 12,000 Polish and 13,000 Hungarian workers are temporarily employed in East Germany.

The SED is now intent on increasing the birth rate. For this purpose child care allowances and financial aid to newly-wed couples are offered. Such couples also receive preferred treatment in housing. A program has been initiated to give 99-year leases on suburban plots to families wishing to build houses of their own.

As a particular concession, mothers with three or more children are allowed to work 40 instead of the normal 45 hours per week. It should be noted that the male-female ratio in the GDR stands at 100 : 117 and that 79 percent of the women between the ages of 16 to 60 are gainfully employed. As of 6 December, this rate had risen to over 80 percent. Military service mostly affects 18-year-old males, but substantial numbers of young females are given military training, including target practice. There is a growing incidence of disease among females. The divorce rate has been reported to have increased from 1.6 to 1.8 per 1,000 people, approximately 50 percent higher than divorce in the Federal Republic (ibid., 7 December).

External Affairs. *Strategy Toward West Germany.* GDR strategy is based on a concept originally presented by Ulbricht to the SED's Seventh Congress in April 1967. The concept was approved by Leonid Brezhnev through his presence and incorporated in the GDR constitution of 1968 (Article 8/2). The resolution issued by the International Meeting of Communist and Workers' Parties at Moscow (17 June 1969), entitled "Tasks at the Present Stage of the Struggle against Imperialism and United Action of Communist and Workers Parties and all Anti-Imperialist Forces" (see *YICA, 1970,* pp. 799–821), is another source of current strategy.

Ulbricht's concept—which superseded the earlier notion that Germany should be reunited by means of a confederation—involves a three-stage progression for the reunification of Germany under SED dominance. It envisages a long period of peaceful co-existence of the two German states and the special political unit of West Berlin. The first step is to develop united actions between the working classes (i.e., the communist and socialist parties) of the GDR and the FRG. The second step consists in transforming the FRG from an "imperialistic" state into a peaceful and progressive anti-nazi democracy (i.e., the FRG is to be ruled by a left-socialist or a socialist-communist regime). The third step is to reunite Germany as a peaceful, anti-imperialist and progressive state. (See Eric Waldman, *Die Sozialistische Einheitspartei Westberlins und die Sowjetische Berlin Politik,* Boppard am Rhein, 1972, pp. 19–39.)

Treaty Making. In December 1969 Ulbricht explained that a treaty based on international law between the GDR and the FRG, which would involve the mutual acceptance of state frontiers, full equality of the two states, and mutual diplomatic recognition, would be regarded as the first step toward leading "the entire German nation on the road into a future of peace and socialism," as called for by the GDR constitution. But Ulbricht was insisting on his terms. As mentioned, GDR negotiations with the FRG moved more smoothly after Honecker came to power. Yet Honecker, too, needed some prodding from Moscow. The Crimea meeting of communist and workers' parties of the socialist countries (21 August) seems to have provided the final impetus. The ruling communist parties did not think explicit diplomatic recognition by the FRG of the GDR was all that important, provided relations could be normalized and the socialist German state were admitted to the United Nations.

In the end, the GDR-FRG treaty which was ratified on 21 December 1972 fell short of mutual recognition, but the deficiency was purely formal. FRG minister Egon Bahr, who had negotiated the treaty on the West German side, declared during the final ceremony: "Good neighborly relations should lead to cooperation, peaceful existence next to one another, and then to an existence with one another." This paraphrased Ulbricht's statement of 18 April 1967. But it seems hardly likely that Bahr meant to endorse Ulbricht's strategic concept.

The compact itself is entitled "Treaty on the Bases of Relations Between the Federal Republic of Germany and the German Democratic Republic." It calls for "normal good neighborly relations on the basis of equality," rules out the threat or use of force, and obligates the signatories to respect their common borders. The preamble talks about the "two German states." The operative text stipulates, inter alia, that permanent missions will be established in the two capitals. The signatories also promised to support negotiations for a reduction of armed forces and armaments in Europe. In addition, they agreed to establish new crossing points and to ameliorate conditions along the borders. (The GDR sold West Berlin 20 acres of land for $9.6 million. The transaction is to ease traffic problems in the center of town. See *NYT*, 20 July.)

The full instrument includes a supplementary protocol, a protocol note, a statement concerning the extension of the agreements and arrangements to West Berlin, a statement on political consultation, correspondence on applications for membership in the United Nations, correspondence on the reuniting of families, facilitation of travel and improvements in noncommercial goods traffic, correspondence on working conditions for journalists, correspondence on the opening of four new border crossings, correspondence on postal services and telecommunications, and correspondence with the text of notes to France, the United Kingdom, the United States, and the U.S.S.R. The treaty also was related to a four-power accord which stated that applications by the two German states for U.N. membership would not affect the prerogatives of the four powers.

The GDR initialed the treaty with the FRG on 6 November, just 13 days before general elections took place in West Germany. This timing was achieved by a united action between the West German SPD and the East German SED, and it was undoubtedly designed to influence voting behavior. In the belief that it puts an end to the "cold war," the West German electorate did, in fact, endorse the treaty. At the same time it returned Brandt's coalition government to power, with an increased majority.

Two basic disagreements, however, were visible from the start. Chancellor Willy Brandt of the FRG argued that East Germany is *not* a foreign country, and that the treaty "helps the concept of one German nation to endure." In contrast, the GDR views the treaty as an international agreement between two different states and as the legal basis for the GDR's continued existence. Furthermore, the FRG regards West Berlin as part of the Federal Republic, albeit under exceptional arrangements. The GDR denies that West Berlin is a constituent part of the FRG: it insists that West Berlin possesses "special political status" and hence must not be governed by the FRG. On 23 November Honecker reiterated, once again, that recent four-power agreements refer only to West Berlin. This version appears to be at variance with interpretations in Paris, London, and Washington and, at any rate, ignores the special ties and connections which do exist between West Berlin and the FRG. (See Honecker's interview with C. L. Sulzberger, ibid., 23 November.)

Socialist Internationalism. SED strategy includes diplomatic operations, largely in the form of negotiations with the FRG. It also includes political operations that are addressed to the *internal* politics of the FRG. The peculiar popular-united-national front structures of the GDR and SED provide convenient handles and covers for offensive political undertakings.

Hermann Axen wrote (*WMR*, January) about a "new type of international relations." As the SED spokesman sees it, those relations are based on the "general democratic principles of respect for territorial integrity, sovereignty and independence, equality, noninterference in internal affairs, and the right of nations to self-determination." But the new type of communist foreign policy also involves the "new and decisive principle" of "proletarian socialist internationalism," which aims at the "formation of a world community of the free nations." Thus while interference in internal affairs is ruled out on a state-to-state basis, this norm does not apply to cross-border relations between political parties.

In the execution of internationalist policy, the CPSU remains "the universally recognized vanguard of the world communist movement." Axen quoted Honecker to the effect that the attitude to the Soviet Union and the CPSU "has been, is, and always will be, the main touchstone of fidelity to Marxism-Leninism and proletarian internationalism," that the guidelines of the CPSU's Twenty-fourth Congress are "of universal significance," and that the SED will "assimilate the vast theoretical and practical experience of the Soviet Union and apply it in adaptation to our concrete conditions."

"The leading role belongs to those who pioneer human progress," Axen volunteered. Who, then, pioneers what? In a statement published by *Pravda* (10 May) Axen explained that "collective formulation of strategy and tactics and joint actions . . . have become an objective necessity." He added that the GDR stands for the *"acceleration and broadening* of the revolutionary process on a *world-wide* scale" (emphasis added). Since the SED is responsible for the German area, Axen seems to have suggested that the revolutionary process should be accelerated in the FRG, that the SED should pioneer "human progress" in West Germany, and that the USSR will provide the required strategic cover. On 9 July the Sixth Plenum resolved to engage in "further persistent struggle" to stimulate the "advance of all revolutionary forces" and to ensure "the most favorable international conditions for socialist and communist construction."

Those theoretical concepts were given more explicit meaning by Colonel General Heinz Kessler, deputy minister of national defense, who on 22 February asserted that an "irreconcilable class struggle" is raging in the FRG. He described the FRG as imperialistic and militaristic, and endorsed a strategy of consistently frustrating the opponent. (FBIS, 28 February, p. E 5.) Admiral Waldemar Verner, another deputy minister of national defense and head of the Main Political Administration of the armed forces, on 28 February asserted that the GDR is "struggling for a comprehensive, continuous and mounting superiority over the imperialist aggressor" (ibid., 2 March, p. E 5). Army general Hoffmann told the Eighth Plenum about international détente and the GDR's *military* strengthening. He added:

> "It will be the task of the entire army . . . to prepare themselves thoroughly for the armed struggle so as to be always capable, standing side by side with the soviet armed forces and the armed forces of the other fraternal armies, to fulfill our tasks and do our utmost to increase battle strength and combat readiness. This is and will unalterably remain our class task. The fulfillment of this class task requires above all constant and close cooperation with . . . the Group of Soviet Armed Forces in Germany." (Ibid., 21 December, p. 24.)

Honecker stressed to the same plenum that the ideological positions of the FRG and GDR are "incompatible." To emphasize the point, he quoted Brezhnev's recent utterance in Budapest: "A struggle is a struggle." "Our mode of thinking," Honecker explained, "differs from that of the representatives of the bourgeoisie, because we are fundamentally changing the world and human existence. . . . We are shaping a different world, the socialist world. . . . With . . . our socialist ideology we will belong to the *victors of history.*" (Ibid., pp. 46 and 48. Emphasis added.)

The National Question. This problem forms an integral part of the struggle about Germany's ultimate fate and the party's quest for victory. The SED line has always been that the solution of the national problem in Germany is, above all, a task for the class struggle. According to Ulbricht, the GDR is the "socialist state of the German nation." This reminder of the medieval-style "Holy Roman Empire of the German Nation" was meant to be conceptual and informative, not facetious. The survival of the German socialist worker-peasant state, as Stoph described the GDR on 16 October (ibid., 2 November, p. 29), is guaranteed by the U.S.S.R., more specifically, by Soviet military power and the Brezhnev doctrine. It is furthermore to be ensured by widespread international recognition and by the GDR's future membership in the United Nations.

In Ulbricht's words, the German national question "is a question of socialism, democracy and peace, *or* monopoly capitalism, neo-nazism and imperialist expansion, i.e., war." (Ulbricht's views are summarized by Waldman, op. cit., pp. 23–30.) Thus, the SED regards the conclusion of the treaty with the FRG as just one step in the struggle toward transforming the FRG into a "parliamentary democracy with anti-militarist . . . character and opposed to neo-nazism," to quote Ulbricht once more.

Honecker has so far been mostly quiet on these problems. Thus, Ulbricht's statements seem to retain their validity.

However, a change may be in the offing and may have been disclosed by a new party line on the German national question. On 3 July, Albert Norden, Politburo member and secretary in charge of propaganda, in an address to leading cadres rejected the notion that there is one German nation. According to him, the socialist nation is growing in the GDR and the old capitalist nation continues to exist in the FRG. "There are no two states of one nation but two nations in states with different social orders." Quoting Stalin's criteria for nationhood, Norden explained that there is no common territory, economy, and culture. Psychological and moral characteristics differ, and so do emotions. There is a different historical tradition. There still remains a common language. But since, besides in the GDR and the FRG, German is spoken in Austria, and in parts of Switzerland, Luxembourg, and eastern France, "the argument about common language leads into dangerous proximity to Hitler's concept of a Greater Germany." Hence the FRG's notion of a special relationship between two German states is designed to place the GDR under "Bonn's imperialist yoke." (*Deutschland Archiv,* November, pp. 1223–25.) Honecker, too, is on record as stating to a People's Army audience that the FRG is a foreign country "and, moreover, an imperialist foreign country" (*Neues Deutschland,* 7 January).

The line about two nations is a departure from Ulbricht, who believes that there is only one German nation (see Oldenburg, op. cit., p. 80). Fundamental SED texts on the history of Germany and the German labor movement are being rewritten and the 1963 party program is to be amended to conform to the new version (ibid., p. 81). These data suggest that a major policy is to be modified and that the changes are under dispute. The new policy would still commit the SED to assist the West German revolutionaries under communist leadership to effect a "socialist" takeover. But the corollary of West German revolution, namely, that once both the GDR and the FRG live under identical social systems, reunification would follow, is being discarded. The contradiction between the SED requirement and wish to be a national party and its "internationalist duty" toward the CPSU is transparent.

"Cultural Revolution" and Propaganda. To promote united actions by the "working class" in both Germanys, the SED wants to kindle a cultural revolution the purpose of which, as stated by Hager before the Sixth Plenum (*Neues Deutschland,* 8 July) is to fill "young people completely with the socialist spirit." Hager supposedly has been working since 1967 on "cultural revolution" and its applicability to Germany. Under his influence, the SED seems to be willing to depart from the rigid lines that were laid down during the Stalin era and to allow for a variety of art forms in addition to "socialist realism." Cultural production still must be inspired by *partiinost* (partyness), but the existence of personal conflicts under socialism may now be recognized. The artists were invited to pay more attention to humor.

Pending the ultimate emergence of cultural and artistic originality, the Politburo on 7 November (i.e., during the ratification period) decided to step up propaganda activities. The purpose is to confront imperialism, defeat anti-communism, develop "socialist personalities," and prevent ideological contamination that may result from contacts with the FRG. There is to be no cease-fire in the ideological struggle against imperialism, anti-communism, and Maoism.

These matters were discussed at length at a Central Committee conference on agitation and propaganda (16–17 November). Addressed by Honecker and Lamberz, it debated a propaganda plan which had been issued on 7 November but remains unpublished. This plan seems to have assigned first priority to ideological activity and "the international fighting partnership for the revolutionary renewal of the world," as Honecker put it. (FBIS, 27 November, p. E 10; also ibid., 17 November, pp. E 3–14.) On 30 November, in amplification of the propaganda conference themes, Norden called for "socialist patriotism and internationalism" and suggested that the SED-GDR create a "socialist fatherland." (*Die Welt,* 1 December.)

Trade. The East European communist countries, and in particular the USSR, have an overriding requirement for improved economic relations with the FRG. They are most anxious, through the GDR-FRG connection, to obtain stronger economic ties with the enlarged Common Market. The GDR needs increased trade with the FGR more urgently than anybody else: only 7 percent—or, according to Honecker, only 10 percent—of East German trade is with West Germany, whereas 70 percent is with the bloc. The GDR has good economic chances for enlarged trade with the West. If it exploits opportunities in a businesslike manner and avoids political complications, the GDR may become a major trade and transport link between Western and Eastern Europe. Except for massive GDR purchases of consumers' goods toward the end of the year, actual progress was slow during 1972. Nevertheless, the GDR ran up a debt of 2.3 billion FRG marks. It became clear that trade expansion necessitates the granting of substantial credits from the FRG for the East Germany economy.

Major Foreign Policy Thrusts. The main recent effort of GDR foreign policy has been to break out from isolation and obtain diplomatic recognition by as many countries as possible. Implementation was proceeding successfully. By the end of 1972, the GDR had been recognized by some 55 governments.

During 1972, the GDR achieved membership in UNESCO and the World Health Organization. On 8 March, through an accord on nuclear safety controls with the International Atomic Energy Agency, the GDR signed its first agreement with a U.N. organization. (The GDR is building a large nuclear energy plant which will increase production of electric power by about a third.) Late in November, the GDR obtained observer status with the United Nations (*Neue Zürcher Zeitung,* 24 November). U.N. membership is expected in 1973.

The GDR maintained active diplomatic relations with other governments of the socialist countries in Eastern Europe; with the Council for Mutual Economic Assistance (CMEA), and —in connection with their possible affiliation—with Iraq, Chile, and Finland; also with Guinea, Syria, and Bangladesh. Foreign trade state secretary Gerhard Beil visited the United States to discuss economic problems. Party-to-party relations were cultivated with the ruling parties of Eastern Europe, including Yugoslavia, and also with Socialist Unity Party of West Berlin and the ruling parties of Mongolia, North Vietnam, and North Korea. In addition, there were contacts with other friendly parties in Belgium, Chile, Cyprus, Denmark, France, Guinea, Italy, Japan, Morocco, South Vietnam, and Sweden.

On 12 May, Honecker and Stoph signed a 20-year treaty of friendship and alliance with Romania.

The GDR has been intensifying its relations with all CMEA member states. It concluded agreements with Poland and Czechoslovakia on unrestricted travel among the three countries, put into effect during January, which resulted in considerable tourism and large purchases. Reportedly about 10 million Poles visited the GDR during the year, largely for bulk buying of consumers' goods. Some 5 million East Germans supposedly vacationed in Czechoslovakia and indulged in heavy purchases. More than 6 million East Germans traveled to Poland, and increasing numbers of Czechs visited the GDR. There may be some doubt about these official figures. In particular, it is likely that foreign travel by East Germans was much smaller.

Yet the travel streams were larger in 1972 than ever before. This unexpectedly dense traffic resulted in friction between tourists and host populations, as well as monetary dislocations which necessitated regulation. On 27 November the GDR decreed that Polish visitors would be restricted to a maximum expenditure of 200 marks. Tough customs controls were introduced and merchandise in excess of 200 marks, which the Poles wanted to take home, had to be returned. It was promised, however, that in 1973 Polish visitors could spend up to 1,000 marks. Since their purchases emptied shops even in large cities and thus aggravated the supply problems of the East German population, free monetary exchange between "socialist" countries suffering from different types of shortages seems to be impractical.

East-West Travel in Germany. A treaty on transport questions, agreed upon 12 May by the GDR and the FRG, took effect on 17 October. According to Kohl, this was the GDR's first treaty with the FRG which "accords with international usage." The agreement deals with goods traffic on railroads, roads, and waterways; tourist traffic; and visiting rights "in urgent family cases." Telephone facilities were augmented between West Berlin and East Germany. After considerable vacillation the GDR, in addition to allowing commercial and cultural visits, gave permission to West Germans to visit friends and relatives in East Germany for 30 days a year. (*NYT,* 18 October.)

In both countries, the two FRG-GDR treaties aroused *one* major popular interest: that extensive travel between the two German states would be resumed and normally continued, that contacts between families be permitted, and that families be reunited. More specifically, great hopes were entertained that the Berlin Wall and the barbed wire fences running along the entire frontier would be eliminated and border crossings normalized, in the same way as had been done among the GDR, Poland, and Czechoslovakia.

The physicist Robert Havemann, who represents the opposition to the communist true-believers, remarked that the SED reported "happily that 99 percent of the citizens went to the polls. Nevertheless, the authorities have to lock the frontiers to prevent our people from escaping." (FBIS, 28 January, pp. U 1–2.) Havemann shared the same Nazi prison with Honecker, had been the SED's leading theoretician on dialectics, was excluded from the party, and, when offered the opportunity to emigrate, refused to leave the GDR. Havemann asserted that opening of the Berlin Wall would not lead to mass flights, provided the population were convinced the border would remain open forever. Since living standards have improved, and adaptation to the GDR regime has occurred, Havemann may have a point. But the authorities do not agree with him and their point may be stronger.

Since the Wall went up in 1961, some 300,000 citizens have left the GDR (*NYT,* 29 October). This is 1.8 percent of the total GDR population. Half of those people departed legally, but virtually all legal émigrés were sick, old, and "useless." The other half displayed tremendous ingenuity and courage, escaping illegally through one of the most heavily guarded borders that ever existed. Most illegal escapees were young and highly qualified.

The FRG Interior Ministry disclosed (*Die Welt,* 10 January 1973) that 6,782 GDR citizens left the GDR illegally during 1972. The incidence of escape rose by some 50 percent over 1971. These 6,782 refugees are those who reported to FRG refugee welfare organizations. There is an additional unknown number of refugees who went directly to their relatives and did not report to reception facilities. In addition, 11,627 persons moved legally from the GDR to the FRG. Those legal émigrés are mostly unable to work. Thus, altogether 18,309 persons left the GDR in 1972, or 0.1 percent of the GDR population. (The U.S. equivalent would be an emigration of 225,000 people.)

West German authorities observed the death of 96 persons who were killed by GDR frontier guards along the FRG-GDR border during 1972. An additional 127 persons, while trying to escape through the border obstructions, were wounded by mines and rifle fire. These figures do not include the casualties that occurred along the GDR-West Berlin border. Furthermore, according to evidence available to the West German authorities, GDR courts convicted 522 persons for attempting to leave the GDR without authorization. (Ibid., 5 January 1973.)

While the treaties were moving from signature to ratification, the border was being equipped with new types of automatic weapons that have a particularly high density of fire. These deadly devices are to eliminate the possibility that GDR border troops might not always desire to hit a person who wants to flee. In addition, the old wall construction was being replaced by an 850-mile, 9-foot-high fence of heavy steel screens attached to concrete posts. To prevent tunnelling, the barrier was being extended several feet underground. While the border was in this way militarily strengthened, a measure of a different kind was also taken: on 16 October all persons who had left the country without permission were amnestied. Theoretically, this means that they are allowed to visit their relatives in the GDR and to return again to their residences abroad. (*NYT,* 17 October.)

Before the traffic agreement entered into force, the GDR relaxed traffic controls during the Easter and Whitsun holidays. But there were repeated difficulties before red tape on visas could be overcome. By the end of 1972, to judge from the Christmas traffic, most hindrances and annoyances seemed to have disappeared, but the handling of holiday travel may remain the exception and not the rule. The GDR retains full authority to reduce intra-German travel to levels it finds acceptable, or even to eliminate it altogether.

According to *Neues Deutschland* (6 October), about 5 million West Germans and West Berliners visited East Germany during the first ten months of 1972. During the same period nearly 900,000 East Germans visited West Germany. About two-thirds of the West Berlin population went into East Germany during the Whitsun holiday alone. As reported by UPI, between 3 June and the end of the year, the GDR had granted about 2 million passes to West Berliners. Obviously, these figures refer to trips, and many persons made several trips. Even so, the figures are surprisingly high. According to the *New York Times* (19 November, citing a decree published in *Neues Deutschland*), the Central Committee was calling for vigilance. By that time, about 6 million West Germans and West Berliners had visited East Germany. The unexpected difficulty emerged that one-day visits which supposedly are permissible without visas were not feasible except by automobile. GDR railroads were braked, so to speak, to reduce traffic volume. The technique had worked before to contain the "invasion" of Polish tourists.

The SED dubbed social democracy "another evil form of imperialism" and instructed its party members and GDR functionaries *not* to receive relatives from West Germany. This edict applied to more than 2 million GDR citizens, including some 265,000 members of the armed forces and police, nearly 400,000 state employees, and about 66,000 party bureaucrats. (*Vorwärts,* 1 December.) By early December, the West German press reported that authorizations for travel by East Germans to West Germany were being kept to a minimum. At the end of the year, the chief of the GDR travel bureau announced that in 1973 GDR tourists would travel to socialist countries but not to the FRG or other Western countries (*Die Welt,* 3 January 1973).

GDR security agents stimulated an alleged voluntary move by personnel in plants and businesses not to invite visitors from the FRG. Others were asked to sign security pledges and, upon threat of punishment, report on any contacts with Westerners. The printed security pledge lists 10 legal stipulations bearing on the violation of GDR secrecy provisions, including several which envisage the death penalty for serious contraventions. (Ibid., 7 December.)

Publications and Broadcast Media. The official organ of the SED Central Committee, *Neues Deutschland,* is the most important daily newspaper in East Germany (circulation about 800,000). The SED also publishes the *Berliner Zeitung* (circulation 500,000) and dailies in major cities of the GDR. In addition, officially approved material appears in publications of the other National Front parties and mass organizations. The SED deals with party questions in the semimonthly *Neuer Weg* and with the theory and practice of scientific socialism in the monthly *Einheit*. A new radio station, "Stimme der GDR" (Voice of the GDR), began transmission on 15 November 1971 and simultaneously "Deutschlandsender" as well as "Berliner Welle" ceased broadcasting.

Hoover Institution   Stefan T. Possony
Stanford University

Hungary

Hungarian communists formed a party in November 1918 and briefly held power. After 1919 the movement was proscribed, and it then virtually disappeared. Near the end of World War II communists organized again and gained control of the country in 1947, taking the name Hungarian Workers' Party in 1948. On 1 November 1956 the name was changed to the Hungarian Socialist Workers' Party (Magyar Szocialista Munkáspárt; HSWP). Current party membership is estimated at 724,000 out of a total population of 10,402,000. For party organization and leadership see *YICA, 1972,* p. 38.

Party and Ideology. HSWP policy continues to follow the pragmatic middle-of-the-road line elaborated in the early 1960s, and there has been no change in the top leadership. The Politburo is comprised of György Aczél, Antal Apró, Valéria Benke, Béla Biszku, Lajos Fehér, Jenö Fock, Sándor Gáspár, János Kádár, Gyula Kállai, Zoltán Komócsin, Dezsö Nemes, Károly Németh, and Rezsö Nyers; members of the Secretariat of the Central Committee are Kádár, Aczél, Biszku, Komócsin, Nyers, Miklós Óvari, and Árpád Pullai. In 1972 the undisputed head of the party, First Secretary János Kádár, reminisced in a mellow mood on the occasion of his 60th birthday party on 25 May: "In 1956, a very serious and critical situation presented itself which is called, scientifically, the counterrevolution. We are aware that this is the scientific definition of what took place in 1956. But there is also another concept which we all might accept: it was a national tragedy. A tragedy for the party, for the working class, for the people, and for the individual. We lost our way, and the result was tragedy. And if we have overcome this now—which we can state with confidence—this is a very big thing." (*Társadalmi Szemle,* June.) Since it was a finally settled question that a people's democratic system existed in Hungary, with time and tolerance "we will find ways and means for believers and nonbelievers to work together for the common socialist goal." "As far as the pace of the revolution goes," continued Kádár, "the important question here is how much we should consume today and how much we should leave for the future."

Earlier in the year, Kádár had told the Budapest party committee that in line with the resolutions of the party's Tenth Congress, measures had been taken to suppress all anomalies that had offended the people's sense of justice and concerned public opinion: "Thus measures have been implemented to better coordinate group and social interests, abolish certain wage anomalies, ensure greater moral and material appreciation of people working decently and well, regulate secondary and part-time jobs, levy heavier taxes on socially unjustifiable high incomes, and prevent building plot speculation; we have increased the severity of the penal code as well" (*Népszabadság,* 13 February). Addressing the same meeting, Politburo member Károly Németh noted certain problems: "While a generally favorable ideological situation prevails in Budapest, erroneous and hostile views also manifest themselves and have an effect on smaller or larger circles. A more ardent, unequivocal, resolute and persuasive attitude is necessary in our ideological struggle against nationalism, anti-Semitism, and middle-class liberalism." Reflecting on the work of the work of the basic party organs, Németh warned against unjust, generalized attacks on economic managers as well as against violations of the party's moral norms and unprincipled indulgence in personalities, all induced by the stable political milieu.

The pursuit of détente in Europe has been accompanied in the Soviet sphere by a campaign of ideological consolidation. Writing in the party monthly *Pártélet* (May), the deputy head of the Agitprop Department discussed the nature of imperialist strategy, particularly regarding Hungary. Bridge-building and peaceful engagement were merely new anti-communist tactics. Bourgeois propaganda talking of a radically new "Hungarian model," identifying economic modernization with "capitalization" and socialist democracy with "liberalization," was slanderous and aimed at loosening the links between Hungary and the Soviet Union and the other socialist states. The concepts of polarity and power blocs were equally eroneous; the only meaningful division was between socialism and capitalism. In the socialist camp the differences lay not in basic Marxist-Leninist principles and ultimate goals but only in methods. Therefore the party must actively fight such subversive "revisionism" as well as "leftist sectarian distortions." Other spokesmen admitted that the West's "divide and rule" tactics (and Radio Free Europe's new "objectivity") in alleging Soviet domination and fanning nationalism were misleading many people. It was charged that the status of Hungarian minorities (particularly in Transylvania) was being deliberately distorted and that propaganda alleging Western superiority was effective among Hungarians. At a Central Committee plenum (14–15 June), Zoltán Komócsin warned that the ongoing East-West negotiations on Europe, arms control, and Vietnam simply meant that military clashes are giving way to ideological and economic competition.

Concurrently the validity of Hungary's New Economic Mechanism (NEM) was constantly defended and reasserted by party officials, and there are indications that this was done to counteract criticism both from those who see in it dangerous liberal tendencies and from those who fail to derive immediate material benefits from the system. It was stressed that while there are transitional problems, the NEM is superior to the old command economy and is essential to Hungary's modernization. The secretary-general of the Hungarian Academy of Sciences noted typically that "Leftist tendencies of a kind able to influence important strata would strengthen if the fight against Right-wing bourgeois and petty-bourgeois phenomena were slackened" (*New Hungarian Quarterly,* Spring).

The continuing central role of the party was stressed by Politburo member Béla Biszku in a lecture at the HSWP Central Committee's Political Academy (*Népszabadság,* 2 March). He observed that "we have currently reached a phase of social development in which we are decentralizing," leading some people to fear that this type of socialist democracy would weaken the leadership of the party, and added: "We have seen no indication thus far of the failure of party management to assert itself in making some significant decisions." That is, the Central Committee organs were continuing to provide primary guidance, while communists working in state organs remained politically responsible to the party and subject to moral standards that were higher than the secular state norms. Biszku noted some duplication in the work of state leaders and party organs and recommended that their respective tasks be better delineated. He concluded with the conviction that the significance of party management would not diminish but increase in the coming years.

Widespread political apathy is a matter of concern to the HSWP, and party organs are urged to reach out to those "outside the current" by producing new ideas and initiatives to

arouse their interest. A Csongrád county survey among workers who participate in party education showed substantial indifference to politics and the work of councils; of those under 25
years of age, 63.3 percent reported slight or no interest (*Pártélet,* April). As a result, the
HSWP is refurbishing its agitprop apparatus. Since the mass media allegedly do not provide
sufficiently differentiated propaganda for the various social strata, a plan has been devised to
create political debating circles which will serve as an organized framework for word-of-
mouth propaganda. Small groups with trained leaders will be supplied by the party with discussion material and are to be operational by the fall of 1973 (ibid., July.)

Other shortcomings arousing concern within the HSWP include the lack of collective work
within the leading body of party organizations, self-enrichment by party functionaries, and, at
least in one Budapest district, a decline in the number and proportion of industrial worker
members.

The treatment of a book by the veteran communist writer József Lengyel was illustrative
of the ambivalence of party policy. Entitled *Confrontation,* it deals with Soviet prison camps
(where Lengyel spent some years under Stalin) and the compromises made by many communists. After the inclusion of a preface noting that the work was for guidance only and warning
that it could be used by socialism's enemies, the book was printed in a small edition and circulated to a closed circle of party members.

Government and Mass Organizations. The National Assembly at its 19–20 April session
approved a draft law for the amendment of the 1949 constitution. The initial impetus for this
had come with the assertion at the HSWP's Eighth Congress (November 1962) that with the
collectivization of agriculture the foundations of socialism had been completed. The revision
was seen less as a political program (which was the case with its predecessor) than as a reflection of achievements. Nor is it the final version; that will come when Hungary can be proclaimed a "socialist" republic. The revised constitution states rather obscurely that Hungary is
still only a "people's" republic, as well as being a socialist state.

The preamble to the constitution still pays tribute to the Soviet liberators but now also
takes a longer historical perspective in referring to a "millenium" of the people's struggle. The
earlier discrimination between "working people" and "citizens" is abandoned as no longer relevant. Socialist national unity, said Kádár in the National Assembly, had been achieved:
"Today, Hungarian workers, peasants, and intellectuals, Communists and nonparty members,
believers and nonbelievers, all work together to advance the welfare of the country"
(*Népszabadság,* 20 April). There is provision for the direct participation of all citizens in the
administration of public affairs. The former vague reference to the "vanguard of the working
class" has been replaced by the assertion that "the Marxist-Leninist party of the working class
is the leading force in society." Also noted is the function of mass movements such as the Patriotic People's Front (PPF) and the trade unions in socialist construction. The equal ranking
of state and cooperative ownership is asserted, and private producers are recognized; "however, private property and private initiative must not violate collective interests." The National Assembly is described as the "supreme organ of the representation of the people" and
as the guarantor of the "constitutional order of society." Constitutional lawyers have for years
urged a more explicit definition of the spheres of legislative authority of the Presidential
Council (with its decree-making function) and the National Assembly, but the revised constitution offers scarcely greater precision in this respect. The Presidential Council is now empowered to declare a state of danger to security and create a national defense council invested
with extra-ordinary powers. Finally, a paragraph of the revised document refers to the
strengthening of friendship with socialist countries, and cooperation with all.

The National Assembly meets for less than two weeks annually in the aggregate, and remains essentially a rubber stamp for government policy, though deputies do voice disagreement occasionally on matters of detail. At the Assembly's 11 October sitting, a reply by the education minister on the training of teachers of the subject "Fundamentals of Our World Outlook" was rejected by 43 members. Also in October, the Ministerial Council issued new directives to improve the effectiveness of deputies outside of parliament by enjoining them to keep in contact with constituents and investigate their complaints, and by ordering the administrative organs of state to respond promptly to deputies enquiries (*Magyar Hirlap,* 21 October).

The government's concern with mobilizing political participation was also evident in the activities of mass organizations. At the Fifth Congress of the PPF, (26–28 April), its secretary-general asserted the front's responsibility for implementing party policy and for relaying and interpreting popular opinion and demands; the PPF is to foster discussion and help correct abuses of the NEM. Both the PPF and the Communist Youth League (KISZ) are charged with promoting voluntary social work (involving such tasks as the building of nurseries and kindergartens) and with reviving flagging public interest in such work. The KISZ also helped to organize in October–November the biennial, country-wide student parliaments. A report on KISZ membership indicates that it is growing and now stands at 820,234. Representation of the different strata is uneven; 20 percent of young agricultural workers, 34 percent of young industrial workers, 50 percent of technical students, 68 percent of high school students, and 90 percent of college students belong to the organization. (*Ifjusági Magazin,* October.) Noting that 35–40 percent of young working people have changed jobs in the last three years (twice the proportion of adults), the KISZ leadership has declared that it will study the problem and oppose "unrealistic and unfounded" demands for job changes.

The National Council of Trade Unions (SZOT) carries on active contacts with foreign trade unions, having in recent months sent a delegation to Italy and received visits from West German, Scottish, and Belgian trade unionists. György Marosán, a former Politburo member who had been pensioned off in late 1962 after an intra-party squabble, wrote a series of articles (*Népszava,* 11, 12, 14 March) advocating an improvement in relations between trade unions in East and West Europe. He admitted that the events of 1956 in Hungary, of 1968 in Czechoslovakia, and of 1970 in Poland had alienated many Western workers, but he argued that without the latter there could be no progress toward a European détente. Despite hostile charges from abroad that they were powerless, the East European trade unions were the "true guardians of workers' interests."

The Workers' Militia celebrated its fifteenth anniversary in January. When established in 1957, the national commander recalled, the Workers' Militia had been "instrumental in enabling the working masses, the sincere adherents of socialism, to overcome their fear and uncertainty" (ibid., 20 January). Its purpose remains to defend and strengthen the workers' power. Membership is voluntary and more than half of new recruits do not belong to the party, but most of them take that step eventually, and 82 percent of the total membership are also party members.

The New Economic Mechanism. By the middle of 1971 it had become clear that the Hungarian economy was running into difficulties. Reports on the 1971 plan and budget indicated the strengths and weaknesses in the performance of the NEM (*Magyar Hirlap,* 30 January, 23 June, 1972). On the positive side, productivity improved despite net declines in the industrial (0.3 percent) and agricultural 2.0 percent) labor forces, while expansion in the priority industrial branches—chemical, power, engineering—continued the planned transformation of the production structure. National income rose by 7 percent, and a better balance was claimed between personal income and goods supply. Per capita real wages rose by 2.5 to 3.0 percent, but this concealed certain imbalances, particularly in favor of parts of the agricultural sector, and the president of the National Planning Office took pains to point out that the 1971 rise in peasant income was due to major expansion of pig-fattening on private plots and that for 1972 the rate of increase would be uniform with that of the rest of the population at 5 percent (*Társadalmi Szemele,* January). Industrial production grew by 5 percent rather than the planned 6 percent, and the gross production value of agriculture was up 9 percent, with livestock production up in pigs but down in cattle. Other indicators were more negative. The proportion of unfinished investments rose by 22 percent, and amounted to 80 percent of all investments. The value of exports went up as planned by 8 percent, but imports were 19 percent greater than planned, producing a severe imbalance of trade particularly with the dollar zone. It was pointed out, however, that the largest single component of the import rise was in machinery which in the long run would help to develop domestic production. The failure of industrial enterprises to meet their estimated payments left the national budget with a deficit of 3,300 million forints instead of the planned 2,160 million deficit.

Politburo member Rezsö Nyers reported to the Central Committee on 1 December 1971 that the most unsatisfactory sector was that of investments, and announced a reduction in the growth rate of state investment below the plan; the concurrent reduction through credit controls of enterprise, council, and cooperative investments, and the prohibition of certain low-priority enterprise investments, and he warned of penalties for overspending (*Pártélet,* January). With regard to the trade imbalance, Nyers indicated cutbacks of state support for imports and a stricter application of customs regulations, but he stressed that such reductions would not affect consumers' goods.

Criticisms of the new rich were frequently voiced by officials, by the media, and by the less privileged social strata, and a public opinion survey (*Népszabadság,* 20 August) indicated a lingering dissatisfaction with price fluctuations and with wage differentiation. Speculation in real estate was curbed by a 1971 regulation limiting ownership to one (vacation) building plot per family and by a progressive real estate tax. A more progressive rate of taxation has also been imposed on non-manual workers and on incomes from moonlighting, and stricter controls have been imposed on the ancillary activities of agricultural cooperatives and on the inducements the latter could offer to attract labor. The government issued a decree limiting the acquisition and use of official cars in enterprises.

There is, however, no indication that the government is planning to drastically amend the NEM. Addressing a national agitprop conference on 3 February, Nyers declared the NEM to be a success (ibid., 6 February): "We have every reason to believe that on the basis of the integral unity of central planning and the market mechanism, the current restrictions can be reduced, enterprise management can be allowed more initiative, and methods of central planning can be improved—probably during the period of the next five-year plan." He acknowledged that the rise in the standard of living was uneven, those on fixed salaries receiving raises only every two or three years and many being left behind in the drive for wage differentiation as an incentive to productivity. As for equal distribution, "this is not practicable during the building of socialism because the volume of production is not enough for a truly communist distribution. This would result only in an equality of poverty, would slow down development, and would fail to make the people either contented or happy." In a subsequent article (*Társadalmi Szemle,* June), Nyers argued that the growth rate had been marginally better since the inception of the NEM in 1968 and that economic growth had become better balanced. Further improvements would come from more efficient central control, greater enterprise independence, the modernization of intra-enterprise mechanisms, and better incentive systems. He ruled out any evolution toward a Yugoslav-style management by "works councils" and the breakup of state property into enterprise property, but he acknowledged the sphere of authority of trade unions. Nyers also defended the development of the cooperative sector but noted that "it is necessary to establish a socially accepted limit on the acquisition of property, to set up a system which will regularly siphon off excess income." At its November meeting, the Central Committee decided to maintain the new controls on investments and prices as a corrective to existing "distortions" and recommended the setting up of a new state planning commission under the cabinet to coordinate ministerial actions.

With regard to production efficiency, favorable developments were seen (*Népszabadság*, 27 August) on the macrostructural level, with improvements in agricultural productivity and in the favored industrial sectors, but at the enterprise level modernization was too slow, the resources being used instead to increase capacity. At the same time, the application of the new Basic Wage decree, which aims at a higher floor as well as greater differentiation, was running into problems, for many enterprises lack the financial means to implement it immediately. The problem of fostering enterprise independence after a long period of central planning was made clear in a report on the extended-range (five-year) projections done on request more or less independently by individual enterprises (ibid., 22 January). In the aggregate, these plans proved to be far more optimistic than the national plan in estimating the sources of investment, and they generally overrated the possibilities of growth, according to the report, in projecting a 38 percent increase in industrial labor productivity over the next five years. The managers have become convenient scapegoats for shortcomings of the NEM in the eyes of some of the public, and it has been noted that top-level enterprise staff are generally appointed with little effective exercise of the trade union and party committees' right to advise. The party daily has rejected, however, the charge that the NEM's stress on efficiency is leading to technocracy by arguing that the specialists necessary to run a complex economy are also committeed to socialism and are not alienated from the people (ibid., 23 December 1971).

Even more critical than managerial inefficiency are the implications of a demographic pattern whereby the number of young people coming into the labor force will decline by 1977, from the current 180,000 to 110,000—at which level it is expected to stabilize. Of the total labor force 9 percent is over 55 years of age, and the problem is accentuated in agriculture, where the proportion is 25 percent. Despite the reduction in wage differentials between workers and farmers, it remains difficult to keep young people on the farms, where working conditions are more primitive, there are no individual incentive systems as in the factories, and social benefits are only 73 percent of those enjoyed by urban workers. As for private plot farming, it remains labor intensive and, for young people, relatively unattractive. One remedial measure has been a Presidential Council decree (22 December 1971) providing incentives for men and women of pensionable age (60 and 55 years respectively) to keep on working. On the other hand, the 44-hour work week has been extended to all industrial employees, leaving only 1.5 million white-collar state and service employees on the longer, 48-hour week. The labor shortage would be less critical were it not for the attitude widespread among both intellectual and manual workers that the basic wage warrants only their physical presence, with real work being done for added material incentives. It was in order to spur labor productivity that the Central Committee passed on 1 December 1971 a resolution reasserting the value of "work competition," particularly through the "socialist brigades" that include some 30 percent of industrial workers. The resolution criticized the past shortcomings of such competition, noting that it was often unrelated to economic targets, that the results were inadequately evaluated, that it was regarded by economic leaders are merely a campaign, and that it was overly bureaucratized (*Pártélet,* January). To give it a new impetus, the system will be linked more closely to enterprise plans and will benefit from a more effective input by the economic leaders.

The government continues to encourage private plots, which cover 10 percent of the total agricultural area and supply a disproportionate amount of vegetables and livestock; the short supply of small machinery necessary to rationalize such farming remains a problem. Private garden plots are enjoying a great surge in popularity, and there are reportedly over a million amateur gardeners producing vegetables and fruits. Meat exports represent an important part of Hungarian exports, and the government has finally taken steps to increase the profitability of cattle breeding by raising prices and state subsidies.

The private retail trade has grown steadily under the NEM, with the number of dealers having risen to 11,000 from 8,800 in 1968. The increased competition stimulated by the activities of this sector is officially sanctioned, although the government's primary interest is to encourage private retail outlets in areas where state or cooperative shops prove to be unprofitable (*Magyar Hirlap,* 16 June). There has been criticism of excessive profits by some private retailers as well as by the managers of certain businesses (mainly catering) owned by cooperatives. The government issued a decree in March to control the operations of the latter group, but they retain great independence to maximize profits.

The government is engaged in a concerted effort to extend the use of computers. There are presently 160 in use, and 400 are projected by 1975. Hungary has been granted $2.2 million by the United Nations to establish an international computer technology center. The often promised and postponed nuclear power plant project appears to be on again (ibid., 16 August). Under a new agreement with the Soviet Union within the CEMA integration plan, the first unit is to become operational at Paks by 1980. (See also, below, "Foreign Trade.")

Social and Cultural Affairs. Demographic patterns continue to occasion widespread concern. The rate of natural increase is down to 2.6 per thousand (compared with 3.0 in 1970) and the population is aging; in the preceding decade the number of children under 10 years declined by 400,000. At the April session of parliament, in a debate on the new health bill, the health minister referred to plans to further improve maternity and family benefits. Premier Jenö Fock subsequently observed that greater restrictions might have to be put on abortions (*Magyar Hirlap,* 12 May). Other social problems receiving attention are alcoholism and a rising divorce rate, the latter been attributable in part to the continuing housing shortage and standing at its highest among manual workers. A report on criminal activities in 1971 indicated an increase in crimes against social property and a marginal decrease in crimes against private property (*Népszabadság,* 16 February).

Following reports in the Western press of student demonstrations of a nationalistic and implicitly antigovernment character in the course of celebrations on the 15 March national holiday, *Népszabadság* belatedly (16 April) took note of the event and dismissed it as the puerile behavior of a small group of young people. The police had quickly dispersed the demonstrators as they prepared to assemble in Budapest.

The Central Committee at its June plenum discussed higher education and adopted a resolution setting out long-term goals of modernization and reduction of the curriculum, the laying of a better ideological foundation, and the fostering of the education of manual workers' children. It urged that more attention be paid to "economic and political knowledge, as well as to training for citizenship," and noted: "Our failure to adequately inculcate a political and Marxist *Weltanschauung* derives mainly from the assigning of an overwhelming amount of indigestible material which bears no relation to reality but is purely theoretical." An article on youth and the teaching of history (*Társadalmi Szemle,* October), acknowledged tendencies among the young toward a romantic nationalism often tinged with anti-Sovietism, noted that the party condemned this on "ideological and political" grounds, and urged historians and teachers to stress the primacy of the class struggle. The Academy of Sciences for its part has approved a 15-year plan for research into the ideological and national consciousness of all social groups and its development since 1945.

In the area of cultural policy, Politburo member György Aczél told a group of visiting Soviet youth representatives that "there cannot be freedom for 'art' that preaches alien ideological views, appeals to base instincts, and is anti-humane and the result of 'anti-culture.' " He observed that young people envy the "romance" of the older generation's revolutionary struggles while being at the same time particularly susceptible to bourgeois ideology, against which "we are waging an implacable struggle" (*Komsomolskaya Pravda,* Moscow, 1 July). Bourgeois tendencies are subject to constant official denunciations, and there has been specific criticism of Hungarian theaters for neglecting Soviet and other socialist works. In October the Central Committee's cultural collective issued new guidelines that reflect the current phase of ideological consolidation (*Társadalmi Szemle,* October). The spectrum of criticism had widened in recent years, Marxist critics were threatened by a wave of bourgeois or ideologically neutral literary and artistic criticism, and some divergences have been noted in the interpretation of the unity of national and class perspectives. Critics, editors, and other creative intellectuals are therefore enjoined to return to Marxist cultural principles. *Kritika,* a scholarly monthly devoted to Marxist esthetics, was revamped in February to reach a wider public with cultural interpretations inspired by socialist realism. In its first issue Kádár paid tribute to the memory of the populist writer Péter Veres, praising him for abandoning his old smallholder ideals in favor of collectivism and for his "sincere rapproachement with the communists."

State pressures and few vocations are causing a crisis in the Catholic church, which is facing a steady decline in the number of priests. In the view of the editor of the Catholic weekly *Uj Ember* (2 January), there is still a lack of realistic judgment about Hungarian Catholicism from both sides: "Our state and political leadership should take a further step along the road of realism and should judge us not by mistaken trouble-makers, but by those masses whose honesty, good work, and constructive integrity go hand-in-hand with a well-founded and modern religious belief." The government is meanwhile pursuing its anti-religious policies by creating more "family institutes" that provide civil ceremonies without charge.

Foreign Trade and Policy. After a trade deficit in 1971 of 5,743 million foreign exchange forints, the balance of trade showed substantial improvement in the first nine months of 1972 (*Világgazdaság,* 18 October). Total volume of trade rose by 7.5 percent, exports by 23.3 percent, and imports declined 4.4 percent. In the critical dollar area, imports were down by over 8 percent while exports rose 17 percent. Evidently the restrictions on imports and the export drive launched by the government in late 1971 was bearing fruit. The importance of trade to the economy was evidenced by Hungary's official participation in 41 international exhibitions during 1972.

Hungary's long-term needs for imported raw materials and the role of the Soviet Union as principal supplier were major topics in 1972 and the source of much international comment and speculation that the Kremlin was displeased with the NEM. An article in *Pravda* (3 February) noted nationalistic manifestations, social problems, and petty-bourgeois tendencies in Hungary. Kádár paid an unofficial visit to Brezhnev in mid-February. Then at the end of March Premier Fock returned from negotiations in Moscow to report that the Hungarians had been "unable to get a definite answer at present from the Soviet comrades" regarding the supply of raw materials to 1985 (Budapest radio, 29 March). The Russians claimed that they could not make definite commitments that far ahead. Said Fock: "We had to rack our brains as to what proposals we could make that would greatly interest our Soviet comrades and would not only be good for the Soviet Union, but also useful and necessary for Hungary." The Soviet Union currently provides approximately 90 percent of Hungary's iron ore, oil, and timber, and a high proportion of other raw materials, and the satisfaction of the growing long-term needs for energy and industrial raw materials is understandably a matter of top priority for Budapest's economic planners. The government quickly denied the existence of a serious rift. On the program "TV Forum" (26 April) Rezsö Nyers admitted to disagreements but called them routine and friendly. In an article on Hungary and CEMA (*Pravda,* 13 May), Fock observed that "capital investments made abroad cannot be the sole form of providing our country with raw materials," that "cooperation is particularly important in supplying our country with raw materials," and proclaimed Hungary's readiness to cooperate in providing desirable exports; he also denounced as hostile rumors Western allegations of Soviet irritation.

Indications that the Soviet-Hungarian terms of trade were less than equitable also surfaced. The Soviet-Hungarian aluminum agreement, whereby aluminous earth is exported to the Soviet Union, turned into aluminum by relatively cheap power, and paid for by some of that aluminum, was extended in the course of Fock's negotiations with the Russians, but some Hungarian specialists have argued that the arrangement is not the most economical for Hungary. Reviewing Soviet-Hungarian economic relations, an official of the National Planning Office noted further a "certain deterioration in the goods exchange price ratio" over the past few years resulting from the rise in the price of raw materials, but concluded that there were no alternatives preferable to Soviet supply (*Külgazdaság,* July). In the course of a question-and-answer program on television on 15 September, Deputy Premier Peter Vályi reminded his listeners that it was Hungary's "international duty" to ship uranium to the Soviet Union, and denied that a better price could be had elsewhere.

Whatever inequities may exist in the terms of trade, the basic problem appears to be that the domestic Soviet demand for raw materials and energy is increasing, as is the likelihood that the Russians will export raw materials in exchange for Western products, and as a result Hungary's needs may not receive top priority. On the positive side, the route has been set for a natural gas pipeline to Hungary and the first stage, to be completed by the end of 1974, is expected to satisfy one quarter of current consumption. Nyers led a delegation to the Soviet Union in May, Kádár discussed economic cooperation with Brezhnev and other East European leaders in the Crimea in July, and in October Vályi negotiated an agreement with the Russians that covered various aspects of economic cooperation, including a division of labor in the production of computers. A conference in Budapest (17–20 October) of Soviet and Hungarian economists indicated consensus on the necessity of adapting central planning techniques to the circumstances of individual countries and on the importance of trade expansion to Hungary's economy. Finally, a visit by Brezhnev (27 November–1 December) resulted in "complete mutual understanding" and praise for Hungary's progress and "political maturity." To all appearances Kádár retains the Soviets' confidence (he was awarded the Order of Lenin) and Hungary's economic problems have no hidden political significance.

Premier Fock exhibited cautious optimism in his report on the CEMA's 26th Council session, held in Moscow 10–12 July. On the implementation of the Complex Program adopted last year, he stressed the coordination of long-term economic policies and reiterated that "it is of extreme importance that we make great efforts to solve our raw material problems" (*Népszabadság,* 13 July). Fock noted that it was particularly important for smaller countries such as Hungary that product specialization and cooperative ventures be expanded. The Hun garians maintain, however, their preference for non-compulsory coordination over central direction by a joint planning board, and frequently advocate expanded use of the transferable ruble and the introduction of even partial convertibility to gold. In September CEMA's International Investment Bank granted a 20.5 million transferable ruble credit to the Hungarian State Railways (at 5 percent interest, to be repaid by the end of 1981) for an electrification and modernization program as part of improvements to CEMA's transportation network.

Elsewhere in the socialist bloc, new agreements have been reached to expand border trade with Czechoslovakia and Yugoslavia, the Hungarian-Romanian friendship treaty was officially renewed, and a cultural cooperation agreement was signed by Yugoslavia and Hungary. The *Gastarbeiter* program with East Germany continues; currently some 10,000 young Hungarian workers are gaining experience in East German factories and receiving formal training while helping to alleviate East Germany's labor shortage. Economic relations with Cuba are also being expanded, and a mixed cooperation committee has been established. Fidel Castro made an official visit to Budapest 30 May–6 June. Premier Fock led a delegation in February to North Vietnam, which is to receive new long-term credits as well as military aid from Hungary. In July Fock visited the Mongolian People's Republic and agreement was reached on credits for the completion and initial operation of industrial plant begun with Hungarian assistance. After six years' absence China once again participated in the Budapest International Trade Fair (May), and trade between the two countries rose sharply in 1971.

Relations with the United States were further normalized in the course of 1972. Secretary of State Rogers's visit to Budapest on 6 July coincided with the signing of agreements on consular facilities and scientific cooperation. In October, preliminary agreement was finally reached in Washington on the settlement of private U.S. claims for nationalized and war-damaged property in the amount of $20 million (against an original American claim for $58.1 million). The Hungarians now anticipate Congressional approval for extension to Hungary of most-favored-nation tariff treatment. A delegation of agricultural specialists visited the United States, and Hungary has been granted a $7.5 million credit for soybeans, breeding cattle, agricultural machinery, and licenses. A novel venture was the formation in May of a Hungarian-American joint stock company, "Euroamerican Technocorporation," to develop and market a Hungarian biochemical invention. Another new joint venture is an Italian-Hungarian textile enterprise headquartered in Rome.

Hungarian officials frequently voice complaints about Western economic discrimination. Of the country's exports to this area 33 percent comes under quota restrictions, 41 percent is unrestricted, and 26 percent is subject to the European Economic Community's agricultural regulations. At the April UNCTAD conference in Chile, foreign trade minister József Biró denounced "closed capitalist groupings" and their "discriminatory restrictions" and called for a pan-European integration of power, pipeline, transportation, and pollution-control systems (ibid., 19 April). Hungary has participated in GATT as an observer since 1967 but continues to press for full membership, arguing that the NEM conforms to the criteria of GATT.

In the diplomatic arena, Hungary hews close to the Soviet line, with the main propaganda emphasis currently being on détente and a European security conference. The first deputy foreign minister observed in an article that "the weakening of American influence will tend to increase European détente" (*Társadalmi Szemle*, September). The Central Committee at its June plenum endorsed the agreements between West Germany and the Soviet Union and East Germany. At a meeting with Gustav Husák in Bratislava, 7–9 July, Kádár endorsed Czechoslovakia's insistence that the Munich agreement be recognized by Bonn as being invalid *ab initio;* full diplomatic relations with West Germany appear to be contingent on the settlement of this question. In intra-bloc relations Hungary maintains an orthodox position critical of Romanian-style particularism. Arguing that "no permanent success can be attained by professing sovereignty charged with nationalism," the party's foreign policy expert, Zoltán Komócsin, concluded: "We Hungarian communists do not consider a comradely exchange of opinions or sincere criticism in connection with our problems to be interference in our domestic affairs" (ibid., July–August). At the preliminary talks for a security conference in Helsinki, Hungary sided with the Soviet Union in opposing a Romanian proposal to underscore the equality of states without regard for their membership in a military alliance. Hungary participated in the Warsaw Pact's "Shield 72" military exercises in Czechoslovakia in September. The joint statement issuing from Brezhnev's visit called for a West German–Czechoslovak settlement, urged military cutbacks in Europe, alluded to the "danger inherent in Maoism," and denounced the United States for procrastination in the Vietnam peace negotiations. On every occasion solidarity with the North Vietnamese and the Arabs is proclaimed, while imperialism, neo-colonialism, and racial discrimination are condemned (notably on the occasion of Indira Gandhi's visit to Budapest in June). On 26 September *Népszabadság* announced the creation of a Foreign Affairs Institute, charged with analysis and forecasting, primarily for official consumption.

Publications. HSWP organs include the Budapest daily newspaper *Népszabadság* (People's Freedom); the theoretical monthly *Társadalmi Szemle* (Social Review); and the monthly organizational journal *Pártélet* (Party Life).

University of Toronto   Bennett Kovrig

Poland

The ruling communist party in Poland has been known as the Polish United Workers' Party (Polska Zjednoczona Partia Robotnicza; PUWP) since 1948, when the name was adopted as a result of a fusion in which the Polish Socialist Party was merged with the communists, at that time called the Polish Workers' Party. (The old Communist Party of Poland was dissolved in 1938 by the Comintern, and from 1918 to 1925 had been called the Communist Workers' Party of Poland.)

Although the present constitution dating from 1952 does not give any legal preponderance to the PUWP in the governmental system, the party exercises a virtual monopoly of political control. It rules through various "transmission belts," among which are the parliament (Sejm), Council of Ministers, National Unity Front, comprising two allegedly independent coalition parties, the United Peasant Party and the Democratic Party, along with the PUWP, and the trade unions and other mass organizations.

In the March 1972 elections to the Sejm out of a total of 460 deputies the PUWP elected 255. The rest were divided among the United Peasant Party, with 117; the Democratic Party, 39, and nonaffiliated, 49 (including 10 representatives of Catholic groups). In the Council of Ministers, PUWP members control 25 (out of 35) positions—including the premiership, held by PUWP Politburo member Piotr Jaroszewicz. PUWP control over the State Council is less accentuated: party members occupy only 8 out of 17 seats, including that of the chairman.

Much the same can be said about the Front of National Unity (Front Jedności Narodu; FJN), which is based on an alliance among the three political parties, but also includes representatives of professional and civic organizations. In the past the FJN led a rather lethargic existence except during electoral campaigns. Recently attempts have been made to upgrade its role and make it a consultative body for the elected deputies. Ways of achieving this goal were debated during the 6 April session of its ruling body, the All-Polish Committee of the FJN.

The PUWP has about 2,250,000 members, among the country's population of 33 million (estimated, 1972).

Organization and Leadership. Heading the PUWP as first secretary is Edward Gierek. Through dual roles, 20 men comprise the 15-member Politburo and 11-member Secretariat. The Central Committee, elected at the Sixth PUWP Congress, December 1971, consists of 115 members and 93 candidates. (For changes in the party and government leadership following the shakeup in December 1970 see *YICA, 1971,* pp. 57–58, and *YICA, 1972,* pp. 49–50.)

Mass Organizations. All mass organizations are treated by the PUWP as instruments of its policy, follow its directions, and are in most cases openly controlled by party members. This fact notwithstanding, these organizations also perform the function—though limited—of articulating group interests of their members.

In a special place among the mass organizations are the 22 trade unions, with a total membership of over 10 million, whose activities are coordinated by the Central Council of Trade Unions (CCTU). After a year's delay, the Seventh Congress of the CCTU, was held in Warsaw on 13–15 November 1972. It reelected Władysław Kruczek, a hard-line Politburo member as chairman.

Youth organizations play a vital role in winning young people's support and in providing the party with a reservoir of future members and leaders. The Socialist Youth Union (Związek Młodzieży Socjalistycznej; SYU) and Rural Youth Union (Związek Młodzieży Wiejskiej; RYU) are the most important and most closely associated with the party. Plans are thought to be in preparation for the integration of all existing youth organizations into a single body, modeled on the Soviet Komsomol. This was probably the reason for the indefinite postponement of the SYU congress, originally scheduled for the spring. The Polish Writers' Union held its Eighteenth Congress in Łódź, on 4–5 February. Among the highlights of the meeting, attended by 113 delegates from regional branches, was a discussion on the role of writers in Poland today and the question of censorship.

Another important event occurred when the Polish Lawyers' Association, with about 17,000 members, held its Eighth Congress in Warsaw on 3–4 June. In attendance were 462 delegates, of whom the overwhelming majority (301) belonged to the PUWP. The agenda included a discussion of a report submitted by the association in April to the premier to help the government "guide legislative work."

Interesting personnel changes occurred in the Union of Fighters for Freedom and Democracy (ZBOWiD). On 6 May its Supreme Council elected Stanisław Wroński, minister for culture and the arts, as chairman, replacing General Mieczysław Moczar, who became one of the deputy chairmen. Premier Piotr Jaroszewicz replaced Józef Cyrankiewicz as the chairman of the Supreme Council. These moves indicated Gierek's steady consolidation of control over the organization, which was considered a popular power base for Moczar. The same can be said of the establishment on 8 June of the new Ministry for Veterans' Affairs, which took over many of ZBOWiD's prerogatives.

Party Internal Affairs. The reshuffling of the party leadership which followed the December 1970 riots produced an evident stability at the top of the ruling structure (see *YICA, 1972,* p. 49). The only exception was the case of Józef Tejchma, who—for reasons not fully clarified—was unexpectedly released on 27 March 1972 by the Central Committee from his post of secretary and transferred to the Council of Ministers as one of the deputy premiers. He retained, however, his position in the Politburo. At the same time Zdzisław Żandarowski, head of the committee's Organizational Department, was elected a member of the Secretariat.

Greater personnel changes occurred at lower levels. Four voivodship first secretaries were replaced, and a number of secretaries were transferred. Probably most significant was the appointment of Władysław Kozdra as the first secretary in the voivodship committee of Koszalin. This reputed hard-liner was removed in August 1971 from a similar position in Lublin. More shifts took place at the county level, where during the first six months no fewer than 45 new first secretaries assumed their posts. Without question, the rotation of cadres resulted from a decision of the Politburo which ordered party control commissions to conduct individual talks with about one third of the activists and "apparatchiks." Ostensibly, the purpose of the screening was to find out more about people assigned to important positions and determine whether the tasks given to them were compatible with their abilities. In practice, it resulted in personnel changes in various posts, and even in expulsions from the party. In June, First Secretary Gierek indicated that the purge might be drawing to a close.

In order to rally the party activists to loyal support, the leaders greatly intensified their personal contacts with the party apparatus. The members of the Central Committee were kept currently informed of Politburo and Secretariat activities, and plenary meetings were held more often. On 16 June a central conference was held in Warsaw, chaired by Gierek and attended by members of the Politburo and Secretariat and the heads and deputy heads of Central Committee departments. Participating were the first secretaries of voivodship party committees, deputy premiers, ministers, chairmen of the presidiums of voivodship people's councils, military commanders, leaders of trade unions, youth and women's organizations, directors of industrial amalgamations and representatives of press, radio, and television. The meeting was devoted to a discussion of foreign policy, economy, and ideological activities, with the purpose of evaluating implementation of policy lines laid down at the PUWP's Sixth Congress.

Shortly afterwards, between 25 June and 3 July, a series of party conferences took place in the western and northern provinces. The conferences, proclaimed as a novelty, followed a pattern set up earlier by similar provincial gatherings. They had mainly a business-like character and concentrated on the discussion of regional political and socioeconomic problems. It was characteristic, however, that all of them were attended by Gierek, accompanied by other Politburo and Secretariat members.

The meetings formed a part of a complex system of internal party information, elaborated according to directives issued by the Secretariat in June 1971 and April 1972. A network of "oral information," reaching from the Politburo to secretaries of primary party units and party activists in local communities, was serviced by 6,066 permanent centers (from 58 in the city of Łódź to over 1,000 in the Warsaw voivodship) and by around 30,000 lecturers employed at central, voivodship, and county committees. In addition the system provided for a scheme of written information, consisting of various centrally issued publications, among which a special role is assigned to the magazine *Zagadnienia i materiały* (Problems and Materials). The publishing activities are co-ordinated by the new Central Committee Department of Propaganda, Press, and Publications, created in January by a merger of the Propaganda and Agitation Department with the Press Bureau.

Domestic Affairs. Following approval by the party's Sixth Congress (December 1971), the PUWP leadership in 1972 sought popular confirmation of its mandate by holding parliamentary elections a year ahead of schedule. No doubt, the elections were also intended as a device for the final removal of former first secretary Władysław Gomułka and his followers from the public arena and for the introduction into the Sejm of more amenable deputies. The expectations were fully met, and on 19 March almost 98 percent of the 22,300,000 strong electorate cast the great majority of their ballots (99.53 percent) in favor of candidates from the Front of National Unity. While all 460 "preferred" candidates were elected, the voters— taking advantage of the Polish preferential voting—managed to change the order in which candidates were chosen. Among the affected were a number of high party and government officials, including three Politburo members, who were dropped from first to last places in their respective constituencies. As might have been expected, Gierek's electoral record remained untarnished as he obtained the highest percentage of support (99.8 percent) of all the candidates.

During the first session of the Sejm, 28–29 March, the newly reappointed premier, Piotr Jaroszewicz, presented several personnel and structural changes in the Council of Ministers.

Two of the six deputy premiers in the former government were replaced. Eight former ministries and committees were merged to form five new functional departments, with special emphasis on problems of science and technology, the service industry, ecology, and social problems. It is worth noting that only a minority of present-day ministers are holdovers from the pre-December 1970 government.

Of much broader scope was the administrative reform approved by the Central Committee during its Sixth Plenum, on 27 September. Thus far the plan regulates only the lowest level of rural government, but party leaders made it quite clear that the first step will be followed by others affecting the entire structure of territorial administration. On 1 January 1973 the existing 4,313 rural communities (*gromady*) will be replaced by 2,381 parishes (*gminy*) endowed with greater economic potential and a degree of autonomy. They will be administered from an office headed by a chief (*naczelnik*), appointed by the chairman of the voivodship people's council. Local interests will be represented by the parish council with members elected from each of the participating villages. The essence of the reform lies not only in the creation of necessary conditions for an efficient administrative operation, but also in the formation of a basis for liberalization of an excessively centralized system and for the development of self-government. Perhaps of equal importance is the opportunity to get rid of redundant, poorly qualified, and often counterproductive bureaucrats.

The Economy. As during the previous year, issues of a socioeconomic nature were in the forefront of the party's domestic activities during 1972. The expected comprehensive reform of the economic system did not materialize, however, and the measures recommended in April 1972 by the party-state "Commission on the Modernization of the Economy and the State" caused considerable disappointment. It became clear that the new leadership had decided rather on a gradual approach, introducing only those changes for which—as Gierek has stated —"we are ready."

An example of pragmatic conduct was continuation of measures concerning agriculture. Abolition, after 1 January, of compulsory deliveries of slaughter animals was accompanied by increases, on 1 January and 4 April in prices paid to farmers for deliveries of cattle. As a result, private animal husbandry became profitable and an important improvement, though still insufficient, took place in meat production and in purchases of livestock (e.g., the meat supply in the first quarter of 1972 was 42 percent higher than a year earlier).

The betterment of farmers' incomes—accompanied by the inclusion, since 1 January, of the rural population in the national health service and the earlier 26 October 1971 elimination of difficulties attached to the sale and inheritance of land—is expected to produce far-reaching and beneficial effects. There was a considerable awakening of farmers' interest in acquiring land. At the end of March about 35,000 applicants bid for 120,000 hectares.

Similar steps were taken in regard to the nonagricultural private sector, particularly handicrafts. On 8 June the Sejm approved government bills concerning organization of handicrafts and a social insurance system for artisans. The new laws which replace various professional organizations with the Central Association of Handicrafts and simplify regulations governing the profession, introduced far-reaching tax reductions and exemptions. The system of social insurance provided for more favorable treatment of craftsmen and families in line with principles regulating social insurance of workers. It is expected that improvement of the legal position will result in an increase, by the end of 1975, in the number of artisans' shops (by 16 percent) and in employment (by 27 percent) as well as improvement in the quantity and quality of services rendered by private handicrafts.

Fewer steps have been taken in regard to the system of planning and management. A bill of 1 March, popularly acclaimed as "Charter of Rights and Duties of the Director," only slightly enlarged the autonomy of industrial enterprises by giving managers somewhat greater flexibility in administering wage funds, without making a breach in the present system. On 9 October plans were announced for an experiment in about 30 large economic units. From scant press commentaries it appears that the proposals attempt to achieve two contradictory objectives: to strengthen central planning and to give more autonomy to individual enterprises.

The dominant feature of policy was the attempt to maintain an economic equilibrium under an improved standard of living. The main statistical office report on plan fulfillment in the first half of the year (*Trybuna ludu,* 24 July) showed that this task was basically attained. Total industrial production increased by 12.5 percent, investments by 25 percent, foreign trade turnover by about 20 percent, labor productivity in industry by 7.4 percent, building construction by nearly 10 percent, average gross earnings by 15.6 percent, and average real wages by 5.7 percent. For the first time in many years production of consumers' goods was higher than that of capital goods. The food industry registered the second highest (16 percent) increase in production. Meat supply from commercial slaughter was higher by 28 percent, cured pork products by 19 percent, poultry by 37 percent, and salt-water fish by 15 percent. The total value of agricultural products bought from farmers by state agencies increased about 25 percent. Retail sales of goods were 13.3 percent higher. The general level of retail prices dropped, with the exception of fruits and vegetables.

Despite this favorable overall record, the economy continued to suffer from a number of problems. The growth of labor productivity was slower than the rate of increase in employment, which in the first half year rose by 401,000, exceeding the level anticipated for the whole year (317,000). As a result, the share of labor productivity in the growth of industrial production dropped from about 69 to 62.4 percent. (*Nowe drogi,* July, p. 29.) In this connection, it must be noted that absenteeism in factories, especially in light industry, and poor work discipline were also adverse factors.

Many economic units, mainly connected with the Ministry of Transport, failed to keep costs within prescribed limits. A considerable number of enterprises did not meet their production targets, especially with regard to exports and consumers' goods for domestic markets. The last failure was particularly painful in view of the considerable increase in employment and earnings, notably of the rural population which could only find what it required with difficulty.

To combat negative phenomena, the leadership resorted to a variety of preventive measures, including the old "voluntary production pledges." Early in January the Politburo launched the "Twenty Billion Drive," designed to produce in 1972 an additional amount of goods to that value. It was assumed that the extra production would be achieved mainly through exploiting existing reserves and at only half of normal costs. It appears that official expectations were correct, and a government spokesman indicated on 25 August (PAP, Polish Press Agency, 25 August) that industry had already implemented most of its additional tasks.

Economic goals of the immediate future were presented in the five-year plan for the 1971–75 period. After a long delay (revisions of the Gomułka draft were started in December 1970), the plan was approved by the Central Committee on 27 March and became law with its passage by the Sejm on 8 June. It envisages continuation of two main tasks: improvement of the living standard and development of the national economy. In comparison with goals mentioned earlier (June and December 1971), targets have been considerably raised. Another upward revision has been forecast, and extensive increases are likely to be introduced. Less than a month after the Sejm approved the plan, the Politburo undertook review of a government project to accelerate agricultural output by promoting additional means to achieve a faster growth of animal production and improve utilization of land (*Trybuna ludu,* 4 July).

The way in which the plan was formulated indicated a pragmatic approach, shown by such non-doctrinal features as, for instance, a very small 2.8 percent spread between the rate of increase of industrial production in groups A and B (capital versus consumers' goods), an approximately equal rate of growth of the national income and of per capita consumption (by an average of 1 percentage point per year), and considerable acceleration of investments in connection with consumption and social services (e.g., 786,000 million złoty out of 1,754,000 million were allocated for building construction and installations).

The planned increase in industrial production amounts to a fairly realistic 50 percent, with the highest rate of growth in the electromechanical branch. Production for export should expand by 53 percent, with the electromechanical industry leading the field. Total agricultural production was marked for a 19–21 percent rise (note the above remark about upward revision), with the crucial increase in livestock at 20 percent and the farmers' gross income from sale of goods to the state increasing, over 1970, by 45 percent. The planned increase in average wages, however, was to be only 8 percentage points higher, but it should, during the first two years of the present period, surpass the total gains during 1966–70.

In the housing sector, the plan provided for a modest improvement. The number of constructed dwellings was to increase by about 15 percent, with a somewhat greater growth in usable area (20 percent). Thus the acute housing shortage (100 dwellings per 114 households) will persist, and may worsen due to demographic factors (new marriages, growing numbers of elderly people, migration to the cities), the elimination of "used-up" and substandard dwellings (30 percent of dwellings in use were built before 1918), and the necessity to deconcentrate areas of abnormally high housing density (sometimes 1,200 persons per hectare).

The PUWP leadership is fully aware of the political significance of the problem, and devoted a great deal of attention to it. On 9 February the Central Committee discussed a plan of action, which was then sent for evaluation to higher party organizations and to the experts. Proposals, in three variants, contained a long-range program of construction (up to 1990), with the stress on urban areas and with provisions for raising the quality of dwellings and for increasing their space.

As a result of the debate, which involved about 120,000 persons and produced over 5,000 recommendations, a final draft of proposals was considered by the Central Committee on 10–11 May, at which time the report was delivered by Gierek. His speech defined a series of basic guidelines to be followed in future housing construction. He acknowledged the importance of housing for stabilization and development of family life, promised an independent dwelling unit for each family, and gave assurances that the socialist state "will guarantee full support and legal protection" for privately owned residences. He expressed the conviction that in small towns, settlements, and villages, individual and one-family dwellings should be the fundamental form of housing. At the same meeting, the first secretary of the Lublin party committee suggested transformation of the tenant-type housing co-operatives into ownership-type, and asked that co-operatives start constructing one-family houses.

The draft was approved and then submitted to the Sejm which, after giving it the first reading on 5 July, sent it for detailed analysis to the proper standing commissions. Simultaneously, the Sejm had under consideration two other bills concerned with housing construction. One postulated the exclusion from public administration of one-family houses and flats in co-operative housing developments, thus promoting their purchase by private owners. It was adopted on 6 July.

Relations with the Church. The year 1972 was highly eventful for the Catholic Church. Doubtless the most important occurrence was the decision of the Holy See on 28 June to acknowledge Polish ecclesiastical administration in the so-called Recovered Territories. The Vatican had long hesitated to recognize Polish sovereignty over these lands, but the ratification of the treaty between Poland and West Germany (see below) cleared the previous obstacle. Equally significant for cooling emotional strains, on 26 October the ambassador of the London-based Polish government in exile was notified that the Holy See considered his mission as terminated. Direct contacts between the Warsaw government and the Vatican were maintained and negotiations aimed at resumption of diplomatic ties continued.

Among a number of conciliatory gestures, on 10 February the Ministry of Finance removed a major irritant by abolishing a requirement that the Church maintain inventories of its property for government inspection and tax purposes. Even more significant in demonstrating good will was the benign official attitude toward public religious manifestations, which are held in Poland on a scale unknown in other communist-ruled states of Eastern Europe. Characteristic was approval, perhaps only implicit, of renewed peregrination throughout the country of a replica from the picture of the Black Madonna of Częstochowa. The journey was started in 1966 during celebration of the millenium of Polish Christianity, but was stopped shortly afterwards by the government. Nothing was heard about the matter over the next five years, but in June 1972 the painting started its travels again. A similar conclusion can be drawn from the 28 May pilgrimage of some 150,000 Silesian miners to Piekary Śląskie, where a festive mass was celebrated; from the 15 August country-wide observances of Assumption Day; and from October festivities on the first anniversary of Father Maximilian Kolbe's beatification in Oświęcim (Auschwitz), attended by a number of bishops from the West.

On the other hand such an incident as that at Zbrosza Duża, where in March militiamen demolished a provisional chapel, indicates that real "normalization" of relations awaits resolution of several important issues. Building of churches is among the most complicated and conducive to conflict; also outstanding are the complex question of religious instruction for children, alleviation of taxes, and other problems.

Other Developments. Certainly the main concern of the communist leaders was preservation of positive attitudes toward Gierek among broad segments of the population. Methods used were of the "carrot and stick" variety. Convinced that the 1970 riots had resulted from privations of everyday life, the new leadership made great efforts to satisfy the material needs of the population and remove causes for specific grievances. Preoccupation with the standard of living was supplemented by a number of other popular concessions, such as the already mentioned extension of health insurance to rural inhabitants (about 6.5 million persons), enlargement of maternity benefits (started 1 July), and introduction of uniform sickness benefits for white- and blue-collar workers (to be completed by mid-1974).

The ruling elite also made various attempts to gain or strengthen its support among special-interest groups, seeking in particular to reach a modus vivendi with writers. The climate for an accommodation was not very propitious since the leaders had committed themselves to ideological orthodoxy while the writers demonstrated a growing determination to discard the fetters imposed on them by Gomułka. A conflict appeared inevitable, with the main battle to take place at the February congress of the Polish Writers' Union.

The leadership, however, decided to avoid a confrontation. On the opening day of the congress, 4 February, the party daily *Trybuna ludu* published a long article offering a compromise. Admitting numerous shortcomings in cultural life, publishing policy, and living and working conditions, the article promised their alleviation, removal of "bureaucratic restrictions on cultural activity," and even respect for "controversial opinions" if these were not in conflict with "the most vital interests of the Polish nation and the socialist system."

An olive branch was extended in the opening speech at the congress by the minister of culture and the arts who, while somewhat enlarging restrictions, stated that the new leadership would not "restrict the freedom of creative work in culture" and would take steps to improve the working and living conditions of writers. He ended with an appeal for an accord on fundamental issues. Writers accepted the compromise, though not without caution and even bitterness. As a reward, authorities permitted establishment of two new literary periodicals, *Literatura* and *Teksty*. Their editorial boards, reflecting the mid-course, were chosen from among both liberals and hard-liners. But the spirit of compromise did not last long. At the 2 May conference of "cultural activists," the majority were party members, First Secretary Gierek concentrated on ideological demands smacking of the Gomułka era.

Another group, important in size (almost 500,000 members) and social influence—the teachers—also received notice of leadership appreciation. It came in the form of a law passed by the Sejm in April and known as the "Teachers' Charter." Provisions set up the same legal status for teachers at schools at all levels and provided much improved material conditions for this badly underpaid profession. Starting in May, teachers' salaries are to increase over the next five years by an average of 40 percent to the level of 2,400 złoty monthly for an elementary school teacher receiving at present only 1,400 złoty, and 9,100 złoty per month for a university professor with 16 years' service. Presumably improvements will not only strengthen the party's influence among teachers—in 1971 about 140,000 belonged to the PUWP—but also assure a steady influx of good cadres.

But if Gierek and his team have largely succeeded in resolving problems at hand, their hold on society was still quite weak and the confidence they enjoyed far from complete. Most of the people's doubts centered on economic issues, and they were afraid of a new economic crisis that might destroy the precarious stability. Recently announced price increases for postal and telephone services started widespread rumors that the cost of foodstuffs would follow the trend. In order to defuse tension, the leaders decided on 30 October to prolong the present price freeze for basic food articles until the end of 1973.

The leadership did not hesitate to serve an occasional stern reminder that the party would use force to protect its position. In the August–September political trial at Opole of two brothers accused of acts "hostile to the interests of the state" (*Trybuna Opolska,* 6 September), one was sentenced to death and the other to 25 years' imprisonment.

International Affairs. While attention of the PUWP leadership was primarily focused on domestic issues, matters of foreign policy were also strongly accentuated in 1972. This fact was expressed in a variety of diplomatic activities, ranging from cultivation of ties with the Soviet Union and other communist-ruled states to new international contacts in remote parts of the world. Among the most important events were ratification of the 1970 treaty with West Germany, Vatican recognition of the Odra-Nysa border, and, last but not least, the visit of President Nixon to Warsaw. The varied and extensive nature of these occurrences was hailed by the Polish mass media as a sign of Poland's "growing prestige and authority in international affairs." They also indicated that the new leadership was attempting to exercise a positive role in the community of nations, without jeopardizing special Polish relations with the Soviet Union. Perhaps it is too much to ascribe a major role in these moves to minister of foreign affairs and Politburo member Stefan Olszowski alone.

Soviet Union. In 1972 Poland continued to maintain close ties with the Soviet Union. Warsaw leaders persisted in praising the U.S.S.R. (e.g., Gierek in *Nowe drogi,* August, pp. 5–18) and travelled to Moscow for advice (e.g., "unofficial friendship visit" of Jaroszewicz on 20 June), while Polish foreign policy pronouncements normally echoed those of Soviet officials. As might be expected, the first visit by newly appointed foreign minister Olszowski was with Andrei Gromyko (12–13 January).

At least on one occasion a marked difference in positions—and of interests—became evident. It was demonstrated in connection with the ratification of the 1970 Warsaw treaty by the West German Bundestag, which coupled formal approval with a declaration that the Warsaw and Moscow treaties "do not create any legal foundation for the frontiers existing today." While the Polish reaction was definitely negative, Moscow implicitly accepted the document. It should be added, however, that the disagreement was apparently eliminated during the foreign minister's visit to Moscow on 16–17 May.

The Soviet Union continued to be Poland's most important trading partner, with Polish exports in 1971 amounting to 462,000,000 exchange złoty and imports 478 million. Economic cooperation was associated with extensive scientific-technical collaboration, frequently evaluated at joint meetings of the Polish-Soviet Commission, which held its 12th meeting in Warsaw on 2–3 February.

Perhaps even greater significance could be ascribed to the opening of two new Polish consulates-general, at Minsk in April and Leningrad in July. Although there still exists great inequality (the Soviet Union has 5 consulates for about 374,000 of its ethnic minorities within Poland), this was a definite improvement. Previously, only one Polish consulate at Kiev served about 1.5 million Poles scattered from the Bug River to Kazakhstan.

China. On 18–26 April the joint standing commission of the Chinese-Polish Shipbrokers' Company met in Warsaw. At present, 20 ships sail the Poland-China route. On 28 April the new Chinese ambassador to Poland presented his credentials. Also this year, China took part in the Poznań international trade fair. On the whole, relations between Poland and China remained correct but rather distant, with some criticism of Chinese policies (e.g., *Nowe drogi,* May, pp. 127–31).

Other Communist-Ruled States. A symptomatic relationship, reminiscent of the pre-1968 "northern tier" concept, continued among Poland, Czechoslovakia and East Germany. In addition to political aspects, however, now economic and technical co-operation is strongly accentuated. Frequent visits of higher party and government officials underline growing ties among these three key states of Eastern Europe.

In 1972 especially close bonds developed with the German Democratic Republic (GDR), despite the ratification of the Warsaw Treaty with West Germany. Official friendship was manifested in June by an especially cordial meeting of Polish and East German leaders, headed by Edward Gierek and Erich Honecker, respectively. But the attempts to bridge old divisions were not restricted to the elites alone. About 9 million Poles and 6 million East Germans crossed the border on the basis of a 1971 agreement permitting visa-free travel and practically unrestricted shopping. Tourists were aided by the semi-official newspapers, *Berliner Zeitung* and *Życie Warszawy,* which published special foreign-language editions for them. Unfortunately, the open-door experiment, unique in Eastern Europe, ended on a sour note. Polish tourists discovered that East Germany represented a commercial heaven in comparison with their own country and started a "run" on GDR shops. Understandably, this caused difficulties for the local population and resulted in a number of unfriendly incidents. To prevent other consequences, authorities reimposed customs and currency regulations on 27 November, but visa-free travel remains.

Relations with other communist-ruled countries followed the usual pattern of visits, declarations of friendship and, in most cases, agreements on economic and technical cooperation. The list of partners with whom Poland dealt in 1972 was extensive, ranging from the other East European states—including Albania, with which a trade protocol was signed in Warsaw on 18 January—to such remote places as North Vietnam, North Korea, Mongolia, South Yemen, and Cuba. Perhaps most unusual among all the dealings was a rather disappointing visit of Cuban premier Fidel Castro to Warsaw on 6–13 June. Official talks appear to have been kept to the bare minimum and no formal communiqué was issued at the end. There was, however, a visible desire for an increase in trade. In February a Polish delegation visited Cuba and shortly afterward a two-year agreement was signed which is expected to double the present turnover by the end of 1973.

Poland again promised assistance to "strengthen the defensive potential" of North Vietnam. The nature of the Polish commitment and its financial value were not revealed. It is known, however, that Polish exports during the 1966–70 period exceeded those of North Vietnam to Poland by about $72 million.

A highlight of 1972 was the visit of Yugoslavia's President Tito with his wife and an impressive retinue of officials to Poland on 19–23 June. Tito's stay offered an opportunity for an extensive exchange of views with Gierek and agreements on a number of issues, including support for a European security conference. Several differences on "socialist construction" were registered but allegedly represent "no obstacle to a favorable development of friendly relations." An accord on increased trade, expected to top $200 million for the year, was signed on this occasion.

Relations with the Federal Republic of Germany. In mid-September 1972, subsequent to the May ratification of the 1970 Warsaw treaty, Poland became the third Warsaw Pact state (after the Soviet Union and Romania) to establish diplomatic relations with West Germany. The decision was announced during a visit to Bonn by Foreign Minister Olszowski on 13–14 September. It was followed by an exchange of ambassadors. Thus an important step was taken on the long, uneasy road to normalization of relations.

Among serious problems that remain to be solved is the resettlement of ethnic Germans from Poland. While the Germans accuse Poland of failing to live up to its obligations and holding up to a quarter of a million applicants, the Polish side maintains that the problem is already solved and points to the dropping rate of exit permits issued. These declined by half in comparison with 1971, when 25,243 ethnic Germans left Poland. It appears that the controversy, in addition to the emotional factors involved, centers on the similar desire of one side to retain and the other to gain a skilled labor force. The whole question is under continuous review by representatives of respective Red Cross organizations, who frequently meet in either Polish or West German cities.

Two more issues occupied public attention in 1972. One was compensation for the victims of Nazi medical experiments in concentration camps; the other, revision of school textbooks. In both areas significant progress was recorded. A big step was taken in July with a decision by the West German government to pay indemnification in the sum of about $100 million. Fruitful efforts were reported by a joint commission of scholars and experts on textbooks, engaged in elimination of historically distorted facts from accounts of relations between the two countries. It was agreed in Brunswick on 12–15 April that maps should carry official names in force of the country in question. The task is expected to be finished in two years.

Many other exchanges took place between Poland and West Germany. On 5–10 February, the chairman of the Social Democratic Party parliamentary group in the Bundestag visited Warsaw in response to an invitation and was received by Gierek, Jaroszewicz, and Olszowski. On the Polish side, perhaps most consequential was the visit by seven members of the Catholic "ZNAK" group, who were received in West Germany in a manner befitting an official delegation. More exchanges will undoubtedly be promoted by other mutual efforts, of which the establishment of a West German-Polish Society in Hamburg is a beginning.

In the area of economic relations, an additional protocol on exchange of goods for 1972 was signed early in January, giving Poland better chances to increase its export of machines and other industrial goods. The trade turnover between the two countries rose in the first quarter by 52.6 percent over the same period in 1971 (*Rynki zagraniczne,* 22 June). West Germany became Poland's biggest trade partner in the West, and Poland was West Germany's second largest partner (following the Soviet Union) among the East European countries.

Relations with Other States. Polish relations with non-communist countries aside from West Germany might be depicted graphically as two concentric circles. Within the smaller, embracing France, the Scandinavian countries, and Austria, Polish policies were motivated by two desires: implementation of Soviet foreign policy in regard to détente with the West and satisfaction of a genuine Polish desire for peace. Within the bigger area, which included the above-mentioned states as well, Polish diplomatic activities seemed to be directed by a desire to expand trade.

Traditional friendship with France has been revitalized and strengthened by close and large-scale cooperation in commercial, technical, and cultural fields. Trade protocols for 1972 gave Poland a greater chance for export of investment goods and thus improved the structure of existing turn-over. France granted Poland credit on favorable terms to finance French imports. This should help to preserve, or perhaps improve, France's position as Poland's fourth most important (following West Germany, Britain, and Italy) trade partner in the West, with total turnover in 1971 reaching some $158 million.

Official visits to France included the 2–5 October trip of First Secretary Gierek, who held a number of top level talks. A joint declaration was signed, together with a new ten-year economic agreement.

Reciprocal contacts between Poland and the Scandinavian countries included visits to Poland by the foreign ministers of Sweden in March, and Denmark in April, and of the defense minister of Norway in April, reciprocated by the Polish deputy foreign minister's visit to Iceland in May, the defense minister's trip to Finland in June, and Foreign Minister Olszowski's visit to Norway, 25–29 June. Olszowski had visited Austria on 12–15 June.

Relations with the United States were highlighted by President Nixon's visit to Warsaw on 31 May–1 June. A joint communiqué issued at the end expressed, among other things, U.S. satisfaction with the 1970 Warsaw treaty, "including its border provisions." This passage was widely interpreted as de facto U.S. recognition of the Odra-Nysa border. At the same time, a consular convention was signed by U.S. Secretary of State Rogers and Foreign Minister Olszowski which regulated the treatment of U.S. citizens of Polish descent in Poland and the opening, as of 1 December of new consulates in Kraków and New York.

The American secretary of commerce visited Poland on 1–2 August and held official talks which resulted in establishment of a Polish-U.S. Commission on Trade. On 17–18 September Foreign Minister Olszowski visited Washington and was received by President Nixon and Secretary of State Rogers. Taking advantage of the East-West détente, the Polish leadership was anxious to expand trade and scientific-technical co-operation with the United States. A number of important licensing contracts have been signed and others are being negotiated. In 1971, Polish imports from the United States amounted to only $73 million dollars, while exports came to $107 million.

International Party Contacts. When discussing relations between ruling communist parties, it is difficult to distinguish where party matters end and government business begins. With this in mind, it is possible to say that the pattern of PUWP international contacts generally paralleled the course of Polish diplomatic activities. The most lively exchanges took place with Moscow, visited by at least half the Politburo. These peregrinations were highlighted by the trip of First Secretary Gierek to the Crimea conference of East European party chiefs (31 July). A five-man Politburo delegation led by Gierek attended the December 50th anniversary of the Soviet Union. High-ranking CPSU visitors to Warsaw were limited to only one Polit-buro member, Victor Grishin, who arrived to help commemorate the same jubilee. Province party leaders from both countries and members of the respective apparats exchanged visits on several occasions, for the purpose of strengthening ties and standardizing administrative practices.

Relations with other ruling communist parties of East Europe were also quite active. In addition to lower-level contacts, Gierek met in June with East German leader Erich Honecker. In July, during the Crimea conference, he held a separate meeting with Czechoslovak party chief Gustav Husak. The Bulgarian leader Todor Zhivkov saw Gierek at Warsaw, who revisited him in Sofia on 5 August. Gierek also conferred at length with Marshal Tito during the latter's stay in Poland. During 5–7 July, a Polish delegation took part in an ideological conference organized by the monthly *Problems of Peace and Socialism* at Prague.

Contacts with non-ruling communist parties were less frequent, but rather extensive in their territorial scope. They ranged from participation in various congresses (Lebanon, Italy, Finland, and France) to visits by foreign communist leaders from Denmark, Norway, Ecuador, and Peru.

Publications. The daily organ of the PUWP is *Trybuna ludu* ("People's Tribune"), with a circulation of 480,000 copies. The monthly theoretical journal is *Nowe drogi* ("New Roads"). *Życie Warszawy* is an important, semi-official Warsaw daily with the appearance of a popular, non-party paper.

University of Windsor   Vincent C. Chrypiński
Canada

Romania

The Romanian Communist Party (Partidul Comunist Român; RCP), according to official histories, was founded on 13 May 1921, following the splintering of the social democratic party. From its founding the party was harassed by government authorities; in 1924 it was banned. Lacking popular support because of its official sympathy for the return of Bessarabia to Russia and the non-Romanian character of much of its membership, and plagued by internal dissensions, the party was unable to exploit the economic crisis of the 1930s with any real success. The growth of fascist elements in Romania led to further police activity against the illegal party.

With its leaders either incarcerated in Romania or in exile in the Soviet Union, the RCP had a limited role during the early years of World War II until the defeat of the Nazis on the eastern front and the arrival of Soviet troops in Romania reversed its fortunes. On 23 August 1944 the pro-German government was overthrown in a coup d'état and a coalition came to power. In October 1944, under communist leadership, the National Democratic Front was established. The elections of November 1946, which were held under legislation highly favorable to the RCP, resulted in an overwhelming victory for the front and further strengthened the Communists. On 30 December 1947 the king was forced to abdicate and the People's Republic of Romania was proclaimed. In February 1948 the RCP and the Social Democratic Party were merged into the Romanian Workers' Party. At the same time the National Democratic Front was replaced by the People's Democratic Front, in which the new party had predominant influence.

In July 1965 the RCP name was resumed as a concomitant step to the elevation of Romania from a "people's democracy" to the status of a "socialist republic." In 1968, when Romania opposed the Soviet-led invasion of Czechoslovakia, the party sought to mobilize mass support, and the Front of Socialist Unity was created to replace the largely inactive People's Democratic Front. The reorganized front includes trade union, youth, and women's organizations, and organizations representing the various national minorities in Romania. The RCP is the only political party. The front provides for mass participation in politics at all levels.

On 30 June 1972 party membership reached some 2,231,000, or about 15 percent of the adult population. Of this total, 1,023,000 (46 percent) were workers, 534,000 (24 percent) were peasants, and 511,000 (23 percent) were intellectuals and officials (*Scînteia*, 20 July). The most significant change in structure was the decline in peasant membership from 28 percent in 1969 to less than 24 percent. In part this reflects the difficulty of attracting the rural population, but more fundamentally it mirrors the decline in the rural population itself, as Romania's growing industry draws manpower to urban areas. The ethnic composition of the party in June 1972, approximately the same as that of the country as a whole, was 88 percent Romanian, 8 percent Hungarian, and 3 percent German. The striking increase in ethnic German party members from 1.4 percent as of 31 December 1971 to 3 percent six months later was undoubtedly due to the policy of discouraging their emigration and attempting to integrate them more closely into Romanian social and political life.

Organization and Leadership. The party is organized into basic units or cells in factories, on farms, and in smaller political subdivisions. In 1972 there were some 64,500 such units. The next higher organizational step is represented by the party organizations in communes (rural territorial subdivisions) and municipalities, in which there are 2,702 and 235 organizations, respectively. Finally, there are party organizations for each of the 39 counties and for the municipality of Bucharest, which oversee the lower-level organizations within their territory. (Figures from *Scînteia,* 20 July). Each of these units is directed by a party committee headed by a secretary or a first secretary who is responsible for the activity of the unit.

According to the party statutes, the supreme authority of the RCP is the party congress, which is held every five years and to which delegates are elected by county party organizations. However, the real power is wielded by the Permanent (Standing) Presidium, the Secretariat, the Executive Committee, and the Central Committee. The Permanent Presidium (created in 1965 to replace the old Politburo) is the highest body in the party, and its members are the most influential persons in Romania. Eight of the present members were elected at the Tenth Congress, in August 1969: Nicolae Ceauşescu, Emil Bodnăraş, Ion Gheorghe Maurer, Paul Niculescu-Mizil, Gheorghe Pană, Gheorghe Rădulescu, Virgil Trofin, and Ilie Verdeţ. In February 1971, at a plenary session of the Central Committee, Manea Mănescu was also elected to this body.

The Secretariat, composed of the secretary-general and a number of Central Committee secretaries, is responsible for various spheres of party activity; its members are also powerful figures in the party. Nicolae Ceauşescu is the secretary-general, elected as such by the party congress, while the other secretaries are elected by the Central Committee. During 1972 a series of major changes affected the Secretariat, and only three of the eight secretaries in office at the year's end had been in office at the beginning: Mihai Gere, Gheorghe Pană, and Dumitru Popescu. At a short working session of the Central Committee on 16 February, Cornel Burtică was elected to the Secretariat and Vasile Patilineţ was removed and made Minister of Forestry Administration and Construction Materials, following a series of irregularities in the security and military sphere for which he had been responsible. At a Central Committee plenum on 18 April Niculescu-Mizil, formerly the party secretary responsible for foreign affairs, was released from the Secretariat and made a deputy premier (Maurer is premier), and Ştefan Andrei, Iosef Banc, and Ion Dincă were appointed secretaries. At a plenum on 20–21 November Mănescu, who a month earlier had been appointed a deputy premier and chairman of the State Planning Committee (see below), was released from the Secretariat, and Miron Constantinescu was appointed in his place.

By these changes a number of powerful figures in the party were removed from the Secretariat and put into government posts, while several relatively junior men in the party hierarchy were promoted to the Secretariat. It is possible that those removed were in opposition to Ceauşescu or his policies, but the fact that they continue to hold high positions in the government and party would seem to indicate that they have not fallen completely from favor. The policy of merging party and government, which Ceauşescu has been advocating for some time, may also be a partial explanation, and it is possible that the secretary-general, who directs the Secretariat, may be bringing the next generation of political leaders into his inner circle in anticipation of the departure of his current colleagues.

The Executive Committee was created at the Ninth Congress, July 1965, primarily to give

Ceauşescu a leading party body in which his own supporters would predominate, since at that time the Permanent Presidium was composed largely of older leaders not beholden to the new party head. The Executive Committee stands midway between the Permanent Presidium and the Central Committee in authority and prestige. Among its 21 full and 17 alternate members are the members of the Permanent Presidium and the Secretariat, and leading government and state officials.

The Central Committee is a body selected by the party congress to direct party affairs in the periods between congresses. It meets in plenary session every two or three months to consider and approve programs and policies. At the beginning of 1972 the Central Committee was composed of 165 full and 115 alternate members. In July the national party conference (see below) decided to add 20 new full and 20 alternate members, for the stated purpose of giving greater representation to persons engaged directly in economic activity and to women. Among those added as full members was the wife of the secretary-general. (For the newly elected members see *Scînteia,* 22 July.)

Party Internal Affairs. Between party congresses, the Central Committee is empowered to convene the National Party Conference, which is on the same scale as a congress except that there are no foreign party delegations and its authority is slightly inferior to that of a congress. A conference is usually convened to deal with specific problems, while the congress concerns itself with general policy. The first such conference of the RCP since the party consolidated its power in Romania was held in December 1967 to consider and adopt a series of administrative and economic reforms. The second took place on 19–21 July 1972, in Bucharest. Its main purpose was to draw up a balance sheet on the economic reforms decided upon at the earlier conference in 1967, as was clearly stated in the 18 April plenum decision to convoke it. However, at the conference no balance sheet on the reforms was presented, and it was announced that the deadline for implementing them had been further postponed, until 1973. The speeches and resolutions indicated a predilection for administrative and organizational reshuffling rather than structural or institutional reform.

The main thrust of the conference in the economic sphere was for upward revision of the targets of the 1971–75 five-year plan. This was the third upward revision since the draft plan was adopted in June 1969. A slogan, repeated frequently and approved by Ceauşescu, called for completion of the plan in four and a half years, and although this proposal was enthusiastically accepted by many of his supporters, there were also obvious signs of discontent. A number of county party secretaries did not pledge to meet these higher targets even when prodded by Ceauşescu to do so. No less a figure than Premier Maurer had earlier delivered a speech, at Cluj, telling party and economic leaders to produce less but better (*Făclia,* Cluj, 25 June), on the same day that Ceauşescu was telling a similar group in Bucharest that raising the targets of the plan was desirable and possible (*Scînteia,* 25 June). Although by the year's end less was heard about completing the five-year plan six months ahead of schedule, there were still enthusiastic exhortations to fulfill it ahead of time. In his speech to the National Party Conference, Ceauşescu specified that the increased targets were to be met through greater efficiency and higher productivity, not through higher investments. He called for better utilization of existing capacities, increased labor productivity, cutting down delays in meeting supply deadlines, adopting more advanced technological processes, and modernizing production methods; also he expected benefits to accrue from cooperation with Western countries in production and technology. While calling for greater industrial output without further investment, he also pledged to improve the standard of living through higher wages, more housing construction, and an increased supply of consumers' goods.

A number of laws and resolutions were approved by the conference, which were to be discussed publicly and improved upon before being submitted for adoption by the Grand National Assembly (parliament). A new draft bill on "Remuneration According to the Quality and Quantity of Work Performed" was proposed which unified existing legislation and established detailed provisions to utilize wages as an economic lever to encourage greater worker interest in the efficiency and quality of production (text in *Scînteia, 29* July). A draft labor code, in preparation since 1967, was also presented (text, ibid., 30 July). The code establishes the rights and duties of employees and workers, the conditions and regulations relating to employment which must be observed by the management of economic enterprises, and provisions on safety, child and female labor, and trade unions. A draft bill on finance was also presented which codifies all legislation relating to the creation and distribution of financial resources, the system of financial accounting and planning, financing and credit, state insurance, personal savings, and the state budget (text, ibid., 28 July). The conference approved a law on planning which establishes the principles on which economic planning is to be based and defines the responsibilities and relationships of the various agencies involved in drawing up, implementing, and checking fulfillment of the plans (text, ibid., 27 July). This law and certain conference resolutions expanded the scope of the economic plan to include the entire socio-economic development of the country. The conference approved the creation of a new body, the Supreme Council for Socio-Economic Development, which will be attached to the State Council and headed by Ceaușescu. Most of these draft bills were discussed and amended after their presentation at the conference, and were adopted by the Grand National Assembly in December.

The speeches and resolutions at the conference stressed the need to strengthen the leading role of the party in all areas of Romanian life. In this regard the party continued the line introduced with the cultural-ideological campaign initiated in the previous July (see ibid., 7, 10 July 1971). Ceaușescu reiterated his concern that party functionaries acquire experience in state positions and vice versa, and again proposed rotation of officials in order to broaden their horizons. The concern to strengthen party control over the economy in order to increase discipline and efficiency was reflected in Ceaușescu's instructions to the party leaders at the conference to become directly concerned with production, and in his proposal that leading factory managers be added to the Central Committee. The cultural and ideological policy instituted in the summer of 1971 was given the imprimatur of the party conference.

During the conference Ceaușescu and a number of other speakers discussed Romanian foreign policy and the role of the socialist nation under contemporary conditions, and resolutions on these topics were approved (Ceaușescu speech, ibid., 20 July; text of resolutions, ibid., 23 July). Although no new formulations or policies were introduced, the party's position on these matters was solidly reaffirmed. The importance of the nation in the contemporary era —it was said to be under attack not only from imperialists but also in Marxist-Leninist circles —was reaffirmed. A distinction was made between the "socialist nation" and the "bourgeois nation," the former being a qualitative step above the latter and hence progressive. It was explained that there could be no difference between true national interests and socialist internationalism, because "one cannot be an internationalist if one does not love one's own nation and struggle to . . . build a new socialist and communist nation." The speeches and the resolution on foreign affairs reaffirmed the principle of state sovereignty and the Romanian view that international relations must be based upon "sovereignty, equality, independence, and non-interference in the internal affairs of other nations." The desire to maintain good relations with *all* socialist countries, with the developed Western states, and with the developing countries was reaffirmed.

Merging of Party and State. Ceaușescu has frequently expressed the desire to bring about a closer relationship between party and state, in order to avoid parallelism and secure better implementation of the party's policy. This theme was reiterated in his speech to the National Party Conference and on several other occasions during the year, and a number of steps were taken to put this policy into practice. Ceauşescu, as leader of the party, had assumed the position of president of the State Council (head of state) in December 1967, and at about the same time the party first secretaries of the county party organizations also became heads of the county People's Councils (the county government units). This practice has since been extended to communes and municipalities. As noted earlier, on 18 April Niculescu-Mizil, a member of the Permanent Presidium and until then a party secretary, became a deputy premier and in October was also appointed minister of education. At the October 11 Executive Committee session two other members of the Permanent Presidium and former party secretaries were also made deputy premiers and given specific responsibilities: Trofin became minister of internal trade (responsible for supply of consumers' goods and food to the population), and Mănescu became chairman of the State Planning Committee. This means that of the nine members of the party's leading body (the Permanent Presidium), six are members of the Council of Ministers. These changes at the highest levels of the party have been accompanied by similar changes on the local level. At a conference with county party officials in the fall, Ceauşescu suggested (ibid., 10 September), and at the plenum on 20–21 November the Central Committee decided, that county party secretaries responsible for economic problems and those responsible for propaganda matters should become vice-presidents of the People's Councils, and that county party secretaries in charge of organizational problems should be elected secretaries of the corresponding units of the Front of Socialist Unity (ibid., 22 November). This merging of party and state appears to be an attempt to eliminate the parallel existence of party and government organizations at all levels, by having the party take over the government. The fact that these measures are being taken on the local as well as the national level strongly indicates that the shifting of Permanent Presidium members into government functions is not a demotion for them, but involves the implementation of Ceauşescu's concept of the relationship between party and government.

Domestic Affairs. *The Economy.* Figures on plan fulfillment during the first six months of 1972 indicated that targets for the total value of industrial production during that period had been exceeded by 1.9 percent, and that in comparison with the same period in 1971 industrial output had increased by 12.6 percent. Above-average growth was achieved in the machine-building and light industries, and average gains were recorded in the electric power, chemical, and food industries. The plan provisions were seriously underfulfilled in the production of chemical fertilizers and meat, however. Investment from central state funds was 12.1 percent above the same period in 1971, but in view of the 15 percent goal set for all of 1972, the figure for the first half year appears to be low (*Scînteia*, 16 July). The provisions for the 1973 plan reflect the drive to fulfill the five-year plan ahead of schedule. Industrial output is scheduled to grow by 16.2 percent and agricultural production by 9.2 percent, while total national income is to grow by 14 percent.

Despite heavy rainfall and adverse weather conditions between August and October, agricultural output for 1972 was satisfactory. The grain harvest was particularly good, and Romania apparently agreed to provide a half million tons of wheat to the Soviet Union. Reports that this would be the best harvest in Romania's history (Agerpres, Romanian news agency, 15 November) will probably hold true for grains, but delays in harvesting caused by the adverse weather resulted in serious losses of vegetables and fruits. Romanian agriculture is still faced with problems caused by a lack of incentive for agricultural workers and organizational difficulties. These issues, among others, were discussed during the Second Congress of the National Union of Agricultural Production Cooperatives, 21–23 February. In an address to the congress, Ceauşescu was critical of administrative shortcomings, emphasized the importance of increasing agricultural efficiency, and stressed the need to extend the irrigation system and expand the use of chemical fertilizers. He also noted that 50 percent of the country's livestock is to be found on private plots, and he called on agricultural administrators to take measures to provide the private sector with greater assistance in order to expand its production (*Scînteia*, 22 February). Proposals to increase wages of farm workers and to reduce the gap between the income of peasants and that of industrial workers were announced. In an attempt to provide better mechanical assistance to agriculture, a reorganization of the Agricultural Mechanization Enterprises (which replaced the former Machine Tractor Stations in 1968) was effected (ibid., 25 March).

A number of measures were taken during the year to deal with a major economic problem —supplying the population with consumers' goods and food. A draft bill on internal trade was approved by the party Executive Committee for presentation to the Grand National Assembly. However, it did not contain any innovations with regard to the domestic trade system, and appeared to be little more than a codification of existing procedures. (Text, ibid., 18 March.) Two other changes which may have a greater impact on this problem were the appointment of Permanent Presidium member Trofin as vice-premier and minister of domestic trade and the creation of a new "Council on Supply and Service to the Population," which he will also head (ibid., 7 November). The provisions of the 1973 plan call for increased output of consumers' goods and provide for greater investment in this sector, although the envisioned increases are relatively modest.

In the early 1970s large credits from Western countries fell due, and various difficulties inhibited an increase in exports; therefore, Romania launched a campaign to reduce imports and expand exports. Preliminary foreign trade figures for 1972 indicate that this program was quite successful. In the first six months of the year exports rose by 14.7 percent and imports by only 10.9 percent, and by year's end it was calculated that the export surplus in convertible currency would exceed 900,000,000 lei ($150,000,000). This led Ceauşescu to conclude that the country would achieve an external payments balance by 1973–74.

Problems of economic management and organization continued to be of concern to the party. A conference of managers of centrals and enterprises in February provided an occasion to express strong criticism of specific branches of the economy and introduce limited measures to strengthen individual enterprises at the expense of the centrals. However, few steps were taken to further implement the economic reform, and the emphasis on party control of the economy led to greater confusion. The party's continued insistence upon a command economy and its reluctance to make alterations in the system to permit such economic levers as prices to influence economic decisions led to more problems.

Culture and Education. The oft-postponed Writers' Union Conference was finally held on 22–24 May, following delays caused by differences between the writers and the party leadership over the cultural-ideological campaign launched in July 1971. By adopting a calculated policy of halfhearted concessions and threats, the party succeeded in winning over a proportion of the writers. Contrary to previous practice, this conference was open only to delegates elected by the various local writers' associations, not to the entire membership, and thus a number of potentially dissident writers were excluded from participation. The strengthening of party control over cultural life was contested by some writers at the conference, but Ceauşescu insisted in his address that literary life must be infused with revolutionary ideology, and the directives adopted by the Writers' Union regarding its future activity reflected the party leader's view. The 91 members of the union's council included writers of liberal as well as conservative persuasion, but the majority of the leaders elected are willing to compromise with the party. (*România literară,* 25 May.) The cultural scene generally continued to be marked by the uneasy compromise between party, which controls privileges and the purse, and writers, who would prefer less emphasis on ideology. The theater proved to be the area in which the ideological tightening was most strongly felt. The interdiction of a daring production of Gogol's *The Inspector General* was followed by major changes in the leadership of the theater involved, and this served to emphasize the party's insistence upon ideological conformity.

The reorganizations affecting education intensified by the ideological campaign continued with the appointment of Permanent Presidium member Niculescu-Mizil as vice-premier and minister of education. The drive to link education more closely to the needs of the economy was intensified, and the importance of strengthening ideological education was stressed at a meeting of social science teachers (*Scînteia,* 11 November). Ceauşescu previously had called for more militant combating of religious ideas (ibid., 3 October). (A "Central Commission for the Dissemination of Scientific Knowledge" was established in May for the purpose of carrying out such a campaign on a scientific level—see *Scînteia Tineretului,* 30 June.)

Internal Security and Military Affairs. In mid-February Western newspapers reported that Romanian General Ion Şerb had been executed for spying for the Soviet Union. Although no official Romanian statement was made, later reports indicated that Şerb, though not executed, had lost his military position, and later a by-election was held to select a new Grand National Assembly deputy to replace him (*Buletinul Oficial,* 8 August). At about the time the reports on Şerb began to circulate, a number of personnel changes took place in the armed forces. Earlier (in January) Vasile Patilineţ, the party secretary in charge of security and military affairs, was appointed minister of forestry administration and construction materials, and was shortly thereafter released from his post in the Secretariat. His responsibilities for military and security affairs were not transferred to anyone else until April, when party secretary Ion Dincă assumed them. In February the State Security Council, which deals with internal security matters, was reorganized (ibid., 28 February), and in April it was decided to merge the council into a newly reorganized Ministry of the Interior (ibid., 19 April). Completing the series of changes in this area was the reorganization of the Ministry of Defense, which is now subordinate directly to the State Council (of which Ceauşescu is president), and only incidentally to the Council of Ministers (ibid., 30 November). Although these developments in military and security affairs pointed to the existence of apparently serious problems in this sector, there are indications that they were resolved, at least for the time being. The fact that Ceauşescu made a four-week tour to Africa during March, as changes were taking place, would indicate that he was confident of control.

Foreign Relations—Communist Party States. *The Soviet Union.* Relations with the Soviet Union improved during 1972, after the war of nerves and the deterioration in relations that had followed Ceauşescu's visit to China the previous June. The most visible indication of this improvement was Ceauşescu's participation in a conference of East European leaders in the Crimea in late July. (The Romanian leader was conspicuously absent from a similar gathering a year earlier.) After the joint talks, Ceauşescu met separately with Brezhnev (*Scînteia,* 2 August). The Romanian party leader also went to Moscow in late December to attend the celebrations marking the 50th anniversary of the creation of the Soviet Union, and had talks with other East European leaders. This improvement was also reflected in the economic sphere when the joint Soviet-Romanian Commission on Economic Cooperation met in late July (ibid., 29 July). Not only was it decided to start coordinating the 1976–80 plans of the two countries much earlier than usual, but it was also agreed that Romania would invest, with other members of Council for Mutual Economic Assistance, in a cellulose plant and a metallurgical complex to be built in the Soviet Union. The two countries also worked out details on the construction of a hydroelectric and irrigation project on the river Prut, which forms part of their common border. But despite these obvious signs of improving relations, there were no indications that either country had altered its position on foreign affairs. The Soviet Union, in cryptically worded broadcasts to Romania and articles in Soviet publications, seemed anxious to achieve greater coordination in foreign policy and to secure Romanian conformity with Soviet desires. Romania, on the other hand, continued to reiterate its insistence that relations among states—even socialist ones—must be based upon the principles of sovereignty, absolute equality, independence, and noninterference in internal affairs. Romania's actions at the Helsinki preparatory talks for a European conference on security and cooperation and at the United Nations—actions which were in conflict with Soviet policy—reaffirmed its intention to pursue its own course despite improved relations with the Soviet Union. In the present circumstances both countries apparently see no advantage in emphasizing the differences between them.

The same policy of cooperating within limits and minimizing differences marked Romania's relations with other Warsaw Pact and CMEA countries. At the meeting of Warsaw Pact leaders in Prague in February, the Romanian delegation included Ceauşescu, Premier Maurer, and other high-ranking party and government officials. Marshal Ivan Yakubovsky, the Warsaw Pact commander, visited Bucharest not long before this conference was held. However, Romania continued its policy of not participating in military maneuvers on foreign soil, as was emphasized by the fact that the Romanian defense minister attended the September joint maneuvers in Czechoslovakia as an observer, and no Romanian troops took part. Romania continued to improve its economic relations with the East European states through CMEA, but, it emphasized that there is no supranational planning within this economic grouping and that each state maintains full sovereignty in economic matters. In recent years Romanian cooperation with CMEA has increased because of a growing fear of the consequences of being left out of the organization's plans and also because it is easier to market manufactured goods in the East than in the West. One indication of this was that Romania decided to join the CMEA Ball Bearing Association, which was founded in 1964 and which it had refused to join until this year (ibid., 6 April).

Eastern Europe. Among the states of Eastern Europe, Romania continued to maintain the closest relations with Yugoslavia. In addition to a constant exchange of middle-level party and government delegations between the two countries, Premier Maurer paid an eight-day official visit to Yugoslavia on 12–19 September, before which Tito and Ceauşescu met on 16–17 May to inaugurate the Iron Gates hydroelectric and navigation system on the Danube. The Iron Gates project, initially discussed in 1956 and put under construction in 1964, has already led to faster and safer navigation of the Danube and will ultimately provide each of the two countries with an average of 5.2 billion kwh. of electric power annually. In addition to this huge project, economic cooperation between the two countries has made considerable progress in the past few years, and there are reports that they will cooperate in the manufacture of a jet fighter/trainer aircraft (*Flight International,* 17 August).

The series of treaties between Romania and the other states of the Warsaw Pact was completed with the signing of new 20-year treaties of friendship and alliance with Hungary and East Germany. This series was initiated in July 1970 when a Soviet-Romanian treaty was signed, to be followed by similar documents with Bulgaria and Poland. (A treaty with Czechoslovakia was signed in August 1968 as an indication of support for the Dubček government, just five days before the Soviet-led invasion of that country.) The strained relations between

Romania and its Warsaw Pact allies in the summer of 1971 as a result of Ceauşescu's visit to Peking delayed the signing of the Hungarian and East German documents. (Hungary had taken the lead in verbally attacking Romania in the summer of 1971.) By March 1972, however, conditions had improved sufficiently for Hungarian party leader János Kádár and Premier Jenö Fock to come to Bucharest for the treaty signing. Despite the improved relations, the treaty was signed only by the two premiers, and not by the two party leaders, though both were present; this indicates that differences on the party level were still significant. (Treaty text in *Scînteia,* 25 February.) The general improvement in East European relations with the Federal Republic of (West) Germany, however, brought the Warsaw Pact states more closely into line with Romania on this issue. The treaty with East Germany was the first such document between the two countries. East Germany was not among the countries with which Romania signed bilateral treaties immediately after the war, and relations between them were poor in 1967, when bilateral treaties with East Germany were signed by the other Warsaw Pact states; but in 1972 East German party leader Erich Honecker and Premier Willi Stoph came to Bucharest, and both party and government leaders signed the document. (Text, ibid., 13 May.) Relations with Poland and Czechoslovakia were correct and friendly, following much the same course as relations with the Soviet Union, though lacking the genuine warmth of Romania's relationship with Yugoslavia.

Contacts with Bulgaria were intensified following Romania's participation in the Crimean summit. Ceauşescu met with Bulgarian party leader Todor Zhivkov in Romania (9–10 August), and a few weeks later the two met again in Bulgaria (27–28 September). These visits prepared the way for serious planning on a joint hydroelectric project on the Danube, and steps were taken toward further economic cooperation. Numerous other high-level visits were exchanged between the two countries. Both were interested in intensifying cooperation among the Balkan states, and both sought to improve bilateral relations with their Balkan neighbors. Ceauşescu took a multilateral approach in July, at the National Party Conference, when he suggested creating a permanent organization to further political and economic cooperation in the region.

Asian Communist-Ruled States. With the exception of Albania, Romania is the East European nation most friendly to China. However, the very warm relationship between the two, which reached its climax with Ceauşescu's visit to Peking in June 1971, seemed to lose some of its intensity as both countries became preoccupied with foreign questions of more immediate concern—China with its position toward the United States and Japan, and Romania with the question of a European security conference. High-level visits continued with exchanges of numerous ministers and other lesser government and party officials. Emil Bodnăraş, a member of the Permanent Presidium, led a military delegation to Peking (29 April–4 May), and other delegations of military personnel and patriotic guards were exchanged.

Relations with North Vietnam and North Korea continued warm and friendly. Deputy premier and Permanent Presidium member Rădulescu visited Hanoi and pledged continuing Romanian support to the North Vietnamese (10–18 March), and Bodnăraş led a delegation to Pyongyang (23–28 April).

Cuba. Cuban premier Fidel Castro paid a five-day visit to Romania (26–30 May) as part of his extended tour of Africa and Eastern Europe. Although no agreements were signed during the visit, relations between the two countries, which have encountered problems in the past, appeared to be improving.

Foreign Relations—Non-Communist States. *The United States.* Relations with the United States were focused on two principal problems. The foremost of these, in Romania's eyes, was the need to expand economic relations, and particularly to increase Romanian exports. Repeated requests that Romania be given most-favored-nation treatment were not fulfilled. Although the U.S. Export-Import Bank was authorized in November 1971 to guarantee credit for trade with Romania, and President Nixon officially stated that he favors extending most-favored-nation treatment, the U.S. Congress did not approve a bill to this effect. Romania's public support for and aid to North Vietnam appear to have been one of the obstacles to Congressional action. In an attempt to promote improved economic relations, Manea Mănescu, a leading economic adviser to Ceauşescu and a member of the Permanent Presidium, visited the United States (19–29 March) to discuss economic cooperation with administration officials and business leaders. The president of the Export-Import Bank visited Romania in order to resolve problems in connection with extending credits.

The second problem in the relations between the two countries was Romania's fear that the United States might reach some agreement which would affect Romania's fate without taking its interests into consideration. After President Nixon's visit to the Soviet Union, U.S. Secretary of State William Rogers was dispatched on a quick tour of several European capitals, including Bucharest (5 July), to reassure the Romanians that the two superpowers had made no agreement at Romania's expense. During his visit Rogers also signed a consular convention.

Western Europe. Relations with West European states focused on two problems, the first of which was also the concern to expand trade. The most significant step in this regard was Romania's official application to the European Economic Community to be granted the generalized trade preferences given developing countries. Despite numerous exchanges of views between Romanian officials and those of EEC member countries (Mănescu visited Paris in March, the French planning minister visited Bucharest in April, Ceauşescu himself visited Belgium and Luxembourg in October, and the Italian foreign minister visited Bucharest in November), Romania's application was not acted upon favorably by the EEC because of French and Dutch objections. This question was still pending at year's end. Romania had also sought to expand its bilateral relations with West European states by passing a new law on foreign trade in 1971 permitting the establishment, in Romania and abroad, of companies owned jointly by Romania and Western firms. During 1972 serious attempts were made to encourage joint ventures with Western firms, but the response was cautious; only firms in West Germany, the United States, and Japan seemed interested in initiating serious negotiations.

The second problem was the question of a conference on European security and cooperation. Romania was anxious that any European security conference not abandon Eastern Europe to Soviet domination, but that it reaffirm and ensure the right of all states to sovereignty and noninterference in their internal affairs, and put an end to the use or threat of force in international relations. Romania also sought to ensure a prominent role for small states in any such conference. In bilateral contacts with West European states, the Romanians actively sought support for their point of view, in the anticipation that a preliminary conference would be held to prepare for a full-scale one. The most overt act of this nature was the signing of declarations by Ceauşescu and government leaders during his visits to Belgium and Luxembourg, reaffirming the principles Romania maintains must govern international relations. These declarations appear to foreshadow the type of document Romania would like to see the security conference adopt. (Texts, ibid., 27, 29, October.) When the preparatory talks on the conference opened in November, Romania's delegation held up the proceedings for several days by insisting on certain changes in the procedural rules which would affirm the equality of states and the fact that the conference was taking place outside military alliances.

United Nations. Romania's activity in the United Nations complemented its policy toward European security. As on many other occasions in recent years, the position of the Romanian delegation differed from that of the Soviet Union and the other Warsaw Pact states. It proposed a resolution to the U.N. General Assembly on security, participated actively in the debate on a definition of aggression, and in talks on disarmament criticized both the Soviet Union and the United States for failing to achieve tangible progress.

Developing Countries. During the year serious efforts were made to identify Romania with the developing countries, and in April at the UNCTAD conference in Santiago, Chile, Romania specifically sought designation as a developing country. This desire stems primarily from economic motives. Not only does Romania seek the same trade preferences from the EEC as it extends to developing countries; it also joined the International Monetary Fund and the World Bank, with the apparent intention of securing loans for economic development projects. In addition to seeking developing-country benefits from the developed states, Romania sought to expand its trade exchanges with countries in Africa, Asia, and Latin America. Trade with these areas has expanded to the point that in 1970 they were the recipients of over 10 percent of Romanian exports. A number of trade exchanges were negotiated with various developing countries (Algeria, Brazil, Chile, Iran, Iraq, Libya, Peru, and Syria), and a visit by Ceauşescu (11 March–6 April) to eight African states (Algeria, Central African Republic, Congo-Brazzaville, Congo-Kinshasa, Zambia, Tanzania, Sudan, and Egypt) was also heavily oriented toward trade and economic cooperation. A similar visit to Latin America is planned for 1973.

In the political sphere Romania sought to maintain friendly relations with all states. Unlike the other members of the Warsaw Pact, it did not establish diplomatic relations with Bangladesh immediately, but did so only on the eve of talks between the leaders of India and Pakistan (28 June), some six months after Bangladesh had declared its independence. This policy of maintaining good relations with all states is nowhere indicated more clearly than in the case of the Middle East. During his African tour, Ceauşescu visited three Arab states (Algeria, Sudan, and Egypt), and within a month of his return played host to Israeli premier Golda Meir (4–7 May) in Bucharest. Romania made no attempt to mediate the Arab-Israeli differences, and apparently was only interested in showing that it maintained good relations with all states. The reestablishment of diplomatic relations with Syria (18 October) and a planned visit by Egyptian president Anwar Sadat to Bucharest in early 1973 reaffirmed the balance of Romania's policy toward states in this area.

Publications. *Scînteia* is the official daily of the RCP Central Committee. The party's monthly ideological review, *Lupta de clasă,* ceased publication with its August issue, and a new party fortnightly entitled *Era socialistă* appeared in September, with a format calculated to appeal to a broader readership. In September the party also began publishing another fortnightly, *Munca de Partid,* which deals with organization and methods of conducting party activity, as well as with questions of party policy. Other important publications include *Informaţia Bucureştiului,* the daily of the Bucharest party committee and the municipal People's Council; *Munca,* the daily of the trade union federation; *România liberă,* the daily of the Front of Socialist Unity; *România literară,* the weekly of the Writers' Union; and *Scînteia tineretului,* the daily of the Union of Communist Youth.

Radio Free Europe   Robert R. King
Munich, Germany

Union of Soviet Socialist Republics

The Communist Party of the Soviet Union (Kommunisticheskaia Partiia Sovetskogo Soiuza; CPSU) derives from the Russian Social Democratic Labor Party, founded in 1898, which split into Bolshevik ("majority") and Menshevik ("minority") factions at its Second Congress, in 1903. Following the 1917 revolution which brought them to power, the Bolsheviks changed the title of the party at its Seventh Congress in March 1918 to the "All-Russian Communist Party (Bolsheviks)." After the country was renamed the Union of Soviet Socialist Republics, the party in 1925 became the "All-Union Communist Party (Bolsheviks)." The present designation was adopted in 1952 at the Nineteenth Congress. The CPSU is the sole political party given legal recognition in the U.S.S.R.

In February 1972 party membership was reported to be 14,631,000 (including 522,000 candidates). This represented an increase of fewer than 180,000 since the Twenty-fourth Congress, April 1971. Another indication of the policy of restricting party growth is the fact that in 1971 only 493,000 persons were accepted as candidate members. This was 88,000 below the 1970 figure and considerably under the average of 600,000 admitted annually between 1966 and 1971. Among those who joined in 1971, workers accounted for nearly 57 percent, the highest such proportion during the last 40 years. This brought their total representation in the party up slightly, to 41 percent. White-collar occupations accounted for 44 percent. Only 15 percent of the party membership worked directly in agriculture. Women, numbering over 3.3 million in the party, constituted nearly a fourth of the CPSU membership, although they comprise more than half the population and half of the labor force. No new statistical information has appeared on the ethnic composition of the party since the 1971 congress. At that time 63 percent of all members were Russians, who made up only 53 percent of the population according to the 1970 census (listing 91 nationalities). In view of the increasing official complaints against "bourgeois nationalism" since the congress, it seems reasonable to conclude that the Russians have maintained, if not enhanced, their predominance in the party.

Membership in the Communist Youth League (Komsomol), the party's youth auxiliary, climbed to over 30 million during 1972. Komsomol members made up 56 percent of all those admitted to the CPSU in 1971. This was 16 percent higher than in 1966 when the party rules were revised, making the YCL the only route to party membership for Soviet youths between the ages of 18 and 23. The CPSU membership of 14.6 million included just under 6 percent of the 246 million population, or 9 percent of all adults at the beginning of the year.

Organization and Leadership. Though the party controls and directs public life, it is formally distinct from the parallel structure of state administration. The government forms a hierarchy of some 50,000 soviets (councils), with each of the 15 Union Republics and 20 Autonomous Republics headed by its own supreme soviet. At the apex is the Supreme Soviet of the U.S.S.R. During the June 1971 general elections for republic and lower-level soviets, only 45 percent of the 2 million deputies chosen were party members, with the percentage rising substantially at higher levels (see *YICA, 1972,* p. 78). The CPSU has a broad base of primary party organizations which numbered more than 375,000 in September (*Partiinaia Zhizn',* no. 17). The structure includes intermediate party committees, the 14 Central Committees of the Union Republics (there is no separate party organization for the Russian Republic), and finally the CPSU Central Committee. The last body is elected at the party congress; according to the statutes, it functions as the highest party organ between congresses. The locus of power lies in the Politburo, which meets weekly to decide basic questions of domestic and foreign policy; and in the Secretariat, which supervises implementation of party directives by departments of the Central Committee and controls key personnel appointments.

The main issue of the year in intra-party affairs centered on the question of further strengthening CPSU ranks and improving their qualitative make-up. In a lecture delivered before the Higher Party School at the beginning of the year, Ivan V. Kapitonov, the secretary in charge of organizational matters, acknowledged that this was becoming "increasingly urgent" because of the growing demands and greater complexity of building communism (*Kommunist,* no. 3). Similarly, greater stress was given in the press to the principle that CPSU growth was not a spontaneous but a regulated process; it was not to be an end in itself but a means by which to maintain the vanguard character and leading role of the party in Soviet society (ibid., no. 13).

The primary means by which the CPSU leadership has sought to exert greater regulatory influence and to root out undesirable elements is through the reissue of party cards. The last exchange of cards took place in 1954, but their validity formally expired in 1970. Since no space remained to record payment of dues, the central Secretariat printed up special sheets for this purpose. Though it ordered a new exchange of party documents, the 1971 congress failed to set any date. Only in May 1972 did the Central Committee announce the operation for 1973 and 1974. It stressed that the exchange would not be a technicality but "an important organizational and political measure." *Pravda* (24 June) also emphasized this in an editorial. Indeed, prominent attention was given throughout the year to the words of General Secretary Brezhnev at the May plenum that the exchange of documents had "a fundamentally political character." According to the editors of the party's main organizational journal, it was to be "a sort of review of our forces and a strict and penetrating check on how each party organization is implementing the decisions of the Twenty-fourth Congress" (*Partiinaia Zhizn',* no. 13). The aim of the re-registration drive, therefore, is to enhance the vanguard role of the party in all sectors of Soviet life and socialist construction. At the same time, however, the leadership has tried to allay concern that issuance of new cards may signal a massive purge such as decimated the party in the 1930's.

On 23 June a meeting was held at the CPSU Central Committee where Politburo member and cadres chief A. P. Kirilenko and Secretary Kapitonov provided general instructions for regional party officials and political commissars of the armed forces. Similar instructional conferences and seminars were then organized in the various republics at all levels of the party hierarchy. *Partiinaia Zhizn'* (July) included a new section devoted to the course and content of preparation for the exchange. Similarly, *Pravda* began to publicize the campaign. In mid-November Kirilenko and Kapitonov again led a three-day conference of heads of general departments from the union republic central committees and lower-level party committees. Many CPSU committees began comprehensive studies and discussions of party life and organization.

In order to be able to cope successfully with the technical demands of the exchange, party committees at all levels added new workers to their party records departments.

The re-registration is to be conducted on a strictly individual basis, primarily through personal interviews with the respective party first secretary and in an "atmosphere of mutual preciseness." The talks are to be such that they will leave "a deep impression on the minds" of members and candidates and lead to a rise in their production activity and socio-political responsibility, according to a *Pravda* (24 June) editorial; for them to achieve their purpose, the paper added, it may be necessary to interview some persons several times. Brezhnev himself warned at the May plenum that there must be no "competition" regarding who finishes the work first. Since the re-registration will take two years to complete, it may be in part intended to maintain and prolong the pressure of a "permanent purge." Special targets will be those who are passive in party life, guilty of shortcomings in personal conduct or work, or not concerned about ideological and professional improvement, or who have incurred party penalties. The last group was increasingly singled out as preparatory work entered its final stages toward the end of the year (see *Pravda*, editorial, 14 November).

From the discussion in the press, it also became evident that certain mistakes were being made during preparations for the exchange of documents. *Pravda* (19 July) warned that "elements of formalism, document mania, and ostentation must be persistently eliminated." Some interviews began to assume the form of a campaign, as party organizations tried to hold conversations with all communists without exception rather than principally with those against whom there had been complaint (*Sovetskaia Estoniia,* 2 November). The practice by some party committees of establishing special interrogation commissions and devising detailed questionnaires was sharply denounced by the editors of *Partiinaia zhizn'* (June). Demanding written accounts from communists was also criticized as "incorrect." In all, despite efforts by the leadership to keep the forthcoming exchange of cards rational, the operation itself showed signs of developing irrational elements along with a logic and momentum of its own. Another issue that gained prominent attention during the year was that of enhancing party influence and control over all aspects of society and the economy. "The party proceeds from the premise that control and verification of execution can not be based solely upon the actions of special supervisory agencies," wrote I. Kebin, the first secretary of the Estonian Communist Party, in *Kommunist* (no. 10). Improvement of administrative activity and successful implementation of party and government directives were simply "inconceivable," he stressed, without constant party concern with development and refinement of control functions by all party, government, and economic bodies. Here the chief focus was on strengthening the role of the primary party organization (PPO), the party's vigilant eye and mobilizing nerve in every collective and organizational cell throughout the Soviet system. On one level, effort was devoted to improve the structure of the PPOs by breaking them down into more manageable units and creating party committees in shops and sections having more than 500 communists. Previously such committees had been formed only in party organizations with more than 1,000 members and candidates. By February there were already 363,000 shop party organizations and 460,000 party groups in the CPSU, according to a report by organizational secretary Kapitonov (*Kommunist,* no. 3). In some primary organizations numbering over a thousand communists, party committees have been elected on a trial basis with an expanded staff and bureaus have been formed in them to handle current matters. Unified party organizations were also created in some production associations, construction trusts, and trade facilities in order to ensure party presence and more influence.

The main thrust of leadership efforts, however, centered on intensifying the control functions of PPOs. Prior to the 1971 congress, only party organizations in factories and farms had enjoyed the right of surveillance and control over administration activities. The congress, however, extended this right to primary party organizations in transport, communications, and supply as well as in all "planning organizations, construction bureaus, scientific research institutes, educational establishments, cultural, medical, and other institutions whose administrative functions do not extend beyond the framework of their own collectives." (See *YICA, 1972,* p. 79.) The significance of this measure is clearly seen by the fact that it involved over 170,000 PPOs or 45 percent of all party organizations and more than 4 million members or one-third of the total membership (*Partiinaia zhizn',* no. 12, 1971, p. 36). Since the congress, considerable mention has been made in the press as to how this right should be interpreted and implemented in practice. From these discussions aimed at defining and delimiting properly the function of control, it is possible to glimpse the new avenues of activity and forms of party influence that have developed.

In scientific research institutes, for example, the PPOs have begun to exercise closer supervision over research projects and the proper use of scientific and financial resources. They have also gained greater influence in the appointment, promotion, and dismissal of staff. For instance, in many Moscow institutes, besides the deputy directors and heads of scientific subdivisions, the senior scholars and research workers have been brought into the *nomenklatura* or appointments list of the party committee or of its bureau. V. Yagodkin, secretary of the Moscow City CPSU Committee, reported (*Kommunist,* no. 11) that a new salary scale had been instituted for scientists that is designed to tie wages more closely to actual performance. A new bonus system is also being introduced in all of the capital's institutes, whereby additional pay is given only at the end of the year instead of quarterly as in the past. It is argued that only then is it possible to gain "complete and impartial" views of a scientist's work. In addition, there has also been an effort to develop and expand "socialist competition" in scientific establishments along much the same lines as in industry. Above all, enhanced party control is manifested in intensified indoctrination among scientists. Again the party authorities in Moscow, the citadel of Soviet science, seem to have taken the lead and set up a number of inter-institute seminars in which scientists from all fields can acquire the proper ideological outlook. According to Yagodkin, a primary purpose for this ideological education is to inculcate in the scientific-technical intelligentsia a spirit of militant irreconcilability toward any sign of bourgeois ideology. "Experience has taught us," the Moscow secretary noted, "that this is the ground on which the seeds of poisonous ideological changes, apoliticism, and lack of principle can sprout." For the scientific community there is simply "no place for neutralism, compromise, or any kind of rest." (Ibid.) In sum, then, the aim of heightened party supervision is not only to curb dissidence and deviance in this critical sector of society but also to increase efficiency in scientific research and to bring science closer to production in order to speed Soviet technological progress and economic growth.

Similar developments also have occurred in party control over educational institutions. The extension of supervisory rights to the PPOs here has provided a powerful additional disciplinary weapon to deal with errant students and established research workers alike. Enhanced party influence is also discernible in the field of personnel management. At the Tashkent State Pedagogical Institute, for example, a list of official positions was recently placed for the first time on the *nomenklatura* of the party committee. This list includes vice-chancellors, deans and their deputies, social science department teachers, and the chiefs of various sections and services. Henceforth, people cannot be reshuffled or appointed to vacant positions on this list without approval of the party committee. (*Pravda vostoka,* 24 February.)

Equally important, party units in such high-level agencies as ministries and state committees also received growing attention. Though they do not enjoy the same supervisory rights over administration as other PPOs, the 1971 congress did, nevertheless, instruct them to "exert control over the work of the staff in fulfilling party and government directives and observing Soviet laws." Indeed, it has been increasingly emphasized that they play a major role in improving the activity of the state apparatus. Efforts to activate the work of these party organizations were not without effect. In Estonia, for example, the party organization of the republic's Ministry of Food Industry initiated a special 22-hour study course for ministry workers aimed at improving their knowledge in the field of administration. The party organizations of the Estonian Ministry for Provision of Everyday Services and of the Finance Ministry were also singled out by I. Kebin, the Estonian party first secretary, for exemplary work in probing and improving the administrative activity of their respective state institutions (*Kommunist,* no. 10). The first secretary of the Baku City CPSU committee, on the other hand, strongly criticized party organizations in republic ministries and state agencies of Azerbaidzhan for not exercising enough their supervisory and surveillance rights. He particularly attacked the PPOs at the republic Ministry of Rural Construction and the Azerbaidzhan supreme court. (*Bakinskii rabochii,* 5 November.) In an editorial, *Pravda* (24 June) noted more generally the failure of many primary party organizations to implement the decisions of the 1971 congress in the area of CPSU control. It also emphasized that this was to be a major criterion for evaluating individual and organizational performance during the forthcoming exchange of party cards. The growing importance of this issue in the minds of party authorities also had been acknowledged by Central Committee secretary Kapitonov in February, when he stated flatly that the expansion of control by primary party organizations was an "urgent requirement" for the present stage of Soviet development. Basically at issue here, however, is the much broader and more complex question of the proper functions of and relations between party and state in the political system.

Significantly on the leadership level, the year witnessed the first changes since 1968 in the top political command. In May, Politburo member Piotr Shelest was made a deputy premier and released from his position as first secretary of the Ukranian Communist Party. That this was a demotion is unmistakable, since there are two first deputy premiers (Mazurov and Polyansky) above him and nine other deputy premiers alongside him. While there is no precedent for a deputy premier's having Politburo status, Shelest still retained his seat on that organ at the year's end. Vladimir V. Shcherbitsky, premier of the Ukraine and fellow Politburo member, was elected to the post of Ukranian party first secretary. In May, Boris N. Ponomarev, a secretary of the Central Committee, was brought into the Politburo as an alternate member. Vasili P. Mzhavanadze, on the other hand, was dropped from this position at the December plenum of the Central Committee. His removal from the Politburo was only a formality as he had been replaced in September as first secretary of the Georgian Communist Party after nineteen years of ruling that republic. Politburo membership at the end of the year is shown in the accompanying list.

POLITBURO

Members:

Brezhnev, Leonid I.	General secretary, CPSU Central Committee
Podgorny, Nikolai V.	Chairman, Presidium of the U.S.S.R. Supreme Soviet
Kosygin, Aleksei N.	Chairman, U.S.S.R. Council of Ministers (premier)
Suslov, Mikhail A.	Secretary, CPSU Central Committee
Kirilenko, Andrei P.	Secretary, CPSU Central Committee
Pel'she, Arvid Ia.	Chairman, Party Control Committee

Mazurov, Kiril T.	First deputy chairman, U.S.S.R. Council of Ministers
Polyansky, Dimitri S.	First deputy chairman, U.S.S.R. Council of Ministers
Shelest, Piotr E.	First secretary, Ukrainian Central Committee (to May); thereafter: deputy chairman, U.S.S.R. Council of Ministers
Voronov, Gennadi I.	Chairman, U.S.S.R. People's Control Committee
Shelepin, Aleksandr N.	Chairman, All-Union Central Council of Trade Unions
Grishin, Viktor V.	First secretary, Moscow City Party Committee
Kunaev, Dinmukhamed A.	First secretary, Kazakh Central Committee
Shcherbitsky, Vladimir V.	Chairman, Ukrainian Council of Ministers (to May); thereafter: first secretary, Ukrainian Central Committee
Kulakov, Fedor D.	Secretary, CPSU Central Committee

Candidate members:

Andropov, Yuri V.	Chairman, Committee of State Security (KGB)
Ustinov, Dmitri F.	Secretary, CPSU Central Committee
Demichev, Piotr N.	Secretary, CPSU Central Committee
Rashidov, Sharaf R.	First secretary, Uzbek Central Committee
Masherov, Piotr M.	First secretary, Belorussian Central Committee
Ponomarev, Boris N.	Secretary, CPSU Central Committee

On balance, these changes appear to have strengthened the position of Brezhnev. The downgrading of Shelest, a powerful rival and apparent opponent of some of his détente-oriented foreign policy initiatives, the promotion of Shcherbitsky, long his protégé, to the top Ukrainian party post, and the elevation of Ponomarev, another member of the Secretariat, to alternate status in the Politburo all serve to tip the scales of power more in favor of the general secretary. On a different level they indicate that growing economic troubles and nationalist restiveness in the provinces are gradually being felt throughout the party hierarchy, including the Politburo.

The composition of the 9-man Secretariat of the Central Committee remained unchanged until December when V. I. Dolgikh, first secretary of the Krasnoyarsk Regional Party Committee since 1969, was made a member of this body. Headed by the general secretary, the members are as follows: Brezhnev, Suslov, Kirilenko, Kulakov, Ustinov, Demichev, Ponomarev, Kapitonov, Katushev (Konstantin F.), and Dolgikh. The first four are Politburo members, the next three are alternates. The addition of Dolgikh does not alter the ethnic composition of the Secretariat, which continues to be run entirely by Russians.

As a result of the removal of Shelest and Mzhavanadze from command of their respective republic party organizations, there have been important leadership reshuffles in both the Ukraine and Georgia. In the former, Aleksandr P. Liashko was transferred from the chairmanship of the Ukrainian Supreme Soviet Presidium to the chairmanship of the Ukrainian Council of Ministers, Shcherbitsky's old post. In turn, Ivan S. Grushetsky, chairman of the Ukrainian Party [Control] Commission since 1966, took over Liashko's former duties as "president" of the republic. In October Valentin Yu. Malanchuk, an expert and hard-liner on Soviet nationality policy in the Ukraine, became secretary of the republic Central Committee in charge of ideology. The party bosses in Kherson and Rovno were also replaced in the wake of Shelest's fall from power. In Georgia important changes of command preceded and followed Mzhavanadze's political downfall. Following a CPSU Central Committee decree in March on "shortcomings" in the Tbilisi party organization, Otar Lolashvili was dismissed in July as first secretary of the Tbilisi City party committee. His successor was Eduard Shevardnadze, the former Georgian minister of interior. Two months later Shevardnadze became head of the entire republic CPSU organization, replacing Mzhavanadze as the Georgian party first secretary. Judging from reports in the Soviet press, the vigorous campaign that has been launched by Shevardnadze to root out corruption, mismanagement, and Georgian nationalism has all the hallmarks of a massive purge in the making. It is also important to note that the promotion of Shevardnadze is reminiscent of the police-style leadership methods introduced in Azerbaidzhan following the election of KGB chief G. A. Aliev as party boss of this Transcaucasian republic in 1969. It also follows the pattern established by Brezhnev of installing police officers in party posts when a republic organization is giving serious trouble.

Other republic first secretaries remained unchanged: Anton I. Kochinian (Armenia), Geidar A. Aliev (Azerbaidzhan), Piotr M. Masherov (Belorussia), Ivan G. Kebin (Estonia), Dinmukhamed A. Kunaev (Kazakhstan), Turdakun U. Usubaliev (Kirghizia), Augustus E. Voss (Latvia), Antanas Yu. Snechkus (Lithuania), Ivan I. Bodiul (Moldavia), Dzhabar Rasulov (Tadzhikistan), Mukhamednazar Gapurov (Turkmenistan), and Sharaf R. Rashidov (Uzbekistan).

Domestic Policies. This year marked the 50th anniversary of the U.S.S.R. Mounting nationalist unrest among the non-Russian republics, growing discontent and dissent in society, and creeping and crippling stagnation of the economy, however, provided ground for official unease rather than jubilation. Premier Kosygin in his 1973 New Year's Day message to the nation recalled, "We have lived through a special year." Similarly General Secretary Brezhnev admitted on 21 December that "The Soviet Union is advancing toward communism. We know the way there will not be easy." Growing official realization of complexities and difficulties in domestic development did not result in any fundamental change of approach or policy, however, for a solution to troubles, party authorities relied essentially on the old and familiar remedy of strengthening discipline, organization, and control. Within this context, it is symbolic and perhaps not by accident that they chose to hold the 50th anniversary celebration nine days early on 21 December, i.e., Stalin's birthday. Brezhnev's speech on the occasion was noteworthy for its particularly harsh tone, hard-hitting attack against bureaucratic evils and "social sores," and relentless demand for greater vigilance and militancy from all. In this respect, it was also reminiscent of his speech to the December 1969 Central Committee plenum in which he criticized heavily the state bureaucracy and called for enhanced party control over all sectors of communist construction. Indeed the question of the nature and degree of party control essential to attainment of official socioeconomic goals remained a central issue of concern and contention among the leadership. This and the related issue of the proper role of and relationship between party and state in society were pinpointed most succinctly by Brezhnev himself when he reminded the Central Committee in May that the party's leading role was "no abstract concept." (*Moskovskaia pravda*, 21 July).

Ideology. The leadership has concentrated its efforts on adapting Marxism-Leninism to the requirements of the modern age and making ideology a more effective tool for mobilizing and managing an increasingly complex and mature industrial society. This was the subject of an All-Union conference of ideological workers convened by the CPSU Central Committee in June. The title of the editorial in *Partiinaia zhizn'* (no. 14) about the conference— "Ideological Work Must Be Raised to the Level of Contemporary Demands"—captures well the main concern and desire of the leadership.

In general, the thrust of official policy has been to organize and orient ideological work more and more around the concept of "developed socialism." (See *Kommunist,* no. 1; *Mirovaia ekonomika i mezhdunarodnye otnosheniia,* no. 6). This is the term that has been coined to describe the Soviet Union at its present historical stage. It is based on a recognition of the fact that socialism represents a more or less lengthy phase in the development toward communism. The need to study pressing problems and dynamic processes of a developed socialist society and the ways and means for gradual transformation into communism was the theme of Suslov at the June ideological conference. He was merely echoing, however, statements he had made the preceding fall at another national meeting on "The 24th CPSU Congress and the Development of Marxist-Leninist Theory." (See *YICA, 1972,* p. 83).

In effect, the search for a model of developed socialism signifies an attempt by the leadership to fill an important ideological void that increasingly complicates political practice. The problem involves not only the failure of Marx to depict in any detail the future communist order but also his emphasis on the essentially primitive, repressive, and transitory character of the socialist phase of development. In his eyes the dictatorship of the proletariat was not a model of a mature socialist society, nor is it taken to be such by the ideologues in Moscow today. Under Khrushchev little effort was made to elaborate such a model, particularly along the lines of perpetuating the existing system and structure of power as is now being done. On the contrary, power considerations and his own ideological outlook led Khrushchev to stress the building of the future communist order, the withering away of the state superstructure, and the growth of public participation in administrative affairs. Though he himself always admitted that this was to be a long-term process, he tended, nevertheless, to push its development much faster than the ruling elite desired. This "great leap" mentality and the "prematurity" of his populist schemes and concomitant curtailment of the state machinery in building socialism have been condemned by his successors (see *WMR,* no. 8, 1971; *Mirovaia ekonomika i mezhdunarodnye otnosheniia,* no. 6, 1972). Instead they accentuate the need to avoid discontinuity and harmful disruptions in moving from the dictatorship of the proletariat to the "state of the whole people." A conservative thrust behind the current ideological line and the present rather than a futurist orientation are in the idea stressed by Suslov that socialism grows into communism, gradually, step by step (*Social Sciences,* Moscow, no. 1:7). Equally important but on a different level, this preoccupation with "developed" socialism reflects growing institutionalization of the regime and the rise to dominance of a bureaucratic oligarchy that is anxious to preserve the system which it has come to embody and to command.

The leadership realizes, however, that economic success and political survival in an age of scientific and technological revolution require more sophisticated tools of social engineering and system maintenance. Such tools are provided, *Pravda* (21 January) notes, by developing the social sciences and adopting modern methods of management and computer technology, popular in the West. Indeed *Kommunist* (no. 1) called the social sciences the "party's combat weapon in building communism." The need to strengthen their role in communist construction was emphasized forcefully at an all-union meeting of heads of social science departments at higher educational establishments in late December 1971. A few days earlier, the CPSU Central Committee had criticized the serious neglect of social science methods and the backwardness of research at the important Economics Institute of the U.S.S.R. Academy of Sciences. The Academy presidium was ordered to redefine the main directions of Institute activity. Henceforth, its primary task will be to elaborate on the economic problems of a developed socialist society (*ibid.*). In June, *Voprosy ekonomiki* (no. 6) announced that its editorial policy was being adjusted accordingly. More attention will be paid to such areas as scientific management, automated control systems, and the methodology of long-term planning and socio-economic forecasting. At about the same time, *Voprosy filosofii* (no. 7) outlined similar trends and tasks in the field of philosophy. Party and Soviet history were criticized for neglect of social science tools (*Pravda,* 13 October). Steps were also taken by the Defense Ministry to enhance the role of social sciences in military training and at military-political academies (*Kommunist vooruzhennykh sil,* no. 10).

Though it recognizes the urgent need for modern techniques that have been developed largely in the West, the ruling elite is also aware and afraid of the dangers of indiscriminate borrowing. Emulation of foreign methods must not result in the imposition of alien models on Soviet society. This is particularly so with regard to Western methods of organization, management, and control. Fishing in these muddy waters, some scientists "scoop up a cupful of conceptions, terms, and categories without any attempt to connect them with our realities," according to one authority (*Novy mir,* no. 7). This source warns against "attempts at mechanical adoption of some particular organizational idea or method without due consideration of our own experiences, of the differences in principle not only in the social but also in the organizational structures, forms, and methods of management in socialist and capitalist countries."

Fear that borrowing advanced methods from the West will plant all kinds of dangerous seeds in the ideological soil of socialist society has led to intensified struggle against bourgeois ideology and anti-communism. At the June ideological conference Suslov said that this struggle "must be active, resolute, specific, and uncompromising." *Pravda* (15 August) also stressed that the study of developed socialism needs to be closely combined with militant and offensive criticism of modern bourgeois theories and revisionist concepts.

The need for intensification of ideological tempering and economic education of officials and ordinary workers alike was cited throughout the year in a variety of publications. The entire system of party-political education was refashioned in order to accelerate technical progress, improve economic management, and raise labor productivity. Economic studies are being expanded in light of a CPSU Central Committee resolution "on improving the working people's economic education." (See ibid., 6 September). Scientific management courses were introduced into the curriculum of universities of Marxism-Leninism for workers in republic ministries and departments as well as for lower-level executives (*Partiinaia zhizn',* no. 14). It was also decided to run such a course at the CPSU Higher Party School and to broaden the program of leadership training there (*Kommunist,* no. 16). "Now it is a question of a qualitatively new stage in economic education," said *Pravda* (6 September). This requires the creation of a differentiated system to ensure training and retraining of various categories of white and blue collar workers. In addition, attention to questions of CPSU nationality policy has been intensified at party schools (*Partiinaia zhizn',* no. 17). Better ideological training among the armed forces was called for repeatedly in party military journals (*Krasnaia zvezda,* 2 June and 1 November). The problem of ideological indoctrination among the scientific and cultural intelligentsia was also aired, particularly in the Central Asian republics where a campaign against bourgeois nationalism was actively waged (See *Kommunist Tadzhikistana,* 29 April; *Kazakhstanskaia pravda,* 22 July).

Closely related to these developments was the announcement of a modernization program for the educational system more generally. The chief aim is to make the schools more responsive to changing demands of the economy in science and technology as well as more effective in inculcating a proper Marxist-Leninist world outlook. A shortage of semi-skilled workers to meet the needs of a growing industrial complex and a declining manpower pool to work the farms have led to a reemphasis on the "polytechnical" approach of Khrushchev and an expansion of vocational training at the high school level (see *Pravda,* 29 June). The deteriorating quality of the educational system was also a contributing factor behind the reforms. In February, M. Lavrentiev, a vice-president of the U.S.S.R. Academy of Sciences, charged that in recent years the average secondary school had been marking time while higher education had "gone into reverse." The dissident physicist, Andrei Sakharov, also criticized severely the poverty of rural schools in a postscript written in June to his famous memorandum of March 1971 to the party leaders. The reforms in higher education (according to *Pravda,* 30 July) are aimed particularly at improved training of specialists in the fields of scientific management, engineering psychology, industrial esthetics, and computers. More rigorous standards for selection of faculty and students as well as in the granting of degrees are directed at not only improving academic quality but also curbing intellectual dissidence and preserving ideological purity. According to new regulations, adopted in September, academic degrees may be revoked if their holders are found guilty of "immoral and unpatriotic acts." Still another innovation in educational policy has been to lower the age for starting school from seven years to six. This is being done to make better use of the child's "underutilized capacity for learning." according to the U.S.S.R. minister of education (*Christian Science Monitor,* 6 October).

Finally, mention should be made of another current in official thought that may forshadow important trends in ideology of the future. Early in the year a new department on theory and methods of ideological work was formed at the Social Sciences Academy attached to the CPSU Central Committee. A special section for research into the effectiveness of party propaganda and political information was also established (*Partiinaia zhizn',* no. 14). This indicates mounting concern among the leadership over performance in this sector and a search for better methods of ideological indoctrination. Just what shape they will take remains to be seen. Significantly, however, in June (*Kommunist Sovetskoi Latvii,* no. 6) the head of this new department advocated essentially the creation of a nationwide computerized system of thought control in the U.S.S.R. In any case, his remedy reflects the growing magnitude not only of deviance in society but also of the drastic measures the leadership is willing to use in order to stamp out dissension and preserve ideological purity.

Dissension and Control. Though Brezhnev declared (*Pravda,* 22 December) at the 50th U.S.S.R. anniversary celebrations that the national question had been "settled completely, finally and for good," nationalist rumblings throughout the country denied his claim. In fact, even he acknowledged that "nationalistic prejudices, exaggerated or distorted national feelings, are extremely tenacious and deeply embedded." Ukrainian national sentiment continued to pose the most formidable challenge due both to its long tradition and to the number of the Ukrainian minority which follows the Russians in size, with 41 million people. Cause for further alarm and aggravation was the fact the Peking began broadcasting to the Ukraine and an allegedly pro-Chinese group has arisen among the nationalist dissidents there (*Radjanska Ukraina,* 26 February). The extreme sensitivity of the Kremlin to Ukrainian nationalism was underscored by both the number of arrests—estimated at more than 100—and the severity of punishment imposed on republic intellectual dissidents and nationalists. Prominent among those arrested in January were the journalist V. M. Chornovil and the literary critics Ivan Svitlychny, Evgen Sverstyuk, and Vasyl Stus. For copying some of the pages of Ivan Dzyuba's *Russification or Internationalism,* Alexander Sergienko was charged with "anti-Soviet activity" and sentenced to 7 years at hard labor. Dzyuba himself was expelled from the Ukrainian Writers' Union in March (*Literaturna Ukraina,* 3 March). At Kiev two members of the republic's Institute of Philosophy were arrested for writing letters to the CPSU Central Committee and to the KGB denouncing repressions and objecting to russification. V. Ivanisenko was expelled on similar grounds from the Institute of Literature, the Ukrainian Writers' Union, and the Communist Party, according to a *samizdat* source. A better-known writer, Ivan Gonchar, was also deprived of his party card. Yuri Shukhevich, who has already spent 20 years in prison, was again sentenced to 10 more years at hard labor. He is the son of Stepan Bandera, the former Ukrainian insurgent leader. The young historian Mykhailo Braychevsky, whose work *Annexation or Reconciliation* resembles Dzyuba's book, was arrested but later released after publicly confessing his "errors." Similar recantations by Zinoviya Franko (*Radjanska Ukraina,* 2 March), Mykola Kholodny (*Literaturna Ukraina,* 7 July), and Leonid Seleznenko (*Robitnycha hazeta,* 8 July) served to generate an atmosphere of fear reminiscent of Stalin's rule. Failure to repress adequately this nationalist upsurge in the republic also probably contributed to the fall of Shelest from the Ukrainian party leadership.

In Georgia, too, the rising wave of nationalism was responsible in large part for a major change in political command. Prominent among the "shortcomings" of the Tbilisi City Party Committee, noted by the CPSU Central Committee, was its handling of the so-called "Sidamonidze affair." (See *Pravda,* 6 March; *Zarya vostoka,* 27 April). V. I. Sidamonidze, a historian at the Georgian Academy of Sciences, wrote a book in which he essentially whitewashed the Georgian Mensheviks and called the declaration of Georgian independence "a progressive act." The fact that the work was not severely condemned or suppressed, but indeed approved and favorably reviewed by Georgian authorities, until Moscow intervened, indicated that historiographical "revisionism" was rife in the republic and even in its party organization. Subsequently, responsible persons at the Party History Institute of the Georgian CPSU Central Committee and the History Institute of the Georgian Academy of Sciences, the entire editorial board of *Literaturnaia Gruziia,* and the Kalinin and Ordzhonikidze district party committees have all been criticized in connection with the case.

Tension was heightened by nationalist unrest in other republics, particularly the Baltic states. In Lithuania, for example, Vaclav Sevruk, a lecturer in sociology at the University of Vilnius, was arrested in January for nationalist activity and "unacceptable Marxist views." Four months later, the self-immolation of a student, Roman Kalanta, in protest against Russian oppression provoked bitter clashes between the KGB and thousands of youths shouting "Freedom for Lithuania." The suicide took place in Kaunas Park, where Soviet rule over Lithuania was proclaimed in June 1940. Ultimately Soviet paratroopers and militia units had to be called in to put down the rioting. Tensions flared again during the international handball tournament, held in Vilnius (11–18 June). Over 150 students were arrested for jeering the Russian players, refusing to stand during the Soviet anthem, and hanging anti-Soviet posters and Lithuanian flags in the streets (*NYT,* 5 July). The underground newsletter, *Chronicle of Current Events,* reported (no. 5) the existence of an "Estonian National Front," which seeks a referendum on the self-determination of Estonia. It also recorded the publication in May of a new samizdat journal called *Eesti Democrat,* which carries the Estonian Front's program. An appeal to the leaders of several Western communist parties from 17 Latvian communists drew attention to the growth of nationalism in another Baltic republic. Detailing the nature of russification and destruction of cultural traditions in Latvia, the authors charge that "Great Russian chauvinism is the deliberate policy of the leadership of the CPSU, and that the forcible assimilation of the small nations of the U.S.S.R. is regarded as one of the most urgent and important aims of state policy." (See *Soviet Analyst,* 2 March, 13 April).

The plight of Soviet Jews and the issue of their right to emigrate to Israel received continuous attention. A change in exit visa policy was introduced by a new decree on 3 August, which requires emigrants to repay sums spent by the state on their education, ranging from $5,000 to as much as $30,000. Since Jews are almost the only category of citizens allowed at present to emigrate, the decree is directed primarily at them and is designed principally to prevent a "brain drain" and the exodus of top specialists and scientists. The decree provoked widespread protests throughout the world. A group of U.S. senators sponsored—

unsuccessfully—an amendment which would block confirmation of the Soviet-U.S. trade agreement unless Moscow rescinded the emigration levy. Protest against the "education tax" was also registered by members of the unofficial Soviet Human Rights Committee (*NYT,* 13 September).

A growing interest in religion and the spread of samizdat religious literature led to intensification of "atheistic education" and a militant antireligious struggle (See *Pravda,* 14 January, 2 April). Indeed, the Evangelical Baptists—one of the most determined dissident religious groups—appear to have somehow established the first underground printing press reported from Russia since pre-Stalinist times (*NYT,* 10 September). Especially in Byelorussia, the Ukraine, Kazakhstan, Transcaucasia, and Siberia local newspapers frequently reported activity and arrest of unregistered Baptists and Seventh-day Adventists. The link between religion and nationalism received mounting stress (*Pravda,* 15 September). The press intensified in this regard its attacks against Cardinal Slipij, metropolitan of Galitch and archbishop of Lvov (*Pravda Ukrainy,* 11 August). Roman Catholic Lithuania posed a special problem. In January, over 17,000 Lithuanian Catholics signed a protest memorandum to Brezhnev against religious repression. The issue became so sensitive that *Sovetskaia Litva* (14 August), the republic party paper, warned communist officials against causing "irreparable damage" by antagonizing Catholic believers. Particularly disturbing to the ruling elite was the stubborn survival of religious feeling among the armed forces (*Krasnaia zvezda,* 22 August, 22 October) and party members (*Pravda,* 15 September). Equally disquieting to the Kremlin were the growing ties between religion and the intellectual dissidence movement. This was most dramatically symbolized by Alexander Solzhenitsyn's taking up the cause of religion. In a letter to Patriarch Pimen, written in March, he accused the head of the Russian Orthodox Church of passively allowing Christian faith in the Soviet Union to be smothered by an atheist state. Bitterly attacking the church leadership, Solzhenitsyn noted: "The Russian Church is concerned about any evil in distant Asia or Africa but on internal ills it has no opinion to offer."

Significantly, the leadership mounted its most determined and repressive campaign to date against dissidence among intelligentsia. A decree issued by the CPSU Central Committee on 30 December 1971 ordered suppression of the leading illegal publication of the dissidence movement, *Kronika tekushchikh sobytii* (Chronicle of Current Events) (see *NYT,* 4 February). This set in motion a wave of arrests and searches by the KGB in Moscow, Leningrad, Kiev, Lvov, Vilna, Novosibirsk, and Khabarovsk. Despite these efforts, the Chronicle continued to appear more or less regularly throughout the year. Yet the regime did succeed largely in ridding itself, either by imprisonment or exiling abroad, of a number of the leading and most active members in the movement. Vladimir Bukovsky, for example, was sentenced in January to a total of 12 years in prison and exile. Pyotr Yakir was arrested in June and ultimately forced to inform on his fellow dissidents. Other prominent figures and civil rights supporters arrested included Kronid Liubarsky, Viktor Krassin, Yuri Melnik, Leonid Pelyushch, and Alexander Rybakov. Among those forced to leave the country were Iosif Brodsky, Alexander Yesenin-Volpin, Yuri Glazov, Yuri Titov, and Valery Chalidze. The last man had been secretary of the unofficial Human Rights Committee, led by Academician Andrei Sakharov. Bulat Okudzhava, well-known writer and ballad singer, was expelled from the CPSU in June for "political mistakes." In March, Alexander Galich, another composer of popular protest songs who had already been expelled from the Soviet Writers' Union, was virtually deprived of all means of livelihood and lay seriously ill, according to the Chronicle (no. 24). Yuri Galanskov, the editor of *Phoenix,* died in November at a labor camp. Major General Pyotr Grigorenko, imprisoned in a psychiatric hospital, was reexamined in January by a medical commission and had his confinement prolonged.

Academician Sakharov and Nobel Prize winner Solzhenitsyn, however, remained free and continued to fight the establishment. In June, Sakharov penned a postscript to his 5 March 1971 memorandum to party leaders, repeating the call for sweeping political reforms. He pointed out "with pain and alarm" that "there is once again an extension of restrictions on ideological freedom, of attempts to cut off all sources of information which is not controlled by the state, of persecution for political and ideological reasons, and a deliberate sharpening of national problems." Soviet society, he complained, was infected with "apathy, hypocrisy, narrow-minded egoism, and hidden cruelty." And he confirmed that "the single true guarantee of the preservation of human values in the chaos of uncontrollable change and tragic shock is the freedom of the convictions of man, his moral striving for good." Among his proposals for reform were those he had offered earlier—amnesty for political prisoners, restoration of rights to exiled nationalities, freedom of information, further economic reform, elimination of single slate elections, and removal of internal passport regulations. He also proposed some new remedies which in official eyes must smack of "creeping capitalism." Thus, he called for expansion of the private sector in agriculture and broader opportunities for private initiative in the service sector, public health, and small-scale trade. On the sensitive question of nationalism, he advocated passage of a law to guarantee any Soviet republic the right of secession. (See *Christian Science Monitor*, 24 June.) As for Solzhenitsyn, *Literaturnaia gazeta* (12 January) denounced him for alleged anti-Soviet trends in his new novel *August 1914* which had appeared in the West during the summer of 1971. In the underground literature, however, it was being warmly received and reviewed before year's end (see *NYT*, 20 November).

At the same time that Sakharov was proposing his reforms for greater intellectual freedom and political liberalization, Suslov was lecturing the All-Union ideological conference on the need for implacable struggle against Western bourgeois ideas and revisionist recipes for "perfecting" socialism. The concerted campaign by the KGB to repress intellectual dissidents was part of a more general drive to tighten discipline and root out decadent trends in the arts. This was the avowed aim of a CPSU Central Committee decree "On Literary and Art Criticism," published at the beginning of the year (*Pravda*, 25, 26 January). "It is not only talent which is important but the direction in which talent is displayed," contended a cultural spokesman for the regime (*Moskovskaia pravda*, 25 October). Consequently, a number of plays were criticized for unflattering portrayals of contemporary life, like A. Khazin's "Distant Relative." *Pravda* (7 September) complained about "despondent coloring" by writers and playwrights who concentrated on the dark side of reality. The film industry was similarly rebuked by the CPSU Central Committee for the low level of its ideological and artistic standards. It was also found guilty of "uncritical borrowing of methods from foreign film-makers which are alien to socialist realism." (Ibid., 22 August.) The journals *Novyi mir* and *Literaturnaia gazeta* were also singled out for official criticism (ibid., 7 September).

To counteract these trends, party authorities took a number of steps to enhance supervision over various dissident sectors. Mention has been made about extension of surveillance and control rights to primary party organizations in scientific, academic, cultural, and medical institutions where members of the intelligentsia are employed. Other measures strengthened party control over information media in the cultural sphere. In January, TASS was upgraded to a state committee of the U.S.S.R. Council of Ministers. It was also given "union-republic significance," which increases Moscow's control over all news and information in the non-Russian republics. In August, the state committees for press and cinematography were similarly transferred into union-republic committees with their chairmen entitled to seats on the Council of Ministers. Further evidence of increased and open interference by the party in the cultural field was the announcement at the end of August that a new newspaper, *Sovetskaia kultura* (Soviet Culture), will be published by the CPSU Central Committee, beginning in January 1973. The existing paper of that name is the organ of the culture ministry and the cultural writers' union. The new publication will give the party a direct channel for its narrow cultural policies. On the international level, Moscow called on the United Nations to arrange an international convention limiting future satellite television broadcasts to foreign states *(NYT, 23 August)*. All these changes are dictated not only by rising dissidence and discontent at home but also by the growing ideological struggle between capitalism and socialism in the international arena. Fearful of a breaking of the cultural wall that genuine détente would bring about, the Kremlin has stressed that expansion of technological cooperation and trade with the West requires not relaxation but intensification of the ideological struggle. Other important changes designed to strengthen control included putting the militia under KGB jurisdiction and a program of modernization and computerization for police organs, revealed by U.S.S.R. minister of internal affairs Shchelokov *(Kommunist,* no. 8).

These measures were not without effect. By the end of the year, the dissidence movement was in considerable disarray and more on the defensive than at any time since the mid-1960s. Some of its members admitted that the cause of human rights now stirs much less interest among the scientific and cultural intelligentsia. The heavy hand of the regime has led to a sense of despair and impotence as prospects for liberalization appear increasingly more bleak *(NYT,* 11 December). The limited amnesty announced by the Presidium of the U.S.S.R. Supreme Soviet on 28 December in honor of the 50th anniversary of the Soviet Union was little more than a token gesture. Since it applied only to those who had been convicted for a term of up to five years and who had not previously served in corrective labor institutions, the amnesty did not release the main activists or dissident leaders presently behind bars, in mental hospitals, or Siberian exile. At the same time, there was cause for even greater alarm in the Kremlin. The dissidence movement itself seemed to be on the verge of a significant shift of emphasis away from a narrow and dominant focus on civil liberties and judicial rights to a broader discussion of the political, social, and economic problems plaguing the system and its people. As the political gap has steadily widened between authorities and dissenters, the latter have tended to sharpen and broaden their criticisms and to seek wider public support (see ibid., 10 September). Particularly disturbing to the authorities was distribution in Moscow mailboxes during June of over 1,000 mimeographed pamphlets calling on workers to strike and demonstrate for better living conditions. This was an appeal not to the intelligentsia but to ordinary workers and presents a threat of a different order and a new force on the political scene. It also dramatizes the magnitude of the growing ills of the economy.

The Economy. Clearly the most worrisome concern of the year was posed by poor performance of the economy. Agriculture again proved to be the "Achilles heel" of the system. A cold, snowless winter followed by the worst drought in a century in the traditional grain growing areas of the country produced a gross grain harvest of only 168 million tons. This was 22 million tons short of plan. State purchases of grain amounted to 60 million tons or 18 million below plan. *(Pravda,* 22 December). Only after a two-week barnstorming trip by Brezhnev through the virgin lands and bringing in thousands of tractors, machine operators, and railroad cars from across the country did Kazakhstan manage to produce a record grain crop of 27 million tons to offset in part the national disaster. On top of last year's harvest, which fell 14 million tons short, this year's failure virtually puts beyond reach the average annual target of 195 million tons of grain called for by the ninth Five-Year-Plan (1971–1975). Similarly, it excludes the possibility of achieving the 21.7 percent increase of gross agricultural product, projected by the plan over 1966–1970. The only bright spot in the agricultural picture was the record cotton crop and 7,300,000 tons in state purchases, the largest in history (*ibid.*). This, however was greatly overshadowed by the fact that during its 50th anniversary Moscow was forced to turn to the capitalist West—notably the U.S.—and purchase over 2 billion dollars worth of grain to feed its citizens.

The setbacks in agriculture had significant repercussions throughout the economy. Premier Kosygin disclosed (*Kommunist,* no. 17) that the rate of economic growth based upon national income was the lowest since the catastrophic crop year of 1963. National income grew by only 4 percent instead of the 6 percent planned. It was the second time in two years, moreover, that the growth rate had fallen, reflecting the general economic slowdown since last year. Contributing to the decline was the continuing lag in planned growth of labor productivity. Through November, it had risen by only 5.4 percent as compared with a scheduled rate of 6.1 percent. The 6.9 percent growth rate planned for industry as a whole did not materialize, because natural gas, oil, electric power, and construction industries failed significantly to meet their goals. In fact, in every major indicator the plan remained unfilled (See *Los Angeles Times,* 30 January 1973).

As a result of these disappointing developments in industry and agriculture, *Pravda* announced on 18 December not only a scaling down of targets but also a significant reordering of priorities. For example, national income, originally scheduled to increase by 7 percent during 1973, is to rise only 6 percent. Total industrial output is to grow by 5.8 percent, about 2 percent below the previously planned goal. The main victim, however, is the Russian consumer. The ninth Five-Year-Plan was the first in the history of Soviet economic planning to set a higher rate of growth for consumers' than for producers' goods. For 1973 these rates were to be 8.1 and 7.6 percent, respectively. The revised plan, presented by the Gosplan chairman Baibakov to the Supreme Soviet (*Pravda,* 18 December), reduces the growth for industry as a whole from an initial rate of 7.8 to 5.8 percent and reverses priorities between the two principal industrial sectors. Output of heavy industry is now scheduled to grow by 6.3 percent or 1.5 percentage points less than before, while consumer goods production is planned to increase by only 4.5 percent or a cutback of 3.6 percent. Real income per capita is also to rise 4.5 percent instead of the previously programmed 7.3 percent. Average monthly earnings are to grow 2.7 percent instead of 4.8 percent. Though the budget and planning committes of the Supreme Soviet amended (ibid., 19 December) the Gosplan draft plan to include roughly 128 million rubles worth of additional fabrics, knit goods, and other consumer items, this was of little consolation to the average citizen. The new plan, on the other hand, maintained the ambitiously high grain production goal (197.4 million tons) to make up for this year's losses. To achieve this target, total farm investment is to be increased by 13 percent over 1972. The bulk of capital investment will be directed toward land reclamation and the construction of production installations. Agriculture will also be supplied with considerable new equipment, including 328,000 tractors and 224,000 trucks (*Kommunist,* no. 17). As for military expenditures in the budget, they are to remain at the level held constant since 1970, namely 17.9 billion rubles (*Pravda,* 18 December). In presenting his economic report to the Supreme Soviet, Baibakov attributed the decline in industrial growth not only to the shortage of farm produce but also to the excess of unfinished construction. Here, he said, the problem lay not with the weather but with the conditions of economic organization and industrial management. Another major area of concern for the leadership had been admitted.

Generally speaking, party authorities sought to overcome existing shortcomings and to speed economic development by improving administration and planning, on the one hand, and strengthening labor discipline and supervision, on the other. Premier Kosygin lectured (*Planovoe khoziaistve,* no. 11) the Gosplan in September on the need for greater bureaucratic rationality in its operations. Two months later, he aired the same concerns with respect to the economic system more broadly in a major article *Kommunist* (no. 17). Brezhnev, too, hammered incessantly on the need to modernize the administrative apparat and professionalize officialdom. At the Fifteenth All-Union Congress of Trade Unions, he stressed (Moscow Domestic Service, 20 March) the importance of learning modern methods of labor, economics, and administration. He returned to this theme in his 50th anniversary report. "The central task today," he said (*Pravda,* 22 December), "is to effect a radical change of orientation, to switch the accent to intensive methods of economic management." As the poor performance level of the economy became increasingly apparent, the authoritative *Kommunist* (no. 13) quoted prominently Brezhnev's statement of 1970: "The science of victory is in essence the science of management." Mention has already been made of the considerable attention given to the need to train and retool officials at all levels of the administrative hierarchy in modern management methods and computer techniques. At the same time, the inadequacies of existing leadership training programs were constantly recorded in the press. Discussions of personnel policy more generally revealed growing dissatisfaction with present practices of recruitment, placement, and promotion of executives (*Partiinaia zhizn',* no. 12).

Above all, there was mounting stress that the party bore primary responsibility for rationalizing the structure and functioning of administration. In an editorial entitled, "Perfect the Style and Methods of Executive Leadership," *Kommunist* (no. 11) reminded its readers in July that improving administration was "an important and component part of the entire activity of the party in its leadership of the economy." Two months later, the editors reiterated (Ibid., no. 13), that "perfection of the system of economic administration at the contemporary stage is one of the burning questions of CPSU economic policy." In essence, such formulations constituted pleas and provided justification for greater party intervention in the area of administrative rationalization and control. In fact growing party interference and presence were reflected in the intensified supervisory activity by primary party organizations in ministries and state agencies, already discussed. Underlying the whole rationalization issue, however, was the vexed question of the proper function of party and state in society as well as particular nature and direction of administrative modernization. The main task remained that set by the 1971 CPSU congress: "To combine organically achievements of the scientific and technological revolution with advantages of the socialist economic system and to develop extensively our own particular forms of combining science with production, forms which are inherent in socialism." The proper means of marrying science with socialism, however, continued to evade and divide the leadership.

Efforts were also made to increase efficiency and raise productivity by tightening discipline and mobilizing mass labor enthusiasm. A nationwide "socialist competition" and production campaign to overfulfill plans and pledges was organized in honor of the 50th anniversary. In all, over 3,000 worker collectives won jubilee badges of honor for outstanding labor heroism (*Pravda,* 22 December). Hoping to avoid another disastrous crop year, the authorities announced that another all-union militant socialist competition in agriculture will be held during 1973 to increase production and procurement of grain and other products. The red banners and pennants to be awarded winners carry prizes of rubles and automobiles. (Ibid., 5 December). In industry a campaign of stringent saving and search for hidden reserves continued unabated. Reflecting official concern over wheat shortages, a save-the-bread campaign was mounted during the summer, urging people to cherish each crumb of bread. In Moscow, cinemas screened a documentary film, "The Battle for Bread." To effect better utilization of work time and cut down on losses due to loafing, tardiness, and absenteeism, the CPSU Central Committee adopted in February a special decree on labor discipline. (*Partiinaia zhizn',* no. 4).

In June a "decisive and steadfast struggle" was launched against drunkenness and alcoholism. The output of hard liquor is to be curtailed, while production of soft drinks will increase. The number of stores selling alcoholic beverages will be cut and their operating hours shortened (Moscow Domestic Service, 16 June). New "anti-drunkenness laws" were passed in the RSFSR making offenders subject to fines, public censure (comradely courts), and administrative sanctions. Recidivists can be deprived of their production bonuses and "privileges." (*Sovetskaia Rossiia,* 20 June). A drive against crime and corruption, including the death penalty for swindlers and embezzlers, received press publicity.

The tone and thrust of Brezhnev's speech (*Pravda,* 22 December) on the 50th anniversary radiated well the atmosphere of heightened struggle and vigilance generated by these mobilization efforts. Complaining of the existence of "social sores," such as unconscientious attitudes toward work, slackness, and grubbing, the general secretary warned of identifying laggers publicly, a kind of "reverse emulation" of socialist competition. "It so happens that everybody knows the winners," he declared, "but there seem to be no losers. This kills the very idea of emulation." Lest the nation forget, he reminded forcefully, "We are, comrades, building not a land of idlers where rivers flow with milk and honey, but the most organized and most industrious society in human history."

International Views and Policies. Foreign policy in 1972 continued to pursue with "unflinching determination" (*Pravda,* 26 March) implementation of the blueprint for action outlined by Brezhnev at the Twenty-fourth CPSU Congress in 1971, which has since been widely advertised as the "peace program" of the Soviet Union. In the Soviet view, the contemporary system of international relations is based on the "correlation of forces between the two systems" (*Kommunist,* no. 9). This attachment to the configurations of the bipolar system and a reluctance to admit to the emergence of a more complicated system of relations explains Moscow's embarrassment with China's changing status in the world community.

The nature of the relationship between the two systems further called for a Soviet policy which, in the words of one commentator, represents a "combination of firm rebuff to imperialism and support for the revolutionary liberation movement with a consistent course toward peaceful coexistence of states with different social systems" (TASS, 31 December). This policy passed a severe test in the spring, when the U.S. decision to mine North Vietnam harbors touched off a major debate within the CPSU leadership concerning President Nixon's visit to the Soviet Union.

The debate was settled at a plenary session of the Central Committee on 19 May. A strongly-worded resolution on the international situation issued at the end of this meeting asserted: "The plenum entrusts the Politburo of the Central Committee with the task of further unfailingly carrying out the peace program worked out at the Twenty-fourth CPSU Congress and, in accordance with the concrete situation, to make use of various forms and methods for its implementation, to link organically the solution of the current and immediate tasks of the present time with the long-term perspective and objectives of the struggle for peace, and freedom and security of peoples, social progress and socialism."

This decision cleared the way for a Soviet-U.S. rapprochement. It also necessitated explanations, started by Brezhnev in a speech at a dinner for Tito in Moscow on 5 June. Brezhnev declared: "The foreign policy of the Soviet Union has always been and always will be a socialist, class, internationalist policy. We want détente. We want durable peace. And precisely because of this we are resolutely opposed to any acts of aggression, to any attempt to suppress the struggle for liberation by the peoples, any attempt to interfere in their affairs, to infringe upon their rights." *New Times* (no. 24, June) commented on Brezhnev's statement: "Hence, to ask which it is that takes precedence in Soviet foreign policy—the struggle against imperialism or the promotion of relations with the capitalist countries on the basis of peaceful coexistence—would be to proceed from utterly false premises. . . . The unity of the two principles of Soviet foreign policy is a dialectical unity. Consistently observed, they are not counterposed to one another. They are mutually complementary."

Moreover, the progress of détente in Europe marked by the conclusion of negotiations destined to open the way for a European security conference, together with the positive development in Soviet-U.S. relations, were to demonstrate that the concept of "peaceful co-existence" not only excludes ideology from its field of action but also presupposes as a corollary intensification of the ideological struggle. Suslov, addressing a congress of "Znanye" (an organization disseminating the official propaganda line) on 20 June in Moscow, declared: "The struggle in the field of ideology, the field where there is no, and cannot be any, peaceful co-existence between socialism and capitalism, has sharpened." Brezhnev, speaking at a reception for Fidel Castro a week later, said: "After having strengthened the principle of peaceful co-existence, we realize that successes in that important matter do not offer possibilities of relaxing the ideological struggle. On the contrary, we must be ready to see the struggle intensify, become an ever sharper form of antagonism between the two social systems." *Pravda* (8 July) wrote: "Peaceful co-existence between states with different social systems . . . does not mean the discontinuation of the class struggle between the two systems, but only renunciation of the use of military methods in that struggle." Brezhnev on 27 June further reflected the optimism now pervading Soviet activity in foreign affairs, when he said: "And we have no doubt as to the outcome of this antagonism, for the truth of history, the objective laws of social development are on our side."

Relations with the United States. Preparations for President Nixon's visit to the Soviet Union on 22–30 May were stepped up following Dr. Henry Kissinger's talks in Moscow. Brezhnev, speaking to the congress of Soviet trade unions on 20 March, defined the official attitude toward the "dialogue" which was on the point of beginning between the world's two most powerful nations as follows: "We approach the forthcoming Soviet-American talks from business-like, realistic positions." Stressing the importance of state relations between the two countries, he added: "That is why we consider it our duty to find fields in the relations between the U.S.S.R. and the U.S. which would make it possible, without retreating from the principles of our policy, to establish a certain degree of mutually advantageous cooperation in the interests of the Soviet and American peoples as well as in the interest of peace."

The Soviet leadership acknowledged later that it had faced opposition in its decision to go ahead with summit talks shortly after the U.S. mined North Vietnam harbors. A commentary in *Pravda* (15 June) said that the summit talks had gone forward "despite obstructionist actions by rightist and leftist opponents of relaxation." The newspaper also said that it was to the credit of the Politburo that the "dialogue took place despite the complexity of the international situation and in the face of the sometimes direct opposition by those who like to warm their hands by fanning the fire of hostility and tension."

Without identifying the presumed opponents of "dialogue" at that time, *Pravda*'s allusion to the role of the Politburo pointed to a direct relationship between the existence of an opposition and the Central Committee plenum of 19 May which entrusted the Politburo "with the task of further unfailingly carrying out the peace program of the Twenty-fourth CPSU Congress." Moreover, the release of P. E. Shelest, an influential member of the Politburo and known for intransigent views, from his post as first secretary of the Ukrainian communist party a day after the plenum suggested that he had played a major part in the opposition.

According to the same commentary, the main debate seems to have run along the following lines: "The spirit of the Moscow talks, which were based on a principled position compatible with reasonable tactical compromises, was fully in line with these positions; it was not a sign of weakness or softness, but a duty for all those who are guided by the true interests of peace and socialism, and not by revolutionary phrases." *Kommunist* (no. 9, June) saw no reason why the United States should be excluded from the field of action of a policy based on the principle of peaceful co-existence. It also pointed to "objective factors" which, despite all serious differences in social systems, ideology, and approach to world politics, create common interests between the U.S.S.R. and the United States, primarily in averting the dangers of a global military conflict and a 'cold war' atmosphere. *Kommunist* insisted that for this reason the Soviet Union considered possible and desirable establishment of "not only good but also friendly relations, of course, not to the detriment of a third country."

Soviet reaction to intensification of U.S. air raids over North Vietnam, following the deadlock in peace negotiations during December, was fully in line with the policy endorsed at the 19 May plenum of the Central Committee. Brezhnev, speaking on the 50th anniversary of the U.S.S.R. (21 December), confirmed that the series of Soviet-U.S. agreements signed during President Nixon's visit to Moscow further helped establish a solid basis for improvement of the political climate between the two countries. There was, however, a new and cautious note of warning in Brezhnev's statement: "It should be stressed with all clarity that much will depend on how events develop in the near future, and in particular on the turn which the question of the end of the war in Vietnam will take." But the last issue of *New Times* (no. 52, December) reflected a reluctance of the Soviet leadership to envisage a setback in relations at this stage, when it claimed without hesitation that the Soviet-U.S. summit in May "will go down in history as a big step forward in developing relations between the two countries."

The series of agreements signed during President Nixon's visit included a 12-point statement on Basic Principles of Relations (ibid.). Other agreements specified a limitation on anti-ballistic missiles and an interim ceiling on strategic arms; environmental cooperation; joint medical research; cooperation in the exploration and peaceful uses of outer space; cooperation in science and technology; and prevention of incidents on the high seas and above them. In addition there was an agreement on a $750 million grain shipment to the U.S.S.R. in July, and two accords were signed on trade and settlement of the Soviet wartime lend-lease debt in October. These latter accords called for an increase of trade to at least $1.5 billion and for Soviet payments of $722 million for World War II debts.

Europe. The successful outcome of the four-power negotiations over Berlin on 3 September 1971 and signing on 17 December 1971 of an East-West German agreement regulating access to West Berlin gave a new impulse to Soviet efforts toward convocation of a conference on European security, an 18-year old project first advanced by V. M. Molotov in February 1954.

Warsaw Pact leaders meeting in Prague on 25–26 January 1972 repeated their previous call for a speedy convocation of the conference. A "Declaration on Peace, Security and Cooperation in Europe" issued at the end of the meeting expressed a conviction that it could be held in 1972 and reaffirmed readiness of participants to appoint delegates for multilateral preparatory consultations. The Soviet Union and its allies committed themselves to the general recognition and practical implementation of seven basic principles of European security which, in their opinion, must represent the basic content of the agenda for a European conference. These principles were: inviolability of frontiers, renunciation of force, peaceful co-existence, good-neighborly relations and cooperation in the interests of peace, mutually advantageous relations among states, disarmament, and support for the United Nations. The declaration also pointed out the "fact" that forces interested in maintaining tension continue to be active in Europe.

At the same time the Soviet Union launched a propaganda campaign, apparently designed to appeal to people in Western Europe over the heads of their governments. Originally undertaken by front organizations, such as the World Peace Council (WPC), the campaign was ostensibly entrusted to national committees concerned with promoting European security formed with WPC help (see World Peace Council).

Following the conclusion of the East-West German traffic agreement on 26 May and implementation of the Four Power Berlin agreement on 3 June, the Soviet leaders in September agreed with Dr. Henry Kissinger to open talks on Mutual and Balanced Force Reductions (MBFR) in Europe. This removed the final obstacle to the beginning of multilateral preparations for the European security conference at Helsinki on 22 November.

With preparations for the conference on the point of entering a final and decisive stage, attention increasingly focused on one issue which had been brought up by Western governments in the course of bilateral consultations, namely, the question of the free movement of people, ideas and information on the continent. This demand stemmed from a conviction among the architects of détente in the West that one of the ways of breaking down existing barriers of distrust was to encourage greater freedom of movement among the people of Europe, beyond the traditional pattern of cultural exchanges.

Western demands for greater freedom of movement in Europe, although couched in conciliatory terms, provoked sharp reaction from East European communist leaders. (See, for example, the Hungarian view in *The Times,* London, 19 May.) Still relying as they do on a strict monopoly of information in order to preserve the integrity of their system, they resented the move as an attempt to undermine their posture at home and bargaining position at the conference table. In anticipation of this danger, they embarked on a campaign explaining their concept of peaceful co-existence while tightening internal discipline.

Moscow presented its case in *International Affairs* (October). Answering a statement by the NATO general secretary (*Newsweek,* 10 July), which insisted on the need for a "freer exchange of persons and ideas and the dismantling of artificial barriers that separate the two halves of the continent," the Soviet journal claimed that the NATO chief and his colleagues were "haunted by the dream of the restoration of the capitalist order where its very foundation has been liquidated" and were "aiming at one-sided concessions froɪɪ the socialist countries, getting rid of all barriers which stand in the way of the ideological and political subversion of imperialism." *Izvestia* (8 October) reflecting these remarks said: "It has long been known that certain Western circles which advocate the 'free exchange of information' are in fact engaged in disinformation and wage an active ideological struggle against the socialist states, hoping for 'convergence.' "

The first hint that the Soviet Union was preparing to face the issue at the conference table came in a major article in *Kommunist* (no. 16, November) written jointly by two deputy chiefs in the CPSU Central Committee's international department. While repeating main themes of the campaign against the Western proposal, they said that the "Soviet Union and the other countries of socialism, while struggling against imperialism and revanchism, against an ideology hostile to the cause of peace and international cooperation, support the broadening of exchanges in the field of culture and in the field of information." At the same time, "we have come out and are coming out against this kind of exchange being used in any way to the detriment of the principles of peaceful co-existence among states with different social orders and contrary to these demands for European cooperation that follow from the UN statute."

Brezhnev, alluding for the first time to the greater flow of information and people in Europe in his speech on the USSR anniversary (21 December), said that the Soviet Union was in favor provided that it will take into account the "respect for sovereignty, laws and customs of each country and will serve the mutual spiritual enrichment of peoples." He also said that he favored tourism, youth exchanges, and traveling by citizens "on a collective or private basis."

The first round of multilateral preparatory consultations, which witnessed Soviet-Romanian disagreement over procedural matters recessed for a month on 15 December, without reaching accord on the conference agenda.

By the end of the year, the Soviet Union had not yet replied to a NATO invitation of 16 November to open negotiations on mutual and balanced force reductions in Central Europe. But Brezhnev indicated on 21 December that the Soviet Union was in favor of "serious preparation and effective conduct" of these negotiations. A first analysis of the problem from the Soviet point of view was set forth in *Mirovaya ekonomika i mezhdunarodnye otnosheniya* (June). The article replied to Kissinger's statement on mutual force reductions of 29 May during Nixon's visit to the Soviet Union, to the effect that any agreement would have to go beyond a simple cut back in forces. Rejecting asymmetric troop reduction and rejecting the geographic factor, the journal contended that the "only possible principle is the principle of equal reduction."

Soviet relations with East European countries were exempt from major complications. *Kommunist* (no. 13, August) recalled that the "policy of strengthening cooperation among the countries of socialism stays at the center of CPSU attention." The question gained added significance because of implications which Moscow's policy of peaceful co-existence, in particular in relation with Western Europe, may have on the cohesion of the "socialist community."

The Soviet view of the issue was stated again in all clarity by an article in *International Affairs* (March). After recalling the decisive role played by the coordinated policy of the socialist nations in "frustrating the adventurist plans of the imperialists" in Europe as well as in other parts of the world, the writer said: "The effectiveness of the policy of each brother nation and of the community as a whole depends on the level of foreign policy coordination, economic potential, the scope of economic cooperation among them, and, at the current stage, also the level of socialist economic integration. These processes constitute the characteristic features of socialist international relations at the present time." Reaffirming the special role of the Soviet Union in the camp, he indicated that the "criterion of one or another progressive political movement consists in the first place in its relation to our country—its objective approach to the evaluation of the internal and external policy of the Soviet Union, the bulwark of peace and socialism on earth." He also admitted that the "process of aligning positions and of working out common lines on problems of world policy, including European affairs, is, it seems, not simple." Coordination demands, he said, "a scientific approach to the problems, considerable efforts, great skill, a full and thorough calculation of internal and external factors."

The Twenty-sixth session of CMEA in Moscow on 10–12 July was said to represent a "new important step in the implementation of the program of integration of the socialist states." Cuba was admitted into the organization on that occasion. The Warsaw Pact, which met at summit level on 25–26 January to agree on further moves toward peaceful co-existence in Europe was said to be the center for coordination of foreign political activity of the socialist countries (*International Affairs,* no. 3, March).

Developments in the "socialist community" were highlighted by Brezhnev's visit to Hungary on 27 November–1 December. A communiqué at the end of the visit declared that the two sides shared "an identity of views on all matters," implicitly denying persistent rumors of differences on bilateral economic relations. Efforts by Gierek in Poland and Husák in Czechoslovakia toward further strengthening the communist regimes in their countries continued to enjoy Soviet support. *Pravda* (19 August), coming out in favor of the current process of "normalization" in Prague, defended the trials staged against supporters of Dubček on 19 July–8 August and accused "organs of bourgeois propaganda" of carrying out a "slanderous campaign planned according to all the rules of psychological warfare." Romania's continuing critical attitude toward the state of relations among the countries of the "socialist community" was reflected in Ceausescu's address to his party's conference in Bucharest on 19 July. Calling for improved relations through a "better definition of the principles and norms that should guide relations among all socialist countries," he said: "These norms should be settled exclusively by negotiations, consultation and, most emphatically, ruling out any kind of encroachment."

President Tito of Yugoslavia visited Moscow on 5–10 June for talks with Soviet leaders. A final communiqué noted the "vitality" of the principles set forth in previous joint declarations. Both sides stated that they were applying socialist principles "in line with the specific peculiarities of their own countries." They observed that "conditions exist for expanding trade between the two countries and agreed on the advisability of strengthening the "legal basis" of mutual relations. Soviet-Albanian relations failed to improve, despite repeated calls by Moscow for the restoration of normal ties between the two countries (*Izvestia,* 28 November; *New Times,* no. 47, November).

Relations between the Soviet Union and West European countries focused on preparations for a European security conference, while the CPSU continued to feel the impact of "normalization" in Czechoslovakia in its contacts with West European communist parties. The first indication that Moscow was revising its hostile stand toward the European Economic Community (EEC) came from Brezhnev on 20 March. Speaking at the congress of trade unions in Moscow, the Soviet leader said that the U.S.S.R. was "far from ignoring the existing situation in Western Europe, including the existence of . . . the Common Market and its evolution." He added that future relations between the EEC and CMEA would depend on how far the former accepted "realities existing in the socialist part of Europe, specifically the interests of CMEA member countries." Brezhnev, in his U.S.S.R. anniversary speech, envisaged the possibility of "some forms of business relations" between the two economic organizations. Gromyko's trip to the Netherlands, Luxemburg and Belgium (5–12 July) offered an occasion to publicize Soviet views on European security. Italian premier Andreotti visited the Soviet Union on 24–29 October.

Soviet-Chinese Relations. Brezhnev's speech on the U.S.S.R. anniversary, 21 December, confirmed the failure of efforts to improve relations with China during 1972. The war of words between Moscow and Peking intensified during the same period, as both sides maneuvered to secure influential positions in the perspective of an imminent settlement of the Vietnam conflict. Ideology played a minor part in the polemics, which have mainly become the reflection of a struggle for power between the two countries. President Nixon's visit to China in February inspired an exhaustive critique of Chinese policy by the Soviet Union. In the Soviet view, China has now become an accomplice of the "imperialists." At the same time Moscow displayed growing concern with the "ever greater part" which Europe is coming to play in "Peking's subversive, splitting and adventurist foreign policy" (*International Affairs,* April).

Little transpired from Sino-Soviet border talks, which have continued to be held in Peking at regular intervals since 20 October 1969. On the eve of their resumption in the spring after a six-month recess since November 1971, Brezhnev, on 20 March, referred to Chinese insistence that relations with the Soviet Union be conducted on the basis of peaceful co-existence. He declared that "if the people in Peking are not expecting more in relations with the socialist states, we are ready to develop relations on that basis too."

The first indication that the negotiations were not making progress came on 10 August, when *Izvestia* issued a lengthy attack on a new Chinese atlas that restated Chinese claims to 1.5 million square kilometers of "age-old" Soviet territory. It complained: "Despite the numerous initiatives of the Soviet delegation, it has not been possible to bring the Peking negotiations to a successful conclusion." According to Brezhnev on 21 December, one of these initiatives consisted of a proposal first made on 15 January 1971 to renounce the use of force in the settlement of pending issues between the two countries. An unusually detailed historical survey of the evolution of the much debated border between China and the Soviet Union (*International Affairs,* June 1972) suggested that the ability of the two sides to reach an agreement remained much in doubt. But the simultaneous denial by Peking and Moscow on 21 December of rumored incidents along the border at the end of November pointed to the intention on the part of both sides not to let a still tense situation get out of hand.

An article in the official monthly organ of the Chinese Communist Party *Hung ch'i* (August) publicly accused the Soviet Union for the first time of having been involved in the alleged plot by the late Chinese defense minister Lin Piao to assassinate Mao Tse-tung. The 27th U.N. General Assembly witnessed a harsh verbal duel between the Soviet and Chinese delegates when the latter opposed a Soviet proposal for a world conference on disarmament and the admission of Bangladesh to U.N. membership. On 23 September the Chinese delegate accused the Soviet Union of having provoked the Indian-Pakistani conflict in 1971, "with a view to expanding Soviet influence on the Asian continent." A Soviet message to Peking on the anniversary of the Chinese People's Republic on 1 October congratulated the Chinese people but accused Mao Tse-tung of "theoretical incompetence" and said that his leadership had taken the Chinese "away from the path of Leninism."

Brezhnev, summing up with unusual frankness Soviet grievances against China aired in Soviet media in the course of the year, said on 21 December: "Essentially, the only criterion now determining the Chinese leaders' approach to any major international problem is their aspiration to inflict as much harm as possible on the U.S.S.R. and damage the interests of the Socialist community." At the same time he reiterated an offer to sign with China a treaty on the non-use of force. He also indicated that Peking's intransigence would not deter the Soviet Union from pursuing a policy which, he said, was "based on a sober account of reality today and in the future."

The only tangible, although rather modest, progress in Sino-Soviet relations came in the economic field with the signing of a trade and credit agreement which called for almost doubling of trade from $153 million in 1971 to $290.5 million in 1972. These figures still are far from comparing favorably with the all-time record of $2.1 billion in 1959.

Asia. The Soviet Union in 1972 pressed with growing insistence for the installation of a system of collective security in Asia on the pattern of the one which it has been advocating in Europe for a number of years. The idea was first advanced by Brezhnev at the conference of communist parties in Moscow during June 1969. At that time it was strongly opposed by China and coolly received by most Asian nations, reluctant as they were to let themselves be dragged into Sino-Soviet polemics. Moscow's renewed interest in this proposal was spurred by Asian developments in the course of the year: the improvement in Sino-U.S. relations, normalization of Sino-Japanese relations, and increased prospects for a Vietnam settlement.

Brezhnev on 20 March reiterated the principles on which such a system should be based: renunciation of force in relations between states, respect for sovereignty and inviolability of borders, non-interference in internal affairs, and widespread development of economic and other cooperation on the basis of full equality and mutual benefit. An article in *Pravda* (28 March) casting doubt on the motives behind the Sino-U.S. rapprochement, saw justification for the idea of an Asian collective security system in fresh evidence of the determination by U.S. "imperialists" to pursue a "policy of the gendarme" in Asia and of Peking's "hegemonic pretensions." An article in *Izvestia* (12 October), entitled "An Urgent Task," commented: "Daily experience demonstrates that such a system is vitally necessary, if it is desired not to transform the Asian continent into a source of unrest." The creation of such a system was said to require "collective efforts on the part of all Asian countries." But at the same time the writer indicated that the Soviet Union was taking a long-term view of the issues: "The situation surrounding implementation of this objective is more complex in Asia than in Europe and, possibly, in Africa." Brezhnev on 21 December confirmed that "some capitals" still see in his Asian security proposal an attempt to "contain and encircle China." He insisted that China was intended to be a "full and equal participant in such a system."

The Soviet Union endeavored to preserve an influential position in the communist regimes of North Vietnam and North Korea while seeking to multiply contacts with a wide range of non-communist Asian countries. In an apparent attempt to exploit North Vietnamese apprehension over Nixon's visit to Peking, Moscow intensified its attacks against Chinese policy toward North Vietnam, denouncing the "escalation of Maoist perfidy as regard to one of the socialist countries" (Novosti press agency, 3 February). Simultaneously it went on reminding the North Vietnamese of the attitude of the Soviet Union, which remained "true to its internationalist duty" (*Kommunist,* no. 5, February). The "brotherly friendship and solidarity between the Soviet Union and North Vietnam" was hailed as a "convincing manifestation of the new type of inter-state relations developing in practice among the socialist countries" (Ibid., no. 3, February).

Podgorny went to Hanoi on 15–18 June, after Nixon's visit to the Soviet Union, to reaffirm support for North Vietnam's "just struggle against aggressive imperialism." The joint communique issued at the end of the visit indicated that talks "took place in a frank, friendly and comradely atmosphere," a formulation which usually points to existing disagreements. Signs of Hanoi's displeasure over Chinese and Soviet interests in improving relations with the United States were detected in the official North Vietnamese communist party organ (*Nhan Dan,* 18 August), which sharply rebuked the U.S. "policy of reconciliation toward a number of big powers." A new Soviet-North Vietnamese trade and credit agreement was signed on 9 December. The resumption of U.S. air raids over North Vietnam, after failure of negotiations on a ceasefire agreement in South Vietnam, drew relatively moderate reaction on the part of the Soviet Union. Soviet public statements continued to call for an early settlement of the conflict and pledged further aid to Hanoi while condeming intensification of the bombing. Soviet preference for a negotiated settlement of the whole Indochinese conflict also found reflection in Moscow's satisfaction with the continuation of peace talks between Pathet Lao and the Laotian government.

A Soviet delegation headed by K. F. Katushev, secretary of the Central Committee, visited North Korea at the beginning of September on the occasion of the 24th anniversary of the Democratic People's Republic of Korea. During the talks, which according to a final communiqué were held in a "warm and friendly atmosphere," the two sides were said to have discussed relations between the CPSU and the Korean Workers' Party, problems of inter-party cooperation, and other unspecified "questions of mutual interest." Moscow reacted positively to resumption of contacts between the two Koreas in August.

Japan and the Soviet Union agreed on 27 January to open negotiations on a peace treaty in the course of the year. The announcement was contained in a joint communiqué issued at the conclusion of Gromyko's visit to Tokyo on 23–28 January. Formal talks started during the visit of the Japanese foreign minister to Moscow on 23 October. It was agreed that they would be continued at a later date. A commentary in *Pravda* (17 December) termed Japan's claim to Soviet-occupied Kurile Islands "absurd and a major barrier" to the signing of a peace treaty. Soviet commentators continued to insist that the Japanese left could exert a decisive influence on Japan's foreign policy, if able to overcome divisions and resort to popular front tactics. *Kommunist* (no. 9, June) was convinced that "objective conditions" existed for creation of a united front of all Japanese "democratic forces." In April a CPSU delegation, visiting Japan at the invitation of the Japanese Socialist Party, agreed to strengthen relations between the two parties "in the interest of intensifying the anti-imperialist struggle" (*Pravda,* 10 April). Advances of the Japanese Communist Party in the general elections (see Japan) was welcomed by Soviet commentators as an encouraging sign of the evolution of Japanese public opinion.

The Indian subcontinent, in the wake of last year's Indian-Pakistani war, continued to require much Soviet attention in 1972. The Soviet Union agreed to provide Bangladesh with large-scale economic assistance and to strengthen its political ties with the government, following a visit of President Mujibur Rahman to Moscow on 1–5 March. A joint declaration on 3 March paved the way for regular political consultations and contained a Bangladesh endorsement of the Soviet position on various international issues.

A delegation of the Bangladesh communist party, headed by its secretary general, held talks with CPSU leaders in Moscow on 31 July and 4 August. A joint communiqué pointed to the existence of a good basis for "unity of all democratic forces" in that country (*Pravda,* 5 August).

Pakistan's President Zulfikar Ali Bhutto conferred with Soviet leaders in Moscow on 16–17 March, in an effort to improve bilateral relations impaired by Soviet support of India and Bangladesh. A joint communiqué on 18 March agreed to renew ties and revive assistance agreements disrupted last year. The two sides arranged to "hold regular exchanges of views on questions of mutual interest."

Direct peace talks among India, Pakistan, and Bangladesh were urged in a joint Indian-Soviet communiqué issued on 6 April following a visit to Moscow by the Indian foreign minister. The statement said that India and the Soviet Union were "convinced that every effort should be exerted to make the subcontinent an area of peace, friendship and good-neighborliness."

The visit of Malaysian premier Tun Abdul Razak to the Soviet Union on 25 September–5 October, the first such visit by a prime minister of that country, was of significance in view of Moscow's continuing disenchantment with Indonesia and neutralist leanings of Malaysia.

Soviet satisfaction with the victory of the Labor Party in the Australian general election on 2 December reflected a growing interest in the "region between the Indian and Pacific Oceans" (*Pravda,* 4 December). A similar consideration may have led Moscow to recognize the existence of the two rival communist parties in Australia.

Middle East and Africa. The gradual deterioration of Soviet-Egyptian relations which climaxed in the ouster of Soviet military advisers from Egypt in July 1972 mainly determined the evolution of Moscow's policies toward the Middle East. Significant course corrections were made by the Soviet Union, while major objectives remained unchanged.

The crisis in Soviet-Egyptian relations had been latent for over a year. Egyptian President Sadat said (24 July) that his differences with the Soviet Union had first emerged after his visit to Moscow in March of last year. Differences deepened rapidly in the course of intensive consultations which opened with Sadat's visit to Moscow on 3–4 February. A mounting campaign of recriminations in the press on both sides sharply contrasted with optimism of official statements. A communiqué at the end of Sadat's talks in Moscow said only that the two sides had "considered measures" in the area of "further strengthening" Egyptian military capabilities against Israel and "outlined a number of concrete steps in this direction." According to the Cairo newspaper *al-Ahram* (30 March), Soviet military aid to Egypt thus far totaled $3 billion.

Sadat returned to Moscow for two days of talks with Brezhnev on 28–29 April. A joint communiqué said that the two sides had "reached agreement on the further strengthening of military cooperation" and had taken unspecified "appropriate measures in that direction." It was also stated for the first time that, because of the continuing deadlock in negotiations on a Middle East settlement, the "Arab states had every reason to use other means as well to regain the Arab lands captured by Israel."

A commentary released by Novosti, the Soviet news agency, on 30 May to mark the first anniversary of the Soviet-Egyptian friendship treaty of 27 May 1971 referred to "new plans for the future which will strengthen our friendship more and more actively." On 18 July, Sadat announced that he had ordered the immediate withdrawal of Soviet "military advisers and experts" from Egypt. (Three days before, Egypt's premier cut short a visit to Moscow after one day of talks on 14 July.) Sadat indicated that Egypt had encountered difficulties in obtaining all the Soviet arms it wanted for its confrontation with Israel. He also suggested that President Nixon's talks in Moscow had influenced his decision. At the same time he proposed a Soviet-Egyptian meeting to "decide the next phase of operations."

Moscow reacted coolly with a statement on 19 July saying that the Soviet advisers had completed their training of Egyptian forces and that they "had been sent to Egypt for a limited period." The statement also quoted Sadat as remarking that the move "in no way affects the foundation of Soviet-Egyptian friendship." This was the first time that Moscow had disclosed the nature of its military assistance to Egypt. Talks on 16–18 October were inconclusive: the joint communiqué did not mention the Soviet pledge of military aid or other assistance to Egypt.

Earlier, Moscow had been looking for an alternative to a policy which had made Egypt the cornerstone of Soviet influence in the region. The decline of Egypt's prestige in the Arab world, the rise of fiercely anti-communist regimes in Libya and Sudan, and the loss of credibility for non-alignment no longer seemed to justify a choice made over a decade ago. *International Affairs* (July), shortly before Sadat's 18 July decision, said that "the role of Egypt in inter-Arab relations, its geographic situation at the junction of the Asian and African continents, and the international stature of Egypt as one of the founding countries of the non-alignment movement gave Cairo's foreign policy a special significance." But for the present, the journal indicated, the significance "popularity" of Egypt's policies depended on the degree of "sharpness of their anti-imperialist character."

While disenchantment with Sadat's policies grew deeper, Moscow moved to seek closer ties with Iraq, Syria, and South Yemen in an attempt to broaden the basis of its influence in the Arab world. An unusually frank article in *New Times* (no. 41, October) admitted that it had been a mistake to seek the unity of "anti-imperialist forces" throughout the Arab world before this unity had been achieved at the national level. Calls for all-Arab unity were "very important and necessary," but the unity of "anti-imperialist forces" on an all-Arab scale could "only be achieved on the basis of strengthening these forces in each separate country." Iraq, Syria and South Yemen were singled out as countries in which there was a "dialogue" between "anti-imperialist and progressive forces," including Marxists, at the national level. This had already led to "remarkably positive progress" toward better cooperation between these forces.

The policies of Iraq and Syria toward Western oil companies were opening new perspectives in the struggle of the Arab peoples "against the forces of imperialism and for a strengthening of their national economies" (*Izvestia,* 2 June). Closer ties with these countries and South Yemen also offered advantages of access to the Asian subcontinent. A review of relations with Arab countries in *International Affairs* (October) dealt at length with Iraq and Syria, while scantily alluding to Soviet-Egyptian cooperation.

An Iraqi delegation, headed by the vice-president of the Revolutionary Command Council, visited the Soviet Union on 10–17 February. A joint communiqué said that the Soviet Union would provide Iraq with more military assistance and that regular ties would be established between the CPSU and the Iraqi Ba'th Party. Kosygin visited Iraq on 6–10 April to attend dedication of the Soviet-financed nationalized North Rumelia oil field. On that occasion a 15-year treaty of friendship and cooperation was signed in Baghdad, similar to the Soviet-Egyptian treaty a year earlier. *Izvestia* disclosed on 21 July that the two countries had signed an economic agreement on 7 June, to aid Iraq in development of its oil industry. The president of Iraq visited the Soviet Union on 14–19 September and, in the final communiqué, the two sides agreed on "concrete measures" for further reinforcement of Iraq's defense potential and "gave their full support to the struggle being carried out by the Arab peoples of the Persian Gulf to frustrate aggressive imperialist plans which endanger their freedom and independence." At the same time, it was affirmed that the people of the area "should be given the right to solve their problems without outside interference." *International Affairs* (October) revealed that CMEA was drafting a plan for more effective assistance to Iraq.

A Soviet economic and military delegation headed by First Deputy Premier Mazurov visited Syria on 21–26 February. According to a communiqué at the end of the visit, the Soviet Union agreed to supply Syria with more arms. A protocol was signed on 25 February providing for Soviet cooperation in carrying out Syria's economic development program. On 10–13 May Marshal Grechko visited Damascus, where he concluded a new arms deal with the Syrian government. The Soviet Union further promised Syria more economic and military aid, according to a joint communiqué at the close of the visit by the Syrian president to the Soviet Union on 6–8 July. This statement also pledged closer relations between the CPSU and the Syrian Ba'th Party. An agreement on economic aid and technical cooperation and a second agreement establishing a joint commission in these fields were signed on 8 July. Syria's defense minister visited the Soviet Union on 6–10 December. The Syrian president, however, told the Beirut newspaper *al Bairaq* (5 December) that the Soviet Union was not helping Syria as much as it could.

South Yemen's head of state visited the Soviet Union on 21–25 November. In a final communiqué, the Soviet Union expressed satisfaction with his government's efforts toward "normalization of relations between the two Yemeni governments" and agreed further to contribute to the strengthening of South Yemen's defense capacity.

Podgorny's visit to Turkey on 11–17 April and the reception of the Shah of Iran in the Soviet Union on 10–21 October offered an occasion to dispel apprehensions about the Soviet Union's current Middle East policies, while reaffirming the importance which it attaches to good-neighborly relations on its southern flank. The Soviet Union and Turkey signed a declaration of such relations on 17 April. The final communiqué on the Shah's visit, stating that "problems concerning the region of the Persian Gulf should be solved by the bordering states in accordance with the U.N. Charter without interference from the outside," confirmed Moscow's intention to stay above the Iranian-Iraqi conflict over territorial rights in the Gulf.

The visit by a delegation of the Palestinian Liberation Organization, headed by its chairman Yasir Arafat, to the Soviet Union on 17–27 July did not affect the course of Moscow's relations which, according to a final communiqué, remained based on Soviet recognition of the "just struggle of the Palestinian people against imperialist and Israeli aggression for the legitimate rights of the Arab peoples."

International Affairs (October) reported that Soviet relations remained "friendly" with Lebanon, Morocco, Tunisia, Jordan, and Kuwait, while Algeria deserved special mention for the progress in Soviet-Algerian economic cooperation. Libya, despite its continuing militancy against communism, was mentioned together with North Yemen and Mauritania for the "anti-imperialist" character of its policy. A Soviet-Libyan economic cooperation agreement was signed on 4 March. Sudan, however, received no mention.

The absence of any significant development in Soviet relations with Africa reflected Moscow's reluctance to engage too deeply in the affairs of the continent, in view of the complex nature of the African political situation at the present time.

The difficulties encountered by Soviet analysts in trying to draw valid conclusions from their observations of the African scene were evident from a frank discussion of national liberation movements in Africa published by *International Affairs* (July). While indicating that a "new powerful tide" was not succeeding the "low ebb" of the past year, this survey warned against hasty generalizations in view of the "extreme complexity and contradictory character" of the movements. The "anti-imperialist" front was said to be gaining strength in better coordination of the armed struggle against Portuguese colonies and the white regime in Rhodesia, through the Organization of African States, and in the growing role played by the African states at the United Nations. But at the same time the continent was witnessing an unprecedented "activation of the forces of colonialism and neo-colonialism," which were using ever "more perfidious and refined" methods to achieve their aims. The "extremely negative role" which the Maoists played in Africa was denounced with vigor. Finally, the study pointed out a "certain eclectism" in the "ideological concepts" of African communism.

Latin America. Growing nationalist feelings and moves against U.S. financial concerns in a number of Latin American countries continued to stimulate Soviet interest. An article in *International Affairs* (October) exclaimed: "Never have the contradictions between Latin America and the U.S. been so sharp as today!" But at the same time it did not exclude the possibility of eventual setbacks for the "progressive" forces: "The danger of counter-revolution at the instigation of local reaction and U.S. imperialism is intensifying."

Soviet ideologists continued to show a marked preference for the Chilean model over most others—considered irrelevant or impractical at the present stage. The efforts of the Popular Unity coalition government of six groups, including communists and socialists, were followed with great attention. The formation of the coalition was regarded as the "clearest embodiment" of the task facing Latin American communists, namely, "to rally all progressive, democratic forces and lead them in the fight for an anti-imperialist, agrarian, popular-democratic revolution that will end domination by U.S. imperialism and the power of latifundists and the bourgeoisie" (*New Times,* no. 5, February). Another article declared: "The evident success of the anti-imperialist struggle in the countries of Latin America, in particular the achievements of the Popular Unity bloc in Chile as well as the experience accumulated during the processs of the formation of large political unions of workers in other countries, are evidences of new possibilities for solid and active coalitions of patriotic and democratic forces." (*International Affairs,* April). Local communists, "marching in the vanguard of these coalitions," were called on to justify the correctness of these tactics at the risk of accentuating dissent among themselves. Aware of the significance of the Chilean experiment with popular front tactics, advocated at the Twenty-fourth CPSU Congress, the Soviet Union offered its political and financial backing to the Allende government during a visit by the Chilean leader 6–10 December in Moscow.

Fidel Castro's visit on 26 June–6 July was an occasion for Brezhnev to reaffirm the special links existing between Cuba, now considered a "solid component of the world socialist system," and the Soviet Union and to remind his guest that revolutionary work should mainly consist in his case of solving problems of administration (*Pravda,* 27 June). Cuba was admitted to CMEA on 12 July.

In March, Bolivia expelled 49 members of the Soviet Embassy in La Paz who were accused of plotting the overthrow of the government. The charge was denied by the Soviet Union.

Publications. The main CPSU organs are the daily newspaper *Pravda,* the theoretical and ideological journal *Kommunist* (appearing 18 times a year), and the twice-monthly *Partiinaia zhizn',* a journal on internal party affairs and organizational party matters. *Kommunist vooruzhennikh sil* is the party theoretical journal for the armed forces, and *Agitator* is the journal for party propagandists, both appearing twice a month. The Komsomol has a newspaper, *Komsomolskaia pravda* (issued six times a week); a monthly theoretical journal, *Molodoi kommunist;* and a monthly literary journal, *Molodaia gvardia.* Each U.S.S.R. republic prints similar party newspapers and journals in local languages, and usually also in Russian.

Hoover Institution
Stanford University
and
Radio Liberty
Munich, Germany

Paul M. Cocks
and
Jean F. Riollet

Yugoslavia

The Communist Party of Yugoslavia was founded in June 1920.[1] At the party's Sixth Congress, in November 1952, the name was changed to League of Communists of Yugoslavia (Savez Komunista Jugoslavije; LCY). The LCY is the only political party in Yugoslavia and holds a monopoly of power through its leading role in the Socialist Alliance of Working People of Yugoslavia (Socijalistički Savez Radnog Naroda Jugoslavije; SAWPY), an organization which includes all mass political organizations and also individuals representing various social groups.

Leadership and Membership. According to the LCY statute, the Congress, to be convened every fifth year, is the League's supreme body which determines the programmatic orientation and policy of the League on essential questions of the country's domestic and foreign affairs. The last, Ninth LCY Congress (March 1969) replaced the Central Committee with an annual Conference which elaborates and defines the League's policy between congresses. The Conference is composed of 367 permanent delegates. At the Ninth LCY Congress, the League's Presidium was enlarged to a 52-member body composed of seven representatives from each of the six constituent republic party organizations, three from each of the two autonomous region party organizations, three from the armed forces and Tito as its chairman (presidents of the central committees and first secretaries of the communist parties in the republics and regions belong ex officio to the Presidium). The Presidium operates on the basis of the political guidelines of the Congress and conclusions of the Conference, is responsible for their implementation, passes the necessary political decisions and coordinates the entire activity of the LCY. The President of the LCY, Josip Broz-Tito, guides the work of the Presidium, which elects a more restricted political organ, the Executive Bureau. According to the LCY statute the Bureau operates within the framework and tasks laid down by the Presidium and is responsible for its work to the Presidium. The Executive Bureau which in the period 1969–71 had 15 members, was reorganized at the Second LCY Conference (January 1972) and now has 8 members who come from the republics and regions. Each member is charged with a specific sector of LCY work. The members are: Krsta Avramović (b. 1928), Serbia, industrial management; Jure Bilić (b. 1922), Croatia, party discipline; Stane Dolanc (b. 1925), Slovenia, foreign policy and inter-party relations; Kiro Gligorov (b. 1917), Macedonia, foreign trade; Stevan Doronjski (b. 1919), Vojvodina, agriculture; Todo Kurtović (b. 1919), Bosnia and Herzegovina, economy; Fadilj Hodža (b. 1916), Kosovo, nationalities; Budislav Šoškić (b. 1925), Montenegro, press and propaganda. Secretary of the Executive Bureau is Stane Dol-

1 Yugoslav communists claim April 1919 as the date of party establishment, when a unification congress in Belgrade temporarily established a Socialist Workers' Party of Yugoslavia (Communists). It included both communist and non-communist elements, but the organization broke up in June 1920.

anc, who played a major role in LCY policies during 1972 and emerged as one of the most powerful party leaders. Despite the fact that the present Bureau includes some younger and relatively unknown persons, and that some party stalwarts (Edvard Kardelj, Vladimir Bakarić, Krste Crvenkovski, Mijalko Todorović, and Veljko Vlahović) were dropped from membership in January 1972, the new organ increased its powers and acted as a political bureau.

The LCY claims a membership of 1,025,476 (*Nedeljne Informativne Novine, NIN,* 8 October). The population of Yugoslavia is 20,770,000 (est. December 1972). Social composition by percentage of the LCY is: workers (28.8); intelligentsia (13) from the fields of education, science, culture, and health; technical professions (5.2); administrative personnel (12.1); agriculture (6.3); directing personnel (7.5); social security services and the army (8.1); retired (8.9); students (3.6) and pupils (1.6); private craftsmen (0.4); unemployed (1); housewives (3.7). Women comprise 19.5 percent of the membership (*NIN,* 8 October).

Party Internal Affairs. Internal LCY turbulence, which in December 1971 climaxed with the purge of the party leadership in Croatia (see *YICA, 1971,* pp. 101–104), continued throughout 1972. Its gravity was depicted by Dolanc: "We are presently going through a revolutionary stage which is extraordinarily difficult, perhaps the most difficult since the beginning of our revolution" (*Borba,* 22 October).

The Two LCY Conferences. Originally scheduled for November 1971, but postponed because of events in Croatia, the Second LCY Conference took place in Belgrade on 25–27 January. Tito opened it and offered the concluding speech while 92 delegates participated in the three-day debates. A lengthy Action Program was adopted. It hailed as a new, significant LCY victory the "political offensive against all reactionary and anti-selfgovernment forces" launched by the LCY Presidium in early December 1971. The main parts of the Program discussed the necessity of strengthening the role of the working class in the system of selfgovernment, insisted on stabilization of the economy, and proclaimed the indispensable necessity of enhancing the political role of and internal discipline within the LCY (*Borba,* 29 January). In his concluding speech, Tito attributed the "slight crisis" through which the League was passing to the incorrect activities of certain leaders, but insisted on the LCY's basic political health. He reproached Conference delegates for omitting to mention the dictatorship of the proletariat "which exists in our country and must continue to exist." Tito also extolled the virtues of democratic centralism and stressed that there could not exist several party centers but only the one and unified LCY. He complained that the LCY, as vanguard of the working class, had an insufficient number of workers in its ranks, and declared that the League and not the Army was the "main guardian of accomplishments of the revolution." Tito approved the purge of the Croatian party leadership but warned against any "witch hunt" in that republic (*Ibid*).

While this Second LCY Conference followed the upheavals in Croatia, the Third Conference, held in Belgrade on 6–8 December, convened shortly after major leadership shake-ups in Serbia and several other republics (see below). These new purges and their underlying causes certainly contributed to the radicalized tenor of the main report delivered by Krsta Avramović, to unisone and tough interventions of more than 100 speakers at the Conference, and to the wording of the eight-part final resolution. Entitled, "The LCY Struggle for the Socialist Orientation and Active Participation by the Young Generation in the Development of a Self-Managing Socialist Society," it ended the Conference which had been devoted to problems of youth. Large parts of the resolution described "ideological disorientation" and shortcomings within existing youth organizations. It denounced "a broader penetration of bourgeois, petty-bourgeois, technocrat-bureaucratic and dogmatic concepts into the minds of the young people, a strengthening of the influence of anarcho-liberalism, spurious leftwing behavior and demagogic ultra-radicalism, and a spread of nationalism among certain sections of youth." To combat these and similar negative phenomena (such as "spread of sheer commercialism," "dissemination of trash literature and other forms of anticulture," "reactionary activity by a section of the clergy," "advocating the concept of a multiparty system in various forms"), the resolution called for "a revolutionary revival and consolidation of the leading role of the LCY in society" in order to insure "the leading role of Marxist and socialist-revolutionary thinking in the system of education." In the same spirit, the resolution stressed a need for "thorough reform of the overall system of education and upbringing" to parallel the struggle "in all spheres: politics, economics, social sciences, cultural and artistic life, sports, education, publishing activities, press and radio and television." Leaving to the Tenth LCY Congress (scheduled for 1974) systematic elaboration of all points raised, the resolution proclaimed that "there can be no place in educational institutions for people who oppose or act against the system of socialist self-management." It announced the need to reform two main organizations, the Youth Federation and the Federation of Students, in order to insure "linking-up, rapprochement and ideological-political unity of young people within Yugoslavia." Likewise, the resolution emphasized the necessity for youth organizations to participate in "all aspects of defense preparation" adding more specifically the need for "more comprehensive preparation and massive involvement of girls in all forms of resistance, including armed struggle." Revival of long neglected "voluntary youth work activities" was also advocated by the resolution (*Borba,* 9 December).

In his concluding speech Tito agreed with the general thrust of the Conference and its resolution. He insisted on the need to fuse student, working, and village youth "into a single united socialist youth organization." He paid special attention to the "more than 300,000 people subject to military conscription who are abroad. They are young people; that is three large armies." Since this number included many skilled workers and potential officer cadres, he stressed the necessity to find jobs for those people in Yugoslavia, especially because the all-people's defense required specialists (*Ibid*).

Tito-Executive Bureau Letter of 18 September. In the interval between the Second and Third LCY Conferences, several events occurred indicating that unity had not been achieved by the leadership in January and explaining the radicalism of the December gathering. Rumors about continuing conflicts at the top and in republic parties, even after the purge in Croatia,[1] circulated during the spring and summer or were hinted at in speeches of LCY officials. They obtained confirmation at the Executive Bureau meeting with Tito present, held on 18 September in Belgrade. The meeting produced a "Letter to all LCY Organizations and Members," signed by Tito and Stane Dolanc on behalf of the Executive Bureau. The fact that the Letter was not issued in the name of the LCY Presidium—as articles 61, 65, and 67 of the party statute would require—indicated that a majority of members opposed Tito and Executive Bureau policies and intentions. The Letter itself was read and discussed at first in closed meetings of LCY organizations, and its contents were not publicly revealed until a month later. The Presidium approved the Letter retroactively on 30 October after the purge

---

[1] On 8 May, the central committee of Croatia unanimously expelled from the League four ex-leaders, who had resigned their posts in December 1971: Miko Tripalo, former member of the LCY Presidium and its Executive Bureau as well as the State Presidency; Savka Dabčević-Kučar, former president of the Croatian central committee; Pero Pirker, secretary of the Croatian executive committee; and Marko Koprtla, member of the same committee and president of the central committee's commission for nationwide defense. The funeral of Pirker, who died 1 August at age 45, precipitated a public demonstration during which several people were arrested (*Borba,* 9 August).

of communist leaders in Serbia, Slovenia and Macedonia (see below). Explaining indirectly the unusual way in which the Letter had been issued, Jure Bilić stated in a speech that "the ideological, political and action unity" of the LCY was threatened because of the emergence of "six or eight political and ideological platforms" reflecting the existence of "various factions and groups" within its component parts. Therefore, communists had to be informed that "something significant, not to say extraordinary, is taking place in society or in the party" (*Vjesnik,* Zagreb, 1 October).

The Letter went to the heart of the matter. It assailed persistent weaknesses in the economic system, denounced glaring social differences in the country, criticized the work of information media and the courts, but its essential target were "manifestations of ideological-political and action disunity, including attempts to renew and to consolidate, either in old or new forms, factionalism, splitting activity and struggle among cliques for positions of power." Violently attacking the tendency to transform the LCY "into an unstable coalition of republican and regional organizations," the Letter pleaded for the very opposite: transformation of the LCY "into the kind of organization of revolutionary action that is capable of translating its stands and policy into life more efficiently." The corollary to this appeal for unity and discipline, based on the principle of democratic centralism, was the Letter's request for "removal from LCY ranks of all elements alien to our ideology and policy." Only a purge of "corrupted individuals, people with petty-bourgeois mentality, supporters of bureaucratic arbitrariness, opportunists, career-seekers" could make the LCY "more ideologically united, capable and attractive to class-conscious workers and young people" (*Politika,* Belgrade, 19 October).

Tito vs. the Serbian Leadership. The Letter, which for the rest of the year remained the key party-line indicator, reflected Tito's own views, anger, and frustration. In a lengthy and remarkably candid interview given in early October, Tito concentrated on the theme of LCY weaknesses and the necessity to eliminate them radically. "We must get organized. . . . There is absolutely no place for any kind of liberalism or any kind of compassion here. . . . We do not have to have more than a million members in the LCY. We can have several hundred thousand less." What seems to have particularly irked Tito was the attitude of many party leaders which he summarized as follows: "Let him [Tito] talk, we shall continue in our own way." The most significant part of the interview was his contention that LCY disarray had its origin in the atmosphere and decisions of the Sixth Party Congress (November 1952), long considered the cornerstone of the Tito anti-Stalinist liberalization: "The party lost prestige after the Sixth Congress, because people wanted to eliminate it as the most important element in the process of developing socialism . . . Just before the Sixth Congress, and in particular, right after it, there was a kind of euphoria that wanted to democratize each and every thing to such an extent that the role of the party was subdued on all important questions concerning social life. The party was only left with the task of giving ideological guidance" (*Vjesnik,* 8 October).

A few days after the interview Tito, accompanied by Dolanc and Gligorov, convoked a meeting of the Serbian "Political Aktiv," i.e. some 80 persons representing the highest party and state offices. The meeting, held behind closed doors in the hall of the federal government building in Belgrade lasted four days (9–13 October). After a three-day recess it reconvened for Tito's concluding speech. On that occasion, he settled accounts with the Serbian leadership and particularly with its president, a former foreign minister and ambassador to the United States, Marko Nikezić. It had been an open secret that Nikezić viewed the basic problems of the party and economy in a different light than Tito and Dolanc (see, for example, his interview in Ljubljana's *Delo,* published also in *NIN,* 10 September). The Tito-Nikezić confrontation must have been a difficult one because the Serbian party chief enjoyed strong support.

The usually well informed British foreign correspondent, Paul Lendvai, reported that "only eight out of 80 people attacked Mr. Nikezić" (*Financial Times,* London, 28 November). Likewise, a special commission of the Serbian central committee whose task was to recommend ways for implementing Tito's Letter of 18 September could not be held on 24 October, "because only ten out of 40 members of the commission came for the meeting" (*Borba,* 25 October).

Tito's political influence, however, prevailed over Nikezić, and his concluding speech of 16 October clearly indicated that the days of Nikezić and his supporters were numbered. From his lengthy, harsh, repetitive, and at places emotional speech, one may extract and condense seven, in Tito's eyes unpardonable, political transgressions of which the Serbian leaders were guilty: hiding ideological differences with the LCY leadership; belittling the struggle against anarcho-liberalism and the class enemy; failing to implement constitutional amendments; indulging in political intrigues ("who will outwit whom"); turning the party into a discussion club; fostering factionalism and splitting activities; being afraid of self-criticism (*Politika,* 18 October). After making his speech, Tito left the Serbian central committee to draw the proper political conclusions.

On 21 October, a plenum of that committee accepted the resignations of Marko Nikezić and Latinka Perović, secretary of the central committee. Five days later, Nikezić was replaced by Tihomir Vlaškalić, professor of economics at the Belgrade University, member of the Serbian central committee since 1968, but not a prominent communist leader. The new secretary of the central committee, Nikola Petronić, once a worker, is an even less known party functionary. Resignations of other highly placed persons followed: on 28 October, Bora Pavlović, secretary of the Belgrade city party committee, resigned; he was followed on 1 November by Mirko Tepavac, Yugoslavia's foreign minister; a day later Koča Popović, a leading partisan commander during World War II, former foreign minister and chief of the General Staff and, together with Nikezić, the most prominent Serbian communist leader resigned his post in the collective Presidency of the Republic.

Purges in Other Republic and Regional Parties. In some basic respects, the purge of top Serbian leaders resembled the elimination of most prominent Croatian communists a year before. Despite the different thrust of Tito's accusations against them (the Croats being guilty of lack of vigilance against nationalism and the Serbs of tolerating anarcho-liberalism), in both cases the purges amounted to breaking up of experienced and younger leaderships, with strong party followings, more attuned to local needs and interests, more willing to tolerate pluralistic stirrings of a developing society, and more aware of the necessity to find new and realistic solutions for an ailing economy at the crossroads between the partly dismantled statist structure and the still feeble system of self-government.

The 1972 purge was not, however, limited to Serbia. On 27 October, Slavko Milosavlevski, secretary of the Macedonian party resigned his post. He is considered a close political ally of the most prominent Macedonian communist leader, Krste Crvenkovski. The latter had been under attack by hardliners since the 1971 events in Croatia. On 29 October, Stane Kavčič, Slovenian premier and LCY Presidium member, also resigned. Supporter of greater Slovenian autonomy and proponent of introducing a shareholding system, he has often been at odds with Tito and Edvard Kardelj. A week after his resignation, he was blamed at a Slovenian LC central committee plenum of being "uncritical . . . of the phenomenon of nationalism in Croatia, as well as of the phenomena of technocratism and liberalism elsewhere in Yugoslavia" (Yugoslav News Agency Tanjug, 4 November). Kavčič is also considered as having been the target of Kardelj's attack against some unnamed people in Slovenia, who favored a "one-sided linkup with Western Europe or Bavaria" (*Borba,* 23 September). On 18 December, the president and the secretary of the Vojvodina regional party committee, Mirko Čanadanović and Miloš Radojčin, both reputed to be Nikezić followers, resigned. Purges of lower echelon party officials took place also in Kosovo (Tanjug, 20 October).

In Bosnia and Herzegovina, the intra-party feud took a different character. Here, four prominent leaders were expelled (Osman Karabegović, once republic premier) or censured (Hajro Kapetanović, former cabinet member) or warned (Avdo Humo, a former premier; and Čedo Kapor, former cabinet member and Spanish civil war veteran). Their public criticism of the republic leadership appeared in a resolution of the Bosnian central committee, held on 27 November, as "spreading unacceptable views concerning the situation in the League of Communists of Bosnia-Herzegovina and in Yugoslavia generally" (*Borba,* 2 December).

Domestic Affairs. Uncertainties about Tito's further course of action following the purge in Croatia and since September, 1972, reassumption of a commanding role by the LCY, had a profound impact on the country's domestic life. In a broader sense, problems and difficulties facing a complex Yugoslav society, were discussed by Stane Dolanc in an interview printed by the Ljubljana daily *Delo* (1 January 1973). He stated that "the most diverse conflicts, shortcomings and problems which, since introduction of self-management have had various forms, emerged during 1972." What certainly did not help to overcome them was party recentralization which runs counter to the spirit and letter of two basic texts and institutions: the 1971 constitutional reform and self-management system, both introduced on the basis of decentralization. Moreover, replacement of experienced, better known and more popular leaders, by new ones who are less so but are expected to perform with enhanced authority—while being completely dependent on one man, the LCY President [1]—is another factor of overriding and yet unpredictable significance. And the fact that a constitutional commission, under the perennial chairmanship of Edvard Kardelj, again during 1972 worked to further amend the constitution, points up a Yugoslav domestic situation in flux.

Problem of Social Inequality. The problem, particularly in the second part of the year, most heatedly vented in public utterances and in the press was that dealing with social inequality among individuals and groups. An uproar occurred after estimates had been published that the number of Yugoslavs with wealth in excess of one billion old dinars, or $600,000, is between 156 and 182 (*NIN,* 24 September; see also *New York Times,* 3 October, and *Christian Science Monitor,* 21 October). While the identity of the billionaires was not revealed (investigation into the origins of savings deposits and other forms of wealth being illegal), two things attracted particular attention: first, the discrepancy between average monthly earnings of a worker—1,700 new dinars or $100—and those on the other end (managers of big enterprises, top soccer players, architects, technicians, engineers, some private businessmen and artisans, with commercial representatives at the top), whose income is five to six times larger; second, the "conspicuous consumption" of rich people with luxurious villas in cities and on the sea, two or three cars, hydrofoil boats, etc. (*Vjesnik,* 8 October). Worse yet, as Tito remarked on 4 September, addressing the shipyard workers in Rijeka: "Among the ranks of the League of Communists there are very rich people whose wealth does not amount to only tens of hundreds of millions, but to a billion old dinars. It is impossible to earn so much" (Radio Belgrade, 4 September).

Aware of the serious political implications from such a state of affairs, the Tito-Executive

---

[1] To what extent Tito still rules, despite his 80 years, as the supreme initiator and arbiter, may be seen from the following words of Branko Pribićević, chairman of the party committee at Belgrade University: "Whenever critical situations in society or party arise, nobody with the exception of Tito has the political courage to say the right word" (*NIN,* 22 October).

Bureau Letter of 18 September insisted on the necessity to "energetically suppress and check those currents in real life which lead toward dividing society into rich and poor." The Letter criticized the inadequacy of existing laws on taxing excessive earnings and advocated rapidly passing laws to regulate and tax incomes acquired from the sale of land and real estate. It criticized also the prosecution and courts for failing to punish adequately those guilty of bribery, corruption and unlawful usurpation of property, proclaiming that people who acquired property contrary to the law and socialist morality could not be LCY members.

The problem of social inequality and conflict was amply discussed at a large symposium of sociologists held at the beginning of the year in the Slovenian Adriatic town of Portorož. Two different views were crystallized at the meeting: one, that the conflicts within Yugoslav society are the result of contradictions among state, self-management system, and market economy, and the other that they stem primarily from economic differences (*Vjesnik,* 17 February; *NIN,* 20 February). On a different level, the campaign launched in September against the well-to-do had a negative effect on the business of banks. It worried state officials planning to create more jobs through expansion of small private enterprise and to attract savings of Yugoslavs at home and abroad (*New York Times,* 3 October).

Arrests, Trials and Resignations. Stormy developments in Croatia reverberated throughout the year. Student leaders and prominent intellectuals arrested at the turn of 1971–72 (for details see *YICA, 1971,* p. 104), accused of nationalist separatism and other subversive or political opposition acts, were brought to trial and sentenced to prison terms of one to four years. Thus, Vlado Gotovac, former editor of the banned weekly *Hrvatski Tjednik,* received the longest of these sentences on 27 October. In a still unclear episode, a group of young armed Croatians, some of them coming from as far away as Australia, entered the country illegally from Austria in early July but was liquidated by the army in Western Bosnia. Other violent acts perpetrated by extreme nationalist Croatian groups against Yugoslav government officials, mainly in West Germany, Sweden and Australia, provoked bitter comment in the Yugoslav press and diplomatic protests that foreign authorities were too lenient in dealing with anti-Titoist activities.

The regime struggle against nationalism and separatism, which mainly had been conducted in Croatia, extended into Serbia during 1972. While the Serbian communist leadership was not accused of nationalist proclivities, prominent individuals and institutions in Serbia were targets of such accusations. The prestigious literary publishing house, Srpska Književna Zadruga, was compared to Matica Hrvatska (Croatian literary-cultural organization and main target of regime attacks last year) and accused by the secretary of the Belgrade party committee of harboring political ambitions, as well as being directed by known Serbian nationalists (*NIN,* 22 October). As a consequence its director, a well-known novelist, Dobrica Ćosić, who in May 1968 had been expelled from the Serbian central committee for nationalism, was forced to resign. On 17 July, Mihajlo Djurić, professor of law at Belgrade University was sentenced to two years in jail for speeches and articles undermining "fraternity and unity" of the peoples in Yugoslavia. On similar charges, former president of the Yugoslav Bar Association attorney Slobodan Subotić was sentenced on 26 June to fourteen months in jail. Miodrag Vulin, lecturer at a workers' university in Sarajevo, on 9 August received a three-year prison term.

Three students at Belgrade University were arrested in March as members of an illegal Trotskyist organization and sentenced in July to terms of 18 months to two years (*Borba,* 21 July).

Tensions in State-Church Relations. The Serbian Orthodox Church has also come under strong attack, particularly its official bi-monthly organ *Pravoslavlje.* A report submitted to the intra-national relations commission of the Serbian central committee stated that "spreading of nationalist passions has become a favorite theme by a large part of the Serbian Orthodox Church supreme leadership" (*NIN*, 22 October). Before that, the Holy Council of the Serbian Church had openly complained that legal and constitutional rights of churchmen have been jeopardized in recent times (*Pravoslavlje*, 1 June). Significantly enough, the Federation of Associations of Orthodox Clergy which, since its inception after the war has been favorably inclined toward the new regime and has often been at odds with the Church hierarchy, in a semi-official communiqué published on 1 May strongly attacked policies of the Holy Council and even threatened to sever itself from the official Church leadership. An editorial in the Federation organ *Vesnik* (15 June) accused the Church hierarchy of spreading the spirit of great Serbian chauvinism in its publications.

In Croatia, the views of Archbishop Franjo Kuharić that parents have the right to educate their children freely without interference from authorities were sternly criticized in the press (*Vjesnik*, 1 April). Later in the year attacks were directed against the Church's alleged intention to assume the role of a political opposition. One edition of *Glas Koncila*, the largest Catholic weekly in Yugoslavia with a circulation many times that of most daily papers, was banned (*Economist*, London, 4 November).

In Vojvodina a proposal was made to reexamine, in the spirit of the 18 September Tito-Executive Bureau Letter, the work of all republic and regional commissions for relations with religious communities (Tanjug, 13 November). In Kosovo, too, communist authorities have been attacking "hostile activities" of both Orthodox and Catholic priests (Radio Belgrade, 5 July; *Rilindija*, Priština, 6 July).

Intellectual Dissent and Repression. In recent years, intellectual dissent in Yugoslavia has largely been tolerated by the authorities, although occasionally the most objectionable books, individual issues of magazines and newspapers, records and films have been temporarily or permanently banned. This may be explained in part because dissenters have had connections —and thus have enjoyed tacit support—within the factionalized party republic and regional leaderships. Last year's purge in Croatia had shaken but not destroyed that pattern. However, the 18 September Tito-Executive Committee Letter and ensuing purges indicated that persistent intellectual dissenters, having lost their party protectors, will become victims of what an editorial in the *New York Times* (14 January 1973) called a "mini-cultural revolution almost reminiscent of Peking's experiment."

The first half of the year witnessed often strong criticism about the situation in Yugoslavia from sociologists, philosophers, and political scientists. Articles in three reviews were especially critical and provoked punitive reaction by the authorities. Thus, the second issue of *Filosofija*, organ of the Serbian Philosophical Association—banned by court decision on 8 September—contained several texts extremely critical of the regime (including the indictment of Professor Mihailo Djurić, as well as his defense). The most mordant was an editorial which claimed that "aspects of repression had become more and more numerous and ominous," and then warned the power-holders that "silencing the people and insisting on their own monopoly over the truth inescapably leads to creation of a pogrom atmosphere."

Then, the May–August issue of the internationally known review *Praxis*, published at Zagreb by the Croatian Philosophical Association contained several articles which prompted the authorities to ban it temporarily. Besides protesting the sentence of Professor Djurić, member of *Praxis'* advisory board, the same issue contained an article by Belgrade Professor Svetozar Stojanović which criticized Tito's "personality cult" and called de-Stalinization in Yugoslavia a "Stalinist de-Stalinization." (It should be noted that *Praxis* criticizes the regime in the name of Marxist humanism, or from leftist positions. That did not prevent the new Croatian party secretary, Josip Vrhovec, to call it "totally anti-socialist and anti-Marxist" in *Vjesnik,* 25 July. See in this connection, "Marxists against Marxists," *Neue Zürcher Zeitung,* 29 July.) Likewise, in the May–June issue of the revue *Gledišta,* published by Belgrade University, a young assistant professor (later expelled from the party) castigated the arbitrary behavior of party leaders who at will every second year had shaken the constitutional order to its roots.

During the last three months of the year, a much tighter control over universities and the press—two favorite targets of Tito's attacks—was imposed. A series of prominent professors at Belgrade University either have been expelled from the party or recieved warnings. A resolution of the party university conference threatened that "those individuals who are acting against self-government, national equality and the ideology of the LCY cannot be educators" *(NIN,* 15 October; see also *New York Times,* 2 January 1973). On 26 October, the editor-in-chief of the most popular Belgrade weekly, *NIN,* Frane Barbieri resigned, followed on 7 November by Aleksandar Nenadović, chief editor of the most prominent Belgrade daily *Politika* and on 12 December by the editor-in-chief of the Belgrade evening paper, *Politika Ekspres,* Miodrag Marović, former Moscow correspondent of *Politika,* who in the past had criticized some anti-Yugoslav Soviet practices.

Economy. Stabilization of the economy was assigned top priority in the 1972 economic plan, adopted by the Federal Assembly in January, as well as by the Second LCY Conference. That this goal could not be achieved during the year became clear after a session of the LCY Presidium on 30 October at Tito's island residence of Brioni. Stabilization of the economy was again proclaimed as the most pressing problem to be solved. But if persistent shortcomings endured, there were also positive economic results.

Achievements. Industrial production was 7.7 percent higher than in 1971, over 2 percent more than officially expected (Tanjug, 15 January 1973). Agricultural output included a bumper harvest of corn (about 8,400,000 tons), the best in Yugoslavia's history. As for wheat, some 4,800,000 tons were produced, or 400,000 less than in 1971 when the wheat harvest reached its highest level *(Borba,* 24 September). The balance of payments was considerably improved, with exports amounting to 38,020 million dinars ($2,236 million)—an increase of 18 percent compared with 1971, and imports totalling 54,800 million dinars ($3,223 million) —or 5 percent less than in 1971. This means that Yugoslavia's foreign trade deficit amounted to about 16.5 billion dinars (just below $1 billion), compared with 25.5 billion dinars in 1971 (just over $1.5 billion) (Tanjug, 26 December 1972 and 8 January 1973). Invisible earnings also increased considerably due to remittances by Yugoslav workers temporarily employed abroad. While they amounted to $652 million in 1971 *(Politika,* 10 June), in 1972 they reached $805 million *(Večernji List,* Zagreb, 19 January 1973). Gains from foreign tourism and remittances from permanent emigrants also increased. Two sets of figures may be quoted concerning employment: the number of the newly employed in the social sector was 4 percent higher than in 1971; on the other hand, in November there were still 327,000 unemployed in Yugoslavia *(Politika,* 19 January 1973). The Yugoslav economy also obtained credits and loans, either from the Soviet Union (see below) or banks in foreign countries, such as the Export-Import Bank of Japan, the East German Bank for Foreign Trade and several U.S. banks *(Quarterly Economic Review,* Yugoslavia, no. 3). Finally, there has been rapid introduction of electronic computer systems in scientific and economic fields.

Shortcomings. Despite government efforts to control prices, the inflation rate did not abate and remains one of the highest among all European countries. Living costs went up by 16.6 percent over 1971, with food prices increasing 19 percent, and those for clothing and shoes by 15 percent (Tanjug, 8 January 1973). Other serious economic shortcomings stressed in the 18 September Tito-Executive Bureau Letter, included a lack of liquidity, increasing operational losses, and financially uncovered investments of enterprises. At the second conference of the Trade Union Confederation held in March, its chairman emphasized that the most important socio-economic problem was illiquidity, "because of which a large number of workers do not receive their wages regularly" (*Borba,* 23 March). At the end of the year 360 economic enterprises unable to make good their losses amounting to 1,260,000,000 dinars were facing court action as well as possible bankruptcy (Tanjug, 27 December). Reduction by one fifth of their wages prompted the workers at an electronic plant in Niš (Serbia) to strike and then demonstrate before the city hall (*Borba,* 5 November). However, *Le Monde* on 7 November wrote that thousands of workers were demonstrating in the streets of that city and that the system of workers' self-management in the plant was a "pure formality." Addressing the 30 October LCY Presidium meeting, Kiro Gligorov stressed the urgency of finding adequate solutions, otherwise "illiquidity and losses in the economy will become an insoluble problem." (*Vjesnik,* 1 November). In a similar vein, speaking about the economic situation, Stane Dolanc, in the above quoted New Year's Day 1973 interview, said that 1973 "will be a difficult one" requiring "firm discipline and self-denial in many things." He was in fact echoing government plans, approved by the trade unions, to reduce in January 1973 salaries of nearly one million workers, and to freeze wages of 1.2 million (Tanjug, 18 December).

Yugoslav Workers Abroad. In September, about one million Yugoslav citizens were working abroad, some 800,000 in West European states and another 200,000 in countries overseas (*Borba,* 1 September). While their remittances represent an asset to the Yugoslav economy, the export of manpower continues also to be a serious problem with many negative aspects—ideological, political, economic. In this last category, there were 150,000 skilled workers among those who have sought employment abroad, about 10,000 of whom are experts (*NIN,* 13 August). Pavle Savić, president of the Serbian Academy of Sciences and Arts, bitterly complained about such a drain and explained why the scientists were leaving the country: "Our creative and social climate is chasing those people into the world. A working atmosphere does not exist here, there is no competition, no scientific criteria, no polemics . . ." (*Borba,* 9 August). Before the end of the year, a draft law was submitted to the Federal Assembly trying to remedy the most unfavorable aspects of the worker exodus.

Adoption of 1971–75 Economic Plan. After 18 months of dramatic parliamentary debates and republic confrontations, the Federal Assembly approved on 28 June the 1971–75 plan for economic and social development. Its aims are to assure a more balanced growth of the economy, to bring into play unused mineral resources, natural energy, and the manpower Yugoslavia possesses, to adjust production to the market mechanism and the system of workers' self-management, to bring per capita income levels of the poorer republics closer to the richer ones, and to secure a higher standard of living (*Quarterly Economic Review,* no. 3, pp. 6–7).

Enhanced Powers of LCY Executive Bureau. Preoccupied with the gravity of the economic situation, the 30 October meeting of the LCY Presidium decided to establish a special working body of organs and organizations at the federal, republic and region levels whose task would be to "find solutions to outstanding problems in our economic system and development, problems whose solution will insure economic stabilization on a more long-term basis" (*Vjesnik,* 1 November). The LCY Executive Bureau was empowered by the Presidium to form and supervise such a body.

Foreign Affairs. *The Soviet Union.* Since the September 1971 trip of Leonid Brezhnev to Belgrade (see *YICA, 1971,* p. 111), Soviet-Yugoslav relations have significantly improved on both the state and party levels. This was conspicuously confirmed by Tito's official visit to the U.S.S.R. during 5–10 June, his tenth stay in the Soviet Union since the May 1955 Khrushchev-Tito reconciliation. Tito was greeted in Moscow with extraordinary ceremony, awarded the highest decoration—the Order of Lenin, offered a special gift by the CPSU Central Committee—a Soviet marshal's saber, and profusely hailed by Soviet leaders. Thus, Nikolai Podgorny, chairman of the Supreme Soviet, called Tito at a Kremlin banquet "a prominent leader of the international communist and working class movement, an outstanding leader of the working people of socialist Yugoslavia, friendly to the Soviet Union." Brezhnev stressed the "qualitative change for the better in relations between our countries [including] contacts between parties" (*TASS*, 5 June). Tito himself spoke of "sentiments of exceptional honor and pride" for being awarded the Lenin Order and declared that "for our party, the LCY, Lenin's thoughts and deeds were always the source from which we drew our strength and in which we found encouragement for new endeavors and actions" (Tanjug, 5 June).

On 10 June, at the end of Tito's stay in the U.S.S.R., which included a visit to Riga, a joint communiqué was issued. It noted the continuing viability of the Belgrade Declaration (2 June 1955) as well as the Moscow Statement (20 June 1956), and stressed the "great importance" of the 25 September 1971 Soviet-Yugoslav statement adopted in Belgrade. The communiqué emphasized CPSU-LCY relations, the two parties being "guided by the teaching of Marx, Engels and Lenin and creatively applying it in accordance with distinctive features of their countries, [and continuing] to act in the spirit of internationalist traditions." The extension of further party, state and government contacts was projected, to include even "developing direct friendly and business ties between the republics, towns and enterprises" of the two countries. The review of international problems—the future all-European conference on security and cooperation, disarmament, Vietnam, the Arab-Israeli conflict, Berlin and relations between the two German states—showed a basic identity of views. The Soviet side proclaimed also its support for "the anti-imperialist trend in the policy of the non-aligned countries" (*Pravda*, 11 June).[1]

While Soviet leaders and the press ostensibly refrained, during and immediately after Tito's visit, from making any criticism of Belgrade affairs, Yugoslav commentators did not fail to mention the persistence of differences between the two countries (Radio Belgrade and Zagreb, 10 June). Moreover, there were hints that at the Brioni LCY Presidium meeting of 12 July, which heard and approved Tito's report on his Moscow visit, some leaders—notably former premier Mitja Ribičič—were critical of the new Soviet-Yugoslav closeness. In a TV interview, later reproduced by the daily *Delo* (Ljubljana, 15 July), Ribičič spoke of "constructive criticism" expressed at the Brioni meeting and of the necessity to have "a deeper strategic study and discussion of the foreign political field." He also observed that all progress achieved by Yugoslavia had been attained "without allowing anyone to interfere in our internal affairs and without giving in to pressure from big powers or permitting foreign bases to be set up."

Tito's visit to Moscow was followed by extensive Soviet-Yugoslav economic negotiations which brought tangible results in the fall. On 2 November a credit agreement between the two countries was signed in Belgrade. The agreement pertains to the building and expansion of 38 plants in various branches of Yugoslav industry, the transportation system and agriculture. The value of the envisaged deliveries will amount to $540 million, with 2 percent interest. Accord has also been reached for the Soviet Union to deliver to Yugoslavia by the end of

---

[1] It should be noted, however, that if in the communiqué both sides agreed on the desirability of preparing and holding a European security conference, nothing more precise was said about its agenda and concrete objectives. Likewise, Soviet approval of one aspect of nonalignment was certainly not identical with the Yugoslav understanding of its entire meaning.

1984 equipment for additional eleven plants, totalling $450 million (*Borba,* 3 November; *Komunist,* Belgrade, 16 November).

It should also be noted that events within the LCY, particularly after issuance of the 18 September Tito-Executive Bureau Letter as well as the increased number of Soviet-Yugoslav contacts, received favorable treatment in the Soviet press. *Pravda* (1 November) analyzed at length the Letter and other internal party developments, especially those in Serbia, and approved reassertion of the LCY's leading role in the life of the country. In a typical sentence, this article summarized the new situation: " 'The communist, the Marxist-Leninist must be an active builder of the new life—such is the demand of the times.' These words are now being uttered at meetings in cities and villages, in all corners of the country." Along similar lines, though referring to the development of Soviet-Yugoslav economic relations, a correspondent of the Soviet news agency Novosti, ended his dispatch this way: "Moscow-Belgrade, Belgrade-Moscow. Every day aircrafts fly, trains travel, and heavy trucks trundle in both directions along these busy routes. An intensive exchange of delegations, specialists and tourist groups between the two socialist countries is continuing. The flow of freight and various commodities is increasing in both directions. Friendship and cooperation draw the peoples closer and reduce distances" (*Sovetskaia Rossiia,* Moscow, 29 November).

Eastern Europe. The Soviet-Yugoslav rapprochement, hailed by all East European governments (with the exception of Albania), had other bloc-wide repercussions. For the first time since the beginning of Yugoslavia's associate membership in the Council for Mutual Economic Assistance (CMEA),[1] premier Džemal Bijedić headed a Yugoslav delegation to the 26th CMEA session, held in Moscow on 10–12 July (at previous meetings Yugoslavia was represented by deputy premiers). Bijedić was invited personally by Soviet premier Aleksei Kosygin. The delegation from Belgrade signed an agreement "by which Yugoslav enterprises participate in implementation of part of the 'complex program' for increasing cooperation and socialist integration among CMEA countries as is in their mutual interest" (Tanjug, 15 July). Insisting that such participation in integrative projects by no way means a change in Yugoslavia's position vis-à-vis CMEA, Yugoslav spokesmen showed an interest in expanding trade relations with East European countries. During the first ten months of 1972, some 34.8 percent of exports went to Eastern Europe (compared with 37.5 percent for all of 1971); and 24.5 percent of imports came from Eastern Europe (23.3 percent in 1971). Further trade increases are planned over the next three years (Radio Zagreb, 13 December; *Ekonomska Politika,* Belgrade, 11 December).

A few days after his U.S.S.R. trip, Tito paid an official visit to Poland (19–23 June). His last visit to Warsaw had been in 1964. In the meantime, particularly after Polish participation in the invasion of Czechoslovakia during 1968 and the workers' riots along the Baltic coast in December 1970, followed by the resignation of Władysław Gomułka, Yugoslav-Polish relations were cool. The 1972 meeting between Tito and Edward Gierek, first secretary of the Polish United Workers' Party confirmed the rapid improvement in relations between the two governments and parties. A joint Yugoslav-Polish communiqué stated that " differences in the ways of building socialism in the two countries are not an obstacle to successful development of mutual relations." Both sides expressed "identity or similarity" of views on major international issues, and appraised with satisfaction the constant growth of their trade relations "which should reach a level of almost $200 million in 1972," a 20 percent increase over 1971 (Tanjug, 23 June).

[1] The cooperation started in 1964. Since then Yugoslavia has had a permanent representative at CMEA headquarters in Moscow, who takes part in the work of its executive committee. Members of Yugoslavia's permanent delegation participate in 12 of the organization's 24 specialized commissions (*NIN,* 2 July).

There were also signs of an improvement in the Yugoslav-Bulgarian relations, a consequence of the Moscow-Belgrade rapprochement. Both governments agreed to simplify passport formalities and ease movement of persons living along borders. Scientists and educators exchanged visits and, more significantly, a high level Bulgarian party delegation visited the Yugoslav Republic of Macedonia on 31 August—the first such visit since 1948. On several occasions, the Skopje daily *Nova Makedonija* (25 January; 15 March; 5 December) noted with satisfaction the fairness with which the Bulgarian press had been reporting Yugoslav affairs.

Yugoslav-Romanian relations continued close and friendly. Party and government delegations were exchanged often; Romanian premier Ion Maurer paid an official visit to Yugoslavia on 12–19 September; Tito and Nicolae Ceauşescu, Romanian head of the government and party, met on 16–17 May to inaugurate the huge Iron Gates hydroelectric and navigation complex on the Danube.

Strengthening of Yugoslav-Albanian economic and cultural ties continued throughout 1972, although suspicions of Tirana's irredentism concerning Kosovo persisted in Belgrade. The Yugoslav press reacted sharply to Albanian denunciation of Tito's visit to Moscow.

West and Central Europe. Two royal visits to Yugoslavia, in September (20–23) by Queen Juliana of the Netherlands and Queen Elizabeth of Britain in October (17–21) were marked by official cordiality. A British-Yugoslav communiqué hailed the "good and friendly" relations existing between the two countries and expressed hope for "consolidation and expansion of these relations in all spheres of mutual interest and benefit." It also stressed that "the two countries' views are quite similar, particularly regarding future cooperation in Europe" (Tanjug, 21 October). Official relations with France and with the Federal Republic of Germany remained friendly, despite protests against the activities of extreme Croatian nationalist groups in West Germany. Yugoslav officials and press warmly greeted the electoral victory of Chancellor Willy Brandt in November.

Relations with Italy, on the other hand, took a turn for the worse. In two major speeches during December, Tito strongly attacked Italian irredentist organizations which "continually whet their appetites for our territory" (i.e., Istria, Zadar, and Dalmatia). He also expressed regret over the slackness of the Italian government in disassociating itself from "these revanchist appetites" (Tanjug, 12 and 29 December). Yugoslav-Austrian relations deteriorated even more. While the official communiqué of 14 April, issued during the visit of Yugoslav premier Bijedić to Austria, spoke of "good neighborly cooperation," noting with satisfaction the quality of human contacts in border areas (i.e., Slovene and Croatian ethnic groups in Austria), the minority issue later became a point of contention. Infiltration of Croatian terrorists into Yugoslavia from Austria in July (see above), contributed to mounting tension, which the official visit of Austrian president Franz Jonas and his talks with Tito in Belgrade during mid-September failed to dissolve. A stern protest note was handed on 8 November to the Austrian ambassador, in which the Yugoslav government expressed its "deep anxiety over continuation and intensity of the anti-Slovene and anti-Yugoslav campaign" in Austria, which allegedly represented "a serious threat to the further development of Yugoslav-Austrian relations." The note charged the Austrian Republic with not fulfilling its international obligation to protect the rights of Slovene and Croatian minorities, assumed under the 1955 Austrian state treaty (Tanjug, 8 November). In his 12 December speech, Tito complained that the Austrian government had not answered that note and repeated his earlier accusation that fascists were destroying bilingual signs in Carinthia. He also took issue with the Austrian chancellor's reply that there were no fascists in that country. Many social organizations in Slovenia and Croatia protested Austrian treatment of minorities.

Extensive and often critical coverage as well as interpretations given by the Western press and information media to domestic events in Yugoslavia, met with utmost displeasure on the part of the highest LCY leaders. Tito, in a speech made on 29 December, denounced "the very strong campaign of slander and attacks in the West." Stane Dolanc stated that, for many Western analysts, criticism of Yugoslavia had become " a matter of class struggle [for which reason they] have undertaken an all-out offensive against Yugoslavia" (*Delo,* 1 January 1973).

European Economic Community. Expansion of Yugoslav participation in CMEA continued parallel with a search for closer links to the European Economic Community. (EEC countries absorb about 40 percent of Yugoslavia's exports, and furnish about 50 percent of its imports.) In July, the Yugoslav government requested preliminary talks concerning a new nonpreferential trade agreement with the EEC Executive Commission, the present three-year arrangement expiring in April 1973. From the Yugoslav view, a future agreement should include the new members of EEC—Britain, Denmark, and Ireland. It should also improve Yugoslav-EEC industrial and technical cooperation and facilitate Western credits as well as terms for West European investments (Tanjug, 10 October; *Quarterly Economic Review,* no. 3). To pursue further negotiations with high Yugoslav officials, EEC Executive Commission president Sicco Mansholt visited Belgrade in mid-December.

The United States. Secretary of State William Rogers visited Yugoslavia on 7–9 July. He held a long talk with Tito on bilateral and international topics. The Secretary told a group of Yugoslav newsmen that relations between the two countries were "excellent" (Tanjug, 9 July). President Nixon's decision in March to extend operations of the Overseas Private Investment Corporation (OPIC) to Yugoslavia opened perspectives for a more rapid inflow of American capital into the Yugoslav economy. On 8 July, Washington granted Belgrade $40 million in commodity credits for purchase of farm surpluses (wheat, edible oils, and fodder). In mid-June the U.S.S. "Springfield," flagship of the Sixth Fleet, visited Dubrovnik.

However, paralleling the purge of "rightist" LCY leaders, an intensified campaign against Western ideological and cultural influences saw a renewal of anti-American propaganda. In his 8 October interview for *Vjesnik* Tito termed impermissible any exchange of LCY functionaries with the United States. He assailed the Yugoslav trade network for marketing imported and even Yugoslav-made U.S. military badges and insignia which many youths wore on their sleeves. In his 29 December speech, Tito attacked renewed American bombing of North Vietnam as a "barbarous, imperialist game of chance." A dispatch to the *New York Times* (2 January 1973) reported that "scholars and officials suddenly find it a stigma to have studied in the United States."

Nonalignment. Speculation at home and abroad that a series of events and measures (Tito's visit to Moscow, closer Yugoslav cooperation with CMEA, Soviet credits, tighter party discipline and control, ideological exclusiveness with anti-Western overtones) indicated steps toward rejoining the Soviet bloc, elicited categorical denials by top LCY leaders, including Tito. In his Ljubljana speech of 12 December, he answered those who were saying this by declaring: "Yugoslavia is going nowhere. Yugoslavia is staying where it is. We want to have good relations with all countries. We want to cooperate economically with both the Soviet Union and the Western countries . . . Yugoslavia is not a pendulum, going one way and then the other . . . We do not waver; we continue along the same road." On the same issue, Dolanc stated in mid-November that "Yugoslavia will not submit to any influence and is firmly standing by the policy of nonalignment" (Tanjug, 14 November). And indeed, a large number of Yugoslav foreign political initiatives and contacts during 1972 corresponded to the Titoist concept of nonalignment.

In an interview granted the Zagreb weekly *Front* (24 April), Tito made several specific points on the current status of nonalignment and about the role he wanted Yugoslavia to play in this respect. To him nonaligned countries represent "the conscience of mankind," because they incarnate the aspirations of people in every country. Unfortunately, in his view, with the exception of a successful decolonization campaign in the United Nations, the activity of nonaligned countries practically died out after the Third Conference of Nonaligned Countries at Lusaka, Zambia, in September 1970. The alleged reason was that imperialist forces had exerted strong pressure against many nonaligned countries which turned inward. Thus, the nonaligned showed little activity during the Middle East crisis, events on the Indian subcontinent, escalation of the war in Indochina, aggression in Cambodia, etc. Now, when the major powers were reaching agreements among themselves, it was time for the nonaligned to become more active and to insure that no agreement would be made at the expense of small and medium-size countries. Tito stressed that an increasing number of states, especially in South America, wanted to be counted among the nonaligned. For Tito the only criterion is lack of membership in any existing bloc. Moreover, disintegrating pacts like CENTO or SEATO should not hinder a country such as Pakistan from belonging to the nonaligned. As for Yugoslavia, it is "providing the initiative for greater activity of nonaligned countries." [1]

With these general principles in mind, a Yugoslav delegation headed by Mirko Tepavac attended the conference of foreign ministers of nonaligned countries at Georgetown, Guyana, during 8–11 August. According to a special Tanjug correspondent, this conference (in the opinion of many) was characterized by a certain radicalization of the movement and by a rising tide of "leftist orientations and strivings" among the nonaligned. Tepavac, in an interview, spoke of the movement's "regeneration." He supported admission of the Provisional Revolutionary Government in South Vietnam as a member with full rights and the decision that Cambodia should be represented by Prince Sihanouk's exile regime (decisions which, incidentally, provoked a walkout by Indonesia, Laos, and Malaysia). For Tepavac, this represented "the liberating aspect of solutions in crisis areas" (Tanjug, 14 August). He minimized the extent and importance of differences at the conference.

Among the large number of high level contacts with individual non-aligned countries, those with Egypt, Ethiopia and India received the greatest coverage by the Yugoslav press. On 4–5 February president of Egypt, Anwar as-Sadat, paid an unofficial visit and had long talks with Tito. Radio Belgrade hinted that this exchange of views concerned not only the Middle East situation but also the position of nonaligned countries at the time of superpowers negotiations. At the end of May, Egypt's foreign affairs minister visited Yugoslavia, while on 3–8 October premier Bijedić travelled to Egypt. A joint statement following the visit emphasized the deep concern of the Yugoslav government over the Middle East crises, caused by "Israel's stubbornness and expansionist designs." It also reconfirmed the Yugoslav stand on the Arab-Israel conflict, namely withdrawal of Israeli forces from all occupied territories and respect for the national rights of the Palestinian people in accordance with U.N. resolutions.

During the visit to Yugoslavia by Emperor Haile Selassie of Ethiopia (25–30 June), "great similarity of views" was achieved in discussing current international problems and the role of nonaligned policy. In early September, the Ethiopian premier also came to Yugoslavia. On 5–9 July president of India, Varahagiri Venkata Giri, paid a state visit and had talks with Tito. The statement following his visit stressed deep friendship between the two countries, but

---

1 In his Ljubljana speech of 11 December, Tito made the following observation: "It is being said that because of alleged internal strife, Yugoslavia lost the opportunity of working among the nonaligned countries. The fact that Yugoslavia as a country with great prestige is one of the main factors among the nonaligned countries, obviously doesn't suit someone's book. This is why they conduct propaganda against Yugoslavia and tell tales that it has lost its prestige."

expressed anxiety of both governments because new policies of the great powers, with all their positive elements, had not yet contributed to solving problems "in the centers of world crisis" (Tanjug, 9 July). Both sides then expressed a need for further strengthening the activity of nonaligned countries. On 14–19 July, Prince Norodom Sihanouk made an official visit to Yugoslavia. He received a warm reception. His views on the problems of Indochina and their solution were fully endorsed by the Yugoslav government. At the end of October, the foreign minister of Bangladesh also visited Belgrade.

International Party Contacts. The LCY has maintained a great variety of contacts on both leadership and cadre levels with other communist parties in Eastern Europe. Among the non-ruling parties the most important visits were exchanged with Italian and French communist parties. Stane Dolanc led an LCY delegation to the Thirteenth Congress of the Italian Communist Party which met in Milan, 13–17 March. In an interview, he hailed new principles of cooperation for the international communist movement, as experienced at the Milan congress: equality, independence of each party, mutual cooperation, and frequent contacts (Radio Belgrade, 18 March). On 11 December a delegation from the Italian Communist Party met in Belgrade with LCY representatives to discuss the situation in the Mediterranean. Deputy secretary general Georges Marchais headed a top-level group from the French Communist Party that visited Yugoslavia for 10 days in October. The communiqué stressed agreement by both parties on a series of questions concerning their joint struggle and that they would step up cooperation in the future (Tanjug, 13 October). An LCY delegation attended the Twentieth Congress of the French Communist Party in December. Representatives from the Communist Party of Japan held top-level talks with the LCY in mid-October, and a group from the Communist Party of Iraq visited the country during 18–22 December. LCY Presidium member Veljko Vlahović attended an international communist conference on Georgi Dimitrov held at Sofia in June, with emphasis on the latter's contribution to the concept of the popular front and on contemporary applications.

Publications. The chief organs of the LCY are *Komunist,* a weekly magazine, and *Socijalizam,* a theoretical monthly. The important daily newspapers are *Borba* (Belgrade) and *Vjesnik* (Zagreb), organs of the SAWPY bodies of Serbia and Croatia respectively, and *Politika* (Belgrade). The *Vjesnik* publishing house also puts out a weekly, *Vjesnik u srijedu.* The Yugoslav communist youth organization publishes a weekly, *Mladost.* Tanjug is the official Yugoslav news agency.

Hoover Institution   Milorad M. Drachkovitch
Stanford University

WESTERN EUROPE

Austria

The Communist Party of Austria (Kommunistische Partei Österreich; KPÖ) was founded on 3 November 1918. The KPÖ enjoys legal status, but plays an insignificant role in Austrian political affairs; it has been without representation in the parliament since 1959. Estimated membership is 15,000. The population of Austria is 7,400,000 (estimated 1970).

The schism within the party that erupted following the Soviet-led invasion of Czechoslovakia in 1968 continues to produce a complicated picture of the communist movement in Austria. Those members expelled from the KPO in 1969 and 1970—the "progressive faction"—remain under the leadership of Franz Marek and publish their own party organ, *Wiener Tagebuch* (see YICA, 1972, p. 117).

The Communist Youth of Austria (Kommunistische Jugend Österreichs; KJÖ), headed by Otto Podolsky, is closely associated with the KPÖ and continues to provide a major source of new party members. The KJÖ was founded in May 1970 to replace the party's Free Austrian Youth organization (Freie Österreichische Jugend; FÖJ), which supports the Marek faction. Otto Podolsky is chairman of the KJÖ. The KPÖ also controls the Trade Union Unity organization (Gewerkschaftliche Einheit; GE), under the leadership of Anton Hofer. The GE works within the influential Austrian Trade Union League in an effort to more effectively influence trade union members.

Members of the KPÖ and the KJÖ are active in several auxiliary organizations, such as the Anti-Fascist Solidarity Club for Progress and Peace, the Children's Youth Guard, the Democratic Women's Association, the Initiative Committee Against Income Tax Robbery and the Austrian-Soviet Society. (See *YICA, 1972,* pp. 117–18.)

Leadership and Organization. During 1972 no changes were announced in party leadership and no congresses were held. Franz Muhri remained party chairman, serving also in the 10-member Politburo and 5-member Secretariat. Erwin Scharf is secretary of the Central Committee, which has 64 members.

Party Internal Affairs. During the year the KPÖ conducted a series of "ideological indoctrination courses" for its members, believing it "necessary to be concerned more critically . . . with theory" in view of the schism within the party that resulted from the invasion of Czechoslovakia. This period since 1968, according to the party's theoretical journal, has been "marked by much confusion, insecurity, and pseudo-Marxism" (*Weg und Ziel,* January 1972).

The themes discussed in party seminars were "The Communist Manifesto Today," "State-Monopolist Capitalism in Austria," "Enterprise Work," "Current Problems of the Communist Movement," "Ideological Conflict Today," and "The Political Development in Austria." The KPÖ recommended a series of works available in the party's bookstores throughout Austria to be used as background for the seminars and discussions, such as Hans Kalt's *Hired Labor and*

Capital and Walter Wachs' *For a Class-Oriented Social Policy.* The party also recommended "daily reading" of its newspaper, *Volksstimme,* to be supplemented by study of the articles contained in the theoretical journal. (Ibid.; *Volksstimme,* 30 January.)

Erwin Scharf acknowledged in March that the party was having "an extraordinarily hard time" because its "modest publication organs" were burdened with explaining "the new functions" of the Austrian Socialist Party (Sozialistische Partei Österreichs; SPÖ) "within the framework of state-monopolist capitalism" as well as with opposing "the anti-communist untruthfulness of the mass media." The party had, however, "liberated itself from the forces which, under the name of communists, spread anti-Soviet and anti-communist ideas." (Ibid., 17 March, 5 April.)

The KPÖ believed that the latest national elections, October 1971, in which the number of votes it received increased in comparison with the previous election (see *YICA, 1972,* pp. 117–21), had "ended the internal party crisis" and confirmed "the correctness of the policy resolved by the 21st Party Congress." A resolution of the Central Committee plenum in January concluded that "the struggle [against] the supporters of the former rightist opportunist group in the party" had substantially "changed from an internal party conflict to a struggle by our party against forces which are attacking us from the outside." But party members were called on to strengthen "the role of the basic party organizations," to found new organizations, to recruit new members and readers of the party periodicals, and to appear as often as possible in public. (*Volksstimme,* 25 January.)

Although the KPÖ may have considered the influence of the "rightist opportunists," led by former Politburo member Franz Marek and Ernst Fischer (who died in August at the age of 74), to have "largely" declined, Marek continued to publish the *Wiener Tagebuch* monthly. In an article by Erich Koerner in the March issue of that journal, the KPÖ was accused of being "an agency of Moscow (Neo-) Stalinism, whose functionaries can only point to their unconditional and fully uncritical loyalty to the 'leadership center' as their highest qualification." Koerner charged that the KPO had deliberately undermined the resolutions of the "still valid 19th Party Congress," and had reduced the party "not only to a *quantité négligeable,* but also, and primarily, to a *qualité négligeable,* both as to the level of its political-ideological argumentation in its publications, and as to its purely propagandist election slogans."

Koerner suggested that "at least for the next few years" those "progressive comrades" remaining within the KPÖ would be unable to change the party's course, citing these reasons: (1) the decline in the number of "cadres who would normally have the decisive role (leadership and promotion of reform efforts) in this process," (2) the "special mechanisms of decision-making and voting" within the party would render ineffective the efforts of those seeking reforms; (3) the number of "comrades 'whose communist conviction is based on unconditional agreement with everything coming out of the Soviet Union' " would increase. Koerner therefore proposed a "union of the independent leftist forces in Austria on a common platform for the purpose of information and cooperation, from which there could then be formed, in the medium or long run, an autonomous socialist organization." It would be necessary, he believed, "to tear down certain barriers in the consciousness, among other things to slaughter that sacred cow in the thinking of many leftists, namely the schematic conception that the present CP is in any case, and in its totality, an integral component of the Left."

The KJÖ held two conferences during 1972 that were of significance. In January the first Viennese provincial conference of the KJÖ was held, attended by 60 "workers, students, and apprentices." "Active participation" by all KJÖ members for "income tax reform" was characterized as the primary task for the immediate future. For the long term, emphasis was to be placed on "agitation" on all appropriate issues. (*Volksstimme,* 23, 26 January.)

In June the KPÖ, KJÖ, and KPÖ-controlled GE sponsored a "youth meeting" in Vienna under the slogan, "Against Capital and Reaction—Worker Youth for Socialism." Forty percent of the 300 participants were under the age of 20. The delegates "unanimously" determined that there was "only one alternative [for Austria's] working youth: socialism." Extensive discussions considered problems facing "youth at work, in the army, in training and in leisure time." (Ibid., 21 May, 4 June.)

KJÖ chairman Podolsky declared in his opening address that the meeting "should yield suggestions and proposals as to how to raise and improve the working youth's class consciousness" and "how to develop social struggle in our country of ostensible social peace," in contrast to the SPÖ's policy of "social partnership." He stressed that "a final solution to all questions . . . in the interests of worker youth" would be possible "only with the downfall of capitalism and the establishment of a socialist society." The conference endorsed neutrality for Austria, called for "freedom" for U.S. communist Angela Davis, and condemned U.S. involvement in Southeast Asia. The delegates demanded "introduction of apprentice compensation on a percentage basis" in Austria, urged "gradual abolition" of the Austrian army and "complete elimination of educational privilege," and called for equality for women and more "moderate-income housing." Franz Muhri told the conference that the "basic problems confronting the younger generation cannot be solved by mere reforms in the framework of capitalism." He emphasized that "socialism [is] a historical necessity in Austria," and that "therefore the young people belong in the communist party." (Ibid., 4, 6 June.)

Domestic Attitudes and Activities. The KPÖ criticized the "social partnership policy in favor of profits" of the SPÖ under Chancellor Bruno Kreisky and endorsed "actions of unified struggle by workers and employees" (*Weg und Ziel,* January 1972). It condemned the SPÖ for following "in essence the same anti-social policy" as the previous government of the Austrian People's Party (ÖVP), and for being "among the most sharply defined anti-communist and anti-Soviet social-democratic parties in Europe" (*Volksstimme,* 5, 21 April).

Only "a strong communist party," Chairman Muhri believed, offered "the true alternative [to] the capitalist class policy of the ÖVP and the "opportunistic policy" of the SPÖ (ibid., 21 April). The KPÖ believed, however, that "new possibilities [to] decisively restrict the influence of the social partnership ideology" did exist. An article dealing with the party's first theoretical conference suggested that the "confrontation of reality" under SPÖ leadership "with the expectations" of the working class would "become the impetus for release of movements by the workers themselves." (Ibid., 30 January.) Muhri welcomed "a greater tendency" within the SPO "to discuss ideological questions of principle," but opposed the SPÖ's "attempt to use abstract ideological discussions to distract attention from actual problems." It was "not just a coincidence" that the SPÖ opposed "joint action" with the KPÖ, for the SPÖ was aware "that such cooperation might endanger the continuation of its present policies and could force changes." (Ibid., 12 March.)

Politburo member Franz Hager outlined the bases for the party's position on domestic issues, stressing "the necessity and real possibilities of the struggle against the state-monopolist reform strategy and for anti-monopolist reforms within the framework of our orientation toward a socialist Austria," and calling for "political and ideological actions by workers and employees." Throughout 1972 the KPÖ conducted a campaign against higher taxes, specifically a value-added tax, and "galloping inflation," and for job security. (Ibid., 2, 26, 27 April, 16 June) and endorsed "educational reform," "a social and democratic solution to the housing problem," "elimination" of the Austrian army, legalized abortion, equality for women, and "the abolition of all privilege [of] a small upper class (ibid., 4 June; *Weg und Ziel,* January, April.)

In June, Muhri declared that it was the KPÖ's responsibility "to drive big capital back, and finally take away its power, and to eliminate the exploitation of man by man." He believed that the "profound social upheaval" necessary for "the establishment of a socialist society" could be attained "only in revolutionary ways, not just by ballots, votes, and parliamentary combinations, but in broad and resolute mass and class struggle, not by a minority but only by the voluntary, conscious support of the majority of the working class and all working people." He stressed that "the containment of social democratic reformism in the Austrian worker movement is a prerequisite for the liberation of the working class," but that the KPÖ "rejects terrorism, anarchistic sectarianism and all similar concepts that consider the class struggle a matter for the 'revolutionary elite.'" (*Volksstimme,* 4 June.) A theoretical article declared "bourgeois parliaments" to be "historically outdated," but also noted that it would be "an extraordinary political folly" to reject participation in the Austrian parliament, in view of the KPÖ's success in the last parliamentary election (*Weg und Ziel,* January.)

Members of the KPÖ were active in over 200 offices and posts of the Austrian police, according to *Volksstimme.* In the personnel elections, held in December 1971, the KPÖ was able to put one member on the Technical Committee of the "Viennese Security Guard" and increased its representation in police departmental committees from 3 to 14 (13 on committees for "criminal policy" and one on the administrative committee). The KPÖ representatives, who are also members of the GE, attributed their election to "continued and consistent political and trade-union work" and to their "correct position on the question of working hours in the security guard." (*Weg und Ziel,* May.)

The KPÖ was especially critical of the government's cooperation with the European Economic Community, which threatened a "sell-out of key Austrian industries through foreign capital." Cooperation with the EEC, the KPÖ believed, increased "the dangers [for] the economic and political independence of neutral Austria." In addition, this "policy for the benefit of domestic and foreign big capital" was financed by "ever increasing burdens on the workers" through low salaries and higher taxes. (*Volksstimme,* 12 March.) The KPÖ Politburo passed a special resolution in September condemning the effects of association with the EEC on the Austrian economy (ibid., 15 September) and Muhri called for a referendum on the government's agreements with the EEC (ibid., 29 September).

International Views and Positions. The KPÖ endorsed a policy of "active neutrality" for Austria, which meant in particular, "recognition of the German Democratic Republic" and support for a "conference on European security and cooperation" in 1972 (*Volksstimme,* 5, 22 April, 23 November; TASS, 29 September.)

The EEC was criticized as "the economic basis of the Western military bloc," from which would eventually emerge "an economic, political and military power bloc" that would violate Austria's neutrality and be detrimental to its economy (*Volksstimme,* 23 February). The frequent statements condemning Austria's association with the EEC culminated in the aforementioned resolution, which asserted that Austrian association with the EEC aimed at "an intensified imperialist integration in the European region rather than at an all-European détente" (ibid., 15 September.)

The KPÖ urged Austria's recognition of the People's Republic of China, the Democratic Republic of Vietnam, and the Democratic People's Republic of Korea (*Weg und Ziel,* January; TASS, 29 September). It welcomed U.S. President Nixon's visit to Peking in February as a contribution toward peaceful co-existence, but warned of "collusion" between China and the United States directed against the Soviet Union. The party cautioned that any other interpretation "replaces the immovable fronts of class membership" with "power combinations" that would not "bring humanity greater security, but greater dangers." (*Volksstimme,* 18 February.) It welcomed the communiqué issued by the two governments following the visit, but criticized China's refusal to normalize relations with the Soviet Union, which indicated that the Chinese government had selected a path leading "still further away from the community of socialist countries and the communist world movement" (ibid., 29 February; *Weg und Ziel,* April).

The KPÖ Politburo issued a special appeal to citizens in May calling for "neutral Austria to protest most emphatically against the U.S. war policy" in Indochina (*Volksstimme,* 10 May). The West German parliament's ratification of the treaties with the Soviet Union and Poland was praised as a contribution toward "a lasting peaceful order in Europe," as was the four-power agreement on Berlin (ibid., 19 May.)

Soviet author Alexander Solzhenitsyn was criticized in an editorial (ibid., 7 April) for placing more value on "the privileges which the church has lost . . . than the struggle of hundreds of millions of people for equality and long urgent social changes." The SALT agreement was endorsed as a contribution toward détente and in the "primary interest" of the Soviet Union; for the United States it was deemed "admission of the fact" that President Nixon was "governing a country with very limited possibilities" (ibid., 28 May). The King of Jordan's plan for settlement of the difficulties in the Middle East was criticized as "a legalization and perpetuation of the illegal division of 1949" (ibid., 16 March).

The KPÖ welcomed President Nixon's visit to Moscow in May as "the end of an era in U.S. policy" since the United States had recognized "the reality of the power of the socialist camp and the peaceful co-existence of differing social systems" (ibid., 30 May). But it carefully pointed out that "peaceful coexistence does not imply a contradiction to solidarity with the national wars of liberation," and declared that the Soviet Union would continue to aid Vietnam (ibid., 31 May). The agreements concluded in Moscow did not mean that "imperialism" had "changed its essence," but that the United States was forced to acknowledge "the principle of peaceful co-existence accompanied by non-intervention in the internal affairs of third nations" (ibid., 4 June). On his journey to Moscow, President Nixon met with Chancellor Bruno Kreisky in Salzburg. The KPÖ said that this meeting recalled "the worst times of the American occupation in our country" (ibid., 28 May).

The KPÖ praised the Czechoslovak government under Gustav Husák and condemned the Austrian government for pursuing a policy of "cold war" with Czechoslovakia in violation of Austrian neutrality (ibid., 29 August). Franz Marek, however, as well as other writers for the *Wiener Tagebuch,* remained critical of Soviet policy toward Czechoslovakia and of KPÖ support for that policy of "normalization"). Marek considered the KPÖ to be "the closest" of all Western communist parties to the Communist Party of Czechoslovakia. It therefore stood "discredited because it has lost all independence vis-à-vis the parties in neighboring countries" and "does not dare to adopt any policy that differs in any way" from that of the Soviet government. (*Action,* Paris, June-July.) Another writer in the *Wiener Tagebuch* (September) declared that " 'normalization' and the Brezhnev Doctrine of limited sovereignty for the socialist states" had brought "a decisive defeat for the international workers' and revolutionary movement [and] for socialism" : "The myth of a unified, monolithic world movement and a 'world socialist system'. . . is dissolving in the light of the new world situation. . . . namely, an increasing differentiation and division of the power groups and systems, a transition from bi-polarity to multi-polarity . . . a process of disintegration in the communist and revolutionary world movements, which can be held back by no 'normalization.' " (See also *Wiener Tagebuch,* April.)

With reference to the achievement of socialism in capitalist countries the articles appearing in the *Wiener Tagebuch* were especially pessimistic. Marek wrote in the March issue that "a far-reaching ideological crisis in the capitalist world" had coincided "with an intellectual crisis in the revolutionary worker movement, which makes the creation of a socialist alternative extremely difficult in the countries which are still capitalist."

International Activities and Party Contacts. The KPÖ Central Committee on 8 March passed a resolution stating that "the most important condition for strengthening the contribution which the communist and workers parties make to the solution of the problems facing the peoples consists of raising the unity of the communist movement itself to a higher level, corresponding to the current circumstances" (*Weg und Ziel,* April). Concern with the unity of the communist movement was evident in numerous contacts with foreign parties.

Central Committee secretary Erwin Scharf led a delegation to the congress of the Italian Communist Party in March, where he emphasized the "solidarity" between the two parties, which were "working passionately for the unity of the world communist movement" (*Volksstimme,* 17 March). The same theme of "unity of action of the working class" appeared in the address Politburo member Franz Hager delivered to the congress of the Finnish Communist Party (ibid., 5 April).

At the invitation of the KPÖ a delegation of the Polish United Workers' Party (PUWP) visited Austria on 10–17 April. In a final communiqué the parties expressed their resolve to further develop bilateral contacts and declared their opposition to "all anti-Soviet tendencies leading to the weakening of the common anti-imperialist front" (PAP, Polish Press agency, 17 April). In June KPÖ Politburo member Friedl Fuernberg traveled to Moscow to receive the Order of the October Revolution in recognition of his contribution toward "the implementation of socialist ideals" for the working class and "the great respect of the Soviet people" for the KPÖ (TASS, 28 June). In April a KPO delegation attended the 25th-anniversary celebration of the Iraqi Ba'th Party (*Volksstimme,* 22 April). A delegation from the Hungarian Socialist Workers' Party visited Austria on 5-10 June at the invitation of the KPÖ. (ibid., 11 June). In May a delegation of the Soviet Komsomol visited Austria at the invitation of the KJÖ. In a joint communiqué the organizations stated that their cooperation would be "intensified over the next few years." Both urged support for the 10th World Youth Festival, condemned U.S. involvement in Southeast Asia, and endorsed an all-European security conference. (ibid., 26 May.)

Publications. The official KPÖ organ is the newspaper *Volksstimme,* published daily in Vienna with circulation estimated at 40,000 on weekdays and 70,000 on Sunday. The theoretical organ *Weg und Ziel* appears monthly. Erwin Scharf is in charge of the journal's "editorial collective."

Standpunkt, the KPÖ organ directed toward police officers, is published irregularly in editions of several pages. The KPÖ-controlled GE has published for 19 years *Der Demokratische Polizeibeamte,* also directed to police officials and constabulary officers; it appears monthly in editions of 6 to 8 pages.

The *Weiner Tagebuch* was formerly the official journal of the "communist intellectuals" until its staff under Franz Marek was evicted from the KPÖ party building in Vienna in late 1969. It appears as "an independent Marxist monthly publication directed at the Austrian left, including the Socialist Party." The "Association of the Friends of the Wiener Tagebuch" publishes a weekly press bulletin.

*   *   *

The Marxist-Leninist Party of Austria (Marxistische-Leninistische Partei Österreichs; M-LPÖ) was established in Vienna in May 1966. It is pro-Chinese in orientation and enjoys legal status. Franz Strobl is first secretary. Its members number about 500. (See *YICA, 1971,* pp. 125–26.)

The party organ, *Rote Fahne,* was critical throughout 1972 of both the KPÖ and the Austrian government. The M-LPÖ believed that the KPÖ did not understand "the essence of Leninist policy of peaceful co-existence . . . which the Chinese Communist Party always recognizes, follows and defends, and that capitulationist and counter-revolutionary falsification of this policy which the Khrushchev-Brezhnev clique pursued and continues to pursue." The M-LPÖ therefore condemned Soviet criticism of the Chinese government on the occasion of President Nixon's visit to Peking. (*Rote Fahne,* no. 3.) The M-LPO was also sympathetic to the Albanian Party of Labor and held a series of discussions during the year concerning problems of "socialist reconstruction" in Albania and the Albanian party's "struggle against revisionism" (ibid., no. 2).

*   *   *

A "Communist Students Union" was founded in October at the University of Vienna to "fight for the social and political rights of the students [and] against the existing policy in higher education when it becomes a prerogative of certain classes." It intends to study the construction of socialist societies in general and "popularize" the "achievements" of the socialist countries. The first issue of its newspaper, *Rote Perspektive,* appeared in November. (TASS, 5 November.)

Hoover Institution   Dennis L. Bark
Stanford University

Belgium

The Communist movement in Belgium is represented by three parties. The oldest and largest is the Communist Party of Belgium (Parti Communiste de Belgique; PCB), founded in 1921. Dissidents from the PCB formed a party of the same name (hereafter referred to as the PCB-II) in December 1963, and dissidents from this party established the Marxist-Leninist Communist Party of Belgium (Parti Communiste Marxiste-Léniniste de Belgique; PCMLB) in November 1967. The latter was called the Communist Party (Marxist-Leninist) of Belgium until the current name was adopted 28 June 1970. In addition to these three parties, there is a Trotskyist movement represented by the Socialist Young Guards, a group aligned with the United Secretariat of the Fourth International. All four organizations enjoy legal status.

Although none of the above parties publishes figures, Western sources estimate that the PCB has between 11,000 and 12,500 members. The PCB-II and PCMLB are believed to have at most 50 and 150 members, respectively. The JGS has a growing membership, which in 1972 was estimated at more than 500. The population of Belgium is about 10 million (estimated 1970).

Two of the communist parties, the PCB and the PCB-II, participated in parliamentary elections of 31 March 1968. No PCB-II candidates were elected. The PCB polled 3.3 percent of the vote for the Chamber of Representatives, losing one seat but retaining five. In the Senate, the PCB obtained 3.5 percent of the vote, retaining its two seats. On 24 September 1971 the Belgian premier dissolved the parliament and called for elections on 7 November, advancing the normal date from May 1972. His government was returned to power. The PCB obtained 163,785 votes (3.2 percent) and held its five seats in the Chamber of Representatives. It lost one of its two seats in the Senate. Again no PCB-II candidates were elected. There are no communist ministers or secretaries of state in the new cabinet, which was sworn into office 21 January 1972.

The PCB was the only communist party to participate in the local elections of 11 October 1970, in which it "suffered reversals," with one exception.

The PCB. Organization and Leadership. Since 1966 the PCB has been divided into two branches, Walloon and Flemish; each directs implementation of policy in its own region. Marc Drumaux, 50, head of the PCB since 1968, died on 15 November after a long illness. The leaderships meet every year to make joint decisions, with each having veto power. The ratio of Walloon to Flemish members in the party is, however, five to one, and all PCB parliamentary representatives are Walloons. Party policy regarding national and international affairs is decided at PCB congresses, normally held annually, with the exception of 1969 and 1970.

The PCB leadership during 1972 was elected by the Twentieth Congress, held in March

1971 at Charleroi. At the first session of the 60-member Central Committee, it reelected party chairman Marc Drumaux and vice-presidents Jean Terfve (president of the Walloon branch) and Jef Turf (president of the Flemish branch). Jef Turf is political director of the party's Flemish-language weekly, *De Rode Vaan*. Robert Dussar is political director of its French-language weekly, *Le Drapeau Rouge*.

The PCB directs a youth organization, the Communist Youth of Belgium (Jeunesse Communiste de Belgique; JCB), and a student group called the National Union of Communist Students (Union Nationale des Etudiants Communistes). The party does not have its own labor union, but exerts some influence in the country's largest trade union, the General Workers' Federation of Belgium (Fédération Générale du Travail de Belgique; FGTB).

Domestic Views and Policies. In 1972 the PCB continued to push for unity with other left-wing forces, though it focused less attention on the Belgian Socialist Party (PSB) and more on a general program of alliance, especially on the local level. A program of united action was formulated and published in March in a booklet, "What Do the Communists Want? —Thirty Questions and Answers for a Loyal Debate." The "program," which is "but a beginning," repeatedly calls for full, open debate on the questions and answers presented, in the hopes of furthering dialogue. Chairman Drumaux foresaw an avant-garde role for the PCB by remaining unified against rightist and leftist opportunism, and maintaining and developing ties with "the most combative and most far-sighted elements in the democratic workers movement."

The thirty questions are grouped in three divisions: the new type of opposition, proposals for an action program, and democracy and socialism. The new type of opposition is defined as that "capable of bringing all progressive opposition groups together into one single movement whose first positive effect would be to clarify the situation"—no single party or leftist opposition group can by itself constitute the desired opposition. The alliance would be comprised of any individuals or organizations with "a clear will to combat traditionalist policy with a view toward substituting a truly progressive policy for it." Drumaux envisioned an alliance of communists, socialists, Christian Democrats, and even those currently supporting the government. This new united front would not be under the banner of one single party, and participating organizations would be permitted to retain their identity and autonomy. The role of the PCB is to prove its intentions by working diligently toward the alliance, and by its very nature it will have "a stimulating capacity"; the PCB gave guarantees that its "indispensable function" would not mean a "leading role," but added: "we are convinced that, without the presence of the party, the political struggle risks becoming less effective."

Despite its leadership, the PCB emphasized that it will enter all discussions and negotiations without preconditions. The alliance would confront all political and social struggles, especially elections at all levels. Once power was achieved, a domestic program would be implemented, to include the nationalization of all key sectors of the economy, with the notable exception of small and medium-sized businesses. The immediate objective of "workers' control" is co-determination rather than self-management, which is considered utopian. Eventually, the alliance will "govern the country in spite of the capitalists and finally without them." In all matters and on all occasions, it will seek "the most progressive solution, the anti-capitalist solution."

In discussing the autonomous role of the leftist parties in the alliance, the booklet criticizes the hesitancy of the Socialists, who are necessary for large-scale action against capitalism: "[While] we wait for the Socialists' rightist leadership to abandon its present attitude, we definitely can no longer stand by without making a move in the direction of the other progres-

sive forces, particularly the Social Christians." In the interim the PCB will work on its immediate objectives, which include workers' control, regional autonomy, and European security.

The first concrete step to make the principles of the booklet a reality was the formation of
the Democratic Progressive Union (UDP) in Mons. This coalition includes the Social Christians, leftist groups, and the PCB, but not the Socialists. The Mons coalition offered an example
to workers in Charleroi area, in Tournai and Liége, where contacts have been initiated and a
structure, patterned after the UDP, was started. A similar alliance was formed in Marcinelle,
but with the participation of the Christians, communists, the FGTB, the Confederation of
Christian Trade Unions, and some Socialists: "Commitment to a broad alliance should not entail any break with the mass organization to which they belong. . . . The UDP is very important to the extent that it becomes a political means of uniting people of diverse opinion but of
common purpose in opposing concerted policies carried out at the national level and also to the
extent that it offers alternatives to these policies. This brings us back to the notion of unity, so
familiar to the Communists."

Belgium's long-standing language and regional disputes were somewhat mitigated in 1972
due to constitutional changes implemented in 1971 which divided the country into Flanders,
Wallonia, and Brussels, and gave each a degree of autonomy in economic, cultural, and political affairs, to be determined by enabling legislation. The PCB continued its attacks on the
governmental reorganization plan, charging that these principles had not been effectuated, and
that the regional interests were being subjugated.

International Views and Policies. The PCB continued to support policies which stressed
the importance of the struggle against anti-communism and anti-Soviet attempts to isolate
communists. It considered that the most ardent proponents of anti-sovietism in Belgium were
the Zionists (communiqué, 20 September). The PCB supported Soviet proposals for disarmament, the convocation of a conference of nuclear powers, and the mutual reduction of forces
in Europe. At the same time, it maintained the PCB's autonomy, stating in the aforementioned booklet: "Enriched by all the experience of the international workers' movement, the
Belgian workers' movement will follow its own path to socialism, based on the unique historical conditions of our country."

The booklet strongly criticizes Belgian participation in NATO and advocates: "get Belgium out of NATO and NATO out of Belgium." The PCB was no less critical of participation in the Eruopean Economic Community, "an anti-democratic bureaucratization of
European technocracy" (communiqué, 19 October). The party repeatedly called for the convocation of a European security conference and the participation by the two Germanys in the
United Nations and other international groups (see *Cahiers Marxistes,* January-March 1972,
pp. 71–76).

International Party Contacts. Meetings and talks were held in Moscow 16–18 February
1972 between CPSU Central Committee and Politburo members, and the PCB delegation led
by Drumaux. The PCB was represented by Drumaux at the Thirteenth Congress of the Italian
Communist Party, at Milan in March. A PCB delegation visited Bulgaria in June.

Publications. The PCB publishes a weekly, *Le Drapeau Rouge.* A four-page bulletin,
PCB Informations, appears three times weekly. The party also prints a weekly in Flemish, *De
Rode Vaan.* Its quarterly, *Les Cahiers Marxistes,* seeks to "contribute to the clarification of
the unresolved problems of socialism and the international communist movement."

*   *   *

The PCB-II. Internal difficulties of the small PCB-II were reflected in the frequency of its publication *La Voix du Peuple*. During 1968, it appeared weekly with 20 pages; it became a bimonthly in 1970, and the last issue of that year had only four pages; in 1971 it came out irregularly, with an issue number but no date. In 1972, issues were published only in January and February, containing eight pages, with the page size halved. The PCB-II does not publicize its party internal organization or leadership. Indications are that Jacques Grippa serves as secretary of the Central Committee. The PCB-II continued its criticism of the Chinese Communist Party leadership as "neo-revisionist Maoists who seized control in the August 1966 coup."

The PCMLB. The PCMLB is recognized by the Chinese Communist Party. It controls the Belgium-China Association (Association Belgique-Chine) and what appears to be a small youth group, the Marxist-Leninist Communist Youth of Belgium (Jeunesse Communiste Marxiste-Léniniste de Belgique). Support for the party apparently originates in the Borinage mining region. The PCMLB adheres to strict Maoist interpretations, and its weekly organ, *Clarté,* frequently prints articles praising China.

* * *

The Trotskyist movement in Belgium is primarily represented by the Socialist Young Guards (Jeunes Gardes Socialistes; JGS—in Flemish, Socialistische Jonge Wacht; SJW), a student group which in 1969 asked to be recognized by the United Secretariat of the Fourth International as a "sympathizing organization." The JGS-sponsored Revolutionary League of Workers (Ligue Revolutionnaire des Travailleurs; LRT), is the official Belgian section of the United Secretariat. *La Gauche,* a weekly Brussels publication of the United Secretariat, is considered the official organ of this group.

American Enterprise Institute Kay McKeough
for Public Policy Research

Cyprus

The Communist Party of Cyprus (Kommounistikon Komma Kiprou) was founded in August 1926 while the island was a British Crown Colony. Outlawed in 1933, it was revived in April 1941 as the Reconstruction Party of the Working People of Cyprus (Anorthotikon Komma Ergazomenou Laou Tis Kiprou; AKEL). AKEL was outlawed again in 1955, when political organizations were proscribed by the British, but has been legal since the proclamation of the Cypriot Republic in 1959. Potentially the strongest and by far the best-organized political party in Cyprus, AKEL currently has between 12,000 and 14,000 members. The total population of Cyprus is 639,000 (estimated 1971), which makes the proportion of party members to national populace second only to its Italian counterpart among non-ruling communist parties. Virtually all AKEL support comes from among the Greek Cypriot majority (about 80 percent) on the island.

Despite the party's overall strength and the generally tolerant attitude of Archbishop Makarios, the president of the republic, AKEL has never held any cabinet posts and, for tactical reasons, has chosen to play down its strength at the government level in recent years. In the July 1970 parliamentary elections the party contested only nine of the 35 seats reserved for the Greek—Cypriot majority. In winning all nine seats, it received an aggregate 39.7 percent of the actual popular vote, or 30.2 percent on the basis of the total Greek Cypriot registered electorate. Some 29 percent of the eligible Greek community voters did not turn out, while it may be assumed that AKEL mobilized most all its members and sympathizers on election day. The apathy of the nationalist Greek Cypriots was a significant factor in the communist success at the polls in 1970. While the leading nationalist parties underestimated AKEL's organized following, they also suffered from fragmented voting since President Makarios did not express a preference among the parties.

AKEL's reluctance to make a genuine showing of its ability to win parliamentary seats takes into consideration two realities: first is the fact that the 1959 Zurich and London agreements provide for the guarantor powers to intervene against a communist threat; second is the probability that a legal push for power by AKEL would unite the right-wing parties. Domestically, AKEL has continual frictions with the four non-communist parties. Highlighted in 1968 by the Warsaw Pact intervention in Czechoslovakia, the ideological difference between the right and left were further emphasized during 1971 by the Soviet Union's increasing interest in Cypriot affairs, and again in 1972 by the renewed threats from underground pro-Athens militants led by General George Grivas. In recent years the party has suffered embarrassment from improved Soviet-Turkish relations and has taken wavering positions on such questions as conciliation between Greek and Turkish Cypriots. Moreover, on 23 August 1972 the People's Republic of China was recognized; it established an embassy in Cyprus, which may offer support for the small "Maoist" faction of AKEL.

Leadership and organization. The leading figures in AKEL are the general secretary, Ezekias Papaïoannou, in that office since 1949, and his deputy, Andreas Fantis. Both were re-elected in 1970 at the party's Twelfth Congress. The Politburo of the Central Committee includes Pavlos Georgiou, M. Poumbouris, Andreas Ziartides, Yiannis Sofoikli, and Yiannis Katsourides. Secretariat members include Georgiou, Katsourides, and Dinos Konstandinou. A notable feature of the party collective leadership is its stability and the comparatively advanced age of each individual.

The total figure for all elements within the AKEL apparatus, including various fronts and allowing for overlapping memberships, is estimated at some 60,000. AKEL controls the island's largest trade union organization, the Pan-Cypriot Workers' Confederation (Pankiprios Ergatiki Omospondia; PEO), which has some 37,000 members—or 49.3 percent of all those holding membership in labor unions—and is an affiliate of the communist-front World Federation of Trade Unions. Many businessmen prefer to deal with PEO because it is well run and usually not excessive in bargaining demands. Andreas Ziartides, a labor leader since 1943, is the PEO general secretary.

The party also sponsors the United Democratic Youth Organization (Eniaia Dimokratiki Organosis Neolaias; EDON), which is headed by Panikos Paionidis. EDON claims to have 10,000 members and is believed also to operate a branch in England. Thru a long-established sports and social program, EDON extends its influence to more than thrice its young membership. The EDON organization of secondary school students—known as PEOM—has an estimated 2,000 members, who are also members of EDON. EDON holds a seat on the Executive Committee of the communist-front World Federation of Democratic Youth.

Other AKEL-dominated fronts include the Pan-Cypriot Confederation of Women's Organizations (Pankiprios Omospondia Gynekon Organosen; POGO); the Pan-Cypriot Peace Council (Pankiprios Epitropi Erenis; PEE), which is a member of the communist-front World Peace Council; the Cypriot-Soviet Association; and the Cypriot-German Friendship Society. An adjunct to AKEL in the United Kingdom, the "Union of Cypriots in England," has an estimated 1,250 members.

While there are no professed communists within the Turkish Cypriot community, some young people, especially those enrolled in Turkish universities, are Marxist influenced. AKEL has made continual overtures for membership to the Turks in Cyprus and also has tried to infiltrate the one Turkish Cypriot labor union. As yet, these gestures have reaped little obvious success. On the other hand, of the estimated 20,000 Turkish Cypriots who reside in England, a few are open members of the Communist Party of Great Britain and many others are undoubtedly crypto-communists. Some of the leftist tension occurring in mainland Turkey is thought to be abetted by Turkish Cypriot communists living in London.

Domestic Attitudes and Activities. AKEL has consistently exploited anti-colonialist sentiment in its protests against the restrictions placed on Cyprus by the Zurich and London agreements and against the continuing presence of the two British bases in the island. On the other hand, because as a mass party it seeks to attract the Turkish minority as well as the Greeks, AKEL has demonstrated in its recent history little more than halfhearted support of the purely Greek objective of enosis—the union of Cyprus with Greece. Knowing that under the present government in Athens enosis would probably result in the outlawing of AKEL, the party has preferred to use the unqualified phrase of "self-determination" in its slogans. Prior to the 1967 coup in Greece, AKEL's strength as a national party was for some time precariously balanced because it could not openly espouse enosis. Thereafter, AKEL began to stress its "patriotic" orientation and took credit for rising above partisan consideration to back Archbishop Makarios against pro-enosis extremists. An outbreak of hostilities on the island, between the extremists and pro-Makarios forces, seemed imminent in 1969 and the situation loomed as a possibility again in early 1972. The communists were also happy to support Makarios's advocacy of a "feasible" solution to the island's nationalities problem. In contrast to this stand was the "desirable" solution, envisaging a workable accommodation between Greek and Turkish Cypriots with at least a temporary abandonment of the goal of "instant enosis." Firmly opposed to the 1967–68 talks between Athens and Ankara, which unsuccessfully sought to impose a settlement on Makarios, AKEL later endorsed the first round of inter-Cypriot discussions which began in June 1968 and ended in the fall of 1971. AKEL current line on the Cyprus negotiations—now expanded to include representatives of Greece, Turkey, and the United Nations as well as the two communities—was reaffirmed by General Secretary Papaïoannou in mid-1972:

> A settlement based on [the] complete independence, territorial integrity and unity of the Cypriot state is the only correct and realistic settlement that can be achieved by peaceful means. This settlement is sought not only by the government of President Makarios and our party, but also by the great majority of the Cypriot people, both Greek and Turkish.

He added that "such a settlement can be achieved only through peaceful talks between Cypriot Greek and Cypriot Turks, provided the pressure and interference of foreign states are terminated and the Cypriot people are enabled to settle their problems themselves and determine their future." (CTK, Czechoslovak press agency, 17 May.)

AKEL frequently addressed itself to alleged external designs to provoke conflict between Cypriots—between left and right, and between Turk and Greek. A familiar theme was played by Papaïoannou when he declared in a Czechoslovak newspaper interview that the causes of the crisis in Cyprus "stem from foreign interference and the attempts of imperialists to incorporate Cyprus into NATO and turn her into a military base serving their aggressive plans in the Middle East." He then went on to summarize his view of the West's grand design for the island: "The chief aim of the imperialists is to sever Cyprus from the camp of non-aligned states and turn her into an unsinkable aircraft carrier of NATO." To achieve this aim the "imperialists" were "making use of all means, including conspiracy, corruption of people, pogroms on communists and attempts on the life of President Makarios." (Ibid.)

This view was consistent with AKEL's earlier denouncing of Britain's decision to transfer its forces from Malta to Cyprus. The Central Committee charged that not only should the transfer be prevented but also that "CENTO's presence in Cyprus be canceled, that the British military bases be abolished, that the island be demilitarized, and that all foreign troops be withdrawn" (*Kharavyi,* 11 January).

Events in Cyprus in early 1972 probably reenforced for the communists their long-held charge that foreign elements were plotting to impose an "undemocratic solution" on the government of President Makarios. In late January a large consignment of arms from Czechoslovakia, including mortars and bazookas, secretly arrived in the island for use by the Greek Cypriot police. When the disclosure was finally made, the government of Greece demanded that the arms be turned over to the National Guard. Makarios's refusal brought to a head a dispute that had been seething between the two governments since the previous summer. AKEL was quick to defend Makarios: "No patriot, no objective person can dispute the right of the state, the lawful government—not the groups in the hideouts—to strengthen the security forces, to consolidate the principle of popular sovereignty, to protect the free institutions, to consolidate the feeling of security and of course to produce or import arms" (ibid., 4 February). The reference to the "groups in the hideouts" was for the followers of the fanatical anti-communist General George Grivas, who had not yet emerged publicly after landing on the island the previous September. AKEL itself was accused of forming armed groups during the crisis with the help of mainland Greek communists, but a spokesman vehemently denied this, saying that "only the state was entitled to possess arms" (reported in *Cyprus Mail,* 5 March). On 11 February the Greek government sent Makarios an ultimatum to hand over the Czechoslovak arms to the U.N. forces, to disarm his police and their supporters, and to set up a government of "national union," which was to include General Grivas. The public nature of the note precluded any diplomatic negotiations and precipitated the most severe crisis between Athens and Nicosia. On 13 February an editorial in *Kharavyi* attacked Greece for its blunt measures:

> The action of the military government in handling such a note to the president of the republic raises the most important question as to whether Cyprus is recognized by all, without exception, as a sovereign state and an equal member of the United Nations which must enjoy full respect. This note gives the impression that Cyprus is a sort of tributary or is under the sovereignty of others who have the right to determine the nature and the composition of its government.

The next day, the fourth regular plenary session of AKEL's Central Committee and Central Control Committee met to discuss "the critical phase of the Cyprus problem and the internal situation." In a speech, Papaïoannou declared: "All the forces of AKEL are in the service of the state, the legal government of the country, and the people's choice as president of the republic, Archbishop Makarios." The unanimously adopted resolutions stressed that the "note of the Athens military government to President Makarios is an unprecedented act of interference in Cyprus's internal affairs, a gross infringement of the sovereignty of the Cypriot people, undermining the republican government's position at the coming round of talks between the two island communities." The meeting stated further that "the only way to save Cyprus is to strengthen the unity and cohesion of all patriotic forces of the Cypriot people on the basis of the policy approved at the 1968 presidential election, the policy of resolving the Cyprus problem within the framework of an independent, democratic, peaceful and united Cypriot state." (Ibid., 16 February.) On 3 March, a "militant mass mobilization of the people" was organized by AKEL to demonstrate the "unity and determination of the Cypriot people to raise an impregnable wall around their elected President and not to allow the imposition of imperialist solutions on Cyprus" (*WMR,* July).

In this particular crisis President Makarios found himself fighting an enemy which appeared in several forms. In addition to the stern "recommendations" from the government of Greece, he was defied by the Greek army officers in Cyprus who influenced his National Guard; his resignation was demanded by the three bishops in his own Holy Synod; he received votes of no confidence from his internal political rivals, and he faced outright insurrection from General Grivas and the diehard supporters of union with Greece.

The only daily newspaper that consistently expressed whole-hearted endorsement of Makarios throughout this crisis was AKEL's journal *Kharavyi.* This tactical show of loyalty was probably welcomed by him. The archbishop has made it clear that his power base as president is dependent mainly on the support of the nationalists. AKEL enjoyed some of its best relations with the government during 1972 and this may explain the rather mild—though far from naïve—comment Makarios made during an interview with a correspondent from the Athens newspaper *Eleftheros Kosmos:*

> The view is expressed by some that Communism in Cyprus has grown in recent years. I do not share this view. I must also say that Communism in Cyprus is peculiar. All members of the left-wing AKEL party are called communists. However, they are not communists in the true sense of the word, since their vast majority are deeply religious and know nothing of the materialistic theories of Communism. (Reprinted in *Cyprus Bulletin,* 7 May.)

The Soviet Union was far from indifferent to the 1972 crisis in Cyprus. A Soviet correspondent in Nicosia charged at the beginning of the year that extremists "incited by NATO circles" were "demanding unification of Cyprus with Greece or a so-called double enosis"—between Greece and Turkey (Moscow radio, domestic service, 23 January). In February there were authoritative reports that two Soviet warships were anchored in international waters 17 miles off Cape Andreas. It was not known whether the ships were there because of the trouble brewing on the island or if they were just there coincidentally. The presence of Soviet ships was also observed at the same anchorage during some of the rotations of the Turkish contingent in the past and no international incidents resulted. (*Elevtheria,* Nicosia, 23 February.) In March, the Soviet Union was more explicit of its regard for Cyprus when it expressed to Greece a "determined interest" in support of the archbishop's government and warned against any schemes to depose him. (This was the third such warning to be given within three weeks. The other two came after the government of Greece sent its note to Makarios.) The increasing Soviet concern for perserving the status quo in the island most likely emanates from a fear that the removal of Makarios would push Cyprus deeper into the NATO orbit and simultaneously place the members of AKEL in serious jeopardy at the hands of right-wing zealots.

By May, the crisis precipitated by the Czechoslovak arms delivery was over and Makarios had emerged as the winner in his test of resolve with the Greek government. He did this by granting just enough concessions to all his adversaries. He first gave the United Nations custody of the arms; then he made certain changes in his cabinet to satisfy Greece. Also he personally met with General Grivas and later gave amnesty to citizens who had advocated enosis. The easing of tensions paved the way for the resumption of the inter-communal talks, augmented by advisers from Greece, Turkey, and the United Nations. While Makarios undercut, by ecclesiastical parliamentary maneuvers, the opposition he had received from the bishops in his Holy Synod, the year came to an end with his rejecting the demands that he run for reelection in February 1973. The AKEL general secretary direly predicted that while Makarios had won the first round, "the creators of the crisis had not given up their plans," and were "regrouping for a fresh round" (*WMR,* July).

AKEL was indoubtedly relieved when a new series of inter-Cypriot talks was announced to begin in July. The party earlier had specifically expressed reservations, however, over the inclusion of Greek and Turkish advisers in the forthcoming talks (*Kharavyi,* 21 December 1971). But when Makarios accepted the mainland advisers, AKEL apparently backed off of its previous position and accepted the fait accompli. Papaïoannou described his current view of the expanded talks in these general terms: "A peaceful democratic solution to the Cyprus problem can be achieved only at the conference table and provided the sides concerned display good will" (TASS, 28 May). This shift by AKEL demonstrates its concern for the one overriding internal factor which forces the communists to support Makarios: opposition to the politico-religious leader of Cyprus would relegate any political party to inconsequential minority status, if not outright condemnation. On the eve of the talks the party stressed that it would "do everything possible to help a rallying of the progressive forces of the Cypriot people in the name of saving Cyprus" (ibid., 2 July). Toward the end of the year Papaïoannou said that AKEL was "striving to do its utmost to ensure the successful completion of the talks in which definite progress was made over the recent period" (ibid., 13 November).

No doubt due to the crisis in the early part of the year, there were fewer Cypriot communist delegations sent to Eastern Bloc countries than in previous years. Still, AKEL members visited Czechoslovakia in May, the Soviet Union in July, and Romania in September. The visits were made on the invitation of the communist parties of the various countries and were usually described as an occasion to exchange views on "current issues of international life"

(Agerpress, Romanian press agency, 17 September). While the AKEL members ostensibly carry out the stated purpose, it is widely believed that such visits are normally made to receive the latest Soviet party line in a first-hand manner. It may be interesting to note that General Secretary Papaïoannou, who did not go on the September trip to Bucharest, made an individual four-day visit there in November (ibid. 19 November). One explanation for his trip could have been the tense situation that developed in the island as a result of anti-Makarios demonstrations on 27 and 28 October. Allegedly, Grivas followers had "received a large number of weapons which were smuggled into Cyprus with the help of certain NATO countries" *(New Times,* Moscow, no. 46, November). While these developments could have necessitated a change in AKEL's tactics at the time, the year ended without a clash between government forces and the underground groups.

International Views and Positions. AKEL consistently follows the Soviet policy line on Middle Eastern and Mediterranean affairs. The communist press in Cyprus parrots the Soviet allegation that the United States is the main force preventing peace throughout the world, and consistently repeats the charge that the United States and Great Britain intend to militarize Cyprus under the NATO umbrella. The main international development on which AKEL expressed an opinion in 1972 was on the announcement that Piraeus would become the home port for the U.S. Sixth Fleet. In a *Kharavyi* editorial (27 January) AKEL used the opportunity to attack both the "military regime" in Athens and the "dependence" the United States now has on Greece for "defense of the area." The editorial stated that there is "nothing to be proud of" in having the "threat of nuclear death . . . exist permanently in Greek territorial waters." What the editorial tried to debunk was the idea that "the establishment of a permanent base for the 6th Fleet" was being regarded by Athens as a "national deed" made necessary by the increasing Soviet danger in the Eastern Mediterranean. It concluded by claiming that the United States was studying a plan to establish bases in other areas of the Mediterranean, hence "our good American may also knock on our door in Cyprus."

An article by Papaïoannou (*WMR,* July) tried to reaffirm that Cyprus still "belongs to the anti-imperialist camp, the camp of newly independent states that do not want to fall prey to NATO imperialist designs." He continued that Cyprus must develop its relations with the "peace-loving countries" and that this would also include the "socialist countries that stand consistently by its side." As a result, the position of Cyprus would be "immensely strengthened" and would "promote the interest of its liberation struggle":

> The liberation struggle of the Cypriot people is part and parcel of the liberation struggle of the peoples of the Middle East fighting against imperialism, for independence, democracy and social advance. It merges with the struggle of the Mediterranean peoples for a nuclear-free zone, for peace and security in Europe.

The article went on that the NATO strategy "aims at the creation of a buffer between the socialist countries on the one hand, and the Arab countries on the other," to be composed of Greece, Turkey, Cyprus, and Israel, with the "real incentive" behind this plan being the "black gold of the Middle East, petrol." Thus Cyprus would play the role of a "war bridgehead and air missile base" against "the Arab peoples and the peoples of the socialist countries." In order to impose this plan, certain domestic obstacles had to be overcome. The "putschists," therefore, decided to "brandish the Communist bogey" in Cyprus and force Makarios to "bow obediently and blindly to the 'national center' of Hellenism or to be overthrown and brushed aside." The plan had failed because the Soviet Union "warned in no uncertain manner that it cannot and will not remain indifferent to foreign threats of invading

Cyprus." This threat could not be taken as empty rhetoric, because the Soviet Union was "not in the habit of throwing words to the wind." When the "putschists" met the determined resistance of the people in Cyprus, "they had to change their mind and looked like the well-known popular saying of the fox with the grapes."

In European affairs, AKEL was undoubtedly pleased to see that Cypriot ties with the German Democratic Republic (GDR) were finally raised from the commercial to the diplomatic level in December. In the same month, there was little communist comment on Cyprus's signing its intention to become an associate member of the European Economic Community, which AKEL had opposed in the past.

Within the international communist movement, AKEL seldom veers from the Soviet line. The party is on record denouncing the "splitting policy" of the Chinese communist leadership, which it said had been, for a decade, a "serious, detrimental phenomenon," weakening the anti-imperialist front in Asia and throughout the world, inciting "U.S. imperialism," and inviting organized "aggression, conspiracies, and coups in Vietnam, Ghana, Indonesia, and the Near East." (Article by Papaïoannou in *Pravda,* 20 February 1970). Nonetheless, AKEL— consistent with its current tactic to support the Makarios government completely—made little adverse comment about Cyprus's giving diplomatic recognition in 1972 to the People's Republic of China.

Publications. AKEL enjoys influential press channels. Its central organ is the daily newspaper *Kharavyi* ("Dawn"), but there are sympathetic writers and editors on most of the island's periodicals. AKEL's theoretical organ is *Theoritikos Dimokratis* ("Theoretical Democrat"). The party also publishes a quarterly review, *Neos Dimokratis* ("New Democrat"); a monthly journal, *Nea Epochi* ("New Epoch"); and a weekly, *Neoi Kairoi* ("New Times"). The PEO publishes a weekly newspaper, *Ergatiki Vima* ("Workers' Step"). EDON publishes a newspaper, *Dhimokratia,* and a monthly, *Neolaia* ("Youth").

University of Virginia   T. W. Adams
Northern Virginia Regional Center
Falls Church, Virginia

Denmark

The Communist Party of Denmark (Danmarks Kommunistiske Parti; DKP) emerged from the left wing of the Social Democratic Party (SDP) midst the social ferment and distress following World War I. Organized on 9 November 1919, it has been legal ever since, except during the German occupation of World War II. The DKP has about 7,000 members, out of a total population of over five million. It draws principally from industrial workers, farm laborers, and leftist intellectuals in Copenhagen and other urban centers.

Communist fortunes have gone steadily downhill in Denmark since their electoral zenith in 1945 (a peak due largely to the DKP's effective role in the Danish Resistance). The expulsion of the colorful Aksel Larsen (party chairman, 1932–58) for "Titoist revisionism" in 1958 and the subsequent formation of the Socialist People's Party (Socialistisk Folkeparti; SF) in 1959 decimated DKP ranks. The emergence in 1967 of the Left Socialists (Venstresocialisterne; VS), a radical splinter from the SF, further whittled away the communist constituency. At the last election on 21 September 1971 the DKP received only 1.4 percent of the vote. It thus fell short of the 2 percent needed to qualify for parliamentary representation. The Social Democrats—with 70 places in the 179-member Folketing (Parliament), with one vote each from Greenland and the Faeroes, and with the tacit backing of the SF (17 seats)—took power. They remained in office throughout 1972, though leftist labor leader, Anker Jørgensen, did replace Jens Otto Krag as prime minister on 5 October. Krag surprised all but his closest confidants by resigning immediately after the Danish referendum on entry into the European Economic Community.

Leadership and Organization. Knud Jespersen, named DKP chairman in 1958 and reelected to that post at the party's Twenty-third Congress in 1969, remained in charge. The Central Committee has 39 full and 13 candidate members. The Control Commission has 5 members and 2 auditors. Though the triennial National Congress is theoretically the highest party authority, the chairman and select members of the Central Committee are omnipotent in practice. The Twenty-fourth Congress is to be held in Copenhagen on 12–14 January 1973. Ib Nørlund, veteran member from the Resistance, remains the party's leading theoretician and tactician.

The Communist Youth of Denmark (Danmarks Kommunistiske Ungdom; DKU) was established in 1920 as a party affiliate. Jørn Christensen, a 28-year-old machinist, is DKU chairman. Largely because of competition further to the left, the DKU has failed to attract more than 2,000 members. Radical young people have tended to turn to such splinter organizations as the Communist League–Marxist-Leninist (Kommunistisk Forbund-ML; KFML), Communist Youth–Marxist-Leninist (Kommunistisk Ungdom-ML; KUML), Communist Labor Circle (Kommunistisk Arbejdskreds; KAK), the KAK-endorsed Communist Youth League

(Kommunistisk Ungdoms Forbund; KUF), Socialist Youth League (Socialistisk Ungdoms Forbund; SUF), and Revolutionary Socialists (Revolutionaere Socialister). All such groups con-
cur in rejecting the policies of the "traitorous" Social Democrats and the "revisionist" SF and
DKP. An exchange between Maoist Benito Scocozza and party secretary Ib Nørlund exemplified conflicting views on alleged "reformism" in the DKP (*Land og Folk,* 25 and 31 August
1972). All these radical factions remain miniscule in number and negligible in political
power.

The DKP does not control any national labor union, though communists were elected to
the Council (Jørgen Jensen) and Executive Committee (Svend Drejer) of the Danish Metalworkers' Union at its congress, 3–9 September. What little influence the party retains in the
labor movement is mostly among lower paid dockworkers and manual laborers. The communists send delegates to the "Workers' Conferences of the Baltic Countries, Norway, and Iceland," held annually in Rostock, East Germany.

Domestic Attitudes and Activities. The communists continued in 1972 their struggle
against "monopoly capital" in behalf of the "social and democratic rights of workers." With a
minority Social Democratic government beholden to the Marxist SF and vulnerable to the appeals of the SDP's own left wing, the DKP was often hard put to outflank the "Establishment"
with its domestic platform. Its two most notable successes were in youth and labor organizations.

DKU chairman Christensen was elected vice-president of the Joint Council of Danish
Youth (Dansk Ungdoms Faellesraad; DUF) at that organization's congress in May. A resolution condemning the escalation of the Vietnam war by the United States was presented by the
DKU and adopted by the meeting. Young communists also supported a resolution sharply condemning the Danish government's plan to reduce funds for assistance to underdeveloped countries and the proposal that the DUF participate in the Student and Youth Festival to be held
in Berlin in 1973. (*Land og Folk,* 16 May 1972.) Christensen noted that such DKU priority
issues as European security, cooperation with socialist countries, recognition of the German
Democratic Republic (GDR), and support for national liberation movements have become
"established parts of the work of the Joint Council" (ibid.).

The communists managed to nudge the Metalworkers' Union—Denmark's most important
labor organization—leftward at the union's September congress, in both leadership and policy
line. The communists helped swing the union presidency to Paulus Andersen because of his
newly proclaimed opposition to Danish entry into the European Economic Community. Jørgen Jensen, the communist candidate for that office, dropped out of the race when Andersen
announced his anti-EEC stand. He was subsequently elected to the union's Council—a first
for Danish communists. Besides spurring the union's surprisingly strong 281–82 vote against
Danish EEC membership, the DKU helped secure adoption of a resolution criticizing U.S.
policy in Southeast Asia.

Although the DKP's strong campaign against EEC membership failed (Denmark approved
entry by a two-to-one margin in a binding national referendum on 2 October), it may well
have persuaded many voters. Chairman Jespersen stressed after the referendum that over a
million Danes had voted "no" and that the negative turnout had been especially high (58.8
percent) in Copenhagen, where the working class is concentrated (TASS, 3 October). Jespersen told a TASS correspondent that the results of the referendum only intensified divisions
within Denmark and that the "referendum had been carried out in conditions of propaganda
pressure on the part of big capital unprecedented in the history of Denmark" (ibid.).

Besides agitating within other Danish organizations and campaigning against EEC entry, the DKP launched some frontal attacks against alleged domestic grievances. In an "Open Letter to the Ruling Parties" Jespersen charged the government with turning its back against society's weakest—old people and children. He proposed that Prime Minister Krag "move against those responsible for the 'difficulties' in affluent Denmark—big capital, its profits and power." (*Land og Folk,* 14 April.) Jespersen called for the government to halt the "arms race insanity," reduce the length of required military service, cancel new weapon purchases, confiscate all profits from speculation, control foreign trade, halt foreign exchange transactions, institute a genuinely progressive tax reform, expand public works, guarantee the right to work, lower the age limit for pensions, expand compulsory education, revise labor court legislation, and support an effective cost-of-living increase for workers. Many of these proposals recurred in a document intended as a basis for discussion in the DKP newspaper *Land og Folk* and in preparation for the party's Twenty-fourth Congress (ibid., 19 May). Besides the specific points already noted, that paper stressed that economic growth in Denmark had primarily enriched "big capital" and that workers must resist such "neo-reformist" concepts as the "economic democracy" put forth by the SDP and SF.

International Views and Positions. Opposition to Danish entry into the EEC dominated DKP activity on the international front. Jespersen stated flatly: "We cannot improve the Common Market and we have nothing to gain by entering it" (*Land og Folk,* 1 January 1972). The Central Committee, meeting on 8 January, criticized the SDP as hurting the working class through espousal of EEC membership; it advocated instead more Nordic economic cooperation (ibid., 12 January). Communists were conspicuous among the eleven contributors to a book touted by the communist press, *A Clear "No" to the Common Market.* When two-thirds of the nation in fact said "yes" to the EEC, the DKP pledged to use the one third who did not as the basis for a continuing "struggle against monopolies" (Central Committee statement reported by TASS, 6 October). Representatives of the communist parties of Denmark, Finland, Norway, and Sweden met in Copenhagen on 9–10 November to assert that they would resist efforts to turn Denmark into a bridge to the north for the promotion of EEC interests.

Promotion of a "Conference on Security and Cooperation in Europe" (CSCE) was another strong DKP theme in foreign policy. Central Committee meetings in May and October underscored the contention that such a conference would "open the road to security and cooperation by all European countries" (TASS, 8 October). On related issues, the DKP continued to plead for recognition of the GDR, and for guarantees of Danish neutrality and recognition of Denmark as a "non-nuclear, militarily-reduced area" in a new European security system (e.g., *Land og Folk,* 19 May). NATO remained on the DKP blacklist.

Opposition to U.S. policy in Southeast Asia continued to figure prominently in DKP agitation—though anti-war demonstrations were fewer and tamer than in the late 1960's. Writers for *Land og Folk* led a campaign to get governmental and popular support in protest against the treatment of political prisoners in South Vietnam. A plenary session of the DKP Central Committee, 20 November, adopted a statement demanding that the United States end its "aggression" in Vietnam and immediately sign an armistice agreement with the Democratic Republic of Vietnam (TASS, 20 November). Perhaps most significant for the sake of U.S.-Danish relations, Prime Minister Jørgensen opened an international "War Crimes Tribunal" in Copenhagen, 10–16 October. Backed in part by communists, the "tribunal" condemned alleged terror bombing by U.S. planes in Indochina.

International Party Contacts. There was little in 1972 to indicate that the DKP has swerved from its traditional loyalty to Moscow—a fact which has dimmed the party's appeal to young leftists in the last decade. A five-member DKP delegation of—Knud Jespersen, Poul Amanuel, Ib Nørlund, Ingmar Wagner, and Jørgen Jensen—met in Moscow, 23–26 January, with members of the Central Committee of the Communist Party of the Soviet Union (CPSU), including, most notably, Suslov and Shelepin. Main topics for discussion were the proposed CSCE and international labor cooperation. Both delegations stressed the importance of ideological cohesion in the international communist movement and emphasized that the "great power, chauvinist policy of the Chinese leaders and ideology of Maoism showed completely that they oppose Marxism-Leninism and are hostile to the interests of the revolutionary and national-liberation movement of the peoples" (TASS, 27 January). Both parties underscored the solidarity of their opposition to U.S. policy in Vietnam and to enlargement of the Common Market (*Land og Folk,* 5–6 February). DKP Chairman Jespersen followed up the January session by meeting with Boris Ponomarev, alternate member of the CPSU Politburo and secretary of the CPSU Central Committee, in late October.

A five-member delegation of the East German Socialist Unity Party (SED), led by Harry Tisch (first secretary of the SED in Rostock) visited Copenhagen in mid-January. The communiqué at the end of the visit stressed that "favorable conditions exist for convening an all-European security and cooperation conference in 1972" and declared that the time was ripe for the immediate diplomatic recognition of the GDR (*Neues Deutschland,* East Berlin, 18 January). Both, too, rejected the "anti-Soviet" policy of Peking. As in the case of DKP-CPSU relations, Jespersen made a follow-up visit, meeting with Erich Honecker, first secretary of the SED Central Committee, 3 November. He told Honecker that the Danish people supported the immediate establishment of diplomatic relations with the GDR, and interpreted their sentiment as an important contribution toward relaxation of international tension (*Land og Folk,* 7 November). Ib Nørlund, Politburo member and secretary of the DKP Central Committee, visited the GDR on 8–16 November. He spoke before SED leaders on the struggle of Danish communists "for the cohesion of all leftist forces against the power of the monopolies and against the policy of the EEC and NATO" (*Neues Deutschland,* 16 November).

Publications. The DKP's newspaper *Land og Folk* ("Nation and People") has dropped from a daily circulation of 60,000 in 1945 to about 6,000. Largely because of its financial difficulties (common to most Danish newspapers), the DKP in February 1972 cut back publication to five times per week. In October a special campaign to raise money netted over 765,000 kronor (*Land og Folk,* 24 November). The party continued to publish *Tiden* ("Times"), a monthly theoretical journal. The DKU publication is *Fremad* ("Forward").

Finland

Exiled leftist Social Democrats—"reds" taking refuge from Finland's bloody civil war—established the Communist Party of Finland (Suomen Kommunistinen Puolue; SKP) in Moscow on 29 August 1918. From then until 1930, the SKP operated through a variety of front organizations. During the 1930s, weakened by internal friction and prohibited by the Finnish government, the SKP reverted to illegal activities. It became a legal political party only in 1944, as required by the Finnish-Soviet armistice of that year. The SKP has an estimated 49,000 members—a figure that may have been inflated by intra-party factions competing for maximal representation at the 1972 party congress—in a population of 4,685,000. Communist strength is concentrated in Finland's northern and eastern districts, with their traditional frontier radicalism, as well as in industrialized urban areas to the south.

Through an electoral front established on 29 October 1944, the Finnish People's Democratic League (Suomen Kansan Demokraattinen Liitto; SKDL), the SKP has consistently received between a fourth and a fifth of the vote in elections since World War II. The SKDL registered minor gains in two elections in 1972. It won 17 percent of the vote in the parliamentary election of 2–3 January (behind the Social Democratic Party with 25.8 percent and the National Coalition Party with 17.6). The party edged up to 17.3 percent (423,000 votes) in the municipal elections of 1–2 October.

Though the communists won 37 seats in the Eduskunta (Parliament) in the January election, they did not participate in any of the several governments which ruled during 1972. They last shared power in the center-left coalition headed by Ahti Karjalainen, 15 July 1970 to 17 March 1971. Largely because of its internal division and preference for staying in opposition during the decision on Finnish affiliation with the European Economic Community, the party took part in neither the minority Social Democratic government (22 February–19 July) nor that of the coalition of Social Democratic, Swedish People's, Center, and Liberal parties (4 September–present).

Leadership and Organization. Arne Saarinen, a former union leader who was first elected SKP chairman in 1966, was reelected at the party's Sixteenth Congress, 31 March–2 April, 1972. Arvo Aalto, a liberal, retained the post of Secretary-General which he had won from Stalinist, Ville Pessi, at the Fifteenth Congress, April 1969. The relative strength of the "liberals" and "Stalinists" was established at an extraordinary SKP Congress in February 1970, when the ratio of liberals to Stalinists was set at 20–15 in the Central Committee, 9–6 in the Politburo, and 5–3 in the Secretariat. For other top officials see *YICA, 1972,* pp. 140–41.

Internal Party Affairs. The split between the more moderate revisionists or "liberals" and the hard-line "Stalinists" within the SKP continued in 1972. Based on the ideological turmoil

139

following the 1956 "de-Stalinization" congress of the Communist Party of the Soviet Union, the division within the SKP was sharpened by the questions of principle posed by the Soviet-led invasion of Czechoslovakia in 1968 and vacillating party fortunes inside Finland. That internal tension wreaked havoc at the SKP congress in 1969. Seven of the eight "Stalinist" delegations stormed out of the proceedings to hold their own "convention" elsewhere. Largely because of Soviet pressure to restore unity, the SKP held the extraordinary congress in 1970 which patched up some differences. Despite subsequent progress, hopes that a unified party would emerge from the Sixteenth Congress proved illusory. That meeting, in fact, formalized the existence of two parties within the SKP and sealed the ratio of power formulated in advance. Although the liberal majority retained control, Stalinist influence grew. Given the serious illness of several liberals and the traveling responsibilities of party leaders, the way was left open for the Politburo to meet with a Stalinist majority. Stalinist strength was apparent in the congress's decision to give access to the party news bureau (Democratic News Service) to the two main hard-line newspapers, *Tiedonantaja* and *Hämeen Yhteistyö*. Points of divergence on central party tasks and the interpretation of Marxist-Leninist principles, spelled out early in the year in *Tiedonantaja* (15, 18, 20, 22 January), remained unresolved and provided fodder for much acrimonious debate.

The spillover from SKP tension affected the SKDL more conspicuously than ever. *Tiedonantaja* (8 January) singled out the electoral front and its leader, Ele Alenius, for severe criticism. It scored Alenius's book, *Sosialistiseen Suomeen* ("Toward a Socialist Finland") as a "work of opportunism" and accused Alenius of leading workers into "petty-bourgeois dilettantism" and so strengthening capitalism. Later (15 June), it condemned the SKDL for "going its own way" and departing from the direction intended by the SKP. The SKDL, normally a rubber stamp for the party, indicated its independence from Stalinist views by its unprecedented rejection of an SKP decision on a parliamentary vote in May. The Stalinist faction of the SKP made clear in its press and its political maneuvering that it hopes to increase its leverage on the SKDL leadership by the time the front holds its congress in 1973.

How party friction affect another internal matter is not clear. The SKP announced that it plans a purge in January–May 1973, when every member must acquire a new card. An estimated 10,000 members could be scratched from the rolls. (*Helsingin Sanomat,* 28–29 October.)

Domestic Attitudes and Activities. The SKP emphasized throughout 1972 that, without communist participation, there could be no stable government serving the interests of workers. Nevertheless it did not join any of the governments in power. It preferred to improve its position by remaining in the opposition while difficult domestic economic decisions were made. Central to these was what developed as a "package"—including ratification of Finland's free-trade agreement with the EEC, the extension of President Kekkonen's term of office, and approval of certain counter-cyclical economic legislation. The SKP remained on record as firmly opposed to an agreement with the EEC, considering any such arrangement to be in conflict with a foreign policy based on the treaty of friendship, cooperation, and mutual assistance with the Soviet Union. The SKP did not consider the legislative counterbalances required by the Social Democratic Party sufficient to eliminate the danger posed by an EEC agreement. Though the SKP favored the extension of the president's term, it demanded that this matter and the EEC issue be kept separate. If pro-Kekkonen and pro-EEC forces should unite, the SKP would find itself in a politically embarrassing situation. In June, the SKP stated that Kekkonen's tenure of office should be extended by the Eduskunta (*Kansan Uutiset,* 5 June). In

December, the party Politburo endorsed a proposal by the premier that the Electoral College from the 1968 presidential elections be convened in order to extend Kekkonen's term until 1978.

An issue drawing vigorous party activity was that of pensions. The SKP Politburo demanded that the generous pension plan approved by parliament on 27 June, over the strong objections of the Social Democrats, be carried out. It severely condemned the compromise put forward during governmental negotiations whereby proposed expenditures for the pension plan were halved (ibid., 23 August).

The SKP continued to thrash out the issue of cooperation with the Social Democratic Party (SDP). SKP-SDP relations vacillated between overtures for cooperation and mutual recriminations. The Sixteenth Congress emphasized the development of cooperation between workers and workers' parties, stressing that the "building of cooperation is a question of party conviction and principle" (ibid, 27 April). Further, the SKP presented offers for negotiations to the congresses of the SDP and the Workers and Smallholders Social Democratic League (Työvaen ja Pienviljelijäin Sosialidemokraattinen Liitto). By autumn, relations seemed to chill. SKP chairman Saarinen stated: "[We] must seriously reexamine problems associated with relations between the two parties." (*Helsingin Sanomat,* 24 September). In November, however, the SKP made a new offer to work out joint lines of action with the SDP. Saarinen stated that it was regrettable that the Social Democrats had not found it necessary to conduct talks on a joint program as proposed earlier by the SKP.

The fluctuations in SKP-SDP relations continued to be reflected in the labor movement, where the two parties have traditionally battled for preeminence. The congress of the Central Federation of Finnish Trade Unions (SAK), 29 June–2 July 1971, had reaffirmed the 8–5 ratio between Social Democrats and liberal communists on its Executive Committee. Social Democratic relations with the SAK deputy chairman and second secretary were good, largely because both men are moderate communists. The congress of the Finnish Metalworkers' Union (the country's largest union), 9–12 December 1971, adhered to a comparable formula for inter-party rapport and elected communists as second chairman and second Secretary.

International Views and Activities. For the most part, the SKP in 1972 focused on the same issues and took the same stand as its Nordic counterparts: opposition to EEC affiliation, criticism of U.S. involvement in Southeast Asia, support for recognition of the German Democratic Republic (GDR) and support for a European security conference.

As elsewhere, the EEC question drew the sharpest fire. The SKP Politburo issued repeated statements against any Finnish affiliation. Finland initialed, but did not sign, an industrial free-trade agreement in Brussels on 20 July. The SKP asserted that such an agreement would contradict the national foreign policy line which is based on the Soviet-Finnish agreement of friendship, cooperation, and mutual assistance, and would "limit the possibilities for implementing an independent economic policy and contribute to its submission to the policy of the West European monopolies" (Moscow domestic service, 30 November). Chairman Saarinen stated that, while it was difficult to say whether the present situation could be compared to that in 1948, there were "many indications that the continuity of Finnish foreign policy" was in danger (*Kansan Uutiset,* 19 November). He warned against rightist pressure for precipitant acceptance of the EEC agreement. Doubtless encouraged by the Soviets, the communists pressed to secure a Finnish agreement with the Council for Mutual Economic Assistance (CMEA)—either instead of or as a counterbalance to any EEC affiliation. The SKP applauded Norway's rejection of EEC membership in its September referendum and expressed confidence that this would make "still more effective the actions of the working people of Finland to keep their country from being drawn . . . into the sphere of the Common Market" (TASS, 29 September).

Due in part to agitiation by the SKP, Finland moved in 1972 to extend full diplomatic recognition to both German states. On 8 December Finland and the GDR signed an agreement to establish diplomatic relations.

Communist efforts in behalf of a European security conference were, in part, rewarded when multilateral preparatory talks on this subject began in Helsinki on 22 November. On a related issue, the SKP approved the discussions between the United States and the Soviet Union. It stressed that such talks "were even more imperative, since a united front against the Soviet Union has already been in the making between China and the USA for a long time." The party excused the Soviet Union for receiving U.S. President Nixon while the Vietnam war was still in progress by claiming that "the Vietnam question will not be resolved by Moscow's refusal to receive Nixon." (*Tiedonantaja*, 6, 8, 11 July.)

International Party Contacts. Despite alleged Soviet sentiments toward different factions in the SKP, the Finnish communists remained loyal to Moscow. There were frequent visits by communist delegations between Finland and the Soviet Union in 1972, most notably those of the SKP led by Chairman Saarinen to Moscow in January and February.

The SKP continued to repudiate Maoist ideology and the Peking leadership. Vice-chairman Taisto Sinisalo emphasized that "the watershed in the recognition of proletarian internationalism has been and is the attitude toward the U.S.S.R. and its Communist Party" (*Tiedonantaja*, 9 March). In response to the Maoist contention that the main conflict now is between the "superstates" or between the people and "social-imperialism," he stressed that "the watchword 'superpowers' is totally foreign to the class attitude." Sinisalo particularly criticized Chinese policy toward South Asia and the United States: "China's attitude toward India's policy and the struggle of Bangladesh, as well as the enthusiasm with which China is now trying to better relations with the United States have especially offended youth, especially when the U.S. is brutally bombing the Democratic Republic of Vietnam and is applying open measures of force and violence against progressive forces at home" (ibid., 15 February).

The Stalinist wing of the SKP made a point of defending the Prague trials (see *Czechoslovakia*). Its journal stated: "No one has been convicted for his political views—only for his practical deeds aimed at violating the country's laws. There are no political trials in Czechoslovakia." (Quoted in *Pravda*, 13 September). The anniversary of the Soviet-led invasion was hailed as "a day of victory for the socialist world organization, a day of victory for the people of Czechoslovakia, a day of victory for proletarian internationalism" (*Tiedonantaja*, 22 August).

The communist-oriented World Peace Council continued to have its international headquarters in Helsinki, where its affiliate is the Finnish Peace Defenders (Suomen Rauhanpuolustajat).

Finnish communists, together with their counterparts from Denmark, Norway, and Sweden, met on 9–10 November in Copenhagen to discuss problems of the working class in northern Europe and to call for the relaxation of tension in Europe.

Publications. *Kansan Uutiset* ("People's News") is the SKP central organ, published daily in Helsinki. *Kommunisti* is the party's monthly theoretical journal. The Stalinist faction controls such papers as *Tiedonantaja* and *Hämeen Yhteistyö*. *Folktidningen*, published weekly, is addressed to the Swedish-speaking minority in Finland.

France

The French Communist Party (Parti Communiste Français; PCF) was founded in December 1920. Although challenged by other small Marxist-Leninist organizations (see below), the PCF remained in 1972 the largest and electorally strongest left-wing party in France. Official details on party membership continued to remain unpublicized. At the party's Twentieth Congress, held in December, Secretariat member André Vieuguet reported that in 1972 the PCF's treasury had sent 454,640 membership cards to the party's federations and that more than 48,000 new members had joined the party (*L'Humanité,* 18 December). Vieuguet did not reveal, however, the number of membership cards actually distributed by the federations, or give any figures on how many party members had left the PCF during the year. Earlier in the year—in an unprecedented move—a meeting of the Central Committee (16–18 May) decided to publish details on party finances. On the basis of information revealed at that time, the dissident communist monthly *Unir-Débat* (Paris, no. 66, 10 June) estimated that total party membership at the end of 1971 had been not higher than 250,000. In December 1971 the non-communist fortnightly *Est & Ouest* (16–31 December) had estimated a total of 295,000. While exact figures are difficult to compute, it would appear that in 1972 the PCF had an actual membership of about 300,000. The population of France is about 52 million (estimated 1972).

In the latest elections to the National Assembly, held in June 1968, the PCF obtained 4,-435,357 votes (20.03 percent); 34 communist candidates (including one representative from the Guadeloupe Communist Party) were elected to the 486-seat Assembly. The most recent elections to the Senate were held in the fall of 1971, at which time a third of the 283-seat Senate was up for election. The single PCF candidate who faced reelection won and the party kept its 18 seats. New elections to the National Assembly are scheduled for March 1973.

Leadership and Organization. A new national leadership of the PCF was elected at the party's Twentieth Congress, held on 13–17 December 1972. The Central Committee numbered 90 full and 28 candidate members (for names see *L'Humanité,* 18 December). The Central Committee, in turn, elected the following to the Politburo: Gustave Ansart, Guy Besse, Jacques Duclos, Etienne Fajon, Benoît Frachon, Georges Frischmann, Henri Krasucki, Paul Laurent, Roland Leroy, Georges Marchais, René Piquet, Gaston Plissonnier, Claude Poperen (previously a candidate member), Georges Séguy, André Vieuguet, and Madeleine Vincent (previously a candidate member). Three new candidate members were elected: Mireille Bertrand, Jean Colpin, and Guy Hermier. Not presenting themselves for reelection were François Billoux, Raymond Guyot, and Waldeck Rochet (all three former members of the Politburo). There were no changes in the Secretariat, which consisted of: Etienne Fajon, Roland Leroy, René Piquet, Gaston Plissonnier, and André Vieuguet. Georges Marchais was elected secretary-general of the party, assuming a post that he had in fact held de facto since at least 1970, when he was appointed deputy to the ailing Waldeck Rochet. The latter was elected honorary president of the party.

At the time of the congress, the PCF claimed to have 19,520 cells in its 97 federations. Of these, 5,376 were industrial, 5,225 rural, and 8,919 local. (ibid., 18 December.)

Auxiliary Organizations. The PCF's primary auxiliary organization is the General Confederation of Labor (Confédération Générale du Travail; CGT), the largest trade union in France. During 1972 the CGT claimed a membership of 2,330,056; independent sources, however, placed the total at approximately 1,700,000. The CGT is led by PCF Politburo members Georges Séguy (secretary-general) and Benoît Frachon (president).

The other major PCF auxiliary organization is the Movement of Communist Youth (Mouvement de la Jeunesse Communiste; MJC), which comprises four groups—the Union of Communist Students of France (Union des Etudiants Communistes de France; UECF), the Union of Young Girls of France (Union des Jeunes Filles de France; UJFF), the Union of Communist Youth of France (Union de la Jeunesse Communiste de France; UJCF), and the Union of Farm Youth of France (Union de la Jeunesse Agricole de France; UJAF). The most recent congress of the MJC was held in December 1970; at that time the following secretary-generals were elected: Roland Favaro (MJC), Gérard Molina (UECF), Nicole Garrand (UJFF), Gérard Lanternier (UJCF), and Michel Larrat (UJAF). No changes in this leadership were reported in 1972.

Other prominent PCF organizations active in 1972 included the Union of French Women (Union des Femmes Françaises; UFF), the Peace Movement (Mouvement de la Paix), and the Movement for the Defense of Small Farmers (Mouvement de Défense des Exploitants Familiaux; MODEF).

Among students the PCF controls a splinter group of the National Union of Students of France (Union Nationale des Etudiants de France; UNEF). This splinter group, originally referred to as UNEF-Renouveau, was designated simply as UNEF during 1972. The contending UNEF, which represented French students at international gatherings, was led by Trotskyists (see below). The principal PCF-controlled high-school organization during the year continued to be the National Union of High School Action Committees (Union Nationale des Comités d'Action Lycéenne; UNCAL), a body formed in 1968.

Party Internal Affairs. By December, when the PCF held its Twentieth Congress, dissension within the party—epitomized by the expulsions in 1970 of prominent personalities, such as Roger Garaudy and Charles Tillon (see *YICA, 1971,* pp. 160–62)—appeared to have been overcome. While there were reports of a power struggle between Georges Séguy, secretary-general of the CGT, and Georges Marchais, the latter was elected secretary-general unanimously. In an apparent demonstration of unity, Séguy presided over the closing session of the congress, which was marked by his rival's election to the party's leading post.

In his closing speech to the congress, Marchais stressed that the PCF paid "constant attention . . . to the movement of life and to the evolution of the situation in the country and throughout the world," and added: "Yes, the PCF is changing and does not stop changing" (*L'Humanité,* 18 December). One of the thrusts evident in party renovation was its concern to retain the allegiance of its young members and its appeal to women. Out of the 1,236 delegates to the congress, 72.6 percent had joined the party since 1958, and 39.5 percent since 1968. The average age of the delegates was thirty-three. Women represented 27.3 percent of the participants (6 percent more than at the Nineteenth Congress, February 1970). A number of young persons, including representatives of the new generation of communist intellectuals, were elected to the party's leading bodies. Thus, Guy Hermier (32 years old), a professor from Dijon, was elected to the Politburo, and Paul Boccara (40) and Philippe Herzog (32), both university lecturers and deputy editors in chief of the journal *Economie et Politique,* were elected candidate members of the Central Committee. Jean-Michel Catala (30), deputy secretary-general of the MJC, was also elected candidate member of the Central Committee.

At the same time, certain traditions remained unchanged. Georges Marchais's federation, the Val-de-Marne (which earlier, under the name of Seine-Sud, was also the late PCF leader Maurice Thorez's base), continued to wield considerable political weight in congressional decisions. Charles Fitermann, secretary to Marchais, and Marcel Trigon, mayor of Arcueil, both of them delegates from the Val-de-Marne, were elected candidate members of the Central Committee.

Domestic Views and Policies. With only some 20 percent of electoral support, the PCF's bid for power continued to rest on the party's ability to persuade other elements of the left-wing opposition to coordinate their actions with communist policy. During the year the PCF focused its attention on the Socialist Party (Parti Socialiste; PS), the largest of the non-communist left-wing groups formed in June 1971 following the union of the traditional socialist party—the Section Française de l'Internationale Ouvrière (SFIO)—with the Convention des Institutions Républicains (CIR) and unaffiliated socialist groups.

PCF-PS negotiations culminated on 27 June in the adoption of a 60,000-word joint program—the first such agreement on common policy since the Popular Front, in the mid-1930s. Relations between the two parties, however, waxed and waned throughout the first half of the year and were tenuous even after the ratification of the program by special conventions of the two parties in July.

The Socialist Party's draft program was made public in early January. The PCF's response was guardedly negative; although PCF spokesman René Andrieu accused the Socialists of having "retreated" from a number of positions agreed upon with the PCF (*L'Humanité,* 12 January), the party's deputy secretary-general, Georges Marchais, stated: "It is impossible, for the time being, to make a comprehensive evaluation of the Socialist program because, according to the Socialist leaders themselves, such a program does not exist as yet but is only a draft" (speech at PCF Central Committee meeting, 20–21 January, *L'Humanité,* 22 January). While stressing that the PCF did not wish to "engage in any polemics," Marchais claimed that "on certain decisive issues" the options presented by the Socialists were "insufficient or unclear" (ibid.).

The PS was scheduled to issue a final program at a special convention in early March. In the meantime, relations between the two parties were acerbated by two additional problems. The PCF's highly qualified opposition to the Soviet-led invasion of Czechoslovakia in 1968 and the subsequent "normalization" policies carried out in that country had been a constant source of friction in the party's relations with the Socialists. In February, the PS urged the PCF to participate in a protest against political repression in Czechoslovakia. In a lengthy letter addressed to the PS's first secretary, François Mitterrand, Marchais turned down the Socialist suggestion, claiming that the Czechoslovak party leader, Gustav Husák, had promised the PCF that no political trials would take place. At the same time, Marchais added:

> One cannot help wondering about the significance of an initiative like yours. The latter, by reinforcing a campaign with very evident anti-communist overtones, cannot but tend to raise new obstacles in the path of unity, to seek new pretexts to delay once again the time for a political agreement taking the form of a joint government program. (*L'Humanité,* 19 February; see also *Le Monde,* Paris, 20–21 February.)

Polemics over Czechoslovakia continued throughout the month, only to be eclipsed by a second source of conflict—the funeral on 4 March of a young Maoist, René-Pierre Overney. The PCF was the only left-wing party not to be represented in the funeral procession, which comprised some 100,000 persons, including representatives of the PS (see below). The PCF newspaper (*L'Humanité*, 6 March) described the funeral procession as "an indecent demonstration" against the CGT and the PCF and expressed its surprise that the "Socialist Party leadership thought it necessary to delegate a few of its people to participate in a demonstration of whose openly anti-communist orientation there was not the shadow of a doubt at the outset." PCF attempts to persuade the Socialists to organize a joint demonstration to counteract the effect of the Maoist-Trotskyist–sponsored funeral procession was rejected by the PS. According to a press statement issued by PCF Politburo member Etienne Fajon, the Socialist leadership "persisted in trying to impose the condition that leftist groups be allowed to participate in such a joint action," despite PCF insistence that these groups be excluded (ibid., 11 March).

The Socialist Party national convention met on 11 March and adopted the party's program. While expressing coldly critical appraisal (ibid., 13 March), the PCF nonetheless declared its willingness to proceed in the two parties' quest for "unity of the left." On 16 March, however, President Georges Pompidou issued a call for a referendum on the ratification of treaties under which Britain, Ireland, Norway and Denmark were to join the European Economic Community. The referendum, interpreted by many as a vote of confidence for Pompidou's government, was opposed by both the PCF and the PS. However, whereas the Socialists, given their basic approval of the expanding EEC, were unwilling to go beyond abstention (an action that would not hamper European unity), the PCF called for a straight "no" response. Polemics between the two parties continued right up to 23 April, the date of the referendum. In many respects the issue of the EEC became a secondary element; rather, the confrontation became one of partisan political will. In a revealing commentary on the PS-PCF controversy, PS Secretariat member Claude Estier stated:

> For many years, the Communist Party has monopolized the discussions on unity of the left. It has been clear for a number of months now that it does not like any other party to challenge its dominance in the name of this union. . . . It would, however, be a good idea if the Communists would get used to one thing. They who consistently denounce the power of the monopolies should know that they themselves have no monopoly right on unity of the left, and that the Socialist Party has given abundant proof that it needs no lessons in this regard. (*Le Monde*, 1 April.)

The rift between the two parties was partially healed by the results of the referendum. Although the referendum was approved, abstention was twice the rate of the most recent major electoral expression (the presidential elections of 1969), and the PCF, the only significant political formation to have recommended a rejection of the proposition, was pleased by the "no" vote, which was 32 percent of those cast, a considerable increase from the communist vote in 1969, which had been 21.27 percent. PS-PCF polemics, however, did not cease entirely, and were, in fact, rekindled by Marchais's comments on the results, which stressed that the vote had confirmed that the PCF's influence was "increasing throughout the country" and that the party was "the determining force of the opposition to the government and its policy." At the same time, Marchais added: "By refusing to form a left-wing alliance on the basis of a 'no' vote, the non-communist left-wing organizations have prevented us from transforming the setback suffered by Pompidou into a real rout." (*L'Humanité*, 24 April.)

At its Central Committee meeting on 16–18 May, the PCF appeared to be taking a harder line in its attitude toward the Socialists. Politburo and Secretariat member Gaston Plissonnier accused the Socialists of engaging in discussions with the Radical Party, led by Jean-Jacques Servan-Schreiber, in "an attempt to channel the popular discontent into a false outlet and to make the Communist Party a complementary force" (ibid., 17 May). The next day, Marchais reiterated Plissonnier's claims and added: "We have already said this before and we repeat it now: it is clear that under no circumstances can the PCF be relied upon to participate—in any form whatever—in any political arrangement which would include the centrist reactionary politicians" (ibid., 18 May). The Executive Bureau of the Socialist Party, in turn, issued a statement underlining the "lack of seriousness and the unacceptable nature of the analyses and allegations made by the Communist Party leaders" (*Le Monde,* 19 May).

In an apparent move to demonstrate its political strength, the communist-controlled CGT called a general strike on 7 June. Although there were large demonstrations, the strike was in general unsuccessful. From then on, rapprochement between the PCF and the PS seemed to accelerate. As noted earlier, the final agreement for a joint program was signed on 27 June, with both parties withdrawing from positions defined in their respective programs (for the PCF program see *YICA, 1972,* p. 149). The PCF reduced the number of new nationalizations of industry that it demanded, while the PS increased its figure. The Socialists dampened somewhat their previous vigorous support for the institutions of the EEC. While both parties attacked NATO, military union was agreed upon when necessary for defense. The PCF agreed to retire from power should it be defeated electorally. On a general level, the new program covered no medium- or long-range prospects and was restricted to the five-year term of the next national legislative assembly. Finally, the program's preamble stated that the document was being submitted to "other democratic parties and organizations."

During the second half of the year, the PCF, the PS, and a splinter group from the Radical Party—the Radical-Socialist Left (Gauche Radicale-Socialiste)—campaigned on the basis of the program. The campaign was not without problems. The independent daily *Le Monde* (14 October) noted that Marchais had on several occasions appealed to party workers not to restrict themselves to the communist viewpoint, "but to work more readily and openly in a spirit of unity" with their new allies. At grass-roots level, many PCF members were reportedly loathe to believe that the Socialists had conclusively broken with their past and their traditions of collaboration with the moderate parties of the center, and even of the right. Certain Central Committee members, even, echoed these sentiments at their meeting on 28–29 September. On the other hand, there was the need to preserve the identity of the party. In an editorial in the PCF's theoretical journal, *Cahiers du Communisme* (October 1972), François Billoux stated:

> It is important for us to be on our guard against two dangers. One mistake would be to think that since we are working with a joint program, everything ought to be done jointly with the other democratic organizations which have rallied to the program. A matching error, and one just as harmful, would be to decide that from now on everything ought to be done with our party, since the consistency and the key measures in our own program are embodied in the logic and the provisions of the joint program.

In general, the PCF took the initiative in making political use of the joint program, repeatedly pressing the other two parties to organize joint campaigns. The Socialists and left-wing Radicals, however, had their own problems. The former had many militant members in the French Democratic Confederation of Labor (Confédération Française Démocratique du Travail; CFDT), which was generally critical of the joint program. The Radical-Socialist Left, a small party, was primarily concerned with maintaining the appearance of an independent political entity.

From October through December, public opinion polls showed growing support for the left-wing coalition, which by mid-December was estimated to have 46 percent of the vote, while the Gaullists held only 38 percent. The PCF became all the more concerned with preserving the coalition. Thus, in November, when it was announced that the Socialist Party would sponsor a conference on repression in Czechoslovakia, the PCF's response was notably guarded. Marchais claimed that he had insufficient information about the conference, and added: "I fervently wish Left parties would respect the pledge they have taken together—to avoid polemics, any quarrel that would harm the success of the joint program" (*L'Humanité*, 6 November). On several occasions, and most notably at the Twentieth Congress, the PCF appeared to be stressing its independence of the Soviet Union and a commitment to French nationalism. In his opening speech at the congress, Marchais evoked two statements made by former PCF leaders. Maurice Thorez, he recalled, had stated: "We are not the party of raised fists, we are the party that stretches out its hand to the French people"; and Waldeck Rochet, Marchais noted, had said: "The Marseillaise is the national anthem of the French people; the tricolor is the good of the whole French nation" (ibid., 14 December).

International Views and Policies. Traditionally aligned with the policies of the Soviet Union and its communist party—the CPSU—the French Communist Party has been handicapped by this allegiance in respect to its domestic policies. Although the PCF had expressed some disapproval of the Soviet-led invasion of Czechoslovakia in 1968, the nature of its opposition, which was highly qualified, and its virtual acceptance of the "normalization" in Czechoslovakia continued to plague the party in 1972.

As mentioned above, the issue of Czechoslovakia was a major bone of contention between the PCF and the Socialists in February. The PCF's position was not helped by the publication in *Le Monde* (11 February) of a secret report by a Politburo member of the Communist Party of Czechoslovakia, Vasil Bil'ak, which did not mention the PCF among those parties which had not "revised their original unilateral opinion" concerning the invasion or their "reservations about the present line" of the Czechoslovak party. In response, *L'Humanité* (14 February) published an editorial entitled "The Generally Known Views of the PCF," which reiterated the party's reservations about the invasion and indicated that PCF Secretariat member Roland Leroy had been sent to Czechoslovakia. A PCF Politburo statement four days later claimed that Leroy had been given a "formal assurance" that the "time of contrived and prefabricated trials is definitely over" (*L'Humanité*, 18 February). An editorial in *L'Humanité* on 26 February reported and concurred with an article published in the Czechoslovak party newspaper, *Rudé právo,* which claimed that the "few dozen people" arrested recently in Czechoslovakia had been engaged in "criminal activities and lawbreaking."

The issue of Czechoslovakia came to the fore once again shortly after the signing of the joint PCF-PS program. Mass trials in Prague and Brno prompted the Gaullist youth movement, the Union des Jeunes pour le Progrès, to draw attention to the French left's silence on the subject and to suggest that the Socialist leader, François Mitterrand, had been "politically gagged" by signing the joint program with the PCF. On 27 July the Socialist Party journal *L'Unité* carried an article by Mitterrand condemning the trials and accusing the Czechoslovak leadership of "making international communism walk backward." At the same time, however, Mitterrand stated that he would not hold the PCF responsible for what was happening in Czechoslovakia. The PCF Politburo then published a statement (which it had formulated at a meeting on 25 July) announcing that the party intended to make representations to the Czechoslovak leaders. While noting that the trials were indeed political and were therefore contrary to the PCF's principles, the Politburo statement continued to endorse the Czechoslovak party's goal of "defeating and isolating the enemies of socialism" even though the methods used were not acceptable (*L'Humanité,* 29 July). The CGT, also, issued a statement a few days later, which noted assurances that had been given that there would not be any political trials, and added: "The trials now in process, the political nature of which is obvious, contradict the assurances given, and the CGT deplores them most energetically" (ibid., 3 August).

Throughout the rest of the year, the PCF remained on the defensive with regard to Czechoslovakia, at the same time expressing solidarity with "socialist construction" in Eastern Europe and reiterating its contention that the issue of Czechoslovakia was being used by "reactionaries" to further an anti-Soviet campaign (see, e.g., ibid., 6 September).

The PCF's public pronouncements on Soviet foreign and domestic policies attempted to conciliate international communist solidarity with the priorities of domestic politics. With the increasing consolidation of the PCF-PS coalition, pro-Soviet sentiment became correspondingly guarded. In mid-February, the veteran PCF leader Jacques Duclos was awarded the Order of Lenin; on that occasion, he stated: "One cannot attack the homeland of the October Revolution without sliding toward anti-communism. . . . Even among those who support communism with words there are some who join these attacks. Yet, anti-Sovietism is inseparable from anti-communism." (*Le Monde,* 20–21 February.) By September, however, Georges Marchais—in a television debate—indicated that the position of the PCF was different from that of the CPSU on cultural matters (ibid., 15 September). At the party's Twentieth Congress, which was attended by a high-level CPSU delegation, led by Mikhail Suslov, Marchais spoke of "the errors and mistakes of the socialist countries," and added: "Our country's working people will build socialism with a consideration for the general principles which characterize it, the experience of other people, and our own traditions and national conditions. For there is not and cannot be a 'model' for socialism which can be transposed from one country to another." (Ibid., 14 December.) However, even though Suslov's presence at the congress was not given prominent coverage in the French communist media, and the Soviet media reciprocated with relatively low-key reports on the congress, PCF-CPSU relations do not appear to have been affected in any significant degree. In a section on the PCF's "international responsibilities," Marchais had referred to "differences of opinion on certain subjects," but had added:

> While retaining our critical judgment, our line of conduct is, and always will be, that of resolutely avoiding polemic and ensuring that such differences do not hinder joint action or lead to a weakening of the fraternal bonds which naturally unite all communist parties. (Ibid.)

In conformity to its alignment with the CPSU, the PCF continued to be highly critical of the Maoist leadership in China. While approving China's diplomatic overtures, the French communists claimed that "anti-Sovietism" continued to "characterize Chinese policy" and that it was leading "the Peking government to take measures harmful to itself and to the struggle of the peoples" (ibid., 2 October). In contrast to the attitude taken by the Italian Communist Party, the PCF was critical of U.S. President Nixon's visit to China, viewing Sino-American reapprochement as collusion against the Soviet Union. An article in *L'Humanité* (21 February) stated:

> Despite the perversion of words, one understands what Mr. Nixon hopes for from China. For him, it is essentially a matter of exploiting the Chinese leaders' break with the international communist movement, and to profit from their anti-Sovietism.

At the PCF congress, Marchais characterized as "deeply regrettable and harmful to the popular fight against imperialism that the Chinese Communist Party—which turned down, along with the Albanian Workers' Party, our invitation to participate in this 20th congress—stands apart from the world communist movement, delivering constant attacks against it and directing all its efforts against the Soviet Union" (ibid., 14 December).

Primarily through its auxiliary, the Peace Movement, the PCF organized a number of demonstrations over the issue of the war in Indochina. The largest of these, officially sponsored by the Peace Movement's parent organization, the World Peace Council, was the "World Assembly in Paris for Peace and Independence of the Indochinese Peoples," held on 11-13 February. It was attended by some 1,200 delegates from 84 countries, including representatives from 48 French organizations. Among the latter, the only significant absentee was the Trotskyist-controlled Indochina Solidarity Front (see below), which was refused admittance. The PCF itself played host at the end of July to a meeting of European communist parties on the issue of Vietnam. The gathering was attended by 27 foreign parties from Eastern and Western Europe (for listing see *L'Humanité,* 28 July).

With regard to French foreign policy, 1972 marked the first major attack by the PCF against the government for a number of years. Since, in the past, Gaullist foreign policy had been supported by the Soviet Union, the PCF's criticisms had been relatively muted. Contrasting President Pompidou's attitudes toward Vietnam (ibid., 6 January) and the Atlantic alliance (ibid., 12 January) with those held by the late President De Gaulle, Georges Marchais claimed that the Pompidou government was engaging in an "accelerated sliding toward Atlanticism, closer links with Washington, and a closer integration of French foreign policy with the general strategy of U.S. imperialism" (ibid., 6 January). The motivation for this strong attack appears, however, to have been primarily one of attempting to create a rift among Gaullist ranks by portraying Pompidou as being unfaithful to De Gaulle's legacy. Following the announcement in December of Pompidou's intention to visit the Soviet Union in January 1973, Marchais expressed his party's hopes that the trip would encourage the French government to "play a more active and independent role for the benefit of détente in Europe, put an end to its refusal to take part in disarmament negotiations, and strengthen Franco-Soviet cooperation." Marchais also added: "It is ridiculous to claim, as certain commentators are doing, that this meeting [between Pompidou and Brezhnev] could embarrass French communists because it is a few weeks before the parliamentary elections." (*L'Humanité,* 7 December).

International Party Contacts. In January, Etienne Fajon led a delegation to the fiftieth anniversary of the Communist Party of Chile; Raymond Guyot attended the Third Congress of the Lebanese Communist Party; and André Vieuguet met with leaders of the Italian Communist Party in Rome. In February, Roland Leroy made his aforementioned investigative trip to Czechoslovakia and Georges Marchais conferred with the communist leadership in East Germany. François Billoux was the PCF delegate at the Thirteenth Congress of the Italian Communist Party in March; during the same month, Gyorgy Aczel, secretary of the Hungarian Socialist Workers' Party, met with PCF leaders in Paris. In August, Gaston Plissonnier visited Poland, while Marchais was in Hungary. In September, Giorgio Napolitano, of the Italian Communist Party Political Office, met with PCF leaders in Paris, as did Edward Babiuch, Politburo and Secretariat member of the Polish United Workers' Party. The Polish party leader, Edward Gierek, conferred with the leadership of the PCF in Paris, in October; also, in the same month, Marchais was in Yugoslavia, while Fajon visited the Soviet Union. In November, Marchais met with leaders of the Communist Party of Great Britain in London. Finally, at the PCF's Twentieth Congress, in December, there were 58 foreign communist party delegations and 18 groups representing foreign "democratic and national" organizations —a total number which, according to Marchais, was "unprecedented" (*L'Humanité,* 18 December).

Publications. The main publications of the PCF in 1972 were: the daily newspaper *L'Humanité;* the weekly *France Nouvelle;* the monthly theoretical organ *Cahiers du Communisme;* a popular weekend magazine, *L'Humanité Dimanche;* a peasant weekly, *La Terre;* an intellectual monthly journal, *La Nouvelle Critique;* a literary monthly, *Europe;* a bimonthly economic journal, *Economie et Politique;* a philosophically oriented bimonthly, *La Pensée;* and a historical quarterly, *Les Cahiers de l'Institut Maurice-Thorez.* In addition the party has a number of provincial newspapers. The MJC published *Nous les Garçons et les Filles;* the UJCF's journal was *Le Nouveau Clarté,* a monthly. For intra-party work the Central Committee published *La Vie du Parti,* a monthly dealing with organizational, propaganda, educational, and other problems.

*   *   *

During 1972 there appeared to be a resurgence in support for heterogeneous views of the small groups that challenged the PCF from the left. This was exemplified by reaction to the death of René-Pierre Overney, a supporter of the Maoist Proletarian Left (see below), during a demonstration on 25 February at the Renault factory in the Paris suburb of Boulogne-Billancourt. Overney was reportedly shot by a factory guard. An initial protest demonstration three days later, organized primarily by Maoists and Trotskyists, brought out some 30,000 persons; on 4 March, Overney's funeral procession saw the most impressive left-wing demonstration in France since the traumatic events of May 1968—some 100,000 participated, including representatives of virtually all left-wing parties. The notable exception was the PCF. In a speech at Strasbourg on the evening after Overney's death, Georges Marchais referred to the murder as a "great boon to those in power" and evoked the specter of another May 1968. "I ask the question: Are we going to start all over again as in 1968? And I reply: No, that must not start all over again." On 28 February, the PCF Politburo issued a statement that noted the rise in "leftist" activism and claimed: "These are not isolated incidents, but rather a vast undertaking of political provocation benefiting the establishment!" The party denounced "the government's ill intention toward the people of France through manipulation of leftist groups" and called on its supporters to "outwit the establishment's plot." (*L'Humanité,* 28 February.)

The nature of resurgence among groups to the left of the PCF was difficult to determine. The February-March demonstrations were not followed by any other significantly large ones. On the other hand, the potential for, at least a temporary, coalition of contending groups was demonstrated. Moreover, the nature of the PCF response engendered an additional unifying force. A statement by a number of left-wing intellectuals, published in *Le Monde* (17 March), concluded: "The real struggle against the capitalist system of bondage is, henceforth, inseparable from the struggle against the French Communist Party in its endeavor to pervert the communist idea."

During 1972, there continued to be over a dozen extreme-left organizations that challenged the PCF. With the apparent decline in Maoist sentiment, Trotskyism represented the most significant orientation.

Trotskyists. The two principal Trotskyist movements were: the Communist League (Ligue Communiste), aligned with the United Secretariat of the Fourth International; and the Internationalist Communist Organization (Organisation Communiste Internationaliste; OCI), which, together with its youth movement, the Alliance of Youth for Socialism (Alliance des Jeunes pour le Socialisme; AJS), and a so-called Federation of Workers' Alliance Committees

(Fédération des Comités d'Alliance Ouvrière), was affiliated with the International Committee of the Fourth International. Although opposed to one another, both groups trace their origins to an erstwhile united Trotskyist movement, founded in 1938.[1]

In 1972 the Communist League claimed a membership of 6,000. In contrast to other extreme-left organizations throughout the country, support for its views appeared to be growing significantly. In addition to the veteran Pierre Frank, the most prominent spokesmen of the League during the year were: Daniel Bensaïd, Gérard Filoche, Alain Krivine (who, in 1969, was candidate for the French presidency—obtaining 239,000 votes), Charles Michaloux, Michel Recanati, Pierre Rousset, and Henri Weber. They were all re-elected to the leadership of the League at the latter's Third Congress, held the beginning of December. The League is active through a number of auxiliary organizations. The principal ones during the year were: the Indochina Solidarity Front (Front Solidarité Indochine; FSI), which was formed in 1971 and which, at its first national assembly in December 1972, claimed 162 affiliated committees (61 from Paris and its suburbs and 101 from the provinces); the National Federation of Struggle Committees (Fédération Nationale des Comités de Lutte; FNCL), organized in 25 universities; and the High School Front of Red Centers (Front des Cercles Rouges Lycéens; FCRL). The Communist League publishes a weekly newspaper, *Rouge*. François Maspero, owner of a major publishing house, is a member of the League. In 1972 Maspero published the League's 172-page program—*Manifeste de la Ligue Communiste*.

The Internationalist Communist Organization and its affiliates had an equal number of members. Unlike the Communist League, however, they tended to stay apart from the actions organized by other extreme-left groups that opposed the PCF. In fact, in 1972, the OCI appeared to be aligning itself closely with the communist-socialist bid for power (see, e.g., *Informations Ouvrières*, 26 April–3 May). During the year the most prominent leaders of this branch of French Trotskyism were Pierre Lambert, Stéphane Just and Charles Berg. The movement has a certain impact among students by virtue of its control over UNEF. Pierre Nesterenko and Jean-Claude Boksenbaum, secretary-general and international vice-president of UNEF respectively, represented French students at the Executive Committee meeting of the pro-Soviet International Union of Students, held in Warsaw on 26–29 January. They were both expelled from Poland after denouncing "normalization" in Czechoslovakia. Subsequently, the OCI and the AJS organized numerous protest meetings (see ibid., 2–9 February and subsequent issues). The AJS has a student affiliate, the Alliance of Revolutionary Students (Alliance des Etudiants Révolutionnaires; AER) and a high school organization, the Union of High School Centers (Union des Cercles Lycéens; UCL). The principal publications of this Trotskyist movement are: *La Venté*, a bi-monthly journal of the OCI; *Jeune Révolutionnaire*, the monthly organ of the AJS; and *Informations Ouvrières*, a weekly newspaper of the Federation of Workers' Alliance Committees. Since the 1971 split in the International Committee, which pitted the OCI against the British Socialist Labour League, the French Trotskyists also have been issuing *La Correspondance Internationale*, an irregular bulletin of the International Committee. The OCI has its own publishing house, Société d'Edition, Librairie Informations Ouvrières (SELIO).

Maoists. Support for pro-Chinese groups continued to wane, despite the mass demonstrations organized following the death of Maoist René-Pierre Overney (see above).

---

[1] For historical background on the French Trotskyist movement, see Pierre Frank, *La quatrième internationale* (Paris: François Maspero, 1969), a book written from the point of view of the United Secretariat; Stéphane Just, *Défense du Trotskysme* (published in two parts—in a special issue of *La Verité*, September 1965, and in a separate book entitled *Révisionnisme liquidateur contre le Trotskysme* [Paris: SELIO, 1971]), an analysis presenting the views of the International Committee; and, for the more recent past, *YICA, 1968* to *1972*.

Orthodox pro-Chinese orientation was centered around the weekly newspaper, *L'Humanité Rouge,* which represented the views of former members of the Marxist-Leninist Communist Party of France (Parti Communiste Marxiste-Léniniste de France; PCMLF), a group dissolved by government decree in June 1968.[1] During the year, *L'Humanité Rouge* gave broad coverage to international developments—from a pro-Chinese perspective—and issued polemical critiques of other extreme-left organizations (see, e.g., "Face au Fauchisme Moderne," a ninety-five page supplement to *L'Humanité Rouge,* no. 155, 1972). The group's supporters were active in the Franco-Chinese Friendship Association (Association des Amitiés Franco-Chinoises) and in the Franco-Albanian Friendship Association (Association des Amitiés Franco-Albanaises), which sponsored various solidarity meetings. The group's leading spokesman during 1972 continued to be Jacques Jurquet. The militants of *L'Humanité Rouge* were the only ones claiming to be Maoist who had relations with the People's Republic of China.

The only other significant Maoist grouping during the year was the one centered around the weekly *La Cause du Peuple,* published by philosopher Jean-Paul Sartre, and whose supporters included most of the former members of the Proletarian Left (Gauche Prolétarienne), an organization banned in May 1970 (see *YICA, 1971,* pp. 168–69). The leading spokesman for this violence-oriented group was Alain Geismar. Some of the supporters of *La Cause du Peuple* were active in a clandestine "army" known as the New Popular Resistance (Nouvelle Résistance Populaire; NRP). On 4 March 1972 NRP militants kidnapped Robert Nogrette, an assistant personnel director at the Renault auto plant where Overney had been killed. Although Geismar called the kidnapping "logical and normal," the action was condemned by most of the other extreme-left organizations. Nogrette was released on 10 March.

Hoover Institution
Stanford University

Milorad Popov

---

[1] Reports in 1971 (see *YICA, 1972,* p. 156) and in 1972 (see *Le Monde,* 15 March and 1 August) indicated that the PCMLF was still operating underground and clandestinely publishing its original newspaper, *L'Humanité Nouvelle.*

Germany: Federal Republic of Germany

The reestablishment of a communist party in the Federal Republic of Germany (FRG) was announced on 22 September 1968 under the name, German Communist Party (Deutsche Kommunistische Partei; DKP). The preexisting Communist Party of Germany (Kommunistische Partei Deutschlands; KPD), founded on 31 December 1918, had functioned with little effectiveness from 1933 to 1945; reconstituted in the Western sectors of occupation in 1945, it was outlawed on 17 August 1956 as having purposes and methods incompatible with Article 21/2 of the FRG constitution.

When the DKP was founded, the KPD still existed as an underground party. In fact, a campaign was started in 1967 to set aside the 1956 judgment. In 1968, a new KPD program was promulgated and top KPD personnel reentered the country. In the summer of that year, the DKP was organized. Its congress in 1971 called for legalization of the KPD, and a committee continues to pursue this goal.

According to its chairman Kurt Bachmann, the DKP is no substitute for the KDP. Yet virtually all DKP founding members and numerous officials of the party are KPD graduates. KPD chairman Max Reimann, who returned to the FRG in 1968, was elected honorary president of the DKP on 25 November 1971. It is not known whether he or any DKP official resigned from the old party. The KPD, which supposedly counted 7,000 underground members in 1968, seemingly was not engaged in newsworthy activity in 1972.

Evidently the top leadership decided that a legal communist party was needed in the FRG, but that the KPD should be kept in reserve. There appear to be several reasons for this decision. (1) Probably because of the U.S.S.R.'s troubles with Czechoslovakia and China, and the danger that an effective Maoist party might suddenly emerge in the FRG, reestablishment of an active party was an urgent matter. (2) To win a court case, reformulations of the KPD program and denials of past practices would have been required. This was unacceptable. (3) The judgment against the KPD is still in force and may serve as a precedent for outlawing the DKP. Consequently, to ensure its own survival, the DKP must work for voiding of the judgment, and it must do so on constitutional grounds. This operation is apt to advance communist purposes, but it requires a live DKP and a resurrectable KPD. The DKP does not have the word "Deutschland" in its name, and therefore its responsibilities are restricted to the Federal Republic; the dormant KPD remains available to play an all-German role. This parallel existence within one country of two communist parties, both recognized by the Soviet-oriented international movement as regular parties in good standing, represents an anomaly. But it conforms with the general line that "fraternal parties" must never split, though they may pursue different approaches whenever those fit their particular situation. (For the general background see Helmut Bärwald, *Deutsche Kommunistische Partei—die Kommunistische Bündnispolitik in Deutschland,* Cologne, 1970.)

Leadership and Organization. At the time of its First Congress (Essen, 12–13 April 1969), the DKP claimed a membership of 22,000. The Second Congress (Düsseldorf, 25–28 November 1971) put the number at 33,410. By February 1972 the figure stood at 34,000 and during the FRG elections the party picked up some 2,200 new members for a total of 36,233. Some 63 percent are over 40 years of age. The party organ, *Unsere Zeit,* claims a circulation of 40,000 copies.

The DKP headquarters is in Düsseldorf. The party is organized into 14 districts, covering all of West Germany. By November 1972 there were some 1,300 industrial and residential cells. In addition, there were about two dozen DKP-affiliated groups in universities. The following may be regarded as DKP affiliates: German Union for Peace (Deutsche Friedensunion; DFU); Young German Democrats (Deutsche Jung-Demokraten; DJD); Young Friends of Nature (Naturfreunde-Jugend); Union of Independent Socialists (Vereinigung Unabhängiger Sozialisten; VUS); Union of Those Who Refuse Military Service (Verband der Kriegsdienstverweigerer), which is affiliated with War Resisters' International; South German Peasants' Assembly (Süddeutscher Bauernkonvent), which may not be a consistent collaborator; Societas Populorum Progressio, an ecumenical action group of politicized Christians who seem to entertain an intermittent relationship; and Union of Persecuted by the Nazi Regime (Vereinigung der Verfolgten des Naziregimes; VVN), which is affiliated with the Union of Anti-Fascists (Bund der Antifaschisten).

The German Socialist Workers' Youth (Sozialistische Deutsche Arbeiterjugend; SDAJ) was founded on 4 May 1968, just prior to the creation of the DKP. It reportedly has 10,000 or more members.

Student organizations are politically the most influential adjunct of the DKP—notably the Spartakus Marxist Student Union (Marxistischer Studentenbund Spartakus) founded in May 1971 at Bonn. (Spartakus, with "k," must not be confused with Spartacus, with "c," which is a Trotskyite competitor.) In 1971 Spartakus claimed 500 members; during 1972 it grew to 2,000 and possibly 3,000 members, dispersed among some 40 universities and colleges. By 1972 it had interlocking directorates with the National Union of Students (Verband Deutscher Studenten; VDS) and with student groups operating openly under the DKP label. Spartakus also was linked with the Social Democratic University Union (Sozialdemokratischer Hochschulbund; SHB), originally an organization of the Social-Democratic Party (SPD). In June 1972 the SPD decided that the SHB was no longer entitled to use the party name; its expulsion was confirmed in court on 29 November. For all practical purposes, the SHB has fallen —at least temporarily—under DKP guidance.

DKP Leadership. At the end of 1972 all the top officials elected by the Second Congress were still in office. Kurt Bachmann is party chairman, Herbert Mies deputy chairman, and Max Reimann honorary president. (For other names see *YICA, 1972,* p. 159.) There is a 15-member Presidium (i.e., Politburo) and 7-member Secretariat. The *Parteivorstand* (Central Committee) has 91 members. The party also has a 9-member Arbitration Commission and a 7-member Review or Control Commission, which handles finances and perhaps carries additional responsibilities. Rolf-Jürgen Priemer is chairman of the SDAJ; Christoph Strawe runs Spartakus.

Finances. West German authorities have estimated that in 1970 the party's income was 800,000 marks. This estimate was inaccurate, if one is to believe a Control Commission statement to the Second Congress that in 1969 the party had an eight-month income of nearly 2.5 million marks and a twelve-month income in 1970 exceeding 6 million marks—the latter attributed to "the fact that the income from membership fees rose by nearly 40 per cent and the income from donations by 64 per cent." The source of donations was not divulged, nor was information on expenditures. It was stated that income did not suffice to discharge future tasks. (*Protokoll des Düsseldorfer Parteitags der Deutschen Kommunistischen Partei,* Hamburg, 1971, pp. 57 ff.) West German authorities estimated that 1970 expenses were 16 million marks; if so, the deficit was 10 million marks. It is unlikely that 1972 income from membership fees much exceeded 2 million marks—at the most, 4 million if each member paid 10 marks per month. The party has had about 100 full-time employees, at monthly salaries of 800–1,000 marks (*Der Spiegel,* no. 24, 1971). Assuming that the number of employees did not increase, fixed salaries alone would cost about 1 million marks: income from fees should suffice, at best, to pay salaries, office expenditures, rent, and some transportation. Part of the cost for the Düsseldorf congress was covered by a special 20-mark assessment and by collections, but it is not certain that a deficit was avoided.

Thus, the large operational expenses for education, printing, propaganda, postage, posters, meetings, demonstrations, and "actions" must be covered by donations, of which only a small fraction can possibly originate from members and sympathizers in the FRG. Pointing to the obvious, namely, that the party's successes depend in large measure on adequate funding, Bachmann in an interview (*Komsomolskaya pravda,* Moscow, 20 October 1972) complained about monetary difficulties. Since the party displayed considerable energy throughout 1972, a broad stream of donations must have been flowing in from outside.

West German election campaigns require substantial outlays for posters, advertising, TV, brochures, leaflets, and postage. The four major parties expended 220 million marks on the 1972 national elections. Most of this came from the SPD, but even the small Free German Party spent 17.5 million marks. (*Dialog,* Bonn, no. 1, 1973, pp. 14 ff.) The DKP remained visible during the entire campaign, and its expenditures must have been considerable.

Basic Principles. The First Congress adopted a charter which is carefully written to avoid constitutional difficulty. It expostulates a wide-ranging program dealing with peace, imperialism, disarmament, European security, social insecurity, rightist and "nazi" policies and parties, the goal of progressive and expanding democracy and of democratic rejuvenation for state and society, education improvements, better living standards, and cultural progress. (See *Grundsatzerklärung der Deutschen Kommunistischen Partei,* Hamburg, 1969.) Couched in pseudo-democratic terminology, the party charter restates communist orthodoxy without significant modernizations.

Party Internal Affairs. Little is known about intra-party disputes, if any, on ideology, tactics or personalities. But the party was, of course, confronted with several serious problems.

Terrorism. On the one hand, the DKP must regard all young extremists as potential recruits. Throughout the year it, accordingly, tried to extend its hold over the whole extra-parliamentary movement and, largely through Spartakus among students, achieved surprising success in these endeavors.

The extremist camp, though largely under DKP influence, includes elements dedicated to terrorism and "adventurism." This generated bad publicity for the party. It is most unlikely that the DKP or any secret agency of the German Democratic Republic or the U.S.S.R. was involved with the terrorist Mahler-Meinhof-Baader gang (which the West German police had emasculated by mid-1972). The leaders of this group considered themselves communists and took the name "Red Army Fraction" (RAF), asserting that their tactics had been employed by Lenin which is quite true. They frequently criticized the DKP as cowardly, opportunistic, and revisionist. RAF plainly wanted to create chaos in the FRG. Whenever it committed an outrage, the German public—without listening to learned disquisitions about the fine distinctions among communists—put the blame on the DKP.

To make things worse, the RAF—a small group of not over 50 persons, half of whom were women—enjoyed the support of a far larger circle of "radical chic" sympathizers. Moreover, the RAF had links with foreign terrorist groups, all of whom also claim to be fighting under the flag of communism.

During May the RAF, due to lax internal security, became more active than ever and in three weeks of political violence at Frankfurt, Munich, Karlsruhe, Augsburg, Hamburg and Heidelberg killed 4 persons and wounded 40. On 20 May the DKP Central Committee took a strong position against terrorism. It recommended "democratic struggle actions" instead of terror, and declared: "The aims and methods of sectarian adventurers and provocateurs have nothing in common with the labor movement and are unequivocally condemned" (*Unsere Zeit,* no. 22, p. 30). On 2 June the RAF used bomb threats to halt traffic in the center of Stuttgart. During June most gang members, including the leaders, were arrested.

The outrage at the Olympic games reactivated the issue because, according to the London *Times* (6 September), the Black September terrorists had been in touch with the RAF and reportedly coordinating operations since February. (According to some sources, the RAF housed the Arab terrorists, helped them to remain physically fit, and supplied the weapons.) At an earlier time, RAF personnel had been trained at Al Fatah camps in the Middle East. Further investigations disclosed links, through a coordinating office at Zurich, of Black September and the German RAF with the Red Army Fraction of Japan, the Tupamaros of Uruguay, the IRA of Ireland, and the Jura Liberation Front of Switzerland.

These interrelationships remain largely obscure. Nevertheless, it is known that Arab terrorists have repeatedly traveled to the GDR. Al Fatah weapons reportedly were obtained from the Soviet bloc. In the U.N. General Assembly, U.S.S.R. foreign minister Gromyko decried the terrorism at the Olympics, but the Soviet bloc voted against effective measures to stop international terrorism. In this respect, then, the image of the DKP, and especially of Spartakus, remains ambiguous.

Constitutional Status. By the end of the year, the party also ran into legal difficulties. The DKP claim that its objectives are compatible with the FRG constitution was rejected by the Administrative Court at Bremen in November. This tribunal also dismissed the contention that DKP members are legally entitled to civil service posts. (*Die Welt,* 3 January 1973.) The judgment explained that since the DKP bases itself on Marx, Engels, and Lenin, and wishes to emulate the U.S.S.R. and GDR model, where there never were free opposition parties nor free elections, it must necessarily regard the dictatorship of the proletariat as the indispensible prerequisite for realization of its goals. Although specific objectives like the "socialization" of the means of production might be constitutionally permissible, no dictatorship can be reconciled with a free and democratic order.

Elections. The DKP Central Committee met in plenary session on 24–25 June; coincidentally, on 24 June Chancellor Willy Brandt announced that there would be general elections in November. The DKP decided to participate in the elections, on the grounds that communists were needed in the Bundestag and that parliamentary work, being linked with mass movements and the democratic activity of the population, should be prepared and influenced by extra-parliamentary actions. In particular, DKP participation was meant to prove that the SPD and its coalition partner subordinated the interests of the workers to those of the monopolists. (*Unsere Zeit,* no. 28, p. 5.) In other words, although "dialectic politics" of having it both ways tends to weaken credibility, the DKP upgraded splitting without abandoning *Bündnispolitik* (policy of united actions).

On 29 September another plenary session decided to base the DKP campaign on the notion that the CDU and CSU were parties of the right, that German democracy was menaced from the right, and that the SPD was a center party which had made its peace with capitalism. By this adjustment of perspective, the DKP shifted the center of the German political spectrum toward the left. As a result, the DKP—together with all other communist groups— occupies the left wing, the leftists can be pitted against the center, and left and center groups oppose the right. This concept of a leftward moving middle seems to have been persuasive to many Germans, and it may remain significant far into the future. By contrast, the communist line that a Christian Democratic Union (CDU/CSU) government would place the Federal Republic under the rule of "U.S. imperialism" and that a strong DKP vote would force the SPD into accepting workers' demands proved less convincing.

Bachmann explained (*Komsomolskaya pravda,* 20 October) that the DKP pursued three major goals: to bloc the CDU/CSU; to put pressure on the SPD; and to broaden the DKP audience. He added that the party had candidates in all 248 electoral districts and that the candidates included representatives from SDAJ and Spartakus. The campaign, which reflected the 44 theses of 1971 and concentrated on foreign and social policy, was conducted aggressively.

The DKP voting potential must be estimated at a minimum of 2 percent. In 1953, the KPD attained 2.2 percent, down from a peak of 5.7 percent in 1949. In 1969, the DKP did not participate in the elections, but set up the *Aktion Demokratischer Fortschritt* (Action for Democratic Progress). This organization did not have much time to make itself known to the electorate, yet some 200,000 votes (0.6 percent) were secured. In comparison with those results, the election of 19 November 1972 turned into a disaster: the DKP secured only 114,000 ballots or 0.3 percent of the vote. The party made only a slightly better showing in the Länder elections of Lower Saxony and Hessen during October. A handful of communists occupy uncertain seats in a few municipal legislatures.

The plenary session on 20 November voiced its dissatisfaction and called for stronger efforts in the future. Bachmann explained that the low number of votes did not reflect the political influence of the party and that many potential DKP voters, to keep the CDU/CSU out of power, had voted for the SPD-FDP coalition. Bachmann was probably correct on the first count, but there is no way to prove that communists in any substantial numbers endorsed the SPD ticket. (FBIS, 21 November, p. U 2.) The DKP probably committed a tactical error in competing for the Bundestag and departing from the role of prompter, pioneer, initiator, and protagonist of united actions. East German leader Walter Ulbricht's concept of 1969, according to which it should be possible to create a Marxist-Leninist combat party in West Germany to force the Federal Republic to peaceful coexistence with the socialist camp and to unite all classes against "West German imperialism" (see Bärwald, op. cit., p. 79) turned out to be utterly impractical in 1972. The DKP had no power to "force" West Germany into anything and, unable to break out into a really modernized version of socialism, it did not prove a credible persuader.

Domestic Views and Activities. The Second Congress approved 44 theses on which the propaganda of 1972 was based (*Protokoll des Düsseldorfer Parteitags,* pp. 298–358.) The plenary sessions of the Central Committee dealt mostly with current priorities and elaborations. The session of 26–27 February propounded the slogan that no problem can be solved without or against the communists; ever stronger opposition against rightist organizations was advocated; great interest was shown in furthering the trends of changing public opinion, especially with respect to the supposedly unjustified fear that there could be any Soviet threat to Western Europe. The party was instructed to claim credit for its "major contributions" to the treaty negotiations between the FRG and the Eastern bloc. These themes of high policy were interwoven with propaganda for bread-and-butter issues—wages, prices, job security, public works, nationalization, support of peasants, and so on. Proposals for reforms were advocated together with the proposal that financing should be achieved through armaments reduction by installments of 15 percent, until the military budget would be reduced by half. The DKP also pushed for the prosecution of tax delinquents and financial manipulators, cessation of capital exports, cancelation of subventions to monopolies, and higher taxation on higher incomes.

Much of this repertory was reconfirmed by the session of 20 May, but at that time propaganda about the Eastern treaties was given highest priority. Advantages which would accrue to the FRG from economic and cultural relations with the bloc were highlighted. The treaties, it was argued for the benefit of party members, would facilitate the change of force and class relationships within the FRG. They would favor the "democratic" camp and improve the chances of the "struggle by the working class." The DKP also called for withdrawal of U.S. troops.

United Actions. One of the main purposes of DKP propaganda was to effect united actions, notably with "Jusos" (young socialists within the SPD), students, and trade unions. In varying degrees these three groups have been moving in the direction of left radicalism.

The DKP believes that without a resolute initiator, student organizations, Jusos, young and old unionists, and unorganized juveniles would not attend demonstrations and other actions in the streets. It proposes to be that catalyst, to bring about joint actions by all anti-monopolistic forces, and in the end gather them together in one "democratic association." During 1972 several united actions were promoted by the DKP inside and outside the universities. In most instances, those actions were designed to embarrass and paralyze the SPD leadership. As the DKP had hoped, these initiatives intensified the class struggle.

United actions were developed in connection with strikes in the transportation, metal, and chemical industries. During the April crisis, when the Brandt government was almost overthrown and the FRG-U.S.S.R. treaty nearly scuttled, "warning strikes" were launched to intimidate the CDU/CSU opposition in parliament. A noisy demonstration was mounted at Bonn. Widespread insurrectional activity was threatened in case the treaty were to fail and the government fall.

These DKP moves were coordinated with communist threats from the outside. As early as 3 March, Valentin Bereshkov, Russian vice-president of the Soviet-West German Friendship Society, suggested that rejection of Bonn's treaties with Moscow and Warsaw might lead to a new round in the cold war and possibly to a hot war. Soviet foreign minister Gromyko on 12 April, before the Supreme Soviet, voiced concern about the possibility of "a profound crisis of [Soviet] confidence in the policy of the Federal Republic, with all the resultant consequences." On 17 April CPSU Politburo member M. A. Suslov indicated the FRG "would lose its significance for the Soviet Union as an important economic partner." On 25 April East German party chief Honecker added warnings. Although the strikes were not on a large scale, they unquestionably rendered the threats more ominous.

Prior to the national elections in November, posters appeared in South Germany which, in the name of the SPD-controlled trade unions, called for a general strike in case the CDU/CSU should win. It appears that the unions did not originate the posters. There were mutual recriminations between SPD and CDU/CSU about this forgery. Some observers believe that the DKP, in fact, was preparing for massive counter-actions against a "rightist" electoral success. The DKP may have been the culprit, but initiatives by dissident radical groups within the SPD and the unions were just as likely.

In December the party, once again, criticized "left opportunists" and "sham revolutionaries:" the idea of instant revolution through terrorism was rejected—revolution must be accomplished by stages. The left deviationists were preventing the emergence of "revolutionary scientific consciousness regarding the laws of social development" and, thus, betraying the revolution. In order to prevent antagonism between the DKP and the "deviationists" in the FRG, the point was made by an SED-organ in the GDR. (*Horizont,* East Berlin, 4 December.) By the end of 1972, when it was a matter of reactivating Juso opposition to SPD leadership, substantial pressure was generated and student unrest flared up again.

The DKP also seemed intent upon united action of a less radical type: through Spartakus, SDAJ, SHB, and VDS, it obtained agreement from the Jusos and the trade union youth group (DGB-Jugend) to participate in the tenth World Youth Festival, planned for 1973 in East Berlin. The participation of DGB-Jugend was predicated on a number of conditions which may or may not be fulfilled, and an invitation to the Falcons, the SPD's very large youth organization, had not been acted upon by 29 December. Success or failure of this venture will provide clues on the effectiveness of the DKP's *Bündnispolitik*.

DKP-SPD. Already in 1972 some of the limits of this policy became visible. For example, during the third plenary session of the DKP Central Committee, Bachmann took credit for saving the Brandt government in the spring. The party had indeed been active, but the majority of the strikers and demonstrators were trade union or SDP members. The actions were not initiated by the DKP but, apparently, by the Jusos, with at least tacit approval from SPD leaders. If indeed, Bachmann's claim were justified, the DKP would have kept the rightist SPD leadership in power, which otherwise it wanted to eliminate. SPD leaders were conciliatory during 1972 and in crucial test cases, including anti-American demonstrations, it was the SPD which benefited from DKP support. The SPD was practicing the united actions which the DKP had preached.

The DKP analysis of the SPD and of the DGB (Deutscher Gewerkschaftsbund—German Trade Union Association) is correct: the social democrats are split into a moderate reform group, which in 1972 held the majority, and the 200,000-odd Jusos, some of whom are moving into party power positions. If, then, the SPD were to join a united front with the DKP, the moderate majority would have to move strongly to the left, which is possible but unlikely; or the Jusos would have to transform the SPD and place it under radical control. The chances of such an occurrence are slight. Besides, a takeover by unreconstructed Jusos probably would split the SPD and ruin the project of uniting the left.

For a while, there occurred experimentation with symbiotic arrangements: Juso individuals were repeatedly invited to participate in DKP meetings, and DKP members attended SPD meetings and possibly took part in intra-party votes. (Bärwald, op. cit., p. 127.) As could have been expected, the experiment failed.

It is widely believed that the DKP has been infiltrating the SPD successfully. Many self-styled communists went from radical revolutionary groups into the SPD and swelled Juso ranks. But the DKP needs all the members it can attract within its own organization; Jusos, who become highly radicalized and turn against democracy, are perhaps entering the DKP. At the 1971 congress, a group of former Juso officials presented a declaration against the SPD. The 25 signers promptly joined the DKP (*Protokoll des Düsseldorfer Parteitags,* pp. 565 ff.).

The DKP and the Jusos do not identify with one another. For example, the DKP supports Juso willingness to fight against "fascism" and also favors the transfer "of monopoly enterprises to the utilization and responsibility of society as a whole." But it disagrees with democratic socialism, which the Jusos do not care to abandon. As of 26 December, the Jusos, in a formal discussion about the SPD's long-range program, declared their willingness to engage in class struggle, but they also reiterated their commitment to democratic socialism. (*Die Welt,* 27 December.) However, the most radical Jusos believe that preservation of the free enterprise system is less important than reunification of Germany, which is to be achieved through linked changes in both German states, especially the establishment of democratic socialism and emasculation of conservative elites in the FRG. (Ibid., 17 January 1973.) But the SED/GDR rejects changes, and the CPSU/U.S.S.R. want, no German reunification.

In any event, it would be a misinterpretation to think that the DKP infiltrates by sending its own members into the SPD, although this may happen in a few key instances. Ideological persuasion remains the essence of infiltration and the chief purpose is to obtain as many Jusos as possible to support, or acquiesce in, overall communist policy.

A large percentage of the Jusos has been veering more and more toward communist positions in social, economic, military, and international areas. But the broad mass is hardly interested in helping the communists to the detriment of their own party. The SPD would like to establish the workers as the "formative social force in the state," but there is no reason to assume that it wants to abdicate in favor of the DKP. The fact is that SHB was evicted by the SPD because it engaged in a "people's front" with Spartakus. The SPD decided, in February 1971, against united action with the communists, and Chancellor Brandt confirmed this line on 20 August 1972. Nevertheless, by the end of the year, united actions were instigated by the Jusos, and the SPD leadership voiced no objection. (Ibid.).

Instead of being a pace-setter, the DKP, so far, has proven to be little more than an echo and an amplifier. The truly strategic initiative for *Bündnispolitik* has not been in DKP hands. This may change, but the presumably durable obstacle to this policy is that the DKP cannot afford to promote a break-up of the SPD.

Education. The DKP conducts a training program, Marxist Workers' Education, in Frankfurt; the Institute for Marxist Studies and Research, also in Frankfurt; and the Karl Liebknecht party school, in Essen.

International Party Contacts. During 1972 the DKP maintained customary relations with the international movement. There were contacts with the "fraternal parties" of Denmark, Finland, France, Greece, Israel, Italy, Lebanon, Spain, and Turkey. The DKP played host to delegations from the United States and Chile. Bachmann visited Poland in September, and he and other party leaders were guests in the Soviet Union and the East European countries. Visits by DKP personnel to the GDR are routine.

Publications. The DKP party organ is the weekly *Unsere Zeit,* published in Düsseldorf. The party also issues *Bonner Korrespondenz—DKP Informationsdienst; Landrevue,* on agricultural problems; *Marxistische Blätter,* a theoretical organ published in Frankfurt; and "Marxistische Taschenbücher," a book series of theoretical texts. In Dortmund, the SDAJ prints *Elan,* a weekly with a circulation of 20,000 copies. *Frontal,* organ of the SHB, and *Offen und Frei,* a communist weekly, have indirect links with the party.

As of February 1972, the party reportedly published 326 district papers with a total distribution of 500,000 copies, 235 local papers with a total of 150,000 copies, and 408 factory papers with an undisclosed circulation. The party operates at least 18 bookstores and controls one publishing firm.

*　　*　　*

Rival Communists. In 1971 the Bonn government identified some 250 leftist groups, of which 130 were described as "orthodox-communist." There were 20 Maoist, 5 Trotskyite, and 5 anarchist organizations. Since the leading groups often used different names at various locations, the effective number may have been smaller, aside from the fact that this total reflects a large number of splits. The Trotskyite groups comprised 400 members; there were 800

Maoists and 80 anarchists. The extremist grouplets published 420 newspapers, with a total circulation of 2 million, including 320 papers (1,650,000 copies) which espoused the "orthodox" communist line. During 1970, a million copies of revolutionary journals were printed each month. (Gerd Langguth, *Protestbewegung am Ende,* Mainz, 1971, pp. 61 f.)

The Communist Party of Germany (Marxist-Leninist)—KPD/ML—was founded on 31 December 1968. At one time, it was the leading Maoist group. However, since it praised Stalin, the KPD/ML, along with all other "Marxist-Leninist" groups of the "extra-parliamentary opposition" (APO) can best be described as "Maoist-Stalinist." The KPD/ML opposed the DKP on the grounds that "its founding was due to agreements and collusions with the reactionary and bourgeois system." The aim of this Hamburg-based Maoist movement, which included a Red Guard youth group, was to smash the bourgeois state apparatus. It was led by Ernst Aust, formerly associated with the outlawed Soviet-oriented KPD. In June 1970 the Bochum-based KPD/ML split off and gave birth to a third group, which subsequently joined the KB/ML (see below). On 31 December 1971 the Hamburg-based KPD/ML held a congress and dissolved itself into "liquidators, conciliators, and Austists."

There also existed a KPD/ML-Bolschewiki, a KPD/ML Neue Einheit (New Unity), a KPD/ML-Revolutionärer Weg (Revolutionary Path), and a Kommunistischer Arbeiterbund KAP/ML. The Kommunistische Bund/Marxisten-Leninisten (KB/ML) operated largely in West Berlin. To judge by the name, it seemed to be Titoist or Old Left-Marxist, but it also adhered to democratic centralism. The Proletarische Front, created in February 1970 and related to the tricontinental movement, appeared to be both anti-Soviet and anti-Maoist. A descendant of the West German SDS, enigmatically entitled Proletarische Linke-Partei-Initiative or PL/PI, preached a Soviet type of democracy—in this context the term "soviet" meant a workers' parliament in the style of 1905 or 1917.

The KPD Aufbauorganisation (KPD/AO)—meaning organization to rebuild the KPD—was founded in 1970 by students, after the demise of SDS. It assumed the name KPD in July 1971. This is, or was, a Stalinist group.

Finally, there are two main Trotskyite groups which under the motto "class struggle instead of people's war," hope to build up the Fourth International. Internationale Kommunisten Deutschlands (IKP)—the group which runs Spartacus (with "c") and has among its leaders Peter Brandt, son of the FRG chancellor—competes with Gruppe Internationaler Marxisten (GIM). (Langguth, op. cit., provides information on publications, biographies, and lists additional "parties." Various programs are reprinted in *Die Partei Aufbauen, Plattformen, Grundsatzerklärungen,* Berlin, 1971.)

Mental unrest continues in the midst of much revolutionary oratory, and almost any skilled organizer, if he has a little money and much energy, should be able to give birth to a "combat party." Few would-be *Führers* ever fail to baptize the new infant with the customary names. In earlier times German youngsters disguised themselves as Indians and cowboys, and reenacted the "Wild West." During the 1960s and early 1970s, they have posed as bearded Marxists and played revolution. If there is a dramatic and emotion-charged political crisis, most of the extremist splinter groups and substantial numbers of non-organized revolutionaries are at the beck and call of the DKP or the Jusos—whoever calls first.

Hoover Institution   Stefan T. Possony
Stanford University

Germany: West Berlin

The Socialist Unity Party of West Berlin (Sozialististische Einheitspartei Westberlin; SEW) was founded on 27 November 1958, in response to a Kremlin decision to attempt the transformation of West Berlin into a "free city." On 26 April 1959, organizations of the Socialist Unity Party of Germany (SED) which operated in the western sectors of Berlin assumed a status of independence, and on 24 November 1962, a statute was promulgated for the new party, which styled itself Socialist Unity Party of Germany—West Berlin (SED-W). The term "Germany" was dropped in 1969. This change was to indicate that only the SED—the ruling party in the German Democratic Republic (GDR)—is responsible for the whole of "Deutschland" and that the other German communist parties merely accomplish tasks within certain areas like West Berlin and the Federal Republic of Germany (FRG). Put differently: the SEW is subordinate to the SED.

The SEW adopted its statute formally during its First Congress, 21–22 May 1966. The Second Congress took place on 22–24 May 1970. The Third Congress was an event of 1972 (see below). It reelected the existing leadership.

Leadership and Organization. Gerhard Danelius and Erich Ziegler serve as party chairman and deputy chairman, respectively. (For Politburo and Secretariat members see *YICA, 1972*, pp. 27–28.)

During 1971, SEW membership was estimated at about 7,000. In the elections of 14 March 1971, the party polled some 34,000 votes, or 2.3 percent of the West Berlin total. About 70,000 West Berliners demonstrated in the streets on 1 May 1972, but this was a "united action" in which several leftist organizations participated. The SEW cannot claim a followership of such magnitude. It is, however, probable that SEW membership grew during 1972.

The SEW's subsidiaries include the Free German Youth (FDJ-West Berlin), which also has units for children. Peter Klaar is in charge of youth activities. Other SEW organizations are the Society for German-Soviet Friendship (DSF—West Berlin), Democratic Association of Women (DFD-West Berlin), Union of Persecuted by the Nazi Regime (VVN-West Berlin), Permanent Committee for Peace, National, and International Understanding, as well as Berlin Community of Tenants. (See Eric Waldman, *Die Sozialistische Einheitspartei Westberlins und die Sowjetische Berlinpolitik,* 1972, pp. 101–9.) The SEW has its own university groups and is linked to Action Community of Democrats and Socialists (ADS).

The SEW is an artificial creation of the Communist Party of the Soviet Union (CPSU), which previously had established the SED, the SEW's foster parent. The political and strategic importance of this party must not be measured by its miniature size. During 1972 it demonstrated ideological cleverness and tactical skill. It is possible that under certain circumstances this seemingly insignificant party may move into the center of a major international confrontation.

Party Internal Affairs. The SEW exhibits a great deal of organizational ability. The party is based on Lenin's principle of "democratic centralism," and strong discipline seems to be observed. Many of the leaders graduated from SED schools and higher party schools in the U.S.S.R. A large percentage of officials and candidates for public office are full-time employees of the party, its subsidiary and front organizations, and its commercial enterprises (mostly, printing and publishing); others work for the GRD railway system.

The SEW exacts high membership dues, and it may be making some money from business ventures. But it is running up huge deficits to pay employees, maintain organizations, and conduct ambitious propaganda campaigns. The deficits are covered by "donations" which, according to widespread belief, come from the GDR. The SEW has been a costly project.

The SEW has been worried by the fact that its membership and leadership groups are growing old. Strenuous efforts are made to recruit young people, but the average membership age is still above 50 years. However, the SEW is proud of the fact that more than four-fifths of its members are "proletarian" by origin, while reportedly no more than 1 percent come from the intelligentsia. Whatever the roots, in terms of *current* occupations, industrial workers account for less than half of the SEW membership. Hardly one-third are white-collar employees, and about one-tenth are of the professional class. Actually, as individual biographies are checked, information on social origin is often unavailable. If a member has temporarily lived from manual labor, the event is presented like a medal in a contest. The important fact is that the leadership group as a whole is highly educated and is living from and by intellectual endeavor. Hence, the contention that the SEW is a true workers' party reflects a dubious sociological perspective.

During 1972, in preparation for the Third Congress, the SEW held party elections. Representatives of cells in enterprises and residential areas were elected between 15 March and 15 May; representatives of precincts and delegates to the congress were chosen between 1 September and 15 October. Otherwise, except for the demonstration on 1 May, the party seems to have concentrated largely on propaganda activities, though presumably it also conducted clandestine operations and was involved in "extra-parliamentary" undertakings.

Throughout the year, the SEW political line was repeatedly reasserted. Generally speaking, the party operated within the framework of resolutions adopted by the Moscow Conference of 1969, the Twenty-fourth Congress of the CPSU, and the Eighth Congress of the SED. Addressing the SEW leadership, Danelius stated that West Berlin must regulate its relations with all states on a basis of independence and must contribute to "productive cooperation between countries with different social orders." He added that "anti-imperialist" mass actions were one of the conditions for the realization of peaceful co-existence. (*Unsere Zeit,* 18 February.)

In the August issue of *Konsequent,* one of the party's ideologues reminded readers that, during the 1848 revolution, to "fight for and win democracy" was considered by Marx and Engels to be the "first step in the workers' revolution." In the current era, however, he said, democracy means "the possession or acquisition" of "political power by the working class in alliance with other working classes and groups." Since "democracy and socialism form a historical unity," the proletarian-democratic upheaval initiates the socialist upheaval. Both socialism and democracy stand in a dialectic relationship to one another: democracy cannot be realized without socialism. It is, therefore, necessary to deprive the "monopolists" of the use of the term "democracy." It might be added that the SEW usually finds it prudent to avoid references to dictatorship. Yet in *World Marxist Review* (January, 1972, p. 41), Hermann Axen, the SED ideological expert—who also speaks for the SEW, pointedly quoted from Lenin's *State and Revolution:* "The transition from capitalism to communism is certainly bound to yield a tremendous abundance and variety of political forms, but the essence will inevitably be the same: the dictatorship of the proletariat."

Danelius held the party to the Stalinist line on internationalism. "Our party is not of the opinion that criticism of the socialist countries is the criterion of a consistent revolutionary but rather of unconditional solidarity." (*Die Wahrheit,* 31 August). Surprisingly, he went back to Marx's theory of increasing poverty and suggested that the contemporary rise of prices was worsening the worker's material position. He emphasized the importance of the youth movement, which should be led by its communist vanguard; furthermore, the Extra-Parliamentary Opposition (APO) and the New Left must be brought under full party control.

Danelius also expressed the belief that the party had been making considerable progress, but in an article (reprinted in the SED's *Neues Deutschland,* 2 September) he admitted that the great task of "raising the class awareness of the workers and the working youths" had not yet been completed.

In *Die Wahrheit* (27 September), Moscow graduate and propaganda expert Karlheinz Kniestedt criticized the radicalism of "pseudo-leftist splinter groups" and said that organized class struggle should replace "petty bourgeois radicalism and anarchism." Kniestedt, who appears to be the SEW specialist on APO questions, explained in strong language that "spontaneity and individual terrorism" serve as "an instrument for provocation against the working class and against the anti-imperialist movement." "Peaceful coexistence," he added, is "a specific form of the socialist class struggle against imperialism on a world-wide scale." Another writer (in ibid., 6 October), stressed that only mass work counts "not the screaming of some fashionable communists, no matter how revolutionarily they behave" and stated that the goal of the SEW is "to shake fundamentally the foundations of the present situation of power." Still another (in ibid., 18 October) criticized left socialist thinking but called for the preparation of "uniform concerted action" between communists and social democrats.

Third Congress. The SEW's outstanding public action during 1972 was the holding of its Third Congress, 20–22 October. This meeting was attended by 418 delegates, 156 guest delegates, and representatives from the communist parties of the U.S.S.R., GDR, Poland, Czechoslovakia, West Germany, France, and Italy. It was preceded by a meeting of the SEW and SED on 26 September, chaired by East German party leader Erich Honecker, apparently to coordinate action on GDR-West Berlin relations. In the main, the congress debated how the SED could contribute toward a détente in Central Europe and prevent the further use of Berlin for cold war purposes—that is, how anti-communist activities could be subdued and stopped. SED Politburo member Paul Verner, who attended for the parent organization, asserted that "socialism prospers in peacetime." (Speech in FBIS, 31 October, pp. U 6-10). Anatoly Skochilov, representative from the Soviet Union, averred that the CPSU has a "constructive approach to international problems which are ripe for solution." (Ibid., 25 October, p. U 4.)

The SEW claimed credit for the four-power agreement on West Berlin which, in the communist version, brought the city closer to international status. This claim was not accepted by foreign observers, including Verner and Skochilov, but they agreed that the SEW's contributions had been important.

Danelius told the Congress that preservation of peace remains "the cardinal question in the world of today" and noted new possibilities in Europe "for the struggle for peace, democracy, and socialism." The SEW supports a European security conference and admission of the

GDR into the U.N. One's attitude toward the Soviet Union, he added, "is the primary and decisive test for each communist." (Ibid., 25 October, pp. U 1–3.)

Danelius discussed mundane tasks also—the party's advocacy of higher wages and salaries, increased social benefits, full employment, rent control and tenant protection, and enlarged workers' rights. The SEW, he said, wants fixed prices for public services and more steeply progressive taxation; party work related to women, youth, and education must be stepped up.

Danelius summed up the results of the Third Congress to the effect that it had confirmed the correctness of party policy. "We outlined new tasks for stepping up the struggle for peace and security in the center of Europe, for the establishment of normal good neighborly relations between West Berlin and the GDR." (Ibid., 1 November, p. F 8.)

Domestic Attitudes and Activities. Before the Congress, Danelius insisted on class struggle, some of which must be directed against the right social democrats who "had concluded a peace treaty with capitalism." The SEW, he explained, favors a democratic order, which he defined as public ownership of big enterprises, control by workers, participation by workers in economic management, and East-West relations on a basis of equality, non-interference, and mutual benefit. According to Danelius, SEW goals can be achieved by parliamentary and extra-parliamentary actions along the "single path" of eliminating the power of capital through class struggle.

Skochilov stated that the SEW was "doing active work under the special conditions of West Berlin and is successfully rebutting both the right-wing opportunists and the ultra-left groupings." The reference to "right-wing opportunists" applied mainly to the Social Democratic Party (SPD), which governs West Berlin. Since there is no chance to break the SPD hold on the electorate, the SEW's task is to criticize socialist politicians and further the party careers of left-wing and young radical socialists within the SPD. The "ultra-left groupings" are the numerous "new left" organizations in West Berlin—Maoists, Trotskyites, anarchists, dissident socialists, and left communists—largely composed of university and high school students, and, in their baffling ideological disparity, "united" only in their rejection of parliamentary methods. They tend to cooperate under concepts such as "Marxism," "Marxism-Leninism," anti-imperialism, and anti-militarism. In Germany, the entire kaleidoscopic set of emerging and disappearing radical groups and grouplets has been placed under the APO label. The term "APO" is a generic term and does not describe any single organization or orientation.

The SED operates on the doctrine that communist revolutionaries must employ *both* parliamentary and extra-parliamentary means, and that they must achieve representation in parliamentary bodies in order to facilitate extra-parliamentary activities from inside the legislature. Given such an arrangement, it becomes the function of the APO to put psychological and physical pressure on the legislators.

It is unlikely that, save perhaps for one or two exceptions, the SEW or other Soviet-dominated communist organizations have established any of the ultra-leftist groups that proliferate in West Berlin. But the SEW may have helped with financing of propaganda, especially the distribution of leaflets. Moreover, the SEW regards ideological struggle as its most important assignment and is trying to save the APO from what Lenin called the "infantile disease" of left radicalism. The SEW's ultimate purpose is to bring all extra-parliamentary activity under its direct or indirect control. The rule is that SEW organizers should take the lead in all "progressive actions" and should exploit political contests to strengthen "socialist consciousness."

In the APO struggle, special emphasis is given to placing West Berlin's universities under communist control. Members of ADS are frequently sent to Moscow for 8-week courses. The SEW-oriented students are committed to use legal means in the struggle for the universities, in contrast to the Maoist Communist Student Group (KSV) which is dedicated to "militant class struggle." (*Die Welt,* 12 December.)

During 1972, SEW/ADS strengthened positions in student self-government and the Academic Senate. They also managed to exercise major influence over departments of social sciences and the various philosophical disciplines. KSV supposedly had only 300 members but, despite this numerical weakness, achieved some popularity. Its aggressive policy was in conformity with the mood of the students who were more interested in striking than studying.

International Views and Activities. All these efforts are of great significance on the Berlin scene. SEW experiences also are instructive to those communist parties elsewhere which wish to acquaint young radicals with the "correct actions," and to weaken the impact of Maoist influences.

It remains, in fact, one of the foremost problems of the international communist movement to establish how radical tendencies among the young can be channeled into applications useful to revolution. It is also necessary to recruit young blood into aging parties. West Berlin is a unique laboratory where methods may be learned on how to induce wayward leftists to adhere to the general line promulgated by Moscow. Successes by the SEW in establishing order within the West Berlin chaos of left radicalism could substantially advance communist fortunes in the FRG.

Another SEW function is to support U.S.S.R. and GDR policies through actions in West Berlin. Such actions seek to give the impression that communist policies find grass roots support there and that West Berliners yearn for the departure of Western "occupation forces" and for the suppression of pro-Western and "anti-socialist" elements. The SEW precipitates genuine or fake actions which are reported and broadcast by GDR and other communist media. Much of this make-believe has been successful. However, the SEW has not succeeded in getting enough votes to obtain a foothold in the West Berlin Senate. The vocal help which East Berlin radio broadcasts gave to the SEW during the elections of 1971 confirmed the suspicion of voters that the SEW is not an indigenous and independent party.

Nevertheless, in line with the policy which the U.S.S.R. has pursued in Germany since 1945, the SEW continues to work for a popular front with the socialists. For this purpose the SEW places special emphasis on contacts with "Jusos" (young socialists) through whom it wants to influence SPD policies. If the Jusos can be enabled to take over the SPD, the government of West Berlin might fall under indirect communist dominance. Otherwise the SEW hopes for a popular front which under communist leadership would include the socialists, liberals and democrats, and ultimately a national front which additionally would embrace "progressive" nationalist elements. A "parliamentary democratic republic" in the image of the GDR is the major intermediate goal. At one level or another the SEW and parties affiliated with it might be merged with parallel and "fraternal" groupings in the GDR or FRG, or both. The party statute of 1969 makes explicit reference to possible dissolution or merging with other parties.

So long as the party line is forcefully articulated by non-party leftists in the legislature, the absence of SEW representatives from the Senate may help rather than hinder. But to advance from an organization excelling in penetration and infiltration to a real political force the SEW does need to become a "mass party"—at least, a party of small "masses." In 1972 this goal remained distant.

Publications. Much SEW activity is of a literary nature. Party publications include a quarterly, *Konsequent.* This untranslatable title means something like "Persistent Consistency." The magazine argues Marxist-Leninist theory and is mainly addressed to students and new left theoreticians. The party organ, *Die Wahrheit* ("Truth"), supposedly has about 9,000 subscribers and is issued four times weekly in 12,000–15,000 copies printed on presses owned by the SEW. Twice weekly the SEW publishes a miniature, unofficial paper, *Berliner Extradienst,* which is mainly for "revisionists" among the new left. Several subsidiary organs issue publications, usually on an irregular basis. The party exerts influence on some organs published by or for industrial firms.

Hoover Institution   Stefan T. Possony
Stanford University

Great Britain

The Communist Party of Great Britain (CPGB) was founded in 1920. Although the oldest and largest representative of communism in Great Britain, the CPGB continued in 1972 to be faced with increasing competition from other parties and groups advocating Marxism-Leninism (see below) and from a vocal and active "new left" movement.

The CPGB is a recognized political party in Great Britain. In 1972 the CPGB confirmed that it had approximately 28,803 members—which was the figure given in an Executive Committee report at the party's Thirty-second Congress, in November 1971. This showed a decline since the previous congress, in November 1969, when the party had a membership of 30,607—the latter figure also reflecting a downward trend since 1964. The population of Great Britain is 55,347,000 (estimated 1971).

Communist party candidates contend in elections for both national and local offices, although there have been no members in the House of Commons since 1950. In local elections in May 1972, the party defended three offices, all successfully.

The CPGB. Organization and Leadership. The National Congress is the supreme authority and policy-making organ of the CPGB. It meets biennially when called by the Executive Committee, but a special congress can be convened under extraordinary circumstances. The Thirty-second Congress was held on 13–16 November 1971 (the next congress will be held on 10-12 November 1973). The National Congress elects the 44-member Executive Committee (the highest authority between congresses), which in turn elects the party officers and the Political Committee. The Executive Committee meets every two months, Political Committee usually weekly or when the need arises. Below the leadership level, are district committees, area and borough committees, and finally party branches. Wales and Scotland do not have separate parties but have area branches of the main party.

John Gollan is the general secretary of the CPGB and Irene Swann the chairman. (For Political Committee members, and department heads see YICA, 1972, p. 170.)

The most popular member of the Executive Committee, judging from the voting to reseat him on the committee at the 1971 congress was James (Jimmy) Reid, who led the Upper Clyde Shipbuilders in the "workers' takeover" in August 1971 and was elected rector of Glasgow University in October. Reid is considered to be a potential leader of the CPGB.

The Young Communist League (YCL), affiliated to the CPGB since the latter's founding, is the party's youth organization. In 1972 the YCL was headed by Tom Bell, national secretary. Like the CPBG, the YCL has declined in membership, from 3,850 in 1969 to 3,000 in 1972.

The CPGB derives its greatest strength from the trade union movement and exercises perceptible influence there. Although increasingly challenged by the Socialist Labour League

(SLL), a Trotskyist party, the CPGB continued in 1972 to contribute actively to industrial agitation with a measure of success disproportionate to its size and electoral support. During the year the party continued in its attempts to attain influence within the Amalgamated Union of Engineering and Foundry Workers (AUEW), Britain's second-largest union (about 1,280,000 members). The party was also active in promoting its Liaison Committee for the Defense of Trade Unions (LCDTU), an "umbrella organization" for unofficial rank-and-file bodies set up in many parts of the country and in key industries, which was founded in 1966.

Party Internal Affairs. During 1972 the CPGB was concerned with three issues; the Warsaw Pact invasion of Czechoslovakia in 1968, the declining circulation of the party organ, *Morning Star,* and the drop in party membership.

At the 1971 congress a minority dissented from the party's condemnation of the invasion, which has not changed since the statement issued on 24 August 1968: "The Executive Committee of the Communist Party of Great Britain deeply deplores the military intervention in Czechoslovakia on Tuesday, August 20th by troops of the Soviet Union, Hungary, Poland, Bulgaria, and the German Democratic Republic. . . . This is a gross violation of the democratic rights of the Czechoslovak Communists."

The dissenters, led by the Surrey district organizer, criticized the leadership largely for its position on the intervention and subsequent events and for its "over-critical" attitude toward the Soviet Union. But they could only secure 18 percent of the delegates' support. The series of trials in Czechoslovakia during the summer of 1972 was criticized by the party and an editorial in the *Morning Star* (10 August) stated: "The current series of trials only increases the concern already expressed by Communists in other countries including France, Italy and Britain."

In 1971 there had been a loss of nearly £19,000 on producing the party organ, and as costs were continuing to rise it was decided to increase the price. The circulation problems of the party organ were reflected in the editor's remarks: "Rapid and substantial rises in costs face the Morning Star with very serious financial problems, and the need to take crucial decisions in the near future. The prospect for 1973 and 1974 is of still greater difficulties." (*Morning Star,* 28 November). Throughout the year the paper made daily appeals for funds and donations which brought in a total of £23,000. This was still not sufficient to meet running costs. On 5 March a rally was held in London on the occasion of the paper's forty-second anniversary in an effort to increase support for it.

The declining party membership was the principal topic at a meeting of the party's London district congress on 18–19 November. While the national figure had shown a decline, it was reported that party membership in the London district was moving upward for the first time in eight years and had reached 4,973. Proposals adopted by the congress called for 5,500 members by June 1973. The district was to make "more conscious efforts to recruit black and other minority groupings of workers," and there was also to be a campaign "for the maximum involvement of women in organisations of the Party." (ibid., 20 November.)

The party's image of non-violence was damaged when Noel Jenkinson, an admitted communist, was charged in October with murdering seven people in a bomb explosion at Aldershot Barracks in February (see *Ireland*).

The CPGB's youth wing followed closely the policies of the adult party. The YCL has a 40-member Executive Committee of which the principal members are Tom Bell, national secretary, and Pete Kavanagh, chairman.

According to the YCL organ (*Challenge,* no. 7), on the domestic front the organization's principal aim was to work for the removal from office of the Conservative government, to achieve greater representation in the student movement, and to develop "pupil power," or what it calls "democracy in school." But industrial relations remained the main area of activity: "Where there is an increase in militancy we see young trade unionists in the thick of it. The YCL looks on this as a most encouraging development." (ibid., no. 8.) On international issues the YCL differed little from the policies of the adult party. Countries visited by YCL delegations included the Soviet Union, Finland, Ireland, and Chile. A Soviet delegation (see below) on its visit to the CPGB had talks with members of the YCL Executive Committee.

Domestic Views and Policies. During 1972 the CPGB continued to adhere to its policy of attaining power by parliamentary means. Its domestic activities were largely concentrated on the trade union movement (including industrial relations and incomes), housing, and student affairs. On 14 August the government's Industrial Relations Act—an attempt to introduce a labor code into British industry—became law. The CPGB's policy toward the Act was expressed by Bert Ramelson, its industrial organizer, in a party document first published in November 1970: "The Industrial Relations Bill 1970 is the most vicious piece of politically motivated class legislation [since] the early 1700s." To defeat the bill, Ramelson urged trade unions to launch "a relentless, mounting campaign culminating in actions of General Strike (1926) dimensions." On the industrial level, conflict between the government and organized labor was manifest during 1972 in several strikes, lock-outs, and picketings in the fuel and transport industries and on the docks. The party's influence was clearly discernible in the docks dispute over "container" shipments when a party member, Bernie Steer, leader of the unofficial National Ports Shop Stewards' Committee (which organized the nationwide "blacking" of container trucks in July), was jailed by the National Industrial Relations Court and released a few days later after the decision was rescinded by the House of Lords. "A great ovation welcomed dockers' leader Bernie Steer at the London rally called by Communist Party last night (3 August)," reported the *Morning Star* (4 August). The paper went on: "We are not interested in amending the Act. It must be totally repealed."

The LCDTU is "a militant movement within the trade unions which gives expression to the demands of rank and file workers" (*WMR,* July 1972). On 10 June a LCDTU conference in London was attended by some 1,200 militants representing shop steward committees, trade unions, and trade councils. The aim of the conference was "to make the Industrial Relations Act inoperable and to challenge the credibility of many elected representatives of the trade union movement." Seventy-two CPGB industrial leaders were present; the conference issued a declaration of support for a campaign "to ignore and defy institutions set up under the Act, to mobilise solidarity for those attacked by the State, and to wage national industrial action against the measure." (*Morning Star,* 12 June.)

Attempts in October and November by the government, the Trade Union Congress, and the Confederation of British Industry to reach agreement on a wages and incomes policy were attacked by the party. Bert Ramelson stated that such attempts "should be resisted and fought by every possible means, including industrial action" (ibid., 4 November); John Gollan, general secretary, called for "all-out action to defeat the freeze" (ibid., 11 November); the party's national organizer attacked the government proposals as "being a major attack on the working peoples living standards" (ibid. 13 November). The tripartite talks were inconclusive.

In April, the Housing Finance Act was introduced by the government, aimed at increasing the rents of state-owned houses and some private dwellings. A party document issued in January stated: "The Communist Party says 'Kill the Tory rent bill.' " Much of the protest against the Act was carried out by a communist front organization, the National Association of Tenants and Residents (NATR—founded in 1948 and reconstituted in 1954). Demonstrations were conducted at several government offices throughout the country. The NATR organized a conference in London (29–30 July) at which "delegates raised the fist of defiance against the Government's Housing Finance Act" (ibid., 31 July).

CPGB activities in educational matters increased during the year. Government proposals on the future of student unions published in November 1971 were attacked: "The Tory Government is determined [to] cripple the student unions . . . and students will need to be alert, vigilant and determined not to submit, as are their counterparts in the trade unions" (*WMR*, July). Most of the militancy against the proposals was generated by the mainly Trotskyist Liaison Committee for the Defence of Student Unions (LCDSU), formed in November 1971. The CPGB's student organizer called for a "united, determined and resourceful response to [the proposals] of the student movement" (*Morning Star*, 2 November). But by mid-November there were signs that within the student movement the LCDSU was itself faced by opposition from a more radical group of International Socialists (IS). The IS decided to leave the LCDSU and stated: "It is unlikely that serious mass opposition . . . will develop with or without the intervention of the LCDSU" (*Time Out*, 10–16 November).

At the level of junior education the YCL participated in the London demonstrations (8 and 17 May) of the Schools Action Union (SAU), a mainly Maoist organization. But for the rest of the year the SAU's acitivities were desultory and received little support or publicity. It was not taken seriously by the education authorities.

The CPGB's representation in official positions in the trade unions was unchanged (see *YICA, 1971*, p. 173) except for the appointment of a communist to the executive of the Union of Construction, Allied Trades and Technicians (UCATT).

International Views and Policies. The CPGB position on international issues was expressed by political committee member Tony Chater in a report to the Executive Committee, 8–9 July. Five subjects were considered: (Vietnam, the Middle East, SALT talks and disarmament, European security, and the Common Market.

"Ending US aggression in Vietnam remains priority number one in the fight for peace," wrote Chater. In support of this the party's front organisation, British Council for Peace in Vietnam (BCPV) held several rallies, vigils, and demonstrations at the U.S. Embassy. On the Middle East, Chater reported that "a special campaigning body has recently been set up in Britain to campaign in support of the UN resolution, [but] much more needs to be done to involve the trade union movement in this campaign." Disarmament was termed "an essential part of the struggle for peaceful co-existence." The report welcomed proposals for a European security conference and charged that "powerful reactionary forces in Western Europe, including the Tory Government, are intent on holding it up and sabotaging it." The major point of the report was opposition to the Common Market. Chater wrote that the Common Market, "as we have always maintained, consolidates the division of Europe." A resolution passed by the Executive Committee at the session stated: "Entry to the Common Market will make every economic problem facing the British people worse. . . . The Common Market is designed for big business. The Treaty of Rome is for the preservation of capitalism." In conclusion it called for a "consistent unrelenting struggle against Britain's entry, outright opposition to the Common Market in principle and committment to unconditional withdrawal if the Tories take us in." (*Comment*, 15 July.)

Toward the violent conflict in Northern Ireland the CPGB's position in 1972 was consistent with its policy document of November 1971, which offered a four-point plan. withdrawal of British troops from the Catholic ("anti-Unionist") areas, disarming of the Unionists, ending of internment and the release of detainees, and enactment of a Bill of Rights at Westminster conceding the demands of the Civil Rights movement (which is communist-dominated).

Among the major visits abroad by CPGB members, John Gollan visited Hungary on 16–20 March at the invitation of the Hungarian Socialist Workers' Party. Gollan visited Romania and Bulgaria in July. In Bucharest he was the guest of the Romanian Communist Party. CPGB representatives also visited Chile, Japan, Belgium, Somalia, Czechoslovakia, and France. Reciprocal visits were paid by the French and Japanese parties. The most important delegation to visit the CPGB was that headed by I.V. Kapitonov, secretary of the Central Committee of the Communist Party of the Soviet Union (CPSU), 9–20 April. The visit was an indication of the acute problems which beset the CPGB. *Pravda* (19 April) reported that the "aim of the trip is to study closer the work of British communists and the life of British working people," with a view to strengthening "cooperation between the CPSU and the British Communist Party." Both the declining membership and the relatively independent line of the CPGB may have given that CPSU cause for concern at the party's position.

Publications. Besides its London daily newspaper, the *Morning Star,* the CPGB's major publications include *Comment,* a fortnightly magazine; *Marxism Today,* a monthly theoretical journal; and *Labour Monthly,* which provides commentary on political events. The YCL has an irregular monthly journal, *Challenge,* and a monthly theoretical organ, *Cogito.*

*   *   *

The SLL. Among the numerous Marxist-Leninist parties and groups that challenge the CPGB's leadership in the British communist movement, the largest and most influential (particularly in the trade union movement) is the Socialist Labour League. The SLL was founded in 1959 and is an affiliate of the Trotskyist International Committee of the Fourth International.

The SLL has a membership of 1,200. Its youth movement, the Young Socialists (YS), claims 20,000 members and is the largest Marxist-Leninist youth group ever to have existed in Great Britain.

The SLL is led by Gerry Healy as national secretary. Other prominent members in the SLL (which does not publish complete information on the composition of its leading bodies) are Michael Banda, editor of the SLL's daily newspaper, *Workers' Press,* and Tom Kemp and Cliff Slaughter, editors of *Fourth International,* a quarterly organ of the International Committee of the Fourth International, published in London. The YS is led by John Simmance. It publishes a weekly, *Keep Left.*

The SLL controls the All Trade Union Alliance (ATUA), a group similar to the CPGB-controlled LCDTU. The main line of SLL domestic policy in 1972 continued to be directed toward industrial agitation. The SLL's approach to organized labor differed from that of the CPGB. While the latter focuses on the trade union movement at executive levels, the SLL concentrates its activities among the rank and file and the stop stewards. For both, the main target areas were the engineering industries, particularly the motor sector.

The SLL fought actively against the Industrial Relations Act and favored the use of strikes for this purpose. The ATUA held its fifth annual congress in Birmingham (a major-car-building area) on 22 October. Some 2,000 workers from every major industry attended and it was believed to be the largest congress the ATUA had held. Discussion took place on a resolution which charged the ATUA and the SLL with the task of building a "revolutionary party to take the working class to power in Britain" (*Workers Press,* 24 October).

The YS was also active in promoting SLL policies in the trade unions. Beginning in March, the YS organized a series of regional right-to-work marches which continued through the year. A rally supporting this activity, held in London on 12 March, was attended by 8,500 supporters. "The Right-to-Work marchers will be campaigning to build the Young Socialists and set up Councils of Action in all areas they pass through" said *Keep Left* (17 June). In 1972 the YS was successful in recruiting members due largely to its attractive program of discothèques, sports, and weekend camps in holiday areas. Like the CPGB, the SLL and the YS were short of funds and frequent appeals were made in their respective organs for donations.

*   *   *

In addition to the CPGB and the LL there are numerous Marxist-Leninist groups in Britain. None of these has been able to muster numerically significant support. There are two main groups, the International Marxist Group (IMG) and the International Socialists (IS). The IMG is the British section of the United Secretariat of the Fourth International. The IMG's national secretary is Pat Jordan, who is also editor of the group's monthly publication, *International.* The principal organ of the IMG is the fortnightly *Red Mole,* which has an editorial committee of seven amongst whom are Tariq Ali and sociologist Robin Blackburn. In 1970 the IMG founded a youth group, the Spartacus League, which was only fitfully active during the year.

The IMG was active on several fronts but did not operate consistently on any particular issue—it tended to follow rather than to anticipate or lead events. It campaigned on Vietnam, Ireland, student affairs, industrial relations, immigration, the Third World, and the Common Market.

The Spartacus League was relatively quiescent and confined itself mainly to organizing discussions, seminars, and talk-ins. Its activities suffer somewhat from the absence of an effective publicity organ.

The IS (led by Tony Cliff and Paul Foot) is mainly active on the industrial front and has branches throughout the country. The IS outlined its platform in the party's weekly organ *Socialist Worker* (25 November): "We believe in independent working-class action for the abolition of capitalism and its replacement by a classless society with production for use and not for profit. . . . We are firmly committed to internationalism." There is considerable animosity between the IS and the IMG, mainly over which movement is the correct representative of the Fourth International. The IS is considered anti-Trotskyist and Stanlinist by the IMG (*Red Mole,* 7 August).

The Communist Party of Britain (Marxist-Leninist) (CPBML) was founded at an inaugural congress in April 1968. This pro-Chinese party is led by Reg Birch. It claims a membership of 400 and is the only pro-Chinese party in Great Britain whose activities are publicized by the People's Republic of China. Beginning in June, its organ, *The Worker,* became a fortnightly.

Though small in numbers the CPBML operated intensively in the engineering industry, in campaigns aimed at destroying the Industrial Relations Act. The campaigns took the form of occupations of factory premises and rallies: "Occupations lend themselves admirably to the present phase of guerrilla struggle. . . . Every guerrilla struggle is a rehearsal for the final confrontation when it will not be individual factories occupied tactically but the whole employing class expropriated strategically." (*The Worker,* mid-July). Reg Birch forecast that his party would become increasingly more militant: "We will fight for our rights. . . . We'll take it out into the open and we'll have a civil war about it" (ibid.).

London, England   D. L Price

Greece

The Communist Party of Greece (Kommounistikon Komma Hellados; KKE) celebrated its 54th anniversary in November 1972, although it did not become a member of the Third International until 1920. The party as originally established in November 1918 was known as the "Socialist Workers' Party of Greece" and in ideological orientation was basically social-democratic. In 1947 the KKE was outlawed as a result of the guerrilla campaign it launched in 1946. Following the defeat of the insurgency in August 1949, most of the KKE leaders and a large segment of the most active cadres escaped into Eastern Europe. Today, the party is fragmented into several conflicting factions receiving varying degrees of support from some 100,-000 Greeks who left the country at the end of the 1946–49 guerrilla war. The various factions claim a total membership of approximately 27,000 in Greece and 15,000 abroad. These figures cannot be verified. The population of Greece is 8,800,000 (estimated 1972).

The KKE operated between 1951 and 1967 through the "United Democratic Left" (EDA), a leftist, "progressive," communist-dominated party. The EDA, like all other political parties, was proscribed in April 1967 by the present government established by the military junta under George Papadopoulos.

The central element in the activities of the communist movement in Greece during 1972 was the continuing fragmentation of the pro-communist left into several factions, namely, the Koliyannis KKE, the KKE (Interior), the KKE "Organization of Marxist-Leninists," and the Nea Aristera (New Left). Efforts to form a "united patriotic front" with other non-communist forces against the Papadopoulos government have had little success. Such efforts, supported separately by the KKE (Koliyannis) and the KKE (Interior), were opposed by the Marxist-Leninists. The Nea Aristera favors such cooperation but faces the competition of such leftist non-communist leaders as Andreas Papandreou, who draw support from the same type of ideological constituency.

Leadership. At present two major factions claim to be the legitimate spokesmen for the Communist Party of Greece.

(1) The Koliyannis KKE is nominally headed by 80-year-old Apostolos Grozos as chairman, with Kostas Koliyannis as secretary-general. It includes among its leading cadres many of those who emerged into the party's leadership in 1956 shortly after the Twentieth Congress of the Communist Party of the Soviet Union, de-Stalinization, and the fall of Nikos Zakhariades (the KKE's "leader" since the early 1930s). Most of the members of this faction have been absent from Greece since the collapse of the KKE's guerrilla campaign in 1949. Two members of its Politburo, Grigoris Farakos and Nikolaos Kaloudhis, were captured in 1971 when they attempted to enter Greece and organize local "resistance groups" against the government. Other known members of the Politburo include Leonidas Stringos (a high-rank-

ing party theoretician since the early 1940s), Panayiotis Mavromatis, and candidate members Kostas Tsolakis and Gerasimos Stefanatos. The Grozos-Koliyannis faction appears to have the formal backing of the Soviet Union. On the other hand, the group appears to be at odds with EDA's leaders; of the eleven full members of EDA's Executive Committee, only one, Mina Yiannou, has sided with Koliyannis.

(Addendum: As this essay was being completed, the KKE (Koliyannis) held the 17th Ple.ıum of its Central Committee somewhere in Hungary in late December. The plenum removed from the Polibureau Kostas Koliyannis, Apostolos Grozos, and Leonidas Stringos. The official explanation for the removal of the party's secretary-general and its chairman (Grozos) was that they resigned for reasons of health. Koliyannis was replaced by a rather unimportant communist known as Florakis. It is very likely that the move was engineered by the Soviet Union on the advice of former EDA leader Elias Eliou in the interests of party unity. Eliou, who recently returned to Greece after a four-month stay in the Soviet Union, remains in the background. The resolutions of the 17th Plenum do not contain any startlingly different policies from those previously advocated by Koliyannis. It is too early at this stage to predict what the effect of these changes will be on party unity.)

(2) The faction known now as the KKE (Interior) resulted from the intra-party feud which surfaced in February 1968 during the KKE Central Committee's 12th Plenum, in Bucharest. At that time the Koliyannis-dominated Central Committee removed from the Politburo veteran communists Dimitrios (Mitsos) Partsalides, Zisis Zographos, and Panayiotis Dimitriou—presumably because they had questioned Koliyannis's effectiveness in conducting the "struggle" against the military regime in Greece. Four days later, the truncated Politburo expelled those three leaders from the party altogether. The Partsalides group refused to accept the decisions of the 12th Plenum; in its defiance the group received the implied support of the so-called Bureau of the Interior (composed of Central Committee members residing and operating clandestinely inside Greece). The Bureau of the Interior rejected the decisions of the 12th Plenum because of legal "irregularities." Of the three leading members of the Partsalides group, Zographos is now dead. His body was found in August 1971 in Bucharest floating in the river, apparently the victim of foul play. Partsalides is now in a Greek prison, sentenced on 4 May 1972 to life imprisonment for his role in the 1946–49 guerrilla war. (In November the deputy prosecuting attorney asked that the conviction be set aside because of the statute of limitations. The case is still pending.) He was captured in October 1971 in Athens together with 16 other communists—including Kharalambos (Babis) Drakopoulos, former first secretary of EDA's Executive Committee and secretary-general of the KKE (Interior) Central Committee at the time of his arrest—when the group tried to enter Greece illegally. The Partsalides group had accepted the leadership of the Bureau of the Interior in April 1968, and had formed the KKE (Interior) in April 1969, when they established a Central Committee with 15 regular and 9 alternate members, most of them residing in Greece. This faction was strengthened by the support it received from composer Mikis Theodorakis (nominal leader of EDA's "Lambrakis Democratic Youth" organization) and from a majority of EDA's Executive Committee, including Antonios Brillakis, Nikos Karras, Babis Drakopoulos, Leonidas Kyrkos, Potis Paraskevopoulos, Vasilis Sakellaris, and P. Katerinis.

In addition to these two rival factions which claim to speak for the KKE, a group known as Nea Aristera (New Left) has made its appearance. It claims to be free of foreign tutelage and promises to respect basic democratic principles such as freedom of expression, parliamentary democracy, and human rights. Manolis Glezos, a veteran communist and one of EDA's principal spokesmen prior to the 1967 coup, is considered a leading proponent of the Nea Aristera movement. He is known to have been critical of both rival factions of the KKE. Another possible leader is Elias Eliou, former EDA leader, who has remained aloof from the intra-party rivalries. Mikis Theodorakis, who has now left the KKE and wants to return to Greece and resume his career as a composer, may also play a leading role in this emerging group.

A fourth group, the KKE Organization of Marxist-Leninists, is now engaged in an effort to capture the most radical elements in the Greek left. This group is openly siding with Communist China in its feud with the Soviet Union. Up until now it has received rather limited support from the Greek communists at home and abroad. In April this group convened its "First Conference" somewhere in Eastern Europe (no place was identified in its published reports), and established a "Central Leadership Organ for the Organization of Greek Marxist-Leninists." The conference openly attacked the Soviet Union as the mainstay of the "revisionists and opportunists." The names of those who presumably formed the "Central Leadership Organ" were not made public. In fact, no prominent communists or leftists have been mentioned in connection with this group.

Internal Affairs. During 1972 the intra-party quarrels continued unabated. The Koliyannis KKE, in a long statement broadcast over its "Voice of Truth" radio transmitter on 3 and 4 January, attacked the "Bureau of the Interior"—the KKE (Interior)—for "splitting the struggle against the junta." At the same time, it blamed the "party's failure to translate the people's resistance into a concerted and effective struggle against the dictatorship" on the "refusal of the bourgeois parties to join in a common effort on the basis of a minimum common program of action."

In the early months of 1972 the Koliyannis group intensified its efforts to convene the party's Ninth Congress. The Eighth Congress was held in October 1961, when the party was fairly united and effectively dominated by Koliyannis. Obviously, a congress convened in the party's current fragmented condition will be denounced by all those who disagree with Koliyannis and will have little practical significance.

The failure of the party's "resistance" and the arrest of key communists in October 1971—including Partsalides and Babis Drakopoulos—further deepened the party's malaise in 1972 as the KKE (Interior) accused the Koliyannis group of betraying its opponents to the Greek authorities. In March the KKE (Interior) suffered another serious setback when Mikis Theodorakis, while visiting Melbourne, Australia, made public on 6 March a letter he had sent five days earlier to the Politburo of the KKE (Interior). In his letter, Theodorakis declared that the party's following had "shrunk" and its influence waned. He asked his colleagues in the Politburo: "Is an organization viable, I wonder, when it has [in Greece and abroad] only one single organ and even that organ does not function properly?" "Around the six of us," he went on, "I find only a void, and this void becomes increasingly greater." Then he added: "Even worse, the majority of our forces has surrendered to discouragement and apathy." Theodorakis had decided to make this letter public because, the day before, the Politburo of the KKE (Interior) had issued a long statement dealing with the decision of Theodorakis to resign from the Politburo. His colleagues were particularly incensed by his attacks not only on Koliyannis but also on the KKE (Interior). In fact, Theodorakis challenged the legitimacy of both factions.

Theodorakis's disaffection was long brewing. He had voiced his dissatisfaction with the policies of the KKE (Interior) for the first time in January 1971, but the disagreement had remained largely a family secret. His views were discussed in March of that year and an open break was averted. Theodorakis resumed his criticism in October 1971 following the failure of the Partsalides-Drakopoulos mission. On 27 February 1972, four members of the Politburo of the KKE (Interior)—K. Zevgou, N. Karras, A. Brillakis, and P. Staveris—addressed a letter to Theodorakis criticizing his public statements, which they found to be in opposition to the group's previous declarations and decisions. They were particularly annoyed, they implied, by his disclosures on "delicate matters concerning the party's illegal work." They concluded on a rather conciliatory note and asked for a private meeting "to clear any misunderstandings." The letter Theodorakis made public in Melbourne was his reply. With this, he severed all organized ties with the party.

The Koliyannis KKE, while rejoicing at the "deep crisis of the revisionists," leveled a fierce attack on Theodorakis for his remarks on the party's "dogmatic and undemocratic methods." He was referring to the KKE (Interior), but his charges applied no less to the Koliyannis group. Besides, his disclosures on the lack of popular support hit a raw nerve. In its statement the group accused Theodorakis of "opportunism and anti-party struggle," "surrender to the class enemy," and "desertion."

During the rest of the year Theodorakis made no effort to rebuild any bridges with his former colleagues in the KKE (Interior). In October he even expressed his willingness to return to Greece "legally" and resume his work as a composer. In an interview published in the Italian journal *Mondo* (quoted in *Ethnikos Kiryx,* New York, 13 November), he defended his views against "the Greek communists in Russia who accuse me of weakness and cowardice," terming the charge "stupid and dishonest." In justifying his resignation he said: "Today the party is divided into two irreconcilable factions and into at least four different trends. It does not have any real influence in Greece. Many of its leaders and a large part of its cadres have been living abroad for more than twenty years. They have practically no understanding of the country's realities." While he repeated his intention to concentrate on his work as a composer, Theodorakis went on to say that through his music he was hoping to give expression to leftist and revolutionary ideas. This last statement is likely to prevent the Greek government from giving him permission to reenter the country and resume his career there.

Unable to bring together a reasonably representative gathering for a Ninth Congress, the Koliyannis group convened instead, during the latter part of June, the 16th Plenum of its Central Committee, presumably in Bucharest. The previous plenum had met in February 1971. The most significant element in the 16th Plenum's resolutions was the faction's bid for broad support from non-communist groups. To promote such a "united front from above," the plenum reasserted that the "revolution" in Greece would not have a "socialist" character at first, and instead would start as a "bourgeois-democratic" type of revolution. This was presented as a major "concession" for the sake of a "common struggle against the junta." In spite of this concession, cooperation with other "resistance groups" is rather unlikely, especially for as long as the current intra-party divisions continue.

The "united front" appeal of the Koliyannis KKE was echoed by the "decision" of the Politburo of the KKE (Interior) which was issued in July under the title "Steadfastly and in an Organized Manner at the Front of Opposition and United Struggle in the Path of Resistance." In its decision, the Politburo expressed support for a "National Political Committee" similar to the one proposed recently by EDA's "Patriotic Anti-dictatorial Front," and stated that it "considers at this moment as the most pressing need an understanding and an exchange of views among all the political forces and the resistance organizations with reference to the immediate prospects of the anti-dictatorial struggle, to pursue on this basis a united position."

The Maoist organization of "Marxist-Leninists" is, in contrast, violently opposed to a "united front" policy. Its organ *Laiki Foni,* published somewhere in Europe, contained in its July edition several attacks on non-communist Greek politicians, including Andreas Papandreou, and Const. Karamanlis. It reserved its highest accolades for Mao, Stalin, and Lenin.

During the year a half-hearted effort by the Communist Party of the Soviet Union to promote a reconciliation at least between the Koliyannis KKE and the KKE (Interior) met with no success. The Soviet authorities did not press the matter because, apparently, they see no immediate use for the KKE, whether united or split in rival factions. Koliyannis has dutifully supported all Soviet policies, including the intervention in Czechoslovakia, which incidentally was criticized in 1968 by the Partsalides group and the Bureau of the Interior. Since a reconciliation of the two main factions would likely require the dumping of Koliyannis, little can be expected in this direction. (Needless to say, the Maoists with their open criticism of the Soviet Union, and the Nea Aristera with its bent for "independence from foreign tutelage," hold little attraction for the Soviet policy-makers.) In the circumstances, it is safe to predict that Moscow will continue to sanction the Koliyannis group as the legitimate leadership of KKE. This attitude was reflected in the awarding of the Order of the October Revolution to Grozos on his 80th birthday in June, a message of congratulations on the same occasion by the Central Committee of the East German Socialist Unity Party, and a meeting between Stringos and Tsolakis representing KKE and Jan Debrouwere and Edouard Florent representing the Belgian Communist Party last February. In contrast, the KKE (Interior) could only find another dissident group, the Communist Party of Israel (MAKI), to hold talks in March.

In summary, the fragmentation of the party became even greater in 1972, while apathy seemed to erode the ranks in both factions. At the same time, efforts to form a "united front" with other organizations opposing the present government in Greece failed to make headway.

Domestic Views and Activities. Reflecting the party's fragmentation, a survey of KKE's domestic views must by necessity focus on the respective positions of the Koliyannis KKE, the KKE (Interior), the KKE group of Marxist-Leninists, and to some extent the Nea Aristera, although this latter group does not claim to speak for KKE.

Koliyannis KKE. The views of the Koliyannis faction were restated in the resolutions of the 16th Plenum, June 1972. Denying any "crisis" in the ranks of KKE, the plenum simply spoke of difficulties caused by the "revisionists," "splinters," and "anti-Soviet elements." These attacks revealed by indirection that Moscow's effort to reconcile the feuding factions had failed. Koliyannis reiterated the thesis previously presented in the "Theses of the Central Committee for KKE's Ninth Congress." He declared:

> The danger to our Party comes from the efforts of a faction in the Party's leadership and ranks to revise its revolutionary character and transform it from a Marxist-Leninist party to a petty-bourgeois social-democratic party incapable of fulfilling its historic mission. The danger also comes from the efforts of this faction to revise the Party's line on the leadership role to be played by the working class in the anti-imperialist democratic revolution. The danger comes from the effort of this faction to subjugate the working class to the liberal bourgeoisie, take the Party down to the road of anti-internationalist ideology, weaken its ties with the sister Marxist-Leninist parties, and in general separate the country's democratic movement from its most decisive allies and defenders, the Soviet Union and the other Socialist countries. (*Enimerotikon Deltion* [Information Bulletin—a collection of communist documents and broadcasts, published and distributed monthly to a limited number of recipients by the General Secretariat of Press and Information, Athens], no. 12, July, p. 9.)

This assessment of the intra-party feud was clearly designed to claim for the Koliyannis faction exclusive representation of Marxist-Leninist ideology in the Greek context, and to secure the blessing of the Soviet Union. In this regard, the Soviet authorities face a dilemma, at least to the extent they care about the Marxist-Leninist movement in Greece. Koliyannis's KKE is operating mostly outside Greece, while the rival KKE (Interior) is active within the country and therefore much more relevant to any future developments. It appears, however, that for the time being, and as long as the Soviet leadership sees no reason to take an aggressive stand on Greek political affairs and adopt a policy of outright hostility to the ruling power, support to Koliyannis is more likely because it tends to be somewhat academic, while an identification with the other faction might involve certain rather hard choices.

While claiming a "leading role" and rejecting the subjugation of "the working class to the liberal bourgeoisie"—a position hardly conducive to cooperation with other non-Communist forces—the 16th Plenum renewed the effort for a "united front from above." It reemphasized the theme of the draft program (written in anticipation of the yet-to-convene Ninth Congress) with regard to the "character" of the revolution. The revolution, it said, will be of the "anti-imperialist, democratic" variety, as contrasted to a "socialist" type. The shift from a commitment to a "socialist" revolution had been prompted in 1970–71 by the expectation that such a "softer" stand would facilitate cooperation with other non-communist groups in a joint effort to overthrow the government in Greece. Such cooperation did not materialize, and the Plenum put on the "bourgeois forces" the blame for the failure to achieve any notable results. Repeating some of the arguments made at the 15th Plenum in February 1971, Koliyannis said in his report that the bourgeois elements, including Andreas Papandreou, fear "the working class and its party, the KKE," and have so far rejected any effective cooperation with KKE in a "common struggle against the junta." In light of this negative stand of the "bourgeois elements," the 16th Plenum resolved that the party must concentrate its efforts "to strengthen and expand the Party's illegal organizations" in Greece "by recruiting new members." Echoing previous resolutions, the plenum complained again that "the organizational-political problem remains very acute." The plenum attributed the failure to attract dedicated members to a number of reasons. The party organizations, it said, are "closed," have not gone beyond "the propaganda stage," "do not care as much as they should about the problems of the working people," and, most importantly, "hesitate to draw to the Party ranks the fighters who have the qualifications to become party members." (Ibid., p. 10.)

One finds no originality in the plenum's resolutions dealing with the party's "conspiratorial, illegal work." The party members operating inside Greece are admonished to use "all the semi-legal and legal possibilities for action, working in the mass organizations, the trade unions, the cooperatives, the cultural clubs, etc.," but at the same time they are warned "against violating or downgrading the conspiratorial methods of struggle" and to "base all illegal work on the principles of decentralization, secrecy, and vigilance." The resolution noted: "In this sector we find many weak spots, from the local organizations all the way up to the Central Committee and the Politburo." These instructions seem to be rather pro forma, since the Koliyannis faction appears to have a rather difficult time communicating with communists in Greece and competing effectively for support with the rival KKE (Interior). For this reason, the plenum paid special attention to the "emigrants," primarily the Greek workers employed by European industry (mostly in West Germany): "The Central Committee underlines the necessity to strengthen our Party's work among the emigrants, our main aim being to develop joint anti-dictatorial work together with other anti-dictatorial forces . . . and educate our members in the rules and methods of struggle." Such efforts, however, are seriously handicapped by the apathy of most emigrants and the proliferation of "anti-dictatorial" organizations which compete for support. (Ibid.)

The 16th Plenum again called on the party members to intensify their work within EDA's Patriotic Anti-dictatorial Front (PAM), which has branches in Greece and throughout Europe. But the resolution was actually referring to that part of PAM which adheres to Koliyannis because ever since the party split PAM has also been divided into pro-Koliyannis and anti-Koliyannis factions. Similar exhortations were addressed to the communists who operate within the clandestine EDA, in the Lambrakis Democratic Youth, and in the KNE (Communist Youth of Greece).

While the Koliyannis group claims a leading role, at the same time it makes a bid for a popular front with other "anti-dictatorial forces on the basis of a minimum program of action." Such a minimum program would include plans for a concerted effort to "overthrow the junta" and then move to a "democratic, anti-imperialist revolution which will free our people from the clutches of American imperialism and local oligarchy." On this point the Koliyannis KKE tries to appear moderate, to open the way to a broader cooperation of "all resistance forces." However, it cannot move too far away from its revolutionary commitments because to do so could blunt its own fight against the KKE (Interior), which is being accused precisely of being "revisionist" and petty-bourgeois. One may safely forecast that the popular front sought by Koliyannis KKE will not materialize.

KKE (Interior). The KKE (Interior) has continued to attack the resolutions issued by the Koliyannis group since 1968, especially those which contain attacks on "other Communist parties such as the Communist Party of China, the Yugoslav League of Communists, the Romanian Communist Party, the Albanian Workers' Party, and others." These resolutions, it says, "are invalid and in no way bind KKE." The implication is that the KKE (Interior) does not toe the Soviet or any other line. This independent stand was also reflected in the decisions of the "Extraordinary Plenum of the Central Committee of the KKE (Interior)" in July 1972 (*Enimerotikon Deltion,* no. 14, September, pp. 4–8). The Extraordinary Plenum avoided in its published statements any laudatory references to the Soviet Union or any other communist country. Instead, it renewed the call for a united "patriotic front" against the present government in Greece.

The July meeting dealt extensively with the claim of the Koliyannis group to direct the activities of the party and give orders to those "who have carried the burden of struggle within the country." It further attacked the Koliyannis group for its habit of reaching decisions without the participation of party members who are active in Greece, for "the centralization, the bureaucratic methods and distortions which have taken place in the peculiar conditions of émigré politics," and for its "deeply-rooted dogmatic-sectarian mentality," the "increasing estrangement of the party leadership from the rapidly changing reality," and the "inability of the leadership to evaluate properly the correlation of forces and chart a course in keeping with existing realities in the country."

The insistence of the Koliyannis group on imposing its will from afar was bound to lead to intra-party friction. "The crisis was brewing for a long time," according to the Extraordinary Plenum, "and it came into the open when the dictatorship revealed the serious errors in the party's policies against the fascist danger." The Koliyannis leadership, "unable to see the complexity of the realities in Greece, spent itself mouthing grandiose 'revolutionary' phrases, in automatically repeating some basic principles but in reality pushing the movement back to the tail end of life by keeping it unprepared politically, organizationally, technically, but surrounding it with a peculiar legalism . . . and imposing its will with the most undemocratic of methods." The main argument of the KKE (Interior) is that the forces of change have matured in its ranks, that the Koliyannis group no longer represents "the living party," and that the time has come for KKE to reassess "its place and role in the international Communist movement." Since the Soviet Union continues to regard the Koliyannis KKE as the legitimate party, the statements of the plenum are clearly anti-Soviet.

KKE (Marxist-Leninists). The third group, KKE (Marxist-Leninists), in the "decisions" of its First Conference, April 1972, and in several articles—in *Laiki Foni* ("People's Voice"), *Anaghenissi* ("Renaissance"), and *Espanastatis* ("Rebel"), communist papers published outside Greece in Europe—takes a clearly anti-Soviet and pro-Mao position and attacks both factions of KKE and all other leftist groupings as "revisionist." "We must understand," the First Conference warned, that "the struggle is between the true revolutionary Communists on the one side, the Marxist-Leninists of the entire world under the leadership of the Communist party of China and the Communist party of Albania, and on the other the revisionists and opportunists of every ilk led by the Communist party of the Soviet Union. . . . Today's revisionists are above all the defenders of a new bourgeoisie, the bourgeoisie of the social-imperialist Soviet Union." The First Conference also rejected any thought of a "united front from above." (*Enimerotikon Deltion,* no. 14, p. 14.)

International Views and Positions. In dealing with the international developments of the preceding months, the 16th Plenum of the Koliyannis KKE expressed full support for the U.S.-Soviet rapprochement: "Of special importance are the Nixon visit to Moscow, the joint Soviet-American communiqué—this most significant document which defines the relations between the two countries on the basis of the Leninist principle of peaceful coexistence—and the other agreements. . . . All these constitute a victory of the peace policy followed by the Soviet Union . . . and became possible because of the tremendous increase in economic, political, and military power achieved first of all by the Soviet Union and the entire Socialist system." The last remark is evidently designed to reassure the party members who are confused by this gradual dismantling of the cold war rhetoric. The Greek communists have taken this rhetoric rather seriously through the years and apparently find it difficult to grasp the reasons behind this improvement in the relations between the Soviet Union and the U.S. "imperialists." In the decisions of the 16th Plenum the Koliyannis group argues that Moscow remains always loyal to its Marxist-Leninist ideology and that the improvement was made possible because of U.S. "concessions." (*Enimerotikon Deltion,* no. 12, pp. 8–10.)

With regard to Cyprus, the Koliyannis group follows the Soviet policy of support to President (Archbishop) Makarios and to Cypriot independence, which presumably is threatened by the machinations of Washington and Athens. By contrast, the organization of the Marxist-Leninists has taken a clearly anti-Makarios stand. At the same time, this group has leveled fierce attacks against AKEL (see *Cyprus*) which is accused of using the slogan of "unity around Makarios" merely to "prepare the ground for the implementation of the designs of the imperialists . . . and the easier infiltration of Soviet social-imperialism" (ibid., no. 14, p. 24).

International Communist Movement. The fragmentation of the Greek communist forces is in effect a reflection of the current conditions in the international communist movement. The Koliyannis KKE is totally committed to the Soviet leadership and, in spite of occasional difficulties, continues to parrot the Soviet line on every issue, including the awkwardly normal relations between the Soviet and Greek governments. The KKE (Interior), in contrast, is currently assuming a posture of independence from the international communist movement by taking a rather even-handed attitude toward the two major camps, the Soviet and the Chinese. The Nea Aristera has yet to develop a coherent and comprehensive program, but from what it has already published one may assume that it, too, will try to remain independent of the international communist movement in all its warring factions. The KKE (Marxist-Leninists) is, of course, upholding the Maoist line. Not surprisingly, communist parties which have taken a rather independent stand in their relations with the Soviet Union tend to give their support to the KKE (Interior). This is particularly true of the Romanian and Italian parties. Other European communist parties tend to ignore the schism and, pro forma, maintain contacts with the Koliyannis group. The Marxist-Leninists turn for financial and other assistance to the Albanian communists and also to the Romanians, who allow one of the largest organizations of this faction to operate among the Greek communists living in the city of Orantea. It may be added that the group's headquarters is reportedly located in Bucharest. In any event, these various factions are handicapped by the ambivalent policies of their patrons toward the present government in Greece.

Party Media. There are three categories of communist publications: (1) those published abroad by the émigré groups, such as *Rizospastis* ("Radical") and the theoretical review *Neos Kosmos* ("New World"), (controlled by the Koliyannis group), and other local newspapers such as *Elefteria* ("Freedom") in Bulgaria, *Laikos Agonas* ("People's Struggle") in Hungary, *Laiki Foni* ("People's Voice") (Marxist-Leninists), *Anaghenissi* (Marxist-Leninists), *Neos Dromos* ("New Roads") (by the Greek communists in Tashkent, U.S.S.R.); (2) the clandestine newspapers published inside Greece, such *Adhouloti Athina* ("Unconquered Athens") *Odhiyitis* ("Guide"—a KKE-Interior version of *Rizospastis), Lefteria* (pro-Koliyannis), *O Makhtis* ("The Fighter"), and two versions of *Eleftheri Patrida* ("Free Motherland"), one pro-Koliyannis, the other pro-Interior; and (3) pro-communist books published openly in Greece by various publishing houses, of which in 1972 more than 54 titles appeared, including books by Che Guevara, Marcuse, Trotsky, and Engels. The KKE radio station, "Voice of Truth," thought to be based in Leipzig, East Germany, broadcasts frequently to Greece.

Howard University   D. George Kousoulas

Iceland

Most Icelandic communists belong to the People's Alliance (Altýdubandalagid; AB), a socialist labor party so named since 1968. The first communist party in Iceland sprang from a secessionist left wing of the Social Democratic Party in 1930 and has been legal ever since. On 24 October 1938—now considered the birth date of the Icelandic communist party—that original party was reorganized to include more radical Social Democrats and renamed the United People's Party–Socialist Party (UPP–SP). By the late 1940s pro-Soviet members had assumed control of the UPP–SP. In 1956 communists and leftist Social Democrats tried to join forces again. The result was an electoral front known as the People's Alliance (PA). In November 1968 the front became an explicit "Marxist political party," divorced from the two other main factions in the Icelandic communist movement—Hannibal Valdimarsson's important Organization of Liberals and Leftists (OLL) and the pro-Soviet, politically insignificant Organization of Icelandic Socialists (OIS). The number of hard-core communists affiliated with the PA remained around 2,000 to 2,500 in 1972, out of a total population of 207,300. The PA continued to draw its support from a disparate amalgam of labor union members, radical teachers and students, die-hard nationalists, and disgruntled Social Democrats.

Despite its changing names and constant internal strife, the PA has been uniquely fortunate and important among West European communist parties. It is one of the few to participate in democratically elected government. It has polled between 12 and 20 percent of the Icelandic vote since World War II. In the last parliamentary election, June 1971, it received 17.1 percent of the vote and 10 of the 60 seats in the Althing (Parliament). The PA thus joined the OLL (9 percent of the vote and 5 seats) and the Progressive Party (25 percent and 17 seats) to form a left-center government. Two communists—Ludvik Josefsson and Magnus Kjartansson—joined the seven-man cabinet. That coalition, under Progressive Prime Minister Olafur Johannesson, replaced the decade-old leadership of the Independence and Social Democratic parties. Throughout 1972 it continued to make its mark, with strong PA urging, on Icelandic fishing rights and the pledge to oust the U.S.-manned Icelandic Defense Force (IDF) from the Keflavk base by 1975. The hard line of Josefsson, communist minister of fisheries and commerce, was largely responsible for the new "cod war" with the United Kingdom which started on 1 September when Iceland unilaterally extended its fishing limits from 12 to 50 nautical miles.

Leadership and Organization. Ragnar Arnalds, former leader of the anti-NATO National Opposition Party, remained PA chairman. First elected in November 1968 to succeed long-time leader Einar Olgeirsson, Arnalds was reelected at the PA congress held on 19–21 November 1971. The party's female vice-chairman, Adda Bara Sigfusdottir, also retained her position. Olafur Einarsson was elected chairman of the Management Council by the Central

Committee on 19 January 1972. The council, which meets weekly, is the party's highest authority between meetings of the Central Committee. At a meeting on 21–22 October the PA Executive Council elected a new 32-member Central Committee. Although party regulations permit only a three-year term, five old members stayed on—the chairman and vice-chairman, and Jon Snorri Thorleifsson, Ludvik Josefsson, and Magnus Kjartansson.

Party Internal Affairs. Factionalism has always plagued Icelandic communists. In fact, the parliamentary strength of the PA has more often fluctuated because of intra-party strife than through changes in popular support. The power struggle between the communists and the "Hannibalists" for control of the PA in 1968 was the clearest case in point. Hannibal Valdimarsson—the pivotal force in Icelandic politics, who now heads the OLL but once chaired the PA—kept control during 1972 of five seats in the Althing which might normally have gone to the communists.

Within the PA itself, the rivalry between the two communist cabinet ministers sharpened in 1972. Ludvik Josefsson seemed eager to score immediate political points despite the cost in governmental stability or international good will, whereas Magnus Kjartansson tried to formulate more moderate positions with long-term validity. Their differences were clearest on the issue of fishing limits and the approach toward foreign investment and domestic economic development. Josefsson, with his apparent intransigence toward the British on fishing rights, often antagonized the rest of the Johannesson cabinet and came close to precipitating the fall of the government.

Despite its internal division, the PA had previously managed to escape the challenge from the "left" which the Sino-Soviet split brought to so many communist parties elsewhere. That changed when the "Communist Organization of Marxist-Leninists" held its founding congress, 5–7 August. The organization intends to stress the teachings of Engels, Lenin, Stalin, and Mao. According to Sigurdur Jon Olafsson, the movement's spokesman, the group traces its heritage back to the early days of communism in Iceland, before the established party "converted into a half-bred social democratic party" (*Visir,* Reykjavik 9 August 1972). The Central Committee consists of Gunnar Andresson as chairman, Hjalmtyr Heiddal, and Einar Andressson.

Domestic Views and Activities. Leaders of the People's Alliance stress that theirs is a "socialist labor party which fights for socialism and increased democracy in every field" (*Thjodviljinn,* 22 October 1972). It claims to fight for "a new social makeup where social concern, equality, and democracy are most important" (ibid.). With that philosophy in mind, the PA Executive Council emphasized at its October meeting that Iceland's persistent economic problems will not be solved until basic changes are implemented in the nation's economic system. The council asserted that the "overhead" in society must be cut down, while at the same time well-organized state planning is carried out (*Timinn,* 24 October). The council stipulated that economic measures be taken to assure full employment and guarantee increased purchasing power for low wage-earners.

Tax reform was another focus for the PA's domestic program. The party stressed that the tax system should be reviewed in order that the tax burden be divided more justly. It specified that it is a PA policy to abolish uniform taxes and those on below-average earnings and to increase real estate taxes. (*Thjodviljinn,* 30 January).

The PA continued to play a leading role in the labor movement. Edvard Sigurdsson headed the General Workers' Union, Iceland's largest single labor union.

International Views and Activities. Proclamations on economic reform notwithstanding, the PA clearly concentrated in 1972 on one issue that had both domestic and international implications—fishing rights. Because Iceland depends so heavily on fish exports for its livelihood and because most Icelanders agreed that fishing limits had to be extended to protect the dwindling stock, the question was a politician's dream. Minister Josefsson proceeded to take a hard line on the unilateral extension of Iceland's fishing limits from 12 to 50 nautical miles —effective 1 September—no matter the consequences. His firm stand had been largely responsible for the first "cod war" with the British, in 1958–61, and lay behind the outbreak of incidents between Icelandic and British trawlers in the autumn of 1972. Unlike his colleagues in the government, Josefsson resisted efforts to compromise on an interim agreement with London. The PA Executive Council affirmed at its October meeting the objective of adhering to the new 50-mile limit, "without giving an inch, until a complete victory has been achieved" (*Thjodviljinn,* 22 October).

Icelandic membership in NATO and the U.S.-manned IDF at Keflavík continued to be prime PA targets. The party demanded repeatedly, as in previous years, that Iceland leave NATO and that it rid itself of all military bases by 1974, when Iceland will celebrate the 1100th anniversary of its founding. For most of 1972, the Johannesson government did not act on its announced objective to review the 1951 Defense Agreement with the United States and seek a phased withdrawal of the IDF during the coalition's four-year term of office. The PA appeared to be the most energetic of the three governing parties in acting on that plank of the government's platform. The PA urged all "anti-occupationists" to support the ouster of the IDF as a "great victory in the country's fight for independence" (ibid., 20 January). On a related issue, the PA continued to condemn the U.S. operation of a TV station at the Keflavík base as a campaign to "capture the minds of Icelanders" and weaken their powers to resist foreign encroachment (ibid., 5 March).

Though entry into the European Economic Community did not dominate public discussion in Iceland as elsewhere in Scandinavia, it was an international concern of the PA. The party clearly sided with EEC opponents throughout the Nordic area. It did so not only because it opposed Icelandic affiliation with the enlarged Common Market, but also because it believed that Icelanders could expect most understanding from EEC opponents on Iceland's fishing rights and the withdrawal of the IDF. The party warned that Danish and Norwegian EEC membership might end Nordic economic cooperation and let the Americans "close their fist tighter around Iceland" (ibid., 18 February).

International Party Contacts. Icelandic communists have generally stood aloof from international party contacts and debates. The PA has tended to put national considerations above the dictates of Marxist-Leninist ideology. That trend continued in 1972, with the PA limiting its recent inter-party contacts to talks with the Romanian Communist Party and to sending a few messages to gatherings of West European communists. When a four-man Romanian delegation visited Iceland in June there was little reference to inter-party ties; stress was put instead on sovereign relations between independent nations.

The current PA leadership has broken away from most vestiges of a pro-Soviet orientation. Continuing criticism of the Soviet-led invasion of Czechoslovakia in 1968 exemplified its independent stand in inter-party dealings. An editorial in the party newspaper stated: "The trials and sentences now taking place in Czechoslovakia on account of political acts are completely opposed to all socialistic ideas and are still a further attack on the struggle being waged by all those who honor socialistic ideas in word and deed" (*Thjodviljinn,* 17 August).

A delegation from the World Peace Council, based in Helsinki, visited Iceland on 6–12

May. The visitors included Romesh Chandra, director; Kazimierz Kielan, secretary; and Matti Kekkonen, member of the directorate and son of Finnish President Kekkonen. The council representatives announced complete support for Iceland's position in the fisheries dispute (ibid., 9 May).

Publications. The PA's central organ is the daily Reykjavík newspaper, *Thjodviljinn* ("Will of the Nation"). The party publishes a biweekly theoretical journal, *Ny Utsyn.* The publication of the new Maoist organization is *Stettabarattan* ("Class Struggle").

Ireland

The Communist Party of Ireland (CPI) was founded in 1921, but its initial existence was short lived. It was refounded in 1933—a date adopted by present Irish communists as the original year of the party's founding. The organizational structure of the CPI was disrupted during World War II, partly as a result of the fact that the Republic of Ireland, in the south, declared itself neutral while Northern Ireland participated in the conflict. In 1948 the communists in the south founded the Irish Workers' Party (IWP), and those in the north the Communist Party of Northern Ireland (CPNI). At a special "Unity Congress" held in Belfast on 15 March 1970, the two parties reunited, founding once again the united Communist Party of Ireland. The party now based in Dublin, held its Fifteenth Congress on 16–17 October 1971 in Belfast.

The CPI is estimated to have a strength of about 300 and has more supporters among northern Protestants than among southern Catholics. The population of the Republic of Ireland is 2,921,000 and that of Northern Ireland is 1,500,000 (1971 census). On 24 March 1972 the British Government imposed direct rule on Northern Ireland and suspended the powers and authority of the Stormont government (*YICA 1972*, p. 189) for at least one year.

Although the CPI is not strong in either the north or the south and holds no seats in any legislative body, it wields influence in Irish politics disproportionate to its small size because of its association with the "Official" wing of the Irish Republic Army (see *ibid.*, pp. 189–91, and for further details *The Ulster Debate*, report of a study group of the Institute for the Study of Conflict, London: Bodley Head, 1972) and to a lesser extent with the Northern Ireland Civil Rights Association (NICRA) (Edwina Steward general secretary)—the latter an uneasy coalition of a wide range of political groups (but which has communists in several key positions) opposed to British policy in Northern Ireland. The CPI controls a small youth organization, the Connolly Youth Movement (CYM), formed in 1965 and led by Madge Davison. The CPI has minimal strength in the labor movement.

Leadership and Organization. In its current form of CPI's leading body—the Executive Committee—is divided into two branches representing the north and the south. The party's founding congress in March 1970 elected Michael O'Riordan as general secretary, Andrew Barr as party chairman, and James Stewart as assistant general secretary. (For Executive Committee and Secretariat names see *YICA, 1972* p. 189.)

Domestic Views and Policies. The fundamental goal of the CPI is to create a 32-county (26 in the south and 6 in the north) united socialist republic in Ireland. To accomplish this, the party advocates the formation of a "national liberation front" in which it seeks the participation of Protestants as well as the predominantly anti-Unionist Catholics. But Protestants in the north are opposed to unification since it would mean losing the majority position they have enjoyed there. The CPI therefore, seeks to aim at those issues which are not mutually antagonistic to both sects. The CPI attempts to unite the two communities through the labor movement and around common grievances—principally inadequate housing, increased living costs, unemployment, and opposition to the Common Market. In its view the present situation, north and south, is a consequence of British "colonial" policy. It maintains that economic underdevelopment accentuated by "exploitation" can be overcome by socialism.

The CPI considers the situation in the north as being extremely complicated but one that does not call for the indiscriminate violence of the "Provisional" IRA and some extremists of the People's Democracy or *Saor Eire*. In 1972 the CPI was concerned almost exclusively with the conflict in northern Ireland, which intensified during the year. Its pronounced policy of non-violence was compromised by its association with the Official IRA; the latter admitted responsibility for a bomb attack on Aldershot Barracks (British Army headquarters) on 22 February in which seven persons died. As most of the terrorist violence was committed by the Provisional IRA (republican, non-communist, and Catholic), that group was strongly and steadily attacked by the CPI. "They [the Provisionals] rely in the most non-political manner on such campaigns as bombings, the net effect of which is to obstruct the development of the mass movement and the pre-requisite of establishing unity between the Catholic and Protestant sections of the working people" (Michael O'Riordan in the Communist Party of Great Britain [CPGB] organ *Morning Star,* 4 December).

The British Government's policy toward the Ulster conflict was treated with hostility. The CPI expressed suspicions of a tacit alliance between the British Army and the northern Protestants, and although these were unfounded the CPI remained mistrustful: "The British Tory Government and the British Army would . . . break all effective working-class organisations" (James Stewart, ibid., 30 October).

The CPI Executive Committee issued a statement on the northern conflict on 8 November which called for a boycott of the plebiscite (British proposals for local government elections and a border agreement), the enactment of a Bill of Rights, the repeal of the Special Powers Act, and the release of all internees: "The Communist Party calls for the creation of democratic conditions that will permit the election of a Democratic Assembly" (ibid., 9 November).

The Official IRA generally supported the policy of the CPI. In an interview Cathal Goulding, chief of staff of the Official IRA, stated "No elite will ever develop a revolutionary struggle. . . . Our future policy . . . is twofold. First of all to continue the mass struggle for democratisation [and secondly to secure] national liberation by campaigning for working-class solidarity which would lead to socialism and a socialist republic in Ireland." (Ibid., 15 November.)

International Views and Positions. In contrast to its domestic activities, the CPI was only fitfully active in 1972 on international issues, of which there were mainly two—Ireland and the Common Market, and Irish-Soviet relations. The CPI opposed the Common Market; a southern area congress of the CPI on 25 November adopted a resolution which urged that "all efforts should be made . . . for a common fight against the EEC monopolists."

Attempts by the Soviet Union to establish trade and diplomatic relations with the Republic of Ireland were unsuccessful. While no official reasons were given by either the British or Irish governments, Michael O'Riordan called for the "rejection of British Tory pressures which have intimidated the Dublin Government from establishing normal trade and diplomatic relations with the Soviet Union and other socialist countries" (ibid., 4 December).

The CPI's youth wing, the Connolly Youth Movement, closely followed the CPI's program. At its Second Congress, in Dublin, October, the CYM's national secretary, Madge Davison, pointed out that the party continued to play a "vital and progressive role in Northern Ireland working to end sectarian splits between Protestant and Catholic youth, and for a Bill of Rights to end discrimination against the Catholic minority" (*Challenge,* organ of the CPGB's Young Communist League, no. 11).

The CPI undertook few visits in 1972, the major one being that of James Stewart, who visited Bulgaria in June for the ninetieth anniversary of Georgi Dimitrov. Edwina Stewart, of the CPI's northern branch and secretary of NICRA, was a frequent visitor to Britain.

The CPI and the CYM have to contend with several left-wing, extra-parliamentary groups which exist in Ireland—in 1972 at least twenty-three such groups existed, among them the Communist Party of Ireland (Marxist-Leninist), which is Maoist; the Trotskyist Revolutionary Marxist Group; the eclectic People's Democracy; and the League for a Workers' Republic. But the urban conflict in the north obscured orthodox radical political activities in the country.

Publications. The CPI distributes three publications: *Weekly Bulletin, Irish Socialist* (monthly), and its theoretical journal, *Irish Socialist Review*. The CYM organ is the fortnightly *Forward*.

London, England   D. L. Price

Italy

The Italian Communist Party (Partito Comunista Italiano; PCI) was founded in 1921. In recent years the PCI has been confronted with marginal competition from a number of small parties and groups adhering to Marxism-Leninism of differing shades of interpretation. During 1972, as in 1971, the main challenge to the PCI leadership within the extreme left continued to originate from the Manifesto group (see below).

The PCI is the largest non-ruling communist party in the world, with some 1,521,000 members. The party's youth auxiliary, the Italian Communist Youth Federation (Federazione Giovanile Comunista Italiana; FGCI) has between 90,000 and 100,000 members. (*World Strength of the Communist Party Organizations,* Washington, D.C., 1972, pp. 22–23.) The population of Italy is 55,338,000 (estimated 1972).

On 15 January the center-left coalition government of Premier Emilio Colombo resigned. On 18 February, after several unsuccessful attempts, Giulio Andreotti, one of the Christian Democrat leaders, formed a new government with an entirely Christian Democrat cabinet. The new single-party government did not receive the vote of confidence from the parliament, and President Giovanni Leone, for the first time in the history of the Italian Republic, dissolved the parliament before the natural close of the term of the legislature and called for national elections. In the general elections for the Chamber of Deputies and the Senate held on 7–8 May, the Christian Democrat party (Democrazia Cristiana; DC), though plagued by disunity and under attack from both right- and left-wing parties, held its position, obtaining 12,943,675 votes (38.8 percent) in the Chamber, with 267 deputies (out of 630), and 11,457,746 (31.1 percent) in the Senate, with 135 senators (out of 322). The Italian Socialist Party (Partito Socialista Italiano; PSI) maintained its seats in the Chamber (61 deputies) obtaining 3,209,503 votes (9.6 percent), but lost 4 seats in the Senate, getting 3,224,778 votes (10.6 percent). Also the Italian Social-Democratic Party (Partito Socialdemocratico Italiano; PSDI) maintained its positions both in the Chamber with 1,716,197 votes (5.1 percent) and 29 deputies, and in the Senate with 1,612,880 (5.4 percent) with 11 senators. The Italian Republican Party (Partito Repubblicano Italiano; PRI) obtained 973,681 votes (2.9 percent) in the Chamber, with 14 deputies, and 917,392 votes (3.0 percent) in the Senate, with 5 senators. The Italian Social Movement (Movimento Sociale Italiano; MSI) did not get the massive support that it expected to obtain, but doubled its seats. It made an electorale alliance with the Italian Democratic Party of Monarchic Unity (Partito Democratico Italiano di Unità Monarchica; PDIUM) and the combined votes totaled 2,894,789 (8.7 percent) in the Chamber for 56 seats and 2,763,719 (9.2 percent) in the Senate for 26 seats. The gains made by the MSI were at the expense of the Italian Liberal Party (Partito Liberale Italiano; PLI), which suffered a big loss in the Chamber, obtaining 1,300,074 votes (3.9 percent), with 21 deputies, and lost 8 seats in the Senate, collecting 1,317,909 votes (4.4 percent) and placing 8 senators. In the vote for the Chamber of Deputies the PCI slightly increased its 1968 poll, getting 9,085,927 votes (27.2 percent) and gaining 2 seats for a total of 179. In the voting for the Senate the leftist "unitary list," comprising the PCI and the Italian Socialist Party of Proletarian Unity (Partito Socialista Italiano di Unità Proletaria; PSIUP) obtained 8,308,283 votes (27.6 percent) and 91 senators—a loss of 10 seats compared with the 1968 elections. The Senate losses were blamed on the PSIUP, which also lost all its seats in the Chamber.

The elections showed small numerical changes from the 1968 figures, but the outcome put an end to the center-left coalition that had led Italy for the past ten years. On 26 June, after several weeks of unsuccessful consultations, Giulio Andreotti formed a center-right coalition government comprising the DC, PSDI, and PLI, with the external support of the PRI. The PLI participated in the government after 12 years of opposition from the right.

The administrative elections held in some parts of Italy on 26 November showed an increase in PSI support.

Organization and Leadership. In 1972 the PCI was structured as follows: 109 federations, 18 regional committees, some 11,000 sections, and about 25,000 cells, together with a large number of youth clubs. The party established also federations abroad (Belgium, Switzerland, Germany, and Luxemburg). The unpaid or part-paid directive committees of these organs numbered more than 80,000 persons. There were probably more than 1,000 full-time paid officials of the federations and sections, with some 200 to 300 at party headquarters in Rome (not including those engaged in the party press).

The directive organs of the PCI are elected at the party's congresses. The Thirteenth Congress, held in Milan on 13–17 March 1972, elected the Central Committee (196 members), Central Control Committee (52), and Directorate (34), the latter working largely through two executive committees, the Political Office (17) and the Secretariat (7). In addition there is a small audit board.

Luigi Longo was elected president of the party, after holding the post of secretary-general since 1964. Enrico Berlinguer was elected secretary-general; he is also member of the Political Office and of the Secretariat. Other leading members of the party elected at the congress are Giorgio Amendola, Gerardo Chiaromonte, Pietro Ingrao, Emanuele Macaluso, Giorgio Napolitano, Alessandro Natta, Agostino Novella, Alfredo Rechlin, and Aldo Tortorella (members of the Political Office), and Paolo Bufalini, Armando Cossutta, Fernando Di Giulio, Carlo Galluzzi, Giancarlo Pajetta, and Ugo Pecchioli (members of the Political Office and of the Secretariat). Gianfranco Borghini is the secretary of the FGCI; he may participate in meetings of the Political Office. Aldo Tortorella is the director of *L'Unità* and Luca Pavolini the co-director. Gerardo Chiaromonte is the director of *Rinascita* (the party's weekly political organ) and Romano Ledda the assistant director.

The PCI dominates the largest of the three main Italian trade union organizations, the General Confederation of Italian Labor (Confederazione Generale Italiana del Lavoro; CGIL). The secretary-general, Luciano Lama, is a PCI member. The CGIL has collaborated closely with the DC unions in the Confederazione Italiana Sindacati Lavoratori (CISL) and the PSDI-PRI unions affiliated with the Unione Italiana del Lavoro (UIL). Efforts toward unification into a single confederation (see *YICA, 1972,* pp. 193–94) went ahead in 1972, though hampered by political events. On 24 July at a joint session of the general councils of the CGIL, CISL, and UIL a federation pact of the three trade union confederations was signed.

Party Internal Affairs. No significant changes came out of the PCI's Thirteenth Congress. The 72-year-old former secretary-general Luigi Longo was given the new and honorific post of party president. His successor, the 49-year-old Enrico Berlinguer, has been his deputy since 1969 and de facto leader during Longo's prolonged ill-health. The nomination of Berlinguer showed the unity of the PCI and meant that the party intended to pursue the "centrist" policy inspired by Giorgio Amendola and implemented by Berlinguer in recent years.

Among the 1,042 delegates at the congress, 145 were women; 146 were young persons under 25 years of age, and 171 between 26 and 30 years—an increase in youth representation of 8 percent compared with the Twelfth Congress. There were 247 delegates between the ages of 31 and 40. The average age of delegates was about 37 years, two years younger than that registered at the previous congress. By occupations, 391 were industrial workers, 45 were agricultural workers or day laborers, 36 were small farmers and sharecroppers, 96 were students, 43 were technicians, 191 were professionals and intellectuals, and 20 were artisans and merchants. The congress was also attended by 122 delegates of the FGCI, by representative of all democratic Italian parties and mass organizations, and by 50 delegations from foreign communist and workers' parties and revolutionary and progressive movements.

At the congress, the Autonomous Socialist Movement (Movimento Socialista Autonomo; MSA) announced its merger with the PCI. Its secretary, Dino Fioriello, was elected to the Central Committee.

On 16 July the Italian Socialist Party of Proletarian Unity (Partito Socialista Italiano di Unità Proletaria; PSIUP) held its fourth and what may have been its last congress and decided to dissolve the party. About two-thirds of the membership opted to join the PCI, and about 8 percent rejoined the PSI. The rest, however, decided to maintain the party's separate identity.

Domestic Views and Policies. PCI interest in 1972 centered upon Italy's economic and political crisis, the May general elections; the gains of the fascist party, the end of the center-left coalition and the formation of a center-right government, and the ups and downs in the process of trade union unification.

The Thirteenth Congress was the first PCI congress to take place during an electoral campaign. "The first task of the Congress," said Berlinguer in his opening report, "is to define the program and the political proposal which are presenting to the electorate." Stressing the need to "give a new political direction to the country," Berlinguer declared: "In a country like Italy a new perspective can only come about through collaboration between the three great popular currents: Communist, Socialist, and Catholic." On the question of the participation of communists in government or in a parliamentary majority, he said: "Such participation is admissible under two conditions: either the necessity to face a reactionary attack which creates a situation of emergency for the future of democracy, or the existence of conditions which allow the implementation of a program of renewal which has the conscious and active support of the broad masses and tends to reinforce the unity of the workers and their political and ideal representatives." He then added that "the nature of the Italian crisis is such today that these two conditions tend to coincide." Berlinguer also explained what the PCI meant by participation in the government: "The alternative . . . that we propose has nothing to do with an enlargement of the Center-Left. It means going beyond the Center-Left and requires the elimination of all anti-communist discrimination." The building of an alternative government, he indicated, required the "defeat of the Christian Democrat party" for "setting the Catholic democratic and popular forces free and opening them up to contact and collaboration with the Communist and Socialist forces." (*L'Unità,* 14 March.)

The PCI strategy remained the one indicated by Giorgio Amendola starting in 1969 and still confirmed by him: "The PCI as a government party is not an election slogan. It implies participation in the country's political leadership" (*L'Espresso,* 19 March). On the same question Alessandro Natta explained the party's position: "The political prospect for a new majority, for a democratically oriented administration, thus appears quite a bit more complex and articulated than any other 'bloc' or 'front' scheme of the left wing forces, to which some people often try to reduce it . . . The cardinal point in a political turnabout is the unity of the left-wing forces, the transition [from] albeit significant and relevant convergence, on individual issues, to a very fundamental understanding on the great topics of national policy." Discussing the significance of the party congress, Natta emphasized that "If we want to single out one relevant aspect . . . we might point up the powerful resurgence and the broad range of the entire Gramscian topic complex dealing with moral and intellectual reform." (*Rinascita,* 17 March.)

On the elections results Berlinguer commented: "Forty per cent of the electorate voted for the left. Unfortunately, the positive results registered by the PCI and the PSI have been accompanied by the fact that the PSIUP has not obtained representation in the Chamber of Deputies. This is in part due to the dispersal of votes caused by the running of disturbance candidates and the action of certain extremist groups. . . . The DC, although it took votes away from its center allies, has not succeeded in reaching its 1968 percentage. The prospects for a centrist solution have been politically defeated." (*L'Unità,* 9 March.)

In an interview (*Népszabadság,* Budapest, 23 July) Berlinguer stressed the PCI's disagreement with Italy's new center-right government: "This government constitutes a break from and an open challenge to the entire workers' movement, the people's mass. With its composition, as regards both the participating parties and individual politicians, it obviously opens the doors to the right and encourages the right wing. This government is the logical consequence and result of the rightist turnabout made by leading groups of the Christian Democrat party in the spring of 1971, which led to the fact that the party has unilaterally repudiated the political alliances it had entered into previously. It has terminated its alliance with the PSI in order to revive, after 15 years, its ties with the PLI. . . . This government relies on a parliamentary majority which, with regard to numerical conditions, is one of the scantiest of all governments formed since the establishment of the republic: on barely one and a half dozen votes in the Chamber of Deputies and only four votes in the Senate." Berlinguer then added that the PCI would "wage a resolute and consistent struggle of opposition . . . to bring to maturity a positive alternative. By uniting all leftist and democratic forces, such an alternative is both feasible and necessary."

On trade union unification, Berlinguer blamed the DC and other parties for the difficulties met in the unification process: "They (the DC, PSDI, and PRI) have done and are doing their best to slow down, and, at times, actually sabotage trade union unification. And at the same time, while they talk about autonomy, they heavy-handedly interfere in the life of the unions. Their ends are evident: to prevent unification and, in any event, to deprive the union movement of its class nature; to convince the workers to forget about the political struggle. . . . Full recognition of trade union autonomy is an integral part of our conception of the process of renewal of society." Criticising the center-left administration, he declared: "It is not resources that are lacking in Italy. It is how they are being used that must be changed. The reforms are also a way of creating new resources." (Ibid.)

In its election program the PCI proposed a wide range of reforms, among them lowering the voting age to 18 years and the shortening of the period of compulsory military service. It also formulated a new economic policy which aimed at achieving "full employment at the highest technological levels historically reached; elimination of existing imbalances, and primarily, solution of the Southern question; satisfaction of the primary needs of all citizens for schools, health, housing, transportation, and protection of the environment." The PCI contributed to the introduction of divorce in Italy in 1970, and in 1972 it presented to the Parliament a reform of family law, comprising also a reform of the divorce law. The party also took officially a position for the first time on the problems of women's liberation. In his report to congress Berlinguer declared that "the condition of women is also a question at once social and ideal. Woman's fight for a civil dignity equal to man's is linked, first of all, to her entrance into production activity and social life. . . . Women are used as occasional reserves of manpower, exploiting the objectively weak bargaining position of the female labor force." He also said that women should be "stimulated and organized to systematically and rationally reject their continued subjection to that form of 'hidden exploitation' represented by domestic slavery." (*L'Unità*, 14 March.)

International Views and Policies. In 1972 the PCI maintained a position of autonomy with regard to the views and policies of other communist parties. The party emphasized its independence and its right to criticize socialist regimes: "the full freedom of judgment which we express regarding the events and experiences of the socialist countries and the workers' movement" (*L'Unità*, 18 March). At the party congress only two foreign delegations, those of North Vietnam and the Soviet Union, were allowed to deliver their messages of greeting from the podium; all the others submitted theirs in writing for publication in *L'Unità*. The message of the Communist Party of Czechoslovakia, was published with a critical introduction expressing disagreement: "In the spirit dictated by an internationalism which allows not only for diversity but also for deep divergences and a method which for us is a question of substance, we publish in full the message of the delegation of the Czechoslovak CP, expressing the positions of that party-position which we do not share, but which we believe it right to bring to the knowledge of our comrades" (*L'Unità*, 16 March).

In his concluding speech to the Thirteenth Congress, Berlinguer stated that the PCI had reconfirmed its "basic position which unites internationalism and internationalist solidarity with the full autonomy of our Party, not only in the elaboration and conduct of its policy in Italy, but also in that other facet of our autonomy which expresses itself in our full freedom of judgement on the events and developments of the Socialist countries and the working class movement. . . . We want to take Italy out from under the subordination to a foreign imperialism in which it has been placed by its ruling classes. We want to restore Italy to independence, sovereignty and security, so that it can play the role of a great and free nation within the West, a role of European and world scope" (*L'Unità*, 17 March).

Berlinguer proposed that 1972 become "the year of a great mobilization for the defeat of U.S. aggression [in Indochina] and to force the Italian government to recognize the People's Republic of China." On U.S. President Nixon's visit to China he commented that "this visit definitively consecrated the failure of twenty-three years of U.S. policy toward People's China." Charging that Italian foreign policy was dependent on that of the United States, he declared: "It is becoming increasingly evident that the 'special relations' created with the United States have become an obstacle to the existence of an Italian foreign policy capable of expressing . . . the basic interests of our country." (Ibid., 14 March.)

International Party Contacts. On 8–15 January 1972 a delegation of the French Communist Party (PCF) made a study visit to Italy. On 18 January Luigi Longo received Vladimir Bakarić member of the Executive Bureau of the presidency of the League of Communists of Yugoslavia. In February Paul Niculescu-Mizil of the Romanian Communist Party Central Committee visited Rome and was received by Giorgio Amendola. On 21 April, in Paris, Berlinguer conferred with the leaders of the peace talks delegations of North Vietnam and the Provisional Revolutionary Government of South Vietnam. On 6 June a delegation of the Portuguese Communist Party met in Rome with Enrico Berlinguer. On 20 June an Iraqi delegation including leaders of the Ba'th Party, Iraqi' Communist Party, and Kurdish Democratic Party visited the PCI. A delegation of the Communist Party of Greece visited on 6 July. A PCI delegation was received in Paris on 12 July by the PCF. On 7 August a PCI representative met in Moscow with B. Ponomarev of the Central Committee of the Communist Party of the Soviet Union (CPSU). On 24 July the PCI welcomed a CPSU delegation in Rome. A PCI representative met with Nicolae Ceausescu in Romania on 6 September. In September, Gheorghe Pana, Romanian Communist Party Central Committee secretary, visited Italy. On 18–19 September a PCI delegation met with a Belgian Communist Party delegation in Brussels. A Yugoslav delegation met with PCI leaders in Rome on 6–18 November.

Publications. Among the many PCI publications, the principal ones are *L'Unità*, a daily newspaper; *Rinascita,* a weekly political journal, and *Critica Marxista,* a bimonthly theoretical organ. The party also controls a Rome daily, *Paese Sera.* The CGIL publishes *Rassegna Sindacale,* and the FGCI publishes *Nuova Generazione. Giorni-Vie Nuove* is a popular illustrated weekly published by the PCI.

*   *   *

In 1972 the so-called ultra-leftist groups that have proliferated in Italy since 1968 appeared to undergo a crisis. A great number of young people apparently preferred to join the FGCI. Examining the reasons of the crisis of the Italian splinter groups, a PCI writer commented: "The high-water mark of an alleged 'Leninist' revival coincided with the loss of one of the fundamental Leninist lessons, which teaches us constantly to subject revolutionary action to practical analysis of a practical situation. . . . Their sudden separation from the reality of the social struggle in Italy plunged the splinter groups into crisis. . . . In the driver's seat is not policy, but 'ideology' in the negative sense Marx put upon it; the inspiration is not reflection relating to living experience, but their own plan for defence, for their own survival. Isolation and with it the loss of any vestige of a mass line, becomes inevitable. . . . Out of direct counterposition to the organized movement grows the now prevalent rejection of organization of any kind on the one hand, and on the other, criticism of politics as such, as the science of society, as a movement of synthesis and mediation." (*Rinascita,* 31 March.)

The three main "ultra-leftist" organizations in 1972 were still the Manifesto, Worker Power (Potere Operaio), and Continuous Struggle (Lotta Continua) groups (see *YICA, 1972,* p. 198). The Manifesto underwent a big electoral failure when it presented its first candidacy in the May elections.

The most important Italian pro-Chinese parties were the Communist Party of Italy–Marxist-Leninist (Partito Comunista d'Italia–Marxista-Leninista), the Organization of Marxist-Leninist Communists of Italy (Organizzazione dei Comunisti Marxisti-Leninisti d'Italia), and the Union of Italian Communists (Marxist-Leninist)—Unione dei Comunisti Italiani (Marxista-Leninista). The last of these groups changed its name on 15 April to Italian Communist (Marxist-Leninist) Party according to *Servire il Popolo,* Milan, 22 April. The main Trotskyist organization was the Revolutionary Communist Groups (Gruppi Comunisti Rivoluzionari), affiliated with the United Secretariat of the Fourth International. (See *YICA, 1972,* p. 199.)

Milan, Italy   Carla Liverani

Luxembourg

The Communist Party of Luxembourg (Parti Communiste de Luxembourg; PCL) was established in January 1921. The PCL enjoys legal status and is strongly pro-Soviet. It is the only communist movement in Luxembourg. Membership figures are not published by the PCL, but Western sources place its strength at 500 to 1,000 persons. The population of Luxembourg is 400,000 (estimated 1970). Pro-Chinese sympathizers are organized in the small Luxembourg-China Society. In several articles that appeared during 1972 in the party organ, *Zeitung vum Letzeburger Vollek* (*ZVLV*), the activities of the "Mao clique" were criticized as "destructive" to the "international workers' movement" (e.g., issue of 6 February).

Major party strength is concentrated in the urban and mining areas of the industrial south. The most significant example of PCL influence is in Esch-sur-Alzette, Luxembourg's second-largest city, whose mayor, Arthus Useldinger, is a member of the PCL Secretariat and Central Committee. In the latest national elections, held in 1968, the PCL successfully elected 6 members to the 56-member Luxembourg parliament, representing 12 percent of the electorate (see *YICA, 1972*, p. 200).

Leadership and Organization. During 1972 the PCL presented a strong image of stability and remained without splits or purges. The party leadership is in the hands of the Urbany family. Dominique Urbany, the titular family head, is party chairman and head of the 3-member Secretariat. The other two members are his son, René Urbany, and Arthur Useldinger (no relation to the family). In addition there are more than 10 other family members in the party organization (see *YICA, 1972*, p. 200). The 10-member Politburo is elected by the 35-member Central Committee. No changes in party leadership or in the Central Committee were announced during 1972.

Domestic Attitudes and Activities. During 1972 the PCL reiterated those same issues of domestic policy it had emphasized the preceding year (see *YICA, 1972*, p. 201). In an article in the Soviet journal, *New Times,* Arthur Useldinger concluded that "inflation and higher prices" had continued to erode the living standards of "our working people." He perceived "a general dissatisfaction which marks the whole political climate in the country," but noted that "a significant first breach" had been made in "the government-employer united front" by the nation's bank clerks. The bank clerks had successfully secured a 13 percent salary increase. Much of the credit for this success, he believed, was due the Federation of Private Employees, which had succeeded in "overcoming white-collar arrogance" by joining Luxembourg's two largest labor unions in the formation of a "National Trade Union Council." This event, Useldinger believed, was of "far-reaching significance" and marked "the beginning of a broad united front of [the] workers which can become strong enough to shatter the anti-popular plans of Big Business." (*New Times,* February.)

Criticism of the government's domestic policies was not limited to alleged collusion with "Big Business." The PCL also claimed that Luxembourg's farmers were "bitterly dissatisfied with the policies of the Common Market" and that the country's pensioners were being "neglected" by the government. Only the PCL and the Luxembourg Socialist Workers' Party (Parti Ouvrier Socialiste Luxembourgeois; LSAP), had taken steps to pressure the government to institute a "partial system of adjustment of pensions to wage levels." (Ibid.)

Special emphasis was placed by the PCL on municipal government as "a sector of the state apparatus." Party members stressed that "it would be utopian to believe that the path to socialism" could ignore the towns, since "the influence of the people on their elected representatives is strongest there." Citing the example of Esch-sur-Alzette, where he is mayor, Useldinger urged that "town policy should play a prominent part" in party work since "the town councils take the role of the trade unions in the enterprises." They represent, he believed, "not merely a political school for the great mass of the people, [but] also a political school for the party, its militants and supporters." (*ZVLV,* 30 September.)

The PCL paid special attention to "the unity of the broad masses of workers and their political and trade union organizations" in Luxembourg, as "a prerequisite to new decisive successes in the struggle for social ascent, for securing and expanding democratic rights and freedoms, for peace and socialism." Under the slogan "The Enemy Stands to the Right," the Executive Committee of the PCL met in July to discuss problems of "the unity of progressive forces in the struggle for political renovation in our country." The committee concluded that "the split in the ranks of the workers" must be overcome, and that "the working class [must] be mobilized for the common struggle." The necessity for unity was declared "the basis for the communists' cooperation with socialist and non-partisan workers" in the trade unions. (Ibid., 4 July.)

To achieve the "replacement of the capitalist system . . . with the socialist social order" the committee approved 9 "primary tasks": (1) to encourage "mutual efforts" by the PCL and LSAP, for which the "joint program" of the communists and socialists of France was cited as an example "that such efforts can lead to success"; (2) to raise the standard of living; (3) to achieve "a democratic tax reform"; (4) to create a national insurance and a "modern health service for all, at the cost of the large capitalist companies and the state"; (5) to achieve "democratic and progressive reform" of the educational system; (6) to secure and expand "the rights of the workers and employees, their committees and organizations in the enterprises and administrations"; (7) to secure "the deciding voice of the workers and employees in economic processes through freely elected representatives to the administrative councils of the companies;" (8) to expand "the powers of the Chamber of Deputies and the community councils"; (9) to secure "effective control of the executive organs by the elected representatives of the people" (ibid., 6 June, 4 July).

International Views and Positions. The foreign policy positions taken by the PCL did not change from those presented during 1971 (see *YICA, 1972,* pp. 201–2). The PCL maintained emphasis throughout the year on "peaceful co-existence between nations." In June party chairman Urbany termed U.S. President Nixon's visit to Moscow "an important stage in the fight to ensure peace," in a speech to the PCL Central Committee. He also cited the ratification by the West German parliament of the Federal Republic's treaties with Poland and the Soviet Union, the four-power agreement on "West Berlin" (sic), and the traffic agreement between East and West Germany, as clearing the path for an all-European security conference and for the "development of normal, peaceful relations between the European states." (*ZVLV,* 6 June.)

Throughout the year the PCL criticized the involvement of the United States in Southeast Asia (TASS, 5 July, 6 August). Chinese support for Pakistan in the conflict between India and Pakistan was condemned as detrimental to world peace. Chinese leaders were also criticized as "enemies of the international working class" for their opposition to the four-power agreement on Berlin and to the treaty between West Germany and the Soviet Union (*ZVLV,* 6 February). The PCL declared its support for the "cause of the Arab peoples struggling for liquidating the aftermaths of . . . Israeli aggression and for establishing a just and lasting peace in the Middle East (TASS, 6 August).

As was the case in 1971, the PCL consistently praised the leadership of the Soviet Union in the world communist movement in our time" (*ZVLV,* 6 June). The PCL called for recognition of the German Democratic Republic as a contribution toward détente, noting that "the world balance of strength in favor of socialism is making the capitalist countries to realize the usefulness of a policy of détente, particularly in Europe" (ibid.; *New Times,* February).

In addition to general criticism of "American imperialism," (*ZVLV,* 23 August), René Urbany delivered a lengthy analysis on "current questions regarding anti-communism" at an international symposium on this subject in Prague, 29 February–3 March, sponsored by the Institute for Marxism-Leninism and the Advanced Political School of the Communist Party of Czechoslovakia. Urbany concluded that intellectuals, students, technicians, members of service occupations, farmers, and members of the "middle class" generally were beginning to have more and more interests in common with the "working class," but that they seek socialism "without the dictatorship of the proletariat." He warned that it is the "tactic of imperialism to dress up as ideological reconciliation the international accords wrested from it, thereby creating new possibilities for undermining the socialist camp and the international workers' movement." In this context, therefore, Urbany stressed the importance of carrying on "the ideological dispute with the opponent in popular language, in close touch with the daily struggle, with the problems of the day encountered by plain working people." He concluded by stressing that "anti-communism's ideological war against Marxism-Leninism will demand exceptional efforts from the ideological consolidation of the ranks of communists and the strengthening of their united front," and especially from "the unity and cohesion of the revolutionary world movement with the Soviet Union." (Ibid., 8 March.)

International Activities and Party Contacts. At the above-mentioned seminar in Prague, René Urbany stressed the "lessons of the Czechoslovak crisis" of 1968 and was especially critical of the "revisionists" in Czechoslovakia who had attempted to deny "the leading role of the communist party" and to undermine the "leading role of the U.S.S.R. in the international class war" (*ZVLV,* 8 March).

A bilateral meeting took place on 1–2 April in Luxembourg with a delegation of the Communist Party of Spain, information was exchanged on national problems and those of the international workers' movement. Although "some points of divergence" were acknowledged in the final communiqué, both parties agreed on the "need to work toward unity and toward strengthening the international communist and workers' movement on the basis of Marxism-Leninism and proletarian internationalism." The delegations also stressed that positive results had been obtained in their respective efforts "to achieve unity among all the anti-Franco forces for the reestablishment of democratic freedoms in Spain and to develop unity of action among the progressive forces in Luxembourg for the defense and expansion of liberty and democracy." (Ibid., 8 April.)

In August a PCL delegation consisting of Dominque Urbany, Arthur Useldinger and René

Urbany visited the Communist Party of the Soviet Union. The communiqué at the conclusion of the meeting declared that the two parties were unified on all questions (TASS, 6 August).

Publications. The party organ, *Zeitung vum Letzeburger Vollek,* is published daily at the PCL's publishing house in Esch-sur-Alzette. A second party periodical, *Wechenzeitung,* appears weekly.

Hoover Institution   Dennis L. Bark
Stanford University

Netherlands

The Communist Party of the Netherlands (Communistische Partij van Nederland; CPN) was founded in 1918 as the Communist Party of Holland, but its establishment is officially dated as of 1919, when it joined the Comintern. The present name was adopted in 1936. Party members number about 10,000. The population of the Netherlands is 13,400,000 (estimated 1972).

Originally pro-Soviet, the CPN has in recent years pursued a policy of autonomy within the international communist movement. Small pro-Soviet groups and a number of splinter groups of pro-Chinese tendency were also active in the country during 1972.

The CPN enjoys legal status, but its influence has always been limited. The parliamentary election of 29 November 1972, however, brought the CPN a considerable gain. While in 1971 the party collected 3.9 percent of the votes cast (246,549 votes, six seats), its proportion for 1972 rose to 4.5 percent (329,973 votes, seven seats).

In a commentary on the election results, the CPN stated that progress was made in all parts of the country, particularly in industrial areas, and most of all in the west. This success was attributed to "the CPN policy of reduction of armament and resistance against the American-German domination in NATO and EEC." (*De Waarheid,* 30 November.)

Leadership and Organization. The CPN's Twenty-fourth Congress, held in Amsterdam on 26–28 May 1972, elected a Central Committee of 36 members and 3 deputies. Seven members of the previous committee were reelected owing to inactivity and were replaced by ten new members. The fact that most of the ten are well-known for their activities in industry reflects "the primary orientation of the party toward the work in industry and the wage struggle, and consequently towards the struggle for unity of the working classes" (discussion, 24th CPN Congress, *Politiek en Cultuur,* June–July).

The congress resolution "charged the new party committee with the improvement of the organization of its activities, in such a way that it will be able to direct its main activities to political leadership," and added: "In this connection, it is advisable to set up a secretariat, especially charged with the daily administration of the party's activities, enabling the Executive Committee to devote itself entirely to political leadership."

On 17 June the Central Committee elected the Executive Committee, consisting of the following 12 members: M. Bakker, L. Bosch, R. Haks, H. Hoekstra, K. Hoogkamp, H. Kleuver, F. Meis, W. Nieuwenhuyse, R. Walraven, Jacob Wolff, Johan Wolff, J. Ijsberg. H. Hoekstra was elected party chairman. The Secretariat, set up by the Central Committee is headed by H. Hoekstra (chairman). Other secretaries are K. Hoogkamp (organization), H. Kleuver (finance), W. Nieuwenhuyse (industrial work), R. Walraven (propaganda and ideological training) and J. Ijsberg (administration). (*De Waarheid,* 19 June.)

The Netherlands General Youth Union (Algemeen Nederlands Jeugd Verbond; ANJV) is small, but is the most important of the CPN front organizations, since it is the main source of future party members. Its main activities are directed toward younger workers. As an organization, however, the ANJV is not a closely knit group.

In January the ANJV succeeded in joining with the Algemene Studentenvereniging Amsterdam (General Students Society of Amsterdam) in setting up a "Committee of Young People for Vietnam." The ANJV later organized a massive demonstration, in which approximately 6,000 persons took part, on 29 and 30 April. Attending the demonstration was a representative of the Viet Cong delegation at the Paris peace talks. He suggested the establishment of a Vietnamese Information Center in the Netherlands, but the Dutch government refused permission for it.

The Netherlands Women's Movement (Nederlandse Vrouwen Beweging) is a small organization allied with the CPN. On 30 May it staged a "Day of Womens' Action" to protest against government policies, with the slogan "No Money for NATO, More Housekeeping Money." It further devoted its attention to the Vietnam issue, high taxes and the government education policy. Another allied group, United Resistance 1940–45 (Verenigd Verzet 1940–45), focused its activities on mutual ties of friendship among former resistance fighters and the collecting of information on "neo-fascist" activities in the Netherlands and the Federal Republic of Germany.

Party Internal Affairs. The Secretariat, which had been abolished at the party congress in 1967, was revived in 1972 to serve as the CPN's administrative and organizational center. This resulted in a further centralization of the party organization.

The CPN congress declared that the party's current task was to bring about the unity of the working class and to enhance its organized force. The way to achieve this was through "the organization of all workers in the Netherlands Federation of Trade Unions (Nederlands Verbond van Vakverenigingen; NVV)." Hence, "The communists must aim at stepping up the political and ideological struggle . . . in industry." This struggle was to be conducted by all party groups within the various enterprises.

A recruitment drive, especially launched for the electoral campaign, resulted in approximately 800 new members of the party. The CPN is, however, concerned with the social background of its new members. The percentage of industrial workers is low while students form a high percentage. Local CPN cells are now required to seek permission of the Central Committee for admission of student members since the CPN suspects that "elements hostile to the party" are attempting to infiltrate the party's ranks. For this reason the CPN placed special emphasis on ideological training: "The main cause of the backlog in size and activity of the party, as against its political influence, lies in the failure to raise the ideological level of the party. This is why the symptoms of revisionism are spreading like a cancer in our party." Therefore, the congress resolution declared, "the activity of the party press and propaganda must be intensified."

Domestic Attitude and Activities. Throughout 1972 the CPN sought to revive the "new orientation policy." This policy first advocated at the party congress in 1964 emphasizes the necessity to unite communists, socialists, and "progressive Christians" in a common front. This policy of unity was inspired mainly by the agreement of French communists and socialists to cooperate, and by the opportunity to join the NVV that was offered to Dutch communists in October 1971 (see *YICA, 1972*, pp. 204–5). In the fall of 1972, a manifesto entitled "For a Better Existence," the CPN declared its willingness to give up part of its identity in order to promote the establishment of a "progressive government, based on communist-socialist cooperation" (*De Waarheid,* 1 September). Earlier, the party chairman in a speech at the congress called upon party members to join the NVV "in the interest of a united and forceful struggle against the employers" (*Politiek en Cultuur,* June–July).

With respect to the "wage struggle and intensification of the class struggle" the congress endorsed the formation of active groups in industry which would operate closely with the NVV unions (ibid., April). The CPN succeeded, for example, in organizing an "action committee" during the difficult negotiations with the Industrial Union (Industriebond) of the NVV and the resulting strike in February 1972. Another action took place in April. F. Meis, a member of the CPN Executive Committee, headed the "Peoples' Congress of Groningen" (see *YICA, 1972,* p. 204). This congress discussed the poor employment situation in the northern provinces and urged joint action in the future: "The organization of a Groningen People's Congress is a new episode in the struggle within which unity is created at the base between socialists and communists, industrial and agrarian workers, shopkeepers, intellectuals, farmers, small and medium-size employers" (*Politiek en Cultuur,* April).

The CPN's major efforts during the year, however, were concerned with the election of the Second Chamber of the Dutch parliament. According to the CPN, the election results indicated wide dissatisfaction with the government's policies on wages and prices and also its foreign policy. The election results therefore constituted "a strong stimulant to carry on the struggle for workers, teachers, shopkeepers, the young—all those who have been active last year." But new policies would not be achieved in the Netherlands unless "dissension-sowing anti-communism and admiration for NATO and EEC [were] abandoned." (*De Waarheid,* 30 November.)

International Views and Positions. In connection with its efforts toward achieving a common front of socialists and communists, the CPN late in 1972 altered its proclaimed views concerning such supernational institutions as the EEC and NATO. The party's old demand for the Netherlands to withdraw from these organizations was no longer raised; it was ostensibly considered politically unrealistic. With regard to NATO and EEC, the CPN endorsed a policy that would guarantee the Netherlands the greatest independence possible. This policy position was also reflected in other international views: the party, stressing its interest in "security for the Netherlands in Europe and in the world," demanded the removal of nuclear arms from Netherlands territory, urged reduction of the contributions toward NATO armament, opposed a European nuclear force, and recommended reduction of military service to ten months. The CPN also advocated "an independent position within NATO" and neutrality for the Netherlands, condemned Greece and Portugal "as American fascist puppets," urged refusal to carry out the decisions of the EEC summit conference of October 1972, and called for immediate recognition of East Germany, North Korea, and the Democratic Republic of Vietnam. (*De Waarheid,* 9 December.)

This same "new orientation" policy appeared in strong condemnation of the political trials in Czechoslovakia (ibid., 5 August). The CPN attitude toward West German foreign policy and the victory of Chancellor Brandt's Social Democratic Party was positive, although not without criticism. The CPN approved Brandt's endorsement of détente in Europe, but criticized his support for further integration in the EEC (ibid., 21 November).

The CPN concluded that capitalism faced a crisis and urged socialists and communists to join forces, since the struggle against capitalism and its allies "requires the cooperation of all communist parties and their concentration on concrete actions." The CPN added, however, that "the relations between the parties of the international communist movement should be based on unambiguous recognition of one another's full autonomy." (24th Congress resolution.) Equally, the party emphasized that "the CPN cannot be made responsible for revisionistic misconduct and mistakes made in socialist countries of Eastern Europe" (*De Waarheid,* 1 September).

International Activities and Party Contracts. As in previous years, in 1972 the CPN's concern with the party's independence influenced its relations with the international communist movement. The CPN endorsed "an international, business-like, and scientific discussion based on equality of rights for all (communist parties)" (*Politiek en Cultuur,* April). But at the same time members were advised to "exercise the greatest vigilance, in order to protect the party's unity and policies against hostile interference" (congress resolution).

Fear of the influence of other communist parties was especially felt with regard to the Communist Party of the Soviet Union (CPSU). The CPN interpreted the criticism leveled at the party's former chairman, Paul de Groot, in the Soviet historical magazine *Voprosy istorii KPSS* (January), as "a public attack on the CPN's international views and a malicious misrepresentation of these views" (*De Waarheid,* 5 February). Just prior to the party congress, *Pravda* (12 May) once again criticized the CPN's attitude toward the other communist parties. This criticism apparently prompted the CPN to reconsider its policy of cautious rapprochement with the international communist movement, introduced in 1969. The congress concluded that "sober, business-like discussion" between the CPN and CPSU was desirable. But the congress resolution maintained that "it is not in the interest of international communism when revisionist symptoms are not mentioned" (*Politiek en Cultuur,* June–July). Fearful of finding itself ultimately isolated from the international communist movement as a result of its critical attitude, the CPN declared itself an adherent of proletarian internationalism. In this connection its conflict with the CPSU was described as "differences of opinion of an ultimately temporary nature with CPSU members or committees, which do not alter solidarity with the Soviet people and the Soviet State as the most prominent socialist country and strategic ally of the Dutch people and the CPN" (ibid., April).

Publications. The most important organ of the CPN is *De Waarheid* (The Truth), published daily in Amsterdam. It has an estimated circulation of 15,000. The party committee announced in 1972, as in the previous year, that it required additional financial support. Therefore the mid-week edition was temporarily reduced from six pages to four at the end of the year. Deficits incurred by the CPN, by the party newspaper and other publications continue to be partly offset by the profits of the CPN's two commercial printing enterprises, the Dijkman and Heierman firms. Income is also provided by renting conference rooms in the party-owned building Felix Meritis in Amsterdam.

The Dijkman printing house received a number of commercial orders in 1972, in contrast to that of Heierman, which experienced financial difficulties together with the party bookshop and publishing house, Pegasus. Heierman continued to print all party publications, including the theoretical monthly magazine *Politiek en Cultuur* (estimated circulation 2,500) and the organ of the Netherlands Womens' Movement, *Vrouwen* (estimated circulation 9,500).

*   *   *

The Netherlands-USSR Friendship Society (Vereniging "Nederland-USSR": NU) is a center for dissident pro-Soviet communists in the Netherlands. The Society publishes a monthly journal *Nederland-USSR*. Its membership is approximately 4,000. The Society stresses its cultural activities and devotes minor attention to Dutch politics. Activities in 1972 ranged from local propaganda meetings to demonstrations and exhibitions. A Siberia exhibition was held in Rotterdam in December. Most of these activities took place in consultation with functionaries of the Soviet Embassy. Through the Friendship Society the Soviet Embassy enjoys useful contacts with various persons and groups. During his visit to the Netherlands in July Foreign Minister Gromyko met with Society members, and on its 25th anniversary the Society received a message of congratulations from President Podgorny and was visited by a delegation headed by the chairman of the Union of Soviet Societies for Friendship and Cultural Relations Abroad.

There are several other splinter groups that are also pro-Soviet in orientation. The Society for Cultural Exchanges (Vereniging van Culturele Betrekkingen; VCU), launched a monthly journal—*VCU*—in December 1971, *Communistische Notities* ("Communist Notes") is a monthly published by a former member of the CPN Central Committee, F. Baruch. The paper is sent to CPN members, who are exposed in this way to Soviet criticism of the CPN, such as the aforementioned piece in *Voprosy istorii KPSS*. The Netherlands Committee of Youth for European Security and Cooperation (Nederlands Jongerencomité voor Europese Veiligheid en Samenwerking; NJEVS) advocates the creation of a European security system and maintains contacts with similar committees in other countries. Three members of the NJEVS visited the Soviet Union in June 1972.

The organizational divisions within the pro-Chinese communist movement in the Netherlands (see *YICA,*1972, pp. 207–8) remained virtually unchanged. Several groups became less important and one group strongly increased in importance.

The position of the Communist Movement for Unity in the Netherlands (M-LO Kommunistische Eenheidsbeweging Nederland-Marxistisch-Leninistisch; KEN-ML) declined considerably in 1972, although the KEN-ML did play a role in the big metallurgy strike (mainly by lending their technical equipment for the supply of information). Together with some other organizations, the KEN-ML organized a Vietnam campaign on Marxist-Leninist principles which ended with a demonstration in Rotterdam on 11 November, in which only a few hundred people took part. But it has become a small student group which enjoys few contacts with the working class. Organizational unity was achieved between the Red Youth Marxist-Leninist (Rode Jeugd-Marxistisch-Leninistisch; RJ-ML), a group which detached itself from Red Youth (Rode Jeugd) and the Bond van Nederlandse Marxisten-Leninisten (BNML). But the new organization experienced internal dissension during the year.

A relatively large expansion was achieved by the Communist Party of the Netherlands, Marxist-Leninist (Kommunistische Partij Nederland-Marxistisch-Leninistisch: KPN-ML), which detached itself from the KEN-ML late in 1971. The membership of this organization has doubled within a year's time and has now reached 250. Following its congress, in October, it assumed the name of Socialist Party (Socialistische Partij; SP). The party leaders gave three reasons for this change of name: The old name caused confusion with the CPN and led to discussions on the Sino-Soviet conflict at the expense of party emphasis in achieving socialism in the Netherlands; anti-communist propaganda had successfully given the old party a poor reputation; and the old name gave the party the image of a small sectarian group, which was no longer suitable in view of the party's "fast-growing influence on the masses in districts and factories."

The SP carried out actions primarily through its mass-organizations. The Union of Tenants and Those in Need of Housing (Bond van Huurders en Woningzoekenden) is the most successful of these. The SP's Vietnam action was especially spectacular. Organized by a "Committee from Human Being to Human Being," it consisted of sending postcards with pictures of victims of U.S. bombings in Vietnam to citizens of the United States chosen at random. Persons whose addresses were taken from telephone directories were supplied with the postcards, which were then to be sold to the public. Starting in mid-October, 250,000 postcards reportedly were sent to the United States by the end of the year.

Two other organizations—the Marxist-Leninist Students Union (Marxistisch-Leninistische Studentenbond) and Workers' Power (Arbeidsmacht) were not active to any significant extent during the year.

Relations with Marxist-Leninist groups and parties abroad have been cultivated by the Marxist-Leninist Party of the Netherlands (Marxistisch-Leninistische Partij van Nederland). These determine to a great extent the importance of this organization and appeared to become considerably closer in the course of 1972.

The Hague   Herman J. M. Mennes
and   and
Hoover Institution   Dennis L. Bark
Stanford University

Norway

The Norwegian Communist Party (Norges Kommunistiske Parti; NKP) is small, but far from mighty. Membership estimates range from 2,000 to 5,000 in a total population of about 4 million.

The party first emerged on 4 November 1923 when a few radical politicians and trade unionists broke away from the Norwegian Labor Party (Det Norske Arbeiderparti; DNA). The NKP opted for continuing loyalty to the Moscow-directed Third International. In contrast, the DNA (though still calling itself the "Communist Party" until 1927 when it rejoined the social democrats) refused to conform to Cominterm principles. The NKP started with an inherited 14 parliamentary seats and a membership of about 16,000. Its course has been down hill ever since, except for some electoral success in 1945, due to communist participation in wartime resistance against the Germans and the liberation of northern Norway by the Soviets.

Sandwiched between Norway's strongest political organization—the Labor Party—on the one hand and the Socialist People's Party (Sosialistisk Folkeparti; SF) and a motley collection of extremist splinter groups on the other, the NKP has barely survived. It last won national representation in the Storting (Parliament) in 1957. It polled only 1 percent of the popular vote in the last election in September 1969 (down 0.4 percent from the previous vote in 1965). It attracted 1.3 percent of the vote in municipal elections in September 1971.

Prospects for a better showing in parliamentary elections in September 1973 are meager. Whether the NKP's main rival, the SF, can fare much better is also dubious. Both parties offer a socialist alternative to the allegedly class-collaborationist policies of the DNA. Furthermore, though both espouse a democratic transition to socialism on the basis of Marxism and parliamentarianism, they are too divided on tactics and ideology to form a united electoral bloc. The NKP continues to try to project a separate identity—a "national" image, neutral in the Sino-Soviet dispute and appropriate to the concerns of its main followers. Most members are found among industrial workers in Oslo and low-income groups in the northern province of Finnmark and the eastern region of Hedmark.

Leadership and Organization. Reidar Larsen, former editor of the party weekly *Friheten,* has continued as NKP chairman. He succeeded Emil Løvlien (the NKP's lackluster chairman since 1946) in 1965 and won reelection to the post at the party's Thirteenth Congress, held in Oslo on 23–25 April 1971. Like his Swedish counterpart, Larsen has tried to direct party energies toward national, rather than international communist, political goals. Larsen heads the Secretariat, which includes Arne Jørgensen, Arne Pettersen, Martin Gunnar Knutsen, Rolf Nettum, Kolbjørn Harbu, Leif Johansen, Leif Hammerstad, and Georg Ovesen. The Secretariat is elected by the Central Committee. Congresses, which appoint the party's Control Committee, are usually held every third year, with national conferences convened in intervening years. Members of the Control Committee are Fredrik Bergstrøm, Eivind Wiik, Kaare Karlsen, Ivar Lie, Just Lippé, and Emil Løvlien. George Ovesen heads the NKP youth organization, Communist Youth (Kommunistisk Ungdom; KU).

Though strongest in the labor movement, the NKP does not control any national labor union and has no national officer in the Norwegian Federation of Trade Unions. At the local level, the party is most notable in the construction workers' union and, to some extent, in the metal, wood, transport, and electro-chemical fields. The NKP directs a "Baltic Sea Committee" which sends delegations to the Workers' Conferences of Baltic Nations, Norway, and Iceland, held annually in Rostock, East Germany.

Party Internal Affairs. Born in factionalism, the NKP has continued to suffer from recurring internal dissension, personal and ideological. Its first major conflict pitted those leaders who had stayed in Norway during the German occupation against those who spent the war years in the Soviet Union or elsewhere abroad—hence the split between the followers of Per Furubotn, chairman during the war years, and Emil Løvlien, a wartime expatriate, who seized party control in 1946. Løvlien ruled the NKP with an iron hand. At some cost to internal unity, Larsen, his successor, has tried to shift the party's ideological direction toward a more nationalist, left-socialist course.

Both Muscovite and Maoist factions have chafed at this approach. An intra-party showdown in 1967 led to the expulsion of 12 members of the NKP Central Committee. Those ousted included Jørgen Vogt, who had been forced to resign as editor of *Friheten* because he condemned Chinese policies. Dissent was silenced, and the Larsen line was confirmed at the party's Twelfth Congress, in 1968. But dissent broke out with renewed virulence at the 1971 congress.

Though party leaders have rarely acknowledged internal strains since then, Larsen has continued to face challenges—particularly from the party's extreme left flank. The NKP cannot afford the loss of this predominantly youthful support since the average age of its members is almost sixty.

The nature of the more strictly ideological dispute within communist ranks surfaced most clearly during 1972 in debates between Georg Ovesen, chairman of the KU, and Sverre Knutsen, chairman of the Socialist Youth League (Marxist-Leninist)—Sosialistisk Undomsforbund (Marxistisk-Leninistisk), or SUF(ml). The KU attacked the SUF(ml) for having a sectarian point of departure in its mass activity (*Friheten*, 12–17 June).

Knutsen was chosen to chair the SUF(ml)'s new Central Committee at the group's second congress in early 1972. Originally the youth arm of the SF, it left the parent organization in 1969 and has dedicated itself largely to the study of Mao's thoughts. Knutsen stressed in an interview that the congress had decided to "work toward developing into a communist mass organization for revolutionary youth" (*Klassekampen*, no. 1, 1972). He added that the SUF(ml) would place itself under the leadership of the Marxist-Leninist Groups—Marxistisk-Leninistisk Gruppe, or MLG, chaired by Sigurd Allern—and, only later, under the communist party. He stated: "It is vital not to relax in the struggle against the harmful influence exerted on young people and others by modern revisionism, meaning the ideas of the Socialist People's Party and the NKP" (ibid.).

The issue of Norwegian membership in the enlarging European Economic Community further aggravated differences among Norwegian communists in 1972. NKP leaders faulted the SUF(ml) for not joining immediately the "Popular Movement against the EEC" and for forming instead its own "Workers' Committee in Opposition to the EEC and High Prices" (*Friheten*, no. 27, 3–8 July). Age Fjeld chided the Maoist *Klassekampen* for implying that

NKP leaders were Soviet "lackeys" and revisionists of the worst kind. He warned that "only the truly communist parties which adhere to a sober and balanced political line can win the confidence of the masses." (Ibid.) The SUF(ml) and the MLG countered with condemnation of the "NKP's slavish adherence to the Soviet line and charged that the NKP, just one year away from its fiftieth anniversary, had betrayed the party's revolutionary traditions and lost its roots among the youth (*Klassekampen,* no. 30, 24–29 July). The *Klassekampen* editorial staff cited Soviet policy in East Europe, the Middle East, and Southeast Asia to document its allegation of "Soviet social imperialism" (ibid.). NKP spokesmen disparaged the Maoist leadership of the SUF, MLG and Red Front and dismissed plans for a "new communist party" with the statement, "The working class does not need it" (*Friheten,* no. 32, 7–12 August).

The plenary meeting of the NKP Central Committee on 7–8 October discussed the results of Norway's EEC referendum (see below), the party's tasks for the coming period, and the draft of the new program to be adopted at the party congress in 1973.

Domestic Attitudes and Activities. Under Larsen's leadership, the NKP continued in 1972 to imitate Swedish communists by presenting itself as a national party committed to striving for change within the existing parliamentary system. Unlike its Swedish counterpart, it has changed neither its name nor its democratic centralism. The party had no direct influence on the government, either under Trygve Bratteli or under Lars Korvald, whose mini-coalition of the Christian People's, Center and Liberal parties succeeded Bratteli's minority Labor government on 18 October. Bratteli had promised to resign if Norwegians should vote down EEC accession in the nationwide advisory referendum, 24–25 September, and did just that after the Norwegian "no." The decisive rejection of Common Market membership capped a long, bitterly fought campaign in which the NKP was a key participant. A resolution adopted 20 March by a NKP conference in Oslo stressed that the party's most important task was to organize the resistance of working people against being drawn into the EEC. The conference expressed full solidarity with the "Popular Movement against the EEC" organization. (TASS, 20 March.) Larsen stressed the EEC membership would imperil Norwegian sovereignty, and warned that Norwegian industry would not be able to compete against the Continent. A plenary meeting of the NKP Central Committee on 21 August urged "progressive" forces of the country, especially communists, to step up their campaign against EEC membership (TASS, 21 August).

With the EEC question dominating the Norwegian scene in 1972, there was little other domestic activity by the NKP. The Labor Party, in power most of the year, continued to preempt many of the causes which the NKP might have seized. For example, a new law on industrial democracy—set to go into effect on 1 January 1973—provides for worker participation in company councils.

International Views and Positions. As in 1971, the EEC issue dominated both domestic and international considerations for the NKP in 1972. With Norway blocked from joining the Common Market and the Korvald government opening negotiations for a free trade agreement in Brussels, the NKP remained alert to any slippage during those talks. It is firmly opposed to a "development clause" which might lead over time to full Norwegian membership in the EEC.

In other foreign policy questions, the NKP continued to advocate Norwegian withdrawal from NATO. The 2 September issue of *Friheten* printed an inter-party demand that Norway call off NATO's "Strong Express" exercise if U.S. bombing of North Vietnam persisted. The party remained active in its opposition to the Vietnam war and helped sponsor several demonstrations outside the U.S. Embassy in Oslo during the year.

International Party Contacts. Though the NKP maintained its neutral stand in the Sino-Soviet conflict, it did expend considerable energy considering the implications for international communism of political trials in Czechoslovakia during the summer of 1972. (The party had vigorously disapproved of the Soviet invasion of Czechoslovakia in 1968—the major exception to the NKP's generally restrained commentary on Soviet activity.) On 20 August the NKP Central Committee sent a letter to the Communist Party of Czechoslovakia expressing the concern which the political trials had aroused among Norwegian communists and the NKP's belief that a socialist democracy must assure people freedom of thought and expression (*Friheten,* no. 34, 21–26 August). Some members took sharp exception to the Central Committee's position on "normalization" in Czechoslovakia and asserted that, for the long-term sake of the international communist movement, "the working class itself will undoubtedly when the time comes have to do things it will not like" (ibid., no. 36, 4–9 September).

The NKP received several foreign communist delegations during 1972. A group from the Communist Party of the Soviet Union (CPSU), led by A. Y. Snechkus, visited Norway on 17–24 October. During its stay, the Soviet delegation met with the NKP Central Committee and local party and trade union activists. It described the implementation of decisions from the CPSU's Twenty-fourth Congress. After a visit to Denmark, a Central Committee delegation of the East German Socialist Unity Party (SED), under Harry Tisch, candidate member of the Politburo and first secretary of the SED district of Rostock) arrived in Norway on 19 January. During talks with the NKP and Labor Party officials, the delegation discussed preparations for a "Conference on Security and Cooperation in Europe," prospects for normalizing Norwegian-East German relations, and plans for the UN Conference on the Human Environment.

Publications. The NKP press consists of *Friheten* ("Freedom"), the party's central organ, and several "in-house" publications of a few district organizations. *Friheten,* first published during the resistance, reached its peak circulation of 100,000 in 1945. Subsequently it fell on hard financial times and dwindling demand, and in 1967 ceased daily publication and became a weekly. The KU publishes a bulletin, *Fremad* ("Forward"). The Maoist publications are *Klassekampen* ("Class Struggle"), *Rode Garde* ("Red Guard"), and *Røde Fane* ("Red Banner").

Portugal

The Portuguese Communist Party (Partido Comunista Português; PCP) was founded in March 1921 and has been illegal since 1926. Under vigorous repression by the Portuguese government, the party clandestinely maintains a tight organization and continues to operate both at home and abroad, mainly in Romania.

Within Portugal, PCP members worked until 1970 through the underground Patriotic Front of National Liberation (Frente Patriótica de Libertação Nacional; FPLN), established in December 1962. The front, which has its coordinating center in Algiers, also attempts to rally socialists, liberals, republicans, Catholics, and liberal monarchists. In 1970 the PCP was excluded from the FPLN, which announced that the front would pursue a policy of armed struggle. That struggle has taken the form of terrorist attacks carried out in Portugal through the International Revolutionary Brigades. According to the police, this group is directed from abroad by former journalist Carlos Carneiro Antunes.

The PCP's members comprise mainly urban workers concentrated in Lisbon and Oporto, and, to a lesser degree, middle-class elements including intellectuals. Farm laborers are barely represented, although a few have been enlisted, primarily in the upper Alentejo area. Considerable support reportedly comes from among university students. Western sources estimate PCP membership at 2,000. The population of Portugal is 8,668,000 (official census, 1970).

In addition to the PCP, which has a decidedly pro-Soviet orientation, there appear to exist two small pro-Chinese groups: the Popular Action Front (Frente de Ação Popular) and the United League of Revolutionary Action (Liga de Ação Revolucionária).

In Portugal, a country that has been led by an authoritarian government since 1926, communism has played only an insignificant role.

Leadership and Organization. The PCP maintains a closely knit apparatus and keeps its leadership within Portugal anonymous (see *YICA, 1972,* p. 214). Among the known leaders in exile is the secretary-general, Alvaro Cunhal.

The party claims to provide the principal opposition leadership and to be especially influential among students and labor groups. Its party cells and illegal "Unity Committees" operate within the official corporate trade unions, enabling them, allegedly, to place trusted party members in top spots. The party also professes to be engaged in "anti-Fascist" political activity through the various branches of the Democratic Electoral Commission, a united front formed in 1969 to participate in elections to the National Assembly (see *YICA, 1970,* p. 244). Other PCP organizations include the National Committee for Assistance to Political Prisoners (Comité Nacional de Ajuda aos Presos Politicos; CNAPP) and committees in support of freedom of speech.

Domestic Attitudes and Activities. Portugal in 1972 saw a "sharpening of the crisis of (its) Fascist regime" and an "intensification of the class struggle," according to a PCP Central

211

Committee member who was interviewed in Moscow (Moscow domestic service, 29 August). He contrasted workers' extremely low wages with heavy state expenditures on the colonial war, the police apparatus, and Portuguese participation in NATO, all of which, he said, devoured 43 percent of the national budget. Despite continuing "cruel repression" by the government, he claimed the party played an active role in the nation's political life and was strengthening its influence among the masses.

The Portuguese government asserted there was PCP involvement in various acts of terrorism during the year ("Radio Free Portugal," 30 September). Such terrorism included bombings by a number of secret urban guerrilla groups, who acclaimed their acts as efforts to sabotage the nation's colonial war effort (*NYT*, 20 August).

The PCP continued to deny participation in acts of terrorism and accused the authorities of using the "bogy" of terrorism to justify a wave of repression and arbitrary arrests. The party protested in a broadcast from abroad (ibid.) that it was "well known" that the PCP "firmly condemns terrorist actions." At best, it said, such attempts end in "rapid defeat and physical extermination of their perpetrators" and "arouse the indignation of the masses against the causes which they claim to serve." On the other hand, it defended the revolutionary legitimacy of "violence"—as distinct from "terrorism"—so long as it was linked to an organized political movement (i.e., Marxism-Leninism), with the support of the masses. It upheld one guerrilla organization, the Armed Revolutionary Action (ARA), as a proper complement of, rather than alternative to, the "mass movement."

Alleged plans for violence on May Day were aborted by a government ban on demonstrations on that occasion and by the arrest of a number of persons arriving from France with explosives and subversive pamphlets (Lisbon domestic radio, 30 April). Also captured, according to the secret police, were extensive plans for sabotage by an underground network of subversives. Prominent in the group were students, some of whom were performing their military service and who possessed arms and ammunition purportedly stolen from the military.

The secret police did not succeed in preventing three bombings later in the summer. In July, 13 army trucks were destroyed in a Lisbon suburb, and in August, electric power installations outside Lisbon were damaged, temporarily disabling about 30 percent of the nation's electric communications system. According to a government spokesman, the attack on those facilities appeared to be an attempt to interfere with the live telecast of the ceremony inaugurating Portugal's president for a third term. Lisbon shifted to thermal power and the ceremonies proceeded some six hours after the explosions.

In September, bomb blasts damaged two radio-relay stations near Lisbon. This action was described in an underground broadcast ("Voice of Freedom," 1 October) as "anti-imperialist" because the installations belonged to "an international trust" (the Marconi Company) and "anti-colonialist" because the facilities were essential links in Portugal's communications system with the colonies, South Africa, the United States, and Great Britain.

Only the International Revolutionary Brigades publicly claimed credit for any of the bombing incidents—the ones in July and September (*NYT*, 20 August; "Voice of Freedom," 1 October). That organization was denounced by the PCP as a group of "left-wing adventurers" ("Radio Free Portugal," 30 September). At the same time, strikes by ARA against the "colonialist military apparatus, destroying military equipment and weapons," were endorsed by the PCP secretary-general. Cunhal, interviewed in an Italian communist journal (*Rinascita*, 22 September), pointed out that the resistance movement in Portugal had not yet reached a situation of "revolutionary crisis" but that armed insurrection was the direction in which the "people's struggle" was moving. He said the three main thrusts of PCP activity at present were the unifying of opposition forces, broad reorganization, and "mass struggles for immediate practical objectives." The primary long-term objectives, he reiterated, were the overthrow of the "Fascist dictatorship" in favor of political freedom and true national independence, and the end of the colonial war, with complete and immediate independence for the peoples of Angola, Guinea, and Mozambique.

Cunhal hailed the spreading "mass struggles" and the "deeply rooted" feelings of solidarity among all domestic "democratic" sectors—students, workers, and peasants, including some "progressive" Catholics. He said that students had succeeded, "through aggressive mass action," in keeping the academic associations under their own control, despite repression by the authorities (ibid.). Scores of students were arrested during the year at the Lisbon and Coimbra universities (*New Times,* Moscow, no. 22). When one group seized buildings of a research institute with demands for educational reform, police expelled them, wounding seven and arresting 60 (*Pravda,* 18 May). A student demonstration in October led to the killing of a Lisbon law student and the wounding of several others. The PCP charged that the "murder" was no accident, the secret police having opened fire on the students "after staging an act of provocation." In spite of a police ban on demonstrations at the funeral, "nothing stopped thousands of people . . . from turning the funeral into a powerful expression of protest" ("Radio Free Portugal," 3 November).

PCP Central Committee member Jorge Vieira asserted that trade union activity was also increasingly vigorous (*Partinaya Zhizn,* Moscow, no. 18). He cited in particular union success in forcing the government in January to approve new wages and other benefits for metalworkers despite the threat of a lockout by management. Cunhal pointed out that strikes were frequent but usually brief since they were illegal (*Rinascita,* 22 September). He also referred to the importance attached by the party to rallies as an instrument for the defense of workers' interests, such as an Oporto street demonstration by 40,000 in April protesting the rising cost of living. Cunhal said the inflation resulted from the government's heavy war spending and from Portugal's submission to foreign imperialism's "rape of the national resources." This, in turn, led to a stepping up of labor exploitation and the emigration "en masse" of discontented workers ("a million in the last decade"). The consequence, he said, was a manpower shortage aggravated by the absence of 15,000 young men in the armed forces in Africa.

Cunhal also referred to increasing acts of defiance by Portuguese peasants, such as in refusing to deliver crops to the corporate agencies and their resistance to the confiscation of communal lands (ibid.).

Allegedly inhuman conditions in which political prisoners are kept in Portugal are described in a book published within the country in 1972 by the CNAPP—(*Presos Políticos, Documentos 1970–71*)—which asserts that members of the present PCP Central Committee have spent collectively a total of more than 250 years behind bars. Claiming that its campaigns at home and abroad have "forced" authorities to free several "staunch fighters," the CNAPP points out that, nevertheless, scores of political prisoners are still in jails and concentration camps, many of them urgently in need of medical care.

Antônio Gervásio, a member of the PCP Central Committee, and other communist activists were reported in May to be on trial on the charges of being members of the PCP and of circulating subversive literature (*New Times,* no. 22). Carlos Domingos, a clandestine fighter for a number of years, was arrested in September ("Radio Free Portugal," 3 November).

International Views and Positions. In 1972 Vieira paid tribute to the working people and communists of other countries, to whom the Portuguese communists were "to a large extent indebted . . . for their successes." He said the latter believed that their national mission was "inseparable" from their international commitments in the struggle for socialism and communism. (*Partinaya Zhizn,* no. 18.)

Cunhal (*Rinascita,* 22 September) criticized the aid provided to Portuguese "Fascism and colonialism" by the United States, England, West Germany, France, and Italy. He said this aid was directly proportional to the position of the "monopolies" in the economies of Portugal and its colonies and to the military bases the government permits foreign countries to have on its territory.

The communist world in Portugal and abroad continued to support freedom movements in the Portuguese colonies of Africa. In Mozambique, the Mozambique Liberation Front (FRE-LIMO) has the support of the Soviet Union, while the rival KOREMO is backed by Peking. FRELIMO, which observed its tenth anniversary this year, boasts 20,000 freedom fighters (versus 40,000 Portuguese troops combating them), which, it is claimed, have already "liberated" a fifth of that territory (*New Times,* Moscow, no. 26),

Publications. The PCP official organ is the clandestine monthly *Avante,* founded in 1931. The party claims that it is published inside the country. The PCP broadcasts to Portugal over "Radio Free Portugal," which is believed to be based in Romania. The FPLN's "Voice of Freedom" radio station is in Algeria.

*   *   *

The two pro-Chinese groups in Portugal are small and apparently isolated internationally. The Popular Action Front (FAP) was founded in 1964. The United League of Revolutionary Action (LUAR), was founded in 1966. No activities of either group came to notice during 1972.

Elbert Covell College   H. Leslie Robinson
University of the Pacific

San Marino

The Communist Party of San Marino (Partito Comunista di San Marino; PCS) was founded originally in 1922, then eclipsed by fascism, and refounded in 1940. Although nominally independent (and represented as such at Italian party meetings and international communist party conferences), it is in reality an offshoot of the Italian Communist Party (Partito Comunista Italiano; PCI). The PCS has an estimated 1,000 members. The population of San Marino is a little over 19,000 (estimated 1971).

The PCS is the second strongest party in the republic. With the Socialist Party it stands in opposition to the coalition government of Christian Democrats and Social Democrats.

Organization and Leadership. Ermenegildo Gasperoni is the secretary-general of the party and has held the post since 1940. The Directorate of the party consists of 10 members.

Party Policy. PCS domestic and foreign policies closely follow those of the PCI.

In 1972 at the Thirteenth Congress of the Italian party (Milan, 13–17 March), Gasperoni emphasized the influence of the PCI on the PCS:

> Given the geographical position of San Marino located in the heart of Italy and the heavy restrictions on our sovereign prerogatives imposed first by the Fascists and then by the Christian Democrat cabinets, [the PCI's] decisions directly concern the working class and the San Marino democratic forces engaged in a struggle to put forward a unitary democratic process in the direction of a deep social, political and economic transformation. . . . "The choices, struggles and successes of the PCI, of the Italian working class and leftist forces, affect San Marino and promote the workers' struggles to impose a democratic swing on San Marino.

He added that any attempt from rightist parties to impose themselves would be attenuated "by the presence of a strong Communist Party in the Italian political scene." (*L'Unitá,* 18 March.)

Publication. The PCS publishes an irregular newspaper, La Scintilla.

Milano, Italy   Carla Liverani

Spain

The Communist Party of Spain (Partido Comunista de España; PCE) was founded on 15 April 1920. It has been illegal since 1939. Despite vigorous government enforcement of the ban and periodic arrest and imprisonment of militants, the PCE maintains an active apparatus and is considered one of the strongest opposition forces.

From a claimed peak membership of 300,000 in 1937 the PCE has diminished to its current level, estimated by non-party observers at between 5,000 and 20,000. In 1969, according to its secretary-general, Santiago Carrillo, the PCE had 22,000 members abroad and "two or three times" that number within Spain. The population of Spain is 33,824,000 (1970). The bulk of the PCE membership is drawn from among urban intellectuals and workers in Madrid, Barcelona, and Bilbao, and farm and industrial workers in and around Seville, Cádiz, Córdoba, and Málaga. On the whole, according to Carrillo, the PCE is not influential among peasants, among whom it encounters distrust. The party also derives support from exiles living in France, mainly in Paris and Toulouse.

Dissidence within the PCE since 1969 over international issues, particularly the role of the Soviet Union in the communist movement, culminated in 1971 in the formation of another party using the same name (here identified as the "rival PCE"). This group is believed to have very few adherents within Spain, but it is said to have a following of some 2,000 to 3,000 Spanish exiles, mostly living in Eastern Europe (*NYT*, 27 December 1971). In addition, it reportedly counts on Soviet financial and moral support.

There is also a small splinter group, the Communist Party of Spain, Marxist-Leninist (Partido Comunista de España Marxista-Leninista; PCE-ML), which appears to be divided into two main factions, both of which are pro-Chinese. Still another group is the Revolutionary Communist League (Liga Comunista Revolucionaria; LCR), a Spanish Trotskyite organization formed in April 1970.

The PCE. Organization and Leadership. The PCE is organized in all of Spain's 50 administrative provinces. At the national level are its 7-member Secretariat, 24-member Executive Committee, and 118-member Central Committee, below which are provincial and intermediate-level committees and, finally, the party cells.

Officers are elected and general policy guidelines determined at occasional party congresses. The Eighth Congress—the first since 1965—was held during 1972 at an undisclosed location and time, apparently in October. An organizational change approved at that meeting involved the reestablishment of the "party conference," which can be convened when it is not possible to hold the congress and when it is necessary to make more broadly based decisions than is possible in the Central Committee ("Radio Independent Spain," 6 November). The party organ *Mundo Obrero* (October) described the congress as the "most representative" of all those held since the Civil War, with the great majority of delegates coming from inside Spain. Little is actually known about the PCE leadership active within the country.

The exile PCE leadership is dispersed mainly in France and the Soviet Union, but also in Belgium, Czechoslovakia, and Romania. The PCE chairman is 77-year-old Dolores Ibarruri ("La Pasionaria" of Civil War days), who lives in Moscow. She held the position of secretary-general from 1942 to January 1960, when because of age she accepted the honorary position of party chairman. The secretary-general and actual leader of the party is Santiago Carrillo, who now lives in Switzerland. (For the Executive Committee see *YICA, 1972,* p. 220.) At the Eighth Congress, most Central Committee members, including the chairman and the secretary-general, were reportedly reconfirmed in their positions.

The PCE advocates strong support of rights of self-determination for Spain's three main nationalities, and therefore maintains branches (said to enjoy autonomy in adapting PCE policy to local conditions) in Catalonia, Galicia, and the Basque regions (Euzkadi). Gregorio López is secretary-general of the Unified Socialist Party of Catalonia (Partido Socialista Unificado de Cataluña); Santiago Alvarez has the same post for the Communist Party of Galicia. Since July 1969 the PCE has cooperated with a faction of the Basque independence movement—Basque Nation and Liberty (Euzkadi ta Askatasuna; ETA)—and the Movement of Basque Priests in a common anti-government front. (The ETA is divided into three known groups. The most militant faction advocates armed struggle and is believed to contain Maoists. The second faction, allied to the PCE, is considered small and uninfluential. The largest group, composed mostly of older Basques, is moderate.)

The party's youth organization, the Communist Youth League (Liga Juvenil Comunista; LJC), formed in October 1961, is active in the anti-government Democratic Students' Union (Sindicato Democrático Estudiantil; SDE) and in the illegal labor unions called Workers' Commissions (Comisiones Obreras, or "CC OO"). The SDE operates at the university level; it maintains centers in Madrid, Barcelona, Valencia, Seville, Saragossa, and Santiago de Compostela. The communist youth movement as a whole is not considered very strong.

Within the labor movement, communists occupy influential positions in the Workers' Commissions. Once a faction within the legal, state-controlled trade-union movement, the CC OO have become an independent and powerful center of anti-Franco forces that includes "progressive" Catholics (from the Acción Sindicalista de Trabajadores) and Socialists (from the Unión Sindical Obrera) as well as communists.

Domestic Attitudes and Activities. The lengthy policy resolution of the PCE's Eighth Congress declared that the party should capitalize on the "growing" opposition to the dictatorship and on the emergence of friction among elements of the ruling circles. Accordingly, it called for continuing efforts to broaden support in Spain for a "Pact for Freedom"—that is, an alliance among all opposition forces (mainly communist, socialist, and Catholic, but also including "bourgeois" groups) aimed at overthrowing Franco and establishing a "pluralistic democracy." The latter goal was characterized as an explicit commitment to a broad provisional coalition government, followed by elections—in an atmosphere of democratic liberties—to determine Spain's future social and political system. (*Radio Free Europe Research,* 25 October.)

In her address to the congress, Dolores Ibarruri said the party would disregard the criticism of those who were tied to "the dead letter of Marxism" and that it would abide by this "long-term" policy of alliances, which she insisted was not "opportunistic" (ibid.). This strategy was justified by Carrillo as a "compromise that has to be made with bourgeois and petty bourgeois forces in order to win over the masses" (BBC, 23 October). Especially praised before and during the congress as a "great victory for the working class" and a model for Spain was a unity agreement concluded in June between French socialists and communists (*Mundo Obrero,* 8 July; "Radio Independent Spain," 18 July; BBC, 23 October).

The Congress further called for an "authentic" political revolution in Spain, not through civil war, but by means of a "national strike" involving "the greatest possible number of forces aspiring to political freedom." Micro-models cited for such action were massive strikes earlier in the year in El Ferrol and in Vigo that effectively "paralyzed civil life, without the army intervening in either case in street repressions" (*L'Unità,* Rome, 21 October).

The underground workers' movement was indeed active in early 1972 in Spain's major industrial centers, where it has grown increasingly effective under the direction of the workers' commissions (CC OO). These illegal labor unions reportedly tend to be dominated by communists (NYT, 19 March). A declared aim of the PCE is greater participation by workers in directing CC OO activities since, according to the rationale, it is mainly by an appeal to their self-interest (to get higher wages and other benefits) that more workers can be persuaded to join in the movement ("Radio Independent Spain," statement of the PCE Executive Committee, 22 February).

Communists boasted that not since 1936 had Spain been swept by a class struggle "of such formidable dimensions" as at the end of 1971 and early 1972 (*New Times,* Moscow, March). *Pravda* (9 May) quoted an *Arriba* (Madrid) admission that there were 233 strikes during the first quarter of the year. It was said that the management at some plants preferred negotiating with CC OO representatives rather than with the state-controlled corporate unions (*Christian Science Monitor,* 18 March). Nevertheless, the "national strike" did not materialize during 1972.

To gain peripheral support for the "Pact for Freedom," the PCE issued an appeal to emigrant Spanish workers in Europe to observe a "Day of Struggle" on 30 April (*Mundo Obrero,* 5 February). The day was to be celebrated with meetings and rallies by emigrants throughout the continent in a call for freedom for Spain and an end to Francoism. At one such rally, in Frankfurt, Carrillo suggested that a congress be held to formulate a "charter of the rights of émigré workers," to raise the class struggle from the national to the European level, and to "concert our efforts throughout Europe" against European and American capitalism ("Radio Independent Spain," 2 May). In June the PCE received from Spanish communists in France a pledge to raise money between June and December for the party's "combat fund" (*Mundo Obrero,* 22 June).

Spain's vice-president expressed concern over communist subversion not only among labor sectors but also among students "acting in the service of the enemies of their country" (*Christian Science Monitor,* 18 March). The PCE itself acknowledged that students (in the universities and in secondary schools) and professional people were proving to be important allies of the working class in the revolutionary struggle ("Radio Independent Spain," statement of the PCE Executive Committee, 22 February). However, student leaders are said to be Maoist and leftist Catholic rather than regular communist (*NYT,* 19 March).

Early in the year, students on various campuses clashed almost daily with police, who were resented for their "three-year occupation" of the country's largest universities (*Christian Science Monitor,* 18 March).

Police "repression" and "provocation" were the subject of further PCE condemnation in November. When the French consul in Zaragoza died following a terrorist attack by youths on the consulate, police arrested and reportedly tortured "scores of democrats" and killed or wounded people who failed to obey police commands to stop. Denying charges that the attack was an outrage committed by communist agitators enrolled as students, the PCE countered that it was in reality a "monstrous act of provocation . . . intended to discredit the communists and the ITA"—the Basque Nationalist Movement ("Radio Independent Spain," 9 November). The Zaragoza local chapter of the PCE protested that in fact it did not approve of the terrorist attack on the consulate and that, in its view, actions of this sort "act as a brake" on the struggle of the masses, making it more difficult to attract people to the movement and making it all the easier for the government to "unleash harsher repression against all the forces of opposition" (ibid., 17 November).

The Rival PCE. The Central Committee of the rival PCE was much concerned during the year with finding ways to "speed up the final defeat of the Carrillo sector." Executive Committee member Enrique Lister drafted a report early in the year for the Central Committee which traced at length the development of the "open and irreconcilable confrontation" between the two factions. He reiterated his own party's unquestioning support for the Soviet Union and condemned the Carrillo-Ibarruri group's "revisionist and opportunistic platform," its campaigns against the Soviet Union and other socialist countries, and its "fifth-column work within the international communist movement." Efforts must be intensified, he said, to discredit Carrillo and to "demolish the legend" about the virtues and abilities of Dolores Ibarruri. Also, workers must be made to realize that Carrillo's group is "not truly democratic," having refused to hold a party congress since 1965. (*Mundo Obrero* [dissident], 1–15 May.)

The regular PCE's response at its Eighth Congress, which it convened later in the year, was to assert that the dissident group "has failed and has discredited itself," in spite of the fact that no other faction was as "rich in resources with which to publish leaflets and to travel" ("Radio Independent Spain," 6 November). This was a reference, of course, to support from the Soviet Union.

Earlier in the year, the regular PCE pleaded for proper respect for the "sincerity" of all communists and an end to the "coarse insults, misrepresentations, slanders, and personal affronts" emerging from Líster's group. The dissidents were further lectured for their rigid allegiance to foreign models and for concentrating their efforts on making socialist propaganda "among a small minority." Socialism is not just for an elite, it was said; "it has to be the concern of the great masses." (Ibid., 21 March.)

International Views and Positions. The PCE international policy rationale continued in 1972 to be developed around the theme of "unity through diversity," or "the decentralization of unity." "Diversity" was characterized as the right to differ from other communist parties on policy details and the right to criticize the other parties without such censure justifying charges of interference in their internal affairs. At the same time, differences must not be allowed to so embitter relations as to prevent unity of action on matters where there was agreement ("Radio Independent Spain," 18 February).

A report to the Eighth Congress declared that what was needed was a more creative and daring application of ideas, within the context of varying national situations, so as to give to socialism "the diversifying characteristics needed to attract broad masses" (ibid., 31 October). This attitude derives from the notion that the unity of all socialist parties is impossible on the basis of accepting the Soviet Union as the "touchstone," or material and spiritual center, of the international communist movement (ibid., 19 February).

The PCE's independent line emerged as a direct result of the Soviet-led invasion of Czechoslovakia in 1968 (see *YICA, 1972*, p. 223) and the continuing Soviet domination of that country's affairs. The PCE maintains that criticism of the Soviet Union and of other socialist states (or parties) is justified whenever "we consider that they are subordinating the general interests of the [international] proletariat to particular or momentary interests of state" ("Radio Independent Spain," 22 February). Thus, concern was expressed over continuing arrests and prosecutions in Czechoslovakia despite assurances by the Czechoslovak party's secretary-general that there would be no trials in connection with the 1968 resistance to the Soviets (ibid., 24 February). Spanish communists also deplored the Soviet move in signing a trade agreement with Spain in September that was expected to nearly double the limited trade between the two countries in 1973.

The errant ways of the Soviet Union from "true" Marxism-Leninism and the policy contradictions among the socialist states are attributed by the PCE to nationalism, "a legacy of capitalism" that "has not yet disappeared" in communist countries. This seriously interferes, it was said, with the need to keep "anti-imperialist unity" as the uppermost criterion for tackling problems (ibid., 31 October). An indirect rebuke of the Soviet Union was apparent in the Eighth Congress resolution's assertion that "the touchstone of proletarian internationalism" was active solidarity with Vietnam. Such a definition contradicts the Soviet Union's traditional self-image as the "touchstone of proletarian internationalism." (*Radio Free Europe Research,* 25 October.)

Even though the PCE continued to upbraid the Soviet Union from time to time, party spokesmen repeatedly emphasized the party's commitment to "fraternal relations" and unity among all communist parties, at least in the arena of international policy. The PCE's greetings to the Central Committee of the Soviet party on the occasion of the 55th anniversary of the October Revolution included praise for the Soviet Union as the "decisive force in the struggle against imperialism." Carrillo voiced great concern over the anti-Sovietism he had observed in China during his visit in that country in 1971, and noted that the Soviet-Chinese quarrel was having "dangerous repercussions on the entire communist movement." To overcome frictions, he suggested a demilitarization of broad buffer areas along the border between the two nations and more "open diplomacy" between them so as to reduce public misunderstandings that could lead to war. If socialist countries cannot practice open diplomacy, he said, "with what authority can we come out against imperialist secret diplomacy?" (Ibid., 18 February.)

The need to promote an anti-imperialist unity of action within the international socialist community, not subservient to the nationalist will of any single party or state, was advanced as the justification for the PCE's rapprochement with the Chinese Communist Party (ibid.). It was pointed out that the PCE is one of the few parties that have relations with both the Soviet and Chinese parties and that, in fact, it now has relations with all communist parties but the Albanian one. The PCE's unifying influence in the international communist movement was credited at the Eighth Congress with contributing in large measure to a "substantial" increase in the party's prestige, as reflected in the many greetings received from fraternal parties (ibid., 31 October).

The PCE declared at its congress that it accepts a policy of détente or co-existence between the socialist and capitalist worlds as a necessary expedient to prevent a destructive atomic world war. The party insisted, however, that this must not signify the maintenance of the status quo; the revolutionary process must continue. Forces of imperialism cited as appropriate targets of continuing socialist solidarity and struggle were the Vietnam "aggression," the subjugation of colonial peoples in Africa by Spain and Portugal, and the spread of the multinational firms that are already "the skeleton of European capitalism." Stressed was the need for socialist cooperation in creating international workers' commissions that could become a "new tool for the inter-European class struggle against the monopolies." (Ibid.)

Even while denouncing the "contradictions" of the "capitalist-monopolist" European Economic Community, the PCE reportedly accepts the need for Spain to accomodate itself to the reality of that integration (*L'Unitá,* Rome, 21 October). Accordingly, it was proposed at the

Eighth Congress that an "association agreement with the EEC" would be appropriate for Spain, though not until after the end of the Franco government. The PCE could then unite its efforts with those of other "progressive" forces of Spain and the rest of the continent "to democratize the EEC and transform the Europe of the monopolies into a socialist Europe."

International Party Contacts. The Communist Party of the Soviet Union in June and July 1972 was host to a five-man delegation of PCE officials that included three members of the Central Committee. The group made a three-week, 14,000-mile-long tour of the Soviet Union for a first-hand study of Soviet life and achievements and for an exchange of experiences ("Radio Independent Spain," 6 July). In an apparent attempt at conciliating Carrillo, lest he align himself too closely with the Chinese Communist Party or mobilize a bloc of communist parties "independent" of Moscow, the Soviets stressed to the delegation the "fraternity" of their two parties, reaffirming that the party led by Carrillo and Ibarruri was "the principal force—not the only force but the principal one—of Spain's revolutionary present and of its democratic and socialist future" (ibid., 2 August; *Radio Free Europe Research,* 25 October).

Other PCE visits during the year were made to Romania, Israel, and North Korea, where communist parties also maintain an independent or neutral stance toward the Communist Party of the Soviet Union.

PCE delegations met formally with Romanian Communist Party officials on three occasions during the year at the latter party's headquarters in Bucharest. In May, Carrillo paid a visit to the Romanian party and in August a PCE delegation headed by Carrillo and Dolores Ibarruri conferred with a Romanian party group led by Nicolae Ceaușescu, secretary-general of his party. It was agreed that "the cooperation, friendship, and militant solidarity" between the two parties should be further expanded and strengthened. In June, discussions were held on the occasion of PCE veteran Mariano Bautista's funeral, which was attended by a PCE group (AERPRES, Romanian press agency, 14 May, 3 June, 29 August).

It was declared at the PCE's Eighth Congress that the party would continue "to strengthen its solidarity . . . with the consistent anti-imperialist forces of the Middle East, including the communist party, the Palestine resistance and the revolutionary forces of Israel ("Radio Independent Spain," 31 October). In line with this aim, a Spanish communist delegation for the first time attended a congress held during the summer by the Communist Party of Israel (MAKI).

In November, Carrillo and two PCE Executive Committee members visited North Korea at the invitation of the Central Committee of the Korean Workers' Party (ibid., 7 November).

Publications. The official organ of the PCE is *Mundo Obrero,* published semimonthly in France. *Nuestra Bandera* is the party's quarterly theoretical journal. Party sources claim a circulation of 60,000 to 70,000 for *Mundo Obrero* and 205,000 for *Nuestra Bandera.* Both are published abroad and distributed clandestinely in Spain. Other major PCE publications include the semimonthly *España Republicana,* published in Havana by the Cuban-Spanish Friendship Society, and *Realidad,* a monthly journal published in Rome. According to party sources, there are 32 PCE publications. In addition, the party directs radio programs to Spain through its station "Radio Independent Spain," which broadcasts from Bucharest.

*   *   *

The two pro-Chinese groups in Spain are organized under the name of the Communist Party of Spain, Marxist-Leninist. The original group, which publishes *Vanguardia Obrera,* was formed in 1964. It is believed to be the stronger, and is recognized by Communist China. The other group, which publishes *Mundo Obrero Revolucionario,* was formed in 1965. It is small and seems isolated internationally. Very little is known about the leadership and organization of either group. Pro-Chinese cells are known to exist in Madrid, Asturias, Catalonia, Aragon, the Basque region, and the Canary Islands.

The Trotskyite Revolutionary Communist League (LCR) claimed to play a very important role in student agitation during the year, especially in Madrid. The LCR alleged that the "Action Committees" it rallied and the PCE were the two most important political forces involved in the student struggles in the capital. The Trotskyite group also reportedly cooperated with the PCE and with Maoist groups in mobilizing student rebellion in other parts of the country (*Rouge,* French newspaper of the Communist League, 5 April, translated in *Intercontinental Press,* New York, 1 May). Spanish police concluded that students responsible for incidents in December 1971 at the University of Bilbao were organized in various small groups, called "Red University" and "Barricade," which were aligned with the LCR (*Pueblo Sucesos,* translated in *Intercontinental Press,* 24 January).

Elbert Covell College   H. Leslie Robinson
University of the Pacific

Sweden

The Swedish Communist Party (Sveriges Kommunistiska Parti; SKP) was formed by left-wing dissidents of the Social Democratic Party in 1921. Legal at all times, it simply changed its name to Left Party–Communists (Vänsterpartiet Kommunisterna; VPK) at its 1967 congress. Most support for the VPK comes from organized workers in the urban industrial areas of Stockholm, Gävleborg, and Göteborg and in Sweden's northernmost province of Norrbotten. VPK members are generally unskilled laborers in the lumber, mining, construction, and transportation fields. They number from 16,000 to 18,000 in a total population of 8,129,000 (estimated 1971).

Though the smallest of the five parties in the Swedish Riksdag (Parliament) in membership and popular support, the VPK sometimes wielded the swing vote in 1972. The party held 17 of the 350 seats in the unicameral Riksdag, thanks to polling 4.8 percent of the vote in the last general election, September 1970. The Social Democratic Party (Socialdemokratiska Arbetarparti; SAP), with 163 seats to the non-socialist opposition's 170, sometimes had to seek VPK support on critical votes. For the first time, the SAP relied on communist votes to pass the Swedish defense budget, 28 May. Normally the Social Democrats have tried to effect a compromise on defense planning with the center, liberal, and moderate parties. In like manner, last-minute (30 May) VPK support for a tax reform bill, which substituted a doubling of the employer-paid payroll tax for a rise in the value-added tax, staved off the collapse of Premier Olof Palme's government and early elections.

Such critical roles for the VPK represented a recent change of fortune for the communists. Their performance in national elections since World War II had been spotty at best. They lost five seats in the 1968 elections, held just after the Soviet-led invasion of Czechoslovakia.

Several splinter groups, mostly Maoist, have emerged to the left of the VPK since the outbreak of the Sino-Soviet split. Left-wing students and intellectuals have gravitated to the Communist League, Marxist-Leninist (Kommunistiska Förbundet Marxist-Leninisterna; KFML) —the largest and most active of those groups. Founded in 1967, the KFML polled only 0.4 percent in its first national election in 1970 and so failed to get the four percent of the national vote (or 12 percent of a district vote) needed for parliamentary representation.

Leadership and Organization. The VPK's Twenty-third Congress, held in Stockholm on 26–29 October 1972, unanimously reelected Carl-Henrik Hermansson as chairman. He first became party chief in January 1964, when he succeeded Hilding Hagberg, a long-time Stalinist. As a representative of the VPK's younger revisionist faction, Hermansson has succeeded, to some extent, in reversing the declining communist appeal, which hit its nadir in the 1962 local elections. He has stressed that the VPK is an independent Swedish organization, committed to maintaining democratic institutions and pursuing left-socialist policies.

Theoretically, all important questions of policy and organization are decided at the triennial party congress. That meeting elects the 35-member Central Committee, known since 1964 as the Party Board, which supervises party activities. That board selects the eight-member Executive Committee (Politburo), which controls the party's daily operations.

There are 28 party districts, which correspond to the nation's 28 electoral regions. Below these are the "workers' communes," which are the main local units responsible for coordinating fund-raising, propaganda, and training.

The VPK's youth affiliate, the Leftist Youth League (Vänsterns Ungdomsförbund; VUF), has virtually withered away in the wake of the pro-Chinese Marxist-Leninist Struggle League (Marxist-Leninistiska Kampförbundet; MLK). Formed in 1970, the MLK supports the KFML but maintains an independent organization.

The VPK heads no national trade union. It controls only about 80 of the nation's 9,000 union locals—primarily in the construction, forestry, and mining industries.

Party Internal Affairs. Preparation and the holding of the party congress consumed most VPK members' energies in 1972. Some 230 delegates attended the sessions, which elected party leaders and approved a new party program.

The draft of the "Program of Principles," first published in -Ny Dag on 22 February, unleashed fierce internal debate. The new program was considerably more radical than the "Socialist Alternative" adopted at the 1967 congress. Whereas the 1967 program was calculated to stem the drift of communists toward the Social Democrats, the 1972 draft seemed intended to cover the left flank by appealing to younger, more radical Swedes. It evoked especially strong opposition from VPK members in Norrbotten, traditionally a center for old-line, pro-Soviet constituents. The Muscovites—especially Sven Pjelf, editor of *Norrskensflamman*—shun critical evaluations of the Soviet Union (alleged "anti-Sovietism") made by young radicals and support instead the kind of cooperation between the communists and Social Democrats which they believe Moscow favors. Party leaders of the Norrbotten district supported the program addendum of Executive Committee member Sven Henriksson, which stressed a transition to socialism via parliamentary means (*Norrskensflamman,* 1 March). Henriksson remarked that "with a too negative attitude toward Parliament, we in fact risk agreeing with those eager to join the EEC" (*Ny Dag,* 19 April). Former party chairman Hagberg criticized the new program for being "silent about the peaceful road to socialism" and instead "guided by Mao's line, the people's war" (ibid., 8–9 March).

Jorn Svensson, VPK member of Parliament from Malmö, was one of the program's main proponents. He condemned reaction from Norrbotten as "a survival from the time of directives" (ibid., 25 March–6 April). He and his colleagues supported the new draft as "a revolutionary alternative in the class struggle against the Social Democratic class cooperation policy" (ibid., 12–13 April). The program called for complete abolition of the armed forces; formation of a "people's militia," which would replace the police; destruction of the secret files of the Swedish security police; the confiscation of extensive industrial holdings in the name of the people; and the nationalization of commercial banks and other large companies.

What emerged from this spirited debate and the congress itself was a more revolutionary program. The VPK Action Program, as it was renamed, called for nationalization of the pharmaceutical, insurance, construction, and war materials industries. In his opening speech to the congress, Hermansson demanded an immediate price freeze, lower direct taxes and interest rates, and an end to the value-added tax on food. He condemned the Social Democrats for compromising with capitalism and called for a "red wave" to reverse high prices and unemployment.

Domestic Attitudes and Activities. Despite the anti-Social Democratic rhetoric which emerged at the VPK congress, the party cooperated with Palme forces and kept the young premier in power during 1972. The votes on tax reform and defense policy, already noted as the main events of the spring session of the Riksdag, were key indices to the party's domestic strategy. As usual, the VPK could be counted on to support the Social Democrats, particularly when the alternative was a non-socialist government in Sweden.

Economic issues dominated VPK domestic concerns in 1972. The communists, like the Social Democrats, asserted repeatedly that reduced military expenditures would free funds for social needs. Hermansson made it clear that he considered the VPK's main task to be the "struggle against unemployment and prevention of the burdens of the crisis being placed upon the workers" (*Ny Dag*, 4–8 February). He urged adoption of a new regional policy "since a considerable part of the unemployment is caused by the regional crisis." He repeated demands for improved working conditions, the reintroduction of price control, expanding the rights of workers in industry, and the abolition of the value-added tax (because it "weighs most heavily on the lower income levels"). In the choice between a better-balanced state budget and progress against unemployment, Hermansson opted unequivocally for the latter. Wildcat strikes in Göteborg shipyards in October, inspired by KFML sympathizers, carried this line to its logical, in unintended, conclusion.

Finally, Hermansson declared at the party congress: "Our internal political demands can be summarized in the following program guaranteeing four fundamental rights in the economic and social area"—which he defined as the right to meaningful work; the right to make decisions about one's own working conditions; the right to a healthy working, living, and leisure-time environment, and the right to economic security (ibid., 27–31 October and 1–2 November).

International Views and Positions. As elsewhere in Scandinavia, affiliation with the expanding European Economic Community continued to be a major communist target. Even though the Palme government negotiated only a free trade agreement with the EEC (signed on 22 July), the VPK charged that the government was subordinating national independence to the Brussels bureaucracy. Speaking at Luleå on 25 September, Hermansson called for a referendum on any Swedish tie to the Common Market, a point he underscored at the party congress.

Hermansson set forth the other main points of the VPK international platform in his speech during an earlier Riksdag debate. He stated that "Swedish recognition of the German Democratic Republic would be an important contribution to the efforts to win over a majority for the general [East and West German] treaty and ensure the relaxation of tension in Europe" (*Ny Dag*, 29 March–6 April). He urged East German participation at the U.N. Conference on the Human Environment, held in Stockholm in June.

U.S. policy in Southeast Asia continued to evoke strong communist opposition. The VPK asked that delegates to the U.N. conference in Stockholm denounce U.S. "ecocide" in Vietnam. Hermansson demanded that the Swedish government clearly condemn "the U.S. war of aggression and break off relations with the Saigon junta and establish diplomatic relations with the provisional revolutionary government of the Republic of South Vietnam" (ibid.). Despite the VPK's continuing initiatives on Vietnam-related issues, the party did not derive much political benefit because the ruling Social Democratic Party was at least as advanced as the VPK in its critiques of U.S. policy and offers to grant humanitarian aid to North Vietnam.

So-called "Swedish imperialism" came in for its share of communist criticism. Hermansson scored Swedish trade with South Africa, Greece, and Portugal. The VPK urged the government to take steps leading toward the recognition of North Korea and to work through the United Nations for the withdrawal of all foreign troops from Korea. Only the communists balked at the Riksdag's strong vote, 6 December, against immediate recognition of North Korea.

International Communist Movement. All the internal debate on Muscovite versus Maoist leanings notwithstanding, the VPK remained aloof from the Sino-Soviet rift and retained its independence of both sides. The main exception to this detachment from international ideological debate had been the VPK's condemnation of the Soviet Union for the invasion of Czechoslovakia in 1968. Consistent with that stand, the Executive Committee issued a statement condemning the political trials which took place in Czechoslovakia during the summer of 1972. It cautioned that, though "the socialist state must defend itself against internal and external attack," that necessity "should not lead to the police, courts, and prisons replacing political debate" (*Ny Dag,* 11–17 August).

Despite Swedish displeasure with the Czechoslovakian situation, the Communist Party of the Soviet Union (CPSU) made a point of sending warm greetings to the VPK during its congress. Its message marked an important change in relations between the two parties, which had been chilly since the adoption of the VPK's 1967 program. The *Svenska Dagbladet* (Stockholm, 31 October) speculated that, as far as Moscow was concerned, the VPK showed with its new party program in 1972 that the prodigal son had come home, with Lenin reinstated as parent.

Several visits of some note took place during the year. A CPSU delegation, led by *Pravda* editor M. V. Zimjanin, visited Sweden, 14–20 May, at the invitation of the VPK. Representatives of both parties stressed their unanimous protest against "U.S. aggression" in Vietnam, their solidarity with all peoples fighting for national independence, their support for the proposed "Conference on Security and Cooperation in Europe," and their emphasis on the importance of continued development of good neighborly relations between the Soviet Union and Sweden (*Ny Dag,* 26–30 May).

Following an invitation from the VPK, a Central Committee, delegation of the East German Socialist Unity Party visited Sweden, 12–18 March. Swedish recognition of the German Democratic Republic was one of the main topics of discussion (*Neues Deutschland,* East Berlin, 18 March. Chariman Hermansson and Sven Henriksson visited Cuba in early December.

Publications. The VPK's central organ is *Ny Dag* ("New Day"), published twice weekly in Stockholm and printed under the name of *Arbetar–Tidningen* ("Worker News") in western Sweden. *Norrskensflamman* ("Blaze of Northern Lights"), published in Luleå, is the party's only daily. Its theoretical quarterly is *Socialistisk Debatt*.

The KFML's theoretical journal *Marxistisk Forum* is published monthly in Uppsala. The Executive Committee of Communist Youth started a new monthly paper, *Stormklockan* (Alarm Bell), in September in Göteborg (see *YICA,* 1971, p. 259). A revolutionary splinter of the KFML—the KFML(r)—issues a bulletin called *Klasskampen* ("Class Struggle").

Switzerland

The Swiss Party of Labor (Parti Suisse du Travail; PST/Partei der Arbeit; PdA) was founded in 1921. The party enjoys legal status and is pro-Soviet in orientation. The party organization is based on the principle of "democratic centralism," and is entirely "independent in the determination of its policy and its action." These two principles were reaffirmed by the delegates to the Tenth Congress of the PdA, held in 1971 (see *YICA, 1972,* pp. 231–32).

Estimated membership in the PdA is between 4,500 and 5,000. The population of Switzerland is 6,300,000 (estimated 1970). The PdA occupies 5 seats in the lower house of the Swiss parliament, the National Council. The party is strongest in the cantons of Geneva, Vaud, and Neuchâtel, but has little strength in the German-speaking industrial centers, such as Basel or Zurich (ibid., p. 231). In January 1972 the Organization of Swiss Communists/ Marxist-Leninist (Organization des Communistes de Suisse/Marxiste-Leniniste; OCS/ML) held a constituent congress to establish the Communist Party of Switzerland/Marxist-Leninist. The orientation of this splinter group is pro-Chinese.

Leadership and Organization. No party congresses were held during 1972 and no changes in party leadership were reported. Jean Vincent, a practicing attorney in Geneva, remained party spokesman in the three-member Secretariat, whose other members are Jakob Lechleiter (Zurich) and André Muret (Lausanne). The Executive Committee has 15 members, and the Central Committee, 50.

Organizations within the PdA, designed to appeal to a variety of interests, include the Free Youth of Switzerland, Swiss Peace Movement, Switzerland-DPRK Society (DPRK: Democratic People's Republic of Korea), Swiss-Soviet Friendship Society, Swiss Committee for Aid to Vietnam, Swiss League of Women for Peace and Progress, and Society for the Defense of Tenants.

Domestic Attitudes and Activities. The proposals and policies of the PdA in 1972 continued to advocate domestic programs outlined during the previous year. In May party chairman Vincent presented the party's views on government policy in a lengthy article entitled, " 'Major Lines' and Directives—The Government's 'Four-Year Plan.' " The main concern of the PdA was that the Swiss government had acknowledged that more "planning" would be required in the future to deal effectively with the country's domestic problems.

Vincent considered it a victory for the PdA that the government had announced "plans" to (1) support small and medium-sized enterprises, (2) provide employment and full employment, (3) handle differently the problem of foreign workers, (4) move from "labor peace to participation," (5) provide education "for all," (6) "plan" research, (7) protect the environment, (8) provide for regional development, (9) encourage housing construction, (10) coordinate transportation and communication, (11) provide adequate supplies of power and (12) more efficiently schedule government expenditures. He did not consider that the government had dealt adequately with the questions of social security, public health, and social and preventive medicine. Although Vincent welcomed the government's plans, he emphasized that first priority should be given to "the means" for their realization and the necessary budgetary requirements. (*Voix Ouvriere,* 1 May.)

The PdA continued to urge its members to support the "unity of the left," particularly with the Socialist Party (Parti Socialiste; PS). Although the PdA did not propose to "erase the differences in views" that existed with the PS, conversations were conducted throughout the year with members of the PS to encourage "the formation of a powerful and active leftist movement." The PdA considered "a joint policy" for the two parties to be "completely conceivable" in the areas of property law, tenant protection, housing construction, and social insurance. Therefore, the PdA supported three Socialist candidates, in addition to its own candidate, in local elections at Basel in March, in order to elect "a leftist majority." (*Vorwaerts,* 10 February.)

International Views and Positions. The foreign policy statements of the PdA in 1972 did not reflect any significant departure from previous positions. The PdA remained critical of U.S. involvement in Vietnam, and the party's Executive Committee issued a special declaration to this effect (*Voix Ouvriere,* 20 May). Swiss cooperation with the Common Market was condemned as representing "greater and greater movement . . . in the direction of vast capitalist concentrations" (ibid., 2 September). The PdA expressed solidarity with the views of the communist parties of France and Italy, in condemnation of the Czechoslovak government's continuing prosecution of persons involved in the events of 1968 (ibid., 5 August, 2 September).

Peaceful coexistence and détente were enthusiastically endorsed by the party organs, *Vorwaerts* and *Voix Ouvriere.* The PdA urged "the participation of the broadest circles of public opinion in the realization of European security, the creation of an atmosphere of understanding and cooperation among the peoples of our continent and the entire world." It affirmed solidarity with "the peoples of Indochina" and supported "a peaceful solution of the Middle East conflict" in accordance with the 1967 resolution of the United Nations. (*Vorwaerts,* 10 February.)

The PdA was particularly concerned with "the inalienable right of every people to decide its own fate without any outside interference," with "the development of relations of cooperation and international solidarity among all socialist states and with all communist and workers parties," and with "establishing and consolidating the unity of the international communist movement based on respect for the principles of Marxism-Leninism, proletarian internationalism, equal rights, non-interference in internal affairs, and mutual aid" (ibid.).

U.S. President Nixon's visit to Peking in February was welcomed by the PdA, which viewed the trip as a "sign of a favorable evolution in American public opinion" in contrast to "cold war" attitudes. The PdA warned, however, that the United States sought to increase "the division between the two largest socialist countries," China and the Soviet Union. At the same time the PdA criticized Chinese support of the Pakistan government headed by Yahya Khan, "a creature of American imperialism," and Chinese approval of "the expansion of the Europe of the trusts by Great Britain's entry into the Common Market." (*Voix Ouvriere,* 24 February; *Pravda,* 10 October.)

International Activities and Party Contacts. Inter-party contacts were carefully maintained during 1972. A delegation of the Romanian Communist Party visited Switzerland at the invitation of the PdA on 1–8 February. The delegation participated in discussions with Vincent, Muret and Lechleiter, with members of the Executive Committee, and with leaders of PdA cantonal organizations in Geneva, Lausanne, Zurich, and Basel. The two parties praised the cooperation which has been developed in numerous areas between Switzerland and Romania, and confirmed their desire to extend this in the future "in the interests of both countries." (*Vorwaerts,* 10 February.)

A delegation of veteran members of the PdA visited the Soviet Union for two weeks in April and May at the invitation of the Central Committee of the Communist Party of the Soviet Union. The visitors toured Moscow, Yerevan, and Volgograd, had discussions with members of the CPSU Central Committee's International Sector and participated in the May Day celebration in Red Square. (*Pravda,* 8 May.) During the visit "fraternizations" were initiated with veteran members of the Belgian Communist Party, who were on a similar tour (*Voix Ouvriere,* 20 May).

During February a delegation of the Communist Party of Spain (PCE) visited Switzerland at the invitation of the PdA and met with the leading members of the party. In a final communiqué the PdA and PCE expressed "their determination to contribute to the unity of all communist and workers' parties founded on respect for independence and non-interference in the internal affairs of each party." The PdA representatives declared that their party would make greater efforts in the future "to enlighten and mobilize Swiss public opinion concerning the heroic struggle by the Spanish people to overthrow [the] dictatorship, restore democracy, and promote socialism." (Ibid., 24 February.)

A PdA delegation headed by Jakob Lechleiter visited the Soviet Union on 24 September-8 October at the invitation of the Central Committee of the CPSU. The delegation met with B. N. Ponomarev, CPSU Politburo candidate member, Central Committee secretary, and other members of the Central Committee. (*Pravda,* 10 October.)

Publications. The PdA publishes official organs in three languages. *Vorwaerts* and *Il Lavoratore* appear weekly in Basel and in Locarno respectively. *Voix Ouvrière* is published daily in Geneva.

*   *   *

The Organization of the Communists of Switzerland, Marxist-Leninist (Organisation des Communistes de Suisse/Marxiste-Leniniste) held a constituent congress in early January 1972 to establish the Communist Party of Switzerland/Marxist-Leninist (CPS/ML). The establishment of this party—governed by "Marxism-Leninism" and the philosophy of Mao Tse-tung —was to open "a new and decisive phase in the struggle to have the proletariat of Switzerland gain power, to have the dictatorship of the proletariat replace the dictatorship of the bourgeoisie, and to abolish all exploitation and oppression of the people." (*Octobre,* February; see also *YICA, 1972,* pp. 237–38.) The party organ is *Octobre,* published monthly.

The other major communist splinter group, the Revolutionary Marxist League (LMR) remains limited primarily to the French-speaking part of Switzerland. It appears to have little influence and was relatively inactive during the year.

Hoover Institution   Dennis L. Bark
Stanford University

Turkey

The Communist Party of Turkey (Türkiye Komünist Partisi; TKP) was founded in 1920 in Istanbul. It soon absorbed the remnants of two other early Turkish communist organizations, one formed in Anatolia and the other among the émigrés of Azerbaijan. Illegal since 1925 and severely repressed within Turkey, the TKP has never created a strong organization and is not a significant political force in the country. It is estimated that the TKP has 1,200 to 2,000 members and 10,000 sympathizers. The population of Turkey is 35,600,000 (estimated 1970).

The TKP supports and has apparently infiltrated a number of Turkish leftist organizations in Europe, including the Federation of Turkish Socialists, the Association for Vigilant Turks, and the Front for a Democratic and Free Turkey. Within Turkey, the TKP supports various leftist organizations, the most prominent being trade union, teacher, student, and youth groups such as the Union of Progressive Forces, the Confederation of Reformist Trade Unions (DISK), the Federation of Idea Clubs (FKF), the Turkish Teachers' Unions (TOS), and the 27 May Clubs.

The TKP has to some extent infiltrated the Turkish Labor Party (TLP), whose policies in many respects parallel those of the communists. The TLP, however, has shown wariness of identification with the outlawed communist party; most of its members claim to be either "national communists" or "national socialists" with no interest in the international communist movement. Even so, TLP delegations have frequently participated in communist-oriented international meetings. In the 1969 parliamentary elections, the TLP secured 2.7 percent of the vote and 2 out of 450 seats, down from 3 percent and 15 seats in 1965. In 1969 the TLP lost any possibility of influencing national policy by parliamentary means when it failed to win the minimum 2,500 votes in a constituency to qualify for a party mandate distribution. In 1971 the TLP was outlawed along with many other leftist groups, as an indirect result of terrorist activities.

Leadership and Organization. Overt TKP activity is directed from abroad. Zeki Baştimar, who goes under the alias Yakub Demir, is the party's secretary general. Most if not all of its 13 Central Committee members live in Moscow.

Domestic Affairs. In 1972, martial law in Turkey further weakened TKP support. Meanwhile party news in the Turkish-language edition of *World Marxist Review* (*Yeni Çağ* [*YC*], January) portrayed the TKP as gaining more and more strength despite the government's suppressive measures. TKP elements played a small role in the activities of the terrorist Turkish People's Liberation Army (THKO) and the moderate anti-U.S., pro-Arab Turkish Revolutionary Youth Federation (Dev-Genc), from which the THKO emerged early in 1971. THKO elements are known to have received training with Palestinian "liberation" groups in Syria and Jordan, but their tactics appear to be also inspired by Latin American urban guerrillas, notably the Uruguyan Tupamaros. The THKO has split the Turkish Marxist left. Leftist intellectuals, particularly, blame the THKO for providing authorities with a pretext to intervene in university affairs. The TKP disapproved of the THKO but was reluctant to condemn guerrillas openly, since their cause seems to be the same.

After 1971 all leftist organizations were banned and the majority of the leaders were imprisoned, some sentenced to capital punishment.

TKP activity throughout 1972 was limited to protests against the executions of last year's revolutionaries and the listing of petitions handed to the Turkish government by "progressive" and middle-of-the-road organizations.

The Turkish premier's visit to France, in January, was accompanied by protests from members of the Turkish Student Organization in Paris, who staged a sit-in and a hunger strike. They were joined by socialists and "Atatürkists," and had support from French leftists (ibid.).

The major issue of criticism was the martial law imposed in April 1971. The TKP strongly condemned martial law and the court-martial trials of Turkish citizens, hailing those members and groups within the parliament that were against it, notably a TLP representative and the left-of-center group in the Republican Party (CHP). In spite of this, the TKP directed criticism against the Republicans, whose rising popularity it attributed to the government's repressions and tax policy, and whose leader it criticized for having openly supported the premier.

According to *YC* (February), worker unrest continued in spite of martial law in the shoe and leather factories, and when negotiations for higher wages reached a stalemate, a strike resulted in a confrontation between the military police and the workers.

In February, trials of 229 Dev-Genc members were begun. Thirteen were condemned to capital punishment, and a 15-year sentence was passed for the others. Turkish students abroad demonstrated against these trials.

In March, military police arrested 25 youths, among whom were the president of the Federation of Idea Clubs and a popular film actor. A youth was killed in Ankara in a shootout with the police. A professor of law and former dean of the law school in Ankara was arrested and charged with turning students against the government. (Ibid., March.)

According to the TKP, apart from the trials and arrests of moderate leftists in the major cities there was a far broader campaign and witch hunt in the southeastern parts of Turkey which was not reported by the press. Allegedly, 4,483 Kurdish nationalists were arrested in Diyarbakir, and this was said to be but a small fraction of the general movement by the martial law committee against the Kurdish population, reportedly including detention camps and torture (ibid.). TKP sources stated that the "liberation struggle of the Kurdish minority" in eastern Turkey was helped by the TKP and TLP. Both parties maintained that the Kurdish problem could only be solved within the framework of the "working-class fight for socialism." It is likely that the TKP, TLP, and Dev-Genc were all involved in the establishment of "revolutionary centers" in Kurdish areas in the past few years. Last year both the TLP and Dev-Genc were charged with disseminating communist and Kurdish nationalist propaganda.

A new wave of political controversy was triggered in May with a political execution. The *YC* praised the speech of a senator who declared that executions will not solve anything and that socioeconomic problems should first be solved. In an attempt to stop political executions four Turkish youths hijacked a plane to Sofia. The plane and passengers were returned unharmed, and the hijackers were granted political asylum, even though Bulgaria seemed reluctant to harm her new friendship with Turkey. After other incidents the government position on leftist militants and young radicals hardened once again and new arrests were made. Two prominent journalists were arrested, as were some leftist teachers charged with spreading communist propaganda (CSM 28 October).

On 22 May a new cabinet was formed. This development was seen by the TKP as reflecting a "moral and political bankruptcy of capitalism in Turkey" which was bringing closer the "proletarian revolution." The new cabinet could not muster much support and by October Turkey seemed to be approaching a crisis owing to the government's failure to carry out promised preparations for certain constitutional amendments which would have ended martial law and prepared the ground for general elections due in October 1973. (*Christian Science Monitor,* 7 October.)

Freedom of the press, or the lack of it, was among the targets of the TKP. The congress of the International Federation of Journalists, held in Istanbul in September, adopted a resolution charging Turkey with restricting press freedom. The leader of the social-democratic Republican Party, made a sharp attack on the banning of some books, stating that many publishers were afraid to issue books on social topics (CSM, 18 September). The martial law authorities replied that they had no choice but to restrict the news, fearing a recurrence of the situation faced in March 1971, and emphasized that the present difficulties in Turkey were the direct result of subversive and terrorist activities.

Foreign Relations. Under the headline "A Call to our People" the *YC* (February) reported that Turkey was in great danger due to "U.S. imperialism and its helper NATO." It protested against the new fleet base in Greece which would be "working directly against the socialist aspirations of Turkey, Cyprus, the Arab countries, and the people of Greece."

U.S. President Nixon's visit to China was also noted by the *YC,* which charged that the Chinese were "watering down" the anti-imperialist movement and that Maoists in Turkey worked hand in hand with U.S. Central Intelligence Agency personnel. On 18 March the Turkish premier visited the United States. The TKP considered that Turkey was being sold to "American big business and warmongers." (*YC,* March.)

Publications. TKP pronouncements are broadcast by a clandestine radio station, Bizim Radyo ("Our Radio"), which transmits from East Germany. Party declarations and documents appear in a special supplement to *Yeni Cag* ("New Age"), the Turkish-language edition of *World Marxist Review.* The party occasionally issues pamphlets which are circulated clandestinely in Turkey.

San Francisco,   S. Akpinar
  California

MIDDLE EAST
AND AFRICA

Algeria

The Algerian Communist Party (Parti Communiste Algérien; PCA) was founded in 1920. Initially an extension of the French Communist Party, after October 1936 it existed independently. In December 1962, five months after the declaration of Algerian independence, the party was banned by the Algerian government under President Ahmad Ben Bella. Approximately two years later, and under pressure from the Algerian government, PCA members were instructed by party leaders to join the ruling Algerian party, the National Liberation Front (Front de Libération Nationale; FLN), and the PCA seemingly disappeared as an autonomous party. After the June 1965 coup which brought Houari Boumedienne to power, dissident left-wing FLN elements combined with communist militants to form an illegal opposition party, the Popular Resistance Organization (Organisation de la Résistance Populaire; ORP). On 26 January 1966 the ORP changed its name to Socialist Vanguard Party (Parti de l'Avant-Garde-Socialiste; PAGS), but according to Henri Alleg, one of its leading spokesmen, it continued to attract "communists and former militants of the FLN who were drawn to Marxism-Leninism" (*Daily World,* New York, 16 January 1969).

During 1969 and 1970, PAGS strength was estimated at about 750 members. Membership figures for 1971 and 1972 are unavailable, and one can assume that government restrictive policies have thinned the party's ranks. Even the PAGS former newspaper, *La Voix du Peuple* (the Arabic version is *al-Sha'b*) is now published under governmental aegis.

Support for the PAGS mainly comes from the PCF and expatriate Algerians. The population of Algeria is between 13,000,000 and 14,000,000 (estimated 1972).

Party Affairs and Leadership. The PAGS has had little impact on official Algerian policies. Of the two major organizations through which it clandestinely operated, the General Union of Algerian Workers (Union Générale des Travailleurs Algériens; UGTA) and the National Union of Algerian Students (Union Nationale des Etudiants Algériens; UNEA), the former was brought under government control in 1968 and the latter was dissolved by the Interior Ministry in 1971. In effect the PAGS, like its predecessor the PCA, has been absorbed into the more militant FLN ranks. At home, the party has once more seemingly disappeared.

Simultaneously, FLN policies have coincided with PAGS goals. The government seizure in 1971 of over 51 percent interest in two French oil companies operating in Algeria and its nationalizing of the companies' interests in natural gas resources and oil and gas pipelines won PAGS support (*L'Humanité,* Paris, 26 March 1971). So have the government's agrarian and land reform policies. Youth contacts with socialist countries also have been encouraged. In March 1972 a youth delegation under the leadership of Cherif Belkacem, national secretary for orientation and information, attended the congress of Cuba's "Union of Young Communists" (UJC). On 17 May an agreement was reached between the UJC and Algeria's "National Liberation Youth Front" (JFLN) which promised "to strengthen the relations of sincere friendship, solid fraternity, and militant cooperation between [the] two revolutions" (FBIS, 17 May). Similarly, Algerian-Soviet agreements (October 1971 and February 1972) have increased training opportunities for Algerian students in Soviet technical and industrial enterprises (*El Moudjahid,* Algiers, 29 September). Hence by implementing aspects of the PAGS program as formerly expressed by front organizations such as·student and trade unions, the Algerian government has muffled the PAGS.

Consequently little is known about the present PAGS leadership or organization. In 1969 three party leaders—Bashir Hadj'Ali (former secretary of the PCA) and two leading left-wingers before Boumedienne's rise to power, Hocine Zahouane and Muhammad Harbi—were transferred from prison to house arrest; on 1 November 1970 these militants were given their freedom. Granted amnesty in 1970 but barred from the cities of Algiers, Oran, Constantine, and 'Annabah were Paul Caballero (former secretary of the PCA in Oran), Bouzid Bouallak, and Jacques Salort. The last two had been associated with the now defunct PCA daily *Alger Républican* (*Le Monde,* Paris, 6 March 1970). Since then, little is known of activities by the party leadership, which also included expatriate Larbi Boukhali (former PCA secretary-general who, as late as 1970, was the main PAGS spokesman).

International Views and Party Activities. Although the Algerian government is pro-Soviet in orientation, there was no Algerian delegation at the Twenty-fourth Congress of the Communist Party of the Soviet Union (March–April 1971). Neither were PAGS members present at the congress of the East German Socialist Union Party (June 1971), and there is no available indication of 1972 international activities by the PAGS, whose international stature therefore is seemingly diminished.

Governmental foreign policies apparently are largely responsible for the eclipse of the PAGS in international communist affairs. Public officials have consistently affirmed Algerian solidarity with "progressive socialist states," "our African continent," "our Arab brothers," and "the right and dignity of Palestinians to liberate themselves by fighting." They have reiterated the country's "duty to maintain . . . solidarity" with and support for "all those who are working to recover their independence and their sovereignty," along with "Algeria's obligations to the national liberation movements in the world" (e.g., FBIS, 6 July 1972). On the other hand, the FLN has consistently denounced "colonial despoilers," "Zionist plots," and "racial provocations," as well as "American terrorist attacks against the civilian population and the territory of the Democratic Republic of Vietnam," all of which statements resemble earlier PAGS declarations.

Moreover, the FLN has supported its revolutionary posture with tangible achievements. During 1972, "friendly accords" and "fraternal visits" were exchanged with no less than six socialist states, including the Soviet Union, Albania, and Cuba (ibid., 10 July; *Arab Report and Records,* 16–30 July). On the economic front, socialist states head the list of Algeria's trading partners (*Révolution Africaine,* Algiers 26 March). Since 1966, economic exchanges between Algeria and socialist countries have increased fourfold.

Because government policies have either suppressed or coincided with PAGS objectives, the party's stridency has ceased. In January 1972 *al-Sha'b* criticized the Cairo meeting of the Afro-Asian Peoples' Solidarity Organization on grounds that it was "a propaganda springboard and a testing ground for political maneuvers at the expense of the struggle of undeveloped peoples." The paper's editorial on U.S. President Nixon's February visit to the People's Republic of China, although cautiously optimistic, was likewise derogatory. The visits between Egyptian President Anwar al-Sadat and Libyan head of State Mu'ammar al-Qadhdhafi provided occasions for reaffirmations of Arab solidarity against "the combined enemy, Zionism and imperialism, which threatens the very existence of the Arab destiny" (21 February, 4 May). This compliance with FLN policies leaves the future of the PAGS in doubt.

University of Maryland   B. Marie Perinbam

Egypt

In 1920 an organization was founded which was later to become the Communist Party of Egypt (CPE). It never enjoyed legal status or developed into any formidable organization. Its failure can be attributed to: early domination by non-Arabs (Jews, Greeks, and others); its unpopular attitudes toward Palestine and Arab unity (it followed Soviet policy even when it conflicted with Arab aspirations); fractionalization; competition with more dynamic movements like the Moslem Brotherhood and Nasserism; and repression by the government.

In April 1965 the CPE decided to dissolve itself—reportedly with Soviet encouragement. It urged its estimated 800–1000 members to affiliate on an individual basis with the Arab Socialist Union (ASU), the mass political organization established by Gamal Abdel Nasser in 1962 as the only legal political group in the country.

The influence of individual Egyptian communists was hardly diminished when the CPE ceased to exist. In fact, the new conditions permitted some party members to become absorbed into the mainstream of Egyptian politics by becoming active in the ASU or holding influential positions in the government-controlled press. Some directed their activity into international communist front organizations, in particular the Egyptian branch of the World Peace Council (WPC) and the Cairo-based Afro-Asian Peoples' Solidarity Organization (AAPSO).

After 1965, the best known Egyptian communist was Khalid Muhyi al-Din (the "Red Major"), a Marxist politician of long standing, who has served as secretary-general of the Egyptian National Peace Council and as a member of the Presidential Committee of the WPC. In 1968 Muhyi al-Din became a member of the ASU Central Committee and in 1969 was elected to the National Assembly, the legislative body of Egypt. On 14 May 1971 a leftist organization of the ASU was dissolved by President Anwar al-Sadat for allegedly attempting to overthrow the existing government. Ali Sabri, known as Moscow's friend in Cairo, reportedly led the plot. He and many Egyptian leftists and ex-communists were immediately arrested. Khalid Muhyi al-Din was arrested in August, as was Dr. Ibrahim Sa'd al-Din.

On 27 May a fifteen-year Soviet-Egyptian treaty of friendship and cooperation was signed.

In 1972 some individual Marxists (they prefer that connotation rather than "communists") were politically active. Lutfi al-Khuli, a past CPE leader, was the official representative of the ASU at the Lebanese Communist Party congress held in Beirut early in January. On 16 January President Sadat appointed a new cabinet. It included two ministers known for their Marxist leanings, both of whom were leading members of the CPE before it was voluntarily dissolved. They are Dr. Fu'ad Mursi, responsible for supplies and internal trade, and Dr. Isma'l Sabri 'Abd Allah, minister of state for planning. While both men had previously held high-level governmental positions, this was the first time two Marxist ministers had joined an Egyptian cabinet. Many observers felt that this move reflected new developments in Soviet-Egyptian relations (Nahar Arab Report, Beirut, 24 January).

Another January development was the student riots. There was speculation as to whether these were spontaneous or were incited from outside. A Western reporter said on 26 January that a student had told him: "We have communists, nationalists, Muslim Brothers—everyone; but we are all Egyptians, and we are demonstrating for Egypt." Sayyid Mar'i, secretary of the ASU Central Committee, however, charged that Maoist and Moscow-oriented communists had penetrated the student movement. Soviet involvement seems highly unlikely, in that students have generally been strongly anti-Soviet; but student demands of 19 January were said to reflect Maoist influence. President Sadat, on the other hand, expressed his view that the students, particularly the Ain Shams University movement, was linked with the Ali Sabri group, which has been consistently pro-Soviet.

In February, members of the leftist secret organization within the ASU, the Arab Vanguard, were arrested, allegedly because of their aim "to overthrow the Arab regimes." This group's identity with the communist movement is unclear though the issue certainly indicates the government repression of such organizations, a fate which would likely befall the communists if they had an organized political structure.

In an interview (TASS, 21 June), Kamil Abu al-Majd, first secretary of the Central Committee of the Socialist Youth Organization of Egypt, stated that his organization "seeks to develop relations with the Leninist Young Communist League and strengthen solidarity between Egyptian and Soviet youth in the struggle against imperialism."

Relations between Egypt and the Soviet Union were tense from early in 1972. Numerous delegations were sent to Moscow, none of which seemed to achieve the desired results—Moscow wanted naval bases, a proposal Egypt rejected, while Egypt wanted offensive weapons of high quality, which the Soviets refused to give. The tension reached a climax on 18 July when President Sadat asked that the Soviet military personnel in Egypt (numbering nearly 20,000) leave the country. The Soviets left, hardly protesting the action. Egyptian-Soviet relations remained unstable despite mediation efforts from various sources, including Kamal Jumblatt, the Lebanese socialist leader. In October, Khalid Mohyi al-Din, the previous communist leader, traveled to Moscow as head of the Peace Partisans in Egypt in an unsuccessful effort to heal the breach between the two countries. Some observers expressed their view at the time that the Soviet Union would be willing to restore relations with Egypt only after securing political guarantees similar to those employed in Syria and Iraq, where it relies on the presence of communist and other "progressive" parties operating alongside the ruling party in a national front. Even if this is not so, it is likely that the Soviets are pressuring at least for the release of such pro-Soviet figures, communist and non-communist, as Ali Sabri and Mohammad Fawzi.

Beside military factors and the Egyptian government's detaining of pro-Soviet elements, another issue is certainly clouding relations. This is the Federation of Arab Republics (FAR). It is generally believed that the existing balance between the political right and left in Egypt will be tilted and that the legal left wing within the ASU will be restricted, if not eliminated, if the union is consumated. Libya's president Mu'ammar al-Qadhdhafi is known to be vehemently anti-communist. Syria is finding this to be a serious obstacle to its participation in the FAR. The federation members are supposed to ban all political parties and allow only the ASU, but Syria insists on maintaining its national front government in which the Syrian Communist Party is an active participant.

One further obstacle to Soviet-Egyptian relations was eliminated with the resignation of Egypt's war minister, deputy premier, and commander of the armed forces, Mohammad Ahmad Sadiq, on 27 October. This is thought to have been the biggest step toward reconciliation since the eviction of the Soviet military personnel in July. There has been speculation that closer relations with the Soviet Union may be conditional on the elimination of rightist elements in the country, like Sadiq, from positions of power. Premier Sidqi, who seems to have taken the place of Ali Sabri as Moscow's friend in Egypt, claims that the rightists are few in mumber but are the dominant power in Egypt.

Whether the resignation of Sadiq or other factors prompted the move, in November the Soviet Union agreed to restore the SAM-6 mobile missiles that were removed from Egypt in July.

At the end of the year, relations with the Soviet Union had not significantly improved. Delegations were still being sent to Moscow without result, and late in December it was noted that Sadat had refused for three weeks to grant an appointment to the Soviet ambassador.

The position of the Egyptian Marxists is still unclear. Despite the common affiliation of many with the CPE before it was dissolved, some are now under political arrest while others hold influential positions in government. The worsening of relations between Egypt and the Soviet Union is likely to weaken their position, as is ever-growing Egyptian frustration over the lack of serious Soviet commitment to Egypt's recovery of its Israeli-occupied territory. In addition, the increasing influence of the anti-communist Libyan leadership leaves the Marxists with ever less opportunity for significant influence of their country's affairs.

Edinboro State College   James D. L. Byrnes
and   and
Stanford, California   Patricia Nabti

Iran

Organized communist activity in Iran dates back to 1920, the year of the founding of the Communist Party of Iran. The present communist party, called the Party of the Masses of Iran (Hizb-e Tudeh Iran), or more popularly the Tudeh Party, was founded in October 1941, after an interval of ten years during which no organized communist party existed in the country. The Tudeh Party was banned by the government in 1949, following an assassination attempt on the Shah's life. Nevertheless, overt activities continued until the fall of Premier Mohammad Mosadiq in August 1953. In 1954 suppression of communist activities was ordered, and thousands of Tudeh Party members and collaborators were arrested. Some leaders escaped into exile in Eastern Europe, managed to regroup, and assumed direction of party affairs from headquarters in East Germany. A pro-Chinese faction split off from the pro-Soviet exiled party in 1965 and called itself the Revolutionary Organization of the Tudeh Party. Additional splintering has occurred since.

Illegal, suppressed, and with most of its members in exile, the Tudeh Party has negligible political significance in Iran. Estimates of its total membership have dropped to approximately 500. The population of Iran is 28,662,000 (estimated 1970).

Leadership and Organization. In 1971 Reza Radmanesh was relieved of his duties as chairman of the Tudeh Party. Investigations into the party's organization led the Central Committee to vote for various changes, including the promotion of Iradj Eskanderi to first secretary.

In 1972 the Tudeh Party did not publicize any names of party members or discuss internal party affairs openly (as it had with regard to the Fourteenth Plenum of its Central Committee in 1971). This ultra-secrecy was probably due to the severely repressive measures taken by the government this year against alleged communists. A number of names of persons arrested and accused of communist affiliation were printed in the Iranian press, but it has not been verified whether they were members of the Tudeh Party, of another Marxist group called Siakhal, or without any such affiliation. Despite repression in Iran, the Tudeh Party continued through the year to express opinions on domestic and foreign affairs through its "Iran Courier" radio broadcasts from East Germany.

Domestic Views and Activities. On 6 February a military tribunal in Teheran under the control of SAVAK (the government security organization) began the trial of 20 alleged members of an unnamed communist organization on charges of armed robbery, anti-state activities, and attempts at assassination. Reportedly a group of 23 had been tried on similar charges earlier, and in March another 11 persons were tried. The *Journal de Teheran* (3 February) noted that "according to the law, the fact of being a communist constitutes in itself, even if it leads to no action, a punishable offence." On 1 March press reports noted that 6 alleged communists had been executed and on 13 March, the *New York Times* reported the execution of an additional 9 "communist guerrillas." Although the political affiliation of those executed is uncertain, dissident sources abroad stated that the acts with which they were charged had been organized by two principal groups, one of which was the very small pro-Maoist, Marxist-Leninist group called Siakhal, a breakaway revolutionary organization of the Tudeh Party.

There is no evidence that any of those on trial were members of the Tudeh Party, but clearly the government's policy of repression has severely limited Tudeh activity within Iran and made activity from abroad the only practical means of influencing the Iranian people. In 1972 the Tudeh Party was seriously concerned with the "intensification of anti-communist activities" in Iran. Besides the trials, it noted anti-communist references to socialist countries in the mass media and the government's strong criticism of Iraq for including two communists in its government.

The Tudeh Party strongly criticized the government's agreement of 25 August with the oil consortium, in which the government "colluded with the consortium [by] renewing the period of plundering domination of this colonialist leech until the end of the century." The previous agreement was to expire in only seven years but the new agreement extends the existence of the consortium until 1994. (Radio "Iran Courier," 31 August). The Tudeh Party clearly felt that Iran had nothing to lose if it adopted an independent policy toward oil—it could find Iranian technicians and international markets, and could even expand production and refining to its own benefit.

The Tudeh Party condemned the government's militarization program. In response to a £100,000,000 purchase in August of arms from Britain it made the comparison that the cost of these arms "is the price of a steel mill similar to the one in Isfahan." The article noted that this is only about one-fifth of the total annually spent on arms and asked: "What fool believes that the purchase of $1,300 million worth of arms each year leads to economic growth and the welfare of society?" (Ibid., 7 September).

The party also criticized the government for not giving aid to the waves of Iranians expelled from Iraq in recent years due to severe tension between the two countries, and blamed the government for putting these refugees in the hands of SAVAK. In turn, it charged SAVAK with being a branch of the U.S. Central Intelligence Agency and a pawn used by the United States for infiltrating the government and all aspects of society in Iran (Ibid., 30 December, 1971).

International Views and Activities. The Tudeh Party in 1972 commented profusely on international issues and, in regard to countries with ruling communist parties, clearly indicated its pro-Soviet outlook. It gave the Soviet Union full credit for the agreement reached with the United States on limiting strategic weapons, which it called a "fatal blow to the imperialist policy of the Cold War period" (Radio "Iran Courier," 30 May). On 13 October the party hailed the signing of a fifteen-year treaty on economic and technical cooperation and a five-year agreement on cultural exchanges between Iran and the Soviet Union. Opposing the government's policy toward the German Democratic Republic (GDR), it expressed the view that the government's unwillingness to recognize the GDR was "diametrically opposed to Iran's national interests," particularly on the level of trade and economic development. (Ibid., 8 March.) The party declared its support for the improvement of relations between Iran and China in May, but vehemently attacked China in September for "anti-Sovietism" and pointed derisively to the similarity in views held by the "reactionary" government of Iran and the government of China in their support of the "reactionary" government of Pakistan in its war against the people of Bangladesh; their support of strongly anti-communist governments such as that of Sudan; and their increasing number of mutual friends, including the United States and members of CENTO (ibid., 21 September).

The party aired numerous commentaries on the United States. When President Nixon visited Teheran (30–31 May), its main criticism, as at other times, concerned the U.S. role in the Persian Gulf. It opposed any "presence of U.S. imperialism," particularly the U.S. military base in Bahrain. The Iranian government was seen as blessing this situation "with a silence smacking of satisfaction." (Ibid, 31 May.) The party charged that the new U.S. ambassador to Iran, Joseph Farland, was chosen for the post due to his past connections with the U.S. Federal Bureau of Investigation and experience in other countries where he helped to ensure U.S. influence and dominance through "conspiratorial methods and plots" (ibid., 22 May), and urged the ouster of U.S. military advisers, whose political and legal privileges amounted to "the revival of capitulation" (ibid., 26 October). The party repeatedly condemned the United States for its Vietnamese war policy. In regard to other non-communist states, Britain was criticized for continuing its "imperialism" in Iran and the Persian Gulf through strengthening Iran's military might, and Japan with penetrating the Iranian economy with Japanese monopoly capital, thus trying to exploit Iran through neocolonialism (ibid., 29 August).

On issues close to Iranian soil, the Tudeh Party criticized the Iranian government for supporting the "anti-democratic military regime" of Pakistan, and not recognizing Bangladesh, blaming this policy on ties with the United States and CENTO. A similar issue exists in the case of Baluchistan, which lies partly in Iran and partly in Pakistan. In this case, the party believes that Iran should remain unified but that the legitimate rights of the Baluchis (as well as the Azerbaijanis, Kurds, Turkmens, and Arabs within the country) should be recognized and their language, customs, and traditions be allowed to exist without repression (ibid., 9 June).

In regard to Iranian relations with Iraq, the party urged reconciliation. It expressed support for the "progressive liberation and anti-imperialist movements" in Iraq and that country's "struggle against imperialism and for social progress." However, it condemned the Iraqi government for deporting Iranians, many of whom were second- and third-generation residents of Iraq. The Iranian government was charged with intensifying the strained relations between the two countries through anti-Iraq propaganda even at the times Iraq made efforts toward reducing tensions. (Ibid., 8 January).

Publications. Tudeh publications are illegal in Iran and are printed in Eastern Europe. On 8 February 1971, the party Secretariat issued a special statement to the effect that all official announcements and documents would be published exclusively in the organ *Mardom* ("People") or the magazine *Donya* ("World") or broadcast by Radio "Iran Courier." It warned that "any document issued in the name of the Central Committee of the Iranian Tudeh Party, which is not referred to in the press or propaganda organs of the party, has no connection with the Iranian Tudeh Party." (Radio "Iran Courier," 18 February, 1971.)

Stanford, California   Patricia Nabti

Iraq

The Iraqi Communist Party (al-Hizb al-Shuyu'i al-'Iraqi; ICP) was founded in 1934. It was from the beginning primarily a students'. party, and suffered from the limitations of being weak, internally split, and poorly organized. In 1945 it held its First Congress and adopted a national charter. The ICP has never enjoyed legal status, although periods of severe repression by authorities have alternated with periods when communism was tolerated or even encouraged. During the rule of Lieutenant-General 'Abd al-Karim Qasim, in the early 1960s, communists were in the government and participated in the campaign for suppressing the Ba'thists. Thus when the Ba'thists overthrew Qasim in 1963 the communists were listed among the main enemies of the new government. Repressive measures against them began to ease late in 1969 when the government appointed Aziz Sharif, known to have close links with the communists, to the post of minister of justice. The party's political status improved further in 1970 when the Ba'thists began to talk about the establishment of a national front with the Kurdish Democratic Party (KDP) and the ICP. On 14 May 1972 the Ba'th government of President Ahmad Hasan al-Bakr appointed two communists to the cabinet—the first communist participation in the cabinet since the Qasim government (see below).

The ICP is believed to have about 2,000 members, though the number may have become larger recently due to the stronger ties of Iraq with the Soviet Union and the increasing legitimacy of the party. There are an additional 10,000 to 20,000 supporters or sympathizers, who are selective about the communist causes they espouse but over the years have backed enough of them to have made the ICP one of the more influential of the Arab communist parties. The population of Iraq is 9,400,000 (estimated 1970).

Leadership and Organization. The ICP leadership is composed largely of intellectuals from the professional classes (lawyers, teachers, and doctors). Many prominent members are of Kurdish origin. At its Second Congress, in September 1970, the party reelected 'Aziz Muhammad (also known as Nazim 'Ali), a Kurd, as first secretary. Muhammad has been first secretary of the party since 1964. His leadership is now identified with the aim of working toward a national front government with the Ba'th Party, to the point that success or failure in this respect is likely to determine his future status in the party.

The ICP is pro-Soviet. A dissident group of anti-Soviet communists exists in Iraq and is called the "Communist Party (Central Command)." This group is strongly opposed to the Ba'thist government and has participated in armed struggle against it, and believed to be the moving power behind the creation of the Iraqi National Grouping, comprised of leftist parties opposed to participation in a national front. There are believed to be no pro-Chinese factions within the communist movement in Iraq.

Domestic Views and Activities. When the Ba'th Party came to power in August 1968, it expressed its determination to form a government composed of all progressive political forces in the country, including the ICP. This cooperation was not achieved. The Ba'th charged that the ICP was making impossible demands for a "national front," while the communists accused the Ba'th of suppressive measures against them. As the economic stake of the Soviet Union in Iraq increased, Soviet pressure was put on the Ba'th and the ICP to improve their relations.

On 15 November 1971 President Ahmad Hasan al-Bakr announced the government's "Charter of National Action," appealing in principle for a national front to include all the "progressive forces" in the country. The ICP responded with a statement of basic support for the proposal. At the congress of the Lebanese Communist Party in January 1972, however, 'Aziz Muhammad pointed out that it was "necessary to set up constitutional establishments, prepare a permanent democratic constitution, and end the transition period within a specific time" (Middle East News Agency, Beirut, 9 January). In other statements the ICP insisted that the charter include guarantees eliminating persecution and granting equal freedom of political action for all parties included in the front.

In February, ICP Central Committee member Makram al-Talabani reaffirmed the party's support for the charter "because its concepts and contents oppose imperialism, call for national liberation struggle, and confirm a peaceful and democratic solution to the Kurdish issue." Also its potential importance as a model for unifying national forces elsewhere in the Arab world was noted. (Iraq News Agency, 23 February.) On March 31, a statement marking the 38th anniversary of the ICP stressed that "the Iraqi communists would make every effort with all the national forces and parties to build the national front" (ibid., 2 April.)

Soviet Premier Alexei Kosygin flew to Baghdad in early April to sign the Soviet-Iraqi treaty of friendship and cooperation (see below). He also met with 'Aziz Muhammad. After the meeting Muhammad declared that the ICP was dropping its reservations about the charter, encouraged by the close cooperation of the Ba'th with the Soviet Union.

On 14 May, President al-Bakr announced his appointment of a new cabinet representing all the major nationalist forces in the country, including the KDP and the ICP. Two members of the ICP Central Committee were given cabinet posts: Makram al-Talabani as minister of irrigation and Amir 'Abd Allah as minister of state without portfolio. Though these are not very important cabinet positions, they have significance as being the first held by communists since the overthrow of the Qasim government. Their value to the ICP is questionable: the party has won only minimal gain in prestige and influence in the government at the price of implying ICP support of the Ba'thist government, whatever its policy. Such a situation would become particularly difficult if the Kurdish problem were to flare up and the ICP had to choose between upholding its long-standing support for the Kurds or siding with the Ba'th to maintain its position in the government.

The formation of a coalition cabinet was a major step toward the goal of a national front. However, all participating parties still held to their conditions for its achievement—even the ICP despite its earlier announcement. The ICP, like the Kurds, linked its participation in such a front with demands for amendment of the constitution to give the cabinet a major part of the powers held by the all-Ba'th Revolutionary Command Council, in addition to the conditions in regard to the charter mentioned earlier.

By mid-November, the front had still not been achieved but the ICP continued its support of it in principle. In a statement on the 55th anniversary of the October Revolution the ICP added: "Our party is constantly striving and making efforts to achieve the cohesion of all the anti-imperialist forces of the Iraqi republic in a single progressive front" (*Pravda*, 10 November).

When negotiations between the government of Iraq and the oil companies operating in the country were breaking down in May, the ICP urged a firm stand against the companies, declaring that the party was "fully prepared to stand alongside the nationalist authority to adopt the strongest effective measures against the monopolist companies to safeguard Iraq's interests and to liberate its oil wealth" (Baghdad radio, 25 May). The largest company involved in these negotiations was the British-owned Iraq Petroleum Company (IPC), which had been operating in Iraq since the mid-1930's. A dispute had existed for several years between the government and IPC over revenues and royalties. On 1 June the government decided to end the dispute with its unilateral decision to nationalize the assets and operations of IPC. The communist party expressed strong approval of this decision as did other communist parties in the Arab world.

International Views and Contacts. In January the ICP sent a delegation, headed by Aziz Muhammad, to the Lebanese Communist Party congress in Beirut. The ICP was one of 24 parties which supported the Lebanese party's proposal for a "conference of the Arab progressive patriotic parties and forces to discuss the means to achieve complete solidarity and unity among them" (*Al-Nida'*, Beirut, 10 January).

The ICP expressed its views on the Arab-Israeli issue most clearly through its participation in the Palestinian National Congress, at Cairo in April. An announcement before the conference stated that the ICP would try to "unify the Palestine resistance and oppose the capitulationist plan of King Husain of Jordan." (Baghdad radio, domestic service, 5 April).

The Soviet-Iraq treaty of friendship and cooperation, signed on 9 April, was hailed by the ICP as enabling Iraq to "develop its economic, social, and defense programs for long periods, relying on honorable Soviet aid" (Iraqi news agency, 11 April). Relations between the ICP and the Communist Party of the Soviet Union (CPSU) were very active. In early April, ICP leaders met with a CPSU delegation led by Alexei Kosygin when he came to Baghdad to sign the Soviet-Iraqi treaty. In June CPSU delegation met with ICP leaders in Baghdad. In October an ICP delegation went to Moscow to confer with the CPSU. The main purpose of these meetings seems to have been to resolve difficulties between the ICP and the Ba'th Party in order to form a national front in Iraq. During the year, representatives of the ICP also met with leaders of other communist parties including those of Sudan, Jordan, Czechoslovakia, and Bulgaria.

Publications. In addition to its monthly organ, *Tariq al-Sha'b* ("The People's Road") and the magazine *al-Thaqafah al-Jadidah* ("New Culture"), the ICP Central Committee in June 1972 launched a new publication, *al-Fikr al-Jadid* ("New Thought"), labeled an "organ of the Iraqi Communist Party and of the progressive and nationalist forces and parties" (Iraqi news agency, 22 October). All three publications are distributed in Iraq. ICP information is also regularly disseminated through the publications of the Lebanese Communist Party: *al-Nida'* and *al-Akhbar.*

Stanford, California   Patricia Nabti

Israel

The first communist party in Palestine or anywhere in the Middle East, the Socialist Workers' Party (Mifleget Poalim Sozialistim) was established in 1919. It existed less than a year. Soon after, another group made a fresh attempt to establish a Palestine communist party, working within a left-wing Zionist party—Poale Zion (Workers of Zion)—to gain a legal front. After gaining strength, this group separated from Poale Zion and founded the illegal Palestine Communist Party in 1922. In 1948, after Israel became an independent state, the party changed its name to the Communist Party of Israel (Miflaga Komunistit Isr'elit, or MAKI).

Party policy on the Arabs in Israel and on Zionism has caused dissension within the party since its conception. Generally, the party had opposed Zionism. But in the early 1960's Moshe Sneh led a section of MAKI's Jewish membership in reassessing the Zionist issue, not only as a matter of principle but also in recognition that this was the only way to broaden the party's appeal to the Israeli masses. This move was resisted by MAKI's Arab membership and by an anti-Zionist minority of Jewish communists. A prolonged struggle resulted in a split in August 1965, with each of the two resulting parties claiming to be *the* Communist Party of Israel. The basically Jewish nationalist faction retained the organization and name of the parent party. The predominantly Arab group named itself the New Communist List (Reshima Komunistit Hadasha, or RAKAH) in reference to the separate slate of candidates this faction presented for the 1965 Knesset elections. In 1972 the Israeli courts, responding to the request of MAKI, issued an order banning RAKAH from officially using the name "The Communist Party of Israel"—an order which went unheeded by RAKAH.

Both Israeli communist parties are small. Each has an estimated membership of under 1,500. The population of Israel is 2,900,000 (estimated 1970). The two parties enjoy legal status, but play a marginal role in the politics of the country. In the national elections of October 1969 the MAKI received 15,712 votes (1.15 percent of the total cast) and kept its one seat in the 120-member Knesset; the RAKAH received 38,827 votes (2.84 percent of the total, but a full 30 percent of the Arab vote) and retained its three Knesset seats. RAKAH has also had some success in placing representatives on a number of municipal councils in recent years. In Nazareth it polled almost 40 percent of the vote in municipal elections held in 1970.

Leadership and Organization. (1) MAKI. The Sixteenth Convention of MAKI, late in 1968, elected Moshe Sneh as party chairman and Shmuel Mikunis as secretary-general. Subsequently a rift developed. Sneh's line of "independent, communist Zionism" faced opposition from Esther Vilenska, a MAKI leader (and representative to the Executive Committee of Histadrut, the Israeli labor federation), generally known as the party's most outspoken hard-line communist, and from Shmuel Mikunis, the secretary-general, both of them favoring a more conciliatory attitude toward the Arabs and the Soviet Union.

Late in 1971 a group of Sneh supporters who claimed to represent 70 to 80 percent of MAKI approached the Israeli left-wing labor party MAPAM, seeking to join that party, out of disagreement with the anti-Zionist policy of MAKI's secretary-general and his supporters *(al Hamishmar,* Tel Aviv, 11 February 1972). No decision was taken by MAPAM and the MAKI rift continued. On 1 March 1972 Moshe Sneh died. This loss put into question the viability of the party. A strong supporter of Sneh, Raul Teitelbaum, succeeded him as party chairman. To balance this, Mikunis was given MAKI's one seat in the Knesset (which Sneh had held), though under the advisership of two Sneh loyalists. During the party's Seventeenth Convention, 20–22 April, the Mikunis faction of 20 to 35 (depending on the issue), out of 163 voting delegates, voted against the theses that Sneh had written. On the final vote for the theses as a whole, however, only 21 abstentions indicated that any opposition existed to the Sneh line of MAKI. At the convention, the election of party leadership followed Sneh's policy, in that not even one token Arab member was placed in any of the top bodies and only a few representatives of the Mikunis-Vilenska opposition. Teitelbaum remained as party chairman of Mikunis as secretary-general. Yair Tsaban, editor of the party journal *Kol Ha'am,* was elected secretary of the Central Committee. The Politburo was elected as follows (new members *): Berl Balti, Eliyahu Drukmann, H. Hubermann *, Shmuel Litvak, Shmuel Mikunis (chairman), Y. Newberger *, Ya'akov Silber, Raul Teitelbaum, Pinhas Tubin, Esther Vilenska, and Yair Tsaban. The resolutions of the meeting indicated at least verbal concessions to the minority—in comparison with the resolutions of the 1968 convention, Zionism was less emphasized, annexationist policies were fully rejected, and criticism of the Soviets was muted. In this manner Sneh loyalists prevented an open split in the party and at the same time upheld their own policy-line in all its essentials. During the convention MAKI considered a closer relationship with MAPAM, and suggested a united front of the two parties due to the general similarity of policies.

(2) RAKAH. This party has a combined Jewish and Arab membership. Two-thirds of its electorate are Arabs, the remainder being Jews, and its leadership is also mixed. One of the main leaders of RAKAH is its Jewish secretary-general, Meir Vilner, who led the original split from MAKI in 1965. Other important leaders include two Arabs: Tawfiq Tubi, who heads the Secretariat, and Emile Habibi. Vilner and Tubi are RAKAH representatives to the Knesset. Habibi was the third until February 1972, when he resigned for ostensibly apolitical reasons. It has been considered by some, however, that his withdrawal was part of a crackdown on Arab nationalist elements within RAKAH. This new line is understood to have been dictated by Moscow in order to improve RAKAH's image among the Jewish population in Israel. Prominent members who apparently have been expelled from the party under this new policy include As'ad Makki, Muhammad Khas, and Mahmud Darwish. Habibi was replaced as RAKAH Knesset representative by Avraham Livernbaum (*Zo Ha'derekh,* 10 May). In turn, Central Committee member Benjamin Gonen has replaced Livernbaum as RAKAH representative to the Histadrut Executive Committee.

RAKAH held its Seventeenth Convention on 21–24 June. The main slogan was "Against Occupation of the Arab Territories, for Peace." Some 1,500 delegates and guests attended the convention, representing 67 local party organizations and 17 foreign communist and workers' parties. Tawfiq Tubi, in an address to the meeting, noted that since the 1969 convention party membership increased by 24 percent. Meir Vilner was reelected as secretary-general, and Tawfiq Tubi as head of the Secretariat. The Politburo was elected as follows (*new members): David (Uzi) Burstein, Gonen Benjamin,* Meir Vilner,* Emile Habibi, David Khenin, Tawfiq Tubi, Ruth Lubitz, Salim al-Qasim,* and Emile Tuma.

MAKI has an active youth auxiliary, the Young Communist League of Israel, known as BANKI.

Arab-Israeli Conflict. The Arab-Israeli conflict is the issue which has caused the greatest strain within the Israeli communist movement. On this issue the policies of MAKI and RAKAH are similar on some points. Both parties officially consider the U.N. Security Council Resolution 242 of November 1967 a proper basis for peace. Both demand full democratic rights, by law and in practice, for the Arab population in Israel. Both reject permanent settlement and annexation of the Arab territories occupied in 1967. Both condemn the government's acts of forced eviction and resettlement of Arabs under Israeli rule, and of confiscation of their property and collective punishment. Both made a special issue of policies in 1972 in regard to the Arab villages of Bar'am, Iqrit, and Rafah.

The points of difference between the two parties, however, are considerable. MAKI maintains Israel's right to national defence, including the right, when necessary, as in 1967, to wage "preventive war" (RAKAH was the only Knesset faction that condemned the 1967 action). Consistent with this view, the MAKI convention resolved that it "considers the Israel Defense Forces' operations against the terrorist hideouts an imperative defense action." This was presumably in reference to Israeli operations in Lebanon and Syria. (Jerusalem radio, domestic service, 22 April) RAKAH, on the other hand, is opposed to this policy. It condemned a U.S. agreement to sell Israel more Phantom jets which would sustain such action. (But both parties, in February and September, demanded Israeli withdrawal from Lebanon, considering Israel's presence there an act of aggression.) On the issue of Israeli withdrawal from occupied territory, RAKAH demands such withdrawal unconditionally, while MAKI believes that withdrawal should be implemented when a peace settlement guarantees Israel's borders.

In regard to the major anti-Israeli incidents in 1972—those of Lod airport and the Munich Olympics—both parties strongly condemned these acts, although RAKAH leader Meir Vilner noted at the time of the Lod incident that "Israeli authorities bore some responsibility because the oppression of the Palestinians drove them to extremism" (Jerusalem radio, domestic service, 21 June). It is, in fact, RAKAH's "solidarity" with the Palestinian resistance movement that MAKI attacks most strongly. MAKI views it as sheer terrorism while RAKAH considers it a legitimate resistance movement aimed at "liberation from the Israeli yoke of colonial occupation" (*Israel at Peace,* June).

MAKI, in fact, gives suggestions but expresses little condemnation of Israeli government policy in regard to the Middle East conflict. It places primary blame for the present deadlock on Arab governments. In March it "urged the government to delcare that it recognizes the right of self-determination for the Palestinian people" and "called on the government to declare its readiness to allow a democratic representation of the Palestinians to participate in peace negotiations" (Jerusalem radio, 18 March). In July it called on the government to launch a three-pronged political initiative with Egypt, with the Palestinians, and with the Soviet Union (*Israel at Peace,* August).

RAKAH, on the other hand, uses far stronger terms. It charges that "the Israeli Government systematically frustrates all the efforts aimed at achieving a just and peaceful settlement of the conflict." It also maintains that "American imperialism is using Israel's occupation to blackmail the anti-imperialist nationalist Arab movement." (RAKAH *Information Bulletin,* special convention issue.) RAKAH bluntly pointed, throughout the year, to the injustices done to Arab workers, the low prices given their crops, their low wages in relation to Jewish workers, and the confinement orders and restrictions they face. The RAKAH convention called for a united front of all who oppose the territorial occupation and support the U.N. Resolution 242 to mobilize pressure on the Israeli government to renounce annexation (ibid.).

Domestic Attitudes and Activities. On purely domestic issues, RAKAH and MAKI held quite similar views during 1972. The main domestic issue for both was Knesset debate and later passage of the "Law for the Settlement of Labor Disputes." According to both parties this legislation was against the workers, generally limiting the freedom to strike and prohibiting the workers in many specific sectors of production and the social services from going on strike at all. Both parties' representatives strongly denounced it in Knesset debate in March. And after passage, both hailed the workers of El Al Airlines for going on strike on 10 April in defiance of the law. RAKAH declared: "The live reality has proved now what the communist deputies told the Knesset during the debate on the law: The working people will break this law and will continue their just struggle by all means." (*Zo Ha'derekh,* 12 April.)

Another major issue for both parties was the rising cost of living in Israel. The RAKAH convention noted that "in 1969 prices rose 4 percent, in 1970 12 percent, and in 1971 20 to 25 percent. Food prices and apartment rents rose sharply." (*Information Bulletin,* special convention issue.) A resolution of the MAKI convention attempted to draw the attention of the wage earners to the growing danger of inflation and the increased cost of living. It called on the shop stewards and trade unions to demand the payment of a cost-of-living allowance whenever the index rose by 3 percent or more and to sign new work contracts for one year only (*Israel at Peace,* May). RAKAH seemed to emphasize another aspect of the problem—the proposal of a minimum wage, calling for the specific figure of 650 Israeli pounds.

Unlike MAKI, RAKAH expressed its interpretation of the causes of these social ills, explaining to workers that the drop in the standard of living and the offensive against social and trade unions rights were the result of the "policy of war and of seizing other peoples' territories being pursued by the Zionist ruling circles" (*Information Bulletin,* special convention issue).

One domestic issue seemed of specific concern only to RAKAH. Its convention passed a resolution condemning the authorities for using emergency legislation of the British colonial administration to restrict the freedom of movement of both Arab and Jewish communist party members. In particular it noted that Arab members of the party Central Committee, the editors of the party newspaper *al-Ittihad* (published in Arabic), Arab leaders of the Communist Youth League, members of municipal and local party councils, and many other party activists were prohibited by court orders from leaving the areas of their permanent residence without special police permission.

A MAKI resolution called on the government to "abolish the laws of religious coercion, to allow civil marriages, to allow all religions, all religious trends Jewish and non-Jewish to operate freely," adding: "Religion must be separated from the State" (*Israel at Peace,* May).

International Views and Activities. There were only two international issues which showed similarity of viewpoint between RAKAH and MAKI. Both parties summarily condemned the United States for its policy in Vietnam, and proclaimed their "solidarity with the heroic people of Vietnam" who were struggling to "achieve a full victory in this long bloody struggle against imperialism." Both also welcomed the summit meeting between Russian and American leaders in Moscow, though from different perspectives. RAKAH, in typical loyalty to Moscow, saw it as an indication of the growing strength of socialist and anti-imperialist forces, while MAKI saw it more neutrally as part of a trend toward détente.

Looking at each party separately, RAKAH organized an Israeli-Soviet Friendship Conference on 21–22 January 1972 to develop links between the Soviet and Israeli peoples. Meir Vilner, in his report to the RAKAH convention, applauded the treaties of the Soviet Union and Poland with West Germany as great contributions to the security and ease of tensions in Europe. In another speech to the convention, Tawfiq Tubi greeted the peoples of Iraq and Syria with special praise in connection with the nationalization of the Iraq Petroleum Company assets on the territories of these countries. While U.S. President Nixon's visit to Moscow was praised, his visit to Peking was greeted with suspicion—mainly of China's growing alignment with the West and its strong anti-Sovietism.

MAKI did not differentiate between President Nixon's Peking and Moscow visits, welcoming both as part of the trend toward détente and prevention of a new war between the major powers. It took a similar view of the arms limitation talks. MAKI, again unlike RAKAH, viewed the official visit by Golda Meir to Romania very positively. (RAKAH felt that it indicated tacit approval by Romania of Israel's annexationist policies.) Along this same line MAKI urged the Soviet Union, Yugoslavia, and the other communist countries to reestablish diplomatic relations with Israel, to reconsider their one-sided policy in the Middle East, and to play a constructive role in promoting agreement between the parties concerned (*Israel at Peace,* May). RAKAH also seemed to wish greater ties between these communist states and Israel, but felt the responsibility rested with Israel first to denounce its present policies of annexation and "imperialist" alignment.

International Communist Movement and Party Contacts. The Soviet Union continues to recognize RAKAH as the official Communist Party of Israel, ostensibly because its membership of Jews and Arabs is more representative. This policy was confirmed by the high-ranking delegation of the Communist Party of the Soviet Union (CPSU) at the RAKAH convention and the absence of any representation at the MAKI meeting. In line with this, most of the international communist movement recognizes only RAKAH—17 foreign communist and workers' parties came to its convention and many others sent greetings. Of special interest, delegations or greetings came from the Arab communist parties of Iraq, Algeria, Jordan, and Sudan. The latter two received strong praise from the convention for their perseverance despite terrible oppression. During its convention and throughout the year RAKAH praised the Soviet Union often and supplied ideological justification for all Soviet government and party action, even if such action was clearly a matter of self-interest rather than ideology. At the same time it strongly criticized the Chinese Communist Party, which it charged with trying to undermine the international communist movement and fan up anti-Sovietism. During the year delegations of RAKAH met with their counterparts in Bulgaria, East Germany, and the Soviet Union, among others.

MAKI plays the role of an outcast in the international communist movement. It maintains contacts with communist countries that have an independent outlook on foreign affairs, in particular Romania and Yugoslavia, and with dissenting communist parties, such as the Swedish, Spanish, and Greek parties. In its position as an outcast, MAKI freely expresses its views of the communist world, criticizing Soviet and, more rarely, Chinese policy when it sees fit. The CPSU approached MAKI during the year to improve relations with it. Suspicions were expressed, however, that in reality the Soviets were trying to cause dissension in MAKI, in that their choice of a contact was Esther Vilenska, thereby implying support for her opposition views rather than those of the Sneh-led majority which she opposes.

MAKI bitterness over Soviet support of RAKAH was expressed in a message to "Guests of the RAKAH congress." It said: "When you, representatives of important Communist parties in Eastern and Western Europe, come to glorify, to praise, to worship RAKAH because of its struggle and its policy, you are only strengthening the justified suspicions against all peace programs that are connected in any form whatsoever with the policies of the Arab-Soviet world" (*Israel at Peace,* June).

Publications. The MAKI central organ *Kol Ha'am* ("Voice of the People") is published biweekly. The party's *Information Bulletin* changed its name after the first issue in 1972 to *Israel at Peace.* It has monthly English and French and occasional Spanish and Italian editions. There are also occasional MAKI publications in other languages.

RAKAH publications include the Hebrew weekly *Zo Ha'derekh* ("This Is the Way"), the Yiddish *Der Veg* ("The Way"), the Arabic *al-Ittihad* ("Unity"), the theoretical journals *Arakhim* ("Values") and *al-Darb* ("The Way"), in Hebrew and Arabic respectively; and the party's monthly *Information Bulletin.* In addition, its Young Communist League publishes *al-Ra'id* in Arabic and *Inyan* in Hebrew.

Stanford, California   Patricia Nabti

Jordan

The founding year of the Communist Party of Jordan (al-Hizb al-Shuyu'i al Urdunni; CPJ) is commonly given by non-communist sources as 1951. Communist activity in Jordanian territory on the west bank of the Jordan River, however, can be traced back to 1943 through communist party activities in Palestine. Thus, in November 1968 the CPJ received congratulatory messages on its twenty-fifth anniversary. The discrepancy is due to the fact that the territory of Jordan was limited to the east bank of the river when the country emerged as an independent entity; land on the west bank was acquired only after Israel became a nation in 1948. It was not until 1951 that a communist party for the whole of Jordan was established.

The CPJ and all other political parties in Jordan were outlawed by royal decree in 1957, after an abortive attempt was made to topple the constitutional monarchy. The CPJ has been illegal ever since, although the normally severe repressive measures have occasionally been relaxed. Under a political amnesty granted at the outbreak of war with Israel in 1967, communists were released from Jordanian jails and a period of tacit tolerance of communist activity began. The change was also due both to communist efforts to gain greater respectability and avoid provoking the government, and to the fact that the political significance of the CPJ was so slight as to cause no worry to the authorities. Repressive measures were resumed in earnest in 1972. Party members are believed to number fewer than 1,000 and sympathizers around 5,000. The population of Jordan is 2,418,000 (government figures, 1971).

Leadership and Party Affairs. No more than minimal information is available about the hierarchy of the CPJ. The names of most of the leaders and Central Committee members are unknown. This is due to the suppressive acts of the government against socialist and other "progressive" elements in Jordan. Some names can be cited, however, such as Fu'ad Nassar, a Palestinian who has been first secretary of the CPJ since its inception. 'Isa Madanat and Taisir Barghuti are known to be leaders loyal to Nassar. An opposition group within the party is led by Iayik Warrand and Dr. Ya'qub Zayadin, who advocate giving priority to national issues. Fahmi Salfiti and Rushdi Shahin were two other prominent members but were expelled in 1971 by the Central Committee for their "insistence on following the disgraceful road of secession and sabotage" (*al-Akhbar,* Beirut, 16 May). They formed their own group, the Leninist Cadres.

In 1972 the government ordered a series of arrests and harassments of CPJ members. The communist leader 'Isa Madanat, who is also a member of the World Peace Council, was arrested, as was Fayiz al-Bajjali, a member of the CPJ Central Committee (ibid., 20 May). On July 28 Dr. Ya'qub Zayadin was arrested (ibid., 5 August).

A CPJ delegation participated in the Third Congress of the Lebanese Communist Party (LCP), held at Beirut on 7–10 January. The names of the spokesman and others in the delegation were not released. Fu'ad Nassar was not at the congress because the Lebanese government refused him entry into the country.

Domestic Attitudes and Activities. The CPJ spokesman at the LCP congress declared that the Jordanian government aimed at liquidating the Palestinian Resistance Movement and all other progressive and nationalist elements, and intimated that "U.S. imperialism and its agents" were assisting. But "the disunity of the Palestinian resistance and the absence of a national progressive front," in his opinion, "made it easy for American imperialism to succeed in its efforts." (al-Nida', 10 January).

As in previous years, the CPJ in 1972 put heavy emphasis on forming in Jordan what Fu'ad Nassar had termed in 1971 "a broad national patriotic front of the working class, the peasantry and the national bourgeoisie, primarily the small and middle sections." (New Times, Moscow, 14 April). Such a front would be intended as the nucleus for a new government.

During the first week of April the Central Committee of the CPJ distributed a secret leaflet rejecting King Husain's plan for the establishment of a united state on the both banks of the Jordan River. The leaflet criticized the timing and content of the plan and the manner in which it was declared, charging that it did not contribute to the "struggle against Zionism and imperialism" but rather "added new difficulties and negative factors to the deteriorating situation in Jordan and the entire Arab situation." The leaflet also discussed the general situation in Jordan, noting restrictions on democratic freedoms, economic ruin, and intensified isolation of Jordan from the Arab countries and the world at large. It showed particular concern over "increasing signs of capitulation and abandonment of any kind of resistance of aggression and occupation." (Iraqi news agency, Amman, 5 April).

In regard to the Israeli-held territory of Jordan (the west bank) the CPJ continued to condemn the occupation itself and Israeli plans for changing the features of the occupied territories. The party stated that any plan for a Palestinian entity on the west bank of the river was a conspiracy against the rights of the Palestinian people (al-Akhbar, 15 January).

International Views and Activities. The spokesman of the CPJ at the LCP congress in Beirut called for unity among the communist parties in the Arab countries and expressed his party's full agreement with the report of the LCP Central Committee, particularly the idea that the present main task of the Arab peoples was to confront the "imperialist-Zionist onslaught," compel Israel to retreat and eliminate the consequences of its aggression, preserve and strengthen national and progressive regimes and the Arab liberation movement, and "retrieve the legitimate rights of the Palestinian Arab people" (al-Nida', Beirut, 10 June 1972). The CPJ was one of the organizations which signed the proposal for a conference of Arab progressive and patriotic parties and forces, initiated by the LCP at the congress.

The CPJ participated in mediation efforts to heal the efforts of Fu'ad Nassar. In June, the CPJ acclaimed Iraq's action in nationalizing the Iraq Petroleum Company. The CPJ noted that despite the company's economic pressure on the Iraqi government, Iraq was able to achieve considerable successes: the fighting stopped in northern Iraq, a national alliance of progressive forces was created, and an Iraqi-Soviet treaty of friendship and cooperation was signed. (Iraqi news agency, Amman, 10 June).

The CPJ spokesman at the LCP congress stated that the main reason for Arab capability in halting the "advance of the Israeli aggressors and the imperialist-Zionist onslaught" was the will of the Arab peoples, their joint struggle, and the "huge aid—political, economic, military, and technical—rendered and still being rendered by the USSR and the other socialist countries" (al-Nida', 10 January).

Publications. The CPJ publishes a monthly organ, *al-Jamahir* ("The Masses"), previously called *al-Tuqaddum* ("Progress"). In the west bank area, the newspaper *al-Watan* ("The Homeland") is published secretly. The CPJ also publicizes its news and activities through the LCP organs *al-Akhbar* and *al-Nida'*.

Stanford, California   Patricia Nabti

Lebanon

The Lebanese Communist Party (al-Hizb al-Shuyu 'i al-Lubnani; LCP) was established in 1924 as the Lebanese People's Party. It was reconstituted as the LCP in 1930. During the period of the French mandate it accepted members from both Lebanon and Syria. Khalid Bakdash (see Syria) was elected secretary-general of the party in 1932. What is generally considered the first congress of the party was held under his leadership in January 1944, after Syria and Lebanon gained national independence. It was decided at this congress to establish separate Lebanese and Syrian communist parties, to be organized respectively by Faraj Allah al-Halu and Bakdash. Some Lebanese communists consider that the real independence of their party was not obtained until 1964, since until then it continued to be under the indirect control of Bakdash. In 1965 the party decided to break from its policy of working independently of other Lebanese political groups and chose to cooperate with a front under the leadership of the Progressive Socialists, a party headed by Kamal Jumblat, who was then a member of the Lebanese parliament.

The LCP was banned until 13 August 1970, when it was granted recognition along with other controversial parties by Jumblat, who was then interior minister. His authority to make that decision has been challenged but the party has continued to function openly and without legal restriction. The LCP has thus become the only legal communist party in the Arab world. It is estimated to have 2,500 members. The population of Lebanon is 2,800,000 (estimated 1970).

Leadership and Organization. The 1970 request of the LCP for legalization was signed by Niqula al-Shawi, Artin Madoyan, Yusuf Khattar al-Halu, and Mustafa al-'Aris. It stated that the party's headquarters was in Beirut and that its purpose was "To destroy the capitalist system and the dictatorship of the Bourgeoisie, and to build a socialist society in which the exploitation of man by man will be abolished." (*Arab World Weekly,* Beirut, 15 January 1972).

The Third Congress of the LCP was held 7–10 January 1972. The main purposes of the congress seemed to be to reaffirm the new legal status of the party, to demonstrate its character as a party vitally interested in Lebanese national affairs, and to show the strength of pro-Soviet forces in the Middle East. Some Lebanese leftists termed the congress a bourgeois demonstration with its ostentatious $30,000 budget, its worldwide invitations, and even a cocktail reception at its close. Others felt its openness might make the party vulnerable if it should again become deprived of its legal position. Despite seemingly perennial fragmentation and dissension within the party in the past, in 1972 the party seemed to be unified in its efforts to achieve the apparent goals of the congress.

The leadership of the LCP remained basically unchanged after elections at the final session of the congress. A 24-man Central Committee was elected, which in turn reelected Niqula al-Shawi as secretary-general and chose an 11-man Politburo: Georges Hawi (considered second in authority), Yusuf Khattar al-Halu, Khalil al-Dibs, Rafiq Samhun, Niqula al-Shawi, Nadim 'Abd al-Samad, Ra'if Fayyad, Artin Madoyan, Karim Muruwwah, Faruq Ma'sarani, and Ahmad al-Mir. From the reports they delivered at the congress, the general responsibilities of individual leaders would seem to be as follows: Georges Hawi, the Lebanese political scene; Yusuf Khattar al-Halu, the agrarian reform program; George Hibri, the labor movement; Khalil Na'was, information and publicity; and George Batal, international affairs; while responsibility for organization in various regions was held by Adnan Daghidi (for the Biqa' district), 'Ali al-'Abd (South Lebanon), Mahmud al-Wawi (North Lebanon), Rafiq Samhun (Beirut), and Maurice Nuhra (Mount Lebanon). Plans were announced for holding a congress every four years.

Domestic Views and Activities. The main domestic activity of the LCP in 1972 concerned the parliamentary elections, held in March and April. The party congress, in January, decided to work within the Lebanese political system and to participate in the elections and to form alliances with other left-wing parties in order to defeat the right-wing Phalangist and Liberal parties. The LCP joined in a front headed by Jumblat's Progressive Socialist Party and including also the Nasserites and the Syrian- and Iraqi-oriented factions of the Ba'th (Arab Socialist) Party.

In the 1968 parliamentary elections, the application of LCP party leader, Niqula al-Shawi, to run for the Greek Orthodox seat in Tripoli was rejected on the basis that he belonged to an outlawed party. In March 1972 he sought nomination for the same seat. The Phalangist Party challenged this second application on the basis that the LCP was still illegal. It charged that the interior minister had no authority to make the 1970 decision to legalize the LCP. The government responded by seeking legal opinion on Shawi's nomination and finally decided on its own to accept his nomination. Official reasoning held that the leftists were very weak and would expose that weakness if given the freedom to run in the elections. Their suppression would only inflate the issue and turn them into martyrs. (*An-Nahar Arab Report,* Beirut, 24 April.)

This was not the only obstacle to communist participation in the elections. A "Parties and Societies Bill" was submitted to parliament which would give the government power to authorize or ban the activities of Lebanese parties associated with foreign parties or governments. The Phalangists and other conservative groups pressed to have the bill passed before the elections, while the parties of the leftist front united in action against the bill. No decision was taken before the elections, however, and it was noted that passage of the bill would depend largely on the strength of the leftist presence in the new parliament. "Defense of democratic freedoms" thus became a major issue in the campaign. When the elections were over, the new parliament was still dominated by conservatives, but the leftists had made their most significant gains since independence. How much this gain could be attributed to participation by the LCP is not clear, since no communist candidate was elected.

On the more theoretical level, the report adopted by the LCP congress included an evaluation of the Lebanese internal situation. It attacked the "Lebanese financial clique" as being in collusion with "imperialists" and Arab reaction in a united effort to obstruct the popular and labor movement. The party urged the removal of this clique from power and its replacement by an alliance of workers, peasants, intelligentsia, and locally-based bourgeoisie. It called for the nationalization of foreign companies, the stiffening of government control over the public sector, the restriction of foreign trade, the strengthening of the industrial sector and the implementation of agrarian reform. (*al-Nida',* 11 January.)

The ICP and the Arab World. The position of the LCP regarding the general Arab situation apparently has not changed since its Second Congress, in 1968. The Central Committee report to the 1972 congress stated that "the correct way to guarantee the development of the Arab national liberation movement, to repel the imperialist-Zionist-reactionary attack, and to remove the effects of the 1967 Israeli aggression" was comprised of three main factors: a strong position against imperialism, especially "U.S. imperialism"; cooperation and friendship with the socialist camp, headed by the Soviet Union; and broader and stronger cooperation and coordination among the Arab progressive forces (*al-Nida'*, 11 January).

The congress expressed its support of the Palestinian resistance movement as part of the liberation movement of the Palestinian people and the Arab people in general as well as part of what it called "the world movement for liberation, progress, and socialism." The LCP noted its own participation in the resistance through the "al-Ansar" forces, established through the united efforts of the Lebanese, Syrian, Jordanian, and Iraqi communist parties (see *YICA 1971*, pp. 298–99). At the same time, the party explained that it approved the U.N. Security Council's Resolution 242 and efforts at peaceful solution of the crisis as being in the interest of the Arab liberation movement under current conditions. It is interesting to note that this statement in regard to the U.N. resolution was not included in the LCP's restatement of policy at the time of student uprisings in Egypt at the end of January.

The LCP congress gave major emphasis to a proposal for a conference of Arab "progressive and patriotic parties and forces." Such a conference had previously been suggested by the Socialist Progressive Party as a forum to discuss the means to achieve complete solidarity and unity. Twenty-four parties and organizations from Arab countries which were participating in the congress supported the proposal. They entrusted representatives of the participating Lebanese parties and the Palestinian resistance movement with preparation of the conference, whose stated goal was to coordinate the struggle against the "imperialist-Zionist-reactionary attack."

The LCP commented on a number of events in the Arab world. The congress welcomed the Confederation of Arab Republics between Syria, Libya, and Egypt. It noted, however, its reservations as to the strongly anti-communist regime in Libya. Similar reserved support was expressed in August when Libya and Egypt announced their plan for comprehensive unity of the two countries.

At the end of January a major student crisis arose in Egypt. The Egyptian government accused the LCP of playing an important role in the crisis. Although evidence of this role was not forthcoming, the LCP did publish the first communist comment on the uprising. It supported the students as expressing legitimate concern over the gap between reality and the Egyptian pronouncement of a "year of decision." It also criticized the force used against the students by what it termed reactionary elements in the government. (*al-Nida'*, 29 January.)

In June the LCP announced its support of the Iraqi government's nationalization of the Iraq Petroleum Company.

In July, the Egyptian government ordered the removal of Soviet military advisers from the country. The LCP accused Egypt's military commander in chief General Muhammad Ahmad Sadiq of hostility toward the Soviet Union, charging that he had demanded the ouster of the Russians under the threat that otherwise "the army would impose the measure by direct interference in the country's political affairs" (ibid., 20 July).

The LCP took part in the Palestinian People's Congress in Cairo on 6–10 April, and in the meetings held in Beirut on 7–11 May to prepare for the proposed conference of Arab "progressive and patriotic" forces.

Other International Views and Contacts. The most important event of 1972 providing the LCP with international contacts was the party congress. A large number of parties and organizations, both Arab and non-Arab, communist and non-communist, were invited and either sent greetings or delegations to the congress. The LCP indirectly expressed a major position of the party by the conspicuous omission of invitations to either China or Albania. During the congress, the party strongly attacked the Chinese communists for deviating from the world communist movement, reaching settlements and understandings with the United States, taking a stand against the people of Bangladesh, supporting the massacres in Sudan, and carrying on a campaign of anti-Sovietism. Reportedly the LCP considered inviting an Israeli communist party delegation but the Central Committee decided to table the idea.

The congress strongly condemned the U.S. bombings of Vietnam and reaffirmed solidarity with the "patriots of Vietnam, Laos, and Cambodia" in their struggle against U.S. "imperialist aggression."

The proceedings of the congress clearly indicated the strongly pro-Soviet position of the LCP. In an interview with *L'Orient-Le Jour* (Beirut, 1–7 January, supplement), Niqula Al-Shawi maintained that Arab communists could not and should not expect Soviet support against anti-communist governments. He explained this on the basis that the Soviet Union might determine that aid to such governments would weaken imperialism and thus be justified.

In February the U.S. ambassador to Lebanon conveyed a message from his government reaffirming its commitment to the viability and security of Lebanon. The LCP saw this as an effort both to counterbalance French influence in the country (the prime minister was just then departing for France) and to interfere in the Lebanese parliamentary elections. Thus, it viewed the U.S. move as supporting the interests of Israel and of reactionary forces in Lebanon, and not the interests of the people of Lebanon. (*al-Nida'*, 4 February.)

In June, an LCP delegation in Moscow hailed the results of the recent U.S.-Soviet talks as an important achievement of the Communist Party of the Soviet Union in deterring imperialism. This was in direct contrast with the LCP position on similar talks held earlier between the United States and China.

During the year the LCP sent delegations to various communist countries. Besides the Soviet Union, these included East Germany, Romania, and Poland. Only the joint communiqué with Romania failed to include strong verbal denunciation of "Israeli imperialism" or "aggression against Lebanon and Syria." This is easily explained by Romania's independent policy of relatively friendly relations with the government of Israel.

Publications. The principal publications of the LCP are the daily *al-Nida'* ("The Call") and the weekly *al-Akhbar* ("The News"). Both have been distributed openly for a number of years, even before the party gained legal status. They serve also as general information media for the illegal communist parties of the Middle East.

Stanford, California   Patricia Nabti

Lesotho

The Communist Party of Lesotho (CPL) was founded in 1961, as a result of close cooperation with South African communists. Banned in February 1970, the party has sought to work in a clandestine fashion since then. Its membership remains insignificant, although the government in 1972 released many party supporters from jail.

Leadership and Organization. The CPL has not published any list of office holders, but according to a Soviet source, J. M. Kena is secretary-general (*Political Parties of Africa: A Soviet Study*. Arlington, Va.: Joint Publications Research Service, 1971, p. 191).

Party Internal Affairs; Domestic Attitudes and Activities. CPL policy was laid down in a draft program, "The Lesotho Road to National Democracy," at the 1969 party congress. The goal is a national-democratic revolution, as a steppingstone on the road to socialism. The CPL condemns what it regards as the "imperialist machinations" of the United States and its "allies," including Great Britain, West Germany, Israel, and the Republic of South Africa, the latter being regarded as a fascist state. The party is strongly pro-Soviet and, more than any other African communist movement, has gone out of its way to stress "love for the Socialist Motherland—the Soviet Union" (Tenth Anniversary Statement of the Central Committee of the Communist Party of Lesotho, in *African Communist,* London, no. 50, pp. 18–22).

International Views and Positions. The CPL claims that the Chinese Communists have interfered in the affairs of Lesotho and have done "much harm to the progressive cause," while on the international plane Chinese "ultra-revolutionary slogans have led inevitably to rapprochement with the United States imperialists" (*Ibid.,* p. 21). The party considers its struggle to be part of a wider liberation campaign in Southern Africa. It maintains close links with the South African Communist Party to which it has been connected by ties of history and policy.

Hoover Institution   Lewis H. Gann
Stanford University

Morocco

The Moroccan Communist Party (Parti Communiste Marocain; PCM) was founded in 1943 as part of the French Communist Party. In 1959 it was suspended by the government, and in 1960 was banned for its incompatibility with Islam. Although several appeals to lift the ban were denied, the party continued to operate more or less openly. In 1968, *PCM* secretary-general 'Ali Yata announced the formation of a new party, the Party of Liberation and Socialism (Parti de la Libération et du Socialism; PLS), and declared himself head. By presenting itself as a "national" political organization "strongly attached to the revolutionary traditions of the Moroccan people, the inheritance of Arab thought, and the liberal content of Islam," the PLS was able to register as a legal party. By 1969, however, Moroccan authorities were alerted to the similarities between the PLS and the PCM, and in August of that year 'Ali Yata was arrested. A month later, he was tried and sentenced to ten months' imprisonment for reviving an illegal political party under a new name. Consequently the PLS and its newspaper, *al-Kifah al-Watani,* were banned.

Government restrictive policies represented a setback for 'Ali Yata, who had long urged the formation of a united-front party consisting of all opposition groups. He was further disappointed when, in July 1970, the National Union of Popular Forces (Union Nationale des Forces Populaires; UNFP) and the Istiqlal party announced the formation of the United National Party (Front d'Unité Nationale; FUN), which excluded the PLS. This combination of opposition groups apparently produced few advantages, and opposition parties are still subject of government attacks.

Little is known about PLS membership, which is believed to number not more than 400. The population of Morocco is estimated at 16,000,000.

As a banned party, the PLS has had little impact on Moroccan affairs, although according to 'Ali Yata the attempted coup against the crown on 10 July 1971 has unleashed dissatisfactions and created a more favorable climate for PLS activities. Addressing himself to "workers, peasants, students, and youth in general," he assured his readers that "there can be no doubt" that government restrictions "have not only failed to stop the movement, but on the contrary [have] stimulated it still more" (*IB,* vol. X, 1972, pp. 71–72).

Groups from which 'Ali Yata still hopes to attract adherents include the major opposition parties such as the Istiqlal party, the UNFP, the General Union of Moroccan Students (Union Nationale des Etudiants Marocains; UNEM), the two main trade unions—the Moroccan Labor Union (Union Marocain du Travail; UMT) and the General Union of Moroccan Workers (Union Générale des Travailleurs Marocaines; UGTM), the Democratic Constitutional Party (Parti Démocratique Constitutionnel; PDC), the Popular Democratic Movement (Mouvement Populaire Démocratique; MPD), and even the Popular Movement (Mouvement Populaire; MP), which is the weakest of the opposition parties. Thus far his efforts have yielded few results. While the UNFP has offered limited support, the strongly nationalistic Istiqlal party has openly criticized the PLS.

Leadership and Party Affairs. The leadership of the PLS includes well-known communists such as 'Ali Yata, PCM secretary-general from 1945 to 1968, when he assumed leadership of the PLS; Abdessalam Bourkia, former PCM secretary; Ahmad al-Marrakishi, a chief spokesman of the PLS; Abdallah Hocine Layachi, Abdelaziz Belal, Simon Levy, and Hadi Messaoud. Another leader is Muhammad Chouaib Rifi, a co-signer of the PLS constitution along with 'Ali Yata. He was arrested with 'Ali Yata in 1969 and like him was sentenced to prison. They were both released in 1970.

Despite government restrictive policies, the illegal activities of the PLS have continued. On 6 January 1972 Abdessalam Bourkia was arrested at Casablanca airport as he was leaving for Beirut. He was charged with "reconstituting a banned party and distributing tracts which threated public order," and was sentenced to eight months' imprisonment. On 27 January the editors of the pro-Peking magazine *Souffles,* Abraham Serfaty and Abd-al-Latif Laabi, the latter a lycée teacher, were arrested without explanation, although it was understood that they had been associated with student unrest in universities and schools (*Arab Report and Record, ARR,* 16–31 January).

Domestic Attitudes and Activities. Between January and April 1972, student strikes were endemic in Morocco. The government attributed them to "outside influences." In defense of student actions, 'Ali Yata charged that far from being manipulated by outside influences, student demands legitimately stemmed from "political incompetence" and the "improvisation and degradation of education in the country," and called for an overhauling and the "Moroccanization and Arabization" of the still largely French educational system ("Veritables Causes des Grèves des Etudiants et des Lycèes," broadsheet published in Casablanca, 21 January). He also questioned the "democratic value" of the new constitution which restricted freedom of speech and association (such as the ban on the PLS and its newspapers, *al-Kifah al-Watani* and *al-Bayan*), and called on the Moroccan people to boycott the elections ("Premières Observations sur le Referendum Constitutionnel," Casablanca, 18 February; "Boycotter le Referendum C'est Contribuer à l'Election d'une Assembleé Nationale Constituente Souveraine," broadsheet published in Casablanca, 21 February). Launching similar attacks against the arrest and trial of thirty-three "compatriots including peasants, some unemployed, intellectuals, engineers, professors, pupils from the lycées, and university students," 'Ali Yata claimed that their only "crime" was that their "political opinions differed from those of the government, and that they attempted to express them" ("Les Trente-trois Inculpés de Marrakech Doivent être Acquittés," broadsheet published in Casablanca, 21 March).

On the labor front, 'Ali Yata congratulated the congress of the Moroccan Labor Union for participating in the struggle against the government, despite the latter's pressures. He also encouraged union members to continue "the politicization of the workers" and their solidarity with "the Palestinian and North Vietnamese anti-imperialists." He exhorted the world's proletarians to unite for their own and the peasants' protection against the common enemies, imperialism and feudalism, and that they ought to culminate the "national democratic revolution by marching arm in arm toward socialism." ("Le Ve Congrès de l'Union Morocaine du Travail," broadsheet published in Casablanca, 16 March.) 'Ali Yata deplored the banning of the PLS—"despite the fact that it is the party of the working classes, the poor peasants, and revolutionary intellectuals, and even although it is animated by an ardent and incontestable patriotism, and very close to Moroccan national realities" ("L'Union, Unique Voie de Salut," broadsheet published in Casablanca, 31 August).

International Views and Positions. Understandably the PLS has not been very active on the international scene. In December 1971 a Moroccan delegation attended the Sixth Congress of the Polish United Workers' Party, at which their spokesman, outlining PLS international policies, reaffirmed the party's pro-Moscow commitment. U.S. policy in Southeast Asia has often been criticized by PLS spokesmen, and in May 1972 'Ali Yata denounced President Nixon's decision to bomb North Vietnam and to mine the harbors. By way of contrast, in July, he congratulated Premier Kim Il-song of the Democratic People's Republic of Korea for concluding an accord with the government of South Korea and praised him for bringing a stabilizing element to the unsettled affairs of Southeast Asia.

Publications. Until the party was banned in September 1969, the PLS published a weekly, *al-Kifah al-Watani* ("The Patriotic Struggle"). Efforts to revive the paper in 1972 met with failure.

University of Maryland   B. Marie Perinbam

Nigeria

The Nigerian communist party, known as the Socialist Workers' and Farmers' Party (SWAFP), was founded in 1963. The Party is illegal but continues to operate through a number of subsidiary organizations, including the Nigerian Trade Union Congress (NTUC), which is one of several labor unions, the Youth Thinkers' Club, and various "Friendship" societies that seek to promote good relations with individual communist-ruled countries. Its influence remains negligible.

Organization and Leadership. The SWAFP abstains from publishing current lists of officials. Dr. Tunji Otegbeye has served as general-secretary in the past and remains the party's leading personality. The following were NTUC chief officers in mid-1972: Wahab O. Goodluck, president; Hudson Momodu, deputy president; S. U. Bassey, secretary-general; Ade Salawu, deputy secretary; S. Oduntan, assistant secretary; Moroudiya King, administrative secretary (*Advance,* 14–20 August). Ideological training is centered at the Patrice Lumumba Labour Academy, directed by S. A. Dada (Ibid., 5–11 June).

During 1972, the government released a number of prominent communists from prison, including Otegbeye, Goodluck, and Bassey.

According to British reports, the SWAFP remains numerically weak and heavily dependent on Soviet subsidies. The Soviet Union is said to have provided funds for the offices of the Socialist Publishing House, which publishes the journal *Advance,* and scholarships for study in communist-ruled countries; these have been channeled through the NTUC, thus bypassing government procedures.

The communist movement is split by serious dissensions. These are said to have involved disagreements between Otegbeye on the one hand, and Goodluck and Bassey on the other. In June 1972 the Nigerian Trade Union Congress journal *Advance,* which previously had been published by Goodluck, with Sylvester O. Z. Ejiofoh as acting editor, was taken over by the Otegbeye faction. Dada became publisher of the paper and Nati Iwuagwu its editor. Dapo Fatogun, formerly editorial adviser, ceased to be associated with the journal. Goodluck lost his position as patron of the Youth Thinkers' Club. By August, the struggle had affected the trade union movement. A "Revolutionary Council" was founded, with headquarters in Benin, headed by P. A. Arobeme. The latter accused Bassey and Goodluck of unconstitutional procedures in removing Dickson Ohikhena from his position as local chairman. (Ibid., 14–20 August). These dissensions were characterized by an unusual proclivity for public debate and open airing of internal differences.

Domestic Views and Policies. In a statement published in September 1972, Otegbeye called for working-class unity and establishment of a central organization for all Nigerian trade unions. He deplored the manner in which formation of numerous small trade unions had allowed employers to exploit workers. He argued that "indigenization" of the economy is progressive to the extent to which "it prevents the exportation of profits by foreigners and enhances the expansion of Nigerian participation in the economy." On the other hand, indigenization "transferred the machinery of capitalist exploitation from foreigners to indigenous Nigerians." Hence, workers must defend their class interests by creation of thrift and consumers' societies. Cooperatives should take part in education and in promoting low-cost housing. Trade union legislation must be amended to permit only wage earners to become union members (*Advance,* 18–24 September). The NTUC gave limited support to the Nigerian government during the year, but looked to a wider national-democratic revolution as a stepping-stone on the road to socialism.

International Views and Policies. The NTUC continued to follow a rigidly pro-Soviet policy. Its journal, *Advance,* expressed strong hostility toward the policies pursued by the United States, its NATO allies, and Israel, and condemned South Africa, Portugal, and their Western backers. The journal fully supported the Soviet Union and its East European allies, especially the German Democratic Republic, and almost never alluded to the People's Republic of China, whose policies it practically ignored.

Publications. The official NTUC journal is *Advance,* which calls itself a "socialist weekly." It is published in Lagos. Circulation has been assessed at about 3,000 readers.

Hoover Institution   Lewis H. Gann
Stanford University

Réunion

The Réunion Communist Party (Parti Communiste Réunionnais; PCR) was founded in 1959 by the transformation of the Réunion Federation of the French Communist Party into an autonomous organization.

The PCR is legal. In 1967 the party claimed to have 3,500 members; a recent Western estimate put the active membership at 500 (*World Strength of the Communist Party Organizations,* Washington, D.C., 1972, p. 123). No new figures were released at the party's Third Congress, held in Le Port on 14–16 July 1972.

Although its membership is small, the PCR succeeds in mobilizing considerable electoral support, particularly among the island's sugar workers and in certain towns. It is the only party with a local organization; electoral candidates of other parties are normally French, without permanent organizations in Réunion (which is one of France's overseas departments and an integral part of the French Republic). The PCR, however, has no representatives in the French Assembly or Senate. On the 36-member General Council it is represented by five party members, its secretary-general, Paul Vergès (for other names see *YICA, 1972,* p. 283). In local elections in 1971 the PCR, which until that time had little influence in municipal government, gained control in three towns: Le Port (where secretary-general Vergès is mayor), Possession, and Saint-Louis (whose mayor, although not a party member, is a sympathizer and heads a largely communist government).

Vergès was reelected secretary-general at the Third Congress but, no leadership lists were printed in the party organ, *Témoignages.*

The PCR controls the largest trade union, the General Confederation of Labor of Réunion (Confédération Générale du Travail de la Réunion; CGTR). The party is influential within the Réunion Front of Autonomous Youth (Front de la Jeunesse Autonomiste de la Réunion; FJAR) and the Union of Réunion Women (Union des Femmes de la Réunion; (UFR).

Departmental and National Views and Policies. In 1972, as with previous years, the issue of Réunion's self-determination dominated all others. The PCR congress, which allocated most of its time to this problem, reaffirmed the party's previous position—and that adopted at Morne-Rouge (Martinique) in August 1971 by 16 representatives of the autonomy movement in the overseas departments, including Vergès. The PCR calls for "free and democratic elections," with universal suffrage, to elect an assembly specifically for the purpose of defining and deciding a statute that presumably would separate Réunion from France in all respects that imply French domination, leaving a body representing Réunion and France on a basis of equal authority to coordinate such affairs of mutual interest as the administration of French financial and technical assistance for Réunion's development.

The PRC was active in joining other pro-autonomy groups in the overseas departments and territories, meeting twice in 1972 with similar French organizations in Paris, 30 May and 15 November. The first session resulted in an agreement (*Témoignages,* 3 June) on a common program much the same as that proposed by the PCR. While the conference received relatively little publicity in the communist press of Guadeloupe and Martinique, it was given very large coverage by *Témoignages* and was further popularized by a series of conferences throughout the island by members of the PCR. The second meeting set up a permanent coordination committee to ensure concerted action by all those working for self-determination of the overseas departments and territories.

Following the May meeting—according to the PCR, as a result of it—the French secretary-general of the overseas departments said that the French government agreed to "grant autonomy or even independence" to the overseas departments if the majority of the population desires it" (*ibid.,* 16 June).

The accord for parliamentary cooperation signed by the French communist and socialist parties, published on 26 June (see France), was also given close attention by the PCR, which emphasized its significance for the overseas departments. *Témoignages* advised its readers of various promises that would be carried out once the leftists attained a majority in the National Assembly: recognition of the right of self-determination for the peoples of the overseas departments and territories, elections in these areas for assemblies to elaborate new statutes for each, and increased French aid for their development (ibid., 29 June).

Matters not directly relating to the autonomy issue included alarm (reportedly voiced at the Third Congress) over ideological deviations within the party. In 1968 Vergès stated that the party was limiting its numbers in favor of improving the members' ideological quality (*Tricontinental,* Havana, March–April 1969). Reporting on the congress, *Témoignages* (5 August) revealed that, because the party was "not isolated in the society," the influx of persons from the middle class, who have not been able to rid themselves completely of former influences, had allowed "opportunist currents" of the left and right to penetrate the party and affect its direction. The congress appealed to party members to combat such manifestations.

The PCR also attempted to appeal to the unemployed and those severely affected by increases in the cost of living and low salaries by waging campaigns in their behalf. On 10 September the party sponsored a rally of undetermined size to call attention to the problem of unemployment, considered by the PCR to be foremost domestic concern. According to the party spokesmen, the numbers of unemployed reached 50,000 in 1972 (about 10 percent of the population), of whom 75 percent were said to be young persons (ibid., 11–12 September).

International Views and Policies. In international communist affairs the PCR has shown a tendency to adopt independent stands on various issues—divorcing itself from an earlier alignment with the Communist Party of the Soviet Union. This tendency was evident in 1968 and was dramatized at the Moscow Conference in June 1969 (see *YICA, 1970,* p. 317). At about the same time the PCR began to exhibit differences with the French Communist Party, but relations appeared to be warmer in 1972.

The PCR expressed support for leftist movements in sub-Saharan Africa during a convention of "democratic forces" at Tananarive, Malagasy Republic, on 19–22 June. It opposed the admission of Great Britain, Ireland, Norway, and Denmark to the European Common Market, but argued that, despite the "nefarious consequences" of the Common Market for Réunion's agricultural and industrial employment, the decision should be left to the French people, and not to those who considered themselves outside of French sovereignty. The party campaigned for abstention in the deciding referendum in April, and expressed satisfaction that only 49 percent of those eligible in Réunion voted, of whom 42 percent were reported as having voted in favor of admission (*Témoignages,* 15 April).

The PCR has been generally very active in making contacts with other leftist parties, and during 1972, though somewhat diminished from previous years, these contacts were continued through numerous trips abroad—particularly to France—by Vergès and other party leaders. At the Third Congress, a Central Committee member of the French Communist Party made an address. The Communist Party of the Soviet Union attempted to send three delegates and the Romanian Communist Party two, but both were met by refusals to issue visas. In December, however, Vergès met P. N. Demichev, a candidate member of the CPSU Central Committee in Moscow (FBIS, 13 January 1973).

Publications. The daily organ of the PCR is *Témoignages.* It claims 6,000 subscriptions. *Jeune Réunion* is the weekly publication of the FJAR.

California State University, San Jose   Eric Stromquist

South Africa

The Communist Party of South Africa, founded in 1921 but officially banned in 1950, reconstituted itself as the South African Communist Party (SACP) in 1953. The SACP and its allied organizations—the African National Congress (ANC), the South African Indian Congress (IC), and the South African Coloured People's Congress (CPC)—are banned by the government. The party is mainly an exile group, but illegal cadres have attempted to operate in South Africa, and a number of prosecutions have taken place.

Leadership and Organization. John B. Marks, party chairman, died in August 1972 at Moscow. The party does not publicize names of its leaders. It is known, however, that prominent Marxist-Leninists adhering to a pro-Soviet orientation include: Moses M. Kotane, a veteran communist who serves as ANC treasurer-general; Hilda Lilian Bernstein, World Peace Council member; Ruth Slovo (who publishes under her maiden name as Ruth First); Dr. Y. M. Dadoo, president of IC; Brian Bunting and others. Party publications are printed in London, main headquarters for the exiles.

In 1970 an enlarged meeting of the Central Committee determined that the SACP should be recast into an organization of professional revolutionaries (*African Communist,* no. 43, p. 54). The SACP sees the role of the congresses as a mass organizations dedicated to the task of effecting a national-democratic revolution; this revolution will serve as a steppingstone on the road to socialism.

According to the SACP, South Africa combines the features of monopoly capitalism with those of a colonial state. South African monopolists, working in cooperation with the United States, West Germany, Israel, and other Western countries, allegedly have established a fascist state which must be overthrown by means of armed struggle.

Resistance initially must be based on well-armed full-time guerrilla groups, beginning in the countryside, with urban groups in an ancillary capacity. These armed forces at all times must remain subordinate to the political leadership. The initial concentration on rural areas does not mean that the population in the countryside is the most significant revolutionary force, though its support must be won.

By far the most important among the congresses is the ANC, which is said to maintain offices in London, the main center, Algiers, Cairo, New Delhi, Dar es Salaam, and Morogoro (in Tanzania). Key leaders are the president, Oliver Tambo, and the secretary-general, Alfred Nzo. Other exiles include Reggie September, Gobrizona Mugquikana, and Godfrey Motsepe, all of whom live in London. (*Africa Confidential,* London, 4 February, p. 5). The ANC apparently comprises both orthodox Marxist-Leninists and African nationalists, including adherents of Black Power doctrines, who assert that all Africans form a single oppressed people. The ANC, like the SACP, stresses the interconnection between what it regards as the colonial systems of South Africa, Portuguese Africa, and Rhodesia. It thus rejects the "domino theory," according to which the Portuguese colonies should be liberated first and South Africa last.

ANC spokesmen admit that armed struggle in South Africa is impeded by the lack of a military sanctuary to the rear of the South African forces, the presence of a well-armed and numerous white population, the existence of a highly developed communications system and the most advanced industrial economy in Africa, and the lack of possible base areas where supply depots and training camps may be set up in secrecy (Sobizana Mnquikwana, "Southern Africa," *Sechaba,* VI, no. 6, June 1972, 2–6). But these difficulties allegedly can be overcome, especially by strengthening ANC contacts with black workers. "Multi-racial" unions have failed, as white immigrant workers have become supporters of the white minority ideology and as whites always seek to gain control over these organizations. According to some ANC sources, even the SACP suffers because it started as a white party and has never become an African organization. (Interview with Tennyson Makiwane of the ANC, *Il Manifesto,* 6 January 1972.) The ANC has made no serious progress in promoting underground warfare throughout South Africa. No permanent guerrilla bases have been established south of the Zambezi. Inside the country, the ANC attempts to cooperate with the South African Congress of Trade Unions (SACTU), a small labor organization headed by Mark Williams-Shope, also an ANC member (*Sechaba,* special edition, 1972). London representative for SACTU is John Gaetsewe. SACTU, however, remains without political significance. Members of the SACP and of the ANC also have played an active part in the Anti-Apartheid Movement in London. Views of the latter organization on South African and international questions essentially reflect those of the ANC.

International Views and Positions. The SACP and ANC both follow a pro-Soviet course. ANC works in alliance with the South West African Peoples Organization (SWAPO), Zimbabwe African People's Union (ZAPU), Frente de Libertação de Moçambique (FRELIMO), Movimento de Libertação de Angola (MPLA) and Partido de Independência da Guiné e Cabo Verde (PAIGC), all of which are pro-Soviet in their outlook.

Tambo attended, on behalf of ANC, the fifth conference of the Organization of Solidarity of Asian and African Peoples, held at Cairo in January 1972 (*Advance,* Lagos, 17–23 January). The ANC participated later in a six-day seminar on "imperialism, independence and social transformation of the contemporary world," convened at Delhi by the World Peace Council and the Afro-Asian Peoples' Solidarity Organization (*Sechaba,* VI, no. 6, June, 15). ANC observers also took part in the fourth conference of Non-Aligned Nations at Georgetown, Guyana, in August. Observers represented SWAPO (Namibia), FRELIMO (Mozambique), Pan-Africanist Congress (South Africa), Organization of Afro-Asian Solidarity (AAPSO), according to *Africa Research Bulletin,* 1–31 August, p. 2583. Nicolae Ceauşescu, secretary general of the Romanian Communist Party, held meetings with Alfred Nzo, as well as with leaders of FRELIMO and SWAPO during a visit at Dar es Salaam, Tanzania, in March (FBIS, 30 March).

In November an ANC delegation, headed by Tambo and Nzo, traveled to East Berlin. Here they conferred with a delegation of the Socialist Unity Party Central Committee (FBIS, 16 November).

Publications. The SACP publishes the *African Communist,* a quarterly. The ANC journal, a monthly, is entitled *Sechaba.* Both are published in London. In addition, the ANC puts out *Mayibuye,* a fortnightly bulletin, and *Spotlight on South Africa* (formerly called *News Di-*

gest). The Anti-Apartheid Movement publishes *Anti-Apartheid News,* a monthly, printed in London.

Hoover Institution
Stanford University

Lewis H. Gann

Sudan

The Sudanese Communist Party (SCP) traces its origins to 1944. Its implication in the attempted coup d'état of 1971 led to its liquidation by the Sudanese government (see *YICA 1972*, pp. 290–92). Most of its leading functionaries were jailed or hanged. The SCP has been reduced largely to a small group of exiles.

Leadership and Organization. Following the disaster suffered by the party in 1971, the SCP was reconstituted in exile, mainly in London. Muhammad Ibrahim Naqud was elected secretary-general (*Arab World,* Beirut, 12 October 1971). Other leading personalities include Politburo member Dr. 'Izz al-Din 'Ali Amir, SCP secretary for foreign relations Mahjub 'Uthman, and Ibrahim Zakariya. Communists and "progressive trade unionists" said to be imprisoned in Sudan under the most distressing conditions include 'Awad Allah Ibrahim, president of the Sudanese Trade Union Federation; al-Hajj 'Abdal-Rahman, assistant secretary of the federation; and at least 16 members of the federation's Executive Committee. Among incarcerated "intellectuals, communists and democrats" are Mrs. Su'ad Ibrahim Ahmad, former lecturer at Khartoum University, and former civil servants Salah Maziri, Karib Allah Muhammad Hamid, and Wazid Muhammad Salih. (*African Communist,* London, no. 50, p. 90.)

Attempts to rebuild the party's cadres in the Sudan do not as yet appear to have met with much success. In February 1972 the government arrested a group established for the purpose of circulating instructions from the party's secret leadership. (*An-Nahar,* Beirut, 20 March). Yusif Abd al-Majid, allegedly a member of the party leadership, was arrested on a charge of distributing arms (FBIS, 31 March). The government has stated that communists should join the governing Sudanese Socialist Union as individuals and that no communist organizations of any kind will be permitted (ibid., 16 January).

Domestic Attitudes and Activities. A great deal of controversy has centered on the place of the 1971 coup attempt in SCP history and that of Sudan at large. In 1972 Vasil Bilak, a Presidium member and Central Committee secretary of the Communist Party of Czechoslovakia put forward the official Soviet interpretation. According to this version, former SCP secretary-general 'Abd al- Khaliq Mahjub staged the military uprising, which was badly planned, lacked support of the Sudanese masses, mistakenly was directed against progressive officers of the government, and in its preparation was not made known to fraternal parties (*Middle East and Maghreb Topics,* February). The journal of the pro-communist Nigerian Trade Union Congress went further by arguing that the uprising had been engineered by the U.S. Central Intelligence Agency in order to eliminate Sudanese progressives (Alex Chima, "Background to the Coup in the Sudan," *Advance,* Lagos, 27 September–3 October 1971). The SCP, on the other hand, warmly defends its role, asserting that the party took no part in the original planning but strongly backed the movement once it began. The attempted seizure of power allegedly had been no ordinary uprising, but was rather "a positive movement, offering a new model of government whose seeds will eventually flower" (*African Communist,* no. 50, p. 91). A statement, ostensibly issued by SCP, announced that the party when it gains power will slay without mercy all those guilty of having murdered its former leaders (Janis Sapiets, "Sudan Communists Vow Vengeance," BBC, 24 February). According to the SCP, the existing government in Sudan is subject to the "criminal and hysterical madness of the Head of State," General Numairi, who allegedly seeks to strengthen his position by appealing to the extreme right wing, including ultra-conservative rural elements and supporters of Islamic theocracy (*African Communist,* no. 50, p. 91).

International Position. The former SCP policy has been disavowed by the Soviet Union. It is even more isolated from China, which maintains friendly relations with the Sudan government and, according to a government spokesman, backed the government while subversives operating under leftist slogans were plotting against it. (*Novaya Vremya,* Moscow, 1 January 1972; FBIS, 12 January.)

The SCP strongly opposes the Federation of Arab Republics and calls for withdrawal of Sudan from association with Libya and Egypt, which helped suppress the 1971 uprising. (*Arab World,* 15 February). Other critics argue that the Sudan, whose blacks comprise 61 percent of the population, should lay no claims to membership in a racial Arab union and that Numairi is in fact an "Arab chauvinist" backed by Libya (*Advance,* 14 August).

The SCP was represented at the third congress of the Lebanese Communist Party, held in January at Beirut, where Zakariya acted as its principal spokesman.

Hoover Institution   Lewis H. Gann
Stanford University

Syria

The Syrian Communist Party (al-Hizb al-Shuyu'i al-Suri; SCP) is an offshoot of the Lebanese Communist Party (LCP) which was established in 1924. During the French mandate over Syria and Lebanon, membership in the LCP was open to communists from both states. Syrian elements became dominant in the party, particularly through the leadership of Khalid Bakdash, a Syrian Kurd who was secretary-general of the party from 1932 until 1944. National independence was granted to Syria and Lebanon in 1944, and in that year the party separated into two components. Bakdash assumed leadership of the newly formed Syrian Communist Party. Separation of the two parties occurred under amicable conditions. The Syrian leadership, in fact, maintained its strong influence over the LCP until the mid-1960s.

French authorities proscribed all communist activity in 1939. This ban continued after Syria's independence. Despite illegality, the SCP has enjoyed several periods of considerable political freedom. The last began in 1966 when a communist was named to a cabinet post for the first time by the extreme left wing of the Ba'th (Arab Socialist) Party. The communist position improved even further after a bloodless coup in November 1970 gave control of both the Ba'th Party and the government to Lieutenant General Hafiz al-Asad. As a result of changes brought about by al-Asad, two communists held cabinet posts in 1971 and eight were members of the People's Council, the newly established 173-seat Syrian legislature. In March 1972 the SCP gained de facto legality through its participation in the "National Progressive Front" formed by al-Asad (see below). In July, however, the government ordered a crackdown on the party's activities and arrested a number of its members, forcing the party again to operate by clandestine means.

Leadership and Organization. Membership in the SCP is believed to range between 3,000 and 4,000. The population of Syria is 6,294,000 (estimated 1970). There has been a struggle for party control since mid-1971. At the end of 1972 it is believed that the same leaders remain, though in a very tenuous position. The party is headed by Khalid Bakdash, who is generally considered the most important communist in the Arab world. He has held the post of first secretary—except for a brief interval in 1968—since the party was established. Bakdash was reelected to lead his party in June 1969, when the SCP held its Third Congress. The Politburo chosen at the same time was composed of Bakdash, Ibrahim Bakri, Riyad al-Turk, 'Umar Qashash, Yusuf Faisal, Daniel Ni'mah, and Zuhair 'Abd al-Samad. The last three and Murad Yusuf were named party secretaries. Yusuf Faisal is the minister of state in the Syrian cabinet and 'Umar Siba'i, a member of the Central Committee and chairman of the SCP Control Commission, is minister of communications.

Party Internal Affairs. A dispute within the SCP which apparently had been brewing since early 1971 and began in earnest in April and May of that year came to the surface in

April 1972. Dissidents in the Poltiburo, led by Daniel Ni'mah, took advantage of the absence of party leader Khalid Bakdash (in Moscow for medical treatment) to pass some controversial resolutions and incorporate them in the draft political program of the party. They also accued Bakdash of using methods reminiscent of Stalinism to control the party. In the Politbudirecto, only Yusuf Faisal opposed these moves. When Bakdash returned, he sought support but found that all but two local organizations sided with his opponents.

Early in 1972 an emergency conference of Arab communist parties, meeting in Syria, decided to "freeze" the SCP quarrel to provide time for mediation and efforts to work out a new compromise draft program. But mediation by Arab communists, in particular Fu'ad Nassar, (see Jordan), leader of the Communist Party of Jordan, were fruitless, as was subsequent mediation by Soviet first deputy premier Kyril Mazurov. In March, party elections for the Damascus regional committee gave the dissidents a comfortable victory over Bakdash. In mid-March, the party newspaper *Nidal al-Sha'b,* now firmly under the control of the dissidents, denied in angry terms the reports that there was a serious split, alluding only to democratic debate within the party (*al-Nida',* Beirut, 18 March). On 31 March, Ni'mah's followers held a meeting which they claimed was attended by 70 to 80 percent of the SCP Central Committee. Bakdash countered with his own meeting the next day, and decided to bring the split into the open. He did this in a statement of 3 April (published 5 April) signed by himself and ten members of the Central Committee (exactly half its membership). A series of attacks and counterattacks followed.

At this point the issues of dispute became clear. The dissidents felt that under Bakdash's leadership the party was too closely and uncritically aligned with the Soviet Union. The dissidents, instead, sought greater ties with Syrian as well as Arab nationalism. Their controversial draft program offered no lofty praise of the Soviet Union or disparagement of Communist China. In regard to the Arab-Israeli crisis, it made no mention of the U.N. Security Council Resolution 242, but rather stated the dual goal of the creation of a Palestinian state and the elimination of the state of Israel. The dissidents tended to disapprove of SCP participation in the National Front, knowing that the Ba'th would dominate it. Yet they supported a proposal for dissolution of their party through merger with the Ba'th and Nasserites in an "Arab Socialist Union." They also supported the proposal for merger of Syria with Egypt and Libya. All these stands were in direct contrast to the policies and tendencies supported by Bakdash and his followers, and by the Soviet Union.

On 5 May a meeting of dissident members of the Politbudirector and Central Committee issued an appeal to Bakdash and his principal supporter, Yusuf Faisal, to work toward party unity. It accused them of forming "duplicate organizations" within the party in five provinces of Syria and misusing the name of the SCP in factional bulletins. Early in July the SCP Politburo called for elections at all levels of the party organization. It also called for the holding of the party's Fourth Congress to approve the draft political program. (Middle East News Agency, Damascus, 7 July.) On 21–25 July representatives of both sides of the SCP met in Moscow. Officially, "the meeting expressed its complete satisfaction and unanimously approved the results of this historic meeting" (*al-Akhbar,* Beirut, 9 August). The reported agreements made in Moscow included: reintegration of all party members within the organizations of the party as elected by the SCP Third Congress; withdrawal of all the attacks and counterattacks issued, beginning with the Bakdash statement of 3 April; dissolution of all organizations created by the two factions during the crisis; and establishment of a four-member committee to examine all that led to party dissent (*An-Nahar Arab Report,* 7 August). The dispute was thus not ended but simply returned to the confines of the original party framework.

Later there were hints of continuing efforts at reconciliation in a report (*al-Hayah,* Beirut,

30 August) that the two factions had reached an understanding on the election of a new party first secretary to reestablish understanding and unified action. The SCP was said to have decided to elect Zuhayr 'Abd al-Samad to replace Khalid Bakdash, who, however, would retain his guiding political role. Whether an election took place has not yet been confirmed.

Domestic Attitudes and Activities. An event of major importance in 1972 served to give the SCP de facto legalization while actually restricting its activities. On 7 March, the Syrian president, Lieutenant General Hafiz al-Asad, signed the charter of the National Progressive Front. The SCP described the front as an "alliance" of the progressive forces of the country rather than a "dissolution" of them (in contrast to the Arab Socialist Union in Egypt, where the communist party was dissolved). The ruling Ba'th Party clearly dominates the front, which also includes the Arab Socialist Union, the Socialist Unionists' Movement, the Arab Socialists' Movement and the Syrian Communist Party. The Central Committee of the front is comprised of nine representatives from the Ba'th Party and two from each of the other four parties. The first representation of the SCP was announced to be Khalid Bakdash and Daniel Ni'mah, the leaders of the two SCP factions. It is disputed whether this choice was made to help heal the rift within the SCP or was made by President Asad to perpetuate the contradictions within the SCP and ensure its subservience. Possibly the most serious threat to the SCP is the decree of the National Front charter giving the Ba'th Party the exclusive right to carry on political recruitment, organization, and propaganda within the armed forces and among students, since the main strength of the SCP has been from the universities. Regardless of the new Front, Yusuf Faisal and 'Umar Siba'i remain the two SCP members within the Syrian cabinet.

The major concern of the SCP during the first half of 1972 was the split within the party. Participation in the front took second place, as indicated by the fact that the two SCP representatives on the Central Committee of the front were willing to miss an important meeting of the committee in order to go to Moscow to repair the rift in the party. Toward the end of July the SCP delegation returned from Moscow with a new drive for action. They organized demonstrations in Damascus to commemorate the anniversary of the execution of the Sudanese communist leader 'Abd al-Khaliq Mahjub for his part in the communist coup to overthrow President Muhammad Ja'far al-Numairi in July 1971. The Syrian government reacted with a general crackdown on SCP activities. A number of civilians and military personnel associated with the party were arrested. And the Ba'th government ordered investigations into the party and related organizations. The demonstrations were apparently not the only reason for the government's taking severe measures against the SCP. The state secruity forces claimed to have evidence that in June the SCP had conspired with the leadership of the Popular Front for the Liberation of Palestine and other Arab terrorist organizations in Beirut with the aim of overthrowing the government in Syria (*An-Nahar Arab Report,* 25 September). The ramifications of this charge on the future of the SCP in the National Front and even its very existence are not yet known. Statements issued by the Central Committee of the SCP in September and later made no mention of repressive actions against the party.

A final domestic issue of note was Syria's nationalization of the property of the Iraq Petroleum Company (IPC). The Politburo members opposed to Bakdash sent a cable to President Asad calling the nationalization "a historic victory and an important step toward complete national sovereignty and the liquidation of remaining imperialist features," and an expression of solidarity with Iraq in its actions against the IPC (Syrian Arab News Agency, Damascus, 3 June).

International Views and Activities. Throughout 1972 "official" statements were made by both factions of the SCP. Relations of both with the Soviet Union were centered on mediation efforts. The faction of Khalid Bakdash, however, made several statements urging stronger ties with Moscow. On the fifth anniversary of the 1967 war he demanded an increase in the role of Soviet military experts in Arab armies as one condition for eliminating Israeli aggression (*Arab World Weekly,* 10 June). In July, Bakdash protested vehemently against the Egyptian expulsion of Soviet advisers and threatened to withdraw the SCP from both the cabinet and the National Front if Syria followed Egypt's example (Middle East News Agency, 24 July). In November, in apparent recognition of his loyalty, the Communist Party of the Soviet Union awarded him the Order of the October Revolution on his sixtieth birthday (TASS, 14 November).

In other statements on the international level, the SCP organ, *Nidal al-Sha'b* supported the student unrest in Egypt in February as legitimate criticism of official government behavior in regard to continued Israeli occupation of Arab territory. Iraq was extended high praise by both factions of the SCP in June for its nationalization of the IPC. Later that month the dissident faction called for the strengthening of Syria's cooperation with Egypt in all fields and, in fact, with all progressive Arab countries in the struggle against "imperialism, Zionism, and reaction" (Middle East News Agency, Damascus, 15 June). Strong criticism was leveled at the Sudan by *Nidal al-Sha'b* in August. It charged the Sudanese government with increasing hostility to communism and democracy, and declared that "Sudan has rapidly departed from the progressive and patriotic Arab procession and from interest, even verbal interest, in Arab liberation issues." In September, the Central Committee of the SCP met and issued a strongly worded statement on the "current intensified imperialist-Zionist-reactionary onslaught." It charged that "Saudi Arabian reaction was plotting against Southern Yemen;" that imperialism was enlisting the help of reaction in Iran; and that part of the Kurdish movement was bringing pressure on Iraq to prevent Iraq's battle against Israeli aggression. (*al-Akhbar,* Beirut, 7 October.)

Publications. The party organ of the SCP is the semi-clandestine, semi-monthly newspaper *Nidal al-Sha'b* ("People's Struggle"), printed in Lebanon. The party disseminates most of its news through the two legal publications of the Lebanese Communist Party: *al-Nida'* and *al-Akhbar.*

Stanford, California   Patricia Nabti

Tunisia

The Tunisian Communist Party (Parti Communiste Tunisien; PCT) was founded in 1920 as a branch of the French Communist Party. In 1934 it became independent. Since 1963 it has been banned and party activities have been clandestine. Membership has been small, and the party's influence on front organizations such as the General Union of Tunisian Workers (Union Générale des Travailleurs Tunisiens; UGTA) and the General Union of Tunisian Students (Union Générale des Etudiants Tunisiens; UGET) has been insignificant. Main party support, however, still comes from students, intellectuals, and Tunisian residents abroad, especially those in France.

Leadership and Organization. Muhammad al-Nafa' is secretary of the PCT. Largely because of government restrictions, his activities have been curtailed (*Jeune Afrique,* Paris, 19 January 1971). The PCT therefore has had a limited voice in Tunisian affairs.

Domestic Views and Activities. Despite government policies, PCT influences nonetheless persist in university circles. Demonstrations and boycotts of lectures, especially on the part of students in the fields of arts, humanities, law, and economics, occurred during February 1972. Events which had been building up because of student demands for greater representation were triggered by the government's announcement of sentences passed on Mme Simone Lallouche and on her husband, Ahmad Ben Muhammad Ben 'Uthman, university lecturer, who had both been charged with involvement in the 1968 riots. (*Arab Report and Records,* London, 1–14 February). Premier Hadi Nouira attributed this latest unrest to "a minority of extremist elements," "destructive people [who were] mentally and emotionally sick," and "Zionist plots," and suggested that communists, Ba'thists, reactionaries, and anarchists had inspired student slogans and aggressive rhetoric (Tunis radio, domestic service, 11 February; *ARR,* 1–14 February). Accordingly the government suspended grants of all students in faculties affected by the unrest and announced that the university would be closed until 30 September.

By 18 April, however, after the government had received "apologies from many students" and the number of detainees had been reduced to about ninety, the university was reopened. Admonishing them, the government reminded students of its power to suppress universities and to terminate grants, and the minister of education called on them to reflect that the goal of education was to "convert [students] to a truly Tunisian and Muslim Zeal" (*ARR,* 16–29 February). Since then, student organizations have shown no sign of their earlier unrest.

International Position. The PCT remains pro-Soviet and anti-Maoist. In a recent article, "The Third World in the World Arena," which criticized Western imperialism and paternalism, the "Peking theoreticians," and Israeli "perfiduous aggression," PCT Central Committee secretary Muhammad Harmel revealed the party's policies. Analyzing relationships between "third world" and industrialized countries, he concluded that whereas the latter have sought to impede the development of former colonial territories through "schemes of 'aid' and 'assistance,' " the Soviet Union has provided material and technological aid "without strings," and therefore is "the natural ally" of the third world (*WMR* vol. 15, 1972, pp. 19–21).

Publications. There is apparently no official PCT journal. In 1971 the party's request to publish a periodical entitled *Dialog* was denied by the minister of the interior (*Jeune Afrique,* Paris, 19 April). Earlier publications have included *al-Tariq* ("The Way") and *Espoir.*

University of Maryland   B. Marie Perinbam

WESTERN
HEMISPHERE

Argentina

The Communist Party of Argentina (Partido Comunista de Argentina; PCA) originated from the International Socialist Party (Partido Socialista Internacional), founded in 1918. Its present name was adopted in 1920.

The PCA claims to have 150,000 members (*Nuestra Palabra,* 11 May 1972). Non-communist sources put the membership between 30,000 and 60,000. The population of Argentina is 23,800,000 (estimated 1970).

PCA membership, two-thirds of which is concentrated in the Federal Capital (city of Buenos Aires) and in Buenos Aires Province, is drawn mainly from the urban middle and lower classes. The social composition of the party was reflected in the class distribution of delegates at its Thirteenth Congress, March 1969: 72 workers, 10 persons in the "liberal professions," 6 teachers, 5 writers and journalists, 4 peasants, 2 housewives, and one student. The PCA is believed to be financially well off through its indirect participation in various commercial and banking enterprises. It was announced in August 1972 that the annual fund drive of the party had brought in more than 315 million pesos.

Although the military government of President Alejandro Lanusse, which came to power in March 1971, has legalized most other political parties, the PCA has continued to be an illegal party due to various anti-communist laws still in effect. It operates more or less openly, however, and its participation in the "National Assembly of Argentines" (see below) has not been hindered.

In addition to the PCA, which follows a pro-Soviet line, communist parties in Argentina include the Revolutionary Communist Party (Partido Comunista Revolucionario; PCR), the pro-Chinese Communist Vanguard (Vanguardia Comunista; VC), and a Trotskyite movement, split into several factions, one of which is dedicated to terrorism and guerrilla war.

In recent years other small leftist groups (composed of Castroite or Peronista extremists, or both), have emerged. While not all of these espouse communist ideologies, they share a strategy of armed struggle to seize power. Their total membership, reportedly distributed in about 15 different organizations, is estimated at between 6,000 and 7,500.

The military regime which has governed Argentina under three different presidents since 1966, has been unable to resolve the nation's economic difficulties, and has faced increasing labor pressures and disturbances, but these have come mostly from pro-Peronista sectors; communist influence on national affairs has been negligible thus far. However, the numerous subversive actions carried out by the small leftist groups have forced the government to adopt harsh measures against terrorism. Since the ascension of Lanusse to power in March 1971, the government has been pledged to the reestablishment of a constitutional regime through elections promised for March 1973.

The PCA. Leadership and Organization. The PCA is led by Gerónimo Arnedo Alvarez as secretary-general. Important members of the Central Committee, elected in March 1969, include Rodolfo Ghioldi, Orestes Ghioldi, Vicente Marischi, Alcira de la Peña, Fernando Nadra, Hector Agosti, Pedro Tadioli, Rubens Iscaro, Benito Marianetti, Oscar Arevalo, and Julio Laborde. The party is organized pyramidally from cells, neighborhood committees, and local committees on up to provincial committees and the Central Committee (21 full members and 8 alternates), Executive Committee (11 members), and Secretariat (4 members). In mid-1972 it was announced that the party's Fourteenth Congress would soon be held at an unspecified time and place, but by the end of the year there had been no indication that the congress was held.

The PCA youth movement, the Communist Youth Federation (Federación Juvenil Comunista; FJC) is organized along the same lines as the party. It claimed to have 35,000 card-carrying members in 1972 and thus to have recovered the strength it had in 1967, before the serious defections in that and the following year. The FJC's national conference in March 1972 claimed to have influence among young people in the organized labor and peasant movements, as well as among students. It called upon young people to rally to the "National Assembly of Argentines" (Encuentro Nacional de los Argentinos; ENA), the political coalition organized in 1970 under communist party sponsorship and including dissident Radicals, Christian Democrats, and Conservatives.

The PCA is weak in the labor movement, despite the presence of party units in unions in a number of industries. The major trade union body, the General Labor Confederation (Confederación General del Trabajo; CGT) is controlled by Peronistas, who are very powerful and reject communist support. The communists are strongly opposed to the CGT leadership. The PCA controls the Movement for Trade Union Unity (Movimiento por la Unidad y Coordinación Sindical; MUCS), which represents small regional unions, mostly those centered in Córdoba and Mendoza provinces. PCA Central Committee member Rubens Iscaro is secretary-general of the MUCS.

Although peasant organizations are mostly grouped under the non-communist Argentine Agrarian Federation (Federación Agraria Argentina; FAA), the PCA claims to be an active participant in the Union of Agrarian Producers of Argentina (UPARA), formed in 1969. UPARA is composed of small and medium-sized farmers, and claims to have 60,000 members.

Most PCA fronts, such as the Argentine League for the Rights of Men, the Union of Argentine Women (UMA), and the Argentine Peace Council, are illegal. There is, however, also communist participation in the Argentine Women's League, in MODENA (a group composed of civilians and retired military men seeking to protect national resources), and in MAVIET, the "Argentine Movement to Help Vietnam."

Domestic Attitudes and Activities. During 1972 the PCA showed a consistently hostile attitude toward the Lanusse government, in contrast with some indications of friendliness the year before. In January the Central Committee declared, in a document entitled "Platform of the Communist Party against the High Cost of Living": "Unless the working class and the people as a whole fight to prevent the dictatorship from carrying on a policy which safeguards the interests of the landed oligarchy, big capitalists and foreign monopolies, mostly U.S. monopolies, and puts the burden of the crisis on the working people, the country is bound to head for national catastrophe." The committee's "platform" set forth 19 points "to improve the working people's condition and stabilize the economy." (*IB,* no. 3.)

At the end of March the ENA issued a denunciation of the government, accusing it of "stifling democracy and holding over 700 political prisoners." Early in April the communists took an active part in a virtual revolt in the western city of Mendoza, arising out of a 300 percent increase in the price of electricity and resulting in a general strike led by the local branch of the CGT, in which communists had some influence. The police temporarily closed down the local CGT headquarters.

In May the PCA accused the government of "total intransigency" and of operating "against national interests." It also castigated most other elements in national politics. It denounced a letter which Juan Perón had sent to the CGT leader José Rucci in which the former dictator advised "prudence." It also spoke of "the betrayal of the Ruccis" and the "deals" of the Hour of the People (La Hora del Pueblo) coalition of Peronistas, Radicals, and others seeking to work out conditions for the promised elections of March 1973.

On 6 July a board meeting of opposition parties resulted in the establishing of the Civil Front of National Liberation (Frecilina). The communists participated in this meeting, but as a statement of the Central Committee explained, they were very disenchanted with its results. This statement said that Perón's personal representative in Argentina "had promised earlier that the conference would discuss the holding of the National Day of struggle for the release of political and social prisoners, for an end to tortures, repeal of . . . repressive legislation, and that an open and frank exchange of views would be launched on the ways and forms of establishing a genuine Front of National Liberation. It was on this condition that the Communist Party took part in the conference. It had to walk out of the conference since what had been promised was not fulfilled." (*IB,* no. 16–17.)

This Central Committee statement ended thus: "The Communist Party calls on the workers, farmers, office employees, students, professionals, intellectuals, women and youth to accept its program, the program of *an anti-imperialist, agrarian democratic revolution* and join its ranks. A strong Communist Party is the best guarantee of the unity of workers and the people in the historic battles for democracy, harmonious development of the national economy, for social progress and national independence." (Ibid.)

Early in August, Secretary General Arnedo Alvarez announced that the PCA "considers that it is now necessary to create a broad national front of all patriots of the country capable of changing the present situation and managing to set up a provisional government of democratic civil coalition on the basis of program demands jointly worked out." This government, he said, would call a new constitutional convention and organize democratic elections in which all would be allowed to participate. Arnedo Alvarez ended, "If one were to succeed in achieving the creation of a national political front, we would be able to deal a heavy blow against reaction. We would be able to weaken it, win secure positions, and, in the final analysis, isolate the reaction and defeat it." (*TASS, International,* 4 August.)

Late in August, federal police arrested 48 persons near Characita cemetery in the Buenos Aires region, during a demonstration to protest an official ban on a communist party meeting. Late in September, 15 PCA members who had been arrested in February at a communist meeting in Paraná, called to discuss the party's participation in the March 1973 elections, were acquitted by a military court on the grounds that participation of all opposition parties in the proposed elections was necessary. However, the court refused to declare the country's "anti-communist" law unconstitutional.

Although communists participated during the year in violent confrontations with police in Mendoza, San Juan, Córdoba, and other cities, they were generally in favor of a kind of "popular front" policy. As for terrorism and individual violence, according to the Moscow weekly

New Times (no. 28) "Argentine democrats, especially the Communists, condemn such activities as playing objectively into the hands of the reactionary forces and urge increased mass action using all forms of struggle."

International Views and Positions. During 1972 the PCA continued its traditionally pro-Soviet attitudes. In June a Central Committee delegation of the party visited East Europe and the Soviet Union. In Romania they were received by Nicolae Ceauşescu, and a joint communiqué was issued. In Moscow the delegation visited the grave of Vittorio Codovilla, the PCA's founder and long-time secretary general, who died in the Soviet capital two years before. N. V. Podgorny presented Rodolfo Ghioldi, senior member of the PCA Central Committee and co-founder of the party with Codovilla, with the Order of the October Revolution. A PCA official visited leaders of the Communist Party of India in Delhi in May.

Publications. The PCA weekley, *Nuestra Palabra,* claims a clandestine circulation of 30,000 copies. The PCA also publishes *Nueva Era,* a monthly theoretical journal, and the bimonthly *Cuadernos de Cultura,* catering mainly to intellectuals. Since August 1970 the party has published the *Boletin de Informaciones Latinoamericanos,* a fortnightly report on communist activities and revolutionary events in Latin America. The Communist Youth Federation prints a fortnightly paper, *Juventud.*

*   *   *

The PCR. The Revolutionary Communist Party, formed originally as the Communist Party of Revolutionary Recovery, was created in January 1968 by dissidents from the PCA, especially its youth organization, who rejected the PCA's attempt to create a "broad democratic front" as an effort at "class conciliation" and "conciliation with imperialism." César Otto Vargas is the PCR secretary-general. He and several other leaders (for names see *YICA, 1972,* p. 311) held important positions in the FJC before expulsion from the PCA in 1967.

The PCR advocates armed struggle to gain power, but believes that leadership in the revolutionary movement must be held by the party. The PCR favors only urban guerrilla struggle, contending that the "wide plains" of Argentina and the "highly developed agriculture of the coast" would not permit successful operations by peasant guerrillas.

No PCR activities gained public notice during 1972. The party presumably continued to publish its clandestine periodical *Nueva Hora.*

The VC. The Communist Vanguard, probably founded in 1964, is a pro-Chinese movement that is said to have some influence among student and worker groups. It showed few signs of activity during 1972.

*   *   *

Trotskyism in Argentina is represented by three groups, the Revolutionary Workers Party (Partido Revolucionario de los Trabajadores; PRT), aligned with the United Secretariat of the Fourth International; the Trotskyist Labor Party—Partido Obrero (Trotskista)—which is aligned with the International Secretariat of the Fourth International headed by J. Posadas, an Argentine; and Politica Obrera, apparently an independent Trotskyite group. The PRT and Politica Obrera, endorse Castroite principles on the guerrilla road to power. A fourth group of Trotskyite origins, the Partido Socialista de la Izquierda Nacional, has formally foresworn allegiance to Trotskyism.

The PRT. The PRT was founded in 1964. In 1968 it divided when two-thirds of its members espoused the concept of armed struggle. The views of the majority faction are expressed in its organ, *El Combatiente,* and those of the minority in *La Verdad*. The United Secretariat apparently supports both groups.

The "armed branch" of the majority faction is the People's Revolutionary Army (Ejército Revolucionario del Pueblo; ERP), in existence since August 1970. The ERP is believed to be strong in Córdoba and Rosario, and to a less degree in Tucumán and Buenos Aires. Its principal leaders, Mario Roberto Santucho Juárez and Enrique Harold Gorriaran Merlo, are members of the 11-man executive committee of the PRT. (Captured by police early in 1972, Santucho made a spectacular escape—see below.) The ERP follows a cellular type of organization, with a political commissar in each cell appointed by the PRT. During the year the ERP developed close relations with two other guerrilla groups, the Peronista-oriented Montoneros and the independent Marxist-Leninist Revolutionary Armed Forces (Fuerzas Armadas Revolucionarias; FAR).

During 1972 the ERP engaged in numerous "operations," among which were the robbery of the National Development Bank on 29 January, the kidnapping and murder of several prominent Argentines, and the mass escape from the Rawson prison camp in June. Three ERP commandos, with the help of two employees, got away with the equivalent of $483,000 from the bank; subsequently the ERP announced that the funds thus "expropriated" would be used "to continue developing the revolutionary war." In April the Argentine manager of FIAT was murdered by ERP guards while police attacked the building in a suburb of Buenos Aires where he was being held. Also in April, General Juan Carlos Sánchez, well-known as a leader of the "hard line" faction of the Army, was murdered in a joint operation carried out by the ERP and the FAR in Rosario. On 15 August 28 guerrillas of the ERP, FAR, and Montoneros groups, broke out of the Rawson prison in Patagonia. They seized control of nearby Trelew naval airbase, and ten of them, among whom was ERP leader Santucho, hijacked an Argentine airliner. Landing at Santiago, Chile, they were given political asylum after negotiations with the government of President Salvador Allende; some days later the ten flew to Cuba. The rest of the escapees surrendered, but on 22 August sixteen of them were gunned down at the Trelew base "while trying to escape."

The minority PRT, headed by veteran Trotskyite Nahuel Moreno, at the end of 1971 reached an agreement for merger with the Partido Socialista Argentino (PSA), the most extreme of the three factions into which the old Socialist Party had divided. They joined forces under the PSA name and began issuing a periodical, *Avanzada Socialista*. During 1972 the PSA sought to bring together a number of far-left groups, apparently including the PCR and VC, into a "Workers and Socialist Pole of Regroupment." Looking ahead to the March 1973 election, the PSA sought recognition as a legal party.

The Partido Obrero (Trotskista) of J. Posadas concentrated its activities on its periodical, *Voz Proletaria*. It charged that the kidnaping of the FIAT manager was organized by the U.S. Central Intelligence Agency. The Posadas group continued to announce the immediacy of the atomic war and to urge workers to "prepare" for it.

The Partido Socialista de la Izquierda Nacional, whose principal leader is Jorge Abelardo Ramos, also sought legal recognition in order to participate in the forthcoming election. It joined with several other small groups to form the Popular Left Front (Frente de Izquierda

Popular; FIP), which issued a statement in August urging an "emergency plan to alleviate the hunger and unemployment crisis." At this time, Ramos commented: "We are with revolutionary socialism but we uphold the banners of Peron."

*   *   *

Castroite and Peronista Extremist Groups. Castroite and far-left Peronista groups in Argentina are small and tend to have a brief existence. Among these, the Argentine Liberation Front (Frente Argentino de Liberación; FAL), the Revolutionary Armed Forces (Fuerzas Armadas Revolucionarias; FAR), and the Montoneros continued to be the most prominent. The FAL, formed in 1962, is a Marxist-Leninist group advocating Castroite tactics. Its membership is believed to include many students and persons in professions. It does not seem to have engaged in independent operations during 1972. The FAR, which began to operate in July 1970, has been described as a "conglomeration of ultra-left Marxist groups with sectors of revolutionary Peronismo" (*Analisis,* Buenos Aires, 4–10 August 1970). It advocates Guevarist tactics and at the same time considers itself Peronist. The FAR is closely linked with the Montoneros, a small Peronista guerrilla group. FAR and Montoneros actions during 1972 were frequently coordinated with those of the ERP.

Rutgers University   Robert J. Alexander

Bolivia

The Communist Party of Bolivia (Partido Comunista de Bolivia; PCB) was founded in 1950 and is pro-Soviet in alignment. A pro-Chinese splinter of the PCB became the Communist Party of Bolivia, Marxist-Leninist (Partido Comunista de Bolivia, Marxista-Leninista; PCB-ML) in 1965. The Trotskyist Revolutionary Workers' Party (Partido Obrero Revolucionario; POR) is currently split into three factions. The National Liberation Army (Ejército de Liberación Nacional; ELN) was founded by Che Guevara in 1966. The Movement of the Revolutionary Left (Movimiento de Izquierda Revolucionaria; MIR) was founded in mid-1971 and reorganized after the 21 August 1971 coup in which rightist Colonel Hugo Banzer overthrew the government of leftist General Juan José Torres and seized the presidency for himself.

All of these parties were illegal during 1972. The PCB and PCB-ML are estimated to have 1,500 and 1,100 members, respectively (*World Strength of the Communist Party Organizations,* Washington, D.C., 1972, p. 134.)

The Anti-Imperialist Revolutionary Front. In November 1971 eight Bolivian leftist parties and movements formed the Anti-Imperialist Revolutionary Front (Frente Revolucionaria Anti-imperialista; FRA) in order to coordinate their efforts to overthrow the Banzer government. Among the founding groups were the PCB, the PCB-ML, the MIR, the ELN, and the Lora and González factions of the POR (see below). According to the communiqué issued at their November meeting, the Banzer government was a "Yankee puppet," formed by the combined action of the U.S. Central Intelligence Agency and Brazilian militarists, with the complicity of the Bolivian Socialist Falange (Falange Socialista Boliviana; FSB) and the right wing of the National Revolutionary Movement (Movimiento Nacionalista Revolucionario; MNR) (*Libertad,* San José, Costa Rica, 8 January 1972). In 1972 the FRA proclaimed itself to be a front of workers, peasants, students, teachers, progressive clergymen, and democratic military men against fascism and imperialism (*Unidad,* Lima, 20 July). An FRA statement on 3 March called upon the proletariat to mobilize and lead the masses to a popular insurrection and the establishment of legitimate revolutionary power (*Masas,* April 1972; *Tricontinental Bulletin,* Havana, July 1972).

The PCB. Leadership and Organization. The first secretary of the PCB is Jorge Kolle Cueto. Others prominent in the party include Mario Monje Molina, a former first secretary, Hernán Melgar Justiniano, a member of the Political Commission, and Central Committee members Simón Reyes and Luis Padilla.

The PCB's youth organization, the Communist Youth of Bolivia (Juventud Comunista de Bolivia; JCB), is illegal and is operated clandestinely. Bolivian universities, in which the JCB had previously been active, were closed during 1972. Spokesmen for the group were Jorge Escalera and Carlos Soría Galvarro.

Simón Reyes, the main PCB labor leader and an officer in the illegal Bolivian Mineworkers' Federation, spent most of the year in exile.

The PCB regards itself as the main proponent of Marxism-Leninism in Bolivia, charging that most other parties and groups which profess Marxism-Leninism do so for "purely demagogic purposes." According to Luis Padilla, "the Marxist-Leninist interpretation of our national reality is gaining followers, and proving its superiority over the idealistic and quasi-scientific bourgeois conceptions" (*WMR,* April.)

Domestic Attitudes and Activities. Early in 1972, at a meeting in Prague, Luis Padilla analyzed the political ideologies (aside from Marxism-Leninism) in the Bolivian political spectrum as follows: The bourgeois nationalists try to institute reformist programs in an imperialist-dominated country, thus supporting dependent capitalist development. They are anticommunist and advocate class reconciliation and the elimination of contradictions. They brand all revolutionaries and patriots as "enemies of the revolution" and conduct an ideological offensive against freedom of thought and criticism. The petty-bourgeois nationalists, on the other hand, try to protect the fundamental interests of the country from foreign monopolies. Popular among the middle strata and the patriotic military men, they seek to build an economy with private, cooperative, and public sectors. This force is sometimes progressive and will join in the struggle against imperialism. (*WMR,* April.)

The PCB, which had been active in the "People's Assembly" in 1971 (see *YICA 1972,* pp. 315–16), participated in the FRA during 1972 (see above).

International Views and Positions. The PCB continued to be closely aligned with the Soviet Union, a position which was reaffirmed at the party's Third Congress, held on 11–12 June 1971 (see *YICA 1972,* pp. 315–17). It looks favorably on the revolutionary governments in Peru and Chile.

Publication. The PCB organ, published irregularly and clandestinely, is *Unidad.*

* * *

The PCB-ML. The Communist Party of Bolivia, Marxist-Leninist, established in April 1965, is headed by its secretary-general, Oscar Zamora Medinacelli. A rival PCB-ML was apparently set up in early 1971 by Jorge Echazú Alvarado, though there has been no news of its activities.

The youth group of the PCB-ML bears the name of its pro-Soviet counterpart, the JCB. The PCB-ML leads the Union of Poor Peasants (Unión de Campesinos Pobres; UCAPO), which has seized lands in some areas and seeks agrarian reform and revolution through armed struggle.

Domestic Attitudes and Activities. According to Oscar Zamora, the Banzer government is a puppet of the "U.S. imperialists" and the "Brazilian gorillas," and hence the Bolivian people must struggle against both the puppet government and the imperialists. The mining proletariat is considered the "revolutionary vanguard of the Bolivian people," and peasant struggles, particularly in northern Santa Cruz Province, are said to be of great significance. The PCB-ML argues that "only the armed action of the masses, based on the correct political and ideological unity of the revolutionary forces, can put an end to fascism and liberate the Bolivian people." Thus, "the principal task of the Party and other genuine revolutionary organizations is to unite, organize and prepare the masses for unleashing a revolutionary war in which a people's army will be born." This army will become the decisive factor for victory over the "fascist regime and its imperialist masters." (*Peking Review,* 26 May 1972.) The PCB-ML has been active in the FRA.

Publication. The PCB organ is *Liberación*. Party statements are also found in *Peking Review* and in releases of the New China News Agency.

*   *   *

The ELN. The National Liberation Army was founded in 1966 and became internationally famous in 1967 when under the leadership of Che Guevara. The chief leader of the ELN in 1972 was Osvaldo "Chato" Peredo. Many ELN members were lost by desertions or were killed by government forces during the year.

In an interview with the Cuban news agency Prensa Latina in October, ELN leaders praised the 1971 "People's Assembly" but noted that its activities were based on the mistaken assumption that the government of Juan Torres would survive. Thus it failed to prepare the workers and the people for the "inevitable confrontation." After the fall of Torres the ELN called for the formation of a united front of forces to overthrow the "domestic fascists" and "Yankee imperialists." This type of organization was considered appropriate for the tasks of the hour, though the ELN still maintained that armed struggle was a superior stage of struggle.

The Bolivian government devoted particular attention in 1972 to the elimination of the ELN. The group suffered great losses between the August 1971 coup and early 1972, as Chato Peredo acknowledged (*¿Por Que?,* Mexico City, 23 March). In October, after many more losses, ELN leaders said that "setbacks are unavoidable" and maintained that the important thing was for the guerrillas to keep a high morale.

Throughout the year the Bolivian government charged that the guerrillas received assistance from the Cuban Embassy in Chile. In March and April, during a period of particularly heavy government raids on ELN hideouts, the government charged the Soviet Union with aiding the revolutionaries and declared half of the members of the large Soviet Embassy staff in La Paz personae non gratae.

*   *   *

The MIR. The Movement of the Revolutionary Left was formed in 1971 by the Revolutionary Christian Democracy (DCR), the Sparticus Revolutionary Movement (MRE), independent Marxist groups, and others. It seeks to organize the people politically and militarily and to prepare for revolutionary violence. It is a member of the FRA and has the motto "United we will win." (See interview with an MIR leader in *Punto Final,* Santiago, Chile, 9 May.)

*   *   *

The POR. The Revolutionary Workers' Party is divided into three factions. The first, under Hugo González Moscoso, is aligned with the Trotskyist Fourth International–United Secretariat. The second faction, headed by the well-known political figure and historian of the Bolivian labor movement, Guillermo Lora, and by Philemon Escobar, has contacts with the

Fourth International–International Committee. The third faction, the POR-Trotskyista (PORT), aligned with the Fourth International–International Secretariat (Posadas branch), is led by Amadeo Vargas.

The Lora faction, which participated in the "People's Assembly" prior to the August 1971 coup, was the object of much controversy within the International Committee (IC) during 1972. Some members of the IC charged that Lora had joined the "Stalinists" (the PCB) and reformists in 1971, and condemned him for failing to establish soviets in Bolivia. Other members of the IC defended Lora's actions. (Representative arguments for the two sides are found in *Fourth International*, London, Summer 1972, pp. 153–62, 174–83.) The Lora faction joined the FRA in November 1971. Its monthly organ is *Masas*.

The González faction, which had not participated in the "People's Assembly" in 1971, joined the FRA in November—a move that was soon criticized by the United Secretariat, which did not approve of "multi-class national unity" with "Stalinists," reformists, and bourgeois elements (see *Intercontinental Press,* New York, 21 February, and *Quatrieme Internationale,* Paris, 15 July). The faction has a monthly organ, *Combate*.

Hoover Institution   William E. Ratliff
Stanford University

Brazil

There have been organized communist groups in Brazil for more than half a century. Their fortunes have fluctuated somewhat with major changes on the Brazilian political scene and with schisms in the international communist movement, but they have rarely attracted a large following or exerted significant political influence. Moreover, their opportunities and short-term prospects have seldom been as restricted as they appear at present.

The original Communist Party of Brazil (Partido Comunista do Brasil), which remains the nation's leading Marxist organization, was founded in March 1922. A Trotskyist faction that was expelled and formed a separate organization in 1929 has maintained a precarious existence since that date. In 1960, in an effort to give the pro-Soviet party a more national character, its name was changed to Brazilian Communist Party (Partido Comunista Brasileiro; PCB). The following year a pro-Chinese element broke away, forming a new party in February 1962, the Communist Party of Brazil (Partido Comunista do Brasil; PCdoB). Dissidence within the ranks of these parties between 1967 and 1969 led to the formation of several splinter groups, predominantly of Castroite tendency, that strongly advocated the use of armed violence to overthrow the regime. Important among those that have survived as separate entities are: the Popular Revolutionary Vanguard (Vanguarda Popular Revolucionária; VPR), the National Liberation Action (Ação Libertadora Nacional; ALN), and the Revolutionary Brazilian Communist Party (Partido Comunista Brasileiro Revolucionário; PCBR). Most of the groups on the Revolutionary Left, however, have fragmented, merged, and re-fragmented so frequently that it is difficult to determine their total number and identity. There are believed to be at least sixteen such organizations in Brazil. In the face of effective police repression, the loss of their most prominent leaders, and sustained public apathy nearly all Brazilian Marxist groups have been forced to recognize the inadequacy of terrorist tactics and are attempting to attain their objectives through more traditional methods of propaganda and infiltration of mass organizations.

The communist movement has been illegal in Brazil throughout most of its existence. Although outlawed in 1947, the PCB was allowed to function and its members ran in elections under the label of other parties. During the presidency of João Goulart (1961–64) the PCB succeeded in infiltrating and controlling important labor, student, political, and bureaucratic groups. The military regime which came to power in March 1964 drove the party underground and banned the existing communist-influenced organizations. In September 1969, in an attempt to curb terrorist activities, the government issued laws providing the death penalty for subversive acts.

Estimates of recent PCB membership have dropped from 40,000 in 1964 to about 13,000 in 1972. Members of the PCdoB are believed to number under 750. The Castroite and other groups are estimated to have a total membership of 1,000 to 5,000. The population of Brazil is 100,000,000 (estimated 1972).

The PCB. Organization and Leadership. The PCB apparatus includes a 21-member Executive Commission (some of whose members are resident abroad), a Central Committee (which appears to function chiefly in Rio de Janeiro), various state committees, and local cells in residential districts and places of employment. The Sixth Congress of the PCB, its latest, took place in December 1967.

The defection of Adauto Alves dos Santos, a long-time assistant to the Central Committee, led to the arrest in December of several party officials in Rio de Janeiro. This blow severely weakened the financial and foreign affairs sections of the Central Committee, but apparently had no serious effect on the PCB organization elsewhere in Brazil.

In a series of exposés published in the Brazilian press in December, Alves dos Santos stated that the PCB receives financial support from the U.S.S.R., channeled through the Soviet commercial mission in Rio de Janeiro.

The PCB secretary-general is Luís Carlos Prestes. According to Alves dos Santos, Prestes has resided in Moscow since March 1971. In his absence the party is directed by Giocondo Gorender Dias, who lives in Rio de Janeiro. Other prominent leaders are Oto José Santos, Armando Ziller, Lucas Romão, Alfredo Castro, J. B. Tavares de Sá, Augusto Bento, Olga Maranhão, Jorge Villa, Sabino Bahia, Felipe Rodrígues, and Abel Chermont (also see *YICA, 1972,* p. 320).

The PCB formerly derived considerable support from the National Union of Students (União Nacional dos Estudantes; UNE) and the Workers' General Command (Comando Geral dos Trabalhadores; CGT), both of which were abolished during the mid-1960's.

According to Secretary-General Prestes, PCB "influence is on the upgrade" in the country's biggest labor organization, the National Confederation of Industrial Workers, and "many" of the more than 1,000 peasant unions representing six million members "are under communist influence" (*WMR,* February).

Party Internal Affairs. One of the major themes in the public statements of PCB spokesmen during 1972 was the vital importance of a careful campaign to strengthen the party. The highest priority was given to the task of gaining new members and attracting former members back into the fold. Prestes set the tone of the campaign, repeatedly stressing the long-range nature and difficulty of the task. "Working deep underground . . . the process of accumulating strength is an arduous one. Struggle against the centralized state's strong military-terrorist organization is difficult and long" (*WMR,* February), and "This is a process whose duration cannot be forecast. It cannot yield immediate results. This struggle demands selfless work, patient efforts and a spirit of self-sacrifice, which are typical of true communist activists" (*Rabotnichesko Delo,* Sofia, 25 March).

In the latter article the secretary-general also noted that in its recruitment and indoctrination campaign the PCB is "relying upon the workers' class, and primarily upon the proletariat in large industrial enterprises." One of the casualties of the recruitment drive was Prestes's daughter, who was arrested with 21 others for trying to revive the PCB among workers in Volkswagen plants in the São Paulo industrial area (FBIS, 29 November). There is no firm information about expansion of the party's labor following, but the publicity given this case and the arrests of dozens of other communists organizers in São Paulo, Recife, and Pôrto Alegre during the second half of the year suggests that the efforts to rebuild a strong communist base in the labor movement is taken seriously by the government.

Domestic Attitudes and Activities. The PCB is an orthodox pro-Soviet party which upholds the role of the masses in obtaining power and opposes many of the subversive activities advocated by Castroite elements. Prestes summarized the PCB position in a statement to the Bulgarian press, citing the PCB's Sixth Congress resolution, "The historic appeal to the Brazilian communists is to build a strong and numerous party of the workers class," and adding, "The [Brazilian] communists are convinced that tyranny can be overthrown only with the joint actions of the broad people's masses" (*Rabotnichesko Delo,* 25 March).

The fiftieth anniversary of the PCB provided the occasion for numerous reviews of the party's history which emphasized the lessons learned from the failure of past efforts to seize power by force, and the correctness of its traditional policy of non-violence and cooperation with other "progressive and democratic" forces. With regard to the present situation the public statements of PCB leaders stressed the need to build a broad political front against the military government. After pointing out the handicaps under which Brazilian communists are now working, Prestes observed that the party is "seeking mutual understanding with political movements and leaders, for we know that the task of the hour is to draw up a common program" (*WMR,* February). Elsewhere he boasted that "The political and tactical line of the communists is gaining ground among the broad patriotic and democratic strata, including representatives of the national bourgeoisie in parliament, the Catholic Church, and the armed forces" (*Rabotnichesko Delo,* 25 March). This claim was partially confirmed by Alves dos Santos, who informed the Brazilian press in December that the PCB was currently trying to infiltrate the armed forces, and was taking advantage of traditional channels of penetration to spread communism through the Christian front. There are no indications, however, that through its contacts in political circles the PCB was able to exert any influence on the outcome of municipal and legislative elections in Brazil during 1972.

The PCB's campaign to win back former members reflects its intensified attempt to unite the fragments of the revolutionary left under party leadership. This goal has led to a marked softening of the party's public attacks on its Marxist rivals in Brazil. Although PCB spokesmen still occasionally lash out against them, the extreme invective of recent years is conspicuously absent. For example, J. Gomes states, "At present we are successfully parrying attacks by ultra-Leftists who, essentially anti-communist, are frankly trying to split and dissolve the Communist Party. Though they have grown weaker after the brutal extermination of their leaders by the dictatorship, they are still following their old line" (ibid., April). The kindest treatment is reserved for the student members of Castroite factions, whose errors are attributed to the exuberance of youth, as in the following comment by Secretary-General Prestes:

> We are convinced that most of the ultra-leftists . . . are simply misguided patriots. We did everything we could to win them over to our side, and have been fairly successful, especially among students, who comprised the core of these groups.
> Inexperienced young people despair easily in the face of the gloomy outlook under capitalism. They know nothing of the proletarian teaching and the history of the revolutionary working-class movement and are easily swayed to participate in reckless ventures, for . . . youth is militant and high-minded. (Ibid., February.)

But the unity of the left was not to be achieved by sweet words and moral suasion alone. Alves dos Santos revealed that the CPSU had advised the party to infiltrate radical left organizations in order to control them. He claimed that at least four Castroite factions had been infiltrated, but added that the conflict between the PCB and groups which favor armed struggle had not yet been resolved.

International Views and Positions. The PCB's strongly pro-Soviet position was reaffirmed in 1972. Writing in March on the occasion of the fiftieth anniversary of the party, Prestes stated that the PCB "will spare no effort . . . toward strengthening the unity and cohesion of the international communist movement on the basis of decisions taken by the June 1969 International Conference of Communist and Workers' Parties" (*Rabotnichesko Delo,* 25 March).

Luis Ribeiro reviewed the half-century of PCB experience as an ally of Moscow, describing the party as "a reliable contingent of the world communist movement, supremely devoted to Marxism-Leninism and proletarian internationalism," which had "an active part in the work of the Communist International and in the International Conferences of Communist and Workers Parties," and whose members "energetically support the Cuban revolution, participate in the Latin American solidarity movement and in the great battle against . . . U.S. imperialism" (*WMR,* April).

J. Gomes stressed the anti-Chinese position of the PCB and pointed to the importance of ideological support from the pro-Moscow publication *Problems of Peace and Socialism,* from which Brazilian communists "expect reasoned articles exposing the essence of Maoism and all other forms of modern opportunism" (ibid.).

In June, following U.S. President Nixon's visit to the U.S.S.R., Prestes broadcast to Portuguese Africa on Moscow's "Radio Peace and Progress," praising the Soviet policy of peaceful coexistence with capitalist states, affirming that "there is no other alternative at present" (FBIS, 8 June).

The message from the CPSU to the PCB on the fiftieth anniversary of the Brazilian party dealt with all of the above points of agreement between the two parties and noted further that the PCB "shows fraternal solidarity . . . with the heroic peoples of Indochina . . . with the just struggle of the Arab peoples . . . against Right-wing and Left-wing opportunism [and] for the united action of all anti-imperialist forces in the struggle for peace, democracy and social progress" (*USSR and Third World,* 13 March–17 April).

International Party Contacts. Luís Carlos Prestes, who currently lives in Moscow, was the chief representative of the PCB to other communist parties during 1972. In April he headed a PCB delegation on a formal visit to the German Democratic Republic and took part in (East) Berlin in a conference on international problems. In June Prestes made a "friendship" visit to Bucharest at the invitation of the Central Committee of the Romanian Communist Party. The following month he "rested" in Bulgaria at the invitation of the Central Committee of the Bulgarian Communist Party, and in August he returned to Romania to spend his holidays. Press releases issued on each occasion indicate that Prestes met with the secretary-general and other officials of the host party.

J. Gomes represented the PCB at a discussion seminar arranged by the *World Marxist Review* early in the year. The seminar, held in Prague, dealt with the ideological struggle of Latin American communist parties and was attended by spokesmen for fourteen Latin American parties.

Publications. The PCB's clandestine newspaper, *Voz Operária,* is the party's central organ. According to a statement by Luís Carlos Prestes published in February, the newspaper "is appearing regularly despite tremendous difficulties. The paper is transported across great distances, sometimes exceeding 1,000 kilometres" (*WMR,* February). J. Gomes also notes that the party has been publishing its theoretical journal *Estudos* since 1971, and is now issuing a local edition of *Problems of Peace and Socialism* (ibid., April). Distribution of these publications is limited primarily to party members. To reach wider audiences for important statements and appeals, the party distributes clandestine leaflets.

*   *   *

The PCdoB. Little is known of the organizational structure of the pro-Chinese Communist Party of Brazil. Leading figures are believed to be Maurício Grabois, João Amazonas, José Camargo, and Tarzan de Castro (sentenced in June to fifteen months in prison for attempting to organize a "red" wing of the party). (For other names see *YICA, 1972,* p. 323).

Domestic Attitudes and Activities. The Central Committee of the PCdoB celebrated the 50th anniversary of the founding of the party, and the 10th anniversary of its "reorganization" in October 1971. It released a statement of its future tasks, which were: (1) the numerical strengthening of the party by the recruitment of self-sacrificing and active vanguard fighters from the working class, peasantry, and other exploited and oppressed layers of society; (2) the widest possible dissemination of the party line, Marxist-Leninist thought, and the spirit of self reliance, and the careful indoctrination of militants so that the PCdoB will be a "truly revolutionary and proletarian party"; and (3) the undertaking of broadly-based political activities to extend party ties with the broad masses in city and countryside and the promotion of the "struggle against the military dictatorship and Yankee imperialism" (*A Classe Operária,* Spanish edition, December 1971; freely and incompletely translated in *Peking Review,* 3 March 1972).

The Central Committee argued that armed struggle was "the only road possible to carry the national democratic revolution to victory, to conquer popular power, to install a new regime, and to open the road to the construction of socialism in Brazil" (*A Classe Operária,* December 1971). At the same time the party reissued a 1969 Central Committee statement explaining that laying the groundwork for eventual "people's war" required a period of non-armed mass struggle (ibid.). José Camargo said in a November 1971 interview in Albania that the workers, peasants, students, progressive intellectuals, and some sectors of the national bourgeoisie had to join forces and employ all forms of struggle, legal and illegal, open and clandestine, in order to carry out the revolution (ibid.). Late in 1971 the PCdoB claimed that the communists were in the vanguard of the peasant struggles in the northeast (ibid.) and a year later it expressed solidarity with reported peasant guerrilla activity in northern Mato Grosso (FBIS, 31 October).

International Views and Positions. The PCdoB was the first pro-Chinese communist party formed in Latin America and it has long joined the Chinese Communist Party in condemning "Soviet revisionism." Since mid-1971, however, when U.S. President Nixon first announced his forthcoming 1972 trip to China, the PCdoB has been less outspoken in its praise of the People's Republic. For example, the October 1971 statement (in a passage omitted altogether from the *Peking Review* version) praised the teachings of Marx, Engels, Lenin, and Stalin, but did not mention Mao Tse-tung (*A Classe Operária,* December 1971).

Publications. The PCdoB publishes an irregular clandestine newspaper, *A Classe Operária,* in Portuguese and Spanish editions. PCdoB statements are occasionally carried by Chinese or Albanian publications.

* * *

Castroite Organizations. Like many other Latin American countries, Brazil has seen the emergence of various small subversive groups holding communist and nationalistic views and advocating "armed struggle" tactics as a means to establish a socialist system. Important among these groups are the VPR, ALN, and the PCBR.

These predominantly Castroite groups function at regional and local levels, since they are not organized on a national basis. Support is drawn mainly from students, workers, former soldiers, and, to a much lesser degree, elements of the Catholic Church. According to both government and communist sources, the proportion of students involved in subversive activities is high (estimates range from 35 to 56 percent of the memberships). The average militant's age is twenty-three years. These revolutionary groups receive verbal support from Cuba, and some appear to receive material aid as well. Reportedly there is a coordinating center for Brazilian revolutionaries in Cuba.

No new prestigious figure has emerged to take the place of Carlos Marighella and Joaquim Câmara Ferreira of the ALN or Carlos Lamarca of the VPR, who have been killed by the police in the past three years. Harsh police and army measures undertaken against the subversives have proven successful, weakening the movement considerably and encouraging important defections. As a result, some of the survivors have begun to adopt a "Leninist" policy of "classical political work" and are attempting to form a "Leninist front" of revolutionary groups. Advocates of such a front have held meetings in Chile and France, without notable success (*Latin America,* 4 August).

Except for the senseless assassination of a British sailor in Rio de Janeiro early in the year, the Castroite factions restricted terrorist activities during 1972 to the armed robbery of banks and other business establishments, chiefly in Rio de Janeiro and São Paulo. Such operations were designed to secure funds and to demonstrate the continued existence of the terrorist organizations. None of the existing Castroite groups claimed responsibility for the reported guerrilla activities among peasants in Mato Grosso.

The VPR. Considered the largest and most active group until the death of Carlos Lamarca in September 1971, the Popular Revolutionary Vanguard is said to derive from a small left-wing organization of former army officers (the National Revolutionary Movement) and from PCB and PCdoB dissidents.

Information published in Chile late in 1971 indicates that the VPR took part in 1970 in a "revolutionary front" with the ALN, PCBR, the October 8th Revolutionary Movement (Movimento Revolucionário 8 de Outubro; MR-8), and the Tiradentes Revolutionary Movement (Movimento Revolucionário Tiradentes; MRT), in an attempt to disrupt the legislative elections with coordinated "armed propaganda" activities over a large geographic area of Brazil.

Another type of activity came to light at the trial of eight VPR members in São Paulo in August 1972. Three were sentenced to twelve years in prison and loss of political rights for the armed theft of a truck and about $500 worth of food, which they distributed, with inflammatory leaflets, to the residents of the Bras de Pina slum community in January 1971.

In July 1972 the largest trial of revolutionaries to that date in Brazil occurred in São Paulo, where 55 members of the VPR were brought to court simultaneously on charges ranging from recruitment to kidnapings and guerrilla warfare. Eight were found guilty and sentenced to terms from one to 25 years. The heaviest sentence was given to Ariston de Oliveira Lucena, one of Lamarca's earliest comrades, who had been sentenced to death by a military court in 1971 for revolutionary activities.

During 1972 the VPR was reported to have agreed to form a "Leninist front" with the Palmares Armed Revolutionary Vanguard (Vanguarda Armada Revolucionária-Palmares; VAR-Palmares) and two factions of the Workers Communist Party (Partido Operário Comunista; POC).

The ALN. The National Liberation Action is the second-largest Castroite group. It was founded, possibly in February 1968, by dissident PCB members who became disappointed with the non-violent "conventional models and methods" of the pro-Soviet party and decided to adopt the tactics of urban and rural guerrilla warfare associated with Castroism. Under the leadership and domination of Carlos Marighella, who insisted (in the words of Fidel Castro) that "the supreme duty of every revolutionary is to make the revolution," the ALN became the primary exponent of urban terrorism, although it continued to acknowledge the Cuban and Chinese dictum that rural guerrillas are the basic forces for an army of national liberation. The group's urban guerrilla activities declined markedly following the death of Joaquim Câmara Ferreira in 1970.

During the first quarter of 1972 armed operations by ALN members were reported in Rio de Janeiro, São Paulo, and the Brasília-Goiás area. During the second half of the year at least seven ALN members or associates, including a Dominican priest and three friars were sentenced to prison by military courts in Rio de Janeiro and São Paulo, and another eleven members were awaiting trial in Brasília. In August it was reported that leaders of the ALN were considering the formation of a political party (*Latin America,* 4 August 1972).

The PCBR. The Revolutionary Brazilian Communist Party was founded in April 1968 by Mário Alves de Souza Vieira, Jacobo Gorender, and Apolônio Pinto de Carvalho, all of whom had been expelled from the PCB in 1967. In 1970 it adhered to the "revolutionary front" comprised also of the VPR, ALN, MRT, and MR-8. The PCBR is based in Pernambuco and apparently seeks to exert influence throughout the Northeast. Security forces on Ceará reported in May that members of the PCBR had belonged to a terrorist cell recently dismantled in that state. The PCBR has almost certainly been infiltrated by the PCB.

Other Castroite Groups. Several other minor extremist groups have operated on the revolutionary left in Brazil and still exist at least in name. These include the MRT, which was founded by PCdoB dissidents in 1969. It gained notoriety with the assassination of a São Paulo industrialist in 1971. Most of the militants involved in that assassination have since been tried and sentenced to long prison terms. The MRT was not politically active in 1972.

The MR-8, which derives its name from the date of the death of Ché Guevara in October 1967, was formed in 1968. It took part in the "revolutionary front" in 1970, and claimed to be active through 1971. It is one of the factions—along with the VAR and VAR-Palmares—said to have been infiltrated and subverted by agents of the PCB.

The VAR-Palmares, formed in 1969, has been one of the more extreme urban terrorist groups. In February 1972 a VAR-Palmares cell in Rio de Janeiro assassinated a British sailor as an act of political protest. The cell was dismantled in March, when three of its members were killed by police. The VAR-Palmares is one of the groups that has reportedly agreed to form a "Leninist front" with the VPR and the POC, and to follow peaceful tactics. It is said to have been infiltrated by PCB agents who advocate a non-violent line.

Little is known of the origins of the Communist Workers Party (POC), which appears to be based in Southern Brazil. Two factions of the organization were reported to be adhering to "classical political" tactics in the Leninist front. Sweeping arrests in October decimated POC ranks and led to the trial of 66 members in São Paulo and 37 in Pôrto Alegre, charged with recruitment and distribution of subversive publications.

The Politico-Military Organization of the National Liberating Command (Organização Político-Militar/Comando Libertador Nacional; OPM/COLINA), based in Minas Gerais, appears to be an off-shoot of COLINA, which merged with the VPR in 1969. Brazilian security forces state that the group has Maoist tendencies and engages in political assassination, armed robbery, and subversive propaganda. In April 1972 fifteen of its members were tried and sentenced to prison by a military court for terms ranging from eighteen months to seven years. OPM/COLINA does not appear to have engaged in significant political activity in 1972.

The People's Liberating Movement (Movimento Libertador Popular; MOLIPO) came to public attention in November, when two of its members were killed in a gun battle with São Paulo police. MOLIPO, which engages in armed robberies and attacks, was formed by ex-militants of the ALN. Brazilian security forces state that it receives financial aid from Cuba, where 80 percent of its members received guerrilla training.

On the periphery of the Castroite groups is Popular Action (Ação Popular; AP), which dates from before 1964. Beginning as a radical Catholic student organization advocating agrarian and social reform, AP has moved farther to the left, and since 1964 some of its clerical and student members have urged violent revolution. The military regime regards it as an extremist group, and during 1972 decreed the preventive arrest of 37 AP members and brought more than 100 to trial for subversion. AP's most notorious militant, Manoel Conceição dos Santos, a peasant organizer long active in Maranhão and reported by Amnesty International to have been killed in a Brazilian prison, was arraigned before a military court in Ceará in September on criminal charges.

At least three small Trotskyist groups were also marginally active in Brazil during 1972. These are: the Trotskyist Revolutionary Workers Party (Partido Operário Revolucionário (Trotskista); PORT), associated with the Posadas wing of the Fourth International; a dissident element linked to the French-based Fourth International; and, a Trotskyist faction known as the First of May (Primeiro de Maio). The latter two attempted to form a united "Trotskyist Bolshevik" organization in São Paulo, publish a newspaper, *Voz Proletária,* and conduct political activities among factory workers. The incipient organization was virtually destroyed when seven members were arrested in August. Three of these were sentenced to prison in December.

University of California,   Rollie E. Poppino
Davis

Canada

The Communist Party of Canada (CPC) was founded in 1921. It functions legally and has a membership estimated at 2,000 to 3,000. The population of Canada is 21,830,000 (official estimate, June 1972).

Most CPC members are elderly. Old-age pensioners, manual workers and white-collar employees concentrated in the urban areas of Ontario, British Columbia, and the prairies comprise the bulk of the membership.

The CPC is not represented in the Federal Parliament or the provincial legislatures. On 30 October 1972 it put up candidates in 30 of the 264 federal ridings. Their electoral performance confirmed the party's limited appeal. The total CPC vote was less than 0.1 percent of the votes cast for the candidates of the other parties. A similar fate befell the five CPC candidates in the provincial election in British Columbia on 30 August.

At the municipal level, however, party members and sympathizers who had the backing of pro-communist labor bodies sat on several municipal councils and school boards.

Party members made progress in the trade union field. They controlled the United Fishermen and Allied Workers Union and the United Electrical, Radio and Allied Workers Union, both of which were allowed in December 1972 to join the Canadian Labor Congress, the successor to the trade union centers from which these two unions had been expelled during the cold war period.

Other Communists played a leading role in ethnic organizations of Canadians of East European extraction. The most important of these is the Association of United Ukrainian Canadians.

The Canadian Peace Congress, founded in 1949, felt the repercussions of the resignations of its president, vice-chairman, secretary, and treasurer in December 1971–January 1972. The president charged that "increasing pressure" had been put on him to withdraw because of his attitude toward the Sino-Soviet dispute and the conflict over Bangladesh. The CPC leaders in turn expressed sorrow at the parting of the ways while criticizing him for his views on "behalf of the erroneous positions of the Chinese leaders." (See *YICA, 1972*, p. 325).

A new executive of the Canadian Peace Congress was elected at a conference attended by 129 delegates in May.

The Young Communist League (YCL) of Canada made "modest gains" in 1972 in the face of competition from stronger Maoist and Trotskyist youth groups.

Leadership and Organization. William Kashtan is secretary-general of the CPC. He and others elected at the Twenty-first Convention, November 1971, remained at the helm of the CPC in 1972. (See *YICA, 1972*, p. 326.)

Sam Walsh was re-elected chairman of the Parti Communiste du Quebec (PCQ), which enjoys a certain autonomy within the CPC, at the Fourth Congress of the PCQ, in March 1972. The 45 delegates, nearly half of whom are active in the trade unions, elected a 13-member National Committee, including seven women.

Domestic Attitudes and Activities. The CPC spent much of 1972 preparing for and fighting the federal election. Party leaders, brochures, and editorials and articles in the party press condemned the policies of the Liberals and Conservatives, criticized the stand that the democratic socialists grouped in the New Democratic Party (NDP) had taken on several issues, and put forward the communist viewpoint.

As in 1971, the communists advocated the formation of a democratic, anti-monopoly coalition consisting of the CPC, NDP, trade unions, "the farm movement" and the "people's organizations." They assumed, in the words of William Kashtan, that "there will be no democratic coalition without a strong Communist party and Communist representation in Parliament" (*Canadian Tribune,* 29 November 1972).

At the same time the CPC called for a policy of full employment, the nationalization of the natural resources industry, a crash program of public works, guaranteed prices for farm products, a 32-hour working week, lower taxes, "genuine Canadian independence," and a "fully autonomous and united trade union movement." The right of self-determination for French Canadians was reaffirmed and coupled with the demand for the "adoption of a new Canadian constitution based on equal voluntary partnership of the French-Canadian and English-speaking people in an independent, democratic bi-national state." (Ibid.)

International Views and Positions. The CPC attacked U.S. policies in 1972 and took an active part in the peace movement against U.S. involvement in Vietnam and in the campaign for the freeing of Angela Davis.

Communist spokesmen expressed the hope that the détente between Canada and the socialist states would be followed by the development of cultural contacts and mutually advantageous trade. They urged the Canadian government to recognize Bangladesh, the Democratic Republic of Vietnam, and the German Democratic Republic; to support the calling of a European conference on security and cooperation; and to withdraw Canada from NATO.

The foreign and domestic policies of the Israeli government were attacked on several occasions. An editorial in the *Canadian Tribune* (13 December) insisted that "Israel's increditable masquerade as a defender of human worth can no longer hold back the odoriferous reality."

The Canadian communist press republished articles of Soviet scholars and journalists critical of Chinese diplomacy in and out of the United Nations and of the advice Peking is giving to pro-Maoist groups in the non-communist world.

The CPC and its auxiliary organizations celebrated the fiftieth anniversary of the Soviet Union at meetings and banquets across Canada. The Soviet ambassador in Ottawa and the minister for youth in the Tory provincial government of Ontario attended such a meeting in Toronto, to which the prime minister of Canada sent a good-will message. (Ibid.)

International Party Contacts. During 1972 Canadian communist leaders attended several conferences abroad. A delegate from the PCQ addressed the convention of the Communist Party, USA (CPUSA). The CPC was in attendance at the congress of the Communist Party of Israel, and the YCL at the convention of the Young Workers Liberation League in Chicago and the congress of the Bulgarian party's Communist Youth Union.

CPUSA chief Gus Hall visited Toronto in March and signed with William Kashtan a joint communiqué of "fraternal co-operation" in the struggle against "monopoly and U.S. imperialism." Angela Davis's sister spoke to the session of the CPC Central Committee in May.

A Canadian delegation of 27 persons, consisting of party members and non-communists, attended the "World Assembly for the Peace and Independence of the Vietnamese Peoples," Paris, in February 1972.

Publications. The weekly *Canadian Tribune,* published in Toronto, is the mouthpiece of the CPC. In April 1972 John Weir replaced as editor Mel Doig, who was appointed to the Editorial Council of *Problems of Peace and Socialism* in Prague. The West Coast edition of *Canadian Tribune,* called *Pacific Tribune,* appears in Vancouver. The theoretical journal *Communist Viewpoint* is published six times yearly in Toronto. The fortnightly *Combat* is the organ of the PCQ. The YCL publishes the *Young Worker* in Toronto.

The North American edition of the Prague-based monthly *Problems of Peace and Socialism* is printed in Toronto as the *World Marxist Review.* The fortnightly *Information Bulletin* is its companion publication.

*   *   *

The Communist Party of Canada (Marxist-Leninist). The Communist Party of Canada (Marxist-Leninist), or CPC(M-L), founded in 1970, is the leading Maoist organization in Canada. The membership consists mostly of young persons and includes a fair number of recent immigrants from the United States, the West Indies, and the Indian subcontinent. Leaders include Hardial Bains, chairman of the Norman Bethune Institute, and Robert A. Cruse, national secretary of the CPC(M-L).

The Federal Elections Manifesto of the CPC(M-L) listed "thirteen basic revolutionary movements amongst the Canadian and Quebec people," demanded the "elimination of U.S. imperialist domination of Canada and Quebec," and called for the "ascendancy of the working class as the ruling class." The 52 candidates of the CPC(M-L) won about 9,000 votes, compared to almost 7,000 for the pro-Soviet CPC. All the Maoist candidates lost their deposits and polled fewer votes than members of the CPC when both presented candidates in the same riding.

The CPC(M-L) has launched a number of duplicated bulletins, all of which appeared irregularly. The most authoritative is the *People's Canada Daily News Release.*

*   *   *

The League for Socialist Action/ Ligue Socialiste Ouvrière. The League for Socialiste Action/Ligue Socialiste Ouvrière (LSA/LSO) is the most important Trotskyist organization in Canada. Affiliated to the United Secretariat of the Fourth International in Paris, the LSA/LSO engaged in numerous polemics with the CPC. Members of the LSA/LSO were prominent in the Left Caucus in the NDP and in the peace, student, Gay Liberation, and women's movements. They also agitated within those French Canadian circles that are opposed to the Canadian federal system.

The LSA/LSO contested one riding in the 1972 federal elections. Its supporters and sympathizers stood as candidates in the municipal elections in Ottawa and Toronto. In the latter city the 25-year-old standard bearer of the LSA polled slightly more votes than the secretary of the CPC's Metro Toronto Committee, who was at the bottom of the poll with 0.8 percent of the votes cast.

At a plenary conference of the Central Committee of the LSA/LSO in September, Ross

Dawson was elected chairman, John Ridell executive secretary, and Gary Porter organizational secretary of the LSA /LSO.

A small group of Montreal Trotskyists led by Michel Mill, a member of the LSA /LSO Central Committee, broke away from the organization.

The fortnightly *Labor Challenge* is the organ of the LSA in Toronto. In Montreal the LSO publishes the monthly *Libération*. The mouthpiece of the youth organization of the LSA, the Young Socialists, is the *Young Socialist*.

University of British Columbia   Ivan Avakumovic

Chile

The Communist Party of Chile (Partido Comunista de Chile; PCCh) was first established as the Socialist Workers' Party in 1912 by Luis Emilio Recabarren. The name Communist Party of Chile was adopted in January 1922, following the party's decision in 1921 to join the Communist International. The PCCh was illegal from 1949 to 1958. It is firmly pro-Soviet in its international policies.

A pro-Chinese party, the Revolutionary Communist Party of Chile (Partido Comunista Revolucionario de Chile; PCRCh) was established in May 1966 primarily from members of the "Spartacus" group of communists which the PCCh expelled in late 1963. The Movement of the Revolutionary Left (Movimiento de Izquierda Revolucionaria; MIR) brought together several leftist groups in 1965.

PCCh membership at the time of the party's Fourteenth Congress, in November 1969, was said to be about 60,000. During 1972 party membership increased from 150,000 (Luis Corvalán, 2 January; Julieta Campusano, WMR, April) to 200,000 (Teitelboim, Granma, English ed., Havana, 14 January 1973).[1] In May 1971 Mario Zamorano said that workers comprised 65.3 percent of the membership, peasants 13.6 percent, while-collar workers 8.9 percent, intellectuals and persons of middle-class background 8.1 percent, and artisans 4.1 percent. Some 30 percent of the party members were women. According to Zamorano 30.6 percent of the members were under thirty years of age, 29.1 percent between thirty and forty, 20.7 percent between forty and fifty, and 19.6 percent over fifty (WMR, September 1971). The population of Chile is 10,044,900 (June 1972).

The PCCh holds 6 (out of 50) seats in the national Senate and 23 (out of 150) in the Chamber of Deputies, having added one in the latter in Coquimbo Province in July. In March 1972 the party nominated its candidates for the March 1973 congressional elections and in November it set itself the task of increasing its electoral backing from some 480,000 to approximately 1,000,000 prior to the March 1973 elections.

The Popular Unity Alliance. Between 1956 and 1969 the PCCh allied itself for electoral purposes with the Socialist Party (Partido Socialista de Chile; PSCh) in the Popular Action Front (Frente de Acción Popular; FRAP). In 1969 PCCh leaders repeatedly argued that leftist unity was necessary in order to transform Chile into a socialist state, but concluded that present conditions required an alliance more broadly based than the FRAP. Thus the PCCh played a leading role in founding the Popular Unity (Unidad Popular; UP), a coalition of six

---

[1] Luis Corvalán is said to have claimed there were "250,000 or so communists" early in the year (El Siglo, 13 February), presumably including members of the Communist Youth, whose membership is generally put at 60,000 (see below). Orlando Millas claimed 120,000 members at mid-year (El Siglo, 21 May).

(by the end of 1972 it was eight) leftist parties and movements at the end of 1969. (The UP program is translated in *Tricontinental,* Havana, March–April 1971, summarized in *YICA, 1971,* p. 388.) The PCCh was the best organized, most disciplined participant, in marked contrast to the second major party in the UP, the PSCh under its present Secretary General, Carlos Altamirano.

The UP presidential candidate in September 1970, PSCh member Salvador Allende, won only 36.30 percent of the popular vote and, in accordance with the Chilean constitution, had to be elected by the Chilean Congress in October 1970. The pro-UP vote in the March 1971 municipal elections was 49.73 percent, of which 16.97 percent went to the PCCh. During January 1972 the UP lost by-elections to fill a vacant Senate seat (46.4 to 52.6 percent), to a candidate supported by the two chief opposition parties, the Christian Democratic Party (Partido Demócrata Cristiano; PDC) and the National Party (Partido Nacional; PN), and to fill a vacant seat in the Chamber of Deputies (40.9 to 58.1 percent), to the candidate of the united opposition. As noted above, the UP candidate (PCCh-member Amanda Altamirano) beat the candidate of the combined opposition in a July by-election to fill a vacancy in the Chamber of Deputies in Coquimbo Province, though Altamirano received fewer votes than had UP candidates in the March 1971 municipal elections. Votes for UP candidates in labor and student elections will be noted below.

President Allende had five cabinets during 1972, each with many carry-over ministers. His original cabinet, appointed in October 1970, was reorganized or slightly altered in January, June, November, and December, in response to assorted political crises. For most of the year PCCh members held three top economic ministries (treasury, labor, and public works). Appointed in October 1970, and retained in January 1972, were Américo Zorrilla (treasury), José Oyarce (labor), and Pascual Barraza (public works). PCCh cabinet members between June and November were Orlando Millas (treasury), Mireya Baltra (labor), and Barraza. In November PCCh members in the Cabinet were Millas, Luis Figueroa (labor), and Sergio Insunza (justice). The Chamber of Deputies began impeachment proceedings against Orlando Millas in December on the grounds that he had violated the constitution and failed to live up to agreements which had led to the settlement of a costly, nation-wide strike of businessmen, professionals, truckers, and others in October. Millas was only the last of a series of Allende's ministers to be charged with violating the constitution in 1972, though he was the first PCCh member to be so charged. On 29 December President Allende side-stepped the impeachment proceedings by making Millas acting economy minister.

During 1971 the rightist and centrist parties, most importantly the PDC and PN, began to support single candidates in provincial and other elections in efforts (usually successful) to defeat UP candidates. Opposition and government fronts have been formed to run candidates in the 1973 elections, the former called the Confederation of Democratic Parties (Confederación de Partidos Democráticos) and the latter called the Federation of Popular Unity (Federación de la Unidad Popular).

Several times during the year the unity of the Popular Unity was threatened, most particularly after the electoral defeats in January (see above), during and after the Concepción crises in May and July (see below), and after the October strike.

The Single Center of Chilean Workers. The PCCh and PSCh have long controlled the Single Center of Chilean Workers (Central Unica de Trabajadores de Chile; CUTCh), Chile's only important labor confederation, which has an estimated 800,000 members (*NYT,* 6 June). At its Sixth Congress, December 1971, CUTCh president (and PCCh Central Committee member) Luis Figueroa announced that an election of confederation leaders by the rank and file would be held in 1973. The election lasted for more than a week beginning on 30 May and the official results, after a recount, were announced in July. The PCCh was declared the winner with 173,068 votes, the PSCh second with 148,140 votes, and the PDC third with 147,531 votes; the ten remaining contenders together received less than 80,000 votes. Figueroa was reelected president; Rolando Calderón (PSCh) was selected secretary general; Ernesto Vogel (PDC) was elected first vice-president. Fifty-four positions on the National Leadership Council were filled by the PCCh (18 seats), the PSCh (16), the PDC (16), and three other small groups (4). (*El Mercurio,* international edition, 10–16 July.) Election procedures, which had been challenged in early June, were again attacked by both the PSCh and the PDC in mid-July. The former sought the nullification of the election but finally accepted the results so as not to damage the unity of the workers. The PDC, which took control of the Santiago Provincial CUTCh Directorate, claimed that irregularities prevented its winning the national elections as well, a conclusion reached by some independent observers (e.g., Juan de Onís, *NYT* magazine, 17 December). In November, when Figueroa and Calderón were given cabinet posts, the National Leadership Council refused to let vice-president Vogel assume leadership of the CUTCh; a new president, PCCh member Jorge Uribe, former director of the Education Division of CUTCh, was appointed during the month (*Chile: Summary of Recent Events,* Embassy of Chile, Washington, D.C., 20 November).

Under PCCh and PSCh leadership the CUTCh has always been a firm supporter of UP policies. The 1972 election showed a spectacular increase in strength for the PDC and demonstrated the degree of labor opposition to UP policies.

The PCCh won 6 of 13 leadership positions—twice as many as the runner-up PSCh—in the Confederation of Copper Workers at its Fifth Congress in July (ibid., 3 August).

The PCCh is active in the Ranquil National Peasant and Indian Confederation (*WMR,* September 1971), which was said to incorporate over 130,000 persons, more than 50 percent of the agrarian labor force, in mid-1972 (*Ultima Hora,* Santiago, 10 May).

The Communist Youth. The PCCh-affiliated youth movement is the Communist Youth of Chile (Juventudes Comunistas de Chile; JCCh). Prominent members during 1972 were Gladys Marín (secretary general), Alejandro Rojas, and Antonio Leal. The JCCh reportedly had 50,000 members in January (Corvalán, *Pravda,* 2 January), and 60,000 at mid-year (Orlando Millas, *El Siglo,* 21 May), rising to 75,000 by early 1973 (Teitelboim, *Granma,* 14 January).

JCCh members, working in large part through the Ramona Parra Brigades, have been among the most loyal and enthusiastic supporters of the UP government. Continued support for UP policies and opposition to "fascist sedition" were the main topics at the JCCh's Seventh Congress in early September (on preparations for which ses *Principios,* July–August). The closing session of the congress was addressed by President Allende who called upon the JCCh to be prepared to form Committees for the Defense of the Revolution as proposed several days earlier by the PCCh (*La Prensa,* Santiago, 10 September). Throughout the year the JCCh condemned the "pseudo-revolutionary phraseology" of the "ultra-left," particularly the MIR, in university and national affairs (e.g., A. Leal, *El Siglo,* 20 May).

Several important elections in which the JCCh participated took place during the year. In January Antonio Leal was elected secretary general of the Student Federation at the University of Concepción (Federación de Estudiantes de Concepción; FEC), thus taking this important federation from the control of the MIR for the first time in recent years. At the same university in December the PDC and PN won the posts of rector and deputy rector by a wide margin (55 to 40 percent) over the UP candidates, but a UP-MIR slate won the following election for the FEC.

The University of Chile was the scene of the most publicized university election of the year, one which was widely interpreted as a serious setback for President Allende. The academic activities of the university had ground to a halt in late 1971 due to a power struggle between the opposition-supported rector, Edgardo Boeninger, and the UP-controlled Superior Council (Consejo Normativo Superior). Rector and Council resigned and stood for election on 27 April 1972. Opposing Boeninger was President Allende's hand-picked candidate, former president of the Inter-American Development Bank, Felipe Herrera, and several "ultra-leftist" candidates including Andrés Pascal Allende, President Allende's nephew, from the MIR. Boeninger received 51.87 percent of the vote to Herrera's 43.62 percent; the anti-UP Frente Revolucionario won 54 of the 100 elected seats (65 professors, 25 students, 10 staff) in the 104-member Superior Council, the UP winning 45 and the MIR front taking one. (*La Prensa*, 23 May.) Thus the opposition stunned the PCCh (see *El Siglo* editorial, 29 April) by taking control of both the rectorship and the Council for the first time in recent years. In July Alejandro Rojas was re-elected to the presidency of the Student Federation at the University of Chile with 40 percent of the vote; the UP took five of the ten positions on the Executive Committee, the PDC winning three and the PN two. (*Intercontinental Press*, New York, 31 July.)

The PCCh. Organization and Leadership. The party's secretary general is Luis Corvalán. The leading bodies of the PCCh are the Central Committee (75 members), Political Commission (15 members until the March plenum, then 9), and Secretariat (6 members before March, 7 after). The pre-March Political Commission included Corvalán, Víctor Díaz, Orlando Millas, José Oyarce, Gladys Marín, Mario Zamorano, Manuel Cantero, Rodrigo Rojas, Carlos Jorquera, Volodia Teitelboim, Jorge Insunza, Bernardo Araya, Julieta Campusano, José Cademártori, and Américo Zorrilla; after March it included Corvalán, Díaz (deputy secretary general), Zamorano, Millas, Teitelboim, Marín, Cademártori, Rafael Cortés, and Héctor Corvalán (died in May), with alternates Insunza, Mireya Baltra, and R. Rojas. The Secretariat after the March plenum included Corvalán, Díaz, Cortés, Zamorano, Samuel Riquelme, Campusano, and Jorquera.

Party Internal Affairs. The PCCh celebrated its fiftieth anniversary in January (see *Principios*, September-December 1971; *WMR*, January 1972; *IB*, no. 3, 1972). Plenary meetings of the Central Committee were held in March, June, August, and November. In March the PCCh reduced the size of its Political Commission (reportedly in order to facilitate discussion) and increased the size of the Secretariat, elected new members to these two bodies, released the names of its candidates for the 1973 congressional elections, and carried out an in-depth critical evaluation of its own and the UP's performance in 1971 and early 1972. Orlando Millas charged on 15 March that some Central Committee members and political officials had not tried hard enough to understand the new situation and new tasks and suffered in varying degrees from indolence, passiveness, accomodation, bureaucraticism, class conciliation, and sectarianism. The order of the day for the plenum, he asserted, was "to fight against opportunism and to begin by doing it at home" (i.e., within the PCCh). He greeted the "immense growth" of the party but warned that careful instruction of the new members was essential. ("En pie de guerra," pamphlet, 1972.) "Sectarian mistakes" by party militants were also elaborated at the June plenum. The August plenum was devoted to the agrarian question (see *IB*, October). The November plenum examined tactics for the upcoming congressional elections.

Domestic Attitudes and Activities. The present stage of the revolutionary process in Chile, according to Luis Corvalán, is "anti-imperialist, anti-latifundist and anti-oligarchy" (*WMR*, November). As Luis Padilla explains it, PCCh policy calls for "unity of all revolutionary, democratic, and progressive forces on the basis of an anti-imperialist, anti-oligarchic program, with socialism as its goal" (ibid., March). In several cases Corvalán argues that a distinctive feature of the Chilean process is "revolutionary change in the framework of the constitution" (ibid., November). However, in his book *Camino de Victoria* he wrote:

> We are for the peaceful way, but hold that the workers' and popular movement should discard the constraints of legality and follow not laws and constitutions established by the bourgeoisie, but their own class interests, taking into account the situation at each specific moment. . . . The peaceful way presupposes a class struggle and not class accord, not amicable coexistence between the exploited and the exploiter and not rejection of an armed struggle if such a struggle is required. (Quoted in *WMR*, March.)

Even in late May, however, after the flare-up between the PCCh and most other UP parties joined by the MIR in Concepción (see below), Corvalán insisted that an armed confrontation was not inevitable (*El Siglo*, 19 May).

A secret report of the PCCh Political Commission, prepared immediately after the UP electoral defeats in January, was published by an opposition paper in early February. It mentioned the need to open discussions with the PDC and the weakening of UP policies as a result of dissension within the PSCh and harassment by the "ultra-left." The Political Commission suggested that the party should not give "too much support" to President Allende but rather promote collective support by all UP parties. One of the most serious problems was in the countryside. The PCCh noted that though the UP had "expropriated farms to turn over to the peasants at a rate five-times faster than previous governments," the UP was "not becoming stronger in the countryside." UP agrarian policy was inconsistent, bursting with subjectivism from the "ultra-left." (*El Mercurio*, international edition, 31 January–6 February; also see below.)

According to Corvalán, nationalization had dealt a blow to the "whole system of imperialist domination;" agrarian reform had put an end to the "omnipotence of the latifundist;" state control over important aspects of the economy had "substantially undermined but not completely broken" the "economic might of the financial oligarchy." UP (and PCCh) objectives were still to "break reactionary resistance, extend the state sector, push ahead in agrarian reform, make all state-owned enterprises pay their way, raise production and productivity, develop economic planning, take the offensive against inflation, assure supplies of the things the country needs, improve job discipline," combat bureaucracy, extend education, housing, and public health. (*WMR*, November; and Orlando Millas, *El Siglo*, 5 June.)

On the day of President Allende's Second State-of-the-nation address in May, just after the UP crisis in Concepción, the PCCh lined the streets of downtown Santiago with party militants displaying banners which proclaimed: "With President Allende and the Program of the Popular Unity we defeat the provocations of the Ultra-right and the Ultra-left." Throughout the year the PCCh condemned the "ultra-right," the Chilean "fascists," who were charged with sedition, counterrevolutionary activities, and seeking to set off a civil war (e.g., *IB*, nos. 6-7; Corvalán, *El Siglo*, 19 May). The U.S. government and business community (particularly ITT) were regarded as the allies of the "fascists." An *El Siglo* editorial (19 May) asserted that "imperialism" sought a "confrontation among Chileans" and to this end was waging "a systematic campaign to discredit the UP government, relying in part on the confusion caused by the ultra-left."

Although PCCh leaders sometimes said the "ultra-left" received far too much attention in the news media (e.g., Corvalán in his press conference on 26 May), this political spectrum was condemned, often at great length, in virtually every PCCh speech or statement on domestic affairs. The "ultra-left," chiefly the MIR, but also the PCRCh and other small groups, was repeatedly labeled "petty-bourgeois" or "adventurist" and declared to be the ally of the ultra-right. Jorge Texier stated the PCCh critique of the MIR at mid-year:

> The ultra-Leftists' 'revolutionary' activity manifested itself above all in the countryside. They incited the peasants to seize land and interfered with the procedure of the agrarian reform specified by the Popular Unity, and this tended to turn what was an anti-oligarchic measure into an unwarranted attack on small and medium landholders and to mislead the politically ignorant peasants. The government's intentions were misrepresented, the reactionary press and opposition parties gained arguments in their favor and, indeed extended their social base in some rural areas. (*WMR,* July; also see Texier article in *Principios,* May-June.)

Volodia Teitelboim, one of the most frequent spokesmen for PCCh positions, told a meeting of party militants in early August that every victory for the people was followed by a provocative act by the MIR which enabled the Right to go on the offensive. Indeed, he charged that there were contacts which brought a "link-up of attitudes" between the ultra-left and the ultra-right. (*El Siglo,* 6 August; also see *WMR,* April, *IB,* nos. 16–17, and *El Siglo* editorial, 19 May.)

International Views and Positions. The PCCh is one of the most firmly pro-Soviet communist parties in Latin America. The party's domestic achievements and loyalty to the Communist Party of the Soviet Union (CPSU) have been widely acclaimed by the Soviet Union and its allies. At the 50th anniversary celebration in January, A. P. Kirilenko, a member of the CPSU Politburo, praised the PCCh for "enriching the international arsenal of forms and methods of dealing with socio-economic problems, the treasure-house of Communist and Workers' parties' collective experience" (*IB,* no. 3).

PCCh leaders themselves have denied that the electoral victory of the UP can serve as a "model" for others to follow. Nonetheless, Orlando Millas told a meeting of Latin American communist officials in 1971 that some features of the Chilean experience should be "taken into account regardless of the distinctive characteristics of the revolutionary movement in each particular country." These features, as summarized from Millas's comments by the *World Marxist Review* (July 1971), included

> the guiding political role of the Communist Party, the Communist-Socialist alliance, the unification of the working class in one trade union center, the mobilization of the peasantry to win a radical agrarian reform, the formation of a broad democratic, national revolutionary coalition on the basis of an anti-imperialist and anti-oligarchic program, the consolidation of mass organizations of the population (such as house committees) uniting various segments of the people in the fight for pressing demands, and the campaign for an educational reform.

The Chilean experience with agrarian reform was examined in detail at a conference of Latin American communist parties which convened in Lima on 12–15 June 1972 (see *Voz Proletaria,* 6 July).

PCCh relations with Cuba were friendly during the year. Fidel Castro's trip to the Soviet Union and Eastern Europe at mid-year was said to be of "unquestionable importance for the peoples who are struggling for their freedom and for those who have taken or are trying to travel rapidly down the road to socialism." Cooperation between Cuba and Chile was termed an "inevitable historical necessity" since they were the two countries in Latin America marching toward socialism. (*El Siglo,* editorial, 14 June.)

International Meetings and Contacts. On 12–15 June the PCCh was represented at a meeting of eight Latin American communist parties in Lima.

Seventy countries were represented at the Presidential Committee meeting of the World

Peace Council (WPC) in Santiago on 4–9 October. WPC Secretary General Romesh Chandra presented the Joliot-Curie Gold Medal to Salvador Allende in recognition of his efforts for world peace. Among the speakers were Allende and PCCh members Alejandro Rojas and Olga Poblete, Krishna Menon (India), Ralph Abernathy and Angela Davis (USA). (*El Siglo,* issues between 4 and 10 October.) In Santiago the WPC decided to give the Joliot-Curie award to several other individuals, including Fidel Castro.

The Second Latin American Women's Seminar, sponsored by the Women's International Democratic Federation, attended by 156 delegates and observers from 35 Latin American, Asian, African, and European countries, and from the USA, met in Santiago on 23–28 October. According to the Chilean Sponsoring Committee, the Seminar was intended to "produce a better understanding between Latin American women and to arouse awareness of the need for greater female participation in development and progress in their respective countries" (*El Siglo,* 8 September). President Allende, whose wife played a leading role in the meeting, addressed the closing session.

Among the guests at the 50th anniversary celebration of the PCCh in January were: Andrei Kirilenko (Soviet Union), Jorge Risquet (Cuba), Paul Verner (East Germany), Kazimierz Barcikowski (Poland), Josef Lenárt (Czechoslovakia), Petre Lupu (Romania), Peko Takov (Bulgaria), Arpád Pullai (Hungary), Miroslav Recujlic (Yugoslavia), Nguyen Thanh Binh (North Vietnam), and Henry Winston (United States). Other visitors to Chile included Pompeyo Márquez, of the Venezuelan Movement Toward Socialism, in March, and Enrique Pastorino, a prominent Uruguayan communist who is president of the World Federation of Trade Unions, in August.

Luis Figueroa attended the 20th Congress of the CPUSA in March; Volodia Teitelboim was in Paris in February and in Cuba in September; and Luis Corvalán visited the Soviet Union, Eastern Europe (he received the Georgi Dimitrov award in Bulgaria) and Cuba in November and December.

Publications. The most important of the PCCh publications are *El Siglo,* the daily official organ of the party, edited by Rodrigo Rojas, and the theoretical journal *Principios* edited by Jorge Insunza. The PCCh also controls the daily paper *Puro Chile.* All are published in Santiago.

*   *   *

The PCRCh. The Revolutionary Communist Party is a small organization which was founded in 1966. The party has probably never had more than several hundred active members. Though most party statements are made anonymously, Juan Báez is known to be among the top party members. Unofficial spokesmen include Robinson Rojas, editor of *Causa Marxista-Leninista* and for some time the Chilean correspondent for the New China News Agency. Changes in Chinese Communist foreign policy since 1970 have evidently led to some internal dissension within the PCRCh, to the spread of "petty-bourgeois" and "revisionist" ideas, and to the expulsion of such "renegades" as José Guevara (*En Defensa de la Línea Proletaria,* pamphlet, 1971). The PCRCh claims to be the first party in Chilean history to truly represent the interests of the masses of workers and peasants (*El Pueblo,* 1 May 1972).

In December 1971, immediately prior to the convening of the CUTCh's Sixth Congress, the PCRCh contrasted the "bourgeois" line of the CUTCh under Luis Figueroa to the "proletarian" line it advocated. The former sought to immobilize the workers, turning them away from their "fundamental task: the seizure of power." (*El Pueblo,* December 1971.) The

PCRCh tried to get Clotario Blest to run for the presidency of CUTCh (ibid., March 1972) but when he did not run supported José Reyes V. and, for other offices, PCRCh and independent candidates. Reyes received 3,216 votes and PCRCh got no positions on the National Leadership Council (*El Mercurio,* international edition, 10–16 July).

The PCRCh was also active in the campaign to elect a rector at the University of Chile, supporting Luis Vitale. Though Vitale received only 418 votes, slightly less than one percent of the total, his candidacy was condemned by the PCCh for leading to the confusion and fragmentation of the left in general (*El Siglo,* 29 April).

Domestic and International Positions. The fundamental enemies of the Chilean people, according to a PCRCh spokesman, are "Yankee imperialism, the large industrial, commercial and financial monopolies, and the latifundists." Thus, the great battle of the Chilean people will be to liberate themselves from imperialism and domestic exploitation. *(Causa Marxista-Leninista,* July–August 1971.) Allende's government is merely completing the reformist policies begun more than 20 years ago (*El Pueblo,* 1 May 1972), by early 1972 already falling increasingly under the influence of the military (ibid., March). In order to complete its "historical task," the Chilean proletariat must "accumulate forces through the struggle, basing itself on the worker-peasant alliance, under the leadership of the proletariat, and its Marxist-Leninist party, and with the support of the broad sectors of the rest of those exploited by imperialism and the large national exploiters" (*La situación actual y las tareas politicas del proletariado y su partido,* pamphlet, 1971).

The PCRCh condemns the "modern revisionism" of the CPSU, and praises the Chinese Communists, who have "led the world struggle against revisionism, a struggle which finds expression in the victorious Proletarian Cultural Revolution" (*Peking Review,* 13 August 1971). U.S. President Nixon's trip to the People's Republic was interpreted as an admission of defeat by the United States and was not seen as a Chinese betrayal of its revolutionary ideals (*El Pueblo,* March 1972; *Causa Marxista-Leninista,* December 1971–January 1972).

Publications. The official organ of the PCRCh, issued irregularly, is *El Pueblo.* Party statements, and unofficial PCRCh views, appear regularly in *Causa Marxista-Leninista.* Both are published in Santiago.

*   *   *

The MIR. The Movement of the Revolutionary Left was formed in 1965 and in December 1967 became an avowedly "Castroite" organization advocating the armed road to power enunciated at the Latin American Solidarity Organization (OLAS) conference held in Havana in August of that year. Early in 1969 the MIR went underground and did not surface again until after Salvador Allende's inauguration as president of Chile in November 1970. During 1972 the MIR continued as before to operate on or beyond the left-most fringes of the Popular Unity.

MIR leaders include Secretary General Miguel Enríquez and other members of the National Secretariat, including Humberto Sotomayor, Roberto Moreno, Bautista von Schowen, Nelson Gutiérrez, and Andrés Pascal Allende.

The MIR dominates two leftist university fronts. The most important is the University Movement of the Left (Movimiento Universitario de Izquierda; MUI) at the University of Concepción. In January 1972 the MUI lost the elections for the University Student Federation at Concepción (FEC) for the first time in five years; in a communiqué released after the election the MUI accused the victorious UP slate of having directed its campaign (of "rumor and slander, lies and deceit") against the MUI rather than against the opposition forces of the PDC and PN. The MIR also controls the Revolutionary Students' Front (Frente de Estudiantes Revolucionarios; FER) at the University of Chile in Santiago. The FER candidate for rector in the May election (see above), Andrés Pascal, was highly critical of the UP election strategy (particularly the Herrera candidacy), charging that "a halting, defeatist policy sows confusion among the masses and weakens the revolutionary forces" (*Punto Final,* 11 April). When the FER received less than 4 percent of the vote, the Front, with its professional and staff counterparts, declared that "once again reformism has paved the road to fascism" (*El Rebelde,* 2 May). The FER candidate received 6 percent of the vote in the elections for the University of Chile Student Federation (FECh) in July.

The MIR controls the Revolutionary Workers' Front (Frente de Trabajadores Revolucionarios; FTR), whose candidate for the presidency of CUTCh, Alejandro Alarcón, received some 10,000 of the 560,000 votes cast. The FTR won one seat on the National Leadership Council (*El Mercurio,* international edition, 10–16 July; FTR platform in *El Rebelde,* 23 May.) Other MIR-controlled organizations include the Revolutionary Peasant Movement (Movimiento Campesino Revolucionario; MCR), which is active directing rural land seizures, and the Movement of the Revolutionary Poor (Movimiento de Pobladores Revolucionarios; MPR), which operates in Chile's squatter settlements and urban areas.

The MIR's frequently stated objectives are the uprooting of the Chilean state and social structure—which it charges with serving only the interests of capitalists and "imperialists"—and its replacement by a socialist state which serves the workers. The controversial position of the MIR within the Chilean left does not derive from this long-term goal, however, but from its concept of the proper road to its achievement. According to the MIR, President Allende asked the "big question" in his state-of-the-union speech on 21 May: will the existing institutions be able to "open up the way for a transition to socialism." The UP has generally answered the question in the affirmative; the MIR has always answered in the negative.

The MIR did not support Allende in his campaign for the presidency in 1970. Since his inauguration the MIR has professed its willingness to defend the UP from any attacks originating on the right, though it has remained critical of any effort to make a revolution through the use of existing institutional structures. The severity of the MIR critique of the UP has varied from one time to another and has generally been aimed at the PCCh, which it correctly sees as the most influential single force in the government.

The MIR dispute with the PCCh (also see above) was at a high level most of the year as reflected in the three instances mentioned below. The MIR carried out a form of agitational campaigning which was intended to radicalize the masses for the January 1972 by-elections, particularly in Linares Province, which the PCCh said alienated many of the UP's natural allies and assured electoral defeat (see MIR declaration in *El Rebelde,* 1 February). The conflict came to a head on 12 May when the MIR joined forces with the majority of the UP provincial committees (without authorization from national UP headquarters), in defiance of the PCCh committee and the mayor of Concepción, to carry out a mass demonstration. One leftist was killed when the police broke it up on order from the mayor, a PCCh member. And in July the MIR again joined up with the majority of the Concepción branches of the UP, again in defiance of the Communists, to form a "People's Assembly" (Asamblea Popular), which was to supersede the "reactionary" National Congress. President Allende denounced the action as a "divisionist maneuver" which strengthened the opponents of the UP, and all of the main headquarters of the UP parties in Santiago repudiated it, though not without some dissenting voices. The MIR regularly calls for the promotion of People's Councils (Consejos Comunales) of workers and peasants as a first step toward a People's Assembly on the national level (see, e.g., *El Rebelde,* 2 May).

At a press conference after the first Concepción event (excerpted in *Punto Final,* 6 June, supplement), Miguel Enríquez denounced the PCCh at great length. He rejected the PCCh slogan of the day— "With President Allende . . ." (see above)—and said the MIR sought to go on the offensive with the masses to defeat the reactionaries, to overcome reformism in the ranks of the left, and to end the repression of leftist revolutionaries. (Also see *El Rebelde* editorial, 23 May.)

MIR disputes with the UP over agrarian reform and revolution in the countryside were also directed primarily toward the PCCh. According to the MIR the PCCh has incorrectly analyzed the class structure of the countryside and has become a pillar of support for the "big agricultural bourgeoisie" which it disguises under the name of "middle landlords and farmers." The most serious shortcoming of the "anti-peasant" policy of the PCCh is its failure to take account of the fact that the confrontation in the countryside is between the "big agricultural bourgeoisie" on the one hand and the rural proletariat and poor peasants on the other. PCCh policy "coincides with the policy that imperialism has been promoting in Latin America" since 1959. MIR policy, on the contrary, is aimed at mobilizing the masses in order to destroy the social, economic, and political power base of the big bourgeoisie by legal and extra-legal means. (*La Política del MIR en el Campo,* pamphlet, most of which is translated in *Intercontinental Press,* New York, 17 April and 1 May.)

On 27 August, when the cost of living increase for 1972 reached 100 percent, the MIR called for cost of living benefits of 100 percent for low-income families. After the October strike the MIR issued a statement (8 November) praising the working people, settlers, poor farmers, and students for taking control of production and distribution and paving the way for the construction of popular power. At the same time it criticized the government for fearing the masses and for introducing the military into the cabinet.

Publication. The weekly organ of the MIR is *El Rebelde.* MIR statements are often carried in *Punto Final.* Both are published in Santiago.

*　　*　　*

Among the other Marxist-Leninist organizations in Chile are: a cluster of small groups which were formed largely of MIR dissidents, including the People's Organized Vanguard (Vanguardia Organizada del Pueblo; VOP), which was responsible for the assassination of a former PDC minister in 1971; the "Manuel Rodríguez" Revolutionary Movement (Movimiento Revolucionario "Manuel Rodríguez; MR–2); and two groups which first appeared in 1972, the "Red Flag" Communist Party (Partido Comunista "Bandera Roja"; PCBR), and the National Liberation Army (Ejército de Liberación Nacional; ELN). The only Trotskyist party in Chile is the Revolutionary Workers' Party—Trotskyist (Partido Obrero Revolucionario—Trotskista; PORT), which is aligned with the Fourth International—International Secretariat (Posadas faction).

Hoover Institution
Stanford University

William E. Ratliff

Colombia

The communist movement in Colombia began within the ranks of the Socialist Revolutionary Party (Partido Socialista Revolucionario; PSR) shortly after the party's formation in December 1926. Contacts between the PSR and the Communist International during 1929 and 1930 inspired a group of PSR members to proclaim publicly the creation of the Communist Party of Colombia (Partido Comunista de Colombia; PCC) on 17 July 1930. The party has retained this designation ever since except for a short period (1944–47) during which it was called the Social Democratic Party (Partido Social Democrático). In July 1965 a schism within the PCC between pro-Soviet and pro-Chinese factions resulted in the latter's becoming the Communist Party of Colombia, Marxist-Leninist (Partido Comunista de Colombia, Marxista-Leninista; PCC-ML). Only the PCC has legal status.

The population of Colombia is 23,000,000 (estimated 1972). The PCC is estimated to have 10,000 to 12,000 members and exercises only marginal influence in national affairs.

PCC candidates were allowed to campaign under their own party label in the April 1972 elections for departmental assemblies and municipal councils. The party ran separate slates for assembly in 17 out of Colombia's 22 departments, the Federal District of Bogotá, and the Intendancy of Caquetá. According to unofficial returns, the PCC received approximately 1.7 percent of the total assembly vote (less than 50,000 votes), compared with less than 0.5 percent of the total vote in 1970 when PCC candidates were required to run under the banner of the Liberal Revolutionary Party. The PCC received its highest electoral support in the Department of Meta, obtaining just under 12 percent of the vote. Other departments where the PCC received more than 2 percent of the total vote were Cundinamarca (4.7 percent), Quindío (4.6), Tolima (4.6), Atlántico (2.1), the Federal District (2.5), and Caquetá (7.8).

Guerrilla warfare, although not a serious threat to the government, has been a feature of Colombian life since the late 1940s, the current wave beginning in 1964. The three main guerrilla organizations are the PCC-controlled Revolutionary Armed Forces of Colombia (FARC), the pro-Chinese People's Liberation Army (EPL), and the Castroite National Liberation Army (ELN). Estimates of membership early in 1972 ranked the ELN first with about 250 men, followed by the FARC and the EPL with 150 and 80 members respectively (*NYT*, 23 January 1972). Although guerrilla actions, particularly by the ELN, appeared to be on the increase early in the year, heavy casualities and the mass arrest of suspected urban supporters in mid-year are believed to have reduced substantially the organizational strength of all three movements.

The PCC. Leadership and Organization. The PCC is headed by its 12-member Executive Committee and 45-member Central Committee. Gilberto Vieira is secretary general of the party. Members of the Executive Committee include, besides Vieira: Alvaro Vásquez, Joaquín

Moreno, Jesús Villegas, Roso Osorio, Hernando Hurtado, Julio Posada, Gustavo Castro, Gustavo Osorio, Juan Viana, Manlio Lafont, and Manuel Cepeda Vargas.

The PCC controls the Trade Union Confederation of Workers of Colombia (Confederación Sindical de Trabajadores de Colombia; CSTC), which claims a membership of 150,000. The PCC vigorously opposes a proposed merger between Colombia's two largest labor organizations—the Union of Workers of Colombia (Unión de Trabajadores de Colombia; UTC) and the Confederation of Workers of Colombia (Confederación de Trabajadores de Colombia; CTC). On several occasions in 1972, UTC and CTC officials denounced efforts by the PCC to increase its influence among labor organizations. Similar charges were directed against the Soviet Embassy for allegedly supporting subversive activities within the labor movement. TELECOM, a 9,000-member communications union, and at least three smaller unions, were expelled from the UTC in 1972 for their "marked communist activity" (*El Tiempo,* Bogotá, 18 September). In July government authorities occupied the CSTC headquarters in Bogotá and arrested several leaders to prevent an unauthorized demonstration march to protest the high cost of living. The PCC's principal labor spokesman is Roso Osorio, secretary general of the CSTC.

The PCC intensified its efforts to increase communist influence within the 900,000-member National Peasant Association of Land Users (Asociación Nacional de Usuarios Campesinos; ANUC). Although founded by the government to encourage peasant participation in the development and implementation of agrarian reform, the ANUC has formulated independent policies under its president, Jaime Vásquez. At a Peasant Congress in February, Vásquez exhorted peasant leaders "to foment an open struggle against the huge land-owning class of the country" (*El Tiempo,* 9 February). The PCC opposes both government initiatives and attempts by Vásquez to exercise control over ANUC's policies and activities. The party attacked the latter for heading a "Trotskyite faction" intent on imposing its own control and leadership (*Voz Proletaria,* 20 July). Although unable to control Vásquez' group, the government has attempted to operate through him to combat the influence of independent agrarian sectors organized by the PCC. No clear political orientation emerged from the Second National Peasant Congress held in July. Attempts by Vásquez to proscribe communist participation in the Congress were defeated by a majority of the 107 delegates who attended. Ideological, sectarian, and personalist differences within ANUC hampered the party's effort to expand its influence (*ibid.*). The principal PCC agrarian leaders with membership in the ANUC are Víctor J. Merchán and Gerardo González.

The PCC's youth organization, the Communist Youth of Colombia (Juventud Comunista de Colombia; JUCO) has its own National Directorate, Executive Committee, and Central Committee. The secretary-general is Carlos Romero, a member of the PCC's Central Committee. In a speech on 1 May, Gilberto Vieira stated that the JUCO's principal task was to work toward the formation of a broad youth movement of opposition as an integral part of the Democratic Opposition Front proposed by the PCC (*Juventud,* Bogotá, 25 May). At the June plenary meeting of the Central Committee, plans were discussed to intensify recruitment activities among urban and rural youth. The plenary report attacked the extremist positions of Maoist and Trotskyite groups and reaffirmed the need to combat official measures that weaken student demands for co-government within the university system (*Voz Proletaria,* 22–28 June). Subsequent recommendations called for communist youth to assist in the organization of all revolutionary groups that state their agreement with the PCC's "politics of popular unity." Special attention was directed toward increasing JUCO's contacts among secondary school students by creating new committees of support and consolidating its influence within the National Secondary Students Union (ibid., 6 July). JUCO's Central Committee announced preparations to hold a Second National Seminar on University Reform early in 1973. In October government security forces raided JUCO's national headquarters and arrested 13 members in connection with student disorders in the capital (*El Espectador,* Bogotá, 12 October). The raid followed charges by the minister of education that "paid agitators" within JUCO were responsible for the continued disruption of normal activities at the National University. Communist youth delegations from Latin America and the Soviet bloc countries have been invited to attend JUCO's Third Congress, to be held in 1973. Carlos Romero announced that a special invitation had been extended to U.S. communist Angela Davis (*Voz Proletaria,* 28 September).

The PCC has controlled a peasant guerrilla group since 1966, the Revolutionary Armed Forces of Colombia (Fuerzas Armadas Revolucionarias de Colombia; FARC). In accordance with Soviet policy, the role of guerrilla warfare has been deemphasized by the PCC in recent years (*IB,* no. 1–2). Several minor skirmishes between the FARC and government troops occurred in the departments of Antioquia, Tolima, and Huila in 1972. However, for the most part the PCC limited the scope of FARC's operations to "defense-type actions." The Colombian Army reported the reappearance of a FARC guerrilla unit in the area of Caquetá, believed to be under the command of Germán Roca, a former lieutenant of Januario Valero who was captured in 1970 (*El Tiempo,* 25 February). Manuel Marulanda Vélez continues as FARC's commander in chief. He has official status in the PCC as a member of the Central Committee (*WMR,* February). Rumors of a possible alliance between the FARC and the ELN persisted in 1972, despite the recognized existence of fundamental differences in ideology and tactics (*Intercontinental Press,* New York, 28 February).

Domestic Attitudes and Activities. In line with its policy of combining various forms of struggle, the PCC considers it important to participate in elections. Despite its limited representation in the departmental assemblies and municipal councils, the party is convinced for the present that elective bodies can be used as an effective forum (*WMR,* February 1972).

In accordance with PCC resolutions passed at its Eleventh Congress, the party continues to emphasize the creation of a united front movement as its "most important task" (*Voz Proletaria,* 16 December 1971). While such a movement failed to materialize in time for the April 1972 elections, the PCC's Central Committee approved a proposal for the formation of a democratic opposition front at its plenary session on 20–21 May (*Voz Proletaria,* 25 May). The committee subsequently reaffirmed its determination to reach an understanding with other opposition groups, especially with the National Popular Alliance (Alianza Nacional Popular; ANAPO), the largest opposition party, headed by former dictator Gustavo Rojas Pinilla. Committee member Alvaro Vásquez outlined a course of action which would involve "continuous cooperation among communists, ANAPO members, and other popular segments . . . that would form the foundation for a powerful people's movement" (*Voz Proletaria,* 22 June). The PCC has expressed its opposition to Rojas's views on agrarian reform. It has also criticized him for "ideological confusion" in advocating a "Colombian-styled socialism" which considers capitalism and communism equally imperialistic (ibid., 6 July). Rojas's resistance to any compromise on ANAPO's platform or his unilateral choice of a presidential candidate for 1974 makes an alliance with the PCC highly improbable.

In September leaders from the PCC, the Christian Democratic Socialist Party (PSDC), and the Broad Popular Movement (MAP), comprised of former members of ANAPO, approved the basic platform of a united opposition front (*El Tiempo,* 23 September). Gilberto Vieira termed the coalition "an important step toward building socialism in the country" (*New Times,* no. 43, October). The Coordinating Committee established for the new front, tentatively named the Union of National Opposition (Unión de Oposición Nacional; UNO), made plans in October for a national congress to be held in February 1973. As a minimal basis for UNO's program, the Committee adopted proposals to lift the state of siege, to nationalize subsoil resources, to carry out a "democratic" agrarian reform, to expropriate urban latifundia, to curb monopolies, to reform all educational systems, and to adopt an independent policy of solidarity with "the countries which are struggling for their liberation from foreign aggression" (*Voz Proletaria,* 5–11 October). In November it was reported that the ANUC, CSTC, and other workers' organizations will soon join the front (*Times of the Americas,* New York, 24 November).

Throughout the year the PCC waged an ideological battle against the "ultra-leftist" groups who oppose the party's line and tactics, especially as they relate to Colombia's continuing university crisis. Gilberto Vieira censured the extremist activity of small groups for their "abstract worship of terrorism" and called upon communist youth to combat "adventurism" within the student movement (*Juventud,* 25 May).

The PCC responded editorially to various charges by high-ranking union leaders, military spokesmen, journalists, and assorted government officials of Soviet-supported subversion in Colombia during 1972. In July the Executive Committee called for vigilance in opposing the "fascist" orientation of sectors within the military. The PCC stated that the resurgence of "military fascism" was related to the "hysterical anti-Communist and anti-Soviet campaign" waged following the arrest of alleged urban supporters of the ELN and the deportation of various Soviet officials suspected of espionage activities (*Voz Proletaria,* 27 July). In September Vieira called upon party members to "unmask the reactionary, anti-national content of the anti-Soviet campaign being waged in Colombia by agents of North American imperialism" (ibid., 7–13 September).

To counter the anti-Soviet campaign and to broaden communist influence among labor, student, and peasant groups, the PCC announced plans to hold a National Organizational Conference in late 1972. Other objectives included a national campaign to finance the united opposition front and to increase the circulation of *Voz Proletaria* by 50,000 copies (ibid., 3–9 August).

International Views and Positions. The PCC continued in 1972 to be a firm supporter of the international positions taken by the Soviet Union. Hemispherically, the party expressed continuing solidarity with Cuba and the Chilean Popular Unity government. Party statements lauded visits to the Soviet Union by Fidel Castro and Salvador Allende as "evidence of the internationalist bonds forged between the U.S.S.R. and the peoples of Latin America." The PCC endorsed the independent action taken by Peru and Chile in reestablishing relations with Cuba, although similar plaudits were not extended in the case of Peru's recognition of the People's Republic of China. In May the Central Committee adopted a resolution condemning U.S. "attempts to precipitate economic crises in Chile and Peru by blocking the extension of credit and loans" (*Voz Proletaria,* 18 May). At a meeting commemorating the 20th anniversary of the founding of JUCO, Vieira reaffirmed the party's loyalty to Moscow and its determination "to continue the struggle against U.S. monopolies" (ibid., 5 May). The military assistance pact between Colombia and the United States was also the focus of criticism "for instituting a policy of greater dependency on the United States" (ibid.). The PCC expressed support for the Soviet line in condemnation of Israel and support for North Vietnam (ibid., 29 June).

The PCC continues to press for an expansion of trade and an increase in cultural, technical, and scientific exchange between Colombia, the Soviet Union, and other members of the socialist bloc. Trade delegations from the Soviet Union and various European socialist countries visited Colombia in 1972. Official and private sources have expressed growing concern over "communist infiltration" resulting from expanded relations with socialist countries. Tradé relations with the Soviet Union were also criticized on strictly economic grounds (*El Tiempo,* 12 February; *El Siglo,* 16 February).

International Party Contacts. The PCC was represented at a conference held in Lima on 12–15 June to discuss Latin American experience with agrarian reform. A PCC delegation visited the Soviet Union and Romania in July in order to become acquainted with the work of party and trade union organizations. A second delegation visited Romania on 10–14 August "to further the relations of friendship, cooperation and international solidarity between the two parties." JUCO was represented at the congress of the Communist Youth of Chile, in August, and the congress of the Czechoslovak Socialist Youth Union, in late September.

Publications. The PCC publishes a weekly newspaper, *Voz Proletaria;* a theoretical journal, *Estudios Marxistas;* and a news sheet, *Noticias de Colombia.* JUCO announced plans to edit a special publication, *Tribuna,* to promote its Third Congress and to disseminate theoretical and organizational information. The FARC publishes a clandestine bulletin, *Resistencia.*

* * *

The PCC-ML. The Communist Party of Colombia, Marxist-Leninist is firmly pro-Chinese. Its leadership hierarchy is not clearly known, but important positions have been held in recent years by Francisco Gárnica, Pedro Vásquez, and Pedro Lupo León Arboleda. The PCC-ML has an estimated membership of 1,000. The party was relatively inactive in 1972 and its organizational strength and finances are believed to be declining.

Within the labor movement, the PCC-ML continued to exercise some influence over the Bloque Independiente, a small trade union organization with an estimated membership of 20,000. The Independent Revolutionary Workers' Movement (MOIR), established in 1971, also follows a pro-Chinese orientation. The MOIR joined a loose electoral alliance of leftist movements for the 1972 elections which included Alberto Zalamea's Popular Front (Frente Popular), the Patriotic Youth (Juventud Patriótica; JUPA), and the Front of Revolutionary Intellectuals (Frente de Intelectuales Revolucionarios). The MOIR leadership justified its electoral participation as "an additional means to develop the revolutionary conscience of the masses" (*El Tiempo,* 20 January). The alliance received less than 0.5 percent of the total assembly vote.

The PCC-ML's guerrilla arm, the EPL, was the first pro-Chinese attempt to stage a revolutionary "people's war" in Latin America. Although it derived some support in 1972 from sympathizers among university students, the EPL has not fully recovered from the loss of two of its principal leaders who were killed in a clash with government troops in December 1971. Colombian Army units continued to inflict heavy casualties on the EPL in 1972 and reportedly captured two of the movement's founders (*El Tiempo,* 5 July). At the end of the year surviving units of the EPL were operating principally in Antioquia Department. One source reported the movement had reduced its armed activities and was now intensifying its indoctrination effort in Colombia's larger cities (*El Siglo,* 13 September).

The PCC-ML contributed to university unrest in 1972 with continued support of pro-Maoist groups. The decision by student leaders within MOIR and JUPA to participate in the April elections created internal division within the Maoist ranks. The defection of the most radical Maoist elements has apparently brought an end to pro-Chinese dominance in student associations at some of Colombia's major universities. The existing anarchy within fragmented student groups crippled the university system in 1972.

Publications. The organ of the PCC-ML is *Revolución*. PCC-ML statements are sometimes found in Chinese publications and those of pro-Chinese parties in Europe and Latin America.

*   *   *

The ELN. The National Liberation Army was formed in Santander, in 1964, under the inspiration of the Cuban Revolution. It undertook its first military action in 1965. In contrast to the limited operations of the pro-Chinese EPL and the pro-Soviet FARC, the ELN engaged in a series of attacks on army patrols, kidnapings, and other related activities during 1972. The ELN's dramatic actions early in the year belied government assertions in late 1971 that the movement had been annihilated. On 7 January a group headed by the ELN's founder and highest-ranking leader, Fabio Vásquez Castaño, occupied the small town of San Pablo in Bolívar Department, killing three policemen, kidnaping several ranch owners for ransom, and stealing weapons and food supplies (*El Tiempo,* 8 January). On 16 January ELN units coordinated attacks on three towns and two large farms in the northeastern section of Antioquia Department. These attacks were led by Ricardo Lara Parada and Fabio's brother, Manuel. The combined actions reportedly involved more than 200 guerrillas (*Intercontinental Press,* 28 February).

In April Colombia's commander of the army denied that ELN actions in Antioquia, in which 8 soldiers were killed, represented a resurgence of subversive groups. He announced that the army had increased its activities to curb guerrilla action and described general public order in the country as "normal" (*El Tiempo,* 25 April). At least six ELN members were killed in clashes with army patrols in Antioquia during May and June.

In July a Colombian army patrol gained possession of compromising ELN documents that reportedly were left behind by Fabio Vásquez following an encounter near Otú, Santander. These documents revealed the existence of a vast urban guerrilla network which maintained direct contacts with the ELN. On 12 July Colombia's defense minister declared that "more than 60 members" of the ELN's urban network had been arrested in Bogotá, Bucaramanga, Tunja, Socorro, Aguachica, and Barrancabermeja (Radio Cadena Nacional, 12 July). Subsequent arrests carried out in late July and August brought the number of suspected ELN urban supporters held for trial to 94 (*El Tiempo,* 2 September). Among those apprehended were government employees, priests, professionals, and students. Although minor ELN guerrilla actions were reported in Santander and Antioquia during October and November, it is generally believed that the various ELN units are now forced to operate without benefit of the intelligence and logistics assistance formerly provided by its urban network.

Washington College   Daniel L. Premo

Costa Rica

The Communist Party of Costa Rica (Partido Comunista de Costa Rica) was founded in 1931 and accepted as a full member of the Comintern in 1935. In 1943, following the wartime policy of many Latin American parties, the Costa Rican communists reorganized under a new name, the Popular Vanguard Party (Partido Vanguardia Popular; PVP).

The Authentic Revolutionary Movement (Movimiento Revolutionaria Auténtico; MRA) is a small guerrilla group.

The PVP has been outlawed since 1948. Although in the past few years the party has, in fact, operated openly, its attempts to have the proscribing article of the constitution repealed have failed. In 1970 the PVP was able to elect two members (including Secretary-General Manuel Mora) to the 58-member Legislative Assembly as candidates of the leftist Socialist Action Party (Partido de Acción Socialista; PASO). In preparation for the February 1974 general elections the PASO nominated Manuel Mora as its candidate for the presidency of Costa Rica (*Libertad,* 14 October 1972). The PVP is probably the best organized and most sophisticated communist party in Central America but its aging leadership, small size, and illegal status preclude its having any effective role in present Costa Rican affairs.

The membership of the PVP, which reached a peak of about 3,000 in 1948, is now estimated to number 1,000. The population of Costa Rica as of 30 June 1971 was 1,785,691 (*La Prensa Libre,* San José, 10 February 1972).

Organization and Leadership. Manuel Mora Valverde, founder of the PVP, has been secretary-general of the party from its beginning. The assistant secretary-general is his brother, Eduardo Mora Valverde. The organizational secretary is Arnoldo Ferreto Segura ("Oscar Vargas").

The PVP is active in the labor movement through the General Confederation of Costa Rican Workers (Confederación General de Trabajadores Costarricenses; CGTC) which it controls. The CGTC is believed to have about 2,500 members out of 24,000 unionized workers in Costa Rica. The secretary-general of the CGTC is Alvaro Montero Vega. Recently the CGTC began publishing the newspaper, *El Orientador* the purpose of which is to encourage the "working class to adopt revolutionary positions" (*WMR,* September). The PVP sponsors the United Agricultural Workers' and Peasants' Federation (FUNTAC) and claims to be actively engaged in forming peasant organizations in all the provinces of Costa Rica. In January FUNTAC held its annual meeting with reports that 6,000 agricultural workers and 3,000 campesinos attended. Guests from a number of Latin American countries were also invited. A national incident occurred when the Costa Rican government expelled two Soviet visitors and a Guyanese trade union official as subversives and threatened to prohibit the meeting.

PVP work among youth is carried out through its affiliate, Vanguard Youth (Juventud

Vanguardia de Costa Rica; JVCR) and its university detachment, the University Action Front (Frente de Acción Universitaria; FAU). The secretary-general of the JVCR is Luis Orlando Corrales.

The secretary-general of the FAU is Oscar Madrigal Jiménez. Its weekly organ, *Unidad,* has a circulation of 5,000. The membership of FAU is reportedly quite small and the group has only limited influence within the all-university student organization, Federation of University Students of Costa Rica (Federación de Estudiantes Universitarios de Costa Rica; FEUCR). In anticipation of the FEUCR elections in April, the FAU merged with several other leftist student groups, including the People's Student Front and the Socialist University Student Youth, to form the Student Union of the Left (UNEI). The UNEI was headed by FAU leader Vladímir de la Cruz who was its candidate for president of the FEUCR. He acknowledged the FAU's connection with the PVP, but claimed its only assistance from the communist party was "moral" (*La Nacion,* 9 April). Sixteen of the 18 positions were won by the Labor Party, which described itself as middle of the road (ibid., 15 April). The UNEI received the second largest number of votes.

The PVP is active organizing women, especially housewives, "politically the most backward segment of the population," and claims its monthly publication for women now circulates 5,000 copies throughout the country (*WMR,* September).

Party Internal Affairs. The PVP continues to be pro-Soviet with no apparent ideological splits within its organization. There has been speculation, however, that there is internal disaffection of young, more militant members with the older leadership.

On 21–22 March the PVP Central Committee held its Third Plenum in San José. The plenum report dealt primarily with the possibilities of forming a "democratic and anti-imperialist" front in Costa Rica. In line with its belief that the development of a democratic front must be guided by a "powerful party of the working class, educated in Marxist-Leninist theory" and "linked to the popular masses," the PVP analyzed the nature of its present membership, its cohesion and ideological firmness. According to the report, the party membership had increased four times in the past two years, and this, although encouraging, raised problems, since three fourths of the party militants are "new people with little experience and political maturity" or "party discipline." Of the total membership, 51 percent are agricultural and industrial workers, or 64 percent if peasants are included. Current recruiting drives of the party are aimed at work centers in order to more easily "link the party to the labor movement." (For complete text of the report see *Libertad,* 8 April.)

The Central Committee also reported that the PVP was presently going through a "serious cadre crisis." The party must work to "consolidate its present membership so that it may improve its role as organizer and leader of the masses," which cannot be done with "low quality cadres or with a cadre shortage." (Ibid.) In order to raise the political standard of new members the PVP sponsors classes for "advanced comrades," and "Marxist Discussion Hours" on domestic and international problems (*WMR,* September). The party maintains national and provincial schools to train personnel and the CGTC has a school for training trade union leaders.

Domestic Views and Activities. In its plenum report the PVP declared that Costa Rica was witnessing a "regrouping of political and social forces"; the "bourgeois opposition forces" were "launching their mid-term push" toward unity for the 1974 election campaign and "various sectors of the people, grouped in labor unions, peasants' committees, youth organizations, and neighborhood boards" were strengthening their organization bonds. Thus, the party felt it was an opportune time to concentrate on the formation of a democratic, anti-imperialist front. The basis of such a front, according to the PVP, is the "worker-peasant-student alliance" which is gradually being created in Costa Rica. (*Libertad,* 8 April.)

PVP leader Mario Solis in an article in *World Marxist Review* wrote that United Fruit Company workers in Costa Rica were currently "more militant and active," the students were opposing "imperialist ideological infiltration with increasing resolve," the intellectuals were becoming more vocal, demanding an end to "U.S. monopoly plunder," and many mass organizations were adopting radical positions because they could see imperialism as the "real cause of the people's plight." The party, however, must combat "ultra-Leftist views spread by certain intellectuals" which are concentrated on students who are "politically unsophisticated." The party must also "expose the reformist policies of the ruling National Liberation Party which adheres to a Social-Democratic position and misleads the masses by promising what it cannot give." He declared further that the "reactionaries—foreign imperialism and the domestic oligarchy—have become more active with official connivance" which, by using the media and backed by "certain elements of the Church hierarchy," are intensifying the "anti-communist and anti-Soviet campaign." The article concluded that the PVP program for "promoting and extending democracy" is to be accomplished by "peaceful means" unless the "class enemy" forces the party to adopt "other forms of struggle." (*WMR,* September.)

Early in 1972 the PVP was concerned with what it claimed was a situation bordering on civil war in Costa Rica. Secretary-General Manuel Mora claimed that the Free Costa Rica Movement, a right-wing organization in Costa Rica, was controlled by the U.S. Central Intelligence Agency and, together with other "militaristic groups of Costa Rica," planned to turn Costa Rica into a "base for [their] operations" in Latin America. According to Mora, these forces planned to make Central America into a "federal republic controlled and directed, through the Central American military dictators, by the Pentagon." (*La República,* San José, 22 January.)

In mid-year the PVP sent a representative to a meeting, attended by seven Latin American communist parties, on agrarian problems (see below). He pointed out the "close connection between the Costa Rican people's struggle for genuine agrarian reform and the fight against imperialism" and said the PVP holds that there can be no question of "far-reaching agrarian changes without abolishing imperialist domination." (*WMR,* June.)

In April the PVP Political Commission issued "theses" analyzing the newly established Costa Rican Socialist Movement. The party, it said, viewed the inauguration of the new organization as an event "facilitating the development of democratic and anti-imperialist forces" and therefore "offering broader perspectives for the formation of an anti-imperialist, democratic front." The Political Commission criticized the new group because it failed to acknowledge the importance of the October Revolution and the Soviet Union. (*IB,* no. 10–11.)

International Positions. The PVP regards the Communist Party of the Soviet Union as the "bulwark of the socialist sector and the revolutionary movement of the world." In its April theses the PVP declared that its "internationalist position" did not conflict with its independence, noting that "each country advances to socialism in its own way and each revolution has its own national features" (*IB,* no. 10–11.)

In connection with the aforementioned plot by the Free Costa Rica Movement, the PVP issued a document in March which described the plans of the Central American armies to invade Costa Rica in order to incorporate it into a Central American confederation which in turn would be used as a base from which to launch an invasion of Cuba. Although some concern was generated among the populace, the government denied that such a plan existed and the year passed without incident.

A joint declaration by the PVP and the Honduran Communist Party was issued in September in which the two parties analyzed the international situation. They praised the efforts of the socialist countries, led by the U.S.S.R., to "preserve peace and save mankind from the horrors of nuclear war." They called for withdrawal of the "imperialist troops" from Indochina and demanded recognition of the Arab countries' "right to their independence" and recovery of Israeli-occupied territories. They also praised the accomplishments of the Cuban Revolution, expressed solidarity with the Chilean people and the Popular Unity government, and saluted the U.S.S.R. on its 50th anniversary.

In January Manuel Mora visited Chile for the 50th anniversary celebration of the Communist Party of Chile. The PVP sent a representative to a meeting of communist and workers' parties of Central America, Mexico, and Panama in May (see *Mexico* and *IB,* no. 12) and to a meeting of communist parties in June (see above). On 29 August Eduardo Mora Valverde met with officials of the Romanian Communist Party in Bucharest. Manuel Mora attended the 50th anniversary celebrations in the Soviet Union in December.

Publications. The PVP publishes a weekly newspaper, *Libertad,* which is claimed to have a circulation of 15,000 (*WMR,* September), and a theoretical journal, *El Trabajo.* The PVP distributes *Principios,* a Costa Rican edition of *Problems of Peace and Socialism,* among party members. Enrique Mora Valverde is the TASS correspondent in Costa Rica.

Palo Alto, California   Lynn Ratliff

Cuba

The Communist Party of Cuba (Partido Comunista de Cuba; PCC) was founded in August 1925. In 1944 it became the People's Socialist Party (Partido Socialista Popular; PSP), which it remained until its merger in July 1961 with Fidel Castro's 26 July Movement (Movimiento 26 de Julio) and the small Revolutionary Directorate (Directoria Revolucionaria) to form the Integrated Revolutionary Organizations (Organizaciones Revolucionarias Integradas). This was transformed into the United Party of the Socialist Revolution (Partido Unido de la Revolución Socialista) in 1963. In October 1965 that party was reconstituted along more orthodox communist lines and again took the name PCC.

Although the PCC has not published membership figures, it is generally thought to be the most elitist of all ruling communist parties, including within its ranks less than 2 percent of the country's population. Recent membership figures found in Western communist publications are: about 55,000 in 1969 (Gil Green, *Revolution Cuban Style,* New York, 1970); about 70,000 in 1969 (*Trybuna Ludu,* Warsaw, 16 April 1969); more than 100,000 in 1970 (*Népszabadság,* Budapest, 5 December 1970); and approximately 60,000 between 1965 and early 1971 (*Land og Folk,* Copenhagen, 18–19 April 1971). A U.S. newspaper correspondent who visited Cuba in 1972 reported that there were 250,000 PCC members (*San Francisco Examiner and Chronicle,* 24 September). The U.S. State Department estimated party membership at 120,000 to 130,000 in 1971 (*World Strength of Communist Party Organizations,* Washington, D. C., 1972, p. 142). The population of Cuba was 8,553,395 at the time of the September 1970 census.

Organization and Leadership. Political power in Cuba in 1971 continued to be primarily in the hands of Fidel Castro Ruz and was exercised through his positions as premier, commander in chief of the armed forces, and first secretary of the PCC. Persons wielding varying amounts of secondary but not insignificant power are found in the PCC's eight-member Political Bureau, seven-member Secretariat, and approximately 100-member Central Committee. The Political Bureau is headed by Fidel Castro; the other members are Major Raúl Castro Ruz, Osvaldo Dorticós Torrado, Major Sergio del Valle Jiménez, Armando Hart Dávalos, and Majors Juan Almeida Bosque, Ramiro Valdés Menéndez, and Guillermo García Frias. The Secretariat is also headed by Fidel Castro; the other members are Raúl Castro, Osvaldo Dorticós, Armando Hart, Faure Chomón Mediavilla (former Revolutionary Directorate leader), Blas Roca Caldeiro, and Carlos Rafael Rodríguez (the last two are former PSP leaders). Approximately two-thirds of the Central Committee members are officers in the Revolutionary Armed Forces (Fuerzas Armadas Revolucionarias; FAR)—the designation of the Cuban military.

On 25 November it was announced that pursuant to orientations from the Political Bureau of the PCC, the Council of Ministers had established an Executive Committee of the Council of Ministers, the members of which were:

Major Fidel Castro, chairman of the Executive Committee, in charge of the Ministry of the Revolutionary Armed Forces, Ministry of the Interior, Secretariat of the Presidency and the Council of Ministers, National Institute of Agrarian Reform, Ministry of Public Health, and the Children's Institute;

Major Ramiro Valdés Menéndez, in charge of the Construction Sector;

Major Guillermo García Frías, in charge of the Transportation and Communications Sector;

Major Pedro Miret Prieto, in charge of the Basic Industry Sector;

Major Flavio Bravo Prado, in charge of the Consumer Goods Industries and Domestic Trade Sector;

Major Belarmino Castilla Mas, in charge of the Education, Culture, and Science Sector;

Major Diocles Torralba González, in charge of the Sugar Industry Sector;

Carlos Rafael Rodríguez, in charge of the Foreign Affairs Sector;

Osvaldo Dorticós, president of the republic, in charge of the Central Planning Board, Ministry of Labor, National Bank, Ministry of Foreign Trade, National Institute of Fishing, and Ministry of Justice.

Mass Organizations. The Cuban mass organizations during 1972 were: the Central Organization of Cuban Workers (Central de Trabajadores de Cuba; CTC), the National Association of Small Farmers (Asociación Nacional de Agricultores Pequeños; ANAP), the Committees for the Defense of the Revolution (Comités de Defensa de la Revolución; CDR), the Federation of Cuban Women (Federación de Mujeres Cubanas; FMC), and the Union of Cuban Pioneers (Unión de Pioneros de Cuba; UPC). The Union of Young Communists (Unión de Jóvenes Comunistas; UJC), the University Student Federation (Federación Estudiantil Universitaria; FEU), and the Federation of Students of Intermediate Education (Federación de Estudiantes de la Enseñanza Media; FEEM) were sometimes regarded as mass organizations. In the words of Fidel Castro on 18 November 1971, these organizations are "the instruments of the Revolution" (*Granma,* English, 28 November).

The CTC. The Central Organization of Cuban Workers is headed by its National Committee, under Héctor Ramos Latour as first secretary. At mid-year CTC membership was reportedly 1.1 million (*Latin America,* London, 28 July), including almost 100 percent of urban workers and a high percentage of rural workers. Efforts were reportedly made during the year to increase the rural membership and to raise the status of women in the organization. The January National Plenary Meeting on Labor Justice, called to determine the effectiveness of the January 1971 law on loafing ("a labor law made by a society of workers") [see *YICA, 1972,* p. 353], concluded that it had been successful politically, economically, socially, and ideologically. During 1972 the CTC continued to concentrate on increasing worker efficiency and productivity. On 1 May Castro reported that there were 18 national trade unions in Cuba and that "grass roots" elections had been held earlier in the year, with 1,244,688 workers electing 164,367 leaders in 37,047 trade union locals (*Granna,* English, 7 May).

The ANAP. The National Association of Small Farmers is headed by José ("Pepe") Ramírez Cruz. It regulates the small farmers who retain, under what is called private ownership, approximately 30 percent of Cuban farmland. At the beginning of the year the ANAP had some 225,000 members, drawn from 180,000 small farm families.

The CDR. The Committees for the Defense of the Revolution are headed by Luis González Maturelos; its 13-member National Bureau, which is directly responsible to the PCC

Central Committee, has a central office in Havana which controls a substructure of provincial, district, sectional, zonal, and bloc committees. In early October there were 7332 Zone Committees, over 70,000 CDRs, and 4,236,342 individual members—some 70 percent of the adult population. The Committees have been active in education, public health, construction, ideological work, social work, and, above all, in revolutionary vigilance. On 28 September Fidel Castro commented: "Revolutionary vigilance is absolutely crushing. . . . Who can make a move without the CDRs knowing it? Not even an ant!" (*Granma,* English, 8 October.)

The FMC. During 1972 the Federation of Cuban Women remained under the control of its president, PCC Central Committee member Vilma Espín. At a plenary meeting on 18 December the FMC president reported that there were 1,615,000 FMC members, comprising 63 percent of Cuban women between the ages of 14 and 65 (*Granma,* English, 24 December). In a broadcast on Havana Radio on 23 August she said that the objectives of the organization were to prepare women to live and work under socialism and to be more useful to society. More specifically, the FMC undertakes to mobilize women for agricultural and other work, manages child-care centers, provides general education and technical training, and organizes ideological study groups. A *Granma* editorial on 23 August reported that there were 7,034 FMC-ANAP mutual aid brigades (*Granma,* English, 3 September).

The UPC. The Union of Cuban Pioneers, founded in 1961, was officially recognized as a children's mass organization in February 1971. In early April it had more than 1.4 million members, some 87 percent of the pupils registered in primary schools (Havana radio, 4 April). The Final Declaration of the UJC Second Congress gave "top priority" to working with children, toward "developing children who will conduct themselves in a communist manner" (ibid., 23 April).

The UJC. The Union of Young Communists (sometimes called the Young Communist League) was described by Fidel Castro on 18 November 1971 as a "school for training future Party members" (ibid., 28 November). Jaime Crombet was first secretary until October 1972, when he was replaced by former second secretary, Luis Orlando Dominguez. The UJC held its Second Congress on 29 March–4 April, attended by more than 2,000 delegates representing the 140,000 UJC members (*IB,* nos. 8–9). Repeated mention was made of the low cultural level and lack of good study habits. The slogan of the UJC is "Work, Study, and Defense" (from the Final Declaration of the Second Congress). The UJC is active in or cooperates with all of the mass organizations and the various "columns," such as the Centennial Youth Column (Columna Juvenil del Centenario; CJC), which are active in work and defense.

The Revolutionary Armed Forces. The FAR (Fuerzas Armadas Revolucionarias) is believed to number 200,000 to 300,000 persons, on a percentage-of-population basis one of the largest armies in the world (*NYT,* 8 December). On 1 May Fidel Castro said that Cuba could mobilize as many as 600,000 persons "in a matter of hours" (*Granma,* English, 7 May). He said on 26 July that Cuba spends more than $1 million per day on defense (ibid., 6 August). This figure does not include foreign military aid which does not need to be repaid, valued at $1.5 billion from the Soviet Union alone between 1959 and April 1970 (ibid., 3 May 1970). The Soviet Union has sent Cuba some sophisticated weaponry including, it is believed, MIG–23 jet fighter-bombers (*U.S. News and World Report,* 15 May 1972). Raúl Castro, armed forces minister, stated on 17 April 1971 that "practically all" command officers and 75 percent of FAR officers in general are members of the PCC or UJC" (*Granma,* English, 25 April 1971). In recent years the discipline, organization, and personnel of the FAR have spread into most sectors of Cuban society, as is seen by the make-up of the PCC hierarchy and the recently appointed Executive Committee of the Council of Ministers (see above).

Domestic Attitudes and Activities. According to Fidel Castro on 22 June 1972, the "tremendous power" of Marxist-Leninist precepts has been demonstrated by the development of the Cuban Revolution. Addressing an audience at Charles University in Prague, he noted that the masses in Cuba had not developed a socialist awareness until after "the fundamental principles of Marxism were put into practice" by his government. Reporting that today the Cuban people have a "deep-rooted" political and socialist awareness, he concluded: "We are privileged to live in an epoch in which the laws that govern history have become known and are being followed." (*Granma,* English, 2 July.) On 26 July Castro spoke of the two factors which have "stood out in the consolidation of the Cuban Revolution," namely "having a revolutionary doctrine and applying it consistently" (ibid., 6 August).

Cuban leaders, who have for years shown a decided preference for moral over material incentives, began to acknowledge the value of the latter in 1971 (see *YICA, 1972,* p. 354). This trend continued in 1972. Carlos Rafael Rodríguez told one foreign reporter that the thought of Che Guevara on this issue had been seriously distorted by leftists around the world. Guevara's basic approach, according to Rodríguez, was that it was "necessary to achieve a proper combination of material and moral incentives." (*Ahora,* Santo Domingo, 18 September.) Food and consumers' goods were somewhat less scarce during the year and some appliances and other articles were available through work centers to those who "fulfilled their social duties." The increased sales during the year were encouraged in order to withdraw some 20 percent of the money now in circulation out of the market place. On 3 April, after discussing the many economic difficulties of the country, Osvaldo Dorticós said the one thing that could always be relied upon was the "great wealth of revolutionary pride and fervor of [the Cuban] people" (*Economía y Desarrollo,* July–August).

The Economy. The Cuban economy is generally discussed in terms of before and after the widespread dislocations and failures of 1970 (see *YICA, 1971,* pp. 412–14). During 1972, officially designated the "Year of Socialist Emulation," attention was focused on the general problems of worker absenteeism, indifference, low productivity—and even unemployment (see Dorticós comments in *Economía y Desarrollo,* July–August)—and consequently on the ways and means of increasing efficiency and productivity. This was reflected in such conferences as the National Plenary Meeting on Labor Justice in January and the Second National Meeting on Work Organization and Production Quotas in July.

Sugar. On 30 June President Dorticós said that the 1972 harvest had been a bad one. He announced that all international commitments had been met, however, after the Cuban people made a particularly great effort to increase the yield and after the Soviet Union had agreed to take less sugar than originally planned. (*Granma,* 1 July.) For the first time in recent years the Cuban government did not give the harvest figures; estimates are that the production total fell from nearly 6 million tons in 1971 to approximately 4.5 million tons in 1972. The main reasons for the bad harvest seem to have been the general aftermath of the 1970 dislocations, bad weather, lack of weed killers, too little cane, problems in cutting, transporting, and milling, and low labor productivity. On 30 June and 3 September Dorticós said that in the coming years the government would work for the progressive growth of production year by year so as to assure consistently good harvests, without ups and downs (ibid.; *Granma,* English, 10 September). On 13 December Fidel Castro said 500,000 men devoted all their energy to the cultivation, harvesting, processing, and transportation of sugar.

Social Services. Of all the "basic social services" in Cuba, education is considered the most important. On 4 April Fidel Castro gave a long report on the state of education in Cuba. As in the past, he emphasized the need to "revolutionize the very foundations of the concepts of education," and called in particular for combining study and work at all levels. He presented data on the present educational situation. School attendance ranges from 99.8 percent (8 year olds) to 39.8 percent (16 year olds); some 200,000 in the 13–15 year range neither study nor work. Promotion rates are low; about 720,000 children are two or more years behind. Some 70 percent of the nearly 80,000 elementary- and intermediate-level teachers are themselves "non-graduates." (Ibid., 16 April.) [1]

Refugees. Approximately 700,000 persons voluntarily left Cuba between 1959 and the end of 1972, a quarter of a million on the refugee flights between Cuba and Miami which began in 1965 and ended on 12 May 1972. The flights began again in December when Cuba announced that 3,400 persons were ready to leave the country.

International Views and Attitudes. PCC positions during 1972 can best be found in the speeches of Fidel Castro and other party leaders; in the 1972 report to the United Nations General Assembly by Ricardo Alarcón (see *Granma,* English, 22 October); in the "Resolution of the Central Committee" on Fidel Castro's visit to Africa and Socialist Europe (ibid., 30 July); and in the various joint communiqués issued during the year (see below).

On 26 July Fidel Castro expressed his conviction that "in today's world, where imperialism exists and is strong, leaving as its heritage a series of poor and underdeveloped countries, independence and revolution are impossible without socialism and international solidarity" (ibid., 6 August).

At the Georgetown Conference of Nonaligned Countries in August, Raúl Roa explained Cuban foreign policy: "Cuba's international policy is based on a revolutionary, anti-imperialist, internationalist position without ambiguities or vacillations of any kind. . . . Our main task is to draw up a clear anti-imperialist plan of action that will contribute to strengthening and advancing the peoples' struggle against colonialism, imperialism, and neocolonialism." (Ibid., 20 August.)

Revolution in Latin America. Ever since the overthrow of Fulgencio Batista in 1959, Fidel Castro has called upon revolutionaries in Latin America to seize power in their countries by armed struggle. The urgency of this call, however, and the breadth of its applicability, has varied from one period to another. During 1972 it was relatively low-keyed, though less so than in 1971. The Cuban government was particularly critical of the "fascist tyrannies" in Argentina, Bolivia, Brazil, and Paraguay; it supported armed insurgents in Uruguay, Colombia, and several other countries. Ricardo Alarcón told the 27th session of the U.N. General Assembly: "Throughout the hemisphere, rebellion grows, resistance spreads and the peoples rise to recover their wealth, consolidate their independence, shake off the Yankee yoke and make the revolution" (ibid., 22 October). And yet on 26 July Fidel Castro repeated his 1969 statement on the Cuban attitude toward revolutionary prospects in the Latin American countries: "We are far from being impatient. . . . We will wait and watch as, one by one, those countries . . . make their revolutions. . . . How long will we wait? . . . 10, 20, 30 years if necessary." (Ibid., 6 August.) Indeed on 1 May he said the Cubans "found encouraging any manifestation of contradiction with imperialism, any manifestation of a spirit of national independence that may lead to profound contradictions that may one day launch a revolution" (ibid., 7 May). Cuban leaders acknowledged during 1972 that the most revolutionary policies being implemented in Latin America were those of governments which had achieved power without the use of armed struggle. On 4 April Fidel Castro spoke of Cuba's need to solve the "serious, difficult, and complex" problems of making the first socialist revolution in Latin

[1] On the problem of Cuban statistics see Carmelo Mesa-Lago, "Availability and Reliability of Statistics in Socialist Cuba," *Latin American Research Review,* Spring 1969, pp. 53–91, and Summer 1969, pp. 47–81.

America. Other countries would have to "travel this long road" in the future, he said, and would "turn their eyes in our direction to find out what we did." (Ibid., 16 April.)

Cuban-Latin American Relations. The hemispheric isolation of the Cuban government which followed the 1964 imposition of sanctions by the Organization of American States (OAS) was weakened during 1972. In May, Peru proposed in the OAS that any government be free to establish relations with Cuba at the level it judged convenient. Though the motion was defeated, seven countries supported it (Peru, Chile, Mexico, Panama, Ecuador, Jamaica, and Trinidad-Tobago) and three abstained (Argentina, Venezuela, Barbados). Cuba still showed no interest in the OAS; on 26 July Castro said that Cuba would "never set foot in that putrid, revolting den of corruption" known as the OAS (ibid., 6 August).

In a 12 June editorial on the OAS vote, *Granma* stated the Cuban position on the reestablishment of relations with Latin American countries: "Our country is willing to establish relations with those governments that are independent and are willing to express and to show their conduct in real steps of sovereignty and national independence" (ibid., 18 June; also see Castro speech of 26 July, ibid., 6 August). Whereas at the beginning of 1972 there were only two Latin American ambassadors in Havana (representing Mexico and Chile), at the end of the year five other countries had established diplomatic relations with Cuba (Peru, Guyana, Jamaica, Barbados, and Trinidad-Tobago). Cuban relations were closest with the Popular Unity government of Salvador Allende in Chile and with the military government of Juan Velasco in Peru, though Castro and other Cuban leaders had good words to say at times for the Panamanian and some other governments. Late in December Fidel Castro led a group of Latin American Communist officials in condemning the government of Guatemala for allegedly killing the entire leadership of the communist Guatemalan Party of Labor (see *Granma,* English, 7 January 1973).

United States. The subject of U.S.-Cuban relations came up repeatedly during 1972, particularly at the end of the year when the two countries began negotiations (through the Swiss ambassador in Havana) to reach an anti-hijacking treaty. Fidel Castro expressed his opinions on the subject of U.S.-Cuban relations on 26 July (and many other occasions):

> Our position is perfectly clear: we demand that they [the U.S.] withdraw from the Guantánamo base, lift their blockade and stop their acts of subversion. That's our position, and it's not open to discussion. . . . Cuba's doors will always be closed to Mr. Nixon's [the "x" in Nixon, as always in the Cuban press, is replaced by a swastika] cheap politicking and dirty deals. . . . We are prepared to get along without relations with the United States for another 5, 10, 15, 20, 30 years!

Although he said Cuba could "wait calmly until there is socialism in the United States," he recognized the possibility of talking with the U.S. whenever that government ceased "playing the role of gendarme over the people of Latin America," carrying out subversive and counterrevolutionary policies. (Ibid., 6 August.) Several months later he told a Mexican reporter that the fact that these denials were unconditional did not mean that Cuba would do nothing in return (*Siempre,* Mexico City, 18 October).

After two airliners were hijacked to Cuba in late October and early November, the Cuban government (on 15 November) officially renewed its 1969 offer to negotiate a bilateral anti-hijacking agreement with the United States covering sea as well as air craft (compare the original offer in *Granma,* English, 28 September 1969 and renewed offer, ibid., 19 November 1972). The U.S. government, under pressure from all sides to "solve" the hijacking problem, immediately agreed to begin negotiations.

Soviet Union. Soviet-Cuban relations, very good when 1972 began, were excellent as the year ended. Fidel Castro visited the U.S.S.R. from 26 June through 5 July, his third visit to the Soviet Union but his first since 1964 (for joint communiqué see *Granma,* English, 16 July). On 26 July Castro said that never before had the Cubans found "greater understanding or readiness and determination to cooperate with Cuba, to help Cuba solve its problems" (ibid., 6 August). It was not until Castro's second trip of the year to the U.S.S.R. in December, that it became clear just how cooperative the Soviet Union had decided to be. On 3 January 1973 the Cuban leader announced that the Soviet government, on its own initiative, had offered the Cuban government a five part economic package which had been gratefully accepted. The agreements: stipulated that repayment of Soviet credits to Cuba between 1959 and January 1973 [estimated at over $4 billion, military aid excluded; *New York Times,* 5 January 1973] was to be postponed until 1986, then repayable over a 25-year period without interest; provided credits to cover Cuba's projected unfavorable trade balance with the U.S.S.R. over the 1973–75 period, repayment due over 25 years without interest beginning in 1986; listed bilateral trade and extensive economic and technical assistance and collaboration; pledged the U.S.S.R. during the 1973–80 period to buy Cuban sugar at 11 cents per pound, several cents above the current market price, and to buy Cuban nickel-cobalt products at $5000 per ton, roughly twice the current market price. Further, new credits for investments, particularly in the nickel industry, were made, repayable in 25 years at a "very low interest rate." (*Granma,* English, 14 January 1973.) The admission of Cuba into the Council for Mutual Economic Assistance (COMECON) as a full member in July also demonstrated the incorporation of Cuba into the Soviet economic bloc.

Cuban relations with the countries of Eastern Europe became closer during the year, as indicated by the increase in high-level contacts (see below). Relations with the People's Republic of China continued to improve slowly in spite of the Cuban distaste for China's rapprochement with the United States. Cuba continued to voice constant and enthusiastic support for North Vietnam and the Provisional Revolutionary Government of South Vietnam. Cuba established diplomatic relations with Bangladesh in February, and with several African countries later in the year.

International Contacts. In recent years high-level contacts with pro-Soviet governments and parties have increased dramatically, as have relations with Latin American governments, while contacts with other governments and parties have remained constant or decreased. Indeed, Fidel Castro and top Cuban leaders made more personal contacts with North African and Soviet-bloc leaders in 1972 than ever before, in large part during the premier's two-month tour of ten countries. The Cuban delegation, led by Fidel Castro, included Carlos Rafael Rodríguez, and a battery of military officers, among them majors Juan Almeida and Manuel Piñeiro. The delegation visited: Guinea, 3–7 May (joint communiqué in *Granma,* English, 14 May); Sierra Leone, 7 May; Algeria, 8–17 May (joint declaration, ibid., 28 May); Bulgaria, 16–26 May, where First Secretary Todor Zhivkov presented Castro with the Georgi Dimitrov Order (communiqué, ibid., 4 June); Romania, 26–30 May (communiqué, ibid., 11 June); Hungary, 30 May–6 June (communiqué, ibid., 18 June); Poland, 6–13 June, where Castro received the 30th Anniversary of the Polish United Workers' Party Medal; German Democratic Republic, 13–21 June (communiqué, ibid., 2 July); Czechoslovakia, 21–26 June, where Castro received the Doctor Honoris Causa in Juridical Science at Charles University, Prague (communiqué, ibid., 9 July); U.S.S.R., 26 June–5 July, where Castro was presented with the Order of Lenin (communiqué, ibid., 16 July).

Soviet visitors to Cuba included: Andrei Kirilenko, member of the CPSU Political Bureau, and the ministers of the interior, public instruction, and culture.

Among the visitors from Czechoslovakia were: Jozef Lenart, member of the Political Bureau of the Communist Party of Czechoslovakia, in January. From Bulgaria: Mako Dakov, Deputy Chairman of the Council of Ministers, in October, and others.

Chilean visitors to Cuba included Communist Party leaders Volodia Teitelboim and Luis Corvalán, in September and November, respectively, and leaders of the Socialist Party, the Unitary Popular Action Movement (MAPU), and the Movement of the Christian Left (MIC). Chilean President Salvador Allende visited Cuba in December; he presented the Chilean Order of Merit to Fidel Castro and Osvaldo Dorticós, and received the Cuban National Order of José Marti. From Uruguay, Socialist Party leaders in February and March, and Communist Party Secretary General Rodney Arismendi, in October. Other Latin American visitors included: Gerónimo Arnedo, Secretary General of the Communist Party of Argentina, in January and in July; Juan Mari Bras, Secretary General of the Puerto Rican Socialist Party, in January; and Pedro Saad, Secretary General of the Communist Party of Ecuador, in August–September.

Asian visitors included: Pak Song-chol, member of the Political Bureau of the Korean Workers' Party, in February; Nguyen Thi Binh, Foreign Minister of the Provisional Revolutionary Government of South Vietnam, in July; N. K. Krishnan and Yogindra Sharma, members of the Secretariat of the Communist Party of India, in October; Yumzhagiin Tsedenbal, First Secretary of the Mongolian People's Revolutionary Party, in November.

Other visitors included: General Secretary Gus Hall and Political Committee member Roscoe Proctor, of the Communist Party of the U.S.A. (CPUSA), in March–April; and Angela Davis, CPUSA member, in September–October, and in December; William Kashtan, Secretary General of the Communist Party of Canada, in August; Carl-Henrik Hermansson, Chairman of the Left Party Communists of Sweden, in November–December; the foreign ministers of Sierra Leone, Somalia, and Tanzania; Fatah Ismail, General Secretary of the National Front for the Liberation of South Yemen, in October–November; delegations from the African Party for the Independence of Guinea and Cape Verde (PAIGC) and from the Ba'th Party of Syria; Cécile Hugel, Secretary General of the Women's International Democratic Federation, in March–April; and Romesh Chandra, Secretary General of the World Peace Council, who presented Fidel Castro with the Joliot-Curie Medal, in October.

Cuban visitors to the Soviet Union and Eastern Europe, besides those in Fidel Castro's delegation, included: Carlos Rafael Rodríguez, to the U.S.S.R. in February, April, and October–November, and to Poland, in February, and Romania, in October–November; Héctor Ramos Latour, to the U.S.S.R., in March; Jaime Crombet to the German Democratic Republic, in June, and to Czechoslovakia, in September. Cuban visitors to Latin America included: Jorge Risquet, to the 50th Anniversary of the Communist Party of Chile, in Santiago, in January; Melba Hernandez to the World Assembly of Peace and Independence of the People of Indochina, in Paris, in February, and to North Vietnam and Laos, in November; Raúl Roa to the Third UNCTAD Conference in Santiago, Chile, beginning in April, and to the Conference of Non-aligned Countries, in Georgetown, Guyana, in August; and Osmany Cienfuegos, to South Yemen, in August.

Publications. *Granma* is the daily organ of the PCC; it appears also in weekly editions in Spanish, English, and French. *Juventud Rebelde* is the daily organ of the UJC. Both are circulated nationally. *Verde Olivo* is the weekly organ of the FAR. Two publications of the Cuba-based Afro-Asian-Latin American Peoples' Solidarity Organization are *Tricontinental* (in Spanish, English, French, and Italian editions), which appears four to six times a year, and the monthly *Tricontinental Bulletin* (in Spanish, English, and French). Prensa Latina is the Cuban news agency.

Hoover Institution   William E. Ratliff
Stanford University

Dominican Republic

Intense disagreement over leadership and policy issues, especially since the civil war of 1965, has led to the fragmentation of the communist movement of the Dominican Republic. There are three principal organizations: the Dominican Communist Party (Partido Comunista Dominicano; PCD), which enjoys more or less official recognition by the Soviet Union; the Dominican People's Movement (Movimiento Popular Dominicano; MPD), which is pro-Chinese; and the Revolutionary movement of 14 June (Movimiento Revolucionario 14 de Junio; MR–1J4), which is also pro-Chinese, but is the group most sympathetic toward the Fidel Castro regime. Splits within these groups have created several new factions and parties. These include the Popular Socialist Party (Partido Socialista Popular; PSP), the Communist Party of the Dominican Republic (Partido Comunista de la Republica Dominicana; PCRD or PACOREDO); and the Red Flag (Bandera Roja) and the Red Line (Línea Roja) of the MR–1J4, and the Proletarian Voice (Voz Proletaria). Only the PCD appears to enjoy recognition within the international communist movement.

Communism in the Dominican Republic is proscribed under laws covering propaganda and subversive activities. The present government of President Joaquin Balaguer allows communist parties to issue statements in the mass media and communist student groups to operate more or less uninhibitedly, but maintains strict control over communist activities. In February 1972 Balaguer said that he had no immediate intention of formally legalizing any of the communist groups, judging that the matter required "further study."

All together, the communist groups are estimated to have about 1,350 members, divided as follows: PCD, 470; MPD, 385; MR–1J4, 300; PSP, 40; PCRD, 145 (*World Strength of the Communist Party Organizations,* Washington, D.C., 1972, p. 144). The MPD (according to another source) has the largest following, allegedly "several thousand." The population of the Dominican Republic is 4,300,000 (estimated 1970).

Politically motivated murders seem to be an established feature of the Dominican scene. Although people of all political colors have been victims, most have been members of communist groups and of the major opposition party, the Partido Revolucionario Dominicano. The killings have been attributed both to feuds between communist groups and to actions by paramilitary groups reportedly organized by the military and the police, particularly the latter. Although there were several spectacular political murders in 1972, the number seemed to be declining somewhat during the year (see below).

Sources of support for the communists include universities, secondary schools, and labor unions, and reflect the fragmentation of the movement. At the university level, the student movement has divided into the following organizations: "Fragua," led by the Red Line of the MR–1J4; Juventud Comunista, led by PCRD members; the Comité Universitario "Julio Antonio Mella," led by PCD members; and the Comité "Flavio Suero," led by MPD members.

The powerful Federation of Dominican Students (Federación de Estudiantes Dominicanos: FED), which is said to enroll about 200,000 university and secondary school students, was after 1969 in the hands of non-communist but left-wing students belonging to the Dominican Revolutionary Party (Partido Revolucionario Dominicano; PRD). In 1972, however, the PRD expelled its student group in the aftermath of a scandal indicating that the head of the FED had for some time been a secret police agent (see below). The communist movement at the secondary school level is represented by the Union of Revolutionary Students (Unión de Estudiantes Revolucionarios; UER).

Within the labor movement, communist support is more limited. The "Foupsa-Cesitrado" labor confederation, reportedly in the hands of MPD members, is only one of several central labor bodies. The largest is the Confederación Autónoma Sindical Cristiana, more or less associated with the Christian Democratic Party (Partido Revolucionario Social Cristiano). The powerful "Unachosin" chauffeurs' union includes communist members, mostly of the MPD.

*　　　*　　　*

The PCD. The PCD was founded clandestinely in 1942. As the Popular Socialist Party (Partido Socialista Popular; PSP), it came into the open for a short while in 1946, but was again suppressed by the Trujillo dictatorship. During the military-civilian revolt in April 1965 the party again took the PCD name, which it has used since then. In 1967 the PCD adopted (verbally but not in practice) a Castroite line, advocating the concept of armed struggle in most Latin American countries—a position that did not last for long and did not affect its relations with the Communist Party of the Soviet Union (CPSU).

Leadership and Organization. Narciso Isa Conde is the PCD secretary-general. (For other names see *YICA, 1972,* p. 362.) The party claims to be organized on a national scale, with cells in almost every city and in many regions of the countryside. It has a committee operating in New York City among persons of Dominican origin.

Domestic Attitudes and Activities. The PCD rejects any "illusions about the electoral path" and holds that the political and economic structures of the Dominican Republic can be changed only by revolutionary means. This theoretical position has not prevented it from making conciliatory overtures to the Balaguer government. One issue during 1972 which separated the PCD from other communist groups was that of the agrarian reform program announced by President Balaguer early in the year. On 11 March the PCD issued a statement which, with minor criticisms, generally endorsed the legislation Balaguer had sent to Congress (and which was passed on 29 March). The party hailed the agrarian reform program as a victory for the left and called on all leftist forces to "deepen the reformist phenomenon" so as to avoid "the growing isolation of the revolutionary forces from the popular masses." While noting that "Balaguer is not revolutionary," the PCD summed up its position by saying: "Faced with this reformist policy, the policy that we must follow is different from the one that arose out of the counterrevolutionary origins of the present regime—and especially since it is clear that today the desirable conditions that might cause another violent outbreak do not exist."

The party denounced the PRD's opposition to the program, particularly attacking the PRD's failure to endorse the land distribution provisions of the Balaguer reform. Even so, the PCD did not repudiate the endorsement which it had previously given of PRD leader Juan Bosch's theory of "dictatorship with popular support."

While supporting Balaguer's plans for land redistribution, the PCD also backed efforts of peasants to seize land on their own account, and in September said that the land seizures were taking place because the attorney-general was not sufficiently energetic in enforcing the agrarian reform laws which had been passed months earlier.

The PCD was one of 14 Latin American communist parties whose representatives participated in a "discussion seminar" arranged by *World Marxist Review* in Prague early in the year. The Dominican representative commented: "Present-day revisionism and opportunism are deviations from scientific socialism. . . . Our Party has to contend with two opportunist trends. One of them, the Right deviation, has lost all influence within the Party. . . . 'Leftism,' Maoist conceptions, have proved especially tenacious and we are successfully combating them, notably in the capital." (*WMR,* April.)

Publications. The PCD publishes a clandestine weekly, *El Popular.* Its declarations also appear as paid announcements or as letters to the editor in the independent daily *El Nacional de Ahora,* in Santo Domingo, which also publishes declarations of other communist groups.

*   *   *

The PSP. When the PCD adopted Castroite views and tactics—mostly limited to verbal declarations—in 1967, a split occurred within the party. The more moderate members, proclaiming their support for Moscow and "peaceful co-existence," formed a new party, using the PCD's former name, the Popular Socialist Party. Despite its pro-Soviet stance, the PSP has not been recognized by the Soviet Union, but it seems to maintain friendly relations with other pro-Soviet parties in Latin America. (For party leaders see *YICA, 1972,* p. 363.)

The PSP condemns the Bosch thesis of "dictatorship with popular support" as being "ultra leftist" (*Tribuna Popular,* Caracas, 15 April 1971).

*   *   *

The MPD. The MPD, formed by Dominican exiles in Havana in 1956, originally included even among its leaders many persons who did not have communist sympathies. After the death of Trujillo in 1961 and the return of its founders to Santo Domingo, it quickly took on a Marxist-Leninist orientation.

The MPD became a formal party only in August 1965. It is pro-Chinese, and is considered to be one of the most active and violent leftist groups. It is said to have considerable support among students and slum dwellers, and has some following in the organized labor movement.

Leadership and Organization. Among the leaders of the MPD is Julio de Peña Valdés, who has been secretary-general of "Foupsa-Cesitrado." He and five others (named in *YICA, 1972,* pp. 363–64) were jailed in January 1971 on charges of illegal possession of arms and planning the assassination of government officials, army and police officers, and foreign diplomats. All six were sentenced to 10-year prison terms on 10 February 1972.

Domestic Attitudes and Activities. The MPD proclaims its intention to bring about a seizure of power by the proletariat, peasantry, and other "progressive" forces in order to install a "people's democratic dictatorship." It maintains that the "only road . . . is armed violence," but also argues that present conditions call for overthrow of the Balaguer government and that this can "only come about through putschist coordination with malcontent militarists and with the civilian right." (*Tricontinental Bulletin,* Havana, August 1971.) The MPD's willingness to cooperate with rightist groups has evoked no response from right-wing parties, and has given it a reputation as an "opportunist" party.

In February 1972 the MPD called on all parties and groups of the revolutionary left to emphasize their differences but also to recognize those things which they had in common. In particular, the MPD noted that it had differences with PRD leader Juan Bosch, but stressed that the MPD and PRD were not enemies, but rather were common victims of government repression and had for long fought against the same enemies. The MPD contended that only the government and "imperialism" would be hurt by such unity among the revolutionary parties.

Perhaps this call for unity by the MPD explains why there was less internecine warfare between the MPD and other communist groups, particularly the PCRD, than in previous years. There seem to have been few, if any, murders of MPD members by rival leftists, or vice versa, in 1972. However, in June the National Union of Independent Drivers (UNACROSIN), a union under MPD influence, announced that members of the PCRD were plotting to assassinate UNACROSIN members. In a press announcement, the UNACROSIN said that its leader had to leave his house to avoid murder, with which he had been threatened if he continued to refuse to join the PCRD. The announcement threatened reprisals if anything happened to him.

In April, troops entered the National University campus, allegedly in search of MPD leaders who had been engaged in terrorist activities. The soldiers shot at professors and students who refused to vacate one of the university buildings, and several were wounded. For some weeks the university and the country's secondary schools were closed as a result of this incident. On 24 June an MPD activist was killed by police in Santo Domingo; the MPD officially claimed that he had been killed as part of a general plan by the police to eliminate the party's leadership. On 8 July the police announced the discovery of one of the largest caches of arms found since the 1965 civil war, and stated that the weapons had been in the custody of the MPD. In September, three jailed MPD leaders were formally convicted of participating in the kidnapping of a U.S. military officer two years before.

Throughout the year there was discussion of deporting those revolutionary political leaders held in jail. In August more than two dozen of them announced that they favored deportation over being kept longer in prison; most of these were reported as members of the MPD. In November, President Balaguer announced that he would deport the revolutionary politicians being held in the country's jails.

Publications. The MPD publishes an irregular clandestine weekly, *Libertad.*

*   *   *

The PCRD. The Communist Party of the Dominican Republic was formed by dissidents of the MPD after the 1965 civil war and is considered a very extreme party. The secretary-general is "Pin" Montas (for other names see *YICA, 1972,* p. 365). The membership is limited mostly to the city of Santo Domingo. The PCRD defines itself as a Marxist-Leninist party, "created in conformity with the thoughts of Mao Tse-tung." The party proclaims its major objective to be to install socialism and then communism; its immediate program attempts to "defeat Yankee imperialism and all its Creole lackeys" through a democratic revolution. (Statements by "Pin" Montas, Radio Continental, Santo Domingo, 17 January 1971.) The PCRD seems to have been relatively inactive during 1972. No statements by it on international issues were noted.

The PCRD's official organ is *El Comunista,* an irregularly appearing clandestine weekly.

*   *   *

The MR–1J4. The Revolutionary Movement of 14 June derives its name from an unsuccessful attempt to overthrow former dictator Trujillo on that date in 1959. Although the 1959 invasion came from Cuba and was helped by Castro, many of the early leaders of the MR–1J4 felt that the Cuban leader had betrayed them, and the party was not pro-communist until October 1963 when the government of then President Juan Bosch was overthrown. Soon after that event, the MR–1J4 attempted a military uprising against the de facto government, which resulted in the death of the original leaders of the movement. Those who took over in their wake evolved quickly in the communist direction, particularly toward the Castro version of Marxism-Leninism. The MR–1J4 has subsequently split into several factions. Aside from the main body, there now exist so-called Red Flag, Red Line, and Voz Proletaria groups.

Activities in 1972. The principal student figure in La Fragua, the university branch of the Red Line faction of 14 of June, Selvio Rodríguez, was also secretary-general of the university students' federation, FED. In August, Juan Bosch of the PRD announced that Rodríguez had been accused of, and had admitted, working for the secret police between 1964 and 1966. Soon afterward, he resigned his FED post. Meanwhile, the PRD suspended its university group, the Democratic Socialist University Front (FUSD), for cooperating with Rodríguez and "not following party principles." The Voz Proletaria faction denounced the PRD's action, declaring that it showed the Bosch party's "bankruptcy."

Earlier, when President Balaguer's agrarian reform program was being discussed in Congress, the main MR–1J4 group supported the activities of peasants who were occupying large landholdings and government property on their own account. In April, on the seventh anniversary of the outbreak of the 1965 civil war, the Red Flag, Red Line, and Voz Proletaria factions jointly issued a proclamation to the effect that the best way to honor those who revolted in April 1965 was to teach the history and lessons of that uprising. The declaration also called on "the workers to form a labor party as an indispensable step for the construction of a socialist society." Finally, it urged "all democratic people" to commemorate 1 May by observing partial strikes in support of the striking workers at the Las Minas textile factory. In July the Red Line faction accused the government of launching an all-out campaign to destroy physically the revolutionary movement. In August the Red Flag group declared its opposition to the idea of deporting political prisoners.

Rutgers University   Robert J. Alexander

Ecuador

The communist movement in Ecuador began in 1926 with the founding of the Socialist Party of Ecuador (Partido Socialista Ecuatoriano). In 1928 the party became a member of the Comintern, and in 1931 changed its name to the Communist Party of Ecuador (Partido Comunista del Ecuador; PCE). A pro-Chinese splinter party, the Marxist-Leninist Communist Party of Ecuador (Partido Comunista Marxista-Leninista del Ecuador; PCMLE) dates from 1963.

PCE members are estimated to number about 500. Most are students and workers; a few are peasants. The PCMLE is believed to have about 250 members, mostly students with some workers included.

The Socialist Revolutionary Party of Ecuador (Partido Socialista Revolucionario del Ecuador; PSRE) is a Castroite organization of some 500 members. The Revolutionary Workers' Party-Trotskyist (Partido Obrero Revolucionario, Trotskista; PORT) is of unknown size.

The population of Ecuador is 6,100,000 (estimated 1970).

The military junta that assumed power in July 1963 declared the PCE illegal, but the party was able to remain intact through clandestine activities and its representation in various mass organizations. After 1966, when the government returned to civilian control, the party again began to function openly, although the 1963 anti-subversion laws have not been rescinded. Late in 1971 the PCE and several other small leftist organizations formed the Popular Unity bloc in anticipation of elections promised for June 1972. In January 1972 it was announced that Pedro Saad, secretary-general of the PCE, would be its presidential candidate (*IB.,* no. 3). However, on 15 February the government was overthrown in a military coup led by Guillermo Rodríguez Lara and the elections were canceled. Little news of the Popular Unity bloc has been reported since although in September Pedro Saad stated that there was a "possibility of reorganizing" the bloc and "giving it new life" (*Verde Olivo,* Havana, 24 September).

Organization and Leadership. The PCE has a ten-member Executive Council and a twenty-one member Central Committee. At lower levels are provincial, zonal, and cell divisions. The secretary-general is Pedro Saad Niyaim. Executive Council members include Elías Muñoz, Miltón Jijón, Alejandro Idrovo, Alba Calderón, Efráin Alvarez, Enrique Gil, and René Mauge.

The party's youth organization is the Communist Youth of Ecuador (Juventud Comunista Ecuatoriana; JCE). The most active student organization at the university level, the Federation of University Students of Ecuador (Federación de Estudiantes Universitarios del Ecuador; FEUE), is under the control of leftist students. PCE influence in the FEUE has declined since 1969 while that of pro-Chinese students has increased. On 10 October the FEUE organized a special program to commemorate the death of Che Guevara. The Ecuadorian Federation of Secondary Students (Federación de Estudiantes Secundarios del Ecuador; FESE), an active organization for younger students, has traditionally been considered under the primary influence of the PCE. Since 1970, however, it seems to have split into pro-Soviet and pro-Chinese factions.

The PCE controls the Confederation of Ecuadorean Workers (Confederación de Trabajadores Ecuatorianos; CTE), which until recently was the largest labor organization in the country, with a claimed membership of 60,000. It is a member of the communist-front World Federation of Trade Unions. The secretary general is Leonidas Córdova and the organization secretary is Dr. Bolívar Bolaños. The CTE held its12th Congress in 1972.

Following the takeover of the government by General Rodríguez the CTE in joint action with the other members of the United Workers' Front (see *YICA, 1972,* p. 367) issued a communiqué stating that the government's announced plan for the country included some "national aspirations which the Ecuadorean labor movement, especially the CTE [had] been striving to achieve, such as better wages, the improvement of living conditions, the elimination of unemployment, improvements in the educational system, social security, housing, and so forth." On the other hand the CTE noted that some problems were not satisfactorily dealt with in the government's plan, in particular those "related to the democratic and social rights and role of the labor movement in the revolutionary process."

The CTE has organized two small peasant affiliates, the Coastal Farm Workers' Federation (Federación de Trabajadores Agrícolas del Litoral; FTAL) and the Ecuadorean Federation of Indians (Federación Ecuatoriana de Indios; FEI).

Party Internal Affairs. The PCE Central Committee, meeting in plenary session on 9–10 February 1972, analyzed and approved the creation of a "Patriotic Front." The party's organizational and propaganda activities were discussed with emphasis on the need for "raising the ideological, political and theoretical level of the Party and all its members." Both successes and shortcomings in organizational work were noted. (*IB.,* no. 8–9.) Plenary meetings were also held on 7 May, 23 August, and late December. The plenum of 7 May scheduled the PCE's Ninth Congress for 11–14 November, though no information on that congress was immediately available.

Domestic Views. Immediately following the overthrow of the government on 15 February 1972, the PCE Central Committee issued a communiqué (*El Pueblo,* 19 February; reprinted in *IB.,* no. 8–9) declaring that "the change of government took place in the setting of an acute national crisis, when poverty and unemployment in the country had reached unbearable proportions as a result of the policy of the ruling classes and the imperialist monopolies." At the same time there were "big opportunities for accelerating national progress and rapidly transforming [the] country by utilizing [its] immense national wealth." The PCE expressed support for the declarations of the new government regarding reintroduction of the 1945 constitution, defense of the sovereignty of the 200-mile limit in territorial waters, agrarian reform, placing of the national wealth "at the service of society," defense of working people from the "exploiting oligarchy," recognition of "human rights," and respect for the university and students. These declarations, according to the communiqué, coincided with demands which the PCE had set forth in its "Program of Immediate Action" of July 1971.

When the Rodríguez government issued its "Plan of Government" on 10 March, the PCE noted its positive elements, such as "limiting the enormous benefits accruing to privileged groups, cutting short the abuses in ownership, eliminating the country's dependent status in all respects on the basis of a sound nationalism, and restricting acceptance of foreign cooperation" (*El Pueblo,* 11 March). The PCE was particularly enthusiastic about the government's objectives of seeking "a rise in the national per capita income, a just redistribution of the national income, the establishment of a sovereign system, and the absorption of isolated manpower." On the other hand were "serious shortcomings" such as the plan's neglect of "citizens' guarantees, labor union rights, and freedom of political and union organization," its incorrect position regarding the nationalization of the petroleum industry, and its failure to openly repudiate international treaties which were "detrimental to [Ecuador's] sovereignty."

In September, PCE leader Pedro Saad, in an interview in Havana, reviewed the progress of the new government. In the area of international policy, he said, "a firm stand [had] been taken" but in domestic affairs a more "gradual position" was predominant. In particular Saad noted the need for acceleration in the agrarian reform process and in the nationalization of the petroleum industry. He observed that in the "democratization of national life," the labor, peasant, and student movements and the PCE were able to operate with "complete legality," there being "no restrictions on, nor persecution for any activity." Within the government, however, Saad noted, there were "contradictions" and factors which interfered with its plan, such as some ministers who had "anti-democratic attitudes," military governors who regarded their provinces as "fiefdoms," and the divisive influence of "imperialism." (*Verde Olivo,* 24 September.)

In celebration of May Day the PCE issued a statement on the need for unity of all "patriotic and democratic forces" in the "fight for a people's Ecuador."

International Views and Activities. The PCE is a solidly pro-Soviet party. In commemoration of the 50th anniversary of the U.S.S.R., Pedro Saad hailed that country's "great efflorescence as a multi-national state of the working people" where living conditions improved with every passing day. The U.S.S.R., Saad continued, "helps all other peoples of the world fighting against the intrigues of imperialism" and fosters enthusiasm among all people "striving to save mankind from the danger of war." (TASS, Havana, 8 September.)

In an interview in Prague, Saad discoursed on the influence of the socialist countries in pointing out the "road toward the genuine liberation of the peoples." He said that the overall trend in Latin America, especially the victory of the Cuban Revolution and the success of the Popular Unity in Chile, "significantly affects" developments in Ecuador. (*Rudé právo,* 18 August.)

Regarding the Andean Pact, Saad declared the party's support for Ecuador's membership since the "correlation of forces therein now favors a positive impetus for [Ecuador's] independence from imperialism." The PCE, however, was not in favor of integration for its own sake. (*Verde Olivo,* 24 September.)

During his 12-day visit to Cuba in September, Saad commented that relations between the Cuban and Ecuadorean parties were "normal" for "two fraternal communist Parties with a common cause." He was impressed with the "formidable impetus to the construction of Socialism" which Cuba was providing and with the "human aspect"—the "revolutionary enthusiasm of the Cuban people"—in the country. (Ibid.)

Besides Cuba, Saad visited the Soviet Union, Czechoslovakia, and Poland.

The PCE's attitude toward the People's Republic of China was made clear in a unanimous resolution, adopted at the December 1971 plenary meeting, which condemned the Chinese leaders for "contradicting the scientific theory of Marxism-Leninism, the unity of the international communist movement, the unity of the socialist camp and the struggle of the peoples for national independence and for peace throughout the world." (TASS, 29 December.)

Publications. The official organ of the PCE is *El Pueblo,* a tabloid weekly published in Guayaquil and distributed openly. A weekly magazine, *Mañana,* published in Quito, which had been banned, was resumed in March 1972 following the military coup. It is said to have a circulation of 10,000 (*Democratic Journalist,* Prague, no. 5).

*   *   *

The PCMLE. The Marxist-Leninist Communist Party of Ecuador is an outgrowth of the split which became evident in the PCE in 1963. As a result of ideological disputes and personal rivalries the PCMLE itself had split into three factions by 1968. One of these, led by Rafael Echeverría, has since 1969 been regarded by the Chinese as the authentic PCMLE.

On 12 April 1972 leftist students at the University of Ecuador, Quito, staged an "anti-imperialist" rally in memory of a prominent pro-Chinese student leader who was killed in 1970 (see *YICA, 1971,* p. 434).

The PCMLE analysis of the situation in Ecuador was presented in a "Manifesto" issued on 1 May. Ecuador was said to be in the midst of its worst crisis in history, due to hunger, poverty, misery, oppression, and inequality. The military government was gradually proving to be just another dictatorship of feudal and bourgeois elements. The PCMLE called for a united front of revolutionary forces, making clear that it was not to include "opportunists or traitors," or "the revisionists, led by Pedro Saad" (*En Marcha,* 30 April–6 May).

The party's long-term objectives are an anti-feudal and anti-imperialist national liberation revolution led by the working class in close alliance with the peasants, and with the cooperation of all revolutionary elements of society ("Manifesto," ibid.). An article (ibid.) explained that the task of the working class is: "the conquest of power through armed insurrection, the destruction of the oppressive state apparatus, and the establishment of a dictatorship of the proletariat which will carry out the socialist and communist transformation of society."

The short-term objectives of the workers and their party (the PCMLE) include: the nationalization of petroleum without indemnification; effective defense of the 200-mile offshore territorial limit; and an end to the rising cost of living coupled with an increase in wages ("Manifesto," ibid.).

In late April *En Marcha,* the weekly organ of the PCMLE, again appeared in print after some two years of limited circulation in mimeographed form.

Palo Alto, California   Lynn Ratliff

El Salvador

The Communist Party of El Salvador (Partido Comunista de El Salvador; PCES) was organized in 1925 by communists from Mexico and Guatemala as part of a plan to establish a "Communist Party of Central America." By 1930 the regional concept had been discarded and the PCES was operating as a national body.

The Salvadoran Revolutionary Action (Acción Revoluccionaria Salvadoreña; ARS) and the Salvadoran Revolutionary Party (Partido Revolucionaria Salvadoreña; PRS) are small Castroite guerrilla groups. There have been no recent reports about these groups or their activities.

Since the early 1930s the PCES has been illegal and has functioned clandestinely. Its influence on the political situation in El Salvador is negligible due to the party's weak organization and the government's increasingly successful programs in such areas as education and agrarian reform.

The PCES is believed to have about 100 members. The population of El Salvador is 3,541,000 (estimated 1970).

The PCES has at various times participated indirectly in national politics in El Salvador through alignment with various leftist fronts or coalitions. In 1972 the PCES supported the candidacy of the center-left National Opposition Union (Unión Nacional de Oposición; UNO) in the presidential elections of 20 February. Colonel Arturo Armando Molina was declared president by the Electoral Council on 25 February; the UNO candidate, José Napoleón Duarte, was a very close second. In March, Duarte and an army officer lead an unsuccessful rising against the government. Although President Molina had promised to follow the policies of his predecessor, by mid-year the threat of serious social and political upheaval caused him to reorganize the government. All opposition parties were broken up and reduced to impotence. The PCES was again forced underground and the far left as a whole was silenced or exiled.

Leadership and Organization. The secretary-general of the PCES is Shakik Jorge Jandal. Other prominent leaders include Antonio Pineda, secretary of the Executive Committee, and the poet Roque Dalton.

The PCES controls the United Federation of Salvadoran Trade Unions (Federación Unido de Sindicatos Salvadoreños; FUSS). According to the World Federation of Trade Union publication *World Trade Union Movement* (London, April 1971), there are 12,000 workers grouped in twenty-one national unions which are FUSS affiliates. FUSS objectives include: formation of a communist-controlled central union; trade and diplomatic relations with all countries, especially communist ones; and nonintervention in the affairs of other states.

The PCES is believed to control two small youth organizations: the Revolutionary University Students' Federation (Federación de Estudiantes Universitarios Revolucionarios) and the Vanguard of Salvadoran Youth (Vanguárdia de las Juventudes Salvadoreñas). These groups appear to have only minimal support among students.

In July the government of General Molina ordered the army to occupy university premises in San Salvador and other cities. Many students and professors were arrested for "distributing training manuals on urban guerrilla warfare," and the schools were closed for two months (*Intercontinental Press,* 4 September). Troops also occupied the headquarters of FUSS.

Party Internal Affairs. The PCES has traditionally been pro-Soviet but in recent years some divisions have arisen among party leaders over the proper form of struggle in the present situation. Roque Dalton and Cayetano Carpio are believed to lead a faction advocating immediate violent action. Shakik Jandal leads the soft-line, pro-Soviet faction which appears to still control the party.

In a speech given at a seminar in Prague on the ideological struggle of Latin American communist and workers' parties, PCES member D. Jiménez said that in El Salvador "petty-bourgeois ultra-revolutionary ideology [had] been making some headway, chiefly among university students and factionalists expelled from [the] party." Their target, he continued, was the communist party, the trade unions, and progressive movements and organizations rather than "imperialism and the oligarchy." Drawing their support from students and using "Maoist" phraseology, they maintained that "armed struggle by small underground groups [was] the only way to win power and implement needed structural change," Jiménez added. The PCES was combating these "dangerous views," although its difficulties were many. The party was training "propaganda cadres," strengthening itself "organizationally and ideologically," training trade-union leaders and "activists," and arranging discussion seminars on vital problems. As a result of these efforts, Jiménez concluded, "party influence in the trade unions [was] growing" and there was a "perceptible urge for unity." (*WMR,* April 1972.)

Domestic Views and Activities. Due to its internal weakness and its very small organizational base, the PCES engages in very little political activity. The only known activity in 1972 was its support for the UNO candidates in the election (see above).

The domestic situation was described in part by D. Jiménez at the aforementioned meeting of communist and workers' parties. He noted that the majority of El Salvador's population is engaged in agriculture—a situation now "giving rise to serious crisis phenomena." The "concentration of land in the hands of big landowners restricts the home market and makes the economy increasingly dependent on the Central American market," Jiménez explained. Thus, "large sections of the Salvadoran population, including the bourgeoisie," were increasingly interested in "radical agrarian reforms." In spite of efforts at reform legislation by the government, Jiménez said that due to its "class outlook" it could never settle the agrarian problem "in the interest of the masses." (*WMR,* June 1972.)

Speaking of PCES activity in the countryside, Jiménez said: "The motive forces of the revolution are primarily the proletariat, peasants and middle strata." The party's task, he added, was "steadily to raise their class consciousness, draw them into revolutionary action, and work to form a united front for democracy and progress." To this end, peasant committees had been organized and a worker-peasant alliance encouraged, using "illegal as well as legal opportunities." (Ibid.)

International Positions. Although its traditionally pro-Soviet position has been challenged by dissidents within the party, the PCES remains to all appearances, in the Soviet camp. The

PCES has charged the Chinese Communist Party with obstructing unity in the international communist movement.

In 1971, Shakik Jandal declared that the El Salvadoran people approved Peru's "anti-oligarchical, anti-imperialist process" and many believed it would be a good example for El Salvador to imitate. The Central American Common Market, he also said, was dominated by the North American "imperialists" and "regional bourgeoisie." (*Unidad,* Lima, 8 July.)

The PCES sent a delegation to the Eighth Conference of Communist Parties of Central America, Mexico and Panama, held somewhere in Central America in May 1972 (see *Mexico* and *IB,* no. 12).

Publications. The PCES issues a semiweekly clandestine newspaper, *La Verdad*.

Palo Alto, California   Lynn Ratliff

Guadeloupe

The Guadeloupe Communist Party (Parti Communiste Guadeloupéen; PCG) originated in 1944 as the Guadeloupe Federation of the French Communist Party, which in March 1958 transformed itself into the present autonomous party. In recent years the PCG has been plagued by conflict and expulsions, and the communist left in Guadeloupe is now represented by several diffuse groups in addition to the PCG, of which the most prominent is the Guadeloupe National Organization Group (GONG).

The PCG is legal. It claims to have 1,500 members (*WMR*, April 1972). The population of Guadeloupe is 335,000 (estimated 1970). The PCG is an active participant in Guadeloupe's political life, on both local and departmental levels (as one of France's overseas departments, Guadeloupe is an integral part of the French Republic). In municipal elections held in March 1971, communist candidates—competing with, among others, the ruling Gaullist party, the Union of Democrats for the Republic (UDR)—won in seven of the 34 municipalities of Guadeloupe, including Pointe-à-Pitre, the largest city. The PCG also participates in Guadeloupe's 36-member General Council, where it is represented by nine party members and supported by a tenth, non-communist councilor. The PCG also has participation at the national level: Paul Lacavé of the PCG Politburo has been a member of the French National Assembly since 1968, and within the French Senate the PCG is indirectly represented by a "progressive ally" elected in 1968 with communist support.

Leadership and Organization. The PCG is headed by Guy Daninthe as first secretary (for other names see *YICA, 1972*, p. 373). A new leadership was scheduled to be elected in 1972 following the party's Fifth Congress, 23–25 November.

In his article on Guadeloupe communists (*WMR*, April) Guy Daninthe stated that the party was organized into 11 "sections" and 50 "nuclei." None of its officers were full-time party workers. A large number of its members were said to be workers, many of whom were engaged in the growing of sugar cane, the island's main economic activity. Of members in professions, almost all were of worker or peasant origin.

The PCG has strong influence in Guadeloupe's largest trade union, the General Confederation of Labor of Guadeloupe (Confédération Général du Travail de la Guadeloupe; CGTG), which has some 5,000 members. PCG Politburo member Hermann Songeons continued in 1972 to be the CGTG's secretary-general.

The party's youth front, the Union of Communist Youth of Guadeloupe (Union de la Jeunesse Communiste de la Guadeloupe; UJCG), was established in 1967. Influence among young people, however, appears to be limited. In his article, Daninthe made no mention of the UJCG and only a brief reference to the party's youth activities, but documents of the Fifth Congress referred to a renewed effort to step up communist activity among Guadeloupe's young people (TASS, 28 November).

The party seems to have influence within the Union of Guadeloupe Women (Union des Femmes Guadeloupéens; UFG), which is affiliated to the Soviet-controlled Women's International Democratic Federation. The UFG held its Fifth Congress on 8–9 July.

Departmental and National Views and Policies. The PCG seeks autonomy for Guadeloupe within the framework of an alliance with France. Politically such an alliance would involve a local legislative assembly, an executive organ responsible to that assembly, and a body to determine the details of cooperation with France, as proposed in the Martinique autonomy convention of August 1971 (see *YICA, 1972,* pp. 392–93). Economically, its main goal is an extensive agrarian reform, whose leadership would be in the hands of workers and employees now engaged in sugar production and marketing.

Daninthe (*WMR,* April) admitted that the party's pro-autonomy stance was competing against the "powerful appeal and explosive quality" of the slogan of independence used by those farther to the left. Arguing that the goal of autonomy was more realistic, he cited the danger of complete independence with respect to Guadeloupe's geographic position "in a region where U.S. imperialism never hesitates to crush a people seeking a genuinely democratic regime." Furthermore, there was the prospect of the "democratic forces of France gaining ground."

A conference for the self-determination of overseas departments and territories, held in Paris on 30 May, was attended by Paul Lacavé, representatives of five other departments and territories, the French communist and socialist parties, and a number of affiliated organizations. The PCG approved the resulting document, although it was given relatively little publicity.

The PCG welcomed the accord between the French communist and socialist parties, announced on 26 June (see *France*). The joint program—probably the most important event of the year for the French Communist Party in view of the upcoming legislative elections—lost much of its importance in Guadeloupe when the Socialist Federation of Guadeloupe disassociated itself from its French counterpart and did not adhere to the accord (*L'Etincelle,* 22 July).

The major event of 1972 for the PCG was the convening of its Fifth Congress, at Pointe-à-Pitre in November, attended by 159 PCG delegates. Themes of the congress were the party's concept of self-determination for Guadeloupe and other overseas departments and the means of bringing about this goal; the party's political orientation in the light of the political, economic, and social conditions that have evolved since its Fourth Congress, in 1968; preparation for the 1973 elections to the French National Assembly, for which three PCG members were candidates; and an examination of the party's weaknesses and errors since 1968 in order to enhance its strength, discipline, ties with the masses, "combativeness," and understanding of Marxism-Leninism.

International Views and Positions. The PCG remained in 1972 a strong supporter of the Communist Party of the Soviet Union. Most of the PCG's attention outside Guadeloupe, however, was given to France and its possessions.

The party campaigned for abstention in a referendum in April to determine the admission of Great Britain, Ireland, Denmark, and Norway to the European Common Market. The party contended that without a satisfactory preliminary definition of its relation to France, Guadeloupe should not participate in a decision that concerned French national sovereignty, unless it was a question of self-determination for Guadeloupe (*L'Etincelle,* 15 April).

Among pronouncements on general international issues, the Vietnam war was given greatest attention. On 19 May the PCG organized a rally and march in Pointe-à-Pitre that was marked by police intervention. The Soviet Union was also a frequent subject of articles in *L'Etincelle,* followed by references to Latin American communism, a series of articles on Spain ("The Crisis of the Church and Army"), and reports on East Germany, Bulgaria, Madagascar, and other countries.

Publication. The PCG publishes a weekly newspaper, *L'Etincelle,* with a claimed circulation of 5,000 (occasionally reaching 15,000 during special events). These figures should be considered impressive, according to Guy Daninthe, in view of the high percentage of illiterates in Guadeloupe, where "persuasion by word of mouth is the traditional and more important method" (*WMR,* April). As with party offices, the paper has no full-time editor.

*   *   *

The GONG. Many of the expelled members of the PCG (and apparently also some current members) have associated themselves with a small militant group, the Guadeloupe National Organization Group (Groupe d'Organisation Nationale de la Guadeloupe; GONG), created in 1963 and based in Paris. In 1964 the group espoused a pro-Chinese stand, accusing the PCG of "revisionism." It calls for independence for Guadeloupe by means of armed struggle. There is very little reliable information on the leadership or organizational structure of the GONG.

The group's main publication is a monthly, *GONG.* Another publication, *Verité et Progrès Social,* identified as pro-Chinese, may or may not be associated with the GONG.

California State University, San Jose   Eric Stromquist

Guatemala

The communist party in Guatemala, which since 1952 has been called the Guatemalan Party of Labor (Partido Guatemalteco del Trabajo; PGT), originated in the predominantly communist-controlled "Socialist Labor Unification," founded in 1921. This group became the Communist Party of Guatemala (Partido Comunista de Guatemala; PCG) in 1923 and joined the Communist International in 1924. Increasing communist activities among workers during the mid-1920s were cut off by the end of the decade and were kept at a minimum throughout the dictatorship of Jorge Ubico (1931–44). In 1947 the communists as an organized group reappeared in the clandestine "Democratic Vanguard." In 1949 this group took the name PCG. A prominent communist labor leader founded a second and parallel communist party in 1950, called the "Revolutionary Workers' Party of Guatemala." The two groups merged into a single PCG in 1951. In 1952 the PCG adopted the name PGT, which it has continued to use. The PGT was legal between 1952 and 1954 and played an active role in the administration of President Jacobo Arbenz. It has been illegal since the overthrow of Arbenz in 1954.

There are three guerrilla groups in Guatemala. The Revolutionary Armed Forces (Fuerzas Armadas Revolucionarias; FAR) is the military arm of the PGT. The largest and most active group during 1972 was the Rebel Armed Forces (Fuerzas Armadas Rebeldes; FAR) (see below). A third organization is the 13 November Revolutionary Movement (Movimiento Revolucionario 13 de Noviembre; MR–13) (see below).

The PGT is estimated to have 750 members. The FAR and MR–13 are believed to have only 50 to 100 members each plus several hundred sympathizers. The population of Guatemala is 5,310,000 (1970 census).

The terrorism that has been a serious problem in Guatemala for several years continued throughout 1972, although at reduced levels. Nevertheless, there were still hundreds of incidents, including kidnappings, assassinations, robberies, and other acts of violence. Both left-wing and right-wing groups were responsible, with some evidence, however, that efforts by the government of Gen. Carlos Arana Osorio to curtail leftist-inspired violence was meeting with some success. The rightist groups, such as the Organized National Anti-Communist Movement (Movimiento Anticomunista Nacional Organizado, MANO) and the Eye for an Eye (Ojo por Ojo), continued to operate with apparently little government interference.

There had been expectations that terrorism might increase in 1972 following President Arana's lifting of the state of siege in late 1971, but his government's strenuous campaign against the leftist terrorists was generally credited with holding terrorism to the relatively low levels of 1972. In addition, the disarray in leftist groups, caused in part by the years of government attacks and more importantly by the deaths, disappearances, and arrests of FAR and MR–13 leaders, was a factor in the lessened violence. The most spectacular terrorist incident during the year was the assassination of a prominent right-wing politician in June (the first vice-president of Congress, a leader in General Arana's National Liberation Movement, and a onetime leader of MANO). It was speculated at first that left-wing terrorists were responsible, but later interpretations were that it was the result of "internecine fighting" on the right (*The Economist,* London, 22 July) or an action of the Army (*Latin America,* London, 19 January 1973).

PGT. Leadership and Organization. Little information is available on the leadership and organization of the PGT. The party has long been led by its secretary-general, Bernardo Alvarado Monzón, and Central Committee members Mario Silva Jonama, Carlos René Valle y Valle, Hugo Barrios Klee, Carlos Alvarado Jérez, and Miguel Angel Hernández, all of whom were reportedly arrested in September and later executed (*Granma,* English edition, 7 January 1973). Guatemalan Interior Ministry sources denied that the alleged arrests had taken place, but government spokesmen agreed that the PGT's top leadership had apparently disappeared. The alleged arrests took place two days before the party's 23rd anniversary and were accompanied by a police announcement that "subversive" PGT literature had been discovered "throughout the country." (*Christian Science Monitor,* 26 October 1972.)

The Patriotic Youth of Labor (Juventud Patriotica del Trabajo) is an auxiliary of the PGT. The party controls the clandestine Guatemalan Autonomous Socialist Federation (Federación Autónoma Socialista Guatemalteca), a small and relatively unimportant labor organization.

Party Internal Affairs. The most recent congress of the PGT was held clandestinely in December 1969. There had been speculation that another congress would meet in late 1972, but the disappearance of the party's top leadership in late September put an end to such speculation. Writing in 1970, a party leader said the PGT was "passing through a particularly trying period," when it had to deal with problems of "armed struggle and those of fighting splinters and liquidators" (*WMR,* December 1970; also see *YICA, 1972,* p. 377). Events during 1972 did little to alter this assessment.

Domestic Attitudes and Activities. The PGT reaffirmed its support for armed struggle in 1972. Writing in the *World Marxist Review,* Francisco J. Prieto said that "a revolutionary people's war" is the "principal method of carrying forward the revolution in our country at this stage." (*WMR,* September 1972). But the party supports "all forms of struggle" and the "drawing [of] the masses into it." Prieto said the PGT held that the revolution in Guatemala consisted of "two closely linked stages." One stage dealt with the agrarian, anti-imperialist, popular revolution, the other with the Socialist revolution. The first stage, Prieto wrote, "will witness, among others, certain social changes, primarily in the countryside." This in turn, he added, "should pave the way for the peasants, led by the working class, to move on to the second, socialist stage of the revolution."

Commenting on municipal elections in March, 1972, Prieto wrote that the ruling coalition's victory "was not unexpected." Holding that the coalition, led by President Arana's MLN, "represents part of the agrarian and the industrial bourgeoisie," he added its victory resulted from "terror against democrats, the 'disappearance' of opposition candidates, the intimidation of voters, and patrolling by army units." The PGT, as an illegal party, did not take part in the election.

International Views. The PGT sent a delegate to the May meeting of Communist Parties of Mexico, Central America, and Panama held in Mexico City (see *Mexico*). A party leader wrote at mid-year that the PGT attaches "vast importance to increasing fraternal support from the working people of all countries and to their solidarity with the Guatemalan people's struggle for freedom and democracy" (*WMR,* September).

Publications. The PGT's national organization and its Southern Regional Committee issue the clandestine newspapers *La Verdad* and *Grito Popular,* respectively. The JPT organ is *Juventud;* that of the PGT's Revolutionary Armed Forces is the clandestine *FAR* (not to be confused with Rebel Armed Forces having the same initials). These latter two periodicals are issued very irregularly.

*   *   *

Guerrillas. In December, 1962 the Rebel Armed Forces was formed by members of three existing guerrilla organizations and after a series of shifts and reorganizations became an independent group. The most active early leaders of the FAR were Marco Antonio Yon Sosa and Luis Augusto Turcios Lima, both former Guatemalan military officers who had received training in the United States.

For several years, the FAR emphasized urban activities, the most important of which were political assassinations and the kidnappings of businessmen, politicians, and foreign diplomats—whose safe return was guaranteed only in exchange for the release of "political prisoners" held by the government or the payment of large monetary ransoms, or both. During 1972, the FAR continued its program, but it was on a much reduced level. The lack of clearly defined leadership, as well as strong government measures to locate FAR hideouts and to arrest suspected FAR members, were elements in the decline of FAR terrorism. But given the recent history of Guatemalan politics, the FAR is expected to remain an important element in the terrorist camp and is thought to be currently undergoing a reorganization.

The official organ of the FAR is *Guerrillero.*

The MR–13. The 13 November Revolutionary Movement was formed by Marco Antonio Yon Sosa and other young military officers after an abortive uprising against the government of Miguel Ydígoras Fuentes on 13 November 1960. Yon Sosa commanded the organization until he was killed on 18 May 1970 in an encounter with Mexican troops on the Mexican-Guatemalan border. The organization has seemed to lack direction and effectiveness since his death. It was largely inactive in 1972 and there is some speculation that its remnants may merge, or indeed already have merged, with the FAR.

The official organ of the MR–13 is *Revolución Socialista;* no issues of the publication are known to have appeared in the past year, a fact which suggests to some that the MR–13 itself is largely defunct now that Yon Sosa is dead.

The Christian Science Monitor   James Nelson Goodsell

Guyana

The People's Progressive Party (PPP) of Guyana was founded in 1950. At its first congress, in 1951, it declared itself a nationalist party, committed to socialism, national independence, and Caribbean unity. During the nearly two decades following, the leadership of the PPP claimed to be Marxist-Leninist, but the party was not officially affiliated with the international communist movement. In 1969 the leader of the party, Cheddi Jagan, moved unequivocally to align the PPP with the Soviet Union. In turn, the PPP was recognized by the Soviet leaders as a bona fide communist party.

The Working People's Vanguard Party (WPVP) is a small pro-Chinese organization (see below).

The PPP is legal. From 1957 to 1964 it was the ruling party in British Guiana (which became independent and took the name Guyana in 1966). In the most recent national elections, December 1968, the People's National Congress (PNC) won a clear majority and since then the PPP has been an opposition party. The PPP abstained from running candidates in the local elections of December 1970, charging the PNC with fraud and violence. It is in the nature of politics in Guyana that support for the two principal parties, the PPP and PNC, is based primarily on race. The PNC is supported by the Negro population. The PPP is supported primarily by the East Indian population, representing about 50 percent of the total, and has a membership of some 20,000. The PPP is estimated to have only about 100 confirmed communists at the present time. The population of Guyana is 763,000 (estimated 1970).

In the past few years the PPP has been loosing support and declining in influence. Its appeal has been weakened by the PNC government's policies of nationalization and recognition of Cuba, China, and the Soviet Union, and by internal dissent and defection caused by Cheddi Jagan's ideological alignment with the Soviet Union.

Leadership and Organization. The first secretary of the PPP is Cheddi Jagan. His wife, Janet Jagan, is the general secretary and Ranji Chandisingh is vice-chairman. The Ideological Committee, headed by the Jagans, was established in 1970 to ensure conformity to Marxist-Leninist teaching within the party.

The Progressive Youth Organization (PYO) is the PPP's affiliated youth group which is believed to be a source of strong support for Cheddi Jagan personally. In March, two members of the PYO attended the Second Congress of the Cuban Union of Communist Youth in Havana. The PPP controls the Guyana Agricultural Workers' Union, which is made up primarily of workers in the sugar industry. The PPP maintains a women's group, the Women's Progressive Organization.

Party Internal Affairs. Although Cheddi Jagan and his followers remain in control of the PPP, the party still suffers from internal dissension caused by his commitment of the party to the international communist movement in 1969 (see *YICA, 1970,* pp. 446–48). Many long-time members have left the party, and many have been expelled by Jagan for failing to support his leadership.

In September 1972 the PPP held its Seventeenth Congress. The party reaffirmed its commitments to "socialism based on Marxism-Leninism." Visitors from other Caribbean countries and Romania attended the congress and the Communist Party of the Soviet Union sent a congratulatory message.

Domestic Attitudes and Activities. In January 1972 Cheddi Jagan gave a speech on the current situation in Guyana in which he said that the "ruling forces" in Guyana claimed the country had a "parliamentary democracy," but that in reality the system was "more dictatorial than democratic." Jagan claimed that the Guyanese had "no basic civil rights," were not allowed to travel freely, and could not obtain jobs if they had studied in socialist countries. Furthermore, the rights to organize and strike were "endangered." In particular, he emphasized the difficulties workers had in forming unions which would be recognized by employers, and the danger of the government's proposed bill forbidding strikes. Jagan concluded saying that in Guyana the "struggle for democratic freedom is part of the workers' struggle to increase their standard of living." ("Radio Peace and Progress," Moscow, 7 January.)

An editorial in the PPP journal, *Thunder* (April–June), said that on 15 June the party paper, *Mirror,* had been forced to suspend publication due to a shortage of newsprint brought about by the government's requirement of licenses for its importation. The editor of *Mirror,* it was reported, charged the government with "deliberately withholding newsprint supplies in an effort to gag criticism." Further, the Guyana Civil Liberties Action Council had charged that the delay in issuing licenses showed a "blatant disregard for the fundamental right of freedom of expression" and that the restrictions on newsprint and printing equipment were "petty, unnecessary and arbitrary and aimed at curtailing the freedom of the press in Guyana."

The PPP issued a statement in July, protesting its exclusion from the Guyana delegation to the Ninth Meeting of the Commonwealth Parliamentary Association. The statement claimed the PPP had been kept out in order to prevent it from exposing the "many violations of parliamentary procedure by the government and the misgoverning of the country."

In August Cheddi Jagan issued an 18-point program which he claimed would make Guyana a "democratic state free from foreign control." Among the demands were a call for nationalization of foreign monopolies, close relations with non-aligned nations, and support for all national liberation movements. (Bridgetown radio, Barbados, 13 August.)

International Positions. International affairs were particularly emphasized in Guyana in 1972 due to its role as host for the Third Conference of Non-Aligned Countries, 8–12 August, in Georgetown. The PPP issued a statement to the preparatory meeting for the conference in February in which it said that under the PNC government, Guyana's claim to non-alignment was "highly questionable," and that the government was aligned with "U.S. imperialism." According to the PPP, the government has not treated socialist countries on an equal basis with capitalist ones as demonstrated by its denial of a resident mission in Guyana for the Soviet Union, its non-recognition of the German Democratic Republic, and its shift of position on recognition of the People's Republic of China coincident with that of the United States. The PPP statement further claimed that while the PNC encouraged students going to Western countries, it put "severe restrictions on those going to the Soviet Union and other socialist countries" and "discriminated against them with respect to government employment." Regarding trade, the party stated that the government's 10 percent service charge on goods imported from socialist countries, including the Soviet Union and China, was not imposed on imports from the "capitalist-imperialist" countries. Finally, the PPP stated that the PNC government was "aligned with the pro-imperialist U.S.-Brazil-Nicaragua-Paraguay-Argentina axis" but to keep up appearances it maintained "nominal associations with the anti-imperialist Cuba-Chile-Peru axis." (*Thunder,* April–June.)

On several occasions during the year, the PPP, through its primary spokesman, Cheddi Jagan, issued statements condemning "U.S. intervention in Indochina." Early in the year Jagan traveled to conferences on the Vietnam war in Paris and Helsinki and in August he made a motion in the Guyana parliament urging the government to issue a resolution condemning the United States at the Non-Aligned Conference.

In a speech at the University of the West Indies, Jagan criticized West Indian leaders for "confused thinking" and reminded them that in other parts of the world "white people were fighting for black people" (Guyana Broadcasting Service, Georgetown, 22 February). He devoted most of his speech to praising the development of communist countries, including Cuba.

Jagan issued an appeal for solidarity with Chile's government in April. He denounced the "maneuvers of the U.S. government and monopolies which seek the eventual overthrow of President Allende's government" and said that "attacks against Chile [were] directed at all Latin America." (Havana radio, 26 April.)

The PPP sponsored a conference of Caribbean revolutionary groups and movements in August, attended by organizations from Guadeloupe, Jamaica, Trinidad-Tobago, Surinam, Venezuela, and French Guiana. Three main topics were discussed: new strategy and tactics of "imperialism" concerning Caribbean integration; civil rights in the Caribbean; and ideology of revolution in the Caribbean, the relevancy of Marxism-Leninism, black power; and prospects and tasks. Jagan declared "U.S. imperialism" to be the "main enemy of the Latin American people" and urged the formation of "Marxist-Leninist vanguard parties" in each of the Caribbean territories.

In October Cheddi Jagan addressed the meeting of the World Peace Council Presidium which met in Santiago, Chile. He gave a lengthy analysis of the "state of dependency of the Latin American countries on U.S. imperialism" and declared that the Soviet Union, Cuba, and Chile were examples to follow.

Cheddi Jagan reportedly traveled to Europe and Asia during the year to attend peace meetings sponsored by various leftist organizations.

Publications. The PPP publishes a quarterly journal, *Thunder,* and a daily newspaper, the *Mirror*. Publication of *Mirror* was suspended for some time during 1972 (see above).

*   *   *

The WPVP. The Working People's Vanguard Party (Marxist-Leninist) was founded in January 1969 by Brindley Benn, a former PPP member. Benn questioned Jagan's form of Marxism and held that the PPP was following the path of "opportunism and revisionism." The WPVP is opposed to participation in elections, on the grounds that both the PNC and PPP are "racist" and thus are impeding the unification of workers. Unequivocally giving his allegiance to Mao Tse-tung, Benn has applauded the Cultural Revolution and criticized the Soviet Union as a class-dominated society. The PPP's alignment with the Soviet Union was branded by Benn as "betrayal" of Guyanese and others fighting for national liberation.

Following the Cuban foreign minister's speech at the Non-Aligned Conference, Benn praised the "people's concept of non-alignment" which it expressed. The speech was significant, he said, because it "underlined Cuba's staunch loyalty to the principle of the international solidarity of the working class." (*Granma,* English, Havana, 20 August.)

The WPVP publishes a newssheet, *Creole.*

Palo Alto, California   Lynn Ratliff

Haiti

The Communist Party of Haiti (Parti Communiste d'Haïti) was founded in 1930. It disintegrated the following year when its leaders were forced to flee the country. The year 1946 saw the founding of the Popular Socialist Party (Parti Socialist Populaire; PSP), which was recognized by the international communist movement, and the formation of a second Communist Party of Haiti; but by 1947 both had collapsed.

In November 1954 a new communist movement, the People's National Liberation Party (Parti Populaire de Libération Nationale; PPLN), was formed. The PPLN broke up in July 1965, but reappeared the following year as the Party of the Union of Haitian Democrats (Parti d'Union de Démocrates Haïtiens; PUDH or PUDHA—or in Creole, Pati Union Demokrat Ayisiin, PUDA), a Castroite group that placed strong emphasis on guerrilla tactics. A pro-Soviet movement, the People's Entente Party (Parti d'Entente Populaire; PEP) was formed in 1959. Although the PUDHA and the PEP based their activities on divergent strategic and tactical concepts, they cooperated from 1964 to 1968 in the "anti-imperialist" and "anti-feudal" United Democratic Front of National Liberation. In January 1969 the PUDHA and the PEP merged to form the United Party of Haitian Communists (Parti Unifié des Communistes Haïtiens; PUCH). The combined PUCH is believed to have about 500 members and presumably derives support from elements in and around the capital, Port-au-Prince, and from a very small rural following (although before the merger the PUDHA claimed to be organized in eight of Haiti's nine provinces). The population of Haiti is 5,200,000 (estimated 1970).

All political parties in Haiti have been proscribed since 1949. In April 1969 a law was passed declaring all forms of communist activity crimes against the state, the penalty for which would be both confiscation of property and death. The government's anti-communist campaign which followed decimated the ranks of the newly formed PUCH. François Duvalier, who had been president since 1957, died on 21 April 1971 and was succeeded by his son Jean-Claude, who continued the repression of communists and other anti-Duvalier groups. Most PUCH activity has necessarily been carried on outside Haiti among exiles in Europe (especially the Soviet Union), Cuba, and, to a much smaller degree, the United States.

Leadership and Organization. The leadership of the PUCH is unknown and is believed to be entirely in exile, primarily in Moscow or Havana. During 1972 PUCH members Jacques Dorsilien and Jean Gerard issued statements on behalf of the party. Little is known about the party's organization within Haiti. A youth group, the Union of United Communist Youth of Haiti, is possibly affiliated with the PUCH and is believed to be based outside Haiti.

Domestic and International Views. Early in 1972, speaking from Moscow, Jacques Dorsilien charged that the Duvalier government, while continuing its "demagogies about so-called national reconciliation and liberalization" of its policies, had recruited spies, imported weapons from the United States, and added two battalions of "anti-communist Leopards" (a special army corps which replaced François Duvalier's personal militia, the Tontons Macoutes) to the army. These measures, he said, were in preparation for "another massacre of the population," and for the "murder of those who effectively struggle for freedom and the overthrow of the Duvalierist regime—especially the communists." Dorsilien urged all patriots to rally their co-workers and "form committees of patriotic resistance under the leadership of the PUCH to free the homeland from the Duvalierists and the imperialists." ("Radio Peace and Progress," 7 January.)

Later in the year Dorsilien declared that since 1957 the Duvalierists had "devoted themselves to selling the country to foreign capitalists" at the "expense of the people's sweat." He accused the government of killing people, sending them to prison without trial, and forbidding the formation of trade unions or political parties. (Ibid., 29 May.)

PUCH member Jean Gerard said in a radio broadcast that "women are the most exploited persons in the Haitian semicolonial and semifeudal regime" since they are exploited both as workers and as women. The government's support for women's liberation is "nothing but more demagogy," he added. The PUCH, Gerard explained, "struggles to give women the right to work, to give women the same wages as men in the same position, to build nurseries, kindergartens, boarding schools, and to take a series of other measures to free women from housework." (Ibid.)

In November the PUCH celebrated its fourth anniversary. A broadcast commemorating the occasion declared that the merger of the two Marxist-Leninist parties which led to the creation of the PUCH "represents a completely different stage in the struggle for liberation." The PUCH, according to the broadcast, is the only Haitian "revolutionary political organization which has a program of really revolutionary changes" and is thus receiving "increasing support and sympathy among all Haitian patriots." (Ibid., 29 November.)

In a summary of the year, a PUCH statement declared that "no demagogy about the so-called liberalization or democratization, nor any gaudy amnesty which the Duvalierists have announced will make the Haitian people give up their struggle." The newspaper *Boukan,* which had not been published for some time, was said to have reappeared in 1972 to "guide peasants and workers" and to "denounce all of the plots of the Duvalierists and U.S. imperialists." The statement noted that during the year there had been strikes and protests and increasing unrest among the peasants indicating the possibility of setting up a "revolutionary union" under the leadership of the communists to overthrow the Duvalier regime. (Ibid., 20 December.)

The PUCH is firmly pro-Soviet. It regards the United States as a "chief supporter" of the "hereditary [Duvalier] dictatorship" and other "Latin American cliques" in order to "plunder their natural resources" (ibid., 6 January). The Haitian party has professed its solidarity with the peoples of Indochina and the Middle East, and with the "liberation struggle" of the peoples of Cuba, Chile, and other Latin American nations.

Publications. In 1969 the PUCH began publication of a clandestine newspaper, *Boukan.* It had been suppressed during the past two years, but reportedly it resumed publication in 1972. The PUCH reportedly also publishes *Nouvelle Optique,* a quarterly review, in Montreal, Canada. The party relies heavily on radio broadcasts from abroad; Havana radio transmits 14 hours weekly to Haiti (11 in Creole, 3 in French) and Moscow "Radio Peace and Progress" broadcasts a 30-minute program daily in Creole.

Palo Alto, California   Lynn Ratliff

Honduras

The Communist Party of Honduras (Partido Comunista de Honduras; PCH) was organized in 1927, disbanded in 1932, and reorganized in 1954 (now considered its official founding date). A small group, which became known as the Honduran Revolutionary Party (Partido Revolucionario Hondureño; PRH), broke away in 1961. A dispute over strategy and tactics in 1967 resulted in the formation of two rival parties claiming to be the PCH. In 1971 the Chinese Communists reported the presence of a pro-Chinese Communist Party of Honduras/Marxist-Leninist (Partido Comunista de Honduras/Marxista-Leninista; PCH/ML), possibly the former PRH or a faction of the PCH.

The PCH is estimated to have had some 300 members (*World Strength of the Communist Party Organizations,* Washington, D.C., 1972, p. 149).

Reports on the organization and leadership of the PCH factions are incomplete and often contradictory. Top leaders of the pro-Soviet faction apparently include Dionisio Ramos, as secretary general, and Mario Sosa Navarro; the chief international spokesman for the PCH in 1972 was D. Paz. The rival faction of the PCH is reportedly led by Tomás Erazo Peña (ibid.).

The PCH held its Second Congress in May 1972. The congress approved the PCH's political theses, adopted a new program and rules for the party, and elected new guiding bodies (TASS, 21 May). Dissension within the party evidently continues to be of concern since the message of greetings sent by the Communist Party of the Soviet Union wished the PCH "further success in strengthening its ranks on the basis of Marxist-Leninist principles and proletarian internationalism" (*Pravda,* 21 May). The party frequently condemns "left opportunism," "subjectivism," and "adventurism," all of which "extol guerrilla warfare" and reject the organization of the working class. According to the PCH, this trend, once important among university students, is on the wane. (*WMR,* April.)

The PCH claims that Honduran labor unions are controlled by agents from the United States and that the peasant movement is weakened by widespread "opportunism." The party claims to have given up its previous policy of forming parallel labor and peasant movements and is now working within the "opportunist-led" organizations. It claims some success in overcoming anti-communist prejudices and in increasing class consciousness. (*Ibid.*)

Domestic Attitudes and Activities. The PCH calls for an "agrarian, anti-imperialist people's revolution" which will require a "high level of consciousness and organization of the people" and "unity of all democratic forces and their insoluble link with the masses." The party claims to be preparing for all forms of struggle; under the present conditions it sees a need for the achievement of its revolutionary aims by non-peaceful means, though it warns that "any action undertaken without participation of the masses could be an extremely dangerous political gamble." (Ibid.) The party calls for the formation of a "democratic government supported by the workers, peasants, intellectuals, small and medium manufacturers and traders and expressing their interests" which will "make it possible to change the country's socio-economic structure." The bourgeoisie and big landed oligarchy are said to be at loggerheads except when it comes to suppressing the people. (Ibid., June.)

One of the chief causes of backwardness and poverty in Honduras, according to D. Paz, is "antiquated production relations," largely due to the massive landholdings of the United Fruit Company and Standard Fruit. An agrarian reform decree in 1962, providing for the abolition of the latifundia, was "unable to break the resistance of the latifundium holders and confined itself to settling the lands." The "bourgeoisie's reformist experiment in so-called agricultural cooperatives" in the late 1960s failed as well. The party claims to see, and to have had a role in developing, a "fresh upswing in the peasant struggle," evident in land seizures, demonstrations, and more radical demands on the government. (Ibid.)

According to Sosa Navarro, the "struggle of the Honduran people," especially since 1969, "has forced the leading classes to assume an attitude of relative tolerance." He stated that the PCH would not issue a blanket statement of support or repudiation of the existing government in Honduras, but would support those policies it considered constructive and criticize the others. Ultimately the Honduran political system had to be changed. (Interview on "La Voz de Honduras," Tegucigalpa, 11 January 1973.)

International Views and Positions. The PCH, in a joint declaration with the Costa Rican People's Vanguard Party, condemned U.S. policy throughout the world, particularly in Vietnam and Latin America, and demanded the return of Arab lands occupied by Israel. The two parties praised the governments of Cuba, Chile, and Panama, and sent fraternal greetings to the CPSU. (Havana radio, 3 September 1972.)

The PCH attended the Eighth Conference of the Communist and Workers' Parties of Central America, Mexico and Panama, in May (see *Mexico* and *IB,* no. 12).

Publications. The pro-Soviet branch of the PCH publishes *Trabajo* and *Voz Popular.* Party statements appear in *Vanguardia Revolucionaria,* described as a paper of the Honduran "working class and peasants" (Sosa interview, 11 January 1973).

*   *   *

The PCH / ML. Little is known of the organizational structure of the PCH/ML. It is believed to find its chief support among university students. The party has outlined its objectives as the destruction of the existing government through mass movements and armed struggle, and the establishment of a revolutionary government which would carry out agrarian reform, recover the national wealth, give state power to the people, establish economic independence for the country, and carry out a cultural revolution. The party condemns the PCH as being "right opportunist" and for "betraying" the fundamental principles of Marxism and the interests of the Honduran people. In July 1971 the PCH/ML Central Committee hailed the Chinese Communist Party as the "bulwark of the world revolutionary movement in the struggle against imperialism, modern revisionism and all reactionaries," and reaffirmed the PCH/ML's commitment to armed struggle. It praised the Chinese for their defense of Marxism-Leninism against the Soviet Union's "deviations of modern revisionism." (*Peking Review,* no. 31, 1971.)

Hoover Institution
Stanford University

William E. Ratliff

Martinique

The Martinique Communist Party (Parti Communiste Martiniquais; PCM) traces its founding to July 1921, when a socialist group, the "Friends of Jean Jaurès," adopted a communist ideology. In 1935 this and another Marxist group, the "Common Front," merged, and the new organization affiliated with the French Communist Party the following year. The party was disbanded while Martinique was under the control of the Vichy government in France (1940–43). In 1944 it reorganized as the Martinique Federation of the French Communist Party, and in September 1957 it became the autonomous PCM. The party is legal.

The PCM is estimated to have from 700 to 1,300 members. The population of Martinique is 335,000 (estimated 1970).

The PCM is an active participant in Martinique's political life, on both local and departmental levels (as one of France's overseas departments Martinique is an integral part of the French Republic). Its following, however, has generally been declining over the past fifteen years, partly because one of its leaders, Aimé Césaire, withdrew in 1956 to create the left-wing non-communist Martinique Progressive Party (Parti Progressiste Martiniquais; PPM), and partly as a consequence of the PCM's policy of autonomy for Martinique (see below), which does not have mass support. In contests for the three seats allocated to Martinique in the French National Assembly, the party won 62.5 percent of the votes cast in the 1956 elections (before the PCM-PPM split). In 1968, running separately, the PCM won about 17 percent; the PPM, about 20 percent; and the governing Gaullist party, the Union of Democrats for the Republic (UDR), some 58 percent.

The PCM controls four municipal (or commune) governments in Martinique. The mayors of Lamentin, Saint-Esprit, Morne-Rouge, and Macouba are PCM members. All four were re-elected to their posts in March 1971. In Martinique's 36-member General Council the party had 4 representatives in 1972.

Leadership and Organization. The PCM is led by its 10-member Politburo and 5-member Secretariat, which are elected by the Central Committee, following the latter's election by the party congress. Armand Nicolas is the secretary-general (for other names see *YICA, 1972*, pp. 390–91). The party held its Fifth Congress on 30–31 December 1972; officers were to be elected the following month.

The PCM obtains its primary support from the communist-controlled General Confederation of Labor of Martinique (Confédération Générale du Travail de la Martinique; CGTM), whose secretary-general is a PCM Politburo member. The CGTM, with some 4,000 members, is the largest trade union organization in Martinique.

The PCM has a youth organization, the Union of Communist Youth of Martinique (Union de la Jeunesse Communiste de la Martinique; UJCM). The organization is apparently still led by a "Provisional Committee" formed in 1969 to replace the Central Committee which was disbanded at that time pending a congress to reelect a new UJCM leadership (see *YICA, 1970,* p. 441). During 1972 the organization received little publicity in the PCM newspaper. Until recently, the PCM could count on considerable support from the General Association of Martinique Students (Association Générale des Etudiants Martiniquais), a member of the communist-controlled International Union of Students, but in 1970 controversy between the party and the more radical student organization attained such proportions that cooperation between the two was impossible. Somewhat less support had been derived from the Organization of Anti-Colonialist Youth of Martinique (Organization de la Jeunesse Anticolonialiste de la Martinique), whose relations with the PCM have also appeared to suffer since 1970. The two student groups received only slight mention in the PCM press in 1972.

Departmental and National Views and Policies. While attacking such domestic problems and institutions as industrial unemployment, racial discrimination, the educational system, and the influence of the church, the PCM in 1972 continued to place emphasis on a drive to achieve autonomy for Martinique—an autonomy that would give the island control over its own legislative and executive functions, while maintaining cooperation with France through a body comprising equal representation from Martinique and France, primarily for the purpose of administering financial and technical assistance to Martinique.

In the furtherance of its goals, the PCM is confronted with two major issues—its relationship with the non-communist PPM and the challenge from "leftist" elements who, in contrast to the PCM's call for autonomy, advocate complete independence. Efforts to unite Martinique's "democratic forces," directed mainly toward the PPM, the only other leftist party of consequence, are for the most part limited to election campaign periods and have as their goal the undermining of the UDR. Although in 1971 the PCM and PPM participated together in a number of activities to gain support for the autonomy movement, there were no such joint efforts in 1972. A PCM Politburo communiqué (*Justice,* 3 February) rejected a request by the PPM for a meeting of all groups in French Guiana and the Antilles opposed to a French-sponsored proposal for a regional statute to reorganize the administration of the Overseas Departments. The PCM, which had made a number of similar requests since the August 1971 autonomy convention at Morne-Rouge (see *YICA, 1972,* p. 393), all rejected by the PPM, contended that the PPM suggestion to include "notoriously anti-communist" pro-independence groups constituted a "negative factor capable of creating confusion between autonomy and independence in the minds of the masses."

On 30 May twenty-two organizations representing the autonomy movement in the overseas departments and territories (presumably including the PPM) met in Paris with the "most representative of French leftist forces," including the French communist and socialist parties (*Justice,* 6 July). Secretary-General Nicolas, representing the PCM, expressed satisfaction that in the communist-socialist alliance agreement signed at the meeting (see *France*) the two French parties recognized the right of the overseas departments and territories to choose their own political statute and autonomy.

The draft resolution for the Fifth Congress of the PCM (*Justice,* 26 October) reaffirmed the party's goal of autonomy for Martinique, stating that its efforts should be directed against (1) the "reactionary" forces of the UDR, which oppose the "democratic evolution of society," and (2) the "so-called revolutionaries," who "prevent the political union of the exploited class." Associated with the anti-UDR campaign was the resolution's charge that French monopolies were exploiting Martinique through their control of key sectors of the economy.

Threats to the PCM from the left were manifested in a variety of forms by various small groups whose "ideological contours are rather poorly defined" (ibid., 2 March). In the Rivière-Salée region an organization called the "People's Forces" under the leadership of Louis Pulvar was accused of making "virulent attacks" against the PCM. A second group, identified as Maoist, made its appearance four years ago under the name "National Movement of Martinique Liberation." It soon broke into a number of factions which in turn began to disappear, leaving only one, associated with the bulletin *Forward*. Of greatest concern to the PCM is an alleged Trotskyist group, the "Socialist Revolution," which issues two newspapers, *The North in Struggle* and the *Avant-Guarde Youth,* the latter being the organ of the party's "Revolutionary League of Youth," apparently the source of greatest direct leftist challenge to the PCM. The challenge is said to be presented in the form of young intellectuals who had been recent PCM sympathizers and were now penetrating the PCM in an attempt to weaken it by propagandizing its militants and those of the UJCM against the "dictators" and "Stalinists" of the leadership. In combating the influence of this and other such groups, PCM members were advised to divide the ideological struggle into one against "assimilationism" and one against leftism, and to help clarify the distinctions between the PCM and the independent groups.

International Views and Positions. The international line of the PCM closely follows that of the Communist Party of the Soviet Union on all major issues. The draft resolution for the party's Fifth Congress reaffirmed its position in the Sino-Soviet dispute by condemning the anti-Soviet campaigns of the Chinese leadership. In 1972 Secretary-General Nicolas took pains to defend the Soviet Union against criticism that it had abandoned the Vietnamese communists and had given in to "U.S. aggression." He attempted to explain the Soviet Union's dual role of practicing a "policy of peace" while at the same time supporting the national liberation movements, stating that the Soviet Union was not a "club of 'revolutionaries in easy chairs' or irresponsible fools," but had in its hand the "key to peace and war." In the case of Vietnam, he said, the direction of Soviet policy could clearly be seen in the amount of arms and specialized training given by the Soviet Union to the North Vietnamese. (*Justice,* 18 May.)

The PCM waged an unsuccessful attempt to sway Martinique's vote on 23 April against admission of Great Britain, Ireland, Norway, and Denmark to the European Common Market by arguing that the Common Market made European exploitation of developing countries easier and that the referendum was merely a diversionary tactic that would not help these countries.

In January the PCM sent a representative to the fiftieth anniversary celebration of the Communist Party of Chile.

Publications. The PCM publishes a weekly newspaper, *Justice,* and an irregular theoretical journal, *Action.*

California State University, San Jose   Eric Stromquist

Mexico

The Mexican Communist Party (Partido Comunista Mexicano; PCM) is a small and rather insignificant element in the Mexican political panorama. Its membership of about 5,000 is far below the legal minimum of 75,000 members a party must have in order to be legally registered and inscribe candidates on the printed ballots at national elections. Because of questions of domestic political tactics, as well as international questions, the party has been much beset by factionalism and internal disputes in recent years.

The Setting. The more important left-wing party is the Popular Socialist Party (Partido Popular Socialista; PPS), which does meet the minimum legal number for registration as a party entitled to have candidates on the printed ballot. Indeed, it is quite likely that the minimum figure for registration (which is expected to be lowered during 1973) was originally set deliberately by the government so that the PPS would qualify, because although quite pro-Soviet and well-regarded in Moscow, the PPS usually collaborates with the ruling party of Mexico, the Institutional Revolutionary Party (Partido Revolucionario Institucional; PRI). It normally endorses the PRI presidential candidate although running a partially separate slate for congressional seats. From the point of view of the PRI, the PPS has the function of channeling leftist sentiment in a harmless manner. This function has been less well served since the death in November 1968 of Vicente Lombardo Toledano, long a major and prestigious figure in Mexican politics and founder, leader, and ideological orientor of the PPS. The present PPS leader, Jorge Cruickshank, does not have Lombardo's appeal.

The PRI has always been a very inclusive party, incorporating elements from the far left to the far right of the political spectrum, with the thrust of policy shifting as successive presidents tried to remedy the excesses in one direction or another of their predecessors. The current president, Luis Echeverría Alvarez, elected in 1970, has taken the PRI back to the left in reaction to the conservative and politically repressive policies of his unpopular predecessor. In this policy ("the democratic opening") Echeverría has met with opposition from traditional elements within the PRI and the government, some of which were responsible for organizing an attack by a gang of toughs ("los Halcones") on a student "democratization" demonstration of 10 June 1971.

The rather paradoxical situation of the leader of an incumbent dominant party claiming to be of leftist orientation and trying to encourage opposition has led to a wide divergence in the political positions assumed by the various elements on the left, especially since the group most likely to benefit from the "democratic opening" policy is the moderate conservative opposition Party of National Action (Partido de Acción Nacional).

The PCM itself has supported the idea of democratization of the system, but has opposed Echeverría on the premise that his espousal of that position is insincere and fraudulent, an at-

363

tempt to trick the leftist opposition. The PPS, on the other hand, has taken a "Stalinist" position, condemning the dissident "democratization" movement among students and some workers as a right-wing maneuver. The PPS is thus close to the views of the traditionalists in the PRI who oppose Echeverría or give only lip service to his leadership, such as the long-time leader of the Confederation of Mexican Workers (Confederación de Trabajadores Mexicanos) Fidel Velázquez. It appears likely that elements in the labor movement close to Velázquez were implicated in organizing and financing "los Halcones."

The differences between the PPS and PCM on democratization parallel the differences between them over the Soviet-led invasion of Czechoslovakia in 1968, which was supported by the PPS and opposed by the PCM. The celebrated mural painter David Alfaro Siqueiros was expelled from the PCM in July 1971 for his disagreement with the PCM on these issues and his refusal to follow the party's line in abstaining from voting in the 1970 elections. (He presumably voted for Echeverría.) Support of government policy was also the reason for the expulsion from the PCM of Arturo Orona and six other peasant leaders from northern Mexico in June 1972.

Other elements on the left have taken a middle position on the democratization question, supporting the line taken by Echeverría against both the traditionalist "Stalinism" of the PPS and the skepticism of the PCM. Some have become active in the PRI; the most prominent of these is the new PRI secretary-general, Enrique González Pedrero, a professor of political science and formerly a writer for the now defunct leftist periodical *Política*. Others have joined with Heberto Castillo, a student leader in the disturbances of 1968, in a loose "movement of consultation," professing democratic and socialist views, that attempts to maintain pressure on Echeverría from outside the PRI to persist in the liberalizing and democratizing process. These include two well-known writers, Octavio Paz and Carlos Fuentes, and the leaders of the electricians' and railway workers' unions (including Demetrio Vallejo, imprisoned by previous presidents under now-repealed anti-subversive laws).

The PCM. The positions taken by the PCM during 1972 include the following. The Echeverría government is a repressive government representing the bourgeoisie. However, it is trying to make its task easier by hypocritically taking a reformist line so as to deceive the people. Nevertheless, the PCM opposes those who have abandoned the struggle to promote democratic freedoms and believe armed struggle to be the only means of achieving change. At the same time it is unrealistic to believe that present leaders can be voted out of office as things stand now. The correct line is instead to persevere in education and propaganda work to raise the consciousness of the working classes and to make the true situation clear to all. Specifically, the PCM works to unify opposition and revolutionary elements in the trade union movement and to fight for effective student participation in the administration of the universities. (Through its youth affiliate, the Juventud Comunista Mexicana, the PCM has some influence at the National University, especially in the Faculties of Economics and Medicine. However, Maoists, Fidelistas, anarchists, and democratic socialist followers of Heberto Castillo compete with the JCM for leadership among leftist students.)

The party's position on agricultural questions is that trade unions should be organized in the countryside (at present not permitted by the government). Existing large properties should be broken up and holdings in irrigated areas should be reduced to 20 hectares. The goal for the present should be to unify small and landless peasants in a struggle against large landholdings. Only subsequently, after the success of this struggle, should small holdings be gradually and voluntarily consolidated into cooperatives and state farms. The party rejects the tactics of armed struggle and charges that so-called guerrilla groups have neither a mass base nor a clear-cut political program.

In 1972 the PCM continued its independent line in international relations with visits by party first secretary Arnaldo Martínez Verdugo to China and North Korea. Another party leader, Marta Bórquez, visited Romania in May. However, friendly relations with the Communist Party of the Soviet Union continued and visits to Eastern Europe have included Moscow and Prague as well as Bucharest. The PCM also served as host for a meeting in May in Mexico City of representatives of the Communist parties of Central America and Panama (see below). This flexible attitude contrasted with the traditionally exclusive pro-Soviet position of the PPS, which criticized the conduct of the Chinese in the United Nations for strengthening the "imperialist" campaign against the socialist countries.

The PCM publishes a weekly newspaper, *La Voz de México;* a magazine, *Oposición;* and a theoretical journal, *Nueva Epoca.*

Despite the PCM's relative moderation and opposition to violent methods, many Mexicans persist in regarding it as somehow responsible for the guerrilla movement and the urban terrorism. The PCM was also made one of the scapegoats for the student disturbances that were severely repressed in 1968, and the last of the PCM members jailed at that time were only released in December 1971. Those released at that time included the party's write-in candidate for president in 1970, under the designation Frente Electoral del Pueblo (People's Electoral Front), Ramón Danzos Palomino.

Other Organizations. There are a host of minor splinter organizations of the far left, many of them ad hoc, ephemeral, or letterhead organizations. Apart from the PCM and the PPS, the most active groups appeared to be the Socialist Front (Frente Socialista) led by Víctor Rico Galán, a journalist who was released from prison on 2 March 1972, after serving six years for alleged subversive activities, and two Trotskyite organizations, the Internationalist Communist Group (Grupo Comunista Internacionalista; GCI) and the Revolutionary Workers Party (Partido Obrero Revolucionario). There are also several small urban terrorist groups, and a rural guerrilla movement operating in the state of Guerrero, the mountainous state south of Mexico City whose difficult terrain has often sheltered guerrillas or bandits in Mexican history.

The current leftist bandit-guerrillas operating in Guerrero were led by Genaro Vázquez Rojas until his death on 2 February 1972 in an automobile crash while being pursued by government agents. According to one version, Vázquez was shot after surviving the crash. The guerrilla leader is now Lucio Cabañas. The guerrillas, who engage in ambushes of military patrols, robberies, jail raids, and kidnapings, call themselves the Peasants' Criminal Execution Brigade, the Peasant Brigade for Justice, or the Party of the Poor.

There were no visible ties between Vázquez or Cabañas and other leftist elements—whose attitude toward the guerrillas ranged from support by some students at the National University, to expressions of sympathy with their presumed motives and ideals but criticism of their use of violent methods by Rico Galán and most of the far left, to strong criticism from the PCM, and to a contemptuous evaluation by the independent left-wing magazine, *Siempre,* which portrayed Vázquez as a mixed-up person motivated partly by love of money. There were reports that impatient military men were using counter-terror techniques against the guerrillas and their presumed peasant sympathizers.

Scattered activities by urban guerrilla groups, such as hold-ups, kidnapings, and a plane hijacking, also occurred, especially during the first few months of 1972. Organizations involved were the Movimiento de Acción Revolucionaria (MAR), the Federación de Estudiantes Revolucionarios, the Unión del Pueblo, the Liga de Comunistas Armados, and the Comandos Armados del Pueblo. Some members of the MAR, at least, received guerrilla training in North Korea after having been students in Moscow. The Mexican government expelled five Soviet diplomats, including the chargé d'affaires, in March 1971, on the premise that the Soviet government had facilitated the MAR members' travel to and from North Korea. Arrests seemed to decimate the MAR, and also the Unión del Pueblo.

Statements from guerrilla groups are given sympathetic presentation in the magazine *¿Porque?* The leading Trotskyite publication is the *Bandera Roja* of the GCI.

University of New Mexico   Martin C. Needler

*   *   *

Eighth Conference of Communist and Workers' Parties. In May 1972 representatives of the "communist and workers' parties" of Mexico, Guatemala, El Salvador, Honduras, Nicaragua, Costa Rica, and Panama met in Mexico City for what was designated their Eighth Conference (though there is some discrepancy in the numbering, as the 1971 meeting was referred to as the eighth also). In a communiqué issued by the conference, the parties declared that the area of Central America, Mexico and Panama was "going through a new stage of struggle and sharp clashes with the forces of Yankee imperialism and local oligarchy." The communiqué summed up the results of work done so far by Marxist-Leninists as (1) "joint action by national political forces for democratic programs, against repression, and for the isolation and defeat of despotic camarillas," (2) "stimulating mass participation and organization, especially of the working class, in the struggle to solve cardinal problems of economic and political development," and (3) maintaining "the determination to fight against various manoeuvres of the ruling classes [and] against dependence and backwardness." In spite of these efforts, the conference declared, "imperialism and the local oligarchies" were able to resist because of the area's "socio-economic backwardness," the "habitual dispersal, spontaneity and corruption intrinsic to social and political life," and the "severity of military camarillas" in many governments. Party members were urged to "search for new forms of organization that would enable the proletariat to score new successes and avoid repression," to fight any "sectarianism" and "opportunism," to "strengthen the bonds between all anti-capitalist, popular forces," and to "search for the most effective forms of combining measures of solidarity and mutual assistance." (*IB*, no. 12.)

The conference issued a resolution claiming that there was an accelerated penetration of "U.S. imperialism" in the area, particularly through the framework of the Central American Common Market. Rather than promoting "independent economic development of the member countries," the common market was said to have made conditions "more critical," since "unemployment has grown, the cost of living has gone up substantially, and the real wages are steadily declining." Although the Communist and Workers' Parties of Central America have always advocated "mutual understanding and fraternal solidarity," their resolution rejected the kind of association being "imposed" on Central America through "imperialist exploitation" and "consolidation of the oligarchic domination." The conference called for greater efforts to achieve the following objectives: "(1) elimination of the disadvantageous system of lifting financial impositions on the scale of Central America; (2) liquidation of the San José Protocol, which increases the cost of living and only pursues the aim of granting still greater benefits to Yankee companies operating in Central America; (3) more effective coordination of the movement of working people and popular organizations for their economic, social and political demands, mainly on wages and living and working conditions; (4) extension of the struggle to foil the imperialist integration plans directed against our peoples and, specifically, the plans of military-political integration drawn up with the purpose of stifling the liberation movement and bolstering up economic and political domination on the Isthmus." The resolution concluded with a call for a "democratic, agrarian and anti-imperialist revolution that will open the way to socialism and establish a people's democratic power." (Ibid.)

Palo Alto, California   Lynn Ratliff

Nicaragua

The Socialist Party of Nicaragua (Partido Socialista de Nicaragua; PSN) was formed in 1937 as the result of a split in the "Party of Nicaraguan Workers," within which the communists had operated. In 1944 the government of Nicaragua permitted communists to hold a national congress, and the PSN regards that year as the date of its official founding. The party was outlawed in 1945 and has been illegal during most of its subsequent existence. Although it has occasionally attempted to influence the political situation through front organizations, the PSN at present is almost totally ineffective, owing both to its small size and weak organization, and to the government's suppression of left-wing groups. The PSN is pro-Soviet.

In 1967 an inner-party struggle developed in the PSN which resulted in the expulsion of some party leaders. These dissidents then organized what they claimed was Nicaragua's only Marxist-Leninist party and took anti-Soviet positions (see *WMR,* April 1972). According to a U.S. source, this group identified itself as the "Nicaraguan Socialist Workers' Party" (POSN) until 1971 when it changed its name to "Communist Party of Nicaragua" (*World Strength of the Communist Party Organizations,* Washington, D.C., 1972, p. 153). It is led by Juan Lorio García.

The Sandinist National Liberation Front (Frente Sandinista de Liberación Nacional; FSLN) is a small Castroite organization (see below).

The PSN is estimated to have fewer than 100 members and the rival communist party only about 40. The FSLN has 50 to 60 active members. The population of Nicaragua is 2,000,000 (estimated 1970).

Following the election of a constituent assembly in February 1972, a three-member "National Governing Junta" was installed in place of Nicaragua's former president, General Anastasio Somoza, who nonetheless remained in effective control of the country as commander of the National Guard. It is expected that Somoza will resume the presidency in 1974 when the constitution permits him to again run in the elections. The communists urged a boycott of the election with some apparent success as a large section of the electorate did not vote.

The PSN. Leadership and Organization. Although very little information about the PSN is available due to its clandestine existence, it is known that the first secretary is now Luis Domingo Sánchez Sancho. The last party congress was held in 1966.

The PSN controls only a few small factions within the labor movement. The General Confederation of Labor (Confederación General de Trabajo), which represents a small part of the organized labor force, reportedly supported the PSN in its positions on labor questions during the year.

A "Confederation of Peasants and Agricultural Laborers" was founded by the PSN in 1967. Since the majority of Nicaragua's laborers are agricultural the PSN has been concentrating on their organization. However, according to PSN member R. Pérez, "repressive measures by the government complicate our activity. Terror and sustained massive intimidation notwithstanding, the Party has made some progress in organizing the peasants, especially in the north, where risings have been frequent." (*WMR,* June 1972.)

The PSN maintains a small youth group, the Nicaraguan Socialist Youth (Juventud Socialista Nicaraguense). In a speech given at a seminar held by *World Marxist Review* in Prague, R. Pérez said that the Socialist Youth movement had been "growing steadily and rapidly since 1967." The National University, he added, had become the "scene of an ideological clash between ultra-Lefts and supporters of [the PSN]." The party, according to Pérez, was working toward the "unity of the student movement and its involvement in the common struggle against the dictatorship." (Ibid., April 1972.) It should be noted that on the university level student unrest and disorder during the past few years has appeared to be primarily the result of activities by guerrilla-oriented Castroite groups. Student support for traditional communist policies is slight.

Party Internal Affairs. The PSN remains a weak organization, not only because of repression by the government and exile of its leaders, but also because of the factionalism which split the party in the late 1960s. According to Pérez, the rival communist party (see above) makes "slanderous attacks on the PSN, distorting its assessment of the situation [in Nicaragua], comes out against the CPSU and the international communist movement and tries to penetrate PSN-led trade unions" (*WMR,* April 1972).

Domestic Views. In his speech to the *World Marxist Review* seminar Pérez described Nicaragua as having been under a "reactionary dictatorship" for more than 35 years. In recent years, he said, the "middle strata have joined the workers and peasants in the fight for national liberation and the overthrow of the Somoza dictatorship." Along with more activity from the "progressive intelligentsia and students," some members of the clergy have taken a "patriotic stand," and the "differing ideologies" of these groups complicate the party's work and demand more flexibility. The PSN, according to Pérez, must now work for the "unity of the democratic and progressive forces" and raise the "political consciousness" of the masses by explaining to them the "nature of the present stage of their struggle." (*WMR,* April 1972.)

Regarding the "ultra-Left," as exemplified by the FSLN, Pérez noted that the PSN had "serious ideological differences with it, primarily on the ways and means of restructuring Nicaraguan society." Whereas the FSLN believes this can be done only through immediate mobilization of "all the democratic and progressive forces for armed struggle," the PSN advocates the same method but does not believe the "necessary revolutionary situation" yet exists. (Ibid.)

Pérez termed the national election of February 1972 a "farce staged by the reactionary bourgeoisie" (ibid.). The PSN, he said on another occasion, had "no illusions at this stage about the possibility of participating in elections held by the dictatorship," but was searching for the "most suitable realistic ways and means of uniting the masses" (ibid., June).

During the year Pérez represented the PSN at a meeting of seven Latin American communist parties sponsored by the *World Marxist Review*. In describing the situation in Nicaragua, he noted that agriculture accounts for better than 60 percent of the workers and that "semi-starvation, poor housing, the absence of medical aid, and illiteracy are all part of peasant life." The government, he said, was carrying out a "so-called agrarian reform" through a special "institute" set up under the "patronage of U.S. monopolies," the purpose of which was to "concentrate the land in the hands of big holders," thereby evicting the peasants from their land. (Ibid.)

International Affairs. The PSN continued to hold to its pro-Soviet position. The PSN praised the Soviet Union for its "vanguard role" in the socialist camp, its "struggle against the imperialist aggressor," its policy of "peaceful coexistence and nuclear disarmament," and its "proletarian internationalism" which "raises still higher the authority of the great motherland of working people throughout the world" (*Pravda,* Moscow, 9 April 1971.)

In May Nicaragua sent a delegation to the Eighth Congress of Communist and Workers' Parties of Central America, Mexico and Panama held somewhere in Central America (see *Mexico* and *IB,* no. 12).

Publications. The long-standing PSN organ, *Orientación Popular,* was suppressed in 1967. Its successor, *Tribuna,* met the same fate in 1968. Since then no regular publication has been issued.

*　　*　　*

The FSLN. The Sandinist National Liberation Front is a small Castroite guerrilla organization founded in 1961 by Carlos Fonseca Amador. It is believed to have 50 to 60 active members. Fonseca is believed to have been in Cuba since his release from a Costa Rican prison in 1970. Due to the government's campaign to suppress the FSLN and to Fonseca's exile, the group is able to engage in only limited activity and little was reported about it during 1972. The FSLN issued at least two communiqués during the year, condemning the Somoza government and the February elections. They also appealed for international solidarity with the FSLN in its struggle to liberate the Nicaraguan people.

The FSLN reportedly publishes an organ called *Trinchera.*

Palo Alto, California   Lynn Ratliff

Panama

The Communist Party of Panama (Partido Comunista de Panamá) was founded in 1930. In 1943 the organization was dissolved and the People's Party of Panama (Partido del Pueblo de Panamá; PDP) was founded.

Other left-wing groups in Panama include the Revolutionary Unity Movement (Movimiento de Unidad Revolucionario; MUR), the National Action Vanguard (Vanguardia de Acción Nacional; (VAN), the Panamanian Revolutionary Union (Unión Revolucionaria Panameña; URP) and the National Liberation Movement of 29 November (MLN-29-11) (see below).

The PDP has been illegal since 1953. When the government of General Omar Torrijos Herrera took power through a coup in October 1968 all political parties were dissolved. After a period of intensified suppression of communist and left-wing groups, civil liberties were officially restored in November 1969. In August 1970 Torrijos declared a general amnesty, and in March 1971 he pardoned a number of political prisoners convicted of terrorism, many of whom were exiled. The communist party, however, remained illegal. During 1972 the political climate in Panama become still less restrictive and on 6 August a national election was held. A 505-member Assembly of Popular Representatives was elected to choose a president, and vice-president, and to ratify a new constitution. On 12 October Demetrio Basilio Lakas was inaugurated as president. The assembly also conferred special powers on General Torrijos who clearly retained effective control of the government in Panama.

The PDP is believed to have about 250 members. The population of Panama is 1,464,000 (estimated 1970).

Leadership and Organization. Since 1951 the secretary-general of the PDP has been Rubén Darío Sousa. (For other names see *YICA, 1972,* p. 402). The party officials have been in exile since 1969, probably in Chile.

The University Reform Front (Frente Reformista Universitaria; FRU) is a university-student affiliate of the PDP. The PDP also exerts influence within the 18,000-member Federation of Students of Panama (Federación de Estudiantes de Panamá; FEP), which is made up of secondary and university students and is a member of the communist-front International Union of Students. Although student organizations were dissolved in 1968 following the takeover of General Torrijos, they have been allowed to reorganize during the past two years and on 24–27 May 1972 the FEP held its Eighth Congress—the first in seven years. The congress delegates unanimously agreed that the situation in Panama since 1968 had "opened new horizons for the taking of even deeper roots by the process that will eventually develop into a revolution in Panama." The students were concerned, however, with the existence within the government of a "reactionary, oligarchic and proimperialist" sector which jeopardized its effectiveness. The congress emphasized (1) the need for educational reform which would "shatter the structures of feudal and reactionary education" in Panama, (2) the need to draw closer to the farmers and the working class to form a "broad anti-imperialist and anti-oligarchic front," (3) support for the 6 August elections, and (4) the need for an internationalist outlook in Panama's struggle against isolation. (*Granma*, English, Havana, 11 June.)

In February a delegation representing the FRU, visited Czechoslovakia. In September the FEP was host to a visiting delegation of the National Liberation Front of South Vietnam.

The Trade Union Federation of the Workers of the Republic of Panama (Federación Sindical de Trabajadores de la República de Panamá; FST) is the labor affiliate of the PDP. It has never been a significant influence in Panama and since 1968 its offices have been closed by the government.

Party Internal Affairs. On 1 April 1972 the General Secretariat Commission of the PDP issued a message commemorating the 24th anniversary of the founding of the first communist organization in Panama. The message stressed the necessity for the PDP as a Marxist-Leninist party, to "fulfill the role of [revolutionary] vanguard" (*IB,* no. 10–11). At a seminar in Prague sponsored by *World Marxist Review* a PDP representative, L. Thomas, spoke about the effect of "long years of illegality and ceaseless persecution" on the "normal development of ideological work" in the PDP. (*WMR,* April).

Commenting on the August elections, Darío Sousa said that the PDP won over 50,000 votes, proving that the party was a "genuine political force." However, he continued, the PDP must "take organizational and political measures to ensure better leadership, better coordination of activities, broader and deeper contacts with the masses, heightened vigilance against espionage and infiltration of the party's ranks, [and,] above all, the launching of an offensive against all deviations that could lead to adventurism and sectarianism or to class reconciliation and to the loss of the political class independence of the People's Party as the party of the Marxist-Leninist working classes." (Moscow radio, 10 October.)

Domestic Views. According to the PDP secretary-general, the people of Panama in 1972 had the opportunity of achieving "lawful democratic freedoms and national liberation—the preconditions for them to clear the way to complete liberation and a socialist society by their creative work" (*IB.,* no. 10–11). The PDP supported the government's new labor law, which took effect in April and provided for compulsory union membership for all workers. However the PDP representative at the Prague meeting described Panama as a "semi-occupied country" where the mass media were "controlled by U.S. imperialism." "Liberal-bourgeois reformism," he said, was "misleading the masses" through propaganda centered around the "menace emanating from outside our continent and the consequential need for U.S. troops to 'defend the neutrality of the Canal' and the concept of 'regional development' allegedly in order to prevent internal strife and conflict." Only in close association with the masses, he added, can "we solve all our problems and demolish reformist views and conceptions." (*WMR,* April.)

The PDP has long considered the main political issue in Panama to be Panamanian sovereignty over the Canal Zone and the elimination of "U.S. colonialism" there. In this area the party supports the government's current efforts to renegotiate the Canal Zone treaty with the United States.

The PDP was represented at a meeting of seven Latin American Communist parties on agrarian problems (see *Costa Rica* and *IB,* no. 12). One representative said that the "agrarian problem can be solved only if the latifundium system and foreign monopoly domination are abolished." Another said that the main cause of rural "poverty, high mortality and illiteracy is the inequitable distribution of the land": "U.S. monopolies" owned "vast lands," the exploitation of which brought in "millions of dollars of profits." The present Panamanian government had set out to establish peasant settlements, which were gradually being reorganized into co-operatives receiving the benefit of government technical assistance, medical care, new roads, and "market centers" which fixed prices and bought produce. The PDP was said to have a big role in organizing peasant leagues. (*WMR*, June.)

International Positions. The PDP continues to maintain its traditional pro-Soviet position in international affairs. While visiting Romania in June, Darío Sousa and a representative of the Romanian Communist Party declared their support for the "right of each people to freely decide its development path," and their "sympathy for states that have shaken off the colonial yoke." The two parties emphasized that "unity of action" was a decisive factor in the world-wide fight against "imperialism, colonialism, and neocolonialism," expressed satisfaction with the "progressive course" of the social changes occurring in Latin America and solidarity with the democratic forces fighting for the "economic, social, and cultural transformations" of their countries. (AERPRES, Romanian news agency, 29 June.) The PDP secretary-general led a delegation to Bulgaria on 30 June–4 July. The PDP attended the Eighth Conference of Communist and Workers' Parties of Central America, Mexico and Panama in May (see *Mexico* and *IB*, no. 12).

Publications. The organ of the PDP is *El Mazo*, published irregularly and distributed clandestinely. A new, official biweekly publication entitled *Momento* was reported in 1972.

* * *

MUR and Other Castroite Organizations. The MUR, an organization particularly active during the 1960s, was founded and led by Floyd Britton, who died in prison in Panama in 1969 (see *YICA, 1970*, p. 457). In 1971 the MUR and another Castroite group, the VAN, led by Jorge Turner, joined with some dissidents from the PDP to form the "National Liberation Movement of 29 November" (the date of Britton's death), which advocated guerrilla activities and the armed road to power. Three leaders of this movement were deported in 1971. During 1972 none of these groups were active and their leaders remained in exile or prison.

Palo Alto, California   Lynn Ratliff

Paraguay

The Paraguayan Communist Party (Partido Comunista Paraguayo; PCP) was founded in 1928. A serious split within the PCP occurred in 1965 when the Soviet Union backed the organization of a commission which expelled party secretary-general Oscar Creydt from his long-held position. The "National Committee for the Defense and Reorganization of the Paraguayan Communist Party" accused Creydt of being too lenient with dissident pro-Chinese members of the party and of acting in a high-handed, dictatorial manner in the conduct of party affairs. Creydt, followed by many of his colleagues, then established what he claimed was the legitimate party (here referred to as the PCP-Creydt). The original PCP remained under the control of the pro-Soviet leaders of the National Committee.

The communist party and all left-wing groups have been illegal in Paraguay since October 1936. Under the government of General Alfredo Stroessner, who has been president since 1954, enforcement of the anti-subversion laws has been strict and all opposition groups have been suppressed. The PCP operates from exile in Argentina, Brazil, and Uruguay. It is believed that no more than 10 per cent of its members actually live in Paraguay. Domestic support for the party is insignificant.

The membership of the PCP, including both factions, is estimated to be between 4,500 and 5,000. The population of Paraguay is 2,400,000 (estimated 1972).

Leadership and Organization. Since 1967 the PCP has been under the leadership of Miguel Angel Soler and Obdulio Barthe. Other prominent figures include Hugo Maciel Campos, Gustavo Colman, and Augusto Canete. It is believed that most PCP leaders live in Buenos Aires.

Party Internal Affairs. In April 1971 the PCP held its first congress in 21 years (see *YICA, 1971*, pp. 406–7). After its Second Plenum, in October 1971, the Central Committee reported that since the congress ties with the working class had been strengthened, the number of party members, "allies," and "friends," had grown, the circulation of the party newspaper had increased, and fund raising for propaganda purposes had been more successful than previously. The Central Committee noted, however, that further improvement was necessary in these sectors, and called for better leadership at all levels (*IB*, no. 1–2, 1972).

Early in 1972, at a seminar on the "ideological front" in Latin America sponsored by the *World Marxist Review,* PCP representative A. Alvarez emphasized the need to achieve party unity through revolutionary vigilance and struggle against "left" and "right" opportunists. These elements, he explained, "play into the hands of imperialism and the dictatorship by their continued attempts to split the revolutionary forces, isolate the working class and its Party from its allies in the democratic, agrarian and anti-imperialist revolution" (*WMR,* April).

In 1972 the PCP was to begin publication of a theoretical journal, to be issued every four months, the purpose of which was to "fulfill the tasks brought to the fore by the present acute ideological struggle." The PCP also planned to publish a document "summing up the experience of the ideological and practical struggle that started in the Party with the exposure and expulsion from the Party of the provocateur Creydt." (*IB*, no. 1–2.)

Domestic Views. According to the report of the Central Committee plenum (see above) the "grand fraud of 're-electing' Stroessner in February 1973 is well under way," the country is under a "constant state of emergency," opposition parties have been banned, and "hundreds of patriots are languishing in prisons." In this situation the report stressed the need for the party to "utilize all legal opportunities" to "organize, unite and mobilize the workers and all the people in the most diverse forms," to "expose the farce and deeply criticize the economic, social and political foundations" of the ruling power, to step up the national and international campaign for the release of political prisoners and abolition of "repressive laws," to organize "unitary actions against the regime's abuses, violence, arbitrariness and crimes," and to consolidate workers', peasant, student, and other mass organizations for "isolating the expelling agents of the dictatorship and leaders who try to stem the process." These efforts must be accompanied by the creation of "unitary committees" and "coordinating councils" at all levels in order to organize a "national anti-dictatorial front," the report declared. (*IB*, no. 1–2.)

The plenum concluded that "as yet there does not exist a revolutionary situation," but that economic and political developments were leading to a "national political crisis unprecedented in the history of Paraguay." Thus "communists and all revolutionaries must themselves be prepared and must ready the people for more decisive and radical forms of struggle." (Ibid.)

In December 1972 Soler said that during the year opposition to the government had increased greatly in labor, farmer, and student circles, in the political parties and even in the Roman Catholic Church. He charged that the people were tired of having their country an international center of smugglers, contraband, drugs, and war criminals. The progress of the masses, the discrediting of the government, the disturbing economic and political conditions, led Soler to predict that "the dictatorship will not last another 5 years." (Interview on Havana radio, 20 December.)

In February the PCP issued a communiqué appealing for "solidarity" with Paraguayan political prisoners, some of whom it said had been in jail for more than fourteen years without trials (ibid., 12 February). According to Soler a united mass rally demanding freedom for the prisoners was held on 12 September at Asunción Catholic University; the rally was broken up but the "brutal paramilitary repression" by the government was "unanimously repudiated" by the people (ibid., 20 December).

The PCP denounced the existence of a "secret plan for the construction of a great North American military air base" in the Paraguayan Chaco, where "Yankee oil monopolies have concessions for the exploitation of oil over an area of more than 14 million hectares" (*Tricontinental Bulletin*, Havana, March).

International Positions. The PCP remained solidly pro-Soviet in its international position. At the plenum in October 1971 the party urged that a greater contribution be made toward "consolidating Marxist-Leninist unity of the international communist movement" (*IB*, no. 1–2).

Miguel Soler attended the celebration of the 50th anniversary of the U.S.S.R. in Moscow in December, and travelled to Cuba at the end of that month.

Publications. The PCP issues a monthly newspaper, *Adelante,* which is published abroad and distributed clandestinely in Paraguay.

*   *   *

The PCP-Creydt. Oscar Creydt, for many years the leader of the Paraguayan communists, has been secretary-general of what he claims is the legitimate PCP since the split of the party in 1965 (see above). In the late 1960s Creydt was openly critical of the Soviet Union and adopted pro-Chinese and pro-Castro positions.

Aside from Creydt himself, little is known of the leadership or membership of this faction. Most members are believed to live in Montevideo. Although its actual size is unknown, the Creydt faction retained considerable strength after the division of the party and is believed to have the support of most of the young members.

The PCP-Creydt has condemned the pro-Soviet party as "phony," "revisionist," and "opportunistic," and has tried to align itself with the communist parties of Cuba, China, and North Korea.

No activities of the PCP-Creydt appear to have attracted notice during 1972.

Palo Alto, California   Lynn Ratliff

Peru

The Peruvian Communist Party (Partido Comunista Peruano; PCP) had its origins in the Peruvian Socialist Party, founded in 1928. The present name dates from 1930. Since 1964 the movement has been divided into a pro-Soviet and a pro-Chinese group, each calling itself the PCP.

There also exist in Peru various Marxist-Leninist organizations farther to the left. These include the Castro-oriented Movement of the Revolutionary Left (Movimiento de Izquierda Revolucionaria; MIR) and the Army of National Liberation (Ejército de Liberación Nacional; ELN), and the Trotskyite Revolutionary Leftist Front (Frente Izquierdista Revolucionario; FIR), Partido Obrero Revolucionario (Trotskistas), and Revolutionary Vanguard (Vanguardia Revolucionaria; VR).

The pro-Soviet and pro-Chinese PCP groups have memberships estimated at 2,000 and 1,200 respectively (*World Strength of the Communist Party Organizations,* Washington, D.C., 1972, p. 155). The other Marxist-Leninist groups are small, the MIR and the VR having perhaps the largest membership. The population of Peru is 13,600,000 (estimated 1970).

Communist membership is predominantly urban, mainly drawn from workers, students, and professional groups. The pro-Chinese PCP seems to have the stronger hold in the universities. Communist influence within the trade union movement is exercised mainly by the pro-Soviet PCP, which controls the General Confederation of Workers of Peru (Confederación General de Trabajadores del Peru; CGTP). The FIR and MIR at one time had some influence among the peasants, although in recent years that has been largely dissipated.

A constitutional provision prohibits communist parties from participating in Peruvian elections, but they have been allowed to operate under various degrees of police surveillance and harassment. The present military government led by President Juan Velasco Alvarado, has permitted the pro-Soviet PCP to function freely, but has kept considerable control over other leftist groups and has deported several pro-Chinese and Trotskyite leaders. On 1 December 1971 a law was passed providing for the death penalty and 25-year prison terms in cases of terrorist attacks causing death, serious injury, or property destruction.

The Pro-Soviet PCP. Leadership and Organization. The highest organ of the pro-Soviet PCP is officially the national congress, which is supposed to meet every three years. Its Fifth Congress was held in March 1969. The principal party leaders include Jorge del Prado Chávez, secretary-general; Raúl Acosta Salas, undersecretary general; and Central Committee members Félix Arias Schreiber, Jorge Bejar, Alfredo Abarca, Segundo Collazos, Andrés Paredes, José Reccio Gutierrez, Pompeyo Mares, Magno Falcón, Mario Ugarte Hurtado, and Juan Caceres.

The pro-Soviet party is organized from cells upward through local and regional committees to its Central Committee. Regional committees exist in 22 cities (see *YICA, 1972,* p. 411). Lima has the largest number of local committees, concentrated in low-income neighborhoods and in the slum areas which the government now refers to as "new towns."

The pro-Soviet PCP has a youth group, the Peruvian Communist Youth (Juventud Comunista Peruana; JCP), which is small and operates mainly in the universities. Jorge Tapia continues to be the JCP secretary general. The most influential organization under the control of the pro-Soviet PCP is the CGTP. Enjoying legal recognition granted by the military government, it now claims 350,000 workers in its ranks. The CGTP, while reflecting the domestic positions of the PCP, has actively supported strikes, which have been tolerated by the government.

Party Internal Affairs. During 1972 the pro-Soviet PCP held at least two plenary sessions of its Central Committee, in April and September, which adopted resolutions particularly reiterating and defining its support for the military regime.

Domestic Attitudes and Activities. Given the present situation, in which the Peruvian government has been undertaking since October 1968 various measures to effect social and economic changes to the benefit of the country's lower and middle sectors, the pro-Soviet PCP has adopted and maintained a policy of virtually total support for the government. During 1972 this position was many times repeated, as when the secretary-general stated in an interview (*Caretas,* Lima, 17 April): "The Peruvian Communist Party does indeed support the present government. [This] is because of the proved anti-imperialist and antioligarchic orientation of the present government." Another party leader said (East Berlin radio, 12 April): "The military government did not recognize from the beginning the importance of the masses as a mobilizing force. On the other hand the masses had their reservations. . . . The good experiences of the last three years, however, have changed these views." A PCP representative at a seminar conducted in Prague by the *World Marxist Review* said: "The Peruvian Communist Party sees its main task in winning over the working class and peasantry for active support of anti-oligarchic and anti-imperialist change. . . . But we are not prodding events, our immediate task is to facilitate the process of progressive change." (*WMR,* April.)

The September plenum called for "prompt nationalization of the large mines, large fishing enterprises, and the principal sectors of foreign trade." On the anniversary of the 1968 military coup, 3 October, the party again declared its support of the government: "The Peruvian Communist Party hereby conveys a warm, militant greeting to the working class, armed forces revolutionary government and all leading and progressive men of our fatherland [on] the initiation of the present process of revolutionary transformations, whose achievements reflect important changes in the country's social and economic structure. . . . The PCP fervently appeals to all workers and Peruvians [to] give the best of their energies to defend the revolutionary process [and] exert their utmost efforts to carry out the anti-imperialist and anti-oligarchic tasks of the present stage of the Peruvian revolution."

A cause of concern, however, was the proliferation of the National System of Support for Social Mobilization (Sistema Nacional de Movilización Social; SINAMOS), established in 1971 as a government attempt to "involve" the rank and file of the citizenry in the revolutionary process. Participating in the organization were many former members of various left-wing parties, none of whom had any love for the pro-Soviet PCP. Fears about SINAMOS were particularly acute in regard to the trade union movement (see below). However, the PCP was also upset by the avowed anti-party bias of "some persons associated with SINAMOS" who were allegedly blaming all of the problems of the workers on the political parties (*Unidad,* 4 May).

The PCP professed no hostility to SINAMOS itself. According to Jorge del Prado: "We believe that SINAMOS has a single objective, and a worthy one: that of implementing the organized participation of the masses in the process of bringing about anti-imperialist and anti-oligarchic structural changes. . . . SINAMOS is not planned as an official party nor as an exclusivist and exclusive political organization. . . . We believe that far from entering into competition with our party or with other revolutionary forces, this organization will actually produce a more far-reaching . . . concordance of effort." (*Caretas,* 17 April).

In spite of this declaimer, the April plenum resolved: "There is a danger that must be avoided. . . . Through SINAMOS there might be developed the McCarthyite proclivities of some of its collaborators. . . . For their part, the popular organizations must be vigilant to see that the possibility of a real united front against reaction and imperialism is not torpedoed from within."

The CGTP. The communist-controlled CGTP was formed in 1968 as a rival to the Confederation of Workers of Peru (CTP), which at that time claimed 70 percent of the organized workers of the country, and is dominated by the non-communist Aprista Party. Since its establishment the CGTP has been a great deal more militant than the CTP, because of the tolerance which the communist-controlled group has enjoyed from the military government. Although reliable figures are not available, it is probable that by 1972 the CGTP was approaching the CTP in size.

During 1972 the CGTP, through its National Federation of Mine and Metal Workers continued to organize numerous strikes within the mining sector. Like the PCP it affirmed support for the government throughout the year, though its New Year's greetings to the president included a list of 12 "requests," ranging from "complete reorganization of the Ministry of Labor, with the personnel changes that are being repeatedly requested by the workers," to recognition of Cuba, and to freeing of jailed mining trade-union leaders. It has also demanded nationalization of the large mining enterprises.

The CGTP showed a certain preoccupation with the intention, announced by SINAMOS in August, to undertake the organization of unions. On 12 September the CGTP issued a statement of "its firm decision to prevent interference by SINAMOS in the internal affairs of workers and their organizations and political tasks." The statement argued that it was up to the workers, their unions, and the CGTP to organize new unions, and that the task of SINAMOS should be limited to encouraging such activity. Perhaps as a result of this protest, the labor minister announced on 22 September that the government had no intention of dissolving existing unions, adding that "The workers themselves will have to decide on the unions and on the unions' future role in the enterprises in whose management they are participating."

International Views and Positions. The PCP continued in 1972 to maintain a very close pro-Soviet alignment. In March and April a party delegation headed by Raúl Acosta, visited East Germany, Czechoslovakia, Poland, and Romania. The party also expressed support for positions taken by the pro-Soviet Chilean and Uruguayan parties.

Jorge del Prado suggested that U.S. President Nixon's visits to China and the Soviet Union showed a contrast between the attitudes of the two communist super-powers toward the United States: "Unlike the U.S.-Chinese talks in Peking, the discussion on peaceful coexistence at the Moscow talks did not have any strings attached." (Moscow radio, 5 June 1972.)

Publications. The pro-Soviet PCP official organ is a weekly newspaper, *Unidad*. According to the Moscow *New Times,* (no. 7, February 1972), "two years ago *Unidad* had a circulation of four or five thousand, now the circulation has grown to 10,000."

*　　　*　　　*

The Pro-Chinese PCP. Leadership and Organization. Virtually from its inception, the pro-Chinese PCP has experienced internal dissension and splits. There are at present at least three factions. The one with more or less official recognition from the Chinese Communist Party is headed by Saturnino Paredes Macedo. The so-called Sotomayor faction has its principal center of influence in the southern city of Arequipa. The so-called Red Fatherland (Patria Roja) faction is said to have the largest following of all pro-Chinese groups among the students.

All these factions oppose the military regime. They were undoubtedly influential in organizing a protest march of San Marcos University students through the center of Lima late in June 1972, which was marked by some violence and was one of the few public demonstrations of strong opposition to the government since its establishment in 1968 (except for annual public meetings held by the Aprista Party in February). Aside from this demonstration, the pro-Chinese communists received little publicity. Efforts made during the year to regroup them into an "Anti-Imperialist Democratic Front" do not seem to have borne fruit.

*　　　*　　　*

In addition to the pro-Soviet and pro-Chinese communist organizations, there are a number of Marxist-Leninist parties and groups of Castroite and Trotskyite orientation. These reached their apogee in the early 1960s and are now small in membership, although they maintain ideological influence among young people, particularly students. The Castroite groups include the MIR, the ELN, and a faction of the VR. The Trotskyites encompass the FIR, the POR(T) and the POMR.

The MIR. The Movement of the Revolutionary Left was first organized as the Partido Apra Rebelde in the late 1950s by a group of young people who felt that the country's traditional democratic leftist group, the Aprista Party, had abandoned its early militancy. After the Cuban Revolution it came under Castroite influence and adopted its present name. In 1965 it launched one of the principal guerrilla war efforts, in which its then leader was killed and a large part of the membership were casualties in one way or another. The extent of the current membership is not known, but the movement has some influence in the universities. Ricardo Gadea, brother of Che Guevara's first wife, is the principal MIR leader.

The MIR opposed the military regime during 1972. In February, Gadea argued in the MIR paper *Voz Rebelde* that, "Faced with the fascist conspiracy which threatens our people, the MIR is willing to fight shoulder to shoulder with revolutionary priests and other Christians, the patriotic military opposed to the imperialistic sacking, socialist intellectuals, workers and all those who are being exploited in the city and the countryside."

In an interview (*Caretas,* 22 May) Gadea explained the MIR's opposition: "We do not support the military junta. This revolution is not the revolution of the working class. The spokesmen for the regime themselves admit that this is a non-capitalist, non-Communist process aimed at establishing a third standard which will reconcile the workers' interest with those of capitalism." When asked how much of a mass following the MIR had, he replied:

"The MIR has never sought to be a party of the masses, but rather a vanguard of cadres rooted in the masses. Nor does the MIR seek to represent the entire Peruvian people. It only wishes to represent the working class, its ideology and its historic interests, by organizing the best revolutionary cadres possible."

Although in this interview Gadea commented that "we are obviously not linked with any guerrilla or armed action," the government announced on 4 August that it had captured 15 members of a 22-man armed MIR, group that had participated in a series of assassinations and robberies in northwestern Peru.

The ELN. The ELN, founded in 1962 by former members of the PCP, participated also in the peasant guerrilla movement of 1965. Its main leader, Héctor Béjar, was released from prison on 22 December 1970 in a general political amnesty.

After several years of inactivity, the ELN reappeared to public notice in February 1972. It issued a manifesto which denounced the government as "a bourgeois reformist regime which is modernizing dependent capitalism." At the same time it reported its "expulsion" of Béjar because of his support of the military regime. During 1972 Béjar became an active official in SINAMOS.

The VR. The VR is a Marxist-Leninist party founded by former Aprista Party members in 1965. It advocates armed confrontation as a means of achieving socialism, but holds that its members should have theoretical and practical training before engaging in actual struggle. Although composed primarily of intellectuals, it includes some workers but apparently no peasants. During the late 1960s it was a major force among students, particularly at San Marcos University.

The VR split in 1971. A faction led by Ricardo Napuri formed the Marxist Revolutionary Workers Party (Partido Obrero Marxista Revolucionario; POMR). In an interview (*Caretas,* 8 June) Napuri proclaimed the POMR to be "Leninist-Trotskyite" and commented: "The purpose of the POMR is, obviously, to become the vanguard of the proletariat." The POMR does not have affiliation with any faction of international Trotskyism.

The FIR. The FIR is a Trotskyite party associated with the United Secretariat faction of the Fourth International. It is led by Hugo Blanco, who in 1962 led a movement by peasants near Cuzco to seize land, culminating in an armed uprising. He was jailed after capture and kept in prison until December 1970, when he was released by the amnesty. Because of his criticisms of the government, he was deported in September 1971, after which he traveled extensively in Latin America, denouncing the government's "oppression." In January 1972 the United Secretariat succeeded in mobilizing a group of French intellectuals to protest against "the increased repression in Peru," as demonstrated by the case of Blanco.

The POR(T). The POR(T) is a Trotskyite faction associated with the International Secretariat of the Fourth International, the Posadas faction. It has supported the government since 1968.

On 5 May 1972 a POR(T) leader was arrested on charges of counterfeiting and forgery. Publicity given to this incident in the conservative Lima daily *El Comercio* seemed designed principally to discredit a former POR(T) leader who currently is a leading figure in SINAMOS.

Rutgers University   Robert J. Alexander

Puerto Rico

The Puerto Rican Communist Party (Partido Comunista Puertorriqueño; PCP) is closely associated with the Communist Party, USA (CPUSA) and shares its pro-Soviet orientation. The Puerto Rican Socialist League (Liga Socialista Puertorriqueña; LSP) has close ties to the Progressive Labor Party (PLP) of the United States and, like the PLP, dropped its pro-Chinese orientation in 1971. Together the PCP and LSP probably have fewer than 100 members.

The Puerto Rican Socialist Party (Partido Socialista Puertorriqueño; PSP), formerly the Pro-Independence Movement (Movimiento Pro-Independencia; MPI), with close ties to Cuba, is independent in the Sino-Soviet dispute. It claimed to have about 6,000 members at the beginning of 1972. The Armed Liberation Commandos (Comandos Armadas de Liberación; CAL) is a small terrorist organization with no apparent international orientation.

None of these parties ran candidates in the November 1972 election though their attitudes toward the electoral process itself varied.

The PCP. The Puerto Rican Communist Party was founded in 1934, dissolved in 1944, and founded again in 1946. Little is known of its organizational structure, except that it appears to operate both in Puerto Rico and in New York City. Among its leaders are its secretary-general, Félix Ojeda Ruiz, and Politburo-member Manuel Méndez del Toro. The views of the PCP on domestic and international affairs mirror those of the CPUSA. The party has long been on good terms with the MPI. In 1970 the PCP rejected an appeal by Juan Santos Rivera, at that time the party's secretary-general, that the PCP merge with the MPI. In January 1971 Gus Hall of the CPUSA urged a policy of cooperation with the MPI. Early in 1972 the PCP published a statement welcoming the founding of the PSP and urging the good relations between the two parties, since "the unity of all progressive and anti-imperialist forces" had always been the policy of the PCP (*IB*, no. 3). The PCP ordered its members to support Rubén Berríos, the pro-independence gubernatorial candidate of the Puerto Rican Independence Party (Partido Independentista Puertorriqueño; PIP)—who received 4 percent of the vote—in the November election. While noting the "profound ideological differences" between the PIP and the PCP, the latter declared that "both fight with the same honor and patriotism for the independence of our country and against imperialism." (*Mundo Nuevo*, New York, 4 November.)

Félix Ojeda wrote in the September issue of *Pueblo* that "anti-communism" is the "favorite weapon" of the "imperialist monopolists to keep the colonial and semi-colonial peoples in hand and prevent the growth and liberation of their countries," of "industrialists against their workers fighting for bread and social justice," and of political leaders in Puerto Rico and abroad (*IB*, no. 18–19).

Publications. The PCP publishes the newspaper *Pueblo* and an information bulletin *El Proletario,* both of which appear irregularly. Party information also appears in *Mundo Nuevo,* an occasional Spanish-language section in the CPUSA organ *Daily World,* and other CPUSA publications.

* * *

The LSP. The Puerto Rican Socialist League, apparently operating in both Puerto Rico and New York City, is led by its secretary-general, Juan Antonio Corretjer. The party was pro-Chinese until 1971 when the People's Republic of China indicated its interest in improving relations with the government of the United States. The LSP still calls for "people's war," the revolutionary strategy the Chinese Communists have allegedly abandoned, in Puerto Rico. According to the LSP, Puerto Rican liberation will be achieved only through "people's war, which is invincible and will defeat imperialism and its lackeys and will install a government of the workers—socialism" (*Challenge / Desafío,* New York, 21 September). The party rejects terrorism, putschism, nationalism, alliances with the bourgeoisie, and electoral participation (*Progressive Labor,* New York, August). Thus it is highly critical of the PCP and the PSP, and termed the November election a "farce" (*Challenge / Desafío,* 30 November).

Publications. Party organs, which appear irregularly, are *Pabellón* and *El Socialista.* Major LSP statements are found in publications of the Progressive Labor Party of the USA, *Progressive Labor* and *Challenge / Desafío.*

* * *

The CAL. The Armed Liberation Commandos, led by Alfonso Beal, describe themselves as the "fighting arm of the Puerto Rican independence movement," whose actions are "designed to undermine the stability and colonial peace of the imperialist invaders." The CAL states: "Our combat is anonymous and armed, but we seek the power of the working class, independence, and socialism." (*Tricontinental Bulletin,* Havana, September 1972.) The organization claims to be responsible for various fires and bombings which have occurred in recent years.

* * *

The PSP. The Puerto Rican Socialist Party was formed in November 1971 at the Eighth National Assembly of the MPI. Party members include Secretary-General Juan Mari Bras, President Julio Vives Vásquez, and Jenario Rentas. In January 1972 Mari Bras said the PSP had a 65-member Central Committee and a 12-member Political Commission (*Granma,* English, Havana, 16 January).

Party Internal Affairs. Mari Bras has stated that the PSP was formed before there were "optimal conditions for the development of a revolutionary party" since revolutionaries cannot just sit around until conditions are perfect. The party is Marxist-Leninist and has adopted "dialectical materialism as [its] analytical method and historical materialism as [its] form for examining social processes." Class struggle is considered "the motor by which our entire strategy is mounted." Organizationally the party is Leninist, made up of "vanguard workers and those adequately armed with proletarian ideology and ready to set examples in dedication, combativity and discipline." This, however, was "not incompatible with being a mass organization." Functioning members would fall into two distinct categories: the vanguard, on the one hand, and the affiliates and sympathizers, on the other. (*Tricontinental,* Havana, March–June.) Mari Bras reports that the "worker-student rank and file" make up the "great alliance" that forms the PSP (*Bohemia,* Havana, 7 January).

According to Mari Bras: "Diverse organizations and fronts have to be mobilized and through them a vanguard influence projected, multiplying support for its positions" (*Tricontinental,* March–June). In this category fall the Federation of University Students for Independence (Federación de Universitarios Pro-Independencia; FUPI), the Federation of Students for Independence (Federación Estudiantil Pro-Independencia; FEPI), composed of high school students, the "Central Union of Workers," and the proposed "United Independence Front."

The Marxist-Leninist party is expected to learn from the experiences and writings of contemporary revolutionaries (e.g., Mao Tse-tung, Ho Chi Minh, Ernesto Guevara, Frantz Fanon), but is to apply what is learned with a full understanding of the particular circumstances of Puerto Rico (ibid.).

Domestic Attitudes and Activities. According to Mari Bras, "the Puerto Rican economy is shaped along the line of the interests of the U.S. capitalists which control the life of the country" (*Granma,* English, 16 January 1972). The organizational strategy of the independence struggle is founded upon (1) the organization of the development of a "revolutionary vanguard, the party"; (2) "the development and intensification of the national unity of Puerto Rican patriotic forces, a large united anti-imperialist front which raises the slogans of national independence"; and (3) "the militant solidarity of all world revolutionary and anti-imperialist forces with the liberation struggle of the Puerto Rican people" (*Tricontinental,* July–August).

The United Independence Front sought by the PSP would be a "broad organizational federation of parties, groups and base sectors around the central objective of independence" (ibid., March–June); it would be based on the workers and students, but would also include the petty bourgeoisie, the small businessmen, the farmers, and the self-employed professionals (*Granma,* English, 16 January). The PSP does not consider "colonial elections" a way to take power, but does not reject participation in elections under certain conditions. The party hoped to unite all pro-independence forces for the November elections, largely by reaching an agreement with the PIP. The PIP, however, would not agree to PSP terms, electing instead to run on its own. Though the PSP did not participate in the elections, it did not discourage Puerto Ricans from voting for the PIP candidate. (*Tricontinental Bulletin,* May–June.) At the same time, the PSP insists upon tactical flexibility, for, as Mari Bras puts it: "No revolutionary will ever accept renunciation of the use of violence and the right to armed struggle" (*Tricontinental,* March–June).

International Views and Positions. Mari Bras regards Cuba as "the main ally of the people of Puerto Rico in their struggle for liberation, independence and socialism" (*Granma,* English 16 January). This attitude comes at least in part as a result of Cuba's yearly effort, which achieved a measure of success in 1972, to get the United Nations to consider Puerto Rico a colony of the United States (see *NYT,* 3 September).

The PSP supports the Popular Unity government in Chile, the Velasco government in

Peru, the demands of the Panamanian government for control over the Canal Zone, and the activities of the Tupamaros and other guerrilla groups in Latin America (*Bohemia,* 7 January).

Juan Mari Bras and a PSP delegation visited the People's Republic of China for ten days in January (*Peking Review,* 4 February) and Korea in February.

Publications. The main PSP publication is *Claridad.* Party positions are carried regularly in *The Guardian,* New York, and in several Cuban publications, most importantly *Granma, Tricontinental,* and *Tricontinental Bulletin.*

Hoover Institution   William E. Ratliff
Stanford University

United States of America

The communist movement in the United States includes a number of rival parties, among which the oldest and largest is the Communist Party, USA (CPUSA), founded in 1919. The party became legal in 1967, following a decision by the U.S. Court of Appeals for the District of Columbia (see *YICA, 1968,* p. 834), but electoral restrictions work against it in certain states.

In 1972 General Secretary Gus Hall reportedly claimed a party membership of between 16,000 and 17,000 dues-paying members and from 120,000 to 125,000 "state of mind" communists (*Daily World,* 10 October). This was an increase of 1,000 to 2,000 regular members over the 1971 figure (see *YICA, 1971,* p. 421). In May, the party's youth movement, the Young Workers' Liberation League (YWLL), founded in 1970, announced a goal of 5,000 members by its next convention (*Daily World,* 10 May). Its current membership was reported at 1,250 (*The Militant,* 26 May).

In the U.S. elections for the Presidency in November, the CPUSA polled 25,223 votes, out of some 77,000,000 cast (*NYT,* 22 December); see below. The U.S. population is 210,-000,000.

Organization and Leadership. The CPUSA's 20th National Convention, held at the Towers Hotel in Brooklyn, New York, on 18–21 February 1972, was attended by 254 delegates, representing 36 states and the District of Columbia. The convention elected 60 members to the Central Committee—hitherto known as the National Committee—and 120 to the National Council. (*Daily World,* 22–23 February.) The editor of the magazine section of the *Daily World* set the Central Committee membership at 40 (*Political Affairs,* April 1972, p. 14). The party again chose Gus Hall as general secretary, Henry Winston as chairman, and Daniel Rubin, organizational secretary. Angela Davis (see below) was among those elected to the Central Committee (*Daily World,* 22–23 February).

Other party officials include Eliseo Arroyo, secretary of the National Commission on Puerto Rican Affairs; Alva Buxenbaum, National Women's Commission chairwoman; Matthew Hallinan, education director; James Jackson, international secretary; Arnold Johnson, Political Action Commission chairman; George Meyers, National Labor Commission chairman; Charlene Mitchell, Black Liberation Commission chairwoman and head of the Defense Commission; Victor Perlo, National Economic Commission chairman; Rosco Proctor, Trade Union Department secretary; and Jose Ristorucci, campaign manager for 1972.

The CPUSA continued to be active in a number of organizations which, though professing independence of the party, followed its policy and directives. The leadership of these organizations was composed primarily of party members. The most noteworthy of these is the above-mentioned YWLL. This organization solidified its fraternal ties with the CPUSA when its national chairman, Jarvis Tyner, was nominated as the party's U.S. vice-presidential candidate, teaming up with Gus Hall as presidential nominee. The YWLL held its Second National Convention at the Midland Hotel in Chicago on 5–8 May to formulate plans for the next two years (*Daily World*, 4 May). Out of the nearly 600 participants, 199 were elected-delegates or alternates (ibid., 20 May). Guest speakers who addressed the convention included representatives of the World Federation of Democratic Youth (of which the YWLL is the U.S. affiliate), the People's Coalition for Peace and Justice, the National Collective, and the Vietnam Veterans Against the War (ibid., 6 May). The YWLL announced that its purpose was to "give ideological clarity and unity to the youth movement" (ibid., 12 May). During 1972 the leadership of the YWLL was comprised of Jarvis Tyner, chairman; Matty Berkelhammer, organizational secretary; Carolyn Black, black liberation secretary; Judy Edelman, labor secretary; Roque Ristorucci, publications director; and Victoria Stevens, student coordinator.

The CPUSA continued to be active in a number of organizations opposing U.S. policy in Vietnam. Although the party appeared to have considerable influence in a number of local groups, it did not control any of the major national movements. The most prominent of the latter included the National Peace Action Coalition (NPAC)—controlled by the Trotskyist Socialist Workers Party (SWP)—and the People's Coalition for Peace and Justice (PCPJ). The CPUSA aligned itself with the PCPJ, a coalition comprising groups of a broad variety of political and tactical persuasions. On 17–21 February the PCPJ sponsored a conference attended by 200 persons from more than 35 organizations. The conference was held in Seattle, Washington and its avowed purpose was to devise a "peace strategy" for the coming year (ibid., 1 March). Subsequently the PCPJ engaged in numerous anti-war protests, including demonstrations at the national conventions of the Democratic and Republican parties. The CPUSA resumed its criticism of the PCPJ's rival group—the NPAC—for refraining from active participation in a unity-coalition of anti-war organizations led by the PCPJ during a six-week period that lasted from 1 April to 15 May. It also assailed the NPAC for "stacking speakers' lists" in its favor and for refusing to divide evenly funds collected at joint anti-war rallies (ibid., 22 March).

Within organized labor the party's influence continued to be minimal despite persistent efforts to extend its role, especially among the rank and file. At its national convention, the CPUSA set its goals for the establishment of additional "shop clubs," calling for "20 in steel, 24 in autos, 20 in electrical, and 18 in transport" (*Political Affairs*, April, p. 14). As its chief vehicle for work within the trade unions, the party used the National Coordinating Committee for Trade Union Action and Democracy (TUAD) a body formed in June 1970. The TUAD held an emergency election conference at the Packinghouse Center in Chicago over the 1 July weekend. Plans were made to send TUAD delegations to the Democratic Party's national convention and to the AFL-CIO Executive Council meeting in August. The conference also took steps to establish "Labor Assemblies for Independent Political Action" throughout the country to educate the electorate about the TUAD position on "the war, racism and the wage freeze." (*Daily World*, 5 July.)

Party Internal Affairs. "Right opportunism" was designated by the CPUSA as a major ideological weakness. At the party's national convention, Gus Hall announced that a strenuous effort would be made to combat this phenomenon. The CPUSA considered it to be "the central pivotal problem" in the trade union movement, exemplified by movement leaders' "open working class betrayal," an absence of class consciousness, and white chauvinism. (*Political Affairs*, April.) Commensurate with the theme that the "key to building the Party . . . is involvement of Communists in mass struggle" (*Daily World*, 24 February), the party stressed the importance of its members' becoming more intimately concerned with "workers, women, youth, the Black liberation movement, the peace movement, and students . . . if weaknesses are to be overcome" (ibid., 25 January).

At the YWLL convention, Jarvis Tyner played down the significance of Maoist and Anarchist-Syndicalist trends but conceded that "the Trotskyites remain a real factor among Left youth, particularly white student youth." Tyner also mentioned as ideological problems the existence of sectarianism, narrow nationalism, male supremacy and feminism—currents which were contributing obstacles to the development of a "broad youth front." (Ibid., 12 May.) Convention spokesmen also conceded that insufficient efforts were being made to bring "working youth and working class youth" into the peace movement and the movement to free "political prisoners" (*The Militant,* 26 May).

Domestic Policies and Activities. The CPUSA's National Committee assigned the highest priority to the party's 1972 election campaign (*Daily World,* 19 February). The party platform for the presidential election was adopted at its 20th National Convention. Among the provisions were the following: an unconditional withdrawal of all men, arms, and supplies from Vietnam; an end to all military expenditures ("padlock the Pentagon"); termination of all military and economic intervention in Latin America, Asia, Africa, and Europe; the shutting down of all foreign U.S. military bases and nationalization of the arms, nuclear power, and space industries, together with public utilities; abolition of the Federal Bureau of Investigation and the Central Intelligence Agency; the disarming of all police and forbidding use of police, the National Guard, or the Army to suppress "labor and people's struggles" (ibid., 24 February).

Among the CPUSA's reasons for fielding a ticket of Gus Hall for president and Jarvis Tyner for vice-president were the opportunities that a campaign provided to increase the size of the party and weld a "broad people's anti-monopoly coalition" (ibid., 17 February), to defeat President Nixon and expose more people to the position of the CPUSA on domestic and foreign policy issues (ibid., 4 March), to "legitimize" the party before the nation and promote it as the leader of the American left (ibid., 1 August), and to achieve ballot status for future election campaigns at every level. Gus Hall declared that the 1972 campaign would be the harbinger for election attempts by the CPUSA in "73, 74, and after" (ibid., 22 August). The party acquired ballot status in the District of Columbia and 13 states: Colorado, Illinois, Iowa, Kentucky, Michigan, Minnesota, North Dakota, New Jersey, New York, Ohio, Pennsylvania, Washington, and Wisconsin (ibid., 2 November).

Along with the election, the CPUSA regarded the trial of Angela Davis as of the utmost significance (see *YICA, 1972,* pp. 423–24). "Committees to Free Angela Davis" were established throughout the country as instruments to introduce non-communists of all races to the party as well as to publicize the Davis case (*Political Affairs,* May). Acquitted early in June, Miss Davis announced that after the 1972 elections, she would commit herself to "building up a national defense organization that the Communist Party and other progressive people are projecting. It will be an organization to support and defend political prisoners . . ." (*Daily World,* 30 September.)

YWLL chairman Jarvis Tyner announced at the group's national convention that the "most important task" was "uniting youth into a massive front" (ibid., 12 May). Convention workshops agreed on three central areas of concentration for the time being. Its organization should activate support on campuses to "free all political prisoners," regenerate an effective peace movement, open universities to community people, and demand more administration concessions to racial minorities (ibid., 13 May). While addressing the convention Tyner named five ways to build a united youth front: "a national student union, a national high school student organization, a national youth sector for the national defense movement and [for the] political prisoner movement, and finally a national organization aimed at ghetto and barrio youth" (*Daily World Magazine,* 27 May).

Regarding the black liberation movement, the CPUSA let it be known that it takes a dim view of a "narrow nationalist interpretation," one that views the movement as something apart from the working-class movement. The party conceded that the merger of these two struggles "was in fact the most difficult organizational and ideological task." (*Daily World,* 7 January.) Henry Winston, party chairman, termed the supporters of black capitalism "reactionary nationalists." He contended that the communist party was the "vanguard party" with the responsibility to foster mass action to lead the black liberation struggle (ibid., 3 March). In treating another aspect of the problem, Winston admonished Stokely Carmichael, former chairman of the Student Non-Violent Coordinating Committee, for his idea of Pan-Africanism that advocated a return to Africa. Winston described this concept as defeatism (ibid., 26 May). Although the CPUSA granted that blacks, chicanos, and other racial minorities were "oppressed" as workers, as racial groups, and as peoples, it insisted that only the communist party in its vanguard role could unite them and bring about their "liberation" (*Political Affairs,* January). As part of its 1972 election platform, the CPUSA promised to spend $60 billion on benefits for racial minorities per year and to provide a guaranteed annual income of $6,500 for a family of four, and to punish by "severe terms of imprisonment" all "racist" acts (*Daily World,* 18 March).

CPUSA criticism of the Black Panther Party took the form of a reply to a Panther editorial in which Angela Davis was attacked "for refusing to involve herself with the programs of Black organizations" and for her allegiance to the communist party, which—the Panthers claimed—served the "interests of the reactionaries in Moscow" and not the "Black people in America" (*The Black Panther,* 2 September). In rebuttal Charlene Mitchell, Black Liberation Commission chairwoman, accused the Panthers of denying journalistic support to Miss Davis and for refusing to join the "National United Committee to Free Angela Davis" (*Daily World,* 12 September). Mitchell went on to depict the Panthers as having a "hustler mentality," endorsing black capitalism, and forsaking the working class "to become part of the Black bourgeoisie" (ibid., 13 September). In another context, the CPUSA condoned black groups' attempting to improve the lot of the black community as "a nationally oppressed people." On the other hand, it censured as "Trotskyist" the notion that the Black Panther Party or any other organization (in contra-distinction to the communist party) could establish itself as the exclusive "political" party to advance the cause of the black people. The CPUSA denied the validity of a black Marxist-Leninist vanguard, arguing that the vanguard of the working class "is defined in terms of class—not race." (*Political Affairs,* February.)

Turning its attention to Trotskyism, the CPUSA credited Trotskyites with making advances within the peace and youth movements. The communist party maintained that the "chief foes" of the Trotskyites in the United States were itself and the Soviet Union. The party condemned the Trotskyites for rejecting the "tactics of the united front." Further, the CPUSA denounced them for advocating "Black nationalism as *the* revolutionary ideology among the black people." It contended that they had substituted black people for the working class in their composition of the vanguard for socialism. (*Political Affairs,* June.) In 1972, the party considered the problem of Trotskyism on a par with that of "Right opportunism" and vowed to expose its true character. In this respect, the CPUSA regarded its presidential ticket and electoral endeavors "a most important step." (Ibid., July.)

The Maoists were singled out for special criticism for impeding the alliance between "the labor and black liberation movements." According to Henry Winston, the Maoists stigmatized white workers as "reactionary" and exclusively emphasized the unity of the Third World. (*Daily World*, 22 January.)

International Views and Contacts. The CPUSA continued in 1972 to support the policies of the Soviet Union. Party chairman Henry Winston saluted the Soviet Union as "the strongest force fighting for peace." In a more militant vein, he foresaw a renewed "world struggle led by the U.S.S.R. and the socialist camp" (*Daily World*, 18 January). Winston visited Chile to celebrate the 50th anniversary of that country's communist party (ibid., 11 January), and also visited Poland and Czechoslovakia (ibid., 22 January, 7 June). Gus Hall made a trip to Cuba early in April. He and Jarvis Tyner led an official delegation to Hanoi, North Vietnam, to participate in talks with communist leaders in that country, Laos, and Cambodia. In mid-October Angela Davis returned to the United States from a journey to "the Soviet Union, the German Democratic Republic, Bulgaria, Czechoslovakia, Cuba and Chile" (ibid., 4 November).

Gus Hall attacked the People's Republic of China as "a negative factor in the struggle against imperialism." In his view, the communist Chinese leaders were following an "opportunistic policy" and serving the "interests of imperialism" by using the conflicts between the United States and the Soviet Union for their own national interest. (*Political Affairs*, November.) Specifically, the CPUSA criticized China for placing obstacles in the path of the Soviet Union in its effort to arm the North Vietnamese (ibid.). Among other reasons the communist Chinese were subjected to rebuke for their evident lack of interest in participating in a Soviet-proposed world disarmament conference (*Daily World*, 5 January) and for a feigned comity with Third World powers to pursue anti-Soviet programs (ibid., 6 January).

Publications. The two principal publications of the CPUSA are *Daily World*, a newspaper published in New York five times a week (Tuesday through Saturday), and the monthly theoretical organ *Political Affairs*. Other publications following the party's line include *People's World*, a weekly San Francisco newspaper; *Freedomways*, a quarterly review addressed to blacks; *Labor Today*, a bimonthly trade union magazine; *American Dialogue*, a quarterly cultural magazine; and *New World Review*, a quarterly on international issues. In June 1970 the CPUSA initiated publication of *Jewish Affairs*, a bimonthly newsletter.

*   *   *

The SWP. Founded in 1938, the Socialist Workers Party (SWP) is the oldest and largest among Trotskyist movements in the United States. The Young Socialist Alliance (YSA) acts as the youth arm of the SWP. The three most notable Trotskyist organizations that have split from the SWP appear to be the Workers' League, the Workers' World Party, and the Spartacist League.

The SWP and the YSA continued in 1972 to have numerically few members, yet they have maintained their influence on college campuses and within the movement against U.S. involvement in Vietnam. The SWP announced that its membership had "doubled its size in the last three years" (*The Militant*, 2 June). The party's membership in 1969–70 had stabilized around 1,000 (see *YICA, 1969*, p. 843, and *1970*, p. 489).

Leadership and Organization. The SWP's national committee convened on 11–14 May 1972 and selected James P. Cannon as national chairman emeritus, Jack Barnes as national secretary, and Barry Sheppard as national organizational secretary. The committee reiterated the necessity for "revolutionary socialists" to continue their participation in the National Peace Action Coalition and the Student Mobilization Committee to End the War in Southeast Asia (SMC). The party reaffirmed its commitment to "deepen and extend the collaboration of the SWP in this process of building a world revolutionary movement." (*The Militant,* 2 June.)

In June the Young Socialist Alliance held a national committee plenum in New York City. It was depicted as the largest leadership meeting in the YSA's 12-year history. Both YSA organizers and national committee members attended the meeting. While deliberating how to expand the scope of the organization, the plenum announced its goal: "to become a mass revolutionary-socialist youth organization." In addition to supplying campaign teams for the SWP presidential ticket, the plenum noted particularly the need to "strengthen its campus base" by indicting the U.S. government and U.S. corporations for their "reactionary role" in foreign affairs. (Ibid., 14 July.)

The YSA opened its Twelfth National Convention on 23 November in Cleveland, Ohio, and welcomed 1,200 participants. The four-day convention was presided over by Andy Rose, national chairman; Andrew Pulley, national secretary; and Laura Miller, national organizational secretary. Andy Rose presented the political report, in which he admitted that the current progress of negotiations for a settlement of the Vietnam war made it impractical to schedule anti-war demonstrations for 1973, although he cautioned that this assessment was subject to review. He was optimistic about the prospects for increased radicalism around other issues and planned to "support candidates of the SWP in the 1973 municipal elections, participate in student government elections, conduct speaking tours, and send teams of YSA organizers throughout the country." The report on black liberation stressed the importance of developing a "militant nationalist organization" to lead blacks in day-by-day struggles. The YSA pledged to press for anti-abortion laws and continue to support "independent Chicano parties" while proselytizing among Chicano students in the interests of advancing revolutionary socialism. (*The Militant,* 8 December.) At the time of the convention, the YSA claimed 53 local chapters and "at-large" members in 161 other areas (ibid., 24 November).

Domestic Views and Policies. The SWP heralded its effort in the 1972 national election as a means of defeating the incumbent and winning young radicals to revolutionary socialism (*The Militant,* 10 November). The party nominated Linda Jenness for president and Andrew Pulley for vice-president. The ticket was recognized in 23 states and the District of Columbia (ibid., 17 November). The SWP campaign aimed at acquainting the public and especially young Americans of high school and college age with its political philosophy and program. "Young Supporters of the Jenness-Pulley" (YSJP) teams distributed literature and solicited votes in major areas. (Ibid., 28 April.) The SWP election platform demanded an immediate end to the Vietnam war and the draft, and the closing of all U.S. military bases in the world. Among its domestic clauses, the platform urged confiscatory taxation of incomes of $25,000 and above, and a cessation of taxation for those under $10,000. It promised government ownership of basic industry and "an independent labor party." It also advocated black "community control" over the police and all fiscal programs and institutions in black neighborhoods. Blacks would be permitted to "keep arms and organize themselves for self-defense against all attacks." The platform also favored a "mass black political party" to participate in elections and otherwise seek to win black community demands. Regarding Chicanos, the SWP predicted that burgeoning La Raza Unida parties would grow into popular parties on a national scale. The party called for "student-faculty control of education," that constituted use of educational facilities by the anti-war and women's liberation movements. (Ibid.) During the campaign the SWP accused its ideological competitor, the CPUSA, of entering the presidential race "as a thinly disguised stalking-horse campaign in favor of George McGovern." The SWP claimed that it had made "significant gains" as a result of its electoral efforts. (Ibid., 20 October.)

Anti-war activities remained an important part of SWP operations in 1972. The Student Mobilization Committee (SMC) organized a national student anti-war conference in New York City, 25–26 February, which reportedly was attended by over 1,000 activists representing "124 high schools and 154 colleges." The main purpose of the conference was to prepare for and coordinate protests against the Vietnam war slated for the spring. (Ibid., 10 March.) According to the SMC, its demonstrations at the Republican Party's national convention in Miami Beach in August were utilized to construct new chapters in various parts of the country (ibid., 15 September). In October the SMC held a national steering committee meeting at Boston University to mobilize the student anti-war movement to greater collective efforts before the year ended (ibid., 6 October).

The SWP supported National Peace Action Coalition and criticized the CPUSA-backed People's Coalition for Peace and Justice for discriminating against anti-war groups that did not support the "seven point peace plan," proposed by the "Vietnam liberation forces." The NPAC contended that it did not take a position for or against the plan, but noted that alignment with the proposed plan might entail concessions that U.S. anti-war forces would not wish to make (ibid., 13 October). The NPAC also complained that the PCPJ had done an injustice to the "independent" anti-war movement by committing itself "to ensure the most massive vote for George McGovern" for president (ibid., 20 October).

The SWP was active in the Women's National Abortion Action Coalition (WONAAC) in 1972. This organization was subject to stricture by some women's groups for "ignoring" other feminist questions in its pursuit of free abortions. The WONAAC argued that this particular issue was not only a pressing one in itself because of the "right of women to control their own bodies," but most likely to spark the interest of uncommitted women in other feminist goals (ibid., 11 February). The national coordinating committee of WONAAC decided to postpone the commencement of an international tribune on abortion until March 1973 in order to rally support for the proposed Abortion Rights Act, which remained in a House of Representatives committee (ibid., 22 September).

International Views and Policies. The SWP announced that its presidential nominees, Jenness and Pulley, traveled in 1972 to Ireland, West Germany, Argentina, Canada, Puerto Rico, Mexico, Chile, and Peru (*The Militant,* 3 November).

The Trotskyist view of the rapprochement efforts of President Richard Nixon in Moscow and Peking was aired at the YSA national convention, with emphasis in this connection on the "struggle of the Vietnamese." The party acknowledged that Vietnamese "liberation" had been "the center of [YSA] political activity" for the last seven years. Convention speakers deplored the "détente" between the United States, the Soviet Union, and the People's Republic of China as an impediment to "the completion of the Vietnamese revolution" and a threat to the progress of "the world revolution" (ibid., 8 December).

The SWP stressed the significance of "political prisoners" as an issue in 1972. It chided Angela Davis for siding with the Soviet Union and not speaking out in behalf of 46 Czechoslovakian prisoners accused of "counter-revolutionary" activity. The SWP contended that these persons were socialists and former members of the communist party who were prosecuted for their opposition to the "Soviet puppet regime in Czechoslovakia." (Ibid., 8 September.) The People's Republic of China was not spared, as the SWP accused the present government of illegally imprisoning Chinese communist Trotskyists, allegedly held without trial for the past 20 years. The SWP demanded information concerning their status and called for their release (ibid., 19 May).

Publications. During 1972 the two major publications of the SWP were a weekly newspaper, *The Militant,* and a monthly journal, *International Socialist Review.* The SMC periodically publishes a newspaper entitled *The Student Mobilizer.* The United Secretariat of the Fourth International continued to publish the weekly *Intercontinental Press.*

*   *   *

The PLP. The Progressive Labor Party (PLP) originated in 1962, after expulsion of Milton Rosen and Mortimer Scheer from the CPUSA the year before. The PLP initially had been known as the Progressive Labor Movement. Its present name was adopted by a founding convention held at New York in April 1965. Until 1971, the PLP followed a pro-Chinese Communist line and was described as Maoist. The PLP does not publish details about its organizational structure.

Domestic Views and Policies. According to PLP, one of the advantages of communist leadership of trade union activities is that it sees "the class struggle not as an isolated fight for immediate gain, but as a long-range fight for state power (*Challenge Desafío,* 3 February 1972). The party urged workers to organize revolutionary "caucuses" that eventually would supplant established trade unions and "become the real union." The ultimate purpose of these caucuses, however, is to win "state power": the control of all governmental levels, including "the military, courts, jails, police, etc." (*Progressive Labor,* March.) Two concurrent meetings in February 1972, one attended by 200 persons in Detroit and the other by 80 in San Francisco, culminated in the formation of the Workers Action Movement (WAM). Ostensibly a worker-union body, WAM pledged to endeavor to build rank-and-file caucuses and to fight for control of the labor unions. Its immediate goals were to achieve "30 hour. work for 40 hours pay," to support the PL-SDS (Students for a Democratic Society–Progressive Labor) campaign "against racial education," and to further prison rebellions (*Challenge Desafío,* 16 March).

A PL-SDS West Coast conference was held at San Francisco State College on 19–20 February. The conference called for the elimination of "racist textbooks and professors" and the encouragement of "political trials and prison rebellions" (ibid., 16 March). The "National Convention Against Racism," called by SDS-PL, drew about 1,000 persons between 30 March and 2 April at Cambridge, Massachusetts. The main focus of the meeting was on the rise of "race theories" and "racist ideology" in academic circles (*NYT,* 3 April). Special attention was directed upon four "white supremacist teachers" who had allegedly "recently published articles saying that black people were genetically inferior to whites." The meeting discussed the mounting of campaigns to disrupt the classrooms of these teachers, to get them fired, and to ban their books from college libraries. (*Guardian,* New York, 12 April.)

International Policies. In 1971 the PLP reversed the pro-Maoist policy it had followed since the party's inception (see *YICA, 1972,* p. 428). In 1972 it solidified this new policy by classifying the leaders of the People's Republic of China as "revisionists," "bosses," and "opportunists" in their negotiations with the United States (*Challenge Desafío,* 16 March).

Publications. During 1972 the PLP issued two publications: *Challenge Desafío,* a monthly English-Spanish newspaper, and *Progressive Labor,* a bimonthly journal published irregularly.

*   *   *

The Revolutionary Union and "Venceremos." The proliferation of smaller communist parties claiming to be the true interpreter of Marxism-Leninism includes two groups following the Maoist line: the Revolutionary Union (RU) and the "Venceremos" (we shall overcome).

An "old China hand" who in 1958 was a communist party labor organizer in San Francisco has been identified as the guiding light behind the RU in a government report (U.S., Congress, House, Committee on Internal Security, *America's Maoists: The Revolutionary Union, The Venceremos Organization,* 92d Cong., 2d sess., 1972). He is Leibel Bergman, who was expelled from the CPUSA when he would not go along with Khrushchev's policy of co-existence. He became a "behind the scenes" functionary of the Maoist-oriented Progressive Labor Party. According to the report, Bergman left the PLP to lay the groundwork for a nationwide "revolutionary union" by founding in the San Francisco area the Red Guard, predecessor to the RU. The RU is described in the report as a "national communist organization made up mainly of workers and students, Black, Brown, Asian, Native American and white" and formed in 1968. At the beginning of 1971 a schism occurred in the RU over ideological and strategic differences. One section kept the name RU and continued to be led by "Bergman, Barry Greenberg, Robert Avakian, and Chris Milton." The second group, led by Bruce Franklin (a professor at Stanford University, later fired), separated and established a new organization named Venceremos. (*San Francisco Examiner,* 26 June.) Evidently the two groups differed about the appropriate time to introduce organized violence. The Venceremos organization held that there was sufficient political consciousness to begin the "military or guerrilla warfare phase of the revolution at once," while the RU argued that the masses were not yet ready and lacked the advantage of controlling the "tools of production and the system of communications" in the United States (ibid.).

Publications. The RU currently publishes three monthly newspapers in the San Francisco Bay Area: *Salt of the Earth, People Get Ready,* and *Wildcat.* Venceremos publishes a newspaper, *Pamoja Venceremos* (Together we shall overcome).

Hoover Institution
Stanford University

Edward J. Bacciocco, Jr.

Uruguay

The Communist Party of Uruguay (Partido Comunista del Uruguay; PCU) dates its formation from September 1920, when the congress of the Socialist Party voted in favor of joining the Communist International. The present name was adopted in April 1921. The party has always been legal. It is firmly pro-Soviet.

The Movement of the Revolutionary Left (Movimiento de Izquierda Revolucionaria; MIR) was founded in 1963 and is pro-Chinese. The Revolutionary Workers' Party (Partido Obrero Revolucionario; POR), originally founded in 1944 as the Revolutionary Workers' League, is Trotskyist and is aligned with the International Secretariat (Posadas faction) of the Fourth International. Numerous other leftist organizations operate in Uruguay and display Soviet, Chinese, Cuban, or nationalist leanings or combinations thereof. Among the most important are the Uruguayan Revolutionary Movement (Movimiento Revolucionario Oriental; MRO), the Socialist Party of Uruguay (Partido Socialista del Uruguay; PSU), the Uruguayan Revolutionary Armed Forces (Fuerzas Armadas Revolucionarias Orientales; FARO), and the National Liberation Movement (Movimiento de Liberación Nacional; MLN)—better known as the Tupamaros.

Except for the PCU all these organizations are apparently small though no precise membership figures are known. The PCU is estimated to have 30,000 to 35,000 members, with workers accounting for about 73 percent of the total. The population of Uruguay is 2,900,000 (estimated 1972).

The Broad Front. The electoral strength of the PCU long resided in the Leftist Liberation Front (Frente Izquierda de Liberación; FIDEL), founded by the PCU in 1962 and composed of some ten small political and cultural groups. In an extremely complex electoral system which discourages voting for minority party candidates, FIDEL had never done very well, winning less than 6 percent of the vote in the 1966 election. In 1971 FIDEL took part in the national election as part of a much larger coalition, the Broad Front (Frente Amplio; FA), made up of 17 leftist and anti-government parties and groups, including, in addition to FIDEL, the PCU, PSU, POR, the Christian Democratic Party (Partido Demócrata Cristiano; PDC), a faction of the liberal Colorado Party led by Senator Zelmar Michelini, a faction of the conservative National (Blanco) Party led by Senator Francisco Rodríguez Camusso, and independent leftists led by Carlos Quijano (publisher of the weekly newspaper *Marcha*). The Broad Front, led by retired General Liber Seregni, won 18 percent of the vote (see *YICA, 1972,* pp. 429–31).

On 1 March 1972 Juan Bordaberry was inaugurated president of Uruguay for a 5-year term. Bordaberry, leader of a moderate faction of the Colorado Party, faced a national congress in which no party had a majority. In the Chamber of Deputies were 41 representatives of the Colorados, 40 of the Nationals, and 18 of the Broad Front, among the latter being PCU Executive Committee members Rodney Arismendi and José L. Massera; in the Senate were 13 Colorados, 12 Nationals, and 5 of the Broad Front, among the latter being PCU Central Committee member Enrique Rodríguez. On 27 March José Pedro Cardozo, a member of the FA Executive Committee and the PSU Central Committee, promised that FA deputies and senators would delay, change, defeat, or otherwise fight in a parliamentary manner the Bordaberry programs in congress (Havana radio, 28 March). Differences have appeared among FA members in congress. Senator Enrique Erro (leader of the Popular Union Party), for example, said in a speech on 4 February that terrorism by the MLN was a "legitimate [form of] struggle for liberation from our fascist government and from imperialism" (*Acción,* Montevideo, 5 February). The PCU daily *El Popular* (5 February) published a summary of Erro's speech which omitted all reference to terrorism, a tactic the PCU has long rejected.

The PCU. Organization and Leadership. The PCU's national headquarters administers provincial subdivisions of the party within each of the republic's 19 territorial departments (provinces). The PCU Central Committee has 48 regular members and 27 alternates.

The PCU Secretariat has five members: Rodney Arismendi, Enrique Pastorino, Jaime Pérez, Enrique Rodríguez, and Alberto Suárez. The Executive Committee totals fifteen, consisting of the five Secretariat members and Alberto Altesor, Leopoldo Bruera, Félix Díaz, José L. Massera, Rosario Pietrarroia, César Reyes Daglio, Gerardo Cuesta, Jorge Mazzarovich, Wladímir Turiansky, and Eduardo Viera.

The party's youth organization, the Union of Communist Youth (Unión de la Juventud Comunista; UJC), was founded in 1955. It reported a 1972 membership of 20,000 and claimed to have enrolled 2,000 new members during January–September through UJC recruitment among young Broad Front supporters, in a campaign directed by UJC first secretary Jorge Mazzarovich (*Ahora,* Montevideo, 22 September).

In recent years the UJC has played an important, and sometimes dominant, role in the Federation of University Students of Uruguay (Federación de Estudiantes Universitarios del Uruguay; FEUU), an affiliate of the Soviet-front International Union of Students. The UJC, joined after March by PCU volunteers, cooperated with the Secondary School Student Socialist Brigades (Brigadas Estudiantiles Socialistas de Secundaria; BESS) to combat the anti-communist Uruguayan Youth on the March (Juventud Uruguaya en Pie; JUP). When the JUP in any school voiced support for government policies, programs, or statements, the BESS and UJC helped organize counter-protests and rival statements by leftist students (*El Oriental,* Montevideo, 17 March and 7 April; *La Mañana,* Montevideo, 20 July). On 7 November Havana radio announced that the UJC would instruct other students in united front tactics at the Fifth Congress of the "Continental Organization of Latin American Students" (OCLAE) in Santiago, Chile, in May 1973.

The National Convention of Workers (Convención Nacional de Trabajadores; CNT) was established in 1966. Individual unions in the CNT are largely non-communist, and some non-communists hold high positions in them. The decision-making offices, however, are dominated by officials of the PCU, including Enrique Pastorino, Félix Díaz, Wladímir Turiansky, and Antonio Tamayo. The CNT claims to have some 500,000 members.

During 1972 the CNT fought the government as it has in the past, through work stoppages and workers' demands which made more difficult the government efforts to stabilize the economy. The CNT repeatedly called for the abolition of COPRIN (the government agency for wage and price controls, used by the Bordaberry administration to fight inflation), for the withdrawal of the Uruguayan government from any dealings with the International Monetary Fund, and for strikes in favor of higher wages and pensions. Typical of the anti-IMF positions was the PCU charge that the IMF directly ordered devaluation of the peso in 1972 with the Bordaberry government simply agreeing (*Estudios,* March–May). In April, Luis Iguini, secretary for international affairs of the CNT and a PCU writer on labor affairs, pledged that the workers' federation would maintain solidarity with actions taken by the workers' federations of Chile, Cuba, and North Vietnam, with help promised from PCU leader Enrique Pastorino, who is president of the Soviet-aligned World Federation of Trade Unions.

Domestic Attitudes and Activities. Early in September Rodney Arismendi reviewed the domestic situation in a report to the PCU Central Committee: "The political situation is unstable, yet favorable conditions have arisen for the people's struggle for their political and economic rights. Uruguay is experiencing a deep crisis, with intensification of class struggle and the emergence of a political Broad Front, allowing the PCU to combine dialectically the policy of asserting the role of the proletariat and that of unity with the middle segments of the population in a broad front." (TASS, international service, 7 September.)

On 15 April the Uruguayan Congress voted to support President Bordaberry's declaration of "internal war" against the Tupamaros in response to MLN killings of several prominent Uruguayans. Several days later Jaime Pérez criticized the government action but emphasized that PCU activities did not parallel those of the Tupamaros: "Today the nation understands that we are in a fight for our lives . . . as the government pushes through a fascist bill on the security of the State. . . . Our party [is] an integral part of the FA [and] the working class must speak with the language of the FA." (*El Popular,* 19 April.) The PCU announced in October that the agenda of the party's December meeting would emphasize effective PCU work with FA committees at all levels of national life in order to advance leftist forces "along the political path toward power" (ibid., 17 October).

During the year the PCU made constant use of its position in the labor movement and in Congress. At a Central Committee conference on 22 April, PCU members were urged to carry out work stoppages ordered by the CNT as "legal confrontation of government policies" (ibid., 23 April). In mid-April the CNT led a two-day general strike in response to a PCU call protesting the deaths of seven party members caught in MLN-police gunfire. In October the PCU helped organize strikes of medical workers, schoolteachers, and employees of the Ministry of Education and Culture. The PCU and CNT urged the Federation of Transportation Workers to hold out for more than the 20 percent raise granted bus, truck, and taxi drivers by COPRIN, apparently with little success (*La Prensa,* Buenos Aires, 18 October).

In the Chamber of Deputies and the Senate the PCU joined other FA congressmen in working for the appointment of a minister of defense who would soften the vigorous coordinated efforts of the police and Army against the Tupamaros. PCU leaders in September devoted much attention to the case of Washington Ferrer, the first deputy in the Congress to lose his parliamentary standing in thirty years. Ferrer was a substitute deputy for the FA under Uruguay's system of electing "suplente" congressmen to serve in case a vacant seat occurs. In June, his principal became ill and Ferrer entered the Chamber. After he praised the Tupamaros on the Chamber floor, security agents began to follow his activities and photographed him leaving an MLN hideout moments before some Tupamaros were arrested. A court in August found Ferrer guilty of violating the new Security Law but left any punishment up to Congress. The Chamber of Deputies voted to cancel Ferrer's status as a member of Congress. Despite the mild punishment for consorting with MLN guerrillas, Ferrer in August and September was portrayed as a victim and martyr in the struggle against the government by various PCU orators and writers. (*Tiempo,* 4 September; Reuters, 15 September.)

This support for Ferrer did not, however, indicate a softening of the PCU attitude toward the Tupamaros. In early October Rodney Arismendi said that though the Tupamaros were sincere, "admirable revolutionaries" who supported the FA in a general way, their basic tactics were nonetheless incorrect. "Parliamentary and labor-management struggles," he asserted, "are the best means toward socialism." (*El Popular,* 2 October.)

International Views and Positions. The PCU has traditionally been firmly allied with the foreign policy positions of the Soviet Union. Early in 1971 Rodney Arismendi wrote that in today's "complex international situation" the foreign policy line of the Communist Party of the Soviet Union was a "distinct and clear-cut guideline for all who defend the cause of peace and progress on earth." Arismendi reiterated the PCU position that "in the unification of diverse anti-imperialist movements the basic role falls to the socialist camp and the international proletariat, against whom Yankee imperialism is directing all its force." (*Pravda Ukrainy,* Kiev, 20 February 1971.)

The PCU retained a friendly attitude towards the Cuban government as reflected in sympathetic coverage of the travels by Fidel Castro at mid-year through the Soviet Union and Eastern Europe. Similarly, the PCU reported on Chilean President Salvador Allende's visit to the U.S.S.R. in December, using the same type of TASS communiqués, telling of the Soviet plans for economic aid to Chile and Cuba. By contrast, the PCU has generally remained silent about China. The PCU interpreted President Nixon's visit to Peking as working against the interests of the U.S.S.R.

During 1972 the PCU accused the Paraguayan government, through its ambassador and embassy in Uruguay, of spying on Uruguayan Marxists, of forming "death squads" to hunt the MLN, of encouraging shock troops acting against communist youth groups, and of financing a weekly paper—*Azul y Blanco*—of "fascist orientation" (*El Popular,* 9 June).

In April, a PCU leader urged that the activities of the International Telephone and Telegraph Company in Chile be widely discussed as an example of "Yankee exploitation" (ibid., 30 April). The PCU, in cooperation with the UJC and CNT, held a "week of solidarity with Chile" at the University of the Republic in Montevideo on 1–7 May, at which the Federation of University Students of Uruguay (FEUU) sponsored the appearance of Chilean students, teachers, writers, labor spokesmen, and others (ibid., 2 May).

Publications. The most important PCU publications are the daily newspaper *El Popular* and the theoretical journal *Estudios.*

*   *   *

The MIR. The Movement of the Revolutionary Left, founded in 1963, is the main pro-Chinese organization in Uruguay. In July 1972 the MIR reportedly reversed its 1971 decision against joining the FA, and endorsed all Broad Front programs (*El Popular,* 23 July).

*   *   *

The MLN (Tupamaros). The idea of the MLN arose among Uruguayan leftists in the early 1960s. The organization made its first raid in July 1963. Since 1969 the MLN has carried out a series of dramatic exploits (e.g., kidnapings, robberies, occupations of small towns and radio stations, mass escapes from government jails) intended to call into question the ability of the Uruguayan government to effectively control the country. The Tupamaros attracted international attention between July 1970 and January 1971 by kidnaping a number of foreign nationals living in Uruguay.

On 14 April 1972 the Tupamaros sought to "raise the level of struggle" by killing three prominent Uruguayans. On 15 April the Congress voted to support the resolution of President Bordaberry for a declaration of "internal war" against the MLN. During the next eight months the combined forces of the Army and the police arrested some 2,500 persons as Tupamaros or active supporters of the MLN and uncovered over 200 hideouts and "safe" houses, some filled with arms and other stores. Of particular importance were the discovery on 27 May of a "people's prison" with two kidnap victims safe inside, and the recapture on 1 September of Raúl Sendic, a founder and top leader of the MLN, who had escaped from prison with 105 other Tupamaros in September 1971. By November almost all significant leaders of the guerrilla organization had been captured, killed, or exiled. The best known Tupamaro still at liberty was Raúl Bidegain.

In an interview published in August in the Chilean leftist journal *Punto Final* a Tupamaro spokesman acknowledged that the MLN had lost the initiative and suffered a "serious reverse" during the first half of the year; the defeat was described, however, as "tactical and nothing more." Efforts to reach an understanding with the Army had failed since the Army terms had been "unacceptable." "Armed struggle," he claimed, was still the proper form of revolutionary activity for Uruguay.

In an MLN document made public by the combined forces on 17 May, the Tupamaros expressed the belief that the 1973 elections in Argentina would increase Peronista nationalism at Uruguay's western border, "working to the advantage of the MLN," and that "similar nationalism in Brazil will help our cause, along with the positive developments in Chile."

The MLN continued to have wide international contacts during 1972. Communist China reportedly contributed some $250,000 to the three dramatic Tupamaro jailbreaks in 1971 and 1972 (Associated Press dispatch, 13 April). British, French, Japanese, Swiss, and United States intelligence agencies in July made available to Uruguay's combined security forces reports on the international activities of the MLN. In Zurich, Beirut, and Tokyo, MLN members with Uruguayan passports met with representatives of the Irish Republican Army, the Palestinian Popular Front, and the Japanese Red Army, to exchange information about guerrilla activities. (*La Nación,* Buenos Aires, 17 July; NYT news service, 15 July; National Council press release, Zurich, 15 July.)

Arizona State University   Marvin Alisky

Venezuela

The Communist Party of Venezuela (Partido Comunista de Venezuela; PCV), the oldest of the extreme leftist groups in Venezuela, was founded in 1931. In December 1970 the party split, one group maintaining the PCV name, and the other calling itself the Movement Toward Socialism (Movimiento al Socialism; MAS). Another Marxist-Leninist group, the Movement of the Revolutionary Left (Movimiento de Izquierda Revolucionario; MIR), originated in 1960 from a split in the Democratic Action Party (Acción Democrática; AD), which controlled the government from 1959 to 1969. A new element in the far left is the Grupo Trotskista Venezolano, organized early in 1972, a Trotskyite group associated with the United Secretariat of the Fourth International. Finally, there remain active remnants of the urban and rural guerrilla movement which had its high point in the early 1960s, when both the PCV and MIR participated, but has had little more than nuisance value since those two parties withdrew from guerrilla activities in 1965–66.

It was estimated that at the beginning of 1972 the PCV had approximately 3,500 members and the MAS some 4,500. (*World Strength of the Communist Party Organizations,* Washington, D.C., 1972, p. 158). No figures are available for the other Marxist-Leninist groups, although their membership is certainly smaller than that of the two major communist groups. The population of Venezuela is 10,800,000 (estimated 1970).

Much of the activity of the Venezuelan Marxist-Leninists in 1972 centered on maneuvers in preparation for the general elections scheduled for December 1973. The PCV had joined early in 1971 with two other opposition parties, the People's Electoral Movement (Movimiento Electoral del Pueblo; MEP) and the Democratic Republican Union (Unión Republicana Democrática; URD) to form the New Force (Nueva Fuerza). During the early months of 1972 extensive efforts were made to attract the Popular Democratic Front (Frente Popular Democrático; FDP) and the dissident communist MAS group to the Nueva Fuerza. However, these efforts failed, and those two named their own candidates. In August the Nueva Fureza convention selected the MEP leader as its nominee, arousing strong resistance in the URD, which by the end of the year had virtually withdrawn from the Nueva Fuerza, leaving it as an alliance of the MEP and PCV.

The PCV. Organization and Leadership. The top leadership body of the PCV is its 13-member Politburo. These include among others, Gustavo Machado, the party chairman, Jesús Faría, the secretary general, and Eduardo Machado, Guillermo García Ponce, Pedro Orega Díaz, Antonio García Ponce, Eduardo Mancera and Alonso Ojeda Olaechea.

Until the split in the PCV in December 1970, the party's Venezuelan Communist Youth (Juventud Comunista Venezolana; JCV) was the largest political group working in the student movement. The split deprived the JCV of most of its leaders and members, and threw it into

400

confusion. It was not until February 1972 that the JCV held its Third National Congress. The PCV described this meeting as "a victory for the efforts to assure the triumph in the [JCV] of Marxist-Leninist principles over opportunism, revisionism and anti-Sovietism instigated by the anti-Party clique," and stated that the JCV had "again become an organization working under the Party's political leadership and solidly united around the correct policy of popular unity." (*IB,* no. 8–9.)

The United Workers' Confederation of Venezuela (Confederación Unitaria de Trabaja-dores de Venezuela; CUTV) is the PCV labor affiliate, established in the early 1960s when the PCV lost virtually all influence in the Confederation of Workers of Venezuela (Confedera-ción de Trabajadores de Venezuela; CTV). The CUTV represents only a tiny fraction of the total labor movement.

During 1972 the CUTV issued several pronouncements which received publicity. One of these urged unified action by Venezuelans to frustrate efforts of foreign oil companies to evade the recently passed law on reversion of petroleum concessions. Another supported the president's decision to renounce the country's commercial treaty with the United States. In August the CUTV held a congress. Among those attending from abroad were representatives of Chilean and Soviet trade union bodies.

The March plenum of the PCV Central Committee decided to cease concentrating com-pletely on trade union activity in the CUTV, and turn instead toward penetration of the CTV. A resolution noted that the CUTV "has made no progress, but on the contrary has become weaker as the result of withdrawal of some trade unions that followed the anarcho-syndical-ists" (ibid.).

The change in the trade union line was evident in January when a Central Committee member said, "We communists are willing to hold labor union and peasant league rallies so that the workers themselves may elect their real leaders," and added that they were "working currently on restructuring the Venezuelan Peasant Movement, so that it can make progress in its struggle for land, credit, water, farm machinery and other benefits covered by the agrarian reform law." (Radio Barquisimeto, 25 January 1972.)

Domestic Attitudes and Activities. The PCV's general political activity during 1972 took place within the context of the Nueva Fuerza. In May the PCV attacked a resolution of the MEP youth which had urged that the Nueva Fuerza select an independent as its presidential nominee. In June the communists urged that the FDP join the Nueva Fuerza. The PCV Cen-tral Committee in June commented that "the policy of popular unity broad and free from sec-tarianism, guarantees the victory of the democratic and anti-imperialist forces in the coming elections." When President Rafael Caldera held a round of meetings with leaders of various opposition parties in June, the communists were included in these meetings.

At a seminar held in Prague in March under the sponsorship of the *World Marxist Re-view,* the PCV's line in participating in the Nueva Fuerza was explained: "Our Party's politi-cal and ideological struggle is directed against bourgeois reformism. And we are now in a bet-ter position to wage that struggle through the Popular Nationalist Front, to which the Party is affiliated." The PCV also coupled its "popular front" line with denunciations of the guerrilla strategy which it had followed in the early 1960s, saying, "Anarchist-type groups advocating guerrilla warfare have an insignificant impact." (*WMR,* April.)

The PCV strongly opposed the candidacy of José Vicente Rangel, sponsored by the dissi-dent communists of MAS. In January Jesús Faría commented that Rangel's campaign was "not helping the New Force in any way." In April Gustavo Machado claimed that Rangel's candidacy divided the opposition and was "not socialist," and accused it of being "favorably viewed by FEDECAMARAS," the Association of Chambers of Commerce and Industry. Once the Nueva Fuerza had chosen Jesús Paz Galarraga as its nominee, the PCV pledged support to his candidacy.

International Views and Positions. The PCV's loyalty to Moscow was underscored in 1972. It was one of 14 Latin American parties participating in the Prague seminar arranged by *World Marxist Review*. In September, Jesús Faría made a trip to Eastern Europe and the Soviet Union, from which resulted joint communiqués with the East German Socialist Unity Party (SED) and the Communist Party of the Soviet Union (CPSU). In the latter it was noted that "J. Faría appraised highly the persistent and selfless work of Soviet people for the further prosperity of the Soviet state and to strengthen its might, as well as the CPSU's class and internationalist position in foreign policy activity." The one with the SED placed emphasis on the "inviolable friendship of the SED and the Venezuela Communist Party with the CPSU and the Soviet Union and [their] loyalty to the principles of proletarian in internationalism."

In February the PCV Politburo issued a denunciation of the Chinese communists: "Mao Tse-tung and his followers are pursuing a policy of anti-Sovietism and are engaged in disruptive activities in the world communist movement contrary to the principles of proletarian internationalism" (TASS International Service, 1 March 1972).

Publications. The principal organ of the PCV is the daily newspaper *Tribuna Popular*. The party issues a theoretical periodical, *Documentos Politicos,* which it had some difficulty in putting out after the MAS split. Another "theoretical" publication is *Teoria y Praxis*.

*   *   *

The MAS. The "Movement Toward Socialism" was formed late in 1970 as the result of the split within the PCV. Its principal leaders include former-PCV Politburo member Pompeyo Márquez, the MAS secretary-general, and Alexis Adam, Eleazar Díaz Rangel, Germán Lairet, Augusto León, Freddy Muñoz, Alfredo Padilla, Teodoro Petkoff, Tirso Pinto, Héctor Rodríguez Bauza and Eloy Torres, one of the principal trade union leaders of the PCV after 1958. The MAS took with it a large part of the intermediary leadership cadres of the PCV, and it seems likely that a majority of the former PCV rank-and-file and virtually all of the JCV joined the new party.

The MAS youth organization, made up largely of dissident members of the JCV, is Juventud Comunista-MAS (JC-MAS), Alfredo Padilla is its secretary-general; Alexis Adam, president of the student body of the Central University in Caracas and a former member of the PCV Central Committee, is president.

The MAS youth group had considerable success in the student organizations during 1972. In elections at the Central University it won a majority of student votes; it also did well in elections in organizations of secondary school students.

The MAS has some influence in the CUTV trade union movement and has major support in the Venezuelan Journalists' Association (AVP) headed by MAS Central Committee member Eleazar Díaz Rangel. It has developed some influence among unionized workers belonging to the CTV, especially among ironworkers in Bolívar State and textile workers in Aragua and Carabobo.

Party Internal Affairs. During the year a factional fight developed between a group headed by Secretary-general Márquez, backed by Youth Secretary Alberto Padilla and José

Germán Lairet, secretary general of MAS in the State of Bolívar; and one led by Teodoro Petkoff. The Márquez group was opposed to breaking all relations with the Soviet Union, whereas Petkoff was in favor of completely independent line. One result of this feud was to force the resignation of Alexis Adam as organizational secretary of MAS in Bolívar State because of his support of the Márquez faction. This growing division within the MAS did not result in an open split in the party, but was somewhat of a handicap for the presidential campaign of the MAS nominee, José Vicente Rangel.

Domestic Attitudes and Activities. Much of the MAS activity during 1972 was concentrated on the presidential campaign of Rangel, who announced his acceptance of the nomination in April. He had informally been campaigning for several months before. Rangel, an independent member of the Chamber of Deputies since 1968, had been one of the younger leaders of the Unión Republicana Democrática to emerge after the overthrow of the Pérez Jiménez government in January 1958. In 1963 he left the URD, together with several other of its left-wing leaders.

A number of other small far-left groups announced their support of Rangel's candidacy, including the Free Press Movement (MPL), Committee of Revolutionary Unity (CUR), Socialist Vanguard, and the new Grupo Trotskista Venezolano.

There was some dissidence within the Rangel campaign ranks. The CUR and other supporters of Rangel complained that the MAS was monopolizing the campaign and using it to foster its own organizational drive. The unhappiness of the collaborators of MAS had the effect of reducing the money available for the Rangel candidacy, since some of the non-MAS figures in the campaign had extensive funds which they might make available but were unwilling to turn over to MAS. The MAS monopoly of the Rangel campaign also served to make impossible the mobilization of the support of the MIR behind his candidacy.

Rangel spelled out his program in an interview with the Caracas magazine *Elite* on 1 September. He noted that "First of all, we propose the nationalization of the Venezuelan state and government. By that we mean that only through a political act that will put full control over activities and absolute command over the economic and social policy in the hands of the state and government of Venezuela will it be possible to take up the great tasks of national development."

The Rangel candidacy received considerable publicity in August, when the Colombian novelist, Gabriel García Márquez, after receiving the Rómulo Gallegos International Prize for Literature from the Venezuelan government, held a press conference at Rangel's home. He announced in this meeting that he was giving his prize money, 100,000 bolivars, to the MAS and the presidential campaign of Rangel. From time to time there was discussion of joining the Rangel campaign with that of the Nueva Fuerza, but an overture from Rangel in August was repudiated by spokesmen of the MAS shortly afterward.

International Views. A trip by Pompeyo Márquez to Eastern Europe, where he spent some time in Romania, gave rise to rumors that the party might receive financial backing there, though there is no evidence of any such aid forthcoming subsequently. The MAS remained without formal links with Marxist-Leninist groups in other countries. The anti-Soviet positions of the Petkoff wing of the MAS are of long standing (see *YICA, 1971: Venezuela*).

Publication. The MAS has an official organ, *Bravo Pueblo,* which appears from time to time.

*   *   *

The MIR. The Movimiento de Izquierda Revolucionaria was established in 1960 by dissidents from Acción Democrática, including most of that party's youth movement. In 1962 it joined the PCV in launching a guerrilla effort, which lasted for about three years. Like the communists, the MIR withdrew from guerrilla activity in 1965–66. Unlike the PCV, the MIR has not sought to obtain legalization, which it lost after participating in a military insurrection in 1961.

On several occasions during 1972 there was public discussion of the possibility that the MIR would seek legal recognition. However, no such effort was actually made. Also, on at least two occasions, in April and September, leaders of the MIR met with the chiefs of the Nueva Fuerza concerning the terms and conditions under which the MIR might support the presidential campaign of the Nueva Fuerza, but apparently no agreement was reached. MIR sources in the state of Lara denied in April that the party had any intention of participating in the 1973 election campaign.

The principal organ of publicity of the MIR is *Al Margen.*

*   *   *

The Trotskyites. Until 1972 there had never existed a Trotskyite movement in Venezuela, although persons of Trotskyite sympathies had some participation in the split of the MAS from the PCV in late 1970. Early in 1972, however, a new organization, the Group Trotkista Venezolano, was established. It became associated with the faction of International Trotskyism known as the United Secretariat of the Fourth International, although the United Secretariat has not as yet had a meeting at which the affiliation of the Venezuelan group could be formally accepted.

The group publishes an occasional periodical, *Voz Marxista.*

*   *   *

The Guerrillas. During 1972 there was some resurgence of extreme-leftist guerrilla activity after the decline in previous years resulting from the "pacification" policies of the government, which has sought to get the subversive groups to return to participation in normal national political activity. The resurgence, however, did not reach major proportions.

In January, scattered guerrilla activities were reported in six states. In the following month the National Guard was said to be looking for Jesús Márquez Finol, or "Commander Motilón," a leading guerrilla figure. In the same month a brewery in Caracas was attacked by an urban guerrilla group which succeeded in taking 250,000 bolivars.

The major guerrilla operation of the year came in June, when a wealthy industrialist was kidnaped by guerrilla forces who received $1,135,000 as ransom for his return. Four groups claimed to be in charge of this operation and there were some rumors that Douglas Bravo, who in the early 1960s was leader of the Furezas Armadas de Liberación Nacional, the guerrilla force of the PCV and MIR, and then broke with the communist party when it withdrew from guerrilla operations, took part in the kidnaping.

Another group active in 1972 was the so-called Point Zero (Punto Cero). Two of its leaders were reported killed on 3 June 100 kilometers from Caracas. It was reported that they had received training either in Cuba or with the Tupamaros in Uruguay. Guerrillas continued to be active in July. The governors of Lara, Yaracuy and Falcón reported that some signs of their presence had been found in the mountainous area shared by these three states. Little was heard of the guerrillas during the rest of the year.

Rutgers University   Robert J. Alexander

ASIA AND
THE PACIFIC

Australia

After the Soviet invasion of Czechoslovakia in 1968, the leadership grew more and more sharp in its criticism of both past and present Soviet methods. The refusal to accept Soviet experience and methods as a guide to action in Australia was reflected in the Statement of Aims made at the Twenty-second Congress of the party, in 1970: "The Communist Party regards as of vital importance the strengthening of fraternal relations between the socialist-based states. We declare that conflict between them, or any attempts to infringe national sovereignty are a departure from socialist principles." (See *YICA, 1972*, pp. 446–49.)

While the overthrow of the Dubček government has continued to be the main bone of contention between the CPA and the Communist Party of the Soviet Union (CPSU), resulting in an exchange of recriminations and, in the case of the CPA, frequent publication of material in favor of Dubček (see, for instance, the party's weekly *Tribune,* 8–14, 15–21 August 1972), the CPA's rejection of Soviet methods has also taken other forms: most significant in 1972 were the development of a theory which made the CPA "the envy of other parties," and a reconsideration of some of Trotsky's criticisms of the Soviet Union in the *Tribune*.

Large sections of the party were deeply disturbed by the apparent lèse-majesté which resulted from the CPA leadership's determined drive toward a complete intellectual, moral, and practical autonomy. After its 1970 congress, and particularly in 1971, the leaders started to group themselves into factions to oppose the "Trotskyite" criticism of the Soviet Union by other sections of the party.

The first group formed in New South Wales around two former CPA Central Committee members and set up "Socialist Publications," whose paper *Australian Socialist* opposed the emancipation of the CPA from CPSU tutelage. In 1971 a "Socialist Unity Committee" was formed in Newcastle. Both groups, and individual dissidents in New South Wales and Queensland, were expelled. A second and much more important group then formed in the party after much patient and thoughtful work, and with considerable moral support from the Soviet Union. Combined, these dissidents were far too numerous to be expelled without thought, and at National Committee meetings throughout 1971 the leadership resolved to be conciliatory and if possible prevent a split without a fundamental departure from the independent line the party had been evolving since the early sixties. For example, the leading dissident, W. J. Brown, was given several chances to abide by future party decisions and avoid expulsion.

Instead Brown counterattacked by laying charges that Laurie Aarons, the national secretary, had breached party rules by encouraging "Trotskyism," among other things, although the charges were bound to fail and thus were merely disruptive (*Tribune,* 22 September 1971). Representatives of the dissident groups, finally meeting at Ultimo in New South Wales in September 1971, constituted a "Representative Continuing Committee" and decided to support Socialist Publications. A significant number of leading communist trade-union officials in New

South Wales attended this meeting. It became clear that more than 100 seamen and water-siders in the largest and wealthiest CPA branch, the Maritime branch, wanted a split, while the Australian Socialist group and the bulk of the membership in Victoria opposed a split and held meetings to oppose such action. CPA branches in Randwick-Coogee, Janalli, Cronulla, Cabramatta-Fairfield, and Port Kembla also condemned the "splitters," who ignored attempts by the CPA to reform the Maritime branch and disperse its members, and organize a second meeting for 5 December (*Sunday Review,* Sydney, 4–10 December). At this meeting they carried a decision to split the CPA by 33 votes to 21, with about 30 abstentions, and elected an executive board. (*Tribune,* 8 December).

It is probable that about 400 communists left the party to join what became known in 1972 as the Socialist Party of Australia. While it is doubtful that this party will replace the CPA as the strongest communist party in Australia, the SPA is without doubt strong and rich. A significant number of its members are trade union officials and it controls as "fronts" the Trade Union Education and Research Centre, the organization through which its members began their activities in 1969; the Centre for Young Unionists, with about 50 members; the Union of Australian Women; and the Trade Union Socialist Activities Association, which arranges frequent trips to the Soviet Union and elsewhere for members (*Modern Unionist,* Sydney, March, April, June 1972). The SPA publishes the *Australian Socialist* and the *Australian Marxist Review.*

The SPA's main strength is in New South Wales and South Australia, and in both states it followed in 1972 the traditional policy of working with the Australian Labor Party (ALP), especially in the trade unions. This has led to rather close association with right-wing ALP officials, such as the assistant secretary of the New South Wales Labor Council, who speaks at SPA-sponsored meetings. There is no evidence that its supporters are increasing in number, but the SPA is certainly healthy despite initial difficulties over who should control the newspaper. Its creation probably reduced CPA activists to about 2,500 at the beginning of 1972, whereas some years ago the party had 4,000 to 5,000 active members. (A. Davidson, *Communist Party of Australia,* Hoover Institution, 1969, p. 171; *Sunday Review,* 4–10 December 1971; *Praxis,* Sydney, June 1972, p. 2).

The CPA therefore began 1972 facing considerable difficulties. Aarons admitted: "It would be blind to assert that the long struggle in the CPA over fundamentals, and the formation of a new breakaway party have had no weakening effect, just as earlier divisions internationally did" (*Australian Left Review,* March, p. 9). The loss in trade union support is probably less important than the loss in members. When the CPA met for its Twenty-third Congress, in April, it appeared to be struggling ineffectively to stay a decline which had been going on for some years. John Sendy, the incoming national president, declared: "The party faces a very critical testing time. It has been split for a second time in ten years, it has aged, it has lost some vitality because of years of difficulties, divisions in the international communist movement, and because of ideological and theoretical unsureness, and slowness to adjust thinking and action and methods to new situations and new problems. It is somewhat bewildered by the strength and depth of some young radicals' criticism of the Party and the way such youth by-pass the Party." (*Tribune,* 4–10 April.)

The congress reaffirmed the Statement of Aims of 1970, introduced a new constitution and elected a 9-member National Executive including Sendy (national president) and Aarons (national secretary). More than a third of the new 33-member National Committee are trade unionists, a quarter are women, and seven are in their twenties. The major innovation in the constitution came after rank-and-file pressure for proportional representation on national bodies and more particularly to counterbalance the numerical preponderance of New South

Welshmen on the National Committee: now there is de jure proportional representative for minorities like women and young people, and a clause which provides that the National Secretary can only hold that office for six years (*Constitution and Rules* 1972, pp. 8, 10).

Since the *nadir* reached in early 1972, the party fortunes have revived somewhat. In September a member of the National Executive stated to the present writer that finally the party's policies had started to pay off.

Policy. The party's policy remained basically what it had been at the 1970 congress. It was Gramscian rather than "Trotskyite," despite SPA accusations. It started from the proposition that the working class, widely defined, was the main revolutionary class and the development of "workers' control" and a "self-managed and self-acting workers' movement" would encourage the practical and theoretical autonomy necessary for the establishment of a hegemony of socialist ideas. "In Australian conditions, the main revolutionary task is to shake and finally destroy the hegemony of capitalist ideology" (*A Left Challenge for the '70s: A Policy Statement adopted by the 23rd Congress of the Communist Party of Australia, April 1972*, p. 14). To complement the practical emancipation of workers' control, the party would therefore concentrate on education in socialist theory through the *Tribune* and *Australian Left Review* and bring this actively into the working class. This was not the elitism of the past but a genuine attempt to unite practice and theory.

Workers' Control and the Unions. Until April 1972, CPA policy contributed negatively to the creation of the SPA. After April, despite having some opponents on the National Committee, it started to pay off. The CPA started to meet significant success in the policy of workers' control in New South Wales, where it advanced in 1971–72 the view that only "grass roots" action by unionists could control the anti-social activity of irresponsible capital (*Modern Unionism and the Workers' Movement, 22nd Congress, 1970*).

Particularly active in bringing about success using this method was the flamboyant New South Wales state secretary of the Australian Building and Construction Workers' Federation ("AB and CWF," formerly Builders' Laborers' Federation), Jack Mundey. Mundey has encouraged the members of his union to intervene en masse to control the destruction of parks, historical buildings, and the environment generally, sometimes working with the most "blue-blooded" groups in Sydney. His success in forcing real estate developers to desist from anti-social enterprise through violent intervention and destruction of developers' property has not only doubled union membership but also earned him the persecution of the state government, which was to bring him to trial on a contempt of court charge in an effort to curb his activities. Mundey represents a new type of communist trade-union leader, intent not on capturing high union positions but stimulating grass roots autonomy. Indeed it is said that in 1973 he will resign his office and work as a simple laborer, to avoid "bureaucratic degeneration." At the 1972 congress he declared: "Workers live 24 hours a day and unions, to be relevant, have to involve themselves in every aspect of life affecting the workers. It isn't much good improving wages and conditions if we are choking to death in polluted and planless cities, devoid of parks and denuded of trees." (*Tribune,* 4–10 April).

The high point in the success of the workers' control movement came in May when the owners of South Clifton colliery decided to close it after they lost a lucrative contract. At the behest of communist shop-stewards the miners occupied the mine and worked it successfully for some days, forcing the owners to find them other jobs and to promise to reopen the mines as soon as possible. The widespread publicity which followed encourages similar, briefer actions elsewhere, breeding a feeling that the world of men is not irreversibly separated into "muscular-nervous" and "cerebral" categories. In Victoria there are beginnings as well and the CPA is. also working with students, influenced by the dissident *Il Manifesto* communists in Italy, who are active as the *Link* group in the Amalgamated Engineering Union (*Link,* Melbourne, August 1972). Joe Palmada's theoretical contributions to the theory of workers' control have been of high quality (*Australian Left Review,* October).

Recruitment and the Press. It was already obvious in 1971 that young workers were attracted by this new activism, which met such success. Of the 41 members recruited in the Sydney CPA District (where Mundey was president) in August-November 1971, 32 were under thirty-five and 33 were workers (24 from industry). Overall, among the 77 new members recruited in Sydney in 1971, 44 were under thirty and half were Young Communist Movement members. At the YCM conference at Minto in April 1972 there were between 55 and 65 persons in attendance. (*Praxis,* February, p. 10; *Tribune* 2–8 May.) Among students and intellectuals the party was meeting poor response until the middle of 1972. Then students, attracted by the sophistication of CPA policy, the success of "workers' control," and the failure of Maoism, also began to join, especially in Victoria, where the defunct university branches were reestablished at Melbourne and Monash universities. At these two campuses the communists are now the most active of all left groups and Monash's *Lot's Wife* has an editor who is on the CPA National Committee. Several of the best young left intellectuals in Australia, disillusioned by the New Left's lack of organization, also joined the CPA and started to work on the *Tribune* and *Australian Left Review.* The declining sales of the first have now been stemmed and in 1972 the second has become the most widely read left journal in Australia. While the Tribune regularly includes obituaries of older party members, these losses are compensated by new recruits: the party is becoming younger.

Migrant Communities. The CPA could draw further heart from developments in the migrant communities in 1972. Faced with worsening economic conditions and the unemployment of which they are especially victims, the migrant communities, usually regarded as firmly anti-communist, have become more radical and are expected to favor the ALP in the December federal election. A CPA Portuguese branch publishing *O Lusitano* has been created, and a new Greek branch has been set up since the middle of the year (*Tribune,* 30 May–6 June; *Greek-Australian Review,* September). Particularly important have been developments in the Italian community, dominated to this date by the Roman Catholic Church and the right-wing Democratic Labor Party. Reports of appalling conditions in migrant camps prompted the Italian Communist Party (PCI) paper *L'Unita* to send Diego Novelli to Australia to examine conditions here. His reports to the PCI in Rome confirmed the stories and the matter was raised in the Italian parliament, which made representations to the Australian government (*L'Unita,* 16 November 1971). Meanwhile branches of both the Christian Democratic and Neo-Fascist parties of Italy were established here. Finally the Australian government permitted the formation at a conference in Melbourne of an "Autonomous Federation of the Italian Communist Party in Australia." Some 40 delegates from all eastern Australian states and South Australia attended this January conference, which elected a 7-member executive board and sent a representative to the PCI congress in Rome. A paper, *Il Progresso,* has been taken over, and the new party has started "grass roots" activity among migrant workers, especially in the arch-conservative Australian Workers' Union. Although it refused to ally itself with the CPA against the SPA and the CPA(M-L)—see below, many of the new party's members are CPA members and it follows an almost identical line. Its estimated 200–300 members, while formally owing first loyalty to the PCI, thus almost compensate the CAP for losses to the SPA (*Constituzione della federazione autonoma del PCI in Australia,* [Sydney?] 1972).

Elections. The CPA candidates thus faced the December elections advising second preference for the ALP, and claiming to regard their campaigns as mere forums for the CPA's extra-parliamentary activism, with the possibility of some success. (*Praxis,* July–August).

The party improved its share of the vote marginally, to between 1 and 2 percent of the national vote, and Aarons, benefiting from the "donkey" vote (because of alphabetical order), received about 4 percent. Competitors from the SPA were resoundingly worsted. So there has been a decided qualitative improvement in CPA fortunes which Laurie Aarons predicted at the party congress, but no real increase in popular support. Many old members have either gone to the SPA or have died, and the younger party is more in tune with contemporary trends and capable of attracting the youth of Australia. Its main problem is that party organization has become too lax for the "party of activists" which it seeks to become. To utilize its new strength and new talent in a rapidly improving economic and social situation which, the CPA thinks, may become as critical as that in France in 1968, it must organize. Since February 1972 strong criticism of the contemporary structure of the party, with its tendency to isolate branches from each other and create "morbid branch structures," has been made without anything being done.

Activity to overcome the "church social" atmosphere at CPA branches, where the elders sit at one table and the "youth" at the other and sing the *Internationale, Auld Lang Syne,* and *April Showers* without fervor, will be one fundamental task in 1973.

The CPA (Marxist-Leninist). This year's increasing student disillusion with the local Maoists' lack of theoretical sophistication has favored CPA growth. The early attraction of Maoist activism gave way in 1972 to criticism as the lack of realism of the Maoists resulted in a lapse from activism into violence, born of futility. Typical of mindless violence is the policy of the Worker Student Alliance (WSA), the main student "front" for Ted Hill's CPA (Marxist-Leninist), toward "Nazi" bomb outrages against Maoist bookshops in Melbourne. "We believe that [the Nazis] should be dealt with violently and [we] invite other groups to join with us in taking this stand," said the WSA's *Struggle* (Melbourne, 29 May). The WSA is thus having difficulty in retaining recruits for its 17 branches in Melbourne, Newcastle, Adelaide, and Perth. (*Struggle,* 12–16 June; B. Taft, "Maoism in Australia," *Australian Left Review,* p. 9.)

Student disillusion with Maoist futility has forced the WSA to become more theoretically sophisticated and conciliatory to stay the decline of WSA strength in the universities. The CPA (M-L), which still has Ted Hill as its chairman, has advocated a policy of a united front "from below" more and more forcefully (*Some Ideological Questions* and *More on Ideological Questions,* CPA(M-L) pamphlets). Though the demand not to be "sectarian and dogmatic" has not been put into practice by Hill or his 50 staunch followers, this year many younger Maoists and WSA members have been prepared to practice what Hill preaches, partly because their own attitude to him is not so uncritical as it was. Since the views in Mao-tse-tung's *On Practice,* which Hill advances, are not very different from those of Gramsci advanced by the CPA, there is a basis for future unity: "To build the revolution is to build the anti-US imperialist united front. This means uniting with all those who can be united with." (Monash WSA Eight Points for Unity.) Already there has been that sort of reconciliation among some Maoists and other leftists summed up in the words of one of the present writer's Maoist students: "We are all revolutionaries, but some of you won't get obituaries in the *Peking Review* if a bomb lands among us." Drawing the groups together has been common hostility towards local fascism after bomb attacks by "Nazis" on the Brisbane CPA headquarters and two Maoist meeting places in Melbourne.

Hill continues to produce the newspaper *Vanguard* and the journal *Australian Communist* and to control the "AB and CWF" on a national level, and still has some influence with the tramways' and waterside workers' unions in Melbourne. He and his followers have unsuccessfully tried to replace the CPA in the anti-war movement, which is now in decline, but they have gained effective control of the Australia-China Society in Victoria. This branch practically carries all the others in Australia and has organized several lucrative tours of China this year (news bulletin, Victoria branch, Australia-China Society, June 1972). We can expect the CPA(M-L) to meet some success as Australian relations with China become closer.

Monash University
    Melbourne

Alastair Davidson

Burma

The Burma Communist Party (BCP) was established on 15 August 1939 with probably 13 members and Thakin Soe as secretary-general. After participating in the struggle for the liberation of Burma under the leadership of the "Anti-Fascist People's Freedom League" (AFPFL), the communists more and more disagreed with the socialists in the AFPFL. In March 1946, Thakin Soe and some followers split from the BCP, where Thakin Than Tun had taken over the leadership, and founded the Communist Party of Burma, also known as the "Red Flag" (here designated the CPB-RF). The Red Flag soon went underground and its armed insurrection against the British resulted in its being declared an unlawful association in January 1947.

The BCP or "White Flag" communists (BCP-WF) under Thakin Than Tun collaborated for some time with the AFPFL, though without much success, and soon after 4 January 1948, the day Burma achieved independence, the White Flag stated that "the AFPFL had become the tools of the British imperialists" (Hugh Tinker, *The Union of Burma,* 4th ed., London, 1967, p. 34). With arrest threatening, the communist leaders escaped and went underground at the end of March 1948. Although the BCP-WF was declared illegal in October 1953, some communist activities could still be carried on legally within other organizations until the Burma Socialist Programme Party (BSPP)—founded after the coup of 2 March 1962 by General Ne Win—was declared the only legal party in Burma on 28 March 1964.

Between 1948 and 1950 the armed insurrection by both factions of the communists, together with other groups, brought the Burmese government of Prime Minister U Nu near to collapse. On 29 July 1948, the "People's Volunteer Organization" (PVO), a paramilitary troup organized by General Aung San during the independence struggle, joined the communists, and in August some parts of the Karen, one of the ethnic minorities in Burma, also joined them. The three groups associated in different short-term alliances between 1948 and 1950. In the following years communist actions were confined to certain areas (especially the Irrawaddy delta, the Pegu Yoma, and the Shan State) and therefore were a local, but constant, harassment to the Union government. Large-scale counter-insurgency operations of the Burmese army, in cooperation with the local "People's Militia," resulted in reducing the communist strongholds in the delta and the Pegu Yoma to unimportant rebel camps. Only the support received from the People's Republic of China—in an irregular and clandestine way from the beginning of the 1950s and openly since at least 1967–68—helped the White Flags to overcome the attacks and to regenerate parts of their strength during the latter year.

The Red Flags, whose main base was in the Arakan region, did not reach any major importance. Labeled as Trotskyist by the other communists, the CPB-RF had no relations with communist parties outside Burma. Cooperation with the BCP(WF) was restricted to a very few joint actions and a silent agreement on areas of influence. The capture of Thakin Soe and the loss of other leaders at the end of 1970 critically weakened the CPB(RF). The Arakan Communist Party, a CPB(RF) splinter group, has lost even the small local importance it was able to claim during the past years.

Figures on the membership in the communist parties in Burma have always been guesswork. Although it is hard to tell whether any Chinese are fighting in the Northeast as BCP(WF) members and if so, how many, or to what extent members of minority groups have joined the communists, a total of about 5,000 (*YICA, 1972*, p. 451) could still be considered correct, in spite of losses in 1972. The population of Burma is about 28 million (estimated 1972).

Leadership and Organization. After the purges and deaths in the past four years, the leadership of the BCP(WF) seems to have consolidated again in 1972. As no new names have become known, the Central Committee is thought to consist of Thakin Zin (chairman), Thakin Ba Thein Tin (first vice-chairman and head of the group's permanent delegation in Peking), Thakin Chit (secretary and Politburo member), Bo Thet Tin (Politburo member), Aug Myint, Ba Myint, Kyaw Mya, Naw Seng (leader of the "Northeast Command"), Thakin Pe Tint (second representative in Peking), and Than Shwe. An article in the *Guardian* (Rangoon, 13 August) stated that the Central Committee "has only four members: two at the so-called headquarters on the Pegu Yoma and two abroad"—that is, the Thakins Zin, Ba Thein Tin, Chit, and Pe Tint. It could be that the government newspaper purposely does not mention others newly appointed because the loss of members is used as proof of the constant disintegration of the communists. The organizational structure extends from the Politburo, through the Central Committee, divisional committees, and district committees, down to the township committees and the fighting units. Divisional committees are thought to exist, at least in name, in all parts of Burma, and district and (especially) township committees only in the regions where the BCP(WF) is active. Its "People's Army" is structured along traditional communist lines with party political cadres superior to military commanders at all levels.

Hardly anything is known about the CPB(RF). The slight information available indicates a further disintegration due to lack of support from outside, shortage of food, and decreasing cooperation from the people.

The Karen National Union Party (KNUP), strongly pro-communist and based in the Western Irrawaddy delta and the Pegu Yoma, is an important military ally of the BCP(WF). The KNUP chairman, Brigadier Kawtha (alias Saw Kyaw Mya Than) died of heart disease on 27 April 1972 (Burma Broadcasting Service, 17 June). This could strengthen the grip of the BCP(WF) on these Karen insurgents, and it will surely try to place a man of its choice as new chairman.

Party Internal Affairs and Program. The purges of "revisionists" which began in 1967 and brought the BCP(WF) to the edge of total disintegration seem to have diminished, but internal rivalry is still sharp. This surely not only concerns the two leaders Thakin Zin and Thakin Chit, whose feud "is now nearly 11 years old" and "has grown in intensity and dimension, with resulting clashes making themselves felt at every opportunity," although the two "work together in close cooperation in matters in which they share common interests" (*Guardian,* Rangoon, 13 August 1972). Some cases of continuation of the 1967 policy of "demote-dismiss-destroy" were reported in 1972. Thus "Commander Bo Lwin of the 4th 'Ever-Victorious' Battalion of the Burmese Communist Party (BCP) was shot in the back and killed on 1 August between Pyu and Zeyawaddy" (*Botataung,* Rangoon, 16 August). These circumstances caused Chairman Thakin Zin to call for party unity in his speech on the thirty-third anniversary of the BCP and to allude to inner-party quarrels:

> The question of perpetuating communism is whether or not to entrust the cause of communism in the hands of Marxists or in the hand of revisionists. The question is a matter of life and death for the party. Some comrades mistakenly believe that children of revolutionary comrades are heirs of communism, regardless of whether they are children of revolutionaries or not. Even if a person is a child of a revolutionary, he cannot join if he does not undertake revolutionary tasks or undergo training. (Radio "Voice of the People of Burma," 20 August.)

At the same time Thakin Zin emphasized that the recruitment of new members was one of the most important tasks. However, he recommended a special scrutinizing, for there were obviously misfits and even government agents among those recruited during past years.

Contrary to the traditional line of other communist parties, the BCP(WF) was ready to make "a [temporary?] alliance with the national bourgeoisie":

> For military victory and the seizure of power, the party must construct a united front composed of armed forces and revolutionary forces. This united front must be strengthened. Hence, the party of the working class must form a revolutionary united front, led by the working class, which is united with revolutionary nationalities. This united front must organize those representing urban petty-bourgeois and national bourgeois. . . . Efforts must be made to be united with them. They are victims of the evil period. (Ibid.)

The government tries to counter this policy, in part by presenting student returnees from White Flag camps in press conferences from time to time so that their experiences, if true or not, can be made known to the people. The BCP(WF) attitude regarding an alliance is due to the difficulty in finding the right position to take toward the socialist government of U Ne Win, which has to fit into the dualistic scheme of communist struggle. Thakin Zin continued: "At present the basic enemies of the Burmese people and nationalities are imperialists, landlords and bureaucrat-capitalists." Hence the BCP(WF) leader laid down "political policy to seize power and to win the revolutionary war against the Ne Win–San Yu military government, which represents the three major enemies." Being aware that the White Flag group is far from being strong enough "for military victory and the seizure of power," especially as they now have to operate in territory inhabited by minority groups, Thakin Zin stated that alliances with insurgent minorities was another main task: "The formation of an alliance with the nationalities, who are waging an armed struggle, is an important factor in an armed revolution and the establishment of leadership of the proletariat." However, the communists possessed military strength only in the area covered by the "Northeast Command," where they have been heavily supported by China. In the other regions the nationality groups seem to be stronger and the BCP(WF) apparently has difficulty in securing leadership of them:

> The party has won the leadership in the NDUF. However, the belief that not one part of the NDUF leads and organizes the people and that the leadership must be jointly held still exists. We must realize that the establishment of party leadership is our first and foremost duty. (Ibid.)

The NDUF—"National Democratic United Front"—was founded in 1959. It united leftist rebel groups, especially the "Karen National Union" and the weak "Mon Pythit Party," under the ideological leadership of the BCP(WF).

Domestic Attitudes and Activities. In 1972 the communists continued their policy of armed struggle against the "mercenaries" (Burmese army) and the "tools" (People's Militia) of the "Ne Win–San Yu military clique." Broadcasts of the White Flag's clandestine radio station, "Voice of the People of Burma" (VPB), therefore often end with an appeal for revolution:

> The Ne Win–San Yu government will be buried if the people as a whole participate in the struggle in the military, political, organizational, economic and other fields. Hence, we solemnly call on the people to rise up and continue their struggle until the Ne Win–San Yu military government is completely crushed. The people are certain to be victorious. (VPB, 26 September.)

The success of the armed struggle has varied from region to region. Fierce fighting seems to be going on still in the northern Shan State—the area between Lashio and Bhamo and the Chinese border. Late in 1972 a BCP(WF) broadcast declared:

> According to an incomplete report, the people's armed forces fought 28 large or small battles in the Namhkam district, 75 in the Kutkai district, 27 in the Kokang district, and 27 in the Wa state—a total of 157 battles.
>
> The Ne Win–San Yu mercenary army lost 111 commanders and troopers and 248 more were wounded in these battles. The people's armed forces captured 40 more; hence, a total of 399 members of the mercenary army were annihilated in the battles. Moreover . . . a total of 706 members of the defence forces [People's Militia] were annihilated in the battles.
>
> The people and people's armed forces of northeast Burma during this 10-months period annihilated a total of 1,105 enemy troops. . . . In April . . . an enemy jet fighter was shot down, along with its pilot. (VPB, 9 November.)

According to other figures the main battles must have been fought early in the year. The fighting forced the government to work out a relief program for refugees from this area:

> The government is carrying out a relief program for the people of southern and northern Wa state who have arrived in the Tangyan township because of the insurgent threat. The relief department will distribute 15,000 yards of cloth worth over 30,000 kyats, 3,000 pieces of warm clothing worth over 300,000 kyats and over 300,000 kyats worth of rice to the Wa refugees. (Loktha Pyeithu Nezin, 22 October.)

Although no official figures have been published by the Burmese government on its losses in the area, the figures given by the communists could be quite accurate, however with the reservation that nearly half of the "annihilated troops" were only wounded. The communist losses during the same period can be estimated at about equal to the government's.

Fighting continued in varying intensity during 1972 in other areas. (1) In the Laukhaung district (northeast of Myitkyina) the BCP(WF), probably together with Kachin rebels, evidently built up a stronghold which they consider as "liberated zone." Here 30 battles were fought during the first nine months of the year and "a total of 170 [enemy troops] were annihilated" (VPB, 2 November). (2) In the southern end of the Arakan Yoma (especially Gwa, Lemyethna and Ngathainggyaung townships) pro-communist Karen National Union Party (KNUP) units, of about 200 or 300 men, staged some attacks with varying success. The BCP(WF) itself is obviously nearly wiped out in this region and completely annihilated in the delta. (3) In the Pegu Yoma, especially at the southern edge between Daik-u and Pyu, the railway tracks leading from Rangoon to Mandalay were blown up several times. (4) In the Moulmein and Tenasserim area minor clashes occurred. Government forces made repeated offensives in all these regions and in the western and eastern Shan State. Although no figures on the results have been published, they seem to have been quite successful except in the northern regions.

The White Flag continued to enforce cooperation with and infiltration into insurgents from minority groups. In October 1971, Thakin Zin and Thakin Chit formed a special fighting unit under the name of "Victory Battalion" to which also a KNUP unit belongs. Its objectives, according to an article in the *Guardian* (13 August 1972) are: to turn the area around the source of Yenwe Chaung into a CPB-RF guerrilla base in the Pegu Yoma; to put an end to the government's timber extraction work in the Pegu Yoma; to control the Pegu Yoma and the area between the railway lines and the motor road; gradually to turn the KNUP unit into a fighting unit which completely accepts CPB-RF leadership and takes orders from CPB-RF leaders. The last objective reveals the difficulties of the White Flags in their alliance with the KNUP. In the "National Democratic United Front" (NDUF) the KNUP seems to have the military leadership whereas the BCP(WF) strives for the ideological leadership.

In the Shan State joint actions with the Shan State Nationalities Liberation Force have been made several times. However, reiterated claims of the BCP(WF) for leadership indicate that the relations between the two groups are not without tension either. For instance, a broadcast on combat news from Kentung included this: "The people in this area realize from their experience that they need the leadership of the Communist Party. They have seen with their own eyes that they can win continuous victories if they fight the enemy bravely under the leadership of the party." (VPB, 26 October.)

In November, "expatriate Tet Tun conferred with Aung Than of the Burmese Communist Party traveling in the communist-held area" (Loktha Pyeithu Nezin, 5 November). The initiative for this meeting came from some members of the "National United Liberation Front" (NULF), which rightist former Prime Minister U Nu founded in 1970. (For background see Richard Butwell, "U Nu's Second Comeback Try," *Asian Survey,* IX, 1969, 868–876; Klaus Fleischmann, "U Nus Come-Back-Versuch," *Saeculum,* XXIII, 1972, 203–220.)

Whereas U Nu left the NULF in April 1972, Mahn Ba Zan—the leader of the "Karen National Union Front" (KNUF)—has obviously tried to re-ally himself with the communists. (The KNUF, which is generally regarded as rightist, split from the "Karen National Union" in June 1968. During the peace talks offered by the Ne Win government in 1963, Mahn Ba Zan headed the delegation of the NDUF.)

In their actions the communists and their allies concentrate on the one hand on the destruction of roads, bridges, trains, tractors, and schools, etc. thus undermining the governmental development work and preventing its further implementation for the areas concerned so that the propaganda against the lack in government's efforts should become more basic. On the other hand, they try to win the villagers' cooperation through intimidation by looting homes of selected persons or the newly established cooperative stores (through which the government attempts to escape the distribution problem) and by killing village headmen and especially Security and Administration Committee, Peasants' Council, or People's Militia chairmen. In most cases the communists ask for taxes or tributes from the villagers, in a process which is described by statements to the effect that they "visited the villages . . . and organized and agitated the people" (VPB, 14 September). In this way they also get sympathizers in different places who warn them of army attacks. The government tries to resettle endangered villages without being able to solve the problem as farmers often go back to their former acres to collect the harvest.

The "Voice of the People of Burma," the propaganda organ of the BCP(WF), attacked the Ne Win government on a few special occasions. On 20 April 1972, General Ne Win and 20 other high-ranking officers resigned from the army "to serve the country more effectively." At the same time the Revolutionary Government was reconstituted; U Ne Win retained the office of prime minister, and General San Yu, just promoted to the rank of general and chief of staff of the armed forces, became deputy prime minister and minister of defense. The number of ministries was reduced to 15. (For details see Klaus Fleischmann, "Birmas renovierte Regierung," *Internationales Asienforum,* III, 1972, 591–94.) Commenting on the changes in the government, the White Flag radio stated:

1. The Ne Win–San Yu military government speaks about anti-imperialism and self-reliance, but in fact is dependent on aid from world imperialists and reactionaries. They serve world imperialists, led by the United States, as running dogs and depend on social-imperialist and international reactionaries.
2. The Ne Win–San Yu military government has declared that it has abolished feudalist-landlordism. However, in practice it is building feudalist-landlordism and imperialist-capitalism. The Ne Win–San Yu government is exploiting the peasant councils.
3. The Ne Win–San Yu military government under the slogan of nationalizing imperialist investments has set up bureaucratic capitalism. The working class continues to [suffer] under their system.
4. The Ne Win–San Yu government is still carrying out its reactionary and unjust civil war. As a result of these reactionary policies, the people are suffering. The changes in the army and government will not improve their situation.

As mentioned earlier, the strictly socialist course of the Ne Win government makes it difficult for the communists to develop a contrasting program. Hence, their propaganda becomes vague and replaces a convincing argumentation by general accusations of tricking and deceiving the people. The preparations for the partial or total resignation of Ne Win from politics, in which light the changes in the government should be seen, were interpreted as a "serious dogfight among them":

> The recent changes within the military government are not minor. The change in which Ne Win was forced to hand over the post of chief of staff and defence department to San Yu shows the seriousness of the power struggle (VPB, 7 May 1972).

A similar accusation was repeated when U Shwe and U Sein Mya were dismissed. (On 22 September 1972, the Revolutionary Council announced the dismissal of U Shwe as a member of the Revolutionary Council and as minister for industry and for labor, and of U Sein Mya as minister for home and religious affairs. No reasons have been given.) However, San Yu, designated successor of Ne Win, is never personally attacked in those broadcasts except in the connection "Ne Win–San Yu clique." This could indicate that China, which is obviously behind the "Voice of the People of Burma," expects a more pro-Chinese attitude from a San Yu government.

International Views and Positions. The BCP(WF) has been firmly aligned with the People's Republic of China during the past several years. Especially the Northeast Command was heavily subsidized from the other side of the border. Since the resumption of full diplomatic relations between the Union government and China in 1970–71, the BCP(WF) is kept at more distance than before. Coverage of White Flag activities in the *Peking Review* stopped during 1972 and, when mentioned, the Burmese communists were ranged behind the communists of Thailand, Indonesia, and Malaysia. Nevertheless, the White Flag party is allegedly still supported from China and the "Voice of the People of Burma" (inaugurated on 28 March 1971) can be considered as mouthpiece for the anti–Ne Win propaganda of Peking:

> The BCP's faithful adherence to Peking's ideological line is clearly expressed in the VPB's doctrinal sessions. The puppet radio station usually closes its broadcasts with quotations from Mao Tsetung's thought. Special articles on Mao's teachings, particularly those calling on the people "to uphold the policy of armed revolution . . . to unite for the seizure of power by military victory," are featured regularly. The VPB also finds occasions to justify Communist China's domestic and foreign policies, particularly in respect of Chinese diplomatic moves to improve relations with countries of different political systems. (S.E.A.T.O., *Trends and Highlights,* 1 April 1972, p. 28.)

The 51st anniversary of the Chinese Communist Party (CCP) was greeted with the vow that the Burma Communist Party in its armed struggle to "crush the Ne Win–San Yu military clique" would

> . . . study and follow the good historical traditions of the CCP, put them into practice correctly, and consolidate them in accordance with their revolutionary experience. We, who are marching along the road covered with the blood of thousands of heroes sacrificed in the struggle for the liberation of the people of Burma, will fight until final victory, despite terrible sufferings, with the revolutionary zeal of the CCP and Chinese people led by Chairman Mao. (VPB, 29 June.)

Attacks against "Soviet revisionism" were maintained. In regard to Southeast Asia, on the occasion of Malaysian premier Razak's visit to Burma on 16 February, the BCP-WF declared:

> The imperialist running dogs and enemies of the people such as Ne Win and Razak will never be able to create a new peaceful and independent Southeast Asia. A peaceful and independent Southeast Asia can emerge only from the solidarity of Southeast Asian people, which is the result of the revolutionary struggle. (Ibid., 20 February.)

In the same broadcast Burma, Indonesia, Malaysia, the Philippines, and Thailand were accused of calling for the neutralization of the area.

Rodenkirchen-Weiss   Klaus Fleischmann
Federal Republic of Germany

Cambodia

Communism first came to Cambodia in late 1930, when the Communist International instructed the Vietnam Communist Party to change its name to Indochinese Communist Party and to expand its activities into Laos and Cambodia. In 1945 the party was "officially" dissolved, but it continued to function covertly. The movement surfaced in 1951 with the creation of three ostensibly independent parties—representing Vietnam, Laos, and Cambodia; however, the Vietnamese made it clear in their internal party documents that the distinction was only tactical and that a single party would again be formed when the situation was favorable (see P. J. Honey, *Communism in North Vietnam,* Cambridge, Mass., M.I.T. Press, 1963, p. 25). The Cambodian communist movement founded in 1951 was the People's Revolutionary Party of Cambodia (Dang Nhan Dan Cach Mang Cao Men; PRP), which was led by Sieu Heng, a *Khmer kron*—one of the perhaps 1,000,000 ethnic Cambodians living in South Vietnam, where he had been a member of Vietminh headquarters (see J. L. S. Girling, "The Resistance in Cambodia," *Asian Survey,* Berkeley, California, July 1972, pp. 552–53). Both the name and statutes of the PRP were originally set forth in Vietnamese and later translated into Cambodian. Following the 1954 Geneva conference on Indochina, Cambodian communists sought to escape the label of "Vietnamese puppets" by forming a front, the Khmer People's Party (Pracheachon Party; PP), in 1955. The PP won 4 percent of the vote in the 1955 elections, and remained active—in the face of increasing government opposition—until the arrest of 14 key leaders (including the party's secretary-general) in 1962 (ibid., p. 554). The PP was banned later that year; little has been heard of it since. In 1970 the PRP became more active and today appears to be the sole Marxist-Leninist organization in Cambodia.

The PRP is illegal and its membership strength is unknown. It is thought to have at least 1,000 members and the support of several thousand sympathizers. The Cambodian communist armed forces—the Khmer Rouge (once known as Khmer Vietminh)—have grown in strength from an estimated 3,000 in 1970 to perhaps 30,000 in 1972 (*New York Times,* 6 November 1972). The Cambodian government places their number at 15,000 to 20,000 (Cambodian Press Agency, Phnom Penh, 18 October). The large majority of communist military forces fighting in Cambodia are Vietnamese, both North Vietnamese Army regulars and South Vietnamese Viet Cong. The population of the country is slightly over 7,000,000 (estimated 1972).

On 18 March 1970 the Cambodian National Assembly voted unanimously to depose the chief of state, Prince Norodom Sihanouk, who was at the time in Moscow trying to obtain the assistance of Soviet leaders in his attempt to force the Vietnamese communists to reduce their activities on the Cambodian side of the Cambodia-Vietnam border. There had been widespread dissatisfaction with Sihanouk over a number of issues, but none was more crucial than the open violation of Cambodian territorial integrity by the Vietnamese communists. The deposed Sihanouk went to Peking, where he received a warm welcome from Premier Chou En-lai and a promise of support in his attempt to return to power. On 23 March Sihanouk announced the formation of the National United Front of Kampuchea (NUFK, sometimes identified as FUNK) to unite all elements willing to support him in his attempts to regain power. In May, Sihanouk proclaimed the formation of the Royal Government of National Union (RGNU, sometimes identified as GRUNK) and sought international recognition as the sole legal ruler of Cambodia. He has admitted that the majority of the members of the RGNU are Khmer Rouge leaders, and that the power is in the hands of the Cambodian communist party (*New York Times,* 26 September 1970). The NUFK appears to be similarly controlled by PRP members, and all significant communist activity in Cambodia during 1972 was carried out in the name of one or the other of the two groups.

There were reports in late 1972 that Sihanouk had lost all of his power among the Cambodian contingent in Peking, and that Ieng Sary and other Cambodian communists were forcing Sihanouk and his wife to attend "self-purification" sessions. These reports received additional support from an American journalist who interviewed Sihanouk in Algiers and reported being told by the former chief of state that he was allowed to retain the title "Head of State" only because "they" thought he was still of use to them (*Far Eastern Economic Review,* 5 August).

Leadership and Organization. The senior Cambodian communist residing in Peking is apparently Ieng Sary. Among those reported to be in Cambodia, Khieu Samphan appears to be in operational control. He is a member of the NUFK Politburo, RGNU vice prime-minister and minister of defense, and commander in chief of the Cambodian People's National Liberation Armed Forces (CPNLAF). Along with Hou Youn and Hu Nim, Khieu Samphan has been identified by Sihanouk as a key leader of the PRP. He has also received special emphasis in communist radio broadcasts concerning Cambodia (for example, NCNA radio broadcast, 24 March 1972). Although not highly publicized, Tou Samouth has been identified as president of the Cambodian communist party.

A list of NUFK Politburo members and RGNU ministers can be found in the 1972 *YICA* (p. 458). Of the 21 RGNU ministers, 11 are reported to reside in the "liberated areas" of Cambodia and the other 10 in Peking. All but one of the 11 inside Cambodia have been identified by Sihanouk as Khmer Rouge leaders (see Sihanouk interview in *Jeune Afrique,* Paris, 26 August 1972). He has also admitted that "the communists predominate and supply cadres for the popular army" (ibid.).

NUFK organization in the "liberated areas" is virtually identical to that practiced by the Vietnamese communists. At each administrative level (hamlet, village, district, and province) there are three, five, or seven-man NUFK committees. Each committee member is responsible for one or more functions—political affairs, military affairs, security, economic matters, cultural activities, education, and so forth. According to NUFK leaders, all the committee members are "elected democratically from the representatives of all strata of the population" (see Ieng Sary interview, *Le Monde,* Paris 15 January 1972). The committees maintain control of the population in the "liberated areas" through various mass organizations which are members of the NUFK. These include the Peasants' Union, the Association of Democratic Youth, the Association of Patriotic Teachers and Intelligentsia, the Writers' League, the Democratic Women's Union, the Trade Labor Union, and the Cambodian People's Movement of United Resistance.

The NUFK also claims to have established NUFK committees "in the regions which are provisionally controlled by the enemy," including a Phnom Penh committee chaired by Prince

Norodom Phurissara, a member of Sihanouk's royal family (*L'Humanité,* Paris, 22 July 1972).

Domestic Attitudes and Activities. Since the Cambodian communists declared their support for the NUFK and RGNU, almost all statements on domestic matters have been made in the name of one or the other of these Peking-based organizations. As in years past, a great deal of attention was devoted to efforts to rally the masses to the communist cause. Appeals to unity were common, and special attention was given to intellectuals, youth groups, and followers of the Buddhist religion. Buddhist "bonzes" are held in high esteem in Cambodia, not only because of their religious position but also because of their "intrasigent nationalism" under the French (see Girling, p. 552). It is therefore not surprising that during May 1972 (the month of Buddha's 2,516th birthday anniversary) the "Patriotic Monks' Association" issued a well-publicized appeal urging other monks and citizens in "nonliberated" areas to struggle "to annihilate the Lon Nol–Sirik Matak–Son Ngoc Thanh monsters, the U.S. imperialists and their Saigon and Bangkok sub-masters" (AKI, Cambodian Information Agency, clandestine, 11 May). While some of the NUFK programs followed traditional communist methods of gaining popular support, such as carrying out an "agrarian reform" (*Jeune Afrique,* 26 August), an effort was made to win the support of wealthier elements of Cambodian society as well. Thus, RGNU information and propaganda minister and PRP leader Hu Nim described as a major feature of life in the "liberated zone" the "guarantee of private ownership, including land, dwelling houses, property and plants." He stated: "The NUFK has never infringed upon this right." (Radio "Voice of the NUFK," clandestine, 25 March.)

On the military front, while exaggerating the extent of their control, Cambodian communists were nevertheless generally successful during 1972. An inherent consequence of relying on inflated statistics is that claims must be magnified with the passage of time in order to avoid apparent failure. At the end of 1971 Cambodian communists were already claiming control of 80 percent of the territory and 5 million of the 7 million population. In order to reflect their military successes during 1972, they were forced to claim control of 85 percent of the territory (NCNA, 13 July) and seven-tenths of the population (*L'Humanité,* 22 July) by mid-year, and "almost 90 percent of the national territory" (NCNA, 8 November) and six-sevenths of the population (AKI, 25 November) by the end of the year. Cambodian government officials insisted that the NUFK controlled "only one-third of Khmer territory and one-seventh of Khmer population" (*New York Times,* 30 October), while U.S. journalists credited them with as much as 60 percent of the population and most of the territory outside of major towns and population centers (ibid. 5 November). Since much of the territory claimed by NUFK consists of hills, mountains, savannahs, and forests—with an average population of only two or three inhabitants per square kilometer (Girling, p. 549), it is misleading to speak of "occupation" by either side.

One factor contributing to communist successes in Cambodia may have been South Vietnamese government success against North Vietnamese Army units engaged in the "spring-summer offensive" which began in April (see *Vietnam: Republic of Vietnam*). Several North Vietnamese divisions were reported to have been driven into Cambodia shortly before a major attack on the district town of Angtassom (47 miles south of Phnom Penh), in early July (*Far Eastern Economic Review,* 15 July). The attack began with the biggest heavy-weapons bombardment of the two-year-old war.

There is considerable evidence that Indochinese communists hoped to stage a coordinated offensive throughout all three countries beginning in late March or early April. On 24 March Khieu Samphan, as commander in chief of the CPNLAF, issued an appeal to "ceaselessly intensify attacks against the enemy everywhere, around Phnom Penh and inside Phnom Penh" and to "tire out his forces and eliminate them partially or totally unit by unit." According to Khieu Samphan, "the entire Indochina front is likewise attacking the enemy without respite." ("Voice of the NUFK," 28 March.) On the same day, the Voice of the NUFK issued an appeal calling for the population of Phnom Penh to "rise up and unite to strike and demonstrate to overthrow the traitorous Phnom Penh clique and recapture power" (ibid. 24 March). Ten days later, in a follow-up broadcast, the campaign was identified as a "nationwide general offensive," but it was stressed that "the attacks on the front in and around Phnom Penh are the most outstanding" (ibid. 3 April). There were rocket and mortar attacks and small-scale sapper attacks on the capital city for several weeks to come, but in June Sihanouk asserted that Phnom Penh was not an immediate objective. He predicted that it would be taken "after a five-year period," and stated: "We do not plan to attack Phnom Penh this year." (Agence France Presse, AFP, 2 June.)

Communist military successes contributed to a general decline in morale among Cambodian soldiers and supporters of the Lon Nol government. Western press reports saw "no hope" for the Lon Nol government, asserting: "It is virtually impossible to find anyone here optimistic about Cambodia's future" (*San Francisco Sunday Examiner and Chronicle,* 8 October). Few Western journalists have had the opportunity to cover the war from the communists' side, and thus most are unaware of the extent of hardships and failures confronting them. The fact that the Cambodian government suffered from heavy casualties and serious internal problems does not necessarily imply a reduction in problems facing the communists. Indeed, the increase in American air operations in Indochina apparently presented serious difficulties to the Cambodian communists, who must rely on the "Ho Chi Minh Trail" for much of their logistical support. In answer to a journalist's inquiry about when he would return to the "liberated areas" of Cambodia, Sihanouk explained that the risk to his life by traveling the trail was considered too great. He explained: "The only way from Peking to the Cambodian liberated area is the Ho Chi Minh Trail, which is intensively bombed day and night by U.S. aircraft. Those who travel by this trail have a 50 per cent risk of being harmed." (AKI, 29 November.)

Cambodian communists continued to emphasize "armed struggle" during 1972, explicitly refusing to participate in peace talks with the Cambodian government and refusing to be bound by the terms of any agreement between the North Vietnamese and the United States. A resolution of an NUFK meeting in Peking explained:

> We are convinced that the armed struggle, the use of lofty revolutionary violence, with no compromise or retreat and with no negotiation with the traitors, is the only correct way, the only just position by which our people and youths in the areas temporarily controlled by the enemy can achieve liberation and live in freedom, genuine democracy and justice. (NCNA, 6 May.)

As rumors of an impending Vietnam cease-fire increased immediately prior to the U.S. presidential election, Sihanouk announced: "We will be by no means tied by an eventual cease-fire in South Vietnam because we, the NUFK, have the sacred duty of pursuing the armed struggle until the total and irreversible annihilation of the traitors who are presently governing Phnom Penh" (AKI, 29 October). Along the same lines, although Cambodian government officials expressed an interest in a possible coalition government with the Khmer Rouge (*New York Times,* 23 October), Sihanouk refused to consider this proposal: "The place of Lon Nol, Sirik Matak, Hang Thun Hak, and their principal collaborators will be in front of the gallows of our people's armed forces and not within our national liberation government" (AKI, 29 October).

During 1972 the Cambodian government held a constitutional referendum and three major elections. On 30 April a referendum was held which approved the proposed constitution by a reported 97.45 percent (Phnom Penh Domestic Service, 10 May). Three days earlier, the NUFK radio warned citizens to boycott the polls under threat of death: "There are only two choices for you; life or death. If you insist on serving the Lon Nol–Sirik Matak–Son Ngoc Thanh clique you are sure to be killed. On 30 April you should find a way to save yourselves. The way to survival is as follows: do not turn out to vote on the referendum. . . . Do not turn out to man voting booths either." ("Voice of the NUFK," 27 April.) On referendum day, Sihanouk announced: "Lon Nol's referendum and constitution are two crimes of high treason. . . . Those who voluntarily participate in one way or another in these crimes will be harshly punished by our people when Phnom Penh is liberated." (AFP, 2 May.)

On 4 June, a presidential election was held in which Lon Nol received a reported 60.76 percent of the vote against two opponents (*New York Times,* 7 June). A week before the election the RGNU issued a statement from Peking, which said in part: "The Royal Government of National Union of Cambodia rejects in advance the results of these fradulent elections commanded by the U.S. imperialists; for this reason, the results will have no political or other effect on the Cambodian people and the Cambodian people's national liberation armed forces" (NCNA, 28 May). Lower and upper house legislative elections were conducted on 3 and 17 September, respectively, and both were strongly criticized by Cambodian communists (see, for example, NCNA, 3 September).

International Views and Positions. Although Cambodian communists have traditionally been most closely aligned with North Vietnam, and the presence of an estimated 30,000 (*Far Eastern Economic Review,* 20 May 1972) Vietnamese communist troops in Cambodia during 1972 reflected Hanoi's continued involvement, the NUFK and RGNU appear to be more closely attached to the Chinese communists. This appearance may well be the result of an intentional attempt to underplay the North Vietnamese role in the fighting in Cambodia, and to increase the appeal of the Sihanouk "government" to the traditionally anti-Vietnamese Cambodian people. Another contributing factor may be North Vietnam's reluctance to become too closely involved with Sihanouk himself.

Sihanouk and his followers were apparently quite concerned about the February visit by U.S. President Nixon to Peking, and Sihanouk traveled to Hanoi for the entire period. Like communist leaders in Vietnam and Laos, Sihanouk frequently assured his followers that the Chinese were not going to "betray" the Indochinese revolutionary movements. He stated: "China considers that Indochina is our affair. We have the exclusive right to discuss the problem with the United States without an intermediary." (AFP, 17 February.) Australian communist Wilfred Burchett interviewed Sihanouk in Peking shortly after the conclusion of the Nixon visit and told a Japanese journalist that "Chou En-lai told Sihanouk that he had made it very clear to Nixon that if he wanted to settle the Cambodian problem, or that of Vietnam or Laos, he should address himself to the Cambodian, Vietnamese or Laotian resistance movements" (Kyodo, Tokyo, 17 March). In a *Le Monde* article (6 September), Sihanouk was quoted as saying that Chou En-lai had "clearly reaffirmed that China will continue its aid until total victory." The Chinese communists continued to voice support for Sihanouk, and on several occasions criticized the Soviet Union for trying to create a "third force" in Cambodia as an alternative to his return (see, for example, *New York Times,* 20 March).

During 1971 Sihanouk continued to appeal to the Soviet Union for recognition of the RGNU and foreign aid, but by the start of 1972 he had apparently given up all hope. The Soviet Union continued to recognize the Lon Nol government, and there were several reports that the Soviet Union was trying to bring together a "third force" coalition which would be neutral in outlook and which would refuse to allow Sihanouk to return to Cambodia. In July, Sihanouk claimed that "Recently, Moscow offered military aid and to recognize us as a front." According to Sihanouk: "We said no. We have more aid from China (and from North Korea and Cuba) than we need." (*Christian Science Monitor,* 8 July.) Although there was apparently no direct Soviet aid, Cambodian communists were on the receiving end of Russian equipment. Sihanouk told a Japanese journalist:

> We are receiving nothing from the Soviet Union. The Soviet Union gives us nothing at all. However, the Soviet Union keeps its eyes shut when North Vietnam hands its aid material over to us. North Vietnam supplies us with "gifts"—even with Soviet tanks, 133-mm field cannons, 122-mm rocket guns, and armored cars. (Sankei Tokyo, 30 September.)

Soviet criticism of Sihanouk increased during 1972. In a response to an attack by Sihanouk on the U.S.S.R., a Soviet publication charged:

> The prince is apparently indignant because the Soviet Union regards him as the leader of the NUFK rather than as the representative of a royal dynasty. It transpires that Sihanouk is not concerned in the slightest about the real interests of the struggling Cambodian people, who require the aid and support of all progressive forces throughout the world. Royal regalia is much more important to him. (*Literaturnaia gazeta,* Moscow, 12 January.)

Relations between the RGNU/FUNK and Vietnamese communists appeared to remain warm throughout 1972. As in years past, messages of solidarity and congratulations were frequently exchanged. When interviewed in Hanoi about the Nixon trip to China, Sihanouk emphasized that he and the North Vietnamese leaders held "identical points of view on all strategic, tactical, and diplomatic questions" (AFP, 17 February). As a peace agreement in Vietnam seemed to become more probable toward the end of the year, Sihanouk reported having been assured by the North Vietnamese leaders that they would help transport Chinese weapons and supplies through Vietnamese territory to Cambodia "even after a cease-fire in Vietnam" (*Christian Science Monitor,* 31 October). An RGNU statement issued shortly thereafter said:

> The Royal Government of National Union of Cambodia has supported and continues to support the draft agreement elaborated in the Paris negotiations on Vietnam between the Democratic Republic of Vietnam and the U.S. Government for resolving the Vietnamese problem.

The statement went on to stress, however, that "an eventual Vietnamese-U.S. peace agreement should never extend its authority to Cambodia." (NCNA, 8 November.)

Cambodian communist relations with Laotian communists continued to be warm, with frequent exchanges of messages of solidarity and congratulations. The Thai government was the subject of several attacks, none stronger than those concerning the border security agreement signed between the Cambodian and Thai governments in Bangkok on 19 January. As could be expected, the United States government was the target of numerous broadcasts by Cambodian communist communications media. Various peace overtures put forth by President Nixon were denounced, especially the 28 January proposal (see, for example, AKI, 31 January; *Le Monde,* 30–31 January; NCNA, 5 February). The United States was also condemned for sending military equipment to the Lon Nol government (NCNA, 15 November; AKI, 23 November), for bombing North Vietnam (NCNA, 12 May and 18 August; AKI, 17 April), and for mining North Vietnamese ports (NCNA, 14 May).

The RGNU voiced continued support for the "valiant struggle of the peoples of Palestine and other Arab countries who are fighting in defense of their just cause," and condemned the "new crimes perpetrated by the Israeli aggressors" (NCNA, 21 September).

Sihanouk was asked on several occasions about the future of Cambodia after "liberation." In response he usually stressed the theme of "internally socialist, externally non-aligned." He conceded that "real power in the unified royal government would be held by the Communists" (*Washington Star,* 11 June), but explained:

> What interests me is not whether Cambodia will be Communist or non-Communist after the war. What interests me is Cambodian independence in the international sense. You know, you may have a Communist Cambodia in home affairs but an independent Cambodia on the international level. Look at North Vietnam. You have also Romania in Europe. And finally you have Yugoslavia. It is not only independent vis-à-vis the Soviet Union but it is nonaligned.
> We may have a Yugoslavian Cambodia. (*Washington Post,* 5 September.)

By the end of 1972 the RGNU claimed either de jure or de facto recognition by some 60 states (AFP, 4 September; NCNA, 6 December). It received an important boost on 10 August when the conference of foreign ministers of non-aligned countries in Georgetown (Guyana) unanimously approved the admission of the RGNU to conference membership as the only legal representative of Cambodia (NCNA, 11, 17, and 19 August).

During 1972 Sihanouk made his first trip to Europe and Africa since being deposed in 1970, visiting Romania, Albania, Algeria, Mauritania, and Yugoslavia. In Asia, besides North Vietnam, he visited North Korea.

Hoover Institution
Stanford University

Robert F. Turner

Ceylon (Sri Lanka)

The first Marxist party in Ceylon was the Ceylon Equal Society Party (Lanka Sama Samaja Pakshaya; LSSP), formed in 1935. Its founders were young Western-educated intellectuals, including N. M. Perera, Colvin R. de Silva, S. A. Wickremasinghe, Philip Gunawardena, and Leslie Goonewardena. In 1939 the LSSP rejected the Stalinist line of the Third International in favor of Trotskyism, and in 1940 it expelled a small Stalinist group led by Wickremasinghe. This group immediately formed the United Socialist Party, which in 1943 became the Ceylon Communist Party (Lanka Kommunist Pakshaya; LKP).

A number of splinter groups have been breaking off from the original LSSP since 1950, when Philip Gunawardena led such a group to form the Viplavakari ("revolutionary") LSSP which is now called the People's United Front (Mahajana Eksath Peramuna; MEP) and is still headed by him. The original LSSP, led by N. M. Perera and Leslie Goonewardena, was expelled from the Fourth International in 1964 at the behest of a breakaway Trotskyist faction called the LSSP-Revolutionary (LSSP-R) headed by P. Bala Tampoe. The LSSP-R itself produced further splinters: the Revolutionary Samasamaja Party (RSP), led by Edmond Samarkoddy, and, in 1968, the Revolutionary Communist League (RCL) led by Keerthi Balasuriya.

The predominantly pro-Soviet LKP suffered a split in 1963 when a pro-Chinese faction broke away following the expulsion of its leader, Nagalingam S. Sanmugathasan. In 1964 each LKP group held its own "Seventh Congress of the Ceylon Communist Party," and each has continued to use the LKP name. However, through a splintering process within the pro-Chinese wing of the LKP, by 1969, the People's Liberation Front (Janata Vimukthi Peramuna; JVP) had emerged on the scene. In March–April 1971 the JVP, led by Rohana Wijeweera, staged the armed uprising. (See *YICA, 1972*, pp. 464–69; *Asian Survey*, February, March 1972).

The parties representing the core of leftist forces in Ceylon are: the LSSP, the pro-Soviet LKP, and the moderately socialist Sri Lanka Freedom Party (SLFP), led by Mrs. Sirimavo Bandaranaike. The SLFP, except for a brief period in 1960, was the island's ruling party from 1956 to 1965, either by itself or as the dominant member of a leftist coalition. All three parties, which had formed the United Front (UF) in 1968, again became partners in a coalition government after the May 1970 general elections.

In 1972 Ceylon became a republic and took as its name the ancient designation Sri Lanka (see below). The population of Ceylon is 12,800,000 (1971 census).

*　　　*　　　*

The Ultra-Leftist JVP. Immediately after the start of the abortive insurrection by the JVP in April 1971, the UF government led by Mrs. Bandaranaike outlawed the movement, which had attracted considerable support among middle-class youths and others of all political persuasions, but primarily unemployed high school and university graduates. The government suppressed the uprising and put between 16,000 and 18,500 youths suspected of active involvement in the movement either in police custody or in detention camps. The government's plan to rehabilitate the "misguided" youths, involving the creation of rehabilitation camps and schemes to deploy them in agricultural production work, has proven to be difficult and financially burdensome. A number of Ministerial Committees deal with matters such as rehabilitation, the grievances of the people in the affected areas, and police and army excesses. A Special Investigating Unit has been set up to undertake inquiries. Moreover, the government is seeking to give a new orientation to the system of education and formulate an employment-oriented economic plan. (*Asian Survey,* March 1972.)

Leadership and Organization. Rohana Wijeweera, the 28-year-old leader of JVP (under trial by the Criminal Justice Commission along with thousands of others during the second half of 1972), developed his strategy of a "one-day revolution—a military seizure of political power" during the late 1960s while he was still a full-time activist in the pro-Chinese LKP. For this, he had been denounced as being "anti-Maoist" by the small faction in that party. Within the context of developing ideological strains within the pro-Chinese LKP, Wijeweera made a futile attempt to seize control of the party's Youth League Federation. This had brought about his expulsion from the party and his decision to organize the clandestine revolutionary movement. Subsequently, Wijeweera was joined by another group with sizable following in the pro-Soviet LKP and led by "Castro" Dharmasekera. The Wijeweera-Dharmasekera combination had sought to "take over" the left parties, working through their youth bases. The movement started organizing activities on a mass scale, exploiting issues such as caste, racial, and religious prejudices among the Sinhalese petty bourgeoisie.

With the struggle for leadership of the movement surfacing (the significant reasons for which were: Wijeweera's appointing people of his caste—Karawa—as regional organizers even in non-Karawa areas, and his call for a violent seizure of power in April 1970), the Wijeweera-Dhrmasekera alliance disintegrated. Wijeweera emerged as the leader of the revolutionary movement. The JVP conducted secret study classes and military training in the jungles and promoted the collecting of guns and dynamite and the manufacture of hand bombs. It began to hold public rallies in which the UF government was attacked for its parliamentary socialism.

The ideology of the JVP was a strange mixture of Marxism-Leninism, "patriotic socialism," Maoism, fascism, and communalism. It had extrolled the petty bourgeoisie, youth, and students as the motive force, while denying a leading role for the working class in a revolutionary transformation of society—both in theory and in practice. JVP leaders openly denounced the methods employed in the Russian, Chinese, and Cuban revolutions. The organization administered an oath at the time of recruitment of its cadres, and demanded absolute secrecy from them. The movement indoctrinated and trained the cadres through "five lectures," delivered by trained tutors, covering topics such as Ceylon's economic crisis, Indian communalist expansion (calculated to appeal to the anti-Tamil emotions of the Sinhalese majority), the failure of the left in Ceylon, and the need for military seizure of power. A majority of the insurgents, except the Wijeweera faction of the JVP, had actively supported the UF parties in the general elections of May 1970. But they had become critical of the UF government's delays in introducing promised reforms, such as nationalization of the industry and combating the country's severe unemployment. (*Asian Survey,* March 1972.)

Domestic Attitudes and Activities. In mid-March 1972, Mrs. Bandaranaike enforced an island-wide security alert to thwart the possibility of the insurgents' embarking on a series of new attacks exactly a year after the abortive uprising. On 6 April the parliament adopted the controversial Criminal Justice Commission (CJC) Bill, providing for trials of revolutionary insurgents and foreign currency manipulators in which evidence such as confessions and hearsay—normally inadmissible—would be used and no right to appeal the verdicts would be allowed. This bill brought about an open rift between the pro-Soviet LKP and the SLFP, partners in the UF government.

The UF government officials seemed to take the view that a third of the 16,000 and more detainees were guilty of nothing more than attending one or two revolutionary lectures. It feared that after a year in detention camps, where they were supposedly being rehabilitated, the youths might emerge more revolutionary than ever. The government therefore was aiming at convicting and jailing 700 hard-core rebels, who might otherwise get off for lack of evidence, and paroling the thousands of others. (*NYT*, 9 April.)

In early June, the government finally began the first of what were to be thousands of trials of those who took part in the April 1971 uprising. Soon thereafter, 34 rebels escaped from the tight security prison at Anuradhapura; two other breakouts took place within four days. Although some of the persons being tried in absentia had either been killed in combat or were believed to be in hiding, at least half of the more than 16,000 insurgents once held in prisons or detention camps were still in custody. Charges against those facing trial included conspiracy to wage war against the state. (Ibid., 18 June, 23 July.)

By September, the number of suspects in detention had decreased to 6,000—many releases having been made just before the CJC began its trials. Nearly 3,000 more suspects were to be released by the end of that month, and most of these were then to be charged before the normal courts with offenses ranging from murder to illegal possession of arms and explosives during the insurrection. This would help the government in closing down two of the largest camps. The core leaders of JVP were to be tried by the CJC on charges of planning and execution of the insurrection and abetment to it. (*Ceylon Daily News*, 8, 11 September.) On 28 September there was a large-scale break-in and escape from the Anuradhapura prison camp, involving 35 insurgent escapees. A massive man-hunt by the police and units of armed forces ensued. Subsequently, some of the escapees were arrested. (Ibid., 30 September, 3, 7, 18 October.) In his trial, Wijeweera continued to raise several questions, including those regarding the legality of the CJC Act (ibid., 8 September, 2 October.)

*   *   *

The Pro-Soviet LKP. A resolution by the pro-Soviet LKP's Central Committee condemned the April 1971 rebellion by the JVP for its "ideology" as well as its strategy and tactics. The hand of "reaction" was seen in the insurrectionists' effort to "disrupt the United Front and its government and drive the Left out of the government." The resolution called for normalization of the situation, inquiry into police and military excesses, early determination about those in custody, a program of radical socio-economic measures in favor of and involving the masses, nationalization of estate supplies and managing agencies, restrictions of foreign firms and investment in Ceylon, and a vigorous land reform involving "land to the tiller." (See *New Age*, organ of the Communist Party in India, 14 November 1971.)

Leadership and Organization. The party is headed by its 8-member Politburo and 37-member Central Committee (25 full members, 12 candidates). The party entered 1972 with the Politburo composed of S. A. Wickremasinghe (president and founder of the party), Pieter Keuneman (general secretary since its inception, and its parliamentary leader), L. W. Panditha (deputy secretary, and head of the Ceylon Federation of Trade Unions). K. P. Silva, P. Kumaraswamy, H. G. S. Ratnaweera, Sarath Muttetuwegama, and V. A. Samarawickrema (national organizer). Considerable changes occurred in September (see below).

The party's major base of power is its association with trade unions and youth organizations. It controls the Ceylon Federation of Trade Unions (CFTU) and the Public Service Workers' Trade Union Federation (PSWTUF), each of which has more than 100,000 members. Smaller unions affiliated with or led by the party are the Ceylonese Women's Association and the All-Ceylon Federation of Communist and Progressive Youth Leagues. The party was claiming in November 1972 that the number of its "candidate members" had increased as much as 15 percent in the past two months due to the party's greater appeal to students (party-backed students had captured power at all the student councils at all four university campuses), trade unions, and rural masses through what it called its new, radical line and realistic and constructive approach to problems facing the masses. It also claimed that the party paper *Aththa* had more than doubled sales during the same two months. (*Ceylon Daily News,* 17 November.)

Domestic Attitudes and Activities. In early 1972, with the economy stagnated, virtually no foreign and domestic investments, a severe drought affecting the rice crop, high unemployment, and foreign debt standing at $1.5 billion, domestic discontent against the UF government was mounting. (*NYT,* 9 April.)

Protests against the state of emergency were surfacing in the youth groups of the pro-Soviet LKP, which openly charged the government with having broken all its pledges to the voters. The *Aththa* was critical of the government on issues such as the rising cost of living and various curbs on liberties. The PSWTUF initiated a campaign for return to a "democratic system of government" and reestablishment of the rights of the trade unions. The Ceylonese Compositors' Union, affiliated with the PSWTUF, asked the Soviet Union, China, and other socialist states to stop all economic and military aid to Ceylon until the government fulfilled the election promises, such as nationalization of major industries. (*Intercontinental Press,* New York, 24 January.)

In March, the Criminal Justice Commissions Bill created an open rift between the partners in the UF government. In the parliament, the members of pro-Soviet LKP joined with the more rightist Opposition (i.e., the UNP) to attack the new legislation. The president of the pro-Soviet LKP, S. A. Wickremasinghe, accused the government of forgetting its pledges and its supporters (probably a reference to some insurgents who worked in behalf of the UF in the 1970 elections), and *Aththa* described the bill as "fascist." On the other hand, the SLFP-oriented newspaper *Nation* questioned the pro-Soviet LKP's sincerity, citing its poor record of concern for human liberties under Stalinist regimes in the U.S.S.R. and elsewhere, and in Czechoslovakia in 1968.

When the bill was passed in early April, only one of the pro-Soviet LKP MPs (a junior minister of education, B. Y. Tudawe) voted for it. Wickremasinghe and Sarath Muttetuwegama abstained, and Aelian Nanayakkara and M. G. Mendis were absent for the vote. Pieter Keuneman who is Minister of Housing and Construction in the UF government, was in Singapore at the time. This voting performance by the pro-Soviet LKP members in the parliament came in the context of the party Central Committee's decision (taken after Mrs. Bandaranaike had told the Government Parliamentary Group that she expected all the members to support the bill) that the party MPs should abstain. (Tudawe, who voted for the bill, was suspended from the Central Committee by the party Politburo on 11 April a decision which the committee reversed on 20 April, "subject to inner party censure.") On 11 April the Politburo postponed a decision on the "concurrence" reportedly given by Keuneman to the bill. On 20 April the Central Committee proposed a "summit conference" of the three UF partners to settle their differences, but Mrs. Bandaranaike rejected this proposal in a letter to Keuneman reminding him that he had approved the bill when it was originally discussed in the cabinet. When Muttetuwegama, Nanayakkara, and Mendis explained to Mrs. Bandaranaike that their failure to vote had been dictated by the party decision, she replied that loyalty to the United Front must come before loyalty to the party—clearly relying on the fact that even without the support of the pro-Soviet LKP, her government would have a solid two-thirds majority. She was also receiving help from unexpected quarters. The leader of the Opposition, J. R. Jayawardene (of the United National Party; UNP), had advocated support for the UF government on internal issues. He was also rumored to be willing to join the UF government. For this, he barely escaped expulsion from the UNP, and received scathing criticism from Wickremasinghe, who characterized him as an "imperial ghost."

Schism within the Party. The pro-Soviet LKP's handling of the CJC Bill revealed the disagreements within the party. One group, led by Wickremasinghe, was seemingly looking for an opportunity to force Keuneman's hand and break with the UF coalition, while Keuneman and his followers preferred to continue working with the government. In the eight-man Politburo, Wickremasinghe had the stronger following, but Keuneman apparently was able to reassert control of the party machine on his return from Singapore. Moreover, he still controlled the substantial union vote. (*Asian Analysis,* July.)

After weeks of crisis within the party, in a showdown on 3 September, Wickremasinghe was elected general secretary by the Central Committee, replacing Keuneman. K. P. Silva was elected as chief organizer and D. Gunasekera as treasurer. In retaliation, Keuneman declined the presidency of the party. His group had become outnumbered in the Central Committee and the Politburo, apparently he had lost the support of certain stalwarts. It seems that Wickremasinghe then decided to leave the presidency vacant for some time. Reportedly, he was finding his new post too arduous and was desirous of getting back to the presidency. Meanwhile he eased his burden through an arrangement whereby K. P. Silva, a leading "hard-liner," acted as the party's deputy secretary, although there was no such formal post in the party. When Kueneman refused to accept any office on the ground that he had no authority to hold a responsible position in the party's top rank, the Wickemasinghe group responded by taking away from the Keuneman group the function of representing the party at the future meetings of the UF government's Central Coordinating Committee; however, Keuneman was not to be asked to resign his cabinet post. (*Ceylon Daily News,* 11 September.)

While the pro-Soviet LKP was facing this internal rivalry between the "hard-line" Wickremasinghe group and the "soft-line" Keuneman group, essentially in relation to the united front tactics of the party, it was working out a formula acceptable to the UF leadership, in order to get a repeal of an order which had expelled the four party parliamentarians and to facilitate their rejoining the Government Parliamentary Group. The formula laid down procedures for resolving differences on government policies or official positions on political questions between the parties in the UF government. The agreement stipulated that (1) each party will abide by cabinet decisions and decisions arrived at the Government Parliamentary Group; (2) every party will follow the whip in the matter of voting; (3) if any of the constituent parties in the coalition wanted time to consider a question which came up for discussion in the cabinet, it would ask its representatives in the cabinet to ask for a postponement of the question until that party had thrashed out the issue in its policy-making body; and (4) whenever differences arose in any matter which did not come within the purview of the cabinet, any party could refer an issue for discussion and decision to the UF Joint Committee leaders—whose decisions are binding on all parties. The UF leadership required each expelled pro-Soviet LKP MP to write a letter of explanation to the chief whip before accepting them back in the Government Parliamentary Group. (Ibid., 27 September.)

The Wickremasinghe group also initiated a purge of 20 "soft-line" (of the 43 full-time) workers in the party, and had the Central Committee appoint a committee of inquiry to investigate charges of misconduct made against a number of trade unionists in the party. The charges leveled by the "hard-liners" in a Central Committee meeting in October included the following of an "anti-party" line by *Satan Maga* (the weekly paper of CFTU, headed by Panditha), started and continued without party approval), and the participation by Panditha and Mendis in silver jubilee celebrations for Keuneman. The latter charge seems to have been dropped subsequently, since Wickremasinghe also attended the celebrations. Earlier, the "soft-liners" complied with the party's request to cease the publication of another newspaper, *Satana.*

Further action on the report of the committee of inquiry was held back by the "hard-liners" until Wickremasinghe returned from his second trip to Moscow during the year. On the protest of the "soft-liners" that the committee of inquiry was made up of three men openly critical of Panditha and Mendis, the membership of the committee was changed—but to another three from the anti-Keuneman group.

By mid-October there were prospects of a split within the party between the two groups. Tudawe, Mendis, Panditha, Samarawickrema, and others had lined up with the Keuneman group, which was talking of breaking away if a compromise could not be reached. Younger members of the "hard-line" group were seeking to reconcile the differences. The party was in financial straits, and the party newspaper *Aththa* was facing a shortage of paper.

The issues dividing the two groups had by now become fairly well crystalized. The "hard-liners" seemed anxious not to lose the party's identity or have the party outflanked by the more militant groups on its left. They wanted to maintain the party's pressure on the UF government in order to bring about rapid and radical reforms. On the other hand, the "soft-liners" wanted to associate the cooperate with the UF government—the first taste of power in the existence of the party. While the "soft-liners" were in favor of the proposed Press Council Bill, the "hard-liners" were opposed to it. In the recent by-elections although the results did not threaten the UF's position in the National Assembly, they indicated considerable voter dissatisfaction with the UF. The pro-Soviet LKP, under the "hard-line" leadership, had not officially entered the hustings, and had not asked any of its MPs to participate actively in the UF's campaign. For this, the SLFP leaders had criticized the party (as well as the LSSP) for its "lukewarm support at the grass-roots level." The UF government also withdrew its advertising from *Aththa,* which had adopted the "hard-line" stance.

Following the Eighth Congress of the pro-Soviet LKP in August (where the "soft-line" had prevailed in the adoption of the political resolution drafted by Keuneman, then general secretary), the party seems to have decided that an editor and editorial board acceptable to the party should be in charge of the *Satan Maga.* This symbolized a victory for the "hard-line" position. (Ibid., 23 October.)

In the context of the increasingly critical stance by the "hard-liners" with regard to UF policies, the party Central Committee decided on 6 December to expel Panditha and Samarawickrema from the party for what was described as gross violation of the "principles of democratic centralism and the norms of party discipline." This decision was taken in the absence of Keuneman and another member of the "soft-line" group. In response, Panditha and Samarawickrema argued that they were expelled without any charge sheet and without opportunity to defend themselves, and stated that they planned to submit an appeal to the Control Commission elected at the Eighth Congress. The two regretted "deeply" that Wickremasinghe had "allowed himself to become a prisoner of an ultra-leftist, adventurist group including some others who are out to destroy the United Front." (Ibid., 8 December.)

A formal split now seemed imminent. Although Keuneman had not participated in the meetings of the Panditha group, and his position with regard to these developments was not known, the "soft-line" group was talking about forming a separate "Sri Lanka Communist Party" in the very near future. Associates of Panditha were predicting a sharp division in the trade unions affiliated with the party. *Satan Maga* was to be continued, and made a daily as a rival of *Aththa*. The prospects for reconciliation between the two groups were very slim. Yet, paradoxically, both (even with a separate party in the making) were anxious to remain in the UF. (Ibid., 9 December.)

International Views and Positions. The warming up of Ceylonese-U.S. relations during the early part of 1972 (*NYT,* 10 April) and the continuation of cordial relations between Ceylon and China, together with the factional rivalry in the pro-Soviet LKP, seem to have posed a dilemma for the Soviet Union. But apparently the Keuneman line (externally pro-Soviet and internally pro-UF) was considered the acceptable in the political circumstance of Ceylon. The head of the Soviet delegation to the Eight Congress (20–24 August) advocated a line basically in keeping with the stance taken by the "soft-liners":

> "The victory of the united front parties with the participation of the communist party has demonstrated the political defeat of the external and internal reaction. . . . In the course of the general elections, the people have clearly spoken out for broad social and economic reforms proclaimed in the united front's program." (FBIS, 23 August.)

However, continued dissidence in the party must have caused concern. In November, Moscow withdrew its annual grant to the party, which found itself with a deficit of about $16,000. It is a fair assumption that the Soviet leadership was expressing disapproval of the "hard line" of the Wickremasinghe group. The Soviet Union seemed interested in having the party give full support to Mrs. Bandaranaike's government despite her declining popularity, and it wanted Keuneman in the UF cabinet to defend Soviet interests vis-à-vis China's deepening involvement in Ceylon on the one hand and Mrs. Bandaranaike's visible shift toward the United States on the other. (*Far Eastern Economic Review,* 4 November.)

In the first half of the year, Mrs. Bandaranaike allowed U.S. as well as Soviet warships to visit Ceylonese ports, and permitted the strengthening of the Soviet diplomatic mission in Ceylon, including a military attaché. But it seemed highly unlikely that Ceylon would grant naval facilities to either of the superpowers at the Trincomalee port, especially in the context of its persevering efforts for having the Indian Ocean declared a "zone of peace."

To possible strains associated with the April 1971 insurrection was perhaps added one more when police revealed in mid-year that subversive literature printed in Cuba and North Korea was arriving through the diplomatic bags of the Soviet Embassy in Colombo (*Christian Science Monitor,* August 17, 1972).

In mid-September, a North Korean delegation led by a deputy minister visited Ceylon and had informal talks with the deputy minister for external affairs without firm decisions being made on any issue. The North Korean deputy minister sought but was not granted an interview with Mrs. Bandaranaike, reflecting the estrangement between the two countries over the complicity of North Korea in the April 1971 uprising. On the other hand, the UF government gave permission for South Korea to open a trade mission in Ceylon, without opening a reciprocal mission in Seoul. (*Ceylon Daily News,* 15, 28 September.)

In its first offer of aid since 1965, the Soviet Union agreed in June to supply Ceylon construction equipment for housing and other building works. It was to provide technical assistance in installing the equipment and instructing personnel in its use, and a grant for sending Ceylonese to the Soviet Union for training. Apparently the Soviet Union was attempting assiduously to improve its relations with Mrs. Bandaranaike's government, as were the East European countries which had been criticized by the Ministry of Planning for occasional "switch trading"—getting goods from Ceylon under barter agreements and then selling them to third parties for hard currency (*Far Eastern Economic Review,* 27 May). In August, it was announced that Ceylon was to receive vast economic assistance from the Soviet Union, Poland, East Germany, Czechoslovakia, and Hungary. The greatest aid was to come from the Soviet Union, which would help in building a rubber factory, a flour mill, and the second stage of a national metallurgical plant, and in developing the mining industry; also Soviet experts would prospect for oil. (*FBIS,* 3 August.) This aid followed upon Mrs. Bandaranaike's decision to modify the UF government's policy and allow a greater role for foreign investments in view of the deteriorating economic situation in the country (*Far Eastern Economic Review,* 6 May, 24 June).

*   *   *

The Pro-Chinese LKP. This party is dominated by Nagalingam S. Sanmugathasan, a Ceylon-Tamil, who is the secretary-general of the party and of its major union base, the Ceylon Trade Union Federation (CTUF) which had an estimated 110,000 membership in 1971. The party itself has an estimated membership of 500 or less.

After the April 1971 uprising during which Sanmugathasan was arrested, (probably as a preventive measure by the UF government) the pro-Chinese LKP apparently experienced suppression by the government and neglect by Peking. China seems to have decided to woo Mrs. Bandaranaike's government rather than support this small party with a predominantly Tamil leadership. In 1972 the only significant event for the party seems to have been the visit by Sanmugathasan to Albania in early May (*FBIS,* 8 May).

Continuing their warming relationship, China and Ceylon signed a protocol in February under the current five-year trade agreement. China agreed to supply 200,000 tons of Burmese rice, and in turn Ceylon was to supply 39,000 tons of rubber. China also agreed to buy further quantities of rubber, coconut products, and other items from Ceylon, which was very appreciative of the agreement, owing to its economic crisis and the falling prices for such commodities in the international market. China is now Ceylon's second biggest trading partner, following the United Kingdom. Another agreement with China established a joint shipping service.

During her eleven-day visit to China in June, Mrs. Bandaranaike had talks with Chou En-lai and Mao Tse-tung. Among other things, she reportedly was seeking China's assistance in strengthening Ceylon's defense forces and civilian police. Under an agreement on economic and technical cooperation, signed 5 July, China would build a cotton mill in Ceylon and provide Rs. 47 million for a textile complex and Rs. 260 million in aid for flood control, prevention of soil erosion, and development of inland fisheries under the current five-year plan. (*Asian Recorder,* 1972.) China had already granted an interest-free loan in convertible foreign exchange of Rs. 150 million (about $25 million) in the early part of the year, provided two merchant ships, and undertaken to supply the Ceylon navy with five gunboats (*Asian Analysis,* July).

Indicative of Chinese neglect of the pro-Chinese LKP was the fact that Mrs. Bandaranaike's visit came subsequent to Sanmugathasan's public repudiation of the "parliamentary road to socialism." Even so, the party's loyalty to China remained undiluted.

*   *   *

The LSSP. The Lanka Sama Samaja Party (the oldest and largest Marxist political organization in the country) abandoned its Trotskyist character and joined the coalition government of the SLFP and the pro-Soviet LKP in 1964, and is a partner in the present coalition government.

The LSSP-oriented or -controlled trade unions are: the Ceylon Federation of Labor, Government Workers' Trade Union Federation, and the Public Services League. It is the most influential Marxist party in the trade unions.

Led by N. M. Perera (finance minister in the UF government), Leslie Goonewardena (minister of communications), and Colvin R. de Silva (minister of plantation industries and constitutional affairs), the LSSP has worked for far-reaching economic reforms in the country, including nationalization of the plantations and industries. In January 1972 Colvin de Silva announced and implemented the government's decision to nationalize Ceylon's seven best-managed, sterling tea estates, totaling 16,320 acres. These estates represented the bastion of foreign capital in the country. Their nationalization fulfilled a plank in the UF election manifesto of May 1970. The minister assured the parliament that there had been "cordial negotiations" with the owners, who were to be paid compensation equivalent to nearly British 300,000 pounds in Ceylonese rupees on the condition that the money was reinvested in Ceylon. In January the government also took over the island's richest graphite mine, owned by a Ceylonese firm. (*Far Eastern Economic Review,* 8 January.) During the year, other takeovers of tea companies followed.

The proclamation of the Republic of Sri Lanka on 22 May, breaking the old link with the British Crown, was in a significant measure the culmination of de Silva's proposals for constitutional reforms (see *YICA, 1972,* pp. 471–72). This move was acclaimed by the Soviet and Chinese leaders, more vigorously by the latter. (*FBIS,* 23 May; *Asian Analysis,* July.) The old House of Representatives is now called the National Assembly, and the cabinet the "Council of Ministers." The composition of the 20-member coalition cabinet was not affected, and the former governor-general became the first president of the republic. The present UF government can now stay in power for another five years, while the term of the governments in future would be six years. The promulgation of the republic, with Sinhala as the only official language, brought about violent disturbances in the Jaffna peninsula organized by the Manarvar Peravai (student body) movement, agitating for a federal constitution (*Far Eastern Economic Review,* 19 August). The movement is believed to be a spillover from the United Tamil Front (a banding together of the old rivals: the Federal Party and the Tamil Congress).

Colvin de Silva and N. M. Perera were soliciting increased foreign aid to overcome what de Silva described in London as "a steadily maturing financial crisis and an economic crisis [combined with] a balance-of-payments and budgetary crisis" (ibid., 27 May). In order to reduce the budget deficit, the LSSP's Perera, ironically, had to initiate cutbacks in the welfare system. A levy of 25 percent was imposed on outpatients in hospitals. Sugar was rationed, and public transport fares were raised. Perera also brought about a devaluation of the Ceylon rupee (long urged by the International Monetary Fund) by 4.5 percent, and allowed the Sri Lanka currency to float with the pound. Perera's budget for 1973 incorporated the Rs. 2,000 ceiling on monthly income as a part of the compulsory savings scheme. Starting in 1973, free rice was to be denied to about 300,000 persons whose incomes exceeded the limit of $80 per month. During 1972, a landownership ceiling of 50 acres per family released 400,000 acres for landless families. About 350,000 workers in the public sector were given wage increases through the establishment of a minimum wage of Rs. 180 per month. The quickened pace and drastic character of reforms initiated by the UF government were not unrelated to the growing radicalization of demands, particularly within the parties which were coalition partners of the SLFP, and were reflected in the intra-party strains within these parties.

Strains within the LSSP. The Central Committee of the LSSP adopted a political resolution on 25 July for presentation to the party congress in November. The "main task," according to this resolution, was to ensure that the program of the UF and the major changes promised in the joint election manifesto were fulfilled (*Ceylon Daily News,* 13 September).

By October, the discussion of this resolution in the party had brought to surface the growing strains between its relatively moderate and radical groups. In particular, a group of young radicals voiced criticism of the LSSP policy. The group, which had no backing from any of the prominent Politburo members, wanted the LSSP to remain in the UF, but to follow a more independent, critical, and radical line—pushing the UF government more leftward. The reasons for the radical line by this minority within the party were: the youth unrest, dissatisfaction in the trade unions over soaring prices, and the militant line adopted by the *Aththa* under "hard-line" pro-Soviet LKP leadership—resulting in an increase in the influence of that party among the students and the unions at the expense of the LSSP. A resolution signed by the above-mentioned leaders of the minority group and others called for the activization of the party and the masses in a joint struggle for the implementation of an eight-point program by the government. The minority resolution, to be moved at the impending party congress stated: "It is time for the party to act not as a docile agent of the Government before the masses, but as their vanguard, leading them as well as learning from them." (Ibid., 30 October). The eight-point program (canvassed earlier as an 11-point program) called for: participation by organized working class in determining government policies and management in public and private sectors; nominal compensation only for land to be taken over under the Land Reform Act; expropriation of foreign-owned estates and big companies and the nationalization of commercial banks without compensation; encouragement of cooperatives and collectives in the agricultural sector, and formation of peasant committees to carry out land reforms; formation of youth brigades for development work; a new wage structure, with a ceiling of Rs. 1,500 per month; ceiling on inheritable wealth; and restructuring of education in the context of an overall socialist plan to ensure meaningful employment opportunities (ibid., 16 October).

However, due to the pressure brought upon them, most of the signers of the minority resolution withdrew their support of it. The three LSSP Ministers argued that if the minority resolution was passed they would have no option but to resign their portfolios because they could not guarantee the implementation of the program.

The congress passed the milder majority resolution on 6 November by 301 votes to 97, with 33 abstentions. However, the minority resolution group won about 25 places in the elections to the 55-member Central Committee and fared extremely well in the voting. (Ibid., 7 November.) In the 10-member Politburo, the minority resolution group expected to win 3 to 4 seats, but succeeded only in placing D. G. William (the leading figure in the party's trade union organization. This radical group was to meet to decide whether it should formally establish itself as a "faction" within the party—accepting majority decisions but propagating its own views and circulating (officially) an internal bulletin to the members. It remains to be seen whether these fissures in the party will lead to its splintering.

In the elections to party offices, Bernard Soysa was reelected general secretary, but since he is the chairman of the Agency Houses Commission, R. Weerakoon was to act as general secretary. Mr. Wanigatunga is now the party's assistant secretary. Besides these three, Perera, de Silva, William, Leslie Goonewardena, Anil Moonesinghe, Hector Abhayawardhana, and V. Karalasingham make up the new Politburo. (Ibid., 14 November.)

*   *   *

Other Parties. The small Trotskyist parties—the LSSP-R, RSP, and the RCL—appear to have been much less active during 1972. Indeed, the latter two did not figure noticeably during the year before. P. Bala Tampoe, general secretary of the LSSP-R (which openly supported the April 1971 uprising), assumed the role of defense counsel for the JVP suspects and figured prominently in the trial of Rohana Wijeweera. The MEP contested one of the four seats in the by-election but failed to win.

*   *   *

Publications. The pro-Soviet LKP publishes a Sinhalese daily paper, *Aththa,* with a claimed circulation of about 55,000. It also publishes the Sinhalese weeklies *Tarunahanda* ("Voice of Youth"), *Nava Lokaya,* and *Mawbima.* The party's main Tamil publication is *Desabhimani,* also a weekly. It has an English weekly, *Forward.* Two publications, *Kommunist Lokaya* and *Nava Sakti,* appear during campaign periods.

The pro-Chinese LKP publishes a weekly in English, *Red Flag.* It also has two "worker" dailies—*Kamkaruwa* in Sinhalese, and its Tamil counterpart, *Tolilali,* with estimated circulations in 1971 of 3,000 and 2,000 respectively. The party also publishes a Tamil "cultural and general affairs" monthly, *Vasantham.*

The LSSP publishes the weeklies *Samasamajaya, Samadharmam,* and *Samasamajist,* in Sinhalese, Tamil, and English respectively. The MEP publishes the weekly *Mahajana Eksath Peramuna.* The RCL has a Sinhalese publication, *Virodhaya;* a Tamil publication, *Ethirppu;* and since 1969 an English publication, *Asian Marxist Bulletin,* the last being dedicated to the rebuilding of the Trotskyist movement in the Indian subcontinent.

California State University,   Mukund G. Untawale
San Francisco

China

The First Congress of the Chinese Communist Party (Chung-kuo kung-ch'an tang; CCP) was held in Shanghai in July 1921. Mao Tse-tung, the present party chairman, who turned 79 years of age in December 1972, was one of the twelve delegates known to have attended. The party celebrates its anniversary each 1 July.

The People's Republic of China (PRC) was established 1 October 1949. State organs are in all important respects dominated by the CCP, the sole legal party. The party constitution adopted in 1969 stresses the dominance of party over government in these words: "The organs of state power of the dictatorship of the proletariat . . . must all accept the leadership of the party."

The CCP is the largest communist party in the world. No membership figures, however, are available for later than 1 July 1961, when the party daily *Jen-min jih-pao* reported that there were more than 17 million CCP members, a figure that was repeated by the theoretical journal *Hung ch'i* on 16 July 1962. There have been recent estimates of as many as 30 million members (e.g., *Far Eastern Economic Review,* 10 September 1972, special supplement, p. 9), but such figures are only speculative. The population of mainland China is commonly put at 750 to 800 million.

Organization and Leadership. According to the party constitution, the "highest leading body" of the CCP is the national party congress, which is to be convened every five years, although under "special circumstances" the congress may be convened early or postponed. The party congress elects the Central Committee, which in turn elects the Politburo, the Standing Committee of the Politburo, and the chairman and vice-chairman of the Central Committee. The Central Committee elected at the party's most recent national congress, the Ninth Congress (April 1969), consisted of 170 full members and 109 alternates.

Effective policy-making power within the party rests with the Central Committee and at higher levels, particularly the Politburo and its Standing Committee. Of the original 25 full and alternate members of the Politburo elected in 1969 (see *YICA, 1972,* p. 478), only 17 were mentioned in the Chinese press in 1972. One of these, Hsieh Fu-chih, died on 26 March. The most active full members were Mao Tse-tung, Chou En-lai, Chiang Ch'ing, Yeh Chien-ying, Chang Ch'un-ch'iao, Yao Wen-Yüan, and Li Hsien-nien. Chu Teh and Tung Pi-wu, both 86 years of age, played minimal roles. Kang Sheng, who along with Mao and Chou is on the Standing Committee, made a couple of appearances, at funerals in January and September. Liu Po-cheng, 80 years old, also appeared at the September occasion. Both Hsü Shih-yu and Chen Hsi-lien, military commanders of the Nanking and Shenyang regions respectively, reappeared in 1972 despite lengthy absences from public view in the last half of 1971. The three alternate members, Li Te-sheng, Chi Teng-k'uei, and Wang Tung-hsing, were active in 1972.

The death of Lin Piao, the erstwhile heir-designate to Chairman Mao, on 12 September 1971 was confirmed finally on 28 July 1972. Remaining missing from public view are Yeh Ch'ün (Lin Piao's wife), Huang Yung-sheng, and three of Huang's deputies, Wu Fa-hsien, Li Tso-peng, and Chiu Hui-tso. All of these may have been connected with the conspiracy that aborted in September 1971. Also missing is Ch'en Po-ta, who seems to have been purged in 1970, and the fourth alternate member, Li Hsüeh-feng.

Below the Central Committee there is a network of party committees at the provincial, special district, county, and muncipal levels. A similar network of party committees exists within the People's Liberation Army (PLA), from the level of the military region down to that of the regiment. According to the party constitution, primary organizations of the party, or party branches, are located in factories, mines, and other enterprises, people's communes, offices, schools, shops, neighborhoods, PLA companies, and elsewhere as required.

Except within the PLA, the national structure of party organization was shattered in the course of the Great Proletarian Cultural Revolution (GPCR). Reconstruction began in late 1969 and by mid-August 1971 the last of the provincial-level party committees was reestablished. Reconstruction at the lower and intermediate levels appears to have continued throughout 1972. The "revolutionary committees" which were created at all levels during the GPCR in order to provide leadership in the temporary absence of regular party and government organizations remain a part of the emerging institutional structure. However, the revolutionary committees are now subordinate to party committees where these have been reestablished, and to "core groups" within the revolutionary committee where there is still no party committee.

State organization, which was severely disrupted during the GPCR, and which was urged by Chairman Mao to achieve greater administrative efficiency with the call for "better troops and less administration," also continued to reinstitutionalize during 1972. By late October, a total of 17 governmental ministries, 3 state commissions, and 15 special agencies were functioning under the direction of Premier Chou En-lai. Only 13 of these 20 bodies are headed by ministers, nine of whom have military backgrounds. Before the GPCR there were 40 ministries, 11 commissions, and 21 special agencies. Many of the old ministries have been merged, while others have been completely dissolved. By the end of 1972, ministers had not yet been appointed to such key ministries as National Defense, Finance, Commerce, and Public Health.

The retailoring of government administrative machinery is designed not only to promote efficiency of operation in Peking, but is also part of the leadership's continuing effort to find a proper balance between centralization and decentralization of administrative authority throughout the country. Hence some of the reduction in administrative cadre in Peking may be compensated by the shifting of some personnel to the provinces or to local levels. No figures are available to record the rate at which this downward transfer is being done or to help determine if it is being successful or not. Whatever is happening to the personnel involved, it does seem clear that some areas of activity, such as education, for example, have undergone a great deal of decentralization. In the past, education has been a highly centralized operation in China. Before the GPCR, the Ministry of Education made educational policy and determined the curriculum and textbooks to be used throughout the country. In 1972 there still was no new Ministry of Education. There was a Science and Education Group under the State Council which is said to formulate educational policy and guidelines which are recommended to the country. But textbooks and much of the curriculum are left to the provinces to determine. Even at the local level some latitude is allowed for using local experience and materials to make teaching more effective. The hiring, firing, transfer, and promotion of teachers is in the hands of local or community authority rather than a local office of the erstwhile Ministry of

Education. By September, however, there were signs of the reinstatement of some features of education that had been discontinued during the educational revolution which accompanied the GPCR. For instance, examinations were being reintroduced with the obvious intention of promoting academic standards and achievement.

A prominent feature of the Chinese bureaucracy which received much attention in 1972 as a result of the accounts of many visiting foreigners and publicity by the Chinese themselves was the new institution of the "May 7th Cadre Schools." These schools originated with the implementation of Chairman Mao's directive of 7 May 1966 which enjoined the army, the party, and government organizations not only to study their own affairs but also "to raise levels of education and to engage in agriculture and side-occupations, to run small or medium-sized factories, to engage in mass work, and to participate in the struggles to criticize and repudiate the bourgeoisie." Others, in the professions generally, were similarly urged to undertake the same kind of broadening experience. At the outset, the schools absorbed the thousands of cadres who were left without positions during the initial restructuring of government ministries and bureaus. Many of the initial "student" cadres were also among those criticized during the GPCR, so that in the early phase the schools carried the connotation of punishment. By 1972 the schools had appeared throughout the country, and most cadres and professional people apparently were being cycled into them. In Peking, for example, each of the districts and counties of the municipality has its own May 7th Cadre School. The Chung Wen District—the area including Tien An Men Square and the hotels where foreigners stay—has its own May 7th school, situated several kilometers out of the city in a dry and dusty environment. Its students, all drawn from the ranks of cadres, teachers, and other professional workers in the Chung Wen District, built the school from scratch out of the very difficult soil. The "students" spend six months at the school, where they engage in agricultural labor, some industrial work in the small, student-constructed dye-making plant, and the study of politics. They may visit their families in town every ten days for a couple of days. At any one time, a sixth of the total professional population of the district is at the school, so that a cycle has been established in which everyone will have experience at the school, and repeatedly, on a regularly rotating basis. The purpose of this exercise is to maintain and improve political responsiveness, cultivate an appreciation for the value of physical labor and what life is like for those who do such work permanently, raise the level of health of those who otherwise work at desks constantly, and deter "Bureaucratic" or "officious" behavior. Thus the newly designed government structure also is meant to be staffed by rededicated and reinvigorated staff members.

Domestic Party Affairs. Following the fall of Lin Piao the previous September, the principal task confronting the party in 1972 was the need to achieve unity throughout party ranks. Associated with this task was the continuing effort to reestablish party leadership, particularly vis-à-vis the PLA. Rehabilitation of old cadres who had been criticized in the GPCR continued, and the recruitment of new party members increased.

The dramatic and shocking downfall of Lin Piao deeply affected the morale of the entire party, especially since Lin had been the constitutionally confirmed heir-designate to Chairman Mao and had long been regarded as Mao's "closest comrade-in-arms." Hence the successful completion of the formation of provincial party committees in August 1971 was almost immediately compromised by the need to rehabilitate the party's spirit and confidence. The immediate need was to eliminate Lin's influence and the remnants of his support, and this state of affairs continued into 1972.

The joint 1972 New Year's Day editorial of the three major party publications—*Jen-min jih-pao, Hung ch'i,* and the PLA daily *Chieh-fang chün-pao*—was entitled "Unite to Win Still Greater Victories." Emphasizing this policy, it reminded the party of Mao's dictum that "the line is the key link; once it is grasped, everything falls into place." To ensure that the line would be grasped, the editorial announced that "the whole army and the people throughout the country should continue to carry out deep-going education in ideology and the political line, strengthen party leadership and deepen struggle-criticism-transformation on all fronts." The way in which to conduct such educational work in ideology and the political line, and the unfolding of a movement to criticize revisionism and rectify style of work (*p'i-hsiu cheng-feng*), was an important consideration: "Practice Marxism, and not revisionism; unite, and don't split; be open and aboveboard, and don't intrigue and conspire." This was to be the approach for dealing with, among other matters, "Liu Shao-chi and other swindlers" who, because they were "extremely isolated," could "only resort to intrigue and conspiracy, rumor mongering and mud slinging."

However isolated the troublesome remnants might have been, the tasks of unifying the party and of asserting its dominance could not have been easy. The Politburo, as noted above, was truncated and may not have been particularly viable. Moreover, in consequence of the GPCR, the PLA had established itself pervasively throughout the governing structure. The military presence does not seem to have abated by 1972. According to a 1972 estimate (*Studies on Chinese Communism,* Vol. 6, No. 4, 10 April), it increased sharply, from 34.5 percent in revolutionary committees to 60 percent, in the party committees at the provincial level. Among the 29 party first secretaries in the provinces, 22 are professional military men. As earlier noted, 9 of the 13 government ministers have a military background—including the new Minister of Public Security, Li Chen. It is also of interest that while such signal dates as 1 May and the anniversary of the party on 1 July went relatively uncelebrated, there was a rather large celebration in Peking on 1 August, the anniversary of the founding of the army.

Despite the pervasive presence of the military there was a concerted campaign throughout the year to assert party control. The Chinese press gave the party more attention than it did the army. Calls for unified and collective leadership were aimed ostensibly at making the military members of revolutionary and party committees responsive to the views of civilian party members. A new slogan enjoining the PLA to learn from the people was implemented. Some PLA members of revolutionary committees acknowledged to visitors that they were performing their assignments to such committees in civilian institutions or organizations partly for the purpose of learning from society. However, the idea of the PLA as a school for Mao's thought continued to complement this new tack. The *p'i-hsiu cheng-feng* campaign, directed mainly against Lin Piao remnants, also served the purpose of reminding the military of its proper role. The considerable emphasis during the year on the need to study Marxism-Leninism and the thought of Mao Tse-tung, while it may also indirectly have helped put Mao's thought back into perspective, also served to remind the military of its subordinate role to the party.

It should be recognized that it is probably simplistic to overemphasize China's domestic political dynamics in terms of a party-PLA tryst: the PLA has been thoroughly politicized over the years to acknowledge party authroity; a great many party leaders have been prominent military leaders as well at one time or another; it is not easy to draw the line between civil and military interests as the various Chinese participants view these; and Chairman Mao, the ultimate civilian authority, is the chief military commander too, and he is certainly committed to party-military unity under party control. Also the party and the military have cleavages within their own ranks, and it is likely that one faction or another from the military may have more in common with a counterpart faction in the party than with other elements within the military. One observer has described such sympathetic factions in China as "elite interest groups" whose affiliational and corporate interests may be stronger than a more abstract ideological loyalty. His analysis suggests that "civil-military *unity* at the regional level has been more important in explaining China's internal political scene than civil-military *conflict* at the national level." (William Whitson, "The Distribution of Power among Military and Civil Interest Groups in China, 1956–72," paper read at the annual meeting of the American Historical Association, New Orleans, 29 December 1972.) These are useful qualifications, yet there do appear to be problems in party-PLA relationships. For example, it is not clear whether reminders to PLA leaders to defer to civilian party leadership have much meaning when a military man holds both military and civilian posts. Illustrating this point, a Szechuan radio broadcast in June (*China News Analysis,* Hong Kong, No. 893) reportedly said that it was wrong for such men with dual posts to bypass civilian authorities in making military decisions.

However, the military in all probability remains divided in the wake of the Lin Piao affair, at least vis-à-vis the party, and the party's efforts may accordingly be considerably facilitated. In any case, only certain leading military leaders seem to have been implicated with or deeply influenced by Lin Piao and to have been considered a threat to the party leadership, and these men have been removed or neutralized. Finally, the national fear of the Soviet Union during 1972 may have been a more basic cement for unity than any campaign for this purpose, for it would caution against the kind of divisiveness that might increase national vulnerability. Some observers believe that this fear was being manipulated by the party leadership for the purposes of securing unity and dealing with the Lin remnants.

By mid-year 1972 the party leadership felt secure enough to announce publicly what had happened to Lin Piao. This it did initially in a statement issued by the Chinese Embassy in Algiers on 28 July (*Current Scene,* December 1972). The statement indicated that Lin had repeatedly made errors in the past and that Chairman Mao had to struggle against him. "Sometimes," it asserted, "Lin was obliged to quell his arrogance and thus was able to accomplish some useful work." But Lin was "a two-faced man" who "undertook antiparty activities in a planned, premeditated program with the aim of taking over power, usurping the leadership of the party, the Government and the army." His plot was unmasked, and although Mao "made efforts to recover him," Lin "did not change his perverse nature one iota." Instead, "Lin attempted a coup d'état and tried to assassinate Mao Tse-tung." His plot was foiled, and he died on 12 September 1971 while trying to flee toward the Soviet Union in a plane which crashed in the People's Republic of Mongolia.

Details of the events that led to Lin Piao's demise emerged in the form of secret party documents which surfaced outside of China. One of these, a document identified as Central Circular No. 12 was published in the Hong Kong *Sing Tao Daily* on 10 and 11 August. It is said to be a summary of Mao Tse-tung's talks with provincial party leaders just prior to the alleged takeover attempt by Lin Piao in 1971. The document was reportedly distributed to Chinese cadres in March 1972. It reports that a major confrontation took place between Mao and Lin at the second plenum of the Ninth Party Congress in August-September 1970 in the city of Lushan in Kiangsi. Lin reportedly made an unscheduled speech at the time in an effort to "overthrow three items on the agenda." The move allegedly was supported by Ch'en Po-ta, Huang Yung-sheng, Wu Fa-hsien, Li Tso-p'eng, Ch'iu Hui-tso, and Yeh Ch'ün. Mao put down Lin's move, and this dispute, described as a "struggle between the two headquarters," temporarily subsided. No final decisions were reached at Lushan, reportedly so that Lin would be protected. However, Mao may have made up his mind at this point to remove his rivals. In December 1970 Mao reportedly tried to reduce Lin's strength by making changes in the staff of the Peking Military Region.

Another document was captured, translated, and released by the Chinese Nationalist Government Information Service and was reported on in the West (*NYT*, 23 July) just five days before the Algiers announcement by Peking. This document, which is taken to be basically authentic but may have been amended by the Chinese Nationalists, was also circulated among Chinese cadres on the mainland. It too refers to the disagreement between Chairman Mao and Lin Piao and others at the 1970 Lushan conference, which it indicates led to heavier plotting in the winter of 1971. Instead of responding positively to criticism, by February 1971 Lin, his wife, and his son, Lin Li-kuo, "continued to plan for a counter-revolutionary coup in Soochow." Lin Li-kuo then went to Shanghai and Hangchow to seek out comrades and to discuss and draft a plan for the uprising. The plan was drafted by Lin Li-kuo and Yu Hsin-yeh, Air Force deputy director of party affairs. They termed the intended coup the "Five-Seven-One Project."

The plotters allegedly affirmed the use of "revolution by violence to stop any counter-revolutionary evolution which takes the form of peaceful transition." They were aware that Mao was suspicious of their activities, so they decided, "instead of waiting passively for our fate," to "take the great gamble." They hoped to capture Mao (who was given the code name "B–52") and compel him to accept their terms. The plotters recognized the difficulties inherent in the enterprise, but allegedly hoped for Soviet support. They also considered the use of "extraordinary measures, such as poison gas, germ weapons, bombing, car accidents, assassination, kidnapping, small urban guerrilla teams" and what was referred to as "Five-Four-Three," a code name for secret weapons.

Allegedly, a major complaint of the plotters was Chairman Mao's shift toward a policy of "peaceful transition," referring to the easing of tensions within China after the conclusion of the GPCR, and perhaps to the decision to expand diplomatic relations. It seems clear, however, from the dates of the developments described in the document that the plotting began before U.S. President Nixon was invited to visit China during Henry Kissinger's visit to Peking in July 1971.

Lin Piao's disgrace is already being reflected in accounts of party history. Issue number 8 of *Hung ch'i* in 1972 carried an article on the famous 1948 Liaohsi-Shenyang campaign during the civil war. The article represents a major revision of China's revolutionary history in that it eliminates Lin Piao's role, except as an obstructionist who attempted to alter Mao's battle plans. The article says that the victory of the campaign "was a victory for Chairman Mao's thinking and a victory of his proletarian line on military affairs over the rightist opportunist line." Earlier historical accounts gave Mao credit as overall commander but highly praised Lin Piao's generalship in executing the campaign. Only the previous October, *China Pictorial,* ironically appearing two weeks after Lin's death, carried pictures of the 1948 battle scenes with a caption indicating that "Comrade Lin Piao assumed direct command of the PLA forces in the Liaohsi-Shenyang and Peking-Tientsin campaigns."

The party in 1972 continued its program of rehabilitation of old cadres who had been criticized and removed from active roles during the GPCR. Several prominent figures reappeared during Army Day festivities. Most notable were Wu Leng-hsi, previously editor in chief of *Jen-min jih-pao* and head of the New China News Agency, and Ch'en Tsai-tao, formerly commander of the Wuhan Military Region. Ch'en was responsible for the famous "Wuhan incident" of July 1967 during which he detained Hsieh Fu-chih and Wang Li. Yang Yung and Liao Han-sheng, respectively the former commander and first political commissar of the Peking Military Region, also reappeared. Both had participated in Ho Lung's alleged "February mutiny" in 1967; thus there was speculation that Ho Lung himself might soon reappear. Other military leaders of note to be seen again were Su Chen-hua, Tu Yi-teh, and

Liu Tao-sheng, respectively the former first political commissar, deputy political commissar, and deputy commander of the navy, and Kan Wei-han, formerly the political commissar of the Chengtu Military Region. Also reappearing on Army Day for the first time since October 1969 was Ch'en Yun, the important economic planner who had been closely associated with Chou En-lai in the past.

Such prominent examples illustrate the general picture, for in many units throughout the country censured cadres were reappearing. Certainly this seems to confirm an adherence to the principle of "curing the sickness in order to save the patient," and it may attest to the efficacy of May 7th Cadre Schools and other reeducation programs. On the other hand, it may also be said to represent a swing to the right, back to the more moderate positions and attitudes that were temporarily set aside during the GPCR, a tendency that was facilitated by Lin Piao's defeat.

Complementing the return to activity of the old cadres during 1972 was the recruitment of large numbers of new party members. The construction and public transportation system of Peking alone was reported to have absorbed more than 10,000 new party members since 1969. Of particular note in recruitment and training programs for new cadres in 1972 was the apparent emphasis given to the recruitment of women and members of the minority nationalities. The New China News Agency reported that 25 percent of new party recruits in Peking were women. It was reported that there were more than 68,000 women cardres in upper-level local party organizations in Tientsin and 900 women in party committees above the hsien level in Kwangtung. A group of U.S. visitors to Wuhan in the spring was told that an ideal proportion of women for political and professional positions was considered to be one third, a proportion still far from realization.

The party does seem to have made progress during 1972 in unifying its ranks, continuing to rehabilitate old cadres, taking in fresh blood, and minimizing adverse effects of the Lin Piao affair. But problems remained at the year's end. Party-military relationships were still not clear. The Politburo remained attenuated. Many posts were yet to be filled. There was as yet no state chairman; aged Tung Pi-wu has been acting chairman. The party constitution of 1969 is obsolete. Many of these and other unattended matters are supposed to be resolved by national and party congresses. That neither the long overdue Fourth National People's Congress, nor a Tenth Party Congress, nor even a third plenum of the Ninth Party Congress was held in 1972 seems to indicate that difficulties remain to be settled before such large bodies can be brought together in order to signal that power is again consolidated.

International Views and Positions. In the field of diplomacy 1972 was a banner year for the People's Republic of China. Peking continued the rapid diplomatic expansion— "Chairman Mao's revolutionary line in diplomacy"—that began in May 1969 (during the GPCR ambassadors were withdrawn from all posts with the exception of Cairo). Through 1970 the emphasis was on restoring the disrupted diplomatic ties, and new relationships were established with only five countries. In 1971 diplomatic relations were established with 12 countries, and ambassadors returned to seven others with which diplomatic relations had been broken. In 1972 Peking resumed diplomatic relations with two countries: Ghana (29 February) and Dahomey (29 December). It established new diplomatic relationships with 17 countries: Mexico (14 February), Argentina (19 February), Malta (31 January), Mauritius (15 April), Greece (5 June), Guyana (27 June), Togo (19 September), Japan (29 September), Federal Republic of Germany (11 October), Maldives (14 October), Malagasy (6 November), Luxembourg (16 November), Jamaica (21 November), Zaire (24 November), Chad (28 November), Australia (21 December), and New Zealand (22 December). The level of diplomatic representation was raised from chargé d'affaires to ambassadors with Great Britain (13 March) and the Netherlands (18 May).

China also played host to an increasing number of visitors. The most important visitor was President Nixon, whose dramatic visit (21–28 February) promised a new era in Sino-American relations. Another important guest was Premier Tanaka Kakuei of Japan (25–30 September), whose visit resulted in the normalization of Sino-Japanese relations. Other prominent government leaders (with dates of arrival in Peking) were Pakistan's president (1 January), Malta's prime minister (2 March), Somali's president (14 May), the prime minister of Sri Lanka (Ceylon) (25 June), France's foreign minister (6 July), Yemen's premier (16 July), Iran's empress (18 September), Zambia's vice-president (17 September), West Germany's foreign minister (10 October), Nepal's prime minister (18 November), and Guinea's prime minister (9 December). It was reported that up to September some 500 delegations of various kinds had visited China from more than 90 countries, while a large number of Chinese delegations visited some 50 countries in return. In the same period more than 500 Americans visited China, as did more than 3,700 Japanese. The number of foreigners visiting China during this eight-month period exceeded the number during the entire year of 1971.

China's foreign trade also continued to develop. Trade relationships were established with more than 130 countries and regions. During the first nine months of 1972 China sent 24 trade delegations and delegates to visit 21 countries and regions, and in return received 84 economic and trade delegations from 30 countries and regions.

Relations with the Soviet Union. There were contradictory elements in Sino-Soviet relations during 1972, but basically the relationship was tense. In the field of trade, for example, a third Sino-Soviet agreement was signed in June which is expected to enable trade to reach $288 million in 1972, as compared with the record low in 1970 of $45 million and the 1971 figure of $154. Talks have proceeded on the border problem intermittently since October 1969, and on border river nagivation, although with little success in either case; the latter talks were adjourned in March without an agreement having been reached.

Relations have remained tense primarily because Peking has largely abandoned its erstwhile "dual adversary" strategy of simultaneously confronting U.S. "imperialism" and Soviet "revisionism and social imperialism." There were occasions during 1972, particularly in the United Nations, when China denounced the two "superpowers," but in the main it was the Soviet Union that was singled out for castigation. This focusing on the Soviet Union as the principal contradiction to be isolated and opposed was especially evident following the Nixon visit to Peking. But China's policy toward the Soviet Union was not inflexibly hostile. One observer (Harold Hinton, in *Current Scene,* November) suggests that especially since the fall of Lin Piao, Peking's Soviet policy has begun to point away significantly from what might be termed "primitive" Maoism toward the direction of "creative" Maoism. The most spectacular indicator of this creative change was Peking's diplomatic overture to the United States. Chou En-lai, the main architect of China's current Soviet policy, "appears to be trying not only to avoid provoking Moscow beyond endurance but to move through the current transitional stage of a 'tilt' toward the United States, in the direction of a better long-term relationship with the Soviet Union as well." A major obstacle in the way of this effort is the intense hostility toward China which pervades the Soviet Union. Despite this, Chou appears to be trying "to move in the desired direction by gradually reducing the ideological content (apart from propaganda polemics designed mainly for domestic consumption and the international left) and the element of direct confrontation in China's relationship with the Soviet Union, as well as with the United States."

The Chinese would appear to have good reason to use all means to diffuse Soviet hostility.

On 9 September U.S. officials in Washington reported (*NYT*, 10 September) that the Soviet Union had added three mechanized divisions to the massive force already deployed along the Chinese border, making a total of 49 divisions known to be in the area, representing nearly a third of the entire Soviet Army (compared with only 15 divisions in 1968). The latest troop movements were regarded as permanent assignments rather than as a temporary shift coincident to the war games which were scheduled for the border region in the fall. The same news story went on to quote the comment of a senior American military official who has had extensive experience in Moscow: "In conversations with Russian officials, especially senior officers, it quickly becomes clear they are nearly paranoiac about the Chinese. We might be talking about the missile race, NATO, even Vietnam, and they don't get very excited. But as soon as the conversation turns to China, almost invariably they become very agitated and emotional. It's amazing to witness this reaction." Aware of this attitude on the part of Soviet officials, the Chinese can be seen to be concerned about the situation. This apprehension can only have been increased as a result of successes in Soviet leader Leonid Brezhnev's policy of détente in Central Europe, such as ratification by the West German Bundestag of the treaties with the Soviet Union and Poland on 17 May. A major purpose of this détente is to provide the Soviet Union with a freer hand in dealing with its China problem.

For its part, China has responded to the increasing Soviet threat by making a major shift in its defense posture. A mid-year assessment by William Beecher (*NYT*, 24 July) was based on four indicators. (1) China had tested a number of relatively small nuclear weapons ranging from 10 kilotons to 30 kilotons each that can be delivered by a tactical Chinese-designed fighter-bomber known in the West as the F–9. (2) China is mass-producing the F–9 at a rate of about 15 a month. Two hundred of the 300 produced in the past two years have already been assigned to operational squadrons. (3) China is apparently abandoning the old defensive concept of deploying poorly equipped militia and paramilitary units along the border in order to draw Soviet divisions deep into Chinese territory before they would engage regular troops, with the guerrilla units remaining behind to attack from the rear. (4) Instead, China has been moving several first-line army divisions and air force squadrons to forward positions. This suggests an intent to challenge more seriously any Soviet advance before it could penetrate deeply into China. Some analysts believe that the Chinese are preparing to employ nuclear weapons if they are forced to do so. In such an event there would be a need to keep major Soviet troop concentrations in sparsely settled border areas, in order to reduce nuclear fallout and other damage to larger Chinese population centers in the interior.

Beecher reported (ibid., 9 September) Pentagon officials as saying that China has been working on at least four types of liquid-fueled missiles, some of which have been deployed in limited numbers. They have ranges respectively of 600 to 1,000 miles, 1,500 to 2,500 miles, 3,500 miles, and 4,000 to 6,000 miles. Modest numbers of the two shorter-range missiles have been deployed at missile test launch pads. Some are kept in man-made caves from which they can be rolled out and fired; some are in steel-and-concrete silos. In addition to these sites associated with test facilities, the first "field" deployment of medium-range missiles has been spotted recently in Manchuria, pointed in the general direction of Vladivostok. These sites are within range also of key rail hubs on the Trans-Siberian Railroad and key airfields behind the Soviet border, both of which would be necessary to support a sustained Soviet ground attack into China. China also has conducted tests of missiles in about the 2,200 miles range, impacting in Sinkiang Province. Some believe that these missiles if fired at full range could reach major Soviet cities, including Moscow. It is not known if any such long-range missiles have been deployed.

The Chinese have also made extensive defensive preparations in many of the urban centers of the country. A number of Western visitors to China in 1971 and 1972 were shown extensive underground networks, which had been excavated out of fear of a Soviet attack.

Given the psychological situation in each of the two countries with regard to each other and the tense situation along the border, it is apparent that armed clashes are likely to break out from time to time. According to Chinese estimates, there were in fact about 1,000 border incidents a year between 1964 and 1969. But there have been no reports of such incidents since 1969. An exception therefore was a report that was initially circulated in confidence among selected Soviet journalists on 27 November 1972, a few days after such a firefight took place. The report did not appear in the Western press (*Honolulu Star-Bulletin*) until 11 December. According to the secret Soviet report, a number of armed intruders entered Soviet Kazakhstan from China's Sinkiang Province, attacked a group of Soviet shepherds and tried to withdraw into China. The invaders reportedly killed five Red Army soldiers and an unknown number of shepherds before fleeing across the border with a large number of sheep. One Chinese was captured, but there was no disclosure regarding the number of Chinese who may have been killed. Moscow protested the intrusion to Peking, but Peking, according to this report, rejected the protest, saying that the marauders were bandits and were of no concern to the Chinese government. There was speculation that the Soviet government believed that the Chinese were more than ordinary sheep rustlers. It was noted that on 29 November, only two days after the report was circulated, Leonid Brezhnev took time out in a speech at an Hungarian industrial complex to accuse China of being "openly hostile" toward the Soviet Union (ibid.). Later, a Chinese Foreign Ministry spokesman denied reports that five Soviet soldiers had been killed, saying that such an incident might have occurred but that accounts of it given in reports from Moscow were, "as far as we know, fabricated" (*Honolulu Advertiser,* 11 December). Impartial observers tended to be dubious about certain elements in the Moscow reports. Some found it difficult to believe that a Chinese army unit would deliberately enter Soviet territory at a time when the Chinese are convinced that they are threatened by the Soviet Union and are massively building air raid shelters. Also, it seemed somewhat implausible that there would be "uncontrolled bandits" on Chinese territory, and even more so that the Chinese government would admit their existence. Presumably, this kind of pressure from the Soviet Union and the limited Chinese capacity to meet the challenge, despite shifts of military strategy and the digging of bomb-shelters, accounts largely for China's diplomatic offensive to win new friends, and in particular for the abandonment of the dual adversary strategy.

Relations with Eastern Europe. China continues to be successful in encouraging anti-Soviet proclivities in Eastern Europe, particularly in the Balkan communist countries. Chinese rhetoric on peaceful co-existence, national autonomy, and national equality as well as outspoken criticism of undue Soviet influence and interference strikes a responsive chord in these countries and stands in rather heartening contrast to the Brezhnev doctrine of "limited sovereignty" which they have denounced. Yugoslavia's "revisionism" seems a faint memory in Peking, and trade between the two countries veritably zoomed; only $7 million in 1971, it was expected to exceed $100 million in 1972. A Sino-Yugoslav civil air transport agreement was signed on 14 April. On 6 August, a 130-member song and dance ensemble from Belgrade arrived in Peking for a tour.

The new Romanian envoy arrived in Peking on 12 January. On 2 March, a Sino-Romanian agreement on radio and television cooperation was signed in Bucharest. On 14 March, a protocol of the 14th session of the Sino-Romanian Joint Commission on Scientific and Technical Cooperation was signed in Peking. On 6 April, a Sino-Romanian agreement on civil air transport was signed in Bucharest. On 8 July, a Chinese labor delegation left Peking for a visit in Romania. On 29 April, a Romanian military delegation arrived in Peking for a visit.

The delegation was led by the vice-president of the Romanian State Council, on his second visit to China in less than two years. China's vice-minister of foreign affairs visited Romania on 20–21 November and spoke with party secretary-general Nicolae Ceauşescu.

There had been speculation that because of the Nixon visit to China, Albania's friendship had cooled. Whatever truth there may have been in this interpretation of Albania's reaction, from all accounts in the Chinese press in 1972 the differences were easily resolved. (Incidentally, both Yugoslavia and Romania praised the Nixon visit to Peking.) As for Albania, there continued to be a great deal of traffic between Tirana and Peking, including most notably a visiting military delegation in November. Its leader, the Albanian minister of people's defense, affirmed that "neither in the past nor in the future can any force on earth do the slightest harm to the great friendship between the Albanian and Chinese peoples." Two weeks later Chairman Mao sent congratulations on the 60th anniversary of the independence of Albania and the 28th anniversary of its liberation, also referring to the "indestructible" friendship between the two countries, their parties, and their people.

The "northern tier" or more "contained" bloc nations also appeared to be improving relations, particularly in trade. Czechoslovakia, Hungary, and Poland doubled their trade with China in 1972. China participated in the trade and industrial fairs of Poland and Czechoslovakia as well as of Yugoslavia during the year. Hungary held a machinery and motor vehicle exhibition in Tientsin in August. On 16 May a Sino-Hungarian scientific and technical cooperation protocol was signed in Peking, the first of these agreements, which before the GPCR had been routine, to be renewed outside the Balkans. These are examples of the inroads that China has managed to make into the rest of Eastern Europe from the Balkan base. While the increased activity has not had much political effect, it demonstrates the Chinese effort to extend contacts into the Soviet Union's own satellites.

Relations with the United States. The outstanding development of the year, and of a generation for Sino-American relations, was the visit to China of President Nixon. The dramatic visit culminated a process that had begun with an invitation that was extended by Chairman Mao in 1970, the advent of "ping pong diplomacy" in 1971, the two preparatory visits of Henry Kissinger in July and October 1971, and the advance party visit of General Alexander Haig, presidential deputy assistant for national security affairs, 3–10 January 1972. The latter visit looked into security arrangements, medical, and communications facilities.

President and Mrs. Nixon, accompanied by a large staff and a retinue of news correspondents, visited China on 21–28 February. The visit received widespread news coverage both abroad and in China; some 60 million Americans are reported to have watched live satellite-relayed television coverage of the event. The President met with Chairman Mao on 21 February, the first day of the visit, confirming the fact that Chairman Mao himself was behind or in agreement with the policy which the presidential visit highlighted. The two leaders were reported to have had "a serious and frank exchange of views on Sino-U.S. relations and world affairs." The President had a number of separate discussions with Premier Chou En-lai, termed "extensive, earnest, and frank," on the normalization of relations between the United States and the People's Republic of China, "as well as on other matters of interest to both sides." (*Peking Review,* 3 March).

President Nixon and his retinue visited Peking, where they viewed cultural, industrial, and agricultural sites, and also toured Hangchow and Shanghai, where continuing discussions were held with Chinese leaders.

A joint communiqué was issued on 27 February in Shanghai (ibid.) which stated that the leaders of both countries had "found it beneficial to have this opportunity, after so many years without contact, to present candidly to one another their views on a variety of issues." The two sides "reviewed the international situation in which important changes and great upheavals are taking place and expounded their respective positions and attitudes." Each side acknowledged that there "are essential differences between China and the United States in their social systems and foreign policies." However, both sides "agreed that countries, regardless of their social systems, should conduct their relations on the principles of respect for the sovereignty and territorial integrity of all states, non-aggression against other states, non-interference in the internal affairs of other states, equality and mutual benefit, and peaceful coexistence." Disputes are to be settled on this basis "without resorting to the use or threat of force." With these principles in mind, the communiqué stated that progress toward normalization of relations between the two countries is in the interests of all countries, that both countries wish to reduce the danger of international military conflict, that neither should seek hegemony in the Asia-Pacific region and that each is opposed to efforts by any one else doing so, and that neither is prepared to negotiate on behalf of any third party or to enter into agreements or understandings with the other directed at other states. Both sides agreed that collusion between countries against others or division of the world into spheres of interest by the major countries would be against the interests of all.

Long-standing serious disputes between the two countries were reviewed. China reaffirmed its position: "The Taiwan question is the crucial question obstructing the normalization of relations between China and the United States; the Government of the People's Republic of China is the sole legal government of China; Taiwan is a province of China which has long been returned to the motherland; the liberation of Taiwan is China's internal affair in which no other country has the right to interfere; and all U.S. forces and military installations must be withdrawn from Taiwan. The Chinese Government firmly opposes any activities which aim at the creation of 'one China, one Taiwan,' 'one China, two governments,' 'two Chinas,' and 'independent Taiwan' or advocate that 'the status of Taiwan remains to be determined.' "

For its part, the United States acknowledged "that all Chinese on either side of the Taiwan Strait maintain there is but one China and that Taiwan is a part of China." "The United States Government," it went on to say, "does not challenge that position. It reaffirms its interest in a peaceful settlement of the Taiwan question by the Chinese themselves. With this prospect in mind, it affirms the ultimate objective of the withdrawal of all U.S. forces and military installations from Taiwan. In the meantime, it will progressively reduce its forces and military installations on Taiwan as the tension in the area diminishes."

Both sides undertook to facilitate the further development of mutually beneficial people-to-people contacts and exchanges in such fields as science, technology, culture, sports, and journalism. They also agreed to facilitate the progressive development of Sino-American trade.

Both sides agreed to stay in contact through various channels, "including the sending of a senior U.S. representative to Peking from time to time for concrete consultations to further the normalization of relations between the two countries and continue to exchange views on issues of common interest." The ambassadors of both countries stationed in Paris were designated as the diplomatic channel to be used. Meetings were held subsequently between the two ambassadors to discuss trade and cultural exchange matters.

Among the many U.S. visitors during 1972 were Senators Mike Mansfield and Hugh Scott, who spent three weeks in China beginning 18 April in response to an invitation from Chou En-lai. While this visit was not an official mission, it was, considering the role that these men play in the U.S. Senate, something more than people-to-people. House Representatives Hale Boggs and Gerald Ford visited China for two weeks beginning 26 June. Following their return to the United States, they stated that the Chinese desired a continuing U.S. military presence in the world as a counter-balance to the Soviet Union. The Chinese subsequently categorically denied having made such a statement. Henry Kissinger made his fourth visit during 19–23 June. He reported to the press that on this occasion he discussed the Vietnam war, trade, and cultural exchanges with Chou En-lai.

Chinese visitors to the United States during the year were far fewer in number than Americans going to China. A table tennis delegation visited a number of places in the United States during 12–30 April. A medical delegation, comprising 10 physicians and 5 others, toured six U.S. cities beginning 12 October. A delegation of scientists visited from 20 November to 16 December. The Shenyang Acrobatic Troupe, 55 persons in all, began a tour of four cities on 16 December.

A number of business deals were concluded during 1972. China purchased the satellite ground station built by RCA Global Communications in Shanghai for use during the President's visit for $2.2 million. In September, the Chinese contracted to buy ten Boeing 707 jets, including spare parts, and to provide for the training for pilots and maintenance men, at a cost of $125 million. China would pay 30 percent down and the rest on deliveries during 1973 and 1974. Also purchased were 40 additional spare engines from United Aircraft Corporation for $20 million, for deliveries beginning in mid-1973. Following the aircraft agreements, China made four large agricultural purchases, including some 2,000 tons of linseed oil, more than a half million tons of wheat, 300,000 tons of "noodle wheat," and 300,000 tons of corn. About 40 American businessmen attended the Canton trade fair in March, the first ever to do so. About 100 were present at the fair in November.

There were some discordant notes in this warming relationship. On 6, 7 and 8 May, U.S. warships and aircraft reportedly attacked two Chinese merchant vessels off the coast of North Vietnam. On 10 May, U.S. aircraft damaged the office of the Chinese economic mission in Hanoi. On 22 August, U.S. aircraft destroyed a lifeboat from a Chinese merchant vessel, killing the five crew members. On 20 December, another Chinese merchant vessel was damaged during an air attack on Haiphong. However, Peking's reaction to these untoward events was subdued. It was apparent through 1972 that China was not anxious to disturb seriously the new relationship with the United States. While the continuing war in Indochina may have slowed developments somewhat, not even the unprecedented heavy bombing of the Hanoi area by B–52s in late December noticeably cooled China's posture toward the United States, aside from routine rhetorical protests.

Relations with Japan. In early 1972 China continued to express concern over apparent renewed Japanese militarism. In April, Peking claimed that increases in the Japanese defense budget were to be allocated for developing missiles and nuclear weapons. On 2 June the *Peking Review* criticized Japan's "exploitation," "plundering of raw materials," and "economic infiltration" in Southeast Asia. China displayed anxiety over the disposition of the oil-rich Tiaoyu Islands (Senkaku Islands), particularly at the time of the reversion of Okinawa to Japanese control in May, and a number of statements asserted China's sovereignty over the area. China also expressed alarm over attempts at rapprochement between Japan and the Soviet Union. Peking condemned the visit of Andrei Gromyko to Tokyo in January as an attempt by the Soviet Union to collude with Japan against China by offering as bait to the Japanese the return of the Kurile Islands and a large-scale joint development project for exploiting the Soviet Tyumen oil field (*Peking Review*, 11 February, p. 20). Nevertheless, Peking rejected any suggestion of coming to an understanding with the Sato government, which seemed particularly disposed to such an achievement following the Nixon visit to China.

In the meantime, Peking continued to develop support for normalization of relations by cultivating key Japanese political and business groups. In March, the Democratic Socialist Party of Japan changed its policy of supporting Taiwanese self-determination to affirming that Taiwan was part of the People's Republic of China. Trade with China continued to grow rapidly. By July, eight of the ten largest Japanese trading companies were given the status of "friendly firms." The remaining two, Mitsui and Mitsubishi, finally accepted Chou En-lai's four principles of trade, requisite to "friendly" status, within the next couple of months. Tanaka Kakuei won the premiership largely on the basis of a pledge to normalize relations with China. In mid-July, Chou En-lai extended an invitation for the new premier to visit China. Prior to Tanaka's visit, Japan's new foreign minister declared that his country would accept the three Chinese principles of normalization. These included recognition of the People's Republic of China as the only government of China, and of Taiwan as an integral part of China. He indicated that the 1952 peace treaty with Taiwan would be automatically abrogated once relations were normalized. (*Japan Times Weekly,* 5 August.)

Premier Tanaka's visit to China on 25–30 September was second in importance only to the visit of the U.S. President. The joint statement of 29 September affirmed the traditional friendship of Japan and China and declared that the termination of a state of war between them would open a new page in Sino-Japanese relations. Japan acknowledged responsibility for "causing enormous damages" to the Chinese people in the past," for which it "deeply reproaches itself." Japan recognized the People's Republic of China as the only government of China, and Taiwan was acknowledged as an integral part of China. Diplomatic relations were established. For its part, China renounced its demand for war indemnities. Both countries renounced the seeking of hegemony in the Asia-Pacific region and opposed such ambitions by any other country. The two countries would hold negotiations to aim at the conclusion of a treaty of peace and friendship. They would also hold negotiations to reach agreements on trade, navigation, aviation, fishing, and other matters. (*Peking Review,* 6 October.) The Tiaoyu question was not addressed.

A few days after this normalization of relations, Tanaka announced that the increased five-year defense plan would be implemented. It was disclosed in mid-December (*Honolulu Star-Bulletin,* 14 December) that during Tanaka's visit Chou En-lai had indicated that he welcomed " a reasonable growth" of Japanese strength as a counterweight to the Soviet Union's "aggressive designs" in Asia. Chou allegedly even speculated on the possibility of Chinese military aid to Japan if the latter were to be attacked by the Soviet Union (ibid.). This allegation was later denied by Peking.

Japan and China reached agreement on yen-yuan exchange, and the Japanese extended long-term credit to China in December. China articulated support for Japan's claim to the Soviet-occupied "northern territories," the four islands of Habomai, Shikotan, Kunashiri, and Etorofu.

Relations with North Korea. On 9 July *Jen-min jih-pao* hailed the surprise joint statement issued by North and South Korea on 4 July as "a good beginning for the cause of the independent peaceful reunification of Korea." The editorial quoted Kim Il-song: "The Korean question must be left to the Korean people so they may solve it by themselves on the principle of national self-determination without any interference of outside forces."

Peking termed South Korea's proclamation of martial law on 17 October "an evident sign that the south Korean rulers fear the south Korean people . . . an act designed to dampen their desire and aspiration for the peaceful reunification of the country, and to further intensify the suppression of the people demanding democratic rights and freedom" (*Peking Review,* 27 October).

The Chinese foreign minister, visiting North Korea on 22–25 December, had a "long and cordial talk" with Kim Il-song, and discussed with the North Korean foreign minister "the question of further strengthening and developing the friendly relations and co-operation between the two countries and on international questions of common concern" (*Peking Review,* 13 October).

Relations with South Asia. Much of China's policy toward South Asia in 1972 appeared to be related to a continuing fear of Soviet efforts toward extending its hegemony into the area. China's representative told the U.N. General Assembly on 3 October that "because of the meddling of the Soviet Union, the turmoil on the South Asian continent has failed to subside" (ibid.).

Pakistan remained important in China's relations with the area. As earlier noted, the president of Pakistan in January visited Peking, where he met with Chairman Mao. Reportedly, Pakistan was dissuaded from an early recognition of Bangladesh and was refused its request for an alliance treaty with China that would correspond to the Soviet-Indian alliance of August 1971.

Indian initiatives toward a rapprochement were rejected by Peking. China claims that India invaded and occupied East Pakistan, and that no settlement can come about until the Pakistani prisoners of war have been released. India claims that it withdrew its troops in March, but Peking has not accepted this claim. In August, China accused India of carrying out "interference, subversion, and expansion in Tibet." At the United Nations in November China accused India of being responsible for the Tibetan refugee problem.

Sri Lanka's prime minister, as noted, visited China in July. (During the visit Chairman Mao revealed the circumstances of Lin Piao's disappearance.) Sri Lanka received a large interest-free loan. Aid also took the form of three additional multi-purpose, medium-class patrol boats in January, and after the signing of a trade protocol in February and a joint Sino-Ceylon shipping agreement in April, two merchant liners—one of these sailed for China, loaded with rubber, on 24 November.

The prime minister of Nepal visited China in November. China had pointedly publicized a reported attack by about 100 Indians on a Nepalese village on 24 August (*Peking Review,* 15 September). During this visit the Chinese announced that they "greatly admire and appreciate Nepal's spirit of defying brute force and daring to struggle."

Relations with Southeast Asia. As a result of China's détente with the United States and as part of its new diplomacy which emphasizes state-to-state relations and plays down armed insurrection, Indochina has become less important in China's overall program. Relations have continued to be outwardly cordial between China and North Vietnam; China received many Vietnamese visitors during the year; continued to give aid, including the negotiation with Hanoi of a new agreement in late November which will provide yet more aid; and issued many statements of support for the people of Indochina and of condemnation of U.S. actions. Nevertheless, China did not respond substantially to the U.S. naval blockade and mining of North Vietnamese harbors in the spring, nor to the heavy bombing at the end of the year. Nor did she cooperate in any special way in facilitating Soviet shipments to North Vietnam. Clearly, China seemed anxious to see a negotiated settlement of the war as early as possible, as well as a limitation of the extension of Soviet influence into the area. Within the Indochina area, China may be concerned about containing the extent of North Vietnamese influence. There were reports in the autumn of Chinese troops in Laos which might have been moved in for the purpose of limiting the westward thrust of Vietnamese forces.

For its part, North Vietnam has asserted its independence by pursuing its own policies. The large-scale offensive in April hardly had Peking's approval, and the same can be said for Hanoi's establishment of diplomatic relations with India.

China continued to support Prince Sihanouk of Cambodia in Peking and gave him a good deal of publicity during the year, including much press coverage of his travels in China and to North Korea. China's policy of support to Sihanouk contrasted sharply with the Soviet Union's continuing to maintain an embassy in Phnom Penh.

Throughout the rest of Southeast Asia the results of the Sino-American détente, the Chinese emphasis on formal international relationships rather than encouragement to wars of national liberation, and China's concern to limit Soviet influence in the area became evident. Each country of the area seemed to be interested in promoting relationships with China. Trade with Malaysia, Singapore, Thailand, and the Philippines improved. However, fear persisted that diplomatic relations with Peking might encourage and lead to support of local communists; hence formal recognition was still not accorded Peking by countries in the area in 1972.

United Nations. In 1972 China played a full and active role in the United Nations, beginning with a hard line on the issue of Taiwan. On 7 January, China succeeded in having Taiwanese reporters expelled from the U.N. premises. China also asked that U.N. development funds for Taiwan be stopped. By August, it was indicated that all mention of Taiwan in U.N. official reports would cease.

On 3 March, China supported a laissez-faire policy before the U.N. Committee on the Peaceful Uses of the Sea-Bed and the Ocean Floor beyond the Limits of National Jurisdiction, holding that each nation should determine its own area of jurisdiction depending upon its economic and environmental needs. This contrasted with the position in 1958, when China maintained a 12-nautical-mile claim, as do most Western states. The new policy sanctions Latin American claims extending 200 nautical miles and accords with Chinese claims to the Tiaoyu Islands. China failed to condemn nuclear testing on the high seas, while agreeing with most nations that they should be subject to international study and jurisdiction. In April, China's participation in the third conference of the U.N. Committee on Trade and Development was limited to giving moral support to the developing nations, criticizing the "superpowers," and reiterating a policy of self-sufficiency for developing nations. An attempt to gain representation in the "Group of 77," an alliance of the poorest nations, was rejected on the grounds that China was already affluent. In June, at the U.N.'s first Conference on the Human Environment, in Stockholm, China opposed a resolution banning atmospheric nuclear testing, but held that total prohibition and destruction of nuclear weapons is required.

At the General Assembly's 27th session China expressed firm support of the Arab cause in the Middle East, and on terrorist activities took the position of not condoning them, while opposing their punishment. China avoided making an issue of Uganda's expulsion of Asians.

The Chinese positions on Bangladesh and on the Soviet Union's proposal for a world disarmament conference were unpopular. Soviet and Indian complicity in Bangladesh was charged, and on 26 August China exercised its first veto in the Security Council against Bangladesh's membership application. The Soviet disarmament proposal was termed a fraud.

Publications. The official and most authoritative publication of the CCP is the newspaper *Jen-min jih-pao* ("People's Daily"), published in Peking. The theoretical journal of the Central Committee, *Hung ch'i* ("Red Flag"), is published approximately once a month. The daily paper of the PLA is *Chieh-fang chün pao* ("Liberation Army News"). The weekly *Peking Review* is published in English and several other languages. It carries translations of important articles, editorials, and documents from the three aforementioned publications. The official news agency of the party and government is the New China News Agency (Hsinhua).

University of Hawaii   Stephen Uhalley, Jr.

India

Indian communists give December 1925 as the founding date of the Communist Party of India (CPI). Although the Western sources usually put the founding in December 1928, there were regional Marxist groups in various parts of India earlier than this.

After the death of CPI secretary-general Ajoy Ghosh in 1962 and the Sino-Indian border conflict of the same year, the struggle between the right and left factions within the party became intensified. This culminated in a formal split in 1964, when two separate congresses were held, each claiming to be the Seventh All-India Party Congress. Since that time, two parties have existed independently. One is commonly referred to as the "right" or pro-Soviet party, and the other as the "left" or "independent" party. They call themselves, respectively, the Communist Party of India (CPI) and the Communist Party of India (Marxist), or CPI(M). In 1969 a new, Maoist communist party, the Communist Party of India (Marxist-Leninist), or CPI(M-L), was created, largely by defectors from the CPI(M). This group derives its inspiration from the peasant revolt it instigated in 1967 in Naxalbari, West Bengal; its members, along with other numerous but smaller Maoist organizations, continue to be referred to popularly as Naxalites.

On a nationwide basis the two large parties, the CPI and the more militant CPI(M), have until this year competed against each other on more or less equal bases of strength. Active membership is probably between 80,000 and 100,000 in each, although the parties themselves claim a much higher figure. The population of India is about 547 million (1971 census, provisional figures).

While the strength of the CPI(M) is concentrated heavily in Kerala and West Bengal, that of the CPI is more widely distributed—in Bihar, Andhra Pradesh, Kerala, West Bengal, Uttar Pradesh, and Tamilnadu.

In parliamentary strength, the March 1971 elections gave the CPI and CPI(M) almost equal shares (about 4 percent for each) of the seats in the Lok Sabha. The CPI had 23 MPs in the Lok Sabha, compared with CPI(M)'s 25. In the fifth general elections for the state and union territory legislative assembly seats, held in March 1972, the CPI won a total of 112 seats while the CPI(M) won only 34. Compared with the CPI's 110 seats and CPI(M)'s 160 at the end of 1971, this marked a drastic decline in the electoral support and strength of the CPI(M).

The CPI(M-L), the most militant of the three communist parties, opposes parliamentary methods and does not participate in any elections. Its membership (estimated at 10,000 in 1972) has declined sharply during the last two years due to the government's armed campaign against it, the increased popularity of Prime Minister Indira Gandhi's government, and the emergence of Bangladesh (which as East Pakistan was believed to provide a sanctuary and a channel for arms for the Naxalites).

In addition to these three, there are a number of smaller communist parties—generally to the left of the CPI. These include the various Naxalite factions which are scattered throughout the country and several parties (such as the Revolutionary Communist Party of India, West Bengal) with limited significance and purely local influence.

The CPI and the CPI(M) operate legally, although members of both parties have been arrested or detained from time to time. The intense government campaign against members and followers of the CPI(M-L), which went underground shortly after its establishment in April 1969, continued with increased vigor in 1972.

Other national parties in India are: the Indian National Congress or the Congress(R), the moderate socialist party led by Indira Gandhi; Congress(O), the breakaway conservative ("Syndicate") faction of the Indian National Congress; Swatantra, a conservative party; Bharatiya Jan Sangh (often referred to as the Jan Sangh), a militant Hindu-Nationalist and conservative party; the Socialist Party (formed by the merger of the Praja Socialist Party and the Samyukta Socialist Party in August 1971), which seeks to develop the image of a moderate socialist party; and the Dravida Munnetra Kazhagam, or DMK, an ardently sub-nationalist party of Tamilnadu, which has now split into two factions, the breakaway faction calling itself the Anna-DMK (for the former leader of the party, Annadurai, who died recently). The conservatives within the Congress(R), the Congress (O), Swatantra, and the Jan Sangh have consistently been the targets of severe criticism from the communist parties in India.

*   *   *

The CPI. Estimates of active membership in the Communist Party of India vary so much as to be of limited significance. The party claims have ranged in the recent past from 172,902 members (February 1968) to 243,238 (during 1970). The active membership of the party is probably between 80,000 and 100,000. During the first half of 1972, the CPI organ (*New Age,* 23 January, 7 May) claimed that several thousand members of the CPI(M) had resigned their membership in that party and joined the CPI. In February, the party's general secretary, C. Rajeswara Rao, claimed a membership of 280,000 in the CPI (ibid., 20 February).

Leadership and Organization. The central leadership of the CPI, elected at its Ninth Congress, includes the party chairman, Sripad Amrit Dange; the general secretary, C. Rajeswara Rao; the Central Secretariat (chairman, general secretary, and 7 Secretaries), the Central Executive Committee (25 members), the Control Commission (9 members), and the National Council (101 full members and 10 candidate members). There are also party secretariats and state councils in each state in India.

Chief among the CPI's major fronts is the All-India Trade Union Congress (AITUC), in which the CPI and the CPI(M) exercised joint leadership until the two parties' differences led to a formal split of the AITUC in 1970. The CPI retained control of the original AITUC, leaving the CPI(M) to form a new organization. CPI Chairman S. A. Dange is the secretary-general of the AITUC; the president is S. S. Mirajkar.

Another important front, the All-India Kisan Sabha (Peasants' Association; AIKS) split in 1969 into two separate organizations—one controlled by the CPI and the other (the larger one) controlled by the CPI(M), both continuing the AIKS name. The AIKS of the CPI is led by Z. A. Ahmed, the organization's secretary-general, who is also a member of the CPI's Central Executive Committee. Other major mass organizations dominated by the CPI include the All-India Youth Federation (AIYF); the All-India Student Federation (AISF); the National Federation of Women; and for agricultural laborers, the All-India Khet Mazdoor Union.

The AITUC (CPI-controlled), the Indian National Trade Union Congress (INTUC; controlled by the ruling Congress Party), and the Hind Mazdoor Sabha (Indian Workers' Organization; controlled by the Socialist Party) signed an agreement in New Delhi on 21 May to establish a National Council of Trade Unions to promote mutual understanding and cooperation.

Domestic Attitudes and Activities. The party's long-range goal is the establishment of a "national democracy" (following Soviet guidelines) composed of a coalition of "left and democratic forces" led by the communist party and based on a worker-peasant alliance. This coalition would be composed of the "patriotic" elements of the national bourgeoisie, the intelligentsia, the peasants (including the "rich peasants"), and the workers, with the working class gradually rising to a position of leadership under the guidance of the communist party, ultimately forming a "genuinely socialist" society. The CPI claims that it had made a major contribution to the formulation of the concept of "national democracy" in the 1960 Moscow document, in the preparation of which Ajoy Ghosh participated. (See Bhabani Sen Gupta, "China and Indian Communism," *China Quarterly,* no. 50, April-June 1972, pp. 280–81.)

The coalitions envisaged by the CPI have been only partly successful, and only at the state level. At the national level, the CPI has not yet been able to form a single alliance with another party, despite constant appeals for a coalition of "progressive" parties in the Lok Sabha. The CPI seeks to utilize parliamentary methods as well as extra-parliamentary devices such as "mass struggles," including "bandhs" (moratoriums), "hartals" (strikes), and demonstrations, in achieving its goal.

To help bring about a shift toward the left in India and to simultaneously create a "left and democratic unity," the CPI Ninth Congress (1971) put forth a 27-point "broad program" providing the basis for a mass movement. Among the salient demands of this program were those for nationalization of "monopoly concerns," expansion of the public sector of the economy, radical land reforms, repeal of "repressive laws," greater autonomy to the states, abolition of privy purses and privileges for the former rulers of princely states, a moratorium on foreign debts, and stronger links with communist countries (not including China).

State Assembly Elections. The CPI thinking, with regard to the general elections to the state legislative assemblies in March, was reflected in an article by Rajeswara Rao, captioned "Basic Issues" (*New Age,* 23 January). He argued that the "hiatus between words and deeds of ruling Congress must go." Despite the adoption of some progressive amendments to the constitution, he saw the "concessions to the monopolists and the imperialists . . . continuing in the name of increasing production and self-reliance," while the government was "enacting anti-working class legislations, restricting the right of the workers and the employees to strike in defense of their living standard." He blamed the Congress for its "pro-hoarder" and "anti-people" policies, and for "pursuing the futile path of capitalist development" to solve the burning problems of poverty, unemployment, and rising prices, as well as to develop a self-reliant economy. Rao urged the Congress to discard the path of "capitalist development" and to take the "national democratic path of non-capitalist development, ending monopolies, landlordism, and imperialist loot." The CPI, he wrote, had "consistently pointed out that there are powerful left and democratic forces in the Congress"; and that the party had "consistently sought to unite with these forces on issues of the livelihood of the masses, as well as in the battle over progressive policies."

The party manifesto stated that the CPI would strive to secure economic self-reliance and prosperity through "radical structural reforms," including constitutional and land reforms. It would "spare no efforts to unite the Left and democratic forces including those in the Congress." The promises of the party to the electorate included: seeking a moratorium on foreign debts, cancellation of collaboration agreements between the private sector and foreign monopolies, a freeze on PL 480 counterpart funds, and promotion of comprehensive economic relations with the Soviet Union and other socialist countries. It called for the nationalization of the wholesale trade and reorientation of the bank credit policy. The party would seek a national need-based wage, drastic lowering of the ceilings on holdings, ownership rights for tenants on the Kerala pattern, taxation of the rural rich, and guarantees of remunerative and stable prices for agricultural commodities. It would seek to eradicate unemployment through policies including the securing of statutory insurance for the jobless, banning of lock-outs and closures, and taking-over of all closed industrial units. It would promote autonomy for tribals within the states or as states, and would distribute land and provide facilities for their better health and education. It would guarantee free education up to 14 years, bring about drastic educational reforms, and end all acceptance of funds by universities and educational institutions from the United States, West Germany, and the United Kingdom and from "imperialist foundations." It would seek to consolidate and develop relations with the Soviet Union, socialist states, Bangladesh, and other neighboring states, and seek to secure diplomatic recognition of East Germany, North Korea, and the Provisional Revolutionary Government of the Republic of South Vietnam (the Vietcong). (*New Age,* 30 January 1972, supplement; for summaries of manifestoes of all the major parties see *Asian Recorder,* 1972.)

The CPI criticized the manifesto of the ruling Congress party for lack of positions "against the foreign and Indian monopolies who hold the nation to ransom" and with regard to the "need to stop the outflow of huge amounts of foreign exchange in the shape of debt repayments and remittances of profits, etc." The party deemed the Congress manifesto "incomplete" on the "two key questions of the path to self-reliance and the realization of radical land reforms," and "deliberately silent" on major critical issues as well as "wobbly and evasive on other important points." It also castigated the manner in which the Congress lists of nominees were being drawn up and the "accommodation of all types of reactionaries within that organization." (*New Age,* 30 January, supplement.)

Although the CPI manifesto had made no mention of the electoral alliances (involving mutual agreement on distribution of seats) and "adjustments" (understandings), the party worked out alliances with the ruling Congress party in West Bengal and electoral adjustments in six states (including Bihar, Punjab, Rajasthan, and Madhya Pradesh) and in the union territory of Delhi.

In January, India had reorganized the Northeastern region and created three new states and two new union territories, to make a current total of 21 states and 8 union territories. The newly created states were Meghalaya (carved out of the Garo, Khasi, and Jaintia Hill districts of Assam), Tripura, and Manipur (the latter two being raised from union territories); the union territories were Arunachal (the former Northeast Frontier Agency) and Mizoram (comprising the area of the Mizo Hills).

In these general elections, the representatives to the Lok Sabha were not involved, having been elected in March 1971. The elections were held in 16 out of the 21 states and in the union territories of Goa and Delhi. In all, there were 2,727 seats in 16 states and in the two union territories (the states of Kerala, Nagaland, Orissa, Tamilnadu, and Uttar Pradesh and the union territory of Pondicherry were not involved). The CPI fielded 324 candidates and won 112 seats. The Congress(R), the ruling party at the center, won 1,926 seats; Congress(O), 88; the CPI(M), 34; the Socialist Party, 57; Swatantra, 16; Jan Sangh, 105; and other parties, 163. In Haryana, Himachal Pradesh, Jammu and Kashmir, Meghalaya, and Goa, the CPI had failed to elect a single candidate. Its largest gains, 35 seats in each, were in West Bengal and

Bihar. (See Rajni Kothari, "Democracy in Perspective: Significance of Recent Elections in India," *Indian and Foreign Review,* 1 April, pp. 13–28, et seq.; also *Asian Recorder, 1972.*)

In these assembly elections the Congress(R), which had run on the slogan "garibi hatao," meaning eliminate poverty, won a sweeping victory in all states and territories excepting Meghalaya, Manipur, and Goa, and including the states like West Bengal, Bihar, Punjab, and Tripura where it had been out of power since 1967. It won a two-thirds majority in 12 states and in Delhi, and almost two-thirds in two other states. It lost only in the newly formed small states of Meghalaya (where the All-Party Hill Leaders' Conference, A-PHLC, with which it had a poll alliance, won) and Manipur (where it has emerged as the largest party but failed to get a clear majority), and in the union territory of Goa, including Daman and Dieu (where the Maharashtravadi Gomantak party had won).

These results were politically disastrous for Congress(O), Swatantra, Jan Sangh, and the CPI(M), particularly because these parties had suffered severe defeats in areas considered their strongholds. The landslide victory of the Congress(R) increased the prospects of political stability in the Indian states, and greater center-state cooperation in seeking to resolve the grave problems in the country—exacerbated by around 2.5 percent annual population growth, massive unemployment, sluggish advances in the public and private sectors, rising external debt-repayment burden, and severe droughts threatening to negate the fruits of India's "green revolution." (See *Far Eastern Economic Review,* 22 April, 16 September.)

In the context of increasing political demands, Indira Gandhi publicly admitted in early December that the implementation of the Plan programs was "slanted," and that their benefits did not substantially reach the poorest sections of the people in India (*Times of India,* Bombay, 3 December).

In late 1972, India experienced large-scale agitation and disturbances over the "mulki" issue in Andhra and Assam. The Indian army had to intervene in Andhra to bring the situation under control.

West Bengal Assembly Elections. In West Bengal, which had experienced acute political instability and violence in the past five years, the Congress(R)-CPI alliance contested in all the 280 constituencies against the CPI(M)-led West Bengal Left Front—which included the Revolutionary Socialist Party, Forward Bloc (Marxist), Workers' Party and the Biplabi ("Revolutionary") Bangla Congress, the Socialist United Center of India, and the Revolutionary Communist Party of India. The CPI won 35 seats to Congress(R)'s 216; the CPI(M) won 14 seats, and the Revolutionary Socialist Party, three. The victory of the Congress(R)-CPI alliance involved a severe setback for the CPI(M)—for long a stronghold of the CPI(M) and the CPI(M-L) factions and a scene of political terrorism by the latter (see *YICA., 1972,* pp. 498–99). During the elections there were spates of political violence in West Bengal and Bihar (an estimated 30 killed); however, there had been greater violence in the past elections.

The results of the assembly elections led to the formation of a Congress(R)-CPI Progressive Democratic Alliance government in West Bengal. Starting with the middle of the year, the CPI was demanding stringent land and urban property ceilings, the nationalization of foreign oil companies and the 75 monopoly houses in India (estimated officially to have owned over half of the entire private, corporate sector's assets in 1967–68). As the CPI's national campaign intensified, the alliance in West Bengal became strained. The CPI—and also the CPI(M)—embarked upon vigorous mass campaigns and bandhs nationally during the second half of the year, occasionally resulting in police firings and deaths. The CPI was seeking to have the central government fulfill promises made to the people in the 1971 and 1972 elections by the ruling Congress party.

In West Bengal, a faction within the CPI advocated opposition to the alliance and greater collaboration with the non-Congress leftist parties, not excluding the CPI(M). This was turned down by the party's State Council by an overwhelming majority. But the Council announced a 4-week program of mass rallies, demonstrations, and "gheraos" (physical encirclement to gain quick justice) of government offices to prevent the Congress party from sliding back on the pledges under the pressure of "monopolists and feudalists." (*Times of India,* Bombay, 14 September.)

Kerala Coalition Government. The CPI-led coalition government in Kerala (the "United Front") includes the Congress(R), Muslim League, Revolutionary Socialist Party, and the PSP faction which had resisted merger with the newly formed Socialist Party in August 1971. It is headed by the CPI's C. Achutha Menon as chief minister, although the party is numerically in a minority position in the assembly. The already shaky coalition government experienced considerable strain during the year, but it managed to survive.

In early January, the United Front government, in a joint statement, put the blame for the communal riots at Tellicherry during the closing days of 1971 on the Jan Sangh (and the Rashtriya Swayamsevak Sangh, or RSS—a militant, paramilitary Hindu organization strongly oriented toward the Jan Sangh) and the CPI(M) (*New Age,* 16 January).

According to the CPI, the UF coalition in Kerala had decided to propose a "time-bound" program to achieve the following during the year: (1) nationalization of all foreign-owned plantations in the state; (2) bringing all private major road-transport routes under government ownership, in a phased program to be completed in four years; (3) a moratorium on sanctioning of new schools and colleges in the private sector; (4) completion of the distribution of "pattas" (woven mats) to all hutment dwellers, bestowing of rights to all tenant holdings in the state in the next three years, completion of surplus land distribution in the next two years, and organizing of small cultivators into agricultural cooperatives; and (5) giving prime importance to industrial and agricultural development to ensure increasing job opportunities to the unemployed multitude (ibid.).

By August, strains had developed between the coalition partners. The Congress(R) was accusing the Muslim League of being "communalist." There was rift between the Congress(R) and the CPI—their ministers were leveling complaints of interference in their respective portfolios at each other. Rivalry at the trade union level had also emerged. (See *Economic and Political Weekly,* August 1972, special issue, pp. 1481–85).

Tamilnadu Electoral Alliance. The CPI broke off its one-year-old electoral alliance with the DMK on 20 March. It gave as the reason for this break the DMK's siding with the "capitalist exploiters." However, the CPI continued its alliance with DMK in Pondicherry. (*New Age,* 2 April.)

Internal Reforms. In August the CPI was proposing to reform its organization to fight "bourgeois tendencies," careerism, and individualism within its rank and file. The organizational reforms were to begin at the top. The party leadership at the central and state levels was to try to set an example to the cadres. A central school was to be started to train party workers. The National Council of the party also considered a report which suggested that revolutionary slogans would not strengthen the party's hold on the masses. (*Times of India,* 28 August.)

The Mass Campaign. The party's "extra-parlimentary" mass campaign continued throughout the second half of the year. The Central Secretariat called for a 3-day satyagraha beginning 3 October throughout the country, and the party claimed that 200,000 volunteers would court arrest by peaceful violation of prohibitory orders, thus seeking to resist the central government's policies whenever they were "against the masses." The party appealed for support to the satyagraha movement against high prices, unemployment, and the "capitalist policies" of the central government from all "democratic-minded and progressive Congressmen" as well. The protest campaign finally ended with the party claiming that about 50,000 volunteers had been arrested. (Ibid., 28 August, 28 September; *Far Eastern Economic Review,* 14 October.)

Following the campaign (in which one CPI leader was shot in Aurangabad), the Central Executive Committee, in a review of the political situation, called for a "frontal fight against chauvinist forces in Assam" and "specific measures to root out the CIA [U.S. Central Intelligence Agency] influence," and "immediate nationalization of foreign oil companies." It called upon the party members to observe 13 November as "Oil Companies Nationalization Day," with demonstrations in front of petrol pumps of foreign companies and at the office of the Petroleum and Chemicals Ministry. The party leaders also took to task those denouncing the Soviet intelligence agency, arguing that "it was ridiculous to equate in this matter the U.S.A. with the Soviet Union, which had proved itself India's most reliable and trustworthy ally." (*Times of India,* 29 October.)

Rajya Sabha Elections. In the elections to the 73 seats in the Rajya Sabha, which ended on 8 April, the Congress(R) increased its strength from 103 to 116, but failed to secure an absolute majority. The CPI won 3 seats, thus raising its strength in the upper house of India's parliament to 11.

International Views and Attitudes. The CPI is a staunch supporter of Soviet positions and policies with regard to the international communist movement, despite differences that have occurred from time to time. The Soviet Union, in its efforts to win the friendship of the Indian government, has at times been more conciliatory toward the government than toward the CPI.

In the recent India-Pakistan conflict involving Bangladesh, the CPI sided fully with the Indian government, supporting India's assistance to the independence movement in Bangladesh and later urging immediate recognition of Bangladesh by the Indian and other governments. At least initially, there had been some attitudinal differences between the CPI and the Soviet Union with regard to the Bangladesh issue (see *YICA, 1972,* p. 501).

The CPI Central Committee passed a resolution on Bangladesh in January, lauding the "selfless participation" of the communists in East Pakistan, "jointly with other progressive and democratic forces," and welcoming the victory of the independence struggle, which it termed a "component part of the world struggle against imperialism and for the right of peoples to be free." The resolution stated that the CPI fully shared "the gratitude of the people of India and Bangladesh to the great Soviet Union for its backing unlimited support." The events were said to have "exposed the base deal between Washington and Peking":

> The greatest disgrace of the Chinese Government is that it teamed up with U.S. imperialists in order to support the Islamabad military junta against the just national liberation struggle of the Bangladesh people and provoke war against India.

The committee also expressed support of Prime Minister Gandhi, who was seeking normalization of relations with Pakistan. (FBIS, 7 January.)

A delegation of the CPI National Council visited Bangladesh, 23–28 April, at the invitation of the Central Committee of the Communist Party of Bangladesh (CPB). They met with CPB leaders and expressed "identical views on the issues concerning the international communist movement" and fully agreed on the "historic significance of the ever-growing friendship and cooperation between Bangladesh, India and the Soviet Union in the common struggle against imperialism." (*New Age,* 7 May.)

The CPI's hostile attitude toward China was reflected in comments on the CPI(M), which it viewed as being more pro-China than "independent."

Welcoming the U.S.-Soviet agreements in May, C. Rajeswara Rao called them "an important step on the way to international security, and development of fruitful cooperation." He saw them as "creating better conditions for India and other third world countries for economic independence and progress." (*Pravda,* 2 June.)

On the Vietnam issue, the National Council adopted a resolution condemning "the barbarous bombing raids of the U.S. Airforce" on North Vietnam and demanded "an immediate end to the aggression and withdrawal of all the U.S. troops." (FBIS, 9 June.)

A CPI delegation visited Moscow on 20–28 June and met with Leonid Brezhnev and other leaders of the Communist Party of the Soviet Union (CPSU). A joint statement, the first of its kind between the two parties, expressed the readiness of both to "develop and strengthen in every way their relations of fraternal friendship on the basis of the principles of Marxism-Leninism and proletarian internationalism." They demanded "an end to the U.S. aggression in Indochina" and hailed "Soviet-Indian friendship and cooperation" as "an example of international relations on the basis of equality between a socialist state and a liberated country." While the CPI commended the Soviet Union for its "constant support to the national liberation movement in Indochina," the CPSU "solidarity with the CPI's activity in uniting the leftist, democratic forces of the country in the struggle to strengthen national independence and for economic and social progress and in the defense of the vital interests of India's working class." (FBIS, 21, 22, 30 June, 6, 18 July.)

The Indian government accorded full diplomatic recognition to the German Democratic Republic (GDR) on 8 October, but apparently not because of the insistent demands of the CPI and the CPI(M) for it. The government had taken this decision some time before; the formal announcement had been withheld in consideration of West Germany's concern over the issue. (*Times of India,* 9 October.)

In an unusual gesture, the Council for Mutual Economic Assistance on 10 October, expressed willingness to welcome India's participation in it as a full member or as an observer. The Soviet Union indicated that it would back India in any form of association the latter would like to develop with the CMEA. (Ibid., 11 October.) However, nothing came out of this offer during the year.

*   *   *

The CPI(M). The Communist Party of India (Marxist) claimed a membership of 106,841 at its Ninth Congress (27 June–2 July 1972), where the secretary-general admitted that the party had been able to increase its influence only in Kerala and West Bengal. He revealed that the membership in 1968 was 76,425 and that in 1970–71 it increased from 84,886 to 105,049.

More probably the membership is between 80,000 and 100,000. According to the claims of the CPI (noted before), thousands of CPI(M) members have switched to the CPI. Furthermore, the CPI(M)'s strength in West Bengal has been reduced drastically. Its test of strength in Kerala, in the normal course, will come in 1975; it could come sooner if the CIP-led coalition government there were to collapse. The CPI(M)'s assembly strength in Kerala at present is 31 seats, as compared with the CPI's 16 (*NYT,* 2 April).

Leadership and Organization. The CPI(M) leadership consists of Secretary-General P. Sundarayya, Chairman Jyoti Basu, the Politburo (9 members), the Central Committee (31 members), and the state secretariats and committees.

The Politburo members, elected at the Ninth Congress, in Madurai (Tamilnadu), are P. Sundarayya, B. T. Randive, M. Basavapunnaiah (editor of the party organ, *People's Democracy*), E. M. S. Namboodiripad, A. K. Gopalan, Jyoti Basu, Pramode Das Gupta, Harkishan Singh Surjeet, and P. Ramamurthy. These leaders are also on the new Central Committee, whose membership was raised from 28 to 31 at the congress.

The CPI(M) acquired its own trade union federation in 1970. A CPI(M)-dominated "All-India Trade Union Conference" in May 1970 created a new organization, the Center of Indian Trade Unions (CITU). B. T. Randive and P. Ramamurthy (who were leaders in the undivided AITUC) are president and general secretary, respectively. The CITU probably has a membership approaching a million.

The CPI(M) has been until this year somewhat stronger than the CPI in organizing the peasantry. The party's AIKS probably has about a million members, with close to two-thirds of the membership in West Bengal. Its leadership includes the Politburo member A. K. Gopalan as president and Central Committee member Harekrishna Konar as general secretary. The CPI(M) also controls an agricultural laborers' union which probably has a membership of about 300,000. The CPI(M)'s former student organization (All-India Student Federation; AISF) was reorganized in December 1970 as the Students' Federation of India.

Domestic Attitudes and Activities. The CPI(M) emerged out of the split of the CPI in 1964. Initially it was more militant than its parent organization in supporting armed revolts by workers and peasants, and it was oriented toward, but not a partisan of, China. In the first year of its existence it had no agreed-upon ideology. In 1966 the Chinese Communist Party (CCP) attempted unsuccessfully to have at least a strong minority of CPI(M) leadership adopt the Maoist line and break away from the parliamentary tradition of the CPI. Instead, in 1967, the CPI(M) opted for the "parliamentary path"; although some of the CPI(M) leaders functioning in West Bengal and Kerala opposed the parliamentary line and exalted peasant rebellions. (See Bhabani Sen Gupta, op. cit., pp. 281–83).

With the adoption in 1967 of the "Madurai line," the CPI(M) assumed an internationally "independent" policy—abandoning its pro-Chinese sentiments and the ramifications of these domestically. It has adopted a stance in recent years which has been "anti-revisionist," and "anti-dogmatist," as well as against "left-wing opportunism."

Since 1969 it has not held positions in the governments of Kerala and West Bengal, and has been placing an even greater emphasis on extra-parliamentary methods and activities. The alliances the party advocates are more exclusive than those advocated by the CPI. The CPI(M) has constantly criticized the CPI for the latter's willingness to form coalitions with various "reactionary" parties. However, the CPI(M)'s practice in making alliances has not been inflexible; consequently, it has had to face counter-criticism from the CPI on this issue.

The CPI(M)'s long-range goal is the establishment of a "people's democracy" in India. The views and positions of the party with regard to this central concept are still evolving. In the political resolution adopted on 1 July by the Ninth Congress, the CPI(M) took the position that "the traditional Marxist concept of self-determination by nationalities was not applicable in the Indian context and that in the interests of the working class the unity of the country should be preserved." According to this resolution, the party would oppose secessionist and separatist trends. However, it deemed that the real threat to unity arose from the increasing centralization of powers by the present Congress government. Thus the party would also support "real autonomy" for all nationalities—aimed at strengthening the unity of the people and based on the party's perception of the voluntary character of the Indian Union: "real equality and autonomy" for the various nationalities that have found expression in the form of linguistic states, combined with the party's opposition to centralization and its repudiation of separatism. Clarifying the concept of autonomy further, the political resolution had stated that except for defense, currency, foreign affairs, communications, centralized economic planning, and inter-state relations, all subjects should remain within the jurisdiction of the states. In terms of party tactics, the political resolution proposed the continuation of the "parliamentary path," the revival of united fronts, and for the present, *not* an armed struggle.

The Ninth Congress adopted several resolutions. One attacked the central government for its alleged failure to "end social oppression and inhuman exploitation of scheduled castes and tribes," and asked the party units to fight "against the social and political oppression and the policy of economic disinheritance practised by the Government and upper classes against Harijans and Adivasis [aborigines]." Another criticized the lack of fixed targets in the Planning Commission's document on approach to the fifth five-year plan, arguing that the greater reliance on import of foreign capital and the increased tax burden on the poor and the middle class would further intensify the crisis in the economy; and that "all the slogans of garibi hatao and increased jobs" would become a hoax. Another resolution criticized the ruling Congress party's approach to the question of ceilings on urban property, and demanded foolproof legislation to ensure real reduction in the disparities in income and wealth. Still another accused the Congress government of having enforced repressive measures in several states, and called upon "all parties, mass organizations and all sections of the people to unitedly resist reactionary policies which are meant to serve vested interests and take the country towards one-party dictatorship." Sundarayya, summing up the achievements of the Ninth Congress, stated that the party had overcome threats from "right deviationism and left adventurism from within" and succeeded in projecting to other "left and democratic parties" in the country an "alternative line to the ruling classes." (See *People's Democracy,* 16 July; ibid., 30 April supplement; *Asian Recorder, 1972; Times of India, 3 July).

The State Assembly Elections. Early in the year, the party Central Committee had proposed a program for "united action" during the elections. This was later adopted as the party program. It included: (1) a complete recasting of the nation's foreign policy with a view to "carrying the struggle against American imperialism" to its logical conclusion; (2) implementation, in practice, of the policy of dispensing with foreign aid and relying on internal resources to carry out the plans of development; (3) withdrawal of the CRP and army, stoppage of mass terror in West Bengal, and repeal of other "repressive" government legislation; (4) basic changes in the constitution to eliminate monopolist and landlord exploitation, ensure "real autonomy" for the states, and ensure the right to work and civil liberties; (5) need-based minimum wage for the workers and employees, stoppage of wagefreezes and lockouts; (6) vigorous measures against the rise in prices, inflation, and heavy taxation; (7) radical land reforms in the interest of the peasantry; (8) immediate introduction of free education up to the secondary stage in all states, and the right of students to participate in the management of educational institutions and academic bodies; (9) drastic steps against those who indulge in outrages against scheduled castes and tribes; (10) safeguards for the rights of the Muslim minority; and (11) equal status and opportunities for women in all fields. (*People's Democracy,* 23 January, 5 March.)

The election efforts of the CPI(M) were heavily concentrated in West Bengal, where it had worked out electoral alliances with leftist parties within a West Bengal Left Front. The front adhered to the 32-point program of the former United Front, which came to power in 1967 and 1969 in West Bengal; and it put forth an 8-point priority plan. The manifesto stated that the front followed strictly a line opposed to "Congress, reactionary, and communal forces." It promised radical land reforms, stable prices, and free primary education. Before the elections, virtually every issue of *People's Democracy* carried headlines calling for the defeat of the ruling Congress. The CPI(M) suffered a severe setback in the elections. It won only one seat each in Andhra, Himachal Pradesh, Maharashtra, and Punjab; 16 seats in Tripura, 14 in West Bengal, and none at all in the remaining 16 states and two union territories. In West Bengal, although the CPI(M) received 27.63 percent of the electoral vote (compared with 8.42 percent for the CPI), it won only 14 seats against CPI's 35. The CPI(M) charged repeatedly that the elections in West Bengal had been "rigged" by the party's "class enemies." In that state, in a massive campaign against the "semi-Fascist methods of the Congress regime," the party observed 11 May as "Anti-Terror Day." (Ibid., 28 May.)

On 16 May the CIP(M) started a massive campaign for radical land reforms and called for a general strike in all factories and industrial establishments. A. K. Gopalan led a "struggle" for the occupation of surplus land in Kerala starting 25 May, under the Action Council of Peasants and Agricultural Workers. According to the party, some 14,000 volunteers were arrested in the first 19 days of the struggle. (Ibid., 11 June.)

In October the party organized a rally in Calcutta against "high prices, unemployment, acute distress, eviction of peasants, chaos in education, and terror and police repression." Similar agitations were launched in Maharashtra, in alliance with other parties. The campaign for the occupation of surplus land was reactivated in mid-November in Kerala. In late November the party alleged that the Youth Congress, Kerala Students' Union, and the Naxalites were combining their activities to terrorize other parties and suppress their "peaceful struggles" (*Times of India,* 24 November.)

Toward the close of the year, the CPI(M) and Akali Dal alliance in Punjab was reported to be on the verge of breaking up. The Punjab unit of the CPI agreed to attend a leftist convention if the Akalis and the Jan Sangh were kept out of it, and the CPI(M) likewise agreed to do so (ibid., 23 November).

Thus, during the second half of the year, there were some indications of overlap between the tactical maneuvers of the CPI(M) and the CPI, as well as parallelism between these two communist parties subscribing to the "parliamentary path."

International Views and Attitudes. The CPI(M) maintains a policy of independence and refuses to be aligned with either the CCP or the CPSU, neither of which has accorded international recognition to it. Since 1967 the party has condemned with equal intensity the errors of Chinese "left-sectarianism" and Soviet "revisionism." The party centers its efforts on establishing relations with "like-minded" communist parties in Cuba, North Korea, Romania, and North Vietnam.

During the year, U.S. involvement in Vietnam and policy in the Bangladesh crisis came under repeated and heavy criticism from the CPI(M). However, China and the Soviet Union were also occasionally castigated. The party Politburo issued a statement in early January denouncing "barbaric air attacks by U.S. planes on North Vietnam." It charged, further, that "the American imperialists are conspiring to unleash an attack on the Democratic People's Republic of Korea," called upon the people and government of India to "denounce these attacks" on North Vietnam; urged the government to "demand withdrawal of all American forces from the soil of Indo-China and Korea," and appealed to China and the Soviet Union to "come together at this critical period and join their efforts to meet this blatant attack" (*People's Democracy,* 2 January). The release of Sheikh Mujibur Rahman by the Bhutto government in Pakistan, over which the party expressed "happiness," was deemed as "another blow to the conspiracy of U.S. imperialists" (ibid., 23 January).

Welcoming the decision of the Indian government to raise the status of its diplomatic relations with North Vietnam to the embassy level, the Central Committee of the party again referred to U.S. "imperialism" in relation to Bangladesh and the resumption of bombing in North Vietnam.

The U.S.-Chinese communiqué in February brought forth a statement by the Politburo which was highly critical of the United States, but which also blamed China for compromising its "position as a firm supporter of the armed struggle of the people of Vietnam against U.S. imperialism" (ibid., 2 April).

The CPI(M), which had campaigned in 1971 for the recognition of Bangladesh by India and castigated China for failing to support Bangladesh, produced a lengthy statement by the Central Committee on "The Party and the Struggle of the Bangladesh People" (ibid., 13 February).

The party welcomed the agreement between Indira Gandhi and Z. A. Bhutto to hold an Indo-Pakistani summit. It put the blame for bad relations between India and Pakistan since their independence on "machinations of imperialism, specifically U.S. imperialism." (Ibid., 7 May.)

The Politburo statement of 30 May on the Soviet-U.S. communiqué accused the U.S. side of declaring "high-sounding principles" with "unmatched cynicism and no serious intent." It added, however, that "The leaders of the Soviet Union also cannot escape the charge of extreme cynicism and opportunism in signing a statement on equality of nations with Nixon who is raining bombs on Vietnam and trying to wipe out the freedom-fighters." It went on to charge that "as in his visit to Peking, in his Moscow negotiations also, Nixon has done his best to exploit the Sino-Soviet differences in the interest of American imperialism, without making any real concessions. (*Ibid.,* 4 June.)

The draft political resolution of the Ninth Congress invited the "sympathy, support and co-operation of all progressive individuals and parties for breaking away from the British Commonwealth and for a really independent, genuinely anti-imperialist, progressive and peace-loving policy." It called for "all-out support" to the people of Vietnam in their "struggle against American imperialism," and recognition of the Provisional Revolutionary Government of South Vietnam; for the recognition of the government of Cambodia headed by Sihanouk; for the "withdrawal of U.S. occupation forces from South Korea" and for peaceful unification of the Korean people; and for full diplomatic recognition to North Korea and East Germany. It had also called for the restoration of trade and closer relations with "Socialist Cuba"; for extending support to the African people fighting against the "racist Governments of South Africa, Rhodesia and against Portuguese imperialism" and to the people of Latin America and other nations "fighting for their liberation"; for friendly relations with "our neighbors," Bangladesh, Pakistan, Nepal, and others; and for friendly relations with the People's Republic of China and closer ties with the Soviet Union and all other "Socialist countries." (Ibid., 25 June).

At the Ninth Congress, the CPI(M) leaders criticized the Soviets and the Chinese in several resolutions. One of them called upon the Soviet Union and China to "forge a united front, despite all their ideological differences," and join hands in "effectively intervening in the war in Vietnam and compelling the aggressors to withdraw." It called upon "all communists, all democratic and freedom-loving people throughout the world to make this demand on the leaders of the Soviet Union and China." The resolution argued that both China and the Soviet Union should have canceled President Nixon's visit to their countries and refused to talk with the Americans who were waging war on a socialist state. (Ibid., 16 July.)

Both China and the Soviet Union were also criticized for their assistance to the Ceylonese government in suppressing the April 1971 uprising. China came under sharp criticism for having "supported the Naxalites who were murdering our comrades and disrupting the movement," as well as for having backed Pakistan in the Bangladesh crisis. (Ibid.)

At the Ninth Congress, the CPI(M) received messages of greetings from the communist parties in North Korea, Romania, and Cuba—but seemingly not from North Vietnam.

The CPI(M-L), or Naxalites. The Communist Party of India (Marxist-Leninist) was formed on 22 April 1969 by the left-extremist elements of the CPI(M) who later left, or were expelled from, the parent organization following the 1967 peasant uprising in Naxalbari (West Bengal) led by these dissident extremists. The CPI(M) had attempted to suppress this uprising.

The CPI(M-L) emerged as a party when its predecessor organization, the All-India Coordination Committee of Communist Revolutionaries (AICCCR) established in 1968, suffered a split between its West Bengal base and its important branch, known as the Coordinating Committee, in the state of Andhra Pradesh. The Andhra group further splintered; and one of its constituents, the Srikakulum Committee led by Tarimela Nagi Reddy, did not join the CPI(M-L) when the AICCCR decided to dissolve its loose organization in favor of creating a new revolutionary party led by Kanu Sanyal and centered in West Bengal—the CPI(M-L). The Reddy group assumed a new name: Andhra Pradesh Revolutionary Communist Committee (APRCC).

Charu Mazumdar, who had been expelled by the CPI(M) in 1967, became the main theoretician and secretary-general of the Maoist CPI(M-L) upon its formation, while Kanu Sanyal, who had led the revolt in Naxalbari, assumed the role of party strategist. The party was recognized by the Chinese Communist Party and referred to by it as "the only communist party in India." The Chinese-oriented Naxalite movement had attracted a number of unemployed college graduates, university students, landless peasants, and workers in tea plantations. Although the Naxalites were and still are to be found in many states of India, they were and continue to be more numerous in West Bengal and Andhra Pradesh.

The CPI(M-L) advocated the organization of peasants for armed struggle to seize power. It condemned the CPI as "revisionist" and the CPI(M) as "neo-revisionist." The latter had been criticized for its readiness to enter into coalition governments at the state level with the CPI and other "bourgeois" parties in West Bengal and Kerala. Ideological as well as physical attacks (the latter in the form of political assassinations) by the CPI(M-L) against CPI(M) reached acute proportions in the late 1960s. More recently, the politically motivated murders in Calcutta alone have been estimated at 10 per day. The CPI(M)'s Central Committee's draft political resolution for the Ninth Congress claimed that the Naxalites had murdered 650 party cadre and supporters between 1970 and 1972 (*People's Democracy*, 30 April).

Since their emergence, the Naxalites have engaged in acts of violence in West Bengal, Andhra Pradesh, Bihar, Orissa, and Kerala—including forcible occupation of land and the looting of harvests and warehouse grains in the rural areas, and destruction of schools, libraries, theaters, and buses in the urban areas. However, there are differences about strategy and tactics among them.

Virtually since its creation, the CPI(M-L) has been plagued with differences within it, and it has not succeeded in uniting all of the CPI(M) defectors or Maoist sympathizers. The CPI(M-L) advocated armed offensive action by small guerrilla groups and the selective "annihilation of class enemies," whereby the "class enemies"—landlords, moneylenders, and policemen, and later the CPI(M) members as well—would be forced to flee the countryside, and the establishing of "revolutionary committees" on the Chinese model in the "liberated" rural areas where the state machinery had been destroyed.

The APRCC, on the other hand, advocated starting the "liberation struggle" with an agrarian revolutionary program and the creation of a mass-based "red army." The Reddy group viewed the "blind violence" of the Mazumdar group as "Guevarism" rather than Maoism, and believed that ideological preparation was necessary for armed struggle. Although the Reddy group claimed to be more faithfully Maoist, the CCP formally recognized only the Mazumdar group.

In early 1970, the CPI(M-L) under Mazumdar's leadership shifted its emphasis from rural to urban areas, particularly in West Bengal. Industrialists, judges, and Congress party members were added to the list of "class enemies." However, the "annihilation" of CPI(M) members gave rise to dissentions and fragmentation within the party. It also brought forth retaliation from the Indian government, with disastrous consequences for the party. At this juncture, the CCP, reportedly, leveled "bitter criticism" of the "style of work" and the tactical concepts of Charu Mazumdar and of the CPI(M-L) leadership generally. The CCP argued that Mazumdar was wrong in concentrating his activities in the Calcutta urban area and neglecting the rural areas; that he had failed to consolidate the gains made in the rural areas during 1967–69; and that he had been guilty of too much centralism as well as of sectarianism. (See Bhabani Sen Gupta, op. cit., pp. 293–94, and the *Statesman,* 11 October 1972.)

Perhaps because of this Chinese criticism, the CPI(M-L) reverted to its original rural emphasis in mid-1970. Late in that year, the West Bengal state committee of the party split into two groups. The Mazumdar group now labeled the other dissident group led by Ashim Chatterji as "revisionist" for its subscription to the orthodox Maoist strategy of establishing "liberated zones" by means of peasant revolts. The differences between these two groups were also exacerbated because of their positions in relation to the situation in East Pakistan. While Mazumdar had maintained that a popular movement for independence in East Pakistan should not be opposed by the party, Chatterji denounced the Bangladesh movement as "bourgeois" and demanded that the party, in accordance with the Chinese government's policy, should actively support the Yahya Khan government in Pakistan by carrying out sabotage operations against the Mukti Bahini ("liberation forces" in East Pakistan). (See *Keesing's Contemporary Archives,* 1972).

Chatterji was arrested by the government on 3 November 1971 apparently on his way to the party Central Committee meeting, somewhere in Bihar. At the meeting, which was not attended by Mazumdar either, the Central Committee on 7 November expelled Mazumdar from the CPI(M-L) for pursuing "a Trotskyite adventurist line" and elected Satya Narayan Singh (party secretary from Bihar) as general secretary.

The split in the party created a fratricidal situation in which several members of the party were killed in clashes between the two factions. The ideological and personal rivalries, which had led to the split, also affected relations between the party and the smaller Naxalite organizations—leading to a gang warfare in late 1971 between the supporters and opponents of Mazumdar. Due to the government's campaign against the Naxalites (starting in 1970) and the split within the party, the decline in the Naxalite movement (already started in the second half of 1971) was further accelerated. Reportedly, in February 1972 about 4,000 Naxalites were serving prison sentences in West Bengal; over 2,000 in Bihar; about 1,400 in Andhra Pradesh; and 1,000 in Kerala, Uttar Pradesh, and other states. Many disillusioned Naxalites were said to be returning to the CPI(M) in West Bengal and Kerala, and to the CPI in Andhra Pradesh. (Ibid.) Another estimate, in August 1972, put the number of Naxalite activists arrested during the year at more than 2,000 (out of an estimated 10,000) and those killed in police encounters in "hundreds" (*NYT,* 5 August 1972).

Nagi Reddy, arrested in Madras in December 1971, was found guilty and sentenced to four years' rigorous imprisonment. Kanu Sanyal was arrested and jailed, along with a number of second-ranking Naxalite leaders, early in 1972.

Mazumdar was arrested in Calcutta on 16 July along with others, including a member of the CPI(M-L) Central Committee. Upon Mazumdar's arrest, the chief minister of West Bengal claimed that the government had "complete control" over the Naxalite movement. His police forces had orders to "shoot on sight" in dealing with Naxalites trying to incite violence and murder. He had also visited Bangladesh on 10–11 June and conferred with Prime Minister Sheikh Mujibur Rahman on the reported smuggling of arms by the Naxalites from Bangladesh. When this area was East Pakistan, it was believed to provide a sanctuary and a channel for the supply of arms from Peking to the Naxalites. Thus, the emergence of Bangladesh appears to have been a major factor in the decline of the Naxalite movement. Mazumdar, who had been suffering for many years from cardiac asthma, died on 28 July of a heart attack in a prison hospital.

Although some trusted followers of Mazumdar are still at large, and many Naxalite cells still active, a demoralization has set in among the Naxalites. In seeking to preserve unity, they are reported to be abandoning their tactic of "individual liquidation of class enemies." Reddy's views are reported to have been changing in the direction of the view that the "class character" of the present government could be exposed through various other means, such as a movement for rigid implementation of the land reform laws; however, he is also said to be "thoroughly disillusioned" with the role of the CPI(M) in the last few years. The Indian government has, in turn, stepped up its efforts to apprehend and bring to trial the Naxalite leaders, and it has been trying to prevent the escape of Naxalites to Bhutan. (*Times of India,* 11 September; also issues of 19, 31 July.)

*   *   *

Publications. The communist parties and groups in India have a network of dailies, weeklies, and monthlies, issued in English and various vernacular languages. The central organization of the CPI publishes the English weekly *New Age* in New Delhi (1971 circulation, 7,500). It also publishes the weekly *Party Life,* and has dailies in five states: two in Kerala and one each in Andhra Pradesh, West Bengal, Punjab, and Manipur.

The CPI(M) central organ is the English weekly *People's Democracy,* published in Calcutta (1971 circulation, 9,000 to 10,000). The CPI(M) also publishes dailies in Kerala, West Bengal, and Andhra Pradesh and weeklies in Tamilnadu, Karnataka, West Bengal, Punjab, and Jammu and Kashmir.

The CPI(M-L)'s English monthly, *Liberation,* and Bengali weekly, *Deshabrati,* were banned in March 1970, but they continued to appear clandestinely until recently. Other extremist publications were: in English, the monthly *People's Path* and biweekly *Commune,* and in Hindi, the weekly *Lok Yuddha* ("People's War").

California State University,   Mukund G. Untawale
San Francisco

Indonesia

Indonesian communism today consists primarily of scattered, intermittent, underground propaganda activity in Java and Bali, and of more overt guerrilla-style resistance in Indonesian West Kalimantan (Borneo) in conjunction with the armed bands of the North Kalimantan Communist Party (see *Malaysia*). Additionally, in Moscow and in some East European capitals like Prague, and in India and Ceylon, there are Indonesian communist exiles following a pro-Soviet ideological line in their policy statements. In Peking there is a self-styled "Delegation" of the Indonesian Communist Party Central Committee, while in Tirana, Albania, an ideologically related group of exiles is connected with the publication of the pro-Maoist *Indonesian Tribune*. Throughout 1972, as in recent years, the Indonesian government called attention to the persistent but unspecified threat of communist subversion in the nation, as arrests and trials of suspected communists, including some in the Indonesian armed forces, continued.

History. The oldest such party in Asia, the Communist Party of Indonesia (Partai Komunis Indonesia; PKI) formally came into existence on 23 May 1920 as an outgrowth of the "Indies Social Democratic Association" founded six years previously by Dutch Marxists. Affiliated from its inception with the Third International (Comintern), the PKI was banned after it launched unsuccessful revolts in West Java and West Sumatra in 1926–27, and its principal leaders took up residence in Moscow or with the Chinese communists, or else acted as roving functionaries for the Comintern in Asia. In October 1945, two months after the Indonesian independence declaration, the PKI embarked on a new, legitimate existence. But on 18 September 1948 some party and front-group leaders and Army sympathizers staged an abortive coup d'état in Madiun, East Java. The direct cause of this action was the attempt by the Indonesian government and army leadership to disband communist paramilitary units; probably it was indirectly inspired by the Communist Youth Conference at Calcutta in February 1948, in the aftermath of which insurrections occurred elsewhere in Southeast Asia.

Not formally banned again after the Madiun rising, the PKI made a remarkable comeback under new, younger leaders, headed by D. N. Aidit, winning a little over 16 percent of the popular vote and achieving the fourth largest parliamentary delegation in Indonesia's first national elections, in 1955. Communists gained steadily in influence during the late fifties and into the sixties under President Sukarno's protection. On 30 September 1965 Aidit and a few other party leaders, in conjunction with dissident Army and Air Force officers and backed by party front-group personnel and a number of Army units, staged an unsuccessful coup in Djakarta and areas of West and Central Java. General A. H. Nasution (unlike six fellow Army generals) escaped communist assassin squads and with the commander of the Strategic Reserve, General Suharto, succeeded in quickly quelling the insurrection. In the weeks following, Aidit was killed, along with thousands of communists and suspects in a massive Army-inspired purge. On 12 March 1966 the PKI was formally banned and on 5 July the study and teaching of Marxism-Leninism, except in the context of academic discussion, was declared forbidden also.

During 1967–68 underground PKI armed units launched a new revolt, eventually centering on a short-lived "Indonesian People's Republic" headquartered near Blitar, East Java. The Indonesian army crushed the insurrection, making hundreds of arrests, of civilians, officials, and military men, among them those suspected of complicity also in the 1965 coup attempt. Since the end of 1968 Indonesian communist guerrilla activity has been confined primarily to the boundary area between Indonesian West Kalimantan and the Malaysian state of Sarawak.

Organization and Tactics. Since the 1967–68 debacle little has been known of the underground PKI organization in Java, its shadow Politburo, and the operations of its armed units like the "Indonesian People's Liberation Army" (Lasjkar Pembebasan Rakjat Indonesia; LPRI), or of the East Java-based "Surabaya People's Guerrilla Movement" (Persatuan Gerilja Rakjat Surabaja). Indonesian Army intelligence sources estimate the number of underground party activists at around 4,000. These are supervised by a loose network of "project committees" or *kompros*. Intense government surveillance, combined with continuing arrests of suspects and deep popular suspicion, has made communist operations or infiltration extremely difficult. No formal or informal party or front organization could hope to exist for very long under present circumstances. During 1971 the Djakarta Military Command alone arrested 224 persons for alleged involvement in the 1965 coup attempt (Antara, Indonesian news agency, Djakarta, 29 December).

Estimates of political prisoners in Indonesia (most of them alleged communists, erstwhile party sympathizers, or participants in the 1965 rising and in subsequent underground activity) continue to fluctuate widely, ranging from 39,000 according to an estimate by a spokesman for KOPKAMTIB ("Command for the Restoration of Security and Order") (Antara, 14 October 1972), to "not far in excess of 23,000" (Amnesty International *Annual Report 1971–72*, London, 1972, p. 33). Early in 1972 KOPKAMTIB declared that up to 1 January 1972 some 125,000 political prisoners had been released, presumably since arrests began in late 1965, and that only 18,570 of those arrested for participation in the 1965 rising and in the Blitar insurrection of 1968 were still being detained, among them 2,494 so-called Class A or "hard core" communist prisoners awaiting trial. The remainder—Class B prisoners who could not be tried "for lack of evidence"—were being "rehabilitated" on the island of Buru in eastern Indonesia. (Bernama, Malaysian national news agency, Djakarta, 6 February). Later in the year, however, a KOPKAMTIB spokesman said there were some 29,000 Class B prisoners "in several parts of the country" (Antara, 9 October). Earlier in 1971 the remainder of some 50,000 relatively innocent Class C prisoners had reportedly been set free.

Treatment and living conditions of the prisoners, particularly on Buru, continued in 1972 to be controversial, for government officials insisting that improvements have been made (contrast, e.g., *Journal of Contemporary Asia,* vol. 2, no. 1, pp. 112–20, with *Antara Daily News Bulletin,* vol. 24, nos. 1482 and 1569, 30 May and 11 September). During the year the escape of three detainees from Buru who killed a guard in the process led the Indonesian government to formulate new, stricter security measures (Antara dispatch, Ambon, 25 October).

Unlike the preceding year (see *YICA, 1972,* p. 509), there were no arrests of prominent underground communist cadres in 1972. On 29 July, however, the Indonesian Defense and Security Department announced the arrest of an unspecified number of senior officers for "possible involvement" in the 1965 coup attempt, and on 4 August General Sumitro, KOP-

KAMTIB deputy commander, announced that the "purge of elements involved in the abortive Communist coup in 1965 in the ranks of the Armed Forces and government bodies" was continuing. On 26 October Indonesian Air Force Marshal Suwoto Sukendar said that a special operation was being undertaken to "purge the Air Force of Communist elements" (*Antara Daily News Bulletin,* vol. 25, no. 1608, 26 October). In view of previous reports of underground communist infiltration of Javanese mystical sects, the announcement by the Central Java Military Commander, General Widodo, on 22 August that caution should be observed in respect to *dukun* (village soothsayers and healers) because "they are likely associated with attempts aimed at a communist comeback" attracted attention. Widodo cited the case of a recently arrested *dukun,* with a sizable following (among them an Army colonel) who had organized a week-long circumcision festivity near Djokjakarta, highlighted by the showing of propaganda films provided by the Soviet Embassy in Djakarta (ibid., vol. 24, no. 1553, 22 August). These and similar arrests in the past have served to strengthen the impression that current underground communist tactics in Java may be focused on winning sympathizers among military dissidents, restive both during the Sukarno era and under the present government of President Suharto, and among nativistic religious groups or leaders standing in an aura of relatively inviolate sanctity in the rural areas.

Outside Indonesia, rival groups of PKI exiles and sympathizers, split along Moscow-versus-Peking ideological lines, continue to frame tactical directives for the Indonesian communist movement. During 1972 the directional relationship between these exile groups and the PKI underground and its Politburo in Indonesia, if any, was not readily evident.

In Peking, the "Delegation of the Central Committee of the PKI" is led by Jusuf Adjitorop, who before the 1965 rising was a member of the party's Politburo and who being then in Peking for medical treatment remained there, thus escaping the anti-communist purge. Djawoto, the former Indonesian ambassador to Peking, is now secretary-general of the Peking-sponsored Afro-Asian Journalists' Association in the Chinese capital. He links the "Delegation" with other "Delegation" or Chinese party front-groups, most of them little more than paper organizations, like the "Federation of Indonesian Students" and the "Indonesian Organization for Afro-Asian People's Solidarity," the latter headed by Ibrahim Isa. The total Indonesian community in and around the "Delegation" now numbers at the most around 300. It includes students, former diplomats and officials and their families, journalists, and PKI front-group cadres who have escaped since 1965. Ideological rifts—resulting in part from student contact with some East European countries—and personal rivalries have made for attrition of the group. Since 1971, Ali Hanafiah, formerly Indonesian ambassador to Ceylon and originally identified with the "Delegation," has resided more or less permanently in Moscow, with a rival group of PKI exiles there.

In Tirana, Albania, there are about 40 Indonesian communists, of whom about half are connected with a largely paper organization, the "Indonesian Students' Association in Albania." The Albania-based group frequently appears to act as a spokesman for the Peking-domiciled PKI exile faction.

At the close of 1971, the Albania-based PKI exile group issued a statement which recalled the *Otokritik* (self-criticism) made by the "Politburo of the PKI Central Committee" in September 1966, and its further statement of 23 May 1967, both of which have since served as the ideological rationale of the pro-Peking Indonesian communist faction abroad, and in particular of the "Delegation of the Central Committee of the PKI" led by Adjitorop. Stressing the importance of armed struggle, and claiming that the "peasants have started to rise up in struggle against feudal power and foreign capital in the countryside" and against the "Suharto fascist dictatorship" generally, the Albania-based PKI exiles reaffirmed their "New Three

Banners of the Party": (1) the building of Marxist-Leninist party free from "subjectivism, opportunism and modern revisionism," (2) the promotion of "the armed people's struggle," specifically of "the peasants in an anti-feudal agrarian revolution" under the leadership of "the working class," and, finally, (3) the fostering of "the revolutionary united front" based on a worker-peasant alliance and also led by the "working class" (*Indonesian Tribune,* Tirana, vol. 5, 1971, no. 4, pp. 3–7).

During 1972 the Albania PKI exile group continued its attacks on the Suharto government, noting, in particular, the allegedly adverse effects of the influx of foreign capital in Indonesia:

> As a result of the intensified plunder of Indonesia's natural resources by foreign capital, as well as the bankruptcy of an increasingly large number of national business enterprises (caused by their inferior strength in competition with foreign companies), Indonesia's economic crisis has grown worse. . . . The rapine of Indonesia and the fleecing of its people are being carried out not only by US monopoly capital, but also by Japanese capital and that of other countries. . . . While the people have to live a growing miserable life, the small handful of national traitors, such as those fascist generals and civil authorities who have turned bureaucrat capitalists, are getting richer and richer. (Ibid., vol. 6, 1972, no. 1, p. 5.)

Meanwhile, on the international scene, the group discerned brighter prospects:

> The world anti-imperialist and anti-social imperialist front has grown mightier than ever. The struggle of countries against domination and bullying by the two superpowers, US imperialism and Soviet social-imperialism, have swept the world more vigorously. . . . The days when US imperialism could impose its domination upon its allies at will have gone forever. . . . Tormented by difficulties both at home and abroad, Soviet social-imperialism is in a terrible plight. Those countries under its sway are no longer willing to trail after Moscow readily. (Ibid., pp. 3–4.)

"Armed struggle" and "people's guerrilla resistance" are the proper path to overthrow the "Suharto fascist military regime," according to the Albanian group. Meanwhile, the "Indonesian Students' Association in Albania," the corollary of the Peking-based "Federation of Indonesian Students," continues in its own publications to excoriate Suharto ("the butcher of hundreds of thousands of people"), whose government is alleged to have encouraged "the cruellest forms of feudal exploitation and oppression in the countryside," as rice production meanwhile stagnates, peasants are "slaughtered" or jailed, public health conditions generally worsen, and political freedoms are destroyed (*Api Pemuda Idonesia,* Tirana, October 1972, pp. 1–4).

The Moscow-oriented PKI exile groups, some of whom reside in India and Ceylon, others in Czechoslovakia and the Soviet Union, in the course of 1972 issued statements under the name "The Committee Abroad of the Communist Party of Indonesia." The group's earlier name, "Marxist-Leninist Group of the PKI," now appears to have been abandoned, at least formally. Secretary of the "Committee Abroad" is Tomas Sinuraja, a minor PKI functionary in Sumatra who fled the country before the 1965 rising. The previously named Ali Hanafiah is another prominent member of the "Committee Abroad," whose members consist of about 100 students, PKI refugees, including a score of pre-1965 East Java party branch leaders who were able to escape the anti-communist pogrom in November 1965 (allegedly with the help of Soviet diplomatic personnel in Indonesia), journalists, including former personnel of the Indonesian news agency Antara, and a few former Indonesian diplomats who deemed it wiser not to return from abroad after Suharto assumed power. The extent to which the Moscow-oriented "Committee Abroad" is in touch with the PKI underground in Indonesia is not known, but is believed to be slight. During 1972 the "Committee Aboard," usually over the signature of

Sinuraja, reaffirmed the analysis of the PKI's pre-1965 mistakes as being caused by a "petty-bourgeois malaise" in the party. This analysis was made by pro-Moscow Indonesian communist exiles (i.e., the "Marxist-Leninist Group of the PKI") in 1966, and was further amplified by the same group's 1969 policy statement, "Urgent Tasks of the Communist Movement in Indonesia."

During 1972 the Suharto government was described by the "Committee Abroad" as converting the Indonesian economy into "an appendage of the US and other imperialist economies," with foreign capital being "used chiefly to build tourist facilities, office buildings, and military installations." Workers were described as being denied the right to strike, while the peasantry's plight was made worse by the "massive terror campaign" launched by the "feudals and rich farmers." The July 1971 general elections were but a "farce," with the government intimidating and terrorizing any opposition. As for foreign policy:

> Though Indonesia is not a member of military alliances, it actually cooperates with the imperialist powers on military matters. Indonesian officers are trained in West Germany and the US, the Indonesian army is being equipped with American and Australian material, there have been joint naval exercises with Malaysia, the Philippines and Japan, American instructors—the Green Berets known for their atrocities in South Vietnam—train Indonesian officers in anti-guerrilla warfare. (Thomas Sinuraja, "Indonesian Communists Continue the Struggle," *WMR*, June 1972, pp. 20–22.)

The "military clique" in Indonesia, according to Sinuraja, will not yield power voluntarily. In accordance with the 1969 policy statement "Urgent Tasks of the Communist Movement in Indonesia," the government will only be overthrown if "indefatigable mass activity" and national unity of all "patriotic forces," are combined with "resolute and systematic preparations for armed struggle" to overthrow the "reactionary" government, thus bringing to power "a government of the national-democratic front with Communist participation." (Ibid., p. 22.)

Despite the call for a preparation for "armed struggle," the leadership of the "Committee Abroad" cautions against precipitate violent action which, it alleges, Indonesian Maoists are recommending:

> The Communists of Indonesia who lost many of their comrades and leaders during the white terror campaign, are working deep underground. At a time when the Party is still weak, the country's Maoists want to continue their adventurous policy, that is "to throw the remnants of the Party against the bayonets of the generals, although no revolutionary situation exists at present and, after their defeat, the revolutionary forces are in a state of despondency and disorganization." Indonesia's Marxist-Leninists declare, indeed, that the Communists' main task at this stage of the struggle is "to restore and unite an unencumbered and independently thinking Communist Party on the foundation of Marxism-Leninism, to revitalise its role of vanguard in our country, its role of fighter for national independence and socialism." ("Advancing under the Banner of Marxism-Leninism," *IB*, Prague, 1972, no. 4–5, p. 68.)

The "Committee Abroad" claims "always" to receive "manifestations of solidarity" not only from the Communist Party of the Soviet Union, but also from the Communist and Workers' parties of Bulgaria, Hungary, Poland, East Germany, Czechoslovakia, Mongolia, North Vietnam, France, Italy, the U.S.A., and other countries. It has, therefore, criticized a recent statement of the Communist Party of the Netherlands which said that the CPN had, in Europe, "remained in isolation" when it called for assistance in saving the lives of Indonesian communists who had been condemned to death by the Suharto government (ibid, no. 10–11, pp. 74–76). The plight of captured Indonesian communists and the political prisoners in Indonesia generally continues to be periodically highlighted in the pages of the media of the world's Moscow-oriented communist parties. A recent "letter from Indonesia" again called attention to the "physical tortures" as well as the "unbearable moral torture" to which political prisoners of the "reactionary military regime" of Suharto were said to be subject (Martopo, "Freedom for Patriots," *WMR,* March 1972, pp. 48–49). Attempts to polarize world opinion against the Suharto government by accentuating its incarceration of political prisoners continues to be a major PKI emigré tactic.

Domestic Developments. It is difficult to assess the validity of the ceaseless warnings about and allegations of underground communist activity in Indonesia by government, including military, spokesmen. President Suharto on 5 October 1972, Indonesia's "Armed Forces Day," warned that the remnants of the PKI, though "no longer" possessing "any meaningful physical strength," were nevertheless "continuing with their underground subversive activities," including spreading of false rumors and "instigating us against each other and other undermining activities" (Djakarta radio, domestic service in Indonesian, 5 October, 1315 GMT; Foreign Broadcast Information Service, 10 October). Eight months previously Suharto had issued a smiliar warning, declaring that underground communists were trying to make a comeback in the country (*Djakarta Times,* 23 February).

Throughout 1972 such various developments as unrest and rioting among Djakarta *betja* (pedicab) drivers, exploitation of gambling and prostitution, conflicts among ethnic and religious groups, a severe fire in Tandjong Priok harbor near Djakarta which cost the lives of 81, malversations in the use of public funds in a number of rural areas in Java, circulation of "subversive" pamphlets of foreign origin, and various instances of sabotage, including of railways, were all attributed by government officials to the communists, or else it was suggested that communists might be involved in them (Antara dispatches, Djakarta, 4 April and 30 May; Medan, 25 May; Semarang, 26 June; Ujungpandang, 18 October; Reuter's dispatch, Djakarta, May 29). Although even sympathizers of the Suharto government have questioned its use of "red scare" tactics, military spokesmen, like Central Java military commander Major General Widodo, have denied that there is an exaggerated "security orientedness" in Indonesia, pointing out that there is "sufficient proof of subversive activities," from railway sabotage to exploitation of Indonesian youths, to indicate that "the communist threat is in no way imaginary" (*Antara Daily News Bulletin,* vol. 24, no. 1543, 9 August).

The so-called "New Left" had taken the place of the banned communist party, according to Widodo, while the Indonesian foreign minister, Adam Malik, in October appealed to Indonesian students abroad to help Indonesia's foreign missions and diplomats to combat the "remnants" of the PKI and of the 1965 coup plotters who, he said, were continuing their subversion against the Indonesian government (Antara, Djakarta, 20 October). The periodic public burnings of "communist books" (as occurred for example in Djambi, South Sumatra, by the public prosecutor's office—ibid., vol. 25, no. 1588, 3 October) have further underscored an official demand for "special attention" to the elimination of the remaining members of the PKI, as outlined in the Indonesian National Defense Development Plan for the period 1974–78, as has President Suharto's characterization of the 1965 coup attempt as "the blackest page in our history of independence, inflicting very deep wounds in the body of the nation" (Antara, Djakarta, 4 October and 16). The long-term strategy of the "remnants" of the 1965 coup movement, according to North Sumatra military commander Brigadier General Yasir Hadibroto, includes arson and other forms of sabotage in order to force a rise in prices and to create maldistribution in the supply of basic commodities (*Antara Daily News Bulletin,* vol. 25, no. 1600, 17 October).

As in previous years, giving added depth to official expressions of concern over the domestic communist threat have been the trials of suspected participants or leaders of the 1965 coup attempt. On 22 September 1972, after a month long trial, a special military tribunal in Djakarta condemned to death former Air Force colonel and Air Force intelligence chief Sudijo for his involvement. He admitted that for a year before the coup attempt he had been in contact with the PKI, and confirmed that former Air Force staff chief Marshal Omar Dhani (already tried and convicted) had also been involved (Antara, Djakarta, 26 August and 22 September). Earlier in the year public attention was drawn to the trial of Pono, a principal leader of the PKI's Biro Chusus (Special Bureau) that had allegedly masterminded the 1965 rising. He testified that former party chairman D. N. Aidit himself had set the date for the coup attempt of 30 September 1965 (*Antara Daily News Bulletin,* vol. 24, no. 1375, 15 January). Meanwhile, the trial was proceeding of former Lieutenant Colonel Pratomo, former commander of the Pandeglang Military District, who admitted providing training to the communist "liberation army" during the PKI's "counter-government" at Blitar, East Java, in 1968 (*Api Pantjasila,* Djakarta, 20 July).

In view of the tight military control over these and similar trials in the past, there has been some public skepticism about the value of the evidence and testimony presented, as well as suspicion that the trials are less revealing of any real domestic communist threat and are more a tactic of the present Suharto government to stabilize its position.

On the other hand, in at least one area of the country, West Kalimantan (Borneo), adjacent to Sarawak, Indonesian government forces are confronted with a more open, if relatively small-scale, communist agitational activity backed by guerrilla insurgency. On 8 March 1972 an Indonesian Defense and Security Ministry spokesman declared that in the 1971–72 period, just ended, 41 "communist guerrilla troops" were killed in West Kalimantan, 43 had surrendered, and 7 had been captured by Indonesian forces (*Antara Daily News Bulletin,* vol. 24, no. 1416, 8 March). During most of 1972, however, there were few armed clashes with government forces, and underground communist dissidents appeared to be concentrating more on propaganda work and on preparations for future campaigns. On 1 February the Indonesian Army chief of staff General Umar Wirahadikusumah issued a new call to his forces to "destroy down to its roots" the Kalimantan rebel movement, and on 17 April the Antara news agency reported from Kuala Lumpur that Indonesia and Malaysia would step up "cooperation in suppressing Communists along the West Kalimantan–Eastern Malaysian border," a cooperation to be structured by a new joint "Committee on Border Affairs" headed by Indonesian Defense and Security Minister General Panggabean and Malaysian deputy premier Tun Ismail. On 22 July, after allegedly communist brochures calling on the populace to raise arms against the government had been discovered, more than "150 underground communists" were reportedly arrested in West Kalimantan, on orders of the Indonesian military commander of West Kalimantan province, Brigadier General Soemadi. A month later Soemadi revealed that those arrested had been particularly active near the towns of Sambas and Sekura and that among them were the "financiers" of the movement, who were identified as "residents of Chinese descent and holders of foreign passports" (*Antara Daily News Bulletin,* vol. 24, no. 1556, 25 August).

Soemadi's reference to Chinese "financiers" underscored the predominantly Chinese character of the entire West Kalimantan communist movement, similar to the Chinese complexion of the Paraku–PGRS movement in neighboring Sarawak (see *Malaysia*), with which the West Kalimantan insurgents and the PKI underground activists are believed to be allied. On 25 April Soemadi reported that 20 West Kalimantan Chinese had been arrested "on charges of collaborating with communist rebels in Sarawak, Eastern Malaysia." The arrested Chinese were said to have attempted to help Sarawak Chinese communists enter West Kalimantan (ibid., no. 1456, 25 April). Two months later, two Chinese girl students of secondary schools in Pontianak, West Kalimantan, were arrested for "spreading anti-government pamphlets" and for hoisting PKI flags (Antara, Pontianak, 3 June). The relative porousness of the jungly Sarawak–West Kalimantan border has facilitated continuous movement and interaction between dissident and/or communist Chinese on both sides of the frontier, and on 11 July Soemadi announced that the areas of Indonesian West Kalimantan bordering Sarawak's First, Second, and Third Divisions would henceforth be "closed" to all non-Indonesian Chinese intending to settle there. The decision was taken to check the infiltration of Chinese immigrants who are not Indonesian citizens or whose nationality is "doubtful" and who, on the basis of evidence, might be linked to Paraku or the PGRS (*Sarawak Tribune,* Kuching, 28 July). On the other hand, West Kalimantan Chinese who are known to be loyal to or who have collaborated with the Indonesian government have, according to an earlier statement of Soemadi, been the target of underground communist terrorist killers. (Antara, Pontianak, 31 December 1971).

Indonesian authorities appear to be aware of the need of socially integrating the troubled Chinese community of West Kalimantan in an effort to undercut communist appeals among them. On 2 May, on the occasion of handing over a check for 10 million rupiahs for the development of Pontianak University, Soemadi said that the "consolidation process" of security in West Kalimantan would continue and he noted that a total of 600 persons had died "as a result of operations against communists" (since what date was not disclosed) (*Antara Daily News Bulletin,* vol. 24, no. 1460, 2 May).

Despite stepped-up joint Malaysian-Indonesian anti-insurgent operations and the continuing arrests of communist suspects in West Kalimantan there is no indication that either Paraku–PGRS operations have diminished (see *Malaysia*), or that the interaction of these operations with Chinese dissidents in West Kalimantan, also in conjunction with the PKI underground of the area, is noticeably declining. Army staff chief Umar Wirahadikusumah asserted at the close of July 1972 that the border terrorists were "keeping in touch" with PKI "remnants" as the latter were attempting to "reactivate" the party (Bernama dispatch, Djakarta, 27 July).

It does not appear that the insurgent groups in West Kalimantan have an organization of their own, distinct from the PKI underground or the Paraku–PGRS organizations. During 1971 there were no major ambushes of, or attacks on, Indonesian government patrols or security posts (unlike developments in Sarawak), although there were occasional skirmishes and exchanges of rifle fire (and a few casualties) with fast-retreating bands of insurgents at the Sarawak border, according to Indonesian Army intelligence. Spreading propaganda leaflets; holding covert anti-government meetings, especially among younger Chinese; stashing supplies of weapons (a number of arms and supplies caches were discovered at the border during a joint Malaysian-Indonesian patrol activity in early October—*Antara Daily News Bulletin,* vol. 25, no. 1595, 11 October), presumably in preparation for more sustained and regular attacks later on: these have been the principal concerns of the border communists in West Kalimantan during the year.

International Implications. Although, from time to time, Indonesian government spokesmen have mooted the desirability of reviving Sino-Indonesian diplomatic relations (suspended though not formally broken since 1967), such spokesmen throughout 1972 continued to stress that Peking is not only actively aiding anti-Suharto PKI remnants abroad, but is generally promoting internal subversion in Indonesia itself. "China has to stop helping subversive activities launched by Communist remnants or Overseas Chinese and stop launching negative issues through the press and radio propagated by Indonesian Communists living in exile in Peking,"

Indonesian foreign minister Adam Malik reportedly declared in mid-September (*Antara Daily News Bulletin,* vol. 24, no. 1571, 13 September). Earlier, on 16 April; in an address to the Foreign Correspondents Association of Singapore, Malik charged that China was continuing to interfere in Indonesia's internal affairs, and that until it stopped supporting communist insurgents in the country a dialogue was impossible (*Far Eastern Economic Review,* 22 April, p. 4; *Free China Weekly,* 30 April, p. 3).

One of the aims of the agreement reached between Malaysia and Indonesia at the close of September 1972 on joint sea patrols in the South China Sea was to stop the supply of weapons coming "mainly from China" (according to Indonesian and Malaysian military officials to the Kalimantan communist insurgents (*Angkatan Bersendjata,* Djakarta, 28 September). On 7 June, the Antara news agency reported from Medan, North Sumatra, that Indonesian officials had seized 250 bales of books and magazines from China. The Chinese publications had been inserted into English and French publications in an effort to smuggle them into Indonesia. Meanwhile Peking media continue to excoriate what are termed the "reactionary Malaysian and Indonesian troops and police" and their "cruel means in their frantic attempts" to break up the "close links" between the Dayaks of Kalimantan and the "people's armed forces" at the Indonesia-Sarawak border areas (*Peking Review,* 17 March, p. 17).

Despite allegations by Indonesian government spokesmen, the exact extent of Chinese Communist aid today to West Kalimantan insurgents or to the PKI underground generally is not known.

Relatively, the Indonesian government has been less vocal in its suspicion of any Soviet support for the Indonesian communists, although the Russian Embassy in Djakarta has been accused of supplying Soviet propaganda films to communist agents in the country (*Antara Daily News Bulletin,* vol. 24, no. 1553, 22 August). In March and April 1972, Soviet Aeroflot planes landed at Kemajoran airport near Djakarta with cargoes of foodstuffs and medicines for the political prisoners on Buru Island. The Indonesian Red Cross, to which the goods were addressed, claimed to be unaware of the sending, and the whole incident was interpreted in Indonesian press circles as a Soviet ploy to embarrass Indonesia (*Angkatan Bersendjata,* Djakarta, 28 April). Soviet comment on the incident began by referring to recently published Soviet party May Day slogans and went on to identify the Soviet people with the "Indonesian democrats" (George Avrin, commentary over Moscow radio, in Indonesian, to Indonesia, 20 April, 1972, 1130 GMT; Foreign Broadcast Information Service 25 April):

> One of the May Day slogans says: Fraternal greetings to the brave fighters in the struggle against imperialist and colonial slavery and for the freedom of nations and socialism and to those fighters suffering in fascist jails and torture chambers. Freedom to the prisoners of capital!
>
> Our Indonesian radio listeners are aware that the slogan reflects the thoughts and feelings of all the Soviet people who have always come forward to support their brothers of the same class in all capitalist countries including the Indonesian patriots.
>
> The press has published statements of the Central Executive Council of the AUCCTU, Committee of Soviet Women, Committee of Youth Organizations of the USSR and the Soviet Committee for Solidarity with Asian and African Countries, expressing solidarity with the Indonesian people's struggle. The statements emphasize that the persecution of Indonesian national democratic forces, first of all, harmed national interests and weakened Indonesia in its struggle against new imperialist attacks, designed to liquidate the people's democratic achievements. Soviet organizations have asked Indonesian authorities to release from jails and concentration camps all workers, farmers, and representatives of the intelligentsia who have been persecuted merely for their progressive views. . . .
>
>   A number of Aeroflot planes have arrived in Djakarta with large shipments of vitamin-rich food, clothing, and medical supplies from the Soviet Union. In this way, the Soviet people have

shown with concrete steps their solidarity with the Indonesian democrats. This solidarity is of great importance. It has revived the spirit and confidence in the Indonesian people.

Publications. The PKI underground in Java issues an irregularly appearing publication, *Mimbar Rakjat* ("People's Forum"), but no issues appeared during 1972. Some underground pamphlets circulating in West Kalimantan were named *Front Pembangunan* ("Development Front"). The principal media of the Mao-oriented "Delegation of the Central Committee of the PKI" are the bimonthly *Indonesian Tribune* and the quarterly *API* (*Api Pemuda Indonesia*—"Flames of Indonesian Youth"), both published in Tirana. The "Delegation" front group, the "Indonesian organization for Afro-Asian Solidarity," has its own irregularly appearing publication, *Suara Rakjat Indonesia* ("Voice of the Indonesian People"). The Moscow-based "Committee Abroad of the Communist Party of Indonesia" now appears to rely chiefly on the Prague-published *World Marxist Review* and *Information Bulletin,* although it has its own irregularly appearing Indonesian-language organ, *Tekad Rakjat* ("The People's Will"). The Moscow group's youth publication *O.P.I.* had only one issue in 1972.

Peking radio, the new China News Agency, and *Peking Review* frequently carry the statements of Jusuf Adjitorop and of the "Delegation of the Central Committee of the PKI." During 1972 Moscow radio, not even in its regular Indonesian-language broadcasts, did not carry statements of the "Committee Abroad of the Communist Party of Indonesia," though pronouncements by the "Committee's" secretary, Tomas Sinuraja, are frequently publicized by the Soviet press and by Soviet-oriented party media around the world.

University of Bridgeport   Justus M. van der Kroef

Japan

The Japan Communist Party (Nihon Kyosanto; JCP) commemorated the fiftieth anniversary of its founding with ceremonies in Tokyo and other cities during July 1972. In December the JCP reached an all-time high in parliamentary representation by electing 38 candidates to the 491-member House of Representatives. Although the party did not achieve the goals of membership and circulation for the party newspaper which had been hoped for, the 300,000 members represented a new record, as did the 500,000 daily and 1,900,000 Sunday circulation for *Akahata* (Red Flag), the party organ. The JCP's rise is remarkable, especially in view of the fact that it has been able to operate legally only since the war and that from 1950 to 1955 it lost most of its leaders—to purges, the underground, defection, and electoral defeat. JCP representation in the national parliament, which was 35 in 1949, was wiped out in 1952, and party membership dropped from 150,000 in 1949 to 40,000 in 1958.

Today the JCP follows the Italian Communist Party as the next largest non-ruling communist party in the world. The population of Japan is approximately 105,000,000.

Besides the 38 seats in the House of Representatives that the JCP won in the 10 December elections, the addition of two other successful candidates—one who ran on a "Reformist Coalition" ticket and the other a member of the Okinawa Peoples Party—brought the total representation claimed by the JCP to 40 seats. This was well above the 1949 peak, when the party elected 35 candidates, and for the first time in history gained third position in the lower house, after the Liberal Democratic Party (LDP) and Japan Socialist Party (JSP), as well as the right to introduce legislation. Since the JCP already controlled 10 seats in the upper house (House of Councillors) as a result of elections in 1971, the total Diet representation of the party mounted to 50, the greatest parliamentary strength achieved by the JCP in its fifty years of existence.

Off-year elections for local assemblies had already brought enough gains for the JCP to become the third party in number of seats held in local assemblies: 2,545 as against 2,501 in the 1971 local elections.

Leadership and Organization. In 1972 there were no important changes in JCP leadership. Miyamoto Kenji continued to be the undisputed leader and, although, as we shall see, there was some dissension among certain elements of the party, especially the youth, over policies followed by Miyamoto, he showed his ability to overcome opposition and to assert strong control. Fuwa Tetsuzo, youthful (42) chief of the Central Committee Secretariat, became ever more prominent as a party spokesman and when significant and authoritative statements of policy were made or published, he was usually the author.

In October minor changes were announced in the Secretariat, the addition of four persons, "in order to consolidate the party structure in preparation for the coming general elections."

Miyamoto is chairman of the 7-member Standing Committee of the Presidium. Nosaka Sanzo, one of the party founders and now 81, continues to hold the largely titular honor of chairman of the 156-man Central Committee and appears prominently at the most important party functions. (For other leaders see *YICA, 1972,* p. 516.)

Party Organizations and Front Organizations.   *The Youth Movement.* The Democratic Youth League (Minseido), has existed under one name or another since shortly after the founding of the JCP in 1922. Traditionally Minseido was tightly controlled by the party, the relationship being regarded as that of a parent and child. Recently problems have arisen to plague the organization, and for a time the authority of the JCP was threatened.

The Twelfth Congress of Minseido, first scheduled for November 1971, was postponed three times and only finally held on 27–29 September 1972. The principal reason for the consecutive delays was a growing group of dissenters within the League which finally embraced a third of the members of its Central Committee. The issue was what the JCP called "new opportunism,"—a dissatisfaction with the Miyamoto parliamentary line, accompanied by demands for action instead of protest. The dissenters complained that there was "no passion" in the JCP; they called for a "dynamic struggle" and criticized the JCP for paying so much attention to party expansion that it neglected fighting against aggression, against the Okinawan reversion treaty, and was diluting the "vanguard spirit of the party" with "proletarian humanism." They noted that Lenin's admonishment to study had been made *after* the revolution whereas Japan was now in a period *before* revolution. In this case, struggle was more important than study. The "new opportunists" criticized the party for paying too little attention to the dangers of a revival of Japanese militarism and rejected JCP statements that militarism could not be revived so long as the "peace" constitution remained in effect and no conscription existed.

Over a period of many months, party officials concentrated on the problem of ridding Minseido of its "anti-Miyamoto group." Numerous articles appeared in *Akahata,* including three major ones: "Characteristics of the New Opportunism" (19–20 June), "Okinawa Struggle and the New Opportunism" (28–30 June), and "The New Opportunism and the Theory of Japanese Militarism as the Major Enemy" (3 August). Party spokesmen reacted aggressively to criticisms of JCP policy, which were denounced as "foreign-inspired." Little doubt was left that the offending "foreign power" was China.

The anti-JCP elements obviously thought during the first half of 1972 that they had a good chance to dominate Minseido, profiting from general dissatisfaction over the highhanded attitude of the party toward the youth group and also from the December 1971 decision of the Central Committee's Sixth Plenum that the age limit of members would be lowered. Of the 108 members of Minseido's Central Committee, 90 were over 30 years of age and would be retired from the organization. Their discontent was expected to support the new opportunists. All in all, many members sensed a contradiction between the "smiling image" propagated by the Miyamoto line and the iron discipline imposed on the organization by the parent JCP.

By September the party had obviously succeeded in bringing the dissidents into line and the Twelfth Congress could finally be safely held, without fear of disruption. The most meticulous care and advance planning were utilized to guarantee that the congress went off without a hitch and without the change of a line in the predetermined program. The guilty were dealt with in different ways; some confessed their sins after reflection and were duly reinstated. Others were punished in varying degrees.

The congress decided to limit membership henceforth to persons between the ages of 15 and 25 years. Minseido probably has about 170,000 members, although the number was announced at the time of the congress as 200,000. The makeup of the organization was as follows: workers, 70 percent; university students, 20 percent; high school students, 10 percent.

The JCP-affiliated National Federation of Students Self-Government Associations (Zengakuren) held its Twenty-third Congress in Nagano on 26–30 July with an attendance of 2,500. The JCP maintained the strictest discipline throughout, permitting no questioning of the agreed agenda and no controversy. Such measures were apparently necessary to prevent any manifestations of the "new opportunism" from disrupting the proceedings. Zengakuren has had as many as 335 self-governing associations in 169 universities, but expansion has recently been at a standstill, particularly in the large private universities.

Worldwide attention was drawn to the series of brutal killings perpetrated during the early months of the year by the United Red Army (Rengo Sekigun) terrorist youth group, and again to the mass murders committed in the Tel Aviv airport on 30 May by members of the same faction, acting in concert with the Palestine Liberation Front. The JCP immediately denounced the "savage, criminal acts" of this terrorist faction, connecting it directly with the ideology of "violent revolution" perpetrated by Mao Tse-tung. Describing the activities of the United Red Army as "popular war, Chinese style," *Akahata* in a running series of articles during February and March—and continuing throughout the year—denounced the terrorists as Trotskyites and "blind groveling followers of Mao Tse-tung" who "should be eradicated without a trace." To prove the point, the newspaper cited articles in the Peking *People's Daily,* quoted Mao and Chou En-lai at length, and published an article by an officer in the pro-JCP Japan-China Friendship Association (*Akahata,* 22 February, 2 May). In early March, the *Yomiuri* newspaper, in discussing the incidents associated with the United Red Army, referred to the mysterious, as yet unexplained "lynching incident" of 1933, implicating Miyamoto himself in the torture and death of a communist party member. Not unexpectedly, *Akahata* rose to Miyamoto's defense, explaining the incident in several articles, but in greatest detail in a three-quarters page spread headlined: "Record of Truth and Justice." Miyamoto's defense was that one of two spies discovered in the party's Central Committee had suddenly died of shock during questioning because of an inherent physical condition and in spite of every effort at resuscitation. Miyamoto was imprisoned for the crime but exonerated after the war ended. The 1933 case was a notorious one and took place in a period when communist violence was not uncommon (see George M. Beckman and Okubo Genji, *The Japanese Communist Party 1922–1945,* Stanford, Calif., 1969, p. 244; John K. Emmerson, "The Japanese Communist Party after Fifty Years," *Asian Survey,* July 1972, p. 572).

Peace Movement. The JCP-sponsored Japan Council against Atomic and Hydrogen Bombs (Gensuikyo) held its annual meetings in Tokyo, Hiroshima, Nagasaki, and Okinawa between 5 and 16 August. The principal assembly, the "Eighteenth World Anti-Bomb Rally," 5–7 August in Tokyo, drew 5,600 persons.

In previous years North Korea had been willing to send representatives only to those "anti-bomb" or "peace" meetings conducted by the JCP-affiliated Gensuikyo. Since the Japanese government consistently refused visas to North Korean delegates, the representation was carried out by the pro-JCP Korean organization in Japan, Chosen Soren. This year, however, North Korea announced that it would send delegates to the meetings of both Gensuikyo and the JSP-affiliated People's Council against Atomic and Hydrogen Bombs (Gensuikin). The JCP had never before accepted representatives from any source participating in the meetings of the rival JSP movement. This time the JCP did not wish to worsen relations with North Korea and did not rule out dual attendance, but apparently made efforts to get North Korea to refrain from sending delegates to JSP events. North Korea then announced that it would not send delegates to either and, when the government refused visas as usual, that Chosen Soren would not this year be permitted to represent North Korea.

Attention in Gensuikyo speeches was more on stopping U.S. "imperialist aggression" in

Indochina than on banning nuclear weapons or memorializing the victims of the bombing at Hiroshima and Nagasaki. There were also the expected calls to rid Japan of the security treaty with the United States and of U.S. military bases (*Koan Joho* [Public Safety Report], August, monthly magazine published by Social Problems Research Institute, Tokyo, and utilizing material from government security agencies.)

Quarrels between the JCP and the JSP caused the formation of separate peace organizations in 1964. Apart from the original differences, conflicting evaluations of the present situation in Asia have deepened the rift. The JSP welcomed U.S. President Nixon's visit to China and the meetings between representatives of North and South Korea as signs of diminishing tension. The JCP furiously attacked the "beautification of Nixon" and took a cool attitude toward North-South rapprochement in Korea.

Gensuikin, which is sponsored by the Japan General Council of Trade Unions (Sohyo) as well as the JSP, held what was called its Twenty-seventh Congress, opening on 12 July with an attendance of 6,500. A third organization, the People's Congress to Ban Nuclear Weapons and Establish Peace (Kakukin) is sponsored by the Democratic Socialist Party (DSP). Its "Conference of Representatives" drew an attendance of 480. Several ultra-radical groups sponsored meetings in Hiroshima and Nagasaki on 6 and 9 August respectively.

Labor. The JCP's Eleventh Congress, in 1970, laid down a labor program of "flexibility in principle" and the party has, as a result, tried alternating "hard" and "soft" policies. Behind the "smiling strategy" (cooperation with companies and championing freedom of workers to support the party of individual choice) was a strong "struggle strategy" which became especially evident in 1972 at the time of the annual "spring struggles" to increase wages, and often took the form of strikes and demonstrations. The JCP has put great energy into extending its influence into the labor unions, by getting more party members in the unions and electing JCP members to positions as union officials. Condemning control of unions by political parties, the JCP has tried to influence workers, under its leadership, to further a united front, and for this reason has propagated the idea of "freedom of party choice" for union members. The strategy is obviously directed at Sohyo, traditionally under JSP influence, and the Japan United Congress of Labor (Domei Kaigi), affiliated with the DSP.

Organized activity to expand JCP influence within the trade unions has been accelerated during the past two years. It has been helped further by decisions taken at the Central Committee plenum in December 1971 to ease entry into the party.

Not surprisingly, this aggressive campaign has aroused some angry reactions. JCP supporters found themselves outvoted at Sohyo's Forty-fourth Congress, which met in Tokyo 7–11 August. The JCP organized its own group of members at the congress to push party positions and met with determined opposition from the JSP. While the "freedom of choice" policy found some support, criticism of the JCP spread throughout the congress, with disagreement surfacing on many issues. The JCP group refused to compromise and presented their own resolution which received only a few votes and was then erased from the record.

Other Fronts. The General Federation of Korean Residents in Japan (Chosen Soren) functions under the aegis of the Korean Workers' Party, the ruling party of the Democratic People's Republic of Korea (DPRK). Chosen Soren claims to represent the majority of Koreans resident in Japan and has 26 affiliated associations and business organizations with a combined membership of 280,000. The members of Chosen Soren alone total some 85,000. (*Sayoku Hyaku Shudan* [One Hundred Organizations of the Left], Shiso-Undo Kenkyu-Jo [Thought Movement Research Institute], Tokyo, 1972, pp. 228–29.)

In early 1972 Chosen Soren conducted a "150 Days Campaign" which began November 1971 and was to culminate in a great celebration of Kim Il-song's 60th birthday on 15 April.

The objective was to tighten ties with the DPRK and at the same time aid those revolutionary elements in South Korea who might promote the North Korean line for unification of North and South. Also "birthday" gifts of machinery for the economic development of North Korea were to be provided. (*Koan Joho,* May.)

The joint communiqué issued 4 July after meetings between representatives of North and South Korea, announcing agreement on further talks to lead eventually to unification, was immediately acclaimed by Chosen Soren as epoch making and as a "victory of Kim Il-song's thought." The organization embarked at once on a nationwide campaign to influence Japanese opinion favorably toward the communiqué. Mass meetings were held in 43 cities and towns throughout Japan; the rally in Kyoto drew a crowd of 13,000.

Because of the recent significant changes in the relations between the United States and China, Japan and China, and the two Koreas, Chosen Soren is expected to emphasize ideology less and realistic politics more. As Japanese interest in trade with North Korea mounts, Chosen Soren will be ready to facilitate the process; it has the necessary contacts. (Ibid., August.)

The marked difference in the attitudes taken by the JCP and Chosen Soren toward the Korean joint communiqué suggests a cooling of relations between the two. The JCP (*Akahata,* 5 August) stated that socialist countries should not unconditionally support the communiqué. The argument is that the Korean question cannot be evaluated without considering that South Korea and its "imperialist" backer, the United States, make any agreement between the two sides totally unrealistic.

Party Internal Affairs. In 1972 the JCP Central Committee met in July, September, and December. The Seventh Plenum, 5–6 July, concentrated on party expansion, the position and tasks of the party in the new international situation, and the elections for the House of Representatives which were likely to be held before the end of the year. Miyamoto Kenji exhorted the members to greater efforts to strengthen and expand the party, not only by the date of the fiftieth anniversary on 15 July but throughout the year.

The plenum adopted a new party emblem and a flag, both proposed by Nosaka Sanzo—a step in harmony with the desire to change the party's image to one with broader appeal and less frightening connotations. Although no proposal seems to have yet been made to change the name of the party organ *Akahata* ("Red Flag"), no longer will the JCP flag be called *Akahata,* but rather the "party flag." Superimposed upon the red flag will be the party emblem, a blue cogwheel out of which a golden stalk of rice protrudes, symbolizing the union of workers and farmers.

The Eighth Plenum, 11–12 September, was primarily concerned with the elections, discussing in particular the character of the Tanaka cabinet, the significant and contradictory forces of the forthcoming elections, the basic policy of the JCP, and the consolidation of a revolutionist united front. Miyamoto closed the meeting with the comment: "Just now it is important to give priority to expansion through the general elections and to push, without ceasing and in coordination, the tasks of mass movement and party buildup to achieve victory in them." (*Akahata,* 13 September.)

The Ninth Plenum, 20–21 December, met to review the party's new parliamentary status as a result of the 10 December elections and published a resolution calling for unremitting zeal to further the party's expansion, looking toward the Twelfth Congress in 1973 and the upper house elections in 1974. (*Akahata,* 24 December.)

Party Policy. The JCP has energetically pursued its policy of seeking power through parliamentary means, of eschewing violence and any image of violence, and of proclaiming its objective to be the establishment of a democratic coalition government. To this end the party has instituted vigorous membership campaigns and tried to attract voters through platforms with grassroots appeal. The remarkable showing made by the JCP in the House of Representatives elections of 10 December testified to the success of the policy.

While continuing to quarrel with its erstwhile benefactors, the communist parties of the Soviet Union and China, the JCP has focused upon international issues that find a popular response in Japan and, what is more important, has posed as the party most genuinely interested in the welfare and well-being of the average citizen. Japanese voters, like those in many other countries, habitually choose candidates on their stands on the day-to-day problems which concern the rank and file, not on great foreign policy questions.

During the year the JCP faced much criticism from within the party—especially from the youth organization (see above for Minseido's problems) and from elements in the labor movement—directed upon the extraordinary emphasis given to party expansion and to the lack of zeal in condemning the revival of Japanese militarism. The intensive campaign to rid the party of this "new opportunism" and its success in Minseido, the élan of the celebrations of the fiftieth anniversary, and, finally and most importantly, the resounding victory in the general elections have probably suppressed, at least temporarily, the proponents of the "new opportunism." Certainly the elections instilled confidence in the party leadership and must have made the goal of a democratic coalition government seem nearer than ever expected.

Fiftieth Anniversary. Celebration of the fiftieth anniversary of the founding of the JCP on 15 July was to be the high point of 1972, and much of the party's activity during the first half of the year was directed to this event. The occasion was to be used to break out of the stagnation into which the party had fallen, inspire and accomplish the expansion of membership long planned, and to stop the internal disturbances which had brought disaffection and dissatisfaction, particularly in the party's youth and mass organizations. The leadership may also have had in mind trying to destroy the unfortunate image of "independent isolation" in the international environment and to capture broader political support, with the forthcoming general elections in mind.

These objectives were partly achieved. The membership reached 300,000 instead of the 400,000 specified as a goal. The "new opportunists" in Minseido were brought under control by September, and, since the party's international position has not in fact changed, it seems questionable that a substantial change can have been achieved in the image of "independent isolation." Still, the elaborate and spectacular anniversary festivities, in Tokyo, together with the new party history and the special editions of the party magazine *Zenei* and numerous other publications, must have carried the JCP message to a wide audience.

The Tokyo events began with a youth assembly on 13 July, attended by 5,000 persons. Given the normal mobilizing power of Minseido (which should have been able to muster 10,000) this turnout could not be termed a success (*Koan Joho,* July). Two meetings were held on the anniversary day, 15 July, one in the afternoon attended by 2,200 and an "invitation only" special meeting in the evening. Those invited to the latter included foreign delegates to the Conference on Theory (see below); the ambassadors of the Soviet Union, Yugoslavia, Poland, Bulgaria, Czechoslovakia, Hungary, Rumania, Cuba, Algeria, Egypt, and Nigeria; a representative of Chosen Soren; the governor of Tokyo; representatives of the JSP, labor unions; and journalists. On 18 July a commemoration assembly was held in the presence of 2,800 persons, mostly central and local party leaders and representatives of JCP-affiliated organizations. The governors of cities and prefectures elected with JCP support (Tokyo, Osaka, and Kyoto, and Saitama Prefecture) and the foreign representatives attending the Conference on Theory were present. Nosaka Sanzo, Miyamoto Kenji, and the four governors addressed the meeting and, according to reports, stressed a "democratic coalition government as a bright goal" (ibid.). The final celebration was held on 29 July with a cultural evening of music, dance, and poetry at which JCP candidates for Tokyo districts in the forthcoming elections were introduced.

Celebrations were also held in the prefectures, and in North Vietnam and North Korea where meetings in Hanoi and Pyongyang took place on 14 July under ruling-party auspices.

Domestic Attitudes and Activities. *United Front.* It was announced early in 1972 that the JSP and JCP would not join to support the same candidates in the expected general elections. After the spectacular communist victory and the considerable Socialist advance in the December elections, responsible officials of both parites announced that their future strategies would include great emphasis on close JSP-JCP collaboration. During the months preceding the election, a united front of these two parties had been more conspicuous for failure than success. Except for "one-day struggles" in which they cooperated, the parties engaged in a series of bitter exchanges over national issues. The JCP, fully conscious of its newly found Diet strength, may decide in 1973 that cooperation with the JSP in the business of the House of Representatives can be so productive that inter-party squabbles should be at least temporarily suppressed. The JSP, on the other hand, may not be able quickly to rid itself of the deep-seated "communist phobia" which it has traditionally harbored and which may now take the form of an even greater fear of a threatening JCP.

As usual, the JCP and JSP managed to stage several "joint one-day struggles" during the year, on the occasions of "Okinawa Day" (28 April), the day of the reversion of Okinawa to Japan (15 May), "Anti-Security Treaty Day" (23 June), and "International Anti-War Day" (21 October). For a time it appeared that the annual "Okinawa Day" joint protest demonstration would not be carried out. Sohyo determined on 18 April that the rally could not be held because of a general strike which was to be in effect on both 27 and 28 April. However, the JCP succeeded in arranging a joint demonstration of 12 organizations which in the end included the JSP, labor, peace, and "people's" fronts. Because of the concurrent strike no mass meeting was held in Tokyo, but a demonstration took place in front of Shibuya Station, and rallies were held in 12 prefectures. The protest meetings on 15 May called attention to the opposition by the "reformists" to the Okinawa reversion treaty as signed: the rally in Tokyo brought out an estimated 50,000 while meetings in 25 prefectures were said to draw crowds totaling more than a million for the entire country.

JCP-JSP disputes arose principally over the antecedents of the radical-terrorist United Red Army and the divergence in world view held by the two parties. The JCP charged that in 1968 and 1970 prominent members of the JSP made statements which tended to foster the growth of the terrorist group (*Akahata,* 24 March), and also mentioned the Japan-China Friendship Association (Orthodox), to which several JSP members belong, as being subservient to Mao Tse-tung "in the same way as the United Red Army faction" (*Mainichi,* Tokyo, 19 April). The JSP replied in its party organ (*Shakai Shimpo,* 2 April) by counterattacking the JCP as the origin of all New Left groups and claiming that all such radicals had belonged to it in the past. The quarrel over an evaluation of the international situation continued intermittently from February through August, the JSP having welcomed U.S. President Nixon's visit to Peking as proof of the "failure of American imperialism" and as having contributed to a lowering of tension in the area. The JCP sprang to the attack, denying that tensions had been decreased and laying out all the arguments about the "beautification of Nixon" and the "deceitful, conspiratorial splitting techniques of American imperialism."

In the fall when protests arose over the repair of U.S. military vehicles for shipment to

Vietnam and access roads to repair shops were blocked, the lukewarm cooperation between the JSP and JCP illustrated the difficulty in forming an effective united front. The JSP organ reported that while JSP representatives sat on the street to bar passage of the vehicles, JCP people watched from the sidelines. "They will go into action only when the police abandon the use of force. What kind of battle is that?" (*Shakai Shimpo,* 3 August.) The JCP retorted: "When the JSP would not join hands with the democratic forces and fight together with us, the united front broke down on the spot" (*Akahata,* 21 August). Some observers remarked that if the JSP and JCP could not truly cooperate on a made-to-order issue like this, one could scarcely imagine a long-term, solid united front.

Elections. As noted before, the JCP's unprecedented success in the elections of 10 December 1972 brought it 38 seats in the House of Representatives and the election of two supporters increased the JCP seat count to 40. Having captured more than 20 seats, the party now possesses the coveted right to introduce legislation in the Diet. Because the two middle-of-the-road parties, the Komeito and the Democratic Socialists, suffered major setbacks (from 47 to 29 and from 31 ro 19 seats respectively), the JCP took its place in the newly constituted House of Representatives as the third party (after the LDP and the JSP).

In the total popular vote, which was more than two million beyond that of 1969, the JCP garnered 10.88 percent (5.7 million votes); the LDP, 46.85 percent; and the JSP, 21.90 percent (11.5 million votes). While more than half of its successful candidates came from urban areas (22 from Tokyo, Osaka, Kyoto, and Kanagawa Prefecture, the capital of which is Yokohama), the JCP also did well in the countryside, electing candidates from 13 prefectures and bringing, with the two "reformist" representatives, its nationwide representation to 19 out of 47 prefectures. (*Akahata,* 12 December.) The average age of the successful JCP candidates was 50.7 years (55.5 for the candidates as a whole); half were in their 40's and one was 36. As for professional background, party specialists, lawyers, and "intellectuals" of local reputation made up much of the JCP contingent—in contrast with the LDP and JSP, which are heavily represented by bureaucrats and labor union officials respectively. Sixty percent of the newly elected representatives were university graduates; of LDP members, the percentage with some kind of higher education was 87; the JCP followed with 76 percent, or 29 out of its 38 candidates. ("The Election in Graphs," Part 2, *Asahi,* 13 December.)

In an analysis of the origins of the large JCP vote, the Tokyo *Asahi* newspaper concluded that only 57 percent of the vote came from JCP members or consistent party supporters; of the rest, 26 percent was thought to come from a "floating vote" of those without direct party affiliation and 16 percent from supporters of other parties ("The Election in Graphs," Part 3, ibid., 14 December). One high-ranking government official was quoted as saying: "In many families, the husband votes LDP but his wife votes JCP." Fuwa Tetsuzo of the JCP Secretariat was supposed to have stated: "I won because of LDP votes!" ("The Change in the Opposition Parties," Part III, ibid., 14 December.)

The secret of JCP success was probably a combination of the vote-pulling power of the "soft" and "independent" party line, the extraordinary organizational strength of the party, the power base established in local assemblies, and the reputation for achievement on the local level. Party officials contrast the situation now and in 1949 when the JCP captured 35 seats in the elections that year. In 1949 the JCP had only 3 seats in prefectural assemblies and 400 in city, town, and village bodies; in 1972 the JCP held a total of 2,545 seats in all local parliamentary bodies. Principally because of the strong local base, some observers predict continued expansion for the JCP, unless the LDP, the JSP, or both, should considerably improve in drawing power at the polls.

Much more direct confrontation between the JCP and the LDP is expected within the Diet in the future. Whether the relationship between the JCP and JSP will be characterized more by competition than by cooperation remains to be seen. With the great diminution of strength of the Komeito and the DSP, the only possibility of an effective united opposition lies with the JCP and JSP, but the mistrust and "communist-phobia" of the latter is still so great that close and effective cooperation may well be hampered.

International Views and Policies. *International Conference on Theory.* Although the JCP invited communist parties of 11 countries to participate in its Conference on Theory, 9–11 July 1972, only six parties sent representatives: those of Great Britain, Spain, Italy, France, Australia, and East Germany. Since the government did not ban the entry of any delegation, the small attendance was presumably due to the party's "independent" line, which has alienated it internationally. In a 30 June press interview, Miyamoto stated that the purpose of the conference was to "exchange reports on the outstanding features of the situation and party struggles in the advanced capitalist countries, and to learn from each other through exchanges of experience." The party probably wanted to use the conference to prove publicly that independence did not mean international isolation, to propagate an "international mood" among its members, and to solidify the changes in theory brought about by the new Miyamoto line, such as "a party system with more than one party." (*Josei Shiryo* ["Documents on the Situation"], Tokyo, 5 August.)

Among the subjects considered at the Conference on Theory were the tactics of a united front in revolutionary actions in capitalist countries and experiences in the use of constitutions and parliaments. The conference also addressed itself to the problem of opposition parties in a socialist system; structural reform; the prospects of "peaceful revolution," with emphasis on the changes in the international situation since Lenin's time; how to encourage the emergence of a socialist society out of the democracy of a capitalist society; and the translation in various languages of the term "dictatorship of the proletariat."

The JCP strove during the year to work itself out of the stigma of "international isolation" which its quarrels with the Chinese and Soviet communist parties had brought upon it. By trying to cultivate relations with parties in other advanced capitalist countries, such as Italy and France, and with parties not closely affiliated with either Peking or Moscow, the JCP sought to counteract the injurious comparisons made between it and other Japanese opposition parties enjoying Chinese and Russian favors. Miyamoto's last-minute decision to approve Premier Tanaka's official visit to Peking testified to the intensity of public pressure on the China question, since to hold out against the trip would have seriously damaged the JCP's image and confirmed its international isolation.

The world view of the JCP, particularly in its Asian aspects, was radically different from that held by the Socialist and other Japanese opposition parties. Refusing to join the chorus of approbation for the "relaxation of tension" supposed to have been brought about in Asia both by the Nixon and Tanaka pilgrimages to Peking and by the seeming rapprochement between North and South Korea, the JCP denounced the Chinese for the "beautification of Nixon," continued to harp on "U.S. imperialism" and its translation into the Vietnam war, and reminded readers of *Akahata* continually that the bombing of Vietnam belied all talk of relaxed tensions. The talks between North and South Korea were regarded as meaningless so long as the South was tied to the United States and had American troops on its soil. As for the Soviet Union, the JCP asked how its leadership could shower with hospitality the responsible head of U.S. imperialism while he was blockading Haiphong harbor and had intensified his bombing of a fellow socialist country, North Vietnam.

Out of the JCP world view came the inevitable conclusion: U.S. imperialism was the principal enemy. Thus the "new opportunists" were berated for underestimating the dangers of this imperialism and overestimating the menace of a revival of Japanese militarism. Lacking a new issue in foreign affairs, the JCP tied all issues to the American threat. Thus, the party opposed the Okinawa reversion agreement because it did not accomplish the withdrawal of U.S. military bases. Extension of this line to condemnation of Japanese military efforts, including the Self-Defense Forces and all defense appropriations, was an easy step. The JCP championed related causes: abolition of the United States–Japan security treaty and withdrawal of all U.S. bases and forces from both Japan and Okinawa, disbandment of the present Self-Defense Forces (the JCP has long maintained the position that if it were in power a "People's Defense Force" would be established) and cancelation of the newly approved Fourth Defense Build-up Plan. That such stands on defense questions were popular was confirmed by a public opinion poll which showed more than 35 percent of the respondents favoring complete cancelation of the Fourth Build-up Plan, with the money spent on housing and welfare (*Tokyo Shimbun*, 24 November).

Meanwhile the polemic exchanges between the JCP and the Chinese Communist Party (CCP) became even more heated, and JCP relations with the Communist Party of the Soviet Union (CPSU) continued to be cool, with occasional blunt criticism published by the JCP.

JCP-CCP Relations. The dispute between the Japanese and Chinese parties continued unabated throughout the year, with extended and repetitive elaborations in *Akahata* of the same arguments which had already been deployed by the JCP in 1971. President Nixon's trip to Peking in February and Premier Tanaka's visit in September inspired party spokesmen to renewed attacks which, especially in the case of the President, fueled the polemics with color and detail. Disagreement with the socialists over the results of Nixon diplomacy was responsible for some of the bitterest tirades in which the JCP could attack the CCP by proxy and at the same time destroyed the chances for much consistent cooperation with the JSP. U.S. imperialism remained the principal target, however, and *Akahata* editorialists did their best to prove that, contrary to generally accepted opinion, U.S.-Chinese rapprochement had not produced a relaxation of tension in the Asian-Pacific area but had, on the contrary, revealed the black depths of U.S. deceit and dangerous intentions.

The day after the issuance (28 February) of the Shanghai communiqué, the chairman of the JCP Foreign Policy Committee issued a statement to annouce that the Nixon visit to China had proved the JCP's previous assessments to have been correct: the President was received by the Chinese not as the "prime mover of aggression" but as chief of state of a friendly country who came "flying the Stars and Stripes and the Nixon Doctrine, and not a white flag at all" (*Akahata,* 29 February).

In March, after enough time to study the effect of the trip and of the communiqué had elapsed, the *Akahata* editorialists produced a series of detailed indictments of the United States, the CCP, and all those who disagreed with the JCP position, particularly the Socialists and the splinter pro-Maoist Japanese groups. A seven-part series running from 11 to 19 March, entitled "What Has Changed? U.S.-China Conversations: Falsity and Reality," discussed all phases of the international situation in Asia, from the war in Indochina ("U.S. does not stop bombing") through the Taiwan question ("U.S. withdrawal of troops is a meaningless gesture") to the Sino-Soviet conflict ("U.S. seeks to profit from the dispute"), to China's changeable attitude toward the United States ("anti-U.S. flag goes up and down"), to the United States-Japan security treaty ("great importance—to Nixon—of a strengthened security pact"). On 25 March a two-page spread in *Akahata* went over all the old arguments, with embellishments, in one of the most comprehensive attacks on China issued during the year. Nixon's objective was seen as diverting public attention to China and away from the war in Indochina, and the Chinese were criticized for receiving him "warmly" in spite of continued "aggression in Indochina" and in spite of U.S. non-abandonment of the "two Chinas" theory. Chou En-lai was excoriated for belying his own words—that the Indochina question must be given top priority—by receiving the President while the bombing continued. The meeting and the communiqué proved that Nixon could "carry out the war of aggression . . . without fearing the worsening of Sino-American relations." The agreement for the withdrawal of U.S. troops was criticized as so hedged by conditions as to be completely illusory. In short, the Chinese, by failing to condemn U.S. aggression in the joint communiqué tacitly accepted it and thereby actually "beautified American imperialism."

Meanwhile the Chinese took every opportunity to express the clear contempt which they felt for the JCP. In March Chou En-lai told a Japanese delegation headed by a JSP Dietman that the "revisionism of the JCP is out of the question" (*Asahi*, 30 March, evening edition). Again, in August, after Tanaka Kakuei had succeeded Sato Eisaku as premier, and the question of diplomatic relations between Japan and China had reemerged as a burning issue, Chou En-lai castigated the JCP, lumping it and the conservative wing of the LDP and the Chiang Kai-shek government in Taiwan together as "ultra-rightist" forces opposing the normalization of Japan-China relations. Fuwa Tetsuzo, chief of the Central Committee Secretariat, both in a press conference and in an *Akahata* article, replied to Chou's arguments by proclaiming that the JCP had consistently over 23 years demanded the restoration of diplomatic relations between Japan and China. Chou, according to Fuwa, was either totally ignorant of Japan or, in order to attack the JCP, was willing to throw away truth and resort to every kind of sordid slander and insult. Fuwa called Chou's action "an outrageously inexcusable intervention in our party." (Kyodo Press Service, 22 August; *Akahata*, 23 August, *Japan Times*, Tokyo, 24 August).

When Premier Tanaka announced his intention to visit Peking for the purpose of normalizing Japan's relations with China, the JCP faced a quandary. Although, as party leaders had repeatedly stated, the JCP had historically advocated the renewal of government-to-government relations, yet to favor a concept in the abstract was one thing and to support an LDP government leader was another. Furthermore, the JCP had directed its most violent invective at President Nixon for his trip to China and had stated, with regard to Tanaka's plans, that the normalization of Sino-Japanese relations was not the top priority matter for Japan's foreign policy at that time. Still, with a general election in the offing and sensing the prevailing "China mood" in the country, the JCP leadership decided that it could not hold out as the sole dissenter on this issue. Consequently on 9 September Chairman Miyamoto announced in a press conference that the JCP "approved the policy for reestablishing diplomatic relations between Japan and China being pursued by the Tanaka cabinet." Miyamoto went on to mention Japan's maintenance of the security treaty with the United States, the 1969 Sato-Nixon joint communiqué which included the "Taiwan clause" (recognition that the security of the Taiwan area was important to the security of Japan), and Chinese interference in Japan's revolutionary movement as violations of China's "Five Peace Principles," the nullification of which was most important (*Asahi*, 10 September). On 21 September Fuwa met with the chief cabinet secretary, Nikaido Susumu, to present a six-point program to guide Tanaka in his negotiations in Peking: (1) establish diplomatic relations on this visit; (2) confirm the position "one China"; (3) accept the Five Peace Principles as the basis of the relationship (mutual respect of territory and sovereignty; mutual non-aggression; non-interference in internal affairs; equality and reciprocity; and peaceful co-existence); (4) clearly recognize the termination of a state of war; (5) break diplomatic relations with Taiwan; and (6) revoke the government view on the "Far East clauses," especially the Taiwan clause, in the Sato-Nixon communiqué of 1969.

After Tanaka's return from Peking, the JCP learned that he had recounted to a group of

LDP Diet members in Tokyo on 30 September how he had admonished Chou En-lai "not to shake hands with the Japanese communists." Infuriated, the party jumped immediately to challenge the premier. The Central Committee filed a protest note, while Fuwa, accompanied by the vice-chairman of the Secretariat and the chairman of the Policy Committee, called on Nikaido to protest "conduct which should never be tolerated in a chief of state." Nikaido later in a press conference stated that Tanaka had not referred to the JCP by name in conversation with Chou En-lai, but had told the Chinese premier that the Japanese people feared the export of revolution from communist countries. Tanaka the same day denied to the press that he had referred to the JCP in his talks with Chou En-lai. (Ibid., 3 October.) Although some press reports indicated that Nikaido had apologized for Tanaka's remark (Kyodo News Service, 5 October; Moscow radio, 8 October), the incident cannot have enhanced the prospects for future cooperation between the JCP and the LDP government.

An issue which could plague Japanese-Chinese relations in the future is the sovereignty of the Senkaku Islands, eight uninhabited islets with a total area of less than five square miles, which have since the war been administered as part of the Ryukyus, but which suddenly came into the news because of suspected oil deposits. The governments of both the Republic of China on Taiwan and of the People's Republic on the mainland have claimed the Senkakus as Chinese. On 30 March the JCP, in another demonstration of Japanese nationalism, announced full support of the Japanese right to the islands, denouncing the Chinese claims as completely groundless. The official party view traced the history of the Senkakus to justify Japanese ownership and to show that by neither act nor statement had the Chinese ever taken any step to proclaim sovereignty over the islands until their very recently announced claims. (*Akahata*, 31 March.)

It remained to be seen whether, with their new-found power due to the December elections, the JCP would temper or change its attitude toward the CCP. By year's end there was no sign that this was to happen and indications were that the quarrel would go on. On the Chinese side, the *People's Daily*, in reporting the December Japanese elections, took pains to note that the JCP was still in the control of the "Miyamoto revisionists."

JCP-CPSU Relations. After Soviet foreign minister Adnrei Gromyko's January visit to Tokyo and the resulting agreement to negotiate a peace treaty "within the year," the JCP sought to remind the public of its position on the northern territories claimed by Japan and held by the Soviet Union. An editorial in *Akahata* (28 January) traced the history of the Kurile Islands, described the Soviet-Japanese negotiations of 1956, and repeated the JCP position that while the Habomais and Shikotan should be returned to Japan as soon as a peace treaty was signed, the Soviet Union should return *all* of the Kurile Islands, including the northern Kuriles (which are not now claimed by the Japanese government), when Japan abrogates the security treaty with the United States.

While the JCP has been more circumspect and far less vituperative in its attitude toward the CPSU than in its treatment of the CCP, nevertheless the party has not refrained from criticism, either implied or direct. For example, the party did not welcome President Nixon's visit to the Soviet Union, and although it did not indulge in the tirades which the Nixon trip to Peking inspired, some of the same charges of "Big Powerism" and the "divide-and-rule policy of American imperialism" were clearly aimed at the Soviets. The JCP returned to the accusation that a great socialist nation was emphasizing peaceful co-existence with U.S. imperialism while belittling the significance of the Indochinese peoples' genuine struggle for peace. Part of the attack was carried on through denunciations of Shiga Yoshio (see below) and his deviationist, pro-Soviet "Voice of Japan" party. (Ibid., 23, 26, 27 May.) After the joint U.S.-Soviet communiqué was published 29 May, the chairman of the JCP's Foreign Affairs Committee evaluated it for the party: "A view that closer contacts between the U.S. and the Soviet Union would contribute to the establishment of peaceful co-existence between socialist and capitalist systems is wholly baseless. Warm treatment given to [Nixon] only helped to make him grow impudent." (Ibid., 31 May.)

United States. The JCP continued to propagandize its line that Japan has become a dependency of "American imperialism," tied through the security treaty and as a consequence pressured toward a revival of militarism, manifest by the Fourth Defense Build-up Plan, the continued U.S. occupation of military bases in Japan and Okinawa, the dispatch of the Self Defense Forces to Okinawa by agreement with the United States, the visits of nuclear-powered submarines to Japanese ports, landings of B–52 bombers in Okinawa, and the repair of military vehicles destined for Vietnam. The JCP called for the abrogation of the security treaty— no new stance for the party—and in April appealed stridently to the Soviet Union to cancel President Nixon's visit to Moscow because of the bombing of Hanoi and the bombing and mining of Haiphong harbor. Nixon's reelection was interpreted as meaning a "more treacherous and cunning pursuit of his dual policy grounded on the line of aggression and intervention, exploitation and extreme conservatism" (Tokyo Joint Press Service, 9 November). The party also stated that it was "an illusion to think President Nixon's victory will lead to a relaxation of tensions" (Kyodo News Service, 8 November).

International Party Contacts. In January 1972 a JCP delegation attended the fiftieth-anniversary congress of the Communist Party of Chile in Santiago, 2–8 January, and was received by Chilean President Allende along with other foreign delegations. En route to Chile, the JCP delegation stopped in Paris where the members on 29 December 1971 called on the Central Committee of the French Communist Party.

In February the JCP joined with the JSP, Sohyo, and numerous peace, women's and other organizations to send a delegation of 46 representatives to attend the "World Conference for Peace and Independence for the Peoples of Indochina" in Paris.

The JCP accepted an invitation from the Communist Party, USA to attend its congress in New York, 18–21 February, and announced that the delegation would be headed by Nosaka Sanzo, chairman of the Central Committee. This was the first time the party had been invited to a congress of the U.S. party, although it would have been Nosaka's second visit to the United States. However, the U.S. government refused visas to the delegation.

In March a JCP delegation attended the congress of the Italian Communist Party, 13–17 March. In March–April a JCP group attended the congress of the Communist Party of Australia. In October JCP representatives visited fraternal parties in the United Kingdom, Yugoslavia, and East Germany. The JCP was represented at the congress of the French Communist Party, 13–17 December.

Several foreign parties sent delegations to Japan during the year. A delegation of the Australian party, headed by Laurie Aarons, national secretary, visited the JCP on 9–12 June. A delegation led by Paul Niculescu-Mizil member of the Presidium and Executive Committee of the Romanian Communist Party visited Japan on 15–27 September. Reflecting the compatibility between party lines and gratitude for the hospitality extended to Miyamoto and his associates in 1971, the JCP went to greater lengths than usual to extend every courtesy to the Romanians, including conferences with JCP chairman Miyamoto and meetings with the Central Committee (*Akahata,* 13, 18, 19, 20, 26, 28 September).

Publications. The circulation of *Akahata* is estimated at 500,000 daily and 1,900,000 for the Sunday edition. *Zenei* ("Vanguard"), a monthly party magazine, is published in approximately 100,000 copies. The Minseido's weekly *Minsei Shimbun* ("Democratic Youth News") is reported to have a circulation of 280,000—a gain over the 240,000 of 1971. Circulation figures for certain other publications put out by JCP affiliates are as follows: *Shinfujin Shimbun* ("New Woman's News"), a weekly, 200,000; *Zenkoku Shoko Shimbun* ("National Commerce and Industry News"), weekly organ of the Federation of Commercial and Industrial Organizations, 200,000; *Gakushu no Tomo* ("Friends of Learning"), a monthly intended for the education of young factory workers, 130,000; *Heiwa Shimbun* ("Peace News"), weekly organ of the Japan Peace Committee (Nihon Heiwa Iin-kai), 32,000; *Sekai Seiji Shiryu* ("World Political Documents"), bimonthly, 30,000; *Gekkan Gakushu* ("Studies Monthly"), 115,000; and *Dokusho no Tomo* ("Reader's Friend"), 10,000. Zengakuren publications are *Sokoku to Gakumon no Tame ni* ("For the Sake of Fatherland and Learning") and *Gakusei Shimbun* ("Students' News").

*   *   *

Splinter Parties. There are two principal Japanese communist parties which oppose the present policies of the JCP. The Voice of Japan (Nihon no Koe) is pro-Soviet, and the Japan Communist Party (Left)—Nihon Kyosanto (Saha)—is pro-Chinese. These groups formed after the JCP's splits with the CPSU and the CCP. The Voice of Japan was organized by Shiga Yoshio, one of the founders of the postwar JCP, following his expulsion from it in 1964. The JCP (Left), which officially came into being in 1966, grew out of the already somewhat dissident Yamaguchi Prefecture Committee. In 1972 both parties celebrated the fiftieth anniversary of the JCP in July and both used the occasion to attack "Miyamoto revisionism."

Although never impressive in membership (reports suggest between 300 and 500), the Voice of Japan has remained a major irritant in relations between the JCP and CPSU. The Voice of Japan celebrated the JCP anniversary and the eighth anniversary of its own publication of *Nihon no Koe* by holding mass meetings in Osaka on 3 July and in Tokyo on 14 July. The attacks on the Shiga group appearing in *Akahata* can be considered a kind of barometer of the prevailing relations between the JCP and the CPSU. In both 1968 and 1971 the JCP thought that the promise of the CPSU to withdraw all support and encouragement to the "Voice" group was valid, but the degree of public protest in 1972 suggests that JCP-CPSU relations are still tenuous. President Nixon's trip to Moscow and the resulting U.S.-Soviet arms agreements provided the impulse for the most notable series of attacks and counterattacks to appear in the columns of the Shiga group's periodical and of *Akahata*. The JCP accused the "Voice" of defending to the letter every position and act of the Soviet Union and of trying to widen the cleavage between the JCP and CPSU, berating the JCP on every issue on which the attitude of the two parties diverged, such as the nuclear non-proliferation treaty, the invasion of Czechoslovakia, the Kurile Islands question, and, most recently, the Nixon visit to the Soviet Union. A major article in *Akahata* (27 August) castigated the Shiga group for inconsistency in condemning Nixon's trip to Peking while praising his journey to Moscow; it rebutted Shiga's criticism of the JCP demand that Moscow cancel the invitation to Nixon by insisting that the JCP had the right to express "hope" to a fraternal party—such an expression was made in a brotherly spirit and was in no sense a "slander" as the "Voice" had stated. The article concluded: "We cannot ignore the fact that the Voice of Japan, the legacy of Khrushchev's interference, continues in its evil character to exist and be active and to influence relations between our two parties. In order to expand the aid of the Japanese people to the people of Vietnam, we must fight to destroy absolutely those who would beautify Nixon and give second place to the Indochina question; we must wipe out completely the heir of Khrushchev's interference."

As a fraternal party of the CCP, the JCP (Left) benefited from the strong "China mood" which prevailed in Japan during much of the year. The party claims to maintain prefectural committees in 11 prefectures. Total membership has been estimated at 2,000. Its Central Committee met on 15–16 January in Yamaguchi prefecture, the birthplace of the group and source of most members. The chairman of the JCP (Left) is Fukuda Masayoshi.

After the United Red Army attracted nationwide and world attention by the atrocities committed by its youthful members, the JCP began a campaign to relate the JCP (Left) to this terrorist band. By quoting the rules of the Fukuda group's youth organization, which incorporate Mao's pronouncements on "violent revolution" and "political power comes from the barrel of a gun," the JCP labeled the JCP (Left) the "founder of the anti-communist assassination band" and denounced it for sharing the terrorist ideals of the United Red Army (*Akahata,* 15 March.) From June on, the *Jinmin no Hoshi* ("People's Star"), organ of the JCP (Left), carried on a consistent campaign to declare that "Miyamoto revisionism" had prevented the JCP from maintaining its revolutionary tradition.

The pro-JCP Japan-Soviet Association, with 10,800 members in 1972, was founded in 1957 after Japanese-Soviet diplomatic relations were established. Reflecting the split which produced the Voice of Japan, the Japan-Soviet Friendship Association formed in 1965 as a breakaway group from the JCP, with the stated objective "to promote mass movements, independent of political parties." Members of the LDP, DSP, and Komeito thereupon joined the association and the Soviet Union supported it. Its membership in 1972 was reported to be 100,000. (*Tokyo Shimbun,* 1 March; *Sankei Shimbun,* 12 March.)

The Japan-China Friendship Association (Orthodox) supports the People's Republic of China and is near the JCP (Left) in outlook and character. The fact that JSP members belong to it has aggravated the recent JCP-JSP confrontation. Encouraged by the efforts of the other opposition parties to seek rapprochement with China and by its admission into the United Nations in 1971 and President Nixon's visit in 1972, the Japan-China Friendship Association (Orthodox) became more active. On 25 February the organization staged a mass rally in Tokyo with such slogans as "Break the Japan-Taiwan Treaty" and "Normalize Relations between Japan and China."

Hoover Institution   John K. Emmerson
Stanford University

Korea: Democratic People's Republic of Korea

The Korean communist movement began in the Russian Maritime Province and Siberia in 1918. It was then spread to the Korean peninsula. The Korean Communist Party (Choson Kongsan-dang; KCP) was formed at Seoul in 1925 during the time of Japanese rule; in 1928, due chiefly to suppression, it ceased to function. Shortly after World War II, a revived KCP appeared briefly in Seoul. The center of the communist movement soon moved to the northern part of the country, then occupied by Soviet forces, and under Soviet auspices the North Korean Central Bureau of the KCP was formed in October 1945. At that time, the Korean Independence League (later renamed the New Peoples' Party) also existed, led by returnees from Yenan, China, who had received training there since 1941 from Chinese communists. In July 1946, these two groups merged, creating the North Korean Workers' Party. This fused movement absorbed the leadership of the South Korean Workers' Party (also formed in Seoul in 1946), and on 24 June 1949 the Korean Workers' Party (Choson Nodong-dang; KWP) was established in Pyongyang. The KWP is today the ruling party of the Democratic People's Republic of Korea (DPRK).

Kim Il-song, Korean-born but Soviet trained, was installed as head of the North Korean government by the Soviet occupation authorities. Kim had been an anti-Japanese communist guerrilla leader in southern Manchuria in the 1930s but had played no part in the movement in Korea. Subsequently trained in the Soviet Union, he returned in September 1945 in the uniform of a Soviet army major. The Soviets, who had not forgotten the factionalism of the "domestic" Korean communist movement in the past, turned a cold shoulder toward both the domestic "mainstream" group and the returned communists from Yenan, and put pro-Soviet Koreans in key positions. Kim Il-song consolidated his power by eliminating opposed factions, and today his Manchurian partisan group (the Kapsan faction) holds unassailable supremacy in the North Korean leadership.

The number of the KWP members has not been revealed since the party's Fifth Congress, November 1970, but is estimated at 1,700,000. The population of the DPRK is about 14,-000,000. KWP members presumably comprise about 12 percent of the population, which may be the highest ratio of any communist party.

Leadership and Organization. North Korea has a typical communist administrative structure. The center of decision-making in the KWP, the government (cabinet) merely executes party policy. All important leaders hold concurrent positions in the party and government. The party secretary-general, Kim Il-song, is also DPRK president and supreme commander of the armed forces. For names of the KWP Political Committee and Secretariat, as elected at the party's Fifth Congress, November 1970, see *YICA, 1972*, p. 530. The 13-member Political Committee (created during the Fourth Congress, 1961) and 10-member Secretariat constitute the core of important decision-makers in the DPRK and act as a controlling nucleus for the Central Committee (117 regular and 55 candidate members).

The new DPRK constitution, adopted on 28 December 1972 at the first session of the fifth Supreme People's Assembly, created a 25-member Central People's Committee as the highest organ of executive power with Kim Il-song as president and Choe Yong-kun and Kang Yang-uk as vice presidents. (For details of the new DPRK constitution see *Dong-A Il-Bo,* Seoul, Korea, 28 December 1972.) Its membership includes all the other leaders who have been either members of the KWP Political Committee or cabinet ministers. The new premier is Kim Il, who had been the ranking vice premier in the former Kim Il-song cabinet. The new DPRK cabinet, called "Administrative Council," consists of premier, 6 vice premiers and 22 ministers and committee chairmen. (The old cabinet consisted of 31 ministries, 5 commissions, and one committee.)

The first session of the fifth Supreme People's Assembly in December 1972 also elected Choe Hyon, O Chin-u and O Paek-yong as vice chairmen of the National Defense Council, Hwang Chang-yop as chairman of the Standing Committee of the Supreme People's Assembly; Pang Hak-se as president of the Central Court; and Chong Tong-chol as procurator general of the Central Procurator's Office.

The KWP controls a number of mass organizations, of which the most important are the two-million-member General Federation of Trade Unions of Korea (GFTUK), and the 2.7 million-member League of Socialist Working Youth of Korea (LSWY; formerly known as the Korean Democratic Youth League). Other major mass organizations are the Union of Agricultural Working People and the Korean Democratic Women's Union, the latter headed by Kim Song-ae, the wife of Kim Il-song. These organizations appear to be autonomous but in reality are what the KWP calls "transmission belts for maintaining the ties between the party and the masses." General Federation of Korean Residents in Japan (Chongnyon; known also by its Japanese name, Chosen Soren) competes with the organization of the Republic of Korea residents in Japan for the loyalties of the more than 600,000 Korean nationals residing in that country.

At least two subordinate political movements under the tight KWP control exist in North Korea: the Korean Democratic Party (Choson Minju-dang) and Young Friends' Party of the Chondogyo Sect (the sect being the Society of the Heavenly Way—Chondogyo Chong-u-dang). No membership figures are available on these movements. Their function is to enhance acceptance of the United Democratic Fatherland Front (Choguk Tongil Minjujuui Chonson), created by 71 political and social organizations in June 1949, which is assigned the task of uniting "all the revolutionary forces of North and South Korea" under the leadership of the KWP, in order to implement the "peaceful unification and complete independence of the country." The KWP also controls the "Committee for the Peaceful Unification of the Fatherland," established in May 1961 and consisting of representatives from the KWP, the subordinate "democratic" parties, and the mass organizations.

Among ruling-party heads, Kim Il-song has held concurrently the highest positions in both his party and government longer than any other political leader in the communist world of the post-World War II period. His authority is absolute, his personality all-pervading. During the 27 years of his rule, his personality cult has continued to grow, until it now surpasses the Mao cult in China (which seemed to be subsiding in 1972). All North Korean publications describe Kim as "the sun of the nation," who is adored by "world revolutionary people," and so on. Kim's birthplace near Pyongyang is the "cradle of the world revolution," and his family is being canonized: his grandfather is said to have led a group that sank "the U.S. imperialist pirate ship General Sherman," his father is described as the foremost leader of the anti-Japanese resistance movement in Korea after 1919, and his mother is credited with the founding of the Korean women's movement.

Kim's younger brother, Kim Yong-chu, is a member of the Political Committee and the Secretariat. Kim Yong-chu, whose earlier life is wrapped in obscurity, has moved up from 47th position in the party hierarchy in 1961 to 24th in 1967, 20th in 1968, and 12th in 1969. This 49-year-old brother appears slated to be the successor to Kim Il-song. As director of the Organization and Guidance Department of the Central Committee, he is in charge of all party personnel matters.

Kim Il-song's 60th birthday (according to Oriental belief, the most auspicious moment in life) was celebrated by the nation on 15 April 1972 and was hailed in terms such as these, from a five-hour speech by a Secretariat member:

> The revolutionary thinking of the great Marxist-Leninist Kim Il-song is an encyclopedic idea which gives comprehensive scientific answers to all the theoretical and practical questions covering all fields of revolution and construction—politics, economy, ideology and culture— which have been arising in different stages of the revolution, and shows the concrete ways and means for their implementation. [It is] an idea giving the most correct and overall answers to all new theoretical and practical problems and fundamental needs of our time. (*Pyongyang Times*, 15 April.)

In further celebration the DPRK erected a statue of Kim and built the "Grand Korean Revolution Museum" on a high hill in Pyongyang, where an unveiling of the statue and inaugural of the museum drew crowds of over 300,000.

The "teachings of Kim Il-song," similar to "Mao Tse-tung Thought" in China, are upheld by the KWP as having "creatively applied and further developed" Marxism-Leninism. The core of this ideology is the concept of *chuch'e* (self-identity or national identity) which can be translated into more specific programs of political independence, economic self-reliance and self-sufficiency, and independent defense capability:

> Establishing *chuch'e* means, in a nutshell, having the attitude of master toward revolution and construction in one's country. This means holding fast to an independent position, refraining from dependence on others and using one's own brains, believing in one's own strength and displaying the revolutionary spirit of self-reliance, and thus solving one's own problems for oneself on his own responsibility under all circumstances. It means adhering to the creative position of opposing dogmatism [of China and revisionism of the Soviet Union] and applying the universal principles of Marxism-Leninism and the experiences of other countries to suit the historical conditions and national peculiarities of one's own country. (Kim Il-song's report to the conference of the KWP on 5 October 1966.)

Domestic Attitudes and Activities. Almost all aspects of life in North Korea are pervaded by Kim Il-song's efforts to build a powerful industrial state with a self-sufficient modern industry, developed rural economy, blossoming socialist national culture, and an invincible defense power, in compliance with his "unitary ideology" of *chuch'e*. The personality cult is becoming increasingly employed to mobilize the entire population to achieve these objectives. In his 10 January 1972 interview with journalists from the Tokyo *Yomiuri Shimbun*, Kim said:

> You asked me about the essential points of our policy based on the *chuch'e* idea. All the internal and external policies of our Party [and the DPRK] are based on the *chuch'e* idea and proceed from it. What underlines our specific measures as well as our lines and policies in all fields of politics, economy, culture and military affairs is the *chuch'e* idea. (KCNA, 15 January.)

Kim constantly reminds the North Koreans that their country should maintain its self-respect and self-confidence—that it never goes hat in hand to the big powers for essentials. North

Korea has received economic and military aid from the Soviet Union and China in the past, but this fact is largely pushed to the background.

In 1972, North Korea is in the second year of the current six-year-plan (1971–1976). Probably in consequence of the mixed achievements and failure of the preceding seven-year-plan (1961–67), which was extended three years (to the end of 1970) because of initial set-backs and a drastic increase in defense spending, the planned growth rates for the current plan are substantially lower. Annual average rates of growth in national income and gross industrial output are to be 10.3 and 14.0 percent respectively, as compared to 15.2 and 18.1 percent in the previous plan. Agriculture continues to be the weakest link in the economy; the growth rate in gross agricultural output is apparently lower than the 10.3 percent planned for national income. There are still eminently respectable goals, however, and their achievement would make the DPRK economy one of the world's fastest growing. (For details see *Nodong Shinmoon,* 3, 10 November 1970; Joseph S. Chung, "The Six Year Plan (1971–76) of North Korea," *Journal of Korean Affairs,* July 1971, pp. 15–26; Harald Munthe-Kaas, "Progress under Kim," *Far Eastern Economic Review,* 1 July 1972, pp. 37–38; and *Washington Post,* 2 July, p. 3C.)

The plan stresses rapid industrialization, especially through fast growth in heavy industry (at the expense of light industry and agriculture), probably not only for defense reasons but because of economic nationalism. Heavy industry is to receive 40.7 percent of total state (government) investment, as against 8.3 percent for light industry and 20 percent for agriculture. The DPRK's estimated gross national product just before the inauguration of the current plan was $2.7 billion ($208 per capita). An 80 percent increase in GNP is projected. Steel production is to reach 3.8 to 4 million tons (2.2 million tons in 1970); coal production, 50 to 53 million tons (27.5 million tons); electricity, 28,000 million to 30,000 million kwh (16,500 million kwy). Light industrial output is to increase by 160 percent at the end of the plan; this would include raising textile production to about 60 million meters of cloth.

The current plan seeks a self-sufficiency rate of 60 to 70 percent in all industrial sectors by substituting domestic raw materials. The DPRK is well endowed with most of the resources necessary for industrialization—lacking only oil, which it now imports from the Soviet Union. The weakest sector of the industrial base is to be strengthened by assigning priority to the development of power and extractive industries, identified as bottleneck sectors during the previous plan. The intensive search for oil in North Korea is a good example of this effort.

By the end of the current plan, in 1976, grain production is to reach between 7 million and 7.5 million tons, and fertilizer production around 3 million tons annually. Since only 20 percent of the KPRK is arable and this land is already utilized to near maximum, the plan calls for raising output per acre through technical improvements such as double cropping, further mechanization, irrigation, and increased use of better-quality chemical fertilizers.

The DPRK is showing considerable interest in improving overseas trade with Western and other countries, particularly Japan. Recently its foreign trade has been in the neighborhood of $400 million annually; 80 percent has been with the communist bloc, and 70 percent of that with the Soviet Union.

As happened under the previous plan, heavy defense spending may emerge as a major factor against the attainment of goals, although Kim Il-song told a Japanese journalist in 1971 that defense costs had been "drastically reduced." (*Asahi Evening News,* Tokyo, 28 September). The DPRK allocated 31 percent of its 1971 government budget for military development—about $620 million. In an annual budget report to the Supreme People's Assembly in April 1972, the finance minister said that North Korea would devote 17 percent of its 1972 budget to national defense—about $550 million (KCNA, 29 April). Total active armed forces in 1972 are believed to number around 410,000 (including 26,000 security units).

South Korea. The development of the DPRK's unification strategy since the Korean War —North Korea's attempt to bring South Korea under communist control by force—can be divided into three time periods: During the first period, 1953 to 1960, the Pyongyang government was preoccupied with reconstruction and rehabilitation of its war-torn country and consolidation of its rules; the reunification issue was largely pushed into the background and official announcements concerning reunification were rather moderate, as exemplified by a proposal for establishing a unified government in Korea through general elections held under the supervision of neutral nations. But the DPRK was adamant in insisting upon withdrawal of U.S. forces from South Korea. In the second period, the DPRK in 1961 began to advocate simultaneous destruction of the anti-communist regime in Seoul and defeat of the U.S. forces in South Korea, and in 1966 launched a campaign of subversion and terror in South Korea which was maintained until April 1971 (see, for example, Kim Il-song's speech to the KWP Central Committee, November 1970, *Journal of Korean Affairs,* April 1971). Paralleling this militant position on reunification were efforts to instill nationalistic sentiment in the North Korean people under the *chuch'e* slogan and put domestic affairs on a wartime footing.

In the third period, since April 1971, the DPRK has modified its bellicost posture toward the South and shifted to softer tactics in seeking reunification. This shift was due probably to a number of factors, among them the Sino-American détente, Chinese-Soviet animosities, the Nixon doctrine, strong anti-communist sentiment and economic development in South Korea, the efforts by East and West Germany to work out a framework for better relations, the need for successfully accomplishing the current six-year Plan through reduced defense spending, and the DPRK's fear (shared by the South) that a big-power directorate would once again settle Korean problems behind its back.

In April 1971 North Korean foreign minister Ho Tam made an eight-point proposal for peaceful unification before the Supreme People's Assembly (see *YICA, 1972,* p. 533). On 6 August Kim Il-song said that he was ready to talk with all political parties, including the ruling party of the South, the Democratic Republican Party, on reunification. He reiterated this position in an interview with the editor of the Tokyo *Asahi Shimbun* on 25 September (see *Journal of Korean Affairs,* October) and in his 1972 New Year Address (KCNA, 1 January; *Pyongyang Times,* 1 January).

On 12 August 1971, meanwhile, the president of the South Korean National Red Cross unexpectedly and dramatically proposed to the North Korean Red Cross that direct negotiations be held to search for ways to reunite separated families in North and South Korea. (It is estimated that 10 million of the 50 million Koreans are separated from family members. Five to six million of these are North Koreans who fled to the South.) Two days later, 14 August, the head of the North Korean Red Cross replied that the proposal was "in accord with the reasonable proposals consistently advanced" by the DPRK (KCNA, 14 August). He suggested that the questions of travel and the exchange of letters also be discussed. Preliminary contacts between the North and South Korean Red Cross officials began in Panmunjom on 20 August and were followed on 20 September by preparatory talks for full-scale Red Cross meetings.

In his 10 January 1972 interview with Japanese journalists, Kim Il-song proposed North-South negotiations on a peace treaty—without withdrawal of U.S. forces in South Korea as a precondition (*Yomiuri Shimbun,* 11 January; *People's Korea,* 26 January 1972). According to Kim, a peace pact should be concluded in four stages: first, a peace pact (presumably a mutual non-aggression treaty) would be signed between the North and South under existing circumstances; then each would declare that it would not attack the other; next U.S. forces would be withdrawn from the South; lastly, both would reduce their respective arms to 10,000 or fewer. The next day (11 January) he proposed that North and South Korea should hold direct talks on an "autonomous and peaceful unification" of the two areas right away (*Shakai Shimpo*, Tokyo, 26 January). In his 26 May interview in Pyongyang with *New York Times* correspondents, Kim stated that he would not support reunification by force; rather, the two Koreas should come together peacefully, by mutual decision and under conditions that would permit co-existence of different systems and ideas (presumably confederation or federation) (*NYT,* 31 May). In his 21 June 1972 interview with the correspondent for the *Washington Post,* Kim said for the first time that he was willing to meet with South Korea's President Park Chung-hee to discuss possible easing of tensions between the two states (*Washington Post,* 26 June).

The goal of peaceful reunification of the divided Korean peninsula was made explicit in Article 5 of the new DPRK constitution adopted on 28 December at the first session of the fifth Supreme People's Assembly. The new constitution also made it clear that the North Korean regime claimed jurisdiction only over the northern part of the peninsula, with Pyongyang as its rightful capital. (South Korea's new constitution, adopted in late December, indicated that the Seoul government would claim jurisdiction only over the southern half of the peninsula. In short the timing and the content of the two new constitutions suggested that the two Koreas agreed, at least tacitly, to recognize each other's authority and to define a political basis for direct negotiations on reunification.)

In the summer of 1972 a series of secret meetings between high-ranking North and South Korean officials were held. Lee Hu-rak, director of the Central Intelligence Agency of South Korea, secretly visited Pyongyang between 2 and 5 May to hold talks with Director Kim Yong-chu of the Organization and Guidance Department of the KWP. While there, Lee talked directly with Premier Kim Il-song. Second Deputy Premier Pak Song-chol—acting on behalf of Kim Yong-chu, who was believed to be in need of a medical operation—made a secret visit to Seoul, 29 May to 1 June, and talked directly with South Korea's President Park Chung-hee. Following these secret talks, a joint North and South Korean communiqué was made public on 4 July simultaneously in Seoul and Pyongyang. In this statement the two Koreas agreed to work toward peaceful reunification by "transcending differences in ideas, ideologies and systems" and spelled out seven goals: (1) peaceful reunification without external interference, overcoming differences in ideologies and political systems; (2) renouncement of armed provocations; (3) exchanges between the North and South in various fields; (4) cooperation aimed at the early success of the North-South Red Cross talks; (5) installation of a direct telephone line between Seoul and Pyongyang; (6) establishment of a North-South coordinating committee co-chaired by Lee Hu-rak and Kim Yong-chu; and (7) adherence to terms of the agreement. (KCNA, 4 July; *NYT,* 5 July.) An hour after the communiqué was announced a telephone "hot line" linking Seoul and Pyongyang was installed in the offices of Lee Hu-rak and Kim-Yong-chu.

As noted already, in September 1971 preparatory talks began in Panmunjom for meetings that were to discuss the technicalities for reuniting the separated Korean families. On 16 June 1972 both sides approved an agenda which provided for discussion of (1) tracing and issuing notifications of the whereabouts and fate of dispersed families and relatives in the South and North; (2) facilitating free visits and meetings between members of dispersed families and relatives; (3) furthering free exchange of correspondence between members of dispersed families; (4) reuniting members of those families, according to their wishes; and (5) other humanitarian matters. On 10 July, six days after the joint communiqué, it was agreed at the 21st session of preparatory talks that delegations to the projected Red Cross meetings would be composed of seven members each and that the meetings would be held alternately in Seoul and Pyongyang.

In the first—and mostly ceremonial—meeting in Pyongyang on 30 August, the two sides confirmed the five-point agenda and agreed to take it up at the second meeting, scheduled for Seoul on 13 September. That meeting, also largely ceremonial, lasted five minutes, but it was agreed that the third session, in Pyongyang, 24 October, would start substantial discussions of the agenda items. The third meeting was concluded without any agreement or progress toward reuniting families, but the fourth in Seoul on 22 November produced an agreement in principle to set up a joint Red Cross committee to trace divided families as the first step in the efforts to reunite them, and to set up a "North-South Red Cross project office" at Panmunjom as a communication center for family contacts.

The Red Cross meetings are expected to parallel those of the North-South Coordination Committee, established under the 4 July communiqué, which is to oversee all détente moves between the two Koreas. Taking control of the Red Cross talks, it separately began discussions of reunification. The first meeting of the North-South Coordination Committee was held in Panmunjom on 12 October. Lee Hu-rak headed the five-man South Korean delegation, and Pak Song-chol the five-man North Korean delegation. "Various problems" were discussed. At the second meeting, in Pyongyang on 2–4 November, the two sides signed an "agreement on the composition and operation of the North-South Coordination Committee" and agreed to stop propaganda broadcasts and leaflet distribution, including psychological warfare activities through loudspeakers in the demilitarized zone, as of 11 November (KCNA, 4 November, which also gives the full text of the agreement). The third meeting, in Seoul, 30 November–1 December, was said to have involved a discussion of how to carry out the 4 November agreement in specific programs; also plans were announced for establishing a secretariat and holding monthly meetings of an executive panel at Panmunjom.

Thus, the two Koreas agreed to end their 27 years of bitterly hostile relations by opening a "dialogue of reconciliation" in two forums, the one seeking arrangements to reunite families separated by the division of Korea and the other aimed at eventual political reunification. Each side spent considerable time probing the other's negotiating posture, and talks at both levels hardly went farther than the discussion of procedural matters. The suspicion between the two governments remained a formidable obstacle. What was more important, it was evident that each had the ultimate objective of reunifying the Korean peninsula under its own political system and domination. That is to say, the strategies of both Pyongyang and Seoul on reunification were the same as before; only the tactics had changed.

In the two forums, South Korea appeared to favor step-by-step progress on non-political or humanitarian issues to build mutual confidence before the political issues at the core are raised. Ever wary of the North's intention, Seoul demands that Pyongyang prove its sincerity (or good faith) first by taking a constructive attitude in the Red Cross talks, which deal with non-political or humanitarian issues that are practical and feasible. From there, Seoul suggests, discussions could move into the more comprehensive political realm. (A close observer of the talks has commented, perhaps correctly, that "implicit in this strategy is an effort to break the North Korean political will.") The North Korean approach may be described as "radicalism" (as opposed to South Korea's "gradualism"): a speedy political agreement must come first because humanitarian, economic and cultural agreements must ultimately rest on a political solution. Pyongyang is apparently confident that its totalitarian system will eventually give it an edge over a "decadent" South.

International Views and Positions. In 1972 the concept of *chuch'e* and the achievements allegedly based on it were given considerable international publicity by the DPRK, apparently to improve its image, win friends, and gain international acceptance. This was done partly by inviting a number of foreign journalists to North Korea (with traveling expenses paid in most cases) and placing large advertisements in foreign newspapers.

For most of the post-World War II decades, North Korea had been among the most seemingly hostile and isolated nations anywhere on earth. But after the summer of 1971— following U.S. President Nixon's surprising rapprochement with mainland China—the DPRK began gingerly opening windows and doors to make contact with the outside world.

The DPRK has supplemented its efforts on the reunification issue by becoming extremely active on the foreign policy front, partly to undermine the international position of its rival in South Korea and partly to develop world support for North Korean policies. Parliamentary, trade, and other good-will missions have been dispatched abroad and invited to North Korea, and friendly diplomatic gestures have been made to every corner of the earth, particularly the Afro-Asian "third world." As of December 1971 the DPRK was recognized by 34 nations (South Korea by 85), though at least four or five of the 34 nations followed a "two Koreas" policy by maintaining diplomatic relations with both Seoul and Pyongyang. During 1972 North Korea established diplomatic relations with Cameroun, Rwanda, Chile, Upper Volta, and Pakistan.

The DPRK exchanged various good-will delegations with the Afro-Asian countries. In January, for example, a delegation of the North Korean Committee for Asian-African Solidarity attended the fifth meeting of the Afro-Asian Peoples' Solidarity Organization, and the same committee sponsored a mass meeting in Pyongyang to mark a "Week of International Solidarity with the Asian, African and Latin American Peoples." Pyongyang also signed many agreements with the Afro-Asian countries on trade, technical cooperation, cultural exchange, and science. Strong propaganda support was given to the Arab struggle against Israel and Zionism. (For details see "Chronicle of Events," *Journal of Korean Affairs,* April, July, October.)

In relations with the communist bloc, North Korea continued to avoid leaning toward either the Soviet Union or China, in accordance with the *chuch'e* principle, and to maintain or seek warm, friendly relations with all of the communist-bloc countries and all leftist revolutionary groups of the world.

In 1972 North Korea gave strong propaganda support to the Vietnamese communists and other Indochina revolutionary groups against "U.S. aggression." On 10 May, for example, the DPRK declared that "it was fully prepared to render all forms of assistance, including the dispatch of volunteers," at any time to North Vietnam. In April, Cambodia's deposed Prince Norodom Sihanouk and his party were lavishly welcomed in North Korea by KWP and government officials and the masses.

In Western Europe the DPRK has maintained cultural missions in Austria and France, and trade missions in Finland and Sweden. Lately the Scandinavian countries have been given special attention, and a decision was made in 1972 to establish an information bureau in Norway. In April the Scandinavian countries were visited by a North Korean parliamentary group led by the chairman of the North Korean Central Broadcasting Committee, and in May a Swedish women's delegation led by the chairman of the Left Union of Women of Sweden visited Pyongyang. The DPRK apparently believes that the Scandinavian countries can and will play a key role in helping to change international attitudes toward North Korea, both inside and outside the United Nations.

Relations with the Soviet Union. Currently, the DPRK's *chuch'e* policy is exemplified by its opposition to both Soviet "revisionism" and the "left opportunism" or "dogmatism" of China. But relations with the Soviet Union continued in 1972 to be warm and cordial. The Communist Party of the Soviet Union (CPSU) sent a congratulatory message to Premier Kim Il-song on the occasion of his 60th birthday. Following DPRK foreign minister Ho Tam's visit to Moscow in February, *Pravda* (26 February) reported that the Soviet Union pledged full support for Pyongyang's effort for the peaceful reunification of Korea on the basis of full withdrawal of U.S. troops from South Korea, and that it greeted "with deep understanding and solidarity" North Korean proposals for substituting a peace treaty for the current truce agreement with Seoul and for opening talks with South Korea. (The DPRK's 1972 policy on reunification is close to the tactics that Moscow has long been urging on the militant Pyongyang leadership.) In party affairs, a KWP delegation visited Moscow in July, and a CPSU delegation attended the celebrations in North Korea, in early September, of the 24th anniversary of the founding of the DPRK. On 13 March a 1972 trade protocol was signed in Moscow by North Korea and the Soviet Union. There were the usual exchanges of greetings on anniversaries.

Relations with China. The simultaneous announcement by the Chinese and the United States governments on 15 July 1971 that President Nixon would visit China came as a deep shock to the DPRK, and Pyongyang expressed displeasure with Peking's move for reconciliation with Washington. But Premier Kim Il-song gradually changed his tune and began praising the prospect of a Sino-American détente, as when he predicted that a welcome relaxation of tensions in Asia might result (*Asahi Evening News,* Tokyo, 28 September).

On 4 March 1972, North Korea broke its silence on President Nixon's trip to mainland China, stating in *Nodong Shinmoon* and over Pyongyang radio that Nixon went to Peking to repair past failures, and that "The trip signified the complete failure of the U.S. containment policy against China."

Pyongyang appeared later to have lost some of the apprehension it initially showed over Peking's new policy of contact with the United States. Uncompromising pronouncements on questions at stake with the United States by Premier Chou En-lai and other Chinese spokesmen and by official publications seem to have gone far toward reassuring Pyongyang that China plans no sellout of North Korean interests. Equally important, Premier Kim is keenly aware a small country like North Korea usually has little choice other than to accommodate itself to the changes in great-power relationships.

Relations with Pyongyang and Peking continued to be warm and cordial. On 5 July, the New China News Agency published without comment full details of the talks between North and South Korea, possibly indicating that Peking knew about the secret negotiations between the two Koreas and welcomed them. On 9 July *Jen-min Jih-pao,* the official newspaper of the Chinese Communist Party, said that the results achieved by the high-level talks were "a great victory of the line pushed by North Korean Premier Kim Il-song and the KWP concerning the reunification of the country." The paper welcomed Kim's "attitude" that the Korean question must be left to the Korean people so they may solve it by themselves on the principle of national self-determination and without any interference by outside forces. In short, Peking pledged full support of Kim Il-song's policy on reunification. It also urged the annulment of what it described as the illegal U.N. resolutions regarding Korea, which included authorization for U.S. troops to serve there under the U.N. flag.

In 1972 North Korea and China exchanged various goodwill delegations and many greetings on anniversaries. A 1972 trade protocol was signed in Pyongyang on 31 December 1971. In April 1972 an agreement on mutual cooperation in fisheries was signed.

Relations with Japan. In 1972 North Korea appeared to be ending its long isolation by taking a more flexible posture simultaneously toward South Korea, Japan, and even the United States.

Anti-Japanese feeling is still strong in North Korea, due to the Japanese occupation from 1910 to 1945. Since the fall of 1971, however, the DPRK has softened its approach to Japan. On 10 January 1972 Kim Il-song modified his usual reference to Japan as being bent on militaristic expansion by asserting that he did not think the Japanese people would allow militarism to revive in their country (*Yomiuri Shimbun,* Tokyo, 11 January). On 11 January he brushed aside another traditional North Korean stipulation by suggesting that the 1965 friendship treaty between South Korea and Japan need not necessarily be abrogated before DPRK-Japanese relations could be normalized (*Shakai Shimpo,* Tokyo, 26 January). Since the fall of 1971, meanwhile, countless visits to North Korea have been made by Japanese editors, newspapermen, broadcasters, public figures, politicians, and a few businessmen.

Motives in North Korea's softening attitude toward Japan would seem to be (1) to cause the conservative-controlled Japanese government to change its present exclusive involvement with Seoul and to enter active relations with Pyongyang; (2) to ease Japan's tight restrictions on travel to and from North Korea by Korean residents in Japan; (3) to promote expanded trade and gain access to Japanese industrial machinery and technology needed to develop the North Korean economy rapidly; and (4) to sow seeds of dissent between, as well as within, Japan and South Korea to prevent a Japanese return to the peninsula (Pyongyang is ever suspicious that a solid defense treaty might bud between South Korea and Japan).

Along with the pursuit of rapprochement with mainland China in 1972, Japan was also inching toward better contacts with North Korea. But the conservative-minded government in Tokyo was proceeding cautiously, partly because each seemingly friendly move to Pyongyang has drawn sharp protests from Seoul and partly because North Korea is well down on the priority list of Japan's foreign policy. Japan made a few hesitant gestures toward North Korea —slightly easier travel to the northern half of the peninsula by Korean residents in Japan, talks on expanded trade, and visits of many Japanese journalists (but none yet from North Korea to Japan).

In January a "memorandum agreement for the promotion of trade," modeled after the semi-official connection maintained by Japan with China in the past, was signed in Pyongyang by the North Korean Committee for Promotion of International Trade, a delegation of the Japanese Dietmen's League for Promotion of Japan–North Korea Friendship, and the Japan–North Korea Trade Association (KCNA, 23 January). According to this agreement, two-way trade between Pyongyang and Tokyo would reach $390 million within the next five years (the grand total of two-way trade between the two countries in 1970 was $57.5 million, about one-twelfth of that with South Korea.) North Korea is expected to provide Japan with pig iron, anthracite coal, and iron ore, and Japan would provide North Korea with industrial plants for the manufacture of such products as automobiles and oil refining machinery (*Washington Post,* 22 January).

Relations with the United States. Although "U.S. imperialism" has been the most hated demon in North Korean life, in 1972 Premier Kim Il-song appeared to desire to steer North Korea into some new relationship with the United States. In part, by opening up limited contacts he presumably hopes to weaken domestic support in the United States for its continued troop presence in South Korea.

For the first time, the DPRK permitted newspapermen and a scholar from the United States to visit North Korea—Selig S. Harrison of the *Washington Post,* Harrison E. Salisbury and John M. Lee of the *New York Times,* and Jerome Alan Cohen, director of East Asian Legal Studies at the Harvard Law School. On 26 May Premier Kim told Salisbury and Lee that the Korean conflict was still technically in a state of cease-fire, but he expressed the hope that the relationship between Pyongyang and Washington might be eased and improved if the United States withdrew its forces from South Korea (*NYT,* 31 May). In early March, meanwhile, a spokesman for North Korea in Japan suggested in interviews with U.S. journalists in Tokyo that such troop withdrawal need not necessarily precede improvements in people-to-people relations between the United States and North Korea, though he reaffirmed that normalization of government relations would not be possible until the forces were withdrawn. (ibid., 12 March; *Washington Post,* 7 March). In the summer there was said to have been an approach to a group of U.S. businessmen for building an aluminum plant and a shipyard in exchange for mica, tungsten, coal, and even gold (*U.S. News and World Report,* 31 July). Earlier, however, a U.S. Department of State spokesman said that North Korea had set conditions for the normalization of relations that were "manifestly unacceptable" to Washington and Seoul, and that the continuing vigorous anti-U.S. propaganda campaign made it evident that the DPRK was not interested in a "serious dialogue" with the United States (*NYT,* 1 June).

United Nations. Branded the aggressor in the Korean War by the United Nations, North Korea has condemned all U.N. actions in Korea during the conflict as illegal and since then (1953) has continuously condemned the United Nations as an "external force" which obstructs the independent and peaceful reunification of Korea by interfering without jurisdiction in Korean internal affairs.

In 1972 Premier Kim Il-song changed his tune and suggested that, if invited, the DPRK would participate in a debate on the Korean question at the U.N. General Assembly. He stated also: "It is high time . . . to take the caps of the U.N. forces off the U.S. troops stationed in South Korea under the cloak of the U.N." (*Washington Post,* 26 June). Immediately following the announcement of the 4 July joint communiqué, the DPRK viewpoint was expressed thus: "Now it is clear that none of the outside forces can find any excuse for interfering in the internal affairs of our nation. . . . The U.S. imperialists must no longer meddle in the domestic affairs of our country. They must withdraw without delay, taking with them all their forces of aggression." (KCNA, 4 July.) At a banquet given by the DPRK cabinet in honor of a delegation from The Yemen Arab Republic government, North Korea's first deputy premier Kim Il said that the United Nations should nullify "its old, illegal resolutions on Korea" and "stop the discriminating treatment of one side only" (ibid., 27 July). Later, China's chief delegate to the United Nations said: "The root cause of the prolonged division of Korea and a serious obstacle to its independent and peaceful reunification is the continued interference in the internal affairs of the Korean people carried out in the name of the U.N." He added that "the U.N. must take positive measures to eliminate this interference." (*NYT,* 21 September.) This view was supported by other communist delegations and a number of non-aligned Afro-Asian nations.

In the latter part of September, pro-North Korea members, led by China and Algeria, reopened the campaign to place the question of reunification of Korea on the agenda of the General Assembly, but this effort was beaten back. Britain's proposal to defer discussions of the Korean question for another year was supported by the United States, Canada, and Japan, and was approved by the General Committee in a vote of 16 to 7, with one abstention (ibid., 21, 23 September). Those supporting it held that a U.N. debate might jeopardize the negotiations under way between North and South.

Publications. The KWP publishes a daily organ, *Nodong Shinmoon,* and a journal *Kulloja.* The DPRK government publishes *Minju Choson,* the organ of the Supreme People's Assembly and the cabinet. The *Pyongyang Times, People's Korea,* and *Korea Today* are weekly English-language publications. The official news agency is the Korean Central News Agency (KCNA).

Washington College   Tai Sung An

Laos

The communist party of Laos is the Lao People's Party (Phak Pasason Lao; PPL). The PPL operates under the cover of the Lao Patriotic Front (Neo Lao Hak Xat; NLHX—sometimes NLHS). In terms of pre-1954 Vietnam, the PPL corresponds to the Vietnamese Workers' Party, with whose history the PPL has been intimately bound up and with which it maintains close ties today, while the NLHX corresponds to the Viet Minh (see *Vietnam: Democratic Republic of Vietnam*).

Although NLHX broadcasts and publications occasionally distinguish between "the Party" and "the Front," the PPL is never identified as such. However, estimates of PPL membership range from 12,000 to 14,000 (*World Strength of the Communist Party Organizations,* Washington, D.C., 1972, p. 79). The military arm of the NLHX, the Lao People's Liberation Army (LPLA), better known as the Pathet Lao, probably numbers more than 43,000 troops (ibid.). A dissident neutralist element called the Patriotic Neutralist Forces (PNF), about 2,000 strong, allied itself with the LPLA in 1964 (ibid.). For further data on the history, organization, and leadership of the PPL, NLHX, LPLA, and PNF see *YICA,* 1972, pp. 537–538.

Events in Laos during 1972 continued to be largely dominated by the fighting in neighboring Vietnam and by the efforts to find a settlement at the Paris talks. While the opposing forces moved back and forth over much the same ground that has been fought over in Laos for the past 10 years in accordance with the dictates of the dry and rainy seasons, neither side made strategic gains at the expense of the other. North Vietnamese forces operating in Laos behind the slim cover of the Lao Peoples Liberation Army (LPLA), better known as the Pathet Lao, maintained open the Ho Chi Minh Trail, Hanoi's lifeline to its forces fighting in South Vietnam, despite heavy U.S. bombing.

At the end of the year a ceasefire in Laos hung in the balance of a negotiated ceasefire in South Vietnam. An Indochina-wide ceasefire had long been a part of the publicly stated American negotiating position, and in the secret talks between Dr. Henry Kissinger and Le Duc Tho the former reportedly won an assurance that a ceasefire in Laos represented no insuperable problem (Hanoi's insistence that it has no troops in Laos representing one of the great fictions of the Second Indochina War). On 22 November, however, Prince Souvanna Phouma, the premier, declared that he had a commitment from the United States to continue the bombing in Laos until a ceasefire in Laos is agreed upon. "We have no hope for peace as long as the Vietnam question is unsettled because the Pathet Lao is following North Vietnam in this matter," he said. "Their proposed peace program is exactly like the North Vietnamese program." (*NYT,* 23 November.)

Elections were held in government-controlled territory on 2 January. The NLHX boycotted the elections, calling them illegal, as it has done in the case of every election since its ministers in the tripartite coalition government left Vientiane in 1963 and 1964. The newly elected National Assembly voted to renew confidence in Prince Souvanna Phouma's government.

The year opened with a heavy North Vietnamese offensive against the government base at Long Tieng in northern Laos. Because of the use of long-range Soviet 130 mm. guns for the first time in Laos, the civilian population of Long Tieng was evacuated on 10 January. Severe fighting developed in the following days on the ridgelines surrounding the base with its airstrip, but the Meo defenders of General Vang Pao's irregular army managed to hold out and launch a counteroffensive which had carried them as far as the Plain of Jars by the end of February. In southern Laos also government positions in the Mekong Valley came under severe communist pressure. The North Vietnamese renewed their offensive against Long Tieng during March, but were unable to capture the place.

While the fighting around Long Tieng was raging, the NLHX observed the 16th anniversary of its founding on 6 January. Prince Souphanouvong, half-brother of Prince Souvanna Phouma and the chairman of the NLHX Central Committee, made the following claim on the occasion:

> The liberated zone now extends from the northern to the southern tip, comprising three-fourths of Laos and bordering with China, Vietnam and Cambodia. Over one million people in the liberated zone have established a democratic administration, and genuinely occupy the country. The security in the liberated zone shows that the strength of our people cannot be defeated by any enemy. The liberated zone is the firm guarantee for the final victory of the Lao revolution, and the symbol of Laos in the future, that is a Laos with peace, independence, neutrality, democracy, unity and prosperity. We also have a large number of qualified political, economic, educational and public health personnel. The strength of our personnel has been rapidly extended. Their qualification in political and specialized fields is increasingly excellent. Amidst the revolutionary flames our personnel are growing stronger, and have come to possess heroic fighting spirit, and become more competent in all fields. They are organized into many closely-knit independent groups under the direction of the NLHX Central Committee. (Pathet Lao radio, 6 January.)

In Vientiane, the preliminary talks between Prince Souvanna Phouma and Prince Souphanouvong's special emissary Tiao Souk Vongsak, secretary of state for public works in the coalition cabinet, which had begun in 1970, continued through the early months of 1972 in a cordial atmosphere, although without signs of basic progress on the central issue of finding a way to reconstitute the split "Government of National Union" (established on 23 June 1962, and signatory of the Geneva Accord of 1962 on Laos).

Prince Souvanna Phouma had on numerous occasions offered to discuss the NLHX five-point proposal of 6 March 1970 (see *YICA, 1970,* p. 623), which had become the basic NLHX negotiating position. He repeated this offer in a message to Souphanouvong dated 24 July (Lao Presse bulletin, Vientiane, 30 July 1972). On 8 October occurred the well-known breakthrough in the Paris talks between Kissinger and Le Duc Tho (*NYT,* 27 October), and on 14 October, showing perfect coordination, a 14-member delegation representing the NLHX and its allied party, the Patriotic Neutralist Forces (PNF), disembarked at Vientiane Airport from the regular Aeroflot flight from Hanoi.

That the delegation meant to conduct serious business rather than propaganda drill was evident from the high rank of its leader, General Phoune Sipraseuth, deputy commander in chief of the LPLA and a member of the Standing Committee of the NLHX Central Committee. In a statement at the airport, General Phoune declared:

> If the Nixon Administration is willing to cease its policy of aggression and intervention in Laos and the Vientiane side regards the national interest as the most important thing, it is certain that

the Laos question will be conveniently solved in the forthcoming talks between the two sides. (Pathet Lao radio, 15 October.)

Besides General Phoune, the NLHX-PNF delegation to the talks included Tiao Souk Vongsak; Maha Kou Souvannamethi, a PNF official specializing in Buddhist affairs; Sot Petrasy, the permanent NLHX representative in Vientiane; Lieutenant Colonel Pradit Thiengtham, LPLA; Lieutenant Colonel Cheng Sayavong, PNF officer; Boutsabong Souvannavong, NLHX; Somsak Soukhavong, a former NLHX chief of Savannakhet Province; Phao Bounnaphoh, PNF; Khamsone Vannasongkha, NLHX. Delegation members believed to be members of the Laotian People's Party (Phak Pasason Lao; PPL), the secret communist party at the core of the NLHX, were General Phoune, Tiao Souk Vongsak, Sot Petrasy, Colonel Pradit, and Somsak Soukhavong.

By 17 October, when the first negotiating session was held between the NLHX-PNF delegation and the government delegation headed by Interior Minister Pheng Phongsavan (it was agreed the sessions would be held regularly every Tuesday), Kissinger was on his way from Washington to Saigon (via Paris) to consult with President Nguyen Van Thieu about the draft peace agreement that was shaping up. Procedural matters that had long served as pretexts for delaying the Lao talks, such as the protocol of how the sides would address each other (the NLHX not recognizing the formal jurisdiction of Prince Souvanna Phouma as premier but merely as head of one of the Lao factions), were quickly swept aside as the two sides sat down in the first negotiations since the tripartite consultative commission charged with implementing the terms of the 1962 ceasefire agreement had fallen into disuse.

Prince Souvanna Phouma received a first-hand briefing on the progress of the Paris talks from William H. Sullivan, a former U.S. ambassador to Laos and a member of Kissinger's team, on 20 October, the day the prince departed for his annual visit to Paris and Washington. He thus was fully informed as to where matters stood and no doubt warned not to make any public revelations (in October 1968 the irrepressible prince had been the first person to disclose to the world, following a meeting with Ambassador Sullivan, that President Johnson had decided to halt the bombing of North Vietnam). On October 27, Souvanna Phouma was received at the White House by President Nixon.

The NLHX delegation in Vientiane was further bolstered by the arrival there on 28 October of Phoumi Vongvichit, the NLHX secretary-general and minister of information and tourism in the tripartite coalition. Souvanna Phouma returned to Vientiane on 9 November and held a 90-minute meeting with Phoumi the following day, after which Phoumi departed to return to Sam Neua via Hanoi. Meanwhile, the weekly Lao talks began marking time as it became obvious further negotiations in Paris would be necessary before a Vietnam ceasefire agreement could be arrived at.

During this time military developments were taking place in southern Laos and around the royal capital of Luang Prabang, which was reported closely encircled by communist forces. In late October government forces managed to reoccupy the southern provincial capital of Saravane, which had been in North Vietnamese hands for a year. On 14 November a North Vietnamese attacking force drove the government occupiers out of the town again, but were themselves again driven out on 22 November after a week of heavy fighting with casualties reported heavy on both sides. Meanwhile, government troops also reoccupied Dong Hene, situated on Route 9 east of Savannakhet, which had been in North Vietnamese hands for some time; this occurred on 12 November. Exactly a month later, on 12 December, government troops advancing eastward toward the region of the Ho Chi Minh Trail entered Muong Phalane, occupied by the North Vietnamese since early 1970.

On 12 December, following resumption of the Kissinger-Le Duc Tho talks in Paris on 4 December, the NLHX-PNF delegation at the regular weekly meeting of the Vientiane talks advanced a new comprehensive political-military proposal. The proposal involved a ceasefire, to be followed within 90 days by a withdrawal of all foreign troops, the prohibition of all reprisals, the prohibition of introduction of military supplies into Laos, and the closing of all refugee centers. The draft agreement assumed the dissolution of the present Vientiane government, including the National Assembly, and the city of Vientiane would be declared a neutral zone. The two sides would form a mixed commission to supervise the ceasefire, assisted by the existing three-nation (India, Canada, and Poland) International Control Commission. Until general nationwide elections could be held—and the draft did not say when this would be—a coalition "Political Consultative Council" comprising four equal delegations (one each from the NLHX, PNF, Vientiane government, and Vientiane neutralists) would be established within 30 days of the signing, preparatory to the ultimate formation of a coalition government. A government spokesman termed the proposal "interesting" and the cabinet took it under study. (*NYT,* 13, 14 December.)

The provisions regarding withdrawal of foreign troops from Laos would presumably result in the tacit withdrawal of the some 60,000 North Vietnamese troops in Laos at the time of writing, and also of the some 6,000 Thai troops fighting on the government side. There are no U.S. ground forces in Laos, but a halt to the U.S. bombing would presumably be covered by the terms of the ceasefire.

Prince Souvanna Phouma has repeatedly declared that the adequate basis for a peace settlement in Laos is a return to the Geneva Agreement of 1962. There would appear to be nothing in the 12 December NLHX-PNF proposal that contradicts the letter or spirit of the Geneva Agreement. North Vietnam also, by referring to the Geneva Agreement of 1962 in the U.S.-North Vietnam draft agreement announced by Hanoi on 26 October, has lent its support to a return to this agreement with respect to Laos. Hanoi is of course interested in advancing the cause of its Lao client, the NLHX, but its central interest remains what happens in South Vietnam.

International Relations of the NLHX. During 1972 the NLHX continued to maintain its contacts with like-minded parties abroad, especially with North Vietnam, China, and the Soviet Union. The occasions of anniversary celebrations, solidarity months, and so forth, were used to exchange messages of resolute support in the common struggle against "U.S. imperialism." Prince Souphanouvong is believed to have visited Peking at the end of September. There appeared to be no change in the prince's undisputed titular leadership of the NLHX, which some observers of Laos affairs feel guarantees that the movement will not entirely become the North Vietnamese puppet that it certainly would under the control of members of the Central Committee such as Kaysone Phomvihan (who is half-Vietnamese) or Nouhak Phoumsavan.

University of Maryland   Arthur J. Dommen

Malaysia

During 1972 Malaysian authorities issued important new warnings about domestic communist insurgent dangers facing the country, both in East Malaysia (Sarawak and Sabah) and along the western border with Thailand. Additional security measures and stepped-up counterinsurgency policies were implemented, in cooperation with Indonesia and Thailand. At the same time an increase in the radio and other propaganda efforts of Malaysian communists, relayed and amplified by media of People's China, was to be observed.

History. Chinese in Singapore, and in Penang and other major towns on the Malay Peninsula organized the first covert communist organizations in the area, which on 28 April 1930 merged into the Communist Party of Malaya (CPM). Some CPM branches had earlier formed the basis of a "Communist Party of the South Seas," established in 1928, which was initially conceived as the principal central command post of Southeast Asian communist movements under the control of the Comintern. Organizational difficulties and especially objections from Philippe communists who desired their own national party organization were among the reasons leading to the formation of the Malay Peninsula and Singapore-oriented CPM. Ineffectual in winning significant trade-union following in the thirties, the CPM did not become prominent until the Second World War, when it played a major role in organizing the anti-Japanese resistance.

With the coming of peace and British assurances of independence the party floundered ineffectively until 1948 when, particularly with the support of young radical Chinese, it began a protracted guerrilla struggle against British authority, concentrated in the jungly interior of Malaya. This so-called "Emergency" period lasted until 1960. But well before then communist appeals had been undercut by CPM inability to win over the Malay population group in its struggle, and by the formal creation of the independent Federation of Malaya. Scattered CPM remnants went underground in the poorly patrolled, densely forested Thai-Malaysian border, where since the middle sixties it has launched a new guerrilla campaign, based on the support of local Chinese and exploiting the ethnic grievances of Muslim Malays on both sides of the frontier.

Domestic Developments. Formally outlawed since 1948, the CPM today is estimated by Malaysian Army intelligence to have about 2,500 to 3,000 formal members, with an informal support base of about 5,000 among Chinese and a few Malays in states like Penang, Selangor, and Negri Sembilan. Additionally, Malaysian premier Tun Abdul Razak has also termed the "communist threat" to be "very real" in the states of Kedah, Perlis, Perak, and Kelantan (*Straits Times,* Singapore, 29 June 1971). The party's border guerrilla force (usually designated as the Malayan National Liberation Army—MNLA—in the CPM and Peking media) is estimated at about 1,000 "regulars" by Malaysian Army intelligence sources, drawn from both formal members and informal supporters. At the end of June 1971 Razak said there were "more than 1,000" communist insurgents operating in the border states (Bernama, Malaysian national news agency, Kuala Lumpur, 28 June). Subsequent estimates have put the number at 1,200 to 2,000 plus a trained but unarmed cadre of "several thousand" on the Thai side of the border (*New York Times,* 7 March 1972).

In Sarawak, another 1,000 insurgents and terrorists (ibid., 5 September 1971), generally believed to be drawn from the estimated 3,000 core members of the Sarawak Communist Organization (SCO) and its 5,000 or so informal supporters in the Sarawak Chinese community, have been engaged in anti-government guerrilla operations for nearly a decade. There are no formal or publicized connections between the CPM and SCO, although covert liaison is widely assumed in official circles. Since the late sixties communist activity in the state of Sabah has been negligible. But late in May 1972 Sabah's chief minister, Tun Datu Haji Mustapha warned that there were "small groups" in the state interested in control by "Communist terrorists" and warned that "all out" action would be taken against them (*Sarawak Tribune,* Kuching, 29 May). Discovery of a fortified and camouflaged insurgent camp near Chemor, south of Sungei Siput in Perak state, in mid-June, 1971, triggered a new spate of government counterinsurgency announcements and the publication on 1 October 1971 of a new government "white paper" entitled *The Resurgence of Armed Communism in West Malaysia.* Already two years previously Tun Abdul Razak, then Malaysian deputy premier, had warned that the communist insurgents along the Thai-Malaysian border were planning a "comeback" and that "total war" would be waged against them (*Malaysian Digest,* 31 October 1969). In an address to district officers and military and police personnel of the four border states (Perak, Perlis, Kedah, and Kelantan) at the close of June 1971, Razak (now premier) ordered "total psychological warfare" against the insurgents. At about the same time Razak announced formation of a "National Action Committee," composed of military, police, and civil administrative officers, with subordinate state "action committees" to coordinate the government's anti-communist drive. On 6 July 1971 the government announced that the communists were determined to disrupt implementation of the new second national development plan for 1971–75. In this second plan M\$2.2 billion was provided for defense and internal security (as compared with M\$1.3 billion in the first, 1966–70 national development plan) (*Keesing's Contemporary Archives,* 16–23 October 1971, p. 24878). In the Malaysian parliament government spokesmen justified the increased security expenditures by pointing to the seriousness of the terrorist upsurge.

Throughout 1972 one dimension of the government's psychological warfare campaign attracted particular attention. This was the house-to-house distribution in the border areas of questionnaires by Information Department officers in an attempt to obtain reliable intelligence on the scope of local insurgent activities and its supporters. Government spokesmen declared increased information was thus becoming available from a cooperative public (Bernama dispatch, Ipoh, 3 June). The questionnaires ask for the names of shops which supply food to the terrorists, how the food is taken to the enemy, and where the insurgents' supply bases are. Through the state-level "Action Committees," and in cooperation with state information departments, public performances of "anti-communist" plays specially written and produced for the government's psychological warfare campaign, have been given in the rural areas of the border states. Simultaneously, tens of thousands of leaflets have been distributed, especially in the jungle area of Perak, to induce terrorists to surrender. The leaflets are in fact printed with a safe-conduct pass (*New Nation,* Singapore, 3 July).

At the same time a similar campaign got under way in the First Division of Sarawak, aimed at the SCO. By the close of July the Sarawak government was also offering M$1,000 cash bonuses to any terrorist who "self-renews" (i.e., surrenders) with a Bren or light machine gun, while terrorist couriers supplying letters or other information were promised a reward in accordance with the importance of the intelligence they supplied (*Sarawak Tribune*, 27 July). More controversial has been the government's decision to resettle or regroup villagers suspected of giving aid to the insurgents into closely watched "new villages" and the construction of ten-foot chain-link fencing (connected with watchtowers) around other hamlets within which inhabitants are confined during curfew (*New York Times*, 7 November 1971).

Government spokesmen have sought to ridicule CPM charges that the government "hates" the fenced-in villages, and have emphasized instead that the fencing is there to protect inhabitants from terrorist attacks (*Mirror*, Singapore, 13 March 1972). Government spokesmen also professed particular concern over allegedly new CPM tactics advocating "co-existence" between communism and religion, especially Islam, in the underground party's drive to broaden its ethnic base and enlist more support from the Malay and Indian population groups. (Of Malaysia's 10,187,000 population at the end of 1961, 4.7 million were Malays and other indigenous people, 4.3 million were Chinese, and 0.9 million were of Indian or Pakistani extraction—Malaysian Embassy release, Washington, D.C., January 1, 1964.) CPM propagandists continue to attempt to exploit the dissatisfaction among ardent Muslims on both sides of the Thai-Malaysian border with their respective governments, fostering the image of a secessionist Islamic state comprising both Thai and Malaysian Muslims. While there are units of Muslim Malays in the MNLA, the strongly anti-communist character of Islam renders CPM interracial tactics uncertain of success. CPM following among the Indian-Pakistani group is negligible.

With the cabinet reshuffle effective as of 1 January 1972, Dr. Lim Keng Yaik, a graduate of Queen's University, Belfast, who had played a major role in the resettlement of Chinese villagers in communist-infested areas during the 1948–60 "Emergency," was appointed "Minister with Special Functions" to coordinate the psychological warfare and the "new village" program. Dr. Lim called on CPM terrorist and insurgent leader Chin Peng to surrender, declaring that the "increasing number of terrorists fleeing the red camps" was rendering the communist campaign meaningless. On 10 January deputy premier and home affairs minister Tun Ismail informed parliament that between 1969 and 1971 alone 348 "communist terrorists" had been killed or captured by Malaysian security forces. But although arrests of suspected communist insurgents and supporters were stepped up (in Kedah state alone more than 100 suspects had been detained in a government drive during the previous weeks, according to a statement of the Kedah chief minister—*Sunday Times*, Kuala Lumpur, 16 April), and although Tun Ismail subsequently announced that border security forces had broken up concentrations of insurgents who were now scattering to safety (Bernama dispatch, Bangkok, 30 May), CPM tactics, meanwhile, continued to focus on recruitment in the Malay communities. Government spokesmen also stressed new communist attempts to win a following among students and other young people, and Premier Razak warned that "communist agents" were continuing to infiltrate villages as well as towns (Bernama dispatch, Ipoh, 20 February; *Sunday Times*, 9 April). By June, 1972 a Home Affairs Ministry spokesman declared in the Malaysian parliament that recently 75 youths had been recruited by the CPM in West Malaysia; some allegedly had become cadres and were infiltrated into the urban areas, others were still undergoing training (*Mirror*, 5 June). In September and October intensified government surveillance in Kedah yielded more than a score of arrests of communist suspects. In some Thai-Malaysian border areas the terrorists were sufficiently in control to impose "curfews" of their own in the regions in which they operate (Bernama dispatch, Malacca, 28 July).

CPM Tactics. CPM and terrorist tactics, according to the government's latest "white book" (October 1971) have since 1970 focused on "long-range infiltration for which the secrecy of jungle movement is obviously necessary." Especially the states of Kedah, Perak, and Kelantan were said to have been deeply penetrated in consequence of this new tactical focus. Concomitantly, the CPM was reported to be downgrading open, "united front" activity in conjunction with such communist-infiltrated allied organizations as the Labour Party of Malaya and the "Malayan People's Party" or Partai Rakyat Malaya (now also known as the Partai Sosialis Rakyat Malaya). Indeed, according to the Malaysian government the CPM had permitted the LPM and PSRM "to wither," and had generally become less active in the labor field in line with its "toning down" of all "open" activities.

Instead, Communist organizational efforts, according to the government's "white book," appeared to concentrate on the formation of a covert "mass base," composed of workers and peasants, as a support for "armed struggle." A number of underground groups were being formed by the communists in different parts of the country, and there was "irrefutable evidence of central direction to ensure coordination" among student groups. The Malayan Communist Youth League apparently acted as the coordinating agency, although, according to evidence cited by the government "white book" itself, other underground student organizations, like the "All Penang Revolutionary Students Union," appear to have broad discretionary powers for independent agitational action. Finally, the Malaysian government declared, the new CPM and terrorist tactics seemed to have been drawn from the communist experience in Vietnam: "Vietcong tactics have been used extensively by CT [i.e., communist terrorist] infiltration groups for both offensive and defensive purposes. Jungle areas and paths have been indiscriminately seeded with landmines and booby traps to hamper SF [security force] movements, regardless of the danger they pose to rural folk who seek their livelihood by extracting jungle produce." A captured terrorist, according to the government "white book," testified that Vietcong tactics and theories on the Vietnam war were specific subjects of CPM training lectures which he had attended. (*The Resurgence of Armed Communism in West Malaysia,* Kuala Lumpur, 1971, esp. pp. 5, 10–11, 22–23, 25, 27.)

The preceding government analysis of current CPM tactical concerns is confirmed to a degree by CPM policy statements, including those made over its clandestine radio station, the "Voice of the Malayan Revolution." During 1971, for example, party pronouncements had already stressed the importance of armed revolution (*YICA, 1972,* pp. 545–46), and captured CPM documents cited in the above-named government "white book" are replete with admonitions to cadres to urge adoption of the "armed struggle of the masses" (since the "so-called 'peaceful road' " is but a "sham"), to "surround the cities from the countryside and capture political power by force of arms," and so on. In a New Year's message broadcast on 1 January 1972, the "Voice of the Malayan Revolution" declared (Foreign Broadcast Information Service, 7 January):

> With the support of all nationalities in the countryside, our army intensified its military activities by mounting various offensives, thereby smashing the enemy's encirclement and suppression operations and achieving good results through valiant fighting. This has further consolidated our base and guerrilla areas on the Malay-Thai border. . . . According to preliminary statistics our army wiped out over 300 men of the Malayan and Thai reactionary forces, wiped out over 30 secret agents and running dogs, damaged two fighter bombers; destroyed three military vehicles, and captured a large quantity of weapons, ammunition and food supplies. . . .

> Under the incentive of the revolutionary armed struggle, which is continuously expanding, the political awareness of the people of various strata was further enhanced. They realized . . . that only by encircling the cities from the countryside and seizing political power by armed force

could they implement the program of the new democratic revolution promulgated by the Communist Party which represents the interests of the people of various strata.

In a broadcast on 29 April, commemorating the forty-second anniversary of the CPM, the "Voice of the Malayan Revolution" declared that "nearly twenty-seven of the forty-two glorious years" of the party had been years of the "great revolutionary war," adding that "Our people . . . grasping the gun firmly and fighting courageously" would gain new victories as the MNLA advanced (*Peking Review*, 26 May). In another "Voice" broadcast, on 17 June, being an editorial commentary on the "Struggle for the Development of People's War," identical themes are found. Stressing that without arms it would be impossible to "expand the people's revolutionary force and create a revolutionary situation as favorable to the people as it is today," the commentary noted that "The violent flames of the armed struggle are constantly spreading," especially in Perak, Kelantan, Kedah, and other states. "To accomplish the new democratic revolution," the statement emphasizes further, "we must follow the path of encircling the cities from the countryside, and seizing political power by armed force." (Foreign Broadcast Information Service, 27 June.)

In subsequent months during 1972 both the "Voice" and clandestine CPM pamphlets in Chinese and Malay repeated the absolute necessity of "armed struggle" in the "liberation war" of "all the nationalities" in Malaya against what was termed the "Razak clique." Additionally, "Voice" broadcasts sought to depict a broadening social base for CPM-led revolutionary action. Thus, in its earlier cited 1 January 1972 New Year's message, the "Voice" declared that people "of all strata" were launching a struggle for equal rights "among the races in all fields," adding that "poor people and petty traders in the cities," and "handicraft workers," as well as "the fishermen," students, "various nationalities," and "peasants" striving to abolish the "feudal" and "semi-feudal" agrarian system were all joining in a great expression of revolutionary unity behind the national "liberation" army.

CPM Organization. The emphasis on the "unity" of races and nationalities in CPM statements is to a degree reflected in the major leadership levels of the CPM, although Chinese continue to dominate the organization. The principal CPM leader of the 1948–60 guerrilla war, Chin Peng, is generally believed to be still party secretary-general, a post he has now held for a quarter of a century. (Though reportedly in ill health, Chin, to all intents and purposes, *is* the CPM, especially in its foreign contacts.) The offices of party chairman and vice-chairman, largely though not wholly honorary, are held respectively by two Malays, Musa Ahmad and Abdul Rashid bin Maidin (the latter is in prison). There is also a ten-man Central Committee and a four-man Politburo, including agitprop section Chairman Chen Tien and control commission (i.e., party discipline) chairman Li On Tung. Seven of the Central Committee are Chinese, two Malays, and one Indian. There is reportedly a "resident" CPM group in Peking which assists in the largely Chinese Communist–financed "Voice of the Malayan Revolution" operations and the printing of CPM publications. According to Malaysian Army intelligence sources, the CPM in early April 1972 announced complete state party hierarchies in Kedah and Kelantan, but names of cadres have not been released.

The MNLA is divided into three "operational" units and one "reserve and training" unit. The "Tenth Regiment," predominantly Muslims and Malays, is active around Weang, on the Thai side of the border and in Kelantan state. Members of this regiment, unlike other operational units, have done double duty as propagandists in remote village areas, moving about in groups of ten or twenty, attending mosque services, helping villagers with ploughing and tapping of rubber trees, and seeking generally close identification with the "masses" (*Straits Times*, 30 June 1971). The MNLA's "Eighth Regiment" is reportedly based near the Thai town of Sadao, operating from there into Perlis and Kedah states. The "Twelfth Regiment," believed to be the strongest and best equipped, reportedly has its headquarters near Betong, in Thailand's Yala Province, but operates primarily in the Perak and Kedah states of Malaysia. According to Malaysian police sources, there has been growing cooperation between the MNLA and the underground Thai Communist Party (*Australian Financial Review,* 8 March 1972). With the new stress on building a broad-based "peasant-workers' alliance" and student support organizations, the MNLA's and CPM's alliance with an infiltration of the Labour Party of Malaya and the Partai Sosialis Rakyat Malaya has greatly declined, as has identification with other fronts like the Malayan National Liberation League. The Malayan Communist Youth League (MCYL) has now become the principal front organization and with its affiliates in other states, like the "All Penang Revolutionary Students Union," a principal source of new MNLA recruits. The new MNLA "reserve and training" regiment, based on a number of shifting Thai-Malaysian border camps, has (according to Malaysian Army intelligence sources) developed a network of regular courier communications with underground MCYL chapters in West Malaysia's major cities and in some village areas.

Organization and Operations of SCO. The Sarawak Communist Organization (SCO) has a core personnel of about 3,000 and an additional 1,000 in guerrilla forces. SCO is the generic name given to an aggregate of banned undergound organizations, including the North Kalimantan Communist Party (NKCP—successor to the Sarawak Liberation League of the thirties in the town of Sibu), the Sarawak Advanced Youth Association (SAYA), and the Sarawak Farmers' Association (SFA). The guerrilla or "terrorist" force comprises two organizations, the North Kalimantan People's Army (Pasokan Rakyat Kalimantan Utara, or Paraku) and the Sarawak People's Guerrilla Force (Pergerakan Gerilja Rakyat Sarawak; PGRS). Neither Paraku nor PGRS—both drawn almost entirely from the urban dissident Chinese youth of Sarawak—appears to have stable cadres or memberships. A number of cadres of both organizations are believed to have trained originally in military and paramilitary camps in Indonesian West Borneo during the Indonesian "confrontation" campaign against Malaysia (1963–66).

The SCO structure is informal, with principal recruiting responsibility and organizational reliance being placed on units and branches of SAYA (for youth work), SFA (for rural inhabitants) and Paraku (terrorism). The NKCP reportedly has a central committee, but except for its secretary-general, Wong Kie Chok (see below), its membership is not known. In July 1970 a principal legal support organization of the SCO, the Sarawak United People's Party (SUPP) whose left wing was communist-infiltrated, began partcipating in the government at the Sarawak state level and subsequently in the national cabinet, and its value to the SCO as an ally has been greatly reduced. Overwhelmingly popular among Sarawak's more than 300,000 Chinese (about a third of the state's total population), the SUPP won nearly 29 percent of the vote in the 1970 elections, and its appeal clearly reached to Malay, Dayak, and other Sarawak population groups as well, most of which are generally strongly anti-communist (R. S. Milne and K. J. Ratnam in *Journal of Southeast Asian Studies,* March 1972, pp. 111–22). Both Paraku and PGRS operate in "batallions" of about forty to fifty men (and some women), and are assumed to maintain ties with the banned, underground Indonesian communist movement. A former Indonesian communist party Central Committee member, M. Sofian, heads Paraku's ideological training. Paraku's chief commander, however, is a Maoist-Oriented Sarawak Chinese, Wong Kie Chok, who reportedly served in the early sixties as an employee in the Chinese Embassy in Djakarta. During 1972 some PGRS units merged with Paraku, which, according to Indonesian military sources, has today become the principal guerrilla force operating on both sides of the Sarawak-Indonesia border.

Early in February 1972 the Malaysian government published a new "white paper" on the SCO. According to this document, the threat of armed communism in Sarawak in the past two years has assumed "serious proportions," with regular infiltration taking place into the state from the Sarawak-Indonesia border areas of West Kalimantan (Indonesian Borneo). The NKCP, according to the "white paper," is "dedicated to the violent pursuit of political power in order to establish communist hegemony in North Kalimantan." Particular attention was called in this "white paper" to: (1) the communist control system imposed upon some 500 families living in the remote Nonok region of Sarawak, complete with communist "village committees," a system recently broken up by government counterinsurgency measures, (2) the influx into Sarawak of SCO agents charged with the establishment of permanent guerrilla bases from which sustained "armed struggle" would be launched, (3) the SCO's intensified efforts to shed its "Chinese" character by winning recruits from both the native Dayak and Malay population groups, including instruction to cadres in indigenous Dayak languages, (4) the active collaboration between Indonesian communists and the SCO leading to the formation of a joint guerrilla group, known as the "Bara Force," which was eventually absorbed into the PGRS, and (5) the help flowing to the SCO and its component units from families and friends of SCO members: "Most of the SCO members coming as they do from small closely-knit rural communities, have maintained their personal ties for the purpose of exploiting sentiment in order to secure support." ("The Threat of Armed Communism in Sarawak," *Malaysian Digest*, 15 February 1972.)

Commenting on the significance of the Sarawak "white paper," Malaysian home affairs minister Tun Ismail declared that Malaysian security forces in Sarawak the previous year had killed 85 terrorists, captured 36, and accepted the surrender of 40 more. Some 60 guerrilla camps were found, and nearly 700 "active supporters" of the SCO were arrested. Tun Ismail also declared at this time that the answer to the communist problem lay in the economic development of Sarawak for which the government had "plans in hand." (Ibid.)

There has been evidence throughout 1972 that SCO cadres are stepping up recruitment. In the Chinese village of Sungei Bedut, near Sibu, SCO activists feel free to "walk into schools" and "deliver lectures," with attacks on the "decadent West" apparently being a favorite theme (James Morgan, "Battle for Sarawak," *Far Eastern Economic Review*, 5 February 1972). A principal SCO propaganda tactic, as in the past, remains that of fostering secessionist sentiments in Sarawak, holding out the image of an independent state free from Malaysia in which the Sarawak Chinese community, because of its prominence in the state's financial and business life, would be dominant. Despite repeated efforts by government security forces to seal off all possible infiltration routes (see, e.g., *Sarawak Tribune*, 14 February) Paraku-PGRS elements still are able to move back and forth across the jungly Sarawak-Indonesia frontier, eluding pursuers, just as the CPM and MNLA are utilizing the Thai-Malaysian frontier in a similar tactic.

According to the Malaysian government, terror remains a major SCO weapon: by mid-1972, for example, the SCO was alleged to have killed 28 civilians so far that year, a rate nearly three times that of "ordinary" murders (ibid., 14 July). In response to these terrorist tactics, Premier Razak announced on 27 March that villagers in the more remote parts of Sarawak would be provided with arms to defend themselves against the SCO, and by the beginning of May special corps of armed civil defense had also been formed in a number of smaller towns and villages in Central Sarawak (Associated Press dispatch, Kuching, 5 May). Sarawak's Third Division was declared a "Special Security Area" and new control measures were to be taken in respect of the private Chinese schools, long a source of SCO recruitment (*Far Eastern Economic Review*, 15 April). On July 27 the Malaysian Home Affairs Ministry reported that 1,500 additional troops would be sent to Sarawak to take the field against the communists. Despite mass arrests (on 23 March the Sarawak "State Director of Operations" against the insurgents, Dato Haji Abdul Rahman Yakub, announced that in the preceding twenty-four hours 124 persons, a majority of them students, had been arrested in a new anti-communist drive—*Sarawak Tribune,* 24 March), and much publicized instances of surrender of SCO cadres (Bernama dispatch, Kuala Lumpur, 19 June), there is no evidence that the insurgency is significantly abating.

However, there are SCO tactical reverses. According to Chinese media, in the "protracted revolutionary struggle" of the SCO, the "people's armed forces have done mass work while fighting," establishing "close relations" with "the people of various nationalities" (*Peking Review,* 17 March). In fact, effective SCO recruitment from among the Dayak and Malay populations, despite strenuous efforts, thus far has been small. No non-Chinese, for example, has been discovered at this time commanding a Paraku-PGRS "batallion," nor are any Malays or Dayaks known to be among the principal leaders of SAYA, SFA, or other SCO constituent groups.

Long-term SCO strategy remains that of developing a true "mass base" of support for the armed insurgents; hence, winning a following among non-Chinese in Sarawak is indispensable. In this connection, current SCO "village welfare" work, such as medical assistance to isolated Dayak communities "which have never seen a doctor before," or help in harvesting or in repairing houses, is giving Malaysian authorities concern (*New York Times,* 15 March). At the same time, Paraku-PGRS guerrilla attacks continue to be focused on government security patrols and outposts, in an attempt to undermine confidence in public authority. For example, on the very day that the Malaysian premier visited Sarawak to announce new emergency measures (26 March), 15 Malaysian rangers were ambushed and killed by SCO guerrillas some sixty miles west of Sarawak's capital of Kuching (*Far Eastern Economic Review,* 15 April).

International Implications. The Soviet Union, which maintains an embassy in Kuala Lumpur and is pushing expanding commercial relations with Malaysia, has kept noticeably silent on the CPM and SCO insurgencies and on intensified Malaysian government efforts at their suppression. Despite significant Sino-Malaysian trade (in 1971 China's imports from Malaysia were valued at US$17.6 million, China's exports at US$45.1 million—*Far Eastern Economic Review,* 30 September 1972), and brisk, if covert exports of Malaysian rubber to China, there are no formal Sino-Malaysian diplomatic relations, and Peking continues to aid (according to Malaysian Army intelligence with funds as well as training of agents) the cause of both the MNLA and Paraku. Peking radio continues to relay, with obvious official sanction, statements of the "Voice of the Malayan Revolution" (which broadcasts from Yunnan Province, in the south of China) and MNLA claims of successes in its "people's war" in Malaysia (Peking radio, 5 January; *Mirror,* 12 June). Malaysian premier Razak, in turn, emphasized his government's support for the entry of China in the United Nations, along with his hope that Peking would observe the UN Charter which "obliges members not to interfere in the internal affairs of others." The communist threat at Malaysia's borders, Razak went on, could in any case not be settled merely on a "quid pro quo basis with China" (Bernama dispatch, Kuala Lumpur, 8 December 1971).

Both ideologically and tactically the CPM-MNLA and the SCO-Paraku-PGRS are Maoist in character, and Peking continues to include "Malaya" in the periodic world surveys in its media devoted to the kind of "armed struggle" of which it approves (see, e.g. *Peking Review,* 21 July 1972). Meanwhile, the Democratic Republic of (North) Vietnam has voiced its support for the communist Malaysian insurgencies also. On February 1, 1972, Hanoi radio lauded the anniversary of the founding of the MNLA, quoting *Quan Doi Nhan Dan,* the DRV Army newspaper, in this connection, and adding that "nothing" could check the advance of the "Malayan revolution." Under the CPM leadership, this North Vietnamese statement went on, a genuinely independent, united, and democratic country would emerge (*Mirror,* 14 February). In keeping with the secessionist sentiments of the SCO and the aspirations of the CPM, the new atlas put out in Peking by the Titu Chupanse publishing house in July, 1972 ignores the term "Malaysia," referring to the country instead as "Malaya."

Reflecting the Malaysian government's heightened sense of public concern over communist activity, new steps were taken in 1972 between Malaysia and Indonesia, and between Malaysia and Thailand, to foster cooperation in border security drives. On 26 December 1971, Djakarta radio announced that a combined Indonesian-Malaysian border operations command had been established in Wangpadun, Sarawak, to combat the Paraku-PGRS. Three days earlier, Djakarta radio announced that two companies of the Malaysian Special Services Regiment (used in counterinsurgency operations) were undergoing training in Bandung, West Java, and that more Malaysian officers would be sent to Indonesia for paratroop training. On 15 March and 17 April expanded joint Malaysian-Indonesian military agreements against communist border insurgents were announced in Djakarta and Kuala Lumpur. The new arrangement was described as a renewal of a pattern of counterinsurgency operations already agreed upon by the two countries in 1967. Under the new agreement Malaysia and Indonesia are to set up a joint Border Committee, with appropriate agencies, to coordinate "joint military operations." Cooperation would be raised from local to inter-governmental levels, with the Indonesian side to be represented by General Maraden Panggabean, state minister of defense and security, and the Malaysian side by Tun Ismail, deputy premier. (*Antara Daily News Bulletin,* 15 March, vol. 24, no. 1424, and 17 April, vol. 24, no. 1449.) On 11 October the Antara news agency in Indonesia announced the "first results" of the new joint border operation, including the killing of one terrorist and the capture of arms and food supply caches and godowns by Malaysian and Indonesian troops and patrols.

On 20 May, Indonesian naval chief of staff R. Sudomo declared that arms were being smuggled by sea to the communist insurgents along the Sarawak-Indonesia border, and that naval patrols around Kalimantan were continuing, inasmuch as last year one vessel, suspected of smuggling arms, had been sunk by the Indonesian Navy in the South China Sea but in Indonesian territorial waters. Chairman Imron Roshidi of the Indonesian parliament's Foreign Affairs Committee charged, meanwhile, that certain cattle vessels from Indonesia to Hong Kong were smuggling arms on their way back to Indonesia (*Sunday Tribune,* Kuching, 21 May; on Indonesian reports of arms smuggling see also *YICA, 1972,* p. 550). In September, Malaysia and Indonesia reached agreement on joint sea patrols in the South China Sea and the Straits of Malacca "directed at subversive activities and Communist infiltration" (*Angkatan Bersendjata,* Djakarta, 28 September).

At first, in April 1972, the West Malaysia military commander, Malaysian general Dato Othman Ibrahim, declared that "coordinated naval patrols" by Malaysia and Thailand had "deterred" terrorist infiltration along the Thai-Malaysian border by sea; no arrest of terrorist suspects and vessels carrying arms had been made since the patrols started two years before (Bernama dispatch, Penang, 25 April). At the end of May, however, Malaysian deputy premier Ismail, shortly before flying to Bangkok to participate in a Thai-Malaysian Border Committee meeting, declared that additional ways had to be found to "curb terrorist infiltration to both countries by sea," and that there was need to strengthen naval patrols, especially along a seven-mile stretch of shallow waters between Thailand and the Malaysian state of Perlis (ibid., Kuala Lumpur, 29 May). In subsequent months, both the Thai-Malaysian Border Committee and the new Indonesian-Malaysian Border Committee stressed the necessity of improved intelligence on insurgent movements. Malaysian police sources have warned of "strengthening liaison" between Malay communists and the underground, but operationally expanding, Thai Communist Party (*New York Times,* 7 March).

Publications. Neither the CPM nor the SCO has regularly-appearing papers or periodicals, although leaflets and mimeographed pamphlets appear from time to time, usually under different names. In London CPM sympathizers publish the *Malayan Monitor and General News,* technically a monthly, but appearing irregularly. The Yunnan-based "Voice of the Malayan Revolution," which daily broadcasts in Chinese, Malay, and Hindi for about six hours, is the CPM's principal news and propaganda medium. Chinese media frequently relay "Voice of the Malayan Revolution" broadcasts. In Sarawak, SCO opinion is articulated through the monthly *Liberation News* (also in Malay edition) and through infrequently appearing newspapers like *Masses News* and *Workers and Farmers News.*

University of Bridgeport   Justus M. van der Kroef

Mongolia

The Mongolian People's Party was founded in 1921 as a fusion between two revolutionary groups. Its First Congress was held in March of that year on Soviet territory, at Kyakhta. Since the Third Congress, held in 1924 at the Mongolian capital city of Ulan Bator (then called Urga), it has been known as the Mongolian People's Revolutionary Party (MPRP). At its Sixteenth Congress, in June 1971, it claimed 58,048 members, or slightly more than 4 percent of the population estimated at 1.3 million in 1970.

Organization and Leadership. The MPRP is organized approximately along the same lines as the Communist Party of the Soviet Union (CPSU). The Politburo has seven full and three candidate members. The Secretariat has five members (four of whom are also on the Politburo as full or candidate members).

The Mongolian premier, Tsedenbal, is also the first secretary and a Politburo member of the MPRP. There are two first deputy premiers (one a full member of the Politburo and the other a candidate) and six deputy premiers (of whom two are Politburo members). The so-called Presidium of the Great Khural (structural equivalent to the U.S.S.R.'s Supreme Soviet) includes a first deputy chairman (also a Politburo member) and two deputy chairmen (of whom one is a Politburo member). A replacement for the former chairman of the Khural Presidium, the deceased Sambu, has not been announced. In all, 16 individuals fill the top 27 party and government positions in the MPR. All 16 occupied very high positions—often the same positions—ten years ago. Experience in economics and planning is a consistent factor in retention of or promotion to high office.

The Mongolian Revolutionary Youth League (MRYL) is the MPRP's organization for young persons. It has about 80,000 members. The Central Council of Trade Unions (CCTU) claimed a membership of 170,000 in 1969–70.

In June 1972 a Central Committee plenum announced the institution of a unified system for state and public control, based on the experience of public control organs of the Soviet Union.

Domestic Attitudes and Activities. Several official announcements in 1972 stated that livestock continues to be the country's most important economic resource, and indicated a goal for 1975 of 25.1 million head. The figure of 25 million head of livestock has been the plan-goal many times in the past thirty years, and seems never to have been attained. A manpower shortage in the rural areas was indicated by the non-voluntary assignment of 50,000 secondary-school graduates to work in those places. The pattern of continued growth of the capital city of Ulan Bator (now some 270,000 population) and also development of smaller "new industrial cities" like Darkhan in the north and Choibalsan in the east continues, even though many places around the country still seem to unite no more than 25 to 50 people living in fewer than a dozen yurts (the Mongolian wood-framed felt tent). But television has come to Mongolia.

Announcements also claim a start on development of mining for molybdenum in the north and copper in the south, with specific negotiations having occurred regarding Soviet assistance and more general discussions concerning Japanese help. Related railroad projects form part of these negotiations. Education continues to serve large numbers in the country, and some 2,000 Mongols were studying abroad in 1972, most of them in the U.S.S.R.

International Views and Positions.

Relations with the U.S.S.R. The basic Mongolian international attitude of undeviating support of the U.S.S.R. continued in 1972. There is no likelihood of the MPR's shifting to China (or to any other country) against the Soviet Union. Soviet troops operate freely throughout Mongolia, and its border with China constitutes the de facto strategic border of the U.S.S.R. Mongolian foreign trade is mainly with the U.S.S.R., and significant Soviet subsidies are granted to the MPR.

Relations with China. In May a particularly virulent Mongolian press attack charged that the Chinese in Inner Mongolia practice "Great Khan chauvinism" and "appalling discrimination and compulsory assimilation." But China continued to have an ambassador in Ulan Bator, and in December discussions were opened concerning the possible return of a few Chinese laborers to Mongolia to finish projects left uncompleted when the Chinese departed in 1966.

Relations with Other Countries. A variety of official and unofficial developments attested to the comparative opening up of Mongolia in 1972, continuing the steady trend of recent years. Tsedenbal visited Cuba in 1972. A Mongolian team participated in the Munich Olympics. Some 1,200 foreign tourists were reported to have come to the MPR in 1970, and undoubtedly the number was much larger in 1972. MPR activity in the United Nations continued in 1972, and diplomatic relations with Japan, Australia, the Netherlands, and others were established. (In January 1973 U. S. press reports indicated that the United States would very likely soon extend recognition.)

Publications. The MPRP publishes a daily newspaper, *Unen* ("Truth"), which has a circulation of about 82,000. The party also publishes a monthly, *Namyn Amdral* ("Party Life"). The MRYL organ, *Zaluchuudyn Unen* ("Young People's Truth"), has 144 issues each year (circulation 60,000); the CCTU organ, *Khudulmur* ("Labor"), has 156 issues per year; and the army organ appearing twice a week is *Ulan Od* ("Red Star"). Montsame is the official MPR news agency.

University of North Carolina,   Robert A. Rupen
Chapel Hill

Nepal

The Communist Party of Nepal (CPN) was founded in Calcutta, India, in 1949 by a small group of Nepalis associated with the Communist Party of India. The CPN was banned in Nepal in 1952. In 1955 the party softened its politically unrewarding anti-monarchic policy, and the ban was lifted the following year.

Background on Leadership and Organization. During the 1950s, as the CPN grew and its policy toward the monarchy was debated, moderate and revolutionary factions crystallized, the moderate faction led by Keshar Jang Rayamajhi and the revolutionary faction by Pushpa Lal Shrestha. The majority faction was Rayamajhi's and drew its strength largely from Kathmandu Valley. The Pushpa Lal faction attracted support in the Valley and in the plains region of Nepal called the tarai. In the parliamentary elections of 1959, the CPN ran candidates in 46 of the 109 constituencies and won 4 seats: 2 in the eastern tarai, one in the western hills, and one in Kathmandu Valley. The party ran strongly in other eastern tarai and Kathmandu Valley constituencies as well.

In 1960, King Mahendra's overthrow of the Nepali Congress–dominated parliamentary government and proscription of political parties brought on a split between the Pushpa Lal and Rayamajhi factions. Pushpa Lal fled to India to organize opposition to King Mahendra's government, while Rayamajhi remained in Nepal to support the king. During 1961 and 1962 Pushpa Lal attempted to work with Nepali Congress exiles in India, but his efforts floundered in late 1962 as a result of the Sino-Indian conflict and the subsequent Nepali Congress decision to terminate its rebel activities. The Sino-Indian conflict contributed to a split within the Pushpa Lal group. Pushpa Lal supported the Indian position in the conflict, while another revolutionary CPN leader, Tulsi Lal Amatya, supported the Chinese and formed his own factional party. In more recent years Pushpa Lal has adopted a pro-Chinese position, and the split no longer appears to exist.

In the meantime, with its major political competitors—Nepali Congress and revolutionary CPN leaders—either in jail or in exile, the moderate Rayamajhi group has prospered. The group's organizational structure of central bodies, regional committees, and a few local cells was kept intact, and the group has functioned more or less openly, with Rayamajhi as the secretary-general. Moderate Communists and their sympathizers ran in the first non-party elections of the king's "panchayat" (assembly) government in 1963 and were reported to have won 15 to 20 percent of the seats in the national panchayat, a considerable improvement over their representation in the parliament of four years earlier. Rayamajhi was appointed by the king to the prestigious but powerless Raja Sabha or royal advisory body, and individuals closely associated with Rayamajhi have been included in most of the ministries formed by the king since 1963. One of Rayamajhi's associates in the past, Shailendra Kumar Upadhyaya, served as home minister in 1970 and 1971. King Mahendra was willing to tolerate the activities of the moderate communists and even to encourage their leaders because he envisaged them as counters to the more popular, more anti-monarchic, and therefore more threatening activists within the revolutionary communist faction and the Nepali Congress.

During the 1960s and early 1970s the three major political forces in Nepal have been the monarchy, the CPN, and the Nepali Congress, with the monarchy dominating. The CPN leaders, particularly Pushpa Lal since his efforts to cooperate with the Congress failed in 1962, and the Nepali Congress leaders have spent considerable time attacking each other. This has been particularly the case since the king released Nepali Congress leaders in late 1968 and revolutionary communist leaders in early 1969, many of whom had been in jail since 1960. Conflict between the two parties was encouraged not only by the adroit politics of the king, but also by the parties' competition for support among the same segments of the population —the students, intellectuals, and, to a lesser extent, villagers. Among the communist leaders released were Shambhu Ram Shrestha and Man Mohan Adhikari. Shambhu Ram had been a moderate member of the CPN Central Committee until the early 1960s, but both he and Adhikari took strong pro-Chinese stands after their release. The moderates have generally been pro-Soviet on international issues and the revolutionaries pro-Chinese, although the major source of conflict between the two factions has always been disagreement about policy toward the monarchy rather than attitudes toward the Soviet Union and China.

Between 1969 and early 1972, revolutionary communist literature circulated widely through Nepal charging Nepali Congress rivals with bourgeois values and association with Indian officials anxious to bring Nepal under their control. The Nepali Congress leaders countered with statements about the growing danger of a communist takeover and subsequent control by China. Some of this rhetoric may have been stimulated by party leaders' hopes of gaining indirect support from foreign powers. In any case, the rivalry between the workers of the two parties has been overt and periodically intense, particularly in some urban centers of the tarai: Bhadrapur, Dharan, Biratnagar, Janakpur, Birganj, and Bhairawa.

Current Domestic Activities. King Mahendra died on 31 January 1972, and his son, Birendra, ascended the throne. Taking advantage of the young king's inexperience, many political leaders began demanding return to a more liberal form of government, with open sessions of the national legislature, direct elections to it, ministers responsible to the legislature rather than to the king, freedom of the press, and a less heavy-handed use of the Public Security Act to stifle political opposition. Until August, King Birendra appeared to be indecisive in responding to these demands, which seemed to encourage politicians to become continually more vocal in their criticism of the panchayat system. Among the most outspoken critics were Keshar Jang Rayamajhi and Man Mohan Adhikari.

Although the moderate communists had found it profitable to support King Mahendra, during the February-August period of 1972 they obviously decided that it was safe to take a more critical stand. In February, Rayamajhi expressed the hope that King Birendra would make a series of political reforms (*Matribhumi* 8 February; note—all sources cited are weekly papers published in Kathmandu). Over the following months he demanded a government elected by adult franchise (*Rashtra Pukar,* 20 April), and fundamental rights for the people and amnesty for political workers in jail or in exile. (*Samiksha,* 8 May). Although Rayamajhi did not state publicly that he favored a return to a competitive political party system, this inference appears to be intended in his various statements.

Adhikari was much more vociferous in his criticisms. He demanded an end to the "anti-people" policies of the government and removal of the ban on political parties (*Matribhumi,* 11

July). He even called upon Nepalis to unite to bring about the downfall of the king's appointed Council of Ministers headed by Prime Minister Kirtinidhi Bista (*Motherland,* 30 August). Adhikari has been perhaps the most popular of all Nepalese communist leaders, and since his release from jail in 1969 he has attempted to use his contacts with both the moderate and revolutionary factions of the CPN to unify the party. His own views are closer to those of Pushpa Lal than to those of Rayamajhi at present. He and Shambhu Ram Shrestha are both members of the Politburo of the Pushpa Lal faction, although it was reported that Shambhu Ram was expelled from the Politburo at its September meeting in Banaras, India (*Naya Sandesh,* 6 October). There has been debate between Adhikari and Pushpa Lal over methods of organizing revolution and its timing. Pushpa Lal appears anxious to launch an armed attack from India into Nepal as soon as possible, while Adhikari insists that it is necessary to take more time and to lay a firm groundwork of organization among the villagers. He has been candid about this debate in his public remarks. In a December interview he said, "Nothing can be achieved as long as we do not work among the peasantry. The recent strikes at Tribhuwan University and students' opposition [to the government] show that only the students have become conscious, not the peasants. Nobody has ever brought about a revolution by staying abroad." He also admitted his failure to achieve a reconciliation with Pushpa Lal because of the latter's insistence on immediate efforts to launch an armed struggle. (*Samiksha,* 6 December.)

In August, King Birendra decided to get tough with critics and since then has been making sweeping arrests, but has not jailed Adhikari, presumably because the government prefers to leave him free to continue his attempts to moderate Pushpa Lal's activities. Indeed, when the Pushpa Lal faction distributed a leaflet in the eastern tarai in December indicating the faction's association with the Indian Naxalites, the revolutionary wing of the Communist Party of India, Adhikari warned that disciplinary action would be taken against CPN members who attempted to use Naxalite support (*Nirmal,* 15 December). However, as a result of his unwillingness to accept a plan for immediate armed revolution, Adhikari has lost support among the most radical communist students. At the fourth annual conference of the Nepal National Independent Students' Union, a "Maoist" group, held in Kathmandu in June, Adhikari was branded a "neo-revisionist" (*Rashtra Pukar,* 29 June).

In September 1971, B. P. Koirala, a Nepali Congress leader and former prime minister, had warned King Mahendra that there would be an armed revolution if he did not return Nepal to parliamentary democracy (*Chetana,* 24 September). On 24 August, 1972 a group of armed men crossed the Indian border into the eastern tarai district of Saptari and attacked the Haripur village police station, killing one policeman. The attack was reminiscent of those conducted by exiled Nepali Congress rebels in 1961 and 1962, and the Nepali Congress appears to have been responsible for the Haripur raid. Because of the apparent revolutionary stance of the Nepali Congress, there has been discussion between Koirala and Pushpa Lal, and reports that the Pushpa Lal faction was supporting Nepali Congress activities (*Weekly Mirror,* 7 August).

The most obvious manifestations of competition between the CPN and the Nepali Congress parties occur at Tribhuvan University on the outskirts of Kathmandu and in the various university-affiliated colleges in Kathmandu Valley and in the tarai. The revolutionary-oriented communist, Maoist, or "progressive" students tend to dominate politics in the colleges of Patan in Kathmandu Valley and Dharan in the eastern tarai. In the university and in most other colleges, the revolutionary communist and Nepali Congress student factions seem fairly equally matched, with perhaps a slight edge for Congress supporters in the past several years. In 1968 and 1970 the communists controlled the major elected offices in the student union at the university and in 1969, 1971, and 1972 these offices were won by Congressites. The student union at Thakur Ram College in the central tarai town of Birganj has been dominated by communist adherents over the past few years; in 1972, however, 24 of the 25 students winning seats on the union's executive committee ran on pro-Congress labels. In the eastern tarai town of Biratnagar, the student union of Morang College had been under the control of pro-communist students for the past three years, but control went to the pro-Congress students in 1972. As already mentioned, the revolutionary communist student organization is the Nepal National Independent Students' Union. The Nepali Congress student organization is the Nepal Students' Union, and the moderate communist student organization is the National Student Union. The latter is only slightly more effective than the moribund pro-government Nationalist Independent Student Union.

The student politics are noisy, with occasional street fights between communist and Congress groups in several tarai towns and periodic demonstrations in Kathmandu. These students are embarrassing to the government because of the publicity they receive in Nepal and abroad, but they are not nearly as threatening to the government as their senior party counterparts. The student politics represent a barometer of attitudes shared by those members of Nepal's small, educated urban elite who do not have government jobs or other profitable relationships with the government. If there is a trend of growing student support for the Nepali Congress, it is probably because students tend to be attracted to the most radical and active party and, at the moment, that appears to be the Koirala wing of the Nepali Congress. Through the student organizations, the parties are able to recruit a few active party workers.

Before the ban on political parties in late 1960, the CPN claimed to have 6,000 members and 2,000 cadets or candidates for membership (*Samiksha,* 11 June 1963). Current estimates are highly problematical. A U.S. government source (*World Strength of the Communist Party Organizations,* Washington, D.C., 1972, p. 104) estimates that there are 10,000 members, but does not indicate relative strength of various factions. It is likely that the revolutionary faction of Pushpa Lal is now stronger, as it has attracted the support of radicalized students, but the core of active workers in each faction remains small.

International Relations. Because Nepal is sandwiched between the two Asian giants, India and China, it is difficult to separate domestic affairs from international relations. This is clearly illustrated in the oppositional activities of the CPN and the Nepali Congress. The moderate CPN faction reportedly receives financial support from the Soviet Embassy in Kathmandu, part of which is undoubtedly used to produce *Samiksha,* the unofficial organ of the faction. The revolutionary faction reportedly receives financial support from the Chinese Embassy in Kathmandu for its activities in Nepal and, through an indirect route, Pushpa Lal is almost certain to receive Chinese support for his operations in India. Likewise, the Nepali Congress activities under Koirala's direction receive funding from sympathizers in India, including (at least in the past) members of India's Socialist Party.

Neither the Pushpa Lal faction nor the Nepali Congress could maintain their party outposts on the Indian side of the Nepal-India border or run their printing presses to produce publicity for circulation in Nepal, if the Indian government were determined to clamp down on this activity. Since 1962 there has been an understanding between the Indian government and exiled Nepalese political leaders that the latter could operate freely in India as long as they did not attempt to carry on armed raids into Nepalese territory. This understanding seems to have been violated for the first time in the raid on the Haripur police station in August 1972. Following the raid, Prime Minister Indira Gandhi reaffirmed the policy of her government (*Dainik Nepal,* 18 December) and Indian border police have moved to tighten border security.

Over the past few years, two communist groups, aside from the Pushpa Lal group, have been operating in Nepal from bases across the border in India—the Tarai Liberation Front and the Naxalites. Of these two, the most active in Nepal has been the Tarai Liberation Front, which was formed in the early 1960s to press the demands of the plains people living in the tarai. Although it has continued to circulate its literature throughout the entire tarai region, most of its organizational efforts have been in the mid-western tarai. It appears its activities contributed at least in part to two brief waves of rioting and looting in the mid-western tarai in 1966 and 1969. Nepalese police allegedly killed two of the group's leaders in 1963 and another in 1967.

In 1967, when the extremist wing of the Communist Party of India gained temporary control of some villages in the Naxalbari region of West Bengal, India, the Indian press claimed that the extremists, later termed Naxalites, were using the tarai as a base of operations and a sanctuary. In mid-1972 there were reports that many Naxalites were retiring to the forest of the eastern tarai to escape a police crackdown in West Bengal. It was also reported that the government of India sought unsuccessfully to persuade the Nepalese government to assist in apprehending the Naxalites (*Sagarmatha,* 27 July). Although there is no evidence that the Naxalites have used their terrorist tactics in Nepal, leaflets circulated in the eastern tarai in late 1972 indicate a possible association between the revolutionary faction of the CPN and the Naxalites. Pushpa Lal undoubtedly hesitates to link himself with the Naxalites for fear that the Indian government will no longer tolerate his presence in India and, likewise, the Naxalites may fear to lose their sanctuaries in Nepal if they associate with Pushpa Lal.

It is not clear what, if any, relationship exists between the revolutionary faction of the CPN and the Tarai Liberation Front. The latter capitalizes upon the resentment which the tarai plains people feel toward the "hill" people who dominate the Nepalese government and administer the tarai. The revolutionary CPN leadership is dominated by hill people of the Brahmin and Newar communities. Man Mohan Adhikari and D. P. Adhikari are hill Brahmins; Pushpa Lal, Shambhu Ram, and Tulsi Lal are Newars. They are unlikely to entertain the Tarai Liberation Front's demand for secession of the tarai from Nepal, as they would someday like to unite Nepal under their own control.

The major international event to which Nepalese communist leaders addressed themselves in 1972 was the Bangladesh crisis. As expected, the moderate leaders took pro-Indian and pro-Soviet stands (*Samiksha,* 7 February), while the revolutionary leaders took pro-Pakistani and pro-Chinese stands. Man Mohan Adhikari was particularly forceful in his condemnation of the Indian army's sweep into Bangladesh. He called this "big-power arrogance" (*Naya Samaj,* 23 January) and warned that "History bears testimony to the fact that Nepal has faced threats only from the south" (*Matribhumi,* 11 January). The moderates welcomed Nepal's recognition of Bangladesh, while the revolutionaries condemned it.

Publications. Until political parties were banned in 1960, the CPN had an official organ called *Navayug* ("New Age"). *Samiksha* ("Analysis") carries the opinions of CPN moderates. *Nepal Patra* ("Nepal Letter") is reportedly published by the Pushpa Lal faction, and *Jana Sangharsha* ("People's Struggle") is a weekly produced by the Maoist students in Patan.

Davidson College   Frederick H. Gaige

New Zealand

The Communist Party of New Zealand (CPNZ) was founded in Wellington at Easter 1921, following a preliminary conference over Christmas 1920. Its influence on New Zealand's political and social development has been small; it has never elected a Member to Parliament, and its membership has never exceeded 2,000—a peak reached in 1944–45, since when there has been a continuous decline.

In the Sino-Soviet ideological dispute the CPNZ is the only Western communist party, among the member parties of the Communist International, to take the side of Peking. Its Moscow supporters split off in 1966 to form the New Zealand Socialist Unity Party (SUP). Besides the CPNZ and SUP, there are the so-called Revolutionary Committee of the CPNZ in Auckland, which was expelled in 1968, and the Wellington District of the CPNZ, expelled in 1970, whose members now describe themselves simply as a Wellington Marxist-Leninist group.

Somewhat apart stand four Trotskyist groups, all of recent origin. The Spartacist League was first in the field, in 1967, followed by the Socialist Action League (SAL) in 1969. A split in the latter, in 1971, led to the formation of the Marxist Labour Group. The Spartacists split early in 1972, with both sides—the Logan and Gager factions—claiming to be the true Spartacists, though Gager's supporters are also using the name of Communist League. There is, finally, a Socialist Party of New Zealand, first founded in 1930, which has given evidence lately of renewed vitality.

The combined membership of these nine groups and parties is between 300 and 400, in a total population of almost three million. This is less than the CPNZ's estimated membership at the beginning of the sixties. The CPNZ and SUP have about 100 to 120 members each, the SAL has 40 plus, and the Socialist Party and the former Wellington District of the CPNZ have about 30 each, while the remaining groups count their active membership on the fingers of one hand. All have legal status.

Organization and Leadership. In 1972 the CPNZ continued its retreat from visible public activity. Its main strength is concentrated in Auckland, where the party has its headquarters; outside Auckland there are only a few branches, whose membership nowhere exceeds a dozen. Although the membership is aging and declining, the CPNZ has been able to gain some young recruits through its influence on the Progressive Youth Movement (PYM), whose Auckland leaders are party members.

The Party Rules provide for triennial national conferences, but no conference has been held since 1966, and there has therefore been no constitutional opportunity to elect national officers. There have been changes in the leadership in recent years, particularly in connection with the wholesale expulsion of the Wellington District, but the composition of the leading bodies—National Committee, Political Committee, and National Secretariat—has not been publicised. V. G. Wilcox as general secretary remains the acknowledged leader of the CPNZ. He has now been joined by Ron Taylor, a dentist who returned to New Zealand early in 1972 after an absence of more than four years in Albania. Taylor's official position in the CPNZ is not clear: two years ago Chinese publications described him as acting national chairman of the CPNZ (e.g., *Peking Review* 24 April 1970), but the party's *People's Voice* in 1970 (29 April) and 1972 (29 March) referred to him merely as a member of the National Committee.

The expelled Wellington District of the CPNZ—the so-called "Manson-Bailey clique," generally described as the "bogus Communists" in the *People's Voice* (e.g., 29 March 1972)—has maintained its separate identity and has succeeded in gaining adherents in other centers, including Auckland. The group has been careful not to come forward as a rival party, because it hopes to draw the majority of the CPNZ to its side and to gain recognition from Peking as the genuine CPNZ.

The SUP has branches in the four main centers but is strongest in Auckland, where its head office is located. Like the CPNZ, it is able to employ a full-time staff which seems out of proportion to the size of its membership. G. E. Jackson, the national secretary, is the party's leading spokesman, but its main asset is the acting president, G. H. ("Bill") Andersen, who is also secretary of the powerful Northern Drivers' Union and one of New Zealand's best-known and most respected (for his ability rather than for his ideology) trade unionists.

The Trotskyist groups came into being independently and not as breakaways from the CPNZ, and this is reflected in their membership, which is very young (mostly under 25) and student-orientated. They are all based on Wellington, but the SAL has also active groups in Auckland and Christchurch. The Socialist Party has groups in Auckland and Wellington, with the main activity in the former.

Domestic Views and Activities. The main domestic issues confronting the Marxist groups in 1972 were their attitudes to Parliament and to trade unions. This was an election year. In the previous general elections, in 1969, the CPNZ and SAL had put forward candidates, but this time their place was taken by the SUP and Socialist Party, who contested the elections for the first time, in each case.

The CPNZ refused to take part in the elections because "with revolution the main trend in the world today, with struggle for both immediate gains and revolutionary policy growing every day in New Zealand, it is apparent that all our forces must be used to strengthen these developments outside the Parliamentary circus" (*People's Voice* 30 August). Any suggestion that the Labour Party was better than the governing National Party was "a step towards revisionism" (ibid.). The CPNZ, together with the PYM, anarchists, and other militant groups promoted a "Radical Election Campaign"—or REC, "pronounced Wreck"—with the object of disrupting political meetings. Their main slogan was "Parliament is a fraud, elections are a farce."

The Revolutionary Committee of the CPNZ, which had long made anti-parliamentarism its main platform, welcomed the CPNZ attitude. "Parliamentary methods have changed nothing," wrote John Dickson. "Workers' Councils are needed and they can start right now by organising the boycott of the Parliamentary elections" (*Compass,* September). The expelled Wellington District took a similar view. "Radicals," they wrote, "ought to work towards developing non-parliamentary activity by the people on the issues vital to the people. . . . What's important is organising—not voting!" (*ML* July/August).

The SAL also refused to stand candidates in 1972, but for different reasons. Early in the year it launched a "Socialists for Labour Campaign" which pledged support for the Labour

Party in the general elections while attacking the party's leadership for its "anti-working class" policies. The Labour Party countered this by banning SAL members from membership in the Labour Party, but the SAL campaign continued, with leaflets, posters, buttons, and pledge cards. To its members the SAL explained that "in supporting Labour to power we in no way give in to parliamentary or social democratic illusions; we emphasize the importance of class politics and a break with capitalism. . . . Socialists for Labour campaign will allow us to get across essentially the same ideas as independent SAL campaigns . . . and probably with more publicity." (*Canta* 11 August.) The Spartacist League (Logan faction), while denouncing the SAL campaign as "obviously bankrupt," put forward a virtually identical policy of giving electoral support to the Labour Party while attacking its programme and leadership (*New Zealand Spartacist*, 2 August).

The SUP put forward five candidates of its own, but it also called for "the defeat of the National Government and its replacement by a Labour Government" (*New Zealand Tribune*, July). While agreeing that a Labour government would not "bring about radical changes of a fundamental nature," it saw possibilities, with Labour in power, of "building a politically active movement in support of a legislative programme to meet the needs of workers today." At the same time it urged voters to vote for SUP candidates as a means of "building the SUP as a future alternative party." (Ibid., October.)

The elections resulted in a landslide victory for the opposition Labour Party. The five SUP candidates gained a total of 444 votes, which was less than one percent of the votes in the electorates contested. The lone Socialist Party candidate polled 83 votes.

While all Marxist groups acknowledge the primacy of the working class in revolutionary politics, the Trotskyist groups, because of the composition of their membership, are only marginally involved in trade union affairs. The SAL in particular, in its paper *Socialist Action*, gives much space to what might be called the "trendy" issues: women's liberation, abortion, high school reform, gay liberation, pollution, and the environment. The SUP, on the other hand, has its main power base in the trade unions and it is here that it clashes head on with the CPNZ. SUP members hold leading positions in several important unions, and SUP candidates, although unsuccessful so far, can count on a quarter of the votes cast in the annual elections for the national executive of the New Zealand Federation of Labour. It is SUP policy to work within the Federation of Labour, which is the sole national trade union center in New Zealand, in support of radical demands: to push the Federation to the left, as far as it can be pushed, but not to step outside it.

The CPNZ, for its part, denounces trade unions as "a vital and necessary part of the capitalist establishment" and urges rank-and-file action, especially "short, sharp, hard-hitting struggles" as a challenge to "bureaucrat unionism" (*People's Voice,* 4 October). One of the few unions in which the CPNZ has been able to exert some influence is the New Zealand Seamen's Union, but a short communist-inspired national seamen's strike in November 1971 ended in defeat and helped the SUP to gain support at the expense of the CPNZ. In the Seamen's Union elections in May 1972, the unofficial leader of the strike, R. Hughes of the CPNZ, was defeated by R. Black of the SUP by 775 votes to 206. The expelled Wellington District of the CPNZ, which has some local union officials among its members, has taken a position very close to the SUP by working within the established union structure, though it is somewhat more critical than the SUP of the policies of the Federation of Labour leadership.

International Positions and Contacts. The CPNZ and its associated PYM give uncritical support to China and Albania. The expelled Wellington District of the CPNZ also supports Chinese policies, and its members work in the Wellington branch of the New Zealand–China

Society, whose national leadership in Auckland is closely linked with the CPNZ. When Rewi Alley, a prominent New Zealander living in Peking, visited his homeland in October 1971, there was speculation that he had been sent to evaluate the rival communist groups, but he unhesitatingly supported the Wilcox leadership, and commended the part it had played in the inner-party struggle. "The outstanding role of the New Zealand Communist Party and the leadership of Comrade Vic. Wilcox in the fight against revisionism and particularly Soviet social-imperialism," wrote Alley, "is very well recognised and highly appreciated in Peking, by the people of China and the true Marxist-Leninists abroad" (*People's Voice,* 22 March 1972).

CPNZ publications are giving an increasing amount of space to material from Albania, especially since R. Taylor's return from Tirana. Other New Zealanders have gone to Albania to take Taylor's place there, and B. J. Holmes attended the congress of Albanian trade unions as a CPNZ delegate. Reporting after his return, Holmes mentioned that he had sat next to a delegate from Ceylon—"where thousands of young people were slaughtered last year by savage state forces" (ibid., 7 June). The SAL paper *Socialist Action* (28 July) pointed out that the Chinese government had supported these "savage state forces," and one political commentator claimed to see signs of a growing estrangement between the CPNZ and China, and re-alignment toward Albania, because of alleged dissatisfaction with Mao's rapprochement with the United States.

Yet in May Day greetings from the CPNZ to both China and Albania, it was the Chinese Communist Party which was described as "the proletarian headquarters of the world's revolutionary peoples", and Mao as "the greatest Marxist-Leninist of our times," providing "inspiration and guidance" to New Zealand (*People's Voice,* 26 April). The CPNZ welcomed U.S. President Nixon's visit to Peking, while it denounced his agreements with Brezhnev as a threat to world peace and "collusion between two imperialist powers to carve up the world by using force and threat of force" (ibid., 24 May).

Following Alley's five-month visit which ended in March, a delegation from the New Zealand—China Society went to Peking, and in July a Chinese table-tennis team came to New Zealand. When E. F. Hill, of the Australian Communist Party (Marxist-Leninist), visited Auckland in August for discussions with the CPNZ, both parties "welcomed the growing development towards revolutionary struggle on both sides of the Tasman [Sea] and stressed this can only be successful with the Marxist-Leninist–Mao Tsetung revolutionary line and activity" (ibid., 30 August).

The SUP is in Moscow's camp. In September it sent a delegate to the first congress of the new Moscow-aligned Socialist Party of Australia, despite protests from the Communist Party of Australia. The remaining groups are uncommitted, as far as the Sino-Soviet ideological struggle is concerned. The Spartacist League is linked with the Spartacist League in the United States, while the SAL, though not formally affiliated to the Fourth International, has close ties with the Socialist Workers Party there. In January it sent delegates to the founding conference of the Socialist Workers League, in Sydney, Australia, and in April to the third national conference of the Socialist Youth Alliance, in Melbourne. The Socialist Party is linked with the Socialist Party of Great Britain and companion parties in other countries.

Ideological differences caused clashes at the Anti-War Conference at Auckland in April, but despite all difficulties the nationwide "Mobilisation" succeeded in getting some 35,000 people to demonstrate on 14 July against the war in Vietnam. Although the CPNZ urged its supporters to join in these marches, it took no part in preparing the Mobilisation, accusing "certain dominant organisers" (mainly Trotskyists from the SAL) of "building a united front for imperialism and not against it" (ibid., 19 July). The central issue, according to the CPNZ, was not withdrawal from Vietnam but "all possible support for the victory of people's war in every country" (ibid.) and struggle against the "main enemy, imperialism, headed by the United States imperialism and the Soviet imperialists" (ibid., 26 July).

Because of this attitude, the Mobilisation organizers refused to allow CPNZ speakers to take part in the final rallies, and the CPNZ was again isolated from the other Marxist groups when it criticized the boycott of French shipping and other services called by the Federation of Labour in protest against French nuclear tests. According to the CPNZ, "opposing French nuclear bomb tests in the Pacific is in line with the policies of the two super-powers—the U.S.A. and the Soviet scab government" (ibid., 7 June).

Publications. All the Marxist groups have their separate journals. The CPNZ publishes the weekly *People's Voice* (under this title since 1939) and a monthly theoretical journal, *New Zealand Communist Review* (under this title since 1960). The SUP brings out *New Zealand Tribune* (monthly, since 1966), the Revolutionary Committee of the CPNZ publishes *Compass* (duplicated, monthly, under this title since 1971), and the expelled Wellington District of the CPNZ began publication of a duplicated irregular bulletin *ML* in March 1972.

Of the Trotskyist groups, the SAL publishes *Socialist Action* (fortnightly, since 1969) and shares a theoretical journal, *Socialist Review* (printed irregularly in Melbourne), with the Socialist Workers League of Australia. The Spartacist League (Logan faction) began publication of the *New Zealand Spartacist* (irregular) in June 1972, while the league's Gager faction produces *Red* (irregular) since November 1971. The first issue of *New Zealand Militant,* a small duplicated bulletin of the Marxist Labour Group, appeared in October 1972, while the Socialist Party began publication of a bimonthly journal, *Socialist Viewpoint* (duplicated), in August 1971.

The circulation of all these publications is kept secret, but within New Zealand *Socialist Action* is probably the most widely read, with a circulation exceeding 2,000 copies.

University of Auckland   H. Roth
New Zealand

Pakistan and Bangladesh

The division of Pakistan in 1971 into two states, Bangladesh and residual Pakistan (former West Pakistan) requires that communism be treated separately for each new entity. So far as is known, links between political groups have also been snapped. This applies with greatest force to the National Awami Party (NAP) faction, of which Khan Abdul Wali Khan was national president. Wali Khan continues to lead the party in Pakistan, which now shares in the governance of the Northwest Frontier Province and of Baluchistan. The former East Pakistan, now Bangladesh, branch is led by a long-time associate of Wali Khan, Professor Muzaffar Ahmad. The Bhashani faction of the NAP had little strength in West Pakistan before division and since has ceased to exist as an organization. The Communist Party of Pakistan (CPP), illegal since 1954, appears to have had little linkage between its covert East and West branches and none are apparent now. In both wings, however, the NAP served as a vehicle for political activity by some members of the outlawed CPP, and continued to do so after the 1967 split into Wali Khan and Bhashani factions.

Bangladesh. The return of Sheikh Mujibur Rahman to Dacca in January 1972 and his immediate assumption of the office of prime minister ushered in a period of domestic politics under the leadership of the "father" of Bangladesh. Mujib moved to set up a government under the leadership of his Awami League. He called for the surrender to the government of arms used by guerrilla forces against the Pakistan army and seems to have received widespread although not complete compliance. The scope of political activity was broadened from that of the Ayub and Yahya administrations permitting open revival of the now renamed Communist Party of Bangladesh (CPBD). The CPBD and the NAP factions had given support to the freedom movement. At the other end of the spectrum "collaborationist" groups, such as the several divisions of the Muslim League and the religiously oriented parties (additionally suspect in a Bangladesh striving toward a secular state), were subject to popular, if not official, restraints.

The communist movement in Bangladesh has continued to show the extreme factionalism of the past year—as if to give credence to an old adage "one Bengali, one political party; two Bengalis, two parties; three Bengalis, two parties with a dissident faction in one." The cluster of parties also shows a division between those operating openly, including the CPBD and the sympathizing NAP factions and those existing covertly which are antithetic to the parliamentary process.

The CPBD which emerged from its clandestine place during 1971 remains a small party. It leader, the septuaginarian Moni Singh, however, has been given a prominent place in the press and has been able to project himself as a supporter of the general policies of the Mujib government—socialism, secularism and democracy. On occasions he has shared the platform with leaders of the Awami League and, more often, with Muzaffar Ahmad of the NAP. The Communist Party of India (CPI) has "recognized" the CPBD as a fraternal party and sent a delegation led by General Secretary Rajeshwar Rao to visit its Bengali confreres. Nonetheless, the CPI is not deluded into believing the CPBD to be a major factor in the politics of Bangladesh and has noted its failure to expand significantly (*New Age,* Delhi, 7 May). Moscow radio and the Soviet press have applauded the role of the CPBD in the freedom struggle and have thereby bestowed apparent blessing upon Moni Singh and his associates, many of whom are Hindus, as he is. The program of the CPBD is anything but revolutionary and goes only marginally farther than that of the Awami League toward nationalization. Large and basic industries would be taken over by the state but small-scale industry would be encouraged to continue and to expand in private hands. Land reform beyond that already carried out in East Pakistan is proposed, along with encouragement of collective farming.

It can be assumed that the CPBD will contest the election expected to be held in 1973, but possibly in alliance with the Muzaffar-led NAP and, should the Awami League split, with the leftist group resulting from the division. Its own weakness makes it unlikely that it would be a major electoral force if it campaigned alone.

The Dacca Bengali-language daily *Sangbad* is the party's principal organ.

The faction of the NAP led by Muzaffar Ahmad has been described as being "pro-Soviet." The NAP itself is a breakaway from the Awami League (see M. Rashiduzzaman, "The National Awami Party of Pakistan," *Pacific Affairs,* 43 [1970], 394–409), having split off in 1957 when, in so far as East Pakistan is concerned, a group of leftists led by Maulana Abdul Hamid Khan Bhashani opposed the policies of H. S. Suhrawardy (and Majibur Rahman). The 1967 division into Bhashani- and Wali Khan-led factions has been described by Rashiduzzaman as one between "pro-China" and "pro-Soviet" alignments although in West Pakistan personality factors were at least as important as those of ideology. During 1972 the Muzaffar NAP has given general support to the Awami League government, although encouraging greater speed in reforms of the economic system along lines similar to those noted above for the CPBD. Muzaffar himself and others in the party have been included in many "all-party" meetings. In April he called for a united front government of "progressive parties" which would implement socialist policies; the parties included in his proposal were the Awami League, the CPBD, and his own. In the face of a Mujib-led Awami League, the Muzaffar NAP has not the electoral strength to be a major factor in the 1973 election. Its hopes therefore rest on either an alliance with the Awami League (cf. the partial alliance of the Congress and the CPI in India in 1971) or a split in the Awami League which might reduce the overwhelming strength of a unified party led by Mujib. On the latter point *Link* (India, 16 April 1972) reported that Awami League Finance Minister Tajuddin Ahmad had supported an alliance, and there have been other reports that Tajuddin along with Foreign Minister Abdus Samad and others might be prepared to part from Mujib to form a "progressive" Awami League. These reports, however, tend to emanate from NAP and CPBD sources and can only be tested when the time for elections approaches.

In addition to the possibly deepening ideological factionalism within the Awami League which serves to raise the hopes of Moni Singh, Muzaffar, and their followers, another potential partner in such an alliance is the Bangla National League. This rather small group has as its leader Ataur Rahman Khan, a former Awami League chief minister of East Pakistan in the pre-Ayub period.

Outside this group of potential allies and in opposition now to the Mujib government stands the venerable leftist Bhashani. Now past 90, he continues to lead his faction of the NAP and in recent months has thundered against the policies of the government and threatened sharp action if changes (often unspecified) are not made. While there is little doubt that Bhashin himself is respected and listened to and well covered by the press, there is no clear information on how much of his organization remains. It is from the Bhashani NAP that many of the followers of the covert communist groups have come, and often the departure was the result of disagreement or impatience with the old man himself. The peasantry has been an area in which Bhashani has worked effectively in the past and in April he reactivated the Krishak Samiti in an effort to draw strength again from that sector. To more orthodox Marxists his slogan of "Islamic socialism" and his use of religious symbols is repugnant, but he recognizes that the base of society in Bangladesh is Islam and this cannot be ignored in the name of Marxism. His more recent statements have tended to be more Islamic and have been interpreted by some to be both anti-India and anti-Hindu (*Ananda Bazar Patrika,* Calcutta, 5 September). He has accused the Mujib government of permitting Bangladesh to be exploited by India and the Soviet Union and added that the CPBD and the Muzaffar NAP are tools of the Soviets, but has also said the government must end its dependence on these two countries and the United States or he may be forced to resort to violence—"even the name of India is hated." As if in contradiction to his apparent anti-Hindu stance, Bhashani has also revived an old plan of his (and others) to unify all of Bengal and Assam under one government. Bhashani has established contacts with the Communist Party of India (Marxist); a delegation of that party attended the conference of the Krishak Samiti. The Awami League has not acted against him, but has responded to some of his speeches, including a reminder that he supported the foreign policy of President Ayub in relation to China and suggesting that Bhashani withdrew support covertly from Miss Fatima Jinnah in her 1965 election campaign against Ayub. What following Bhashani could achieve in violent, agitational, or electoral activities is questionable and the government's permitting him to continue his outburst could suggest, of course, either that they are fearful of the result should he be arrested or that he is no longer effective and need not be incarcerated.

Best known of the former lieutenants of Bhashani who have deserted is the one-time NAP general secretary, Muhammad Toaha. He now leads the covert Communist Party of East Bengal (Marxist-Leninist) (CPEB/ML). Toaha appears to be going it alone, following Maoist doctrines of revolution and waiting for the opportunity to launch a guerrilla campaign against the Awami League. He is said to be certain that the government will collapse and that the present Bangladesh—created by a "counter-revolutionary conspiracy hatched by the imperialists and Indian expansionist" (*New Age,* 9 April)—will be replaced by an "orthodox" revolutionary regime. Possibly more potentially violent is the Proletarian Party of East Bengal (PPEB), led by Siraj Sikdar. Once known as the "Test Tube Group," it advocates the violent overthrow of the bourgeois regime of Mujib. Still another splinter covert group is the Bangladesh Communist Party (Leninist) (BDCP/L) led by another former Bhashanite, Rashid Khan Menon; it reportedly has links with the Naxalite Communist Party of India (Marxist-Leninist). The East Bengal Communist Party (EBCP), also covert and advocating violence, was reported to have split into two factions. All of the covert groups represent potential dangers to the government and it may be assumed that each has some weapons available from those not turned in to the authorities in response to Mujib's call. The danger would increase if there were a loss of legitimacy—or, perhaps more properly, a failure to gain legitimacy—by the Mujib government. Serious disaffection by the people would serve as a breeding ground for the kind of violence advocated by these groups.

Student politics are especially important in the Bengali context, dating back to anti-Urdu demonstrations in the early period following partition and continuing on through the key role played in the events leading to the separation of Bangladesh from Pakistan. In the May elections to the student union at Dacca University the control by the Awami League associated students organization, the Chhatra League, was broken by the Chhatra Union, sponsored jointly by the Muzaffar NAP and the CPBD. The victory was aided by a split in the Chhatra League. Although both factions claim continued support for Mujib, he appeared in July to have favored a section led by Abdul Kuddus Makhan over that led by A.S.M. Abdur Rab. The Rab faction is the more impatient of the two in demanding a reorientation of society and the economy.

Internationally, Bangladesh during 1972 has a "one and one" record with the two major communist powers. China has continued to give support to Pakistan and vetoed the Bangladesh application for membership in the United Nations. The veto was based on the continued presence of Indian troops in Bangladesh (denied by both India and Bangladesh and not accepted by the world press) and the "violation" of the Geneva Convention on Prisoners of War —Bangladesh refuses to permit repatriation of Pakistani prisoners of war held in India pending recognition of Bangladesh by Pakistan. The Soviet Union was the first of the "big three" powers to recognize Bangladesh (on 25 January) and has, along with other Eastern European countries, been prominent in relief (the Soviets, for example, have undertaken the task of clearing the Chittagong harbor) and other assistance and in arranging trade agreements. Mujib visited the Soviet Union at the end of February and Foreign Minister Abdus Samad has visited several Eastern European countries. Nonetheless, Bangladesh has pursued a policy of non-alignment and, following a period of delay, has entered into friendly relations with the United States. Some of the Bengali press, however, has been caught up in the almost hysterical accusations against the U.S. Central Intelligence Agency which have affected Indo-U.S. relations.

Pakistan. The CPP remains under the ban placed on it in 1954, although as noted earlier some members of the banned party continued political activity through the NAP. In both the Frontier and the Punjab the NAP has suffered defections both to the now ruling People's Party of Pakistan (PPP) and to miniscule leftist parties led by members of the CPP. It needs to be noted, however, that the West Pakistan NAP was only secondarily a haven for CPP members. Primarily it was and is a party of regional political forces, forces which were able to win sufficient seats in the 1970 election to permit the party now to participate in governing coalitions in the Frontier and Baluchistan. In neither province can the generality of membership of the NAP be considered "leftist" despite an election manifesto which called for some measure of socialism.

In the Frontier former NAP leader Afzal Bangash has formed a new and militant party which has been a bother to the ruling coalition but appears to have little following that could be translated into votes in another election. In Punjab key party member Mian Mahmud Ali Qasuri defected to the PPP, was elected in a by-election in January 1971 to fill one of the seats vacated by Zulfiqar Ali Bhutto, joined Bhutto's cabinet, and resigned from the cabinet in a dispute over the constitution in September 1972 although continuing as a member of the PPP. Mian Arif Iftikhar, who remained with Bhashani following the December 1967 split in the NAP, has also joined the PPP. Others prominent in the Punjab, including C. R. Aslam and Major Muhammad Ishaq, have left the NAP and gone their own directions with little impact on the political scene. Labor leader Mirza Muhammad Ibrahim appears to have lost his once strong influence in the Lahore labor areas. In Baluchistan a split in the NAP led by Khan Abdul Samad Khan Achakzai, a Pathan, has not been healed, but this has not hindered the party from governing there. In Sind, the NAP appears to be ineffective—although the summer of 1972 saw an internal struggle for control of an almost non-existent party. The

NAP general secretary, Mahmudul Haq Usmani, spent the last half of the year in jail as a result of his position on the Sindhi-Urdu controversy (Usmani is an Urdu-speaking refugee).

There have been assertions that some communists have infiltrated the PPP, but this is difficult to ascertain (one is reminded of the charges leveled at the Congress Party in India especially during the heyday of Krishna Menon). For example, when Meraj Muhammad Khan resigned from the Bhutto cabinet this was welcomed by the leader of the Jamiat-ul-Ulema-i-Pakistan, Maulana Ghulam Ghaus Hazarvi, who said all ministers and legislators "believing in communist philosophy" should resign and welcomed Meraj's departure as a first step (*Pakistan Times,* 15 October). Communists, or at least persons who were associated with the party or a front organization prior to 1954, continue to be prominent in other fields. Several who openly acknowledge such association are on the staff of the Progressive Publications (*Pakistan Times, Imroz*), and a former editor of the *Pakistan Times,* Mazhar Ali Khan, is acting as editor in chief of *Dawn* while Atlaf Gauhar is in jail. (Mazhar Ali Khan's son is the London-based Trotskyite, Tariq Ali.) Two of the accused in the Rawalpindi conspiracy case are in the PPP. General Muhammad Akbar Khan is a minister of state in the Bhutto cabinet, and his divorced wife, Nasim, Jehan, is a PPP member of the National Assembly.

Internationally, Pakistan continued to have close relations with China and mixed relations with the Soviet Union and Eastern Europe. Initially Pakistan instituted a version of the Halstein doctrine by breaking diplomatic relations with countries which recognized Bangladesh. Relations were broken with countries which preceded the Soviet Union in recognizing, but the "doctrine" broke down when the Soviets accorded recognition and relations were not broken. Relations have been restored with other countries. Bhutto said Pakistan must take "a realistic attitude toward the great powers." In March, Bhutto visited Moscow, and while the trip was not an unqualified success it did serve to restore communication between Islamabad and Moscow and during the year economic and cultural relations between the two countries were brought back to those preceding the Pakistani action in the eastern province in March 1971. Other nations in Eastern Europe have generally resumed economic assistance, trade, and cultural programs.

China has continued to give diplomatic, economic and military support to Pakistan. Bhutto visited Peking in January and there was a steady stream of visits in both directions throughout the year. Discussions were held concerning the full utilization of the $200 million credit for economic development given by China in November 1970. There have been reports that China has assisted in rebuilding Pakistan's military capability. For example, the *Sunday Telegraph,* London, reported on 6 February that China told Pakistan it would meet Pakistan's full needs and added that "several" squadrons of MiG—19s and "up to 100" tanks were being supplied. China's veto of the U.N. membership application by Bangladesh has been mentioned above.

In a series of events in November Pakistan established closer relations with communist countries and moved further toward the goal of non-alignment expressed in the PPP election manifesto. It withdrew from membership in SEATO and the United Nations Commission on Korea, and recognized North Vietnam, North Korea and East Germany.

United States Military Academy   Craig Baxter

Philippines

Philippine communism centers around two parties, respectively oriented toward Moscow and Peking, and their front organizations.

History. The oldest and currently, comparatively, the less violent and active is the Communist Party of the Philippines (Partido Komunista ng Pilipinas; PKP), officially proclaimed on 7 November 1930 on the thirteenth anniversary of the Russian Revolution (though organized a month and a half earlier). The PKP's roots lay in the growth of radical and Marxist trade unions, and the party's first secretary-general, Crisanto Evangelista, had taken the lead in organizing on 12 May 1929 the radical new labor federation "Association of the Sons of Sweat" (Katipunan ng mga Anakpawis sa Pilipinas; KAP). Immediate intensification of labor and anti-government agitation led to the official outlawing of both PKP and KAP (14 September 1931) and many of the 3,000 party members resigned or went underground. PKP cadres continued operating through a number of fronts, such as the "League for the Defense of Democracy," and remained in close touch with the Comintern and the Communist Party, USA. On 7 November 1938 the PKP effected a merger with the Socialist Party and its radical "General Workers Union," thus reflecting general Comintern policy at this time as to the desirability of formation of anti-fascist "united fronts" everywhere. Philippine President Manuel Quezon, meanwhile, had granted clemency to a number of PKP leaders (31 December 1936) and the party, as well as the KAP, was regaining a measure of legitimacy.

On 29 March 1942 the "Military Committee" of the PKP's National Anti-Japanese United Front took the lead in organizing an "Anti-Japanese People's Army" (Hukbo ng Bayan Laban sa Hapon, or Hukbalahap; "Huks" for short). The prestige which the PKP thus acquired was quickly dissipated after the war when the Huks refused to disarm and indicated they meant to become a militant political force in the newly independent Philippines. On 6 March 1948 the Huks were outlawed (technically the PKP was not), and on 7 November, 1948 the Huks, led by Luis Taruc, reconstituted themselves as the Hukbo ng Mapagpalaya ng Bayan ("People's Liberation Army"; HMB), becoming in effect the PKP's formal military arm, as the party Poltiburo, meanwhile, began calling for an "armed struggle" against the government of President Elpidio Quirino and set 1 May 1952 as the target date of its overthrow (*The Communist Movement in the Philippines,* SEATO Short Paper no. 46, Bangkok, March 1970, pp. 24–25). Already on 18 October 1950, in a raid on PKP headquarters in Manila, virtually the whole of the party's Politburo (among them PKP secretary general José Lava) had fallen into government hands. In subsequent years combined counter-insurgency operations and land reform policies under Philippine Defense Secretary (and later President) Ramón Magsaysay saw the one-time peak strength of the PKP-HMB, estimated at about 25,000 and more than half of them armed, steadily slink away.

On 17 June 1957, when virtually all top party leaders were behind bars and the Huks had become little more than a conglomeration of furtive bands of terrorists and brigands, the government's new anti-subversion law (Republic Act 1700) formally declared the PKP and HMB illegal organizations. Until his arrest on 12 May 1964, Jesús Lava (José's brother), as secretary-general of the PKP underground remnant, directed his organization in terms of a new "parliamentary" united front strategy. Allying itself with the aspirations of unfulfilled Filipino nationalism, this strategy in the 1960s witnessed the emergence of a number of radical front groups like the "National Youth" organization (Kabataang Makabayan; KM), founded in 1964, the Labor Party (Lapiang Manggagawa; LM), the "Free Peasants Union" (Malayang Samahang Magsasaka, or Masaka), and the "Movement for the Advancement of Nationalism" (MAN), founded in 1967. Particularly the last-named group also attracted prominent non-communist Philippine intellectuals and political figures. Overlapping memberships facilitated emergence of other fronts like the new "Socialist Party of the Philippines" (SPP), founded in 1967.

Among younger PKP cadres the alleged "revisionist" and "peaceful" approach of the Lava united front policy, as well as the need for a communist fighting force free from the taint of the criminality, corruption, and common brigandage into which most of the HMB, still popularly called "Huks," seemed to have fallen, dictated formation of another militant organization. From 26 December 1968 (Mao Tse-tung's seventy-fifth birthday) to 7 January 1969, a "Congress of Re-Establishment of the Communist Party of the Philippines" was held near the town of Capas, in southern Tarlac Province, Luzon. This congress formally established a new party which, according to its constitution also adopted at the congress, is called either "Communist Party of the Philippines (Marxist-Leninist)" (hereafter CPP-ML), or "Communist Party of the Philippines (Mao Tse Tung's Thought)" (*The Maoist Communist Party of the Philippines,* SEATO Short Paper no. 52, September 1971, p. 44). On 29 March 1969, probably also near Capas, at a conference of CPP-ML cadres, a few HBM ideological militants, and other "Red Commanders and Soldiers of the People" there was formed the "New People's Army" (NPA). Currently the NPA is the most active anti-government guerrilla force in the Philippines, engaged in Mao-style "protracted" and "people's war." Meanwhile the PKP, sometime in the middle of 1969, also broke its nominal affiliation with the HMB, largely because of unprincipled gangsterism that had overtaken the Huks, although some Huk commanders in the later sixties like Sumulong (Faustino del Mundo) had vague populist revolutionary leanings. By the end of 1969 the parent PKP had organized its own "National Army" (Army ng Bayan, or AB), with which some armed Masaka members affiliated. The AB has thus far, however, not engaged in violent confrontation with authority. The HMB remnant, some of whose more adventurous members have drifted either to the NPA or AB, continues to operate as a petty criminal organization in the provinces of Pampanga, Tarlac, and Nueva Ecija and in Manila.

Organization and Tactics. The total strength of the PKP is estimated at about 1,500 and that of the AB at about 100. Major additional PKP influence, though not necessarily complete dominance, extends itself to Masaka, the "Democratic Union of Filipino Youth" (M alayang Pagkakaisa ng Kabataang Pilipino, or MPKP, established in 1967 by KM dissidents), MAN, the "Bertrand Russell Peace Foundation" chapters in the Philippines (established since 1964), the "Brotherhood for Our Development" (Ang Kapatrian Sa Ikauunlad Natin, or AKSIUN —an organization of unemployed laborers formed in 1969), and a number of trade unions and labor federations like the "National Workers' Federation" (Pambansang Kilusan ng Paggawa). Hard-core PKP sympathizers in these groups are estimated at about 12,000. A foreign

PKP sympathizer has described these organizations as having "rejected and condemned the Maoist intrigues" (William J. Pomeroy, "The Philippines—Neo-Colonialism in Crisis," *Marxism Today*, March 1972, p. 79). But in the developing NPA offensive in the course of 1972, culminating in the promulgation of nationwide martial law by the government of President Marcos on 22 September 1972 (see below), significant, if informal, support for the CPP-ML and the NPA was generated throughout the constellation of PKP front groups and allies.

A paper Politburo, led by Jesús Lava as secretary-general, nominally directs the PKP; former party leaders like guerrilla tactician Angel Baking and former secretary-general José Lava (both released from prison in 1970) act in a covert, informal advisory capacity. In keeping with its continuing policy of peaceful parliamentarism, PKP tactics currently are focused on winning a widening group of followers, not necessarily party members, in a broad spectrum of organizations, especially trade unions, and identifying as closely as possible with the generalized public dissatisfaction with the existing, allegedly U.S.-dominated, Philippine political system, its inefficiency and corruption, and the sluggish growth and inequalities in the economy. A basic PKP "cell" structure, generally in front or allied organizations, and with some degree of regional centralization exercized usually through friendly labor union officials, comprises the present frame of PKP operations.

The Central Committe of the CPP-ML is headed by José Maria Sison, a former literature and social science teacher at the University of the Philippines, co-founder of KM, and first secretary-general of MAN. Victoriano Corpus, a former Philippine Army lieutenant who, on 29 December 1970, after a daring raid on a government armory at Baguio defected to the NPA, and Bernabe Buscayno ("Commander Dante"), formerly of the HMB, head the CPP-ML's Military Commission, although already by the beginning of 1970 quarrels over tactics between Buscayno and Sison led the latter increasingly to turn to Corpus. Little is publicly known of the CPP-ML organizational structure at the provincial and district level, or of the functions of its Central Committee, probably not least because since its inception the party's whole purpose seems to have been to act as a support group for the NPA. This would be in keeping with the CPP-ML's constitutional directive (article IX, section 3), which defines the NPA as "the main weapon of the Party in the people's democratic revolution and in the subsequent socialist stage." The NPA is commanded in the same article to "create an independent regime by making agrarian revolution, waging armed struggle and building of rural base areas." PKP organs, meanwhile, have excoriated CPP-ML strategy which allegedly "has turned the gun into a fetish and degraded Marxism-Leninism to the level of a cowboy ideology" (*Ang Komunista*, February 1971, p. 13).

Estimates of the size of the CPP-ML, the NPA, and their allies have fluctuated widely. Before the proclamation of martial law (22 September 1972) Philippine government statistics reported an armed core of 570 with additional 1,240 "part-time" guerrillas, and some 4,500 "support troops." Civilian "mass" support was put at 60,000. (Associated Press dispatch, Manila, 25 May 1972.) The NPA itself, however, claimed that it had a following of 400,000 persons (out of a total 37 million Philippine population) and even before its mid-1972 campaign it claimed to have established its "revolutionary committees" in more than 800 villages in 18 out of the country's 67 provinces (*Far Eastern Economic Review*, 13 May 1972, p. 26; Associated Press dispatch, Manila, 25 May). In contrast, a special Philippine Senate Committee, in a report issued on 6 September 1971, estimated NPA strength at only 350 armed men, while President Marcos a week previously had said the NPA numbered about 1,000 front-line fighters with an active support base of about 50,000 (*Keesing's Contemporary Archives*, 25 September–2 October 1971, p. 24852). Apart from its small following of about 200 in Masaka, and an equal number in the Socialist Party of the Philippines, the CPP-ML's principal front group support is derived from student organizations, particularly the 5,000-member KM and its offshoot, the "Democratic Youth Association" (Samahang Demokratiko ng Kabataan; SDK), founded in 1967, with about 1,000 active members. The SDK has allies among some unions of service workers in the Manila area, and also dominates such federations of student workers and peasants as the "Movement for a Democratic Philippines," organized in 1970, but largely inactive through 1972. Overlapping memberships in various front organizations have a tendency to inflate estimates of the following of both the PKP and the CPP-ML. The activists in both parties tend to be predominantly urban-oriented, although in 1972, as some NPA activity shifted from Central to Northern Luzon provinces, the CPP-ML solidified its rural following also, through a network of village "revolutionary committees" (called "Barrio Organization Committees," or BOC), and among the Dumagat tribal people of the Palanan coastal range in Luzon (Justus M. van der Kroef, "The Philippine Maoist," *Orbis*, Winter 1972).

Both the PKP and CPP-ML programs stress that the Philippines is entering a "revolutionary" period. Indeed, PKP publications describe the present condition of the country as "analogous to that in Russia on the eve of the 1905 Revolution," calling attention to the cracks appearing in the "neo-colonial political system" of the Philippines dominated, as it is said to be, by "American imperialists" and the native oligarchy. Workers oppressed by "crooked union officials who preach industrial peace and live in bourgeois luxury," peasants feeling the "backlash of neo-colonial land reform," petty-bourgeois intellectuals "rising in protest"—all these and others are perceived by the PKP as contributing to a "stream of popular revolutionary energy" now running strong (*Ang Komunista*, February 1971, pp. 18–19). One PKP Central Committee member, writing in the international organ of Moscow-oriented parties, declared in April 1972, that in his country conditions had become "extremely complicated and explosive" as a result of the domination of "US monopoly policy" and its minions (Francisco Balagtas, "American Imperialism in the Philippines," *WMR*, April 1972, pp. 34–36).

In its official party program the CPP-ML has set itself "ten guidelines," headed by the "destruction of the forces of 'US imperialism' and 'feudal oppression' " in the Philippines. Other points include establishment of a "people's democratic state," struggle for unity and democratic rights, obedience to "democratic centralism," satisfying the demand for land among the rural population, establishment of a national industry, integration of national minorities, pursuance of a "people's democratic cultural revolution" free from "imperialist" and "feudal" influences, and implementation of a foreign policy based on "proletarian internationalism" (*The Maoist Communist Party of the Philippines*, pp. 14–15).

CPP-ML commitment to the tactical necessity of violent resistance has been frequently affirmed, and the party and the NPA have claimed to be building "revolutionary bases" and "guerrilla warfare zones" as their "revolutionary armed struggle developed rapidly" in both Northern and Southern Luzon (*Peking Review*, 14 January 1972, p. 18). Throughout 1972 CPP-ML media sought to portray the party as being at the head of a revolutionary momentum, "carrying forward an armed, protracted struggle" as party cadres "mobilize and organize the people in their millions for the revolution" (*Ang Bayan*, 29 March, cited in *Peking Review*, 26 May, p. 19).

Domestic Developments. After the 21 August 1971 terrorist bomb attack during a Liberal Party rally which killed 10 persons and wounded 94 more, the Marcos administration increasingly called attention to the allegedly widening influence of the NPA, as meanwhile the president's skeptical opponents in the press and in the opposition Liberal Party accused him of raising a "red scare" to perpetuate himself in office. By December 1971 Marcos was saying that communist "rural sanctuaries" were being established throughout the provinces and Governor Antonio Villanueva of Ilocos Sur Province warned that the NPA under Sison and Corpus was fully operating in Ilocos Sur and Isabela provinces and fanning out to the northern provinces as well (*Manila Times,* 17 December). Though six months later Marcos still claimed that NPA "subversives" had "increased by leaps and bounds" and were now also spreading throughout the southeastern provinces of Luzon in the so-called "Bicolandia" area *(Daily Mirror,* Manila, 20 June 1972), there had been up to that point fewer reports of the kind of NPA assassinations of provincial officials or attacks on government patrols and military bases that were typical of much of 1971 (see *YICA 1972,* p. 575).

In early June 1972, however, reports of clashes between NPA units and government constabulary and troops were again becoming more frequent, and Philippine armed forces spokesmen declared that the NPA was steadily gaining strength, particularly in the Eastern Visayas, where an NPA force under Benjamin Jallores ("Commander Benjie"), composed of 100 armed regulars and backed by a "service support" contingent of 300, was now reportedly operating (*Manila Chronicle,* 22 June, and *Manila Bulletin,* 27 June). Reports that Philippine armed forces retirees were joining the NPA or crime syndicates because of financial straits, that there was evidence of communist infiltration into feuding Christian and Muslim armed bands in Mindanao, and that NPA "Barrio Organization Committees" were rapidly spreading in the central and eastern parts of the country all seemed to lend substance to Marcos's warning that the security problem in Bicol and the Visayas was becoming "alarming" (*Pace,* Manila, 16 June; *Manila Chronicle* 22 and 26 June; *Manila Bulletin,* 24 June). In an interview with a leading Asian news weekly Marcos predicted that "leftist extremists" would resort to open insurrection when he retired late in 1973 (*Far Eastern Economic Review,* 24 June).

In subsequent weeks there were similar warnings concerning the developing consolidation of NPA influence. On 23 July the Philippine News Service reported that a 400-man, well-armed NPA unit was preparing for attacks on military installations in Isabela Province (ibid., 29 July). On 25 August Philippine Constabulary chief Brigadier General Fidel V. Ramos warned of intensifed "urban guerrilla" activities by the NPA, focused on Manila. Ramos's remarks came when a series of bombing incidents in Manila (fifteen such incidents between the middle of July and the middle of September alone), involving stores and public utilities and other government offices, and attributed to the NPA, heightened public tensions. NPA ambushes of and clashes with government patrols in Isabela and Camarines Sur caused military warnings (according to Marcos) that at this rate the communist movement would "overwhelm" the country unless the 650,000-man military establishment (all but 6 percent in the Army) was strengthened (*New York Times,* 9 September). The National Defense and Security Committee of the Philippine Lower House declared on 1 September that the country faced an "alarming" communist threat of subversion. Committee chairman Constantino Navarro said his committee had become convinced of an extensive communist plot as a result of the committee's hearings. However, critics of Marcos, notably Senator Beningno Aquino of the opposition Liberal Party, charged Marcos with importing guns to be planted in select areas so as to heighten public anxiety about the NPA and thus permitting Marcos to put much or all of the country under military rule. Others alleged that the recent Manila bombing incidents were not the work of NPA members but of common criminals seeking to extort money from store owners (*Far Eastern Economic Review,* 30 September). Marcos, meanwhile, charged that in the rural areas fearful government officials, landowners, and businessmen were contributing funds to the "invisible government" of the communists (*New York Times,* 9 September).

Adding to the public confusion over the extent of NPA activity was the mystery surrounding the 90-ton Philippine-owned motor vessel *Karagatan,* which ran aground at Digoyo Bay,

Palanan District, Isabela Province around 4 July, after reportedly delivering arms to local NPA units. Philippine Constabulary, investigating the vessel, came under heavy attack by NPA units, necessitating the calling of naval and air reenforcements, as meanwhile caches, containing hundreds of M-14 rifles and thousands of rounds of ammunition, were discovered by the Constabulary. Where the *Karagatan* got its cargo of weapons (indeed if it had been engaged in any "gun running" at all) became the subject of much controversy in subsequent weeks (*Philippines Herald,* Manila, and *Manila Chronicle,* 10 July; Peter Kann in *Wall Street Journal,* 1 September).

Amid reports of new government skirmishes with the NPA in Isabela and the Bicol area there came bomb explosions at utility stations and a gasoline depot in Manila as the Defense Department, meanwhile, warned that NPA "killer squads" acting according to a "September–October plan" were roaming the city and had scheduled the assassination of top officials and bomb attacks on the Manila airport (*Far Eastern Economic Review,* 9 September). There were also bombings on 19 September at the city hall in Quezon City, site of the Philippine Constitutional Convention. Two days later there was a mass demonstration, reportedly sparked by the KM, at Plaza Miranda in the capital, protesting government "repression" and allegedly impending imposition of martial law, upon which the president at the urging of military commanders was now said to have decided. On the night of 22 September, after the car of Defense Secretary Juan Ponce Enrile was attacked by gunmen (Enrile was unharmed by the shots because he was driving in another escort car), Marcos formally proclaimed martial law throughout the country.

In a nationwide radio address the next day Marcos declared that he was acting in accordance with Article 7 of the Philippine constitution which grants the president the right to place the country under martial law and to suspend habeas corpus. Marcos said he was acting to "protect [the country] and our democracy," and stressed that "this is not a military takeover of civilian government functions." Schools were to be closed, the media controlled, and rallies and demonstrations prohibited, and various reform measures in the structure and operations of government were to be announced shortly. The president said he felt justified in taking all these steps because "a state of rebellion exists in the Philippines," not just ordinary "lawlessness and criminality," in that "battles" were taking place between government forces and "subversives" in many provinces throughout the country.

Marcos, then, in the same address, identified the extent of NPA operations. In Isabela Province alone, he said, the CPP-ML and NPA were now controlling "33 municipalities out of 37," while 207 NPA "Barrio Organization Committees" constituted an "invisible government" and the NPA "had established communal farms and production bases." Other provinces throughout Luzon were also being affected: in six months' time, according to the president, the armed NPA had grown to 10,000 armed regulars and part-time supporters, while front groups, like the KM, had also greatly expanded. KM chapters according to the president, had grown from 200 in 1970 to 317 in July 1972, with a corresponding increase in membership from 10,000 to about 16,000. The SDK, Marcos said further, now had 159 chapters with "1,495 highly indoctrinated and fanatical members." Critical, in the president's judgment, was the evidence of the NPA's new firepower as reflected in the *Karagatan's* supply of arms to the communists. Marcos charged further that the NPA was getting funds and equipment "not only from inside the Philippines but also from outside our country." Moreover, the Defense Department had reported that attempts were being made to infiltrate the armed forces. Also, the "subversives have organized urban partisans in the greater Manila area and they have been and still are very active"; in consequence, the president said, in the greater Manila area "tension and anxiety" had mounted to the point that usually "busy centers" from "cinema houses" to "public markets" were "practically deserted." With the power now in his possession, Marcos concluded, not only "the threat of a violent overthrow of our republic" would be eliminated, but "we must now reform the social, the economic and political institutions in our country." (Text of Marcos speech, Foreign Broadcast Information Service, 25 September.)

In the weeks following this address a spate of presidential decrees and regulations, ranging from the death penalty for violators of a new ban on firearms, and the arrests of prominent politicians and journalists, to massive purges of the civil bureaucracy and the granting of land-ownership (involving a total acreage of 3.75 million) to some 715,000 rice- and corn-growing tenants, descended on the Philippine nation. Despite the curbs on press freedom and partisan political activity, the initial public reaction to the Marcos martial law and attendant reform measures was not unfavorable. This was due in large measure to continuing reports of clashes with the NPA. On October 2 Information Secretary Francisco Tatad confirmed Philippine Constabulary reports of a new shoot-out with NPA elements in Camarines Sur, four days earlier. On October 7 Philippine armed forces intelligence said that NPA units comprising some 350 members were concentrating in parts of Quezon and Rizal provinces for what appeared to be an impending "now or never" battle near Manila; meanwhile skirmishes between government forces and the Maoist insurgents were said to be occurring almost daily since Marcos proclaimed martial law (*New York Times,* 8 October; Associated Press dispatch, Manila, 12 October). On 17 October Tatad announced the arrest of four alleged participants in what was described as a "communist assassination plot" against Marcos. The same day, Marcos in an address marking the opening of SEATO naval exercises declared that the communist threat in the Philippines had grown to such dangerous proportions that he had nearly been compelled to seek the assistance of the United States and other foreign allies (*New York Times,* 18 October). On 21 October it was reported from Mindanao, where Christian and Muslim armed bands have been battling each other, that some 400 Moslems attacked a military camp and occupied the Mindanao State University at Marawi, before the insurgents were driven off. Twenty-six died in the fighting, which according to the government's Information Secretary Francisco Tatad was inspired by "Maoists" (*Times of India,* 23 October).

Not all Filipinos were persuaded by these reports and presidential revelations. Marcos's martial law declaration probably solidified to a degree the whole communist opposition against him, despite internal doctrinal differences. One result of the arrests following in the wake of the martial law decree was the causing of even some non-communist radicals to move toward an alliance with the NPA. Thus, in the provinces, young activists, fearing that they might be apprehended, went into hiding or joined the communist bands in the mountains (*New York Times,* 10 October). In Camarines Sur and Isabela, according to a statement on 26 September by Philippine Cabinet Secretary Alejandro Melcher, tenant farmers, with the aid of the NPA, had occupied large acreages of land belonging to private companies. Some observers viewed Marcos's sweeping land reform measures, granting land to tenants, as a mere ex post facto ratification of a fait accompli, not likely to bring much favor to the president in any case in view of the serious lag in the implementation of earlier measures granting land-ownership to tenants, such as the 1964 Land Reform Bill. (About 46 percent of all Philippine farms are operated by tenants, 37 percent are fully owned by the occupier, 16 percent are partly owned, and 1 percent are under other forms of management. Average rice farm holdings range from two to three hectares. *International Labour Review,* August–September 1972, p. 115.) Liberal Party observers of the NPA and KM have stressed the serious income maldistribution in the Philippines, in which 2.6 percent of families earn 10,000 Pesos (US $1,538) or more a year, while 77.1 percent earn below 3,000 Pesos ($461) (Benigno

Aquino, "Youth in Revolt," *Far Eastern Economic Review,* 10 June 1972, pp. 22–24). Critics contend that it will take more than Marcos's emergency decrees to ameliorate such inequalities and undercut NPA and other radical appeals.

International Aspects. The upsurge of CPP-ML and NPA activity focused new attention on the alleged foreign support for and contacts of the Philippine Maoists, as meanwhile the Marcos government was seeking to improve its official relations with major communist powers, particularly the Soviet Union and China. Philippine press reports, shortly before Marcos proclaimed martial law, that underground Indonesian communists had infiltrated the southern Philippines were discounted by Philippine authorities (*Antara Daily New Bulletin,* Djakarta, 28 September 1972), although in the past such Indonesian communist infiltration had been blamed for much of the radical agitation in Manila (Justus M. van der Kroef, "Philippine Communism and the Chinese," *China Quarterly,* April–June 1967). On 8 April 1972, however, President Marcos himself charged that both Indonesian and Chinese communists had been involved in local communist action against his government, and said that Philippine communist leaders had been trained in China (*Far Eastern Economic Review,* 15 April). Marcos's reaction came only a few weeks after Chinese premier Chou En-lai had personally assured Marcos's own emissary, Leyte governor Benjamin Romualdez, during the latter's secret visit to Peking, that China would not support financially or morally any group which would try to subvert the Philippines (ibid., 26 February). The obvious Maoist orientation of the CPP-ML and the NPA, no less than the earlier vigorous propaganda support given by Peking to the Philippine Maoists (see *YICA 1972,* p. 575), seemed to put the assurances given Romualdez by the Chinese as much into question as the hostile anti-Marcos tone of the Chinese Communist media in 1972 and their continued dissemination of CPP-ML and NPA policy declarations. Thus the celebration of the 12 June 1972 anniversary of the Philippines' national independence day was described in the Chinese media as having taken place in the context of popular opposition to "US imperialist aggression" against the Philippines and of a public demand for "genuine independence" (*Peking Review,* 23 June). The NPA's third anniversary was commemorated in the pages of *Peking Review* (see 26 May 1972 issue) by reprinting excerpts from the NPA's journal *Ang Bayan.* Yet the Marcos government, prior to the martial law declaration of 22 September, had been quietly proceeding with negotiations looking toward establishment of diplomatic relations with both China and the Soviet Union. The previously noted visit to Peking of Marcos's emissary Romualdez had been expected to pave the way for a more formal visit to the Chinese capital by the president's wife, Mrs. Imelda Marcos, who had visited Moscow for talks with Russian leaders on 14 March. Nothing came of the expectations of a Peking visit by Mrs. Marcos, however, although on 7 June the Philippine government announced that it was planning to send two official missions to China and the Soviet Union to examine the possibility of formulating diplomatic relations.

Meanwhile establishment of a Philippine-Soviet Friendship Society in mid-May 1972, with Mrs. Marcos as honorary chairman, the visit to the Soviet Union of Bals Ople, Philippine labor secretary, the following month, and sympathetic press and radio commentaries in the Soviet Union during this period on the Philippines' search for "new ways of development, ways that would be more in the national interest of the Philippines" (Dmitri Borisov, Moscow radio, 30 May; *USSR and Third World,* London, II, no. 6, 310) contrasted with the harsh attacks on the alleged "strangehold" on the Philippine economy and educational establishment by "American imperialists and their agents" in the Philippines and with the charge that the "dominant classes" in Philippine society "are closely connected with imperialism"—charges and attacks to be found in the main international organ of Moscow-oriented communist parties (*WMR*, April, pp. 34–36). Similar criticism continues to reflect the PKP's official position also.

Although in the wake of the Romualdez visit a 16-man delegation of the "Association for Philippine-Chinese Understanding" and a 20-woman delegation of the "Association of Women Doctors of the Philippines" arrived in Peking on 28 and 29 April, respectively, further moves toward a new Sino-Philippine rapprochement have now been suspended. At the end of October 1972, neither Peking nor Moscow had taken an official position on Marcos's proclamation of martial law or on the intensifying struggle of the Marcos government against the NPA.

Publications. The main PKP organ is *Ang Komunista* ("The Communist"), which appears irregularly in both English and "Philipino" (Tagalog) editions. MPKP and AKSIUN issue occasional pamphlets under their names. The CPP-ML monthly is *Ang Bayan* ("The Nation"), published in English and Tagalog. The KM's organ, *Progressive Review,* did not appear during 1972. CPP-ML and NPA statements and *Ang Bayan* articles are periodically excerpted in *Peking Review* or relayed over the Tagalog service of Peking radio.

University of Bridgeport   Justus M. van der Kroef

Singapore

Singapore communists do not have either a formal, or lawful, or even underground party organization of their own; most are nominally affiliated with the Communist Party of Malaya (CPM) and regard the constitutional separation of the state of Singapore from the Malay Peninsula as both illegitimate and undesirable. Singapore communists have opposed both the creation in 1963 of the Malaysian Federation, on the grounds that the real rights of self-determination of the Borneo states of Sarawak and Sabah were being violated, and the subsequent departure in 1965 of Singapore from the Malaysian Federation. Some 1.6 million of Singapore's estimated 2.1 million population are Chinese, and, as is the case both in Eastern and Western Malaysia, Singapore communism has a predominantly Chinese complexion (with some participation of Singapore Indians) and is particularly susceptible to mainland Chinese political influences. In the fifties and sixties the Chinese schools in Singapore were particularly subject to such influence.

Organization and Tactics. Owing to strict government surveillance, the actual structure of Singapore underground communism, if any exists, and its relations with the CPM, are deeply buried and are little known. Political radicalism, especially if suspected to be of communist origin, is quickly nipped in the bud by the government; there are about 100 political prisoners, some of whom have been detained for nearly a decade, although in 1972 no arrests were announced as having been made under the Internal Security Act. (See Amnesty International, *Annual Report 1971—1972,* London, 1972, p. 34). Singapore communism therefore follows a self-protective policy of complex front formation and rapid front dissolution, generally, and of necessity, committed to a politically militant but officially non-violent strategy.

The principal communist front group is the Barisan Sosialis ("Socialist Front"), established on 26 July 1961 by radical dissidents in the People's Action Party (PAP) which has dominated Singapore government and politics since the early sixties. Communist influence, though not control, is also apparent in the "People's Front," formed on 27 March 1971 by Lui Boon Poh, an attorney educated in Britain. The radical Partai Rakyat ("People's Party"), originally founded in 1956 and with a following largely among some 300 or so Singapore Malay leftists, was the Barisan's principal political ally in the sixties, but is now dormant. Additionally, some twenty smaller trade unions (with a following mainly among street hawkers and vendors, shop assistants, clerical workers, and construction workers) have given the Barisan Sosialis electoral support, or are informally allied with it, although most of these unions could not be considered communist front organizations. Barisan support from Chinese secondary school associations and in Nanyang University, quite strong in the late fifties and most of the sixties, has now been greatly reduced.

Barisan members are estimated to number 700 to 800. They are led by a 14-man Central

Committee headed by Lee Siew Choh (re-elected as party chairman since 1961). See Cheng Kiong is the Barisan's vice-chairman and Tai Cheng Kang its treasurer. Exact total formal membership of the "People's Front" is not known, but is not believed to exceed 300. Communist supporters in the trade union movement may be estimated at 6,000 at least, providing Singapore communism with most of its rank and file, and also the backbone of its electoral support. Arrests of prominent Barisan cadres (at least 60 of the approximately 100 political prisoners currently held by the Singapore government are from the Barisan), and periodic dissension over tactics have made for weakness and frequent criticism of alleged leadership ineffectiveness in the party, even in leftist circles. Barisan Sosialis and "People's Front" tactics at present eschew the violent confrontation with authorities through riots and demonstrations that characterized Singapore communism in the fifties and sixties.

Instead, efforts are concentrated on a "parliamentary" process of political radicalization of the public, exploiting existing and allegedly slowly growing dissatisfaction with the PAP government of Singapore premier Lee Kuan Yew. The "People's Front" appears to have been formed to give the radical left and the anti-Lee opposition a legitimate political channel outside the Barisan Sosialis. The latter has been considered in some Singapore leftist circles (especially elements under the age of 30 years) as tainted with too many failures and leadership squabbles. On all major issues, however, such as the need for establishing formal relations with the People's Republic of China, freedom for political prisoners, and the implementation of a "genuinely socialist" economic action program for Singapore, the two organizations see closely eye-to-eye.

In its 17-point "elections manifesto" issued on 4 June 1972, in preparation for the 2 September general elections, the Barisan Sosialis called, among other points, for a "genuinely independent democratic unified Malaya, including Singapore island," freedom of thought and opinion and the release of all political prisoners, changes in the labor and citizenship laws, reduction in taxes and public housing rentals, free movement to and from Malaya across the causeway connecting Singapore and the Malay Peninsula, freedom of education and free medical services for the poor, "promotion of local capital in industries," and "equality for women" (*Plebeian,* 4 June). Explanatory statements in relation to these points stressed the need to break the domination of Singapore by British and American "imperialists," particularly in Singapore's economy and in its defense posture, condemnation of "the LKY (i.e., Premier Lee Kuan Yew) fascists" for their "white terror" of political arrests, and the eradication of the "widespread fear of unemployment" and exploitation of workers "for the benefit of foreign monopoly capital" (ibid.).

Earlier, the Barisan Sosialis had sought to defend itself against attacks by PAP spokesmen that it was "not principled," "self-contradictory," and "without popular support" by attempting to show that it was the PAP which had changed course over the years on such issues as Singapore's merger with Malaya and the release of political prisoners. All the same, as its critics have noted, the Barisan, in 1965, had refused to participate in the Singapore parliament, and in 1968 had boycotted the general elections. Its reason for doing so, according to a party statement in May 1972, was that the "bogus nature" of Singapore independence and democracy needed to be exposed, particularly the "oppressive class nature" of the Singapore parliament. Today, however, according to the same Barisan statement, "circumstances have changed" and it "has become absolutely necessary" to use "all available means possible, including parliament and other forums in the fascist state," to expose the "political deceptions and diabolical machinations" of the Lee Kuan Yew government (ibid., 14 May). Considering tactical possibilities suggested by the unexpectedly large opposition vote to the Lee Kuan Yew government in the 2 September 1972 elections (see below), it seems likely that the Barisan Sosialis, and Singapore communism generally, will continue to stress the path of non-violent parliamentary opposition in the next few months, despite pressures for a more radical course coming from a few militants. The same is true for the "People's Front," whose program in essentials dovetails with that of the Barisan Sosialis. For example, Lui Boon Poh has also called for the creation of a "unified Malayan Democratic Republic" which would join Singapore again with the Malay Peninsula (see Peter Wicks in *New Guinea and Australia, the Pacific and Southeast Asia,* Sydney, September–October, 1971).

Domestic Developments. On 2 September general parliamentary elections were held, in which a total of 136 candidates from six parties and two independent candidates contested 57 seats. The People's Action Party won all seats (additionally, eight PAP candidates had earlier won uncontested seats at the time of nomination), and 522,000 or over 69 percent of the votes cast. Even so, the size of the opposition vote (224,500 or nearly 31 percent) was a surprise to the government, and Premier Lee's spokesman characterized the votes the PAP did not win as more in the nature of protest votes "against the PAP than for the opposition. We have no illusions over this." (*Mirror,* Singapore, 11 September.) Lee himself, meanwhile, claimed that only "good luck" had prevented violence in two electoral constituencies "where race, religion and language were exploited to the fullest." He was referring to areas of Singapore dominated by Malays. Lee also stressed the problem of "getting an intelligent, constructive opposition" in Singapore, characterizing existing opposition parties as mere "fly by nights." Lee said further that the PAP government would pass laws requiring all political parties to open their books periodically to public inspection in line with his earlier accusation that "foreign interests" were backing some opposition candidates. (Associated Press dispatch, 7 September.) Critics fear that such a measure would further inhibit the growth of opposition parties. "People's Front" candidate Leong Mun Kuai, who opposed Lee Kuan Yew in the Tandjong Pagar constituency in the 1972 elections, was arrested on a charge of having urged the assassination of government leaders (*Far Eastern Economic Review,* 16 September, p. 20).

Neither the Barisan Sosialis nor the "People's Front" did well, and the 1972 election clearly tarnished the Barisan's image further. The opposition Worker's Party, led by former chief minister David Marshall and attorney J. B. Jeyeratnam, and with a considerable following in the Indian community, perhaps provided the largest surprise among opposition parties, winning nearly 90,000 votes. The claim of Barisan chairman Lee Siew Choh, that voting irregularities had occurred in his own unsuccessful contest against PAP chairman Toh Chin Chye, was not sustained, and seemed also to some leftists but another expression of Barisan weakness.

During the year the PAP government continued to stress a position of Singaporean nationalism in its educational and press policies. There is a clear implication in government policies that "a-national" or "un-Singaporean" behavior, as determined by the government, is likely to cost the offending culprit, particularly one whose citizenship or residence rights can be called into question, a further stay in the island state; even for citizens life can be made difficult. On 6 July 1972, Premier Lee in an Australian television broadcast declared that his government has been sending "communist students" from Singapore to Australia, Canada, and New Zealand in an effort to break up concentrations of leftists in his country. He said that the students returned home to Singapore "fairly middle class and comfortable," although he claimed they had become "armchair critics." The students' sojourn abroad was designed to bring them under the influence of new ideas. But, the Singapore premier added, "We have not sent any to Britain because there they go to the London School of Economics and come back an even more convinced revolutionary or, even worse, an anarchist." Lee further took note of Singapore's Chinese schools which, he declared, were under communist control and had produced "an endless stream of cadres." He added, however, that the erstwhile communist grip on the predominantly Chinese Nanyang University had now been broken. (*Bangkok World,* 7 July.)

During 1972 there were no charges of communist influence in the Singapore press made by Premier Lee, such as were made in 1971 and previous years. Local press circles, however, continue to complain of strict surveillance over management and all source of origin of working capital. Fear of undue foreign (especially communist or even U.S. financial interest) must be balanced, according to pro-government publicists, by the Lee Kuan Yew government's interest in foreign capital: "the present government is one of the very few governments among the developing nations which has not hesitated to bring in foreign and local experts for consultation, and to help in projects that are now under way in Singapore" (R. S. Bhatal, "Power and Stability," *Far Eastern Economic Review,* 5 August 1972, p. 14).

Although Singapore continues to favor a modest Australian, New Zealand, and British military presence in the island state and its environs, in line with the provisions of the Five-Power Defence Arrangement (which includes the previously named states and Malaysia, and was renewed on 1 November 1971), there is a realization that the British, New Zealand and Australian military commitments to Singapore and Malaysia may rapidly be drawing to a close and that new policy postures, particularly in relation to the Soviet Union and China may become necessary. "Neutralization" of Southeast Asia, as propagated by the Malaysian government, is not viewed as a viable future framework of regional security. Rather, Singapore seeks an active international (though not necessarily military) presence. Premier Lee Kuan Yew has been quoted as saying:

> I would like the US to maintain a sufficient economic and strategic presence in the area to prevent any other single power, or any group of powers, from gaining complete hegemony over the area. But I don't think you need bases and troops to do that. The Russians don't have bases and they are extending their influence all right. (Pang Cheng Lian, "Watching Moscow," ibid., 28 October 1972.)

Further accommodation of the interests of the communist powers (Singapore has diplomatic relations with the Soviet Union, but has little direct trade; it has no diplomatic relations with China but indirectly has a good deal of entrepôt trade) would probably also affect the Singapore government's present domestic hard-line policies toward communism.

International Aspects. Singapore communists have not issued separate statements on international questions, nor are they known to attend communist international gatherings apart from CPM delegations. The reason is that the CPM technically claims control over and speaks for Singapore communists. Both the Barisan Sosialis and the "People's Front" are committed to a union of Malaysia and Singapore in a "democratic" state. Because of the pronounced influence of China and Maoist ideology on the CPM and its front and associated organizations, the international orientation and, to a significant degree, ideological complexion of Singapore communism, generally, may be considered as pro-Peking.

Publications. While there is no distinctive Singapore communist publication, the biweekly *Plebeian* (in English) and the weekly *Chern Sian Pau* (in Chinese), published by the Barisan Sosialis, most regularly and frequently reflect the communists' position. The CPM's principal medium in Europe, the infrequently appearing *Malayan Monitor and General News,* published in London, and the "Voice of the Malayan Revolution," the CPM radio transmitter based in Yunnan, southern China, articulate official Malayan communist policy statements also as they apply to Singapore. Publications like *Mimbar Rakyat* appearing under the auspices of the presently dormant Partai Rakyat ("People's Party") have now become infrequent, as strict government surveillance over the communist front press and over the importation of communist literature has an inhibiting effect.

University of Bridgeport   Justus M. van der Kroef

Thailand

Throughout 1972 communist activities inside Thailand, as in the past, were intermittent and scattered. Except for the contingency of a communist regime in Laos capable of fomenting subversion in the vulnerable northeastern provinces, these fragmented outbursts of local communist action comprised a variety of nuisances to the central government in Bangkok, rather than a serious threat capable of subverting the security of the kingdom. Communist activity in Bangkok by the outlawed Thai Communist Party—TCP—and the Chinese Communist Party of Thailand—CCP(T)—remained dormant and non-violent. Estimates of the size of the TCP remained at about 300 members and the CCP(T) at about 3,000. These minuscule membership figures have stayed essentially unchanged since the early post-World War II period. Factors which continue to inhibit the spread of communism in Thailand are the lack of deep-seated historical grievances, the absence of colonial rule, the traditional loyalty toward the monarchy and Theravada Buddhism, the fear of Chinese domination, widespread landownership, a sense of individualism, and continual economic growth and prosperity.

The only overt communist activity during the year occurred in rural insurgencies in the southern, northern, and northeastern provinces. In sensitive border areas, the interaction between internal provincial grievances and external political and material support abetted dissidence and violence by some 6,000 to 7,000 insurgents operating in 37 of the 71 provinces of the country. (Personal briefing, Communist Suppression Operations Command, Bangkok, 27 April 1972.)

The Southern Insurgency. Communist guerrilla warfare in the southern insurgency continued to be waged by the Communist Party of Malaya (CPM) along the Thai-Malaysian border. This movement of Malaysian Chinese communists comprises the remnants of the insurgent organization, formed during the Japanese occupation in World War II, which fought the British colonial government from 1948 until the mid-1950s. It still obtains much of its financial support from the extortion of wealthy Chinese in Malaysia, and it uses isolated jungle areas on the Thai-Malaysian border as staging bases and rest camps for its paramilitary attacks against Malaysian security forces. With no apparent success, the CPM has sought to exploit the anti-Thai grievances among the Thai-Muslim minority in the southern provinces. Traditional Malay racial hostility toward the Chinese and Islamic opposition to the Marxist-Leninist-Maoist ideology of the CPM have inhibited cooperation between Malaysian Chinese communists active in Thailand and the small terrorist organization of Thai-Muslim separatists seeking the secession of four southern provinces to Malaysian jurisdiction.

The CPM is greatly limited in Thailand by its very small alien political base. Its revolutionary goal likewise is directed against the Malaysian government, not against the ruling power in Bangkok. Its guerrilla warfare activities are confined to the Thai-Malaysian border area, and it engages in military skirmishes with Thai security forces only when its staging areas and rest camps are threatened. Perhaps the most limiting factor for the CPM is its lack of foreign assistance. During the 1960s some unconfirmed reports claimed that Chin Peng and his communist organization had received weapons and supplies from China and North Vietnam. Any external aid of this kind has been on a small scale and of no significant effect in Thailand.

During 1972 small-scale attacks were made by Thai communist terrorists in the central Kra Isthmus. Operating against isolated military and police installations, these guerrilla forces constitute the most recent insurgent group in the southern provinces. Their dramatic raids have occurred near Surat Thani and Nakorn Sri Thammarat, less than 200 miles from Bangkok. In time, this new dissident organization could become a serious security threat. These Thai insurgents in the south are of the same racial and linguistic stock as the dominant Thai majority. Under favorable conditions they could conceivably expand their area of violence and terror. Yet Thai communists in the central Kra Isthmus number only a few hundred, and thus far they have received no widespread popular support.

The Northern Insurgency. Communist activity in the north has consisted of subversive actions by an estimated 400 Thai, Thai-Chinese, and Pathet Lao (see *Laos*) party cadres trained by the Chinese communists at a special base in North Vietnam. These communist agitators have exploited grievances among the Meo and a few other mountain tribes caused by Thai government restrictions on opium growing, smuggling, and swidden (slash and burn) agriculture. Most of the diverse tribal groups in the northern provinces have migrated to Thailand during the past century, while several tribes have moved from insecure areas in Laos and Burma during the past two decades. (J. L. S. Girling, "Strong-Man Tactics in Thailand: The Problems Remain," *Pacific Community,* April 1972, p. 539.) Anti-Thai hostility has been exacerbated in recent years by increasing contacts between southward-moving hill tribes and westward-migrating Thai villagers from economically depressed provinces in the northeast.

Unlike the communists active in the south, the insurgents in the northern provinces have received considerable assistance from China and North Vietnam. Infiltrating party agitators have succeeded in providing small arms and guerrilla warfare training to 2,000 to 3,000 Meo tribesmen. Chinese and Soviet weapons include AK–47 rifles, B–40 rocket launchers, 60 mm. mortars, and plastic mines. Communist-led Meo insurgents have attacked Thai military and police installations with increasing strength since 1968. In 1970 they murdered the governor of Chiengrai Province and two military colonels who were attempting unarmed to negotiate the surrender of a local insurgent group (*Bangkok World,* 21 September 1970). These three men were the highest-ranking government officials killed in any insurgency in the kingdom. By 1972 the insurgents in the north were causing about 1,000 government casualties a year.

In March 1972 the northern insurgents posed a sufficient threat to cause the Thai government to launch the biggest military offensive in the history of the country. Major elements of two army divisions numbering 12,000 men were used against communist terrorists in the three "tri-border" provinces of Phitsanulok, Phetchabun, and Loei (*Christian Science Monitor,* 11 April). The government offensive achieved few concrete results and only a few prisoners and sympathizers were captured. The insurgents had better arms and fought with greater tenacity than expected. Yet the Thai government was generally pleased with this military counter-action. It served as a valuable training exercise and oriented a large part of the Thai military organization from defensive to offensive tactics. It also proved that the Thai army could engage in sustained action over a large geographic area, and it showed that isolated guerrilla bases were no longer inaccessible to government military forces. It likewise had a desirable political effect in showing many people in the northern provinces that the central government was no longer indifferent to their safety and welfare.

The Thai government has received sizable foreign assistance in coping with communist activity in the north. The United States has supplied military equipment, and U.S. military advisers have been attached to Thai army troops deployed in the northern region. Specialized counter-insurgency training at a Thai military base in Phitsanulok has been provided by U.S. military advisers, who are forbidden from accompanying Thai troops into combat areas. The Southeast Asia Treaty Organization since 1965 has maintained a Hill Tribes Research Center in Chiengmai to study the northern tribal groups and to advise the Thai government on special assistance programs designed to improve living standards among these semi-nomadic people. (*The Story of SEATO*, South-East Asia Treaty Organization, Bangkok, 1972, p. 28.) Under SEATO auspices, Australia, Great Britain, and the United States have also provided the services of several professional anthropologists and specialized equipment for this research program. A $3,000,000 pilot project has likewise been inaugurated in the northern provinces by the United Nations to provide the tribal groups with technical assistance in the cultivation of food and cash crops to replace opium growing.

The communist-led insurgency in the north is more serious than the two small communist groups in the south, yet in this region also the spread of dissidence and violence faces many limitations. Communist leaders in the northern provinces have built their movement on a relatively small and highly fragmented non-Thai political base. The only tribal group which has joined in insurgent activity on any considerable scale is the Meo, whose total numbers are estimated at 50,000 to 70,000. Other tribal groups, comprising 90 percent of the tribal population in the north, also have certain grievances against the central government, yet with few exceptions they have not resorted to violence. The primitive culture of the hill tribesmen inhibits the spread of organized political control into lowland areas inhabited by the more advanced Thai people. Tribal insurgents are also untrained for sustained and sophisticated military operations outside the rugged mountainous terrain in the north. The threat of the communist insurgency is limited largely to the area where the territory inhabited by the mountain hill tribes joins the flat plains inhabited by the dominant Thai population.

The Northeastern Insurgency. Thai communist insurgents have operated among disgruntled villagers in the northeast in small groups since the mid-1950s. As in the north, this insurgency has been abetted by Thai communist cadres trained by the Chinese communists in North Vietnam. In December 1965 the Chinese foreign minister called for the violent overthrow of the Thai military regime in Bangkok, and shortly thereafter the communist movement in the northeast formed the "Thailand Patriotic Front" (TPF) (*Bangkok World*, 19 December). During the past seven years this clandestine organization has waged guerrilla warfare against Thai security forces and isolated rural villages. Its size is estimated at 1,500 insurgents and 50,000 sympathizers.

Communist agents in the northeastern provinces have exploited psychological and economic grievances among the Thai-Lao people in this strategic region. A distinct separatist feeling has existed among these people due to the long period of isolation from the dominant Thai population in the central provinces and the negligence of the Bangkok government toward their welfare and development. Economic grievances are caused by the semi-arid soil in the northeast which produces only one rice crop each year. This region has sparse mineral resources and little prospect of industrial development. The population density is higher than in other regions of the country, and the population growth rate of 3.5 percent makes it the most rapidly growing region in the kingdom. Per capita income is less than 50 percent of the national average.

The communist-led TPF has stressed these adverse economic and social conditions in fomenting dissidence and violence against the central government. Since 1970 the TPF has apparently coordinated some of its paramilitary operations with those of communist insurgents in the northern provinces. Four daring small-scale attacks have been made against air bases used by the United States (*Christian Science Monitor*, 4 October 1972). Communist insurgents in the region have received some logistical support from China, although this foreign assistance has been much smaller than that supplied to the northern insurgency. The distance from southern China to the northeastern provinces is greater than to the northern provinces, and the transporting of weapons and supplies to northeastern Thailand is hampered by sizable areas in Laos controlled by the Royal Laotian government and by the Mekong River, patrolled by the Thai river police. Economic improvements and strong countermeasures by the Thai armed forces since 1970 have caused the communist party leaders to curtail overt armed attacks and switch to an effort to build a clandestine political organization in this strategic region. (Girling, op. cit., p. 540.)

The reduced militancy of the communist insurgency in the northeastern provinces contrasts sharply with the dramatic activities of the insurgents in the south and the north. Yet the northeastern insurgency is potentially the most dangerous in the kingdom. Under favorable conditions the skillful exploitation of psychological and economic grievances in this region combined with external military assistance from China or North Vietnam, or both, could cause the expansion of insurgent control over a large portion of Thai territory and people. Without adequate countermeasures this threat could eventually jeopardize the security of the country. Subcultural hostility toward the central government has assumed some initial characteristics of a civil conflict between people of the same race, language, and culture. The potential of the northeastern insurgency to expand is not restricted by non-Thai political bases as in the south and the north. The establishment of political control by communist insurgents over sizable portions of the northeast could lead to more ambitious paramilitary attacks in the heavily populated central provinces surrounding Bangkok.

The threat of the northeastern insurgency has special significance due to its close proximity to Laos where approximately two-thirds of the territory is controlled by North Vietnamese and Pathet Lao military forces. Communist rule over the entire Laotian territory would facilitate the opportunity to spread insurgent activity in northeastern Thailand. (Frank C. Darling, "The Role of Laos in the Defense Strategy of Thailand," *Pacific Community*, April 1972, pp. 516–30.) In effect, Laos could become a vast staging base for Laotian communist agents to infiltrate a vulnerable region containing 12,000,000 Thai-Lao people and constituting a third of the territory of the Thai kingdom. The prevention of communist rule in Laos and the removal of provincial grievances in the northeastern provinces have consequently been key goals of the Thai government.

The official effort to improve economic conditions in the northeast has largely involved the Accelerated Rural Development program, launched in 1965. This government assistance program has employed small technical teams called Mobile Development Units to construct water facilities, sanitary projects, and land settlement schemes in many northeastern villages. The government has also built new roads to assist in opening markets for villagers producing small cash crops. The Ministry of Education has established new schools, and a regional university has been erected at Khonkaen for higher education in the region. These government efforts have met with some apparent success and the provincial feeling of separatism is declining. A sense of identification with the central Thai society is likewise increasing due to modern mass media and growing economic opportunity.

The effort of the Thai government to reduce economic grievances in the northeast which can be exploited by communist agitators has been extensively supplemented by assistance from the United States and other foreign sources. Since the negotiation of economic and military aid agreements with the Thai government in 1950, the United States has spent $588,-075,000 in military assistance and approximately $400,000,000 in economic and technical assistance (*Military Assistance and Foreign Military Sales Facts,* Washington, Department of Defense, April 1972, p. 6.) Since 1961 the bulk of U.S. aid has been devoted to improved security and economic conditions in the northeastern provinces. The World Bank has also provided much developmental assistance in promoting economic advancements in the northeast. About $300,000,000 in loans has been made to Thailand for the construction of railroads, highways, and hydroelectric power projects. The Southeast Asia Treaty Organization has established numerous community development projects and technical training centers in this region. Under the auspices of the Colombo Plan, Australia, New Zealand, and Great Britain have constructed new bridges and roads.

The Role of International Politics. The future strength of communism in Thailand depends heavily on the forces of international politics. The communist insurgencies in the north and northeast especially will be affected by possible changes in the foreign policy of China and other major powers. At the present time there is much ambiguity regarding the future role of China in "wars of national liberation" in nearby noncommunist societies such as Thailand. In his inaugural address before the U.N. General Assembly, the leader of the Chinese delegation declared that his government has "consistently maintained that all countries, big or small, should be equal and that the Five Principles of Peaceful Coexistence should be taken as the principles guiding the relations between countries. . . . No country has the right to subject another country to its aggression, subversion, control, interference, or bullying" (*NYT*, 16 November 1971). Yet three months later the Chinese government articulated a much different view in portions of the Shanghai communiqué issued at the end of U.S. President Nixon's official visit. This document stated: "Countries want independence, nations want liberation and the people want revolution—this has become the irresistible trend of history." It specifically cited China's support for the "liberation" of Vietnam, Laos, and Cambodia. In subsequent months China has undertaken actions to assist subversive activities with communist-led groups in Burma, Indonesia, and the Philippines.

Ultimately the spread of communist contingencies in Thailand depends most extensively on the foreign policy of the United States. Since 1950 U.S. political and material support to Thailand has been the major foreign factor elevating economic standards and deterring military or subversive threats. U.S. assistance has likewise been the dominant factor preventing communist domination in the small adjoining countries of Laos, Cambodia, and South Vietnam. The maintenance of non-communist governments in these strategic societies has been a key factor in the efforts of the United States to terminate its direct participation in the Vietnam conflict under conditions which will reduce the risks of future local insurgencies escalating to the point where they can once more involve the major powers. For several years the United States has been seeking agreements to minimize these risks in its negotiations with North Vietnam and its military suppliers, the Soviet Union and China. Many of these conditions presumably will be included in a peace agreement for Indochina.

As a peace agreement in Indochina is administered, the Thai government would be wise to strengthen its domestic policy. It could use the opportunity provided by U.S. diplomatic and military power as well as economic assistance from various foreign allies to promote a stronger and more unified society. Economic development could be more broadly based and benefit larger segments of the population. Political development could come from the establishment of some form of constitutional rule particularly adapted to the needs and norms of the Thai people. These reforms combined with the continuation of a realistic foreign policy could do much to reduce internal grievances which might again be exploited by communist subversive efforts in the future.

De Pauw University   Frank C. Darling

Vietnam: Democratic Republic of Vietnam

The Vietnam Workers' Party (Dang Lao Dong Viet Nam; VWP) is an outgrowth of the Indochinese Communist Party founded on 3 February 1930. On 19 May 1941 the Eighth Congress of the party created the "League for Vietnamese Independence" (Viet Nam Doc Lap Dong Minh Hoi), which became known as the Viet Minh. While presented as a nationalistic front of all anti-French and anti-Japanese forces in Vietnam, the Viet Minh was in fact completely controlled by communists. For propaganda purposes, the Indochinese Communist Party was officially dissolved in November 1945. Party functions were carried on clandestinely by the "Association for Marxist Studies," under the leadership of Truong Chinh (who had been party secretary-general). On 11 February 1951 the party surfaced and changed its name to Vietnam Workers' Party. Similar parties were created in Laos and Cambodia; however, VWP internal documents indicated this to be a tactical move—the VWP was to maintain secret control over all communist organizations in Indochina. At the same time, the Viet Minh was absorbed into the "United Vietnam Nationalist Front" (Mat Tran Lien Hiep Quoc Dan Viet Nam), better known as the Lien Viet, a front organization created by the communists in 1946. In September 1955 the Lien Viet was absorbed by the Vietnam Fatherland Front (Mat Tran To Quoc Viet Nam), which remains active today. Prior to the Geneva conference of 1954, the VWP and all communist activity in Indochina were illegal. The Geneva agreements recognized communist control of northern Vietnam—the Democratic Republic of Vietnam (DRV)—and since then the VWP has been the party in power there. Small "rubber stamp" parties—the Democratic Party and the Socialist Party—regularly issue statements praising the VWP and supporting all of its policies, but all power in the DRV remains in the hands of the VWP.

Although the 1959 constitution of the DRV vests all legislative power in the hands of the National Assembly, the Assembly's true nature is established by radio and press reports of its activities. Session after session it hears reports from various government leaders which, along with an assortment of resolutions, are always "unanimously adopted" (see, for example, Hanoi radio, 21 January, 27 March, 1 June, and 18 August 1972; *Nhan Dan,* 30 March). In practice the VWP dictates and supervises the administrative, legislative, judicial, military, cultural, and economic activities of the government through parallel but separate hierarchial organizations extending to the lowest territorial level. All key positions in the DRV government are held by senior VWP leaders. In 1972 the VWP claimed a membership of "more than one million members" (ibid., 3 February). The population of North Vietnam is around 22 million.

Leadership and Organization. According to the "Statute of the VWP," the highest leading organ of the party is the National Delegates' Congress. Although the Congress is normally supposed to meet once every four years, the statute provides that when "faced with special circumstances" the Central Executive Committee may postpone its meetings during a certain period. The last such congress was held in September 1960. Between congresses, party activities are to be led by the Central Executive Committee, which in turn elects the Politburo to "lead party activities during the interval between two plenary conferences of the Central Executive Committee." In practice, the Politburo is the most powerful group in North Vietnam.

Between May and September the two alternate (non-voting) members of the Politburo—public security minister Tran Quoc Hoan and army chief of staff Colonel-General Van Tien Dung—were elevated to full membership. Both had been alternates since 1960. Their promotion brought the Politburo to its full strength of 11 voting members as it existed prior to the 1967 death of Senior General Nguyen Chi Thanh and the 1969 death of President Ho Chi Minh. The 11 Politburo members are usually ranked as follows: Le Duan, Truong Chinh, Pham Van Dong, Pham Hung (thought to be in South Vietnam directing COSVN—see *Vietnam: Republic of Vietnam*—and thus frequently absent from lists of Politburo members present in Hanoi on ceremonial occasions), Vo Nguyen Giap (senior general), Le Duc Tho, Nguyen Duy Trinh, Le Thanh Nghi, Hoang Van Hoan, Tran Quoc Hoan, and Van Tien Dung (colonel general). The Central Executive Committee consists of 41 full members and 28 alternates (a list of names can be found in *YICA, 1972,* p. 586).

The most important mass organization is the Vietnam Fatherland Front (see above), of which the VWP is the leading component. Organizations affiliated under the front include the Vietnam General Federation of Trade Unions, the Ho Chi Minh Working Youth Union, and the Vietnam Women's Union.

Party Internal Affairs. Prior to the death of Ho Chi Minh (3 September 1969), it was common for analysts of North Vietnamese affairs to divide the Politburo into factions—usually pro-Chinese and pro-Soviet groups—or into "dogmatic" and "pragmatic" elements. While either approach oversimplifies, both have some merit. Truong Chinh, the former VWP secretary-general and leading theoritician, is clearly more "pro-Chinese" than Senior General Vo Nguyen Giap and more "dogmatic" than VWP First Secretary Le Duan. It is probably a mistake to categorize Vo Nguyen Giap as "pro-Soviet" in any serious sense. He is certainly not a "revisionist," and his military writings show a strong influence of those of Mao Tse-tung. Giap, once a history teacher, who is aware that traditionally Chinese imperialism has been Vietnam's greatest enemy, might more properly be categorized as "anti-Chinese" rather than "pro-Soviet" (although his anti-Chinese feelings have on occasion been manifested by pro-Soviet activities). Truong Chinh (whose party name means "long march" and reflects his pro-Chinese alignment) is apparently convinced that the benefits to be gained by a close association with Communist China far outweigh any possible dangers such an association might bring. He was held largely responsible for a brutal "land reform," conducted along Chinese lines and with Chinese advisers between 1953 and 1956, which is thought to have taken as many as 500,000 lives (see Hoang Van Chi, *From Colonialism to Communism—A Case History of North Vietnam,* New York: Praeger, 1964, pp. 72, 205; *Washington Post,* 3 October 1972). General Giap led the public criticism of the "land reform," which resulted in Truong Chinh being forced to make a self-criticism and to resign his post as VWP secretary-general. This is considered but one of many indications of a virtual vendetta between these two senior VWP leaders.

Truong Chinh has also apparently had strong differences with Le Duan, who became VWP first secretary in 1960 (Ho Chi Minh had held the position of secretary-general following Truong Chinh's demotion in 1956, turning it over to Le Duan at the Third Party Congress under the new designation of "first secretary"). In order to increase agricultural production,

Le Duan had supported a "three contracts" system in which peasant families were allowed to use small plots of land for personal profit so long as they fulfilled certain production requirements on cooperative land. Le Duan realized that the peasants would work harder if allowed to retain some of the profits of their labor. He came under strong attack from the more dogmatic Truong Chinh in 1968 and 1969, and the "three contracts" system was eventually eliminated.

Le Duan is also reported to have something of a vendetta going with Politburo member Le Duc Tho, stemming from a 1951 encounter while both were in South Vietnam and quarreled over the proper strategy to be followed in fighting the French. Le Duc Tho won the argument, and Le Duan was ordered to return to Hanoi. Le Duan returned to South Vietnam shortly after the end of the First Indochina War, and it was largely through his efforts that communist forces in the South were reorganized and committed to the overthrow of the government of South Vietnam.

Perhaps the most important intra-party dispute in recent years has been the question of priorities. All of the Politburo leaders apparently agree on general objectives—to develop North Vietnam's economy and to "liberate" South Vietnam—with Hanoi's limited resources it is not possible to give full attention to both tasks. The three basic choices open to the Politburo are: (1) devote maximum attention to the military situation in South Vietnam with the hope of winning a rapid victory but at the expense of the northern economy, (2) scale down the military struggle in South Vietnam and give maximum emphasis to strengthening the North, and (3) give equal importance to both tasks. The disputing factions have sometimes been labeled the "northern" and "southern" factions, reflecting their relative emphasis on strengthening the North or stepping up the military struggle in the South. Hanoi communications media attempt to hide such disputes, and thus it is frequently difficult to determine Politburo alignment. What evidence there is suggests that Le Duan and Vo Nguyen Giap lead the "southern" faction, while Truong Chinh heads the "northern" group. During most of 1971 (see *YICA, 1972*, p. 589) the two factions appeared to be in general equilibrium, with equal attention being paid to both objectives (this of course oversimplifies, as Hanoi has many other objectives). By the end of the year, however, it appears now that the "southern" priority faction had apparently gained a majority in the Politburo. An indication of this is found in an address to the December congress of the Vietnam Fatherland Front (see *YICA, 1972*, p. 592) by Truong Chinh, which was made public in February 1972. Truong Chinh stated: "At present, to struggle against the Americans for national salvation is the foremost duty of our people" (Hanoi radio, 2 February). If it seems surprising that Truong Chinh would make such a pronouncement, it should be recalled that Le Duan made one of the first attacks on the "three contracts" system (see above)—of which he had been a principle advocate—after the Politburo decided to discard it. Such precedents obviously complicate the task of aligning the Politburo, and have resulted in competent scholars reaching conclusions completely contradictory to those stated above.

During early 1972 there was further evidence that the "southern" priority-oriented members of the Politburo were having their way. A key article in the January–February issue of *Tap Chi Tuyen Huan* (Hanoi) noted that "Fighting the Americans for national salvation is the most sacred duty of our party, of the working class, and of our entire Vietnamese people at present." The VWP military daily editorialized in February:

> Now the Vietnamese revolution is fulfilling two strategic tasks at one time: constructing socialism in the north and liberating the south. The anti-U.S. national salvation undertaking is the most important task for all our people and combatants. (*Quan Doi Nhan Dan*, 3 February 1972).

The emphasis on liberating the South was also apparent at the 20th Plenum of the VWP Central Committee, which reportedly took place "early in 1972." A lengthy broadcast by Hanoi radio (10 April) explained:

> The VWP Central Committee recently held its 20th plenum to discuss and decide tasks related to the anti-U.S. national salvation resistance and to socialist construction in the north. . . . The plenum asserted that the balance of forces has turned increasingly in our favor and to the enemy's disadvantage. . . . We have the proper conditions to take the initiative in attacking the enemy. . . . To completely defeat the U.S. aggressors is the main task of our entire party, armed forces, and people.

Although the full text of the plenum resolution was not made public, it was summarized on several occasions and each time the first point read something like this: "Concentrate overall strength on leading the anti-U.S. national salvation resistance struggle to total victory" (*Thoi Su Pho Thong,* Hanoi, June). While emphasis was also given to the task of building North Vietnam, this was not for the moment the number one priority. The second point in the above-cited summary, for example, set forth the task of "gradually" leading agriculture from small-scale to large-scale production. It is probable that the decision to launch the large-scale offensive in South Vietnam which began in April was taken at the 20th Plenum. The priorities outlined by the plenum resolution were apparent in DRV communications media during the early days of the offensive. The party daily, for example, editorialized: " 'Everything for the south! Everything for the front line! Everything to defeat the U.S. aggressors!' is a slogan of action for every one of us" (*Nhan Dan,* 10 April).

Since the death of VWP Central Committee chairman Ho Chi Minh it has been common for analysts to characterize the DRV rulers as a "collective leadership." The term was in fact used by the North Vietnamese themselves for the same purpose. It should be remembered, however, that even during the height of Ho Chi Minh's rule—at a time when he was clearly the decisive figure in the government—the DRV described itself as having a "collective leadership" (see *YICA, 1972,* pp. 587–88 for more). The term should not be misunderstood to mean that power is equally divided among a handful of key party leaders, or that there are no significant differences of opinion in the party. As noted last year (ibid., p. 588), what evidence there was indicated that Le Duan had at least temporarily established a position of greater strength than any of his rivals. This conclusion is supported by the subsequent shift in priorities described above. It is also reinforced by the frequency with which Le Duan was quoted by VWP media during 1972. A lengthy and important theoretical article in *Tap Chi Tuyen Huan* (January–February) cited various writings of Le Duan fifteen times in seven pages. Even public security minister Tran Quoc Hoan, thought by many observers to be closely aligned with Le Duan's chief rival, Truong Chinh, cited Le Duan's writings in a major article on "struggling against counter-revolutionaries" which appeared in the VWP theoretical journal (*Hoc Tap,* March). Things became less clear as the year progressed, however, and some observers concluded Truong Chinh had considerably increased his power. A key factor in this analysis was the April offensive in South Vietnam—which relied almost entirely on main force North Vietnamese Army elements—and on the strong U.S. response thereto. If the Politburo concluded that the offensive was something less than a big success—and such a conclusion is supported by much of the available evidence—then the "southern" oriented faction of Le Duan may well have been held responsible. It is unlikely that Hanoi anticipated the unprecedentedly strong U.S. response, which included a renewal of bombing throughout North Vietnam and the mining of DRV waterways. These American actions have clearly created serious problems for the North Vietnamese, and it would not be especially surprising if Le Duan were held responsible. In mid-1971 Le Duan spent six weeks in the Soviet Union heading the DRV/VWP delegation to the Soviet party congress. In December 1972, however, it was Truong Chinh who headed the important DRV/VWP delegation which visited Peking and then traveled to the U.S.S.R. While there are other explanations for Le Duan's absence from this delegation, it could be an indication of a shift of power in Truong Chinh's favor.

There are indications that the VWP conducted a minor purge during the middle of 1972. In addition to a number of articles in the Hanoi press concerning the treatment of dissidents and counter-revolutionaries (*Chicago Tribune,* 29 June), there was a Politburo directive on "developing criticism of the press." *Hoc Tap,* the VWP monthly theoretical journal, explained in its April issue:

> Our party Central Committee Political Bureau recently issued a directive on "developing criticism in the press." Our party and president often reminded the party press and party-led press of the necessity of satisfactorily carrying out criticism, and self-criticism in the press is a very important task. . . . Criticism and self-criticism are as necessary to us as air and water are to our life. . . . Not every person at the various levels and branches and not every cadre and party member clearly understands and correctly implements the lines, policies, and laws of our party and state. . . . Unsatisfactory manifestations have been noted . . . in the performance of tasks by cadres and party members. . . . Because of limited personal knowledge, because of the habits and the influence of erroneous thoughts left by the old society or because of conservative thought, our cadres, party members and people may have shortcomings and commit errors. Therefore, we should manifest what is correct and criticize what is erroneous and educate and improve men in a socialist society to constantly develop the revolution in our country and advance our society.

The article continued, however, to warn of wrong kinds of criticism:

> Any criticism inconsistent with these objectives is detrimental and must therefore be avoided. We must be extremely vigilant over malicious "criticism" aimed at attacking individuals, sowing disunity, fabricating stories, distorting facts, defaming our regime, maligning others, using "double talk" or disclosing state secrets. Such "criticism" is inconsistent with socialist ethics and violates state law. We must resolutely eliminate such "criticism."

Although the campaign to recruit the "Ho Chi Minh class of new party members" came to a close in 1971, considerable attention was given during 1972 to recruiting new party members. As was the case in 1971, the year 1972 saw many "shortcomings" in recruiting new party members and the emphasis appeared to be more on quality than quantity (see for example *Hoc Tap,* February).

Domestic Attitudes and Activities. During 1972 the VWP placed primary emphasis on the military struggle in South Vietnam (see above). The "anti-U.S. national salvation resistance" was said to have "entered a new period" on 30 March with the start of Hanoi's major conventional offensive against the government of the Republic of (South) Vietnam (*Nhan Dan,* 23 May). Although the offensive was officially the work of the "National Liberation Front" (see *Vietnam: Republic of Vietnam*), both the army daily and Defense Minister Vo Nguyen Giap admitted that "our northern armed forces" were "supporting" the offensive "with our troops and weapons" (*Quan Doi Nhan Dan,* 16 April; Giap interview in *Vorwaerts,* Bonn, 27 April). Indeed, the offensive could not have taken place without the direct North Vietnamese involvement. Paraphrasing Mao Tse-tung, the *Far Eastern Economic Review* (15 April) noted that "the NLF's political power clearly comes from the barrel of North Vietnamese guns." Two key reasons for the offensive were attributed by non-communist journalists in North Vietnam to "informed sources in Hanoi." Both reasons were more political than military in nature: (1) the offensive was "aimed at showing that sector of South Vietnamese opinion, so long expectant and now questioning, that Vietnamization of the war is a dangerous gamble" (Agence France Presse [AFP], 19 April), and (2) it was necessary "in order to have the seven-point peace proposal of the Provisional Revolutionary Government of South Vietnam and the program of the liberation forces accepted" at the Paris talks (*Yomiuri,* Tokyo, 2 April).

Apparently there were significant elements of the DRV population dissatisfied with the continuing military involvement in South Vietnam, and recruiting new soldiers for the front was sometimes difficult. These problems were not because of the masses' "negative attitude," but "because the leadership and organization still leave much to be desired." The army monthly (*Tap Chi Quan Doi Nhan Dan,* January) explained: "With correct leadership it is possible to motivate the people ideologically and to step up the movement in any place and at any time even though the masses' level of awareness is still low or they are influenced by the propaganda arguments of bad elements." Considerable emphasis was given to countering the influence of such "bad elements," with articles and editorials in many party publications calling for strengthening "order and security" and for countering "counter-revolutionaries" (see for example *Hanoi Moi,* 28 January; *Nhan Dan,* 12 February, 21 July). Perhaps the most important of these were two articles by Minister of Public Security (later to become a full-member of the Politburo) Tran Quoc Hoan, which appeared in the March and May issues of the VWP theoretical journal, *Hoc Tap.* The first of these was by far the stronger in tone, and complained "in our dealings with counter-revolutionary elements in the recent past we have still entertained rightist thoughts and have not properly used violence." It charged that "A great number of cadres and party members have been . . . neglecting the aspects of suppressive violence, believing it is no longer necessary," and concluded:

> In summary, our party's policy is to put the struggle against counter-revolution under the party's close leadership, adequately rely on the working people's massive strength, and, on the basis of thorough ideological understanding, take precautionary measures, actively and continuously launch attacks, firmly hold on to the principle of actively defending oneself, [and] take the initiative in resolutely and carefully annihilating the enemy without letting even one enemy flee . . .

The second article was milder in tone, and was therefore interpreted by some observers as something of a "correction" for tactical reasons. The first article could hardly have lessened resistance to the communists in South Vietnam, where between three and five million people are reported to be on communist "blood-debt" lists for "punishment" in the future (*NYT,* 24 October).

North Vietnam's offensive against South Vietnam was met by strong measures from the United States—including large-scale naval bombardment. As the party daily (*Nhan Dan,* 12 July) noted editorially, "the U.S. aggressors' bombs and shells did cause us some concrete difficulties." Hanoi was compelled to call for a mass mobilization of its work force "to serve in any capacity or any mission assigned them," and warned that those who disobeyed would have to perform up to two years' forced labor (*NYT,* 18 July).

In spite of the added hardships, the DRV continued its requirements of economic orthodoxy at the expense of maximum production. The "three contracts" system (see above) continued to be described as a "shortcoming" of past agricultural policy, in spite of the fact that it contributed proportionally much more to the economy than did the cooperatives (*Nhan Dan,* 29 June). The "free" or "black" market also came under strong attack, but apparently continued to expand in spite of the protest. An editorial in *Hoc Tap* reported: "The free market has appreciably expanded and is not yet managed closely. . . . In the free market . . . almost all material supplies, [including] various types of material supplies and goods which are distributed under ration cards, have been purchased and sold almost publicly without being forbidden." Apparently the North Vietnamese people see little wrong with the black market, as *Hoc Tap* notes: "Some people would like to see the free market develop widely in their localities."

During 1971 North Vietnam experienced its worst flooding in over 25 years (see *YICA, 1972,* p. 590). Possibly in anticipation of a recurrence in 1972, Hanoi radio began charging the United States with intentionally bombing dikes to bring about more flooding. Several broadcasts charged that the "U.S. imperialists must bear full responsibility for the consequences of their wicked scheme" of bombing dikes (Vietnam News Agency [VNA], 13 September; *Quan Doi Nhan Dan,* 24 June). There were no significant floods during 1972.

Late in the year, when it appeared that North Vietnam and the United States were about to sign a peace agreement, Hanoi explained that an agreement would not mean an end to the struggle, but rather a temporary change in struggle methods:

> The collapse of imperialism and the transition from capitalism to socialism and communism are the process of development of history during which the situation does not develop along a straight but a tortuous line. The development of the revolution does not have the same pattern everywhere and at all times.
>
> The problem is that we must firmly grasp the concrete circumstances in order [to] determine appropriate forms and methods of struggle which are beneficial to revolution and which ensure that the revolution makes progress. . . . An important task is to divide the enemy force, and to utterly isolate the main and most dangerous enemy.
>
> The revolutionary struggle remains a protracted, difficult, and complicated undertaking. There is a time for us to advance, but there is also a time for us to step backward temporarily in order to advance more steadily later. We cannot exterminate imperialism at one time and in a single battle. We drive it back step by step and destroy it part by part.
>
> For this reason, we must sometimes alter our fighting style and our struggle methods. Sometimes we must accept a certain agreement with the enemy which must be essentially based on a revolutionary stand, that is, aimed at weakening his forces and increasing our forces. Such an agreement is one of principle and it is basically different from the unprincipled agreement of opportunism. . . . Complete victory is the unchanged path that our party and people are following. (*Hoc Tap,* November.)

Thus it appears likely that a cease-fire agreement will be signed by the North Vietnamese in the first few months of 1973. Whether or not this will lead to peace will probably depend upon whether or not the communists are able to seize control of non-communist Indochina through political and diplomatic struggle. In April, 1966, North Vietnamese Army Lieutenant General Nguyen Van Vinh explained to the Fourth COSVN Congress in South Vietnam: "Whether or not the war will resume after the conclusion of agreements depends upon the comparative balance of forces. If we are capable of dominating the adversary, the war will not break out again, and conversely." (U.S. Department of State, *Working Paper on the North Vietnamese Role in the War in South Viet-Nam,* May 1968, Item 303, p. 14.)

International Views and Activities. On the international front, 1972 was a year of great concern for North Vietnamese communist leaders. At a time when their military escalation in South Vietnam demanded increased external assistance and the closest possible ties with China and the Soviet Union, the DRV leaders watched in anguish as U.S. President Nixon was warmly received in both Peking and Moscow. It was clear that Hanoi was very upset by the activities of the "super powers" (AFP, 16 June), and that these activities were causing "the greatest of difficulties" for the Vietnamese communists. In an interview with a Japanese daily, the editor of *Nhan Dan* explained: "Nixon is capitalizing on the disunity among the socialist countries in one way or other to be free to act. This affects our war and, thus, our fighting has become very difficult." (*Mainichi,* Tokyo, 1 July.) The army daily explained the Nixon policy thus: "We must understand that when Nixon speaks of 'peaceful co-existence' or of 'destroying barriers' he means infiltration of socialist countries, creating peaceful evolution, sabotaging socialist countries and sowing discord among them" (*Quan Doi Nhan Dan,* 22 April). Although Peking apparently tried to reassure the DRV leaders by signing a new aid agreement on 22 January (the two countries had concluded their annual aid agreement only four months earlier), this was insufficient reassurance for the North Vietnamese (*Far Eastern Economic Review,* 26 February, 8 April). Although DRV communications media gave no coverage to the Nixon visit to China, their displeasure was apparent from the pro-Soviet emphasis in their press. This led some observers to conclude that North Vietnam was shifting its traditionally neutral position in the Sino-Soviet dispute to a more pro-Soviet alignment (see for example *Baltimore Sun,* 19 April). As it became apparent that President Nixon would also visit Moscow, however, DRV-Soviet relations cooled noticeably—without a corresponding warming in DRV-China relations. Finally, on 17 August, the party daily *Nhan Dan* featured a 2,000-word "important editorial" which, although it did not mention either country by name, was obviously a strong criticism (by DRV standards) of the two great communist powers. Noting that Nixon had applied "the policy of reconciliation" toward "a number of big powers," the editorial—while acknowledging that under some conditions a policy of reconciliation might be useful—declared: "If out of the narrow interests of one's nation, one tries to help the most reactionary forces avert the dangerous blows, just like throwing a lifebuoy to a drowning pirate, that is a cruel reconciliation beneficial to the enemy and not beneficial to the revolution." In an obvious attack on both the U.S.S.R. and China, *Nhan Dan* said that "the vitality of Marxism-Leninism and proletarian internationalism manifests itself first of all in revolutionary deeds, not in empty words." (*NYT,* 18 August.)

The new Nixon diplomacy brought about an emphasis on "independence" and "self-sufficiency" in VWP publications, but Hanoi continued to call for international unity and assistance at the same time. The Vietnamese communists frequently stressed that neither the U.S.S.R. nor China could negotiate an end to the Vietnam war with the United States, asserting: "The Vietnamese are masters of their own fate, on the battlefield as well as at the conference table" (*Hoc Tap,* July). An article in *Tap Chi Tuyen Huan* (January–February), entitled "Intensify Teaching of the Sense of Independence and Sovereignty to our Cadres, Party Members, and People," stressed that:

> To be loyal to Marxism-Leninism does not mean to copy and memorize every sentence and word in the classic works of Marx, Engels, Lenin, and Stalin but to be thoroughly imbued with the fundamental principles . . . and to creatively apply the Marxist-Leninist methods to the situation in each country in each revolutionary stage. . . . Such a line bears a profound independent and sovereign character and is highly creative.

The article noted, however, that "the socialist camp is a unified entity," and stressed the importance of proletarian internationalism in the face of the new Nixon diplomacy:

> At present . . . Nixon advocates trying to implement the policy of "establishing half of the bridge"—a policy calling for wooing one socialist country after another, sowing disunity among various countries, putting one component against another and carrying out economic and cultural infiltration in order to promote counter-revolutionary peaceful evolution and, thereby, weaken one socialist country after another and ultimately the entire socialist camp. In this situation, the task of firmly maintaining the stand of proletarian internationalism [is] of particular important significance.

In another article dealing with proletarian internationalism, a Hanoi monthly noted:

> We attach the greatest importance to and regard international assistance as an indispensable condition for successfully carrying out the anti-U.S. national salvation resistance. . . . Our party and our people always . . . do their best to help protect the purity of Marxism-Leninism, re-

store the solidarity and unity of the socialist system and of the international communist and workers movement, and [particularly] we strive to consolidate and tighten the bond of unalterable friendship between our country and the fraternal socialist countries, especially the Soviet Union and China. (*Tap Chi Quan Doi Nhan Dan,* May.)

Along these same lines, even though Hanoi was obviously displeased with Chinese and Soviet reactions to the new Nixon diplomacy, consistent efforts were made to improve relations with both countries. There were frequent exchanges of friendship delegations, and messages of solidarity were sent on all appropriate occasions. While the DRV was obviously displeased with the two communist giants, it realized that their continued assistance was "indispensable" and that it therefore could not afford to alienate either of them. Similarly, DRV relations with East European communist nations continued to be warm, and economic and military assistance was received from all of them except Yugoslavia (*Far Eastern Economic Review,* 26 February).

DRV relations with South Vietnamese communists, and those in Laos and Cambodia, underwent few or no significant changes during 1972. The North Vietnamese continued to direct communist activity in South Vietnam as they had in years past, through the "Central Office for South Vietnam" and the "People's Revolutionary Party of South Vietnam (see *Vietnam: Republic of Vietnam*). While President Nixon was in Peking, Prince Norodom Sihanouk, head of the exile Cambodian government group (R.G.N.U.), visited Hanoi and expressions of solidarity were exchanged. Similar sentiments were exchanged with Laotian Prince Souphanouvong. The Thai Communist Party, which celebrated its 30th anniversary on 1 December, was the recepient of warm praise from Hanoi, and the Thai government was frequently attacked as a "main tool of the Nixon Doctrine in Southeast Asia" (*Hoc Tap,* June).

North Vietnam continued to support the "Palestinian people's struggle for their sacred national rights," and to condemn "Israeli aggression" (VNA, 15 May, 20 September). In accordance with this position, *Nhan Dan* blamed the deaths of several Israeli Olympic competitors at the Munich games on "the Israeli and West German authorities," who "had chosen the path of 'treachery and betrayal' " (VNA, 12 September). The article charged that "the U.S. and Israel scheme to make the most of the Munich bloody incident is very perfidious," and concluded: "The Vietnamese people who have seen the true colors of U.S. imperialism . . . are resolved to support the Palestinian people's fight for their sacred fundamental rights till its final victory."

North Vietnam had warm praise for India on several occasions, and on 7 January the two countries upgraded their diplomatic missions to embassy status (ibid., 7 January). On 1 June ambassadorial-level diplomatic relations were established with Chile (Hanoi radio, 1 June), and later in the year with Tunisia, Cameroun, Guinea, Zambia, Pakistan, and Austria (AFP, 31 August; VNA, 31 August, 4 September, 23 September, 8 November, 1 December). This brought to 47 the number of countries maintaining relations with the DRV.

Following another appeal by President Nixon for United Nations assistance in solving the Vietnam situation, North Vietnam again denounced the U.N. and stated: "As everyone knows, the U.S. administration previously and frequently plotted to bring the Vietnam problem before the U.N. . . . Our people's unchanged stand is that the Vietnam problem must be settled at the Paris conference on Vietnam. There is no other way. The U.N. has no right to interfere in the Vietnam problem." (Hanoi radio, 16 May.)

As in previous years, there were frequent expressions of appreciation for the anti-war movements throughout the world, especially in the United States. The "Vietnam Committee for Solidarity With the American People" expressed warm praise for the "U.S. antiwar struggle" (ibid., 24 January), and the party daily gave full coverage to anti-war activities in the

United States (see for example *Nhan Dan,* 26 April, 23 May). Considerable publicity was given to the trial of U.S. communist "sister Angela Davis," who was portrayed as the victim of "the biggest political conspiracy in the United States in recent years" (VNA, 6 June). The extra security measures taken in preparation for the trial were presented as proof that the U.S. administration "intended to condemn Angela Davis prior to her trial" (Hanoi radio, 3 March). Her acquittal was viewed as a victory for the "progressive, democratic, and peace forces" in the United States.

Publications. VWP policy statements and directives are carried primarily in the daily organ of its Central Committee, *Nhan Dan* ("The People"), whose editor in chief is Hoang Tung; in *Hoc Tap* ("Studies"), the VWP monthly theoretical journal edited by Dao Duy Tung; and in *Quan Doi Nhan Dan* ("People's Army"), the daily organ of the army. Other major publications include *Tien Phong* ("Vanguard"), the organ of the Central Committee of the Ho Chi Minh Working Youth Union; *Lao Dong* ("Labor"), the organ of the Vietnam General Federation of Trade Unions; *Cuu Quoc* ("National Salvation"), the weekly organ of the Central Committee of the Vietnam Fatherland Front; *Doc Lap* ("Independence"), the weekly organ of the Central Committee of the Vietnam Democratic Party; and *To Quoc* ("Motherland"), the bimonthly organ of the Vietnam Socialist Party. (*Cong Nghiep,* the organ of the VWP Central Committee Industry Department, ceased publication with the May–June issue in 1972.) International publications include *Vietnam Courier,* a weekly published in English and French by the Committee for Cultural Relations with Foreign Countries, and *Vietnam,* an illustrated monthly published in English, French, Russian, Chinese, and Vietnamese. The Foreign Languages Publishing House in Hanoi publishes close to 50,000 books each year in Russian, Chinese, English, French, Spanish, German, and Esperanto, and regularly sends material to over 60 countries.

Party statements are also broadcast by the Vietnam News Agnecy, which is headed by Dat Tung. Hanoi radio—"The Voice of Vietnam"—broadcasts round the clock on three wavelengths in 10 languages.

Hoover Institution   Robert F. Turner
Stanford University

Vietnam: Republic of Vietnam

Prior to the division of Vietnam at the seventeenth parallel by the Geneva Conference of 1954, the communist movement throughout the country was under the control of the Indochinese Communist Party, renamed the Vietnam Workers' Party (VWP) in 1951 (see *Vietnam: Democratic Republic of Vietnam*). After partition, the party went underground in the South but still received instructions from the VWP leadership in Hanoi. Utilizing the "united front" strategy which had been highly successful for Vietnamese communists during years past, the VWP Central Committee announced in September 1960: "To ensure the complete success for the revolutionary struggle in South Vietnam, our people there, under the leadership of the Marxist-Leninist Party of the working class, must strive [to] bring into being a broad National United Front" (Le Duan, in *Third National Congress of the Viet Nam Workers' Party,* Hanoi, Foreign Languages Publishing House, I, 62–63). Three months later, on 20 December, the National Liberation Front of South Vietnam (Mat Tran Dan Toc Giai Phong Mien Nam Viet Nam; NLFSV or NLF) was founded.

For propaganda reasons, the VWP decided to establish an "independent" Marxist-Leninist party in the South. On 18 January 1962, the Hanoi-based Vietnam News Agency (VNA) announced that the People's Revolutionary Party (Dang Nhan Dan Cach Mang; PRP) had been formally established on 1 January 1962. The relationship between this "new" Marxist-Leninist party and the VWP was made clear by an internal party document captured in Ba Xuyen Province, dated 7 December 1961: "The People's Revolutionary Party has only the appearance of an independent existence; actually, our party is nothing but the Lao Dong Party of Vietnam [VWP], unified from North to South, under the direction of the Central Executive Committee of the party, the chief of which is President Ho [Chi Minh]." Although the two parties disclaim any official connection in their external propaganda, it is noteworthy that the international communist movement does not recognize the independent existence of the PRP, dealing directly with the VWP and North Vietnamese government in matters concerning material aid and supplies. The PRP and all communist organizations are illegal in South Vietnam.

On 8 June 1969 a "Congress of People's Representatives" met in "liberated areas" of South Vietnam and established the "Provisional Revolutionary Government of the Republic of South Vietnam" (PRGSV or PRG). Shortly thereafter, the PRG assumed all state functions of the NLF, internal and external—including the seat at the Paris negotiations. Most nonmilitary communist activity in South Vietnam during 1972 was conducted in the name of the PRG; however, there were indications of a reemphasis on the NLF toward the end of the year (see below). The term "Viet Cong"—a contraction of Viet Nam Cong San, which means "Vietnamese Communist"—is often used to identify the military and political elements of the South Vietnamese communist movement as distinct from the movement in North Vietnam and those North Vietnamese Army (NVA) regulars fighting in the South.

In 1951 the activities of the VWP in southern Vietnam were organized under a six-man "Central Office for South Vietnam" (Trung Uong Cuc Mien Nam; COSVN), and were headed by Le Duan, who is now first secretary of the Central Committee of the VWP in Hanoi. COSVN was phased out in 1954, but its function was assumed by the Nam Bo Regional Committee. In late 1960 Hanoi decided to reactivate COSVN, and sent Major General Tran Luong, a member of the VWP Central Committee, to South Vietnam to be in command. Since then, actual military command of Viet Cong forces has been in the hands of senior North Vietnamese military and political leaders, who are in close contact with the VWP in Hanoi.

Accurate estimates of PRP membership are not available, but the party is thought to have at minimum 40,000 to 60,000 dedicated, hard-core cadres (NYT, 5 November 1972). Estimates of total membership run as high as twice those figures. Viet Cong military forces are thought to number perhaps 80,000, supplemented by at least 20,000 NVA regulars fighting in nominally Viet Cong units. There are another 15,000 or so political cadres—several thousand of which are reported to be North Vietnamese—directing the party's "legal" and "illegal" infrastructure. (The New Yorker, 13 January 1973, p. 74.) According to U.S. intelligence sources, the Viet Cong have to rely on NVA troops to keep traditional Viet Cong guerrilla units up to strength. "In some famous battalions with Vietcong names, only the guides and a few of the officers are native southerners," according to these sources. (NYT, 5 November 1972.) It has been estimated that in a free election in South Vietnam, the communists would receive perhaps 15 percent of the vote (Christian Science Monitor, 12 May). The population of South Vietnam is estimated at about 18,000,000 (Time, 6 November); however, the communist "Liberation Radio" places the population at 17,500,000 (Liberation Radio, 3 November).

Leadership and Organization. As noted above, the PRP is not an autonomous entity, but rather the southern branch of the VWP in Hanoi. Consequently, the senior communist leaders in South Vietnam are actually the VWP representatives in COSVN. The most important communist in South Vietnam during 1972 was Pham Hung, a senior member of the VWP politburo, who reportedly replaced NVA Senior General Nguyen Chi Thanh when the latter was killed in an air attack in South Vietnam in July 1967. Pham Hung's chief political deputy has been identified as Nguyen Van Linh (also known as Muoi Cuc), and his chief military assistant is thought to be NVA Lieutenant General Hoang Van Thai—who reportedly heads the important Military Affairs Committee of COSVN in addition to being a vice-minister of national defense in North Vietnam and a member of the Central Committee of the VWP. Other key COSVN leaders include Lieutenant General Tran Van Tra (reportedly also minister of defense of the PRG under the alias Tran Nam Trung, a name also attributed to Major General Tran Luong and others) and Major General Tran Do.

The announced chairman of the PRP Central Committee is Vo Chi Cong, who is also thought to be known as Nguyen Van Cuc and Muoi Ut. The secretary-general is Tran Nam Trung (NVA Lieutenant General Tran Van Tra?), and the deputy secretary-general is thought to be Nguyen Van Lien. (Names of other reported PRP leaders can be found in YICA, 1972, p. 597).

The NLF is represented at the hamlet and village level by "administrative liberation associations," which themselves are composed of "functional liberation associations" and political parties (see Douglas Pike, Viet Cong: The Organization and Techniques of the National Liberation Front of South Vietnam, Cambridge, Mass., M.I.T. Press, 1966, pp. 109–18). Nominally, authority runs from the NLF Central Committee down through a number of administrative levels to the village administrative liberation associations, but in fact all command authority and reporting passes vertically through PRP channels to COSVN.

The chairman of the Presidium of the Central Committee of the NLF is Nguyen Huu Tho, and the chairman of the PRG is Huynh Tan Phat (for other leaders see *YICA, 1972,* pp. 597–98). Nguyen Cong Phuong (previously listed as "Nguyen Cao Phuong") was reported to have died "because of his advanced age and serious illness" in Hanoi on 21 August 1972. He had been a member of the PRG advisory council since its creation in 1969.

Regular NVA units operating in South Vietnam do not normally report through COSVN. All other communist military elements—main force and paramilitary—belong to the People's Liberation Armed Forces (PLAF). Pham Hung is reported to serve as both commanding officer and political officer of the PLAF.

Another Viet Cong front is the Vietnam Alliance of National, Democratic, and Peace Forces (Lien Mien Dan Toc Dan Cav va Hoa Binh a Viet Nam; VANDPF) formed during the 1968 Tet offensive and announced in April 1968. The VANDPF is headed by Trinh Dinh Thao, who, like most other key VANDPF leaders, holds a position in the PRG or NLF. The VANDPF has announced its "unanimity with the NLF on all subjects." Its purpose is to serve as an alliance of "intellectuals, students, civil servants, and others who despite their different political leanings and religious colors are identified with one another in their hatred for the unbearable rule of the U.S. puppets."

Domestic Attitudes and Activities. Vietnamese communists believe that "the only path to national liberation [is] violent revolution" (Liberation Radio, 25 August 1972)—although the "armed struggle" must be carried out in conjunction with the "political" and "diplomatic" struggles to be fully effective—and in recent years most domestic activities have been directed toward the overthrow of the Republic of Vietnam government (GVN). Throughout 1972 communist publications and radio broadcasts continued to call for "total" or "complete" victory (for example, Liberation Radio, 28 January, 31 December; *Tien Phong,* no. 2; Liberation Press Agency [LPA], 11 April; and *Quan Giai Phong,* as quoted by Liberation Radio on 12 April).

The VWP Politburo apparently decided around the first of the year to give increased emphasis to the task of "liberating" South Vietnam (see *Vietnam: Democratic Republic of Vietnam*) and caused orders to be given throughout Indochina for the launching of a large-scale "spring-summer offensive" commencing on 30 March. The offensive was described by NLF chairman Nguyen Huu Tho as "a follow-up of the Tet 1968 simultaneous attack and uprising" (*L'Humanité,* Paris, 19 May) and was credited by Liberation Radio with scoring achievements in one month "as significant as those scored in a decade" (Liberation Radio, 15 May). The fundamental purpose of the offensive, according to communist spokesmen, was "to demonstrate that the American policy of Vietnamization is bankrupt" (interview with Mme Nguyen Thi Binh, radio "Voice of the GDR," East Berlin, 19 April), and to force the United States to hold "serious discussions" at the Paris conference (*L'Humanité,* 19 May; LPA, 6 July). Following discussions with Romanian communist sources, the *Far Eastern Economic Review* (8 July) concluded that "the communists were forced to mount a sophisticated, conventional— and mainly North Vietnamese—military campaign because they realised they had lost considerable popular support from a war-weary population." According to Liberation Radio, "after nine months of unremitting offensive and concerted uprising," communist forces had "put out of action nearly half-a-million enemy troops, destroyed or seized . . . 11,000 military vehicles . . . 1,500 artillery pieces, 45,000 weapons . . . and downed or destroyed 2,500 aircraft of various types" (Liberation Radio, 31 December). The communists claimed that "many vast areas" had been "liberated," with a total population of "more than five million people" (ibid.; LPA, 30 December). There were, however, indications that the party was less than satisfied with the response of the "masses" to the 15 April "Appeal of the NLF Central Committee and PRGRSV" (for text see LPA, 15 April). Some of the problems were noted by "Cuu Long" (thought to be Major General Tran Do), who devoted a lengthy article in late April to problems of guerrilla warfare in the southern rural areas. "Cuu Long" noted that because of pacification operations conducted by "U.S., puppet and satellite military forces," the "guerrilla force and revolutionary bases in many localities must move temporarily to other localities or be ostracized by the masses, which have been temporarily swayed by the enemy through a newly established system of posts and coercive machinery." He explained that " [the enemy's] main strength lies in his local coercive machineries, of which the cruel, diehard administrative personnel and spies constitute the hardcore force. . . . It is these cruel, diehard agents and units that adversely affect the masses," who are "the great, latent strength of the local people's war in weak hamlets and areas." Unfortunately, according to "Cuu Long," "this strength has been blurred in many localities because of difficulties." The solution to this problem was clear: "It is the duty of the guerrillas to completely or partially destroy the enemy's coercive machinery. . . . By completely or partially destroying the enemy's coercive machinery we can change the balance of forces and cause his foundations to decline and collapse." "Cuu Long" concluded that in order "to destroy or scatter the enemy's coercive machinery it is absolutely necessary to annihilate the top villains and cruel agents. First it is necessary to annihilate the villains and then the enemy's coercive machinery must be destroyed." (Liberation Radio, 21 April.)

"Cuu Long's" instructions did not go unheeded, and as territory was "liberated" during the "spring-summer offensive" the communists proceeded to "annihilate the top villains and cruel agents." Shortly after seizing control of Quang Tri city, a "Provisional People's Revolutionary Committee" was established. It issued the following instructions:

> Officers and men of the puppet army, police agents and puppet administrative personnel, members of the secret service, spy organizations, and of reactionary political parties and sects must report to the revolutionary administration. . . . Anyone who tries to escape to continue to operate for the enemy will be severely punished. (Ibid., 4 May.)

One week later the committee issued a communiqué which asserted:

> The revolutionary administration is determined to punish . . . those who have plotted to assist or have assisted the U.S. aggressors, undermined the revolution, opposed the revolutionary administration, sabotaged the all-people solidarity bloc, disturbed order and security and harmed the people's lives, property and human dignity and the revolutionary administration's property. (Ibid., 11 May.)

Similar instructions were given for newly "liberated" territory in other parts of South Vietnam (see for example Liberation Radio, 19 June, 24 September). The northern part of Binh Dinh Province was in communist hands for nearly three months, during which time an estimated 500 government officials and other "villains" were executed (NYT, 6 August). Although Liberation Radio praised communist forces for "appropriately punishing the U.S.-Thieu clique's stubborn henchmen" (6 April), and noted the "stepped up activities to annihilate tyrants in the newly liberated areas" (24 September), when the GVN and the U.S. government criticized the executions of civilians Hanoi radio (23 August) charged them with having "slandered the communists" and denied that the executions had occurred. Similarly, when the GVN released a captured Viet Cong "death list," it was denounced as a "completely fabricated story" by LPA (Liberation Radio, 25 October).

During 1972 there were approximately 40,000 reported incidents of Viet Cong terrorism —an all-time high for the Vietnam war—and it was estimated that over 10,000 additional incidents went unreported (*The New Yorker,* 13 January 1973). In November the assassination of Cao Dai General Nguyen Van Thanh was attributed to the communists, but was strongly denied by Liberation Radio (2 December, 5 December 1972). It is unlikely, however, that the communists would have claimed responsibility for the assassination of a religious leader with such a large following.

While the "spring-summer offensive" was less than a total success for the communists, it did provide them with substantial territorial gains. By the end of the year they were credited with control of between a third and half of the territory in South Vietnam. Such statistics can be deceiving, however, as much of the communist-held land is dense jungle, mountains, or other sparsely populated regions of the country. In terms of population, the Viet Cong and North Vietnamese Army were thought to control perhaps 10 percent and the GVN 70 percent, with the remaining 20 percent living in contested zones (*Time,* 6 November 1972; *The New Yorker,* 13 January 1973).

According to Liberation Radio (5 July), "immediately after wiping out the enemy's coercive machinery in the newly liberated areas, our compatriots enthusiastically built and consolidated the revolutionary administration." Although the executions of some "reactionaries" and "counter-revolutionaries" were considered necessary to eliminate key opposition and *pour encourager les autres,* the "revolutionary administrations" worked actively to win the support of as many people as possible. In Quang Tri, for example, the "Quang Tri People's Revolutionary Committee" issued ten "commandments" for cadres, personnel, and combatants, calling for them to "promote unity," protect religion, behave "in compliance with revolutionary ethics" (e.g., "be diligent, thrifty, honest, and impartial"), and warning them not to "misappropriate the people's property" or "use the people's property without their approval." Violation of any of the ten "commandments" would "result in severe disciplinary action." (Liberation Radio, 12 May.)

As had been the case in years past, the Vietnamese communists continued to hide most of their Marxist objectives (collectivization of land, political restrictions, elimination of religion, and so forth), relying in their appeals for mass support on those promises calculated to win the hearts and minds of the people. This policy was explained by VWP first secretary Le Duan, in 1960, when he wrote:

> Only by winning over the peasant masses . . . can the working class conquer the leadership of revolution. . . . That is why the Marxist-Leninist parties . . . must have suitable programs, policies, slogans, and styles of work to win over the peasantry. (*On Some Present International Problems,* Hanoi, Foreign Languages Publishing House, 2d ed., 1964, p. 44.)

In line with this policy, Liberation Radio (23 November 1972) announced:

> Struggling for democratic freedoms—physical freedom, freedom of speech, press freedom, freedom of meeting and organization, freedom of political activity, religious freedom and freedom of movement, residence and enterprise—and demanding the right to private ownership, the right of free enterprise and so forth have become imperative for the people of various strata in the temporarily occupied areas. Not only is the struggle for freedom and democracy not separate from the struggle for peace and national independence, but it also creates favorable conditions for the present struggle for the restoration of peace.

In the early days of the revolutionary movement in South Vietnam, much of the popular support achieved by the Viet Cong was the result of the promise of "land to the tiller." In North Vietnam, agricultural collectivization was not mentioned to the people until the VWP was in firm control, because the party realized the importance the people placed on their right to own their own land. Similarly, in South Vietnam the Viet Cong have instructed their cadres to conceal future plans for collectivization—knowing that such a policy would meet with no small opposition (Jeffrey Race, *War Comes to Long An,* Berkeley, University of California Press, 1972, p. 129). In recent years the GVN has attempted to neutralize the effectiveness of the communist promise of "land to the tiller" by conducting a land reform of its own. To the degree that this has been successful, it has become a target for communist propaganda and "armed propaganda" (terrorism) attacks. As was the case in 1971, communist propaganda media continued during 1972 to predict the "complete failure" of the GVN land reform and other pacification activities (see for example Liberation Radio, 25 March).

There were frequent propaganda appeals for unity in the struggle against the Americans and their "puppets" (ibid., 5 February, 7 March, 18 August), and calls for South Vietnamese army (ARVN) soldiers to "save themselves" by deserting (ibid., 7, 9, 23 February, 4, 9 March, 6 April, 12 July). Several of these broadcasts stressed the "lenient policy" of the "Liberation troops" toward "Saigon puppet troops," explaining that "thousands of POW's scattered in the various prisons of the revolution have daily voiced their gratitude to the revolution which has taken care of them, given them medicine when they are sick and comforted them when they are worried" (ibid., 6 March).

Talks continued in Paris between the United States and South Vietnam on one side, and the PRG and North Vietnam on the other. The PRG continued to support the seven-point peace plan first proposed on 1 July 1971 (see *YICA, 1972,* p. 603), clarifying "the two key points" on 2 February 1972. The clarified points required the United States to cease all military activities and set a deadline for the withdrawal of all military personnel, weapons, and war means "without posing any conditions," and to respect "the right to self-determination of the South Vietnamese people" by ending "all its intervention in the internal affairs of South Vietnam." In return, the PRG promised to release all prisoners of war (Liberation Radio, 2 February). The PRG continued to insist on the removal of South Vietnamese president Nguyen Van Thieu (ibid., 7 February; Agence France Presse [AFP], 12 September; *Giai Phong,* 9 November) and on the creation of a coalition government consisting of one-third communists, one-third anti-communists, and one-third "neutralists" (Vietnam News Agency, Hanoi, 11 September). Toward the end of the year, the communists were apparently willing to alter their stand slightly and it seemed as if an agreement would soon be signed. There was some question as to whether this would bring peace, however, and Mme Nguyen Thi Binh—PRG foreign minister and representative at the Paris talks—told a Japanese journalist: "We do not think that this agreement will end the war. Even after it has been signed, we will have to continue our struggle so that it will be fulfilled." (*Akahata,* organ of the Japan Communist Party, Tokyo, 30 November.)

Relations with North Vietnam. As noted above, the communist movement in South Vietnam is an integral part of the Lao Dong Party—the VWP—of North Vietnam. Major decisions are made by the party in Hanoi, and there are VWP Politburo and Central Committee members in the South to handle other problems. This does not mean that there are no differences between those individuals assigned to directing the war effort in the South and their colleagues in Hanoi, or between native "Viet Cong" and North Vietnamese Army soldiers and personnel. Despite continuous declarations of solidarity, there have been indications during recent years of friction between North and South Vietnamese communists over a number of issues. The NVA soldiers often tended to regard themselves as superior in training and discipline to their southern counterparts, and neither liked to be placed under the command of the other. Inadequate supplies of food and matériel increased the friction, as PLAF troops resented the arrival of better-equipped NVA units. There have also been reports of problems between the NVA soldiers and the local population of South Vietnam, which is much more likely to protect or assist local communist guerrillas than soldiers from North Vietnam.

Following the 1954 Geneva Conference, which resulted in Hanoi's temporary abandonment of Viet Minh followers south of the 17th parallel in order to ensure communist control of North Vietnam, there were indications that southern Viet Minh supporters in many instances became bitter and distrustful of the party. It is probable that at least some of the veterans remember Hanoi's willingness to temporarily abandon the struggle, and that rumors of a negotiated settlement have created some concern. Toward the end of 1972 there were indications that the PRG was being pushed into the background in favor of the NLF as a concession made by Hanoi to the U.S. position that there were "two warring parties" rather than two governments in South Vietnam (*The New Yorker,* 13 January 1973). Rumors of a "touchy relationship between Hanoi and the top communist echelon in the South" (ibid.) were strengthened by a *Le Monde* (Paris, 25 November 1972) account of an "unsuccessful coup" launched by over 1,000 dissidents under the command of North Vietnamese General Le Vinh Khoa against NLF/PRG headquarters in South Vietnam. The report, given to a French correspondent by "a reliable and very well-informed source," explained that the rebels were "partisans of continuing to fight to the bitter end," and were led by PRP chairman Vo Chi Cong, NLF Presidium member Tran Bach Dang, and NLF Central Committee member Vo Van Mon. They were reportedly supporting the position held by VWP first secretary Le Duan (see *Vietnam: Democratic Republic of Vietnam*). According to these "sources," the rebellion—which is said to have lasted two days (10–12 November)—was finally put down by PRG defense minister and PLAF commander in chief Tran Nam Trung. NLF chairman Nguyen Huu Tho was reportedly wounded during the struggle. According to the *Le Monde* report, a "people's tribunal" on 16 November sentenced Vo Chi Cong to 20 years in a concentration camp for his part in the attempted coup, Tran Bach Dang to 10 years, and Vo Van Mon to death in absentia. The French correspondent who wrote the account concluded that "this unsuccessful coup has contributed to the strengthening both of the unity and of the independence of the Liberation Front on the eve of a cease-fire." The Liberation Press Agency responded immediately (25 November) by charging the account was "a sheer fabrication" and "a psy-war trick in a bid to distort the fight of the Vietnamese people and fool world public and the American people." An equally plausible explanation—especially since Tran Nam Trung is reported to be NVA Lieutenant General Tran Van Tra, deputy chief of staff of the North Vietnamese Army and an alternate member of the VWP central committee—is that the story was planted by communist propagandists in an attempt to give the NLF a more autonomous image. It appears clear that Hanoi had prior to the time of the attack reached a decision to sign an agreement to temporarily bring the fighting to a halt (see for example *Hoc Tap,* Hanoi, no. 11, November), and it seems unlikely that "three understrength [NVA] battalions" would lead an attack against VWP policy.

International Views and Positions. The PRP expresses no international views of its own, as it is only a branch of the VWP and is not even recognized by the international communist movement. Communist views and positions in South Vietnam generally coincide with those expressed by the VWP in Hanoi, and are reflected in statements made in the name of the PRG and NLF (both of which have considerable international recognition). South Vietnamese communists undoubtedly viewed the 21–28 February visit by President Nixon to the People's Republic of China with at least as much alarm as their comrades in Hanoi; however, in commenting on the upcoming trip they expressed confidence that China would continue its assistance "until final victory over the American imperialist aggressors and their lackeys" (*Revolution Africaine,* Algiers, 24 December 1971). Liberation Radio (5 February) assured its listeners that Chinese premier Chou En-lai had "once again affirmed the position of the Chinese Government and people to do their utmost to support and assist the Vietnamese people's anti-U.S. national salvation resistance." Following the U.S. mining of Haiphong harbor in early May, LPA carried a Chinese statement "severely condemning" President Nixon for the action:

> "This act of war escalation by U.S. imperialism seriously encroaches upon the territory and sovereignty of the DRV, grossly violates the freedom of international navigation and trade and wantonly tramples upon the Charter of the United Nations and international public law. It is a provocation not only against the Vietnamese people but also against the people of the whole world. The Chinese Government and people express their utmost indignation at and strongly condemn it." (LPA, 13 May.)

This condemnation was the extent of Chinese reaction, however, and was not as strong as similar statements in previous years. In the circumstances, it was hardly likely to reassure the Viet Cong, and it suggested that China was more interested in temporarily improving relations with the United States than in helping to "liberate" South Vietnam.

Liberation Radio made no mention of the Nixon visit to the Soviet Union, but Vietnamese communists were undoubtedly displeased that "the number one enemy of all mankind" was being received there shortly following the mining of DRV ports and a major escalation in U.S. bombing. Liberation Radio carried several pledges from Soviet leaders "to assist and support the Vietnamese people in their struggle against the U.S. aggressors until complete victory" (Liberation Radio, 5 February), and LPA (23 March) reported Soviet leader Brezhnev's reaction to the mining of Haiphong and increased bombing:

> "In this struggle, the Soviet people completely stand on the side of the Indochinese peoples. To support the Indochinese peoples is our internationalist obligation and we will certainly accomplish it to the end. The Soviet Union indignantly condemns the piratic bombing by the U.S. Air Force against the territory of the Democratic Republic of Vietnam and the Republic of South Vietnam. We demand the interventionists to withdraw from Indochina. We demand them to let the peoples in this area independently and freely decide their own destiny, without interference and pressure from outside."

Such sentiments would have probably been more convincing to South Vietnamese communists had they been accompanied by a cancellation of the impending Nixon visit to Moscow, which took place without incident. On 20 August the Soviet Union concluded a "month of friendship and militant solidarity with the Vietnamese people's fight against U.S. aggression" (ibid., 22 August), and later the NLF and PRG sent a joint message to Soviet leaders expressing "warmest congratulations" on the occasion of the 55th anniversary of the October Revolution and thanking the Soviet Union for its "precious support and assistance" (ibid., 6 November). Relations with Eastern European communist states continued to be warm, with messages being exchanged on national days and important anniversaries.

As in years past, the NLF and PRG exchanged numerous messages of solidarity with other Indochinese communist movements. In discussing the "spring-summer offensive," LPA asserted (11 April) that "On the three battlefields, the Vietnamese, Lao and Cambodian peoples have coordinated their activities in a harmonious manner." The "Thanom-Praphat reactionary clique in Thailand" was characterized as having "willingly sold themselves out to

Washington and become loyal servants of the U.S.," thus entitling "the Vietnamese people" to "use their sacred self-defense right and make the clique of lackeys in Thailand pay for their debts" (ibid., 9 June). The "Thai people's revolutionary struggle" received strong support from "the South Vietnamese people" (ibid., 7 August). The "pro-U.S. clique in Indonesia" was also attacked for "its dark design against the Vietnamese people": "The way of thinking, statements and deeds of those in Indonesia who style themselves 'neutral' and 'non-aligned' are running counter to the aspirations and interests of the Indonesian people, betraying the national liberation movements in Asia, Africa and Latin America and opposing the interest of peace in Southeast Asia and in the world." (Ibid., 6 December.) The "proposal for settling the Vietnam issue" put forth by the ASEAN (Association of South East Asian Nations) in August was denounced because it "makes no distinction between the U.S. aggressors and the Vietnamese people who are fighting against aggression" (ibid., 17 August). The NLF and PRG continued to support "the just struggle of the Korean people against U.S. imperialism" (ibid., 2 October), and supported moves to reunify the two Koreas (ibid., 10 August). LPA followed the general communist line in the Middle East, condemning the "Israeli aggressors" (14 September, 6 November). In June the NLF observed an "International Day of Solidarity with the South African People" (ibid., 26 June).

Since the start of large-scale U.S. involvement in the war in South Vietnam, the communists have been hoping to achieve victory primarily through the "political" and "diplomatic" struggles, and efforts have been made to exacerbate the "internal contradictions" within the United States by encouraging the "peace" movement. On the occasion of Women's International Day (8 March), Mme Nguyen Thi Binh sent a message to American women urging them to strengthen their solidarity and to play a more important role in "the American people's common struggle for an end to the aggressive war in Vietnam and for social progress in the United States" (ibid., 5 March; Liberation Radio, 8 March). An appeal was also made to members of the Southern Christian Leadership Conference, the Black Panther Party and the National Welfare Rights Organization on the occasion of the "International Day of Solidarity with the Afro-American People" on 18 August (ibid., 17 August). The acquittal of U.S. communist Angela Davis—"after 22 months of illegal imprisonment and brutal torture"—was hailed as "a bitter political rebuff for the Nixon clique" (ibid., 6 June). Both Liberation Radio and the Liberation Press Agency broadcast frequent statements supporting the "anti-war movement in the United States" during 1972 (Liberation Radio, 26 April, 26 September; LPA, 27 April, 4 July), and such support was expressed also by Nguyen Huu Tho in a New Year's "Message to the American People" (ibid., 30 December 1971) and by Mme Nguyen Thi Binh in a letter to the U.S. Congress (VNA, 26 April 1972). The U.S. presidential election received considerable publicity in Vietnamese communist radio broadcasts, which aired numerous quotations from Democratic Party candidate Senator George McGovern and his supporters denouncing President Nixon and his Vietnam policies.

Although communists in both North and South Vietnam have ruled out proposals calling for United Nations action to end the war or U.N. supervision of a cease-fire and elections following an armistice (both the United States and the nationalist "State of Vietnam" had proposed U.N. supervision at the 1954 Geneva Conference, and U.S. efforts to obtain U.N. assistance in ending the war in 1968 were blocked by a Soviet veto in the Security Council), the PRG foreign minister called on members of the United Nations "to raise their voice in this General Assembly to condemn the U.S. extermination war in Vietnam and demand it to end its aggression and withdraw from there all its troops" (LPA, 1 October).

In August the PRG scored a diplomatic victory when it was admitted to the conference of nonaligned nations meeting in Georgetown, Guyana (Liberation Radio, 18, 19 August). During 1972 the PRG established diplomatic relations with Mali, Chile, Guinea, and Uganda.

Publications. The main publications of the PRP are *Tien Phong* ("Vanguard"), and *Nhan Dan* ("The People"), a weekly newspaper patterned after the North Vietnamese party daily of the same name. The "central organ" of the NLF is *Giai Phong* ("Liberation"), and the "official mouthpiece" of the NLF Central Committee is *South Vietnam in Struggle,* published three times each month in English and French. The main PLAF newspaper is *Quan Giai Phong* (Liberation Army).

Viet Cong statements are carried by Liberation Press Agency (LPA)—the official press agency of the NLF (founded on 12 October 1960)—and by Liberation Radio (founded on 1 February 1962). Statements are also frequently carried by Hanoi radio.

Hoover Institution
Stanford University

Robert F. Turner

INTERNATIONAL COMMUNIST FRONT ORGANIZATIONS

Afro-Asian Writers' Permanent Bureau

The Afro-Asian Writers' Permanent Bureau (AAWPB) was originally set up by the Soviets at an "Afro-Asian Writers' Conference" in Tashkent in October 1958. Following a second conference, in Cairo in February 1962, a "Permanent Bureau" was established with headquarters in Colombo, Ceylon. The Chinese communists gained control of the organization at a meeting of its Executive Committee in Bali, Indonesia, in July 1963, and established a new Executive Secretariat in Peking on 15 August 1966. Thus, while the AAWPB is still officially based in Colombo, it operates exclusively from Peking. A pro-Soviet faction—the AAWPB-Cairo—broke away after the Chinese began to dominate the organization. The AAWPB-Cairo, now planning its Fifth Conference, is the more active of the two. The AAWPB-Peking, which has not yet held a third conference, appears to have no activities outside its irregular publication, *The Call,* and occasional statements carried by the New China News Agency.

The AAWPB-Cairo. The pro-Soviet faction of the AAWPB was founded on 19–21 June 1966 at an "extraordinary meeting" attended by delegations from Cameroun, Ceylon, India, Sudan, the Soviet Union, and the U.A.R. Its relatively successful "Third Afro-Asian Writers' Conference," held at Beirut in 1967 and attended by some 150 delegates from 42 countries, was the first serious blow to the pro-Chinese AAWPB. Since then, the pro-Soviet organization appears to have consolidated and augmented its base of support.

The secretary-general of the AAWPB-Cairo is Yusuf el-Sebai (Egypt), who is also secretary-general of the Afro-Asian People's Solidarity Organization and a member of the Presidential Committee of the World Peace Council. The assistant secretary-general is Edward el-Kharat (Egypt). The AAWPB-Cairo has a ten-member Permanent Bureau, with members from India, Japan, Lebanon, Mongolia, the Portuguese colonies, Senegal, South Africa, the Soviet Union, Sudan, and Egypt. There is also a 30-member Executive Committee.

The AAWPB-Peking. The pro-Chinese AAWPB, the continuation of the original body, is led by Frederik L. Risakotta (Indonesia), a member of the Peking-based Delegation of the Communist Party of Indonesia Central Committee, who is identified as "acting head ad interim" of the AAWPB Secretariat. (The former secretary-general, Rathe Deshapriya Sananayake, returned to his native Ceylon in mid-1968; Kinkazu Saionji, who was identified in April 1970 by the NCNA as "acting head ad interim," returned home to Japan the following August.) The AAWPB-Peking claim of affiliates in some 40 countries probably includes individual as well as organizational memberships.

Views and Activities. The AAWPB-Peking was inactive throughout 1972. Early in the year it was announced *al-Ahram,* Cairo, 18 January) that a preparatory committee for the

Fifth Afro-Asian Writers' Conference would meet in Moscow in June, but no further information became available regarding this scheduled gathering.

While AAWPB-Cairo's activities were obviously very limited, its secretary-general, Yusuf el-Sebai, was busy in his role as secretary-general of the Afro-Asian People's Solidarity Organization (AAPSO). In this latter capacity he participated in all AAPSO-sponsored meetings, including the AAPSO Fifth Congress (Cairo, 10–13 January), the "International Emergency Conference in Support of the Indochinese Peoples" (Cairo, 20 May), and the Second Afro-Asian Women's Conference (Ulan Bator, 14–18 August). The activities of Yusuf el-Sebai clearly indicate that he devoted more time to AAPSO than to AAWPB-Cairo; his leadership of both organizations links these two groups by what can be described as an "overlapping directorate." Additional aspects of this linkage are noticeable if AAPSO and AAWPB-Cairo are juxtaposed: both are headquartered in Cairo and both focus on problems of the same geographical area and thus to an extent have analogous functions. The overlap of leadership and function is somewhat unusual; certainly there is no other case among the fronts where anyone has assumed the role of secretary-general in two organizations. In fact, it might be said that the main difference between AAPSO and AAWPB-Cairo is not one of leadership, function or location but of "activity": AAWPB-Cairo has been essentially dormant whereas AAPSO has been busily engaged in sponsoring conferences and seminars and issuing statements on a wide variety of problems. Although no explanation exists for the dormant condition of AAWPB-Cairo, one possibility is simply that the leadership has deliberately shifted its efforts and some of the operational responsibilities of AAWPB-Cairo to AAPSO. The organizational and functional linkage between the two groups allows for and perhaps encourages a transference of these responsibilities, and AAPSO is a broader-based organization which does not have a competing Chinese counterpart—two attractive characteristics from the Soviet point of view.

Publications. The main organ of AAWPB-Cairo is the "literature, arts and sociopolitical quarterly" *Lotus* (formerly *Afro-Asian Literature*), which appears in English, French, and Arabic editions. In addition, books by various "Afro-Asian men of letters" have been published by AAWPB-Cairo in the Soviet Union.

The AAWPB-Peking bulletin, *The Call*, is issued from Peking at irregular intervals in English, French, and Arabic.

California State College,   Paul F. Magnelia
Stanislaus

International Association of Democratic Lawyers

The International Association of Democratic Lawyers (IADL) was founded at an "International Congress of Jurists" held in Paris in October 1946 under the auspices of a para-communist organization, the Mouvement National Judiciaire, and attended by lawyers from 25 countries. Although the movement originally included elements of various political orientations, the leading role was played by leftist French lawyers, and by 1949 most non-communists had resigned.

The IADL was originally based in Paris but was expelled by the French government in 1950. It then moved to Brussels, where it remains; some organizational work has also been carried out from Warsaw.

Membership is open to lawyers' organizations or groups and to individual lawyers, and may be on a "corresponding," "donation," or "permanent" basis. Lawyers holding membership through organizations or individually are estimated to number about 25,000. The IADL claims to be supported by a membership fee and donations; no details of its finances are published.

The IADL holds consultative status, Category C, with the U.N. Economic and Social Council.

Structure and Leadership. The highest organ of the IADL is the Congress, in which each member organization is represented. There have been nine congresses to date, the latest at Helsinki in July 1970. The Congress elects the IADL Council, which is supposed to meet yearly and consists of the Bureau, the Secretariat, and a representative of each member organization and of the co-opted members.

The key officers of the IADL are the president, Pierre Cot (France), and the secretary-general, Joë Nordmann (France).

Aims and Policies. The stated aims of the IADL are to develop mutual understanding among the lawyers of the world, to support the aims of the United Nations, to encourage the study and application of democratic principles conducive to the maintenance of peace, and to promote the independence of all people. In its activities, however, the IADL has devoted itself almost entirely to supporting the policies of the Soviet Union.

Views and Activities. Denis Nowell Pritt (United Kingdom), the honorary president, died on 23 May 1972. He was described as a "dedicated fighter for peace and justice" and a "lifelong champion of friendship with the Soviet Union" (*Tass,* 23 May; *Morning Star,* London, 24 May). During his active career in the "peace movement," he was president of the British Peace Committee, a member of the World Peace Council, and a Lenin Peace Prize winner.

IADL activities in 1972 centered around efforts to observe and criticize "political trials" taking place in various countries. Thus, in May, under the sponsorship of the French Committee for Democratic Liberties and Amnesty in Portugal, two lawyers attended political trials in Lisbon as IADL observers (*L'Humanité,* Paris, 27 May). An IADL observer also attended the trial of the Greek communists (Greek News Agency, 21 February). A member of the Brussels bar was an observer at the trial of U.S. communist Angela Davis; his report was given in Brussels at a conference organized by the *Cercle du Libre Examen* and the Angela Davis Committee (*Le Drapeau Rouge,* Belgium, 24–30 March). Earlier in the year a member of the Paris bar went to Iran to act as an observer at what the IADL described as "political trials"; the Iranian government, however, refused to allow him to attend (*Le Monde,* Paris, 12 February).

IADL delegates attended the "Conference on the Abolition of Dictatorship in Greece," which was held in Paris on 17–19 March (*L'Humanité,* 4 April). Also in March, IADL representatives attended sessions of the Special U.N. Committee on Apartheid and the Permanent Committee of the Non-Governmental Organizations of UNESCO (IADL *Information Bulletin,* no. 2), and in September, the All-India Congress for Peace and Solidarity, Calcutta (*Patriot,* New Delhi, 22 September). (On the Calcutta conference see also *World Peace Council.*)

A delegation comprising Secretary-General Nordmann and a person described as an "international secretary" protested to the U.S. Embassy in Paris about the blockade and intensification of bombing in North Vietnam (*L'Humanité,* 13 May). Protests against U.S. policy in Indochina continued throughout the year.

Two organizations applied for affiliation: the South Yemen Bar and the Bar of Santo Domingo (Dominican Republic) (*Information Bulletin,* no. 1).

Publication. The IADL's two principal publications are the *Review of Contemporary Law,* which is supposed to appear semiannually but does not always do so, and the *Information Bulletin,* which appears irregularly and is frequently devoted to a single topic. Both publications are in English and French. The IADL also issues pamphlets on questions of topical interest.

California State College,   Paul F. Magnelia
Stanislaus

International Federation of Resistance Fighters

The International Federation of Resistance Fighters (Fédération Internationale des Résistants; FIR) was founded in 1951 in Vienna as a successor to the International Federation of Former Political Prisoners (Fédération Internationale des Anciens Prisonniers Politiques). With the name change, membership eligibility was widened to include former partisans and resistance fighters, and all victims of Nazism and fascism and their descendants.

In 1959 the FIR had a membership of four million; no figures have been announced since. On its twentieth anniversary, in 1971, the FIR claimed affiliated groups and representation in every country of Europe (*Resistance unie,* no. 14). The headquarters is in Vienna; a small secretariat is maintained in Paris. In 1972 the FIR was granted Category B Status with the U.N. Economic and Social Council (ECOSOC) (*Informationsdienst,* no. 8).

Structure and Leadership. The organs of the FIR are the Congress, General Council, Bureau, and Secretariat. Until the Sixth Congress (Venice, 1969), the Congress was convened every three years. It was then decided that this body should meet every four years. The Congress elects the FIR president, vice-presidents, and members of the Bureau, and determines and ratifies members of the General Council after they have been nominated by national associations. The General Council is supposed to meet at least once a year. The Bureau supervises the implementation of decisions by the Congress and General Council, and is also responsible for the budget; it is headed by the FIR president, and from among its members it elects the Secretariat.

Arialdo Banfi (Italy) has been FIR president since 1965; Jean Toujas (France) is Secretary-General (for additional information on the leadership see *YICA, 1972,* p. 613).

Aims and Policies. The FIR claims to be independent of all parties and governments, and its charter outlines the following basic aims; to unite the members in order to secure the independence of their homelands and the freedom and peace of the world; to defend freedom and human dignity and to fight against racial, political, ideological, and religious discrimination and any renaissance of fascism and Nazism; to honor the martyrs of underground fighting and to keep alive the memories of their ideals and the horrors of prisons and concentration camps; to represent the material and moral interests of resistance fighters and their heirs; and to work for friendly and peaceful relations between nations in accord with the U.N. Charter.

In spite of these stated goals, the FIR has always subordinated its interests to the policies of the Soviet Union. (For conspicuous instances see *YICA, 1972,* p. 612.)

Views and Activities. FIR activities in 1972 reflected two major preoccupations: the Greek government, and the general improvement in East-West relations.

The FIR continued its criticism of the "fascist" regime in Greece and was represented by its deputy secretary-general at the "Conference on the Abolition of Dictatorship in Greece," Paris, 17–19 March (*Informationsdienst,* no. 4). Later the FIR protested against "tortures of arrested patriots" in Greece and demanded the release of resistance fighters (Greek communist party radio "Voice of Truth," 15 August).

The ratification of the agreements between the Federal Republic of Germany and Poland and the Soviet Union was strongly endorsed (*FIR Declarations,* 25/31 May). The deputy secretary-general attended the congress of the French "National Federation of Deportees and Internees, Resistance Fighters and Patriots" at Royan, 4 June (*L'Humanité,* 5 June). The FIR denounced repeatedly U.S. policy in Indochina, particularly the increased bombing of North Vietnam (*Informationsdienst,* no. 10, September).

The August issue of *La Voix Internationale de la Résistance* taunted the FIR regarding its silence on the replacement of the 1968 leaders of its Czechoslovak affiliate by "Moscow men." A critical letter to Prague from the French affiliate was not published in the FIR organ *Résistance Unie.*

Publications. The FIR publishes a journal in French and German, *Résistance unie* and *Widerstandskämpfer.* News reports are also disseminated occasionally through the French-language *Service d'Information de la FIR* and its German counterpart, *Informationsdienst der FIR.*

California State College,   Paul F. Magnelia
Stanislaus

International Organization
of Journalists

The International Organization of Journalists (IOJ) was founded in June 1946 in Copenhagen. Merging with it at that time were the International Federation of Journalists (IFJ) and the International Federation of Journalists of Allied and Free Countries. By 1952 all non-communist unions had withdrawn in order to refound the IFJ. Since 1955 the IOJ has made unsuccessful overtures to the IFJ for cooperation and for eventually forming a new world organization of journalists. It was for the purpose of bridging differences with the IFJ that the IOJ in 1955 founded the International Committee for Cooperation of Journalists (ICCJ). No IFJ member is known to have affliated with the ICCJ—perhaps because most ICCJ officers are also leading members of the parent IOJ. The IOJ headquarters, originally in London, was moved to Prague in 1947.

In 1963 pro-Chinese journalists established a rival organization, the Afro-Asian Journalists' Association (AAJA; see below).

The IOJ was awarded consultative and information Category B status with UNESCO in 1969. It also holds consultative status, Category II, with UNESCO's Economic and Social Council.

Structure and Leadership. National unions and groups are eligible for membership in the IOJ, as are also individual journalists. The organization claims to have some 150,000 members, representing 67 organizations in 58 countries (TASS, 14 June 1971).

The highest IOJ body is the Congress, which is supposed to meet every four years. The Congress elects the Executive Committee, made up of the Presidium (president, vice-president, and secretary-general), other officers (secretaries and treasurer), and ordinary members. President leaders, elected by the 1971 meeting of the Congress, include Jean-Maurice Hermann (France), president, and Jiří Kubka (Czechoslovakia), secretary-general (for other leaders and details on structure see *YICA, 1972,* pp. 615–16).

Aims and Policies. Although the avowed aims of the IOJ include "defense of the right of every journalist to write according to his conscience and conviction," its duties, according to a Secretariat statement, are to expose the "demagogism of imperialist propaganda," promote the cohesion of all "anti-imperialist" forces, and spread the "truth about the great success of the socialist countries" (TASS, 14 June 1971).

IOJ training schools, drawing mostly journalists from developing countries, are in Hungary, East Germany, and Czechoslovkia.

Views and Activities. The Presidium, meeting in Balatonszeplak, Hungary, 26–28 September 1972, approved the work done by the IOJ since the last Congress. The Presidium expressed support for the 1967 U.N. resolution on the Middle East and for efforts to promote a European security conference, and demanded an early peace in Vietnam (TASS, 30 September; *Mladá fronta,* Prague, 7 October).

Earlier, the IOJ appealed to all journalists to back the activities of the "International Initiative Committee of Journalists for European Security and Cooperation," directed toward the speedy convening of a security conference, the establishment of a permanent journalists' body on European security, and preparations for an "Assembly of European Journalists" (TASS, 8 January; CTK, Czechoslovak news agency, 12 January). After February little mention was made of the proposed Assembly. The IOJ secretary-general indicated that a meeting would be held in Czechoslovakia in February which would be attended by representatives from radio, press, and TV of the socialist countries and from which the IOJ would issue materials on questions of security (TASS, 28 January).

IOJ relations with certain national press federations become subject to some controversy in January as a result of the case of an Italian journalist arrested in Prague. The Italian Press Federation (FNSI) told the IOJ that because of lack of clarification about the arrest it could not continue with the preparations for a "second European meeting of Journalists," due to be held in Italy in June (*Corriere della Sera,* Milan, 18 January). Relations continued to deteriorate between FNSI and IOJ when in February another Italian journalist was arrested in Prague and forced to leave the country. Before departing he was asked to explain his relationship with former leading members of the Communist Party of Czechoslovakia. The Italian Communist newspaper *L'Unità* (9 February) described his expulsion as "absurd." The FNSI accused the Czechoslovak government of preventing the IOJ from functioning, and added that the expulsion was fresh proof of the determination of Czechoslovak authorities to trample on any autonomy of the IOJ (*L'Unità,* 10 February).

The IOJ continued to bring journalists, particularly from developing areas, to its schools. In November 1971 its thirteenth advanced course in journalism began in Budapest, to last nine months; in attendance were 12 journalists from Africa, Asia, and Latin America (*Advance,* Nigeria, 13 December). In October 1972 it was announced that 14 young Bangladesh journalists were receiving training there (Budapest radio, 11 October).

In May, at Prague, the IOJ and representatives of journalists' unions of the socialist countries called on "all democratic journalists" to support the "just struggle of the Indochinese people" and to take an active part in the "mass movement against U.S. aggression" (CTK, 19 May). Later the IOJ promised to give "material help from its solidarity fund" to Vietnamese journalists "struggling against U.S. aggression (ibid., 10 October).

In accordance with a decision of the 1971 Congress, an IOJ delegation visited Latin America during August and September. The five-man group stopped in Cuba, Chile, Peru, and a number of other countries (*El Siglo,* Santiago, 15 August; *Unidad,* Lima, 17–24 August). In messages to the Chilean government, the IOJ condemned the intervention of the SIP (Interamerican Press Society) in Chile's internal affairs, and praised the government's activities against "maneuvers inspired by reactionary forces in the service of foreign imperialism" (*El Siglo,* 5 October).

The IOJ indicated that it was preparing a statement of solidarity with Iraq's decision to nationalize its oil. Because of Iraq's policy the IOJ decided to hold a meeting of its Executive Committee in Baghadad in 1973, described as the "greatest international journalists' gathering in revolutionary Iraq" (*Baghdad Observer,* 17 August).

Publications. The IOJ issues a monthly journal, the *Democratic Journalist,* in English, French, Russian, and Spanish, and a fortnightly *Information Bulletin.*

The AAJA. The Afro-Asian Journalists' Association was set up in Djakarta in April 1963, with an Afro-Asian Press Bureau and a permanent Secretariat. Until the attempted communist coup in Indonesia (1965), the AAJA appeared to represent a possibly serious rival to the pro-Soviet IOJ, particularly in developing countries. At that juncture, AAJA headquarters were "temporarily" moved to Peking. Djawoto, the AAJA's Indonesian secretary-general, who was dismissed from his post as Indonesia's ambassador to China, has since headed the Secretariat in Peking, which has become the permanent seat of AAJA operations.

There is no indication that the AAJA has succeeded in winning over the allegiance of IOJ members or member organizations. Few journalists' organizations and governments have expressed open support for the AAJA or indicated that they would send delegates to an eventual AAJA conference. The AAJA devotes its energies mainly to propagating the Chinese line in international political affairs.

Publications. The AAJA's main publication, *Afro-Asian Journalist,* appears irregularly. Pamphlets on topical issues are published from time to time.

California State College, Paul F. Magnelia
Stanislaus

International Union
of Students

The International Union of Students (IUS) was founded in August 1946 at a congress in Prague attended by students of varying political persuasions. This diversity of political views lasted until 1951, when most of the non-communist student unions disaffiliated because of the IUS's domination by pro-Soviet groups. The 1960s were marked by bitter debates between the pro-Soviet and pro-Chinese students. As a result of continuing Soviet domination of the Union, the Chinese in the middle 1960s withdrew from active participation.

The IUS has consultative Category C Status with UNESCO; applications for Category B status have been repeatedly deferred.

Structure and Leadership. The highest governing body of the IUS is its Congress, which is supposed to meet every two years and to which affiliated and associated organizations send delegates. The Congress elects the Executive Committee, made up of the Secretariat, Finance Committee, and individual members. The national student organizations represented on the Executive Committee are chosen by the Congress, but each designated organization selects its own representative. The Executive Committee usually meets at least twice a year. Dusán Ulcak (Czechoslovakia) is the IUS president; Fathi Muhammad al-Fadl (Sudan) is secretary-general.

Aims and Policies. According to its constitution, the IUS is to defend the interests of students and to strive for (1) the rights of all young people to enjoy primary, secondary, and higher education, (2) the promotion of national culture, (3) the realization of the aspirations of students in colonial and dependent countries, and (4) world peace. Since its founding, however, the IUS has been primarily concerned with political issues and has always supported the policies of the Soviet Union.

Views and Activities. At its meeting in Warsaw on 26–29 January 1972, which was attended by 40 member organizations, the Executive Committee restated the attitude of the IUS on a number of major international issues. It strongly supported the "peoples of Indochina" against "American imperialism," the Arabs against "Israeli aggression" the "national liberation struggles" in Africa and Latin America, and the Soviet proposal for a European security conference. The meeting discussed the organizing of the 10th World Youth Festival, scheduled for August 1973. The Youth Section of the African National Congress of South Africa (ANC) was accepted as a member (*Mladá fronta,* Prague, 27, 28, 31 January).

Internal friction developed at the Warsaw meeting. Two factions of UNEF (National Union of Students of France) were invited: the Trotskyist UNEF-AJS and communist UNEF-Revouveau. The UNEF-AJS delegation asked that the IUS condemn "normalization in

Czechoslovakia," and requested release of all political prisoners in that country. After heated words, particularly with some Latin American delegates, and some blows, the request was refused. The UNEF-AJS group was then excluded from the meeting and asked to leave Warsaw at once. Shortly after their return to France, the UNEF-AJS condemned the "Stalinist methods" of the Warsaw meeting, and read a message of sympathy from former IUS president Jiří‘ Pelikan, who fled to the West after the 1968 Soviet intervention in Czechoslovakia (*Le Monde,* Paris, 12 February).

Support for a European security conference became the main preoccupation of the IUS in subsequent months. Immediately preceding the Executive Committee meeting and also in Warsaw, the IUS along with the Polish Students' Association sponsored an "International Student Meeting on European Security." This gathering attracted some 200 persons, from 60 national unions in Africa, Asia, Latin America, and Europe, and from international organizations. The IUS president, in an opening statement, indicated that the meeting would act on the decisions of the "Youth Conference on European Security" held in Florence the previous December. The final appeal of the conference urged young people to help create a system of security and cooperation in Europe. More specifically it asked for ratification of the pending Soviet–West German and Polish–West German accords, and those between East and West Germany; called for recognition of East Germany; and asked support for the holding of a governmental conference on European security, and for the "Assembly of Representatives of Public Opinion on European Security and Cooperation," scheduled to be held in June at Brussels (*Mladá fronta,* 20 January; TASS, 25 January).

IUS representatives attended a number of preparatory sessions for the Brussels assembly (see *World Peace Council*) and the international youth conference, scheduled for August (see *World Federation of Democratic Youth*). A eight-member delegation represented the IUS at Brussels.

IUS interest in the Middle East was reflected in the attendance by its president and vice-president at the conference of the Afro-Asian People's Solidarity Organization, held in Cairo on 10–13 January. In May an IUS delegation visited Cairo, and in July the IUS along with the General Federation of Egyptian Students sponsored a "World Student Conference of Solidarity with the Struggle of the Students and People of Egypt," which some 50 student organizations and international groups attended (*al-Ahram,* Cairo, 25 July).

In Kerala, India, 15–20 July, the IUS cosponsored with the World Federation of Democratic Youth an "Asian Regional Youth Seminar," as part of its "Youth Accuses Imperialism" campaign. Hosts were the All-India Youth Federation and the All-India Students' Federation. The several papers presented by the IUS dealt with "imperialist" penetration of economic and educational systems, and "the role of youth and students in the struggle for the consideration of national independence" (*New Age,* New Delhi, 23–30 July; *Patriot,* India, 13 July).

Throughout 1972 the IUS denounced U.S. policy in Indochina, condemning the "American imperialists" and urging all students to give their full support to efforts to end the Vietnam war. In the spring it began a new publication, the *IUS Bulletin for Europe,* which in part was designed to strengthen cooperation with anti-war groups in the United States.

The Executive Committee meeting in Warsaw adopted a resolution on Northern Ireland protesting the "oppression" of workers and the general restriction on civil rights. The Committee determined to cooperate with the Union of Students of Ireland (USI) and other "progressive" forces, and instructed its Secretariat, in cooperation with the USI, to organize an international seminar in Northern Ireland in August (*IUS News Service,* no. 5). As part of its "Youth Accuses Imperialism" campaign, the IUS arranged for six representatives of the Irish

Union of Students (Dublin) to visit IUS headquarters in Prague in March; a joint statement condemned the presence of British troops and demanded an end to mass terror (CTK, Czechoslovak news agency, 14 March).

The secretary-general of the World Student Christian Federation WSCF) visited the IUS Secretariat in March. The discussions touched on WSCF's participation in the 10th World Youth Festival and the general strengthening of cooperation between the two organizations (*IUS News Service*, no. 8).

The constituent conference of the International Preparatory Committee of the 10th World Youth Festival was held in Sofia, 19–20 January. The IUS had previously issued a statement declaring that the festival would "give impetus to the world-wide campaign 'Youth Accuses Imperialism' endorsed by the 10th Congress of the IUS" (ibid., no. 23, 1971). The IUS was represented by its president and secretary-general at the meeting and thereafter was represented on the Provisional Working Group for the festival, which met periodically during the rest of the year (*ADN*, East German news agency, 18 February; *Mladá fronta*, 20–21 January).

An IUS statement condemned the state of emergency declared in South Korea (*IUS News Service*, January). On the "International Day of Solidarity with the Students and People of Brazil Fighting Against Dictatorship," the IUS denounced the "fascist" regime in Brazil. Later it expressed solidarity with Bolivians opposed to the government of Hugo Banzer (*El Siglo*, Santiago, 20 August), called for a "day of international solidarity with the people and students of Puerto Rico in their struggle for independence" (ibid., 12 September), and expressed support for Chile, indicating it would call for a day of solidarity with that country (ibid., 24 October). The "Third International and Sixth National 'School of Student Leaders,'" co-sponsored by the IUS and the Federation of Students of the (Chilean) State Technical University, was announced as forthcoming in Chile, with delegates expected also from Guatemala, Uruguay, Peru, and Bolivia (ibid., 2 October).

The IUS secretary-general and vice-president visited New Zealand in August to discuss the possibility of IUS membership for the New Zealand University Students' Association (*The Press*, Christchurch, 10 August).

Publications. The principal IUS publications are a monthly magazine, *World Student News*, published in English, French, German, and Spanish, and a fortnightly bulletin, *IUS News Service*, issued in English, French, and Spanish.

California State College,   Paul F. Magnelia
Stanislaus

Women's International Democratic Federation

The Women's International Democratic Federation (WIDF) was founded in Paris in December 1945 at a "Congress of Women" organized by the communist-dominated "Union des Femmes Françaises". The WIDF was headquartered in Paris until 1951, when it was expelled by the government. It then moved to East Berlin. The WIDF holds Category A status with ECOSOC and Category B with UNESCO.

Structure and Leadership. The WIDF Congress, which meets every four years, is the highest governing body. Next in authority is the Council, which meets annually and is in control between Congresses; it elects the Bureau and the Secretariat. The Bureau meets at least twice a year and implements decisions taken by the Congress and the Council; it is assisted by the Secretariat.

In 1972 Hertta Kuusinen (Finland) remained as president; Fanny Edelman (Argentina) replaced Cecile Hugel (France) as secretary-general.

Membership in the WIDF is open to all women's organizations and groups and in exceptional cases to individuals. Total membership is estimated to be in excess of 200 million and in 1971 included 107 affiliated and associated organizations in 95 countries. The WIDF tries to maintain contact with non-affiliated women's groups through its International Liaison Bureau, which has headquarters in Copenhagen and a secretariat in Brussels.

Aims and Policies. According to its charter, the WIDF aims to unite all the women of the world, regardless of race, nationality, religion, or political belief, so that they may work together to defend their rights as citizens, mothers, and workers; protect children; ensure peace, democracy and national independence; and establish bonds of friendship and solidarity among themselves.

In actual practice, the WIDF has devoted most its efforts to supporting the policies of the Soviet Union. The Chinese, who have not participated in WIDF activities for a number of years, declared in 1965 (NCNA, 8 November) that "certain leaders of the WIDF" had "reduced the Federation to an instrument for the enforcement of the foreign policy of one country."

Views and Activities. During 1972 the WIDF issued statements and took positions on a wide variety of political problems. Of noticeable significance were the stands taken on the European security question and the situation in Northern Ireland. Most of its efforts, however, appeared to be concentrated on improving or expanding its organizational capability, and in general getting women more effectively involved in public affairs, particularly in the developing areas.

Representatives from women's organizations in 80 countries attended the WIDF Council meeting in Varna, Bulgaria, 30 April–5 May. Among the delegates were those from the WFDY and the WFTU. The main report, read by the secretary-general, dealt with the role that women's organizations could play in involving young women in the economic, political, social, and cultural life of their countries. Delegates discussed the participation of young women in public activities, the rights and welfare of women and children, and the urgent need to deal with international issues such as Indochina. Several appeals were adopted: women were urged to struggle for peace in Indochina, for the success of International Children's Day (1 June), and for greater involvement of young women in the affairs of their country. Before closing, the Council supported the convening of the following seminars and conferences: the "Second Seminar of Latin American Women," a "Second Afro-Asian Women's Conference" in Ulan Bator in August, and a seminar in New Delhi on the "Training of Cadres to Combat Illiteracy." The Council decided to hold the WIDF's thirtieth-anniversary Congress in 1975, and to support the Soviet-proposed European security conference (TASS, 30 April; BTA, Bulgarian news agency, 3–6 May). Women's democratic organizations of Bangladesh, Dahomey, and Burundi were admitted into the WIDF at the Council meeting (Sofia radio, 5–6 May).

Shortly after the Council, a seminar of leaders of women's organizations and movements from 28 Asian, African, and Latin American countries was held in Druzhba, Bulgaria, 7–10 May, with the Bulgarian Women's Unions as host, to discuss the life and work of women in socialist countries (ibid., 7–10 May).

Fanny Edelman addressed an All-Africa Women' Conference seminar on "The Role of Women in the Liberation of Africa," held under the auspices of the WIDF in Dar es Salaam, 24–31 July (TASS, 26 July; *Daily News,* Tanzania, 22–31 July).

The WIDF began early in the year to prepare for the seminar of Latin American Women. The first preparatory meeting took place in Havana, 1–3 February. Women's groups from Argentina, Chile, Mexico, Uruguay, and Cuba were represented. The agenda was outlined and included proposed discussions on rights, family happiness, redemption of wealth and cultural patrimony, and peace, national independence, and solidarity (*Granma,* Havana, 7 February).

With the WIDF-affiliated Union of Chilean Women as host and under the presidency of the wife of Chilean president Allende, the seminar, officially entitled "Women Today in Latin America," opened on 23 October (*Women of the World,* no. 3, July; *El Siglo,* Santiago, 8–31 July, 24 October). Present were 156 observers and delegates from 35 Latin American, Asian, African, and European countries. A declaration of solidarity with Cuba was adopted, and the president, speaking at the end of the seminar, said that "without the fighting presence of women, there could be no revolution" (ibid., 28–31 October).

Working closely together, the Afro-Asian People's Solidarity Organization (AAPSO) and the WIDF held the first preparatory meeting in Cairo, 15–20 May, for the Second Women's Afro-Asian Conference (*New Age,* New Delhi, 4 June). On 14 August the conference opened in Ulan Bator. In attendance were delegates from 56 countries and representatives from 9 international organizations. The conference, in a general declaration, stated its determination to fight for further strengthening the "militant solidarity and anti-imperialist unity of all progressive forces." Conference resolutions called for the participation of Afro-Asian women in the "struggle for liberation, independence, and peace"; the withdrawal of U.S. forces from Indochina; and condemnation of "Israeli aggression." The conference also expressed support for Iraq against oil monopolies (TASS, 18 August).

In March the WIDF was represented at the Paris "Conference for the Abolition of Dictatorship in Greece" (*L'Humanité,* 4 April). WIDF delegations visited Cuba (*Granma,* 1 April) and attended India's 25th anniversary celebration (CTK, Czechoslovak news agency, 8 April).

In various statements the WIDF congratulated U.S. communist Angela Davis on her acquittal (ADN, East German news agency, 24 February); expressed solidarity with the women and children of Northern Ireland, and demanded the immediate withdrawal of all British troops and the release of all political prisoners (ibid., 1 August); and condemned "U.S. crimes" in Indochina, supported the "women of the Middle East in their fight against Israel," and encouraged all women and organizations to work for a European security conference (ibid., 31 August). An International Women's Day broadcast to Albania accused the Union of Albanian Women of undermining the unity of the WIDF (Moscow radio, 8 March). A reply (Albanian Telegraph Agency, 8 March) stated that the Albanian women contributed to the "exposing of and fight against the imperialist-revisionist aggressive plots and plans," and to the exposing of the "traitorous line" of the WIDF leadership, which was being manipulated by the "Moscow revisionists."

Publications. The WIDF publishes an illustrated quarterly magazine, *Women of the Whole World,* in English, German, Spanish, French, and Russian, and issues pamphlets and bulletins on specific problems.

California State College,   Paul F. Magnelia
Stanislaus

World Federation
of Democratic Youth

The World Federation of Democratic Youth (WFDY) was founded in November 1945 at a "World Youth Conference" convened in London by the World Youth Council. Although the WFDY appeared to represent varying shades of political opinion, key positions were quickly taken by communists. By 1950 most non-communists had withdrawn and established their own organization, the World Assembly of Youth (WAY). Originally based in Paris, the WFDY was expelled by the French government in 1951. Its headquarters has since been in Budapest.

All youth organizations that contribute to the safeguarding of the activities of young persons are eligible for membership. A total membership of some 100 million persons in 200 organizations in 90 countries was claimed in 1970 (TASS, 12 October).

Structure and Leadership. The highest governing body of the WFDY is the Assembly, which convenes every three years, and to which all affiliated organizations send representatives. The Executive Committee is elected by the Assembly and is supposed to meet at least twice a year. The day-to-day work is conducted by the Bureau and its Secretariat. Roberto Viezzi (Italy) is president; Alain Therouse (France) is secretary-general.

WFDY subsidiaries include the International Committee of Children's and Adolescents' Movements (CIMEA), which organizes international camps and film festivals; the International Bureau of Tourism and Exchanges of Youth (BITEJ), charged with planning and supervising work camps and meetings; the International Sports Committee for Youth, which arranges special events in connection with the World Youth Festivals sponsored by the International Union of Students (IUS); and the International Voluntary Service for Friendship and Solidarity of Youth (SIVSAJ), geared to increasing WFDY influence in developing countries by sending "young volunteers" to work with the people of these countries.

Aims and Policies. The avowed aims of the WFDY are to contribute to the education of young persons in the spirit of freedom and democracy; to raise the living standard of the young; to end colonialism; to ensure peace and security in the world; to promote the active participation of young persons in economic, social, cultural, and political life; to ensure in all countries and for all young persons full freedom of speech, the press, religious belief, assembly, and organization; and to further the spirit of international friendship and support the principles of the United Nations. In practice, strong support of the Soviet Union and its policies has been evident in WFDY statements and actions. Since the emergence of the Sino-Soviet dispute, the Chinese have not participated in WFDY activities.

Views and Activities. Throughout 1972 the WFDY appeared to be primarily preoccupied with promoting a youth conference on European security and preparing for the 10th World Youth Festival.

The Florence "Youth Conference on European Security" (December 1971) laid plans for the convening of a youth conference on European security; the initial "preparatory seminar" for this conference was held in Lillehammer, Norway, 28 February—4 March 1972. The host for the Lillehammer meeting was the Norwegian National Committee (a member of the Council of European National Youth Committees—CENYC). In attendance were 52 delegates from 23 countries and representatives of the WFDY, IUS, and other international organizations (Helsinki radio, 3 March). Other preparatory seminars were held in Brussels and Budapest (*IUS News Service,* no. 8; Warsaw radio, 5 May). In June WFDY representatives attended a seminar organized by the Czechoslovak Union of Socialist Youth at which the youth conference on European security was the main topic (*Mladá fronta,* Prague, 14 June; CTK, Czechoslovak news agency, 23 June).

Official invitations to the youth conference were issued by the Finnish Organizing Committee. Co-sponsored by the WFDY and the CENYC, the "European Youth Security Conference," was held in Helsinki on 26–31 August. In attendance were 400 delegates from Europe, Canada, and the United States. Addressing the conference were the Finnish foreign minister and representatives of the WFDY, IUS, and CENYC (Helsinki radio, 26 August). The final communiqué called for recognition of East Germany, membership in the United Nations for both German states, respect for the sovereignty of all European states, limitation of nuclear weapons, and the convening of a European security conference (ibid., 30 August; TASS, 30 August). Several "conservative" youth organizations apparently refused to sign the communiqué as it related to the recognition of East Germany (*Suomenaa,* 31 August). *Mladá fronta* (30 August) referred to the impossibility of allowing "revanchist, racialist, and militaristic ideas" to be discussed, and added that some views were reminiscent of the cold war. A Soviet notice (TASS, 30 August) referred to disagreements, but indicated that they had been overcome. A representative of the Preparatory Committee of the Finnish youth organizations, reported that the conference "confirmed" that there was not yet agreement on the present European situation (*Mladá fronta,* 1 September).

Although the Helsinki meeting was its major effort in support of "European security," the WFDY also participated in the "Assembly of Representatives of Public Opinion on European Security and Cooperation," the most important conference on this theme sponsored by front organizations in 1972 (see *World Peace Council*).

For the 10th World Youth Festival—scheduled for the summer of 1973 in Berlin with the East German youth organization, the Free German Youth, as host (see *WFDY News,* no. 10, 1971)—a constituent conference of the festival's International Preparatory Committee (IPC) met in Sofia, Bulgaria, on 19–20 January 1972. Some 150 delegates from 60 youth organizations attended. The IPC appealed to "youth in all countries" to promote the festival with the "broadest anti-imperialist cooperation," (inviting) "international and national organizations, all political, trade union, and cultural organizations of youth and students which agree with this appeal" to take an active part in the preparations (*Mladá fronta,* 20, 21, 25 January). The Free German Youth created a national festival committee with Erich Honecker, first secretary of the East German Socialist Unity Party as chairman (ADN, East German news agency, 18 February).

The IPC meeting in Sofia set up a Provisional Working Group to coordinate activities between its sessions. Representatives of the Free German Youth and several international organizations, including the WFDY and IUS, made up the group, which met in East Berlin in

April, Prague in May, Budapest in June, and East Berlin again in August (*Neues Deutschland,* Berlin, 18 April; ADN, 23 August) to make plans for the second IPC session in October and for establishing national preparatory committees. By early in the fall there reportedly were 50 such committees (CTK, 27 September).

The second meeting of the IPC (East Berlin, 5–6 October) stressed that the aim of the pre-festival campaign was to create the widest possible unity of action of the "anti-imperialist forces." The festival's proposed new slogan, "For Anti-Imperialist Solidarity, Peace, and Friendship" was opposed by the British delegation, which determined to campaign under the old one, "For Solidarity, Peace, and Friendship." To work out a draft festival program the IPC elected a 22-member Permanent Commission (ADN, 3, 5, 7 October; *Mladá fronta,* 4, 6, 7 October; CTK, 7 October). During the session, the Provisional Working Group reported on proposals for the festival program (unanimously approved, although subject to amendments). These included "Festival Days" honoring Vietnam, the German Democratic Republic, National Liberation, "Solidarity with Youth and Students Fighting Militarism, Fascism, and Repression"; students, women, and "Action for Peace, Security and Cooperation"; major events devoted to "Indochina, Arab Youth and Students, Portuguese Colonies, Southern Africa and Apartheid"; Japan (anniversary of Hiroshima); the Anti-War and Black Power Movement in the USA, and "Cuba, Chile and other Latin American Struggles"; and an "Indochina Center" and an "Anti-Imperialist Center"; on "Problems of Young Workers, the Rights of School Students and Children, the Environment and Pollution, Student Power, Hunger in the World, and the Technological Revolution," and "the Reform and Democratization of Education" to discuss "education, health, drugs, sexual liberation, and regional issues"; and a conference to discuss "International Student Unity" (*Mladá fronta,* 6 October).

The WFDY participated in the "Asian Youth Seminar" in Kerala, India, 15–20 July. Sponsored by the WFDY and the IUS, with the All-India Youth Federation and the All-India Students' Federation as hosts, the seminar dealt with the socio-economic impact of "imperialist" economic aid to developing countries. Throughout, the differences between "imperialist" penetration and the aid of the socialist countries were discussed. The final resolution expressed solidarity with the "peoples of Indochina against U.S. imperialism," support for liberation struggles in Africa, and support for the forthcoming World Meeting of Working Youth in Moscow and the 10th World Youth Festival (*New Age,* New Delhi, 9, 23, 30 July; *Mladá fronta,* 2 August).

In Latin America, WFDY President Viezzi attended the congress of "Young Communists of Cuba" on 30 March (ibid., 31 March). The WFDY, the IUS, the Federation of Central American University Students, and the Federation of University Students of Costa Rica sponsored a "meeting of solidarity with the peoples of Guatemala and El Salvador" in San José, El Salvador, 27 April (*El Siglo,* Santiago, 28 April). In a telegram to the Chilean government, the WFDY expressed "solidarity with the Chilean people in their fight against the machinations of American imperialism and announced its decision to organize an international campaign to expose the policy of American "imperialism" (*Mladá fronta,* 6 April). In the fall, WFDY Secretary-General Therouse attended the congress of "Young Communists of Chile" (*El Siglo,* 6–7 September).

A WFDY delegation was present at the second congress of the Connolly Youth Movement, in Dublin, 28–29 October. In a policy statement the movement declared that it was "a communist youth group" and that through its affiliation with the WFDY it had built up fraternal relations with Marxist youth organizations over the world (*Irish Times,* Dublin, 30 October).

The first secretary of the Albanian Union of Working Youth reported to its congress on the "ugly phenomena and degeneration characterizing the capitalist world" and said: "the activity of the WFDY and the IUS, which have been placed completely under the control of the Soviet revisionists and have been transformed into tools of their opportunist, counter-revolutionary, and social-imperialist policy, bear witness to all this quite clearly" (ATA, Albanian news agency, 23 October).

The final WFDY meeting of the year took place in Moscow on 10–15 November. Called a major event in the "Youth Accuses Imperialism" campaign, this so-called International Conference on Working Youth in Contemporary Society, brought together 271 socialist, social democratic and Christian youth organizations, WFDY affiliates, and youth sections of trade unions from 115 countries. Also represented were the IUS, WFTU, WPC, ILO, and United Nations (TASS, Telegraphic Agency of the Soviet Union, 10 November; *L'Humanité,* 11 November). Speeches were given by Gennady Yanayev, chairman of the USSR Committee for Youth Organizations, Boris Ponomarev, CPSU Secretary and candidate Politburo member, WFDY president Roberto Viezzi (Italy), and WPC Presidential Committee member Evgeny Fedorov (USSR). In a final statement, the Conference urged young workers to support stronger international solidarity and greater unity among anti-imperialist forces; hailed young workers of the socialist countries; voiced solidarity with youth in developing countries fighting imperialism; and welcomed progress made in preparation for the Conference on European Security and Cooperation (Moscow Radio and TASS, 10–15 November).

Publications. The WFDY publishes a bimonthly magazine, *World Youth,* in English, French, German, and Arabic (new). Its monthly *WFDY News* appears in English, French, and Spanish. Other publications are directed to specific areas of interest, including special magazines and pamphlets to commemorate congresses, festivals, and other events.

California State College,   Paul F. Magnelia
Stanislaus

World Federation
of Scientific Workers

The World Federation of Scientific Workers (WFSW) was founded in London in 1946 at the initiative of the British Association of Scientific Workers, with 18 organizations of scientists from 14 countries taking part. Although it purported to be a scientific rather than a political organization, communists obtained most official posts at the start, and have kept control since. The headquarters is in London, but the secretary-general's office is in Paris.

WFSW membership is open to organizations of scientific workers everywhere and to individual scientists in countries where no affiliated groups are active. The WFSW claims to represent 300,000 scientists in 30 countries; most of the membership derives from 14 groups in communist-ruled countries. (The only large non-communist affiliate, the British Association of Scientific Workers, has 21,000 members.) Scientists of distinction who do not belong to an affiliated organization may be nominated for "corresponding membership." The WFSW has a constitution and a "Charter for Scientific Workers" to which affiliates must subscribe (see *YICA, 1968*, p. 736).

Structure and Leadership. The governing body of the WFSW is the General Assembly, in which all affiliated organizations are represented. Nine General Assembly meetings have been held, the latest in April 1969, in Paris. Between meetings, the Executive Council is responsible for controlling WFSW activities, but the Bureau conducts the day-by-day work. The Bureau consists of the WFSW president, vice-presidents, treasurer, Executive Council chairman and vice-chairman, chairman of the Editorial Board, and heads of regional centers. Dr. Eric Burhop (United Kingdom) is president; Pierre Biquard (France) is secretary-general.

Principles and Aims. The stated aims of the WFSW are to work for the fullest utilization of science in promoting peace and welfare of mankind; to promote international cooperation in science and technology; to encourage the freedom and coordination of scientific work; to improve the professional, social and economic status of scientific workers, and to encourage scientific workers to take an active part in public affairs. Although the aims appear to minimize political involvement, the WFSW has from the start taken an active interest in and stand on political issues, in all cases favoring the Soviet Union.

Views and Activities. In 1972 the WFSW Bureau met on 19 May and the Executive Council on 20–22 May, both in Paris. The Bureau meeting passed resolutions demanding removal of all discrimination regarding invitations to the Stockholm Environmental Conference and calling for the admission of East Germany to the U.N. special agencies. At the Council meeting Burhop pointed to three areas in which the WFSW should increase its activities: international scientific cooperation, development of ties with the main international trade unions, and the development of methods to resolve problems created by the growth of monopolies in Western Europe. The Council agreed to organize a West European conference on problems of research and development (for March 1973), to issue the appeal on the abolition of nuclear weapons which was first drawn up at a conference in East Berlin, November 1971; and to push forward on the "Commission of Inquiry into Chemical Warfare in the Portuguese African Territories," jointly sponsored by the WFSW and the British Society for Social Responsibility in Science. The three French affiliates agreed to coordinate their work within the WFSW and to hold in the fall a seminar on problems of research in France.

In a statement circulated at a summer school in Como organized by the Italian Physics Society, the WFSW condemned U.S. bombing in Vietnam and asked all scientists to take a firm stand against the bombing (*L'Unità,* Rome, 14 August).

WFSW president Burhop was awarded the Lenin Peace Prize (Moscow radio, 3 May).

Publications. The official publication of the WFSW is *Scientific World,* issued bimonthly in English, French, Russian, German, Spanish, and Czechoslovak editions. The WFSW *Bulletin,* issued irregularly and only to members, is published in English, French, German, and Russian editions. "Science and Mankind" is the general title of a series of WFSW booklets that have appeared in several languages. The WFSW also publishes pamphlets on particular subjects from time to time.

California State College,   Paul F. Magnelia
Stanislaus

World Federation of Trade Unions

The World Federation of Trade Unions (WFTU), set up at the initiative of the British Trade Union Congress, held its founding congress in October 1945 in Paris, where its first headquarters was established. Expelled from Paris and next from Vienna for subversive activities, the headquarters has been in Prague since 1956. At Soviet insistence, Louis Saillant (France) was elected the WFTU's first secretary-general. He is generally considered responsible for bringing the WFTU Secretariat and other ruling bodies under communist control. Some non-communist affiliates in 1949 gave up their membership to found an alternative organization, the International Conference of Free Trade Unions (ICFTU).

Structure and Leadership. The highest authority of the WFTU is the Congress; it meets every four years and is composed of delegates from affiliates in proportion to the number of their members. The latest congress, at Budapest in 1969, drew 461 delegates, observers, and guests from 97 countries and was said to be representative of 153 million workers, organized in more than 50 national affiliated organizations and almost as many non-affiliated groups. The Congress, which has no policy-making function and is too large to transact much specific business, elects the General Council, Executive Bureau, and Secretariat. The 1969 meeting elected a General Council of 66 regular and 68 deputy members, representing the national affiliates and 11 "Trade Union Internationals" (TUIs). It chose an Executive Bureau composed of the newly elected WFTU president, Enrique Pastorino (Uruguay), and secretary-general, Pierre Gensous (France), along with 23 others representing various parts of the world; two seats were left vacant for representatives of China and Indonesia. The Executive Bureau, comparable to a politburo, is the most powerful body of the WFTU. It has assumed much of the authority which before 1969 was enjoyed by the Secretariat. The Secretariat was revamped by the Congress and reduced to 6 members, including the secretary-general.

The Trade Union Internationals represent workers of particular trades and crafts. One of the main purposes of the TUIs is to recruit local unions which do not, through their national centers, belong to the WFTU. Though the TUIs are in theory independent (each TUI has its own offices and officials, holds its own meetings, and publishes its own bulletin), their policies and finances are controlled by the WFTU department having supervision over their particular areas. The WFTU General Council in December 1966 decided that each TUI should have its own constitution; this move for bolstering the appearance of independence had the purpose of allowing the TUIs to join international bodies as individual organizations.

A number of subsidiary WFTU organizations deal with specific problems and seek the collaboration of non-communist trade unionists in solving them. One of the most important, the "Special Commission on U.N. Agencies," was established in 1967 to try to expand WFTU activities in the United Nations. The WFTU is permanently represented at the U.N. in

New York, the International Labor Organization (ILO) in Geneva, the Food and Agriculture Organization in Rome, and UNESCO in Paris, and enjoys Category A status with a number of U.N. agencies.

Aims and Policies. The WFTU constitution states that the federation exists "to improve the living and working conditions of the people of all lands." It details the prime purposes of the WFTU as (1) to organize and unite within its ranks the trade unions of the whole world irrespective of considerations of race, nationality, religion, or political opinion; (2) to assist, whenever necessary, the workers of socially or industrially less-developed countries in setting up their trade unions; (3) to carry on the struggle for the extermination of all fascist forms of government and every manifestation of fascism; and (4) to combat war and the causes of war and work for a stable and enduring peace.

The constitution clearly endorses political activity by the WFTU. Non-communist unions have complained that the WFTU is subservient to the Soviet Union and that it supports Soviet causes around the world, while reserving adverse criticism for Western countries or those politically at odds with the Soviet Union. Chinese trade unions have been inactive in the WFTU since 1966.

Views and Activities. WFTU secretary-general Gensous stated the theme of much of the WFTU's activities in 1972 when he wrote that this would be "a year of new steps along the road to unity of action by trade unions of different organizations" (*Trud,* Moscow, 14 January). The emphasis on "unity of action" was repeated at the Bureau meeting in Moscow, 25–26 March, where the first item on the agenda was "Present-day development of international trade union links and unity" (TASS, 25 March) and a resolution urged all affiliated organizations to step up activities to strengthen unity. The resolution called for a joint rebuff by the WFTU, the ICFTU, and the World Confederation of Labor (WCL) to the challenge made by capitalism; took note of existing multilateral initiatives, particularly the planned joint trade-union conferences in Europe, Asia, and Latin America; and urged the widest cooperation among "all trade union organizations to make the work of the International Labor Organization more dynamic." It added: "International unity can and should be expanded in the interests of protecting peace, of aiding the peoples struggling for liberation from colonialism and neo-colonialism, for winning and expanding democratic freedoms." (TASS, 26 March; *World Trade Union Movement,* April.)

The drive for "unity" and "links" with other organizations was clearly visible in the WFTU's efforts to gain greater influence in the ILO and its specialized agencies. This work was seen as rather important since the governing body of the ILO would be reelected in 1972 (*World Trade Union Movement,* January). At Dubrovnik, Yugoslavia, 2–4 February, the WFTU, WCL, All-African Trade Union Federation (AATUF), Standing Congress of Trade Union Unity of Latin America (CPUSTAL), International Confederation of Arab Trade Unions (ICATU), Irish Congress of Trade Unions (ICTU), General Council of Japanese Trade Unions ("Sohyo"), and Confederation of Yugoslav Trade Unions discussed the situation in the ILO Workers' Group and the promoting of joint action among trade unions of differing views at the ILO (*News in Brief,* no. 6).

At Brussels, 11 April, a trade union meeting on unity at the ILO, brought together the same organizations along with the Brotherhood of Asian Trade Unionists (BATU), Latin American Workers Centre (CLAT), and Pan-African Federation of Believing Workers (PAFBW). The purpose of this meeting was to complete "the exchange of opinions already begun within the framework of the preparations for the International Labor Conference to be held in June of this year." It was noted that elections to the Workers' Group on the ILO Governing Body were to be held at the June conference, and that the elections should be prepared through real cooperation among all trade union organizations. (*News in Brief*, no. 16.)

The thrust behind repeated references to the elections and real cooperation was somewhat clarified in an article in *World Trade Union Movement* (April). The WFTU pointed out that the ILO was going through a crisis which could "be overcome only through radical changes in structure, program and practical activities." The way to this radical change was seen as lying in "the widest possible cooperation among all genuine trade union organizations."

The 186th session of the ILO Governing Body met on 2–3 June; the 57th conference of the ILO on 7–27 June, both in Geneva. The WFTU asked the Governing Body to study several matters, including the hanging by the Sudanese government of Shafi Ahmad al-Shaikh, a former WFTU vice-president. The WFTU strongly supported several agreed-upon meetings, including one on the relation between multinational companies and social policy; another was the Fourth African Regional Conference. The WFTU welcomed the ILO's decision to nominate WFTU candidates to a study group on young workers' problems. (*News in Brief*, no. 27/28.)

The WFTU like the other front organizations continued to promote the Soviet-proposed European security conference. This effort involved the mobilization of labor unions, primarily through the WFTU's proposed European trade union conference. In January the WFTU Secretariat after consultation with an East German trade union delegation and Alexander Shelepin (president of the General Council of Soviet Trade Unions) stated that it attached great importance to the convening of an all-European trade union conference and to the "speedy convening of a European security conference" (CTK, Czechoslovak news agency, 7 January). The secretary of the French General Confederation of Labor (CGT) also called for a trade union conference which would include trade unions of the German Democratic Republic (TASS, 16 March). Such a demand paralleled the Soviet insistence that the security conference formalize existing political frontiers (notably of East Germany). Gensous stated that the trade union conference would help strengthen the trend toward unity and cooperation and would logically include joint action for peace and security (*News in Brief*, no. 28). Discussion continued on the proposed trade union conference, but no definite date was decided upon. The WFTU supported and attended the Brussels "Assembly of the Peoples of Europe on Security and Cooperation," which was sponsored by the World Peace Council.

The quest for "unity" was apparent in WFTU activities in Latin America. In the December 1971 issue of the *World Trade Union Movement*, Gensous stated that CPUSTAL, with WFTU support, had contributed to trade union coordination on the continental level. He added that the WFTU was prepared to give its full backing to CPUSTAL's proposed "Latin American Conference of Unity and Solidarity," which according to a February 1972 decision by the CPUSTAL Secretariat would be held in 1973 (*World Trade Union Movement*, May). CPUSTAL can be viewed as the Latin American regional arm of the WFTU.

Early in 1972 the WFTU sought to better its relations with the ICFTU through a letter to the general secretary of that body (*News in Brief*, no. 4). In the fall, ICFTU's rejection of relations and contacts were described by the WFTU as causing embarrassment and incomprehension (*World Trade Union Movement*, September).

The WFTU position on the Common Market underwent a forced change. Initially opposed to an expanded market, the WFTU at its Bureau meeting in Moscow seemed to be preparing for the inevitable when it put forward general proposals for wider European trade union cooperation against multinational companies in a broader Europe (TASS, 25–26 March). At the same time, it continued to publicize, and thus encourage, the existing opposition to an expanded market. The anti-market position of the unions in Denmark and Norway was reviewed in articles in *World Trade Union Movement* (April).

The "3rd World Conference on the Problems of Working Women," Prague, 25–28 April, was organized by the WFTU and the Central Council of the Czechoslovak Revolutionary Trade Union Movement. Some 200 delegates from 70 countries attended. The conference issued an appeal for trade unions "to intensify their struggle for the legitimate demands of working women" and to promote women to "leading positions in the unions" (*CTK*, 25–28 April; *Mladá fronta*, 26 April).

The WFTU Youth Committee, meeting in East Berlin, 11–13 April, declared itself in full support of the proposed 10th World Youth Festival (TASS, 13 April). (See *World Federation of Democratic Youth*.)

The WFTU continued its criticism of U.S. policy in Indochina, condemning the "brutal bombing raids" and the mining of ports (TASS, 27 June) and appealing to all workers and trade unions to observe the "Week of Solidarity with the Peoples of Indochina," called by the Stockholm Conference on Vietnam (*News in Brief*, no. 38).

In maintaining its negative attitude toward Israeli policy, the WFTU condemned the September Israeli air attacks on Syria and Lebanon, and sent "solidarity" messages to the International Confederation of Arab Trade Unions, the General Federation of Workers of Syria, the Lebanese Federation of Workers and Employees, and the Palestinian Trade Union Federation (ibid., no. 37).

The WFTU backed Iraq's decision to nationalize the Iraqi Petroleum Company and was represented at an international trade union conference in Baghdad, 15–19 July, in support of the nationalization (Iraqi News Agency, 19 July).

The WFTU hailed the "victory in the struggle for national liberation" of the working class of Bangladesh (*News in Brief*, no. 5); praised the trade unions in Northern Ireland, condemning those who sought to divide the workers by sectarian demands and calling for the immediate introduction of a bill of rights and the ending of internment without trial (ibid., no. 15); expressed satisfaction at the acquittal of U.S. communist Angela Davis (ibid., no. 23); and on several occasions petitioned the ILO regarding police intervention and the arrest of several trade union leaders in Spain (ibid., no. 26). In a statement on Latin America, the WFTU called on all trade unions to support the Brazilian people against "U.S. imperialism and the Brazilian dictatorship," and extended praise to the Chilean people and government (ibid.).

The WFTU came under criticism from the Albanian Central Trade Union Council, whose president stated that the Albanian Trade Unions have relations with over 100 national trade unions, and that this was "living proof of the failure of efforts of the Soviet revisionists and the treacherous leading clique of the World Federation of Trade Unions to isolate the Albanian Trade Unions." Regarding WFTU promotion of unity in trade union movements of all countries, he added: "One knows that the working class would pay dearly for such unity." (ATA, Albanian news agency, 8 May).

TUI leaders from France and Syria represented the World Federation of Teachers—a TUI—at the "First International Trade Union Meeting of Teachers" in Budapest, 6–8 June, attended by 89 delegates from 41 countries. The theme of the meeting was "Young Teachers' Problems and the Role of Trade Unions in Solving Them." (*World Trade Union Movement*, April; *L'Humanité*, Paris, 8 June.)

On 1–3 November, the 22nd WFTU General Council meeting was held at Bucharest. Attending were representatives from more than 50 countries. Among the major speakers was CPSU Politburo member Aleksandr Shelepin, who stressed that "unity of action by the world in trade union movements is striking roots ever more firmly in the minds and hearts of millions. . . ." The future WFTU task, therefore, should be to seek united action in the battle for workers' vital interests, peace and social progress. In this regard, Shelepin cited increased ties between Soviet trade unions (which he heads) and West German, Swedish, American, and Canadian organizations, and visits to the U.S.S.R. by many ICFTU-affiliated Latin American movements (*Trud,* 3 November). Shelepin, Konstantin Gyiaurov (Bulgaria), and Sandor Gaspar (Hungary) all spoke of the need for cooperation among European trade unions, and indicated that agreement had been reached on the holding of a "European Trade Union Conference" within the framework of the second European regional International Labor Organization meeting in 1973 (Ibid.; Bulgarian Telegraphic Agency BTA, 1 November; *Nepszava,* 3 November). In addition to the question of unity, the General Council reviewed problems relating to Indochina and the Middle East, as well as preparations for the Eighth WFTU Congress, scheduled for October 1973 in Berlin.

Publications. The most important publication of the WFTU is the illustrated magazine *World Trade Union Movement.* It is circulated in some 70 countries in English, French, Spanish, German, Russian, and other foreign-language editions. The monthly bulletin *News in Brief* is published in four languages. Leaflets, pamphlets, brochures, or booklets are issued as activities or interests warrant.

California State College,   Paul F. Magnelia
Stanislaus

World Peace Council

The "World Peace" movement headed by the World Peace Council (WPC) dates from August 1948, when a "World Congress of Intellectuals for Peace" in Wroclaw, Poland, set up an organization called the "International Liaison Committee of Intellectuals." This committee in April 1949 convened a "First World Peace Congress" in Paris. The Congress launched a "World Committee of Partisans of Peace", which in November 1950 was renamed the "World Peace Council." Originally based in Paris, it was expelled in 1951 by the French Government, moving first to Prague and then, in 1954, to Vienna—where it adopted the name "World Council of Peace." Although outlawed in Austria in 1957, the World Council of Peace continued its operations in Vienna under the cover of a new organization, the International Institute for Peace (IIP). The IIP has subsequently been referred to by WPC members as the "scientific-theoretical workshop of the WPC" (*CTK, Czechoslovak news agency,* 16 December 1971). In September 1968 the World Council of Peace transferred its headquarters to Helsinki, while the IIP remained in Vienna. Although no formal announcement was made, the World Council of Peace has reverted to its original name, the World Peace Council.

Structure and Leadership. The WPC is organized on a national basis, with "Peace Committees" in some 80 countries. No figure of the total number of members has ever been disclosed, but the WPC has members from more than 100 countries, most of them representing Peace Committees. The highest authorities of the WPC are its 600-member (maximum) Council, the Council-elected 50-member Presidential Committee, and the Committee-elected 15-member Secretariat. The Presidential Committee and Secretariat exercise control between Council sessions. The executive bodies of the IIP—ostensibly independent of those of the WPC, but in fact elected by the WPC Council—are the 7-member Presidium and 30-member Executive Committee.

A number of structural changes adopted by the 1971 Assembly increased the authority and control of the WPC over the various Peace Committees and even individual members (see *YICA, 1972,* p. 637).

Two new "commissions" became operative in 1972. In January, a "Development Commission" was set up to offer more effective support to developing countries. (*Peace Courier,* March). The new "Cultural Commission" met for the first time in March. Its task was defined as the creation of a large-scale social movement comprising intellectuals to struggle for peace, security, and progress (*PAP,* Polish press agency, 4 March).

Romesh Chandra (India) remained as WPC secretary-general in 1972.

Principles and Aims. The WPC, according to its stated tenets, favors general disarmament; elimination of all forms of colonialism and racial discrimination; and respect for the territorial integrity, popular sovereignty, and independence of every state. From its inception, however, the WPC has defended the policies of the Soviet Union and attacked those of the Western powers in every instance where such issues were at stake. Recent activities have focused primarily upon "U.S. aggression" in Southeast Asia and support of the Soviet call for a new European security system. Increasingly, the WPC is attempting to broaden and coordinate the efforts of its members and affiliates in various parts of the world by linking, as joint objects of attack, what it characterizes as (1) "racism" and "neo-colonialism"—from the United States to the Portuguese colonies and to South Africa and Rhodesia; (2) "imperialism" —the United States, West Germany, and Israel; and (3) "fascism"—Greece, Portugal, and Spain. Although a broad segment within the WPC disapproved of the 1968 Soviet-led invasion of Czechoslovakia, the WPC as an organization has remained firm in its support of the Soviet Union. The People's Republic of China has not participated in WPC activities for several years.

Views and Activities. The lead article in *Peace Courier,* January 1972, set forth the broad outlines of the WPC's activities in 1972. Pointing to the need to step up the struggle for peace, it called for expanded publicity, the inclusion of ever greater numbers of people in powerful campaigns, and the strengthening of existing organizations.

The Presidential Committee meeting in Helsinki, 28–31 January, drew representatives of Peace Committees from some 50 countries. Identified as the main goals of the WPC were "victory over US imperialist aggression in Indochina," "a political settlement in the Middle East" with "full implementation" of U.N. Security Council resolution 242, "a Conference on European Security [and] action to unmask the activities of American imperialism and of NATO in the Mediterranean," "full support to the growing struggles of the peoples of Latin America," and "the intensification of the struggle of the African people against colonialism and racist regimes" (*Peace Courier,* February). The committee also pledged its backing for national liberation movements in Angola, Guinea Bissau and the Cape Verde Island, Mozambique, South Africa, South West Africa, and Rhodesia (*Conference Documents*).

WPC support for a European security conference meant in the first instance support for its proposed "Assembly of Representatives of Public Opinion on European Security and Cooperation." This "assembly," under discussion for several years, was viewed by the WPC and similar organizations as a vehicle to mobilize wide-scale public backing for the proposed security conference. In a series of meetings to prepare for and publicize the proposed assembly, on 11–13 January some 200 persons, mostly WPC members, attended a "consultative" meeting in Brussels (*Peace Courier,* January; *Le Soir,* Brussels, 14 January; TK, 14 January); on 18–19 April in Brussels a "Preparatory Committee" session was attended by some 60 representatives from throughout Europe; and the "European Security Commission," set up at the 8th World Assembly for Peace, East Berlin, June 1969, met in Bratislava on 29–30 April.

The Assembly, in Brussels on 2–5 June, was attended by some 1,000 delegates from 28 countries. Maurice Lambilliotte, who had "managed" the preparatory efforts since 1968 (*Neue Zürcher Zeitung,* 7 May), was chairman of the Belgium-Soviet Society and a leading figure in the IIP; he died on 12 August 1972 (*Le Soir,* 13 August). Besides Chandra, Presidential Committee members attended the assembly from Belgium, the Soviet Union, West Germany, Finland, and France. Also in attendance were high officials of several front organizations. Messages were received from U.N. Secretary General Kurt Waldheim, the heads of state of East European governments, and several cardinals from Western Europe (*Conference Documents; Le Soir,* 4, 5 June).

The work of the Assembly was conducted in three commissions: political, economic and cultural. The central focus of the deliberations of all three bodies was consistent with the stated aim of the Assembly: mobilization of public opinion for a European security conference (*Conference Documents*). Looking forward to post-Assembly activities, "specialized" groups—women, trade unionists, youth, churchmen, and writers, among others—met during the conference and discussed tactics for organizing specific segments of society. Plans were laid or further developed for the holding of an international youth conference on European security in August, a trade union conference later in 1972, and a women's conference in August 1973 (*ibid; Le Soir,* 4, 5 June).

In order to carry on the work of the Assembly, two permanent committees were created. The Working Secretariat, in Brussels, was to assist the "National Committees for European Security and Cooperation" in organizing meetings, supplying documents, and publicizing the aims of the Assembly. The Initiative Committee was transformed into the Committee for Contacts and Coordination, and instructed to seek political implementation of the goals of peace, security and cooperation. Reportedly this latter committee was created as a result of Soviet pressure (*L'Humanité,* Paris, 6 June. *Avanti,* Rome, 13 June).

The WPC continued in 1972 its activity in various conferences, meetings, and protests condemning "U.S. imperialism" in Indochina. By far the major activity of this sort was the "World Assembly for Peace and Independence of the Indochinese Peoples," held in Paris (Versailles) on 11–13 February. Assisting the WPC in preparing for this assembly were the Stockholm Conference on Vietnam and several French organizations (*Guardian,* London, 12 February). In an interview on East Berlin television (20 January) Chandra stated: "US imperialists are desperately maneuvering to lull international opinion. . . . Therefore, the Paris meeting will draw the attention of the entire international community to the fact that Nixon and his friends are lying when they say that they are going to discontinue the war." Attending this meeting were 1,200 delegates from 84 countries and representatives from various front organizations. Besides Chandra, Presidential Committee members were present from Italy, Belgium, Japan, and Guyana (TASS, 1, 12, 14 February; *Mladá fronta,* Prague, 17 February). The report of the assembly's Action Commission called for the cooperation of trade unions, political and cultural groups, and religious organizations in a common struggle against "U.S. imperialism"; urged the coordinated activity of the international anti-war movement and the organization of world-wide rallies in support of the "peoples of Indochina"; and proposed a coordinated campaign of action against big American firms profiting from the war.

The Executive Committee of the Stockholm Conference on Vietnam met in Stockholm on 18 March and in line with the recommendations of the Paris assembly, enlarged itself to include representation for the All-African Trade Union Federation (AATFU), the International Confederation of Arab Trade Unions (ICATU), and the Permanent Congress of Trade Union Unity of Latin America (CPUSTAL). The Executive Committee also formed a Bureau to carry out its activities between sessions (WFTU *News in Brief,* March). (For the relationship between the WPC and the Stockholm Conference on Vietnam see *YICA, 1969,* pp. 942–44.)

Throughout the summer and fall the WPC repeatedly denounced "U.S. imperialism" in Indochina and organized a variety of "protests" on behalf of the peoples of the area, also designating 13–19 March a "Week of Solidarity with Indochina" and 1 August a "day of international protest" against U.S. bombing raids on the dams and dikes in North Vietnam (WPC circular, 28 February; TASS, 2 August).

The third meeting of the "War Crimes Commission," set up by the Stockholm Conference on Vietnam, was held in Copenhagen, 10–16 October, "under the auspices of the World Peace Council and Vietnam."

The "Conference on Peace and Justice in the Middle East," cosponsored by the WPC and the Afro-Asian Peoples' Solidarity Organization and originally planned for late 1971, had been postponed to 1972. On 1–2 March, a Preparatory Conference convened in Rome with representatives from 20 countries present. The participants expressed the wish to hold the conference at Bologna in 1972, but the vagueness of the communications issued at the time left the impression that there were difficulties in getting the conference organized. One possible factor affecting the preparations was brought to light by an Iraqi representative, who stated that political conditions in Egypt and the arrest of the secretary-general of that country's peace committee had adversely influenced the efforts of the preparatory groups (*Baghdad Observer,* 29 February). Information appearing during the spring and early summer indicated that the conference was being postponed again and rescheduled for early 1973. The postponement was confirmed when the International Organizing Committee, meeting in Rome on 24 October, noted in a communiqué the persistence of the crisis in the Middle East and said that as a consequence there was a growing urgency for the development of more effective popular action for a political solution to the conflict. The committee then stressed that the conference would be open to all forces and personalities. No date was set, and the committee arranged to meet again in January 1973 (*L'Humanité,* 30 October; *L'Unità,* Rome, 2 November).

In July it was announced that a joint WPC-AAPSO "Conference of Solidarity with Iraq" would be held in Baghdad on 17–18 August to discuss "the solidarity of world progressive opinion with the severe struggle waged by the Iraqi people against the policy of plunder of the imperialist monopolies" (*Baghdad Observer,* 7 July). Attending the conference were delegates from 45 countries in Africa, America, Asia, and Europe, representing national organizations, international front organizations, and the Palestine Liberation Movement. The conference, opened by the president of Iraq, adopted a political declaration stating that Iraq's decision to nationalize the Iraq Petroleum Company was a historic act which had special significance in the struggle against imperialism and its monopolies. An action program outlining the methods to be employed in support of Iraq was drawn up: meetings, demonstrations, and resolutions were suggested as means of resisting attempts to boycott the importation of Iraqi oil; popular organizations in all peace-loving and non-aligned countries were to be encouraged to press their governments into purchasing Iraqi oil; and the "International Seminar on Oil," to be held in Baghdad, 10–16 November, was pointed to as a weapon against imperialism (Baghdad radio, 18 August). At the final press conference, Chandra indicated that the solidarity conference with Iraq was merely the first round in support of the Iraqi people, and that the next would involve activities directed at the peoples of the United States and Britain so as to create a strong public opinion that would compel these countries to stop their "economic aggression" against Iraq. He also announced that Iraq would explain its battle against the oil companies at an international conference for peace and afro-asian solidarity, in Calcutta, 20–24 September (ibid., 19 August).

In Calcutta, 20–24 September, Chandra inaugurated this "All-India Congress for Peace and Solidarity." The congress was sponsored by the All-India Peace Council and the Indian Association for Afro-Asian Peoples' Solidarity, which merged during the congress to form the All-Indian Peace and Solidarity Organization (*Hindustani Standard,* Calcutta, 23 September).

The 4–9 October Presidential Committee meeting in Santiago, Chile, attended by delegates from some 70 countries, paid special attention to the "struggle of the Latin American peoples against imperialism" (*Conference Documents; El Siglo,* Santiago, 7, 8 October). Chandra hailed Chile as a great example to the whole world and emphasized that beside Chile stood the Soviet Union, the whole socialist camp, and the world's anti-imperialist forces. He then spoke of the importance of bringing into the WPC other organizations "with which a common interest unites us and which we also defend together." Referring to the many organizations which had come out against the war in Vietnam, against Israel's annexationist policy, and for the liberation of Latin America, he said "we must talk with these organizations, we must heed their proposals and they in their turn must heed ours." Extending a general invitation, he asked that political, trade union, and solidarity organizations take part in the forthcoming WPC Congress in Moscow (ibid., 6–8 October). Among other speakers was U.S. communist Angela Davis, who denounced U.S. policy in Vietnam and called the meeting "a demonstration of solidarity and support for the just struggle that Chile is waging for her independence and sovereignty" (ibid., 6–7 October; *Prensa Latina,* Cuban news agency, 9 October). The Soviet-proposed European security conference was among the topics endorsed by the meeting (*Conference Documents; El Siglo,* 9 October).

A WPC "fact-finding mission" visited Northern Ireland in April. Later a member of the mission delivered a petition to the British prime minister, calling for the release of all internees, withdrawal of British forces, and abolition of the Special Powers Act (Moscow radio, 28 April).

Leaders of the WPC and the IIP met in February to discuss future cooperation (WPC letter, no. 10, 9 March). The WPC's Commission on Racism and Racial Discrimination, meeting in Brussels, 29–30 May, condemned white minority regimes in Africa, Israeli policy, and racial discrimination in the United States and Latin America. It recommended increased material aid to "national liberation" movements, the holding of a conference against racism and racial discrimination in 1973, and increased support for a campaign to mobilize world opinion against apartheid in South Africa. (*IUS New Service,* no. 12.) After a visit to Iceland by a WPC delegation, the WPC gave full support to that country in its dispute with Great Britain and West Germany over fishing limits (*Thjodviljinn,* Reykjavík, 6–9 May).

In a statement on 8 September the WPC described the killing of Israeli athletes at the Olympics in Munich as "sad and bloody expression of the tragedy of the Palestinian Arab people."

Publications. The WPC issues a semimonthly bulletin, *Peace Courier,* in English, French, Spanish, and German, and a quarterly journal, *New Perspectives,* in English and French. The WPC also distributes occasionally a *Letter to National Committees,* and a *Letter* to members. Documents, statements, and press releases are issued in connection with conferences and campaigns.

California State College,   Paul F. Magnelia
Stanislaus

BIBLIOGRAPHY

General on Communism

Alberdi, P. G. *Los países socialistas en la historia contemporánea.* Buenos Aires, Ediciones Centro de estudios, 1972. 256 pp.

Antimilitarismus. Aus den Erfahrungen des antimilitaristischen Kampfes der kommunistischen Weltbewegung. Ein Handbuch für den antimilitaristischen Kampf heute. Erlangen, Karl-Liebknecht Verlag, 1971. 250 pp.

Basmanov, M. *Trotskyite Efforts to Win Over Youth.* Moscow, Novosti, 1972. 80 pp.

Beilenson, Laurence W. *Power Through Subversion.* Washington, D.C., Public Affairs Press, 1972. 312 pp.

Blond, Georges. *La Grande armée du drapeau noir; les anarchistes à travers le monde.* Paris, Tallandier, 1972. 445 pp.

Dunn, John M. *Modern Revolutions.* New York, Cambridge University Press, 1972. 346 pp.

Fedoseyev, P. N. *Marksizm v XX veke: Marks, Engels, Lenin i sovremennost.* Moscow, Mysl, 1972. 582 pp.

Fricke, Karl Wilhelm. *Warten auf Gerechtigkeit. Kommunistische Säuberungen und Rehabilitierungen. Bericht und Dokumentation.* Cologne, Verlag Wissenschaft & Politik, 1971. 256 pp.

Garaudy, Roger. *The Crisis in Communism: The Turning Point of Socialism.* New York, Grove Press, 1972. 256 pp.

Ghioldi, Rodolfo. *Lenin y el pensamiento contemporáneo.* Buenos Aires, Editorial Anteo, 1972. 77 pp.

Huberman, Leo. *El ABC del socialismo.* Buenos Aires, Dist. Tres Américas, 1972.

Kapur, Harish. *The Soviet Union and the Emerging Nations.* New York, Humanities Press, 1972. 124 pp.

Kapustin, O. *The World Revolutionary Process at the Present Stage.* Moscow, Novosti, 1972. 192 pp.

Library of Congress. *World Communism, 1964–1969.* Vol. 2. Washington, D.C., Government Printing Office, 1972.

Luard, Evan, ed. *The International Regulation of Civil Wars.* New York, New York University Press, 1972. 240 pp.

Martinet, Gilles. *Los cinco comunismos: ruso; yugoslavo; chino; checoeslovaco; cubano.* Caracas, Editorial Tiempo Nuevo, 1972. 237 pp.

Matthews, Herbert L. *A World in Revolution: A Newspaperman's Memoir.* New York, Scribner, 1972. 462 pp.

Ogurtsov, S. *Modern Trotskyism on Revolution, War and Peace.* Moscow, Novosti, 1972. 80 pp.

Schapiro, Leonard, ed. *Political Opposition in One-Party States.* New York, Halsted Press, 1972. 289 pp.

Skvortsov, L. *Ideology and Social Progress.* Moscow, Novosti, 1972. 176 pp.

Sobolev, A. *The Anti-Revolutionary Essence of the Theory and Policy of Modern Trotsky-ism.* Moscow, Novosti, 1972. 80 pp.

Solovyev, O. *The Socialist Revolution: Facts and Fiction.* Moscow, Novosti, 1972. 208 pp.

Staar, Richard F., ed. *Yearbook on International Communist Affairs, 1972.* Stanford, Calif., Hoover Institution Press, 1972. 708 pp.

U.S. Department of State. *World Strength of the Communist Party Organizations.* Washington, D.C., Government Printing Office, 1972. 159 pp.

Welch, Claude E., Jr., and Taintor, Mavis Bunker. *Revolution and Political Change.* Belmont, Calif., Duxbury Press, 1972. 350 pp.

Wörterbuch der Marxistisch-leninistischen Soziologie. 2d ed. Opladen, Westdeutscher Verlag, 1971. 536 pp.

EAST EUROPE AND THE SOVIET UNION

General

Beck, Carl, et al. *Comparative Communist Political Leadership.* New York, McKay, 1972. 320 pp.

Bender, Peter. *Eastern Europe in Search of Security.* Baltimore, Johns Hopkins University Press, 1972. 144 pp.

Bromke, Adam, and Rakowska-Harmstone, Teresa, eds. *The Communist States in Disarray, 1965–1971.* Minneapolis, University of Minnesota Press, 1972. 363 pp.

Bautina, N. V. *Sovershenstvovanie ekonomicheskikh vzaimootnoshenii stran-chlenov SEV.* Moscow, Ekonomika, 1972. 176 pp.

Carsten, F. L. *Revolution in Central Europe 1918–1919.* Berkeley, University of California Press, 1972. 360 pp.

Dellin, L. A. D., and Gross, Hermann, eds. *Reforms in the Soviet and Eastern European Economies.* Lexington, Mass., Heath, 1972. 175 pp.

Domes, Alfred, ed. *Freiheit des Geistes? Dokumente und Kommentare zu Osteuropa-Fragen.* Bonn, Atlantic Forum, 1972. 88 pp.

Douglas, Dorothy W. *Transitional Economic Systems. The Polish-Czech Example.* New York, Monthly Review Press, 1972. 375 pp.

Frenzke, Dietrich. *Die kommunistische Anerkennungslehre. Die Anerkennung von Staaten in der osteuropäischen Völkerrechtstheorie.* Cologne, Verlag Wissenschaft & Politik, 1972. 280 pp.

Kennan, George F. *Memoirs, 1950–1963.* Boston, Little Brown, 1972. 368 pp.

Kintner, William R., and Klaiber, Wolfgang. *Eastern Europe and European Security.* New York, Dunellen, 1971. 383 pp.

Kolarz, Walter. *Myths and Realities in Eastern Europe.* Port Washington, N.Y., Kennikat Press, 1972. 273 pp.

Kompleksnaya programma dalneishego uglubleniya i sovershenstvovaniya sotrudnichestva i razvitiya sotsialisticheskoi ekonomicheskoi integratsii stran-chlenov SEV. Moscow, Politizdat, 1972. 120 pp.

Kormanov, U. F. *Spetsializatsiia i kooperirovanie proizvodstva stran-chlenov SEV*. Moscow, Ekonomika, 1972. 335 pp.

Kretschmar, Robert S., Jr. and Foor, Robin. *The Potential for Joint Ventures in Eastern Europe*. New York, Praeger, 1972. 153 pp.

Lindner, Walter. *Aufbau des Sozialismus oder kapitalistische Restauration? Zur Analyse der Wirtschaftsreformen in der DDR und der CSSR*. Erlangen, Politladen GmbH, 1971. 100 pp.

Mastny, Vojtech, ed. *East European Dissent, 1953–1970*. New York, Facts on File, 1972. 2 vols.

Petrovichev, N. A., et al. *Partiinoye stroitelstvo*. Moscow, Politizdat, 1972. 496 pp.

Schaefer, Henry Wilcox. *Comecon and the Politics of Integration*. New York, Praeger, 1972. 218 pp.

Schwarz, Fred. *The Three Faces of Revolution*. Washington, D.C., Capitol Hill Press, 1972. 252 pp.

Selucky, Radoslav. *Economic Reforms in Eastern Europe*. New York, Praeger, 1972. 179 pp.

Sinanian, Sylva, Deak, Istvan, and Ludz, Peter C. *Eastern Europe in the 1970s*. New York, Praeger, 1972. 279 pp.

Staar, Richard F. *The Communist Regimes in Eastern Europe*. 2d rev. ed. Stanford, Calif., Hoover Institution Press, 1971. 304 pp.

Tyrmand, Leopold. *The Rosa Luxemburg Contraceptives Cooperative: A Primer on Communist Civilization*. New York, Macmillan, 1972. 287 pp.

Uschakow, Alexander. *Der Ostmarkt im Comecon*. Baden-Baden, Nomos Verlagsgesellschaft, 1972. 486 pp.

Wiener, Friedrich. *Soldaten im Ostblock*. Munich, Lehmanns Verlag, 1972. 208 pp.

Wilczynski, Jozef. *Socialist Economic Development and Reforms: From Extensive to Intensive Growth under Central Planning in the U.S.S.R., Eastern Europe, and Yugoslavia*. New York, Praeger, 1972. 350 pp.

Albania

Albanian Party of Labor. *Geschichte der Partei der Arbeit Albaniens*. Tirana, Institut für Marxistische-Leninistische Studien, 1971. 746 pp.

Hoxha, Enver. *La teoría marxista leninista y la práctica revolucionaria*. Montevideo, Nativa Libros, 1972. 36 pp.

Bulgaria

Oren, Nissan. *Bulgarian Communism: The Road to Power, 1934–1944*. New York, Columbia University Press, 1972. 293 pp.

Czechoslovakia

Bittman, Ladislav. *The Deception Game: Czechoslovak Intelligence in Soviet Political Warfare*. Syracuse, N.Y., Syracuse University Press, 1972. 246 pp.

Czerwinski, E. M., and Piekalkiewicz, Jaroslaw, eds. *The Soviet Invasion of Czechoslovakia: Its Effects on Eastern Europe*. New York, Praeger, 1972. 210 pp.

Kohout, Pavel. *From the Diary of a Counterrevolutionary*. New York, McGraw-Hill, 1972. 307 pp.

Krejci, Jaroslav. *Social Change and Stratification in Postwar Czechoslovakia*. New York, Columbia University Press, 1972. 207 pp.

Kusin, Vladimir. *Practical Grouping in the Czechoslovak Reform Movement*. New York, Columbia University Press, 1972. 224 pp.

Levy, Alan. *Rowboat to Prague*. New York, Grossman, 1972. 531 pp.

Pelikan, Jiri, ed. *The Secret Vysočany Congress*. New York, St. Martin's Press, 1972. 304 pp.

Sik, Ota. *Czechoslovakia: the Bureaucratic Economy*. White Plains, N.Y., International Arts & Sciences Press, 1972. 138 pp.

Ulc, Otto. *The Judge in a Communist State: A View from Within*. Columbus, Ohio University Press, 1972. 307 pp.

Germany: German Democratic Republic

Baring, Arnulf. *Uprising in East Germany: The Events of June 17, 1953*. Ithaca, Cornell University Press, 1972. 194 pp.

Der Marxismus ist kein Dogma, sondern eine Anleitung zum Handeln. East Berlin, Redaktion der Wissenschaftlichen Zeitschrift der Humboldt-Universität, 1971. 140 pp.

Domes, Alfred, ed. *Ost-West Polarität*. Cologne, Verlag Wissenschaft & Politik, 1972. 255 pp.

Dulles, Eleanor Lansing. *The Wall: A Tragedy in Three Acts*. Columbia, University of South Carolina Press, 1972. 105 pp.

Haenisch, W. *Aussenpolitik und internationale Beziehungen der DDR, 1949–1955*. East Berlin, Staatsverlag, 1972. 400 pp.

Hoernle, E. *Zum Bündnis zwischen Arbeitern und Bauern. Ein Auswahl seiner agrarpolitischen Reden und Schriften, 1928–1951*. East Berlin, Dietz, 1971. 654 pp.

Lippmann, Heinz. *Honecker and the New Politics of Europe*. New York, Macmillan, 1972. 272 pp.

Ludz, Peter Christian. *The Changing Party Elite in East Germany*. Cambridge, Mass., MIT Press, 1972. 509 pp.

Mampel, Siegfried. *Die sozialistische Verfassung der DDR. Kommentar*. Frankfurt, Metzner, 1971. 1100 pp.

Mende, Klaus-Dieter. *Schulreform und Gesellschaft in der DDR, 1945–1965*. Stuttgart, Klett, 1971. 153 pp.

Niermann, Johannes. *Sozialistische Pädagogik in der DDR: eine wissenschaftstheoretische Untersuchung*. Heidelberg, Quelle & Meyer, 1971. 112 pp.

Seht, welche Kraft. Die SED—Tradition, Gegenwart, Zukunft. East Berlin, Dietz, 1971. 340 pp.

Hungary

Gadó, O., ed. *Reform of the Economic Mechanism in Hungary*. Budapest, Akadémiai, 1972. 260 pp.

Ignotus, Paul. *Hungary*. New York, Praeger, 1972. 333 pp.

Janos, Andrew C., and Slottman, William B. *Revolution in Perspective: Essays on the Hungarian Soviet Republic*. Berkeley, University of California Press, 1972. 216 pp.

Lauter, Géza P. *The Manager and Economic Reform in Hungary*. New York, Praeger, 1972. 189 pp.

Radványi, János. *Hungary and the Superpowers: The 1956 Revolution and Realpolitik*. Stanford, Calif., Hoover Institution Press, 1972. 197 pp.

Silagi, Denis. *Ungarn. Geschichte und Gegenwart. Eine Landesbiographie*. 2d ed. Hannover, Verlag für Literatur & Zeitgeschehen, 1972. 168 pp.

Szasz, Bela Sandor. *Volunteers for the Gallows: Anatomy of a Show-Trial.* New York, Norton, 1972. 244 pp.

Lithuania
Sabaliunas, Leonas. *Lithuania in Crisis: Nationalism to Communism, 1939–1940.* Bloomington, Indiana University Press, 1972. 293 pp.

Poland
Cieplak, Tadeusz N., ed. *Poland Since 1956: Readings and Essays on Polish Government and Politics.* New York, Twayne, 1972. 482 pp.

Davies, Norman. *White Eagle, Red Star: The Polish-Soviet War, 1919–1920.* London, MacDonald, 1972. 318 pp.

Deschner, Gunther. *Warsaw Rising.* New York, Ballantine, 1972. 157 pp.

Fiszman, Joseph R. *Revolution and Tradition in People's Poland.* Princeton, N.J., Princeton University Press, 1972. 382 pp.

Groth, Alexander J. *People's Poland: Government and Politics.* San Francisco, Chandler, 1972. 155 pp.

Kruszewski, Z. Anthony. *The Oder-Neisse Boundary and Poland's Modernization: The Socioeconomic and Political Impact.* New York, Praeger, 1972. 260 pp.

Laeuen, Harald. *Polen nach dem Sturz Gomulkas.* Stuttgart, Seewald Verlag, 1972. 260 pp.

Pirages, Dennis Clark. *Modernization and Political-Tension Management: A Socialist Society in Perspective. Case Study of Poland.* New York, Praeger, 1972. 260 pp.

Zawodny, J. K. *Death in the Forest: The Story of the Katyn Forest Massacre.* Notre Dame, Ind., University of Notre Dame Press, 1972. 235 pp. Reprint.

Romania
Jowitt, Kenneth. *Revolutionary Breakthroughs and National Development: The Case of Romania, 1944–1965.* Berkeley, University of California Press, 1972. 325 pp.

U.S.S.R.
Adams, Arthur E. *Stalin and His Times.* New York, Holt, Rinehart & Winston, 1972. 243 pp.

Akhmedova, M. *Their Road to Socialism: Transition of the Central Asian Republics to Socialism: General Laws and Special Features.* Moscow, Novosti, 1972. 112 pp.

Barghoorn, Frederick C. *Politics in the U.S.S.R.* 2d ed. Boston, Little Brown, 1972. 384 pp.

Borisov, O., and Koloskov, B. *Socialist Internationalism and Soviet-Chinese Relations.* Moscow, Novosti, 1972. 48 pp.

Brumberg, Abraham, ed. *In Quest of Justice: Protest and Dissent in the Soviet Union Today.* New York, Praeger, 1972. 477 pp.

Chkhikvadze, V. M., ed. *The Soviet Form of Popular Government.* Moscow, Progress, 1972. 253 pp.

Connor, Walter D. *Deviance in Soviet Society: Crime, Delinquency, and Alcoholism.* New York, Columbia University Press, 1972. 327 pp.

Deriabin, Peter. *Watchdogs of Terror: Russian Bodyguards from the Tsars to the Commissars.* New York, Arlington House, 1972. 320 pp.

Dimitriev, S., and Ivanov, V. *Historic Lessons of Anti-Trotskyist Struggle.* Moscow, Novosti, 1972. 80 pp.

Dodge, Norton T., ed. *Analysis of the USSR's 24th Party Congress and 9th Five Year Plan.* Mechanicsville, Md., Cremona Foundation, 1972. 100 pp.

Dornberg, John. *The New Tsars: Russia Under Stalin's Heirs.* Garden City, N.Y., Doubleday, 1972. 470 pp.

Ferro, Marc. *The Russian Revolution of February 1917.* Englewood Cliffs, N.J., Prentice-Hall, 1972. 392 pp.

Gallagher, Matthew P., and Spielmann, Karl F., Jr. *Soviet Decision-Making for Defense: A Critique of U.S. Perspectives on the Arms Race.* New York, Praeger, 1972. 112 pp.

Galler, Meyer, and Marquess, Harlan E., comps. *Soviet Prison Camp Speech: A Survivor's Glossary.* Madison, University of Wisconsin Press, 1972. 152 pp.

Gitelman, Zvi Y. *Jewish Nationality and Soviet Politics: The Jewish Sections of the CPSU, 1917–1930.* Princeton, N.J., Princeton University Press, 1972. 573 pp.

Gorbanevskaya, Natalia. *Red Square at Noon.* New York, Holt, Rinehart & Winston, 1972. 288 pp.

Gorbunov, V. V. *Lenin i sotsialisticheskaya kultura.* Moscow, Mysl, 1972. 340 pp.

Graham, Loren R. *Science and Philosophy in the Soviet Union.* New York, Knopf, 1972. 584 pp.

Grimsted, Patricia Kennedy. *Archives and Manuscript Repositories in the USSR: Moscow and Leningrad.* Princeton, N.J., Princeton University Press, 1972. 436 pp.

Hahn, Werner G. *The Politics of Soviet Agriculture, 1960–1970.* Baltimore, Johns Hopkins University Press, 1972. 311 pp.

Hanak, Harry. *Soviet Foreign Policy Since the Death of Stalin.* London, Routledge & Paul, 1972. 340 pp.

Harvey, Mose L., et al. *Science and Technology as an Instrument of Soviet Policy.* Coral Gables, Fla., University of Miami Press, 1972. 219 pp.

Heald, Edward. *Witness to Revolution: Letters from Russia, 1916–1919.* Kent, Ohio, Kent State University Press, 1972. 367 pp.

Heen, Nancy Whittier. *Politics and History in the Soviet Union.* Cambridge, Mass., MIT Press, 1971. 319 pp.

Hollander, Gayle Durham. *Soviet Political Indoctrination: Developments in Mass Media and Propaganda Since Stalin.* New York, Praeger, 1972. 244 pp.

Hovannisian, Richard G. *The Republic of Armenia, 1918–1919.* Vol. I. Berkeley, University of California Press, 1972. 570 pp.

Hyde, H. Montgomery. *Stalin: The History of a Dictator.* New York, Farrar, Straus & Giroux, 1972. 679 pp.

Jacobsen, C. *Soviet Strategy—Soviet Foreign Policy.* Glasgow, The University Press, 1972. 232 pp.

Jacobson, Julius, ed. *Soviet Communism: The Socialist Vision.* New York, Dutton, 1972. 363 pp.

Jacoby, Susan. *Moscow Conversations.* New York, Coward McCann & Geoghegan, 1972. 287 pp.

Katz, Abraham. *The Politics of Economic Reform in the Soviet Union.* New York, Praeger, 1972. 242 pp.

Kerenskii, Aleksandr Fedorovich. *The Crucifixion of Liberty.* New York, Kraus Reprint, 1972. 406 pp.

Khchikvadze, V. M., ed. *The Soviet Form of Popular Government.* Moscow, Progress, 1972. 252 pp.

Khmel, Alexander, ed. *Education of the Soviet Soldier: Party-Political Work in the Soviet Armed Forces*. Moscow, Progress, 1972. 217 pp.

Kim, M. P. *Sovetsky narod—novaya istoricheskaya obshchnost*. Moscow, Politizdat, 1972. 349 pp.

Krassó, Nicolas, ed. *Trotsky: The Great Debate Renewed*. St. Louis, New Critics Press, 1972. 191 pp.

Kudryavtsev, V. *The 24th CPSU Congress and the Struggle for Peace*. Moscow, Novosti, 1972. 112 pp.

Lazitch, Branko, and Drachkovitch, Milorad M. *Lenin and the Comintern*. Vol. I. Stanford, Calif., Hoover Institution Press, 1972. 683 pp.

Lenin, V. I. *La guerra imperialista*. Rome, Editori Riuniti, 1972. 221 pp.
———. *La rivoluzione d'ottobre*. Rome, Editori Riuniti, 1972. 488 pp.

Levytsky, Boris. *The Uses of Terror: The Soviet Secret Police, 1917–1970*. New York, Coward, McCann & Geoghegan, 1972. 349 pp.

Litvinov, Pavel, and Reddaway, Peter, eds. *The Trial of the Four: The Case of Galanskov, Ginzberg, Dobrovolsky, and Lashkova*. New York, Viking, 1972. 434 pp.

McNeal, Robert H. *Bride of the Revolution*. Ann Arbor, University of Michigan Press, 1972. 326 pp.

Medvedev, Roy A. *Let History Judge: The Origins and Consequences of Stalinism*. New York, Knopf, 1972. 566 pp.

Meissner, Boris, ed. *Social Change in the Soviet Union: Russia's Path toward an Industrial Society*. Notre Dame, Ind., University of Notre Dame Press, 1972. 247 pp.

Morgan, Michael. *Lenin*. Athens, Ohio University Press, 1972. 236 pp.

Nogee, Joseph L., ed. *Man, State, and Society in the Soviet Union*. New York, Praeger, 1972. 224 pp.

Nove, Alec. *An Economic History of the U.S.S.R.* Baltimore, Penguin, 1972. 416 pp.

Page, Stanley W. *Lenin and World Revolution*. New York, McGraw-Hill, 1972. 252 pp.

Radio Liberty Committee. *Sobranie dokumentov samizdata*. Vol. I. New York, 1972.

Rauch, Georg von. *A History of Soviet Russia*. 6th ed. New York, Praeger, 1972. 541 pp.

Reddaway, Peter, ed. and trans. *Uncensored Russia: Protest and Dissent in the Soviet Union*. New York, American Heritage Press, 1972. 499 pp.

Rothberg, Abraham. *The Heirs of Stalin: Dissidence and the Soviet Regime, 1953–1970*. Ithaca, N.Y., Cornell University Press, 1972. 450 pp.

Rothenberg, Joshua. *The Jewish Religion in the Soviet Union*. New York, Ktav, 1972. 242 pp.

Schulz, Heinrich E., ed. *Who Was Who in the USSR: A Biographic Directory of Prominent Soviet Historical Personalities*. Metuchen, N.J., Scarecrow Press, 1972. 677 pp.

Skirda, Alexandre. *Kronstadt 1921: Prolétariat contre bolchévisme*. Paris, Editions de la Tête de Feuilles, 1972. 274 pp.

Smolar, Boris. *Soviet Jewry: Today and Tomorrow*. New York, Macmillan, 1971. 228 pp.

Souvarine, Boris. *Stalin: A Critical Survey of Bolshevism*. New York, Octagon Books, 1972. 690 pp. Reprint.

Suny, Ronald Grigor. *The Baku Commune 1917–1918: Class and Nationality in the Russian Revolution*. Princeton, N.J., Princeton University Press, 1972. 412 pp.

Treml, Vladimir G., and Hardt, John P., eds. *Soviet Economic Statistics*. Durham, N.C., Duke University Press, 1972. 457 pp.

Trotskii, Lev. *Writings of Leon Trotsky*. New York, Pathfinder Press, 1972. 379 pp.

Trotsky, Leon. *The Young Lenin*. Garden City, N.Y., Doubleday, 1972. 224 pp.

Tyazhelnikov, Y. *Soviet Youth*. Moscow, Novosti, 1972. 112 pp.

U.S. Senate, Committee on the Judiciary. *Abuse of Psychiatry for Political Repression in the Soviet Union*. Washington, D.C., Government Printing Office, 1972. 257 pp.

Van den Heuvel, C. C. *Soviet Foreign Policy and Ideology*. The Hague, Interdoc, 1972. 15 pp.

Vasin, V., Gribanov, S., and Undasynov, I. *Communists and Social-Democrats*. Moscow, Novosti, 1972. 192 pp.

Werth, Alexander. *Russia: The Post-War Years*. New York, Taplinger, 1972. 446 pp.

Wesson, Robert G. *The Soviet State: An Aging Revolution*. New York, Wiley, 1972. 222 pp.

Wittlin, Thaddeus. *Commissar: The Life and Death of Lavrenty Pavlovich Beria*. New York, Macmillan, 1972. 566 pp.

Wyndham, Francis, and King, David. *Trotsky: A Documentary*. New York, Praeger, 1972. 204 pp.

Yugoslavia

Johnson, A. Ross. *The Transformation of Communist Ideology: The Yugoslav Case, 1945–1953*. Cambridge, Mass., MIT Press, 1972. 304 pp.

Roberts, Walter R. *Tito, Mihailovic and the Allies 1941–1945*. New Brunswick, N.J., Rutgers University Press, 1972. 368 pp.

WEST EUROPE

General

Böckelmann, Frank. *Über Marx und Adorno. Schwierigkeiten der spätmarxistischen Theorie*. Frankfurt am Main, Makol Verlag, 1972. 204 pp.

Gustafsson, Bo. *Marxismus und Revisionismus*. Stuttgart, Europäische Verlagsanstalt, 1972. 400 pp.

John, E. *Zur Dialektik des Sozialen, Nationalen und Internationalen in der Kulturentwicklung*. East Berlin, Dietz, 1972. 84 pp.

Kriegel, Annie. *Les grands procès dans les systèmes communistes*. Paris, Gallimard, 1972. 192 pp.

Lindenberg, Daniel. *L'Internationale communiste et l'école de classe*. Paris, Maspero, 1972. 352 pp.

Martinet, Gilles. *Les cinq communismes*. Paris, Seuil, 1972. 251 pp.

Über die Partei; Texte der schwedischen und norwegischen Marxisten-Leninisten. Hamburg, Kommunistischer Arbeiterbund, 1971. 16 pp.

Windelen, Heinrich. *SOS für Europa*. Stuttgart, Seewald Verlag, 1972. 228 pp.

Cyprus

Adams, T. W. *The Communist Party of Cyprus*. Stanford, Calif., Hoover Institution Press, 1972. 284 pp.

Finland

Nousiainen, Jaakko. *The Finnish Political System*. Cambridge, Mass., Harvard University Press, 1971. 454 pp.

France

Billoux, F. *Quand nous étions ministres*. Paris, Editions Sociales, 1972. 196 pp.

Brunet, Jean-Paul. *L'enfance du parti communiste, 1920–1938*. Paris, Presses Universitaires de France, 1972. 96 pp.

Clavaud, Fernand. *Les communistes et les paysans*. Paris, Editions Sociales, 1972. 126 pp.

Gross, Babette. *Frankreichs Weg zum Kommunismus*. Kreuzlingen, Neptun Verlag, 1971. 112 pp.

Groupe pour la Fondation de l'Union des Communistes Français. *Première année d'existence d'une organisation maoiste, printemps 70–printemps 71*. Paris, 1972. 216 pp.

Institut Maurice Thorez and Centre d'Etudes et de Recherches Marxistes. *La front populaire*. Paris, Editions Sociales, 1972. 176 pp.

Johnson, Richard. *The French Communist Party versus the Students: Revolutionary Politics in May–June 1968*. New Haven, Conn., Yale University Press, 1972. 215 pp.

Kessel, Patrick. *Le mouvement maoiste en France*. Vol. I. Paris, U.G.E., 1971. 448 pp.

Kriegel, Annie. *The French Communists, Profile of a People*. Chicago, University of Chicago Press, 1972. 408 pp.

Laforge, André. *Convulsions marxistes dans l'église*. Paris, Cercle d'Information Civique et Sociale, 1972. 144 pp.

Leroy, Roland, Casanova, Antoine, and Moine, André. *Les marxistes et l'évolution du monde catholique*. Paris, Editions Sociales, 1972. 255 pp.

Manceaux, Michèle. *Les Maos en France*. Paris, Nouvelle Revue Française, 1971. 254 pp.

Marcellesi, Jean-Baptiste. *Le Congrès de Tours, décembre 1920; études sociolinguistiques*. Paris, Le Pavillon, 1971. 357 pp.

Parti Communiste Français. *Messages des partis communistes et ouvriers et des partis et mouvements démocratiques nationaux*. Paris, Imprimerie Hermel, 1971. 80 pp.

———. *Une politique pour la France; programme de gouvernement démocratique d'union populaire*. Paris, 1971. 46 pp.

Racine, Nicole. *Le parti communiste français pendant l'entre-deux-guerres*. Paris, Armand Colin, 1971. 310 pp.

Schnapp, Alain, and Vidal-Naquet, Pierre. *The French Student Uprising: November 1967– June 1968: An Analytical Record*. Boston, Beacon Press, 1972. 608 pp.

Varfolomeeva, R. S. *Borba Frantsuzskoi Kommunisticheskoi Partii za mir, demokratiyu, sotsializm: 1945–1970 gg*. Moscow, Mysl, 1972. 240 pp.

Germany: Federal Republic of Germany

Angress, Werner T. *Die Kampfzeit der KPD, 1921–23*. Düsseldorf, Droste Verlag, 1971. 272 pp.

Ausgewählte Reden, Aufsätze und Beschlüsse der KPD-Aufbauorganisation. Berlin, Verlag Rote Fahne, 1971. 349 pp.

Der Illegale Kampf der KPD, 1935–1945. Münster, Verlag Kommunistische Texte, 1971. 95 pp.

Deutsche Kommunistische Partei. *Parteitag: Protokoll des Düsseldorfer Parteitags der Deutschen Kommunistischen Partei*. Düsseldorf, 1971. 620 pp.

Die Partei aufbauen. Plattformen, Grundsatzerklärungen der KPD/AO, KPD/ML, KPD/ ML-ZK Linie, KPD/ML-Bolschewik Linie, KPD/ML-Neue Einheit, Rote Garde, KP/ ML, PL/PI, Proletarische Front. Berlin, Verlag für das Studium der Arbeiterbewegung GmbH, 1971. 169 pp.

Duhnke, Horst. *Die KPD von 1933 bis 1945*. Cologne, Kiepenhauer & Witsch, 1971. 608 pp.

Gallas, Helga. *Marxistische Literaturtheorie. Kontroversen im Bund proletarisch-revolutionärer Schriftsteller.* Neuwied, Luchterhand Verlag, 1971. 257 pp.

Hölz, Max. *Vom weissen Kreuz zur roten Fahne.* Frankfurt am Main, Verlag Neue Kritik, 1972. 393 pp.

Kommunistische Partei Deutschlands. Zentralkomitee. Konferenz, 4. Februar 1972. *Rechenschaftsbericht.* Berlin, Verlag Rote Fahne, 1972. 279 pp.

Konze, M. *Für die Befreiung der Frau.* Frankfurt am Main, Verlag Marxistische Blätter GmbH, 1972. 218 pp.

KPD—Verbot; ein Protokoll. Cologne, Pahl-Rugenstein Verlag, 1971. 180 pp.

Kuczynski, Jürgen. *Klassen und Klassenkämpfe im imperialistischen Deutschland und in der BRD.* East Berlin, Dietz, 1972. 568 pp.

Langguth, Gerd. *Protestbewegung am Ende: Die Neue Linke als Vorhut der DKP.* Mainz, Hase & Koehler. 1972. 348 pp.

Marchwitza, Hans. *Sturm auf Essen.* Cologne, Kiepenheuer & Witsch, 1972. 176 pp.

Marxismus und Politik. Dokumente zur theoretischen Begründung revolutionärer Politik. Aufsätze aus der Marxismus-Diskussion der zwanziger und dreissiger Jahre. Vol. I. Frankfurt am Main, Makol Verlag, 1972. 500 pp.

Merkel, Konrad, ed. *DDR-Landwirtschaft in der Diskussion.* Cologne, Verlag Wissenschaft & Politik, 1972. 160 pp.

Nelson, Walter Henry. *Germany Rearmed.* New York, Simon & Schuster, 1972. 354 pp.

Retzlaw, Karl. *Spartakus. Aufstieg und Niedergang; Erinnerungen eines Parteiarbeiters.* Frankfurt am Main, Neue Kritik, 1971. 511 pp.

Schenk, Fritz, ed. *Kommunistische Grundsatzerklärungen 1957–1971.* Cologne, Verlag Wissenschaft & Politik, 1972. 240 pp.

Schulbuchkonferenz der DKP Hessen, Frankfurt am Main, 6. Juni 1971. *Kampf der Verdummung!* Frankfurt am Main, Verlag Marxistische Blätter, 1971. 100 pp.

Tormay, Thomas von. *Der böse Deutsche. Das Bild der Deutschen aus kommunistischer Sicht, dargestellt am Beispiel der ungarischen Massenmedien.* Mainz, Hase & Koehler, 1971. 280 pp.

Turek, Ludwig. *Ein Prolet erzählt.* Cologne, Kiepenheuer & Witsch, 1972. 309 pp.

Waldmann, Eric. *Die Sozialistische Einheitspartei Westberlins und die sowjetische Berlinpolitik.* Boppard am Rhein, Harald Boldt Verlag, 1972. 336 pp.

Weymann, A. *Gesellschaftswissenschaften und Marxismus: zur methodologischen Entwicklung der marxistisch-leninistischen Gesellschaftswissenschaft in der DDR.* Düsseldorf, Bertelsmann Verlag, 1972. 172 pp.

Great Britain

Ferris, Paul. *The New Militants: Crisis in the Trade Unions.* London, Penguin, 1972. 112 pp.

Gallacher, William. *Last Memoirs.* London, Lawrence & Wishart, 1972. 320 pp.

Greece

Clogg, Richard, and Yannopoulos, George. *Greece under Military Rule.* New York, Basic Books, 1972. 272 pp.

Holden, David. *Greece without Columns.* New York, Lippincott, 1972. 336 pp.

Iatrides, John O. *Revolt in Athens: The Greek Communist "Second Round" 1944–1945.* Princeton, N.J., Princeton University Press, 1972. 340 pp.

Italy

Allegato, Luigi. *Socialismo e comunismo in Puglia*. Rome, Editori Riuniti, 1971. 164 pp.

Almanacco Partito Comunista Italiano, 1971. Rome, Direzione PCI, 1971. 223 pp.

Critica Marxista. Cinquantesimo del PCI. *Storia politica; organizzazione nella lotta dei comunisti italiani per un nuovo blocco storico*. Rome, Critica Marxista, 1972. 386 pp.

De Clementi, A. *Amadeo Bordiga*. Turin, Einaudi, 1971. 253 pp.

Del Pozzo, Franca. *Alle origini del PCI—Le organizzazioni marchigiane, 1919–1923*. Urbino, Argalia, 1971. 221 pp.

Gramsci, Antonio. *La costruzione del Partito Comunista (1923–1929)*. Turin, Einaudi, 1971. 563 pp.

Landzardo, Liliana. *Classe operaie e Partito Comunista alla Fiat—La strategia della collaborazione, 1945–1949*. Turin, Einaudi, 1971. 655 pp.

Longo, Luigi. *Le brigate internazionali*. Rome, Editori Riuniti, 1972. 368 pp.

Marramao, Giacomo. *Marxismo e Revisionismo in Italia. Dalla "Critica sociale" al dibattito sul leninismo*. Bari, De Donato, 1971. 440 pp.

Mughini, Giampiero. *Die KP Italiens und die nicht-reformistischen Gruppen*. Berlin, Merve Verlag, 1971.

Pesce, Giovanni, *And No Quarter: An Italian Partisan in World War II*. Athens, Ohio University Press, 1972. 269 pp.

Pozzolini, A. *Antonio Gramsci: An Introduction to his Thought*. London, Pluto Press, 1972. 154 pp.

Probleme des Klassenkampfes und des Kampfes um gewerkschaftliche Einheit in Italien. Frankfurt am Main, Institut für Marxistische Studien und Forschungen, 1971. 360 pp.

Sema, Paolo. *La lotta in Istria 1890–1945—Il movimento socialista e il Partito Comunista Italiano—la sezione di Pirano*. Trieste, Cluet, 1971. 365 pp.

Valiani, Leo. *Azionisti catolici e comunisti nella resistenza*. Milan, Franco Angeli, 1971. 449 pp.

Spain

Angel, Miguel. *Los guerrilleros españoles en Francia, 1940–1945*. Paris, Editions Ruedo Iberico, 1971. 260 pp.

Carrillo, Santiago. *Libertad y socialismo*. Paris, Librairie du Globe, 1971. 151 pp.

Ibarruri, Dolores. *A Dolores Ibarruri en su 75 anniversario: Suplemento a "Nuestra Bandera."* N.p., 1971. 32 pp.

————. *España, estado multinacional*. Paris, Editions Sociales, 1971. 61 pp.

Sorel, Andrés. *Busqueda, reconstrucción e historia de la guerrilla español del siglo XX a través de sus documentos, relatos y protagonistas*. Paris, Librairie de Globe, 1970. 247 pp.

Switzerland

Enckell, Marianne. *La Fédération jurassienne. Les origines de l'anarchisme en Suisse*. Lausanne, Editions L'Age d'Homme, 1971. 148 pp.

Humbert-Droz, Jules. *Dix ans de lutte antifasciste, 1931–1941. Mémoires*. Vol. III. Neuchâtel, Editions de la Baconnière, 1972. 429 pp.

MIDDLE EAST AND AFRICA

General

Cohn, Helen Desfosses. *Soviet Policy toward Black Africa: The Focus on National Integration.* New York, Praeger, 1972. 336 pp.

Ferrara, Francisco, comp. *Asia y Africa: De la liberación nacional al socialismo.* Buenos Aires, Centro Editor de América Latina, 1972. 168 pp.

First, Ruth. *Power in Africa.* Baltimore, Penguin, 1972. 513 pp.

Gibson, Richard. *African Liberation Movements: Contemporary Struggles against White Minority Rule.* New York, Oxford University Press, 1972. 350 pp.

Lenczowski, George. *Soviet Advances in the Middle East.* Washington, D.C., American Enterprise Institute for Public Policy Research, 1972. 176 pp.

Rodinson, Maxine. *Marxisme et monde musulman.* Paris, Seuil, 1972. 699 pp.

U.S. Senate, Committee on the Judiciary. *Communist Global Subversion and American Security.* Vol. I. *The Attempted Communist Subversion of Africa through Nkrumah's Ghana.* Washington, D.C., Government Printing Office, 1972. 215 pp. Reprint.

Egypt

Heikal, Mohamed Hassanein. *The Cairo Documents.* New York, Doubleday, 1972. 360 pp.

Ghana

Howell, Thomas A., and Rajasooria, Jeffrey P. (eds.). *Ghana and Nkrumah.* New York, Facts on File, 1972. 205 pp.

Israel

Chaliand, Gerard. *The Palestine Resistance.* Baltimore, Penguin, 1972. 190 pp.

Schiff, Zeev, and Rothstein, Raphael. *Fedayeen: Guerrillas against Israel.* New York, McKay, 1972. 246 pp.

South Africa

Lerumo, A. *Fifty Fighting Years: The Communist Party of South Africa, 1921–1971.* Toronto, Progress Books, 1972. 216 pp.

NORTH AMERICA

Balawyder, Aloysius. *Canadian-Soviet Relations between the World Wars.* Toronto, University of Toronto Press, 1972. 248 pp.

Communist Party of Canada. *Power of the People: Fifty Years of the Communist Party of Canada, 1921–1971.* Toronto, Progress Books, 1972. 40 pp.

————. *The Road to Socialism in Canada: The Program of the Communist Party in Canada.* Toronto, Progress Books, 1972. 70 pp.

Communist Party, USA. *Toward Chicano Liberation: The Communist Party Position.* New York, New Outlook, 1972. 24 pp.

————. Convention Document. *Our National Crisis and How to Solve It: Main Political Resolution.* New York, New Outlook, 1972. 95 pp.

Forman, James. *The Making of Black Revolutionaries.* New York, Macmillan, 1972. 568 pp.

Hall, Gus. *Capitalism on the Skids to Oblivion—The People's Struggle for a New Beginning.* New York, New Outlook, 1972. 96 pp.

Hercules, Frank. *American Society and Black Revolution.* New York, Harcourt-Brace-Jovanovich, 1972. 435 pp.

Hoar, Victor. *The Mackenzie-Papineau Battalion.* Toronto, Progress Books, 1972. 298 pp.

Kiernan, Bernard P. *The United States, Communism and the Emergent World.* Bloomington, Indiana University Press, 1972. 248 pp.

Leamer, Laurence. *The Paper Revolutionaries: The Rise of the Underground Press.* New York, Simon & Schuster, 1972. 220 pp.

Methvin, Eugene H. *The Rise of Radicalism.* New York, Arlington House, 1972. 385 pp.

Mitchell, Charlene. *The Fight to Free Angela Davis: Its Importance for the Working Class.* New York, New Outlook, 1972. 12 pp.

Rubin, Daniel. *For a Party of Mass Action: New Conditions, New Tasks of the Party in the '70s.* New York, New Outlook, 1972. 24 pp.

Sargent, Lyman Tower. *New Left Thought: An Introduction.* Homewood, Ill., Dorsey Press, 1972. 215 pp.

Sheppard, Barry, ed. *A Revolutionary Strategy for the 70s: Documents of the Socialist Workers Party.* New York, Pathfinder Press, 1972. 265 pp.

Starobin, Joseph. *American Communism in Crisis, 1943–1957.* Cambridge, Mass., Harvard University Press, 1972. 317 pp.

U.S. Congress, House of Representatives, Committee on Internal Security. *America's Maoists: The Revolutionary Union, The Venceremos Organization.* Washington, D.C., Government Printing Office, 1972. 202 pp.

Winston, Henry. *Black and White—One Class, One Fight: The Role of White Workers in the Struggle against Racism.* New York, New Outlook, 1972. 48 pp.

LATIN AMERICA

General

Assmann, Hugo. *Opresión-liberación-desafío a los cristianos.* Montevideo, 1971. 208 pp.

Barbu, Noel, et al. *Revolucionarios de tres mundos.* Buenos Aires, Centro Editor de América Latina, 1971. 157 pp.

Barringer, Richard E. *Patterns of Conflict.* Cambridge, Mass., MIT Press, 1972. 293 pp.

Bingaman, Joseph W. *Latin America: A Survey of Holdings at the Hoover Institution on War, Revolution and Peace.* Stanford, Calif., Hoover Institution Press, 1972. 96 pp.

Bortnik, Rubén. *Dependencia y revolución en América Latina.* Buenos Aires, 1972. 54 pp.

Briones Toledo, Hernán. *El marxismo en sus fuentes.* Santiago, 1972. 96 pp.

Bünting, A., and Moyano, C. A. *¿La Iglesia va hacia el socialismo?* Buenos Aires, Editorial Guadalupe, 1971.

Consuegra, José. *Lenin y la América Latina.* Bogotá, Ediciones Cruz del Sur, [1972?]. 200 pp.

Correa, J. *Los jerarcas sindicales.* Buenos Aires, Editorial Polémica, 1972. 110 pp.

Cristianos por el socialismo. Lima, Dist. Mejía Baca, 1972. 45 pp.

Davis, Jack. *Political Violence in Latin America.* London, International Institute for Strategic Studies, 1972. 35 pp.

Díaz, Jesús. *El marxismo de Lenin.* Buenos Aires, Dist. Siglo XX, 1971. 198 pp.

Dussel, Enrique. *Caminos de liberación latino-americana (seis conferencias).* Buenos Aires, Latinoamérica Libros, 1972. 141 pp.

Espinosa García, Manuel. *La política económica de los Estados Unidos hacia América Latina entre 1945 y 1961.* Havana, Casa de las Américas, 1971.

Fournial, Georges. *L'Amérique latine et le socialisme.* Paris, Inst. Maurice Thorez, 1972. 18 pp.

Gastiazoro, Eugenio. *Desarrollismo o socialismo.* Buenos Aires, 1971. 164 pp.

Gebhardt, Hermann P. *Guerrillas: Schicksal für den Westen: die lateinamerikanische Revolutionsbewegung.* Stuttgart, Seewald, 1971.

Goldenberg, Boris. *Kommunismus in Lateinamerika.* Stuttgart, Kohlhammer, 1971. 639 pp.

Goldhamer, Herbert. *The Foreign Powers in Latin America.* Princeton, N.J., Princeton University Press, 1972. 321 pp.

Guillén, Abraham. *Socialismo de autogestión.* Montevideo, Aconcagua, 1972. 284 pp.

Harnecker, Marta, and Uribe, Gabriela. *Capitalismo y socialismo.* Santiago, 1972. 63 pp.

Hirsch-Weber, Wolfgang. *Lateinamerika: Abhängigkeit und Selbstbestimmung.* Opladen, Leske Verlag, 1972. 170 pp.

Huguet Ribe, José. *Colaboración entre naciones o aniquilación.* México, Costa-Amic, 1971. 316 pp.

Huizer, Gerrit. *The Revolutionary Potential of Peasants in Latin America.* Lexington, Mass., Heath, 1972. 237 pp.

Kadt, Emanuel de, ed. *Patterns of Foreign Influence in the Caribbean.* New York, Oxford University Press, 1972. 188 pp.

Magri, Lucio, and Guevara, Ernesto. *¿Qué es un partido revolucionario?* México, Dist. Porrua, 1972. 178 pp.

Mallin, Jay, ed. *Terror and Urban Guerrillas: A Study of Tactics and Documents.* Coral Gables, Fla., University of Miami Press, 1972. 176 pp.

Mariátegui, José Carlos, et al. *El marxismo en América Latina; antología.* Buenos Aires, Centro Editor de América Latina, 1972. 140 pp.

Max, Alphonse. *Guerrillas in Latin America.* The Hague, Inderdoc, 1971. 100 pp.

Mondolfo, Rodolfo. *Verum-Factum; desde antes de Vico hasta Marx.* Buenos Aires, Ediciones Siglo XXI, 1971.

Needler, Martin. *The United States and the Latin American Revolution.* Boston, Allyn & Bacon, 1972. 167 pp.

North American Congress on Latin America. *Ciencia y neocolonialismo; fundaciones Ford y Rockefeller, CIA, AID, Departamento de Estado y universidades.* Buenos Aires, Ediciones Periferia, 1971.

Plazas Olarte, Humberto. *Lenin, 1870–1970. Con un Capítulo sobre el influjo de sus doctrinas en el Nuevo Mundo y el Proceso Revolucionario iniciado en Cuba, Chile, Perú y Bolivia.* Bogotá. n.p., 1971. 208 pp.

Polantzas, Nicos. *Fascismo y dictadura. La tercera internacional frente al Fascismo.* N. p., 1972. 427 pp.

Ratliff, William E., ed. *Yearbook on Latin American Communist Affairs, 1971.* Stanford, Calif., Hoover Institution Press, 1971. 194 pp.

Ruíz García, Enrique. *América Latina, hoy.* 2d rev. ed. 2 vols. N.p., 1971.

Sacchi, Hugo M. *El movimiento obrero en América Latina*. Buenos Aires, Centro Editor de América Latina, 1972. 109 pp.

Schmitt, Karl M., ed. *The Roman Catholic Church in Modern Latin America*. New York, Knopf, 1972. 225 pp.

Selser, Gregorio. *Los cuatro viajes de Cristobál Rockefeller*. Buenos Aires, 1971. 447 pp.

Serge, Víctor. *Lo que todo revolucionario debe saber sobre la represión*. México, Ediciones Era, 1972. 141 pp.

Solidarity: A Sharpening of the Revolutionary Awareness of Our People. Havana, Political Editions, 1972. 26 pp.

Sweezey, Paul, et al. *Economía política del imperialismo*. Buenos Aires, Periferia, 1971. 110 pp.

U.S. Congress, House of Representatives, Committee on Internal Security. *The Theory and Practice of Communism in 1971*. Parts 2 and 3 (Latin America). Washington, D.C., Government Printing Office, 1972.

Valentini, Alberto. *Cristianismo e marxismo*. Pôrto Alegre, Livraria Sulina, 1971. 143 pp.

Veneroni, Horacio L. *E.E.U.U. y las fuerzas armadas de América Latina*. Buenos Aires, Editorial Periferia, 1971. 186 pp.

Viñas, Ismael. *Capitalismo, monopolios y dependencia*. Buenos Aires, Centro Editor de América Latina, 1972. 135 pp.

Volski, V., et al. *La cuestión agraria y los problemas del movimiento de liberación en la América Latina*. Moscow, Editorial de la Agencia de Prensa Nóvosti, n.d. 157 pp.

William, Eric. *From Columbus to Castro: The History of the Caribbean, 1492–1969*. New York, Harper & Row, 1971. 576 pp.

Argentina

Brignardillo, Luisa A. *El movimiento estudiantil argentino*. Buenos Aires, Ediciones Macchi, 1972. 358 pp.

Codovilla, Victorio. *Trabajos escogidos*. Vol. I. *Marxismo-leninismo en América. Las soluciones auténticas*. Buenos Aires, 1972. 301 pp.

Echagüe, Carlos M. *Las grandes huelgas*. Buenos Aires, Centro Editor de América Latina, 1971. 112 pp.

Eggers Lan, Conrado. *Izquierda, peronismo y socialismo nacional*. Buenos Aires, 1972. 127 pp.

Esteban, Juan Carlos. *Imperialismo y desarrollo económico*. Buenos Aires, 1972. 213 pp.

Ferrero Ameghino, A. J. *¡Alerta, Gorilas!* Buenos Aires, Editorial Bases, 1972. 55 pp.

Ghioldi, Rodolfo. *Lenin y el pensamiento contemporaneo*. Buenos Aires, Edición Anteo, 1972. 76 pp.

Godio, Julio. *Los orígenes del movimiento obrero*. Buenos Aires, 1971. 159 pp.

———. *Socialismo y luchas obreras, 1900–1950*. Buenos Aires, Centro Editor de América Latina, 1971. 142 pp.

Guerin, Daniel. *Marxismo y socialismo libertario*. Buenos Aires, Editorial Proyección, 1972.

Lera, Angel. *Crisis y revolución*. Buenos Aires, Hoy, 1971. 102 pp.

Marini, Alberto. *Estrategía sin tiempo. La guerra subversiva y revolucionaria*. Buenos Aires, Círculo Militar, 1971. 266 pp.

Meléndez, Raquel, and Monteagudo, Néstor. *Historia del movimiento obrero*. Buenos Aires, Centro Editor de América Latina, 1971. 112 pp.

Morelli, Alex. *Libera a mi pueblo*. Buenos Aires, n.p., 1971. 130 pp.

Ramos, Jorge Abelardo. *Revolución y contrarrevolución en la Argentina. IV. El sexto dominio, 1922–1943*. 4th ed. Buenos Aires, Editorial Plus Ultra, 1972. 266 pp.

Ramos, Jorge Abelardo. *Revolución y contrarrevolución en la Argentina. V. La era del bonapartismo; 1943–1972*. 4th ed. Buenos Aires, Editorial Plus Ultra, 1972. 300 pp.

Rotondaro, Rubén. *Realidad y cambio en el sindicalismo*. Buenos Aires, 1971. 426 pp.

Bolivia

Assmann, Hugo. *Teoponte, experiencia guerrillera boliviana*. Caracas, Dist. Librería Historia, 1972. n.p.

Malloy, James M., and Thorn, Richard S., eds. *Beyond the Revolution: Bolivia since 1952*. Pittsburgh, University of Pittsburgh Press, 1971. 402 pp.

Mas, Santiago. *Revolución y contrarrevolución en Bolivia*. Buenos Aires, Centro Editor de América Latina, 1971. 56 pp.

Otros documentos del "Che" en Bolivia. N.p., Ediciones Katari, [1972?]. 78 pp.

Rodríguez, Eliseo Reyes, et al. *Diarios de Bolivia*. [Buenos Aires?], Ediciones Fuerte, 1971. 162 pp.

Rojas, Martha, and Rodríguez, Mirta. *Tania; misión guerrillera en Bolivia*. N.p., Ediciones Katari, [1972?]. 100 pp.

Brazil

Marighela, Carlos. *For the Liberation of Brazil*. London, Penguin, 1971. 191 pp.

Quartim, João. *Dictatorship and Armed Struggle in Brazil*. New York, Monthly Review Press, 1972. 250 pp.

Sacchi, Hugo M. *Prestes; La rebelión de los tenientes en Brasil*. Buenos Aires, Centro Editor de América Latina, 1971. 252 pp.

British Honduras

Hyde, Evan X. *The Crowd Called Ubad: The Story of a People's Movement*. Belize, [1971?]. 90 pp.

Chile

Angell, Alan. *Politics and the Labour Movement in Chile*. New York, Oxford University Press, 1972. 289 pp.

Brodersohn, Víctor. *Chile entre la ley y la revolución*. Buenos Aires, Centro Editor de América Latina, 1972. 251 pp.

Cerda, Carlos. *El Leninismo y la victoria popular*. Santiago, Editorial Quimantu, 1971. 273 pp.

Chile 1971: habla Fidel Castro. Santiago, Editorial Universitaria, 1971. 301 pp.

Chile, hoy. México, Siglo XXI Editores, 1971. 416 pp.

Conferencia Episcopal de Chile. *Evangelio, política y socialismo; documentos de trabajo*. Santiago, Secretariado del CECH, Dist. Librería San Pablo, 1971. 91 pp.

Corvalán, Luis. *Camino de victoria*. Santiago, Editorial Horizonte, 1971. 427 pp.

Debray, Régis. *The Chilean Revolution: Conversations with Allende*. New York, Pantheon, 1972. 201 pp.

Feinberg, Richard E. *The Triumph of Allende: Chile's Legal Revolution*. New York, New American Library, 1972. 276 pp.

Garces, Joan E. *1970: la pugna política por la presidencia en Chile*. Santiago, Universitaria, 1971. 127 pp.

Labrousse, Alain. *L'expérience chilienne*. Paris, Seuil, 1972. 402 pp.

Martner, Gonzalo. *El pensamiento económico del gobierno de Allende*. Santiago, Editorial Universitaria, 1971. 354 pp.

Millas, Orlando. *En pie de guerra para defender nuestra revolución y seguir avanzando*. Santiago, 1972. 18 pp.

Movimiento de Izquierda Revolucionaria. *La política del MIR en el campo*. Santiago, Imp. Bio-Bio, 1972. 39 pp.

Parker, Dick. *La nueva cara del Fascismo*. Santiago, 1972. 167 pp.

Partido Comunista Revolucionario de Chile. *En defensa de la línea proletaria*. [Santiago?, Imp. Bio-Bio?, 1971?] 32 pp.

————. *¡La lucha da lo que la ley y el explotador niegan!* Santiago, Imp. Bio-Bio, [1971?]. 31 pp.

————. *La situación actual y las tareas políticas del proletariado y su partido*. Santiago, Imp. Bio-Bio, [1971?]. 35 pp.

————. *La situación campesina y las tareas del partido*. Santiago, Imp. Bio-Bio, [1971?]. 53 pp.

————. *La situación del movimiento estudiantil y las tareas del Partido Comunista Revolucionario*. Santiago, Imp. Bio-Bio, [1971?]. 47 pp.

Peralta, Ariel. *El mito de Chile*. Santiago, Editorial Universitaria, 1971. 230 pp.

Piga Dacchena, Arturo. *Por qué se rebelan los jóvenes?* N.p., 1972. 237 pp.

Quién es Chile. Santiago, Quimantu, 1971. 129 pp.

Rodríguez Elizondo, J. *Mitología de la ultraizquierda*. Santiago, Editorial Austral, 1971. 108 pp.

Rojas, Robinson. *El imperialismo yanqui en Chile*. Santiago, Editorial ML, 1971. 110 pp.

Viola, Eduardo. *Recabarren; Los orígenes del movimiento obrero en Chile*. Buenos Aires, Centro Editor de América Latina, 1971. 280 pp.

Vuskovic, Pedro. *La política económica del gobierno popular chileno*. Buenos Aires, Siglo Veintiuno Argentina Ed., 1971.

Colombia

Caicedo, Edgar. *Historia de las luchas sindacales en Colombia*. Bogota, Ediciones CEIS, 1971. 233 pp.

Gómez Valderrama, Pedro. *Los ojos del burgués; un año en la Unión Soviética*. Bogotá, Editorial Universitaria Colombiana, 1971. 195 pp.

Ossa, Manuel. *Camilo Torres*. Buenos Aires, Centro Editor de América Latina, 1972. 280 pp.

Torres Restrepo, Camilo. *Revolutionary Priest: Complete Writings and Messages of Camilo Torres*. New York, Random House, 1971. 460 pp.

Cuba

Aguilar, Luis E. *Cuba 1933: Prologue to Revolution*. Ithaca, N.Y., Cornell University Press, 1972. 256 pp.

Bonachea, Rolando E., and Valdés, Nelson P., eds. *Cuba in Revolution,* Garden City, N.Y., Doubleday, 1972. 544 pp.

Canton Navarro, José. *Algunas ideas de José Martí en relación con la clase obrera y el socialismo*. Havana, Instituto Cubano del Libro, [1971?].

Cardenal, Ernesto. *En Cuba*. Buenos Aires, 1972. 370 pp.

Castro, Fidel. *History Will Absolve Me*. Havana, Social Sciences, 1971. 85 pp.

————. *Revolutionary Struggle, 1947–1958* (*Selected works of Fidel Castro*). Vol. I. Cambridge, Mass., MIT Press, 1972. 471 pp.

Fornet, Ambrosio. *Cuentos de la Revolución Cubana.* Santiago, Editorial Universitaria, 1971. n.p.

G.-Calzadilla, Miguel A. *The Fidel Castro I Knew: Biographical Fragments on the Cuban Revolution.* New York, Vantage Press, 1971. 80 pp.

Gadea, Hilda. *Ernesto: A Memoir of Che Guevara.* Garden City, N.Y., Doubleday, 1971. 222 pp.

Hageman, Alice L., and Wheaton, Philip E. *Religion in Cuba Today.* New York, Association Press, 1971. 317 pp.

Haimovich, Perla. *Julio A. Mella: El despartar revolucionario en Cuba.* Buenos Aires, Centro Editor de América Latina, 1971. 196 pp.

James, Daniel. *Che Guevara: una biografía.* México, Editorial Diana, 1971. 479 pp.

Marrero, Levi. *Cuba: la forja de un pueblo.* San Juan, Editorial San Juan, 1971. 123 pp.

Medina Pena, Luis. *El sistema bipolar en tensión: la crisis de octubre de 1962.* México, Colmex, 1971. 114 pp.

Nelson, Lowry. *Cuba: The Measure of a Revolution.* Minneapolis, University of Minnesota Press, 1972. 242 pp.

Russell, Phillip. *Cuba in Transition.* Austin, Armadillo Press, 1971. 57 pp.

Saínz Mont, Ramón. *Cuba en llamas.* New York, 1972. 513 pp.

Suchlicki, Jaime, ed. *Cuba, Castro and Revolution.* Coral Gables, Fla., University of Miami Press, 1972. 250 pp.

Tamburrino, Lina. *Cuba ad una svolta.* Ravenna, Longo, 1971. 183 pp.

Valdés, Nelson P., and Lieuwen, Edwin. *The Cuban Revolution: A Research-Study Guide, 1959–1969.* Albuquerque, University of New Mexico Press, 1971. 230 pp.

Wolpin, Miles D. *Cuban Foreign Policy and Chilean Politics.* Lexington, Mass., Heath, 1972. 414 pp.

El Salvador

Arias Gómez, Jorge. *Farabundo Martí; esbozo biográfico.* San Jose, Costa Rica, Editorial Universitaria Centroamericana, 1972. 157 pp.

Barón Ferrufino, José René. *Comunismo y traición.* San Salvador, Editorial Ahora, S.A., 1971. 459 pp.

Guatemala

Melville, Thomas, and Melville, Marjorie. *Guatemala, Another Vietnam?* London, Penguin, 1971. 310 pp.

Mexico

Allaz, Tomás G. *La iglesia contra la pared ¿hambre o revolución?* México, Editorial Nuestro Tiempo, 1971. 244 pp.

Flores García, José. *Juventud al rojo vivo.* 2d ed. México, Dist. Porrúa, 1971. 232 pp.

Monsiváis, Carlos. *Días de guardar.* México, Ediciones Era, 1971. 380 pp.

Ortiz, Orlando, comp. *Genaro Vásquez.* Mexico, Editorial Dioqeues, S.A., 1972. 277 pp.

Poniatowska, Elena. *La noche de Tlatelolca.* México, Ediciones Era, 1971. 282 pp.

Silva Michelena, H., and Sonntag, H. R. *Universidad, dependencia y revolución.* 2d ed. México, Siglo XXI Editores, 1971. 217 pp.

Silverio Saínz, Nicasio. *El manifiesto del Partido Comunista (notas y comentarios).* México, Editora Univex, 1971. 228 pp.

Stavenhagen, Rodolfo. *Neolatifundismo y explotación, de Emiliano Zapata y Anderson Clayton and Co.* México, Editorial Nuestro Tiempo, 1971. 174 pp.

Tirado, Manlio, et al. *El diez de junio y la izquierda radical.* México, Dist. Porrúa, 1971. 250 pp.

Wences Reza, Rosalio. *El movimiento estudiantil y los problemas nacionales.* México, Nuestro Tiempo, 1971. 152 pp.

Wing, Juvencio, et al. *Los estudiantes, la educación y la política.* México, Nuestro Tiempo, 1971. 176 pp.

Peru

Aguilar Derpich, Juan. *Perú, socialismo militar?* Caracas, Librería Politécnica Moulines, 1972. 260 pp.

Baines, John M. *Revolution in Peru: Mariátegui and the Myth.* University, University of Alabama Press, 1972. 206 pp.

Blanco, Hugo. *Land or Death: The Peasant Struggle in Peru.* New York, Pathfinder Press, 1972. 178 pp.

Guardia, Sara Beatriz. *Proceso a campesinos de la guerrilla "Tupac Amaru."* Lima, Dist. Mejía Baca, 1972. 78 pp.

Mariátegui, José Carlos. *Ensayos escogidos.* Lima, Dist. Mejía Baca, 1971. 248 pp.

———. *Seven Interpretive Essays on Peruvian Reality.* Austin, University of Texas Press, 1971. 301 pp.

Paredes Macedo, Saturnino. *Situación política y tareas del Partido Comunista Peruano.* Montevideo, Nativa Libros, 1972. 146 pp.

Quijano, Aníbal. *Nationalism and Capitalism in Peru: A Study in Neo-Imperialism.* New York, Monthly Review Press, 1971. 122 pp.

Sharp, Daniel A. *Estados Unidos y la revolución peruana.* Buenos Aires, Editorial Sudamericana, 1972. 708 pp.

Tauro del Pino, Víctor H. *Visión del materialismo dialéctico e histórico.* Lima [1972?]. 102 pp.

Uruguay

Actas Tupamaras. *Escritas por el M.L.N. Tupamaros.* Bogotá, Editorial América Latina, 1971. 248 pp.

Acuna, Juan Antonio. *Persecución política, atropello y despojo.* N.p., 1971. 190 pp.

Frente Amplio Independientes. *Documentos.* Montevideo, 1971. 79 pp.

Gilio, María Esther. *The Tupamaros.* London, Secker & Warburg, 1972. 197 pp.

Gómez, Eugenio. *Crisis; violencia y guerra.* Montevideo, 1971. 126 pp.

Labrousse, Alain. *Nous les Tupamaros.* Paris, Maspero, 1972. 243 pp.

Mayans, Ernesto. *Tupamaros, antología documental.* Cuernavaca, Mexico, Centro Intercultural de Documentación, 1971. 492 pp.

Otero, Lisandro. *En busca de Viet Nam.* Montevideo, Ed. Nuestra Tierra, 1971. 167 pp.

Suarez, Carlos, and Anaya Sarmiento, Rubén. *Los Tupamaros.* México, Dist. Porrúa, 1971. 247 pp.

Trías, Vivián. *Imperialismo, geopolítica y petróleo.* N.p., Banda Oriental, 1971. 55 pp.

———. *Imperialismo y rosca bancaria en el Uruguay.* N.p., 1971.

Venezuela

Arnove, Robert F. *Student Alienation: A Venezuelan Study.* New York, Praeger, 1971. 234 pp.

Libro rojo, 1936. Caracas, Librería Politécnica Moulines, 1972.

Partido Comunista de Venezuela. *Aportes a la historia del P.C.V.* Maracaibo, Biblioteca de Documentos Históricos, 1971. 154 pp.

ASIA AND THE PACIFIC

General

Lansdale, Edward Geary. *In the Midst of Wars: An American's Mission to Southeast Asia.* New York, Harper & Row, 1972. 386 pp.

Waddell, J. Robert E. *An Introduction to Southeast Asian Politics.* New York, Wiley, 1972. 305 pp.

Zaharov, V. A., et al., eds. *Southeast Asia: History, Economy, Policy.* Moscow, Progress, 1972. 276 pp.

Zasloff, Joseph J., and Goodman, Allan E., eds. *Indochina in Conflict: A Political Assessment.* Lexington, Mass., Heath, 1972. 227 pp.

Burma

Lvin, Takin. *Istoriya rabochego dvizheniya Birmy.* Moscow, Progress, 1972. 224 pp.

Ceylon

Jayawardena, Visakha Kumari. *The Rise of the Labor Movement in Ceylon.* Durham, N.C., Duke University Press, 1972. 382 pp.

Kearney, Robert N. *Trade Unions and Politics in Ceylon.* Berkeley, University of California Press, 1972. 195 pp.

Mukherjee, S. *Ceylon—Island That Changed.* New Delhi, People's Publishing House, 1971. 135 pp.

China

Ambroz, Oton. *Realignment of World Power: The Russo-Chinese Schism under the Impact of Mao Tse-tung's Last Revolution.* New York, Speller & Sons, 1972. 2 vols.

An, Tai Sung. *Mao Tse-tung's Cultural Revolution.* New York, Pegasus, 1972. 211 pp.

Archer, Jules. *Mao Tse-tung.* New York, Hawthorn Books, 1972. 211 pp.

Centre d'Etude du Sud-Est Asiatique et de l'Extrême Orient. *China After the Cultural Revolution.* Brussels, Université Libre, 1972. 2 vols.

Chai, Winberg, ed. *The Foreign Relations of the People's Republic of China.* New York, Putnam, 1972. 420 pp.

———. *The New Politics of Communist China: Modernization Process of a Developing Nation.* Pacific Palisades, Calif., Goodyear Publishing Co., 1972. 306 pp.

Cheng, Peter P. *A Chronology of the People's Republic of China, from October 1, 1949, through December 31, 1969.* Totowa, N.J., Littlefield Adams, 1972. 347 pp.

Clubb, O. Edmund. *Twentieth Century China.* 2d ed. New York, Columbia University Press, 1972. 526 pp.

Durdin, Tillman, et al. *The New York Times Report from Red China*. New York, Quadrangle, 1972. 367 pp.

Fan, Kuang Huan, comp. *Mao Tse-tung and Lin Piao: Post Revolutionary Writings*. Garden City, N.Y., Anchor, 1972. 536 pp.

FitzGerald, Stephen. *China and the Overseas Chinese: A Study of Peking's Changing Policy, 1949–1970*. Cambridge, Cambridge University Press, 1972. 268 pp.

Fokkema, D. W. *Report from Peking*. Quebec, McGill-Queen's University Press, 1972. 185 pp.

Harrison, John A., ed. *China*. Tucson, University of Arizona Press, 1972. 230 pp.

Hinton, William. *Hundred Day War: The Cultural Revolution at Tsinghua University*. New York, Monthly Review Press, 1972. 288 pp.

————. *Turning Point in China: An Essay on the Cultural Revolution*. New York, Monthly Review Press, 1972. 112 pp.

Karnow, Stanley. *Mao and China: From Revolution to Revolution*. New York: Viking, 1972. 592 pp.

Kau, Ying-mao, ed. *The People's Liberation Army and China's Nation Building*. White Plains, N.Y., International Arts & Sciences, 1972. 225 pp.

Kolatch, Jonathan. *Sports, Politics and Ideology in China*. Middle Village, N.Y., Jonathan David Publishers, 1972. 254 pp.

Kuo, Leslie T. *The Technical Transformation of Agriculture in Communist China*. New York, Praeger, 1972. 290 pp.

Ling, Ken. *The Revenge of Heaven: Journal of a Young Chinese*. New York, Putnam, 1972. 413 pp.

Macciocchi, Maria Antonietta. *Daily Life in Revolutionary China*. New York, Monthly Review Press, 1972. 528 pp.

MacFarquhar, Roderick, ed. *Sino-American Relations, 1949–71*. New York, Praeger, 1972. 267 pp.

MacInnis, Donald E., comp. *Religious Policy and Practice in Communist China: a Documentary History*. New York, Macmillan, 1972. 392 pp.

Mehnert, Klaus. *China Returns*. New York, Dutton, 1972. 322 pp.

Melby, John F. *The Mandate of Heaven: Records of a Civil War, 1945–1949*. Garden City, N.Y., Doubleday, 1972. 278 pp.

Myrdal, Jan and Gun Kessle. *China: The Revolution Continued*. New York, Random House, 1972. 201 pp.

Pye, Lucian W. *China: An Introduction*. Boston, Little Brown, 1972. 384 pp.

Ribao, Renmin, et al. *Breve historia del Partido Comunista de China*. Montevideo, Nativa Libros, 1971. 76 pp.

Rice, Edward E. *Mao's Way*. Berkeley, University of California Press, 1972. 596 pp.

Richman, B. M. *Industrial Society in Communist China*. New York, Random House, 1972. 968 pp.

Scalapino, Robert A., ed. *Elites in the People's Republic of China*. Seattle, University of Washington Press, 1972. 671 pp.

Schell, Orville, and Esherick, Joseph. *Modern China: The Story of a Revolution*. New York, Knopf, 1972. 149 pp.

Seybolt, Peter J., ed. *Revolutionary Education in China: Documents and Commentary*. White Plains, N.Y.: International Arts & Sciences, 1972. 300 pp.

Shabad, Theodore. *China's Changing Map: National and Regional Development, 1949–71*. Rev. ed. New York, Praeger, 1972. 420 pp.

Shewmaker, Kenneth E. *Americans and Chinese Communists, 1927–1945*. Ithaca, N.Y., Cornell University Press, 1972. 387 pp.

Sidel, Ruth. *Women and Child Care in China: A Firsthand Report*. New York, Hill & Wang, 1972. 207 pp.

Snow, Edgar. *The Long Revolution*. New York, Random House, 1972. 269 pp.

Snow, Helen Foster. *The Chinese Communists: Sketches and Autobiographies of the Old Guard*. Westport, Conn., Greenwood Publishing Co., 1972. 398 pp.

Suyin, Han. *The Morning Deluge: Mao Tsetung and the Chinese Revolution, 1893–1954*. Boston, Little Brown, 1972. 571 pp.

Terrill, Ross. *800,000,000: The Real China*. Boston, Little Brown, 1972. 236 pp.

Ting, Jan C. *An American in China*. New York, Paperback Library, 1972. 190 pp.

Topping, Seymour. *Journey Between Two Chinas*. New York, Harper & Row, 1972. 320 pp.

U.S. Congress, Joint Economic Committee. *Economic Developments in Mainland China*. Washington, D.C., Government Printing Office, 1972. 148 pp.

———. *People's Republic of China: An Economic Assessment*. Washington, D.C., Government Printing Office, 1972. 328 pp.

Whitson, William W., ed. *The Military and Political Power in China in the 1970s*. New York, Praeger, 1972. 390 pp.

Wilson, Dick. *The Long March 1935: The Epic of Chinese Communism's Survival*. New York, Viking, 1972. 331 pp.

India

Communist Party of India. *Constitution of the Communist Party of India*. New Delhi, New Age, 1972. 40 pp.

———. *Documents of the Ninth Congress of the Communist Party of India*. New Delhi, New Age, 1972. 420 pp.

———. *Organisational Report and Resolution on Party Organisation*. New Delhi, New Age, 1971. 126 pp.

Mitra, Pratap, and Sen, Mohit. *Communist Party and Naxalites*. New Delhi, New Age, 1971. 130 pp.

Nizami, Taufiq Ahmad. *The Communist Party and India's Foreign Policy*. New York, Barnes & Noble, 1972. 282 pp.

Sen, Bhowani. *The Truth about CPM: A Critique of the Ideological-Political Line of the Communist Party in India (M)*. New Delhi, New Age, 1972. 40 pp.

Sen Gupta, Bhabani S. *Communism in Indian Politics*. New York, Columbia University Press, 1972. 455 pp.

Indonesia

Legge, J. D. *Sukarno: A Political Biography*. New York, Praeger, 1972. 431 pp.

Van Dijk, C. *The Indonesian Communist Party (PKI) and Its Relations with the Soviet Union and the People's Republic of China*. The Hague, Interdoc, 1972. 76 pp.

Japan

Brzezinski, Zbigniew. *The Fragile Blossom: Crisis and Change in Japan*. New York, Harper & Row, 1972. 153 pp.

Langer, Paul F. *Communism in Japan: A Case of Political Naturalization*. Stanford, Calif., Hoover Institution Press, 1972. 112 pp.

Korea

Han, Woo-keun. *History of Korea.* Honolulu, University of Hawaii, 1972. 509 pp.

Kim Il Sung. *On Immediate Political and Economic Policies of the Democratic People's Republic of Korea and Some International Problems.* Pyongyang, Foreign Languages Publishing House, 1972. 46 pp.

Li Yuk-sa, ed. *Juche! The Speeches and Writings of Kim Il Sung.* New York, Grossman, 1972. 271 pp.

Scalapino, Robert A., and Lee, Chong-sik. *Communism in Korea.* 2 vols. Berkeley, University of California Press, 1972.

U.S. Government. *Directory of North Korean Officials.* Washington, D.C., Government Printing Office, 1972. 211 pp.

Thailand

Darling, Frank and Darling, Ann. *Thailand, The Modern Kingdom.* Singapore, Asia Pacific Press, 1971. 122 pp.

Vietnam

Buttinger, Joseph. *A Dragon Defiant: A Short History of Vietnam.* New York, Praeger, 1972. 160 pp.

FitzGerald, Frances. *Fire in the Lake: The Vietnamese and the Americans in Vietnam.* Boston, Little Brown, 1972. 491 pp.

Goldston, Robert. *The Vietnamese Revolution.* Indianapolis, Bobbs-Merrill, 1972. 194 pp.

Race, Jeffrey. *War Comes to Long An; Revolutionary Conflict in a Vietnamese Province.* Berkeley, University of California Press, 1972. 299 pp.

Sainteny, Jean. *Ho Chi Minh and His Vietnam: A Personal Memoir.* Chicago, Cowles, 1972. 193 pp.

U.S. Congress, Senate Committee on the Judiciary. *The Human Cost of Communism in Vietnam: A Compendium.* Washington, D.C., Government Printing Office, 1972. 123 pp.

Van Dyke, Jon M. *North Vietnam's Strategy for Survival.* Palo Alto, Pacific Books, 1972. 336 pp.

Webb, Kate. *On the Other Side: 23 Days with the Viet Cong.* New York, Quadrangle, 1972. 160 pp.

West, F. J., Jr. *The Village.* New York, Harper & Row, 1972. 228 pp.

INDEX

INDEX OF PERSONS